W9-BOK-929

FIFTH EDITION
50 STATES

FIFTH EDITION
90,056
LOCALITIES

FIFTH EDITION
1 BOOK
THAT MAKES SENSE OF IT ALL

The key to understanding differences across U.S. state and local governments lies in the comparative approach of **Governing States and Localities**.

Unlock what's behind the sometimes collaborative, sometimes contentious relations of state and local politics with this fresh perspective that blends scholarship and news-writing style. The **Fifth Edition** examines how states and localities are increasingly assertive in seeking independence from Washington's policy priorities, especially when those priorities clash with their partisan leanings.

CHAPTER-OPENING PEDAGOGY KEEPS STUDENTS FOCUSED

- **Chapter-opening vignettes** capture students' interest with headline-grabbing style through compelling stories that link to the broader themes of the chapter.

- **Chapter-opening comparative questions** prompt students to look systematically for answers using the comparative method.

- What causes some states or localities to change party preferences?
- How do state regulations affect voting?
- How do politicians tune in to what citizens are thinking?

- **Chapter objectives** identify key takeaways for close, focused reading.

Chapter Objectives

After reading this chapter, you will be able to

- describe the role of elections within the U.S. political system,
- identify the different positions for which elections are used, and
- discuss the role of public opinion in elections and representation.

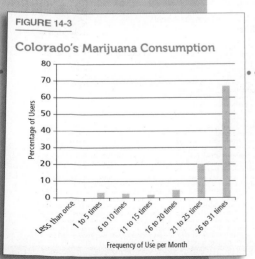

FIGURE 14-3

Colorado's Marijuana Consumption

THROUGHOUT EACH CHAPTER

- A **marginal glossary** defines key concepts as they are introduced.
- More than **80 tables, figures, and maps** provide an intuitively easy way for students to grasp the similarities and differences among states and localities.

Voter turnout
The percentage of voting-eligible citizens who register to vote and do vote

The Latest Research

This chapter has noted at various points the differences across legislatures that can make a difference. Term limits, partisanship and ideology, the sociodemographics of a legislature—all these can make a difference to legislative agendas, policy priorities, and whose political preferences do, or do not, get represented. Given the importance of these differences, it is not surprising that scholars are interested in their causes and consequences.

Below we summarize some of the latest research that employs the comparative method to explore how these legislative differences translate into power and policymaking.

• **Birkhead, Nathaniel A.** "The Role of Ideology in State Legislative Elections." Prepared for presentation at State Politics and Policy Conference, Iowa City, IA, May 23–25, 2013. http://www.uiowa.edu/~stpols13/papers/Birkhead%20ideology%20in%20State%20Legislative%20Elections.pdf.

How much do ideology and voting records actually matter when incumbent state legislators are up for reelection? They may have other interests than those of their district in mind when they vote, such as currying favor with party leaders or interest groups. If a legislator's voting record ends up being more extreme than the views of her district, will she be punished? Incumbent ideological extremity is associated with decreased electoral vote share in congressional elections, but individual state legislators and their voting habits receive less attention. Examining some 1,500 state legislative contests, Birkhead finds that ideological extremity does not seem overall to have a statistically significant effect on incumbents' vote totals, although Republicans (but not Democrats) are rewarded to a minor extent by voters for moderation.

• **Cummins, Jeff.** "The Effects of Legislative Term Limits on State Fiscal Conditions." American Politics Research 20 (2012): 1–26.

One of the themes running throughout this entire book, not just this chapter, is how battered state finances continue to be a major influence on policy and politics. This study analyzes state budgets between 1983 and 2008 and finds that as legislative turnover increases, budgets are more likely to head toward the red. This happens for several reasons. More experienced legislators may be better equipped to handle fiscal crises, in the same fashion a veteran pilot is better prepared for in-air emergencies. Legislators who have short time horizons are less likely to take into account the long-term implications of policy. The findings of this study have particular resonance given that term limits were increasing legislative turnover during and after the Great Recession.

• **Gamm, Gerald, and Thad Kousser.** "Contingent Partisanship: When Party Labels Matter—and When They Don't—in the Distribution of Pork in American State Legislatures." Paper presented at the American Political Science Association annual meeting, Chicago, IL, 2013. http://papers.ssrn.com/sol3/papers.cfm?abstract_id=2300304.

Legislatures often have authority to guide spending projects toward particular areas in a state. Examining budget decisions in six states during the first half of the 20th century, the authors found that states where power was divided between the two major parties were more likely to make spending decisions on a statewide basis, while one-party legislatures were more likely to direct money to specific districts—with the majority, of course, taking a larger share of such spending. In states where there was less competition or polarization between the parties, partisan identity mattered less than seniority or members' voting near the ideological center of the legislature when it came to receiving funds for their districts.

• **Reingold, Beth, and Adrienne R. Smith.** "Legislative Leadership and Intersections of Gender, Race, and Ethnicity in the American States." Paper presented at the annual meeting of the American Political Science Association, Washington, DC, August 26, 2014. http://papers.ssrn.com/sol3/papers.cfm?abstract_id=2487604.

THE LATEST RESEARCH feature highlights cutting-edge scholarship related to each chapter's discussion, providing students with a broader social science understanding of states and localities.

A DIFFERENCE THAT MAKES A DIFFERENCE boxes provide clear examples of how variation among states and localities can explain a wide range of political and policy phenomena. Just some of the new coverage:

- ideological polarization and depressed voter turnout,
- the clout gained by rural localities sticking together, and
- state approaches to setting up health care exchanges.

A Difference That Makes A Difference

Does Ideological Polarization Depress Voter Turnout?

There's a kind of truth in labeling when it comes to contemporary American politics. If you vote for a Democrat, you know what you're going to get in terms of that candidate's positions on issues such as abortion and same-sex marriage. If you support a Republican, you can bet he or she will take a more conservative stance on issues such as gun control and immigration.

In the mid-20th century, political scientists sometimes decried the lack of a "responsible party model," meaning parties that offered voters clear choices. With the parties now so well sorted ideologically—with few elected officials breaking with party orthodoxy on major issues—where does that leave voters?

There's a big academic debate about whether people who don't do politics for a living are as vehement about their disdain for politicians. Some of the most polarized states is [...] dominate at the [...] for president. [...] Democratic pre[...] home to Madi[...] ship county, an[...] tory, including [...]

Some of those areas have voter turnout rates far above the national average. In 2012, Ozaukee County had the highest turnout of voting-age citizens—84 percent—of any county with a population above 50,000. Nearby Waukesha County was second, while Dane County came in fifth. Suburban Brookfield, which gave Republican candidate Romney two thirds of its vote in 2012, had an astonishing turnout rate of 90 percent.

"Strongholds have higher turnout, apparently because people feel like they're more engaged in politics, their neighbors are engaged," said Torben Lutjen, a political scientist at the University of Dusseldorf who has studied polarized communities in Wisconsin. "Given a clear choice, voters in recent election cycles have seemed to prefer candidates who adhere to the party line, often [...]

LOCAL FOCUS boxes spotlight how localities function independently of states, yet are both constrained and empowered by intergovernmental ties. New examples include:

- political participation (or lack thereof) in local politics,
- the price localities are paying for the fracking boom, and
- how cities are addressing climate change.

Local Focus

Cities Seek to Prepare for Local Climate Effects

As is true throughout the Midwest, summer storms have gotten worse in Dubuque, Iowa, leading to flash floods along the Mississippi River. Water speeds downhill toward the Bee Branch Creek, a partially buried waterway that flows beneath several neighborhoods before emptying into the Mississippi. Often, the storms dump so much rain that the creek's concrete channels cannot contain the runoff. Water spills over streets, across backyards, and into basements. It can push open manhole covers, spray out from fire hydrants, and carry away parked cars.

Six times between 1999 and 2014, Dubuque has been declared a presidential disaster area. One storm in 2011 dumped nearly 11 inches of rain on the city in less than 24 hours. The city estimates that since 1999 floods in the Bee Branch Creek watershed have caused $70 million in damage to homes and businesses. Mayor Roy Buol worries that climate change, which has raised the average U.S. temperature by 1.5 degrees since 1895, will only make the storms worse. So Buol and other Dubuque leaders are planning for $200 million in infrastructure improvements to give the city resilience in the face of global warming and natural disasters.

Dubuque is not alone. Cities love their waterfronts, but in an era of fierce storms and rising sea levels, they are investing heavily in infrastructure improvements designed to help them ride out the next storm. It's expensive—Miami Beach is planning to spend $300

million, however. Local governments don't have enough extra money to take on such projects alone. "Everything that Norfolk needs to do is $1 billion," said Lori Crouch, a spokeswoman for that southeastern Virginia city. "We don't have $1 billion."

That's why a lot of cities and counties are drawing up wish lists—so they have projects in mind that they can start working on once they receive federal and state aid after disasters strike. "Every time there is a disaster, you use the money you get from the disaster to build up your long-term resiliency," said Niek Veraart, an infrastructure consultant.

Rebuilding after one disaster offers a unique opportunity to learn and prepare for the next. Still, it would be better to put resilience measures in place before the next disaster strikes, rather than afterward. But while it can be hard to secure funds to prevent bad things from happening, money almost inevitably starts to flow once disasters occur. Cities have learned that they can't simply rebuild what was lost but also have to think about making changes that will prevent repetition of the same type of destruction.

with recommendations—more than 100 so far—including a surface water reservoir. By reducing flooding, the reservoir would help cope with extreme storms, such as the one that dumped 22 inches of rain on Palm Beach County on a single day in January 2014.

Just the first phase of the reservoir could cost $150

Policy in Practice

How Super PACs Supplement—and Sometimes Surpass—Parties

Members of the school board in Elizabeth, New Jersey, made a political enemy, and they paid the price. Several of them backed someone who ran against state Senator Raymond Lesniak, and in 2013 he repaid the favor. Lesniak worked with a super PAC called the Committee for Economic Growth and Social Justice, run by his former campaign consultant. It spent more than $150,000 to unseat members of the school board.

Lots of politicians and wealthy donors have set up super PACs, which are able to spend unlimited funds on political campaigns. Donors to Lesniak's group included his allies in the bail bond and online gambling industries, which would seem to have no natural interest in education policy in a 25,000-student school district in suburban New Jersey. But they were happy to help out Lesniak, who chairs a powerful economic development committee.

The super PAC tied to Lesniak was not alone. In elections," said Daniel Tokaji, coauthor of *The New Soft Money*, referring to his interviews with political consultants. "On some occasions, we got laughs or chuckles when we even mentioned state or local parties."

Wealthy donors have always carried a lot of sway in politics. That they can now spend so freely—and cut out the middlemen by setting up their own political organizations—has some Americans worried that the rich are having an unhealthy amount of influence. Super PACs spent more than $1 billion on elections in 2012, while spending on ballot measures topped $1 billion for the first time in 2014—largely from corporations eager to push or block measures that circumvented the legislative process.

"There are five or six people in this room tonight that could simply make a decision—this will be the next president—and probably at least get a nomination, if...

States Under Stress

Governors Aren't Afraid to Grab Jobs From Other States

As he prepared to leave office, Texas governor Rick Perry had reasons to be satisfied. His state had consistently led the nation in job creation, with its economic growth outpacing the rest of the country's 2 to 1 over the preceding two decades, according to the Federal Reserve Bank of Dallas.

But Perry wanted more. During his last 2 years in office, the Republican seemed to spend as much time outside of Texas as he did in the state, traveling to New York, California, Illinois, Connecticut, and other states to encourage firms to move their operations to Texas.

Governors always want to recruit companies. Perry took an unusually public and aggressive approach, however. Not coincidentally, Perry chose for his tour states that had Democratic governors. He argued that the Texas model of low taxes and limited regulation were better for business. "When you grow tired of Maryland taxes squeezing every dime out of your business, think Texas, where we created more jobs than all other states combined," Perry said in radio and TV ads that ran in the state. "Maybe it's time to move your business to Texas."

When governors of the states he visited objected to both his presence and his policies—pointing out that Texas has large numbers of low-wage jobs and the highest percentage of residents without health insurance—Perry didn't shy away from the fight. When he visited Maryland in 2013, Democratic governor Martin O'Malley not only wrote an op-ed for the *Washington Post* touting his state's virtues over those of Texas but went on CNN's *Crossfire* to debate the Texan. After

O'Malley bragged about the "great companies" in his state, Perry said, "We'll recruit them."

"You're welcome to try," O'Malley said.

For all the media attention Perry's efforts garnered, they didn't always pan out. TexasOne, the public-private partnership that underwrote Perry's travels, claimed that its efforts helped convince companies to announce the creation of nearly 45,000 new jobs in Texas during the governor's last decade in office. But the *Dallas Morning News* noted in 2014 that "not all of those positions eventually materialized."

Perry caught his biggest fish that year when Toyota announced it would move its North American headquarters from California to the Dallas area, bringing with it roughly 4,000 jobs. The company didn't cite Perry's recruitment effort as its motivation for moving, but clearly it didn't hurt. An economic development fund overseen by the governor offered Toyota a $40 million incentive package to sweeten the deal. It beat out a $100 million package from North Carolina, whose commerce secretary told the Associated Press it was tough to compete against the lack of corporate or personal income taxes in Texas.

But Perry couldn't win them all. He missed out in 2014 on the chance to land a $5 billion battery factory planned by electric carmaker Tesla, which is based in California. Perry personally led negotiations with the company and went so far as to drive a Tesla Model S through Sacramento, California's state capital—a move the *Los Angeles Times* described as "stalking"—but Tesla decided to locate its plant in Nevada.

POLICY IN PRACTICE boxes demonstrate how different states and localities interpret and implement legislation, such as:

- the role of super PACs in supplementing or surpassing that of parties,
- the life or death stakes involved in appellate court organization, and
- the challenges of implementing policies like gun control and Common Core standards in education.

STATES UNDER STRESS boxes underscore how budgetary constraints reshape how state and local governments operate, with new material including:

- suing for education funding in Kansas,
- long-term pay freezes in state and local governments, and
- governors seeking to lure jobs away from other states.

---

edge.sagepub.com/smithgreenblatt5e

ⓈSAGE statestats

SAGE STATE STATS is an interactive database that delivers a dynamic and engaging user experience unmatched by other resources. SAGE State Stats features data from more than 80 different government and nongovernment sources and is backed by a rich collection of more than 2,000 current and historical data series on popular topics of research interest.

SAGE State Stats exercises are tied to chapter topics and appear in the book. They are accessible on the student resource center, where links from the exercises to the appropriate data help students formulate a response, allowing them to visualize similarities and differences among states and localities.

Governing States and Localities
by Kevin B. Smith and Alan Greenblatt

Fifth Edition

Student Resources

1. Introduction to State and Local Government
2. Federalism
   - Action plan
   - Learning Objectives
   - Quiz
   - eFlashcards
   - Video and Multimedia
   - Chapter Summary
   - State Stats Exercises
3. Constitutions
4. Finance

State Stats Exercises

SAGE Stats User Guide

1. On average, the federal government contributes around 10 percent, the state government around 47 percent, and local governments around 44 percent to public K–12 schools. How much money, per capita, does your state spend on elementary and secondary education? Is this an example of compact federalism, dual federalism, or cooperative federalism? Why? (http://data.sagepub.com/sagestats /document.php?id=807)

2. What percentage of your state's population is enrolled in Medicaid? How does your state compare to the states around it? How might the Affordable Care Act change these numbers moving forward (http://data.sagepub.com/sagestats/document.php?id=1780)

3. How many immigrants were admitted to New Mexico in 1997? How many were admitted to Arizona in the same year? How might this difference affect variations in policies regarding immigration (http://data.sagepub.com/sagestats/document.php?id=3799)

FIFTH EDITION
SAGE-EDGE

edge.sagepub.com/ smithgreenblatt5e

SAGE edge offers a robust online environment featuring an impressive array of tools and resources, keeping both instructors and students on the cutting edge of teaching and learning. SAGE edge content is open access and available on demand. Learning and teaching has never been easier!

SAGE EDGE FOR INSTRUCTORS supports teaching by making it easy to integrate quality content and create a rich learning environment for students.

- **Test banks** built on **Bloom's Taxonomy** provide a diverse range of test items with **Respondus** test generation
- Editable, chapter-specific **PowerPoint® slides** offer complete flexibility for creating a multimedia presentation for the course
- **Video** and **multimedia content** enhances student engagement and appeals to different learning styles
- **Instructor Manual** summarizes key concepts by chapter to ease preparation for lectures and class discussions
- **Transition Guide** provides chapter-by-chapter outline of key changes to the fifth edition
- A set of all the **graphics from the text**, including all of the maps, tables, and figures, in PowerPoint, .pdf, and .jpg formats, helps instructors produce meaningful class presentations quickly
- **SAGE State Stats Guide** provides information on how to use the SAGE State Stats database for the exercises in the book and on the student study site
- A **common course cartridge** includes all of the instructor resources and assessment material from the student study site, making it easy for instructors to upload and use these materials in learning management systems such as Blackboard™, Angel®, Moodle™, Canvas, and Desire2Learn™

SAGE EDGE FOR STUDENTS provides a personalized approach to help students accomplish their coursework goals in an easy-to-use learning environment.

- Mobile-friendly **eFlashcards** strengthen understanding of key terms and concepts
- Mobile-friendly practice **quizzes** allow for independent assessment by students of their mastery of course material
- A customized online **action plan** includes tips and feedback on progress through the course and materials, which allows students to individualize their learning experience
- **Chapter summaries** with **learning objectives** reinforce the most important material
- Carefully selected **video** and **multimedia content** enhance exploration of key topics
- **SAGE State Stats Guide** provides information on how to use the SAGE State Stats database to complete the exercises in the book and on the student study site

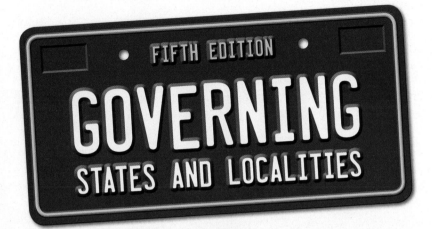

FIFTH EDITION

GOVERNING
STATES AND LOCALITIES

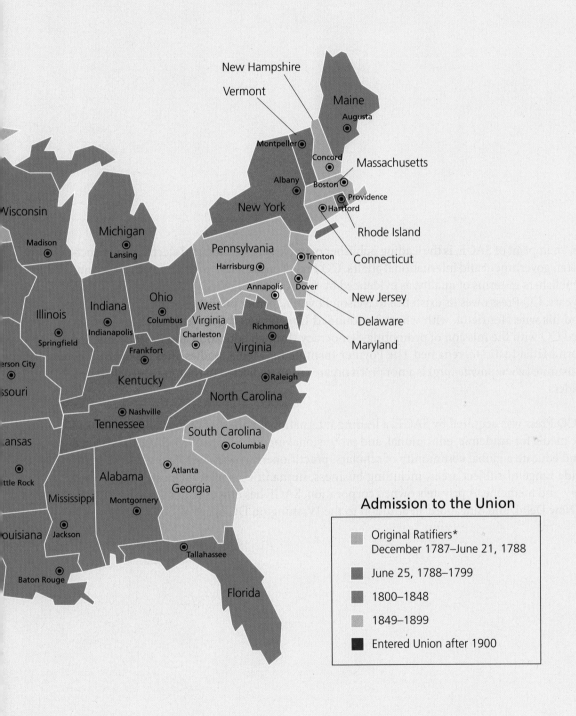

New Hampshire

Vermont

Maine

Augusta ◉

Montpelier ◉

Concord ◉

Massachusetts

Albany ◉

Boston ◉

Providence

New York

◉ Hartford

Rhode Island

Wisconsin

Michigan

Madison ◉

◉ Lansing

Pennsylvania

Harrisburg ◉

◉ Trenton

Connecticut

Illinois

Indiana

Ohio

West Virginia

Annapolis ◉ Dover

New Jersey

◉ Columbus

Charleston ◉

Richmond ◉

Delaware

◉ Indianapolis

Springfield ◉

Frankfort ◉

Virginia

Maryland

erson City

Kentucky

◉ Raleigh

ssouri

Nashville ◉

North Carolina

Tennessee

ansas

South Carolina

◉ Columbia

◉ Little Rock

Alabama

◉ Atlanta

Georgia

Mississippi

Montgomery ◉

ouisiana

Jackson ◉

Baton Rouge ◉

◉ Tallahassee

Florida

Admission to the Union

Original Ratifiers*
December 1787–June 21, 1788

June 25, 1788–1799

1800–1848

1849–1899

Entered Union after 1900

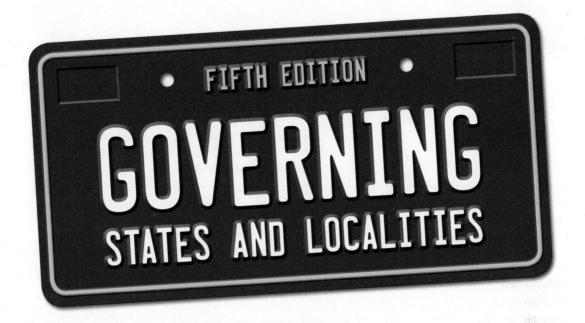

FIFTH EDITION

GOVERNING
STATES AND LOCALITIES

KEVIN B. SMITH
University of Nebraska – Lincoln

ALAN GREENBLATT
Governing magazine

Los Angeles | London | New Delhi
Singapore | Washington DC | Boston

Los Angeles | London | New Delhi
Singapore | Washington DC | Boston

FOR INFORMATION:

CQ Press
An Imprint of SAGE Publications, Inc.
2455 Teller Road
Thousand Oaks, California 91320
E-mail: order@sagepub.com

SAGE Publications Ltd.
1 Oliver's Yard
55 City Road
London EC1Y 1SP
United Kingdom

SAGE Publications India Pvt. Ltd.
B 1/I 1 Mohan Cooperative Industrial Area
Mathura Road, New Delhi 110 044
India

SAGE Publications Asia-Pacific Pte. Ltd.
3 Church Street
#10-04 Samsung Hub
Singapore 049483

Printed in Canada

Cataloging-in-publication data is available for this title from the Library of Congress.

ISBN 978-1-4833-7803-9

Acquisitions Editor: Sarah Calabi
Senior Development Editor: Nancy Matuszak
Digital Content Editor: Allison Hughes
Editorial Assistant: Raquel Christie
Production Editor: Laura Barrett
Copy Editor: Megan Granger
Typesetter: C&M Digitals (P) Ltd.
Proofreader: Sarah J. Duffy
Indexer: Rick Hurd
Cover Designer: Janet Kiesel
Marketing Manager: Amy Whitaker

This book is printed on acid-free paper.

15 16 17 18 19 10 9 8 7 6 5 4 3 2 1

Brief Contents

Contents

AP Photo/The Denver Post, Kathryn Scott Osler

Chapter 1 3

Introduction to State and Local Government: They Tax Dogs in West Virginia, Don't They?

Getty Images

Chapter 2 27

Federalism: The Power Plan

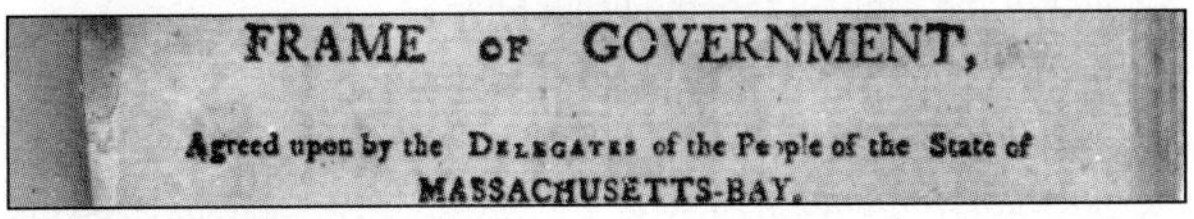

FRAME OF GOVERNMENT,

Agreed upon by the DELEGATES of the People of the State of
MASSACHUSETTS-BAY.

The Granger Collection, New York

Chapter 3 59

Constitutions: Operating Instructions

© JOSHUA LOTT/Reuters/Corbis

Chapter 4   89

Finance: Filling the Till and
Paying the Bills

AP Photo/Erik Schelzig

Chapter 5   117

Political Attitudes and Participation:
Venting and Voting

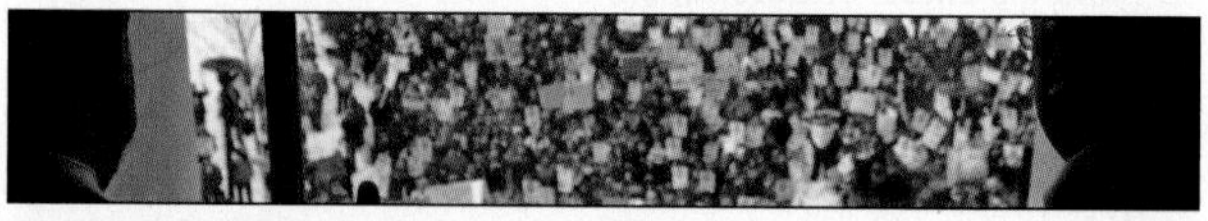

AP Photo/Andy Manis

Chapter 6   155

Parties and Interest Groups: Elephants,
Donkeys, and Cash Cows

https://twitter.com/WendyDavisTexas

Chapter 7   195

Legislatures: The Art of Herding Cats

AP Photo/Arthur D. Lauck, Pool

Chapter 8   239

Governors and Executives: There Is No Such Thing as Absolute Power

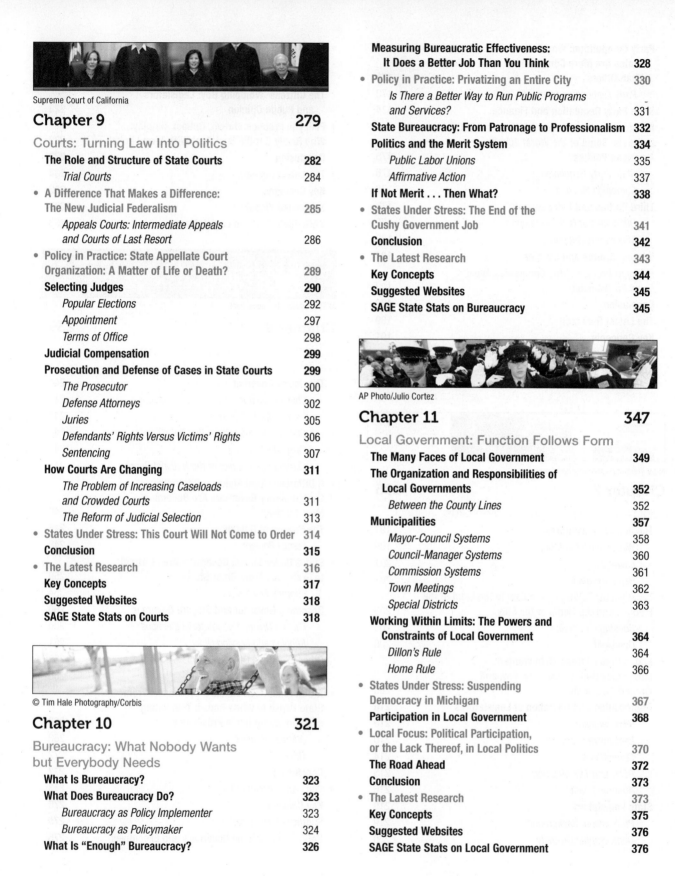

Supreme Court of California

Chapter 9   279

Courts: Turning Law Into Politics

© Tim Hale Photography/Corbis

Chapter 10   321

Bureaucracy: What Nobody Wants but Everybody Needs

AP Photo/Julio Cortez

Chapter 11   347

Local Government: Function Follows Form

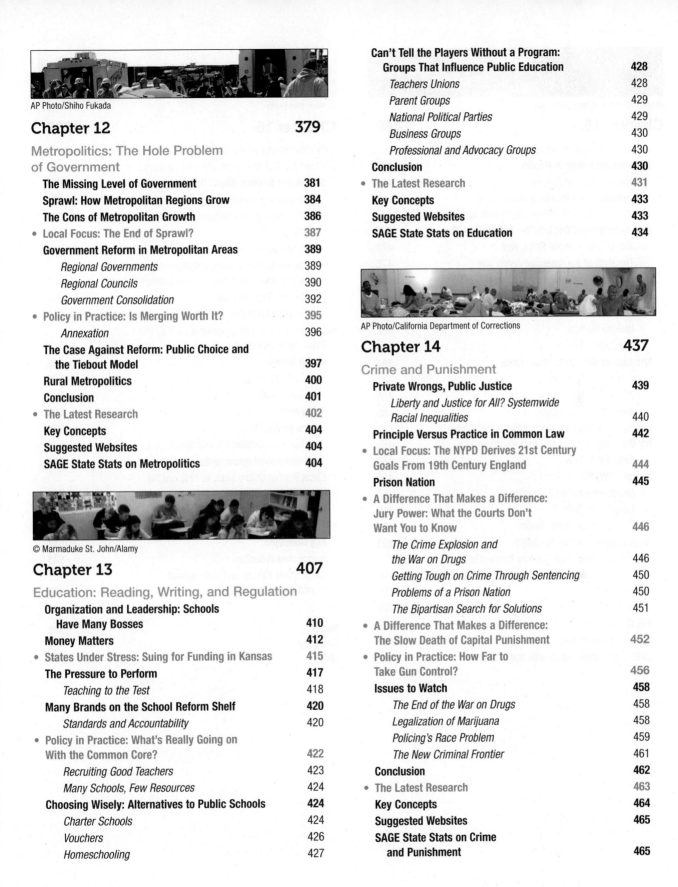

AP Photo/Shiho Fukada

Chapter 12   379

Metropolitics: The Hole Problem of Government

© Marmaduke St. John/Alamy

Chapter 13   407

Education: Reading, Writing, and Regulation

AP Photo/California Department of Corrections

Chapter 14   437

Crime and Punishment

© LUCY NICHOLSON/Reuters/Corbis

AP Photo/Mel Evans

Tables, Figures, and Maps

Tables

Figures

Maps

Preface

The primary goal of this fifth edition of *Governing States and Localities* is to offer a comprehensive introduction to state and local governments and to do it with a difference. This book is a unique collaboration between academic and professional writers that rests on a foundation of academic scholarship, more than two decades of experience teaching undergraduates about state and local governments, and the insight and experience of a journalist who covers state and local politics.

Like its predecessors, this fifth edition aims to provide a fresh and contemporary perspective on state and local politics in terms of coverage and content, as well as in the look and feel of the book. The text deliberately follows a newsmagazine's crisp journalistic style, and the book employs magazine-quality, full-color layout and design. Our intent is to deliver a text that meets the highest academic and pedagogical standards while remaining engaging and easily accessible to undergraduates. *Governing* magazine remains an important partner for this edition, and many of the feature boxes draw directly from the work of its award-winning reporters, bloggers, and correspondents.

This fifth edition contains a number of significant updates and revisions. These include the new "Chapter Objectives" feature, designed to provide a road map for each chapter's primary pedagogical goals and to make assessment readily measurable for instructors. As in the past, we have updated our graphical presentations, offering illustrations that intuitively highlight key points in the text. Only the most useful data are presented, in the most effective displays, to encourage students' visual learning and data literacy.

Students can get more hands-on experience with data through this edition's SAGE State Stats exercises, which appear at the end of each chapter. State Stats, a database featuring data from more than 80 government and nongovernment sources, provides a tool to research key information and trends on the states. Students will be able to investigate reliable, easy-to-use data on areas such as health care, crime, and education, while intuitive mapping and graphing tools encourage them to compare data through visualization. The exercises can be carried out by accessing State Stats through the student companion site, and new instructions on how to use the site are available for both students and instructors.

All chapters have been revised substantially, with the content updated whenever possible to reflect the latest issues, trends, and political changes, including the following:

- Analysis of the results of the most recent legislative and gubernatorial elections
- Discussion of the most important state supreme court decisions and constitutional debates
- Exploration of key changes in campaign and election regulations
- In-depth examination of recent events and issues that have impacted (and in some cases transformed) states and localities, such as the rollout of the Affordable Care Act and the debate over Common Core State Standards in education
- Updates to "The Latest Research" sections at the end of each chapter, where recent scholarship is put into the context of what students have just read

Although these represent significant revisions, the current edition retains the pedagogical philosophy of the comparative method. This approach compares similar units of analysis to explain *why* differences exist. As scholars know well, state and local governments make excellent units of analysis for comparison because they operate within a single political system. The similarities and differences that mark their institutional structures, laws and regulations, political cultures, histories, demographics, economies, and geographies make them exciting laboratories for asking and answering important questions about politics and government. Put simply, their differences make a difference.

The appeal of exploring state and local government through comparison is not just that it makes for good political science. It is also a great way to engage students, because it gives undergraduates an accessible, practical, and systematic way to understand politics and policy in the real world. Students learn that even such seemingly personal concerns as why their tuition is so darned high are not just relevant to their particular situation and educational institution but also fundamental to the interaction of that institution with its state's political culture, economy, history, and tax structure, and even to the school's geographic and demographic position within the state and region. Using the comparative method, this book gives students the resources they need to ask and answer such questions themselves.

Key Features

This book includes a number of elements designed to showcase and promote its main themes. Sets of chapter-opening questions engage student interest and prompt students to look systematically for answers using the comparative method. The idea is not simply to spoon-feed the answers to students but, rather, to demonstrate how the comparative method can be used to explore and explain questions about politics and policy.

Following the comparative questions, each chapter moves on to an opening vignette modeled after a lead in a newsmagazine article—a compelling story that segues naturally into the broader themes of the chapter. Many of these vignettes (as well as many of the feature boxes) represent original reporting.

Chapter objectives appear after the vignettes. Based on Bloom's taxonomy, they present straightforward, big-picture statements of key information students should take away from each chapter. Instructors may easily turn these into class discussion topics or homework assignments.

The feature boxes in each chapter emphasize and reinforce the comparative theme:

- "A Difference That Makes a Difference" boxes provide clear examples of how variations among states and localities can be used to explain a wide range of political and policy phenomena. These pieces detail the ways the institutions, regulations, political culture, demographics, and other factors of a particular state shape its constitution, the way its political parties function, how its citizens tend to vote, how it allocates its financial resources, and why its courts are structured the way they are, to name a few.

- "Local Focus" boxes spotlight the ways localities function independently of the states and show how they are both constrained and empowered by intergovernmental ties. From battles to wrest control of their budgets from the state to constitutional restrictions on how they can tax and spend, the topics addressed in these boxes showcase the rich variety represented in these nearly 87,000 substate entities.

- "Policy in Practice" boxes demonstrate how different states and localities have interpreted and implemented the legislation handed down from higher levels of government, and the consequences of these decisions. Gubernatorial policy innovators, the surprising effects of new e-government tools, and the political and policy challenges involved in tuition hikes are just some of the issues addressed.

- "States Under Stress" boxes demonstrate how the lingering effects of the Great Recession continue to reshape how state and local governments operate. The issues addressed in these boxes include power shifting toward the federal government, the scramble for federal stimulus dollars, and the weakened negotiating stand of public-sector labor unions.

Another key feature that serves the comparative theme is the design and use of graphics and tables. Nearly 30 full-color, 50-state maps, including four unique cartograms, provide a visual representation of and intuitively easy way to grasp the differences among states and localities—whether the sizes of the state economies, the party affiliation requirements for voting in direct primaries, the methods of judicial selection, or state incarceration rates. Similarly, more than 50 tables and figures emphasize how states and localities differ and what these differences mean to politics and policy. State rankings of voter turnout rates, recent regional murder rates, and many other features support comparisons made in the text.

To help students assimilate content and review for tests, each chapter includes a set of highlighted key concepts. These terms are defined in the margins near the places where they are introduced and are compiled into a list at the end of each chapter, with corresponding page numbers. A comprehensive glossary of key terms precedes the book's index.

Organization of the Book

The book is organized so that each chapter logically builds on previous chapters. The first chapter (subtitled "They Tax Dogs in West Virginia, Don't They?") is essentially a persuasive essay that lays the conceptual groundwork for the book. Its aim is to convince students that state and local politics are important to their day-to-day lives and to their futures as professionals and citizens. That is, it makes the case for why students should care about state and local politics. Along the way, it introduces the advantages of the comparative method as a systematic way to explore this subject. In introducing the book's approach, the chapter provides the basic context for studying state and local governments, especially the differences in economics, culture, demographics, and geography that drive policy and politics at the regional level.

The next two chapters cover federalism and state constitutions. These chapters provide a basic understanding of what state and local governments are and what powers, responsibilities, and roles they have within the political system of the United States, as well as a sense of how they legally can make different political and policy choices.

Chapter 4 examines the finances of state and local governments. The key revenue streams for states and localities—income, sales, and property taxes—fell dramatically during the Great Recession. Seven years later, state and local revenues are still not fully recovered, even as demands for their services have increased. This ongoing imbalance between revenues and expenditures continues to be a dominant driver of politics and policy at the state and local levels. This chapter gives students a fundamental sense of the revenues and expenditures of state and local governments and their central importance to virtually everything government does.

Chapter 5 examines political participation with an eye to helping students understand how citizens connect to the core policymaking institutions of government. Chapters 6 through 10 are separate treatments of those core institutions: parties and interest groups, legislatures, governors and executives, courts, and the bureaucracy. There is special emphasis in each chapter on how variations in the structure, powers, and responsibilities of these institutions have real-life implications for citizens of states and localities.

Chapters 11 and 12 focus on local government. Chapter 11 concentrates on laying out the basic structure, authority, and responsibilities of local government. Chapter 12 examines the relations among local governments from a regional perspective. The final four chapters are devoted to specific policy areas—education, crime and punishment, health and welfare, and the environment—that represent a selection of the most critical policy functions of state and local governments.

Ancillaries

http://edge.sagepub.com/smithgreenblatt5e

SAGE edge offers a robust online environment featuring an impressive array of tools and resources for review, study, and further exploration, keeping both instructors and students on the cutting edge of teaching and learning. SAGE edge content is open access and available on demand. Learning and teaching has never been easier! We gratefully acknowledge Jayme Neiman, for developing the ancillaries on this site.

State Stats, a password-protected, interactive database that is part of the SAGE Stats product, delivers a dynamic and engaging user experience that is unmatched in other resources. State Stats features data from more than 80 different government and nongovernment sources and is backed by a rich collection of more than 2,000 current and historical data series on popular topics of research interest.

SAGE edge for Students provides a personalized approach to help students accomplish their coursework goals in an easy-to-use learning environment.

- Mobile-friendly **eFlashcards** strengthen understanding of key terms and concepts.
- Mobile-friendly practice **quizzes** allow for independent student self-assessment of mastery of course material.
- A customized online **action plan** includes tips and feedback on progress through the course and materials, which allows students to individualize their learning experience.
- **Chapter summaries** with **learning objectives** reinforce the most important material.
- Carefully selected chapter-by-chapter **video** and **multimedia content** enhances classroom-based explorations of key topics.
- **SAGE State Stats guide** provides information on how to use the SAGE State Stats database for exercises in the book and on the student study site.

SAGE edge for Instructors supports teaching by making it easy to integrate quality content and create a rich learning environment for students.

- **Test banks** provide a diverse range of pre-written options as well as the ability to edit any question and/or insert personalized questions to effectively assess students' progress and understanding.
- Editable, chapter-specific **PowerPoint®
slides** offer complete flexibility for creating a multimedia presentation for the course.
- **Video** and **multimedia content** that appeal to students with different learning styles.
- **Instructor manual** summarizes key concepts by chapter to ease preparation for lectures and class discussions.
- Chapter-specific **discussion questions** help launch classroom interaction by prompting students to engage with the material and reinforcing important content.
- A set of all the **graphics from the text**, including all the maps, tables, and figures, is available in PowerPoint, PDF, and JPEG formats for class presentations.
- A **transition guide** provides a chapter-by-chapter outline of key changes to the fifth edition.
- **SAGE State Stats guide** provides information on how to use the SAGE State Stats database for exercises in the book and on the student study site.
- A **common course cartridge** includes all the instructor resources and assessment material from the student study site, making it easy for instructors to upload and use these materials in learning management systems such as Blackboard™, Angel®, Moodle™, Canvas, and Desire2Learn™.

In addition, students and instructors alike will find *Governing* magazine's website especially useful for further research and in-class discussion. To help them bring the latest word from the states and localities into their classrooms, adopters may receive a free semester-long subscription to *Governing* magazine.

Acknowledgments

A lot of effort and dedication go into the making of a textbook such as this, only a fraction of which is contributed by those whose names end up on the cover. Allie Curttright and Taylor Thomsen, students at the University of Nebraska–Lincoln, deserve special recognition for their important contributions as research assistants, as do Aine O'Connor of Washington University and Steven Michael Sylvester of the University of Kansas. In addition, we thank Melissa Feinberg, the original author of the chapter on courts, for revising that chapter, as well as John Buntin for his update of the crime chapter.

To Nancy Matuszak, Raquel Christie, Charisse Kiino, Laura Barrett, and Meg Granger—the editorial team at CQ Press and SAGE responsible for much of what happened from game plan to actualization—a single word: Thanks! The word is miserly compensation for their work, effort, and dedication, and in no way makes up for all the trouble we caused. Nonetheless, our thanks are most sincerely meant (again). We heartily thank our many reviewers, past and present, for their careful and detailed assistance with reading and commenting on the manuscript:

Sharon Alter, *William Rainey Harper Community College*

Jeff Ashley, *Eastern Illinois University*

Jenna Bednar, *University of Michigan*

Neil Berch, *West Virginia University*

Nathaniel Birkhead, *Kansas State University*

John Bohte, *University of Wisconsin–Milwaukee*

Shannon Bow O'Brien, *University of Texas–Austin*

Jaclyn Bunch, *University of South Alabama*

Adam Butz, *Marshall University*

William Cassie, *Appalachian State University*

Jennifer Clark, *University of Houston*

Douglas Clouatre, *Mid Plains Community College*

Gary Crawley, *Ball State University*

Warren Dixon, *Texas A&M University*

Nelson Dometrius, *Texas Tech University*

Jaime Dominguez, *DePaul University*

Deborah Dougherty, *Illinois Central College–Peoria*

Nicholas Easton, *Clark University*

Craig Emmert, *University of Texas–Permian Basin*

David H. Folz, *University of Tennessee–Chattanooga*

Patricia Freeland, *University of Knoxville*

Michael E. Greenberg, *Shippensburg University*

Donald Haider-Markel, *University of Kansas*

George Hale, *Kutztown University*

William Hall, *Bradley University*

Susan Hansen, *University of Pittsburgh*

Dana Michael Harsell, *University of North Dakota*

Avra Johnson, *Minnesota State University–Mankato*

Lisa Langenbach, *Middle Tennessee State University*

William Lester, *Jacksonville State University*

Angela Lewis, *University of Birmingham*

Daniel J. Mallinson, *Pennsylvania State University*

Madhavi McCall, *San Diego State University*

Bryan McQuide, *University of Idaho*

Gary Moncrief, *Boise State University*

Scott Moore, *Colorado State University*

Angela Narasimhan, *Keuka College*

Lawrence Overlan, *Bentley College*

David Peterson, *Iowa State University*

Lori Riverstone-Newe, *Illinois State University*

James Sheffield, *University of Oklahoma–Norman*

Kelly Sills, *Washington State University–Vancouver*

Lee Silvi, *Lakeland Community College*

Zachary Smith, *Northern Arizona University*

Kendra Stewart, *Eastern Kentucky University*

Sharece Thrower, *University of Pittsburgh*

Charles Turner, *California State University–Chico*

Kenn Vance, *John Jay College of Criminal Justice–CUNY*

John Woodcock, *Central Connecticut State University*

Heather Yates, *Illinois College*

Stephen Yoder, *Towson University*

We hope and expect that each of them will be able to find traces of their numerous helpful suggestions throughout this final product.

Finally, in general, we express our appreciation to those political scientists and journalists who pay attention not only to Washington, D.C., but also to what is happening throughout the rest of the country.

About the Authors

Kevin B. Smith is professor of political science at the University of Nebraska–Lincoln. He is the author or coauthor of ten books on politics and policy, as well as numerous scholarly articles on state politics and policy. He is also the longtime editor of CQ Press's annual *State and Local Government* reader as well as the former former associate editor of *State Politics & Policy Quarterly*. Prior to becoming an academic, he covered state and local politics as a newspaper reporter.

Alan Greenblatt, a reporter at *Governing*, has been writing about politics and government in Washington, D.C., and the states for more than two decades. As a reporter for *Congressional Quarterly*, he won the National Press Club's Sandy Hume award for political journalism. At *Governing* magazine, he has covered many issues of concern to state and local governments, such as budgets, taxes, and higher education. Along the way, he has written about politics and culture for numerous other outlets, including NPR, the *New York Times* and the *Washington Post*.

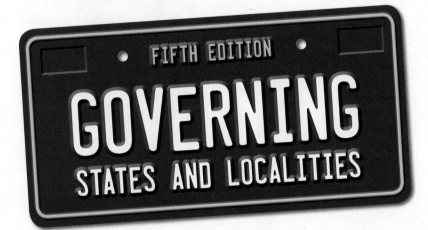

Is government going to the dogs? State and local governments raise revenue in many different ways, including taxing varying levels of income, sales, and property. They can tax virtually anything, including dogs. In some places man's best friend is not only a family pet but also a source of money for government.

Introduction to State and Local Government

THEY TAX DOGS IN WEST VIRGINIA, DON'T THEY?

- What are the advantages and disadvantages of federalism?
- What is the comparative method, and why is it a useful way to talk about state and local governments?
- What role do state and local politics play in determining how much certain services—such as a college education—cost?

M ost college students are much more interested in job prospects than politics—but not Jeramey Anderson. In fall 2013 he was equally interested in both. He was sweating a job application, and his chances for success depended not just on his qualifications and a lot of hard work but also on politics. The Tulane University senior was running for election, and his prospective bosses—the voters of District 110 of the Mississippi House of Representatives—were perusing his résumé carefully. He got the job. On his 22nd birthday, he was sworn in as Mississippi's youngest state lawmaker.

After reading this chapter, you will be able to

- identify the ways state and local governments can affect daily life,
- discuss how the comparative method can help explain differences between states,
- describe the importance of state and local government within the wider context of American government,
- identify the factors that influence how states and localities exercise their independent decision-making authority, and
- summarize how this book will foster your knowledge of the roles and importance of state and local governments.

Anderson, needless to say, is not your typical state legislator. Most state legislators are middle-aged and white (see Chapter 7). Anderson is African American and, at least by the demographic standards of state legislatures, a whippersnapper. Most state legislators don't have to worry about balancing college homework with lawmaking. (You can learn more about Anderson on his homepage, www.jerameyanderson.com.) More important for our purposes, Anderson is also a very unusual college student. He is really into state and local politics; most college students are not. Most college students are not that into politics period. Consider the evidence: In the 2012 presidential election, about 45 percent of 18- to 29-year-olds—the age bracket most college students fall into—actually cast a ballot. That was a decline of 6 percentage points from 2008. In comparison, the over-30 crowd had a 66 percent turnout. It's not just voting. According to one survey of college freshman, only about a third think it's worth bothering to keep up with politics. And even that figure has an alarming gender split—40 percent of male freshman think it's important to keep up with politics, while barely 30 percent of female freshman share that interest in politics (note that Anderson is a typical legislator in at least one way: he is a male). Only a quarter of college freshman discuss politics, and only a fifth attach much importance to influencing society through the political system.[1]

These sorts of numbers present a big potential challenge for a textbook such as this. Sure, we can expect some of our readers to come with an interest and curiosity about state and local politics. The

Jeramey Andersons of the world almost certainly will find their way into classes on this topic. To you all, we say welcome and enjoy the ride—there is a lot for you to enjoy and soak up in what follows. What about the rest of you, though—why should you care? Why should you have an interest in politics? More specifically, why should you give a hoot about politics and government at the state and local level? Fair question. The first goal of this textbook is to answer it. Everyone, and we mean *everyone*, should be interested in state and local politics. Here's why.

The Impact of State and Local Politics on Daily Life

Regardless of who you are, what you do, or what you want to do, if you reside in the United States, state and local governments play a large role in your life. Regardless of what you are interested in—graduating, starting a career, beginning a family, or just good old-fashioned sex, drugs, and rock 'n' roll—state and local governments shape how, whether, and to what extent you are able to pursue those interests. To make things immediately relevant, let's consider your college education. The vast majority of college students in the United States—about 70 percent—attend public institutions of higher education.[2] Public colleges and universities are created and supported by state governments. For many readers of this book, the opportunity to get a college education is possible only because each state government created a system of higher education. For example, California has three major higher education systems: the University of California, the California State University, and the California Community Colleges system. State governments require that taxpayers subsidize the operation of these education systems; in other words, the systems were designed not just to provide educational opportunities but also to make those opportunities broadly accessible, with tuition covering only a portion of the actual costs of a student's education.

Much of the rest comes from the taxpayers' pockets via the state government. When that state subsidy falls, college students inevitably end up paying more in tuition. If you wonder why your tuition bill keeps going up, wonder no more. It is largely because state governments have been financially battered by a slow recovery from the Great Recession of 2008 to 2009. One of the budgetary consequences is that these governments have less money to spend on higher education. What that means is that tuition has to make up a larger portion of university revenues. As recently as the past decade or two, state appropriations covered 30 to 50 percent of the costs of getting a college degree at public institutions. In 2011 to 2012, that proportion was down to less than 20 percent.[3]

State support for some public universities has fallen so low that they have effectively been privatized. For example, the University of Colorado at Boulder and the University of Michigan at Ann Arbor now get only 6 or 7 percent of their revenues from their respective states. Yet at the same time that state appropriations are footing a smaller and smaller fraction of higher education's costs, demand for a college education has skyrocketed. Something has to give in such a situation, and it has: Tuition has gone up, often way up. The impact of state budgetary decisions, though, does not affect just your tuition bill; it might be shaping the entire context of your educational experience. For example, in the past few years at the University of North Carolina, budget challenges have not just upped tuition; class sizes have expanded, 556 class sections have been whacked, salaries have been frozen, admissions to some programs have been reduced, and the university is finding it harder to compete with more well-heeled (especially private) universities for top faculty. If you are enrolled at a public college or university, it is a good bet that you can relate to this sort of thing. As painful as they are, eye-watering tuition increases cannot by themselves make up for shortfalls in state appropriations; so colleges are getting increasingly creative in figuring out how to tap into new revenue streams to keep their operations going. The University of Washington has increased admissions of foreign students who pay full sticker price—about half its enrollment is now from out of state and paying triple the tuition rates paid by state residents. In effect, foreign students rather than state taxpayers are being asked to subsidize a state university. Perhaps the most radical approach to solving higher education's revenue problem has been given serious consideration at the University of California, Riverside: ditching tuition altogether and letting the university take a 5 percent share of students' salaries after they graduate.[4] Over the long term, students will likely end up paying a lot more, but in the short term the idea of no tuition bills seems pretty attractive.

True, the situation is slightly different if you go to a private university, but do not for a minute think you are not affected by state politics. For example, most students at private universities receive some sort of financial aid, and a goodly chunk of this comes from state and local taxpayers. In fact, undergraduates at private colleges receive on average more than $2,500 in state grants or other financial aid from state or local government. Not including tuition, that amount of financial aid is several hundred dollars more than what the average undergraduate at a public college receives from the state.[5]

State governments do not determine just what you pay for a college education. They may also determine what classes you pay for, whether you want to take those classes or not. Some states have curriculum mandates. You may be taking a course on state and local politics—and buying and reading this book—because your state government decided it was a worthy investment of your time and money. In Texas, for example, a state politics course is not just a good idea; it's the law. According

Unlike most college students, Jeramey Anderson is passionately interested in state politics. He was sworn in as the youngest member of the Mississippi House of Representatives on his twenty-second birthday.

to Section 51.301 of the Texas Education Code, to receive a bachelor's degree from any publicly funded college in the state, a student must successfully complete a course on state politics.

Think that's a lot of regulation, a lot of impact on your day-to-day life? The government's role in shaping your college education is actually pretty small. Compared with the heavy involvement of state and local governments in shaping K–12 education, colleges have free rein. Roughly 90 percent of students in Grades 9–12 attend public high schools.[6] Local units of government operate most of these schools. Private grade schools also are subject to a wide variety of state and local government regulations, from teacher certification and minimum curriculum requirements to basic health and safety standards. Whether you attended public or private school—or were homeschooled—at the end of the day you had no choice in the decision to get a basic grade-school education. Although the minimum requirements vary, every state in the union requires that children receive at least a grade-school education.

State and local governments do not exist simply to regulate large areas of your life, even if it sometimes seems that way. Their primary purpose is to provide services to their respective populations. In providing these services, state and local governments shape the social and economic lives of their citizens. Education is a good example of a public service that extends deep into the daily lives of Americans, but it is far from the only one. The roads you use to get to school are there because state and local authorities built them and maintain them. The electricity that runs your computer comes from a utility grid regulated by state government, local government, or both. State and local governments are responsible for the sewer and water systems that make the bathroom down the hall functional. They make sure that the water you drink is safe and that the burger, sushi, or salad you bought in your student union does not make you sick.[7] State governments determine the violations and punishments that constitute criminal law. Local governments are responsible primarily for law enforcement and fire protection. The services that state and local governments supply are such a part of our lives that in many cases we notice only their absence—when the water does not run, when the road is closed, or when the educational subsidy either declines or disappears.

The Comparative Method in Practice: Yes, They Really Do Tax Dogs in West Virginia

Recognizing the impacts of state and local government may be a reasonable way to spark an interest in the topic, but interest alone does not convey knowledge. A systematic approach to learning about state and local government is necessary to gain a coherent understanding of the many activities, responsibilities, and levels involved. In this book, that systematic approach is the **comparative method**, which uses similarities and differences as the basis for systematic explanation. Any two states or localities that you can think of will differ in a number of ways. For example, they really do tax dogs in West Virginia. The state authorizes each county government to assess a fee for every dog within that county's jurisdiction. This is not the case in, say, Nebraska, where dogs have to be licensed but are not taxed.[8] Another example: Texas has executed hundreds of criminals since the moratorium, or ban, on the death penalty was lifted in the 1970s; other states have executed none.

Or consider the electoral differences among states. In recent elections, Kansans and Nebraskans sent only Republicans to the U.S. House of Representatives (in 2014, all seven House members from these two states were Republicans). The people of Massachusetts sent just Democrats (all nine seats were held by Democrats in 2014). Differences among states and localities do not just involve such oddities as the tax status of the family pet or such big political questions as the balance of power in the House of Representatives. Those of you who do something as ordinary as buying a soda after class may pay more than your peers in other states or cities. Some readers of this book are certainly paying more in tuition and fees than those in other colleges. Why?

The comparative method answers such questions by systematically looking for **variance**, or differences, between comparable units of analysis. For our purposes, states are one comparable unit of analysis. Local governments—governments below the state level, such as county boards of commissioners and city councils—are another. Governments at each of these levels, state or local, have basic similarities that make meaningful comparisons possible. One way to think of this is

> Governments at each of these levels, state or local, have basic similarities that make meaningful comparisons possible. One way to think of this is that the comparative method is based on the idea that you can learn more about apples by comparing them with other apples than you can by comparing them with oranges or bananas.

that the comparative method is based on the idea that you can learn more about apples by comparing them with other apples than you can by comparing them with oranges or bananas.

For example, governmentally speaking, all 50 states have a lot in common. Their governmental structures are roughly the same. All have a basic division of powers among the executive, legislative, and judicial branches of government. All have to operate within the broad confines of the single set of rules that is the U.S. Constitution. There's a bit more variety below the state level, with many different kinds and levels of local government (counties, municipalities, townships, and so forth), but broadly speaking all these governments share a basic set of responsibilities and all have to operate within the rules set down within their respective state constitutions. These similarities among states and among local governments make meaningful comparisons possible. Paradoxically, what makes such comparisons meaningful are not the similarities but the differences. This is because even though states share similar political structures and follow the same overall set of rules, they make very different choices. These differences have consequences. Take, for example, college tuition and fees. As noted earlier, there is a direct relationship between the size of a state government's contribution to higher education and a student's average tuition bill. Underlying this relationship is a set of differences that explains why

Comparative method
A learning approach based on studying the differences and similarities among similar units of analysis (such as states)

Variance
The difference between units of analysis on a particular measure

North Dakota is the country's fastest-growing state, with a 7.6 percent population increase from April 1, 2010, to July 1, 2013. The next highest population increase in that time period was in Texas, with an increase of 5.2 percent.

your tuition bill is high (or low) compared with tuition charged by colleges in other states. Simply put, your tuition bill is comparatively higher (or lower) depending on the size of a state government's subsidy to higher education; this is a lesson hundreds of thousands of students have become all too painfully aware of in recent years. These sorts of meaningful differences extend far beyond how much you're paying for your college education. A similar difference explains why some of you will pay more for a soda after class than others will. The sales tax on a can of soda ranges from 0 to 8 percent, depending on the city and state, hence the different prices in different locales.[9] These examples demonstrate the essence of the comparative method—from your tuition bills to the price of soda, differences among political jurisdictions make a difference in the daily lives of citizens.

Such differences can lend themselves to very sophisticated and very useful statistical analyses. For example, exactly how much is a tuition bill influenced by state support of public higher education? A professional policy analyst can use data on state higher education funding and tuition rates at state universities and colleges to provide a precise estimate of the relationship between the contributions from state government and your tuition bill. On average, for every appropriation of $1,000 per student by state government, tuition and fees at public 4-year universities fall by a little more than $200.[10] Of course, the reverse is also true. For every reduction of $1,000 per student in state aid, tuition goes up by an average of $200.

This basic approach of looking for differences that make a difference can be used to answer a broad range of "why" questions. For example, we know that how much a state gives to higher education helps determine how much you pay in tuition.

So why do some states provide more support to higher education than others do? This is a question about one difference (variation in how much state governments spend on higher education) that can be answered by looking at other differences. What might these differences be? Well, they could stem from partisan politics in a state's legislature, a state's traditions and history, or a state's relative wealth, among many other possibilities. As a starting point for using the comparative approach to analyze such questions, consider the following basic differences among states and among localities.

Sociodemographics

The populations of states and localities vary enormously in size, age, and ethnicity. The particular mix of these characteristics, or **sociodemographics**, in a specific state or community has a profound impact on the state or community's politics. California is the most populous state in the nation, with more than 38 million residents. This is a racially and ethnically diverse population, with only 39.4 percent non-Hispanic whites and many first-generation and second-generation immigrants. Roughly 15.3 percent of Californians live in poverty. Compare this with New Hampshire, which has about 1.3 million residents, 91.9 percent of whom are non-Hispanic whites and only about 8.4 percent of whom live below the poverty line.[11] These population characteristics present different challenges to the governments in these two states. Differences in populations are likely to promote different attitudes about and policies on welfare, affirmative action, bilingual education programs, and even the role and responsibilities of government in general.

And it gets better. All these population characteristics are dynamic; that is, they change. From 2000 to 2010, the population of McKinney, Texas, grew by more than 200 percent.[12] During roughly the same time period, the population of Parkersburg, West Virginia, shrank by more than 21 percent. Such population expansions and contractions create very different problems and policy priorities for local governments—the struggle to accommodate new growth in a fast-developing area versus the

Sociodemographics
The characteristics of a population, including size, age, and ethnicity

challenge of maintaining even basic services in a rural county in which there are ever fewer taxpayers to tax. Or consider the population of the entire state of Florida, which was still growing in 2010, but at the slowest annual rate seen in three decades. That gearing down of population growth is expected to influence everything from housing starts to job creation to state and local tax collections.[13]

How might sociodemographics be related to, say, your tuition bill? Consider the age distribution of a state's population, from young to old. There is less demand for college education among those older than 65 than there is among those in the traditional undergraduate demographic of 18 to 24. Given this, states with higher percentages of their populations in older age groups face a different set of education policy pressures than those with higher concentrations in younger groups. States with large aging populations are likely to face less demand for higher education spending and more demand for public programs that address the needs of the elderly, such as access to health care. Why do some states provide more support to higher education than others? At least a partial answer to this question is that different sociodemographics create different demands for higher education.

Study Map 1-1 for a moment. Believe it or not, you are actually looking at the United States. The reason the states look so strange is that this is a special kind of map called a cartogram. Instead of using actual geographical space to determine the size of a particular area represented in the map—the number of square miles in each state, for instance—cartograms use other variables to determine how size is represented. This cartogram

MAP 1-1

Population by State, 2010

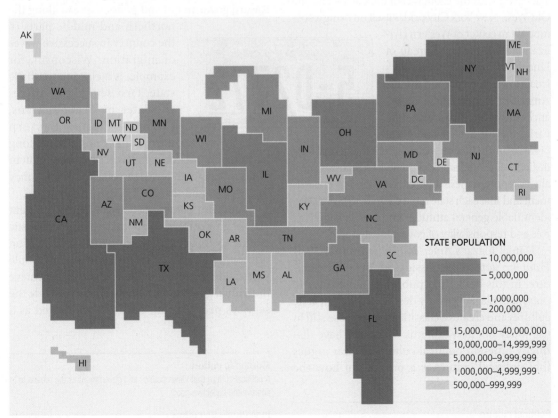

Source: U.S. Department of Commerce, *Statistical Abstract of the United States, 2012* (Washington, DC: U.S. Census Bureau, 2012), "Table 16. Resident Population by Age and State: 2010," 21, www.census.gov/prod/2011pubs/12statab/pop.pdf.

depicts the size of each state's population, another useful way to compare states. Notice that some states that are geographically pretty big, such as New Mexico at 122,000 square miles, are very small on this map because they have small populations. Other states that are geographically quite small, such as Connecticut (with only 5,000 square miles), look much bigger on this map because they have large populations. Some states, such as Virginia, don't look that different in size at all from their appearance on a traditional map.

Culture and History

States and localities have distinct "personalities" that are apparent in everything from the "bloody bucket" shoulder patch worn by the Pennsylvania National Guard to the drawl that distinguishes the speech of West Texas natives. Some states have been part of the Union for more than 200 years and still project an Old World connection to Europe. Hawaii and Alaska became states within living memory and are more associated with the exoticism of the Pacific and the Old West. New York City prides itself on being a cosmopolitan center of Western civilization. The visitor's bureau of Lincoln, Nebraska, touts the city's small-town ambience and Middle American values. These differences are more than interesting variations in accent and local points of pride; they are visible symbols that represent distinct values and attitudes. Political scientists generally accept that these differences extend to government and that each state has a distinct **political culture**, identifiable general attitudes and beliefs about the role and responsibility of government.

Daniel Elazar's *American Federalism: A View From the States* is the classic study of political culture. In this book, first published more than 40 years ago, Elazar not only describes different state cultures and creates a classification of those still in use today but also explains why states have distinctly different political cultures. Elazar argues that political culture is a product of how the United States was settled. He says that people's religious and ethnic backgrounds played the dominant role in establishing political cultures. On this basis, there were three distinct types of settlers who fanned out across the United States in more or less straight lines from the East Coast to the West Coast. These distinct migration patterns created three different types of state political cultures: moralistic, individualistic, and traditionalistic.[14]

States with **moralistic cultures** are those in which politics is the means used to achieve a good and just society. Such states tend to be clustered in the northern parts of the country (New England, the upper Midwest, and the Pacific Northwest). Elazar argues that the Puritans who originally settled the Northeast came to the New World seeking religious freedom. Their political culture reflected a desire to use politics to construct the best possible society. This notion, that government and politics represent the means to the greater good, creates a society that values involvement in politics and views government as a positive force for addressing social problems. This general orientation toward government and politics spread along the northern and middle parts of the country in successive waves of migration. Wisconsin, for example, is a classic moralistic state. First settled by Yankees and later by Scandinavians, Germans, and Eastern Europeans, the state has long had a reputation for high levels of participation in politics (e.g., high levels of voter turnout), policy innovation, and scandal-free government.

States with **individualistic cultures** have a different view of government and politics. In individualistic cultures, people view government as an extension of the marketplace, something in which people participate for individual reasons and to achieve individual goals. Government should provide the services people want, but it is not viewed as a

---

Political culture
The attitudes and beliefs broadly shared in a polity about the role and responsibility of government

Moralistic culture
A political culture that views politics and government as the means to achieve the collective good

Individualistic culture
A political culture that views politics and government as just another way to achieve individual goals

Demographics and culture give each state and locality a unique "personality." Here teenagers celebrate the Chinese New Year by blowing confetti into the air in New York City's Chinatown.

© Oote Boe 3/Alamy

vehicle to create a "good society" or intervene in private activities. Politics in individualistic states is viewed the same as any other business. Officeholders expect to be paid like professionals, and political parties are, in essence, corporations that compete to provide goods and services to people. Unlike those in moralistic states, as long as the roads are paved and the trains run on time, folks in individualistic states tend to tolerate more corruption in government.

Why? In individualistic states, "both politicians and citizens look upon political activity as a specialized one," Elazar writes, "and with no place for amateurs to play an active role."[15] The roots of this view of government, according to Elazar, come from the English, Scottish, Irish, and Germans who initially settled in states such as Maryland, New Jersey, and Pennsylvania. They came to the United States in search of individual opportunity, not to construct some idealized vision of the good society. This "every man for himself" attitude was reflected in politics, and the individualistic culture was carried by subsequent waves of migration into places such as Illinois and Missouri.

New Jersey is a good example of an individualistic state. The state, as political scientist Maureen Moakley puts it, "has always been more of a polyglot than a melting pot."[16] Originally settled by waves of poor and uneducated immigrants in pursuit of the American Dream, in more recent times it has become home to more than a million foreign-born residents and large racial and ethnic minority populations. The result is a fragmented political culture in which many residents feel more connected to their local communities than to the state. Not surprisingly given all this, New Jersey has a long tradition of strong, independent local government, with laws that give the state's nearly 600 general-purpose local governments more power than localities in other states.

In a **traditionalistic culture**, politics is the province of elites, something that average citizens should not concern themselves with. Traditionalistic states are, as their name suggests, fundamentally conservative, in the sense that they are concerned with preserving a well-established society. Like moralistic states, traditionalistic states believe that government serves a positive role. But there is one big difference—traditionalistic states believe the larger purpose of government is to maintain the existing social order. Those at the top of the social structure are expected to play a dominant role in politics, and power is concentrated in the hands of these elites. Traditionalistic states tend to be rural states (at least historically) in which agriculture, rather than a broader mix of competing commercial activities, is the main economic driver.

Traditionalistic culture
A political culture that views politics and government as the means of maintaining the existing social order

A Difference That Makes A Difference

Is It Better to Be a Woman in Vermont or a Gal in Mississippi?

According to the Institute for Women's Policy Research (IWPR), it is better to be a woman in Vermont than a gal in Mississippi.

Why? Well, in an analysis of the status of women in the states, the IWPR had several reasons for ranking Vermont as the best state for women and Mississippi as the worst. For example, in Vermont women had greater economic autonomy and enjoyed greater reproductive rights than did women in Mississippi. This is only a partial answer to the question, however. To learn the rest of it, we must ask: *Why* would women have greater economic autonomy and more reproductive rights in Vermont than in Mississippi?

The comparative approach to answering this question involves looking for other differences between Vermont and Mississippi—differences that might explain the variance in the status of women. Some candidates for those explanatory differences are presented in Table 1-1. This table shows the top five and the bottom five states in the IWPR rankings, the dominant political culture in each state, and the percentage of state legislators in each state who were women in 2014. Notice any patterns?

You may have caught that all the top five states have either moralistic or individualistic cultures, and all the bottom five states have traditionalistic cultures. Therefore, political culture might explain some of the difference in women's status. States in which the dominant political values stress the importance of everyone getting involved might offer more opportunities for women. So might states in which such values emphasize hard work as the predominant basis for getting ahead in life. States in which the dominant political values stress leaving the important decisions to established elites might offer fewer opportunities for women because, traditionally, elites have been male.

Also, take a look at the proportions of women in the state legislatures. On average, about one third of state legislators in the top five states are women. In the bottom five states, that average is halved—only about 16 percent of state legislators are women. This is a difference that can have considerable impact. A number of studies show that women legislators tend to support

TABLE 1-1

Politics and the Status of Women in the States: Some Variables

Five Best States for Women	Dominant Political Culture	Percentage of State Legislators Who Are Women
1. Vermont	Moralistic	40.6
2. Connecticut	Individualistic	28.3
3. Minnesota	Moralistic	33.8
4. Washington	Moralistic	32.7
5. Oregon	Moralistic	30.0
Five Worst States for Women	Dominant Political Culture	Percentage of State Legislators Who Are Women
46. Oklahoma	Traditionalistic	13.4
47. Arkansas	Traditionalistic	17.0
48. Kentucky	Traditionalistic	18.1
49. South Carolina	Traditionalistic	12.9
50. Mississippi	Traditionalistic	17.2

Sources: Amy Caiazza, Misha Werschkul, Erica Williams, and April Shaw, *The Status of Women in the States* (Washington, DC: IWPR, October 2004), http://www.iwpr.org/publications/pubs/the-status-of-women-in-the-states; Daniel J. Elazar, *American Federalism: A View From the States* (New York: Crowell, 1966); National Conference of State Legislatures, "Women in State Legislatures: 2014 Legislative Session," April 1, 2014, http://www.ncsl.org/legislators-staff/legislators/womens-legislative-network/women-in-state-legislatures-for-2014.aspx.

more progressive policies, are more likely to pay attention to women's issues, and are more likely to push these issues into law.[a]

Thus, states that have more women in their legislatures are more likely to respond to issues such as reproductive rights, violence against women, child-support policies, and family-leave benefits. All these factors contribute to the IWPR's calculations. Why is Vermont a better state for women than Mississippi? A comparative answer to that question is that Vermont has a political culture that is more likely to encourage and support political participation by women and also has a greater female presence in its state legislature.

---

[a] Michele Swers, "Understanding the Policy Impact of Electing Women: Evidence From Research on Congress and State Legislatures," *PS: Political Science & Politics* 34, no. 2 (2001): 217–220.

Traditionalistic cultures tend to be concentrated in the Deep South, in states such as Georgia, Mississippi, and South Carolina. In these states, politics is significantly shaped by tradition and history. Like the settlers of individualistic states, those who settled the South sought personal opportunity. The preindustrial, agrarian economy of the South, however, led to a culture that was little more than a variation of the feudal order of the European Middle Ages. As far back as the 1830s, French aristocrat and writer Alexis de Tocqueville, writing about the United States, noted that "as one goes farther south . . . the population does not exercise such a direct influence on affairs. . . . The power of the elected officials is comparatively greater and that of the voter less."[17]

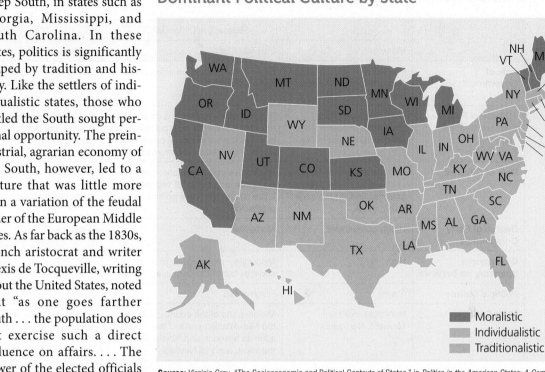

MAP 1-2

Dominant Political Culture by State

Source: Virginia Gray, "The Socioeconomic and Political Contexts of States," in *Politics in the American States: A Comparative Analysis,* 10th ed., ed. Virginia Gray and Russell Hanson (Washington, DC: CQ Press, 2013), 22.

Few states today can be considered "pure" examples of any of these cultures. In other words, most states have elements of two of the cultures or all three. For example, a number of traditionalistic states, such as Florida and Georgia, have seen huge influxes of people from northern states, people who often are not from traditionalistic cultures. The Deep South is also considerably more urban than it used to be. Such changes tend to add elements of the moralistic and individualistic cultures into the traditionalistic mix.

Even with such changes, however, for most states, one of Elazar's three political cultures is likely to be dominant, as Map 1-2 shows. Numerous studies have found that the dominant political culture shapes politics and policy in important ways. Policy change and innovation, for example, are more likely in moralistic states. Individualistic states are more likely to offer businesses tax breaks. Traditionalistic states tend to commit less public money to areas such as education.[18] Faced with similar problems, therefore, the Texas and Wisconsin state legislatures may propose radically different policy responses. These differences are at least partially products of the political cultures that still distinguish each state. In other words, culture and history matter.

These cultural differences certainly are apparent when it comes to supporting higher education. Moralistic states commit considerably more resources to higher education than do individualistic and traditionalistic states. They spend about 13 percent more per capita on colleges and universities than do states with the other two cultures. Because moralistic states are those in which attitudes support higher levels of commitment to the public sector, these spending differences make sense in cultural terms. Why do some states provide more support to higher education than others do? Apparently, another part of the answer is that some political cultures see higher education in more communal than individual terms. See Table 1-2 for a summary of the three political cultures.

TABLE 1-2

Political Cultures at a Glance

	Elazar Classification		
	Moralistic	**Individualistic**	**Traditionalistic**
Role of Government	Government should act to promote the public interest and policy innovation.	Government should be utilitarian, a service provider.	Government should help preserve the status quo.
Attitude of Public Representatives	Politicians can effect change; public service is worthwhile and an honor.	Businesslike—politics is a career like any other, and individual politicians are oriented toward personal power. High levels of corruption are more common.	Politicians can effect change, but politics is the province of the elites.
Role of Citizens	Citizens actively participate in voting and other political activities; individuals seek public office.	The state exists to advance the economic and personal self-interest of citizens; citizens leave politics to the professionals.	Ordinary citizens are not expected to be politically involved.
Degree of Party Competition	Highly competitive	Moderate	Weak
Government Spending on Services	High	Moderate—money goes to basic services but not to perceived "extras."	Low
Political Culture	Strong	Fragmented	Strong
Most Common in . . .	Northeast, northern Midwest, Northwest	Middle parts of the country, such as the Mid-Atlantic; parts of the Midwest, such as Missouri and Illinois; parts of the West, such as Nevada	Southern states, rural areas

Source: Adapted from Daniel J. Elazar, *American Federalism: A View from the States,* 2nd ed. (New York: Crowell, 1972).

Economy

The relative size and health of a state's economy has a huge impact on its capacity to govern and provide public services. The per capita gross domestic product—the state equivalent of the gross national product—varies from about $28,000 in Mississippi to $62,000 in Delaware[19] (see Map 1-3). This means government in Delaware has the ability to tap a greater amount of resources than can government in Mississippi. The difference in wealth, in effect, means that if Delaware and Mississippi were to implement identical and equivalent public services, Mississippi would have a considerably higher tax rate. This is because Mississippi would have to take a greater proportion of its smaller amount of resources, compared with Delaware. These sorts of differences also are visible at the local level. Wealthy suburbs can enjoy lower tax rates and still spend more on public services than can economically struggling urban or rural communities.

Regional economic differences do not determine just tax burdens and the level of public services; they also determine the relative priorities of particular policy and regulatory issues. Fishing, for example, is a sizable industry in coastal states in the Northeast and Northwest. States such as Maine and Washington have numerous laws, regulations, and enforcement responsibilities tied to the catching, processing, and transporting of fish. Regulating the economic exploitation of marine life occupies very little government attention and resources in places such as Kansas and Nevada, although agriculture in the former and gambling in the latter create just as many policy challenges and demands for government action.

Regardless of the basis of a state's economy, greater wealth does not always translate into more support for public programs. States with above-average incomes actually tend to spend *less* per capita on higher education. Why would less-wealthy states concentrate more of their

MAP 1-3

Economy by State, 2012

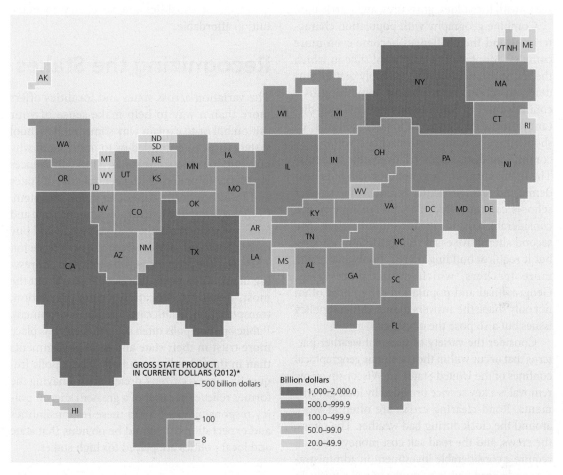

GROSS STATE PRODUCT
IN CURRENT DOLLARS (2012)*
— 500 billion dollars

— 100

— 8

Billion dollars
1,000–2,000.0
500.0–999.9
100.0–499.9
50.0–99.0
20.0–49.9

The relative size of state economies is measured in terms of gross state product. Notice how big states with small economies (Montana and Alaska) compare with small states with big economies (New Jersey and Massachusetts).

Source: U.S. Bureau of Economic Analysis, "Gross Domestic Product by State (millions of current dollars)—All Industry Total, 2012," http://bea.gov/iTable/iTable .cfm?reqid=99&step=1.

resources on higher education? There are a number of possible explanations. Education is a critical component of a postindustrial economy; so states that are less well-off may direct more of their resources into education in hopes of building a better economic future. Citizens in wealthy states simply may be better able to afford higher tuition costs. Whatever the explanation, this example suggests another advantage of employing the comparative method—it shows that the obvious assumptions are not always the correct ones.

Geography and Topography

There is wild variation in the physical environments in which state and local governments operate. Hawaii is a lush tropical island chain in the middle of the Pacific Ocean, Nevada encompasses a large desert, Michigan is mostly heavily forested, and Colorado is split by the Rocky Mountains. Such geographical and topographical variation presents different challenges to government. State and local authorities in California devote considerable time and resources to preparing for earthquakes. Their counterparts in Texas spend comparatively little time thinking about earthquakes, but they do concern themselves with tornadoes, grass fires, and hurricanes.

Combine geography with population characteristics and the challenges become even more complex. Montana is a large rural state in which the transportation logistics—simply getting students to school—can present something of a conundrum. Is it better to bus students long distances to large, centrally located schools, or should there be many smaller schools within easy commuting distance for relatively few students? The first is cheaper. Larger schools can offer academic and extracurricular activities that smaller schools cannot afford. But the busing exacts a considerable cost on students and families. The second alternative eases transportation burdens, but it requires building more schools and hiring more teachers, which means more taxes. Geographical and population differences often not only shape the answers to such difficult policy issues but also pose the questions.

Consider the variety of seasonal weather patterns that occur within the enormous geographical confines of the United States. In Wisconsin, snow removal is a key service provided by local governments. Road-clearing crews are often at work around the clock during bad weather. The plows, the crews, and the road salt cost money. They all require a considerable investment in administration and coordination to do the job effectively. In Florida, snow removal is low on local governments' lists of priorities, for good reason—it rarely snows in the Sunshine State. On the other hand, state and local authorities in Florida do need to prepare for the occasional hurricane. Hurricanes are less predictable and less common than snow in Wisconsin, and it takes only one to create serious demands on the resources of local authorities.

And, yes, even basic geography affects your tuition bill, especially when combined with some of the other characteristics discussed here. Many large public colleges and universities are located in urban centers because central geographical locations serve more people more efficiently. Delivering higher education in rural areas is a more expensive proposition simply because there are fewer people in the service area. States with below-average population densities tend to be larger and more sparsely populated. They also tend to spend more on higher education. Larger government subsidies are necessary to make tuition affordable.

Recognizing the Stakes

The variation across states and localities offers more than a way to help make sense of your tuition bill or to explain why some public school systems are better funded or to understand why taxes are lower in some states. These differences also serve to underline the central role of states and localities in the American political system. Compared with the federal government, state and local governments employ more people and buy more goods and services from the private sector. They have the primary responsibility for addressing many of the issues that people care about the most, including education, crime prevention, transportation, health care, and the environment. Public opinion polls often show that citizens place more trust in their state and local governments than in the federal government. These polls frequently express citizens' preference for having the former relieve the latter of a greater range of policy responsibilities.[20] With these responsibilities and expectations, it should be obvious that state and local politics are played for high stakes.

> Compared with the federal government, state and local governments employ more people and buy more goods and services from the private sector. They have the primary responsibility for addressing many of the issues that people care about the most, including education, crime prevention, transportation, health care, and the environment.

High stakes, yes, but it is somewhat ironic that state and local governments tend to get less attention in the media, in private conversation, and in curricula and classrooms than does their federal counterpart.[21] Ask most people to think about American government, and chances are they will think first about the president, Congress, Social Security, or some other feature of the national government. Yet most American governments are state or local. Only 535 elected legislators serve in the U.S. Congress. Thousands of legislators are elected at the state level, and tens of thousands more serve in the legislative branches of local government.

In terms of people, state and local governments dwarf the federal government. The combined civilian workforce of the federal government (about 3 million) is less than half the number of people working for a single category of local government—more than 6 million people work for public elementary and secondary schools alone.[22] Roughly 5 million state employees and more than 14 million local government employees punch the time clock every day (see Map 1-4). In terms of dollars, state and local governments combined represent about the same spending force as the federal government. In 2011, state and local government expenditures totaled about $3 trillion.[23]

MAP 1-4

Number of Government Employees by State, 2012

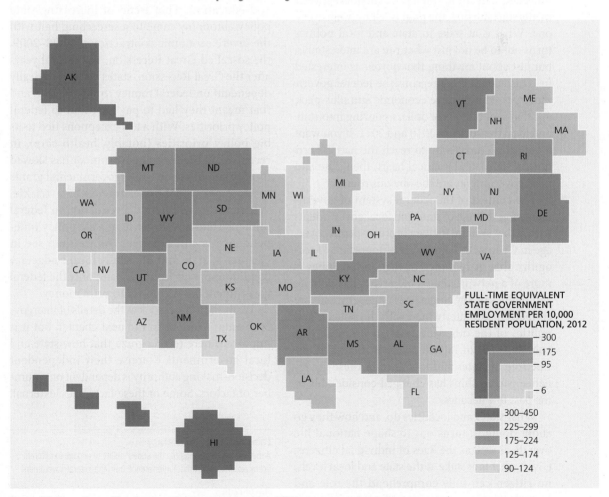

Source: U.S. Census Bureau, "State Government Employment and Payroll Data," 2012, www.census.gov/govs/apes.

The size of state and local government operations is commensurate with these governments' 21st century role in the political system. After spending much of the 20th century being drawn closer into the orbit and influence of the federal government, states and localities spent the century's last two decades, and much of the first decade of the next century, aggressively asserting their independence. This maturing of nonfederal, or subnational, government made its leaders and policies—not to mention its differences—among the most important characteristics of our political system. The Great Recession of 2008–2009 made that importance all too clear. As the economy went south and the budget gaps went north, state and local governments were forced into a painful process of cutting budgets. As pretty much any college student at a publicly supported college or university can attest, when state and local governments start hurting, the pain is felt by, well, everyone. What is at stake in state and local politics turns out to be not just what *you* are interested in but just about anything that *anyone* is interested in. This is one of the reasons the federal government passed a massive economic stimulus package that sent billions of dollars pouring into state and local treasuries in 2010 and 2011. If you want a quick and direct way to reach the nation's economic, social, and political heart, then state and local governments are the obvious routes.

The context of the federal system of government, and the role of state and local governments within that system, is given more in-depth coverage in Chapter 2. For now, it is important to recognize that governance in the United States is more of a network than a hierarchy. The policies and politics of any single level of government are connected and intertwined with the policies and politics of the other levels of government in a complex web of interdependent relationships. The role of states and localities in these governance partnerships has changed considerably in the past few decades.

What states and localities do, and how they go about doing it, turns out to shape national life overall, as well as the lives of individual citizens. Given what is at stake at the state and local levels, no citizen can fully comprehend the role and importance of government without understanding subnational politics.

Laboratories of Democracy: Devolution and the Limits of Government

U.S. Supreme Court justice Louis Brandeis famously described the states as **laboratories of democracy**. This metaphor refers to the ability of states—and, to a lesser extent, localities—to experiment with policy. Successful experiments can be replicated by other states or adopted by the national government. For much of the past 30 years, state–federal relations have been characterized by **devolution**, or the process of taking power and responsibility away from the federal government and giving it to state and local governments. As a result, the states for a time aggressively promoted new ways to solve old problems in such high-profile policy areas as welfare, gun control, and education. That trend of increasing state policy autonomy came to a screeching halt with the severe economic contraction of 2008–2009, the so-called Great Recession. For several years after the Great Recession, states became critically dependent on federal money to stay solvent, and that meant they had to pay attention to federal policy priorities. With a few exceptions tied to its big policy priorities (notably, health care), in recent years the federal government has slowed its program of massive intergovernmental grants to state and local governments to a trickle. Whether this will herald a reduction in federal influence and a resurgence of state policy independence is still not clear. As we shall see in Chapter 4, state and especially local budgetary conditions are far from rosy, and only the federal government has the power to print money.

We'll take a closer look at the details of intergovernmental relations in the next chapter, but it is important here to recognize that how state and local governments exercise their independent decision-making authority is dependent on a number of factors. Some of these factors are external.

Laboratories of democracy
A metaphor that emphasizes the states' ability to engage in different policy experiments without interference from the federal government

Devolution
The process of taking power and responsibility away from the federal government and giving it to state and local governments

It has a local government much like any other major municipality and electoral votes like a state, but it is ultimately ruled by Congress even though it has no representatives with full voting rights in the national legislature. Technically, Washington, D.C., is a federal city, the only political jurisdiction of its kind in the United States.

© Steve Gottlieb/Alamy

The U.S. Constitution, federal laws and regulations, nation-wide recessions, and the like constrain what states and localities can and cannot do. Internal factors, such as the characteristics of a particular state, also play a critical role in setting limits on what the state decides to do.

The big three of these internal factors are wealth, the characteristics of the state's political system, and the relative presence of organized interest groups, those individuals who organize to support policy issues that concern them. Public programs cost money. Wealth sets the limits of possible government action. Simply speaking, wealthier states can afford to do more than poorer states can. For most states, lack of funds is currently the biggest factor limiting independent policy action at the state and local levels. Simply put, many subnational governments do not have the money to launch expensive new policy initiatives. Indeed, in recent years many of these governments have not had the money to keep funding their existing programs and services (higher education, for example) at previous levels. While it is important, however, money is not the only factor that influences policy directions at the subnational level. Political system characteristics are the elements of the political environment that are specific to a state. States in which public opinion is relatively conservative are likely to pursue different policy avenues than are states in which public opinion is more liberal. States in which Republicans dominate the government are likely to opt for different policy choices than are states in which Democrats dominate. States with professional full-time legislatures are more likely to

formulate and pursue sustained policy agendas than are states in which legislators are part-timers who meet only periodically. States in which the government perceives an electoral mandate to reform government are more likely to be innovative than are states in which the government perceives an electoral mandate to retain the status quo.[24] Organized interest group activity helps determine what sorts of policy demands government responds to. Governments in states with powerful teachers unions, for example, experience different education policy pressures than do governments in states where teachers unions are politically weak. These three factors constitute the basic ingredients for policymaking in the states. Specifics vary enormously from state to state, and the potential combinations in this democratic laboratory are virtually infinite.

Localities face more policymaking constraints than states do because they typically are not sovereign governments. This means that, unlike states, local governments get their power from the level of government above them rather than directly from citizens. The states have much greater control over local governments than the federal government has over the states. Yet, even though local governments are much more subordinate to state government than state government is to the federal government, they do not

Local Focus

The Federal City

Riddle me this: It is a city. It is sort of a state. It is ruled by Congress. What is it? It is the District of Columbia, otherwise known as Washington, D.C. It is also the nation's capital—and surely the most unusual local government in the country.

Technically, Washington, D.C., is a federal city. Article I, Section 8, Paragraph 17 of the U.S. Constitution gives Congress the power to rule over an area not to exceed 10 square miles that constitutes the seat of national government; yet it has never been quite clear what that means in terms of governance. Should Congress rule the city directly? Should the citizens of the city be given the right to elect a representative government? If they do this, should the government be subordinate to Congress or should it be counted as equivalent to a state and thus free to make any laws that do not violate the U.S. Constitution?

Throughout the city's history, these questions have been answered very differently. In the early 1800s, the district was a strange collection of cities and counties, each governed by different means. Washington City and Georgetown were municipalities run by a chief executive (a mayor) and a legislature (a council). Depending on the time period, however, the mayors were sometimes appointed by the federal government and sometimes elected. In addition to the two cities, there were also two counties. Maryland laws governed Washington County; Virginia laws governed Alexandria County.

In the 1870s, Washington City, Georgetown, and Washington County were combined into a single governmental unit, a federal territory with a governor appointed by the president and a legislature elected by the territorial residents. This eventually became the District of Columbia, or Washington, D.C. For most of its history, commissioners appointed by the federal government governed the district. It was not until 1974 that the residents of Washington, D.C., gained home rule and the right to elect their own mayor and council.

This mayor–council arrangement, however, is unlike any other municipal government in the United States. The laws passed by the council have to be reviewed and approved by Congress. The laws that govern federal–state relationships treat the district as a state, even though it is not a state and cannot operate like one. The mayor is not considered the head of a federal agency, but he or she is expected to act like one when seeking appropriations from Congress.

This odd hybrid of local, state, and federal governments is reflected in the unique electoral status of Washington, D.C., voters. Voters in the district have a local vote but only half of a federal vote. They can vote for the president but not for a member of Congress. They can vote for a mayor and council, but they have no voting representative in Congress; yet Congress has the power to overturn laws passed by the council. The district now has three electoral votes. Prior to 1963, it had none and D.C. voters could not cast a ballot for president.

All this makes Washington, D.C., the nation's most unusual local government. It is the only municipality that is a creature of the United States rather than of a state constitution, and, as such, it is the only really national city in the country.

Source: Selected material from Council of the District of Columbia, "History of Self-Government in the District of Columbia," 1997, www.dccouncil.washington.dc.us.

simply take orders from the state capital. Many have independent taxing authority and broad discretion to act within their designated policy jurisdictions.

These policy jurisdictions, nevertheless, are frequently subject to formal limits. The authority of school districts, for example, extends only to funding and operating public schools. State government may place limits on districts' tax rates and set everything from minimal employment qualifications to maximum teacher-to-pupil ratios. Even within this range of tighter restrictions, however, local governments retain considerable leeway to act independently. School districts often decide to contract out cafeteria and janitorial services, cities and counties actively seek to foster economic development with tax abatements and loan guarantees, and police commissions experiment with community-based law enforcement. During the past two decades, many of the reforms enthusiastically pursued at all levels of government—reforms from innovative management practices to the outright privatization of public services—have had their origins in local government.[25]

> States and localities are not just safe places to engage in limited experimentation; they are the primary mechanisms connecting citizens to the actions of government.

What all this activity shows is that states and localities are not only the laboratories of democracy but also the engines of the American republic. States and localities are not just safe places to engage in limited experimentation; they are the primary mechanisms connecting citizens to the actions of government. It is for exactly this reason that one of the central federal government responses to the economic crisis of 2008–2009 was to shore up local and state governments financially.

Conclusion

There are good reasons for developing a curiosity about state and local governments. State politics determines everything from how much you pay for college to whether your course in state and local governments is required or elective. Above and beyond understanding the impact of state and local governments on your own life and interests, studying such governments is important because of their critical role in the governance and life of the nation. Subnational, or nonfederal, governments employ more people than the federal government and spend as much money. Their responsibilities include everything from repairing potholes to regulating pot. It is difficult, if not impossible, to understand government in the United States and the rights, obligations, and benefits of citizenship without first understanding state and local governments.

This book fosters such an understanding through the comparative method. This approach involves looking for patterns in the differences among states and localities. Rather than advocating a particular perspective on state and local politics, the comparative method is predicated, or based, on a systematic way of asking and answering questions. Why is my tuition bill so high? Why does Massachusetts send mostly Democrats to the U.S. House of Representatives? Why are those convicted of capital crimes in Texas more likely to be executed than those convicted of comparable crimes in Connecticut? Why are sales taxes high in Alabama? Why is there no state income tax in South Dakota? We can answer each of these questions by comparing states and looking for systematic patterns in their differences. The essence of the comparative method is to use one difference to explain another.

This book's examination of state and local politics is organized into three distinct sections. The first section consists of five chapters designed to set the basic framework, or context, for studying state and local politics. Included here are chapters on federalism, state constitutions, budgets, political participation, and political parties and interest groups. The second section covers the institutions of state and local government: legislatures, executives, courts, and bureaucracy. Although elements of local government are discussed in all these, there are also two chapters in this section devoted solely to local politics and government. The final section covers a series of distinct policy areas: education, crime, health care, and the environment. These chapters not only cover areas of substantive policy interests but also offer concrete examples of how a broad understanding of the context and institutions of state and local governments can be combined with the comparative method to promote a deeper understanding of the politics of states and localities.

The Latest Research

As discussed extensively in this chapter, the comparative method is an important tool used by scholars to understand how state-level differences translate into meaningful political and policy differences. A lot of these differences that make a difference are not static—indeed, some may be changing even as you read this textbook. Recently, some of the most foundational state differences have been the subject of a series of studies that may change our understanding of those differences and their implications.

The "granddaddy" of all differences is political culture, a concept originated by Daniel Elazar that continues to be widely respected for its explanatory power. Yet, however powerful its explanatory capacities, Elazar's classification of state political cultures is not based on intensive statistical analysis; it is much more impressionistic. It is also static—in other words, the basic state classifications of moralistic, traditionalistic, and individualistic have not changed since Elazar defined them nearly half a century ago. In the time that has elapsed since then, large shifts in demographics have taken place as the result of new waves of immigration, population, and other relevant data have become more widely available, and sophisticated statistical analysis techniques have been developed and broadly employed. All this gives state scholars the opportunity to undertake much more fine-grained analyses of regional value systems, how they translate into culture, how that culture might change, and what those changes might mean for state politics and policy.

Related to the renewed interest in studying and tracking cultural changes is a spate of new scholarship that focuses on measuring state-level political orientations and ideology, in effect capturing the political nuances of what makes a "red" state or a "blue" state or even a "happy" state. Several teams of scholars have been developing new measures of state-level policy attitudes and orientations, and these improved measures

of political differences are proving useful for predicting important policy differences.

Below we summarize some of the cutting-edge research on the differences that make a difference.

• •

- **Lieske, Joel.** "The Changing Regional Subcultures of the American States and the Utility of a New Cultural Measure." *Political Research Quarterly* 63 (2010): 538–552.

- **Lieske, Joel.** "American State Cultures: Testing a New Measure and Theory." *Publius: The Journal of Federalism* 42 (2012): 108–133.

Lieske, a political scientist at Cleveland State University, is the scholar most associated with the contemporary study of state political culture. He focuses on what is perhaps the toughest question of culture studies: How can we measure culture? Elazar's classifications are useful but impressionistic, and efforts to quantify those classifications into "yardsticks" to measure degrees of cultural difference often amount to nothing more than putting numbers on Elazar's classifications. Lieske has long argued that regional subcultures may be more expansive than Elazar's threefold classification. In the first study listed above, he uses county-level data on racial origin, ethnic ancestry, religious affiliation, and various indicators of social structure to create a composite statistical measure of political culture. This is a much more sophisticated analysis than that employed by Elazar, and it results in not three primary subcultures but eleven. In Lieske's analysis, for example, moralistic cultures are actually made up of three related but distinct political subcultures—Nordic, Mormon, and Anglo-French, with the labels representing the cultural elements of particular ethnic groups (especially Germans and Scandinavians) and different sects of dissenting Protestantism. In the second study, Lieske puts his new measure to the test, pitting it against Elazar's typology to see which best predicts various indicators of state performance. Lieske's measure does the better job, suggesting that the new measure—which, unlike Elazar's, can at least theoretically be updated with new census data—better captures cultural differences that make a difference to state politics and policy.

- **Berry, William D., Richard C. Fording, Evan J. Ringquist, Russell L. Hanson, and Carl E. Klarner.** "Measuring Citizen and Government Ideology in the U.S. States: A Re-appraisal." *State Politics & Policy Quarterly* 10 (2010): 117–135.

One of the most important differences among states lies in the general political attitudes or orientations of the states' citizens. Scholars consider it critical to tap into those state-level attitudes for many reasons. For example, if we do not know the political orientations and attitudes of citizens, we have no means of assessing whether state lawmakers actually reflect and represent the wishes of their constituents. State-level measures of ideology are incredibly hard to construct. The central problem is that no comparable state-level scientific polls are done in all 50 states at the same time. One way to get around this problem is to infer state preferences by looking at the ideologies and policy preferences of the candidates who win congressional elections. This study employs these kinds of data to create a measure of state ideology that is found to do a good job of explaining differences in various policies, from social welfare to incarceration rates.

- **Carsey, Thomas M., and Jeffrey J. Harden.** "New Measures of Partisanship, Ideology, and Policy Mood in the American States." *State Politics & Policy Quarterly* 10 (2010): 136–156.

This article takes an alternate approach to tackling the same measurement problem Berry et al. (2010) address in the study summarized above. Rather than inferring from lawmaker characteristics, however, Carsey and Harden put together measures of state partisan identification, ideology, and policy mood using data from a series of polls taken in congressional election years from 2000 through 2006. The resulting measures are found to be good estimates of state-level differences on these dimensions.

- **Álvarez-Diaz, Ángel, Lucas González, and Benjamin Radcliff.** "The Politics of Happiness: On the Political Determinants of Quality of Life in the American States." *Journal of Politics* 72 (2010): 894–905.

This is a study of the differences that influence perhaps the most important difference, asking, What political differences influence the quality of life of citizens? The authors examine the ideology and partisanship of state governments and the policies these governments pursue, seeking to correlate them with measures of citizen satisfaction. Some may find the results surprising. States with more generous social welfare policies and more economic regulation—in other words, states that more closely resemble the social democratic countries of northern Europe—tend to have happier citizens who are more satisfied with their quality of life.

- **Pacheco, Julianna.** "Measuring and Evaluating Changes in State Opinion Across Eight Issues." *American Politics Research* (2014). doi:10.1177/1532673X14524819.

The basic question Pacheco is asking is whether differences noted in some of the studies just described are stable or whether they change. What she finds is that state ideology is pretty stable. State partisanship, on the other hand, changes a bit over time. State-level attitudes on some specific issues—such as the death penalty and preferences on education and welfare spending—can change quite a bit over time. These findings have some interesting implications. They suggest that some policy preferences or political attitudes are rooted in deeply stable aspects of the state political system; an obvious candidate for the source of such stable orientations is political culture. Other preferences or attitudes, though, are just as clearly rooted in current events, national trends, or other aspects of politics that likely fall outside of political culture. While political culture almost certainly is a difference that makes a difference, it is just as clearly not the only difference that matters.

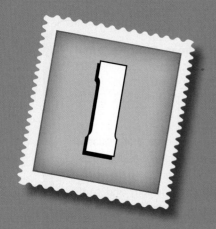

Chapter Review

Key Concepts

- comparative method (p. 7)
- devolution (p. 18)
- individualistic culture (p. 10)
- laboratories of democracy (p. 18)
- moralistic culture (p. 10)
- political culture (p. 10)
- sociodemographics (p. 8)
- traditionalistic culture (p. 11)
- variance (p. 7)

Suggested Websites

- **academic.udayton.edu/sppq-TPR/index.htm.** Data archive website of *State Politics & Policy Quarterly,* an academic research journal devoted to the study of state-level questions.

- **www.csg.org/csg/default.** Website of the Council of State Governments, an organization that represents elected and appointed officials in all three branches of state government. Publishes on a wide variety of topics and issues relevant to state politics and policy.

- **library.cqpress.com/statestats.** A comprehensive and searchable database of state-level information (requires subscription).

- **quickfacts.census.gov/qfd.** U.S. Census Bureau website that lists state rankings on population, per capita income, employment, poverty, and other social and economic indexes.

State Stats on State and Local Government

*Explore and compare data on the states! Go to **edge.sagepub.com/smithgreenblatt5e** to do these exercises.*

1. How many state and local government employees are there in your state? Which state has the most? The least? How have these numbers changed in the past 10 years? Why do you think these changes have occurred?

2. States with which political culture (individualistic, traditionalistic, or moralistic) spend the most, per capita, on higher education? Why might this be?

3. In your state, did the percentage of households headed by single mothers increase, decrease, or stay the same between 2006 and 2010? How might any changes in this percentage influence your state's budgeting decisions? How does this compare to states that neighbor yours?

4. What is the per capita state and the local sales tax revenue in Delaware? What about in the states immediately surrounding Delaware? How are those states able to collect sales taxes? Why wouldn't neighboring citizens just drive to Delaware to do all their shopping?

5. What is the per capita gross domestic product (GDP) in your state? Is it above or below the national figure? Did your state's per capita GDP increase, decrease, or stay the same between 2010 and 2011? What differences between your state and others might explain why your state is above/below the national average?

6. Did the number of state government employees in your state change due to the Great Recession of 2008–2009? Why did it happen or not happen?

States and the federal government, like it or not, need each other. President Barack Obama and Oklahoma governor Mary Fallin may have different party loyalties and different policy preferences, but they had to set aside their differences to work together effectively to help Oklahoma communities devastated by tornadoes in 2013.

Federalism

THE POWER PLAN

- Why does the federal government seem to be gaining power while the states are losing it?
- What are the advantages and disadvantages of federalism?
- Why would some businesses prefer to be regulated by the federal government rather than by state governments?

In 1883 the poet Emma Lazarus was asked to pen a few words that might be donated to a charitable auction. The auction's purpose was to sell works of art and literature to raise money for a pedestal designed to hold a very big sculpture. You might have heard of the sculpture—the Statue of Liberty, which has raised high the torch of freedom over New York Harbor for more than a century and serves as one of the best-known and most iconic symbols of the United States. You might also know at least a few lines of "The New Colossus," the sonnet Lazarus composed for the cause—especially the bit that says, "Give me your tired, your poor, your huddled masses yearning to breathe free." The words express the idea of the United States as a nation of immigrants, founded not on race or religion but on a universal idea of individual liberty. *E pluribus unum* and all that. That sentiment of international roots and values, proudly engraved on a bronze plaque below Lady Liberty's tootsies, has been in pretty short supply in many states and localities over the past couple of years. Indeed, state and local attitudes toward immigration have often been less about welcoming the tired, poor, and huddled masses than about telling them to get lost.

To be fair, the standoffish attitude of many states toward immigration these days is targeted specifically at illegal (or undocumented) immigration rather than at immigration in general. Illegal immigration is an issue that sparks furious controversy. It is also an issue that highlights the often contentious and fractious relationship between state

After reading this chapter, you will be able to

- identify the three systems of government and how they divide power,
- explain what federalism is and why it was chosen as a system for the United States,
- discuss the advantages and disadvantages of federalism,
- describe the ways elements in the U.S. Constitution provide a basis for federalism,
- summarize the different types of federalism that developed over time, and
- discuss the Supreme Court's role in U.S. federalism.

and federal governments. Historically and constitutionally, regulating immigration falls under the jurisdiction of the federal government. During the first decade of the 21st century, though, many states thought the federal government had punted on its responsibilities. By some estimates, nearly 12 million people live in the United States in violation of federal residence laws, many of them from South American countries, seeking to emulate Europeans of an earlier century by immigrating in search of social and economic freedom and opportunity. For many state and local officials, the rising rate of illegal immigration created a massive headache; it increased demand on public services and resulted in a sort of shadow society that posed challenges for everything from law enforcement to tax collections to accurate population estimates. States wanted the feds to do something—it was their job, after all. The feds did nothing. So states decided to take on the job themselves.

> One of the most important questions in the American political system is: Who—the federal government or the state governments—has the power to do what?

One of the most restrictive, and certainly the most famous, of the new state-level immigration laws is Arizona's Support Our Law Enforcement and Safe Neighborhoods Act (SB 1070), signed into law by Governor Jan Brewer in 2010. In a nutshell, SB 1070 made it a *state* crime to be in the United States illegally. Under its provisions immigrants had to carry paperwork proving their legal residence status and law enforcement officers were required to ask for that proof if they suspected someone of being in the state illegally. The law also made it illegal to hire, shelter, or transport those without proper documentation.

The bill, to put it mildly, was enormously controversial. Proponents saw it as an appropriate response to a problem Washington was ignoring. Critics saw it as barely veiled racism. Regardless, it put the state government into a direct confrontation with the federal government. When that happens—and it has happened a lot—the U.S. Supreme Court gets to serve as referee. In 2012 the Supreme Court struck down most, but not all, of SB 1070. The Court essentially ruled that the federal government immigration laws preempt state law, that under the Constitution's supremacy clause what the federal government wants takes precedence. And if the federal government wants to do nothing about illegal immigration, well, tough.

Critically, though, the Court left intact SB 1070's requirement that immigrants carry documents proving they are legal residents of the United States—the "show-me-your-papers" provision. As many other states followed Arizona's lead and adopted immigration regulations, some form of a "show-me-your-papers" law is something many immigrants will now likely have to deal with whether they live in Arizona or not. South Carolina's vigorously enforced Illegal Aliens and Private Employment Act, for example, requires employers to verify that potential hires are legally eligible to work. If the employers fail to do so, the state can suspend their business licenses. Localities have also started to try to regulate illegal immigration. An ordinance passed by the Nebraska city of Fremont in 2010 outlaws renting to illegal immigrants; renters in that city are required to cough up $5 for a permit and swear they are in the country legally. In 2014, the U.S. Supreme Court let stand a lower court decision upholding Fremont's ordinance, clearing the way for other municipalities to adopt similar regulations.

The whole immigration controversy is a good example of how subnational governments are, by design, assigned a central domestic policymaking role. States and localities, in short, enjoy a high degree of independence from the central government. This importance and independence are products of **federalism**, a political system in which national and regional governments share powers and are considered independent equals. An understanding of this system of shared powers is critical to an understanding of the politics of states and localities and the central role they play in the U.S. political system. One of the most important questions in the American political system is: Who—the federal government or the state governments—has the power to do what? In the words of University of Chicago law professor Cass Sunstein, the debate over the distribution of powers between the state and federal levels holds "the ultimate fate of measures safeguarding the environment, protecting consumers, upholding civil rights, protecting violence against women, protecting endangered species, and defining criminal conduct in general and banning hate crimes in particular."[1]

Who gets the power to do what will affect the lives of virtually all citizens in the United States. This chapter provides a basic understanding of federalism, its history and evolution in the United States, and its implications for politics and governance in states and localities.

Systems of Power

We typically think of a nation as being ruled by a single sovereign government—that is, a government that depends on no other government for its political authority or power. This does not mean, however, that every nation has one government. Power and policy responsibility are distributed throughout any given political system in one of three ways, and all typically involve multiple levels of government. (See Figure 2-1.) The first option is to concentrate power in a single central government. Nations in which legal authority is held exclusively by a central government are known as **unitary systems**. Unitary systems typically do have regional and/or local governments, but these can exercise only the powers and responsibilities granted them by the central government. In other words, these governments are not sovereign; how much or how little power they are allowed to wield is up to the central government, not the citizens of the particular localities. The United Kingdom is a good example of a unitary system. Historically, the United Kingdom has a strong tradition of local and regional government; power is concentrated in the nation's Parliament. If it so chooses, Parliament can expand or contract the powers and responsibilities of these lower governments or even shut them down entirely.

In contrast to unitary systems, confederal systems concentrate power in regional governments. A **confederacy** is defined as a voluntary association of independent, sovereign states or governments. This association stands the power

---

Federalism
Political system in which national and regional governments share powers and are considered independent equals

Unitary systems
Political systems in which power is concentrated in a central government

Confederacy
Political system in which power is concentrated in regional governments

FIGURE 2-1

HOW IT WORKS

Systems of Government

Unitary System

Central government grants powers to the regional governments.

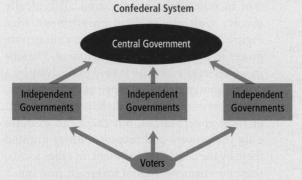

Confederal System

Independent states or governments grant legal authority to central government.

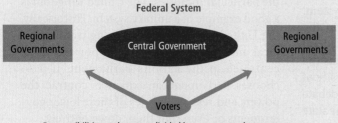

Federal System

Responsibilities and powers divided between central government and regional governments or states; neither level dependent upon the other for its power.

sovereign states. The national government consisted of a legislature in which all states had equal representation. There was no national executive branch, such as the presidency, and no national judiciary, such as the Supreme Court.

This confederal system was adopted during the Revolutionary War and remained in effect for more than a decade. Many of the nation's founders saw its many flaws, however, and wrote its replacement at the Constitutional Convention of 1787 in Philadelphia. The product of that gathering—the U.S. Constitution—was ratified in 1788 and replaced the Articles of Confederation as the basis of the U.S. political system.[2] The second experiment with confederacy began in 1861 at the onset of the Civil War. Southern states seeking to secede from the Union organized their political system as a confederacy. All this ended with the South's surrender in 1865 and the return of the seceded states to the Union.

Federal systems operate in a middle range between unitary systems and confederacies. Responsibilities in a federal system are divided between the two levels of government, and each is given the appropriate power and legal authority to fulfill those responsibilities. The system's defining feature is that neither level of government is dependent on the other for its power. Within its defined areas of responsibility, each is considered independent and autonomous. In the United States, the two levels of government considered sovereign are the federal government and state governments. States are legally equal partners with the national government and occupy a central role in the political system. Although required to operate within the rules laid down by the U.S. Constitution, states are considered sovereign because their power and legal authority are drawn not just from the U.S.

hierarchy of a unitary system on its head. In a confederacy, the central government depends on the regional governments for its legal authority. The United States has experimented with confederal systems twice during its history. The Articles of Confederation was the first constitution of the United States. It organized the U.S. political system as an agreement of union among

Constitution but from their own citizens as codified in their own state constitutions. Local governments are treated very differently than are states. Within their own borders, states are very much like unitary systems; substate governments such as cities and counties get their power from the state, and they exercise only the policymaking authority the state is willing to grant. The specifics of local governments' powers and policy responsibilities are discussed in more depth in Chapter 11.

Why Federalism? The Origins of the Federal System in the United States

The United States is a federal system for a number of reasons. Largely because of their experiences with the Articles of Confederation, the framers of the Constitution rejected the possibility of a confederacy. The national government was so weak under the Articles that prominent figures such as James Madison and George Washington feared it doomed the newly independent republic to failure.

These fears were not unfounded. Following the successful conclusion of the Revolutionary War in 1783, the new United States found itself in the grip of an economic recession, and the central government had little power to address the crisis. Indeed, it actually contributed to the problem by constantly threatening to default on its debts. Independence had brought political freedom, but it also meant that American-made products were now in head-to-head competition with cheap, high-quality goods from Great Britain. This made consumers happy but threatened to cripple American businesses. The economic difficulties pitted state against state, farmer against manufacturer, and debtor against banker. The weak central government really did not have the power to attempt a coordinated, nationwide response to the problem. It could do little but stand by and hope for the best.

As internal tensions mounted within the United States, European powers still active in the Americas threatened the nation's very sovereignty. Spain shut down shipping on the Mississippi River. The British refused to withdraw from some military posts until the U.S. government paid off its debts to British creditors. George Washington believed the United States, having won the war, was in real danger of losing the peace. He said that something had to change "to avert the humiliating and contemptible figure we are about to make on the annals of mankind."[3]

For a loose coalition of the professional classes who called themselves Federalists, that "something" that needed to change was obviously the central government. This group of lawyers, businessmen, and other individuals, drawn mostly from the upper social strata, sought to create a stronger and more powerful national government. Americans, however, were not particularly enthusiastic about handing more power to the central government, an attitude that is not so different from today's. Most recognized that the Articles had numerous flaws, but few were ready to copy the example of the British and adopt a unitary system.

Two events in fall 1786 allowed the Federalists to overcome this resistance and achieve their goal of creating a more powerful national government. The first was the Annapolis Convention. This meeting in Maryland's capital convened to try to hammer out an interstate trade agreement. Few states sent delegates. Those who did show up had strong Federalist sympathies. They took advantage of the meeting and petitioned Congress to call for a commission to rewrite the Articles of Confederation.

The second event was Shays's Rebellion, named for its leader, Daniel Shays, a hero of the recently won Revolutionary War. The rebellion was an uprising of Massachusetts farmers who took up arms in protest of state efforts to take their property as payment for taxes and other debts. It was quickly crushed, but with further civil unrest threatening to boil over into civil war and with mounting pressure from powerful elites within the Federalist ranks, the Continental Congress was pushed to call for states to send delegates to Philadelphia in summer 1787. The purpose of the meeting, which came to be known as the Constitutional Convention, was the rewriting of the Articles of Confederation.

Once convened, the group quickly abandoned its mandate to modify the Articles and decided to write an entirely new constitution. In doing so, the Federalists who dominated the convention rejected confederacy as an adequate basis for the American political system. Their experience under the Articles had taught them that a central government subordinate to the states was not much of a government at all. What they wanted was a government capable of dealing effectively with national problems, and this meant a strong central government whose power was independent of the states.

Some Federalists, notably Alexander Hamilton, were attracted to the idea of a unitary government, but such a system was never seriously considered at the Constitutional Convention. Popular sentiment did not favor a unitary system, which was understandable given that the Revolutionary War had been fought in no small part because of the perceived arrogance of and abuse by a central government toward its regional subordinates (the states were originally colonies of the British Crown). Political realities also argued against pushing for a unitary system. To have any legal force, the new constitution would have to be ratified by the states, and it was highly unlikely the states would voluntarily agree to give up all their powers to a national government. Federalism was thus the only practical option.

Yet a federal system meant more than the political price that had to be paid to achieve a stronger national government. The founders were attempting to construct a new form of **representative government**, in which citizens would exercise power indirectly, on the basis of a paradox. Convention delegates wanted a more powerful national government, but at the same time they did not want to concentrate power for fear that would lead to tyranny. Their solution to this problem was to create a system of separated powers and checks and balances. They divided their new and stronger national government into three branches—legislative, executive, and judicial—and made each branch partially reliant on the others to carry out its own responsibilities. This made it difficult for any single group to gain the upper hand in all three divisions of government and gave each branch the power to check the excesses of the other branches.

The delegates achieved a similar set of goals by making state and national governments coequal partners. By letting states remain independent decision makers in a wide range of policy arenas, they divided power between the national and subnational levels of government. The national government was made more powerful by the new constitution, but the independence of the states helped set clear limits on this power.

The Advantages and Disadvantages of Federalism

Federalism solved a political conundrum for the founders and helped achieve their philosophical aims of dispersing and separating power. Yet federalism is not necessarily better than a confederal or a unitary system, just different. In the United States, the pros and cons of federalism have benefited and bedeviled the American political system for more than two centuries.

There are four key advantages to the federal system. (See Table 2-1.) First, it keeps government

---

Representative government
A form of government in which citizens exercise power indirectly by choosing representatives to legislate on their behalf

TABLE 2-1

Advantages and Disadvantages of Federalism

Advantages	Disadvantages
Allows for flexibility among state laws and institutions.	Increases complexity and confusion.
Reduces conflict because states can accommodate citizens' interests.	Sometimes increases conflict when jurisdictional lines are unclear.
Allows for experimentation at the state level.	Duplicates efforts and reduces accountability.
Enables the achievement of national goals.	Makes coordination difficult.
	Creates inequality in services and policy.

Policy in Practice

Squeezing Lemons

Dan Brochu claimed that his new Oldsmobile Omega traveled well only when it was going up and down a repair lift. Maybe he wasn't exaggerating—inside a year the car went through four transmissions and a complete electrical system failure, and to add insult to injury, the paint started to peel. Thomas Ziemba could relate. His new Chevy Caprice had a skipping engine, a defroster that spewed steam, and a radio that seemed possessed—it would work only if he blew the horn first. Brochu and Ziemba had lemons; they knew it, and in 1982 they wanted the Connecticut state government to know it.

The state government not only got the message; it did something about the problem. The legislature passed Connecticut General Statute 743b, colloquially known as the "lemon law." When it was passed in the 1980s it was a new and innovative policy. The lemon law basically said that if a car was defective and its defects could not be repaired by reasonable effort (defined as four attempts or 30 days in the shop), it was legally a lemon and the consumer could sue the car's manufacturer. The basic upshot was that if someone could prove he or she had a lemon, the manufacturer had to cough up a refund or replace the car.

These days, this sort of law does not seem so innovative or unusual. There's a reason for that. After Connecticut passed its lemon law and it seemed generally effective in making manufacturers stand behind their products and warranty claims, other states, in so many words, said, "That's a good idea. Let's get us a lemon law, too." And they did. Today, all 50 states have some version of a lemon law.

The spread of lemon laws is a good example of one of the key advantages of federalism. By allowing states to experiment, federalism enables them to formulate effective policy innovations, which may then be adopted by other states. Effective policies will spread, while not-so-effective policies will not. While federalism clearly has some downsides, the laboratories of democracy, at least in this instance, were pretty good at whipping up some lemon-aid.

Sources: Better Business Bureau, "Standards of the Connecticut Lemon Law," 2006, http://www.bbb.org/us/Storage/16/Documents/BBBAutoLine/CT-LLsummary.pdf; "Lemon Laws: Mixed Signals," *Newsweek*, May 31, 1982, 50.

closer to the people. Rather than the federal government's imposing a "one-size-fits-all" policy, states have the freedom and authority to match government decisions to local preferences. This freedom also results in the local variance in laws, institutions, and traditions that characterizes the U.S. political system, and provides the comparative method with its explanatory strength.

Second, federalism allows local differences to be reflected in state and local government policy and thereby reduces conflict. Massachusetts, for example, tends to be more liberal than, say, Alabama. California has a much more ethnically and culturally diverse population than does Nebraska. Rather than having the various interests and preferences that spring from state-to-state differences engage in a winner-take-all policy struggle at the federal level, they can be accommodated at the state level. This reduces the friction among interests and lessens conflict.

Third, independent subnational governments allow for flexibility and experimentation. The states, as Supreme Court justice Louis Brandeis famously put it, are "the laboratories of democracy." Successful policy innovations in one state can be adopted by other states and copied by the federal government (see the box "Policy in Practice: Squeezing Lemons").

Fourth, the achievement of at least some national goals is made easier by the participation of independent subnational governments. For example, the federal government's 2010 Patient

Emergency management provides a classic example of how federalism shapes policy. The Federal Emergency Management Agency (FEMA) is a critical component of any government response to disaster, but its effectiveness is tied to its coordination with state and local agencies. Here a FEMA inspector talks to residents of Vilonia, Arkansas, after their home was destroyed by a tornado in 2014.

© CARLO ALLEGRI/Reuters/Corbis

Protection and Affordable Care Act (popularly known as Obamacare) is the most sweeping reform of health care regulation in half a century. The primary goal of Obamacare is to reduce the number of people without health insurance, and one of the law's key provisions is the establishment of health insurance exchanges, basically centralized places where people can buy federally subsidized health insurance packages. As state governments constitute ready-made centralized regulatory bodies geographically distributed across the nation, it makes sense to have them set up and run these exchanges rather than have the federal government do it from scratch.

Along with its benefits, however, federalism confers a set of disadvantages. First, while allowing local differences does keep government closer to the people, it also creates complexity and confusion. For example, if you own a nationwide business, you have to deal with state *and* federal regulations—51 sets of regulations in all. That means, among other things, 51 tax codes and 51 sets of licensing requirements. And many communities have their own restrictions and requirements for businesses as well.

Second, federalism can increase conflict as easily as reduce it. The Constitution is very vague on the exact division of powers between state and federal governments. This results in a constant struggle—and a lot of litigation—to resolve which level of government has the responsibility and legal authority to take the lead role in a given policy area. For example, who should challenge drug companies that make false or misleading claims about their products? In January 2007, 30 states settled with the Bayer Corporation for $8 million over safety concerns about a cholesterol-reducing drug that had since been pulled from the market. But just weeks earlier, the makers of four purported weight-loss drugs agreed to pay $25 million to settle allegations by the Federal Trade Commission that they had made unproven claims about the effectiveness of their products. Similar cases, but one was ruled on at the state level and the other at the national level.

Third, although federalism promotes flexibility and experimentation, it also promotes duplication and reduces accountability. For example, local, state, and national governments have all taken on law enforcement responsibilities. In some areas, this means there may be municipal police departments, a county sheriff's department, and the state patrol, plus local offices of the Federal Bureau of Investigation and the U.S. Drug Enforcement Agency. The responsibilities and jurisdictions of these organizations overlap, which means taxpayers end up paying twice for some law enforcement activities. Also, when these agencies are unsuccessful or ineffective, it can be very difficult to figure out which is responsible and what needs to change.

Fourth, the federal system can make it hard to coordinate policy efforts nationwide. For example, police and fire departments on opposite sides of a state border, or even within adjacent jurisdictions in the same state, may have different communication systems. It is hard to coordinate a response to a large-scale emergency if the relevant organizations cannot talk to each other, but the federal government cannot force state and local governments to standardize their radio equipment.

Finally, a federal system creates inequality in services and policies. The quality of public schools and welfare services, for example, depends heavily on the choices state and local governments make. This inevitably means that some states offer better educational opportunities and do more for the needy than others do.

The Constitutional Basis of Federalism

The relationship between national and state governments is like a sibling rivalry. It is hard to imagine either level of government getting along without the other; yet because each is independent and focused on its own interests, conflict is common. The ink was barely dry on the newly ratified Constitution before the federal government and the states were squabbling over who had the power and authority in this or that policy area. In writing the Constitution, the founders recognized that the differences between states and the federal government were likely to be a central and lasting feature of the political system. Accordingly, they attempted to head off the worst of the disputes—or at least to provide a basis for resolving them—by making a basic division of powers between the national and state governments.

The Constitution grants the federal government both enumerated and implied powers. **Enumerated powers** are grants of authority explicitly given by the Constitution. Among the most

important of these is the **national supremacy clause** contained in Article VI. This states that the Constitution "shall be the supreme law of the land; and the judges in every state shall be bound thereby." In other words, federal law takes precedence over all other laws. This allows the federal government to preempt, or override, areas regulated by state law. In recent decades, the federal government has aggressively used this power to extend its authority over states in a wide range of policy issues, so much so that **preemption** has been called "the gorilla that swallows state laws."[4]

Other enumerated powers are laid out in Article I, Section 8. This part of the Constitution details a set of **exclusive powers**—grants of authority that belong solely to the national government. These include the powers to regulate commerce, to declare war, and to raise and maintain an army and navy. Article I, Section 8, also confers a set of **concurrent powers** on the national government. Concurrent powers are those granted to the national government but not denied to the states. Both levels of government are free to exercise these prerogatives. Concurrent powers include the power to tax, borrow, and spend.

Finally, this same section of the Constitution gives the national government **implied powers**. The basic idea behind implied powers is that the authors of the Constitution realized they could not possibly list every specific power that the national government would require to meet the needs of a developing nation. Accordingly, they gave Congress the flexibility to meet unforeseen challenges by granting the federal government a

---

National supremacy clause
Constitutional clause that states that federal law takes precedence over all other laws

Preemption
The process of the federal government's overriding areas regulated by state law

Exclusive powers
Powers given by the Constitution solely to the federal government

Concurrent powers
Powers that both federal and state governments can exercise. These include the power to tax, borrow, and spend.

Implied powers
Broad, but undefined, powers given to the federal government by the Constitution

---

Enumerated powers
Grants of authority explicitly given by the Constitution

set of broad and largely undefined powers. These include the **general welfare clause**, which gives the federal government the authority to provide for "the general welfare of the United States," and the **necessary and proper clause**, which authorizes Congress "to make all laws which shall be necessary and proper" to carry out its responsibilities as defined by the Constitution. (See Table 2-2 for explanations of these and other provisions.)

The Constitution says a good deal about the powers of the federal government but very little about the powers of the states. The original, unamended Constitution spent much more time specifying the obligations of the states than it did defining their power and authority. The obligations list includes Article IV, Section 2, better known as the **full faith and credit clause**. The clause requires all states to grant "full faith and credit" to each other's public acts and records. This means that wills, contracts, and marriages that are valid under one state's laws are valid under all. Under the **privileges and immunities clause**, states are prohibited from discriminating against citizens from other states. The idea here was to protect people traveling across state boundaries or temporarily residing in a state because of business or personal reasons from becoming the targets of discriminatory regulation or taxation.

The Constitution also sets out an often criticized system for electing the nation's president and vice president. The presidency goes not to the candidate who wins the most votes but, rather, to the one who wins the most states. Article II, Section 1, charges the states with appointing electors—one for each of a state's U.S. senators and representatives—who actually choose the president based on the winner of the state's popular vote. (If the Republican candidate gets the most votes in a state, the state's delegation to the Electoral College is made up of Republican Party loyalists who vote for the Republican nominee.) A presidential candidate needs a majority in the Electoral College, which requires the votes of at least 270 of the 538 state electors, to be named the winner.

Other than these responsibilities and explicitly granting the states the right to enter into compacts, or binding agreements, with each other on matters of regional concern, the Constitution is virtually silent on the powers of the states. This lopsided attention to the powers of the federal government was a contentious issue in the battle to ratify the Constitution. Opponents of the document, collectively known as Anti-Federalists, feared that states would become little more than puppets of the new central government. Supporters of the Constitution sought to calm these fears by arguing that states would remain sovereign and independent and that the powers not specifically granted to the federal government were reserved for the states. As James Madison put it, in writing the Constitution the Federalists were seeking "a middle ground which may at once support due supremacy of the national authority" but would also preserve a strong independent role for the states.[5]

Madison and his fellow Federalists offered to put these assurances in writing. In effect, they promised that if the Constitution was ratified, the first order of business for the new Congress would be to draft a set of amendments that would spell out the limits of central government power and specify the independence of the states. Although Anti-Federalist skepticism remained, the Federalists kept their promise. The First Congress formulated a series of changes that eventually became the first 10 amendments to the Constitution and are collectively known as the **Bill of Rights**.

General welfare clause
Constitutional clause that gives Congress an implied power through the authority to provide for the "general welfare"

Necessary and proper clause
Constitutional clause that gives Congress an implied power through the right to pass all laws considered "necessary and proper" to carry out the federal government's responsibilities as defined by the Constitution

Full faith and credit clause
Constitutional clause that requires states to recognize each other's public records and acts as valid

Privileges and immunities clause
Constitutional clause that prohibits states from discriminating against citizens of other states

---

Bill of Rights
The first 10 amendments to the Constitution, which set limits on the power of the federal government and set out the rights of individuals and the states

TABLE 2-2

The U.S. Constitution's Provisions for Federalism

What It Is	What It Says	What It Means
Article I, Section 8 (commerce clause)	The Congress shall have Power . . . To regulate Commerce with foreign Nations, and among the several States, and with the Indian Tribes.	Gives Congress the right to regulate interstate commerce. This clause has been broadly interpreted to give Congress a number of implied powers.
Article I, Section 8 (necessary and proper clause)	The Congress shall have Power . . . To make all Laws which shall be necessary and proper for carrying into Execution the foregoing Powers, and all other Powers vested by this Constitution in the Government of the United States, or in any Department or Officer thereof.	An implied power giving Congress the right to pass all laws considered "necessary and proper" to carry out the federal government's responsibilities as defined by the Constitution.
Article IV, Section 3 (admission of new states)	New States may be admitted by the Congress into this Union; but no new State shall be formed or erected within the Jurisdiction of any other State; nor any State be formed by the Junction of two or more States, or Parts of States, without the Consent of the Legislatures of the States concerned as well as of the Congress.	Allows the U.S. Congress to admit new states to the union and guarantees each state sovereignty and jurisdiction over its territory.
Article IV, Section 4 (enforcement of republican form of government)	The United States shall guarantee to every State in this Union a Republican Form of Government, and shall protect each of them against Invasion; and on Application of the Legislature, or of the Executive (when the Legislature cannot be convened) against domestic Violence.	Ensures that a democratic government exists in each state and protects states against foreign invasion or insurrection.
Article VI (supremacy clause)	This Constitution, and the Laws of the United States which shall be made in Pursuance thereof; and all Treaties made, or which shall be made, under the Authority of the United States, shall be the supreme Law of the Land; and the Judges in every State shall be bound thereby, any Thing in the Constitution or Laws of any State to the Contrary notwithstanding.	States that federal law takes precedence over all other laws.
Tenth Amendment	The powers not delegated to the United States by the Constitution, nor prohibited by it to the States, are reserved to the States respectively, or to the people.	Guarantees that a broad, but undefined, set of powers be reserved for the states and the people, as opposed to the federal government.
Fourteenth Amendment	All persons born or naturalized in the United States, and subject to the jurisdiction thereof, are citizens of the United States and of the state wherein they reside. No state shall make or enforce any law which shall abridge the privileges or immunities of citizens of the United States; nor shall any state deprive any person of life, liberty, or property, without due process of law; nor deny to any person within its jurisdiction the equal protection of the laws.	Prohibits any state from depriving individuals of the rights and privileges of citizenship, and requires states to provide due process and equal protection guarantees to all citizens.
Sixteenth Amendment	The Congress shall have the power to lay and collect taxes on incomes, from whatever source derived, without apportionment among the several States, and without regard to any census or enumeration.	Enables the federal government to levy a national income tax, which has helped further national policies and programs.
Seventeenth Amendment	The Senate of the United States shall be composed of two Senators from each State, elected by the people thereof, for six years; and each Senator shall have one vote . . . . When vacancies happen in the representation of any State in the Senate, the executive authority of each State shall issue writs of election to fill such vacancies: Provided that the legislature of any State may empower the executive thereof to make temporary appointments until the people fill the vacancies by election as the legislature may direct.	Provides for direct election of U.S. senators, rather than election by each state's legislature.

Most of these amendments set specific limits on government power. The aim was to guarantee certain individual rights and freedoms, and, at least initially, they were directed at the federal government rather than at state governments. The **Tenth Amendment**, however, finally addressed the power of the states. In full, the Tenth Amendment specifies: "The powers not delegated to the United States by the Constitution, nor prohibited by it to the states, are reserved to the states respectively, or to the people." This provided no enumerated, or specific, powers to the states, but those implied by the language of the amendment are considerable. The so-called reserved powers encompass all the concurrent powers that allow the states to tax, borrow, and spend; to make laws and enforce them; to regulate trade within their borders; and to practice eminent domain, which is the power to take private property for public use. The reserved powers also have been traditionally understood to mean that states have the primary power to make laws that involve the health, safety, and morals of their citizens. Yet the powers reserved for the states are more implied than explicit, and they all rest in an uneasy tension with the national supremacy clause of Article VI.

After the Tenth Amendment, the **Fourteenth Amendment** is the most important in terms of specifying state powers. Ratified in 1868, the Fourteenth Amendment is one of the so-called Civil War Amendments that came in the immediate wake of the bloody conflict between the North, or the Union, and the South, or the Confederacy. The Fourteenth Amendment prohibits any state from depriving individuals of the rights and privileges of citizenship, and requires states to provide due process and equal protection guarantees to all citizens. The Supreme Court has used these guarantees to apply the Bill of Rights to state governments as well as to the federal government and to assert national power over state power in issues ranging from the desegregation of public education to the reapportioning of state legislatures.

Tenth Amendment
Constitutional amendment guaranteeing that a broad, but undefined, set of powers be reserved for the states and the people

Fourteenth Amendment
Constitutional amendment that prohibits states from depriving individuals of the rights and privileges of citizenship, and requires states to provide due process and equal protection guarantees

The implied powers of the federal government, the limitations set on states by the Fourteenth Amendment, and the undefined "leftovers" given to the states by the Tenth Amendment mean that the scope and authority of both levels of government are, in many cases, dependent on how the Constitution is interpreted. The Constitution, in other words, provides a basic framework for solving the sibling-rivalry squabbles between the states and the federal government. (See Figure 2-2.) It does not, however, provide an unambiguous guide to which level of government has the primary power, responsibility, and authority on a broad range of policy issues. This, as we will see, means that the U.S. Supreme Court is repeatedly thrust into the role of referee in power disputes between national and state governments.

The Development of Federalism

Although clearly establishing a federal political system, the provisions of the U.S. Constitution leave considerable room for disagreement about which level of government—federal or state—has the power to do what. Disagreements about the scope and authority of the national government happened almost immediately when the First Congress convened in 1789. The issue of a national bank was one of the most controversial of these early conflicts and the one with the most lasting implications. Alexander Hamilton, secretary of the treasury under President George Washington, believed a central bank was critical to stabilizing the national economy, but there was nothing in the Constitution that specifically granted the federal government the authority to create and regulate such an institution.

Lacking a clear enumerated power, Hamilton justified his proposal for a national bank by using an implied power. He argued that the necessary and proper clause implied the federal government's power to create a national bank because the bank would help the government manage its finances as it went about its expressly conferred authority to tax and spend. Essentially, Hamilton was interpreting *necessary* as "convenient" or

FIGURE 2-2

Powers of National and State Governments

National Government Powers

Coin money

Regulate interstate and foreign commerce

Tax imports and exports

Make treaties

Make all laws "necessary and proper" to fulfill responsibilities

Make war

Regulate postal system

Powers Denied

Tax state exports

Change state boundaries

Impose religious tests

Pass laws in conflict with the Bill of Rights

Concurrent Powers

Tax

Borrow money

Charter banks and corporations

Take property (eminent domain)

Make and enforce laws and administer a judiciary

State Government Powers

Run elections

Regulate intrastate commerce

Establish republican forms of state and local government

Protect public health, safety, and morals

All powers not delegated to the national government or denied to the states by the Constitution

Powers Denied

Tax imports and exports

Coin money

Enter into treaties

Impair obligation of contracts

Enter compacts with other states without congressional consent

Source: Adapted from Samuel Kernell, Gary C. Jacobson, and Thad Kousser, *The Logic of American Politics,* 6th ed. (Washington, DC: CQ Press, 2013), Figure 3-2.

"appropriate." Secretary of State Thomas Jefferson objected, arguing that if the Constitution was going to establish a government of truly limited powers, the federal government needed to stick to its enumerated powers and interpret its implied powers very narrowly. He thus argued that the *necessary* in the necessary and proper clause should properly be interpreted as "essential" or "indispensable." Hamilton eventually won the argument, and Congress approved the national bank. Still, the issue simmered as a controversial—and potentially unconstitutional—expansion of the national government's powers.

The issue was not fully resolved until 1819, when the Supreme Court decided the case of *McCulloch v. Maryland.* This case stemmed from the state of Maryland's attempts to shut down the national bank, which was taking business from state-chartered banks, by taxing its operations. The chief cashier of the national bank's Baltimore branch refused to pay the tax, and the parties went to court. The Supreme Court, in essence, backed Hamilton's interpretation of the Constitution over Jefferson's. This was important above and beyond the issue of a national bank. It suggested that the Constitution gave the national government a broad set of powers relative to the states. Key to this early affirmation of the federal government's power was U.S. Chief Justice John Marshall, whose backing of a broad interpretation of implied powers laid the foundation for later expansions in the scope and authority of the federal government.

The full impact of *McCulloch v. Maryland,* however, would not be felt for some time. For the most part, the federal government began to feel its way into the gray areas of its constitutional powers pretty cautiously. Federalism went on to develop in four distinct stages—dual federalism, cooperative federalism, centralized federalism, and New Federalism—and the first of these stages leaned toward the more limited role of the federal government favored by Jefferson.

Dual Federalism (1789–1933)

Dual federalism is the idea that state and federal governments have separate jurisdictions and responsibilities. Within these separate spheres of

Dual federalism
The idea that state and federal governments have separate and distinct jurisdictions and responsibilities

authority, each level of government is sovereign and free to operate without interference from the other. It represents something of a middle ground in the initial interpretations of how the Constitution divided power. On one side of the debate were Federalists such as Hamilton, who championed a nation-centered view of federalism. They wanted to interpret the Constitution as broadly as possible to give the national government supremacy over the states.

On the other side were fierce **states' rights** advocates such as John Calhoun of South Carolina, who served as vice president in the administrations of John Quincy Adams and Andrew Jackson. Supporters of states' rights wanted the federal government's power limited to the greatest possible extent and saw any expansion of that power as an encroachment on the sovereignty of the states. In the 1820s and 1830s, Calhoun formulated what became known as the **compact theory** of federalism. The idea was that the Constitution represented an agreement among sovereign states to form a common government. It interpreted the Constitution as essentially an extension of the Articles of Confederation, a perspective that viewed the U.S. political system as more confederal than federal.

The compact theory argued that if sovereignty ultimately rested with the states, then the states rather than the Supreme Court had the final say in how the Constitution should be interpreted. The states also had the right to reject federal laws and make them invalid within their own borders. This process was known as **nullification**, and the compact theory took it to an extreme. Calhoun argued that states could reject the entire Constitution and choose to withdraw, or secede, from the Union. In the 1820s, national policies—especially a trade tariff—triggered an economic downturn in the southern states, which created wide support for nullification and **secession** arguments. These extreme states' rights views were not completely resolved until the Union victory in the Civil War ended them for good.

Dual federalism walked the line of moderation between the extremes of **nation-centered federalism** and **state-centered federalism**. Basically, dual federalism looks at the U.S. political system as a layered cake. The state and federal governments represent distinct and separate layers of this cake. To keep them separate, advocates of dual federalism sought to limit the federal government to exercising only

> Even at the height of the dual federalism era, state and federal governments were collaborating as much as they were fighting.

a narrow interpretation of its enumerated powers. If the Constitution was to be interpreted broadly, that interpretation should favor the states rather than Congress. This became the central operating philosophy of the U.S. Supreme Court for much of the 19th century and is most closely associated with the tenure of Chief Justice Roger B. Taney, who served from 1836 to 1864. Compared with his immediate predecessor, John Marshall, Taney was much less sympathetic to arguments that interpreted the federal government's powers broadly.

The dual federalism doctrine gave rise to some infamous Supreme Court decisions on the powers and limitations of the federal government. Perhaps the best known is *Scott v. Sandford* (1857). This

States' rights
The belief that states should be free to make their own decisions with little interference from the federal government

Compact theory
The idea that the Constitution represents an agreement among sovereign states to form a common government

Nullification
The process of a state's rejecting a federal law and making it invalid within state borders

Secession
The process of a government's or political jurisdiction's withdrawing from a political system or alliance

Nation-centered federalism
The belief that the nation is the basis of the federal system and that the federal government should take precedence over the states

State-centered federalism
The belief that states are the basis of the federal system and that state governments should take precedence over the federal government

case dealt with Dred Scott, a slave taken by his master from Missouri, a slave state, to Illinois, a free state, and on into what was then called the Wisconsin Territory, where slavery had been outlawed by the Missouri Compromise of 1820. This federal law stipulated which new states and territories could and could not make slavery legal. After his master's death, Scott sued for his freedom, arguing that his residence in a free territory had legally ended his bondage. Scott's case was tied to the Missouri Compromise, which the Supreme Court subsequently ruled unconstitutional. The justices' justification was that Congress did not have the enumerated, or the implied, power to prohibit slavery in the territories. Thus, Scott remained a slave, although his owners voluntarily gave him his freedom shortly after the Supreme Court decision. He died of tuberculosis in 1858, having spent only 1 of his nearly 60 years as a free man.

Cooperative Federalism (1933–1964)

In theory, dual federalism defines and maintains a clear division between state and national governments and sets a clear standard for doing so. If the federal government has the enumerated power to take the disputed action or make the disputed law, it has supremacy over the states in the particular case; if it does not have the enumerated power, then the Tenth Amendment reserves that power for the states, and state preferences take precedence.

The problem was that dual federalism's clarity in theory rarely matched the complex realities of governance in practice. State and national governments share interests in a wide range of issues, from education to transportation. To divide these interests cleanly into separate spheres of influence was not only difficult; in many cases it was impractical and not desirable. Even at the height of the dual federalism era, state and federal governments

FIGURE 2-3

The Varieties of Federalism

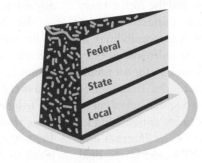

Dual or "Layer Cake" Federalism

Cooperative or "Marble Cake" Federalism

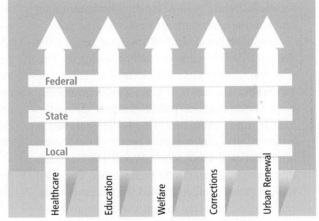

Centralized or "Picket Fence" Federalism

were collaborating as much as they were fighting. The federal government, for example, owned vast tracts of land in the Midwest and West, and it made extensive grants of these lands to the states to help develop transportation and education systems. Many of the nation's best-known state universities got their start this way, as land-grant colleges.

In the 19th century, the federal government also gave out cash grants to support Civil War veterans housed in state institutions, gave money to the states to support agricultural research, and lent federal manpower—primarily U.S. Army engineers—to help state and local development projects.[6] Rather than a layered cake, some experts believe a more appropriate metaphor for federalism is a marble cake, with the different levels of government so thoroughly mixed with one another that they are impossible to separate. (See Figure 2-3.)

Certainly as the nation became increasingly industrialized and more urban, state and federal interests became increasingly intertwined. As the 19th century drew to a close and the 20th century began, the federal government undertook a significant expansion of its policy responsibilities. In 1887, it began to regulate the railroads, a policy area with enormous significance for the economic development of states and localities. In economic and social terms, this was roughly equivalent to the federal government of today announcing its comprehensive regulation of the Internet and software manufacturers. By fits and starts, dual federalism gradually fell out of favor with the Supreme Court. The Court instead began to interpret the powers of the federal government very broadly and to allow the jurisdictions of state and national governments to merge gradually.

Several events accelerated this trend. In 1913, the Sixteenth Amendment was ratified, giving the federal government the ability to levy a nationwide income tax. The new taxing and spending authority helped further national policies designed during the next decades.[7] World War I (1914–1918) resulted in a significant centralization of power in the federal government. During World War II (1939–1945), that power was centralized even further. The need to fight global conflicts pushed the federal government to assert the lead role on a wide range of economic and social issues. Even more important to the long-term relationship between state and national governments was the Great Depression of the 1930s, a social and economic catastrophe that swept aside any remaining vestiges of dual federalism.

The central catalyst for a fundamental change in the nature of state–federal relations was the election of Franklin Delano Roosevelt to the presidency in 1932. In an effort to combat economic and social malaise, Roosevelt aggressively pushed the federal government into taking a lead role in areas traditionally left to the states, and in the 1930s the federal government became deeply involved in regulating the labor market, creating and managing welfare programs, and providing significant amounts of direct aid to cities. The general approach of Roosevelt's so-called New Deal agenda defined the central characteristics of **cooperative federalism**—using the federal government to identify a problem, set up the basic outline of a program to address the problem, and make money available to fund that program, and then turning over much of the responsibility for implementing and running the program to the states and localities. This arrangement dominated state and federal relations for the next three decades.

Centralized Federalism (1964–1980)

Having all levels of government addressing problems simultaneously and cooperatively paid dividends. It combined the need to attack national problems with the flexibility of the decentralized federal system. Cooperative federalism, however, also signaled a significant shift in power away from the states and toward the federal government. The

Cooperative federalism
The notion that it is impossible for state and national governments to have separate and distinct jurisdictions and that both levels of government must work together

The Sixteenth Amendment gave the federal government the power to levy an income tax. Some of the money collected by the federal government in income taxes is returned to the states in the form of grants to support a wide range of domestic policies and programs.

FIGURE 2-4

Key Dates in the History of American Federalism

Revolutionary War starts	1775	1776	Declaration of Independence adopted
Articles of Confederation ratified	1781	1783	Revolutionary War ends
Annapolis Convention	1786	1786	Shays's Rebellion
Constitutional Convention drafts new constitution	1787	1788	U.S. Constitution ratified
First Congress adopts Bill of Rights	1791		
McCulloch v. Maryland establishes that the federal government has a broad set of powers over the states	1819		
Roger Taney sworn in as chief justice; adopts dual federalism as model for federal–state relations	1836	1832	South Carolina attempts to nullify federal law
		1857	*Scott v. Sandford* demonstrates the limits of the federal government
Southern states experiment with confederacy as Civil War starts	1861	1860	South Carolina secedes from the Union in December; hostilities between North and South begin a month later
		1865	Civil War ends with Union victory; Thirteenth Amendment abolishes slavery
Fourteenth Amendment passes	1868		
		1887	Federal government regulates the railroads
Sixteenth Amendment passes	1913		
Great Depression	1930		
		1933	Franklin Delano Roosevelt takes office; Era of cooperative federalism begins
Era of centralized federalism begins	1964		
		1972	Richard Nixon begins revenue sharing
Election of Ronald Reagan and emergence of New Federalism	1980		
		1986	William Rehnquist becomes chief justice; Supreme Court begins to look more favorably on states' rights arguments
Supreme Court decides *Bush v. Gore*; George W. Bush receives Florida's contested electoral votes and becomes president	2000	2008 –2009	Great Recession

key to this power shift was money, specifically federal **grants-in-aid**, which are cash appropriations given by the federal government to the states. An ever-increasing proportion of state and local budgets came from federal coffers. At the beginning of the 19th century, federal grants constituted less than 1 percent of state and local government revenues. By the middle of the 1930s, federal grants accounted for close to 20 percent of state and local revenues.[8]

For the next 30 years, the federal government continued to rely on grants to administer programs, including the 1950s construction of the federal highway system that Americans drive on today. The 1960s marked a shift, however. **Centralized federalism**, ushered in with Lyndon Baines Johnson's presidency, further increased the federal government's involvement in policy areas previously left to state and local governments. It is commonly associated with Johnson's Great Society program, which used state and local governments to help implement such national initiatives as the Civil Rights Act and the War on Poverty. This is sometimes called "picket-fence federalism" because in practice the relationships between local, state, and national governments were centered on particular programs and the agencies that managed them. These policy-specific agencies (bureaucracies dealing with education, transportation, welfare, and the like) were laid across the levels of government like pickets on a three-rail fence.

Those initiatives meant more money—and more regulations—for states and localities. The federal government aggressively began attaching strings to this money through **categorical grants**. Federal–state relations evolved into a rough embodiment of the Golden Rule of politics—he who has the gold gets to make the rules.

Richard Nixon's presidential administration took a slightly different tack. It cut some strings but continued to increase the number of grants doled out by the federal government.[9] In the late 1960s, the administration pioneered the idea of **general revenue sharing grants**, federal funds turned over to the states and localities with essentially no strings attached. Although popular with states and localities—from their perspective it was "free" money—this type of grant-in-aid had a short life span; it was killed by the Ronald Reagan administration in the early 1980s.

Federal grants, strings or no strings, do not sound so bad on the surface. Money is money, and a government can never have too much. The problem was that the grants were not distributed equitably to states and localities, and a central feature of cooperative federalism was the often fierce competition to control and access these revenues. The politics became complex. One form of conflict arose between the states and the federal government over what types of grants should be used for particular policies or programs. States and localities favored federal grants with fewer strings. Congress and the president often favored putting tight guidelines on federal money because this allowed them to take a greater share of the credit for the benefits of federal spending.

Perhaps the most important dimension of the politics of grants-in-aid, however, was the federal government's increasing desire to use its purse strings to pressure states and localities into adopting particular policies and laws. Beginning in the 1960s and 1970s, cooperative federalism began a new, more coercive era with the rise of ever-more-stringent grant conditions. These included **crosscutting requirements**, or strings that applied to all federal grants. For example, one requirement a state or locality must meet to receive virtually any federal government grant is an assessment of the environmental impact of the proposed program

---

Grants-in-aid
Cash appropriations given by the federal government to the states

Centralized federalism
The notion that the federal government should take the leading role in setting national policy, with state and local governments helping implement the policies

Categorical grants
Federal grants-in-aid given for specific programs that leave states and localities with little discretion over how to spend the money

---

General revenue sharing grants
Federal grants-in-aid given with few constraints, leaving states and localities almost complete discretion over how to spend the money

Crosscutting requirements
Constraints that apply to all federal grants

or policy. Accordingly, most state and local governments began writing—and defending—environmental impact statements for any construction project that involved federal funds.

The federal government also began applying **crossover sanctions**. Crossover sanctions are strings that require grant recipients to pass and enforce certain laws or policies as a condition of receiving funds. One example is the drinking age. As a condition of receiving federal highway funds, the federal government requires states to set 21 as the minimum legal age for drinking alcohol.

Increasingly, the strings came even if there were no grants. State and local governments were issued direct orders, essentially were commanded, to adopt certain laws or rules, such as clean-water standards and minimum-wage laws.[10] These **unfunded mandates** became a particular irritant to state and local governments. Even when there was broad agreement on the substance of a mandate, subnational governments resented the federal government's taking all the credit while leaving the dirty work of finding funds and actually running the programs to the states and localities.

Congress eventually passed a law banning unfunded mandates in the mid-1990s, but it is full of loopholes. For example, the law does not apply to appropriations bills—the laws that actually authorize the government to spend money. The National Conference of State Legislatures has estimated that in the 5-year period from 2004 to 2008, the federal government shifted $131 billion in costs to the states in unfunded mandates.[11] Congress, in other words, continues to pass laws that subnational governments must obey, and Congress also passes on the cost of implementing these laws to the states.

New Federalism (1980–2002)

Centralized federalism's shift of power toward the national government always faced opposition from states' rights advocates, who viewed the growing influence of the national government with alarm. By the end of the 1970s, centralized federalism also was starting to face a practical crisis—the federal government's revenues could not keep up with the demand for grants. With the election of Ronald Reagan in 1980, the practical and ideological combined to create pressure for a fundamental shift in state and federal relations.

Reagan was not the first president to raise concerns about the centralization of power in the national government. A primary reason for Nixon's support of general revenue sharing, for example, was the attraction of giving states more flexibility by cutting the strings attached to federal grants. It was not until Reagan, however, that a sustained attempt was made to reverse the course of centralized federalism. Reagan believed the federal government had overreached its boundaries, and he wanted to return power and flexibility to the states. At the core of his vision of state-centered **New Federalism** was the desire to reduce federal grants-in-aid. In return, states would be given more policymaking leeway with the money they did get through **block grants**.

Reagan's drive to make this vision a reality had mixed success. The massive budget deficits of the 1980s made cutting grants-in-aid a practical necessity. We can see this in Figure 2-5, which shows federal government grants to state and local governments in billions of constant dollars from 1940 through 2014. There was a clear upward trend beginning in the 1960s that peaked in about 1978. After that, federal grants to states stayed relatively constant for about a decade—while the federal government was not really drastically cutting grants in the 1980s, in real terms it did not increase them either. At least for a while, the federal government managed to rein in the grant dollars flowing to states and localities. Reducing the federal government's influence over states and localities turned out to be another matter.

Crossover sanctions
Federal requirements mandating that grant recipients pass and enforce certain laws or regulations as a condition of receiving funds

Unfunded mandates
Federal laws that direct state action but provide no financial support for that action

New Federalism
The belief that states should receive more power and authority and less money from the federal government

Block grants
Federal grants-in-aid given for general policy areas that leave states and localities with wide discretion over how to spend the money within the designated policy area

FIGURE 2-5

Federal Grants to States, 1940–2014 (in billions)

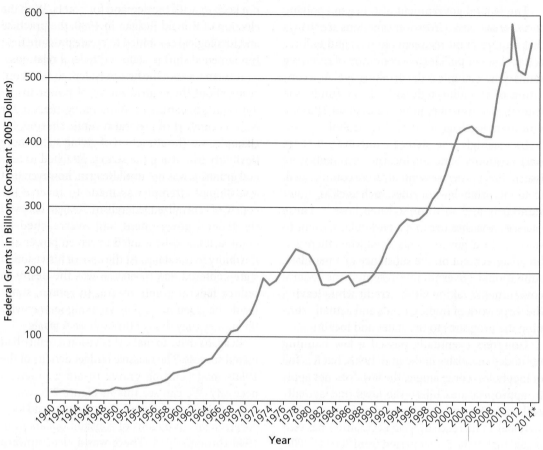

*Data for 2014 are estimated.

Source: U.S. Office of Management and Budget, *Budget of the United States*, Historical Tables, Table 12.2, "Summary Comparison of Total Outlays for Grants to State and Local Governments: 1940–2019 (in Current Dollars, as Percentages of Total Outlays, as Percentages of GDP, and in Constant (FY 2009) Dollars)."

Reagan, like many conservatives, was a modern heir to a states' rights perspective that dated back to the Anti-Federalist movement. This means he believed that government should be as close to the voters as possible—in the city hall or the state capitol—rather than far away in Washington, D.C. Yet believing that government should be closer to the people in the abstract is far different from putting that belief into practice. Taking power from the federal government did advance a core philosophical belief of the Reagan administration, but it also created problems for Reagan supporters, who were not shy about voicing their displeasure.

Such core conservative constituencies as business and industry quickly realized that dealing with one government was much less of a headache than dealing with 50 governments. They almost immediately began to put counterpressure on the movement toward expanded state policymaking authority. The result was something of a push and pull, with the Reagan administration trying to shove power onto the states with one set of legislative priorities and yank it back to the federal government with another. Ultimately, Reagan did succeed in cutting grants-in-aid. He consolidated 57 categorical grants into 9 new block grants. General revenue sharing and another 60 categorical grants were eliminated entirely. This reduced the amount of money sent to the states while increasing the states' ability to act independently.[12]

Yet Reagan also engaged in a number of fairly aggressive preemption movements and backed a number of unfunded mandates. This reduced the independence of states and forced them to fund programs they did not necessarily support.

The seeds of New Federalism had a hard time taking root at the national level, but its roots sank fast and sank deep at the state and local levels. States were caught between the proverbial rock of a cash-strapped federal government and the hard place of the demand for the programs traditionally supported by federal funds. They slowly and often painfully worked themselves out of this dilemma by becoming less reliant on the federal government. States began aggressively pursuing innovative policy approaches to a wide range of social and economic problems. By the 1990s, as one author puts it, there was "a developing agreement among state and national political elites that states should have greater authority and flexibility in operating public programs."[13]

The effort to take power away from the federal government and give it to the states was broadly supported by public opinion, as polls consistently showed that Americans placed more trust in state and local governments than they did in the federal government.[14] In the 1990s, the Clinton administration championed the idea of devolution, an extension of New Federalism that sought a systematic transition of power from the federal to the state level in certain policy areas.

Probably the best-known example of devolution is the Personal Responsibility and Work Opportunity Reconciliation Act of 1996, popularly known as the law that "ended welfare as we know it." The law, which Clinton signed under Republican pressure during the 1996 presidential campaign after vetoing it twice, ended Aid to Families with Dependent Children and replaced it with a block grant. In essence, the law embodied the deal between state and federal governments that embodied devolution—the federal government would provide less money, and the states would get more policymaking authority.

Like its parent, New Federalism, the devolution revolution faced strong resistance, often from an old enemy. Conservatives, at least rhetorically, still were the strongest states' rights advocates. Yet when states' rights conflicted with key portions of the conservative political agenda, conservative groups still fought tenaciously for federal supremacy over the states, just as they had during the 1980s. An example of this contradictory behavior is the 1996 Defense of Marriage Act. This federal law was proposed in the wake of movements in Hawaii and Vermont to legalize same-sex civil unions. Now, remember, the full faith and credit clause means that a contract made under the laws of one state is legally recognized and binding in all states. So if one state made same-sex unions legal, it raised the possibility that the other 49 would have to recognize such civil unions as the legal equivalent of marriages. There was a strong push from many traditional states' rights advocates for the federal government to, in essence, grant states exceptions from their full faith and credit obligations. The Defense of Marriage Act did this. It also put the federal government into the business of defining what constitutes a marriage, an area traditionally left to the states.[15]

Ad Hoc Federalism (2002–Present)

The mixed commitment to New Federalism is perhaps best exemplified by the presidency of George W. Bush. Bush came to the White House from the Texas governor's mansion and, at least on the surface, was a strong supporter of the principles of New Federalism. The policy record of the Bush administration, though, was considerably at odds with New Federalism sentiments. For example, Bush's signature domestic policy was the No Child Left Behind Act, which asserted federal control over important aspects of public education, a policy area traditionally under the jurisdiction of state and local governments. Peter Harkness, editor of *Governing* magazine, summed up the Bush administration's record on federalism thus: "The administration has mandated more, preempted more and run roughshod over state initiatives that didn't conform to its own ideology."[16]

Michigan was the first state to plow its roads and to use the yellow dividing line on its highways.

Part of Bush's departure from the New Federalism philosophy was driven by recession and war. Throughout the history of the United States, during times of crisis, power has become centralized in the national government—it simply is better equipped than the individual states to deal with national economic challenges or international conflict. The Bush administration found itself struggling with a soft economy at the beginning of its term and a disastrous slide into economic recession at the end of its term. In between, much of its focus was devoted to a global war on terrorism in response to the devastating attacks of September 11, 2001.

During the 8 years of the Bush administration, the commitment to New Federalism dissolved more or less entirely. This did not necessarily mean that federal–state relations in the Bush era shifted from a commitment to devolution to a commitment to centralizing power in Washington, D.C. What it meant was that a principled guiding philosophy of state–federal relations—such as dual federalism, cooperative federalism, or New Federalism—was abandoned. Instead a new, more partisan or ideologically based approach to state–federal relations came to the fore, an approach described as **ad hoc federalism.**[17] Ad hoc federalism is the process of choosing a state-centered or nation-centered view of federalism on the basis of political or partisan convenience. In other words, the issue at hand, not a core philosophical commitment to a particular vision of federalism, determines a policymaker's commitment to state or federal supremacy.

This is not necessarily a bad thing for states or localities. For example, when the federal government failed to ratify the Kyoto Protocol, a treaty addressing climate change—an international agreement considered the province of the federal government—more than 700 generally liberal-leaning U.S. cities decided independently to adopt the treaty's provisions. In other words, based on the issue at hand, more liberal cities decided that treaties concerning global warming were within their jurisdiction. Similarly, as we have already seen, when the federal government would not pass an immigration law, more conservative states decided based on the issue at hand that this was within their jurisdiction. States such as Alabama, Arizona, Georgia, Indiana, South Carolina, and Utah, accordingly, passed immigration laws.[18] The big concern of ad hoc federalism is that it treats the key institutional feature of the American political system not as a consistent and stable basis for organizing policy and constitutional responsibilities but as a more incoherent structure that is viewed differently depending on ideological convenience. Thus, conservatives champion states' rights in arguing against the federal government's constitutional authority to mandate the purchase of a health insurance policy, but they conveniently forget states' rights when arguing for the federal government's authority to pass laws outlawing gay marriage. Similarly, while liberals traditionally have been more inclined to downplay states' rights arguments in favor of centralizing federal government power over a wide range of issues, they discover a commitment to states' rights when it suits them (on gay marriage, for example). Ad hoc federalism makes equal opportunity hypocrites of all.

The shift toward ad hoc federalism was, at least temporarily, slowed by the Great Recession of 2008–2009, which shook up state–federal relations and shifted power decisively toward the federal government. This was not so much a premeditated attempt by the federal government to usurp the power of the states as it was a recognition that state and local government revenues were in free fall and only the federal government had the capacity to stem the financial bleeding. The federal government, though, was not going to provide billions of dollars to states and localities without getting its policy priorities attended to. Accordingly, out of budgetary necessity, states and localities found themselves orbiting the policy preferences of the federal government.

Ad hoc federalism
The process of choosing a state-centered or nation-centered view of federalism on the basis of political or partisan convenience

In the past few years, the economy returned to modest growth and the tide of federal grants-in-aid dropped dramatically. Between 2011 and 2012, federal grants to state and local governments plunged by roughly 12 percent in inflation-adjusted terms. As states once more began to stand on their own two financial feet, they almost immediately began trying to assert more independence from the federal government. That trend was accelerated by a series of elections beginning in 2010 that established strongly conservative Republican governments in about half the states that often openly resisted working with the federal government on a wide variety of policy issues. Probably the best example of this was the Affordable Care Act, or Obamacare. Although Obamacare was originally designed to be implemented with broad buy-in and cooperation from the states, governors such as Texas's Rick Perry and South Carolina's Nikki Haley were openly hostile to it. In 2014, the South Carolina legislature actually passed a bill making it illegal for state agencies and employees to implement Obamacare. States were not just trying to resurrect nullification for Obamacare; legislators in Missouri, Alaska, and Kansas tried to push through bills that would effectively make it illegal to enforce federal gun control laws.

This new, more confrontational face of ad hoc federalism raises real questions about the future of state–federal relations and the ability of different levels of government to work cooperatively with each other (see the box "States Under Stress: Two-Speed Federalism").

The Supreme Court: The Umpire of Federalism

Article VI of the Constitution contains the national supremacy clause, which declares that the Constitution, laws passed by Congress, and national treaties are the "supreme law of the land." This does not mean that the states are always subordinate to the national government. Don't forget—the Tenth Amendment also counts as part of that supreme law. However, it does mean that federal courts often have to referee national–state

conflicts. Because it has the final say in interpreting the Constitution, the Supreme Court is, in effect, the umpire of federalism. Its rulings ultimately decide the powers and limitations of the different levels of government.

The Rise of Nation-Centered Federalism on the Court

Throughout U.S. history, the Supreme Court has cycled through trends of state-centered and nation-centered philosophies of federalism. As we have already seen, the early Supreme Court under Chief Justice John Marshall pursued a fairly broad interpretation of the federal government's powers in such cases as *McCulloch v. Maryland*. Marshall's successor, Roger Taney, took the Court in a more state-centered direction by establishing dual federalism as the Court's central operating philosophy. The shift from dual federalism to cooperative federalism required a return to a more nation-centered judicial philosophy. Although the Court initially took a more nation-centered direction in its rulings following the Civil War, it was not until the Great Depression and Roosevelt's New Deal that a decisive tilt in the Court's rulings cleared the way for the rise of cooperative federalism and the centralization of power in the national government.

The shift toward a liberal interpretation of the federal government's powers dominated the Supreme Court's operating philosophy for much of the next 60 years and is exemplified by its decision in *United States v. Darby Lumber Co.* (1941). The substantive issue at stake in this case was whether the federal government had the power to regulate wages. The Supreme Court said yes, but the decision is of more lasting interest because of the majority opinion's dismissive comment on the Tenth Amendment. Once considered the constitutional lockbox of state power, the amendment, according to the Court's ruling, now did little more than state "a truism that all is retained which has not been surrendered." In other words, the Tenth Amendment was simply a basket for the "leftover" powers the federal government had not sought or did not want.

During and after the New Deal era, the Supreme Court also accelerated a trend of broadly

States Under Stress

Two-Speed Federalism

At first glance, the policy topics of health care, homeland security, education, and abortion seem to have little in common. Substantively, that is true enough. Structurally, though, they all share something important in common: Congress and/or the Supreme Court has taken actions intended to guarantee equal and uniform application of laws and policy regulation nationwide. That uniformity seems to be breaking down fast, as there are now large policy differences among the states in all these areas.

Widening differences in state politics and policy priorities, many of them rooted in differences in political culture, are contributing to an increasing policy polarization among the states. These differences are readily apparent in the diverging of public policies originated among the states, whether they be legalization of gay marriage and marijuana use or "stand-your-ground" gun laws and climate-change policies. Recently, however, these yawning ideological gulfs have begun to spill over into the implementation of federal programs as well.

Recent elections brought a good deal of polarization to state governments. In 2014, a single party controlled a supermajority in the legislature in roughly half the states, and almost half had unified Republican control of both the governor's office and the legislature. Concurrent with the emergence of one-party dominance in many states is a growing ideological distance between the two parties that increasingly reflects the yawning divide that characterizes Congress. With a Democratic president who is far from popular with right-leaning voters, conservative Republican governors have not just the incentive but the political muscle to mount serious challenges to federal mandates and policy prescriptions.

At a minimum, growing ideological differences across states clearly help explain wide differences in participation by states in major federal policy programs. For example, the Affordable Care Act intended for states to expand Medicaid (a health care program for the poor) and to set up their own online health care exchanges. More than a dozen states have refused to do either. State participation in federal programs is increasingly reflective of the ideological and partisan composition of state government. What can the federal government do when state governments flat out refuse to work with them, even to the extent of turning down big federal monetary incentives to participate? The answer seems to be, work with the states you have rather than the states you want. Out of necessity, national officials have taken ad hoc federalism to a new extreme by adopting flexible strategies that largely enable states to participate in new federal initiatives as much or as little as their politics permit. These initiatives include the following:

interpreting Congress's powers to regulate interstate commerce. It did this through its interpretation of the **interstate commerce clause**. In *Wickard v. Filburn* (1942), the Court ruled that the clause gave Congress the power to regulate what a farmer could feed his chickens. The case involved an Ohio farmer, Roscoe Filburn, who was growing more wheat than allowed under federal production limits. He wasn't selling the excess wheat but feeding it to his chickens. The Court reasoned that this reduced the amount of chicken feed Filburn would buy on the open market and because that market was an interstate market, which meant interstate commerce, Congress could regulate what Filburn was doing. In *Heart of Atlanta Motel v. United States* (1964) and *Katzenbach v. McClung* (1964), the justices ruled that this clause gave Congress the power to regulate private acts of racial discrimination. These cases involved the owners of a motel and a restaurant, respectively, who wanted to refuse service to blacks. The Court ruled that

---

Interstate commerce clause
Constitutional clause that gives Congress the right to regulate interstate commerce. This clause has been broadly interpreted to give Congress a number of implied powers.

- *Partial preemptions:* These establish a floor but not a ceiling for new regulations, allowing some states to go beyond a federally required level of regulation. California, for example, has long taken advantage of this with the Clean Air Act, which allows states to impose stricter limits on auto emissions than what is federally mandated.
- *Waivers:* These tools have been used for several decades, first in welfare reform and later in Medicaid. States have been able to tailor federal entitlement and grant programs to achieve cost savings, shifts in service-delivery approaches, and other innovations.
- *Opt-outs:* These have allowed conservative states to avoid participating in some federal programs altogether. In the case of regulatory opt-outs, the federal government typically stands by to enforce federal rules in nonparticipating states, thereby ensuring some level of national uniformity. This was most notable with the Affordable Care Act, which allows states to opt out of operating their own insurance exchanges. When states opt out of grants, however, there is typically no federal fallback.

Where is all this leading? No one is quite sure. People increasingly talk of a two-speed European Union where, for example, some EU members adopt the euro while other member nations such as Denmark and Britain opt out and keep their own currencies. It seems as though something similar is happening in the political system of the United States; a sort of "two-speed federalism" is emerging where states opt in or out of federal policy initiatives based on their ideological and partisan leanings. Whether this is good or bad remains to be seen. On the one hand, states could emerge as newly empowered actors in charge of federal programs. On the other, the polarization that gave rise to wide variations among the states could become institutionalized, further segmenting the nation into radically different policy worlds.

Two-speed federalism could also be temporary. If the goals of national programs become more deeply rooted—for example, if people decide they like the expanded health care opportunities associated with Obamacare—it could prompt a push for stronger forms of nationalization of policy programs. In other words, if state governments will not implement policy programs that state citizens decide they want, they might ask the federal government not to take away state options to opt out.

Source: Adapted from Paul Posner and Timothy Conlon, "The Future of Federalism in a Polarized Country," *Governing*, February 2014.

these businesses served interstate travelers, that was interstate commerce, and so Congress had the power to force them to obey federal antidiscrimination laws.

A series of such decisions over the course of more than 50 years led some judicial scholars to conclude that the Supreme Court had essentially turned the concept of enumerated and reserved powers on its head. In effect, the assumption now seemed to be that the federal government had the power to do anything the Constitution did not specifically prohibit.[19] The states and localities were drawn ever closer into subordinate satellite roles in

orbit around the federal government. This situation continued until just before the end of the 20th century. At that point, the Court once again began siding with the states over the federal government.

A Tenth Amendment Renaissance or Ad Hoc Federalism?

By the mid-1990s, the Supreme Court was dominated by justices appointed by New Federalists. Reagan, who had campaigned on his intention to nominate federal judges who shared his conservative philosophy, appointed four. He also elevated a fifth, William Rehnquist—originally appointed as an associate justice by Nixon—to the position of chief justice. Reagan's vice president and presidential successor, George H. W. Bush, appointed two more justices. The end result was a mid-1990s Supreme Court chosen largely by conservative Republican presidents who wanted limits set on the federal government's powers and responsibilities. The justices obliged.

In a series of narrow (mostly 5–4) decisions in the 1990s, the Court began to back away from the nation-centered interpretation of the Constitution that had dominated its rulings during the era of cooperative federalism (see Table 2-3). *United States v. Lopez* (1995) was a significant victory for states' rights and a clear break from a half century of precedent. This case involved the Drug Free School Zone Act of 1990, which made it a federal crime to possess a firearm within 1,000 feet of a school. Following a good deal of precedent, Congress justified its authority to regulate local law enforcement by using a very liberal interpretation of the interstate commerce clause, the basic argument being that the operation of public schools affected interstate commerce so the federal government had the constitutional authority

TABLE 2-3

Key U.S. Supreme Court Rulings Regarding Federalism, 1995–2014

Case	Decision
United States v. Lopez (1995)	Court strikes down a federal law prohibiting possession of firearms near public schools. First time since World War II that Court placed limits on Congress's powers under the interstate commerce clause.
Seminole Tribe of Florida v. Florida (1996)	Court rules Congress cannot allow citizens to sue states in a federal court except for civil rights violations. State claim upheld.
Printz v. United States (1997)	Court strikes down a federal law requiring mandatory background checks for firearms purchases. State claim upheld.
Alden v. Maine (1999)	Court rules that Congress does not have the power to authorize citizens to sue in state court on the basis of federal claims. State claim upheld.
United States v. Morrison (2000)	Court strikes down the federal Violence Against Women Act. State claim upheld.
Reno v. Condon (2000)	Court upholds a federal law preventing states from selling driver's license information. State claim overturned.
Bush v. Gore (2000)	Court overrules a Florida Supreme Court action allowing hand recounts of contested election ballots. State claim overturned.
Alabama v. Garrett (2001)	Court rules that state employees cannot sue their employers in federal court to recover monetary damages under the provisions of the Americans with Disabilities Act. State claim upheld.
Lorillard Tobacco Co. v. Reilly (2001)	Court strikes down Massachusetts laws regulating the advertising of tobacco products. State claim overturned.
Kelo v. City of New London (2005)	Court rules that government can seize private property for public purposes, including economic development. State claim upheld.
Gonzales v. Raich (2005)	Court rules that federal laws outlawing marijuana can be upheld by federal law enforcement officers in states where medical marijuana has been legalized. State law enforcement groups, however, do not have to participate in federal efforts to seize marijuana.
Gonzales v. Oregon (2006)	Court rules that the U.S. attorney general overstepped his authority by threatening to eliminate prescription-writing privileges for doctors who follow state law allowing physician-assisted suicide. State claim upheld.
Arizona v. United States (2012)	Court rules that states do not have the authority to enact and enforce immigration laws; however, it allows states to implement "show-me-your-papers" regulations that require law enforcement officers to determine the immigration status of anyone they stop or detain.
National Federation of Independent Business v. Sebelius (2012)	Court rules that the federal government can require individuals to purchase health insurance and that doing so does not violate powers reserved to the states under the Tenth Amendment.

to ban guns near schools. The Supreme Court disagreed and argued that the commerce clause granted no such authority.

Similar reasoning was used by the justices in *United States v. Morrison* (2000) to strike down the Violence Against Women Act. Congress had passed this law in 1994 out of concern that the states, although having primary responsibility for criminal law, were not adequately dealing with the problem of violence against women. The key provision of the act gave assault victims the right to sue their assailants in federal court. Congress argued that it was authorized to pass such a law because fear of violence prevented women from using public transportation or going out unescorted at night. Such fears, the reasoning went, placed limits on economic opportunities for women. This argument made the connection to commerce and Congress's constitutional authority. The Supreme Court again rejected this broad interpretation of the commerce clause.

At the same time as it was narrowly interpreting the Constitution to limit federal power, the Supreme Court after 1990 began to interpret the Constitution broadly to expand state power. Notably, the Court made a series of rulings that broadly interpreted the Eleventh Amendment's guarantee of **sovereign immunity** to the states. Sovereign immunity is essentially "the right of a government to be free from suits brought without its consent."[20] In cases such as *Seminole Tribe of Florida v. Florida* (1996) and *Alden v. Maine* (1999), the Supreme Court adopted an interpretation of the Eleventh Amendment that limited the right of citizens to sue states for violations of federal law. These rulings not only lessened the power of the federal government over the states but also arguably gave the states more power over their own citizens.

Although these and other rulings resurrected the Tenth Amendment and underlined the independent power of the states, there has been an element of inconsistency to Supreme Court decisions since 1990. In *Bush v. Gore* (2000), the Court abandoned its commitment to states' rights by overruling the Florida Supreme Court and ordering a halt to the contested recount of presidential ballots. Democratic presidential nominee Al Gore indisputably won the popular vote in 2000, but the outcome of the presidential election was decided by Florida's electoral votes. Gore and Bush ran neck and neck in this state, the decision so close that a series of controversial and hotly contested recounts were undertaken with the approval of the Florida courts. In effect, the U.S. Supreme Court overturned the state court's interpretation of state law—which allowed the recounts—and decided the presidency in favor of George W. Bush. Another decision that favored federal power over state power came in *Lorillard Tobacco Co. v. Reilly* (2001). Here, the Court overturned a Massachusetts law that regulated the advertising of tobacco products. The Court argued that federal law—specifically, the Federal Cigarette Labeling and Advertising Act—legitimately preempts state law on this issue.

The Court also trumped 10 states that had legalized the use of marijuana for medical purposes. In *Gonzales v. Raich* (2005), the Court, led by its more liberal justices, ruled that federal law enforcement officers, prosecutors, and judges can prosecute and punish anyone possessing marijuana. This ruling is interesting because, while it upheld federal laws, it did not overturn state laws and left state and local officials free not to participate in any federal efforts to seize medical marijuana.[21] Just 6 months later, however, the Court upheld a state law related to serious illnesses when it ruled in *Gonzales v. Oregon* (2006) against the federal government's challenge of Oregon's law that allows physician-assisted suicide. In recent years, the Court has reviewed a number of preemptions of state law on everything from banking regulation to labor arbitration, and, for the most part, it has sided with federal authority.[22]

This was certainly the case in the Court's 2012 landmark ruling in *National Federation of Independent Business v. Sebelius*, which bitterly disappointed many conservatives. This case decided the federal government's power to enact the Patient Protection and Affordable Care Act (aka Obamacare), in particular the federal government's authority to require individuals to purchase health insurance. Chief Justice John

---

Sovereign immunity
The right of a government not to be sued without its consent

Roberts, appointed by President George W. Bush and typically seen as a member of the Court's conservative bloc, surprised many by voting with the more liberal justices to affirm that power. Yet in another landmark case decided the same year, the Court put caveats on federal supremacy. In *Arizona v. United States* (2012), the case that decided Arizona's immigration law discussed in the opening section of this chapter, the Supreme Court essentially ruled that only the federal government has the power to set immigration policy but affirmed that states have the right to check the immigration status of people within their borders. In other words, the Court sort of split the difference between state and federal claims to power.

So over the past quarter century or so, the Supreme Court has sometimes zigged and sometimes zagged on state–federal relations. In the 1990s its rulings seemed to herald a resurrection of states' rights by conservative justices, but this commitment was never consistent, and something of that inconsistency is seen in the landmark cases affecting state–federal relations in the past few years. Some scholars argue that these sorts of inconsistencies have always been characteristic of the Supreme Court's federalism rulings. Ideology—not a firm commitment to a particular vision of state–national relations—is what ultimately decides how a justice rules in a particular case.[23] Therefore, a Court dominated by conservative appointees will occasionally depart from the state-centered notion of federalism if a nation-centered view is more ideologically pleasing, whereas a Court dominated by liberal appointees will do the opposite. The Supreme Court, like the president, finds it hard to resist the temptations of ad hoc federalism.

> Ideology—not a firm commitment to a particular vision of state–national relations—is what ultimately decides how a justice rules in a particular case.

Conclusion

The Constitution organizes the United States into a federal political system. This means that the states are powerful independent political actors that dominate important policy areas. Many of these policy areas are those with the most obvious and far-reaching roles in the day-to-day lives of citizens. Education, law enforcement, utility regulation, and road construction are but a handful of examples. The independence they are granted under the federal system allows states broad leeway to go their own way in these and many other policy areas.

The resulting variation has a number of advantages, such as making it easier to match local preferences with government action and allowing states and localities to experiment with innovative programs and policies. There are also a number of disadvantages. These include the complexity and difficulty in coordinating policy at the national level. The interests of state and national governments overlap in many areas. Because of this and because the Constitution does not clearly resolve the question of who has the power to do what in these arenas of shared interest, conflict is inevitable.

What is the future of federalism? In the past decade, the federal government's commitment to New Federalism all but collapsed, being replaced by a much more ad hoc approach to state–federal relations. Under the George W. Bush administration, the federal government veered away from the devolutionary trends of the 1990s and made numerous efforts to shift power to the national government. The economic shocks of 2008–2009 caused a significant retrenchment among subnational governments, which suddenly found themselves heavily reliant on the federal government as a major revenue source. As state budgets and an overextended federal government have slowed grants-in-aid, states have been seeking to assert more independence from the federal government. This does not, however, seem to herald a return of New Federalism but more a resumption of ad hoc federalism. This sometimes is taking a particularly confrontational path, with some states opting out, or even seeking to effectively nullify, federal programs and laws. The ideological and partisan divides at the root of ad hoc federalism have clearly grown over the past few election cycles. This creates a situation ripe for continued conflicts between state and federal governments, conflicts that in many cases will have to be resolved by the Supreme Court. The Court recently has exhibited some inconsistency in its own commitment to favoring states' rights in resolving state–federal conflicts. Yet, regardless of how these conflicts are ultimately resolved, the future undoubtedly will find states and localities continuing to play a central role in the U.S. political system, both as independent policymakers and as cooperative partners with the federal government.

The Latest Research

Federalism in the United States is dynamic. The roles and responsibilities of federal and state governments are constantly evolving based on political and economic context, policy demands and innovation, Supreme Court rulings, and the political philosophies, ideological preferences, and partisan fortunes of lawmakers at both levels of government. Current scholars of federalism find themselves in a particularly interesting period in the development of intergovernmental relations. The worst of the recession is over, yet fiscal stresses remain. Federal, state, and local governments are trying to reset their relationships with each other to deal most effectively with what comes next—but no one is sure what comes next.

Below are summaries of some of the most recent research on federalism. Two constant themes emerge from this stream of scholarship: First, intergovernmental relations have undergone and are currently undergoing dramatic changes, and, second, those changes have enormous implications not just for politics and policy but also for the day-to-day lives of citizens.

• • • • • • • • • • • • • • • • • • • •

- **Bowling, Cynthia J., and J. Mitchel Pickerill.** "Fragmented Federalism: The State of American Federalism 2012–13," *Publius: The Journal of Federalism* 43 (2013): 315–356.

  The scholarly journal *Publius* periodically publishes articles by scholars of state politics on the state of American federalism. This article introduces an entire issue of that journal devoted to academic studies of the current climate of state–federal relations. As Bowling

and Pickerill conclude, these relations are, "arguably, more chaotic, complex and contentious than ever before." There seems to be less and less of a broad, coherent philosophy governing intergovernmental relations and more and more marriages of policy convenience when the ideological and partisan stars line up—and the pursuit of bitter and acrimonious divorces when they do not. The bottom-line conclusion here is that increasingly intense partisan and ideological differences are creating gridlock in the federal system just as they have done in Congress. States are seeking to pursue their own policy paths in areas such as gay marriage, fracking, health care, immigration, and gun control—embracing federal guidance when it fits local politics and forcefully rejecting that guidance when it does not. The result is not only a patchwork of policies but heightened intergovernmental conflict.

- **Rivlin, Alice.** "Rethinking Federalism for More Effective Governance." *Publius: The Journal of Federalism* 42 (2012): 387–400.

  In this article, Rivlin argues that the realities of post-recession governance create a pressing need for a reconsideration of the relationship between state and federal governments. In particular, Rivlin pushes for two key reforms. First, she argues that state and federal governments should rethink their job responsibilities. Rather than taking on increasingly shared responsibilities in areas such as education, she suggests, one level of government should take primary responsibility. Who gets the job should depend on who is best positioned

(Continued)

(Continued)

to do that job and who has traditionally had the legal authority to do it (in the case of education, this would be the states). This is essentially an argument that a good dose of dual federalism is not necessarily a bad thing. The second big reform that Rivlin endorses is a fundamental rethinking of how government funds itself. She argues that the existing federal tax system is poorly suited for the 21st century and suggests the implementation of a kind of national sales tax, collected by the federal government but distributed to the states. This would allow states to recapture sales taxes lost to Internet sales as well as provide a more uniform and reliable revenue source for more distinct and defined policy responsibilities.

- **Robertson, David Brian.** *Federalism and the Making of America*. New York: Routledge, 2012.

The two articles described above are analyses of changes in intergovernmental relations more or less as they occur in real time. Robertson's book makes a good companion to these, placing such time-focused studies into perspective by offering a sweeping story of the historical development of federalism in America, from its birth at the founding of the Republic to the red-state–blue-state conflicts of the 21st century. The book is notable for its focus on federalism as the stage on which most of the great policy battles in American history have been fought. Racial relations, economic regulation, social welfare and regulation—all these issues and more have been critically shaped by America's system of intergovernmental relations.

- **Weissert, Carol S.** "Beyond Marble Cakes and Picket Fences: What U.S. Federalism Scholars Can Learn From Comparative Work." *Journal of Politics* 73 (2011): 965–979.

This article is Weissert's presidential address to the Southern Political Science Association, one of the more prestigious professional associations in the discipline. In it Weissert examines an issue critical to readers of this textbook: the comparative method. She argues that while there is no doubt that state scholars put the comparative method to good use, they have a particular blind spot—they fail to learn from scholars of other federal systems that employ the same method. If we want to learn what differences really make a difference—not just in the United States but anywhere at any time—we need to pay attention to differences that make a difference in other federal systems, not just federalism in the United States.

Chapter Review

Key Concepts

- ad hoc federalism (p. 48)
- Bill of Rights (p. 36)
- block grants (p. 45)
- categorical grants (p. 44)
- centralized federalism (p. 44)
- compact theory (p. 40)
- concurrent powers (p. 35)
- confederacy (p. 29)
- cooperative federalism (p. 42)
- crosscutting requirements (p. 44)
- crossover sanctions (p. 45)
- dual federalism (p. 39)
- enumerated powers (p. 35)
- exclusive powers (p. 35)
- federalism (p. 29)
- Fourteenth Amendment (p. 38)
- full faith and credit clause (p. 36)

- general revenue sharing grants (p. 44)
- general welfare clause (p. 36)
- grants-in-aid (p. 44)
- implied powers (p. 35)
- interstate commerce clause (p. 50)
- national supremacy clause (p. 35)
- nation-centered federalism (p. 40)
- necessary and proper clause (p. 36)
- New Federalism (p. 45)
- nullification (p. 40)

- preemption (p. 35)
- privileges and immunities clause (p. 36)
- representative government (p. 32)
- secession (p. 40)
- sovereign immunity (p. 53)
- state-centered federalism (p. 40)
- states' rights (p. 40)
- Tenth Amendment (p. 38)
- unfunded mandates (p. 45)
- unitary systems (p. 29)

Suggested Websites

- **www.nga.org.** Website of the National Governors Association, which includes a section devoted to state–federal relations.
- **www.publius.oxfordjournals.org.** Website of *Publius,* a scholarly journal dedicated to the study of federalism.
- **www.supremecourtus.gov.** Website of the U.S. Supreme Court; includes text of the Court's opinions.

State Stats on Federalism

Explore and compare data on the states! Go to **edge.sagepub.com/smithgreenblatt5e** *to do these exercises.*

1. On average, the federal government contributes around 10 percent, the state government around 47 percent, and local governments around 44 percent to public K-12 schools. How much money, per capita, does your state spend on elementary and secondary education? Is this an example of compact federalism, dual federalism, or cooperative federalism? Why?

2. What percentage of your state's population is enrolled in Medicaid? How does your state compare to the states around it? How might the Affordable Care Act change these numbers moving forward?

3. How many immigrants were admitted to New Mexico in 1997? How many were admitted to Arizona in the same year? How might this difference affect variations in policies regarding immigration?

4. What was the incarceration rate per 100,000 people in Utah in 2010? What was the rate in neighboring Idaho? Why might this difference be concerning?

5. What was the tax levied on agricultural real estate in your state in 1994? What was the amount in a neighboring state? How might these differences affect someone looking to farm?

6. What percentage of the land in Nevada does the government own? What about in Connecticut? How might this difference lead to different relationships between these states and the federal government?

State constitutions differ from the U.S. Constitution in many ways. Some are older—the Massachusetts Constitution, shown here, was written about a decade before the U.S. Constitution was adopted. Most state constitutions are longer, more detailed, and much easier to change than their federal counterpart.

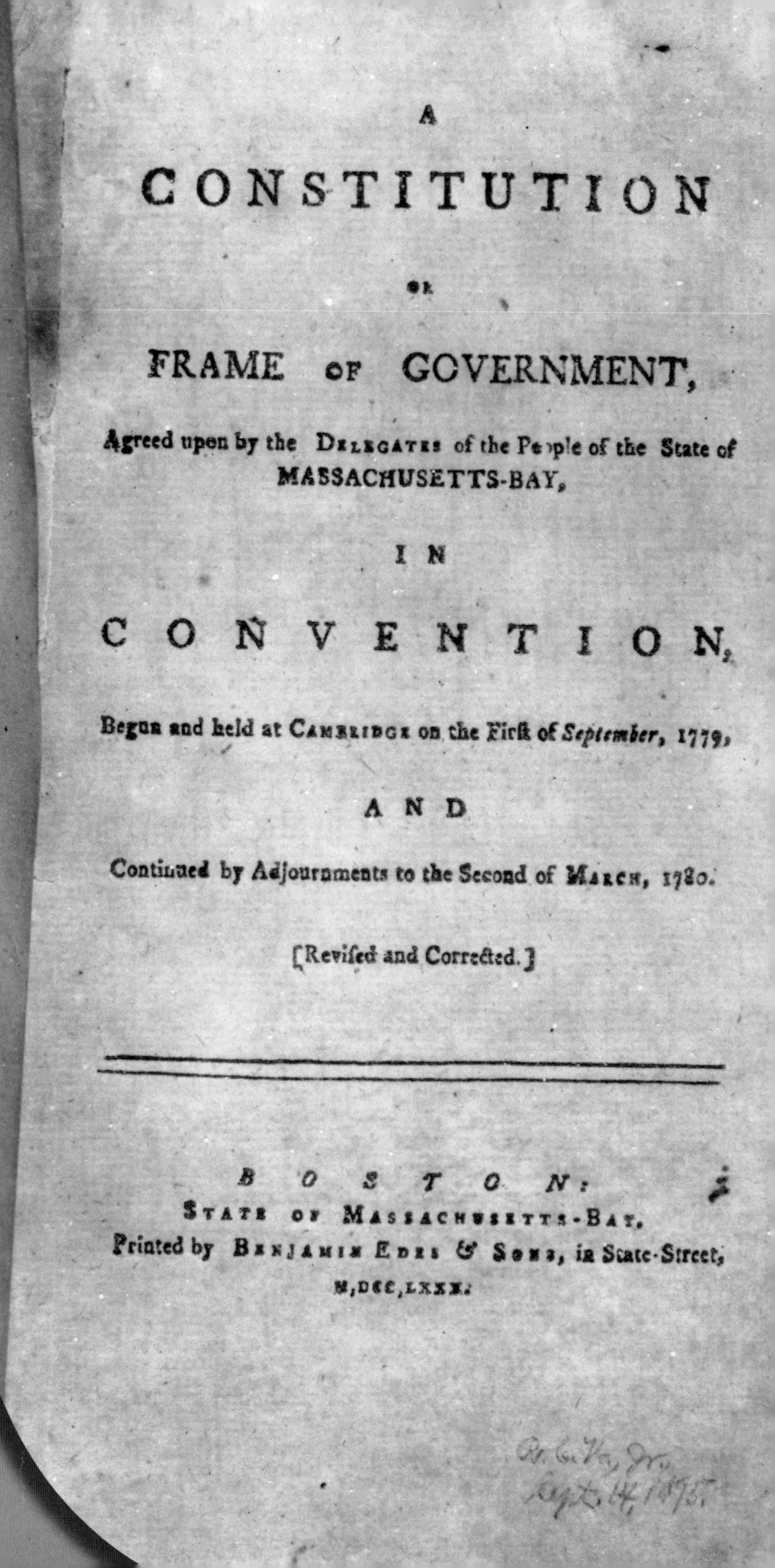
A

CONSTITUTION

OR

FRAME OF GOVERNMENT,

Agreed upon by the DELEGATES of the People of the State of MASSACHUSETTS-BAY,

IN

CONVENTION,

Begun and held at CAMBRIDGE on the First of *September*, 1779,

AND

Continued by Adjournments to the Second of MARCH, 1780.

[Revised and Corrected.]

BOSTON:

STATE OF MASSACHUSETTS-BAY,

Printed by BENJAMIN EDES & SONS, in State-Street,

M,DCC,LXXX.

The Granger Collection, New York

Constitutions

OPERATING INSTRUCTIONS

- What impact do state constitutions have on our lives?
- Why do state constitutions differ?
- How do constitutions determine what state and local governments can and cannot do?

You do not need a PhD to help change the state constitution in Colorado. You just need to be a registered voter. Want to understand what you are being asked to change? Well, keep studying. For that, you really might need a PhD.

Like many states, Colorado has a process of **direct democracy**—in other words, a system that allows citizens to make laws themselves rather than outsourcing the job to elected representatives. This includes the ability to vote on proposed amendments to the state constitution. Voting on amendments is one thing; understanding them is quite another. For example, consider the following proposed amendment (fair warning—prepare to go cross-eyed):

> Concerning reform of the state civil service system, and in connection therewith, modifying the merit principle, exempting certain positions from the system, modifying the number of eligible applicants from which an appointment is to be made, modifying the residency requirement, expanding the duration of temporary employment, specifying the rulemaking authority of the state personnel board and

---

Direct democracy
A system in which citizens make laws themselves rather than relying on elected representatives

After reading this chapter, you will be able to

- describe the role of state constitutions,
- explain how state constitutions evolved in early American history,
- discuss the role of bicameral legislatures in the first generation of state constitutions,
- identify the ways state constitutions can be formally changed,
- identify informal means of changing constitutions,
- discuss why constitutions vary from state to state,
- explain how state constitutions differ, and
- relate the ways local governments may be subject to governing documents such as a constitution.

the state personnel director, allowing the general assembly to reallocate the rulemaking authority of the state personnel board and state personnel director, authorizing a modification to the veterans' preference, and making conforming amendments.[1]

Eh? Don't get it? We don't either—and one of us actually has a PhD. According to one study, the language of policy proposals put to voters in direct democratic processes is written at a 17th-grade level. That means these proposals are, on average, written for people who have at least a college degree. In Colorado, such proposals were written at a 26th-grade level—they are literally written so you need a PhD to understand them (or not—it sure didn't help us make sense of the mouthful in the previous paragraph).[2]

This is important because, as we shall see, state constitutions have an enormous impact on state governments and policymaking—and on us. They affect the education we receive, the employment opportunities we enjoy, the political cultures of the states in which we live, and the rights we do (or don't) have. State constitutions and the rights and powers they provide also vary widely. Thus, it would be nice if we could at least get a plain-English general gist of what these all-important sets of rules and laws mean and what they imply. Ballot initiatives written in dense legalese probably won't get you there, but hopefully we can help you understand the importance of state constitutions and the difference they make—no PhD required.

For example, Colorado, as we have already seen, embraces the idea of direct democracy. In that state the constitution allows the **electorate**, or those individuals who can vote, to take policy matters into their own hands (even if the voters are not quite sure what they are holding). Ballot initiatives and referendums allow Colorado voters to amend the constitution or override the decisions of the state's elected officials—or even remove the officials entirely—with ease. In contrast, New York's constitution does not allow these things. New York politicians are famously insulated from voters' demands, and state-level decisions are made by a handful of senior elected officials.

So here's one difference that can make a big difference—some state constitutions allow direct democratic processes such as ballot initiatives and referendums, and other states do not. That's far from the only difference, though. State constitutions include everything from rules about who can hold elective office (some states have term limits, and others do not) to parking regulations for major municipalities. No two state constitutions are alike. What explains the tremendous variation among state constitutions? A state constitution reflects that state's particular historical experiences, its political culture, its geography, and its notions of what makes good government. We'll look at these sorts of differences and their implications in this chapter.

Electorate
The population of individuals who can vote

Before getting to that, though, it is critical to understand the importance of state constitutions, which serve an underappreciated role not just in organizing state and local governance but in determining individual rights and the operation of the entire federal system. Since the 1990s, the U.S. Supreme Court has made a number of decisions strengthening the role of states in the federal system, decisions that elevate the importance of state constitutions. The Court's insistence on determining the boundaries of federalism and evaluating state laws and regulations—a form of activism sometimes referred to as **judicial federalism**—even gained former Chief Justice William Rehnquist the nickname "Governor Rehnquist."[3]

State supreme courts also are becoming more assertive. In 1977, Supreme Court justice William Brennan, a former justice of the New Jersey Supreme Court, wrote a famous article for the *Harvard Law Review* noting that state constitutions afford their citizens a layer of rights above and beyond those protected in the U.S. Constitution. He urged state courts to pay more attention to these rights and to assert themselves more forcefully. They have. Some state supreme courts, for example, have ruled that their constitutions guarantee equal marriage rights to same-sex couples. (See the box "A Difference That Makes a Difference: State Constitutions and the Right to Marry.") This is an example of assertive state supreme courts finding new rights that exist only in state constitutions. This means that the documents that reflect and determine what state and local governments can and cannot do have become even more important to an understanding of politics in the United States.

What State Constitutions Do: It's Probably Different From What You Think

Mention "the constitution" and chances are good that your listener will think instantly of the U.S. Constitution. The founders have gotten more than 225 years of good press for their work in 1787. Schoolchildren memorize "We the People of the United States, in order to form a more perfect Union . . . " and venerate the document's wisdom. Yet the U.S. Constitution is only half the story. As residents of the United States, we live under a system of **dual constitutionalism**, in which the federal government and state governments are cosovereign powers. Both run in accordance with the rules laid out in their respective constitutions. Despite the important role state constitutions play in establishing our rights and organizing our local and state governments, most people know very little about them.

The U.S. Constitution and all state constitutions have some functions in common. They set forth the roles and responsibilities of the government, describe the basic institutional structure of the government, and establish procedures for the operation of these institutions. Most state constitutions reflect the influence of the U.S. Constitution. They create three primary branches of government (legislative, executive, and judicial) and provide a general governmental framework. Like the U.S. Constitution, they all contain something roughly equivalent to a bill of rights that spells out the rights of citizens and places specific limits on governmental powers. Most state constitutions place these rights firmly in the context of **natural law**, also known as **higher law**, a tradition that holds that these rights are not political creations but divine endowments. Natural law thus holds that basic rights and values, such as those guaranteed by the Bill of Rights, are not created by governments through law. If these rights were created by governments, after all, it would imply that governments could take them away. Instead,

Dual constitutionalism
A system of government in which people live under two sovereign powers. In the United States, these are the government of their state of residence and the federal government.

Judicial federalism
The idea that the courts determine the boundaries of state–federal relations

Natural law or higher law
A set of moral and political rules based on divine law and binding on all people

governments merely "discover" the rights that nature bestows to all people and restrains from interfering with those rights. Constitutions and any subsequent **constitutional amendments**, or changes, thus do not create rights; they are there to make sure those natural rights are not taken from anyone.

Yet in many ways it is misleading to compare state constitutions with their better-known federal counterpart. Consider the important differences discussed below.

Powers Granted to Government. Perhaps the most important and surprising difference between the U.S. Constitution and state constitutions is the scope of the documents. The U.S. Constitution's original purpose was to organize a federal government with sharply limited powers. In contrast, state governments have what is called **plenary power**, which means their powers are not limited to those laid down in the U.S. Constitution or their own state constitutions. As the Tenth Amendment of the U.S. Constitution makes clear, *all* powers not expressly delegated or forbidden to the federal government are reserved for the states. In other words, this is not a limited grant of power in the sense of laying out the specifics of what states have the authority to do or not do. It basically says that states can do whatever they want—they have complete or plenary power—as long as they do not contravene the U.S. Constitution.

That plenary power is vested in the lawmaking bodies of state government—that is, state legislatures. This does not mean that these legislatures can go around arbitrarily breaking the rules laid down by their own constitutions, which can be quite restrictive. What it means is they can act without express permission of the constitution; as long as their actions are not prohibited, they are good to go. Think of it like this: When passing a law, Congress must address the key question, "Is this allowed (by the U.S. Constitution)?" For state legislatures the key question is, "Is this prohibited (by the state constitution)?" That's the difference between limited and plenary powers in the federal system. State legislatures, through the U.S. Constitution and their own state constitutions, have these powers. Congress does not. State constitutions, in short, do not establish limited governments in the same way the U.S. Constitution establishes a limited federal government.[4]

Permanence. The U.S. Constitution is widely seen as the document that created the United States—the embodiment of the founders' wisdom. As such, it is held in the highest regard by politicians and the public alike. It has lasted more than two centuries and has been formally changed only 27 times. In contrast, state constitutions are amended and even replaced much more frequently. Most states have replaced their original constitutions at least once. California is currently on its second constitution. New York is on its fourth. Louisiana is on its eleventh. In fact, one political scientist has estimated that the average state constitution lasts for only about 70 years.[5]

Length. The federal constitution is a relatively short document. At about 7,400 words, it is shorter than most chapters in this book. In contrast, state constitutions tend to be much longer—about 26,000 words on average. Some are much, much longer. New York's constitution and California's ruling document are each roughly 50,000 words long. The longest state constitution, Alabama's, is more than 45 times the length of the U.S. Constitution.[6]

Specificity. Why are state constitutions so much longer than the federal constitution and so much more likely to change? Part of the answer has to do with the different functions of the federal constitution versus those of state constitutions. The U.S. Constitution is primarily concerned with setting up the basic structures and procedures of government. State constitutions do these things, too, but they often set forth procedures and address policies in much greater detail than the federal constitution

Constitutional amendments
Proposals to change a constitution, typically enacted by a supermajority of the legislature or through a statewide referendum

Plenary power
Power that is not limited or constrained

does. Whereas the federal constitution creates a framework for government, state constitutions often get into policy details. South Dakota, for instance, is one of several states that once sanctioned its state prison to produce twine and cordage. Oklahoma's constitution mandates that home economics be taught in school; Maryland's regulates off-street parking in Baltimore. Political scientist Christopher Hammonds has estimated that 39 percent of the total provisions in state constitutions are devoted to specific policy matters of this sort. In contrast, only 6 percent of the U.S. Constitution deals with such specific issues.[7]

> Whereas the federal constitution creates a framework for government, state constitutions often get into policy details. South Dakota, for instance, is one of several states that once sanctioned its state prison to produce twine and cordage.

Embrace of Democracy.
The U.S. Constitution creates a system of representative democracy; it purposefully rejects direct democracy as a basis for governance. The founders went to great pains to check "the whimsies of the majority" by designing a system of checks and balances that deliberately keeps policymaking at arm's length from the shifting winds of popular opinion. During the Progressive Era in the early 1900s, many states revamped their constitutions to do just the opposite. This was particularly true of the newer western and midwestern states, in which old-school politics was less entrenched and political cultures tended toward the moralistic or individualistic.

Progressive reformers believed that old constitutional arrangements were outmoded and that citizens should have the opportunity to participate directly in making laws. Moreover, they worried that state legislatures had been captured by wealthy special interests. In other words, they thought that representative democracy was working for the benefit of a few rather than for the benefit of all. Their solution was to give the people the ability to amend their constitutions and pass laws directly through the use of referendums and ballot initiatives. Thus, in about half the states, state constitutions champion direct democracy in a way that the U.S. Constitution purposefully does not.

Finances.
Congress and the White House can run up as much national debt as they can persuade bond buyers to swallow. In contrast, 32 state constitutions require the legislative and executive branches to balance their budgets. Another 17 states have statutes that mandate balanced budgets. Only Vermont can choose to run up debt as the feds do. Even state constitutions that do not require a balanced budget take a much more proscriptive, or restrictive, view of budget matters than does the U.S. Constitution. California's constitution, for instance, mandates that almost 40 percent of the state budget go toward education, a requirement that has constrained legislators' options when the state has been faced with budget shortfalls.

Other state constitutions mandate a specific style and format for laws that allow the transfer of money to the executive branch. These are known as **appropriations bills**. During the 1990s, some states, including Arizona, Colorado, Nevada, Oklahoma, and South Dakota, amended their constitutions to require supermajorities—two thirds or three fifths of the electorate—instead of simple majorities of the legislature to increase revenues or taxes.[8] Sometimes constitutions get more specific still, prohibiting legislators from attaching "riders" to appropriations bills and requiring a single subject for each bill. (Riders are amendments or additions unrelated to the main bill.) Not surprisingly, state legislators sometimes try to evade these strict requirements. As a result, state judges tend to be much more involved in monitoring the government's budget process than

---

Appropriations bills
Laws passed by legislatures authorizing the transfer of money to the executive branch

Library of Congress

are their federal counterparts. In 2004, for instance, the Ohio Supreme Court reminded legislators that it would strike down any laws passed in violation of the state's single-subject rule.

The Evolution of State Constitutions

The first state constitutions were not technically constitutions at all. Rather, they were **colonial charters** awarded by the king of England. These charters typically were brief documents giving individuals or corporations the right to establish "plantations" over certain areas and govern the inhabitants therein. King James I of England granted the first charter in 1606. It created the Virginia Company of London, which in 1607 established the first English settlement in North America at Jamestown in what is now the state of Virginia.

As the colonies expanded, many of these charters were amended to give the colonists "the rights of Englishmen." Just what those rights were, however, was never entirely clear. Britain's constitution was not (and is not) a written document. It is a tradition

---

Colonial charters
Legal documents drawn up by the British Crown that spelled out how the colonies were to be governed

based on the Magna Carta of 1215 and on a shared understanding of what government should and should not do. From the start, some colonies took an expansive view of their rights and privileges. The Massachusetts Bay Colony, like other English settlements in North America, was organized as a corporation and was controlled by a small group of stockholders. But whereas the charters of the other companies remained in England within easy reach of the British courts, Puritan leader John Winthrop took his colony's charter with him when he sailed for the New World in 1630. This made it difficult for the English government to seize and revoke the charter if the company misbehaved or operated illegally, which it soon did. The Puritans excluded non-churchgoers from local governments, punished people who violated their sense of morals, and generally behaved as an independent polity. This misbehavior eventually incurred the displeasure of King Charles II, who revoked the charter in 1691. Massachusetts then received a new royal charter that provided for a royal governor and a general assembly—a form of governance that lasted until the Revolutionary War, nearly a century later.[9]

When the colonies won their independence, it was clear that the colonial charters had to be replaced or at least modified. It was less clear what should replace them. Some colonial leaders believed that the Continental Congress should draft a model constitution that every state should adopt. Richard Henry Lee, a Virginia politician, explained the idea in a letter to John Adams in May 1776: "Would not a uniform plan of government, prepared for America by the Congress, and approved by the colonies, be a surer foundation of unceasing harmony to the whole?"[10]

Adams thought not. Although he liked the idea of uniform state constitutions in principle, he worried about what would happen in practice. He believed that effective government required a strong executive. The colonists' experience dealing with royal governors, however, had created an aversion to executive power. Adams feared that the Continental Congress would create governments dominated by powerful **unicameral legislatures** or even do away with governors altogether and create a special committee of legislators to handle the everyday business of governing. This would violate what he saw as the wise precautionary principle of the **separation of powers**.

Ultimately, despite being a unicameral body itself, the Continental Congress rejected that particular idea. Instead, it passed a resolution that urged the 13 colonies to reorganize their authority solely "on the basis of the authority of the people."[11] This set the stage for the states to create their own varied blueprints for government.

After independence was declared and secured, the states convened special assemblies to draft new constitutions. Most adopted lightly modified versions of their old colonial charters. References to the king of England were deleted and bills of rights added. In most of the new states, power was concentrated in the legislative branch to diminish the possibility of tyrannical governors' appearing in the political arena.

The First Generation of State Constitutions

This first generation of state constitutions created powerful **bicameral legislatures**—with a few exceptions. Georgia, Pennsylvania, and Vermont opted for unicameral legislatures. Governors and state judiciaries were clearly subordinate in most cases. In fact, legislatures often appointed both the governor and judges. No one envisioned that one day a state supreme court would have the power to overrule the acts of a legislature on the grounds that its laws were unconstitutional. Indeed, the states that did provide for a constitutional review entrusted that function to a special "council of revision" or to "councils of censor."

Nor did the early state constitutions embrace the now commonplace idea of "one person, one vote." Every early state constitution except Vermont's restricted voting access to white males who met certain minimum property requirements. Vermont gave the vote to every adult male. Supporters of a limited **franchise** defended these limitations as essential to the new republic. Without property qualifications, John Adams warned,

> there will be no end to it. New claims will arise; women will demand a vote; lads from 12 to 21 will think their rights are not enough attended to; and every man who has not a farthing will demand an equal voice with any other, in all acts of the state. It tends to confound and destroy all distinctions, and prostrate all ranks to one common level.[12]

Indeed, Adams wanted to restrict the franchise even further by setting still higher property requirements.

In practice, the actual requirements necessary to achieve the right to vote varied widely. Some states, such as New Hampshire, let all white male taxpayers vote. This reflected the fact that New Hampshire was a state of small landowners with a fairly egalitarian political culture. However, even this fair state specified a higher threshold of property ownership that must be met should a man wish to hold office. In Virginia, a state with a more hierarchical political culture dominated by a small group of wealthy landowners and planters, the property qualifications were stiff. Only white males who owned at least 25 acres and a 12-foot-by-12-foot house, 50 acres unsettled, or a town lot

---

Unicameral legislatures
Legislatures that have only one chamber. Nebraska is currently the only U.S. state with a unicameral legislature.

Separation of powers
The principle that government should be divided into separate legislative, executive, and judicial branches, each with its own powers and responsibilities

Bicameral legislatures
Legislatures made up of two chambers, typically a house of representatives, or assembly, and a senate

---

Franchise
The right to vote

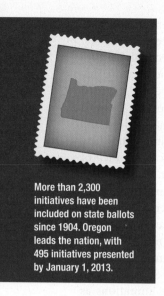

More than 2,300 initiatives have been included on state ballots since 1904. Oregon leads the nation, with 495 initiatives presented by January 1, 2013.

with a 12-foot-by-12-foot house could vote. It is not entirely clear how many people met these qualifications. Most scholars believe that in the more democratic northern states 60 to 80 percent of white males could vote. Needless to say, women and nonwhites could not.

Over the course of the 19th century, the franchise was expanded gradually, although in a very uneven and often unjust fashion. A number of southern states, for example, rewrote their constitutions to allow minorities to vote only when such changes were forced on them as part of the price for their readmission to the Union after the Civil War. African American rights also were enshrined in the Fourteenth Amendment of the U.S. Constitution. Yet, despite these protections, gains for African Americans proved short-lived. In the last decade of the 1800s, African Americans' ability to vote and to participate in all aspects of society were harshly limited by the passage of **Jim Crow laws**. These laws provided for the systematic separation of races, sharply restricted access to the franchise, and permitted the outright intimidation of African Americans.

Women fared only slightly better. Wyoming began to allow women the vote in 1869. By 1912, only 13 states had followed suit. It took the Nineteenth Amendment, ratified in 1920, to secure the right to vote, or suffrage, for all women nationwide. The limitations on the franchise imposed by many early state constitutions did little to promote good governance. State legislatures quickly developed an impressive record of corruption and fiscal extravagance because some of the men who had the legal right to vote also had money to influence politicians, an easy task in many states. But the era of unlimited legislative power did not last very long. New territories entering the Union, such

as Indiana and Mississippi, opted for elected governors, as did older states that began to revise or replace their constitutions in the 1820s. The intention was to create more balance among the branches of government and allow all voters (not just the rich ones) more of a voice in deciding who would run a state. By 1860, South Carolina was the only state with a governor selected by the legislature.[13] In hindsight, the 19th century is seen as a period of tumultuous constitutional change.

Formal Constitutional Changes

Every state constitution provides a method for making changes. Fourteen states actually require citizens to vote periodically on whether or not they want to convene a **constitutional convention**. Voters can decide if they want to amend or replace their state's constitution.[14]

In the early 19th century, suggesting such change could be an exciting—and dangerous—business. In 1841, a patrician attorney and renegade lawmaker by the name of Thomas Wilson Dorr convened an illegal constitutional convention. Its task was to replace Rhode Island's colonial charter with a more modern and progressive constitution. The aged document still limited the franchise to voters owning land valued at $134 or more at a time when other states had long since abandoned such requirements. Dorr's supporters elected him "governor" the following year on a platform that proposed allowing all white males—even Catholic immigrants, a group viewed by the Protestant majority with great suspicion—to vote, which caused the sitting governor to order Dorr arrested and tried for treason. Thus began the Dorr War, or Dorr's Rebellion. Dorr's supporters then attempted to seize the arsenal in Providence but were repelled when their cannons failed to discharge. A month later, Dorr and his followers tried again. This time a

---

Jim Crow laws
Legislative measures passed in the last decade of the 19th century that sought to systematically separate blacks and whites

Constitutional convention
An assembly convened for the express purpose of amending or replacing a constitution

The Peculiar Constitution of Early Pennsylvania

The original American colonies were established for a wide variety of purposes. The Massachusetts Bay Colony, for example, started off as a haven for a persecuted religious sect. The Puritans were determined to create, in the words of Massachusetts's first governor, John Winthrop, "a city upon a hill" to serve as an example of a holy community for all people. Other colonies, such as Virginia, began as business ventures. Still others, including Pennsylvania, were both.

Pennsylvania's first colonial charter reflected the colony's dual purposes as a religious settlement and an investment. It illustrates how state charters were created to serve very particular goals—and how "rights" that Americans now take for granted, such as the right to self-governance, were by no means obvious to this country's founders.

The colony started out as a business venture. In 1681, William Penn received a proprietary interest—the controlling share—in what is now the state of Pennsylvania as repayment for a debt that England's King Charles II owed Penn's father. Penn was already deeply involved in land speculation in North America. He and 11 other investors already owned East Jersey (present-day New Jersey). Soon after buying into Pennsylvania, they acquired a lease on Delaware.

Penn, however, wasn't just a businessman. He was also a devout Quaker, a member of a peace-loving religious group that was often at odds with the official Church of England. Pennsylvania was to Penn "a holy experiment"—a unique chance to found a province dedicated to Quakerism's vision of equality and religious freedom.

William Markham, Penn's deputy, was sent in 1681 to establish a seat of government for Penn's new colony. Penn also instructed his representative to construct a

"City of Brotherly Love"—Philadelphia. One year later, Penn himself arrived in his fledgling colony. His first major action was to draw up a constitution, or charter, for his new colony, which he called the "Frame of Government." His second major act was to establish friendly relations with the American Indians in the area—an unusual action that reflected his pacific religious beliefs.

In many ways, the Frame of Government echoed Quakerism's progressive dogmas. Penn's constitution guaranteed religious freedom to everyone who believed in God. It also set forth a humane penal code and encouraged the emancipation of slaves. In contrast, the early settlers of Massachusetts were interested not in individual religious freedom but in establishing a just Puritan society. As a result, the functions of local churches and town governments were intertwined in early Massachusetts. Indeed, the colony was governed as a virtual theocracy for its first 200 years.

However, the Pennsylvania model was not a uniform triumph of humane liberalism. Penn did use his charter to protect his business interests. The Frame of Government provided for an elected general assembly, but it also concentrated almost all power in the executive branch of government, which was controlled by Penn and the other proprietors.

It was not long before colonists began to chafe at some of the less progressive features of Penn's early constitution. He was forced to return to Pennsylvania in 1701 and issue a new constitution, the Charter of Privileges, which granted more power to the provincial assembly. However, the conflict between proprietary and antiproprietary forces did not diminish until 1776. That year, noted revolutionary Benjamin Franklin led a convention to assemble and approve a new constitution for the state as it struggled for independence from Great Britain.

force of militiamen and free blacks from Providence repelled them.[15] Still, Rhode Island's establishment got the hint. A new, more liberal constitution was quickly enacted.

The amendment process has since become a bit more routinized in most states. Amending or replacing a state constitution is typically a two-step process. First, a constitutional amendment or a new constitution must be proposed and meet a certain threshold of support. Then it must be ratified.

Changes to state constitutions are generally proposed in four primary ways: through legislative proposals, ballot initiatives or referendums, constitutional conventions, and constitutional commissions.

Legislative Proposals

Most attempts to change state constitutions begin with legislative proposals. Forty-nine state constitutions allow the state legislature to propose constitutional amendments to the electorate as a whole.[16] While virtually all state legislatures can propose constitutional amendments to submit to voters for approval or disapproval, what state legislatures actually have to do to make that happen varies quite a bit. In 17 states, a simple majority

vote in both houses of the legislature is enough to send a constitutional amendment on to the voters for **ratification**. Most other states require a supermajority for legislative approval of a constitutional amendment. Some states set the bar even higher. The constitutions of 11 states—Delaware, Indiana, Iowa, Massachusetts, Nevada, New York, Pennsylvania, South Carolina, Tennessee, Virginia, and Wisconsin—require the legislature to vote for a constitutional amendment in two consecutive sessions before it can be ratified.[17] In principle, some state legislatures also can propose completely new constitutions to voters. However, no state legislature has successfully proposed a wholesale constitutional change since Georgia did so in 1982.

Ratification

A vote of the entire electorate to approve a constitutional change, referendum, or ballot initiative

MAP 3-1

Number of Constitutions per State

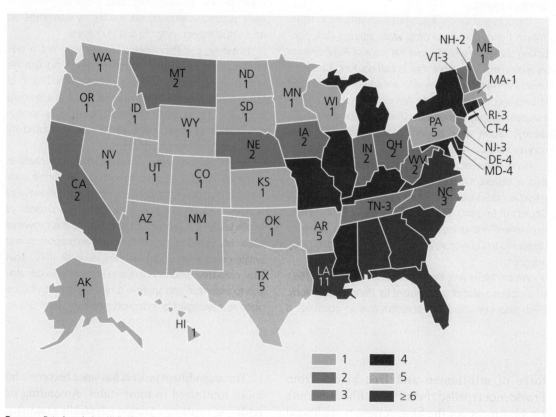

Source: Data from Audrey Wall, "State Constitutions," in *The Book of the States 2013*, ed. Council of State Governments (Lexington, KY: Council of State Governments, 2013), Table 1.1, http://knowledgecenter.csg.org/kc/content/book-states-2013-chapter-1-state-constitutions.

Ballot Initiatives and Referendums

Twenty-four states give voters another way to propose constitutional amendments—through **ballot initiatives** or popular **referendums**. These ballot measures offer citizens a way to amend the constitution or enact new legislation without working through the legislature. South Dakota was the first state to provide voters with the option of ballot initiatives, in 1898, but it was only after Oregon embraced them in 1902 that the push for direct democracy really got under way. In the 16 years that followed, nearly two dozen states followed Oregon's lead. The last of the two dozen states to approve ballot initiatives was Mississippi in 1992, some 70 years after the state supreme court tossed out its first ruling allowing initiatives.[18]

How ballot measures work in practice varies widely from state to state, although there are some common elements to the process. In most states, citizens must first provide the text of their proposal to an oversight body, usually the secretary of state's office or a legislative review committee. Then they need to gather enough signatures to place the proposal on the ballot. This threshold varies widely among states. Wyoming sets the bar high, requiring a number of signatures equal to 15 percent of the votes cast for governor in the most recent election. The bar

Ballot initiatives
Processes through which voters directly convey instructions to the legislature, approve a law, or amend the constitution

Referendums
Procedures that allow the electorate either to accept or reject a law passed by the legislature

MAP 3-2

Number of Amendments Adopted per State

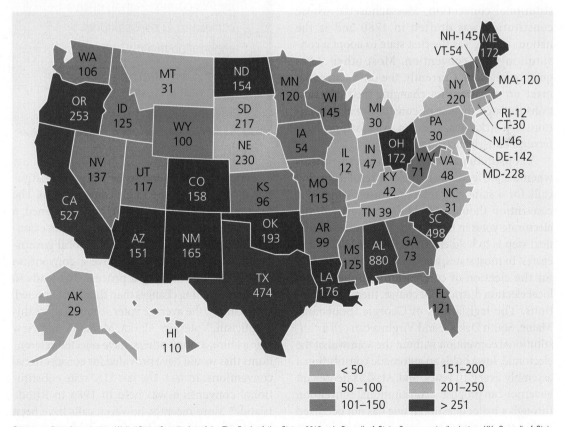

Source: Data from Audrey Wall, "State Constitutions," in *The Book of the States 2013,* ed. Council of State Governments (Lexington, KY: Council of State Governments, 2013), Table 1.1, http://knowledgecenter.csg.org/kc/content/book-states-2013-chapter-1-state-constitutions.

is lower in Colorado, where proponents need only gather signatures equal to 5 percent of the votes tallied for secretary of state in the previous election. The signatures are then verified, again by the secretary of state or the attorney general. Proposals that pass each test make it onto the ballot at the next election.

Ballot measures typically combine the proposal and ratification stages of the amendment process. Once a proposed amendment is on the ballot, it usually requires a simple majority to pass and become part of the constitution, although some state constitutions do require a supermajority. The practical result is laws without lawmakers; the initiative is commonly employed to seek policy changes that, for whatever reason, are not being considered or undertaken by the legislature.

Constitutional Conventions

The most freewheeling approach to changing or replacing a state constitution is to convene a constitutional convention. Massachusetts, whose constitution was drafted in 1780 and is the nation's oldest, was the first state to adopt a constitution via a convention. Most other states quickly followed. Currently, the only states that make no provisions for changing their constitutions through the use of constitutional conventions are Arkansas, Indiana, Mississippi, New Jersey, Pennsylvania, and Texas.

A constitutional convention typically begins when a state legislature passes a resolution that calls for a statewide referendum on whether a convention should be held. If a majority of the electorate votes in favor of the proposal, then the next step is to hold elections for convention delegates. In most states, a law is passed that provides for the election of convention members from local election districts. Of course, there are exceptions. The legislatures of Georgia, Louisiana, Maine, South Dakota, and Virginia can call a constitutional convention without the approval of the electorate. Iowa holds an automatic constitutional assembly every 10 years, and Alaska's lieutenant governor can propose a constitutional convention through a ballot question if one has not occurred within the past decade.

Once delegates are selected, a constitutional convention can convene. The delegates are free to amend, revise, or even replace their state's constitution; a constitutional convention can change the existing document in any way it sees fit or write an entirely new constitution. Ultimately, its handiwork goes before the electorate as a whole to be voted in or cast out.

Or a constitutional convention can do nothing at all. In 1974, Texas convened a convention to rewrite its creaky 1876 constitution. The delegates spent several months drafting a new constitution, but when it came time to put it to a vote, a majority of the delegates unexpectedly came out against it. The next year, the state legislature voted to put the newly drafted constitution to the public anyway as a referendum. The voters turned it down.[19]

> State legislators tend to be wary of constitutional conventions and rarely convene them. The reason for this caution is that, once convened, a constitutional convention theoretically can examine any and all aspects of state and local government.

State legislators tend to be wary of constitutional conventions and rarely convene them. The reason for this caution is that, once convened, a constitutional convention theoretically can examine any and all aspects of state and local government. Lawmakers who approve a convention might end up initiating a process that leads to more far-reaching changes than they had expected. Increasingly, the average voter seems to share this skepticism. Voters in Alaska, Montana, and New Hampshire, among others, have rejected referendums that would have provided for constitutional conventions. In fact, the last U.S. state constitutional convention was held in 1986 in Rhode Island.[20] More recently, however, calls have been heard for a convention to reform California's constitution, which includes a series of contradictory provisions; for example, some mandate spending while others restrict taxation. The irony is, voters approved the amendments that made the document so at odds with itself—and now they may have a hand in forcing its overhaul.

Constitutional Revision Commissions

If constitutional conventions are for the bold and trusting, then **constitutional revision commissions** are often the cautious technocrat's preferred route to constitutional change. A constitutional revision commission typically consists of a panel of citizens appointed by the governor, by the state legislature, or by both. The commission suggests—but cannot mandate—changes to the state constitution. Between 1990 and 2000, seven states—Alaska, Arkansas, California, Florida, New York, Oklahoma, and Utah—convened constitutional revision commissions. Alabama's legislature created a constitutional revision commission in 2011 and charged it with a multiyear effort to recommend piecemeal changes to that state's bloated constitution (see Figure 3-1). As of early 2014, only a handful of recommendations originating from Alabama's revision commission have been submitted to voters for approval, and some of these have been rejected.[21]

Two states go even further in their enthusiasm for constitutional commissions. Florida's constitution requires that a constitutional revision commission convene every 20 years. It also gives this commission a unique power—the right to present proposed changes directly to voters for their approval or rejection. Florida's latest constitutional revision commission met in 1998. It recommended 13 changes to the state constitution, including a provision that would allow local governments to expand their requirements for background checks and waiting periods for firearms purchases. That led the head of Florida's chapter of the National Rifle Association (NRA) to decry the proposal as a power grab and to issue a warning that gun owners might vote down all the proposed constitutional changes, even changes with universal support, should the firearms provision be included.[22] The commission refused to back down. Six months later, more than 70 percent of voters supported the measure.

The other state with an unusual constitutional revision commission is Utah, the only state whose commission is permanent. Members of the Utah Constitutional Revision Commission are appointed by the governor, by the leaders of both houses of the legislature, and by sitting commission members. Unlike Florida's commission, Utah's commission can issue its recommendations only in the form of a public report to the governor. Although it is a permanent body, the Utah commission has not met much lately—it got into hot water for not supporting (or opposing) amendments favored by partisan interests in the state legislature. In response, the legislature passed a law mandating that the commission can meet only if it is specifically requested to do so by the governor or legislature, and neither has proven particularly eager to make such a request.

Ratification

Once an amendment has been proposed and found acceptable, it must be ratified before it can go into effect. In most states, this is a straightforward process. First, the proposed constitutional amendment or new constitution is put before the voting public in the next statewide election. Then, the electorate either approves or rejects it. Two states add a twist to this process. In South Carolina, a majority of both houses of the state legislature must vote to approve a constitutional amendment—after the successful popular referendum—before the amendment can go into effect. In Delaware, approval by a two-thirds vote in two successive general assemblies gets a constitutional amendment ratified. As already discussed, the ballot initiative essentially combines the proposal and ratification stages. Once a proposed amendment is qualified for the ballot, it usually requires only a simple majority to become part of the constitution.

Constitutional revision commissions
Expert committees formed to assess constitutions and suggest changes

FIGURE 3-1

HOW IT WORKS

Alabama's State Constitution: The More Things Change, the More They Stay the Same

Since 1819, Alabama has adopted six different constitutions. The most recent was ratified in 1901 and consists of more than 360,000 words (that's about 45 times longer than the U.S. Constitution). The bulk of this comes from the 835 (and counting) amendments that make it the world's longest operating constitution. It was the product of a constitutional delegation comprising 155 white males who, like convention president John Knox, were mostly large planters. They wished to hold back the industrialization that had left Alabama in great debt. Knox, however, described the constitution's primary purpose as "secur[ing] white supremacy." African American voters were stripped of voting rights, and interracial marriage was forbidden (as recently as 2012 the state's legislature was still working to strip racist language from the constitution). Civil rights advocate Booker T. Washington, among others, condemned the document.

Many of its original provisions are now defunct or have been retracted, but that doesn't mean there are not still big problems with the constitution. Some provisions allow the continuing disfranchisement of many citizens, delay of economic development, and denial of governing powers to localities. Critics have accused the constitution of encouraging unproductive government action; the state legislature spends more than half of its time debating issues that have only local relevance, and two thirds of the constitutional amendments address issues specific to one town or county.

There have been numerous efforts to change Alabama's constitution—six different governors have tried to change the existing 1901 document. In each case, they were met with resistance from the legislature, the state supreme court, or powerful planters and industrialists. The latest attempt at reform involves a constitutional revision commission created in 2011 by the legislature. The job of this 16-member commission is to comb through the constitution and recommend changes. These are recommendations, though, not mandates. Recommendations by the commission can be rejected by the legislature and must be approved by voters before taking effect. So while Alabama's constitution is likely not set in stone forever, the prospects of a start-from-scratch do-over still seem slim.

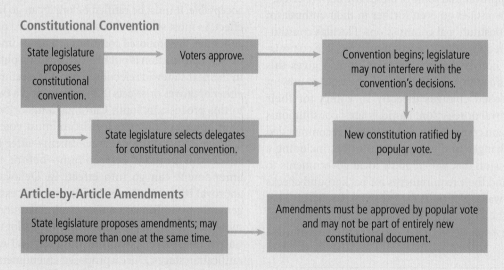

Constitutional Convention

State legislature proposes constitutional convention. → Voters approve. → Convention begins; legislature may not interfere with the convention's decisions.

State legislature selects delegates for constitutional convention.

New constitution ratified by popular vote.

Article-by-Article Amendments

State legislature proposes amendments; may propose more than one at the same time. → Amendments must be approved by popular vote and may not be part of entirely new constitutional document.

Source: Alabama Citizens for Constitutional Reform, www.constitutionalreform.org.

Informal Methods for Changing Constitutions

In recent years, voters and legislators nationwide have generally resisted making major changes to their states' constitutions. However, many state constitutions have changed dramatically in informal ways. The most common route of informal constitutional change is via the state supreme courts. For instance, this is the case when a court interprets an existing constitution in a way that creates a new right, such as the right to an adequate or equitable education (discussed in Chapter 13, on education).

Sometimes constitutional changes also come about from **judicial review**, which is the power of courts to review the actions of the legislative and executive branches of government and invalidate them if they are not in compliance with the constitution. In December 1999, the Vermont Supreme Court directed the state legislature to pass a law that would provide for civil unions. Its rationale? The court found that because the state constitution was "instituted for the common benefit, protection and security of the people," the state government could not refuse to provide the benefit of marriage to gay people. To those who objected that the state constitution, which was enacted in 1793 and at the time was a model of brevity at 8,200 words, said nothing about gay marriage, the court explained that its job was "to distill the essence, the motivating idea of the framers," not to be bound by 18th-century notions of jurisprudence.[23] In November 2003, the Massachusetts Supreme Court went further when it declared the state's ban on same-sex marriage unconstitutional, which prompted efforts to amend not just state constitutions but the U.S. Constitution as well to define marriage explicitly as a union between a man and a woman. While the attempt to amend the U.S. Constitution mostly fizzled, as of 2012 thirty states had amended their constitutions specifically to ban same-sex marriage.

State constitutions also can change when other branches of government successfully lay claim to broader powers. For example, Rhode Island's legislature has used its strong constitutional position—a clause in the state constitution says that the General Assembly "can exercise any power" unless the constitution explicitly forbids it—to take control of functions that most states delegate to governors. This means that in Rhode Island legislators not only sit on the boards and commissions that oversee a range of state agencies, but they also dominate the board that sets the salaries for high-ranking executive branch officials. Not surprisingly, this has given the legislature a great deal of power over executive branch decisions. In short, Rhode Island has just the type of government that John Adams feared.

Southern states such as Florida, Mississippi, and Texas also tend to have constitutions that provide for weak governors. In these cases, this arrangement is a legacy of the post–Civil War **Reconstruction** period. During Reconstruction, the victorious Union army forced most of the former Confederate states to replace their constitutions. Reconstruction ended in 1876, and the Union troops withdrew. With the exception of Arkansas, North Carolina, and Tennessee, the southern states soon abandoned their revised constitutions in favor of new ones that greatly weakened gubernatorial powers.[24] Part of the reasoning for this was that weak governors could be kept from enacting policies that the federal government encouraged but that were contrary to the norms of these traditionalistic states. This had happened during Reconstruction, when the governors of the states that had seceded from the Union were replaced by individuals sympathetic to the federal government in Washington or were forced to cooperate with federal policy in regard to such issues as African American rights. For example, in 1885 Florida passed a constitution that took away the governor's right to appoint his own cabinet; members were elected instead. Although it has been amended many

---

Judicial review
The power of courts to assess whether a law is in compliance with the constitution

---

Reconstruction
The period following the Civil War when the southern states were governed under the direction of the Union army

Procedures for Constitutional Amendment by Legislature

MAP 3-3

Legislative Vote Required for Proposal

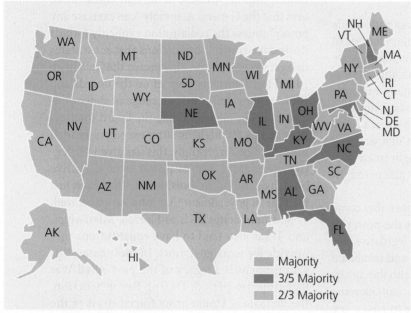

Legend:
- Majority
- 3/5 Majority
- 2/3 Majority

Source: Data from Audrey Wall, "State Constitutions," in *The Book of the States 2013*, ed. Council of State Governments (Lexington, KY: Council of State Governments, 2013), Table 1.2, http://knowledgecenter.csg.org/kc/content/book-states-2013-chapter-1-state-constitutions.

MAP 3-4

Vote Required for Ratification

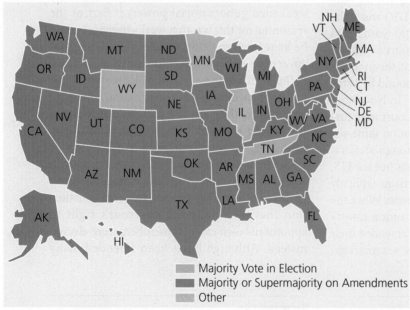

Legend:
- Majority Vote in Election
- Majority or Supermajority on Amendments
- Other

Source: Data from Audrey Wall, "State Constitutions," in *The Book of the States 2013*, ed. Council of State Governments (Lexington, KY: Council of State Governments, 2013), Table 1.2, http://knowledgecenter.csg.org/kc/content/book-states-2013-chapter-1-state-constitutions.

times since, that constitution is still in effect today. As a result, Florida has one of the weakest governorships in the country.[25]

Of course, state legislatures do not always gain the upper hand. In states whose constitutions give governors the edge, some chief executives have been very aggressive in expanding their powers. Although their techniques do not involve written amendments to the state constitutions themselves, they do affect the distribution of powers within state government—a function that is a primary concern of state constitutions.

State constitutions may also be changed in another way—through simple neglect. Sometimes state governments just stop enforcing obscure or repugnant sections of their state constitutions, effectively changing the constitutions in the process. No politician today would dare to argue for denying the vote to individuals simply because they are poor or do not own land or belong to a minority group; yet until 1999 Texas's constitution contained a provision that limited the right to vote to citizens who owned land and paid a poll tax. The state government had stopped enforcing these objectionable requirements long before but had neglected to actually repeal them. Likewise, Alabama's constitution outlawed interracial marriages until an amendment overturned the ban in 2000; the state had informally dropped enforcement of the provision years earlier.

Why State Constitutions Vary

Without a doubt, state constitutions vary widely from state to state. What explains these differences? Four factors seem particularly important: historical circumstances, political culture, geography, and changing notions of good government.

To understand how historical circumstances and culture can create a constitution—and then be shaped by that constitution—consider the case of Texas. The Lone Star State's current constitution was written in 1876, soon after federal troops had withdrawn and Reconstruction had ended. During Reconstruction, a strong Unionist governor backed by federal troops had governed the state, centralized police and education functions in state hands in Austin, and generally defied the white Democrats who had been in power before the Civil War. So Texas followed in the footsteps of other southern states and drew up a constitution designed to ensure that the state would never again have an activist state government. Toward that end, the new constitution allowed the legislature to meet only infrequently, limited the governor's power over the executive branch, and provided for an elected judiciary. The document's sole progressive feature was a provision that for the first time allowed women to continue to own their property after they were married.[26]

White Democrats' antipathy toward Reconstruction explains much of the content of Texas's 1876 constitution. The state's political culture explains why its constitution has endured to the present. Political scientist Daniel Elazar classifies Texas as a traditionalistic/individualistic state that, in his words, "places a premium on limiting community intervention" and "accepts a natural hierarchical society as part of the ordered nature of things."[27] Although Elazar's categories have blurred in recent years, state constitutions continue to bear them out. In short, Texas's constitution is well suited to the state's political culture—a culture that views strong activist government with suspicion.

In contrast, a constitution that allowed the legislature to meet only every other year would suit a moralistic state poorly. Not surprisingly, moralistic states such as Michigan, Minnesota, and Wisconsin allow their legislatures to meet far more frequently than does Texas. Because they envision fairly robust styles of governance, the constitutions in these states allow the legislatures to meet throughout the year, creating what are, for all intents and purposes, full-time professional legislatures.

New England's propensity for short, framework-oriented constitutions is a variation based noticeably on geography. One political scientist has hypothesized that such a variation may reflect the fact that New England states are small and relatively homogeneous and their citizens are thus less inclined to fight to include in their states' constitutions policies they support.[28]

Of course, history, political culture, and geography aren't the only factors that determine the kind of constitution a state will have. Another important factor is the changing sense of what works best. In the early 19th century, many states concluded that a system in which the legislature operates with unbridled power simply did not work well, so they changed their constitutions in ways that strengthened the chief executive. Eighty years ago, groups such as the National Municipal League argued that state constitutions should be more like the federal constitution; that is, they should be much shorter documents that provide a framework for governance rather than long documents that get into the details of policies. That argument gave rise to the **model constitution**, a kind of ideal notion of a constitution that states

> Of course, history, political culture, and geography aren't the only factors that determine the kind of constitution a state will have. Another important factor is the changing sense of what works best.

Model constitution
An expert-approved generic or "ideal" constitution that states sometimes use as a yardstick against which to measure their existing constitutions

A *Difference*
That Makes *A Difference*

State Constitutions and the Right to Marry

"By the power vested in me, by the state of . . . " These words are repeated by wedding officials every day, in every state. States control who can marry and when. In Nebraska, teens younger than 19 need their parents' permission to marry, while over the state line in Kansas, people can walk down the aisle at 18. A number of states prohibited interracial couples from marrying until 1967, when the U.S. Supreme Court declared Virginia's law unconstitutional in *Loving v. Virginia.* Today, debate rages around gay marriage. Currently, 19 states have legalized such unions, while 31 states have amended their constitutions to explicitly prohibit legal recognition of same-sex marriage. Washington, D.C., which is technically a federal city, not a state, allows gay marriage.

Legalization of gay marriage has been achieved through judicial review (e.g., in Connecticut, Iowa, and Massachusetts) and through legislation (e.g., in New Hampshire, New York, and Vermont). Gay marriage has had a less fortunate time at the polls; proposed constitutional amendments to outlaw same-sex marriage have frequently been backed by large majorities of voters. This trend may be reversing, however. Public opinion polls suggest voters are moving toward majority support of same-sex marriage. In 2012 a majority of voters in Maine and Maryland approved referendums on legalizing same-sex marriage. These were the first instances of same-sex marriage proposals' being approved by popular vote, and they were hailed as landmark victories by gay rights advocates.

As of mid-2014, however, the ability of same-sex couples to marry is still very much confined by geography—this is a difference that continues to make a big difference. In some states same-sex couples are, at least legally, treated no differently from heterosexual couples in terms of being able to marry. In other states there is no legal option at all. The bottom line is that the right to marry continues to be almost exclusively something determined at the state level. The problem, of course, is that this right exists in some states and not in others. There are several legal challenges to same-sex marriage currently being litigated in the federal courts, and until the U.S. Supreme Court agrees to hear one of these cases and makes a clear ruling (it declined the opportunity to do exactly this in 2014), legal recognition for same-sex unions will continue to vary across states.

Sources: Jo Becker, "A Conservative's Road to Same-Sex Marriage Advocacy," *New York Times,* August 18, 2009, http://www.nytimes.com/2009/08/19/us/19olson.html; Erik Eckholm, "In Maine and Maryland, Victories at the Ballot Box for Same-Sex Marriage," *New York Times,* November 2012, http://www.nytimes.com/2012/11/07/us/politics/same-sex-marriage-voting-election.html?_r=0; Initiative and Referendum Institute, "Same-Sex Marriage: Breaking the Firewall in California?" *Ballotwatch,* no. 2 (October 2008), http://www.iandrinstitute.org/BW%202008-2%20(Marriage).pdf; Christine Vestal, "Gay Marriage Legal in Six States," *Stateline,* June 4, 2009, http://www.stateline .org/live/details/story?contentId=347390.

interested in "improving" could adopt. During the 1960s and 1970s, many states did revise their constitutions in ways designed to make their governments more effective, although the latest edition of the model constitution was written in 1968.

Since the mid-20th century, however, some political scientists have questioned the assumptions behind the model constitution movement. To these revisionists, the fact that most state constitutions outside New England are long and policy rich is actually a good thing—a healthy sign of an engaged electorate. Revisionists argue that, although Americans have essentially left it to the U.S. Supreme Court to interpret and on occasion to change the federal constitution, citizens have defended their right to participate by shaping their state constitutions.[29]

How State Constitutions Differ

The most obvious ways state constitutions differ involve their length and ease of amendment.

These differences are not simply cosmetic; they almost always reflect the different functions that state constitutions serve. Vermont has the shortest state constitution. Like the U.S. Constitution, its goal is primarily to establish a framework for effective government, not to regulate the details of specific policy matters. This is true to a lesser extent of other states in New England as well.

In contrast, constitutions in other regions of the country tend to be longer and more specific in their policy prescriptions. In most states, voters and interest groups that want to accomplish such goals as increased state spending on education will lobby the governor or the legislature. In California, a state with a long, policy-specific constitution that provides for a high degree of direct democracy, people often attempt to amend the constitution instead. Although the majority of political scientists wring their hands about this tendency, it is undeniable that Californians play a role in shaping their constitution that voters in New England cannot. Also note that these two aspects—length and ease of amendment—not only reflect differences in goals and purposes but also directly influence each other. If a constitution is easier to amend, it makes sense that it is more likely to get amended—and that usually means it gets longer. Again, a difference makes a difference.

Operating Rules and Selection for Office

State constitutions create varying organizational structures and operating rules for the constituent elements of state government. They establish different methods and requirements for serving in state politics. Some of these differences reflect the historical differences among states as well as variations in political culture and geography. Other differences reflect differing notions of what makes good government. Sometimes these notions can be quite quirky. Consider the following, for example. To serve as the governor of Oklahoma, a state of 3.8 million people, you must be at least 31 years old. In contrast, to be the chief executive of California's population of 38 million, you need only be 18. You might be eligible to lead one of the nation's largest states, but don't plan on buying beer or wine, even at your own fundraisers!

In addition, state constitutions differ widely in how many statewide elected positions they create and how those positions are filled. One of the most important of these differences has to do with the judiciary. At the federal level, judges are selected by the president and approved by the U.S. Senate. Things work very differently in the states. Some states elect their judges, some states appoint their judges, many states use a combination of appointment and election, and some states use different selection methods for different types of courts. The details of these various systems and their particular pros and cons are discussed in depth in Chapter 9. What's important for our purposes here is that there are big differences from state to state in how judges end up on the bench, and those differences are products of different constitutional approaches to structuring and staffing the judicial branch of government.

Even seemingly small institutional differences created by different constitutional approaches can have big impacts on how state governments work. For example, if a state's constitution gives the executive strong veto powers, the governor may have an easier time getting a recalcitrant legislature to consider his or her point of view on a particular piece of legislation than would a governor with weak veto powers. Similarly, some studies have shown that elected judges are more likely than those more insulated from the ballot box to uphold the death penalty in cases involving capital crimes.[30] In short, the different operating rules embedded in state constitutions lead to very different types of governance.

Distribution of Power

State constitutions make widely differing decisions about where power should reside. Although all state constitutions make at least a bow toward

Virginia's executive mansion is the oldest continuously occupied governor's residence in the United States. It has been the home of Virginia's governors since 1813.

Rather than raise taxes to cover budget shortfalls, state policymakers have frequently turned to spending cuts. This was certainly the case for Florida governor Rick Scott, who as a candidate promised to reduce spending and followed through by line-item vetoing more than $100 million out of the state's 2012–2013 budget and $68.8 million from the 2014–2015 budget.

MCT via Getty Images

the principle of the separation of powers, in actuality many give one branch of government a preponderance of power. Under some state constitutions, the reins of government are clearly in the hands of the legislature or general assembly. Other states have amended their constitutions to give executives the upper hand.

Traditionally, state constitutions tended to create stronger legislatures and weaker executives. In recent decades, however, even though strong state legislatures are still the norm, constitutional changes in many states have bolstered governors' powers. More than 40 state constitutions now give governors the important power of the **line-item veto**, the ability to veto certain portions of appropriations bills while approving the rest. Exactly what counts as an item, and thus what is fair game for a governor's veto pen, is often unclear. As a result, line-item veto court cases have become a common part of the legal landscape.

Some states go even further. In Wisconsin, for example, the state constitution allows the governor the power to strike out an appropriation entirely and write in a lower figure.[31] During his term in office, Wisconsin governor Tommy Thompson pushed the power of the partial veto to strike passages and even individual words from

---

Line-item veto
The power to reject a portion of a bill while leaving the rest intact

bills that came to his desk. In some cases, Thompson would strike individual letters from bills to create entirely new words, changing the entire meaning of the legislation. Critics came to call Thompson's creative writing "the Vanna White veto." In one case, Thompson used the Vanna White veto and his Scrabble skills to transform a piece of legislation from a bill that set the maximum detention period for juvenile offenders at 48 hours into one that allowed for a 10-day detention period, a move that enraged the Democratic legislature.[32] Voters later amended the constitution to prohibit that particular veto maneuver. Yet, despite the controversies that surrounded such actions, during his record 14-year reign, none of Thompson's more than 1,900 budget vetoes was ever overturned by the legislature.[33]

The power structures set up by the constitutional systems of some states resist easy classification. Take Texas, for example. The fact that the legislature meets for only 5 or 6 months every other year might lead you to think that power in Texas resides primarily with the governor. Not so. In fact, the Texas constitution arguably makes the office of lieutenant governor the most powerful in the state. In Texas, the lieutenant governor presides over the Senate, appoints Senate committees and assigns bills, and chairs the powerful Texas Legislative Council, which is responsible for researching and drafting bills. Indeed, many observers attribute George W. Bush's two successful terms as governor to his close relationship with his lieutenant governor, Bob Bullock, a Democrat.

Rights Granted

State constitutions differ not only in the mechanisms of governance they create and the sets of constraints and powers they give to government but also in the rights they confer on citizens. For example, the U.S. Constitution does not explicitly mention a right to privacy, although the U.S. Supreme Court did define a limited right to privacy in *Griswold v. Connecticut* (1965). In contrast, Montana's constitution states that "the right to individual privacy is essential to the well-being of a free society and shall not be infringed without the showing of a compelling state interest."[34] As a result, courts in Montana—and in Kentucky and Tennessee—have interpreted the state constitution to protect adults' freedom to engage in consensual oral or anal sex, which until quite recently was illegal in many other states.[35]

Even rights that are directly addressed by the U.S. Constitution are often expanded, clarified, or given more specifics in state constitutions. For example, the Second Amendment says, "A well regulated Militia, being necessary to the security of a free State, the right of the people to keep and bear Arms, shall not be infringed." Legal scholars have been arguing over the meaning of this vaguely worded amendment for a long time—is the right purely an individual right? If so, the government has a narrow basis for regulating private ownership of firearms. Or is the right attached to the necessity of a "well regulated Militia"? If that's the case, it suggests a more expansive basis for government regulation of firearms. No such confusion is raised by Nebraska's state constitution, which says that "the right to keep and bear arms for security or defense of self, family, home, and others, and for lawful common defense, hunting, recreational use, and all other lawful purposes, and such rights shall not be denied or infringed."

Representative Government Versus Direct Democracy

One of the most striking differences among state constitutions is the degree to which they have (or have not) embraced direct democracy. Most

Americans celebrate the United States as a democracy, but the founders believed that they were establishing something somewhat different—a representative democracy. This is a form of government in which qualified representatives of the public make the decisions. Most of the founders viewed direct, or pure, democracy with suspicion. A "pure democracy, by which I mean a society consisting of a small number of citizens, who assemble and administer the government in person, can admit of no cure for the mischiefs of faction," warned James Madison, one of the primary authors of the U.S. Constitution, in his famous argument for the document in *Federalist* No. 10:

> A common passion or interest will, in almost every case, be felt by a majority of the whole . . . and there is nothing to check the inducements to sacrifice the weaker party or an obnoxious individual. Hence it is that such democracies have ever been spectacles of turbulence and contention; have ever been found incompatible with personal security or the rights of property; and have in general been as short in their lives as they have been violent in their deaths.[36]

In other words, Madison believed that entrusting a simple majority with the power to carry out its will would lead to fickle and tyrannical behavior and to a government that would teeter between anarchy and autocracy.

The U.S. Constitution's solution to the problem of pure democracy was to create a representative government, or, as Madison saw it, government by a small group of elected officials "whose wisdom may best discern the true interest of their country."[37] In accordance with this belief, the U.S. Constitution created an upper chamber—the Senate—whose members would be selected by state legislatures from among their eminent men. The document also created an electoral college to elect the president. Both of these decisions were made to insulate the federal government from the whims of the majority. The Constitution makes no provision for direct democratic processes. There is not a single federal officeholder *directly* elected by the entire nation. Indeed, as we saw in 2000 with the election of George W. Bush, the Electoral College system can result in a candidate's winning the presidency after losing the popular vote.

Whereas the creators of the federal government took great care to ensure it was insulated from direct democratic processes, many states decided to do just the opposite during the Progressive Era. By giving their citizens the chance to make laws and change their constitutions directly, the Progressives sought to circumvent legislatures and executives they viewed as being beholden to wealthy special interests. As Robert M. La Follette, a leader of the Progressive Party in Wisconsin and later a governor and senator from the state, put it:

> The forces of the special privileges are deeply entrenched. Their resources are inexhaustible. Their efforts are never lax. Their political methods are insidious. It is impossible for the people to maintain perfect organization in mass. They are often taken unaware and are liable to lose at one stroke the achievements of years of effort. In such a crisis, nothing but the united power of the people expressed directly through the ballot can overthrow the enemy.[38]

For politicians such as La Follette, direct democratic mechanisms, such as the ballot initiative and the referendum, represented the general populace's best hope for breaking the power of political bosses and moneyed interests. From 1902 through 1918, direct democracy enjoyed a great vogue in the states. Sixteen states adopted the ballot initiative in that period. After World War I, ballot initiatives lost some of their luster as popular enthusiasm for Progressive ideas waned. Only five states—Alaska (1959), Florida (1968), Wyoming (1968), Illinois (1970), and Mississippi (1992)—have amended their constitutions to allow for ballot initiatives since the end of the Progressive Era.[39] What's more, note where these states are located. The majority of the states that allow direct democracy lie west of the Mississippi River, where the practice fits with much of the West's populist history.[40]

For much of their existence, initiatives and referendums were used sparingly. Then came Proposition 13 in California. In the 1970s, taxpayer activist Howard Jarvis and retired real estate salesman Paul Gann launched what at first seemed a foolishly impractical campaign to roll back California property taxes and cap the rate at which they could grow. Their campaign struck a chord with many Californians. The state's booming economy had sent property values skyrocketing. Higher property assessments led to higher real estate taxes, which created a huge revenue boom for the state and local governments. Indeed, at the time the state government had a $5 billion annual surplus. Yet despite the public outcry for relief from rising property costs, Governor Jerry Brown and the rest of the politicians in Sacramento could not agree on a tax reduction plan.

In 1978, California voters passed Proposition 13 and took the decision out of politicians' hands. It directed the state to roll back real estate taxes to 1975 levels and decreed that property assessments could not increase by more than 2 percent a year, regardless of inflation. Most localities previously had reassessed real estate taxes every 2 years. Proposition 13 decreed that property could be reassessed only when it was sold. The legislation also cut property tax receipts in half and marked the beginning of a nationwide "taxpayer revolt." The revolt culminated in the election of former California governor Ronald Reagan to the presidency 2 years later.

California's political establishment viewed the passage of Proposition 13 with great trepidation. Politicians worried that it would cripple their ability to pay for the schools and infrastructure that had contributed so much to California's post–World War II successes. These fears proved well-founded. In the wake of Proposition 13, California went from having one of the nation's best-funded public school systems (in the top third in terms of per-pupil spending) to having one of the worst (in the bottom third). The proposition put such draconian limits on the ability of local governments to raise revenues that municipalities and counties became increasingly dependent on the state for their funding—so much so that 10 years later, in 1988, California teachers' unions pushed through Proposition 98, which mandated that upward of 40 percent of California's general revenue go to education.[41]

Qwest Field, home of the Seattle Seahawks, was made possible by a ballot initiative that provided $300 million in public financing for construction of the stadium. The team's owner, billionaire and Microsoft cofounder Paul Allen, financed the successful ballot initiative.

AP Photo/Greg Trott

In addition to complicating government finances and drastically reducing the flexibility of lawmakers in California, the success of Proposition 13 revived interest in ballot initiatives in the 24 other states in which they were permitted. In the three decades from 1940 through 1970, an average of 19 initiatives appeared on ballots per 2-year election cycle in the United States. In the 1980s, that number shot up to 50 initiatives in the average election cycle. In the 1990s, it hit 76 per election cycle.[42] Many of these initiatives were proposed constitutional amendments. Their sheer numbers indicate that states allowing ballot initiatives are now engaged in an almost continuous cycle of changing their constitutions. These changes are increasingly less about broad questions of good governance and more about pushing narrow agendas.

In the past two decades, the initiative process has been used to push through legislation on some of the most controversial political issues in the entire country. Oregon voters used a ballot initiative to narrowly (51–49 percent) approve physician-assisted suicide in 1994. In California, voters have used initiatives to impose some of the nation's strictest term limits on elected officials (Proposition 140), to end affirmative action (Propositions 209 and 96), to deny education and health benefits to families of illegal immigrants (Proposition 87), to spend $3 billion on stem-cell research (Proposition 71), and to recall a sitting governor and replace him with an action-movie star. You can check out the latest ballot initiatives and their electoral fates at ballotpedia.org, which keeps a running tally of these proposals and how they fared at the ballot box.

The initiative process has become big business. Hundreds of millions can be spent in a single election cycle on battles waged over ballot measures.[43] Several companies are devoted to gathering the signatures needed to get issues placed on ballots for anyone who can afford their services. Signature gathering can be a pretty lucrative business—in 2010 and 2012 it cost, on average, more than a million dollars to collect enough signatures to get a proposal certified and on a state ballot.[44] Those who have used them successfully see ballot initiatives as tools for circumventing hostile legislatures and acting on the will of the majority. But most political scientists and close observers of state politics have a different viewpoint. They argue that the results of the use of ballot initiatives only reinforce the wisdom of the founders in their decision to keep direct democratic processes out of the U.S. Constitution. A number of those who have examined initiatives have concluded that the process has been hijacked by those with deep pockets and by individuals who use the initiatives to further their own self-interests. Veteran *Washington Post* political reporter David Broder describes ballot initiatives in scathing terms, calling them "the favored tool of millionaires and interest groups that use their wealth to achieve their own policy goals—a lucrative business for a new set of political entrepreneurs."[45]

Exploiting the public's disdain for politics and distrust of politicians, interest groups with deep pockets now have a mechanism through which they can literally rewrite state constitutions to advance their own agendas. For example, in 1997 Microsoft cofounder and Seattle Seahawks owner Paul Allen made an end run around a balky state legislature and spent $6 million on a ballot initiative that required the state of Washington to foot much of the cost for a new stadium for his team. It proved to be a good investment; the initiative passed with 51 percent of the vote. Although this was welcome news for many football fans, most political scientists probably see it as an illustration of the very problem that Madison identified in *Federalist* No. 10. In some ways, the initiative has created a very odd form of governance in which citizens live under laws that are often resisted by their elected governments. With its ability to make sweeping changes in state constitutions, the initiative process could radically change the American system of government in the next few decades.

Constitutions for Local Government?

For the most part, substate governments, such as school districts, counties, and many municipalities, are considered subordinate arms of the state. They may seem like autonomous political units, but they in fact operate under state constitutions and at the discretion of state governments. The courts generally have viewed only the federal government and the states as sovereign entities with the right to determine how their authority should be exercised. The authority and power of local governments is largely confined, if not outright dictated, by the states (these issues are discussed in more depth in Chapter 11).

There are some exceptions to this rule. The **municipal charter** is a key example. In a rough sense, municipal charters are similar to the charters that served as the governing documents for the original colonies. Legally, most municipalities are corporations, and their charters describe the purposes of the municipalities and the processes for achieving these objectives. A charter is not a constitution; rather, it is a grant of authority derived from a constitution or from state law. Some states have **home rule**, which allows municipalities the right to draft and amend their own charters and to regulate local matters within their jurisdictions without interference from the state. Some states have municipal home rule provisions in their constitutions; others grant home rule to municipalities through legislation. Municipal home rule means that some local governments are operated by charters that "can take on many characteristics of a constitution."[46] Even in the most liberal home rule states, however, state constitutions and state law generally take precedence over municipal charters.

Conclusion

Even though you rarely read about them in the newspaper—much less hear about them on the evening news—state constitutions play *the* critical role in defining the possibilities of politics in most states. All state constitutions set the basic structure of government, apportion power and responsibilities to particular institutions and political actors, and determine the rights and privileges of citizenship. State constitutions reflect states' distinctive political cultures and, over time, reinforce or alter those traditions.

Beyond this common core of shared functions, however, state constitutions vary greatly. Some protect and extend the rights of the individual beyond the guarantees of the U.S. Constitution; others do not. Perhaps the single biggest difference among state constitutions is the degree to which they serve as a venue for policymaking. In western

---

Municipal charter
A document that establishes operating procedures for a local government

Home rule
A form of self-governance granted to towns and cities by the state

states, whose constitutions provide for a high degree of direct democracy, advocates and interest groups often attempt to enshrine their policy positions in the state constitutions. As a result, these states have long, detailed constitutions. In contrast, the constitutions of the eastern states, particularly in New England, more closely resemble the U.S. Constitution.

State constitutions tend to have a bad reputation with political scientists, for understandable reasons. Although many function well, in more than a few instances they play an outright disruptive role. In states such as Alabama and Texas, antiquated state constitutions have made it difficult for state governments to promote economic development—a function that most people believe the state government should serve. In California and other states, interest groups have used state constitutions to ensure that the states' general revenues flow toward the pro-

grams they support. In the process, they have reduced—in some areas drastically—the flexibility of legislatures to make independent decisions, a set of constraints that amounts to putting limits on representative democracy.

But, as political scientist Christopher Hammonds has argued from another perspective, the fact that constitutions continue to be a contentious venue for politics in many states is not necessarily all bad. Although it is still theoretically possible to change the U.S. Constitution, for all practical purposes we as a society have given that right over to the U.S. Supreme Court. It takes an extraordinarily contentious issue, such as reproductive rights, to provoke talk about changing the federal constitution. In contrast, citizens continue to exercise their right to tamper with and tweak their state constitutions. Is that all bad?

The Latest Research

State constitutions are one of the most important and understudied aspects of subnational government. While it is not hard to find constitutional scholars in political science, the vast majority of these study the U.S. Constitution, not its state counterparts. More attention is paid to state constitutions in the field of law, but even there scholars focusing on state constitutions regularly lament the relative lack of research available on these centrally important legal documents.

This lack of attention is surprising because, as the studies listed below amply demonstrate, state constitutions are important—not just as the bases for much of the criminal and civil law in the United States but also as documents that reflect deeper philosophical notions of what a government is, what it should do, and what rights citizens should or should not have. These are not just abstract theoretical arguments; your marriage rights, to

take one prominent example, are almost wholly determined by the constitution and the laws it authorizes in the state in which you reside.

Below we summarize some of the more recent and prominent research on state constitutions. All these studies reflect a constant theme: not just the central importance of state constitutions to the American political system but also how those constitutions are constantly changing and creating differences in state-level legal structure that have big, real-world impacts on the lives of state residents.

• •

- **Zackin, Emily.** *Looking for Rights in All the Wrong Places: Why State Constitutions Contain America's Positive Rights.* Princeton, NJ: Princeton University Press, 2013.

(Continued)

(Continued)

The U.S. Constitution is different from those of other nations in that it almost exclusively emphasizes negative rather than positive rights. A negative right means government cannot interfere with your exercise of that right; Congress, for example, is constitutionally prohibited from interfering with your right to speak your mind or practice your religious beliefs. A positive right on the other hand requires government to take positive action, to provide you with a good or service. The Constitution is pretty quiet on what services government owes its people, which has led a lot of legal scholars to conclude that the United States really has no established tradition of positive rights. Zackin's book disagrees, arguing that there is a strong tradition of positive rights in the United States; legal scholars haven't found them because they have looked in the wrong place. She suggests that Americans actually have quite a lot of positive rights—for example, they have a right to a free public education. These positive rights, however, are not found in the U.S. Constitution but in state constitutions. State constitutions, in short, are where we find positive rights.

- **Williams, Robert F.** *The Law of American State Constitutions.* New York: Oxford University Press, 2009.

Williams is one of the most widely recognized scholars of state constitutional law, and this book is one of the most comprehensive and up-to-date scholarly analyses available of the nature and purpose of state constitutions. This work is notable not just for its overview of the historical development of state constitutions, their structure, and their legal implications but for staking out a strong "positivist" position on these documents. Essentially, Williams argues that state constitutions should not be viewed as mini-versions of the U.S. Constitution. Instead, each should be viewed as a unique text and interpreted—by scholars and judges—within that framework. This argument amounts to a strong rejection of the so-called common principles approach, which views and interprets state constitutions basically as a branch of common law—that is, a set of cases or precedents.

- **Krislov, Marvin, and Daniel Katz.** "Taking State Constitutions Seriously." *Cornell Journal of Law and Public Policy* 71 (2008): 295–342.

This is a study of how state constitutions change. In comparison with the federal constitution, state constitutions generally have much less restrictive amendment processes, and even within individual states there may be multiple avenues to constitutional change. While noting the huge variation across states in these amendment processes, Krislov and Katz pay particular attention to direct democratic processes. Their analysis shows that such processes, in particular constitutional initiatives, have become a primary method of amending state constitutions. Yet even among states that allow ballot initiatives, there is substantial variation in the rules and procedures for passage of a constitutional initiative. This study suggests that those differences create different sets of incentives for groups to pursue constitutional change and that the rapid shifts in state constitutional content create particular challenges for the process of state-level judicial review.

- **Lupia, Arthur, Yanna Krupnikov, Adam Seth Levine, Spencer Piston, and Alexander Von Hagen-Jamar.** "Why State Constitutions Differ in Their Treatment of Same-Sex Marriage." *Journal of Politics* 72 (2010): 1222–1235.

This is an interesting companion study to the Krislov and Katz article. This team of researchers examines state-level variation in attitudes toward same-sex marriage and constitutional outcomes. One of the surprising findings of their study is that attitudes correlate somewhat poorly with constitutional amendments on same-sex marriage. Public opinion regarding same-sex marriage does not differ greatly between states with constitutional amendments banning the practice and those without such amendments. The authors find that the differences that do exist are explained, at least in part, by the relative complexity of the rules and regulations associated with constitutional amendment. The fact that U.S. state constitutions differ in the legal status of same-sex marriage has less to do with attitudes on that topic in the states and much more to do with the institutional arrangements established by those constitutions to translate the will of the people into state law.

3

Chapter Review

Key Concepts

- appropriations bills (p. 63)
- ballot initiatives (p. 69)
- bicameral legislatures (p. 65)
- colonial charters (p. 64)
- constitutional amendments (p. 62)
- constitutional convention (p. 66)
- constitutional revision commissions (p. 71)
- direct democracy (p. 59)
- dual constitutionalism (p. 61)
- electorate (p. 60)
- franchise (p. 65)
- home rule (p. 82)

- Jim Crow laws (p. 66)
- judicial federalism (p. 61)
- judicial review (p. 73)
- line-item veto (p. 78)
- model constitution (p. 75)
- municipal charter (p. 82)
- natural law or higher law (p. 61)
- plenary power (p. 62)
- ratification (p. 68)
- Reconstruction (p. 73)
- referendums (p. 69)
- separation of powers (p. 65)
- unicameral legislatures (p. 65)

$SAGE edge™
for CQ Press

Sharpen your skills with SAGE edge **at edge.sagepub.com/ smithgreenblatt5e.** SAGE edge for students **provides a personalized approach to help you accomplish your coursework goals in an easy-to-use learning environment.**

$SAGE statestats

Suggested Websites

- **camlaw.rutgers.edu/statecon.** Website for Rutgers University's Center for State Constitutional Studies.

- **www.iandrinstitute.org.** Website for the Initiative and Referendum Institute at the University of Southern California, a clearinghouse for information about the initiative and referendum processes of the states.

SAGE State Stats on Constitutions

Explore and compare data on the states! Go to **edge.sagepub.com/ smithgreenblatt5e** *to do these exercises.*

1. Some scholars say that unicameral government works best when its citizens are a relatively small, homogenous group. What about Nebraska's demographics and population makes it suited for unicameral government? Are there any states that are more homogenous than Nebraska? Why do they not have unicameral governments?

2. Vermont is the only state that does not have a balanced budget requirement. How does its outstanding government debt load compare to its neighboring states' debt loads? Is this surprising? Why or why not?

3. Recall this chapter's example of a Colorado ballot initiative written at the postgraduate reading level. What is Colorado's percentage of college

graduates? Why might this initiative, as written, be a problem for voters? Are there any states with lower college graduation rates? What are the implications of these numbers?

4. What percentage of the population in California is foreign born? What about Montana? How might differences in the makeup of the electorate in these states impact their laws?

5. What was the percent change in Nevada's population of eighteen to twenty-four-year-olds from 1990 to 2000? How might this type of change influence (or not) the kinds of policies that the citizens want? What does this kind of change generally do to voter turnout? Did this happen in Nevada?

6. California has direct democracy, but Nebraska does not. In the case of these two states, does direct democracy lead to higher voter turnout? Why do you think this is?

State governments aren't the only ones that have had to deal with lingering revenue shortfalls as a result of recession. In the past few years, some local governments have been so financially stressed they've been forced into bankruptcy. In 2013, Detroit, Michigan, became the largest municipality ever to go bust.

Finance

FILLING THE TILL AND PAYING THE BILLS

- What are the differences between progressive and regressive tax systems?
- Why are property taxes so important to communities?
- How does the federal government support state and local budgets?
- Are states' revenue and spending programs sustainable?

A combination of poor economic conditions and bad fiscal decisions had been pushing Detroit, Michigan, toward a financial cliff for years. On July 18, 2013, the city finally fell off the edge—right into the arms of Chapter 9 bankruptcy and the record books. It now has the dubious honor of being the largest city in U.S. history to go bust.

Detroit is far from being the only local government in the United States to find itself in financial straits in the past few years. The economy might have stabilized since the Great Recession, but it certainly has not fully recovered, and the coffers of some governments have not been able to support the wait for better economic times. Harrisburg, the capital of Pennsylvania, went into receivership in 2011. Montgomery County, the largest county in Alabama, filed for bankruptcy the same year. Central Falls, Rhode Island, became insolvent in 2010, and Stockton, California, went bust in 2012.

At the next level of government, the picture is only slightly less alarming. No state has declared bankruptcy—at least not yet—and the budget situation in many states is actually improving compared with a few years ago. No one is popping champagne corks, though, because finances at the state level have managed to advance only from the catastrophic to the very bad. For fiscal year 2013, states faced a combined shortfall of $55 billion.[1] That's

After reading this chapter, you will be able to

- explain what taxes generate revenue to the states,
- identify other state revenue sources,
- discuss why taxing varies between state and local governments, and
- describe the budget process and restraints on budgeting.

a whopping combined budgetary shortfall, but it is still a big improvement over a few years ago when a single state—California—was struggling to close a $50 billion hole in its budget. In other words, states are a long way from the let-the-good-times-roll numbers that policymakers would prefer to see in their balance sheets. Revenues are still struggling to keep pace with obligations, and many states still face uncomfortable choices between cutting spending and raising taxes—or doing both.

Deficits are a bigger problem for state and local governments than they are for the federal government. At the national level, a budget shortfall is an embarrassment, not a crisis. Virtually all states (Vermont is the only exception) are required by law to balance their operating budgets every year, and most local governments are in the same boat. When the bills add up to more than what's coming in at the federal level, Congress is free to borrow to cover the gap. In other words, the federal government can run **budget deficits, or shortfalls**, as much as it likes. Not so for state and local governments. They can delay the inevitable by cooking the books with some fancy accounting tricks and hoping for the best, but even the sharpest of bean counters cannot shield them from the hard fact that the law requires their ledgers to be balanced. When income minus expenditure results in a negative number, they cannot just borrow or print money

and hope the future will somehow provide an easy way out; they have to figure out how to get more revenue and/or cut spending.

Even today, a lot of the financial difficulties of states and localities remain rooted in the Great Recession of 2008–2009, which pushed many states toward a financial implosion because they simply could not manage the revenue/spending balancing act. The **revenues** that keep states functioning—especially income, sales, and property taxes—dropped precipitously, and unemployment rates rose above 10 percent. In a single year's span, between June 2008 and June 2009, state income tax receipts plunged by more than a quarter.[2] At the same time, consumer demand dried up, taking with it state sales tax revenues, and the housing crisis sent property values—and their resulting taxes—tumbling. That all happened just as demand for services and programs that states partially or wholly fund—everything from Medicaid to higher education—jumped.

States were rescued from this crisis by the **American Recovery and Reinvestment Act (ARRA)**, a $787 billion package passed by Congress that was designed to stimulate the economy with targeted tax cuts, job creation, and government investments. Almost $300 billion of the stimulus was used to help prop up state and local government programs, including $87 billion for state Medicaid programs and a $53.6 billion state fiscal

---

Budget deficits or shortfalls
Cash shortages that result when the amount of money coming into the government falls below the amount being spent

Revenues
The money governments bring in, mainly from taxes

American Recovery and Reinvestment Act (ARRA)
A $787 billion federal government package intended to stimulate economic growth during the recession of 2008–2009

User fees
Charges levied by governments in exchange for services. Such fees constitute a type of hidden tax.

stabilization fund, which most states used in 2009 and 2010 to stave off deep cuts to education and emergency services.[3] This massive financial injection made the federal government the single largest source of revenue for state and local governments for a year or two. By 2012, though, the federal government was turning off the tap. This kept states and localities in a tough financial bind; their income sources were slowly starting to rise, but not to prerecession levels, and the federal government was no longing shoveling cash their way. So state and local governments went right on looking for new revenue sources and spending cuts, and resigned themselves to being less hopeful of finding a billion or two of extra federal aid between the couch cushions. The upshot is that these days there is less danger of a massive, widespread fiscal tsunami swamping all states and localities than there is of the odd government being unable to keep treading financial water and thus slipping under a sea of red ink.

In 2011 (the latest figures available), residents of the United States paid about $4,200 in state and local taxes per person.[4] Along with **user fees**, those collections raised about $2.2 trillion.[5] State and local governments use these funds along with federal grant dollars to do everything from financing local schools and state universities to providing health insurance for low-income families and people with disabilities to building highways. The money also helps maintain correctional facilities that house more than 2 million people per year and provides police and fire protection to the remaining roughly 312 million people in the population. In short, state and local taxes pay for the programs that Americans care most about and that most directly affect their daily lives.

There is a tendency to think of taxes and budgets as a bit of a yawn—isn't this topic dry, technical, and boring? We'll be the first to admit that *The Fiscal Survey of States* is not exactly most people's idea of a fascinating read, but this topic is actually among the most important and consequential in this book. Budgets are the subject of some of the most intense political struggles in state and local politics, and not just because people care about money. Budgets are extremely important because they are fundamentally about policy. Indeed, in many ways they are *the* central policy documents

of government. They determine and reflect the policy orientations of elected leaders. If you want to know what your state or local government's priorities are, its budget will tell you.

> Budgets are extremely important because they are fundamentally about policy. Indeed, in many ways they are *the* central policy documents of government. They determine and reflect the policy orientations of elected leaders. If you want to know what your state or local government's priorities are, its budget will tell you.

This chapter discusses how state and local governments raise money, how they decide to spend it via the budget process, and what they spend it on. It examines why state and local governments make such different taxing and spending choices, and it explores the consequences of these varying choices. The chapter concludes with a discussion of how budgetary constraints and challenges are forcing many state and local governments to rethink how they pay for public services.

Show Me the Money: Where State Tax Revenues Come From

More than half of the total revenues of state and local governments in 2008 (the latest year for which comprehensive figures were available), or about $1.9 trillion, came from six primary taxes.[6] These were sales taxes, including **excise taxes**, often referred

---

Excise or sin taxes
Taxes on alcohol, tobacco, and other similar products that are designed to raise revenues and reduce use

to as **sin taxes**, on tobacco and alcohol; property taxes; income taxes; motor vehicle taxes; **estate taxes**, also called death taxes; and **gift taxes**. As states struggled to balance their budgets in the last years of the decade, they increasingly turned to all these taxes for help; they raised almost $24 billion in tax and fee increases in their 2010 budgets alone.[7]

Sales Taxes

In 2008, state and local governments took in $448 billion from **sales taxes**—about 34 percent of total state and local government tax revenues. About 81 percent of the money raised by sales taxes goes to state governments. In addition, most states allow at least some counties and cities to levy additional sales taxes. Currently, about 7,500 localities do. Some states, such as California, return a small percentage of sales taxes to the areas in which the purchases were made. Overall, sales tax revenues account for nearly 16 percent of local government tax revenues nationwide.[8]

State governments and, to a much lesser extent, local governments also take in significant sums from gasoline taxes and sin taxes on tobacco and alcohol. States interpret these taxes in very different ways. Other factors often influence what gets taxed and for how much. North Carolina has a large tobacco-growing industry and a tax of only $0.45 on each pack of cigarettes. New York has no large-scale tobacco industry and levies a tax of $4.35 per pack of cigarettes sold.[9]

Politicians like sales taxes because they tend to be less visible to their constituents than an income tax is. As such, they are less likely to cause voters to retaliate against them at the polls. Economists like sales taxes because they are **focused consumption** taxes that do not distort consumer behavior. That is, sales taxes, even relatively high ones, often do not cause consumers to buy less.

This does not mean that sales taxes do not receive their share of criticism. Many liberals and advocates for low-income people complain that these are **regressive taxes**. If Bill Gates buys a grande latte, he pays about $0.28 in sales tax; a freshman at the University of Washington pays exactly the same. The tax is the same, but the student is paying a much higher percentage of his or her income to the government than Gates is. Put another way, if Gates's income were even a mere $5 million a year and a typical student's income is $2,500 a year, guess how much Gates would have to pay in sales tax on that latte to face the same **tax burden** as a typical student. Give up? His grande latte would cost him a whopping but tax-proportionate $566.20. Of course, as already noted, it doesn't really work that way. If and when Gates goes to a coffee shop, he pays the same price and the same sales tax as anyone else.

States often do attempt to make their sales taxes less of a burden on low-income residents by exempting necessities such as food, clothing, and electric and gas utilities from taxation. In general, however, states that rely heavily on sales taxes tend to have more regressive tax systems than do other states.

Take, for example, Tennessee, a state that relies heavily on sales taxes rather than assessing personal income taxes. Rich and poor alike paid a 7 percent state sales tax at the cash register in 2014. That's bad enough, but local governments can add an extra sales tax on top of that. For example, residents in Memphis have to pay an additional 2.75 percent sales tax; effectively, the sales tax in Memphis is 9.75 percent. The upshot of such a heavy reliance on sales taxes is that low-income residents pay a higher percentage of their incomes

---

Estate taxes
Taxes levied on a person's estate or total holdings after that person's death

Gift taxes
Taxes imposed on money transfers made during an individual's lifetime

Sales taxes
Taxes levied by state and local governments on purchases

Focused consumption taxes
Taxes that do not alter spending habits or behavior patterns and therefore do not distort the distribution of resources

---

Regressive taxes
Taxes levied on all taxpayers, regardless of income or ability to pay; tend to place proportionately more of a burden on those with lower incomes

Tax burden
A measurement of taxes paid as a proportion of income

in taxes than they might if they lived in a state that relies more on income taxes. That makes Tennessee's tax system highly regressive.

Sales taxes have another problem—they simply are not bringing in as much revenue as they used to. In the words of James Hine, a finance expert at Clemson University, relying on the sales tax "is like riding a horse that is rapidly dying." What that basically means is that the sales tax base is slowly eroding. Two factors seem to account for this. First, services have become a much more important part of the economy. In 1960, 41 percent of U.S. consumer dollars was spent on services. By 2000, that amount had risen to 58 percent. Yet most sales taxes are still skewed toward the purchase of products rather than the purchase of services. Buy a robotic massage chair at the Mall of America in Bloomington, Minnesota, and you'll pay $58.20 in sales tax on that $800 item.[10] Hire an acupuncturist for an hour from a holistic medical center in Bloomington, and you'll pay no sales tax at all.

Hawaii, New Mexico, South Dakota, and Wyoming have changed their tax codes so that sales taxes now apply to most professional and personal services.[11] However, most other states have been reluctant to follow suit because taxing services could put them at a competitive disadvantage. For instance, if Illinois were to place a sales tax on accounting services, there would probably be a sudden boom in business for accountants in nearby Indiana.[12]

The second factor behind faltering sales tax revenues is the rise of the Internet and online shopping. In 1992, the U.S. Supreme Court ruled that states could not force companies to collect sales taxes for them in places where the companies had no physical presence. As a result, most online purchases are tax free. A study by William F. Fox and Donald Bruce of the University of Tennessee, Knoxville, found that the overall losses of sales tax revenue from Internet sales were $8.6 billion in 2010, and the researchers predicted losses as high as $11.4 billion per year by 2012.[13] For states such as Texas and Tennessee that don't have income taxes and that rely heavily on sales tax revenue, this trend is a big problem. To make up for the kind of revenue loss that Fox and Bruce have predicted,

Texas would have to raise its current statewide sales tax rate from 6.25 percent to 7.86 percent.[14]

The U.S. Congress has rejected states' pleas to stop exempting online retailers from collecting sales taxes, citing the difficulty the companies would have complying with the wide variety of state sales tax codes. In 2007, Congress extended the moratorium on online taxation until 2014. Absent federal intervention, states have banded together to collect taxes on online sales. Dozens of states have joined the Streamlined Sales Tax Project, agreeing to simplify their tax codes in exchange for the chance to convince retailers to collect the taxes voluntarily. The project went live in October 2005, with 150 retailers signing on in 18 states.[15] By June 2011, more than 1,400 companies were participating in 24 states.[16] Several states, led by New York, jumped ahead of the project by passing laws mandating that Amazon.com and other similar companies collect sales tax on purchases residents make from affiliates located in the state. Amazon challenged the law, but the New York Superior Court upheld it in 2009.[17] After years of controversy and legal battles, in 2012 California also managed to introduce a law requiring Amazon to collect local and state sales taxes. This was a big deal for the cash-strapped state government, which needed the revenue, but not such a good deal for California consumers—it added 7 to 10 percent to the cost of an Amazon purchase.[18]

Property Taxes

The second-largest source of tax revenue for state and local governments is property taxes. In 2009, property taxes raised about 33 percent, or $430 billion, of total state and local government tax revenues.[19] Most sales tax revenues go to state governments, but almost all property taxes go to local governments. As a result, property taxes are by far the most important source of revenue for local governments. About 72 percent of local government tax revenues, but only a tiny fraction (2 percent) of state tax revenues, comes from property taxes.[20]

Just about every local government relies on property tax revenues, but property tax rates vary widely from community to community. Most

Will that be cash or charge? Either way, these shoppers at the Mall of America in Bloomington, Minnesota, got a break from sales tax on their clothing purchases. Minnesota is one of numerous states that consider clothing an essential item and, therefore, waive any sales taxes on it. Other states, such as New Hampshire, have no sales tax at all, which makes their malls and shopping outlets very popular with shoppers from neighboring states.

REUTERS/Andy King

Americans who own homes or condominiums face an effective tax rate of about 1.15 percent.[21] The word *effective* simply acknowledges that some places have exemptions and adjustments that make the effective tax rate lower than the nominal tax rate. You can figure out the nominal tax rate by dividing the amount of tax paid by the amount of taxable income. You find the effective tax rate by dividing the amount of tax paid by the amount of total economic income.

In other words, if you own a condo worth $100,000, you probably pay about $1,120 a year in property taxes. In Manchester, New Hampshire, however, you'd pay $1,900 in property taxes on that same condo. That's because New Hampshire has an effective tax rate of 1.90 percent, which is one of the highest among cities across the country. Why are New Hampshire's property tax rates so high? Largely because the state has no income tax and no sales tax. That limits the state government's ability to raise funds. It also means that the state does not offer its towns the level of financial support most state governments do. As a result, whereas most local governments receive 25 percent of their total revenues from property taxes, local governments in New Hampshire are forced to rely on property taxes for 53 percent of their total revenues.[22]

The Education Connection. Property taxes are important for another reason: They pretty much finance public elementary and high school education. In 2011, education accounted for about a third of direct spending by local government.[23] In most states, where you live determines how many education dollars your children will receive. Wealthy communities with high housing values raise the most money from property taxes. School districts in these areas tend to have the most educational resources. Conversely, school districts in the poorest areas have the fewest resources. In recent years, state and federal governments have stepped in to try to ease these funding gaps by providing more resources to poor schools that cannot compete resource-wise with schools that have strong property tax bases, but the gaps are persistent. For example, the federal government's main effort to reduce resource inequality comes through Title I of the Elementary and Secondary Education Act, which sends billions of dollars to schools that serve socioeconomically distressed students. One analysis of education spending in New York City found that schools in poorer communities make do with less per-pupil revenue even with the help of Title I funds. Some schools serving the poorest communities do so with about 85 percent of the average per-pupil expenditure in New York.

The bottom line is that when schools are heavily dependent on property taxes, it is all but impossible to equalize resources. If states do nothing, schools in areas with high property values will have bigger budgets; if they try to equalize resources, they have to find the money (read: raise taxes), which is never popular and is especially resented if viewed as a tactic to divert money from local schools to nonlocal schools.

The Pros and Cons of Property Taxes. Property owners generally pay their property taxes twice a year in large lump sums. As such, these taxes tend to be highly visible and extremely unpopular with the public. However, local officials like them because property tax receipts are historically less volatile and more predictable than are other types of tax revenues. Local revenue departments assess the values of houses and businesses and then send the owners their tax bills; so the local government knows exactly how much revenue a property tax will yield.

In most instances, taxes seem worse when the economy is bad. Property taxes are the exception. They tend to rise most sharply when a town or city is experiencing an economic boom and housing prices are soaring. In these circumstances, an upsurge in property values can lead to a backlash.

The most famous of such backlashes occurred in California in 1978. In response to years of rising property values and related taxes, Californians passed Proposition 13. This piece of legislation capped the property tax rate at 1 percent of a property's purchase price and froze property assessments at their 1978 levels, until the property is resold. Newcomers to a neighborhood have to pay property taxes based on the actual value of their houses.

To this day, Proposition 13 is hotly debated. Conservatives have long praised the movement that gave rise to it. They say that it was the harbinger of the conservative politics that former California governor Ronald Reagan would bring to Washington 3 years later. Most experts, however, believe that its effects have been devastating, especially to education. Prior to Proposition 13, California was one of the most generous contributors to public education among the U.S. states; in the years since, it has become one of the least generous.

Even the most liberal electorates can be goaded into atypical action by rising property tax rates. In 1980, Massachusetts voters passed Proposition 2½, which capped property tax increases at, you guessed it, 2½ percent. As a result, towns that want to increase spending by more than that, for such needs as increased funding for education, have to hold special override sessions. Towns also have come to rely on user fees (a phenomenon examined later in this chapter).

Many state and local governments have attempted to ease the burden of property taxes on senior citizens and, in some cases, on other low-income individuals. In about 50 Massachusetts towns, senior citizens can reduce their property taxes by performing volunteer work. Cook County, Illinois, limits property tax rate increases by tying them to the national rate of inflation.[24] Despite these efforts, tensions between retirees living on fixed incomes and parents eager to spend more on local schools are commonplace. These pressures can be particularly acute in areas with large numbers of retirees. Indeed, some "active-adult retirement communities" ban families with children altogether.

Another hidden cost of property taxes is worth noting. You might think that commercial and residential property owners are the only ones who pay, right? You're off the hook if you rent, right? Wrong! Most economists believe that landlords pass the cost of property tax increases on to renters in the form of rent increases.

Income Taxes

Personal **income taxes** account for 21.3 percent of all state and local tax revenues.[25] That makes income tax revenue the third most significant source of state and local government income. In some ways, however, this figure conceals more than it reveals. Almost all nonfederal income tax revenues go to state governments.[26] In many states, personal income taxes are assessed on a graduated scale; so higher wage earners pay a greater percentage of their income in taxes. This structure tends to make state tax systems that rely more heavily on the income tax than on the sales tax more **progressive**.

Income taxes
Taxes on wages and interest earned

Progressive tax system
A system of taxation in which the rate paid reflects ability to pay

As with property taxes, states have different approaches to income taxes, with some using such taxes as a primary revenue source and others shunning them altogether. Alaska, Florida, Nevada, South Dakota, Texas, Washington, and Wyoming impose no income taxes at all, and New Hampshire and Tennessee impose taxes only on certain types of income. Your state's reliance (or lack of reliance) on income taxes influences not just how much you take home in your paycheck but also how much stuff costs. This is because states that do not collect income taxes usually rely heavily on sales tax revenues. States that have no sales tax tend to make up the loss by taking a bigger bite out of income. Oregon, for example, has no sales tax and is thus heavily reliant on income taxes (individual and corporate) as a primary revenue source. In 2008 Oregon's income tax provided 75 percent of the state's total tax revenues—the most of any state.[27] Voters in Oregon endorsed, and even increased, the state's reliance on its income tax in January 2010 by approving an increase in the tax rate on the highest-wage earners—the first time they have approved such an increase since 1930.

Two states, Alaska and New Hampshire, have neither income taxes nor sales taxes. How do they manage to function without two of the primary sources of revenue for most state governments? For Alaska, geology is the difference that makes a difference: The Prudhoe Bay oil fields bring in so much money that the state has little need for other revenue streams. The difference for New Hampshire is mostly the residents' hardheaded resistance to taxation. Unlike Alaska, New Hampshire has no big alternate revenue source—it just makes do. According to Donald Boyd of the Rockefeller Institute, New Hampshire's state government simply does less than most state governments. The state relies almost exclusively on local governments to finance elementary and secondary education rather than raising state revenue for this purpose. Unlike many other states, it also has managed to avoid court orders to spend dramatically more on secondary school education. It is able to do all this, in part, because the average New Hampshire resident has one of the highest levels of income in the country. The people of New Hampshire are able to pay for a lot of goods and services for themselves.

These states are the exceptions. On average, Americans pay about $899 a year in state income taxes.[28] However, residents of states with high tax rates, such as Maryland, Massachusetts, New York, and Oregon, pay significantly more in income taxes. (See Table 4-1.)

Other Tax Revenue Sources: Cars, Oil, and Death

Car registrations, deaths, and oil and other natural resources also are major sources of state revenues. In 2008, car registration fees brought in almost $20 billion to state and local governments. Estate taxes, sometimes called death taxes, and gift taxes brought in another $5.3 billion.[29]

Thirty-two states levy **severance taxes** on natural resources that are removed, or severed, from the state. Some states are quite creative about devising severance taxes. Washington, for example, taxes oysters and salmon and other game fish caught in the state. But despite some creative taxing, the only states that raise real money from severance taxes are states with significant coal, oil, and natural gas reserves, such as Wyoming and Alaska.

Show Me the Money: Income From Fees, Charges, and Uncle Sam

The total tax revenues discussed so far add up to a lot of money (nearly $2 trillion), but that covers only about two thirds of the roughly $3 trillion in annual spending that state and local governments racked up in 2012. The rest of the money came from user fees and other charges, insurance trust money, and intergovernmental transfers.

These sources of revenue can be significant. In 2008, state and local governments raised $613 billion from "charges and miscellaneous fees." That is $165 billion more than they raised from sales taxes.[30] Government levies in the form of, for

---

Severance taxes
Taxes on natural resources that are removed from a state

TABLE 4-1

State Individual Income Tax Collections per Capita, Fiscal Year 2012

State	Individual Income Tax Collections per Capita ($)	Rank	State	Individual Income Tax Collections per Capita ($)	Rank
Alabama	$627	36	Nebraska	$994	18
Alaska[a]	$0	44	Nevada[a]	$0	44
Arizona	$475	41	New Hampshire[b]	$62	42
Arkansas	$816	27	New Jersey	$1,257	8
California	$1,453	6	New Mexico	$553	38
Colorado	$946	22	New York	$1,985	2
Connecticut	$2,054	1	North Carolina	$1,070	15
Delaware	$1,307	7	North Dakota	$625	37
Florida[a]	$0	44	Ohio	$782	30
Georgia	$825	26	Oklahoma	$730	32
Hawaii	$1,112	13	Oregon	$1,500	4
Idaho	$763	31	Pennsylvania	$792	29
Illinois	$1,206	11	Rhode Island	$1,029	16
Indiana	$730	33	South Carolina	$659	35
Iowa	$987	19	South Dakota[a]	$0	44
Kansas	$1,005	17	Tennessee[b]	$28	43
Kentucky	$803	28	Texas[a]	$0	44
Louisiana	$539	39	Utah	$870	24
Maine	$1,085	14	Vermont	$956	20
Maryland	$1,214	10	Virginia	$1,254	9
Massachusetts	$1,801	3	Washington[a]	$0	44
Michigan	$701	34	West Virginia	$946	21
Minnesota	$1,489	5	Wisconsin	$1,183	12
Mississippi	$504	40	Wyoming[a]	$0	44
Missouri	$853	25	United States (average)	$899	—
Montana	$899	23			

Source: Tax Foundation, *Facts and Figures 2014: How Does Your State Compare?* (Washington, DC: Tax Foundation, 2014), Table 13, http://taxfoundation.org/article/facts-figures-2014-how-does-your-state-compare.

[a] State does not tax wage income.

[b] State does not tax wage income but does tax interest and dividend income.

example, university tuitions, public hospital charges, airport use fees, school lunch sales, and park permits obviously can make a big difference to the bottom line. Recently, states have increased fees to help close budget deficits and avoid more prominent tax increases. The pattern accelerated as tax revenues fell off in recent years: In 2010 state budgets included $5.3 billion in fee increases.[31] In 2013 state budgets tacked on another $500 million in new fee increases. State and local governments earned another $144 million from utility fees and, yes, from liquor sales and licenses.[32]

Insurance Trust Funds

The amount of money shown on a pay stub before any deductions are taken out can be pretty

Thanks to unprecedented revenues from oil production, North Dakota is expected to have a $2 billion budget reserve at the end of fiscal year 2013. North Dakota recently surpassed Alaska to become the nation's second-biggest oil producer, following only Texas.

impressive; the actual amount of the paycheck can be a bit disappointing. What many wage earners may not realize is that they are not the only ones paying the taxes and fees they see deducted from their paychecks. Their employers often have to match these payroll taxes and deductions. These **insurance trust funds** go to their state governments and to the federal government. Ultimately, the contributions are invested to support Social Security and retirement programs, workers' compensation and disability programs, and other related insurance programs that benefit employees.

Intergovernmental Transfers

The final portion of state and local government revenues comes from **intergovernmental transfers** of money. In the case of state governments, that means transfers from the federal government. In the case of local governments, it means transfers from state governments. In 2011, the federal government provided some $575 billion to state and local governments, making it the single largest source of revenues for these governments.[33] That situation was temporary, however—a good portion of that money from the federal government came from the stimulus funds appropriated by ARRA, as discussed in the introductory section of this chapter. Much of that money was disbursed to states and spent by 2012–2013.

About 90 percent of federal funds go to specific state programs. Medicaid, the joint state–federal health insurance program for low-income people and people with disabilities, is by far the largest recipient. It receives about 64.6 percent of all federal funds that go to state governments.[34] Education (both K–12 and postsecondary school), transportation projects, and public welfare also receive significant federal funding. Most of these funds cannot be used on just anything—states must spend them on certain programs and often in a certain fashion.

During the 1960s, local governments and some neighborhood organizations also received substantial federal funding. Many of these programs have since ended or have been scaled back drastically. Aside from the stimulus bill, local governments get only about 4 percent of their total revenues from the federal government. Adding to the problem for localities is that states have reduced their support for local governments, too, as one tool to help balance their own budgets. Still, intergovernmental revenue transfers—mostly from state governments—account for about a third of local government spending.[35]

Localities generally have welcomed the money, but relationships between state governments and county and city governments have not always been easy. Over the course of the past decade, many city and county governments have found themselves stuck with unfunded mandates. These requirements have been imposed on them by federal or state legislation that forces them to perform certain tasks but fails to provide them with the money to carry out those tasks. Transfers of money and responsibilities, however, continue to be commonplace during economic downturns.[36]

Taxing Variations Among State and Local Governments

Generalizations about state and local finances should not obscure the fact that different states and localities tax themselves in very different ways and at very different rates. As we have been hinting throughout our discussion thus far, differences make a difference. The first and most obvious difference concerns the very different tax burdens that states choose to impose on themselves. In

---

Insurance trust funds
Money collected from contributions, assessments, insurance premiums, and payroll taxes

Intergovernmental transfers
Funds provided by the federal government to state governments and by state governments to local governments

A Difference That Makes A Difference

The Blessing and Curse of a Booming Economy

While many states are pinching pennies, North Dakota is dealing with an economic boom and an overflowing state treasury. What's the secret to North Dakota's good fortune? It's mostly geography. The state just happens to be the location of certain fortuitous events that predate the Great Recession—and we mean *way* predate the Great Recession, like by 417 million years. Somewhere around that time, a large oil deposit formed under what is now the border between North Dakota and Canada. The first well sunk to try to tap that oil was drilled on land owned by a farmer named Henry Bakken; what is now known as the Bakken Formation is believed to hold a massive 4.3 billion barrels of oil.

While the Bakken Formation's potential had been known for a long time, it wasn't until relatively recently that the technology to tap that oil cost-effectively became available. Coincidentally, that technology came online and opened up the taps on the Bakken Formation pretty much at the same time the United States was hit by the worst financial crisis in five generations. Geology was thus a difference that made a big difference to this state. The happy coincidence that the sea of fossil fuel on which it sat was newly open to extraction meant that North Dakota pretty much missed the financial hard times of the Great Recession.

Taxes on oil and gas production netted the state $839 million in fiscal year 2011–2012 and are expected to generate $1 billion a year for the state's bottom line into the foreseeable future. That's a big number for a small-population state such as North Dakota. While other states have been struggling just to make ends meet, North Dakota has been increasing its biennial budgets by 12 percent.

Economically, North Dakota is like some sort of alternate universe compared with many places that are still struggling economically. The state has more jobs than workers—at one point in Williams County there were nine jobs available for every person seeking work. The average oil and gas worker there earns north of $90,000 per year. Average household income in municipalities such as Stanley (population 1,458) has jumped 130 percent in a decade.

While the oil boom means that North Dakota does not have to worry about budget deficits, the effects are not all positive. The state is undergoing a population boom that is straining public services and creating housing shortages. A new two-bedroom apartment can set you back $3,500 a month, and that's if you can find one to rent. The housing shortage is so bad that 25 percent of the high school students in Watford City are considered homeless. State and local governments are frantically trying to build the infrastructure to support the massive growth triggered by the oil boom but are having a hard time keeping up.

Still, states that are struggling to make ends meet might be forgiven if they look at North Dakota's problems with envy. At least North Dakota has extra money to deal with its problems, which is more than many states can say.

Sources: Ryan Holeywell, "North Dakota's Oil Boom Is a Blessing and a Curse," *Governing*, August 2011, http://www.governing.com/topics/energy-env/north-dakotas-oil-boom-blessing-curse.html; Curtis Johnson, "Can a North Dakota Oil-Boom Town Survive Success?" *Governing*, June 2014, http://www.governing.com/gov-institute/voices/col-growth-watford-city-north-dakota-can-oil-boom-town-survive-success.html.

2011, Connecticut residents paid the most per capita in state and local taxes of any state in the country—$7,150. However, New Jersey residents faced the largest tax burden. They returned 12.6 percent of their incomes to state and local governments, the highest percentage of any state in the country. In contrast, residents of Alaska, South Dakota, Texas, and Wyoming faced some of the lowest state and local tax burdens in the country. On average, in 2011 they paid 7.1 percent of their incomes in state and local taxes.[37]

State and local governments do not just choose to tax themselves at different rates; they also choose to tax themselves in different ways.

MAP 4-1

ARRA Funds Awarded by State, 2013

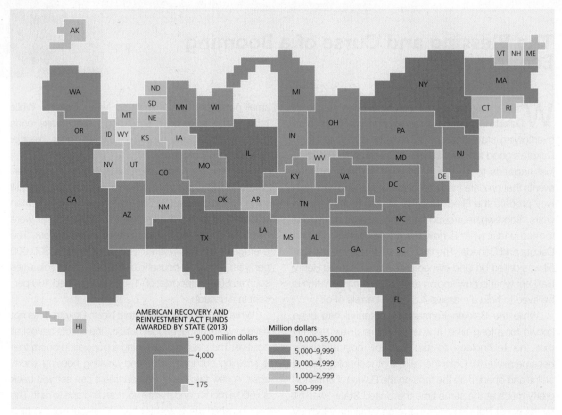

AMERICAN RECOVERY AND
REINVESTMENT ACT FUNDS
AWARDED BY STATE (2013)

— 9,000 million dollars

— 4,000

— 175

Million dollars

- 10,000–35,000
- 5,000–9,999
- 3,000–4,999
- 1,000–2,999
- 500–999

Source: Recovery Accountability and Transparency Board, "State/Territory Totals, as Reported by Recipients," May 1, 2014, http://www.recovery.gov/arra/Pages/textview.aspx?data=recipientHomeMap.

Residents of many Tennessee counties pay sales taxes of almost 10 percent. New Hampshire relies on property taxes to generate 18 percent of its total state tax revenue. In contrast, property taxes do not contribute anything to state coffers in 14 states, although localities rely heavily on them.[38]

In thinking about a state's tax burden, it is helpful to distinguish between its **tax capacity** and its **tax effort**. In Newport Beach, California, for example, many homes are worth more than $1 million—a far cry from the price tags of a few years ago—but on that much value, even low property tax rates are going to bring in serious money. Conversely, Odessa, Texas,

with a median home price of $66,700, is not going to generate a lot of property tax revenue no matter how high its rates are. Newport Beach's tax capacity is high; Odessa's tax capacity is low.

Rather than tax capacity, many political scientists prefer to look at a different measurement—tax effort, which is the aggregate-level equivalent of individual-level tax burden. Basically, measurements of tax effort seek to determine the proportion of its income that a given community chooses to pay out in taxes. A community's tax effort is also a good proxy for its appetite for public services. Some communities are willing to pay for street cleaning; some are not. Some communities, such as Cambridge, Massachusetts, even are willing to pay a government employee to drive around and announce that street cleaning is about to commence.

Tax capacities and tax efforts often diverge markedly. Consider Massachusetts and New

---

Tax capacity
A measure of the ability to pay taxes

Tax effort
A measure of taxes paid relative to the ability to pay taxes

Hampshire. Both are comparatively affluent states. Personal income per capita in 2010 was $51,302 in Massachusetts and $43,586 in New Hampshire.[39] In other words, the two states have similar tax capacities. However, they make very different tax efforts. New Hampshire has the second-lightest tax burden in the country. Its residents pay about $3,769 a year in state and local taxes. In contrast, residents of neighboring Massachusetts pay about $5,586.[40]

Explaining Tax Variations

What accounts for differences in tax capacity and effort such as those found between Massachusetts and New Hampshire? Political culture is one difference that helps explain the difference. New Hampshire prides itself on its rugged individualism. Its motto is "Live Free or Die." Residents tend to want the government to stay out of their way. In contrast, Massachusetts was founded as a commonwealth. The founding document of the Massachusetts Bay Colony describes a single "Body Politic" dedicated to the "general good" of the colony.[41] In this tradition, state and local governments are seen as effective ways of advancing that general good; thus, higher taxes and larger governments are more acceptable.

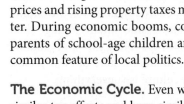

Political culture, however, is not the only important variable that explains the very different tax efforts among states. Factors such as geography, geology, demographics, and history also influence the choices that state and local governments make.

Geography. One obvious, but easily overlooked, factor that influences state tax policies is geography. Some states use sales tax policy as a competitive edge. Delaware proudly recruits shoppers from nearby mid-Atlantic states to its outlet malls with "no sales tax" advertisements. In contrast, Hawaii charges a 4.5 percent tax on nearly everything sold, including many services. How can it get away with the practice? Well, unless residents are willing to fly to the mainland for their sundries, they don't have much choice but to pay up.

Geology. As we have already seen, geology plays an important role in some state economies. This is most notably true in oil-rich and natural-gas–rich states such as Alaska, Wyoming, and North Dakota (see the box "A Difference That Makes a Difference: The Blessing and Curse of a Booming Economy"). Thanks in large part to Prudhoe Bay, state and local governments in Alaska are able to maintain high levels of spending with very low tax burdens. Alaska used its mineral riches to help establish the Alaska Permanent Fund, which is a sovereign wealth fund—basically a state-owned investment corporation. The fund's profits are partially redistributed to state citizens; so rather than the state taxing residents, the fund pays Alaskans for being Alaskans. The fund sends each eligible citizen a yearly **dividend** check; in 2012 the amount per person was about $878.

Demographics. Demographics also play an important role in determining the attitudes of state and local governments toward taxes. This is particularly true at the local level. Consider a city with a strong local economy and rising house prices. Such a city attracts a large number of young workers with children. These are people who might very well want to spend more money on local schools and are willing to deal with rising property tax revenues. However, as mentioned previously, for seniors living on fixed incomes, rising house prices and rising property taxes might spell disaster. During economic booms, conflicts between parents of school-age children and retirees are a common feature of local politics.

The Economic Cycle. Even when states make similar tax efforts and have similar cultures, their state and local finances can still vary widely because states (and even cities) can have very different economies. The national economic numbers that most people are familiar with—unemployment, productivity gains, income, and the like—are not necessarily accurate reflections of state economic conditions.

Dividend
A payment made to stockholders (or, in Alaska's case, residents) from the interest generated by an investment

Depending on the makeup of their economies, states can find themselves at very different points on an economic cycle at the same point in time. For example, industrial states such as Michigan and Indiana tend to experience economic downturns first. Texas historically has had a countercyclical economy. When rising oil prices threaten to push industrial states into recession, Texas tends to do well. The same is true of Wyoming, Alaska, and, most recently, North Dakota.

Demographics, geography, history, political culture, and the swings of the economic cycle are all important, but these variables do not explain all the financial choices that state and local governments make. Take Mississippi, for example. One of the most religious and politically conservative states in the country, Mississippi is the buckle of the Bible Belt. In 1990, however, Mississippi passed riverboat gambling legislation. This legislation allowed casino operators to build full-size casinos on barges moored permanently to the shoreline on the Mississippi River and the Gulf Coast. The goal was to turn the northwestern town of Tunica, which had gained a measure of renown after the television newsmagazine *60 Minutes* profiled it as the poorest city in America, into Las Vegas East.

What's important to keep in mind here is that Nevada and Mississippi have completely different political cultures. Political scientist Daniel Elazar describes Mississippi as a traditionalistic state and Nevada as an individualistic state. In short, Nevada has the kind of political culture that we might expect to produce, well, Las Vegas. Mississippi does not. Today, however, the hamlet of Tunica has more casino square footage than does the East Coast gambling hot spot Atlantic City, in the individualistic state of New Jersey. Clearly, political culture isn't everything.

Debt

The final source of money for state and local governments is debt, generally issued in the form of **bonds**. These are financial instruments with which state and local governments promise to pay back borrowed money at a fixed rate of interest on a specified date. The interest rates paid by a government depend largely on the government's bond rating. Bond ratings are issued by three private companies—Moody's, Standard & Poor's, and Fitch—and are based on the governments' fiscal health; many states' bond ratings have fallen during the current recession. A rating of AAA is the best, and anything lower than BBB is considered "junk bond status" and would send a government's interest rates skyrocketing. No state has ever fallen below a BBB rating.[42]

State and local governments, as well as quasi-governmental entities such as utility and water authorities, use bonds to finance **capital investments**, typically infrastructure upgrades such as new roads, new schools, and new airports. There are two types of bonds: **general obligation bonds**, which are secured by the taxing power of the jurisdiction that issues them, and **revenue bonds**, which are secured by the revenue from a given project, such as a new toll road. For state governments, capital investments are projects such as highway construction, power plant construction and pollution control, and even land conservation. Because the issuance of general obligation bonds must be approved by voters, state and local governments turn to revenue bonds more often.

Local governments use bonds to finance projects such as construction or improvement of schools, sewage and water lines, airports, and affordable housing. Investors like them, too, in part because the earnings from most state bonds are exempt from state income taxes.

In 2012, state and local governments issued about $295 billion in bonds.[43] **Municipal bonds**,

---

Capital investments
Investments in infrastructure, such as roads

General obligation bonds
Investments secured by the taxing power of the jurisdiction that issues them

Revenue bonds
Investments secured by the revenue generated by a state or municipal project

Municipal bonds
Bonds issued by states, counties, cities, and towns to fund large projects as well as operating budgets. Income from such bonds is exempt from federal taxes and from state and local taxes for the investors who live in the state where they are issued.

Bonds
Certificates that are evidence of debts on which the issuer promises to pay the holders a specified amount of interest for a specified length of time and to repay the loans on their maturity

Bonds and Broken Budgets

The story of how Jefferson County, Alabama, waded into budget and bond muck stretches back to 1993, when the Cahaba River Society, a group dedicated to preserving the river that flows through Birmingham, complained that the county's sewer system was discharging raw sewage into waterways. Federal officials issued a consent decree in which Jefferson County promised to upgrade the system.

The county paid for the upgrade by issuing $3 billion in bonds. As sewer service rates rose to meet those costs and Jefferson County struggled under its debt, county officials looked for a way to lessen the loan payments. In 2002 and 2003, they refinanced their bonds with variable-rate and auction-rate securities. (Auction-rate securities are bonds for which the interest rate is reset at auction every few weeks.)

Auction-rate securities were supposed to be safe, but the auction-rate market collapsed in February 2008. Then the bond insurance companies that were backing the county's debt suffered their own fiscal problems and their credit was downgraded. The result: Jefferson County's interest rates skyrocketed, much like the rates of homeowners whose subprime mortgages had just reset. The county's revenue from sewer fees could not cover the borrowing costs. On April Fool's Day 2008, Jefferson County failed to make payment on its debt. Instead, it reached an agreement with its creditors to pay the interest and get an extension on the principal—an agreement that left the county of 660,000 teetering on the edge of bankruptcy.

County commissioners and other Alabama political players developed a variety of ideas to solve the sewer mess—to no avail. Without a solution in sight, the county made massive cutbacks: reducing department budgets by one third, canceling road maintenance contracts, closing courthouses, and laying off hundreds of county workers. "We're having to downsize this government to the point that it may not be able to operate," County Commissioner Bettye Fine Collins said in 2009.

Collins's comments were prophetic. In December 2011 Jefferson County filed for bankruptcy; by that time its debt had ballooned to more than $4 billion, a crushing burden the county simply could not manage. Jefferson County then spent the better part of 2 years caught up in litigation with its biggest creditors, who faced the prospect of losing hundreds of millions of dollars. In 2013 Jefferson County reached a deal with these creditors, agreeing to pay them 60 percent of what they were owed. This allowed the county finally to emerge from bankruptcy.

As discussed in the opening section of this chapter, variations on the Jefferson County story have played out across the country, as the recession significantly weakened local governments' financial footing.

Sources: Adapted from Josh Goodman, "Drained," *Governing*, August 2009; "Jefferson County Reaches Deal to End Biggest U.S. Municipal Bankruptcy," *Governing*, June 5, 2013, http://www.governing.com/news/state/Jefferson-County-Reaches-Deal-to-End-Biggest-US-Municipal-Bankruptcy.html; Karen Pierog, "Default, Bankruptcy Fears Overhang U.S. Muni Market," Reuters, February 16, 2010.

called munis, are generally safe and attractive investments, particularly for the rich. Municipal bondholders usually are exempted from paying federal or state taxes on income they receive from bonds. Sometimes, however, municipal finances go disastrously awry. In 2009, Jefferson County, Alabama, the largest county in the state, announced it would file for bankruptcy after defaulting on $3 billion in bonds to finance improvements to its sewer system.

The Budget Process

Once state and local governments have raised money from taxes, user fees, and bonds, and have received money from intergovernmental transfers,

MAP 4-2

Municipal Bankruptcies as of December 2013

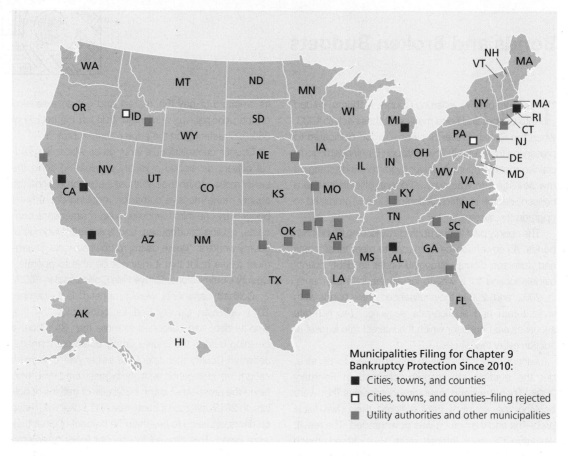

Municipalities Filing for Chapter 9 Bankruptcy Protection Since 2010:

- ■ Cities, towns, and counties
- □ Cities, towns, and counties–filing rejected
- ■ Utility authorities and other municipalities

Source: "Bankrupt Cities, Municipalities List and Map," *Governing*, December 3, 2013, http://www.governing.com/gov-data/municipal-cities-counties-bankruptcies-and-defaults.html.

Note: Only about half of the U.S. states allow municipalities to file for Chapter 9 bankruptcy; laws in other states prohibit such filings. Not all bankruptcy filings were approved.

they must decide how to spend it. These decisions are made during the **budget process**.

Most state and local governments budget for one **fiscal year**. Unfortunately for fans of simplicity in government, the fiscal year is not the same as the calendar year. The federal government's fiscal year runs from October 1 to September 30. Most state and local governments begin their fiscal year on July 1; Alabama, Michigan, New York, and Texas are exceptions. Thus, when legislatures debate the budget, they are almost always debating the budget for the coming fiscal year.[44] Nineteen states pass 2-year budgets.[45]

Budget timelines do vary from state to state, but the budget process itself is quite similar across states. It begins with instructions from the governor's budget office. The executive branch agencies are told to draw up funding requests for the upcoming year. During the fall (assuming the typical fiscal year beginning on July 1), the budget office reviews the spending requests and

Budget process
The procedure by which state and local governments assess revenues and set budgets

Fiscal year
The annual accounting period used by a government

Despite some groups' moral objections to gambling, states have turned to casinos such as this one floating on the Mississippi River in Natchez, Mississippi, to help raise much-needed revenues.

© Kevin Fleming/Corbis

helps the chief executive develop a unified budget for the executive branch.

Most chief executives unveil their budgets in state-of-the-state addresses in January. In 45 states, governors and mayors are required by law to submit a **balanced budget** to the legislature or city council. The legislative body reviews the budget, authorizes spending on certain programs, appropriates the necessary money, and presents its budget to the chief executive to sign into law.

As a guard against fiscal excess and abuse, 49 states have statutory or constitutional requirements that the state legislature must enact a balanced budget. Only Vermont is free to run up debt as it pleases. All but five states also have laws that require lawmakers to save a certain portion of state revenues in so-called rainy day, or budget stabilization, funds. States can draw on these funds during times of recession, when revenues fall. Although rainy-day funds rarely offset the revenue drops that occur during a recession, they do provide some cushion for the lawmakers who have to balance state budgets. In 2009 and 2010, for example, rainy-day funds helped close more than $35 billion of states' budget gaps—funds that would have otherwise had to come from more severe program cuts or greater tax increases.[46] Many local governments face similar requirements because of state laws or their own municipal codes.

There are, of course, exceptions. In states such as Arkansas, Mississippi, and South Carolina,

legislatures take the lead role in formulating the initial budget plan. Legislative bodies also take the lead in county and city governments with weak chief executives, such as Los Angeles, California. In many western states, citizens and special interests have become players in the budgeting process via ballot initiatives.

Expenditures, or Where the Money Goes

As you can imagine, state and local governments spend a lot of money to provide all the services and programs they are responsible for. In fiscal year 2012, state governments alone spent nearly $2 trillion. (See Table 4-2.) In 2013 state and local governments combined spent about $10,019.50 for every man, woman, and child in the country.[47] So where did the money go?

Wages. Salaries are the single largest source of **expenditures** for state and local governments— roughly $800 billion in 2008. State and local

---

Balanced budget
A budget in which current expenditures are equal to or less than income

Expenditures
Money spent by government

TABLE 4-2

State Revenue, Expenditures, and Debt, 2012 (in Thousands of Dollars)

	Total Revenue	Total Expenditure	Debt at End of Fiscal Year
United States	1,912,253,172	1,976,789,593	1,147,933,947
Alabama	28,970,138	27,730,899	8,719,430
Alaska	15,050,413	11,729,460	5,909,456
Arizona	30,947,615	31,232,561	14,182,905
Arkansas	18,439,297	19,618,284	3,568,702
California	250,882,537	267,017,700	152,821,830
Colorado	25,675,544	28,238,168	16,329,530
Connecticut	27,307,921	28,370,101	31,965,511
Delaware	8,015,377	8,315,681	5,796,853
Florida	82,823,985	79,482,176	38,171,049
Georgia	40,505,805	44,751,105	13,400,514
Hawaii	10,600,634	11,565,554	8,398,012
Idaho	8,308,086	8,301,262	3,945,615
Illinois	68,901,523	72,622,240	64,301,765
Indiana	35,284,647	35,832,998	22,511,518
Iowa	20,979,691	20,407,524	6,166,080
Kansas	16,144,318	16,747,356	6,860,094
Kentucky	25,683,865	29,349,094	15,103,515
Louisiana	26,942,887	31,685,604	15,415,488
Maine	8,342,043	9,047,755	5,605,606
Maryland	36,004,081	41,030,733	25,741,733
Massachusetts	48,981,548	56,487,432	79,800,278
Michigan	64,021,268	61,726,982	30,823,672
Minnesota	38,553,800	38,612,582	13,230,223
Mississippi	18,765,201	20,051,298	7,194,251
Missouri	31,065,599	31,360,850	20,385,537
Montana	7,727,604	7,062,896	3,995,366
Nebraska	9,781,249	9,525,518	2,073,385
Nevada	14,317,867	13,477,122	3,896,718
New Hampshire	7,153,139	7,423,747	8,029,849
New Jersey	57,582,037	68,121,744	64,851,557
New Mexico	15,195,673	17,018,829	7,550,084
New York	179,604,728	181,226,180	135,884,070
North Carolina	56,470,410	43,624,402	18,291,688
North Dakota	9,246,488	6,315,436	2,083,611
Ohio	72,465,759	76,524,453	36,521,981
Oklahoma	23,263,487	22,598,865	9,979,234
Oregon	25,059,234	26,862,451	13,782,071
Pennsylvania	78,539,490	87,346,336	46,205,176
Rhode Island	7,946,561	8,325,783	9,211,790
South Carolina	26,106,015	27,791,485	14,854,263

	Total Revenue	Total Expenditure	Debt at End of Fiscal Year
South Dakota	4,351,161	4,424,154	3,607,615
Tennessee	30,803,108	31,497,959	6,167,659
Texas	137,723,080	125,532,786	45,626,393
Utah	15,600,624	17,109,026	7,067,149
Vermont	6,348,888	5,959,260	3,390,961
Virginia	43,103,206	46,761,727	27,799,760
Washington	40,665,155	45,501,471	29,090,132
West Virginia	13,247,295	13,222,912	7,306,756
Wisconsin	35,880,592	36,446,089	22,995,708
Wyoming	6,845,489	5,773,573	1,321,804

Source: U.S. Census Bureau, "2012 Annual Survey of State Government Finances," January 23, 2014, http://factfinder2.census.gov/faces/tableservices/jsf/pages/productview.xhtml?src=bkmk.

governments are the biggest employers in the United States. In 2014, state governments employed 5.1 million people nationwide. Local governments employed another 14.1 million people.[48]

Education. Education has long been the single largest functional spending category for state and local governments. In 2012 state governments alone spent $588 billion on education, the majority of it (about $317 billion) in the form of transfers to schools and school districts.[49]

Despite the big financial commitment by states—they provide about half the funding—primary and secondary education traditionally have been the preserve of local governments. In most states, elected local school boards hire superintendents and principals, select curricula that align with state standards, and develop school budgets. Local governments typically devote about 38 percent of their budgets to education.[50]

State governments also devote a portion of their expenditures to higher education; in 2012 this amounted to a total of about $72.4 billion. That number has been steadily declining, however—in 2007 states spent more than $75 billion.[51] Funding for higher education has been cut largely because it comes out of general revenue funds; that is, it is part of what is known as **discretionary**

spending. In tight economic times, discretionary spending is one of the first parts of a government budget to come under stress—when revenues shrink, legislatures have to reduce annual appropriations, and that means cutting discretionary spending. As publicly supported colleges and universities have ways to deal with spending cuts from state government (read: jacking up your tuition and increasing your class size), higher-education funds have been particularly hard-hit by budget retrenchment.

Health Care. Since the late 1990s, health care spending has surged dramatically. For state governments, spending on health care is now greater than spending for any other single item. Medicaid is the largest and most expensive state-run health program. When it was established in 1965, it was viewed as a limited safety net for the very poor and disabled. However, the numbers of low-income, uninsured Americans have grown, and medical care has become more expensive. The program has grown at an enormous rate as a result. In 1970, state governments spent $2 billion on Medicaid, and the federal government kicked in another $3 billion. In 2008, the states and the federal government spent $311 billion on the program, up from $298 billion just a year earlier.[52] State Medicaid programs provide health insurance to more than 60 million people and account for 23.7 percent of total state spending.[53]

The number of people served by Medicaid is rising dramatically. In 2010 the federal government enacted the Patient Protection and Affordable Care Act—commonly known as Obamacare—which has the explicit aim of extending health insurance coverage to millions of uninsured people. The law is of central interest to the states because one of its central goals is to expand Medicaid eligibility, and Medicaid is a program cooperatively run—and paid for—by both state and federal governments. As such, it is an example of **fiscal federalism,** a system of delivering public services that involves the federal government's picking up most of the costs while states take responsibility for administering the services.

Obamacare was a contentious and controversial law opposed by some state officials, who viewed it not just as federal encroachment on state sovereignty but as a potential budget buster. Though the federal government pledged to pick up the vast majority of the costs of adding millions to the Medicaid rolls, at least in the short term, some state governments worried that the federal fiscal commitment was not forever. The federal government pledged to pay 100 percent of expansion costs for 3 years and after that 90 percent of the costs until 2022. But what about after 2022? Some states were concerned that they could end up being saddled with huge costs at some point in the future.

The sovereignty and budget concerns were addressed in *National Federation of Independent Business v. Sebelius,* a case decided in 2012 by the Supreme Court. The court ruled that the major provisions of Obamacare were constitutional but that the federal government could not force state governments to join in the planned expansion of Medicaid, effectively giving states the right to opt out. As of 2014, roughly 40 percent of states—mostly conservative and Republican—had decided not to participate in the Medicaid expansion. By some estimates, if fully implemented in all states, Obamacare could add an extra 17 million people to the numbers covered by Medicaid, which is an **entitlement** program. This means states and the federal government are obligated by law to provide health insurance to low-income individuals who qualify for the program, regardless of the cost. At least as of 2014, states that were participating had added considerably fewer than 17 million new enrollees to Medicaid. Just how many had been added because of Obamacare was hard to figure out. Estimates ranged from 2 million to 4 million new enrollees through the beginning of 2014—though some of those new enrollees would have been eligible under the old rules and thus should not be considered additions because of Obamacare.

Though it is the biggest health care policy reform in decades, Obamacare is still in the early

Discretionary spending
Spending controlled in annual appropriations acts

Fiscal federalism
The system by which federal grants are used to fund programs and services provided by state and local governments

Entitlement
A service that government must provide, regardless of the cost

stages of implementation and, until it is fully operational several years from now, it will be hard to assess whether or not it has increased state health care expenditures. In the meantime, at least some state officials will remain concerned that they may be left in the lurch at some point in the future, stuck with the obligation of covering the costs of an entitlement program that the federal government is not fully funding.

What is in no doubt is that Medicaid and other health care programs are expensive for both the states and the federal government. In 2012 total Medicaid costs were about $415 billion; states contributed about $176 billion, with the rest coming from the federal government.[54] The Children's Health Insurance Program (CHIP) is another joint state–federal program that helps provide health insurance for children in poor families. In 2009, CHIP was a $10 billion program, with about $7 billion funded by the federal government and the rest provided by the states.

States do have some leeway in determining how generous they want to be with programs such as Medicaid and CHIP. Eligibility for these sorts of programs is typically determined by family or wage-earner income relative to federally established poverty levels. While the federal government sets basic guidelines on those eligibility requirements, states can use more generous guidelines if they choose. For example, in Mississippi children under the age of 5 are eligible for Medicaid benefits in families earning up to 133 percent of the federal poverty level. In Wisconsin they are eligible if their families earn up to 300 percent of the federal poverty level.[55] In other words, whether someone is eligible for Medicaid benefits is dependent not just on how much his or her family earns but also on what state the family lives in.

Welfare. Welfare has been one of the most contentious issues in U.S. politics for a long time. Like Medicaid, welfare is an entitlement program; states have some leeway to determine eligibility, but they cannot deny or restrict benefits to qualified individuals. From 1965 to 1996, women with young children were eligible to receive monetary assistance through a welfare program known as Aid to Families with Dependent Children (AFDC).

In 1996, Republicans in Congress and President Bill Clinton joined forces to pass the Personal Responsibility and Work Reconciliation Act, which abolished AFDC and replaced it with the Temporary Assistance for Needy Families (TANF) program. TANF disbursed federal money to states in block grants and gave them considerable freedom in determining how they wanted to spend those funds. Many liberals predicted that such welfare "reform" would result in disaster. Instead, the number of people on welfare rolls declined dramatically. From 1994 to 1999, the welfare caseload declined by nearly 50 percent, from about 4 million people to 2 million people.[56]

Welfare continues to be a politically contentious issue even though, from a financial viewpoint, it is actually a pretty minor program. In 2011 states spent about $15 billion on TANF, with the federal government kicking in another $15 billion—that's no more than a percentage point or two of total state spending.[57]

Fire, Police, and Prisons. In 2008 state and local governments spent $129 billion on fire and police protection. They spent an additional $73 billion on prisons and correctional facilities.[58] State and local government spending on police protection and prisons varies widely. New York City, with a population of 8 million, employs a police force of 37,000. That works out to 1 police officer for every 216 people. In contrast, Los Angeles, a city of 3.8 million, employees only 10,000 police officers. That equals only 1 police officer for every 380 people.

States also have very different levels of enthusiasm for funding prisons. In fiscal year 2012, Florida devoted 4.2 percent of its state spending to prisons. That is a level of spending more than 1 percentage point higher than the national average and reflects Florida's incarceration rate, which is among the 10 highest in the country. In contrast, West Virginia's state government spent only 1.0 percent of its state budget on corrections.[59]

Highways. In 2011 state and local governments spent about $153 billion on transportation, much of it devoted to highways and roads.[60] Most of this money came from dedicated revenue sources, such as the gasoline tax, but the federal govern-

FIGURE 4-1

HOW IT WORKS

A Year in the Life of a State Budget: Idaho's Budgetary Process

Most folks first hear about state budget priorities through their governor's state of the state address, the forum in which most state budgetary news is presented. In reality, budget planning begins well in advance of this address and involves all three branches of government to some degree. In Idaho, each year in May (after the last of the potatoes have been planted), that state's Division of Financial Management (DFM) starts sowing its own seeds: overseeing the development of that state's budget for the coming fiscal year. This is the beginning of what is really an 18-month process: the planning for fiscal year 2014, for instance, will actually get under way about mid-year in 2012.

This chart shows how the process works in Idaho:

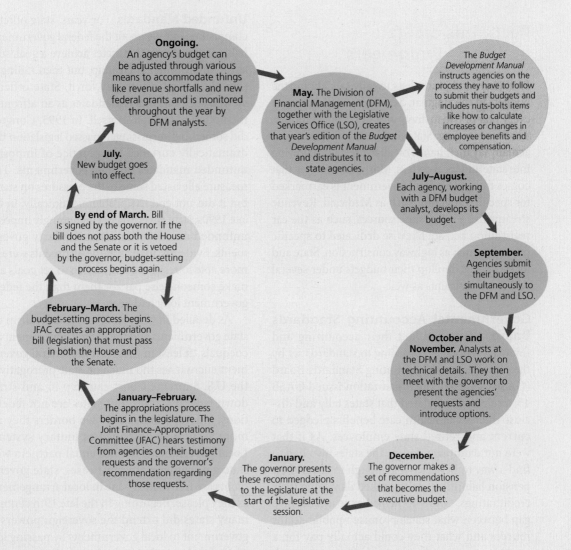

Source: Adapted from Idaho Division of Financial Management, "Budget Process," 2009, http://dfm.idaho.gov/citizensguide/budgetprocess.html.

ment accounted for nearly a third of these funds.[61] The federal contribution to state transportation spending has been unusually high for several years because of ARRA, which channeled billions in federal stimulus money to the states in the form of highway funds.

Not surprisingly, states with wide-open spaces spend more money on highway construction and transportation. In 2012 Alaska devoted 16.8 percent of total state expenditures to transportation. This was the highest percentage of any state in the country, followed by North Dakota at 16.4 percent and South Dakota at 15.9 percent. Nationwide, state governments spent 7.8 percent of total revenues on transportation in 2012.[62]

Restraints on State and Local Budgeteers

Politicians and journalists usually talk about "the budget" in the singular, as if elected officials meet every year or two to divvy up a single pot of money. That's misleading. State and local officials cannot actually lay their hands on all the revenues flowing into state and local coffers. Most of the money that comes from the federal government is earmarked for specific programs, such as Medicaid. Revenue streams from many state sources, such as the car registration tax, are likewise dedicated to specific purposes, such as highway construction. State and local officials develop their budgets under several additional restraints as well.

Governmental Accounting Standards Board. States conduct their accounting and financial reporting according to standards set by the Governmental Accounting Standards Board (GASB). In 2004, the organization issued GASB 45, a rule that mandated that states tally and disclose the cost of health care benefits pledged to current and retired state employees. As if that were not daunting enough, the states also had to find a way to begin saving enough to cover their pension liabilities, or they risked damaging their credit ratings. GASB 45 helped expose a massive gap between what states promised public-sector retirees and what they could actually pay for, a gap that was pushed wider by the revenue crunch of the Great Recession. The basic problem is that while state pension schemes have the funds to pay for promised retiree pensions and health care benefits in the short term, they do not have the money set aside to pay for the expected long-term increases in those costs. As of 2012 the gap between the assets of state pension funds and their financial obligation to cover promised pension and health care benefits was $915 billion. That rises to more than a trillion dollars if you add in the promises made by local governments to their retirees.[63] States have taken some steps to try to close the gap by reducing benefits and increasing employee contributions to those benefits, but even with those reductions it is not clear that states will be able to cover their promises without resorting to getting more from taxpayers.

Unfunded Mandates. For years, state officials complained bitterly about the federal government's habit of mandating that states achieve a goal, such as an environmental cleanup, but then failing to provide any money to pay for it. State officials viewed such unfunded mandates as an affront to the notion of federalism itself. In 1995, Congress did something surprising: It passed legislation that dramatically curtailed the practice of imposing unfunded mandates on state governments. This measure alleviated some of the pressures on states, but it did not end the problem. Ironically, in the late 1990s, state governments increasingly imposed unfunded mandates on county and city governments. Evidently, many state governments were no more able to resist the temptation to set goals and make someone else pay for them than the federal government long had been.

As detailed in Chapter 2, under federalism the state governments and the federal government are coequals, at least in theory. If the federal government encroaches too much on state prerogatives, the U.S. Supreme Court can step in and strike down federal actions. But states are not federations; indeed, within their own borders they are more accurately described as unitary systems. Local governments are not equal partners with state governments. In most cases, state governments are free to intervene in local arrangements as they please. Beginning in the late 19th century, many states did extend the sovereign powers of government to local governments by passing legislation that provided for home rule. Communities could enact charters and ordinances, change their names, and annex their neighbors without the permission of the legislature. They also controlled their own budgets and property taxes.

At the time, California was one of the strongest home rule states. In recent years, however, that has changed. California cities now control less than half of their discretionary spending. The state tells them what they must do with the rest. The situation is even worse for California's counties. They have the final say over less than one third of the money they spend.[64]

Ballot Initiatives and the Budget Process.

California's experience illustrates one of the most significant trends in state finances—the growing use of ballot initiatives to shape and restrain state tax systems. According to Bill Piper of the Initiative and Referendum Institute, voters put 130 tax initiatives on ballots nationwide from 1978 through 1999. Roughly two thirds were antitax initiatives that cut, limited, or eliminated taxes in some way. Of these, 41 passed. In fact, a whopping 67 percent of all antitax initiatives that came up for a vote from 1996 through 1999 passed.[65] The net effect of all those initiatives was to create a massive headache for California's budget makers in the 21st century—in simple terms, they got to control less and less of the state's financial affairs, which were increasingly constrained or just put on automatic pilot.

The big problem with using direct democracy to make far-reaching budgetary decisions is that while citizens generally prefer low taxes, they also tend to favor fairly high levels of spending on a wide range of government programs and services. The end result is that state and local governments are required to do a lot of expensive things, even as they are being legally required to limit their revenues. These same constraints also made it hard for some states to respond effectively to the fast-moving economic hits brought on by the Great Recession. California is just one of a number of ballot initiative states that are choking on tax and spending policies put in place by voters.

At their worst, antitax budget initiatives can paralyze state legislatures and local governments. At least 15 states have passed initiatives or referendums that require tax decisions to gain supermajorities in a legislature to be approved. Assembling those supermajorities—typically two thirds or three quarters of the legislature—is an enormous challenge. In Montana, for example, the required supermajority is three quarters of the legislature. State Senator Roy Brown once commented on the slim chances of changing tax policy with that obstacle in place: "We can't even get a three-fourths majority vote to go to the bathroom."[66]

Conclusion

State and local governments rely on six major types of taxes to fund the operations of government: property taxes; income taxes; sales taxes; sin, or excise, taxes; user fees; and gift taxes. Each of these taxes has distinct pros and cons. Local governments like property taxes because they set the rates and thus control exactly how much revenue is raised. However, when property taxes rise, seniors and people on fixed incomes often suffer. Income taxes tend to be more progressive; sales taxes are more regressive. The exact configuration of taxes in any given state reflects that state's history and political culture. Tax revenues, in turn, support the budget process by which state and local governments set their spending priorities. Increasingly, governments are relying on user fees—collected in relatively small amounts but frequently—to supply key revenues.

State and local government finances can be difficult to unravel. However, this is an area that citizens are highly advised to watch. Not only do the budget decisions of state and local governments determine the services that individuals enjoy and how much they pay in taxes, but this also is often the arena in which the priorities of public life are sorted out. Is it fair or unfair to ask wealthy citizens to pay a higher percentage of their income in taxes? States such as Texas and Florida, which have no income taxes, have in a sense decided that it is unfair. States such as California, which has an income tax, have reached a different conclusion. Should everyone pay more in taxes to extend health care to low-income citizens? Massachusetts's tax policies suggest that its answer is yes. Many states in the Deep South have reached different conclusions. In short, the consequences of budget decisions are very real.

There is another reason to pay close attention to state and local finances. Over the past few years, the recovery from the most severe recession since World War II has been sluggish, and states' revenue systems are not set up to make the most of today's evolving economy. To get consistently back in the black, state financial structures almost certainly will need to change. States such as Tennessee that rely heavily on sales tax revenues face particularly serious long-term challenges. As Internet sales and dollars spent on untaxed services continue to grow, sales tax revenues in particular will most likely continue to falter. This will create a need for new revenue-raising measures. Yet states with ballot initiatives may well find new approaches blocked by antitax sentiments at the voting booth.

The Latest Research

The running theme of this chapter is that state and local budgets are all-important. The process of how subnational governments get their money, spend their money, and keep revenue and expenditures in a legally mandated balance is ground zero for the most important current policy debates in state and local politics.

Academic research typically lags behind current events by several years; so the latest research on taxing and spending is mostly not based on data from the past fiscal year or two. Nevertheless, the latest research has plenty of lessons for states and localities facing tough fiscal decisions and for voters who want to hold policymakers accountable for those decisions. The research discussed below reflects two central themes: (1) the real-life impact of state-level economic conditions and who is or is not held responsible for those conditions and (2) the efforts of states to deal with the effects of taxing and spending limitations.

• •

• **Brown, Adam R.** "Are Governors Responsible for the State Economy? Partisanship, Blame, and Divided Federalism." *Journal of Politics* 72 (2010): 605–615.

One of the long-standing debates in state politics scholarship is who gets held accountable for economic performance: the president, governors, or a combination of both. This is a particularly interesting time to revisit this question, as governors are pursuing different approaches to addressing state-level fiscal problems and President Barack Obama was reelected to a second term despite sluggish economic growth and unemployment rates flirting with double digits. Brown's study is interesting because it shows that voters assign blame or credit for economic fortunes not on state or national economic conditions or the policies of policymakers but on the partisanship of who holds high executive office. Essentially, if the economy is doing poorly, voters who share their governor's partisanship will give the governor a pass—and blame the president if he is from the opposite party. If the economy is doing well, voters who identify with the governor's party will give that official the credit. This has the interesting implication that objective economic conditions are not as important to voters' judgment of the performance of a chief executive's taxing and spending policies as one might think.

• **Bifuloco, Robert, Beverly Bunch, William Duncombe, Mark Robbins, and William Simonsen.** "Debt and Deception: How States Avoid Making Hard Fiscal Decisions." *Public Administration Review* 72 (2012): 659–667.

The vast majority of state governments, as noted in this chapter, are legally required to have balanced budgets. This seems simple enough; doesn't it just mean that revenue has to equal expenditure? Well, sort of. Over the past few years, states have tried all sorts of accounting gimmicks to satisfy the letter if not the spirit of balanced-budget mandates. Some of those gimmicks can obscure the real health of state government balance sheets. Bifuloco and his colleagues examine how several states borrow to finance current operating expenditures—something that seems mighty close to the deficit spending that state governments are supposedly prevented from doing. To make their financial statements look balanced, states underfund long-term obligations, defer payments, restructure debt, and borrow money from designated funds to cover general fund deficits. These moves are largely designed to get state governments cash in the short term while piling up debt obligations in the long term. This study reveals the extent to which this sort of deficit financing in all but name goes on, and raises questions about the transparency of state financial statements.

- **Hong, Sounman.** "Fiscal Rules in Recessions: Evidence From the American States." *Public Finance Review* (2014). doi:10.1177/1091142113515050.

As discussed in this chapter, the vast majority of states are legally required to balance their budgets. This study uses the comparative method to see just how those rules do—or do not—work in practice. What it finds is that the impact of balanced-budget rules depends on political and economic context. For example, balanced-budget rules are more likely to be adhered to in recessionary years than in years when the economy is doing well. Gubernatorial partisanship also seems to be a difference that makes a difference. If there is a Republican in the governors' mansion, states are considerably more likely to cut budgets to meet balanced-budget rules. The size of those cuts, though, is mitigated if there is divided control of state government (i.e., if there is a Democratic legislature and a Republican governor or vice versa). The general takeaway point of this study, then, is that having a balanced-budget rule is one thing. How that rule is enforced, however, is something else and is dependent on the political and economic environment of a state.

- **Kelly, Nathan, and Christopher Witko.** "Federalism and American Inequality." *Journal of Politics* 74 (2012): 414–426.

One of the most contentious issues in current American politics is income inequality. Do the haves get too much and the have-nots too little? If so, should government do anything to balance things out? In an era of tight budgets and bruising arguments over who, if anyone, should be taxed more and how that money should or should not be spent, answers to these questions are contested and controversial. This debate has played out primarily on a national stage, but this study uses the comparative method to show that state-level factors contribute greatly to income inequality. Kelly and Witko look at more than three decades' worth of state-level data and find that factors such as a state's demographics, the degree of unionization in its labor pool, and the partisan makeup of its government are differences that make a difference to income inequality.

Chapter Review

Key Concepts

- American Recovery and Reinvestment Act (ARRA) (p. 90)
- balanced budget (p. 105)
- bonds (p. 102)
- budget deficits or shortfalls (p. 90)
- budget process (p. 104)
- capital investments (p. 102)
- discretionary spending (p. 107)
- dividend (p. 101)
- entitlement (p. 107)
- estate taxes (p. 92)
- excise or sin taxes (p. 91)
- expenditures (p. 105)

- fiscal federalism (p. 107)
- fiscal year (p. 104)
- focused consumption taxes (p. 92)
- general obligation bonds (p. 102)
- gift taxes (p. 92)
- income taxes (p. 95)
- insurance trust funds (p. 98)
- intergovernmental transfers (p. 98)
- municipal bonds (p. 102)
- progressive tax system (p. 95)
- regressive taxes (p. 92)
- revenue bonds (p. 102)
- revenues (p. 90)
- sales taxes (p. 92)
- severance taxes (p. 96)
- tax burden (p. 92)
- tax capacity (p. 100)
- tax effort (p. 100)
- user fees (p. 90)

Suggested Websites

- **www.cbpp.org.** Website of the Center on Budget and Policy Priorities. Founded in 1981, the center studies fiscal policy and public programs at the federal and state levels that affect low-income and moderate-income families and individuals. An excellent source of information on state budget issues.

- **www.census.gov/compendia/statab.** The U.S. Census Bureau provides an online version of the *Statistical Abstract of the United States.* Section 8, "State and Local Government Finances and Employment," provides a wealth of information on state and local government revenue and spending. The Census Bureau ceased publication of the *Abstract* after 2012 as a budget-cutting measure. Subsequent versions have been published by a private company, ProQuest.

- **www.gao.gov.** Home page of the Government Accountability Office, which is tracking the use of ARRA stimulus funds in 16 of the largest states.

- **www.nasbo.org.** Website of the National Association of State Budget Officers.

- **www.ncsl.org.** Website of the National Conference of State Legislatures. NCSL's fiscal program produces periodic state budget and tax updates, and tracks state actions to close budget gaps.

- **www.recovery.gov.** The federal government's webpage dedicated to tracking ARRA.

⑤SAGE statestats

State Stats on Finance

Explore and compare data on the states! Go to **edge.sagepub.com/ smithgreenblatt5e** *to do these exercises.*

1. In 2013 the national per capita federal economic stimulus fund amount was $860. How does your state compare to this average? What might account for some of the variation? Is this the same trend as usual when it comes to your state's receiving money from the federal government?

2. Does your state collect income tax? Sales tax? Which source of revenue does your state most heavily rely on? Do you think that this is a good thing? How does it compare to neighboring states?

3. Mississippi collects a relatively high amount of sales tax revenue per capita. Considering its population, why might some people have a problem with this taxation system? Explain why you agree or disagree. Now, look next door at Alabama. Why might these two neighboring states be so different in terms of sales tax revenue?

4. How much outstanding debt does your state have? If your state mandates a balanced budget, where did this debt come from? How does your state's debt load compare to the states around it?

5. Which state has the most local government direct general expenditures? Which state has the least? Why do you think there is so much variation? Do these expenditures translate into jobs and services in these states?

6. Do any cities near you place an additional tax on meals? What are some cities that do, and what are the types of things this tax pays for?

Members of the Nashville Student Organizing Committee protest in the gallery of the Tennessee House chamber a state law preventing student IDs from being used to vote. Many states have passed controversial laws in recent years that require individuals to present identification before they can vote.

Political Attitudes and Participation

VENTING AND VOTING

- What causes some states or localities to change party preferences?
- How do state regulations affect voting?
- How do politicians tune in to what citizens are thinking?

The most fundamental aspect of a democracy—the right to vote—has become highly controversial. Over the past few years, numerous states have passed new laws requiring citizens to present government-issued identification to vote. That may not sound like such a big deal—most adults have driver's licenses, for instance—but Democrats and civil rights groups have complained that such restrictions are meant to disenfranchise voters who are disproportionately members of minority groups. Supporters of such laws say they are meant simply to safeguard against voter fraud, preventing people from voting where they're not supposed to or from voting multiple times.

Before wading into the particulars of this controversy, it's worth nothing that whatever the intent, these new laws represent a break from a long-standing trend. Since the Voting Rights Act of 1965, the federal government and states had been consistently trying to find ways to make voting easier. Whether allowing people to register to vote automatically when they acquired those driver's licenses, allowing people to vote by mail, or creating early voting days to offer people additional chances to exercise their franchise, all the momentum was in the direction of making voting easier. That's no longer the case.

Democrats complain that the GOP is now trying to limit access for certain demographic groups. "What we see here is a total disrespect and disregard for constitutional protections," said the Rev. William Barber, president of the North Carolina NAACP (National Association for the Advancement of Colored People).[1] Critics such as Barber say that voter ID laws and cuts to the number of hours polling places are open are being driven by desires for partisan gain and are not legitimate attempts to limit voter fraud. Voter fraud, they contend, is a myth—proven by instances such as the Alabama Republican Party's failure to find instances of fraud, despite in 2014 offering a reward of $1,000 to anyone who could help find examples. Justin Levitt, a law professor at Loyola Marymount University, found 31 credible incidents of voter impersonation (someone casting an improper ballot in a way that an ID law could prevent) across the country between 2000 and 2014, out of more than 1 billion primary, special, and municipal election ballots cast.[2] Critics of the voter ID laws argued that Levitt's findings proved that voter ID laws provide a fake fix to a nonexistent problem. "We might have stopped 31 impersonation cases out of 1,000,000,000 votes to the tune of tens of millions of $ to distribute IDs & litigate," tweeted Michael McDonald, an elections expert at the University of Florida.[3]

But judges from the Supreme Court on down have found that voter ID laws are constitutional. North Carolina passed one of the strictest set of voting rules since the 1965 Voting Rights Act, for instance, and in 2014 the Supreme Court ruled that the law was not racially discriminatory. In the closing weeks of the 2014 campaign, in fact—after absentee ballots had already been cast in some states—the Court issued a series of voting rights decisions regarding laws in Ohio, Texas, and Wisconsin, making voting easier in some states and harder in others.[4]

And for all the complaints that such laws are meant to suppress voter turnout, so far there's limited evidence they've had that effect. Some potential voters may have been discouraged, and there have been numerous anecdotal examples of elderly voters being turned away from the voting booth for want of a proper ID. The Government Accountability Office, Congress's investigating agency, released a study suggesting that states that adopted strict voter ID laws saw turnout drop a couple of percentage points more than states that hadn't between 2008 and 2012.[5]

But the number of people unable to vote due to the stricter laws may be limited. Turnout has been relatively strong in recent elections, suggesting that most of those who are motivated to vote are still able to do so. Some voters, at any rate, may have been energized to turn out by the very laws that they felt sought to disenfranchise them. "There's an active pushback going on of people wanting to say, 'Like hell you'll take my vote away,'" said Bob Hall, executive director of Democracy North Carolina, an advocacy group that registers voters in the state.[6]

At any rate, there's been no decline in voting among those groups allegedly targeted. In fact, the U.S. Census Bureau found that about two in three eligible African Americans (66.2 percent) voted in the 2012 election, which was higher than the share of non-Hispanic whites who voted (64.1 percent).[7] That was a first, and the share of Asian and Hispanic voters is rising relative to whites as well.

Who votes matters a lot. Increasingly, the two major parties rely on particular groups for support, with GOP voters typically being more rural and suburban and Democrats relying on people who live in denser areas and minority groups. Support for the Democratic Party is nearly a given among African Americans, while white voters in much of the South gave nearly 90 percent of their support to Republican presidential candidate Mitt Romney in 2012.[8] Minority voters are expected to make up nearly one third of the electorate in 2016—an enormous shift since the days when whites accounted for more than 90 percent of voters (95 percent in 1952).[9] That presents an ongoing challenge to the GOP. One survey in 2014 found that 70 percent of nonwhites viewed the Republican Party unfavorably.[10]

But Democrats have their challenges as well. Democrats have won the popular vote in five out of the past six presidential races but have struggled in recent midterm elections, when their coalition of minority and younger voters has not shown up in the same numbers as during presidential contests. That has less to do with voter ID laws than with voting habits. During the run-up to the 2014 midterm elections, President Obama spoke repeatedly about the "congenital disease" of Democrats' not turning out. "Our voters are younger, more unmarried women, more African-American voters," Obama said at one event in Houston. "They get excited about presidential elections; they don't get as excited about midterm elections."[11]

Voters are split not only by race but increasingly by county. Localities more and more tend to vote for one party over the other—that's one reason there are so few competitive U.S. House or state legislative seats. Still, even in the bluest of blue or reddest of red communities, there are always exceptions. This is why political pros are increasingly borrowing technology and demographic breakdowns from consumer marketers, looking to target voters individually as much as possible. Political data mining has evolved far beyond the old idea that you can guess a voter's partisan leanings by looking at the types of magazines he or she subscribes to. Now, campaigns access all manner of consumer databases, gleaning such near-complete portraits of individuals' habits and inclinations as to threaten the sanctity of the secret ballot, according to Chris Evans, managing editor of the *Minnesota Journal of Law, Science & Technology.* "The goal of these 'digital dossiers' is to profile likely voters and identify traits that predict voting habits," Evans wrote in 2012. "Political data-mining has proven to be a winning election tactic, but the resulting erosion of voter privacy has gone unabated."[12]

The reason for this micro-level attention to voters, of course, is that it is difficult to predict how people will vote based just on where they live. It is a safer bet to examine the issues they care about and the interest groups they belong to. Interest groups, as discussed at greater length in Chapter 6, are organizations that attempt to influence policymakers. Although most people will rarely, if ever, call or write to their members of Congress or state officials, many of them will belong to groups that make the case for particular positions on given issues.

Interest groups can bring resources to a campaign in return for candidates' attention to their issues. But all voters do not belong to interest groups—or think of themselves as being part of any—and politicians know that their careers depend on more than financial contributions from these organized interests. Come election time, they need the support of the vast majority of people who do not belong to such groups and who do not pay close attention to politics on a regular basis.

Given all this, how do politicians figure out what the voters back home are thinking when it seems that the only people they hear from at the capitol or city hall are part of some organized group? How can they pay attention to the needs and desires of the majority of constituents who do not speak out and do not subscribe to *Guns & Ammo,* much less to their local newspaper?

This chapter answers those questions, and also looks at how voters maintain or change the political cultures and preferences of their states and districts over time. Some of the mechanisms for change discussed include elections and the avenues for direct democracy, such as ballot initiatives and referendums. Public opinion—and how and whether politicians respond to it—is another factor that influences political outcomes.

Elections

We have created an odd paradox as a nation. Americans like elections—we hold more of them than any other country on earth—yet we consistently score one of the lowest voter turnout rates of any democracy in the world.

State political cultures are reflected and sustained through elections, when a majority or **plurality** of voters elects officials who more or less share the political beliefs of the majority or plurality. The use of elections to select the holders of public office is the fundamental process of representative democracies. More bluntly, elections are the main way that the will of the people connects to and influences the actions of government. Election laws are set and controlled by the states, and each state must determine what constitutes a valid vote. There has long been a great deal of variation among states regarding how easy or how hard it is for citizens to vote. Some of the differences were smoothed away in recent years by federal laws and court decisions, but many remain and new ones are being created, and these largely reflect the types of political cultures Daniel Elazar describes (outlined in the preceding chapters).

These differences, in turn, affect national politics. The way people vote in their own states—the type of access they have to the ballot—helps determine the success or failure of presidential candidates and the makeup of Congress. With numerous states in recent years enacting voter ID requirements and other restrictions that make it harder for people to register and vote, voting rights have reemerged as one of the most salient issues in American politics.

But differences in election laws are not the only reason one state may tend to vote differently than its neighbors, in partisan terms. For about 100 years after the Civil War, for example, Republicans were not a true national party. They had next to no presence in the South, which still resented Republican intrusions during the Civil War and Reconstruction in support of abolition, suffrage, and economic opportunity for African Americans. That is one reason Democrats held the region for decades. In fact, the Republican Party of the 19th century bore a closer resemblance in some ways to the Democratic Party of today than to its 21st century GOP descendant. Times and political parties change, however. These days, the South is one of the pillars of Republican strength. The region's continuing conservatism now fits well within the GOP.

Southern states and the less populous, heavily rural states of the Mountain West, such as Idaho, Wyoming, and Montana, tilt toward Republican interests. For a time in the 1970s and 1980s, they formed a bloc that helped elect presidents through their disproportionate share of the Electoral College. Each state's Electoral College votes are equal to the size of its congressional delegation. Because each state is guaranteed at least two U.S. senators and one U.S. representative, the Electoral College gives a minimum of three votes to each state, regardless of population. This means that the voting power of smaller states in the Electoral College is disproportionately larger than the states' populations, whereas the voting power of bigger states is disproportionately lower.

For example, in 2012 California had 55 electoral votes to represent a population of nearly 37.7 million. In that presidential election, then, each of California's Electoral College votes represented about 685,000 people. Contrast that with Wyoming, which had the minimum of three Electoral College votes but had a population of only about 568,000. Each of Wyoming's Electoral College votes, in other words, represented nearly 190,000 people. Political analyst Steven Hill, director of the political reform program at the New America Foundation, calls this "affirmative action for low-population states."[13] This is one reason George W. Bush was able to win the presidency in 2000 despite losing the popular vote. This imbalance in the representation of Electoral College votes leads to periodic efforts by groups that want to make sure no one ends up in the White House with fewer popular votes than the opponent—an incredibly tough reform to pull off without amending the Constitution. In recent years,

---

Plurality
The highest number of votes garnered by any of the candidates for a particular office but short of an outright majority

for example, states such as Maryland, Massachusetts, and California have enacted laws that will require them to award their electoral votes according to national popular vote percentages, but those measures won't take effect until a preponderance of states are onboard with the idea.

In more recent elections, however, the larger, more urbanized states have been able to outvote the rest. With Texas being the only highly populous state that votes reliably Republican, Democrats have had the upper hand in presidential voting of late. Perhaps for this reason, in states such as Pennsylvania and Virginia where the GOP controls the legislature but voters have tended to prefer Democratic presidential candidates, legislators have talked about awarding electoral votes by congressional district rather than sticking with the traditional winner-take-all system. Those efforts have yet to meet with success, but Republicans have been able to enact conservative legislation at the state level, since they control the levers of political power in more states than Democrats do.

If there's disagreement between states about the best political approach to take, there's also disagreement within states. Some voters have felt disenfranchised lately because one party dominates state politics and they don't subscribe to that party's platform. That's always the case to some extent—politics is about picking winners and losers, after all—but in this highly polarized system, people in more conservative, rural areas may feel powerless and resentful when their state is dominated by more liberal, urban-voting blocs. That's why smaller counties in states such as California and Colorado have held secession votes in recent years. In other words, they've been so unhappy with state laws regarding issues such as gun control and environmental regulation, they wanted to split off and form their own states. (Don't hold your breath that this will actually happen anytime soon.)

A Voice for the Public

Elections may be how citizens can speak out for their beliefs, and they may give states a voice in national politics, but you wouldn't know it from the interest they generate among the general public. The franchise appears to be diminishing, with the act of voting on the decline. People do not feel

well connected to government; some hate it. Less than half the voting-age population cast ballots in presidential elections. In elections in which congressional or statewide offices are at the top of the ticket, the percentage drops to less than 40 percent. For municipal elections, turnout rates are generally less than 20 percent. Turnout got so grim in Los Angeles that the city ethics commission in 2014 voted in support of the idea of holding random drawings for financial prizes of up to $50,000 to encourage more people to vote.

Voting does tend to pick up for competitive races, when voters feel as though they have a genuine choice and might make a real difference. The major political parties, however, have reconciled themselves to the reality that millions of people feel that their votes don't count. (Sometimes the parties are even accused of suppressing turnout by using negative ads and other means to sour people who might vote for the other side.)

Upset that an estimated 4 million evangelical Christians did not vote in 2000, Karl Rove, President George W. Bush's lead political adviser, designed a reelection campaign in 2004 to motivate these voters through the use of such issues as limitations on stem-cell research and bans on gay marriage. The campaign did use other issues to appeal to other blocs of voters, but it was designed primarily to motivate Bush's base voters rather than to reach across the political spectrum and

> The idea that voters are most easily motivated by appeals to a few core issues is also related to the growing use of ballot initiatives as a means of promoting turnout. For instance, the numbers of conservative Ohio voters who turned out to cast their ballots in favor of a constitutional ban on gay marriage in 2004 are said to have helped Bush carry that year's most contested state.

A Difference
That Makes A Difference

Does Ideological Polarization Depress Voter Turnout?

There's a kind of truth in labeling when it comes to contemporary American politics. If you vote for a Democrat, you know what you're going to get in terms of that candidate's positions on issues such as abortion and same-sex marriage. If you support a Republican, you can bet he or she will take a more conservative stance on issues such as gun control and immigration.

In the mid-20th century, political scientists sometimes decried the lack of a "responsible party model," meaning parties that offered voters clear choices. With the parties now so well sorted ideologically—with few elected officials breaking with party orthodoxy on major issues—where does that leave voters?

There's a big academic debate about whether people who don't do politics for a living are as vehement about their disdain for the other party and its policies as the politicians are. One thing political scientists are arguing about is whether polarization—the differences and lack of cooperation between the parties—is turning off citizens to the extent that they're actually less likely to vote.

There's evidence both ways. One of the most polarized states is Wisconsin, which Republicans currently dominate at the state level but which votes Democratic for president. Wisconsin is home to some of the most Democratic precincts in the country, such as Dane County, home to Madison and the University of Wisconsin's flagship county, as well as some thoroughly Republican territory, including some suburbs of Milwaukee.

Some of those areas have voter turnout rates far above the national average. In 2012, Ozaukee County had the highest turnout of voting-age citizens—84 percent—of any county with a population above 50,000. Nearby Waukesha County was second, while Dane County came in fifth. Suburban Brookfield, which gave Republican candidate Romney two thirds of its vote in 2012, had an astonishing turnout rate of 90 percent.[a]

"Strongholds have higher turnout, apparently because people feel like they're more engaged in politics, their neighbors are engaged," said Torben Lutjen, a political scientist at the University of Dusseldorf who has studied polarized communities in Wisconsin.[b] Given a clear choice, voters in recent election cycles have seemed to prefer candidates who adhere to the party line, often punishing moderates or politicians with a reputation for compromising, particularly during party primaries. "The folks who've worked across party lines are generally being replaced," said Joe Hackney, a former Democratic speaker of the North Carolina House. "The public does ultimately hold the key to that."[c]

But voters often say they want politicians to do the right thing, to put party considerations aside and make the deals that are best for the state or the country. Voters never seem to like the negative advertising often aired not only by both campaigns but by outside groups such as super PACs (political action committees). Enough negativity—or simply the sense that candidates

appeal more broadly. The strategy worked, at least in the short run. Conversely, in the run-up to his reelection bid in 2012, Obama sought to appeal to various Democratic constituencies; for example, he courted Latinos and gays, respectively, by halting federal efforts to deport many younger illegal immigrants and by coming out in favor of same-sex marriage, and he tried to cut into Republican rival Romney's support among working-class voters by accusing him of having sent jobs overseas during his business career.

The idea that voters are most easily motivated by appeals to a few core issues is also related to the growing use of ballot initiatives as a means of promoting turnout. For instance, the numbers of conservative Ohio voters who turned out to cast their ballots in favor of a constitutional ban on gay marriage in 2004 are said to have helped Bush carry that year's most contested state. Two years later, liberals, looking for weapons of their own, ran initiatives for minimum-wage increases on half a dozen state ballots. Some political scientists

and parties are talking entirely past one another—can turn off some voters. "We divide evenly in elections or sit them out entirely because we instinctively seek the center while the parties and candidates hang out on the extremes," Stanford University political scientist Morris C. Fiorina writes in his book *Culture War? The Myth of a Polarized America*.[d]

Jon C. Rogowski, a political scientist at Washington University, found that increasing policy differences between candidates significantly reduces voter turnout, rather than stimulating political participation. Rogowski looked at the positions of U.S. House and Senate candidates and found that where the greatest ideological difference was expressed between candidates, citizens were less likely to vote, even after controlling for other factors such as district demographics. "High levels of campaign conflict—such as that found in negative advertising—may simply turn off voters," Rogowski concludes.[e]

But Rogowski notes that these effects are not uniform. Those who are already the least engaged politically are the most likely to be dissuaded from participating by polarizing choices. Negative advertising can convince voters that a candidate—or even both candidates—is unworthy of office. But it can also convince some people to vote to prevent what they consider to be a bad choice from winning. In a study of the 2004 presidential election, Alan I. Abramowitz and Kyle L. Saunders found that "the intense polarization of the electorate" led to dramatic increases in turnout and other forms of political participation.[f] "Issues that evoke emotional responses can activate normally indifferent voters and increase turnout in certain groups," said Matt Hennessy, a Democratic consultant based in Connecticut.[g]

---

[a] Craig Gilbert, "Far From Creating Fatigue, Partisan Battles Energize Voters," *Milwaukee Journal-Sentinel*, May 10, 2014, www.jsonline.com/news/statepolitics/far-from-creating-fatigue-partisan-battles-energize-voters-b99256305z1-258676961.html.

[b] Phone interview with Torben Lutjen, September 28, 2012.

[c] Alan Greenblatt, "Voters Angry at Washington Gridlock May Want to Look in the Mirror," NPR, October 1, 2012, www.npr.org/blogs/itsallpolitics/2012/10/01/162084449/voters-angry-at-washington-gridlock-may-want-to-look-in-the-mirror.

[d] Morris P. Fiorina, *Culture War? The Myth of a Polarized America*, 3rd ed. (New York: Longman, 2010), xiii.

[e] Jon C. Rogowski, "Electoral Choice, Ideological Conflict, and Political Participation," *American Journal of Political Science* 58, no. 2 (2014): 479–494.

[f] Alan I. Abramowitz and Kyle L. Saunders, "Is Polarization a Myth?," *Journal of Politics* 70, no. 2 (2008): 543.

[g] E-mail exchange with Matt Hennessy, June 18, 2014.

---

have found evidence that controversial ballot initiatives do increase turnout, particularly in nonpresidential election years.[14]

But the idea that most voters are motivated by a single issue, or a handful of issues, oversimplifies things. It is true that the majority of voters remain loyal to one party over the other throughout most of their voting lives; yet they can be convinced to cast their votes—or even to change their votes—by any number of factors. The state of the economy, the health of a state's budget, corruption scandals, or the course of a military conflict may change minds and voting habits. "Each election forces one to revisit such topics as to what's effective in voter mobilization or who you aim at," says independent political analyst Rhodes Cook.[15]

State Supervision of Elections

It seems obvious to say, but elections are fundamental to democracy. They are the source of authority for governmental decisions and power. On these occasions, a majority of eligible citizens presumably give their blessing to officeholders who will determine the course of policy. Elections are the main conduit through which citizens express their pleasure or displeasure with governmental decisions. If voters are unhappy with the decisions their elected officials have made, they can turn them out of office at the next election. For all the system's faults, politicians and parties have to win approval from voters at regularly scheduled intervals if they are to remain in power.

The U.S. Constitution gives states the authority to determine "the times, places and manner of holding elections." In nearly every state, the secretary of state has the practical duty of running elections: setting dates, qualifying candidates, and printing and counting the ballots. In a few states, the lieutenant governor or a state election board oversees these chores. The states, in turn, rely on the counties or, in some cases, cities to run the polls themselves. The localities draw precinct boundaries and set up and supervise polling places. In many cases, they have the main responsibility for registering voters. Following an election, county officials count up the ballots and report the results to the appropriate individual, such as the secretary of state, who then tabulates and certifies the totals.

The styles of the ballots used vary from state to state. California currently uses a random alphabet system to decide the order in which candidate names appear, rotating the starting letter of that alphabet in each state assembly district. The **office group ballot**, also known as the **Massachusetts ballot**, lists candidates' names, followed by their party designations, under the title of the office they are seeking (governor, state representative, and so on). The other major type of ballot is the **party column ballot**, or the **Indiana ballot**, which "arranges the candidates for each office in columns according to their party designation."[16] Fourteen states make it even easier for citizens to vote for party nominees—voters can cast a **straight ticket** vote for all of one party's candidates with one computer click or pull of the lever. This is a practice in decline, however; several states have abolished it, most recently North Carolina in 2014.[17]

Each state's election code determines the specific details about ballots and, perhaps most important, the order in which offices and candidates will appear. This varies considerably among the states. By 1992, about 80 percent of the states had replaced paper ballots with punch cards, machines in which voters pull a lever next to the name of the candidate of their choice, or optical-scan voting machines.[18] Voters in most states now use electronic systems resembling automated teller machines (ATMs), but many states require a paper trail to allow for verification of the electronic results. All but a handful of states tabulate votes for write-in candidates, although victories or even significant showings by such candidates are few and far between.

A few cities, including Minneapolis and San Francisco, use instant-runoff voting (IRV) for municipal elections. Rather than picking one candidate, voters rank all the choices. If one candidate receives more than 50 percent of the first-choice votes, he or she wins. If no one receives a majority of the first-choice votes, the candidate with the lowest number of votes is disqualified and his or her supporters' second-place choices are redistributed among the remaining candidates. This process continues until someone emerges with a majority. The benefit of such a system, supporters say, is that a candidate who is acceptable to a majority of voters will win, as opposed to the outcome in a winner-take-all election in which a candidate with only, say, 30 percent to 40 percent of the vote comes out on top of a large split field. Both the Heisman Trophy winner and the winner of the Academy Award

---

Office group (Massachusetts) ballot
A ballot in which candidates are listed by name under the title of the office they are seeking

Party column (Indiana) ballot
A ballot in which the names of candidates are divided into columns arranged according to political party

---

Straight ticket
Originally, a type of ballot that allowed voters to pick all of one party's candidates at once; today, voting a straight ticket refers to voting for all of one party's candidates for various offices—for instance, voting for all Democrats or all Republicans.

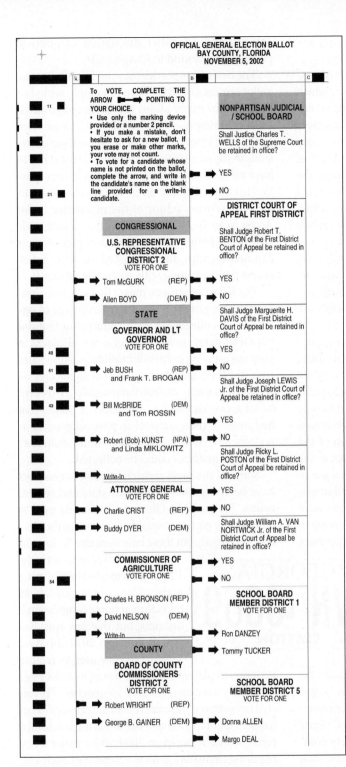

The two main types of ballots are the office group ballot and the party column ballot. These sample ballots from elections in Florida and West Virginia show the differences between the two basic approaches to ballot design. The West Virginia ballot exemplifies the party column ballot, which lists the candidates in columns that indicate their party designations. The Florida ballot, on the other hand, emphasizes office rather than party. This is the key feature of the office group ballot, which lists candidates by name and party under the title of the office they are running for.

for Best Picture are now determined by an IRV or preferential voting system. But IRV has its critics, who say it can result in victories for candidates who were the first choice of few. Jean Quan, for instance, was elected mayor of Oakland, California, in 2010 after being picked as the first choice of just 24 percent of voters. Burlington, Vermont, and Aspen, Colorado, have abandoned the IRV method after complaints that it left voters confused.[19]

Regulating the Parties

A state's authority to print ballots or purchase voting software gives it enormous control over which parties and candidates are presented to the voters. Until the late 19th century, parties themselves printed the ballots, a system that obviously encouraged voters to select a straight ticket of their chosen party's nominees. The advent of the **secret ballot**, also known as the **Australian ballot**, led the states to print their own ballots and, therefore, to determine which parties should appear on ballots. "From there," writes Kay Lawson, a retired San Francisco State University political scientist, "it seemed but a short step to requiring that parties show a minimum level of support to qualify."[20]

The Republican and Democratic parties are themselves regulated at the state level by a bewildering array of varying state laws. Some states provide detailed regulations for party organization, activities, and nominating procedures. Others are silent on many specific matters. According to political scientist V. O. Key, the traditional Democratic one-party control of the South, although now a thing of the past, led to the introduction of the political primary. Voters had no real choice in the general election; so primaries gave them a say in who ultimately would hold an office.[21] For that reason, some southern states—which Democrats once entirely dominated—hold runoff elections when no candidate receives a majority of the primary vote. "They trace their lineage back to an era when there was only one party in politics," said Charles Bullock, a political scientist at the University of Georgia who wrote a book about runoff elections. "Back in the day when the South was one-party Democratic, the runoff was often the determinative election. So you often had more people participating in the runoff than in the original primary."[22] These days, nearly all states hold primary elections to pick party nominees for state offices, although some states, such as Virginia, still nominate candidates at party conventions. (A fuller discussion of political parties can be found in Chapter 6.)

The two major parties may not like all the state ballot regulations they have to comply with, but the rules in many states are designed to favor them over new or minor parties and independent candidates. Prior to a pair of Supreme Court decisions in the late 1960s, it was possible for states to have no mechanism in place to qualify new parties for their ballots. Even today, according to Richard Winger, editor of the newsletter *Ballot Access News,* in 11 states new parties cannot qualify for the ballot before they have picked their candidates, who must be listed on their ballot access petition along with voters' signatures.[23]

The Court's decisions meant that a state no longer could require that a certain percentage of signatures be collected in each county. But that did not mean states could not erect new roadblocks to keep out aspiring parties or candidates. Nine states changed their laws to require that signatures be collected in each congressional district. This kept ballot access elusive for candidates or parties that had most of their support in particular cities or regions. Fifteen states also placed time constraints on when signatures could be collected.

Some of the most restrictive ballot access laws have been repealed by various state and federal courts. For example, Ohio and California used to require new parties to qualify even before the election year began, but these laws were struck down in 2006 and 2012, respectively. Virginia formerly blocked petitioners from gathering signatures outside their home congressional districts, but that law was also struck down in 2012. In West Virginia the law used to require petition circulators who were trying to collect signatures to tell everyone they approached, "If you sign my petition, you can't vote in the primary." That happened not to be true—but it was the law, until a court struck it down in 2004. Why make a law requiring circulators to fib to voters? Well, such a fib benefits the major parties by keeping out the competition, and the major parties write the laws.

These sorts of laws benefiting political parties, if not the democratic process, remain on the books in various places. Texas insisted for years that voters who participated in major-party primaries were

---

Secret (Australian) ballot
A ballot printed by a state that allows voters to pick and choose among different candidates and party preferences in private

Policy in Practice

Vote Counts More Accurate—but Still Not Perfect

Perhaps nothing demonstrates more clearly how much better states and counties have gotten at counting votes than a look at how other entities do it.

Republican presidential caucuses in 2012 were plagued with problems. Several states were embarrassed by snafus following their caucuses, which are run by political parties rather than by public officials.

In Iowa, an 8-vote election-night win for Romney was later converted into a 34-vote victory for Rick Santorum, with party officials admitting that they didn't, in fact, know the actual number. (The state party chair resigned.) Counting of caucus votes was slow enough in Nevada to raise doubts during the delay, while in Maine, the GOP decided to declare Romney the statewide winner even before some counties had held their caucuses. "It's been stunning to watch," said Cathy Cox, a former Georgia secretary of state. "Caucus voting looks like the Wild West of voting."

Election experts agree that vote counting has generally gotten quicker and more accurate since presidential election results in Florida were disputed all the way up to the U.S. Supreme Court in 2000. After that controversy, the federal government devoted billions of dollars to help states modernize their voting machinery, leading to widespread adoption of electronic, touch-screen voting.

But not only has the money from the 2002 Help America Vote Act run out, but the machines it helped buy are nearing the end of their useful life, according to a 2014 report by a presidential commission on voting, which concluded that the nation faces an 'impending crisis in voting technology." The commission recommended that localities invest in tablets so that people can vote on machines similar to what they use every day and governments can make use of the devices between elections. Few places are ready to pony up the millions of dollars required, however.

Voting in the United States is a highly decentralized process. Every state has its own rules, which are then generally implemented separately by individual counties. State and county election officials continue to suffer embarrassing moments, as when New York City found nearly 200,000 uncounted votes a month after the general election in 2010, an oversight Mayor Michael Bloomberg called "a royal screw-up." New York elections since then have also been marked by long lines and legal challenges, with the city moving back to 1950s-style lever machines for its 2013 mayoral election. New York is not alone in having a hard time producing fast, accurate results. In 2014, Washington, D.C., was unable to extract the results from five electronic voting machines, delaying the results of a primary election in which the incumbent mayor was defeated. Despite concerns about electronic voting that were raised from the start, such screw-ups are generally caused by human error.

Problems caused by the improper reading of paper ballots are what spurred innovations in voting machines over the past decade. And concerns remain about electronic voting machines. In at least some polling places in 16 states, machines don't produce any paper trail that can be used as a backup in case of a recount or dispute. And about half the states have systems that are vulnerable to hacking, especially when it comes to military personnel voting overseas, according to a 2012 study by researchers at Rutgers Law School. That means the job of counting votes remains more complicated than it looks—as GOP caucus organizers have found. "If you can't produce pretty instantaneous results, people are going to lose confidence in the results and you're going to open up the floodgates to opportunities for fraud," says Cox, the former Georgia official.

Source: Adapted from Alan Greenblatt, "Caucus System Cracks Revealed during 2012 GOP Primary Season," *Governing,* May 2012, http://www.governing.com/topics/politics/gov-caucus-system-cracks-revealed-during-2012-primary-season.html.

not allowed to sign petitions to get new parties on the ballot; the state also required citizens to know their voter registration numbers and to affix those numbers next to their signatures on petitions. Quick—what's your voter registration number? (Those requirements were eventually tossed out following repeated court challenges.) In its 1971 decision in *Jenness v. Fortson,* the Supreme Court upheld a Georgia law that requires minor parties or independent candidates to collect signatures that represent 5 percent of registered voters. In 1986, the Georgia legislature lowered that threshold to 1 percent for statewide petitions, but that still means more than 50,000 signatures, a bar no one has been able to meet since 2000. Georgia still requires that 5 percent of registered voters sign petitions for district and county offices, which is one big reason no minor party has appeared on the ballot for a regularly-scheduled U.S. House election there since 1942. Other Republican-controlled states such as Alabama, Oklahoma, and Tennessee have passed laws since 2013 to discourage minor parties. "The time, money and energy spent getting on the ballot is more than the time, money and energy spent once we are on the ballot in most of these states," said Phil Huckelberry, co-chair of the Green Party's ballot access committee.[24]

For third-party and independent candidates, then, it can be a real challenge to gain access to the ballot. Of course, how hard or easy it is for these political outsiders to get on the ballot varies from state to state. As with everything else, there are differences that make a difference. Given what we know about Elazar's theory regarding southern, or traditionalistic, states and their hierarchical attitude toward politics, it should not surprise us that states such as Alabama, North Carolina, and Oklahoma have the most restrictive ballot access laws. That does not mean that hundreds of minor-party and independent candidates have not overcome all these hurdles and more to win spots on statewide ballots. A few of them have even won election as governor—for instance, in Minnesota in 1998, Maine in 1994 and 1998, and Rhode Island in 2010 (though note that all three of these examples involve moralistic or individualistic states). Their place on a ballot one year, however, is no guarantee that members of their parties will qualify the next time around. Alabama requires that a minor party poll at least 20 percent of the vote for governor to win an automatic qualification for the next ballot. New Jersey, Oklahoma, and Virginia require at least 10 percent, and Pennsylvania requires 15 percent, or more than 1 million votes. Given all the restrictions, Lawson concludes, "The laws have been effective in keeping minor parties off the ballot in election after election."[25]

Minor-party candidates are concerned about ballot access in more progressive states as well. Since 2008, Washington State has used a top-two or **blanket primary** system, in which the top two finishers proceed to the general election, regardless of party. California voters adopted the same system in 2010. The blanket primary presents a big obstacle to minor parties and independent candidates; primary elections tend to be low-turnout affairs dominated by voters who are major-party partisans. As a result, independents and minor-party candidates rarely—if ever—have the chance to appear on general election ballots. Out of 86 instances in which there were minor-party candidates and at least two major-party candidates running for federal or state office under the top-two voting system leading into 2014, the minor-party candidate qualified for the general election exactly zero times.[26] "It's the biggest threat to independent and third parties in the last 50 years," complained Christina Tobin, a Libertarian Party candidate for California secretary of state in 2010.[27]

Why all the restrictions? Keeping minor parties off the ballot naturally helps the two major parties. Those who are in power control the rules that keep them in power. "VA's D legislature thought the rules up, knowing they would benefit themselves & friends," tweeted Larry Sabato, director of the University of Virginia's Center for Politics, in 2011. "Then Rs, once in power, liked restrictions too."[28]

Blanket primary
An initial round of voting in which candidates from all parties appear on the same ballot, with the top two vote-getters proceeding on to the general election

Restricting Voters

The sense that the rules can rig the game is one reason why restrictions on voters themselves have become controversial of late. States do not just regulate the access of parties to the ballot, after all; they also regulate the interaction of citizens with that ballot. They determine who can register to vote and how they can register. Changes in federal law over the years have removed many of the barriers that states had once imposed to restrict voting rights—those based on property ownership, literacy, race, sex, and age. But there are still differences among states in how easy or difficult it is for citizens to register to vote—a necessary step toward having the chance to vote in every state except North Dakota, which does not require voter registration. Those differences have become more pronounced in recent years, with 17 states passing new laws to tighten registration or voting requirements in 2011 and 2012 alone.

In the early years of the nation, most eastern states required citizens to own property to be eligible to vote. Those requirements diminished over time, in large part because the western frontier states lacked the type of class structure that reinforced them. The eastern states, however, soon came up with the idea of imposing literacy tests. Before they could vote, new immigrants had to demonstrate knowledge of the state constitution or other complex issues to the satisfaction of the local election official.[29] Native whites who were illiterate often were exempted from this requirement. Southern states took up literacy testing as a means of keeping African Americans from voting, as African Americans generally received an inadequate education in schools segregated by race. Literacy tests remained a part of the southern legal landscape until the federal Voting Rights Act of 1965 barred them. Southern states also sometimes imposed poll taxes as a means of disenfranchising African Americans and some poor whites, until the Supreme Court found them unconstitutional in 1966. (See the box "A Difference That Makes a Difference: How Some States Discourage Voters.")

Several amendments to the U.S. Constitution expanded voting rights to include minorities and women. The Fifteenth Amendment, passed following the Civil War, was meant to end discrimination against black men seeking to vote. Until the civil rights movement of the 1960s, however, southern states effectively bypassed the provisions of the amendment for a century through literacy tests, intimidation, and other means. The Voting Rights Act of 1965 gave the federal government the authority to review state requirements for registration and voting. In 1964, the Twenty-Fourth Amendment banned the use of poll taxes meant to keep African Americans and other poor people from voting. Women received the right to vote with the ratification of the Nineteenth Amendment in 1920. The voting age was lowered to 18 by the Twenty-Sixth Amendment in 1971. In 1993, Congress passed what became known as the "motor voter" law, which requires states to allow citizens to register to vote when they take tests to receive their driver's licenses.

Why all the effort to get people registered to vote? The purpose of registering voters is to prevent fraud. Registration is intended to stop people from voting more than once or outside their home jurisdictions. This makes sense, but throughout the nation's history, many states have used registration laws as a means of making voting inaccessible to some.

Voter fraud has become a contentious topic in recent years, with opinion largely split along partisan lines. Republicans say that such measures as requiring each voter to show a form of photo identification are necessary to guard against fraud, while Democrats argue that the GOP is simply trying to block access by poor people and members of minority groups, who are least likely to have such identification—and most likely to vote Democratic. In 2008, the Supreme Court upheld a 2005 Indiana law requiring that anyone seeking to vote produce a government-issued photo ID, such as a passport or driver's license, at the polls. "This notion that somehow voter fraud is a dirty word, I don't understand it, because you're talking about people stealing votes, canceling out legitimate votes," Attorney General Alberto Gonzales testified in 2007.[30]

About 18 percent of the total number of registered voters in Minnesota—542,257—registered to vote on election day in 2008. Minnesota is one of just six states to allow same-day registration.

Political scientist Andrew Hacker wrote after the decision that the justices failed to take into account the hardships that requiring a "license to vote" would impose on the 15 percent of Indiana's voting-age population who had no driver's license or other photo identification. Hacker noted that in Milwaukee County, Wisconsin, 53 percent of African Americans lacked a driver's license, compared with 15 percent of the adult white population statewide. "Requiring a driver's license to vote has a disparate racial impact, a finding that once commanded judicial notice," Hacker wrote.[31]

Voter Turnout

Even as some states are tightening requirements for voter registration, with some now requiring individuals to provide proof of citizenship, others are seeking to make the mechanics of registering easier. California is considering a change that would allow people as young as 15 to "pre-register" to vote when they first receive permits to drive. Other states are looking at other pre-registration ideas so that people will be registered to vote as soon as they turn 18. More states are allowing same-day registration (meaning you no longer have to register weeks in advance of Election Day). In June 2014, Illinois became the 20th state to allow citizens to register to vote online—double the number back in 2012. Washington State in 2012 unveiled an app that allows citizens to register through Facebook using personal data. "In this age of social media and more people going online for services, this is a natural way to introduce people to online registration and leverage the power of friends on Facebook to get more people registered," said Shane Hamlin, Washington's codirector of elections.[32]

But efforts to ease registration do not always lead to higher voter turnout. The motor voter law produced an initial spike in registration, but it had little or no effect on the number of people voting. According to Curtis Gans of the Committee for the Study of the American Electorate at American University, **voter turnout** rates have declined by about 25 percent over the past 40 years.[33] Turnout did spike for the hotly contested 2004 presidential race, but it dropped again in 2006. A record 131 million Americans cast votes in 2008, but that number dropped by about 5 million 4 years later. There are countless reasons voter turnout has decreased, including a general disaffection with politics and government, a measurable decline in civic education and newspaper reading, a weakening of such civic-minded institutions as student government and unions, and the changing role of political parties away from engaging and educating voters and toward raising money and providing services to candidates.

Turnout rates are in decline, but they are not declining uniformly across the states. The percentage of the voting-age population that turned out to vote in 2012 was more than 30 points higher in Minnesota, the best-performing state, than in Hawaii, which was the worst. There are many reasons some states have such disparate turnout rates, most of which are related to political culture, demographics, and party competition.

In general, the closer you live to Canada, the more likely you are to vote. The states with turnout rates of more than 70 percent for the 2008 presidential election, including Minnesota, New Hampshire, and Iowa, were mostly in the northern tier of the country. The states with lower turnout rates, including Arkansas, Hawaii, Tennessee, and Utah, were in the South or far West. (See Table 5-1.) What explains the difference? Culture, for one thing. Elazar's theory about moralistic states appears to hold up, at least as far as voter turnout goes. "You're talking about states with fairly vigorous political parties, communications media that do cover politics and an educational system more geared toward citizen engagement than other parts of the country," says Gans. A big state such as California has a mix of cultures—individualistic and moralistic—according to Elazar.

It is not just political culture that makes a difference. Demographics also matter, and moralistic states tend to be more likely to have demographic profiles favorable to turnout. People are more likely to vote if they are better educated, if they are elderly, and if they are white. "In states with a high

---

Voter turnout
The percentage of voting-eligible citizens who register to vote and do vote

TABLE 5-1

Percentage of the Voting-Age Population Casting Ballots in the 2012 Presidential Election

Rank	State	Percentage of Total Voting-Age Population	Elazar Classification	Rank	State	Percentage of Total Voting-Age Population	Elazar Classification
1	Minnesota	71.3	Moralistic	27	District of Columbia	56.8	
2	Wisconsin	69.4	Moralistic	28	Connecticut	55.6	Individualistic
3	New Hampshire	67.8	Moralistic	29	Idaho	55.5	Moralistic
4	Iowa	67.1	Moralistic	30	Florida	55.2	Traditionalistic
5	Maine	66.9	Moralistic	31	Alaska	55.1	Individualistic
6	Colorado	68.1	Moralistic	32	South Carolina	53.8	Traditionalistic
7	Ohio	65.2	Individualistic	33	Kansas	53.5	Moralistic
8	Michigan	62.0	Moralistic	34	Rhode Island	53.4	Individualistic
9	Montana	61.6	Moralistic	35	Illinois	53.3	Individualistic
10	Virginia	60.8	Traditionalistic	36	New Jersey	53.3	Individualistic
11	Massachusetts	60.4	Individualistic	37	Kentucky	53.2	Traditionalistic
12	North Carolina	60.2	Traditionalistic	38	Indiana	56.0	Individualistic
13	Maryland	59.6	Individualistic	39	Georgia	52.2	Traditionalistic
14	Missouri	59.5	Individualistic	40	Utah	51.4	Moralistic
15	North Dakota	59.4	Moralistic	41	New Mexico	49.5	Traditionalistic
16	Vermont	59.3	Moralistic	42	Tennessee	49.4	Traditionalistic
17	Oregon	58.6	Moralistic	43	Nevada	48.7	Individualistic
18	Washington	58.3	Moralistic	44	Arkansas	47.5	Traditionalistic
19	Delaware	58.0	Individualistic	45	Arizona	46.5	Traditionalistic
20	South Dakota	57.7	Moralistic	46	New York	46.2	Individualistic
21	Mississippi	57.3	Traditionalistic	47	Oklahoma	46.2	Traditionalistic
22	Louisiana	57.1	Traditionalistic	48	West Virginia	45.5	Traditionalistic
23	Pennsylvania	57.1	Individualistic	49	California	45.1	Moralistic
24	Nebraska	56.8	Individualistic	50	Texas	41.7	Traditionalistic
25	Wyoming	56.8	Individualistic	51	Hawaii	40.0	Individualistic
26	Alabama	56.0	Traditionalistic				

Source: United States Elections Project, "2012 General Election Turnout Rates," July 22, 2013, http://elections.gmu.edu/Turnout_2012G.html.

percentage of minorities, you're going to have low turnout," says Steven Hill of the New America Foundation. "States with higher voter turnout, such as Minnesota and Maine, tend to be fairly white states."[34] Such moralistic states historically also have bred strong two-party competition. This tends to increase turnout. Citizens in states or districts dominated by one party tend not to vote as eagerly. Their candidate of choice is certain to win—or to lose if they are "orphaned" voters whose party is weak in their home state or district. What

we see here are differences that interact with other differences to produce variation in turnout.

Voter turnout rates actually have increased in the South, where many of the historical impediments to registration and voting have declined and the major parties have become more competitive than had been the case for more than 100 years. But the region has merely stabilized at a turnout rate that is slightly lower than that in the rest of the country. Its high proportion of African Americans and its historical legacy of suppressing

> Hispanics have long been considered the "sleeping giant" of American politics because of their failure to vote in numbers commensurate with their share of the population. They cast just 6 percent of the ballots in the United States in 2004, barely half as many as African Americans, even though they constitute a larger portion of the national population.

their votes and the votes of some whites keep the South's turnout rates sluggish even though African Americans do tend to vote in greater numbers than do other minorities, such as Hispanics.

Hispanics have long been considered the "sleeping giant" of American politics because of their failure to vote in numbers commensurate with their share of the population. They cast just 6 percent of the ballots in the United States in 2004, barely half as many as African Americans, even though they constitute a larger portion of the national population. Their numbers ticked upward in 2008 but still trailed well behind those of African Americans, who turned out in high numbers in support of Obama. A record number of Hispanics voted in 2010, with their share of the electorate ticking up to nearly 7 percent; still, less than a third of eligible Hispanics cast ballots that year.[35] By 2012, it appeared that the sleeping giant had awakened. Hispanics made up 10 percent of voters that year, and their share of the electorate—and their influence—is considered certain to grow.

But growth in the Latino electorate is still lagging well behind the rate of growth of the Hispanic population as a whole. "Hispanics have voted in record numbers in recent years, but their turnout rate continues to lag behind whites and blacks," the Pew Research Center concluded in 2014.[36] The standard explanation is that Hispanics simply lack the well-established political organizations needed to encourage registration and turnout. But other factors are involved as well. More than 20 percent of voting-age Hispanics are noncitizens and thus not eligible to vote. As Ruy Teixeira, a Democratic polling expert, says, "People who look at the overall size of the Hispanic population and look at the vote think, 'Oh my God, what if these people ever get mobilized?'... But so many of these people can't vote anyway."[37]

Then there's age. The median age of Hispanics in the United States is just 27, compared with a median age of 42 for non-Hispanic whites. A much higher percentage of Hispanics do not vote because they are simply too young. That will change. About 50,000 Hispanics will turn 18 every month for the next dozen years or so. This could mean that Hispanic voting rolls will swell enormously—or it could mean that young Hispanics, just like young Americans of every race, will fail to exercise their right to vote in great numbers. Hispanics, in other words, already behave pretty much like everybody else.

As previously mentioned, many other factors also determine rates of voter turnout. Elderly people tend to vote in high numbers—which is one reason Social Security and Medicare are always important political issues. Young people, by contrast, vote in lower numbers, in percentage terms. People who are wealthy tend to vote more than do the poor, and people with higher levels of education vote much more regularly than do people with limited education. These are some of the reasons a high-income state with an educated population, such as Connecticut, has much higher turnout rates than a low-income state where the population is poorly educated on the whole, such as Hawaii.

A competitive election will draw a crowd even in a state that normally has low voter turnout. When people feel as though they have a real choice, they are more likely to make the effort to vote. A close three-way race for governor, such as the one that took place in Minnesota in 1998, will produce record turnout, whereas a yawner between a popular incumbent and a no-name opponent will make people sit on their hands.

Some states tend to have consistently competitive elections because the two major parties are matched fairly evenly, each getting a roughly equal share of support from the electorate. Other states are one-party states, with Republicans or Democrats being dominant. One-party states rarely have competitive elections—but when they do, voter turnout is certain to go up.

In his best-selling 2000 book *Bowling Alone,* Robert Putnam notes that moralistic states such as Minnesota and the Dakotas have much higher rates of volunteering, attendance at public meetings, and "social trust," as measured by polls, than do traditionalistic states.[38] In other words, voter turnout is just one indication of the overall sense of civic engagement in a place. States with strong "socializing institutions"—anything from membership organizations to news media that still cover politics—are more likely to be places where people are engaged enough to vote.

What Elections Are Used For

Forty-nine states elect a governor and two sets of state legislators: state senators and members of a state house of representatives, delegates, or assemblymen. Nebraska, the only exception, elects a governor and a one-chamber legislature. Beyond that, there is quite a bit of variation among the states in what they allow people to vote for. Many states allow voters to pick a number of statewide officeholders, such as attorney general and secretary of state, whereas in a few places these are appointed positions. Judges are elected at the voting booth in most places but not in about a dozen states. Roughly half the states allow voters to make policy decisions directly through ballot initiatives and referendums.

A look at state elections shows that states have quite different rules about who gets to vote for whom. That, in turn, can affect how a state makes policy. A governor who can appoint his or her entire cabinet is likely to have better success at pushing through policies than is a governor who has to contend with a group of elected officials, each with his or her own agenda.

All this is putting aside local elections, which also vary considerably. Most large cities, such as Chicago and Los Angeles, allow voters to elect a mayor directly. Many smaller cities have what is called a council-mayor format, in which the city council picks one of its own members to serve as mayor, while the city is administered by a city manager, who is not elected. The same holds true for counties. In some places a county commission picks its own leader, whereas in others voters pick a county executive on their own. Local elections are, for the most part, nonpartisan—that is, candidates do not run under a party label. But, again, there are exceptions, such as the highly partisan elections for mayor of New York City.

Electing the Executive Branch

Until recently, New Jersey voters elected only their governor out of all statewide officeholders. This system helped create one of the most powerful governorships in the country. It wasn't always so. For centuries, New Jersey governors were much weaker players than the state's legislatures. They were limited to a single term and had weak veto and appointment powers. County officials in the state also were quite powerful, at the expense of state officials. That all changed, however, with the new state constitution of 1947. The constitution was pushed through by reformers of the moralistic strain that had always been present, although usually not dominant, in New Jersey politics. The reformers got new powers for the state's governors, including the ability to succeed themselves, authority to appoint not just cabinet officials but also about 500 board and commission members, and broad authority to reject legislation. New Jersey's governors now can veto all or part of many bills and can issue conditional vetoes, meaning a governor can reject portions of a bill while suggesting new language for it.[39] Compare all that influence with the limited powers of the governor of Texas. In Texas, the governor is only 1 of 25 elected statewide officials—and he or she is sometimes not even considered the most powerful one among them.

Other states chart more of a middle-of-the-road course, electing a handful of statewide officials. In most states, in addition to a governor,

---

Nonpartisan election
An election in which the candidates do not have to declare party affiliation or receive a party's nomination; local offices and elections are often nonpartisan

A Difference That Makes A Difference

How Some States Discourage Voters

The notion of equal access to the ballot for all—one person, one vote—is a cornerstone of American democracy. But how do you determine whether the person seeking to vote has the right to vote?

That question is at the center of one of the major debates in U.S. politics in recent years. Numerous states have put in place greater safeguards to protect against voter fraud, demanding evidence of identification such as driver's licenses at polling places and sometimes requiring that those wishing to register to vote produce documents such as birth certificates. (See Map 5-1.)

These laws were given the green light by the U.S. Supreme Court in 2008, when it upheld a 2005 Indiana law requiring that voters produce government-issued photo identification at the polls. Kris Kobach, the Republican secretary of state in Kansas and sponsor of his state's 2011 voter ID law, says that requiring voters to show a photo ID is no burden at a time when they have to do the same to board an airplane, enter a federal building, or even "buy the kind of Sudafed that works."

Such arguments have been persuasive, at least with the general public. Polling in recent years has consistently shown that about 70 percent of Americans support voter ID laws.

Still, critics of the laws—mostly Democrats—complain that they amount to attempts at voter suppression. The people least likely to be able to produce government-issued IDs are minorities, the young, and the old—all groups expected to favor Democratic candidates in general. "He's doing a better job as Republican state chair as secretary of state than he did when he was the Republican state chair," Kansas state representative Ann Mah, a Democrat, said of Kobach.

Voter ID laws are a solution in search of a problem, the argument goes. The 41 incidents of improper voting or registration activity for 2010 that Kobach's office cited are mostly accounted for by honest mistakes, Mah argued, such as snowbirds accidentally seeking to vote in two states or felons being allowed to vote although they were ineligible. There was no evidence that Kansas was seeing large numbers of illegal aliens voting, or that there was a conspiracy on the part of any party or group to affect the outcomes of elections, said Chris Biggs, Kobach's Democratic predecessor as secretary of state.

Those findings track those of national studies. An analysis of 2,068 reported fraud cases dating back to 2000, conducted by a Carnegie-Knight investigative reporting project in 2012, found that there had been just 10 cases of alleged in-person voter impersonation since 2000. "With 146 million registered voters in the United States, those represent about one for every 15 million prospective voters," reported *The Washington Post*.[a]

During the 2012 election year, media reports appeared frequently about senior citizens who had voted for decades but had been turned away from the polls when they were unable to produce long-lost documents that were suddenly the key to the franchise. Matt Barreto, a University of Washington political scientist, conducted a survey in 2012 that found that, while most Pennsylvanians believed they had proper ID, 13 percent of registered voters lacked the kind of identification required by the state's new law.[b]

Eric Holder, President Obama's attorney general, likened voter ID requirements to "poll taxes," a long-discredited and abandoned tool meant to disenfranchise African American voters. Despite the Supreme Court ruling, the U.S. Justice Department and other entities challenged numerous voter ID laws in court.

Pennsylvania lawmakers were chagrined when their own attorneys had to concede in court that the state had

Voter ID laws became controversial in 2012. Democrats argued that Republicans were seeking to suppress Democratic supporters, their fears fueled by remarks from Pennsylvania House GOP leader Mike Turzai that a new voter ID law would "allow" Republican presidential nominee Mitt Romney to win the state.

AP Photo/Marc Levy, FILE

Herman Fredrick, a resident of Norristown, Pennsylvania, had to show photo identification to vote in a primary election in April 2012. Pennsylvania was among a number of states that had controversial voter ID requirements in place for that year's presidential election.

no awareness "of in-person voter fraud in Pennsylvania and do not have direct personal knowledge of in-person voter fraud elsewhere." They were even more embarrassed when Mike Turzai, the Pennsylvania House Republican leader, seemed to verify critics' complaints that the state had passed the law for partisan purposes, saying at a June 2012 rally, "Voter ID . . . is going to allow Governor [Mitt] Romney to win the state of Pennsylvania."

But defenders of the law say that Democrats and civil rights groups are too quick to dismiss evidence of voter fraud—and all too eager to try to turn accusations of "voter suppression" into a rallying cry to gin up support from the Democratic Party base. These laws have been in place in some states for multiple elections now, with no evidence as yet that they have reduced turnout.

Much of the debate ultimately swirled around competing visions of election regulation—whether the goal should be to ensure that access to the ballot is strictly enforced to protect against abuse, or whether chances for fraud are too slim to justify denying eligible voters their right to vote simply because they lack certain forms of documentation. Both political debate and court cases turned not only on voter ID requirements but also on efforts to purge voter rolls and limit the numbers of hours polling places would be open.

Most people—and certainly most Republican lawmakers—seemed to feel that protecting the ballot box and insisting that citizens make the extra effort to obtain proper identification was the way to go. During debate over Florida's voter ID law in 2011, Republican senator Mike Bennett said, "I don't have a problem making [voting] harder. I want

people in Florida to want to vote as bad as that person in Africa who walks 200 miles across the desert. This should be something you do with a passion."

Still, plenty of people believed this view of the matter was too harsh, that too many Americans had to endure long lines on election day or, worse, were at risk of being unfairly turned away for lack of knowledge about the new laws and difficulty in acquiring the right kinds of ID. President Obama has repeatedly said that people waiting in long lines to vote is not acceptable in the world's oldest democracy.

Voter ID laws don't even help prevent the most common types of fraud, such as ex-felons voting when they shouldn't or people voting in multiple states, argues political scientist Jonathan Bernstein. "There is a natural trade-off between voting participation and policing fraud," he wrote in 2014. "Build higher walls against fraud, and some innocent voters will be denied access; make full participation the priority, and some crooks are going to find ways to take advantage. What's unusual about asking people to show a photo ID at the polling place is that polling-place voter impersonation doesn't seem to exist, and certainly not without the active collusion of election officials."[c]

[a] Katasha Khan and Corbin Carson, "Election Day Impersonation, an Impetus for Voter ID Laws, a Rarity, Data Show," *Washington Post,* August 11, 2012, http://www.washingtonpost.com/politics/election-day-impersonation-an-impetus-for-voter-id-laws-a-rarity-data-show/2012/08/11/7002911e-df20-11e1-a19c-fcfa365396c8_story.html.

[b] Angela Couloumbis, "Numbers Behind Pa. Voter-ID Law Debated in Court," *Philadelphia Inquirer,* July 27, 2012, http://articles.philly.com/2012-07-27/news/32870331_1_voter-law-form-of-photo-identification-thousands-of-inactive-voters.

[c] Jonathan Bernstein, "Voter ID Still Means Voter Suppression," *Bloomberg View,* May 14, 2014, www.bloombergview.com/articles/2014-05-14/voter-id-still-means-voter-suppression.

MAP 5-1

States Requiring Voter Identification, 2014

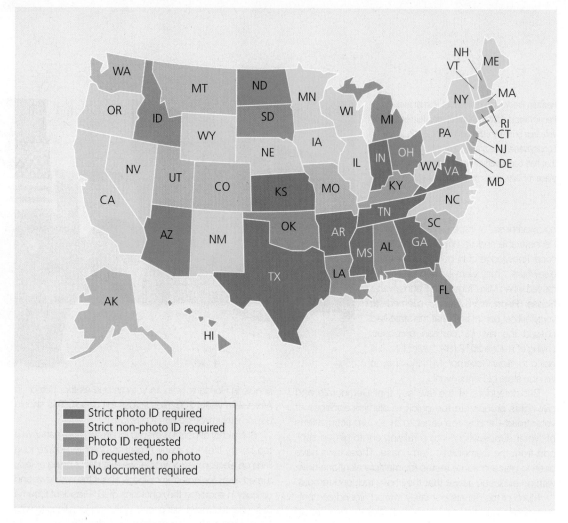

Note: The Arkansas Supreme Court struck down the state's strict voter ID law in October 2014.

Source: National Conference of State Legislatures, "Voter Identification Laws in Effect in 2014," http://www.ncsl.org/research/elections-and-campaigns/voter-id.aspx#map.

voters elect a lieutenant governor, treasurer, secretary of state, and attorney general. A few states elect other officers as well, such as an insurance commissioner. Some observers believe that appointed officials are removed from political concerns and can make decisions without regard to partisan interests. Others believe that having to answer directly to the public makes individual officeholders more responsive to the public's needs and desires. Regardless of which side is correct, the fact that many statewide officeholders

run for office independent of the governor gives them a power base of their own.

Attorneys general, treasurers, and other statewide officials often have aspirations of becoming governor themselves one day. This often leads to conflict with the sitting governor. Some of these fights occur along partisan lines. New Mexico attorney general Gary King, a Democrat, complained in 2012 that Republican legislators were trying to examine his office e-mails in retaliation for his office's investigating the state Department

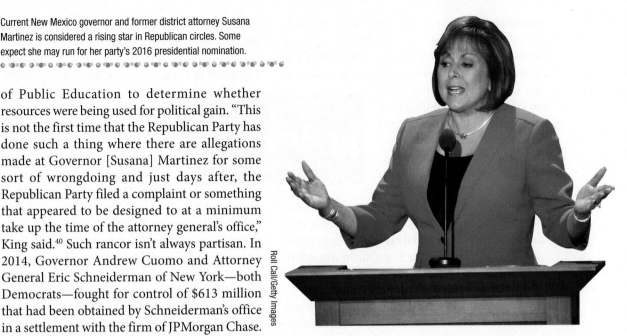

Current New Mexico governor and former district attorney Susana Martinez is considered a rising star in Republican circles. Some expect she may run for her party's 2016 presidential nomination.

Roll Call/Getty Images

of Public Education to determine whether resources were being used for political gain. "This is not the first time that the Republican Party has done such a thing where there are allegations made at Governor [Susana] Martinez for some sort of wrongdoing and just days after, the Republican Party filed a complaint or something that appeared to be designed to at a minimum take up the time of the attorney general's office," King said.[40] Such rancor isn't always partisan. In 2014, Governor Andrew Cuomo and Attorney General Eric Schneiderman of New York—both Democrats—fought for control of $613 million that had been obtained by Schneiderman's office in a settlement with the firm of JPMorgan Chase. The two had already been like oil and water, said observers in Albany, with Cuomo creating a new financial industry oversight agency soon after taking office and giving it responsibilities that overlapped with the attorney general's duties. "It's a pretty big slush fund," one Cuomo ally said of the settlement money. "The question now is whose slush fund is it going to be."[41]

Legal Offices

Voters pay comparatively little attention to candidates running for some state executive branch offices. Races for, say, state treasurer are, for the most part, just not seen as all that exciting. Most often, the party that wins the governorship takes the lion's share of the secondary executive branch offices anyway; so there is not much ticket splitting. These are offices often pursued by legislators or other politicians looking to move up the political ladder. They hope these second-tier positions will firm up their résumés for their future bids for prominent offices such as governor.

But that's starting to change, with more money being spent on elections that were once nearly forgotten. Even the once politically sleepy office of secretary of state is drawing more attention and campaign spending. Maybe it's not surprising that as voting laws have become more contentious, the state official most often in charge of overseeing

them has attracted more attention, with super PACs from both parties hoping to elect favorable election officers. A group called SOS for SOS was formed in 2014 and hoped to raise $10 million that year to support conservative candidates. "Get in the game. We were literally asleep at the wheel," said Gregg Phillips, head of the PAC. "There hasn't been a real effort on our side to support these folks."[42] Competing groups were started that year by Democrats, including former Obama campaign officials.

Big money partisanship started being seen below the gubernatorial level nearly 20 years ago with the office of attorney general, the chief law enforcement officer in the state. For many years, Democrats completely dominated the office in most states, but that began to change in the late 1990s. For one thing, the job came to be seen as a more important stepping-stone to the governorship than in the past; in 2012, eight former state attorneys general were serving as governors. Attorneys general in 10 other states, including Michigan, Pennsylvania, and California, ran for governor in 2010. Republicans, unde®rstandably, became increasingly unwilling to concede this important gateway to the chief executive's office.

Moreover, state attorneys general, who traditionally had concentrated on law enforcement and consumer protection disputes within their states, had joined in a series of multistate settlements that represented important challenges to corporate interests. They forced a series of settlements in 1998, for instance, that pushed the major tobacco companies to change their marketing strategies and to pay states an estimated $246 billion over 25 years. Some Republicans believed that these activist attorneys general were engaging in "government lawsuit abuse"—not targeting criminal behavior but, instead, going after companies to achieve changes in policy and regulation that could not be accomplished in the legislative arena. They founded the Republican Attorneys General Association (RAGA) as a campaign wing to elect members of their party to the office, and they funneled to their candidates contributions from businesses and conservative interest groups that were threatened by the new activism. "Historically . . . attorney general races were off most business people's radar screens," according to Bob LaBrant of the Michigan Chamber of Commerce. In the new environment, he says, "there's greater incentive to get involved in an attorney general race because of the increased involvement of attorneys general across the country in litigation against the business community."[43]

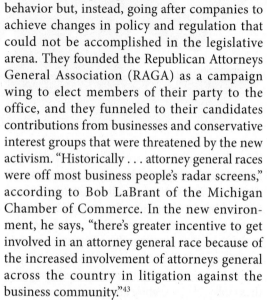

Such interest-group money and influence do make a difference. In 2002, the Law Enforcement Alliance of America, an arm of the gun lobby, ran an estimated $1.5 million late-season ad campaign that helped keep the Texas attorney general's office in Republican hands. This was an expanded version of the U.S. Chamber of Commerce's effort in Indiana in 2000, when a $200,000 ad campaign was widely viewed as a leading factor in driving an incumbent Democrat attorney general out of office.[44] Such numbers, once eye-popping, have become routine. All told, Republicans improved their numbers after RAGA's founding from just 12 attorneys general in 1999 to 20 in 2003 to 27 by 2012. Both parties now believe that campaigns for attorney general will remain more expensive and competitive than they had been historically.

A related phenomenon is affecting judicial elections, which traditionally had been sleepy affairs. All but 11 states hold some type of elections for judicial posts. These are either direct elections by voters or retention elections used by voters to grant additional terms to justices appointed by the governor or the state legislature.

Until the mid-1990s, judicial campaigns were cheap and fairly ho-hum. What campaign contributions candidates did receive came mainly from trial lawyers, along with contributions from unions and other constituencies allied with the Democratic Party. All that began to change, however, when Republicans and their business allies grew weary of seeing their legislative victories in areas such as tort law and workers' compensation overturned by the high courts. (Lawyers, lobbyists, and their firms remain the biggest overall donors.) "Republicans have had a significant amount of success at the state level, not only being elected to offices but implementing bold conservative solutions," said Matt Walter, president of the Republican State Leadership Committee, which helps elect GOP candidates. "Unfortunately, that's running into a hard stop with judges who aren't in touch with the public."[45]

In 2000, candidates in supreme court races in 20 states raised a total of $45.5 million, a 61 percent increase over the previous record. By 2012, it was up to $53.6 million, down from a peak of $63.4 million in 2007 and 2008, according to the National Institute on Money in State Politics. The average cost of winning a judicial election jumped 45 percent between 2002 and 2004, while individual races also kept breaking records, with one Illinois contest nearing the $10 million mark in 2004.[46] Elections for individual, lower-level judgeships have broken through the million-dollar barrier also. Given the flood of interest group money into judicial elections, ads might attack any part of a judge's record, even if the organization sponsoring the ad is mainly focused on business regulation. Tennessee Supreme Court Justice Sharon Lee—one of three justices targeted for defeat in a 2014 retention election that drew millions in spending—complained that she and her colleagues were tarred for their stances on issues that they hadn't even weighed in on. "They'll say we're responsible for UT's losing season and Vanderbilt's winning season," Lee said.[47]

The issue of fundraising by judicial candidates drew attention with the 2008 publication of best-selling mystery writer John Grisham's novel *The Appeal*. Its plot turns on a rigged Mississippi Supreme Court election. The following year, the U.S. Supreme Court ruled in *Caperton v. Massey* that a West Virginia Supreme Court justice who had benefited from a $3 million campaign orchestrated by a coal-mining company with a large case before the court had a conflict of interest. But Chief Justice John Roberts, writing in dissent, noted that the majority had not drawn a clear line in terms of what constitutes the appearance of corruption and that this will lead to further confusion.

Direct Democracy

In addition to electing officials to state and local offices, voters can participate in certain forms of direct democracy. As discussed in Chapter 3, in about half the states, voters can pass legislation on their own through ballot initiatives or referendums, which also are available in hundreds of municipalities across the country. In 24 states, citizens can petition to place a piece of legislation or a constitutional amendment on the ballot for approval or rejection by voters. Also in 24 states—mostly the same states—citizens can petition to review a law passed by the legislature and the governor, which they can then accept or reject. (See Table 5-2.)

When citizens or groups other than elected officials put a measure on the ballot to become a law, this is called a popular initiative. When citizens put a measure on the ballot to affirm or reject an action of the legislature or other political actor, this is called a popular referendum. When the legislature places a measure on the ballot to win voter approval (such as for a constitutional amendment or bond issue), it is called a legislative referendum. Some referendums are nonbinding—expressing the will of the people but not becoming law—but most are binding and do have the force of law once passed.

In all 50 states, the legislature or other government agencies have the power of legislative referendum. In the decades following independence, citizens in several northeastern states ratified new constitutions; Congress subsequently made legislative referendums for constitutional amendments mandatory for all new states entering the union after 1857.[48]

As discussed in Chapter 3, the notion of popular referendums and initiatives really took root because of the efforts of reformers from the Populist and Progressive movements. These individuals sought to give citizens more influence over state political systems that they saw as dominated by moneyed interests such as banks, railroads, and mining companies. A majority of the states that have adopted the popular initiative process (under which citizens can collect a certain number of signatures to place issues directly on the ballot) did so in the late 1800s and early 1900s. Most of these states are in the West and the upper Midwest, which had political cultures that welcomed the idea of populist control. Much of the opposition in the southern and eastern states grew out of racist concerns that giving people direct authority to make laws would give too much power to African Americans or to new immigrants such as the Irish.

Recent ballot initiatives and referendums have covered a wide range of topics, from banning or allowing gay marriage and legalizing marijuana to banning the use of bait, dogs, or traps in bear hunting (a question before Maine voters in 2014). Many initiatives have to do with tax and spending issues. Sometimes voters send contradictory signals. For instance, in Washington State, voters in recent years have approved limitations on property and other taxes while at the same time approving such expensive programs as teacher pay increases and school class size limitations.

Those who favor the initiative process say that it gives voters a chance to control government directly. Voters know that they are voting for an environmental safety program or a campaign finance law, as opposed to voting for candidates who say that they favor these things but may act differently once in office. Initiative states do tend to have lower state spending per capita, but that gap generally is bridged by local spending, which tends to run higher in initiative states.[49]

Critics of the initiative process say that it creates more problems than it solves. Because voters are presented with a straight yes-or-no choice about spending more on, say, elementary and secondary education, they do not take into account other competing state priorities, such as transportation

TABLE 5-2

Avenues for Direct Democracy

State	Popular Referendum	Ballot Initiative	Constitutional Amendment by Initiative	Recall of State Officials
Alabama	No	No	No	No
Alaska	Yes	Yes	No	Yes
Arizona	Yes	Yes	Yes	Yes
Arkansas	Yes	Yes	Yes	No
California	Yes	Yes	Yes	Yes
Colorado	Yes	Yes	Yes	Yes
Connecticut	No	No	No	No
Delaware	No	No	No	No
Florida	No	Yes	Yes	No
Georgia	No	No	No	Yes
Hawaii	No	No	No	No
Idaho	Yes	Yes	No	Yes
Illinois	Yes	Yes	No	No
Indiana	No	No	No	No
Iowa	No	No	No	No
Kansas	No	No	No	Yes
Kentucky	Yes	No	No	No
Louisiana	No	No	No	Yes
Maine	Yes	Yes	No	No
Maryland	Yes	No	No	No
Massachusetts	Yes	Yes	Yes	No
Michigan	Yes	Yes	Yes	Yes
Minnesota	No	No	No	Yes
Mississippi	No	Yes	Yes	No
Missouri	Yes	Yes	Yes	No
Montana	Yes	Yes	Yes	Yes
Nebraska	Yes	Yes	Yes	No
Nevada	Yes	Yes	Yes	Yes
New Hampshire	No	No	No	No
New Jersey	No	No	No	Yes
New Mexico	Yes	No	No	No
New York	No	No	No	No
North Carolina	No	No	No	No
North Dakota	Yes	Yes	Yes	Yes
Ohio	Yes	Yes	Yes	No
Oklahoma	Yes	Yes	Yes	No
Oregon	Yes	Yes	Yes	Yes
Pennsylvania	No	No	No	No
Rhode Island	No	No	No	Yes
South Carolina	No	No	No	No
South Dakota	Yes	Yes	Yes	No

State	Popular Referendum	Ballot Initiative	Constitutional Amendment by Initiative	Recall of State Officials
Tennessee	No	No	No	No
Texas	No	No	No	No
Utah	Yes	Yes	No	No
Vermont	No	No	No	No
Virginia	No	No	No	No
Washington	Yes	Yes	No	Yes
West Virginia	No	No	No	No
Wisconsin	No	No	No	Yes
Wyoming	Yes	Yes	No	No
Total number of states with	25	24	18	18

Source: Data compiled from the Initiative and Referendum Institute at the University of Southern California, www.iandrinstitute.org/statewide_i&r.htm, and the National Conference of State Legislatures, www.ncsl.org/LegislaturesElections/ElectionsCampaigns/RecallofStateOfficials/tabid/16581/Default.aspx.

or colleges, the way legislators must. Voters can say, as those in Washington have, that they want both lower taxes and more services but leave legislators and governors few tools for balancing the budget or responding to economic recessions.

Those opposed to initiatives also say that the idea that they express the popular will better than do elected representatives sounds good in theory but is flawed in practice. In many states—particularly California—initiatives have become big business. They are not necessarily the expressions of grassroots ideals anymore; instead, they are proposed and paid for by wealthy individuals, corporations, or interest groups, such as teachers unions or the owners of gambling casinos. Total spending on ballot measures topped $1 billion for the first time in 2014. "Oil and gas companies in Alaska spent more than $170 for every vote they won in a successful campaign to reject higher taxes" in August 2014, *The Washington Post* reported.[50]

Still the most famous and influential modern ballot initiative is Proposition 13, approved by California voters in 1978, which limited property tax rates and made other changes to the state's tax and spending laws (see Chapter 3). The initiative was copied successfully in Michigan and Massachusetts, and most states soon placed limitations on their own property tax rates. The success of Proposition 13 fueled the modern initiative movement. Only 87 statewide initiatives were

proposed during the entire decade of the 1960s. Since 1978, however, about 300 initiatives have been proposed per decade. Ninety-three statewide initiatives were placed on ballots in 1996 alone. That appears to have been the peak year, with supporters of the initiative process complaining since then that state legislatures have placed new restrictions on ballot access and signature collection. But following a long decline, the numbers of initiatives started going up again in 2012 and are likely to continue to climb, according to Jennie Bowser, a senior fellow with the National Conference of State Legislatures, because there is "an industry" that relies on an active initiative process.[51]

The power of initiatives can be seen in the establishment of legislative term limits, which exist in nearly every state that allows ballot initiatives but in only a couple of states that do not. Term limits have been imposed in virtually every case by voters through ballot measures, not by legislators themselves. In addition, congressional term limits were a popular idea during the early 1990s and were approved in a number of states; however, the U.S. Supreme Court ruled in 1995 that states cannot unilaterally alter the constitutional requirements for holding federal office. State legislators are subject to term limits in 15 states, but the defeat of a term-limits initiative in Oregon in 2006 signaled the end of the movement.

States Under Stress

Protest Movements Achieve Different Levels of Success

Two large-scale populist movements emerged during the first term of Barack Obama's presidency: the Tea Party movement and the Occupy movement. Participants in both were angry about the influence and power of large institutional forces in society. The two movements' platforms were diametrically opposed, however, and the approaches they took to trying to influence American politics were completely different.

The fast-growing Tea Party movement began in 2009, shortly after Obama became president. It was made up of individuals angry about the size of government—a backlash against the president's $800 billion stimulus program, a bank bailout plan that Congress had passed under President George W. Bush to the tune of $700 billion, and a deficit that in 2009 topped $1.4 trillion. "The Republicans for the last two decades have been a party whose litmus tests have been cultural issues, especially abortion," explained conservative columnist Michael Barone in 2010. "The tea partiers have helped to change their focus to issues of government overreach and spending."[a]

Members of the movement also derided Obama's health care legislation, which they saw as obtrusive and a threat to individual liberty, since it mandated that most people buy health insurance. Not surprisingly, then, they aligned themselves largely with the Republican Party—even if many participants in the Tea Party movement insisted that they were independent.

The Tea Party movement, which derived its name from colonial-era protests against British taxation—quickly claimed more than 1,000 different affiliate groups around the country.[b] Tea Party–endorsed candidates prevailed in numerous GOP primaries in both 2010 and 2012. Republican strategists largely welcomed the burst of energy that tea partiers brought to their cause, which had been discouraged by widespread electoral losses in 2006 and 2008.

Some criticized the Tea Party for being too unyielding. Some of the candidates backed by Tea Party groups in primaries were unable to prevail in contests Republicans might have won had they nominated more "establishment" or mainstream candidates. And those Tea Party favorites who did win elections drew criticism once in office for refusing to compromise at all on budget matters, nearly forcing the country into default in 2011.

But while the Tea Party was influencing Republican politicians in Congress and the statehouses, those politicians were trying to co-opt the Tea Party, to harness its energy and enthusiasm without letting its agenda dominate the party's direction. "That's the secret to politics," GOP consultant Scott Reed said in 2011. "Trying to control a segment of people without those people recognizing that you're trying to control them."[c]

During the 2014 primary season, it was tough to see whether the GOP had absorbed the Tea Party or if the reverse was true. Particularly in U.S. Senate contests, the U.S. Chamber of Commerce and other so-called establishment entities heavily supported candidates they thought stood a better chance of winning than others who were Tea Party darlings. Those groups largely succeeded, but many thought the Tea Party had really won by forcing incumbent Republicans to embrace more conservative positions on issues such as immigration and federal spending. "Despite the losing record of the tea folk in Senate primary battles, it's apparent they are winning the war with the Republican establishment by pushing the entire party even further to the right," wrote liberal commentator Ed Kilgore.[d]

Being co-opted seemed to be the main thing the Occupy movement wanted to avoid. The movement began with a protest in September 2011 in a park near Wall Street in Lower Manhattan; the demonstrators complained that too much wealth was concentrated in the hands of too few individuals.

The slogan "We are the 99 percent" went global, as did the idea of protesting by camping in place for 24 hours a day, which quickly spread to hundreds of cities. The issue of income inequality and the question of whether the wealthiest 1 percent held too much power soon became central concerns of the movement.

But Occupy was not able to translate its complaints into a policy agenda. It wasn't clear what the members of the movement wanted to have happen. The mere act of their camping out became problematic as winter set in and issues of sanitation and crowd control grew worse; in many cities, authorities ordered police to remove the protesters from public spaces.

As Rosemary Feurer, a historian at Northern Illinois University, has noted, protest movements typically don't start out with set lists of goals that they want politicians to achieve. The populist movements of the 19th century and early labor union activity began in ways similar to the beginnings of the Occupy movement: An encampment of people came together, found they shared a sense of dissatisfaction with the status quo, and worked to change it. As Feurer has observed, "What starts these movements is a list of grievances. You don't start with a list of goals, but with a sense of what's wrong."[e]

Occupy gatherings sought to run by consensus, with those gathered expressing approval or disapproval of simple items, such as the order of speakers, through hand gestures. The movement, by its nature, was suspicious of leaders. "Don't lose sight of the bigger message of this movement being driven from the bottom up by consensus and not affiliation or deference to any group that's out there," said Ed Needham, a media spokesman for Occupy Wall Street.[f]

As such, Occupy had a hard time finding allegiance even with politicians who might have been sympathetic.

This was exemplified when John Lewis, a Democratic congressman from Georgia and hero of the civil rights movement, showed up at the Occupy Atlanta site. Protesters there praised Lewis but refused to let him speak right away, as that would have disrupted the scheduled agenda.

Lewis, who had other obligations, decided to leave, although he said he took no offense. Recalling his own days as head of the Student Nonviolent Coordinating Committee in the 1960s, he said civil rights groups sometimes reached consensus slowly and refused to be deferential to more established leaders. "It is growing, it is maturing, it will work out," Lewis told reporters, speaking about the Occupy movement at the Atlanta site. "It will come of age."

Just a few months after the protests began, however, it didn't appear that Occupy would have continuing relevance. What were highly visible encampments had already given way to sporadic, sparsely attended marches. Some of its rhetoric is still used by leftist protesters, but while the Tea Party thrives, Occupy is mostly a memory. "Occupy does not have a traditional leadership structure, making it difficult for the movement to engage in conventional political organizing in support of state legislators and members of Congress, like the Tea Party has," *The New York Times* reported in April 2012. "And some activists, angry at politicians across the board, do not see electoral politics as the best avenue for the movement, complicating efforts to chart its direction."[g]

[a] Michael Barone, "Tea Party Brings Energy, Change and Tumult to GOP," *Washington Examiner,* March 14, 2010, http://townhall.com/columnists/michaelbarone/2010/03/15/tea_party_brings_energy,_change_and_tumult_to_gop/page/full.

[b] Peter Katel, "Tea Party Movement," *CQ Researcher,* May 19, 2010.

[c] Quoted in Matt Bai, "'You're Nuts!'" *New York Times Magazine,* October 16, 2001, 44.

[d] Ed Kilgore, "The Tea Party Is Losing Battles but Winning the War," *Talking Points Memo,* August 6, 2014, http://talkingpointsmemo.com/cafe/losing-battles-winning-wars.

[e] Quoted in Alan Greenblatt, "For Wall Street Protests, What Constitutes Success?" NPR, October 14, 2011, http://www.npr.org/2011/10/14/141347126/for-wall-street-protests-what-constitutes-success.

[f] Phone interview with Ed Needham, October 12, 2011.

[g] Michael S. Schmidt, "For Occupy Movement, a Challenge to Recapture Momentum," *New York Times,* April 1, 2012, A21.

Rather than looking to expand term limits, legislators and many others concerned with the effects of term limits on good governance have been seeking to expand the length of time legislators may serve. Term limits are still too popular to repeal, but some people believe that allowing legislators 10 to 12 years in a chamber, as opposed to 6 to 8, will make them more expert in grappling with the complex policies they must address. Even these efforts, however, have proven to be tough sells.

Ballots have become regular battlegrounds for a number of other issues as well. Limitations on reproductive rights, such as parental notification requirements for minors seeking to obtain abortions, have been debated by voters in many states, as have smoking bans and property rights protections. Although many ballot measures involve putting restraints on government—by limiting state spending, for instance, or by holding judges more accountable for their decisions—voters in recent cycles have rejected these ideas. Public officials have been able to make the case that the sometimes rigid restrictions proposed would tie their hands even in emergency situations. Perhaps surprisingly, their arguments have been echoed in many states by organized business groups that, although fiscally conservative, have been concerned that artificial limits on government might affect their own priorities, such as improvements in education and transportation projects.

Since 2004, perhaps the most prominent measures on many ballots have sought to place a ban on gay marriage. Many states had already defined marriage as the union of a man and a woman, but following a Massachusetts court decision that found gays had a right to marry, 30 states have changed their constitutions to ban same-sex marriage. In May 2012, North Carolina voters approved such a ban, but the next day, President Obama said that he was now in favor of legalizing same-sex marriage (while stressing it was a policy best handled by the states). Supporters of gay marriage enjoyed their first successes at the ballot box in November 2012. Minnesota voters rejected a ban on same-sex marriage, while voters in Maine and Washington granted marriage rights to same-sex couples and Maryland voters approved the legislature's decision to allow gay marriage. Same-sex marriage supporters have had great success in the courts, overturning voter-approved bans in a number of states and bringing the total of states that allow same-sex marriage to 30 by October 2014.

As noted earlier, some political scientists have suggested that high-profile initiatives do lead more people to vote. Given the attention a proposed gay marriage ban received in Ohio in 2004, when that state's electoral votes ultimately decided the presidency, there was much coverage in the media that looked at the question of whether the initiative helped President Bush by encouraging social conservatives to vote. "I'd be naïve if I didn't say it helped," Robert T. Bennett, chair of the Ohio Republican Party, told *The New York Times*. "And it helped most in what we refer to as the Bible Belt area of southeastern and southwestern Ohio, where we had the largest percentage increase in support for the president."[52]

Not surprisingly, liberals decided to jump on this particular bandwagon, finding causes to place on ballots in hopes that more progressive voters would turn out as well, causes such as minimum-wage increases, marijuana legalization, and campaign finance restrictions. But there is a school of thought that argues that they need not have bothered. Simon Jackman, a statistician at Stanford University, has shown that same-sex marriage initiatives boosted turnout by about 3 percent in the 11 states that had them on the ballot in 2004. Upon examining data from all of Ohio's counties, however, he concluded that the state's initiative did not boost support for Bush.[53]

Others have noted that it is no accident that high-profile initiatives tend to appear in closely contested states. "The list of [presidential] battleground states almost exactly matches up with the list of controversial ballot measures this year," said Bowser, who tracks initiatives for the National Conference of State Legislatures, in 2004.[54]

Beyond initiatives and referendums is perhaps the ultimate expression of popular dissatisfaction—the **recall**. Recalls of local officials are

---

Recall
A way for voters to oust an incumbent politician prior to the next regularly scheduled election; they collect signatures to qualify the recall proposal for the ballot and then vote on the ouster of the politician

allowed in about 30 states and 61 percent of U.S. municipalities—more local governments than allow initiatives or referendums. Like ballot initiatives, recall laws are mainly by-products of the intention of early 20th century reformers to make state governments more responsive to average citizens. Recalls of state officials are allowed in 19 states.[55] No governor had faced a recall since the 1920s when, in 2003, California Democrat Gray Davis was recalled and replaced by Republican Arnold Schwarzenegger. In 2012, Wisconsin governor Scott Walker, a Republican, survived a recall attempt over labor issues in what became one of the most expensive elections in U.S. history.

These high-profile recalls helped promote growth in recalls at the local level, with everyone from county commissioners to school board members being shown the door. In 2011, at least 57 mayors faced recall attempts—up from 23 in 2009. Not all these recall attempts succeeded, but in recent years, serious recall attempts have been launched against mayors in cities such as Omaha, Kansas City, and Portland, Oregon. The overwhelming recall election loss of Carlos Alvarez, mayor of Miami-Dade County, Florida, in 2011 makes him perhaps the most prominent victim of the recall trend at the local level.[56] Once voters discovered the recall as an option, they seemed to like it. Of the 39 state legislative recall elections since states first allowed them in 1908, 18 occurred between 2010 and 2014, while nearly four dozen local officials faced recall elections in 2014.[57] Colorado voters unhappy with new restrictions on weapons successfully recalled two state senators—including the state Senate president—in 2013, while a third resigned rather than face a recall.[58]

The only governor to be recalled before Davis in California was Lynn Frazier of North Dakota in 1921. Frazier, the state attorney general, and the agricultural commissioner all lost their offices after a grassroots movement swelled against scandals in Frazier's government. The only other governor who has ever faced a scheduled recall election was Evan Mecham of Arizona; the legislature saved voters the trouble by removing him from office in 1987.

California requires a number of signatures equal to only 12 percent of the number of people who voted in the most recent election for the office, whereas most states require 25 percent and Kansas requires 40 percent. Some states have looked at restricting recall attempts as they've become more popular—one such state being Arizona, where state Senate President Russell Pearce was recalled in 2011. Michigan made changes to its law following the ouster of state Representative Paul Scott in 2011, resulting in a big and almost instantaneous drop in state and local recall elections—down from 31 in 2011 to 13 in 2013.

Public Opinion

Randall Gnant, the former president of the Arizona Senate, says that there is quite a contrast between the politics of today and those of the 1800s. Back then, he says, "it seemed that everybody took part in the political process—there were torchlight parades, party-run newspapers for and against candidates." Today, "we're into sort of a reverse kind of period. Now, almost nobody participates in the electoral process—voter turnout rates are abysmally low." But that does not mean that citizens are not paying any attention to the political process. Given the importance of websites, Twitter, and other media that quickly spread public opinion—or at least a share of it—the old idea that voters agree to a sort of contract with politicians whom they elect to 2- or 4-year terms is rapidly becoming dated. Voters are more than willing to express their displeasure about a given policy well before the next scheduled election day. "Try to get somebody interested in electing a candidate and they just don't want to get involved," Gnant points out. "But they are perfectly willing to get involved if somebody does something they don't want them to do."[59]

Citizen opinion usually does not register loudly enough to result in a recall or other formal protest. On most issues that come before policymakers at the state level, citizen opinion hardly seems to exist or be formulated at all. After all, how many citizens are going to take the time to follow—let alone express an opinion about—an obscure regulatory issue concerning overnight transactions between banks and insurance companies?

This lack of interest, or, at the very least, this lack of time, begs an important question. If citizens do not or cannot make their feelings known on every issue addressed in the hundreds of bills that wend through the average state legislature each year, how can legislators know that their votes will reflect the will of their constituents? After all, as V. O. Key writes, "Unless mass views have some place in the shaping of policy, all the talk about democracy is nonsense."[60]

Responding to Opinion

Doug Duncan served for a dozen years as county executive of Montgomery County, Maryland, before giving up the job in 2006. Like many veteran officeholders, he found that one of the biggest changes in his job came in the area of communications. "Doing it is half the job," he says, "and the other half is telling people about it so they know how you're spending their money."[61] The old outlets for government officials making announcements or responding to criticism—local daily newspapers and evening TV news broadcasts—have declined in audience or even gone away completely in some cases. Nevertheless, with the growth of the Internet, more information sources are available now than ever before. "The information's there," Duncan says. "It's just a question of how you make it available."

E-mail, Twitter, and websites devoted to neighborhood concerns or services such as libraries have made it easier for public officials to know what their constituents are thinking—at least those constituents who are motivated enough to make their opinions known on a given issue. And elected officials have become fairly quick to adopt more recent platforms, such as Facebook and Twitter. But let's be realistic—state officials, in particular, cannot know what the majority opinions are in their districts on every issue they confront. Mike Haridopolos, a former GOP president of the Florida Senate, cautions officials against reading too much into what they hear through social media. "I tell my members, just because you get a tweet or an e-mail doesn't mean your whole district is concerned about something," he says.[62] And even multiple e-mails might be the work of just one or two individuals using multiple aliases.

Cities are starting to move away from the old model of holding public hearings, where members of the public show up at a certain time and place to offer their opinions about projects and policies. Surveying citizens by mail or online can yield greater feedback than sparsely attended hearings. St. Paul, Minnesota, for instance, has been using its Open St. Paul site to gauge citizen sentiment on bringing streetcars back to the city and to solicit thoughts on how to make its recycling program more effective. Austin has developed "meetings in a box" that allow groups in the community to use their own meetings to discuss questions that planners wanted asked. The city worked with African American pastors and the Asian Chamber of Commerce, and took out ads on Spanish-language television network Univision to attract participants who didn't usually show up at official city gatherings. The city also used social media to reach younger residents and developed an online site, SpeakUpAustin, to solicit ideas and encourage public feedback on them. More than 18,000 people wound up getting involved in the development of the city's latest comprehensive plan.

A survey of local officials in California in 2013 found something of a participation paradox. Fully 88 percent of respondents said that the public has "ample opportunity" to participate in local decision making—but a vast majority also believed the public to be too busy to participate, too disengaged or ignorant to understand the issues facing their communities, and too angry and distrustful of local officials to be reliable partners.[63] This disconnect is the result of the fact that public officials typically end up hearing—a lot—from a relatively small number of people, often those with a narrow agenda or those accustomed to complaining. On most issues, state legislators and city officials do not hear from any constituents at all. A few high-profile concerns, such as tax increases or the legalization of casino gambling, may lead a newspaper or an interested party to conduct a statewide poll, but even on the rare occasions when polls on state issues are conducted, the resulting data are not broken down by legislative district. Given their lack of specific information about how constituents view particular areas, public officials have to rely on a series of clues.

Some political scientists have taken data from various nationwide polls, broken them down by state, and analyzed how well elected officials have reflected the general ideologies and desires of the public in their states.[64] What they have found is that average state opinion does seem to be reflected in the policy decisions made in individual states. What does *average state opinion* mean? It encompasses the types of things we discussed earlier in regard to Elazar's classifications of the states. Some states tend to be more liberal overall, whereas others are more conservative. The average citizen's desires—whether in a conservative state such as Texas or a more progressive one such as Vermont—tend to be pretty well reflected by state laws on issues from restrictions on abortion services to welfare spending, the death penalty, environmental protections, and gay rights.[65]

> For one thing, elected officials devote an enormous amount of time to trying to gauge how opinion is running in their districts. They may not hear from constituents on every issue, but they pay close attention to those concerns that are registered through letters and phone calls.

How does this happen? For one thing, elected officials devote an enormous amount of time to trying to gauge how opinion is running in their districts. They may not hear from constituents on every issue, but they pay close attention to those concerns that are registered through letters and phone calls. They go out and seek opinions by attending religious services and civic events where they can hear the concerns of constituents directly.

They use surrogates—such as newspaper articles and interest groups—as ways of determining what is on their constituents' minds. Susan Herbst, executive vice chancellor and chief academic officer for the University System of Georgia, spent some time earlier in her career hanging out with legislators in Springfield, Illinois. She found that the media were important in shaping public opinion by giving a voice to average people in their stories. The media also shaped the terms of debate. Herbst noted that people in the capital thought that lobbyists often provided good indicators of how people felt about an issue: "Staffers seem to think that the nuances and intensity of public opinion are best captured in the communications of interest groups."[66] More recently, political scientists at the University of Minnesota have found that media coverage of debates among political elites—those most directly engaged in actual legislative debates, such as trade associations—does help shape mass public opinion on issues.[67]

This is not to say that using interest groups as surrogates can't be misleading sometimes. The National Rifle Association, for example, may call on its state members to send letters to legislators in numbers that dwarf those mustered by gun control advocates—even in places where a majority favors gun control. "Intense minorities can come off potentially sounding like majorities when in fact they're not," says Illinois Wesleyan University political scientist Greg Shaw.[68] Legislators like to think that they have a pretty good sense of whether a mail-writing campaign has sprung up spontaneously or shows signs of having been organized—multiple participants signing their names to the same form letter, for example—but sometimes this is easier said than done. Nowadays, someone actually taking the time to write and mail in a letter—as opposed to tweeting or leaving an angry comment on a Facebook page—will have a disproportionate impact just because old-fashioned letters have become unusual.

Formal interest groups do not represent every constituent. Some people may favor environmental protection but not give money to the Sierra Club or the World Wildlife Fund. Some older people actually resist invitations to join AARP at cheap rates. Still, legislators do gain some sense of how active such groups are in their states and whether they seem to have favorable support at home. A lot of this is inexact, but legislators learn from talking to people whether their constituents are most upset about crime or transportation problems. They are convinced that if they vote for things that voters

Elected officials do not just have to address the issues they campaigned on, respond to views expressed at the ballot box, deal with the demands of special interest groups, and be attentive to the expectations of political parties; they also have to be prepared to deal with the unexpected. Wildfires on the West Coast are a recurring hazard, and other kinds of emergencies, natural and otherwise, happen all the time.

broadly support, such as mandatory sentencing guidelines for drug offenders or limits on welfare benefits, they will be rewarded politically.

Conversely, a legislator's major fear is of being punished politically. Failure to get reelected can be the death knell of a political career. It is important to note, however, that if legislators or governors did not broadly reflect the wishes of the populace that elected them, they would never have won their positions in the first place. In this age of computer-assisted **redistricting**, legislative districts in particular are shaped according to the local political culture, which tends to lean in one ideological direction. Ninety times out of a hundred, a liberal is not going to get elected to a conservative district.

Once elected, legislators who want to get reelected are careful not to stray too far from the public opinion in their districts, as best as they can perceive it. They cannot know what the public opinion is about the specifics of every bill, but the fact that not every individual is paying close attention to state politics does not mean that legislators can do

whatever they want. Political officials recognize that lobbyists and other interested parties are watching their voting records carefully and can use such information against them, if necessary. "Legislators aren't worried about what their constituents know—they are worried about what an opponent might do with their record in the next election," says Paul Brace, a Rice University political scientist. They act, therefore, as if there is someone or some group out there who has a chance of using a potentially unpopular record against them. "Legislation is written in minutiae, but you know if you vote for it, you'll get an opponent who can dumb it down and use it against you in the next election, and you won't do it."[69]

Some states offer less opportunity for using a politician's record against him or her. In a moralistic state such as Minnesota, there are more daily newspapers paying close attention to state policy matters than in, say, individualistic Wyoming. There are more public interest groups and state-level think tanks closely monitoring St. Paul than there are monitoring Cheyenne. Citizens in states with higher levels of civic engagement are more likely to keep their politicians "honest"—reflecting voters' overall policy desires—than are citizens in less engaged states.

In a state such as Idaho or Maryland, one party so completely dominates state politics that only rarely are politicians voted out of office because their records do not reflect public opinion. But even Idaho Republicans or Maryland Democrats

---

Redistricting
The drawing of new boundaries for congressional and state legislative districts, usually following a decennial census

can lose—if only in the party primary—if voters sour on their records. Every state capital has engendered enough of an echo chamber that examines and discusses the work of legislators and other elected officials that an overall sense of their records—conservative or liberal, sellout or crusading—is known to people who care enough about politics to vote. If those records do not reflect local opinion, the jobs will go to other candidates in the next election.

Conclusion

This is a highly partisan era, with little civility or cooperation, it seems, between Republicans and Democrats. But the war between the red and the blue will never be as heated as the war between the blue and the gray—the North and the South during the Civil War. Although voters today are divided, they are not as deeply divided as they have been at other moments in the country's past, such as during the Civil War or at the time of the Watergate scandal.

This fact is reflected in the recent series of contentious but ultimately narrowly won presidential contests, and on down through other levels of government. As with Congress and the Electoral College, state legislatures have been closely divided, with the two main parties switching leads in total number of seats nationwide throughout the early 21st century. The lead among governorships has switched around, too, with Republicans currently up.

The outcomes of recent elections reflect the divided public mood. State and local officials have less ability to control who participates in the political process because of the many changes in voting laws passed at the federal level. They do still maintain a lot of control over whom citizens can vote for through their regulation of political parties and their ability to decide who deserves to get their names on the ballot.

Which state officials citizens get to vote for differs depending on where the citizens live. In most states, citizens vote for several statewide officials such as governor, attorney general, and secretary of state. In others, they might vote for little more than the governor. Similarly, in some localities citizens elect the mayor directly, whereas in others the mayor is chosen by the city council from among its own membership. Some states allow people to vote directly for judges, while in other states judges are appointed to office. Some localities allow residents to vote for school board members; in others, these positions are appointed.

In general, citizens vote for enough officeholders with the authority to control policies that the majority's will becomes law. However, because polling is done far more often at the national level than at the local or even the state level, officeholders sometimes have only an anecdotal sense of what their constituents are thinking. They do pay close attention to the clues they are given and monitor opinion as closely as they can. They are well aware that if they do not create the types of policies that most people want, they are not going to stay in office for long.

The Latest Research

This chapter has explained in some depth the role of state and local governments in structuring elections. As discussed above, what citizens need to do to register to vote, where they vote, when they vote, and the mechanics of how they vote are largely decisions made by state and local governments. States have differences on all these matters, and it should come as no surprise after reading this chapter that these differences make a difference. Tougher registration requirements, for example, tend to result in lower voter turnout.

(Continued)

(Continued)

The studies discussed below represent some of the latest research on how the basic mechanics of elections—for example, deciding what type of ballot to use or where to set up polling stations—can have big impacts on electoral participation. The common theme here is that how states decide to regulate elections is one of the most important, and often overlooked, influences on political participation in local, state, and federal elections.

• •

- **Ahler, Douglas J., Jack Citrin, and Gabriel S. Lenz.** "Do Open Primaries Help Moderate Candidates? An Experimental Test on the 2012 California Primary." Presented at the annual meeting of the Western Political Science Association, Los Angeles, CA, March 28–30, 2013. wpsa.research .pdx.edu/papers/docs/ahlercitrinandlenz.pdf.

In a highly partisan era marked by little cooperation between the parties at the federal or state level, some politicians and advocacy groups are pushing to enact changes in election law that might promote more moderate or centrist candidates. A number of studies have shown, however, that such changes in rules or regulations might have limited effect. This study, for instance, is based on a survey of nearly 5,000 California voters. It found that the state's primary system, in which the top two vote-getters advance to the general election regardless of party affiliation, is not helping elect more moderates to Congress or the state Senate. Voters don't seem to have enough information to distinguish properly between the platforms of extreme and more moderate candidates. Even when the top two finishers were from the same party, there were examples in 2012 of voters preferring the more ideological candidate of the pair.

- **Anzia, Sarah F.** *Timing and Turnout: How Off-Cycle Elections Favor Organized Groups.* Chicago, IL: University of Chicago Press, 2014.

Many municipal elections are held in odd-numbered years, with fewer voters turning out when there are not major races for offices such as governor or president on the ballot. As a result, organized interest groups such as unions or municipal workers are often able to mobilize disproportionate support for candidates of their choice. Members of interest groups with a large stake in an election outcome turn out at high rates regardless of election timing, and their efforts to mobilize and persuade voters have a greater impact when turnout is low. That both helps unions push for advantageous labor terms and helps industries that do business with local government keep contract-granting friends in power. Anzia finds, for instance, that school districts that hold off-cycle elections pay experienced teachers 3 percent more than do districts that hold on-cycle elections.

- **Herrnson, Paul, Michael Hanmer, and Richard Niemi.** "The Impact of Ballot Type on Voter Errors." *American Journal of Political Science* 56 (2012): 716–730.

This study examines how ballot format and type of voting system (paper or electronic) influence voter error. Specifically, the researchers examined two types of error: (1) wrong-candidate error, which happens when a voter mistakenly casts a ballot for the wrong candidate, and (2) unintentional undervoting, which happens when a voter plans to cast a ballot for a particular elective office but does not. They found that there was not much difference in these sorts of errors across voting systems (paper ballots had a slightly higher error rate); however, there was a big difference between standard office group (Massachusetts) ballots and ballots that offered the option of voting a straight ticket. The straight-ticket option led to significantly more errors. For example, voters in elections using ballots with this option were more likely not to vote in nonpartisan races they had intended to vote in (such races would not be included in a straight-ticket option), and, more disturbing, they were more likely to vote unintentionally for the wrong candidate. The error rate was small, generally less than 5 percent, but it was still enough to make a difference in an election, at least in theory.

- **Hood, M. V., III, and Charles Bullock III.** "Much Ado About Nothing? An Empirical Assessment of the Georgia Voter Identification Statute." *State Politics & Policy Quarterly* 12 (2012): 393–414.

As discussed above, among the more controversial reforms of voting regulations in recent years has been the decision by some states to require voters to provide proof of identification before casting ballots. Opponents of these laws worry that they will suppress turnout, especially among certain disadvantaged (particularly racial minority) groups who are less likely to have government-approved IDs such as driver's licenses. This study examines the impact of Georgia's decision to implement a voter ID law beginning in 2007. The researchers did not find that the new law suppressed turnout in any particular racial demographic. However, they did find that the law reduced voter turnout, although not by much; the new regulation was associated with a decrease in turnout of less than half a percentage point.

Chapter Review

Key Concepts

- blanket primary (p. 128)
- nonpartisan election (p. 133)
- office group (Massachusetts) ballot (p. 124)
- party column (Indiana) ballot (p. 124)
- plurality (p. 120)
- recall (p. 144)
- redistricting (p. 148)
- secret (Australian) ballot (p. 126)
- straight ticket (p. 124)
- voter turnout (p. 130)

Suggested Websites

- **fairvote.org.** Website of the Center for Voting and Democracy, which promotes voting and advocates instant-runoff voting and the abolition of the Electoral College.

- **www.lwv.org.** Website of the League of Women Voters. Provides a wealth of voter education information.

- **www.nass.org.** Website of the National Association of Secretaries of State. Secretaries of state typically serve as chief election officials, and their offices have primary responsibility for recording official election outcomes.

- **www.people-press.org.** Website of the Pew Research Center for the People & the Press, which conducts surveys and publishes studies that look at the demographic trends affecting politics.

State Stats on Political Attitudes and Participation

Explore and compare data on the states! Go to edge.sagepub.com/ smithgreenblatt5e to do these exercises.

1. Considering the historical support of African Americans for one political party over the other, if you were running for president as a Democrat, would you be more likely to win in Michigan or West Virginia? Why?

2. If voters in lower income-brackets are less likely to vote than their richer counterparts are, would you expect to see higher voter turnout in Texas or Utah? Why?

3. What is South Dakota's per capita expenditure on welfare programs? What is Maine's? What political variables might account for such a big difference between the two states?

4. The chapter notes that government leadership is not nearly as white and Protestant as it used to be. How did the percentage of the population in your state that is white change between 2000 and 2010? What (if anything) does this mean for politics?

5. Which states have the largest percentage of the population who are marijuana users? How does this correlate with the results of the recent election that legalized marijuana for recreational use in two states? If this trend continued, which states might we expect to see legalize marijuana next? Why?

6. How many legal immigrants were admitted to Florida in 1997? How do you expect that this may have changed the political landscape?

Once seen as a fringe cause, legalization of marijuana use won voter approval in two states in 2012. But demonstrators such as Joe Tremolada in Oakland, California, are still protesting federal enforcement of drug laws.

Parties and Interest Groups

ELEPHANTS, DONKEYS, AND CASH COWS

- Why are political parties weaker than they used to be?
- Why are political parties stronger in some states than in others?
- How do interest groups influence policymakers?

mericans for Prosperity (AFP) has spent millions of dollars in recent years airing television ads critical of Democratic candidates. In 2014, it expanded its efforts to persuade and mobilize voters where they live, keeping a lineup of paid staffers on the ground in no fewer than 33 states. In some places where the group is particularly active, AFP made its presence felt even more dramatically—for example, operating six separate field offices in Iowa alone.

All these activities make AFP sound kind of like a **political party**. Certainly it was seeking to excite its members and casual voters about issues such as lowering taxes, something that political parties also do. But it's not a party. The organization, largely funded by Charles and David Koch—brothers who run Koch Industries, a privately-owned oil services and consumer goods company—is a tax-exempt social welfare organization, forbidden from

---

Political party
Organization that nominates and supports candidates for elected offices

After reading this chapter, you will be able to

- describe the role of political parties in the U.S. political process and government from the 1920s to 1940s,
- compare why some states are more politically competitive than others,
- identify the ways political parties are subject to regulation,
- explain the role of third parties and independents in the political process, and
- discuss the ways interest groups and lobbies influence politics.

explicitly endorsing candidates in the way a party would. Tim Phillips, the president of AFP, says his group pushes issues rather than individual candidates. But he acknowledges that they have a similar mission. "We seek to build a long-term infrastructure, with full-time staff, with strong local knowledge, that goes out and recruits volunteer activists from all walks of life, to help deliver our message and set the tone in a community or in the state."[1]

AFP is a good example of how in today's politics the line between political parties and interest groups—individuals, corporations, or associations that seek to influence the actions of elected and appointed public officials on behalf of specific companies or causes—is becoming increasingly blurred. Historically, political parties have helped select, groom, and promote candidates, who took positions that were largely aligned with their parties' platforms. Today, candidates at both the state and federal level may end up relying more heavily, for financial support at least, on outside interest groups. Such a group may have a broad political agenda that closely mirrors that of a party—helping support and elect more Republicans, for instance—or it may be more concerned with a single issue, such as protecting the environment or keeping taxes low. In either event, political parties—and candidates themselves—have less control over the political agenda than they did even a few years ago, simply because campaign finance is now structured in such a way as to make interest groups more influential. The reason is simple: Candidates and parties need the

money. More than $2 billion is spent on state-level races during every 2-year election cycle. And interest groups themselves are acting more like parties did in the past, helping recruit candidates as well as supporting them financially once they decide to run.

Business and labor groups have long played major roles in politics, protecting their interests by finding and supporting sympathetic allies. But now they have pretty much taken matters into their own hands. The Supreme Court has lifted most limits on political spending by entities such as corporations. Wealthy individuals such as the Koch brothers and Tom Steyer, a hedge-fund billionaire concerned with environmental causes, are pursuing their own agendas, spending millions to support causes and candidates near and dear to their hearts. Michael Bloomberg, the media mogul and former New York mayor, has funded a group to promote gun control. Facebook founder Mark Zuckerberg and other tech titans have launched an advocacy group pushing changes to immigration law. The list goes on and on. "Everywhere you look these days," a *National Journal* correspondent noted in 2014, "wealthy donors are . . . taking a DIY approach to their political activism."[2]

Individual donors or campaign committees known as super PACs are mostly working to support candidates who run under the Democratic or Republican banners. With so much money and organizational talent now outside of their control, parties enjoy much less sway over American political operations than they once did. Aside from having no monopoly over mechanics such

Interest groups
Individuals, corporations, or associations that seek to influence the actions of elected and appointed public officials on behalf of specific companies or causes

Super PACs
Political action committees that can spend unlimited funds on behalf of political candidates but cannot directly coordinate their plans with those candidates

as efforts to get out the vote, the parties can impose less discipline when it comes to stances on issues. Candidates don't have to fear being cut off from party funds and regular donors if they know some billionaire might be willing to underwrite their efforts. That has been especially apparent in recent years on the Republican side, where conservative groups such as AFP and Club for Growth, along with grassroots supporters of the Tea Party, have routinely challenged incumbents and other so-called **establishment** candidates, backed by traditional GOP business interests, in Republican **primary elections**.

All this has led to complaints from old party regulars that politics has become an undisciplined free-for-all. Super PACs are not allowed to coordinate their messages directly with candidates, but sometimes these organizations are run by close allies of candidates, such as former aides. Other times, they have no connection to candidates at all—which leads some observers to worry that such groups can push their own issues and end up dominating the political conversation. Candidates can end up feeling like bystanders to their own campaigns, their efforts at shaping and spreading messages minimized as outside groups spend far more money. Some have complained even about super PAC spending that offered support, saying that they get the blame for, say, negative advertising over which they have no control. "It's one of the major problems with the current campaign finance system," said Democratic consultant Jeff Link. "A candidate is no longer the loudest speaker in his or her own campaign."[3]

In addition to super PACs, so-called dark money groups—organizations whose purposes are nominally educational and are able to spend freely in political campaigns without disclosing their donors—play an increasingly large role in American politics. In the congressional elections of 2014, 55 percent of the money spent by outside groups on broadcast advertisements was paid for by organizations that disclose little or nothing about their donors, compared with 45 percent by super PACs, which file regular disclosure forms with the Federal Election Commission.[4] In the Kansas governor's race in 2014, $3.3 million of the $6.3 million spent on ads a month ahead of the election had been paid for by nondisclosing groups.[5]

Despite all this change, parties still have an important role to play—arguably more important than their role a generation ago. After all, the parties retain strong advantages when it comes to securing spots on ballots. These days, they also serve as strong brand identifiers, letting voters know whether a candidate likely takes a conservative or liberal line on most issues. Parties are less hierarchical now and more of a network than they've ever been, University of Denver political scientist Seth Masket concluded in 2014. "The two-party system is about as strong as it's ever been," Masket wrote. "Any candidate who wants to have even a chance at achieving office has to pick one of the two major parties to run with, and any policy idea needs an affiliation with at least one major party in order to become a law."[6]

This chapter explores the roles political parties play and how those vary by state, as well as the influence of interest groups, not only on elections but also on governance.

A Primer on Political Parties

Political parties are not as dominant in American life as they once were. From roughly the 1820s until the 1940s, political parties constituted a leading organizing force in this country. They not only provided citizens with political identities but also were major sources of social activity and entertainment—and, in many cases, jobs. Today, parties are not as effective as they used to be at getting people out to vote or even at organizing them around an issue. However, they do remain important to candidates, giving them a kind of brand identification and acting as fundraisers.

Establishment
The nexus of people holding power over an extended period of time, including top elected officials, lobbyists, and party strategists

Primary elections
Elections that determine a party's nominees for offices in general elections against other parties' nominees

Although there are two major national parties, the party organizations play larger roles at the state level than they do as national forces. Their respective strength varies widely from state to state and is affected by such factors as the different ways states regulate parties, the differences in the historical roles parties have played within each state, and the amount of competition between the major parties within a given state. In general, the more closely balanced the two main parties are in a state, the more likely that they will have well-funded and well-organized state-level party organizations.

Political parties recruit candidates for offices and provide them with support for their campaigns. They give candidates money or help them raise it and offer logistical and strategic assistance. Just as important, they help coordinate the candidates' messages with those of other candidates running for other offices under the party's banner.

Since the 1850s, the vast majority of candidates for political office in the United States have run as members of either the Democratic or the Republican Party. The Democratic Party as we know it today evolved from **factional splits** in the earliest days of the American republic. The country started without a two-party system, but **factions** soon developed. The Federalists, led by Alexander Hamilton, favored a strong central government with power rooted in the industrial North. The Democratic-Republicans, led by Thomas Jefferson, emerged as the party opposing the Federalists. They argued for states' rights against a "monarchical" rule by the aristocracy and declared that farmers, craftspeople, and shopkeepers should control their own interests without interference from the capitol.

Jefferson's party, which eventually morphed into the Democratic Party, dominated politics throughout the first half of the 19th century. That same period saw the creation of numerous parties: Whigs, Know-Nothings, Barnburners, Softshells, Hunkers, and Free Soilers. They all had some success, but the Democratic Party of Jefferson and Andrew Jackson dominated so completely that, as the main source of political power, the party split into factions, with northern and southern Democrats arguing over the expansion of slavery. That argument created an opening for a new major party.

The Republican Party was formed in 1854 in opposition to slavery. It soon replaced the Whig Party, which had been formed in 1834 to protest the spoils-system politics of Jackson. The Republican Party, also known as the Grand Old Party (GOP), quickly enjoyed congressional success. Following the election of Abraham Lincoln in 1860, Republicans dominated the presidency for decades to come. Their antislavery stance, however, guaranteed that the party remained practically nonexistent in the South until the civil rights era of the 1950s and 1960s. Democrats reemerged as the nation's dominant party in the 1930s, when Republicans took the blame for the Great Depression. The Democrats' New Deal coalition of southerners, union workers, African Americans, the poor, and the elderly drove American politics well into the 1960s but fragmented after that, resulting in a loss of political control.

Long-standing Democratic majorities at the congressional and state levels eroded. Republicans dominated presidential elections from 1968 through 1988, winning five out of the six contests. Since then, however, Democrats have met with more success, carrying the popular vote five of six times. But national elections are still highly competitive. In 2004, Republican George W. Bush became the first presidential candidate since 1988 to win a majority—51 percent—of the popular vote. (He had prevailed in the Electoral College 4 years earlier, despite trailing in the national popular vote count by 500,000 votes.) In 2012, Democrat Barack Obama won reelection with 51 percent of the vote—down from 53 percent in 2008, making him just the third president in U.S. history to have been reelected with a smaller share of the vote than he received during his initial election. (The other two were Franklin D. Roosevelt, whose winning percentage ticked down in both 1940 and 1944, and Jackson, who took less of the popular vote in 1832.) The narrow

---

Factional splits or factions
Groups that struggle to control the message within a party; for example, a party may be split into competing regional factions

margins of presidential victories suggest that, at least at the national level, the two major political parties have spent more than a decade at roughly equal strength.

It is no secret that contemporary politics is highly competitive. Neither side enjoys a consistent advantage nationally. Candidates from either party are capable of winning statewide offices in most states. Overall support for the parties is, however, split along regional lines. Democrats enjoy more support along the West Coast and in the Northeast, whereas Republicans are dominant in the South and the Plains states. The upper Midwest and parts of the Mountain West such as Colorado and Nevada have become the most competitive regions.

Although most Americans are familiar with the Republican and Democratic parties, many may not realize that political parties technically take many different shapes. When people refer to Democrats or Republicans, they are really referring to officials belonging to two umbrella groups that cover a wide variety of parties. Each of the national parties is in reality a consortium of state parties. Party chairs and other representatives from the state parties dominate the national party committees. State parties, in turn, are consortia of local parties. In some states local parties are defined by counties, whereas in others they are defined by congressional districts. Although both the Democratic and Republican parties are active in every state, some state and local parties are more active than others. Parties in densely populated states such as Florida and California are well-funded, professionally run organizations. In less populated states such as Montana and Idaho, the parties have very small full-time staffs and take on more personnel just during the few months leading up to an election.

A given state may have a particularly dominant political party, but overall, the political parties in most of the world's other Western-style democracies are much stronger than those in the United States. For example, in the United States, party leaders are not able to nominate candidates of their own choosing. Most candidates are now chosen directly by the voting public through primaries. In fact, even a party's top nominee—its presidential candidate—may not have been the first choice of party leaders. This is much different from the way party politics operates in, say, Great Britain. There, political parties are much more centralized. Leadership within a party translates more cleanly into leadership in government. The parties, not voters, select the parties' nominees for the office of prime minister.

In the United States, the national Republican and Democratic parties essentially are made up of state parties. The Republican and Democratic national committees are made up almost exclusively of state party chairs and one male and one female representative from each state. Representatives from the territories—Puerto Rico, Guam, and the U.S. Virgin Islands, among others—form the rest of the body for each party. U.S. political parties tend to be regulated at the state level. The ways they raise and spend money, their organizational structures, and the rules they follow to nominate candidates and place them on ballots are all subject to differing state regulations. How much power the national parties have in relation to the state parties shifts over time, as we will see.

> In an era of polarization, in which party loyalties are strongly divided, it's not too strong to say that many Americans not only disagree with but hate the viewpoints of the "other" party.

That is not to say that parties are not collections of interests. Parties are conglomerations of people who share some overlapping ideology, or set of political, economic, and social beliefs. These days, Democrats are supported by pro-choice groups, same-sex marriage proponents, and gun control advocates. Environmentalists, trial lawyers, labor union members, Hispanics, Asian Americans, and African Americans also tend to be Democrats. Republicans gain support from corporate and small businesses and from social conservatives. Party members tend to advocate respect for limited government, private property, and protection of rights for gun owners. Republicans are also more likely than Democrats to attend church regularly. In an era of **polarization**, in which party loyalties are strongly divided, it's not too strong to say that many Americans not only disagree with but hate the viewpoints of the "other" party. Political reporters have delighted in recent years in playing at being pop sociologists and pointing out the differences between adherents to the two parties in everything from favorite baby names to beer preferences. Over the past 50 years, the percentage of people who said they'd be upset if their children married someone from the other party has jumped from 5 percent to 40 percent.[7]

If the partisans on either side are more divided, it's not necessarily the case that parties are able to stifle internal divisions within their own ranks. After Ronald Reagan and other Republicans chipped into Democratic support among certain groups in the New Deal coalition, the Democrats became a famously argumentative group, with various factions within the party struggling to find common cause with one another. As recently as 2006, a Democratic strategist wrote about "the Democratic Party's well-deserved reputation for being a fractious coalition of infighting special interests."[8] But following their poor showing in that year's elections, Republicans began to argue more loudly among themselves about which ideas should prevail within the party—a fractious debate that continued through and after the party's losing presidential campaigns in 2008 and 2012. Conservative, populist, so-called Tea Party groups began holding large rallies in 2009 to decry big government, President Obama's administration, and their more moderate counterparts within the Republican Party. "There is clearly a war going on in the Republican Party," Bob Smith, a Republican and former U.S. senator from New Hampshire, said. "The sooner the party's leadership recognizes that, the better off they'll be."[9] As noted earlier, Tea Party–backed insurgents and establishment candidates have continued to square

off in search of GOP support. In 2014, the establishment candidates mostly won, but they did so by co-opting the issue stances of the Tea Party.

Political parties, however, remain different from other groups that participate in the political process, including interest groups. A political candidate runs under a single party label, such as Republican, Democratic, or Green. The candidate campaigns for office and is nominated as a member of that party. In contrast to political parties, an interest group may support a candidate, but that person's candidacy is not based on affiliation with the group. The interest group, in fact, might be supporting candidates from several parties. Increasingly, however, politically engaged interest groups tend to be associated with one party or another.

Candidates still may rely on parties to serve as conduits to interest groups and voters, but the importance of parties to individual candidates has not been as great recently as in the past. Academics have noted a shift to **candidate-centered politics** over the past 30 years or so. What this means is that parties play less of a role in determining who is going to run for which office. Instead, candidates, in effect, select themselves. Ambitious people interested in politics and government run for the offices of their choice rather than working their way up the party ranks in roles their parties might have chosen for them. Arnold Schwarzenegger decided in 2003 to suspend his acting career to run for governor of California and won the support of the state's Republican Party. In the old days, a party's gubernatorial candidate first would have had to put in years in lower offices. He or she would have had to earn the support of party leaders throughout the state before running for the state's highest office. Today, upstarts may well decide to run against initially better-known candidates with party support. For example, Republican Ted Cruz came seemingly out of nowhere to defeat Lieutenant Governor David Dewhurst in the 2012 Texas GOP Senate primary. Then Republican Dan Patrick prevailed over Dewhurst as he sought reelection in 2014.

Cruz, Patrick, and plenty of other insurgent candidates have given party elders lots of headaches in

---

Polarization
A split among elected officials or an electorate along strictly partisan lines

Candidate-centered politics
Politics in which candidates promote themselves and their own campaigns rather than relying on party organizations

recent years, but they still identify themselves as Republicans. Some Tea Party members describe themselves as conservatives or libertarians but insist that they are not Republicans. For potential officeholders, however, there's little choice but to maintain allegiance to the GOP. Throughout American history, the major parties have proven adept at embracing popular ideas presented by outsiders or third-party candidates. Democratic and Republican candidates in the 1990s took the idea of a balanced federal budget more seriously because third-party challenger Ross Perot had raised the issue. During the 1930s, Franklin D. Roosevelt lifted many of the ideas of Socialist candidate Norman Thomas. When faced with the rare strong minor-party challenge, a major-party candidate can argue that he or she offers the best vehicle for presenting any shared ideals—and stands a better chance of beating the other major-party candidate. Perot's 1992 showing was the best by a third-party candidate since Theodore Roosevelt's in 1912—and neither one of them came close to winning.

The parties not only provide an important way for candidates to identify themselves but are central to governance. However important interest group spending is during an election, parties remain the primary mechanisms for the organization of government. Except for Nebraska, which is nonpartisan, all state legislatures are organized by party. If Democrats have a majority of the seats in the Maine House of Representatives, for example, the Speaker and other top leaders will be Democrats and the party will control each committee as well. As a theoretical ideal, political scientists use the **responsible party model** as a way to measure and assess political parties. The responsible party model holds that political parties should present clear policy options to voters, that voters will cast ballots based on the options they favor the most, that while in office parties try to create and implement the programs they promise,

---

Responsible party model
The theory that political parties offer clear policy choices to voters, try to deliver on those policies when they take office, and are held accountable by voters for the success or failure of those policies

and that in the next election the parties will be judged by their performance in delivering those programs. In short, this model views political parties as connecting the wishes of citizens to government programs and policies, organizing the government to deliver on those wishes, and acting as agents to hold government accountable for delivering on what it promises.

Today, with different factions fighting one another for prominence and power, this concept remains important. During a fight between more moderate Republicans and more conservative Republicans for control of the Kansas Senate in 2012 primary contests, the balance was tipped toward conservatives thanks to more than $8 million spent by groups such as Americans for Prosperity, the Club for Growth, the Kansas Chamber of Commerce, and Kansas Right to Life.[10] The moderates sought their revenge during the next election, with more than 100 moderate Republicans endorsing Democrat Paul Davis's 2014 challenge against GOP governor Sam Brownback. Such an open factional split within a party is unusual, but it demonstrated the importance of the party label. People unhappy with the GOP's conservative drift could vote against Republican candidates during the next election. Although prominent donors such as the Koch brothers and George Soros have become targets in their own right, it's not possible for voters to try to oust their favored candidates in the same way they can choose to vote against Republicans or Democrats. Many of the super PACs that are most active in one election cycle might not even be around a few years later.

That fact—as well as the way a small number of individuals have come to dominate campaign spending (fewer than 200 donors made up 80 percent of super PAC spending in 2012)—has led some to worry that American democracy is at risk of being hijacked. For a study published in 2014, Martin Gilens and Benjamin I. Page analyzed 1,800 policy issues and found that "when the preferences of economic elites and the stands of organized interest groups are controlled for, the preferences of the average American appear to have only a minuscule, near-zero, statistically non-significant impact upon public policy."[11]

FIGURE 6-1

HOW IT WORKS

Democratic and Republican Party Organization in Ohio and Cuyahoga County

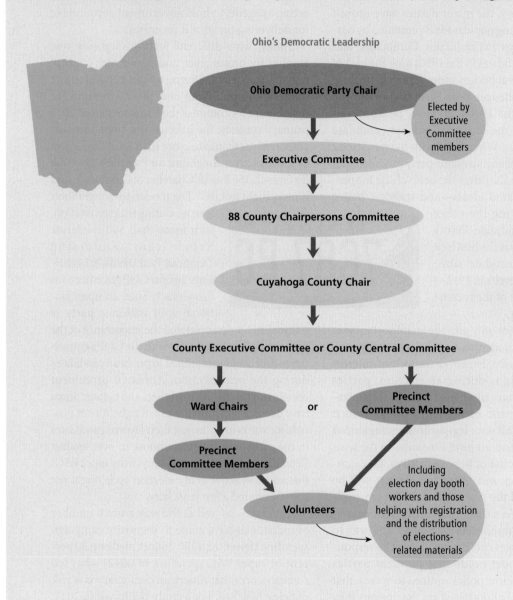

Ohio's Democratic Leadership

Ohio Democratic Party Chair — Elected by Executive Committee members

Executive Committee

88 County Chairpersons Committee

Cuyahoga County Chair

County Executive Committee or County Central Committee

Ward Chairs or **Precinct Committee Members**

Precinct Committee Members

Volunteers — Including election day booth workers and those helping with registration and the distribution of elections-related materials

---

Not everyone believes that the situation is so dire. Politicians are highly attuned to the wishes of voters, as measured by opinion polls and other means. But many people are concerned about how much money is flooding into politics these days, exacerbating perennial concerns about whether the political game is rigged in favor of moneyed interests.

What Parties Were Like

Parties remain important organizers, and party identification offers voters a handy shortcut when it comes to figuring out where candidates are likely to stand on various issues. In their early years, political parties in the United States

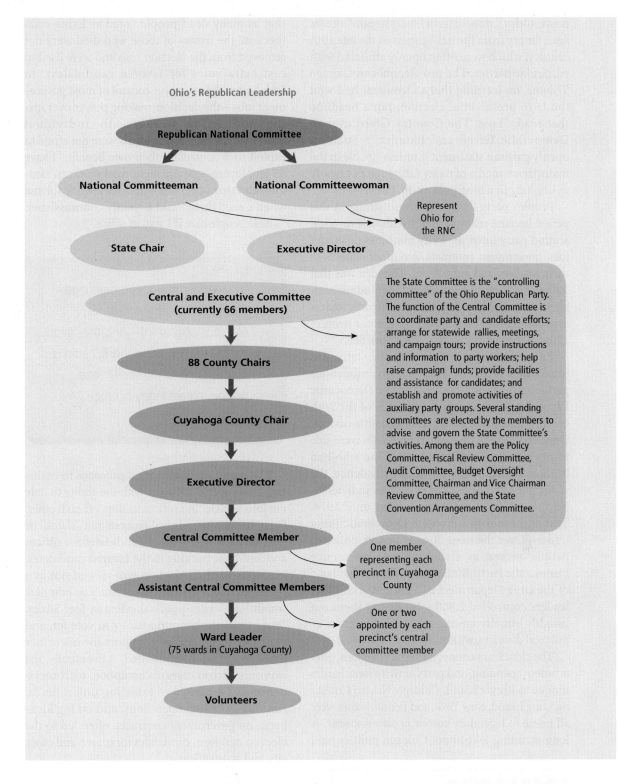

Ohio's Republican Leadership

Republican National Committee

National Committeeman

National Committeewoman

Represent Ohio for the RNC

State Chair

Executive Director

Central and Executive Committee (currently 66 members)

The State Committee is the "controlling committee" of the Ohio Republican Party. The function of the Central Committee is to coordinate party and candidate efforts; arrange for statewide rallies, meetings, and campaign tours; provide instructions and information to party workers; help raise campaign funds; provide facilities and assistance for candidates; and establish and promote activities of auxiliary party groups. Several standing committees are elected by the members to advise and govern the State Committee's activities. Among them are the Policy Committee, Fiscal Review Committee, Audit Committee, Budget Oversight Committee, Chairman and Vice Chairman Review Committee, and the State Convention Arrangements Committee.

88 County Chairs

Cuyahoga County Chair

Executive Director

Central Committee Member

One member representing each precinct in Cuyahoga County

Assistant Central Committee Members

One or two appointed by each precinct's central committee member

Ward Leader
(75 wards in Cuyahoga County)

Volunteers

were a lot more than just brand identifiers and fundraisers. Many of the social services now provided by local governments, such as food assistance and job placement, were the province of political parties throughout much of the 19th century. For all the contemporary complaints about the "liberal media," one-sided bloggers, and the domination of talk radio by conservative hosts, today's nonpartisan "mainstream" media are a far cry from the newspapers of the late 19th century, which were often openly affiliated with particular parties. The pro-Republican *Chicago Tribune,* on learning that a Democrat had won the 1876 presidential election, ran a headline that read, "Lost. The Country Given over to Democratic Greed and Plunder."[12] Such an openly partisan statement is unimaginable in the mainstream media of today (although not nearly as unlikely in a blog post or on Twitter).

People's party loyalties were so strong in this period because many of their livelihoods revolved around party interests. Party machines doled out jobs, government contracts, and other benefits to their workers and supporters. The idea was that "offices exist not as a necessary means of administering government but for the support of party leaders at public expense," as one political scientist wrote of 19th-century party cliques in New York State.[13]

Politics in many cities and some states was totally dominated by these usually indigenous party machines. In Rhode Island, the Democratic Party was dominant through much of the 20th century, and party leaders brooked little dissent. Only a handful of free-agent candidates were able to pry nominations away from those who had been endorsed by the party. In Providence, the state capital and largest city, only three individuals held the office of mayor from 1941 until 1974. Two of those men were state Democratic Party leaders. Over the same 30-year period, only two people served as chairs of the Providence Democratic Party. Both of them doubled as head of the city's Department of Public Works. Party leaders controlled 2,800 jobs, doling them out roughly equally among the various wards, or political districts, within the city.[14]

The close links connecting control of jobs, government spending, and party activity were hardly unique to Rhode Island. Chicago, Nassau County on Long Island, New York, and Pennsylvania were all home to legendary **political or party machines**. A long-standing joke about Chicago politics held that as many dead people voted as living ones (because the names of those who died were not removed from the election rolls and were used to cast extra votes for favored candidates). In Oklahoma, the state gave control of most government jobs—the decision-making power over hiring and firing workers—to individual officeholders. These individuals were not afraid to exploit such control for their own benefit. "I have 85 employees—garage men, road workers, janitors, elevator operators—and they work for me when I need them," said a county commissioner. "These people care if I stay in office."[15]

> "I have 85 employees—garage men, road workers, janitors, elevator operators—and they work for me when I need them," said a county commissioner. "These people care if I stay in office."

The machine system used **patronage** to maintain firm control of power, with the ability to dole out jobs and elective offices feeding off each other. Party machines and rival factions ran "slates," or specific lists, of endorsed candidates for offices and lent their backing to the favored candidates. "Each succeeding election was viewed not as a separate contest involving new issues or new personalities," writes political scientist Joel Sibley, "but as yet another opportunity to vote for, and reaffirm, an individual's support for his or her party and what it represented."[16] Eventually, the exposure of clear cases of corruption, such as evidence that a party was extorting union funds, running gambling operations, and taking kickbacks on government contracts, often led to the election of reform candidates for mayor and other city and state offices.

Political or party machines
Political organizations controlled by small numbers of people and run for partisan ends. In the 19th and 20th centuries, these organizations controlled party nominations for public office and rewarded supporters with government jobs and contracts.

Patronage
The practice of elected officials' or party leaders' handing out jobs to their friends and supporters rather than hiring people based on merit

"To the victor belong the spoils." President Andrew Jackson popularized a system of patronage, insisting that public offices should be filled by supporters of the party in power.

In many states, such as Alabama, Florida, and Michigan, elected officials and party leaders had little opportunity to practice patronage. Therefore, there was little motivation to build up a machine. In some places, such as Texas, 19th-century political parties were weak. They helped administer the election code and tried to remain acceptable to all candidates. In other places, disgust over corruption in politics led to antimachine statutes, such as the imposition of civil service requirements for many government jobs and tougher anticorruption laws. The widespread use of **nonpartisan ballots** for municipal offices was the direct result of reforms imposed in reaction to political machines. These ballots, which do not list candidates by political party, are designed to separate city government from party voting.

California may be the best example of a state that had such a progressive reaction against the machines. The state was hostile toward parties, lacked any type of patronage system, and held nonpartisan elections. Precinct and ward organizations were weak, whereas individual candidates were assertive.[17] Party organizations were once banned from endorsing candidates in primary contests. The law also limited state party chairs to 2-year terms and required the rotation of chairs on a geographical basis every 2 years. In 1989, the U.S. Supreme Court threw out the statute and declared it unconstitutional.[18]

But California was the exception to the rule. Throughout the 1800s, most states essentially treated parties as private associations and chose not to regulate them. This remains the position

CIVIL SERVICE REFORM.

OFFICE-SEEKER. "St. Jackson, can't you save us? Can't *you* give us something?"

Nonpartisan ballots
Ballots that do not list candidates by political party; still often used in local elections

of many other countries today. But during the 20th century, that all changed in the United States. States began to regulate parties as though they were public utilities. Such state regulation of political parties is examined later in this chapter.

Parties in the 20th Century

At the dawn of the 20th century, political machines were generally locally based, and local parties were much more important political actors than were state parties in states where there were powerful big-city machines. Elsewhere, state parties often were funded and controlled by corporate interests—in many cases by just one interest, such as the DuPont Corporation in Delaware or the Anaconda Copper Company in Montana. Following the Progressive Era reforms in states such as California, state parties became little more than empty shells. As late as the 1970s, many state parties lacked permanent headquarters and were run out of their chairs' homes.[19]

State parties lost much of their influence because of the rise of primary elections. In primary elections, voters select the candidates who will represent the parties in **general elections**, the contests between party nominees that decide which candidates will actually win political office. Before primary elections became common, parties picked their nominees through **party conventions**, meetings of a few hundred party officials or supporters. At conventions, party leaders closely controlled most votes and thus had enormous influence over who would or would not become the party's official nominee in the general election. This influence is lost in a primary election; in a primary, members of the general public have the chance to cast secret ballots. This gives party officials less direct control over the nominating process. Some states, such as Virginia, still allow for the option of nominating candidates by party conventions, but every state now has a system in place to nominate candidates through primaries. Every party holds statewide conventions, and many hold conventions at the local or district level as well.

Direct primaries allow rank-and-file voters to choose nominees for public office through means of a direct ballot. This contrasts with the convention system, in which the role of voters is indirect—voters choose delegates to a convention, and the delegates choose the nominee. At the state level, there are three basic types of direct primaries. In a **closed primary**, only registered members of the party holding the primary are allowed to vote, meaning that an individual must be a registered Democrat to vote for the Democratic nominee for office or a registered Republican to vote

for the Republican nominee. This type of primary prevents **crossover voting**, in which a member of one party votes in another party's primary (a Democrat voting in a Republican primary, for instance). This practice is not allowed in all states. In an **open primary**, independents—and in some cases members of both parties—can vote in the primary of any party they choose. In a blanket primary—a type of primary invalidated in 2000 in the U.S. Supreme Court case *California Democratic Party v. Jones*—all candidates from all parties are listed on a single ballot and voters are allowed, in effect, to mix and match the primaries they participate in. That is, a voter could vote in one party's primary for a particular office, then switch to another party's primary for another office. Louisiana holds what is essentially a nonpartisan blanket primary—sometimes called a jungle primary—in which all candidates run in the same primary regardless of party. If no candidate wins an outright majority in the primary, the two top vote-getters—regardless of party—go on to a general election face-off. A **runoff primary** sometimes occurs in some states if no candidate receives a majority of the vote in an initial primary. In that case, the top two candidates face off. Washington State and California voters in recent years have established similar "top-two" primary systems, in which candidates from all parties appear together on a single primary ballot, and the top two finishers, regardless of party, proceed to the general election. Map 6-1 shows a state-by-state breakdown of the main types of primaries.

The opposite of the relative openness of primaries is the "smoke-filled room"—a historic term referring to an area at a convention in which party barons, some puffing on big cigars, would choose

---

General elections
Decisive elections in which all registered voters cast ballots for their preferred candidates for a political office

Party conventions
Meetings of party delegates called to nominate candidates for office and establish party agendas

Closed primary
A nominating election in which only voters belonging to that party may participate. Only registered Democrats can vote in a closed Democratic primary, for example.

Crossover voting
Members of one party voting in another party's primary. This practice is not allowed in all states.

Open primary
A nominating election that is open to all registered voters regardless of their party affiliations

Runoff primary
An election held if no candidate receives a majority of the vote during the regular primary. The two top finishers face off again in a runoff to determine the nominee for the general election. Such elections are held only in some states, primarily in the South.

MAP 6-1

Party Affiliation Requirements for Voting in Direct Primaries, 2012

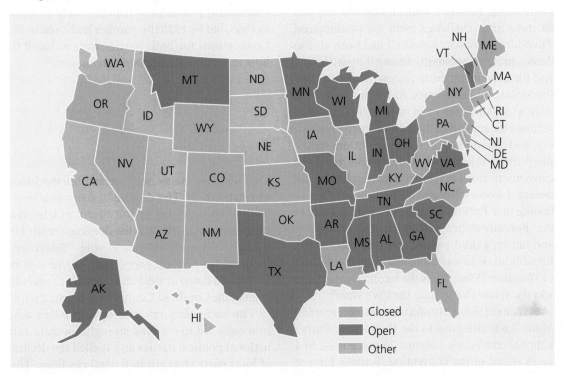

Source: Fair Vote, "Congressional and Presidential Primaries: Open, Closed, Semi-Closed, and 'Top Two,'" February 2012, http://www.fairvote.org/research-and-analysis/presidential-elections/congressional-and-presidential-primaries-open-closed-semi-closed-and-top-two/.

Notes:

Alaska: Closed caucuses for both parties.

California: In 2010, California approved a system in which all candidates compete on the same primary ballot, with the two top finishers, regardless of party, proceeding to the general election.

Idaho: Democrats have a semiclosed caucus, while the Republicans have an open primary.

Iowa: Closed caucuses, but voters may change registration at polls.

Kansas: In the Democratic caucus, independent voters can register as Democrats on caucus day. For Republicans it is a closed caucus.

Louisiana: Primaries are open for congressional elections, as of 2011.

Maryland: Parties can choose to open primaries, but both Democrats and Republicans have chosen not to.

Massachusetts: Registered Democrats and Republicans can vote only for their own party in the primary, but independent voters may decide which party they would like to vote for.

New Hampshire: Closed primaries are in effect, but semiclosed primaries are allowed if a party's rules allow it.

New Jersey: Registered Democrats and Republicans can vote only for their own party in the primary.

North Carolina: A person registered with a party must vote in that party's primary. Unaffiliated voters may choose a party on the day of the primary election.

North Dakota: North Dakota has no voter registration. To vote in the Republican caucus, a citizen must have affiliated with the Republican Party in the last general election or plan to in the next election.

Ohio: A voter must vote in the primary of the same party he or she participated in at the last primary election.

Rhode Island: If voters are registered as "unaffiliated" they may vote in the primary of any party they choose. Once they vote in a primary, however, they are considered a member of that party until and unless they "disaffiliate."

Utah: Currently only Republicans close their primary. Democrats and independents can vote in the Democratic primary. Conventions are held by the political parties prior to the primary.

Virginia: Parties may choose to nominate by convention rather than by primary election.

Washington: The state in 2004 moved to an open, "top-two" primary system, which the Supreme Court upheld in 2008.

West Virginia: Although technically a closed system, all parties allow any voter not registered with an official party to request their ballot for the primary election.

a candidate of their liking. It is one of the classic images in American politics. Examples of such cronyism abound. At the 1912 Republican National Convention, President William Howard Taft had to stave off a challenge from his predecessor, Theodore Roosevelt. Roosevelt had been able to demonstrate his popularity among the party's rank and file by winning every primary that year, save the Massachusetts primary. At the time, however, only a dozen states even held primaries. Taft retained the support of the national party machinery and dominated delegate selection in the nonprimary states. Ultimately, he controlled the convention. Taft was renominated, but he was not reelected. Roosevelt bolted the party, angrily maintaining that Taft's nomination thwarted the will of the "honestly elected majority" of GOP delegates, and ran on a third-party ticket. The split within Republican ranks was enough to allow the election of Woodrow Wilson, only the second Democrat to win the White House since the Civil War.[20]

As late as 1968, party officials selected about 600 of the 2,600 delegates to the Democratic Party's national convention—almost 25 percent—2 to 4 years ahead of the convention. Senator Eugene McCarthy, D-Minn., had made such a surprisingly strong showing in the New Hampshire primary that he drove President Lyndon Johnson from the race. But Johnson's backing was still significant enough to help his vice president, Hubert H. Humphrey, win the support of delegates controlled by party officials. McCarthy believed he had been cheated by the party rules, so he proposed that all delegates to the nominating convention be chosen through "procedures open to public participation" in the same year in which the convention was to take place.[21]

Humphrey recognized that McCarthy and Senator Robert F. Kennedy, D-N.Y., both of whom had campaigned on anti-Vietnam platforms, had taken 69 percent of the primary vote. Respectful of what that number meant, he wanted to reward their followers with a consolation prize. So Humphrey coupled McCarthy's changes with one proposed by Senator George McGovern, D-S.D. McGovern wanted to see delegations demographically match—or at least reflect—the compositions of the states they represented. More and more states threw up their figurative hands as they tried to meet each of these new requirements. Taking the path of least resistance, they decided that the easiest thing to do was to hold popular-vote primaries. Democratic primaries were held in only 15 states in 1968, but by 1980 the number had risen to 35. Conventions for both parties were reduced to little more than coronation ceremonies.[22]

How State Parties Recovered: Campaign Reform in the Late 20th Century

Candidates no longer need hierarchical machines to reach voters. The decline of party machines was followed in time by the advent of televised campaign commercials as the dominant mode for trying to persuade citizens to vote. "Television, that's the big political party," John Coyne said as he stepped down in 1993 after serving 12 years as chair of the Cuyahoga County Democratic Party.[23]

The increasing reliance on campaign ads, ironically, led to restored strength for state and national political parties and spelled the decline of local party strength in federal elections. The move from greeting potential voters in person at party dinners and county fairs to airing TV ads meant that politicians had to run more professional campaigns. They now hire pollsters to figure out which issues will resonate best in their ads. Consultants help shape their message on these issues, and media gurus produce the ads and place them in favorable time slots. Once more changing with the times, state parties became important clearinghouses, connecting candidates with consultants. Eventually, they evolved into important consulting organizations themselves. During the 2006 campaign, when Democrats believed they had a shot at taking control of the Michigan Senate (they failed), their chief strategist sent legislative aides to run campaigns in several close races. Ken Brock, chief of staff to the Michigan Democratic Senate Campaign Committee, paid homage to the idea that candidates with a good feel for local issues were crucial. But he was equally interested in "educating our candidates" about the resources, messages, and tactics he believed would work for them. Lansing strategists provided the lists of voters that candidates should try to contact. Brock summed up his reasoning: "The way I see it is that they're all highly competent people, but they haven't had the experience of running in an expensive, marginal contest."[24]

Every Democratic and Republican state party now has a full-time chair or executive director. Most have other professional staffers as well, who handle fundraising, communications, field operations, and campaigns.[25] In general, Republican state parties tend to be better funded and, therefore, better run than their Democratic counterparts. Democratic state parties, however, often gain support from their allied groups, such as labor unions.

With their massive computer databases, maintained and updated from year to year, political parties help candidates target and reach voters who are sympathetic to their messages. It's common now for candidates to carry iPads and smartphones loaded with the latest voter registration data instead of the old-fashioned clipboards full of paper printouts on which they could scribble notes. There's a race between the parties now in terms of how most effectively to harness "big data" to make predictions about what messages will appeal most to individual voters and motivate them to vote. In 2012, the Obama campaign conducted 5,000 to 10,000 shorter interviews and 1,000 longer interviews with voters every week in each of the most competitive states. "To derive individual-level predictions, algorithms trawled for patterns between these opinions and the data points the campaign had assembled for every voter—as many as one thousand variables each, drawn from voter registration records, consumer data warehouses, and past campaign contacts," a writer for *MIT Technology Review* reported.[26]

Aside from mining data about voters, parties also play an important role in helping interested groups and potential contributors determine which of their candidates have a realistic shot at winning. The major parties are not the voter organizers they were in the machine days, when individuals were encouraged to vote "early and often," but they do still contact up to 25 percent of the electorate in any election cycle. Individuals contacted by parties have a much higher tendency to vote than do people who are not contacted, possibly because they feel as though they were called because their parties think their votes matter, or maybe just because of the helpful reminder. While the national parties typically play a greater role in polling and developing issues, "local and state parties [are] particularly important for registering voters and conducting get out the vote campaigns."[27]

One state chair in the 1950s exemplified the move that parties made toward professionalized consulting services. Ray Bliss took over the Ohio Republican Party after it suffered an electoral drubbing in 1948. He immediately began to identify and recruit better candidates. He also looked at ways to encourage citizens to vote, noting that, in 1948, 140,000 rural Republicans did not vote and 150,000 potential Republican voters in urban areas were not even registered. Following Bliss's registration and get-out-the-vote drives, Ohio Republicans in 1950 reelected a U.S. senator, won three statewide offices, and regained control of the state legislature.[28]

Minority-party members enviously keep close tabs on the governing party, and they alert the public and the press to every perceived misstep and abuse. It also is important for minority parties to avoid being demoralized and to continue to offer voters alternatives so that candidates from their parties will be in place once the public is ready for a change. Quite often, they fail. All too often, candidates are elected or reelected without a fight. With so many districts strongly tilted toward one party or the other, just barely more than half—54.6 percent—of the 6,000 state legislative races in 2014 featured competition between at least two candidates from the major parties.[29]

Still, the two parties remain so closely competitive nationally that political scientists refer to a period of **dealignment**, meaning that neither

---

Minority-party members
Politicians or officials associated with the party that is out of power, for instance, Democrats in a chamber where the GOP holds the majority of seats

Dealignment
The lack of nationwide dominance by any one political party

Policy in Practice

How Super PACs Supplement—and Sometimes Surpass—Parties

Members of the school board in Elizabeth, New Jersey, made a political enemy, and they paid the price. Several of them backed someone who ran against state Senator Raymond Lesniak, and in 2013 he repaid the favor. Lesniak worked with a super PAC called the Committee for Economic Growth and Social Justice, run by his former campaign consultant. It spent more than $150,000 to unseat members of the school board.

Lots of politicians and wealthy donors have set up super PACs, which are able to spend unlimited funds on political campaigns. Donors to Lesniak's group included his allies in the bail bond and online gambling industries, which would seem to have no natural interest in education policy in a 25,000-student school district in suburban New Jersey. But they were happy to help out Lesniak, who chairs a powerful economic development committee.

The super PAC tied to Lesniak was not alone. In 2013, when New Jersey held local- and state-level elections, outside groups spent a record $41 million on campaigns and ballot initiatives. That was 3 times what independent political groups had spent 4 years earlier, and nearly 3 times as much as the Republican and Democratic parties spent.[a]

With super PACs and so-called social welfare organizations far outweighing party and candidate spending in many races, from the presidency to the school board, many people are wondering whether parties are losing their influence on American politics. "The overriding theme was that the state and local parties are just not the important players that they used to be in federal elections," said Daniel Tokaji, coauthor of *The New Soft Money*, referring to his interviews with political consultants. "On some occasions, we got laughs or chuckles when we even mentioned state or local parties."[b]

Wealthy donors have always carried a lot of sway in politics. That they can now spend so freely—and cut out the middlemen by setting up their own political organizations—has some Americans worried that the rich are having an unhealthy amount of influence. Super PACs spent more than $1 billion on elections in 2012, while spending on ballot measures topped $1 billion for the first time in 2014—largely from corporations eager to push or block measures that circumvented the legislative process.

"There are five or six people in this room tonight that could simply make a decision—this will be the next president—and probably at least get a nomination, if ultimately the person didn't win," President Obama said at a 2012 fundraiser attended by executives from Microsoft and Costco. He argued that his advantages of incumbency and extensive online fundraising network might not be available to future candidates operating in the changed campaign finance landscape. "You now have the potential of 200 people deciding who ends up being elected president every single time," Obama said.[c]

The Center for Public Integrity estimated that fewer than 600 people in 2012 had bumped up against federal spending limits that restricted the total amount an individual could give to candidates and party committees. (The total at the time was $123,200 per election cycle.)

party is dominant. In earlier periods of American history, one party or another generally had dominated politics, holding most of the important offices. The two major examples are Republican dominance from the time of the Civil War into the 1920s and the Democratic New Deal coalition, which held power from the presidential election of 1932 into the 1960s. The 1932 election of Franklin D. Roosevelt is the best example of a **realignment**, the switching of popular support from one party to another. Neither party has pulled off a similarly lasting realignment since then, in that voters seem about equally supportive of both major parties. Indeed, Republican hopes of creating a "permanent majority" following George W. Bush's 2004 win were dashed quickly when Democrats took

Realignment
The switching of popular support from one party to another

The Supreme Court abolished such limits with its 2014 decision in *McCutcheon v. FEC*. Massachusetts abandoned its aggregate limits on donations to state-level candidates the day the Court released its decision, with the dozen other states with such limits in place quickly revisiting their policies.

Super PACs are not supposed to coordinate their activities with candidates themselves. There has often been a thin membrane between such groups and the campaigns they back, however, with former top aides to many candidates running super PACs operating on their behalf. A set of e-mails among aides to Republican governor Scott Walker revealed in 2014 showed that such separations are sometimes entirely porous. The e-mails suggested that the governor himself was involved in soliciting large-dollar donations on behalf of Club for Growth, a nominally independent group that had his back during a 2012 recall campaign. Among other transactions, the e-mails revealed that Walker had spoken by phone with Kenneth G. Langone, a cofounder of Home Depot, who donated $15,000 to the Club for Growth that day, as well as meeting with real estate developer Donald Trump, who also gave $15,000.[d]

According to an e-mail from his fundraising consultant to Club for Growth, Walker wanted "all the issue advocacy efforts run thru one group to ensure correct messaging." Many candidates have complained in recent years that they can't pick the issues they want to talk about, since the people running super PACs may have their own agendas. Not all super PACs, after all, are set up by a candidate's buddies. Many are run by interest groups consumed by a single issue, or an individual whose concerns may have little to do with the district or state at hand.

With party spending sometimes dwarfed by super PACs, some people argue that it's time to lift the restrictions on fundraising that parties still operate under. The existing laws have "succeeded in profoundly altering the state of American politics by severely weakening American political parties to the benefit of outside spending groups who may raise and spend unlimited funds in connection with federal elections," election lawyers Neil Reiff, a Democrat, and Donald McGahn, a Republican, said in testimony before a U.S. Senate committee in 2014.

---

[a] Fredreka Schouten, "Federal Super PACs Spend Big on Local Elections," *USA Today*, February 25, 2014, http://www.usatoday.com/story/news/politics/2014/02/25/super-pacs-spending-local-races/5617121/.

[b] Quoted in Peter Overby, "Outside Group Mirrors Successful Strategies of Political Parties," NPR, August 22, 2014, http://www.npr.org/blogs/itsallpolitics/2014/08/22/342354175/outside-group-mirrors-successful-strategies-of-political-parties.

[c] Kenneth P. Vogel, "Big Money, the Koch Brothers and Me," *Politico*, May 29, 2014, http://www.politico.com/magazine/story/2014/05/big-money-the-koch-brothers-and-me-107225.html.

[d] Adam Nagourney and Michael Barbaro, "Emails Show Bigger Fund-Raising Role for Wisconsin Leader," *New York Times*, August 22, 2014, http://www.nytimes.com/2014/08/23/us/politics/emails-show-bigger-fund-raising-role-for-gov-scott-walker-of-wisconsin.html.

---

control of the U.S. Congress in the 2006 midterm elections, followed by Barack Obama's win in the 2008 presidential election. Democrats took a shellacking in 2010, were able to recover to some extent by 2012, and then lost big again at the state and federal levels in 2014. The electorate looks different between presidential and midterm elections, but it's clear that neither party has been able to sustain an enduring advantage in recent years.

Party Competition: Why Some States Are More Competitive Than Others

Historically, most state political cultures have heavily favored one party or the other, as shown in Map 6-2. A well-known example of this is the

MAP 6-2

Interparty Competition, 2007–2011

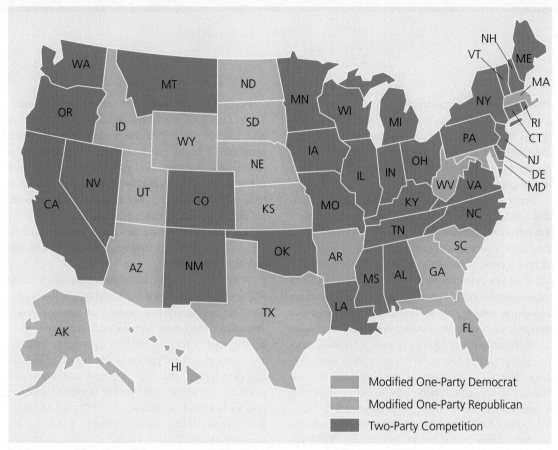

Modified One-Party Democrat

Modified One-Party Republican

Two-Party Competition

Source: Data compiled from Thomas Holbrook and Raymond La Raja, "Parties and Elections," in *Politics in the American States: A Comparative Analysis,* 10th ed., ed. Virginia Gray and Russell L. Hanson (Washington, DC: CQ Press, 2013), 88.

old Democratic "Solid South." For more than a century, most southern voters were "yellow-dog Democrats," meaning they would sooner vote for a yellow dog than for a Republican. From 1880 to 1944, all 11 states of the old Confederacy voted for Democrats in every presidential election—with a couple of exceptions in 1920 and 1928. These states elected only Democrats and a few independents as governor, and they elected only Democrats to the U.S. Senate after popular voting for senators began in 1916.[30] The Democratic hegemony in the South began to break up with the civil rights era that began, roughly, with the elections of 1948.

Party control in individual states has tended to seesaw in most states in recent decades, with either major party having a shot of winning the governorship or control of the legislative chambers. One reason is the increased mobility of the American population. In the past, people put down roots and perpetuated the political cultures of their families, but today the country's population is constantly shifting. The many northeasterners who have moved into the South, for example, do not hold the same cultural memory of the Civil War that kept many conservatives from supporting Republicans. Immigrants to California have made the state more Democratic—Republicans politically misplayed their hand with California Hispanics by pushing an anti-immigrant ballot initiative during the 1990s. But people leaving California have made other states more Democratic as well. Californians made up half of all newcomers to Nevada during that state's recent boom years. In fact, according to the Brookings Institution, people originally from California make up more than 20 percent of Nevada's electorate, compared with 14 percent who are native born.[31] "In the case of Nevada, the spillover effect is pretty clear," said demographer John Pitkin. "Nevada is almost a satellite of California."[32]

But while states don't remain static, more and more they are voting in monolithic fashion, favoring candidates of one party or the other for most elected offices. It's long been tough for a Republican to win in Maryland or Hawaii, or for Democrats to prevail in Idaho or Utah, but single-party control has become common in many states in recent years. Fewer counties vote one way for president and another for U.S. House or state Senate. And the partisan vote in more places has gotten more lopsided. In fact, one of the striking results of the 2012 elections was that, at the legislative level, Republican "red" states got redder while "blue" states elected more Democrats. The result was supermajority control in numerous legislative chambers. In 2014, most of the country got more red. And once a party loses power in a state, it is at a disadvantage in recovering power. Its traditional allies also have a harder time pushing their agendas. We'll discuss the effects of this further in Chapter 7.

Party Factions and Activists

With party leaders prevented from dispensing prizes such as jobs, party activism and various party tasks are now largely carried out by volunteers. And because people seldom work for free unless they believe in something very strongly, political volunteers have become more ideological. People work for candidates and parties because they believe in specific causes, such as handgun control legislation or protections for small-business owners.

Just because jobs are no longer the parties' golden eggs does not mean that politicians and parties do not seek to pluck favors from their constituents through policies or promises. Both major parties court the elderly with assurances of health care benefits, such as Medicare, because senior citizens vote and thus are worth courting. Young people, by contrast, have historically tended not to vote. Only 24 percent of Americans 30 years of age and younger voted in 2006, which was the best midterm showing for the young in 20 years.[33] The young voter turnout increased in the 2004 and 2008 presidential elections—51 percent of the population between the ages of 18 and 29 cast ballots in 2008—but the group's participation continued to trail behind that of older voters by almost 15 percentage points.[34] In 2012, the number of people between the ages of 18 and 29 stayed about the same as in 2008—about 23 million—but because of a decline in voter participation overall, their share of the total electorate ticked up by one percentage point, to 19 percent.

Remember, however, that each party is a kaleidoscope of interest groups and can appeal only so much to any one group before it risks alienating support among other groups. Republican support for abortion and contraceptive restrictions or outright bans has helped solidify the party's dominance among evangelicals and other social conservatives, for instance, but at the cost of alienating many women voters, particularly single women.

It is obvious that one person cannot simultaneously support higher pay for teachers and cutting educational budgets. That is why politicians must perform the neat trick of motivating the true believers within party ranks to support their candidacies during primary elections without pinning themselves down so much that they do not appeal to members of the other party and independents during the general election. It's not always possible to square that knot. Reaching out to broaden appeal while simultaneously tending to current supporters is always a tough trick. Some Republican Party leaders in recent years have argued that the party needs to soften its stance on immigration to appeal to Hispanic voters who increasingly spurn the GOP. The party's current supporters, however, mostly favor maintaining a hard line on the issue.

Both major parties try to appeal to as much of the populace as possible, but their supporters sometimes care more about promoting particular issues than they do about winning elections.

And, as already noted, interest groups now raise their own funds and use them freely to promote their issues in campaigns. In Wisconsin, political races have been dominated for years by issue ads run by the Wisconsin Manufacturers and Commerce and the Wisconsin Education Association Council. Because these two groups care so much about taxes and education, respectively, these issues dominate many races. Politicians and parties have no control over such ads, so they cannot control the agenda. Anything else the candidates might want to emphasize is likely to be drowned out. Nobody disputes that taxes and schools are important, but making them the only subjects in an election detracts from other issues.[35]

Now those groups sometimes find themselves outgunned as well, with numerous organizations from inside and outside the state making their opinions known. This dynamic was heightened with the recall elections that dominated the state's politics in 2009 and 2010. Jennifer Shilling, a Democratic state representative, decided to challenge Republican senator Dan Kapanke in one of several recall contests that took place in 2009 after GOP leaders had slashed budgets and eliminated collective bargaining rights for most public-sector employees. Shilling raised $400,000 for the race, against Kapanke's $1.6 million. But both candidates' treasuries were dwarfed by the millions spent by outside groups that ran independent expenditure campaigns. Shilling won, but she said, "It was just numbing to look at my financial report, knowing what we needed to be competitive and get our messages out."[36]

During the 1980s, it appeared that candidates were fairly free agents. They were rid of the old party machine apparatus and able to set their own agendas and spread their own messages, largely through broadcast ads. Twenty years later, times changed again. Yes, candidates are now more independent, presenting themselves for party nomination and spending sums they have raised to get into the public eye. The campaigns, however, have become such big business that the candidates' funds and self-motivation often are not enough. Plus, candidates need votes, and to get these votes, they must join

ranks with party officials and interest groups that tend to take the ball and run away with it. Candidates become mere pawns in campaigns that have been overtaken by deep-pocketed interest groups. They stand on the sidelines and watch as the parties or other groups run the greater volume of ads, redefining their campaigns for them.

It is easy to become confused about which is the most powerful—candidates, interest groups, or political parties—and in which situations they hold that power. What is important to remember is that all three are vital parts of the political process and their relative importance varies depending on the time and place. It is impossible to illustrate every variation, but none of them is ever either nothing or everything. Their roles are entwined.

State Party Regulation and Finance

It is important to note that the parties do not dry up and blow away once an election is over, although they are obviously most active during campaign seasons. Not only must they plan for the next election—and the one after that and the one after that, in perpetuity—but they also play an important role in actual government operations. Granted, parties no longer are able to run government strictly to perpetuate their own power, as was true to a certain extent in the machine era, but they still help their most important supporters maintain access to officeholders and other officials.

The Nebraska state legislature is organized on a nonpartisan basis (as are most municipal governments), but every other state legislature is organized by party. In other words, if the Republican Party holds a majority of the seats in a state's house of representatives, Republicans not only control the leadership, schedule, and agenda of the house, but they chair the house committees as well. There are exceptions and examples of shared power, particularly when partisan control of a legislature is tied, but these are rare. The more normal state of affairs is for the majority party to rule.

A *Difference* That Makes *A Difference*

Out-Party Loyalists: Some of the Worst Jobs in American Politics

A good candidate in the right year can win in nearly any state, regardless of party affiliation. But some states favor either Republicans or Democrats so heavily that members of the other party barely have a chance. That leaves true believers in a lonely place.

The Sole Republican

Sam Slom calls himself the Lone Ranger. He's the one and only Republican serving in the Hawaii Senate. "When that happened after the election of 2010, I got condolence calls and sympathy calls," he says.

Slom is outnumbered 24 to 1, but as the chamber's only Republican, he gets to serve on all 16 of the Senate's standing committees. He and his staff keep an eye out for drafting errors on bills that will create problems that might undermine their sponsors' attentions. "If you look over the 16 years I've served, you'll find very few bills that have my name on them," he said in 2013. "You'll find a lot more that were my bills originally that my colleagues were so enamored of that they put their name on them."

Rebuilding in Baby Steps

For most of Oklahoma's history as a state, Democrats ruled the roost. Like the rest of the South, however, over the past 20 years the state has increasingly given its support to Republicans at all levels of politics. "Oklahoma's the reddest of the red states, a dubious honor," says Wallace Collins, who is chairman of the state Democratic Party.

His party is completely shut out of the state's congressional delegation, as well as all 13 statewide offices. It also holds few seats in the state legislature. That's why Collins's strategy is to rebuild in "baby steps."

"The way we lost control was a little bit here and a little bit there," he says. "We'll get back the same way."

Hoping to Break Factional Ties

Chris Rothfuss was the Democratic leader in the Wyoming state Senate in 2014. There wasn't a lot of competition for the job. Democrats hold just four seats in the chamber. Republicans have 26.

Wyoming gave a bigger share of its vote to Republican Mitt Romney in 2012 than did any other state, save for neighboring Utah. Democrats might have made some inroads in the southern Rocky Mountain states, but not farther north.

Like a lot of red-state Democrats, Rothfuss represents a university community, in his case Laramie. But he gets a lot of e-mails from Democrats from around Wyoming who are looking to have some kind of voice in the state capitol. "Obviously, even if you're not going to win the vote, it's important to have both sides of the debate presented so you have a better discourse," he says.

Lonely In Rhode Island

Ann Clanton says it can be "quite lonely" being an African American woman who is a Republican. Helping run the party in a state dominated by Democrats makes it worse.

"We're in one of the bluest states in the nation," says Clanton, who is the executive director of the GOP in Rhode Island. "We have an uphill battle getting people to stay engaged with the platform of the Republican Party right now."

As is true throughout New England, Rhode Island Republicans have become nearly an endangered species. Clanton says one of the most difficult aspects of her job is trying to convince candidates that they have a realistic chance of winning if they run under her party's banner. Too often, even those who generally share the party's philosophy find it easier to run as an independent or even a Democrat. And it's hard to make the case to younger voters that the party has anything to say to them. "It's tough going out there and recruiting people," Clanton says. "It's very hard. We have a lot of Democrats who we know are Republican but run as a Democrat—basically so they can win."

State Party Regulation

Remember that states did not regulate political parties until the beginning of the 20th century, when the progressive backlash against machine abuse led states to intervene. Political scientists now refer to parties as equivalent to public utilities, such as water and electricity, in which the public has a sufficient interest to justify state regulation.[37] Political parties, after all, are the main conduits through which elections are contested and government is organized. The legal justifications that states have used to regulate parties revolve around registration requirements—29 states and Washington, D.C., register voters by party[38]—because party names are printed alongside the names of candidates on ballots.

Thirty-eight states regulate aspects of the structure of their state and local parties, often in explicit detail, to prevent antidemocratic, machine-boss control.[39] Some states determine, for instance, how the members of state parties' central committees should be selected and how often those committees will meet. A state might specify which party organization can name a substitute candidate if a nominee dies or withdraws prior to an election. Such regulation is practiced whether in regard to a state party in Minnesota or a local party in Pennsylvania.

A relatively limited number of state parties have challenged the laws regulating parties in the wake of the 1989 Supreme Court decision, mentioned previously, in which the Court ruled that the state of California did not have the authority to dictate how political parties are organized. The major parties in New Jersey did adopt a number of changes in party structure, but for the most part the parties seem satisfied with the way things are being run under the systems imposed on them by the states.

The decision in 1989 was neither the first time nor the last time the U.S. Supreme Court weighed in on concerns related to political parties. The nation's highest court has issued a number of other decisions in recent years to clarify the legal rights of parties. In a series of cases emanating from Illinois during the 1970s and 1980s, the Court made it clear that "party affiliations and support" are unconstitutional bases for the granting of a majority of government or public jobs, except at the highest levels.[40] In 1986, it ruled that the state of Connecticut could not prevent independents from voting in Republican Party primaries if the GOP welcomed them.[41] This precedent, which allowed the parties rather than the state to determine who could participate in the parties' primaries, was later followed in several other states. The parties have not always gotten their way, however. In 1999, the Court determined that states have the constitutional right to regulate elections and prevent manipulation. The ruling blocked a new party in Minnesota from "fusing" with the state's Democratic Party by nominating candidates for election that the Democrats already had nominated.[42]

Campaign Finance

Some think that when it comes to campaign finance, the rules should be changed to allow parties to spend more. They are still subject to campaign restrictions that don't apply to outside interest groups such as super PACs. That distorts the playing field, giving the "least accountable organizations . . . the most leverage over our campaigns," veteran political journalist Thomas B. Edsall concluded in 2014.[43] "The problem is the limits," Tennessee GOP senator Lamar Alexander said at a committee hearing in 2012. "These new super PACs exist because of the contribution limits we've placed upon parties and candidates. Get rid of the limits on contributions, and super PACs will go away."

Congress has attempted to regulate the flow of money into politics at various times in recent decades, notably following the Watergate scandal of the early 1970s (which involved, among other things, funneling of illegal corporate campaign contributions into a presidential slush fund) and in 2002, due to concern over large amounts of spending by parties. The recent history of campaign finance laws, however, has shown that courts are skeptical about attempts to limit political spending, which is viewed as protected speech.

In 1974 and 1976, Congress enacted laws that limited the amount of money candidates could collect from individuals and political action committees. Congress revised the law in 1979 after complaints from party leaders that the new laws almost completely eliminated state and local party organizations from participating in presidential campaigns. The old law, party leaders contended, put too many restrictions on how parties could spend money during a presidential election year. The revised law lifted all limits on what state and local parties could raise or spend for "party-building" activities. These included purchasing campaign materials, such as buttons, bumper stickers, and yard signs, and conducting voter registration and get-out-the-vote drives.[44]

In 1996, the U.S. Supreme Court lifted federal limits on how much parties could spend. Under the new rules, a party could spend as much as it liked to support a candidate, as long as the candidate did not approve the party's strategy or ads or have any say over what the party was doing. The Court decided that no one had the right to restrict **independent expenditures**— that is, funds spent on activities or advertising without the candidate's knowledge or approval. "We do not see how a Constitution that grants to individuals, candidates, and ordinary political committees the right to make unlimited independent expenditures could deny the same right to political parties," wrote Justice Stephen G. Breyer.[45] A decade later, the Court tossed out a Vermont law that sought to limit fundraising and the amounts that candidates could spend on state campaigns.

It quickly became clear that the more lax restrictions were broad enough to allow for the purchase of TV ads and the funding of other campaign-related activities with so-called **soft money** donations, which were nominally meant to support party building. Restrictions on how parties spent soft money, which was raised in increments of $100,000 and more from corporations, unions, and wealthy individuals, were nearly meaningless—as long as the parties did not coordinate directly with candidates in spending the money. Parties violated the spirit, although not the letter, of the law, with state parties acting as virtual soft money–laundering machines for the national parties and for each other. In 2002, Congress revisited the issue and enacted the McCain-Feingold campaign finance law, which blocked the national parties from collecting soft money donations.[46]

Meanwhile, the state parties themselves are no slouches at raising money, as Figure 6-2 shows. Democrats and Republicans at the state level raised more than $500 million during the 2008 election cycle—a slight dip because of the loss of federal party transfers under McCain-Feingold.[47] But no matter what limitations are placed on campaign finance, money finds its way into the system because the U.S. Supreme Court held in its 1976 decision in *Buckley v. Valeo* that political expenditures are equivalent to free speech. In January 2010, in *Citizens United v. Federal Election Commission,* the Court ruled that political spending by corporations in candidate elections cannot be restricted. That finding was at odds with long precedent and the campaign finance laws of at least two dozen states, but in a 2012 ruling, the Court made clear that states cannot ban direct political spending by corporations. Two years later, the Court abolished the aggregate limits that an individual donor can give to federal candidates and parties during any given election cycle. "What followed has been the most unbridled spending in elections since before Watergate," wrote reporter Jim Rutenberg in *The New York Times.* "In 2000, outside groups spent $52 million on campaigns, according to the Center for Responsive Politics. By 2012, that number had increased to $1 billion."[48]

A total of $8,713,918 was contributed to Hawaii's Democratic and Republican candidates and committees in 2012, with $7,414,853 of that going to Democrats.

Independent expenditures
Funds spent on ad campaigns or other political activities that are run by a party or an outside group without the direct knowledge or approval of a particular candidate for office

Soft money
Money not subject to federal regulation that can be raised and spent by state political parties. A 2002 law banned the use of soft money in federal elections.

FIGURE 6-2

State Party Fundraising Over Time

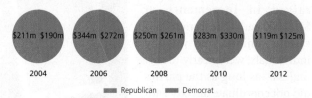

| 2004 | 2006 | 2008 | 2010 | 2012 |

$211m $190m $344m $272m $250m $261m $283m $330m $119m $125m

■ Republican ■ Democrat

Source: Data compiled from the National Institute for Money in State Politics, "Industry Influence," 2013, http://www.followthemoney.org/industry-influence.

Says University of Virginia government professor Larry J. Sabato:

> There is no way to stop the flow of interested money and there will always be constitutional ways around the restrictions enacted into law. What is so fundamental is that politics and government determine the allocation of goods and values in society. Those goods and values are critical to the success or failure of hundreds of interest groups and millions of individuals. Those groups and individuals are going to spend the money to defend their interests, period.[49]

Third Parties and Independents

More Americans now identify themselves as politically independent than at any time in the past 75 years, according to a Pew Research Center survey conducted in 2012. Thirty-eight percent of Americans described themselves as independent, which was an increase from 32 percent in 2008 and 30 percent in 2004.[50] Now, political scientists will tell you that many if not most self-described independents actually tend to support one party or the other, but that begs the question: If millions of people are disenchanted with the Republican and Democratic parties, for a variety of reasons, why isn't there more of a movement toward establishing a viable third, or minor, party as an alternative? Every election cycle seems to find more people dissatisfied with the major parties and more willing to identify themselves as independent.

Still, in 2012 there was nothing resembling a strong third-party movement in the presidential race. If anything, the opposite was true. An organization known as Americans Elect sought to create a place for a strong third-party candidacy, spending $35 million on marketing, social media and other technology tools, and ballot access, and securing a spot on the ballots of 28 states by May 2012. But it shut down its crusade that month, having been unable to persuade a viable candidate to run under its banner.[51]

In most other democracies, numerous parties exist, each with strong support. In countries such as Israel and Italy, the leading party typically does not have enough seats in parliament to construct a government on its own and has to enter into a coalition with other parties. That has never been the case in the United States, for a number of reasons. Democrats and Republicans, as we have been exploring, have established wide networks of contacts and supporters—individuals and groups that have long loyalties to one party or the other. They have officeholders at all levels who can help with strategy and fundraising.

The major parties also have many other institutional advantages. For one thing, the United States favors a winner-take-all system in which the person who receives the most votes in a district wins. In some countries, seats in the legislature are distributed on a percentage basis so that if a party gets 5 percent of the vote it receives about 5 percent of the total seats available. But if a party took only 5 percent of the vote across the United States, it probably would not win a seat anywhere. In 1992, Texas computer billionaire Ross Perot, the most successful third-party presidential candidate in decades, took 19 percent of the vote but did not carry a single state.

For the 1996 presidential race, Perot established the Reform Party, which he called his gift to the American people. Perot used that gift himself, running for a second time but not doing nearly so well. He had a hard time getting on the ballot in some states—rules regarding ballot access differ across states and are often complicated. In the state of New York, for instance, a candidate must collect a certain number of signatures from each of the congressional districts to get on the ballot. Many candidates with more modest financial means than Perot's have had difficulty gaining access to ballots. After the 2012 elections, in which some Democrats won with less than 50 percent of the vote, Republican-controlled legislatures in states such as Arizona, Alabama, and Tennessee enacted laws designed to raise requirements for third parties to reach the ballot, such as requiring additional signatures from registered voters on petitions. In 2014, the Supreme Court denied an appeal by the Libertarian Party of Ohio to have its candidates for governor and lieutenant governor listed on the ballot. They'd been kept off due to faulty candidacy petitions.

Difficulties of Building Support

Many Democrats blamed Green Party presidential nominee Ralph Nader for the defeat of their 2000 candidate, Al Gore. Gore won more popular votes than Republican George W. Bush but was defeated in the Electoral College. Some people believe that a third-party candidate will never be anything more than a "spoiler" who deprives major-party candidates of needed votes. Others believe that third parties help present a real and needed alternative to the Democrats and Republicans. Unless the major parties are challenged, the thinking goes, they will never change. A number of independent and third-party candidates had strong showings in statewide races in 2014, including Bill Walker, an independent candidate who won the gubernatorial election in Alaska, alongside a Democrat who gave up his own nomination to run on a unity ticket as Walker's running mate.

> Some people believe that a third-party candidate will never be anything more than a "spoiler" who deprives major-party candidates of needed votes. Others believe that third parties help present a real and needed alternative to the Democrats and Republicans.

Minor-party candidates have enjoyed some success running for lower offices. Within a state or legislative district, there is a better chance that an individual will enjoy enough personal popularity to equalize the playing field against Democrats and Republicans, who typically are better funded and connected. Still, only seven governors elected during the past 50 years have been neither Democrats nor Republicans. Three of the six before Walker—Walter Hickel of Alaska, Lowell Weicker of Connecticut, and Lincoln Chafee of Rhode Island—had earlier won statewide office as Republicans. Another two were elected in Maine, a state noted for the independent-mindedness of its electorate. The sixth, Jesse Ventura of Minnesota, served only one term, and the would-be successor from his Independence Party finished a distant third in 2002. Certainly, the two major parties make the argument all the time that a vote for a third-party candidate will just be wasted and make it more likely that a worse alternative will win. In 2014, Democrats hoped that independent candidate Eliot Cutler would drop out of the gubernatorial contest in Maine, since his strong showing 4 years earlier had arguably helped elect Republican Paul LePage.

At the legislative level, things are just as grim for third-party candidates. Following the 2014 elections, there were only 25 third-party or independent state legislators in the United States (not counting nonpartisan Nebraska), out of a total of 7,400. Each of these candidates had dedicated followers. But from a pragmatic perspective—say, that of a voter interested in seeing his or her agenda become law—it probably makes better sense to support a Democrat or Republican who has a chance of serving in the majority party than it does to pull for a person who will hold just one vote. "Voters simply have a hard time thinking beyond the two parties they're familiar with," said political scientist John Baughman. "A voter lacking much information about the candidates is often comfortable making a vote choice simply based on their party affiliation, but if it's a candidate outside their party affiliation, making that choice is even harder."[52]

A few minor parties have enjoyed periods of success in certain states, such as the Progressive Party during the 1920s in Wisconsin and the Farmer-Labor Party during the 1930s in Minnesota. Over time, however, these parties have been unable to survive the loss of early popular leaders or have been absorbed by one of the major parties. For example, the official name of Minnesota's Democratic Party is still the Democratic Farmer-Labor Party, in reference to its merger with the defunct minor party. The Liberal Party of New York boasted a New York City mayor in the 1960s named John Lindsay. New York is one of the few states that allow candidates to be listed multiple times on a ballot, as the nominee of, for instance, both the Liberal and the Republican parties. In 1980, U.S. Senator Jacob Javits was denied the nomination of the state's Republican Party and ran as the Liberal candidate. He succeeded only in splitting the votes of liberals, moderates, and Democrats, and helped elect a more conservative Republican. The Liberal Party disbanded in 2003 after failing to garner enough votes in the previous year's gubernatorial contest to maintain its guaranteed spot on state ballots. "Parties, I suppose, have a life span," said Dan Cantor, executive director of the Working Families Party. "They had their heyday in the [19]50s and [19]60s. It looks like they have come to a full stop."[53]

Ultimately, it is the states that publish the ballots and have the authority to decide which parties' nominees are going to be listed on them. It is the states that grant ballot access to parties based on their having won a minimum percentage of the vote in a previous statewide general election. The threshold varies from 1 percent in Wisconsin to as much as 20 percent in Georgia. Such high institutional barriers make minor parties' complaints about two-party dominance of American politics about as fruitless as trying to hold back the tide.

Major-Party Support

One other reason minor parties have trouble gaining traction is that people are not, in the main, terribly unhappy with the major parties. The major parties, after all, do devote themselves to appealing to as broad a range of citizens as possible. That said,

voter identification with the parties has declined. Some states allow voters to vote a straight ticket, meaning they could pull one lever to vote for all the Democratic or Republican candidates on the ballot. Voters are often willing to divide their ballots, a practice called **ticket splitting**. As one voter joked, "I vote for the man for president, and give him a Congress he can't work with." But for many voters, their identification with either the Democratic or Republican Party—or against one or the other—has become sufficiently strong that ticket splitting has come down, with the presidential, congressional, and state legislative maps all increasingly resembling one another.

In 1960, the Gallup Organization found that 47 percent of respondents identified themselves as Democrats, 30 percent as Republicans, and just 23 percent as independents or members of other parties. By the 1990s, those numbers had converged. In 2014, Gallup found that 42 percent of Americans identified as independent—a record high—compared with 31 percent Democratic and 25 percent Republican.[54] As polling by the Pew Research Center and other groups has found, however, most self-identified independents are not true independents. Their preferences generally do lean toward one of the major parties. "Partisan loyalties in the American populace have rebounded significantly since the mid-1970s, especially among those who actually turn out to vote," concluded political scientist Larry M. Bartels.[55] The proportion of pure independents, those who do not lean toward either party, peaked at 16 percent in 1976. Twenty years later, true independents were just 9 percent of the populace.[56] The same 2014 Gallup poll that found that independents far outnumbered partisan voters also found that 47 percent of those self-identified independents leaned toward the Democratic Party, while 41 percent tended to favor the GOP.

Many people may not choose to identify themselves with either major party, but they mostly tend to vote one way or the other, a team of political

---

Voter identification
When a voter identifies strongly with one of the major parties, he or she is considered a Democrat or a Republican; many voters, however, are considered weakly aligned with either major party

Ticket splitting
Voters' or districts' voting for different parties' nominees for different offices—for instance, supporting a Republican for president while supporting a Democrat for Congress

scientists concluded in the 1992 book *The Myth of the Independent Voter.*[57] "Independents have a great pride factor—'I vote for the person, not the party,'" said Jane Jech, a Republican candidate for the Iowa Senate in 2012. "But in truth, they lean one way or the other."[58]

The Republicans and Democrats have dominated American politics for 150 years. They have met every challenge—both ideological and structural—and found a way to preserve their near-total control. As political scientist Jeff Fishel puts it:

> If there's any lesson of history about the two major parties in American politics, it is that they're incredible adaptive survivors. They lost the monopoly they had, particularly on candidate recruitment and finance. That certainly does not mean that they're going out of business, just that they have to compete with other groups.[59]

Interest Groups and Lobbies

Tanning salons promise a "healthy glow," but they're actually not good for your skin. Dr. Brundha Balaraman, a dermatologist in St. Louis, treated a high school student who had developed a melanoma on her leg after frequenting tanning beds. She had never been warned of the risks. No wonder. Balaraman found out that the state of Missouri doesn't regulate tanning beds (most states don't). The dermatologist began a 7-year quest to convince the legislature that some protections were needed, resulting in the passage of a law in 2014 that created fines for facilities that allow minors to use tanning beds without parental consent.

When people don't like a law or regulation, they can ask their legislators to change it. That's what lobbying is all about—the right to petition for redress of grievances. If many citizens are cynical about political parties, they're even more put off by interest groups. It's true that lobbyists representing big companies, unions, and other organizations often push for legislation to promote or protect their own narrow interests. But lobbying is how citizens and private companies make their views known to policymakers between election seasons. Sometimes people even lobby for altruistic reasons, rather than self-interest—college students seeking to influence university investment decisions or citizens advocating for government policies to put pressure on foreign dictatorships, for example.

But such cause campaigns are different in kind than the average work done by interest groups, which tend to have long-standing interests in issues or regulations that affect the groups or their members directly. Often they use the legislative or regulatory process as a means to seek advantage over their professional competitors. As should be apparent by now, interest groups have always been important resources for candidates, providing volunteers and other services as well as money. They have taken on even greater importance in the current era of high-stakes fundraising and super PACs. They are the organizations that take a direct interest in political activity—both in terms of supporting candidates during an election season and in terms of lobbying elected and appointed government officials regarding policy and spending matters. Still, they differ from parties in that politics and elections are not their whole reason for being. As political scientist Frank J. Sorauf notes, "The American Medical Association devotes only part of its energies to protecting its interests through political action. Not so the political party. It arises and exists solely as a response to the problems of organizing the political process."[60] In other words, the American Medical Association may spend millions of dollars annually trying to affect elections and legislation, but it devotes more of its energy and resources to educating its members, promoting good health care techniques, and engaging in other private activities. This difference in focus illustrates a fundamental and obvious trait that separates political parties from special interest groups—political parties run candidates for office under their own labels, whereas special interest groups do not.

Interest groups basically come in five flavors. One is the membership group, such as the American Medical Association or the Sierra Club, made up of individual members with a common interest. A second type is the trade association, which represents individuals or organizations in a particular industry or field, such as the National Restaurant Association or the Alliance of Automobile Manufacturers. The third type of interest group is that consisting of an individual institution; many large organizations, such as Microsoft and General Motors, have lobbyists on staff or devote a significant portion of their executives' time to lobbying. The fourth type consists of government lobbyists (sometimes called legislative liaisons), those who represent the interests of one branch of government to another. Executive branch officials have aides designated to lobby Congress or a legislature on their behalf, and cities, counties, and states hire lobbyists to make their cases in Washington. The fifth, and smallest, category is the interest group made up of private individuals who lobby on their own behalf for a pet project or against a policy that they find reprehensible.[61]

People and organizations have a constitutional right to petition the government for redress of grievances. That means they have the right to complain to lawmakers and regulators about their disagreements with laws and how they are enforced. That is what lobbying is. It is worth noting that the government runs some of the most active lobbies. The White House maintains a lobbying shop to try to persuade Congress of the wisdom of its policies. Municipal governments hire lobbyists and associations to protect their interests in their state capitals. Currently about 40,000 lobbyists are working in state capitals, and the number of associations and related groups has quintupled over the past 50 years. Lobbying in the states is now a billion-dollar business every year.[62]

The Internet has made it easy to track which interest groups are active in which states. Open up a search engine and type in the name of a state and "lobbying registration," and you'll quickly find the website of an ethics commission or other state board with which all lobbyists must register. The National Institute on Money in State Politics (www.followthemoney.org) and the Center for Public Integrity (www.publicintegrity.org) also offer detailed information about campaign finance and lobbying activity in the states, as well as studies about overall trends.

The raw numbers—who is spending what where—tell only part of the story, however. It is often difficult to find out which group has influenced the outcome of a specific piece of legislation. Some interest groups, play a very public game, but others are more secretive, playing an insider game in which influence is a matter of quiet access to legislators.

That is why many interest groups hire **contract lobbyists,** usually lawyers or former government staffers or elected officials who are valued for possessing insider knowledge and contacts within particular state capitals. Contract lobbyists generally have a number of clients, as lawyers do. About 20 percent of lobbyists registered to ply their trade in a given capital are contract.[63] They use their relationships and contacts to convince legislators that they should or should not pass particular bills. And although lobbyists ignore the executive branch at their peril, given that spending decisions and regulatory action are carried out there, more lobbying activity happens in the legislative arena. "You don't change their minds," said a California lobbyist. "You find ways of making them think they agreed with you all along."[64]

Legislators often rely on lobbyists to provide them with information, whether simply data about an industry's economic outlook or their opinions about whether a bill would cost jobs in the legislators' districts. Dr. Balaraman, the dermatologist concerned about tanning beds, conducted a survey she could show legislators that found that, out of the 243 facilities that responded, 65 percent allowed children as young as 10 to use tanning beds, with many of them providing misleading information about the risks.[65]

Legislators are always grappling with many issues at once: the state budget, education, the environment, and so on. It is up to lobbyists to keep legislators and their staffs apprised of who favors a particular bill and who would benefit from or be hurt by it. Lobbyists build up relationships with legislators over time, and legislators come to trust some of them for reliable information, even if they hold differing positions on particular issues. Often, members of trade associations and other groups will seek to inform legislators about their views, without necessarily knowing whether the politicians they're meeting with agree with them or not;

Contract lobbyists

Lobbyists who work for different causes for different clients, in the same way that a lawyer represents more than one client

Policy in Practice

Why Companies Avoid Overt Partisanship

Michael Jordan, the basketball legend, refused to engage publicly in partisan politics. The reason was simple, he explained: Republicans buy shoes, too, and Jordan didn't want to antagonize any potential customers for Nike, whose products he endorsed. Major corporations tend to employ the same logic. They don't want to risk angering potential consumers who disagree with their politics.

When the Supreme Court abolished limits on corporate contributions to political causes, some worried that big corporations would dominate the game. But it turned out that major companies don't want to be associated closely with partisan causes. Most super PAC money comes from wealthy individuals such as owners of privately held companies who don't have to worry about what shareholders or the broader public thinks in the way a major consumer company does.

Target, the big retailer, found itself the target of boycott campaigns in 2010 after it donated $150,000 to a super PAC that supported a gubernatorial candidate who opposed gay marriage. Perhaps more striking, however, was the defection of many major corporations from a previously obscure legislative group that had become the center of controversy in 2012.

The American Legislative Exchange Council, known as ALEC, had long championed conservative legislation. The group brought together state legislators and corporations to craft policy that was then turned into model bills introduced in many states. Much of it had to do with fiscal matters, such as tax policy, or policies that had some direct benefit to the group's corporate members—including prison sentencing laws that helped bring business to ALEC's active private prison affiliates. Roughly a thousand bills based on ALEC language are introduced in an average year, with about 15 percent enacted into law.

For years, liberal advocacy groups decried ALEC's influence, but they were unable to alarm very many members of the public, since the group remained little known. That began to shift, however, in 2011, when 850 model bills generated by ALEC, along with other documents, were published on a website run by the liberal Center for Media and Democracy. That made it easier for journalists and the group's ideological opponents in individual states to compare proposed legislation with language crafted by ALEC.

ALEC was facing some public relations headaches, but its problems really began with the high-profile shooting of Trayvon Martin, an unarmed African American youth, in Florida in February 2012. The man who shot Martin, George Zimmerman, maintained that he was innocent of murder charges thanks to the state's "stand your ground" law, which allows people to use force when they feel they may be at risk.

That type of law had been promoted by ALEC. The group soon backed away from the issue, announcing 2 months after the shooting that it was disbanding the task force that dealt with public safety and elections issues. From now on, ALEC leaders said, they would stick purely to economic matters.

By then, it was too late for many of ALEC's corporate members. Several major companies, including Coca-Cola, Pepsi, McDonald's, and Kraft, had cut their ties with the group. They were joined in 2014 by tech giants such as Microsoft, Google, and Yelp. Some three-dozen corporations and foundations would ultimately make the decision that being associated with ALEC, however effective the group had been in the past, was bad for business.

Source: Adapted from Alan Greenblatt, "ALEC Enjoys a New Wave of Influence and Criticism," *Governing*, December 2011, http://www.governing.com/topics/politics/ALEC-enjoys-new-wave-influence-criticism.html

this is "lobbying as primarily engaged in providing information about constituency views, with groups pressing lawmakers to enact particular policies based on how constituents will respond," as one academic wrote after spending time working on Capitol Hill.[66] Of course, smart lobbyists don't pass up the chance to present their side of things. Often, they can hold tremendous sway over issues,

The Democratic political action committee PA Families First launched attack ads in 2014 against Pennsylvania governor Tom Corbett for cuts to state education funding. Like many candidates running for office, Corbett faced an increase in opposition ads from interest groups, which are now allowed to organize into super PACs and dig into deeper spending pockets.

particularly those that may be little studied by part-time legislators and little noticed by media outlets and the public.

Standing in contrast to contract lobbyists is the **cause lobbyist**, someone who promotes a single-issue agenda, such as medical marijuana or campaign finance reform. A cause lobbyist often plays an outsider's game, using the media to sway public opinion and pressure public officials. Groups that do not have an economic interest in legislative outcomes are able to get away with this tactic because their ideological position is clear for all to see. Major industries also occasionally play outside games as they seek to pressure politicians by stirring up interest through issue advertising.[67] Contract lobbyists, by contrast, engage in **direct lobbying**, dealing directly with legislators in hopes of persuading them. Students trying to get public officials to divest from Sudan earlier in this decade were taking part in **indirect lobbying**, building

support for their cause through the media, rallies, and other ways of influencing public opinion, hoping that legislators would be swayed by the resulting buzz.

Using the media effectively can be trickier for private corporations and other entities directly affected by legislation. The media nearly always portray this third type of lobbyist in a negative light. If a politician sponsors a bill favoring a particular industry and individuals in that industry have made substantial donations to his or her campaign treasury, news stories are bound to be written about that money trail. For instance, when the Tennessee legislature considered revising the legal definition of bourbon and Tennessee whiskey, there were stories about lobbying expenditures and campaign contributions from the major distilleries. Numerous states, including Kentucky, Massachusetts, and Minnesota, have passed ethics laws in recent years that preclude lobbyists, who used to wine and dine legislators, from giving legislators anything of value, even a cup of coffee.[68]

Today, many interest groups try to combine the direct and indirect approaches, hitting up legislators for favors in private meetings while also running public relations campaigns through the media. Groups also are likely to join together in coalitions, hoping that a united front will not only present a more coherent and persuasive message but also prevent any individual group from looking as though it is acting out of narrow self-interest. Interest groups often look for surprising allies who will plead their case. For instance, groups wanting to increase funding for after-school programs will enlist law enforcement agencies to argue that the

Cause lobbyist
A person who works for an organization that tracks and promotes an issue, for example, environmental issues for the Sierra Club or gun ownership rights for the National Rifle Association

Direct lobbying
A form of lobbying in which lobbyists deal directly with legislators to gain their support

Indirect lobbying
A form of lobbying in which lobbyists build support for their cause through the media, rallies, and other ways of influencing public opinion, with the ultimate goal of swaying legislators to support their cause

programs help cut crime by giving young people something constructive to do.

As mentioned earlier, some interest groups, particularly those with ideological agendas, tend to be loyal to one party over the other. Interest groups as a whole, however, do not give most of their support to candidates of a particular party. Rather, they give most of their support to the *incumbents* of either party. One reason for this is that incumbents are reelected the vast majority of the time, so betting on their victory is pretty safe. It makes more sense, pragmatically speaking, to curry favor with someone who possesses power than with someone who does not. Even if the incumbent does not subscribe to an interest group's entire program, the group may find it is able to work with the individual on an issue or two.

Interest groups also favor incumbents because the campaign contributions such groups make are based more on rewarding public officials for positions they already have taken than on trying to persuade them to take new positions altogether. In other words, if a legislator already has demonstrated support for gun owners' rights, the National Rifle Association (NRA) will be inclined to support him or her. The group does not give donations to gun control advocates in the hope of changing their minds. The money follows the vote, in most cases, rather than the other way around. "Someone isn't going to vote one way or the other on gun control based on whether or not they received a contribution from the NRA," says John Weingart, associate director of the Eagleton Institute of Politics at Rutgers University. "But the example we always use here is that if there's a fight

MAP 6-3

State Corruption Report Card

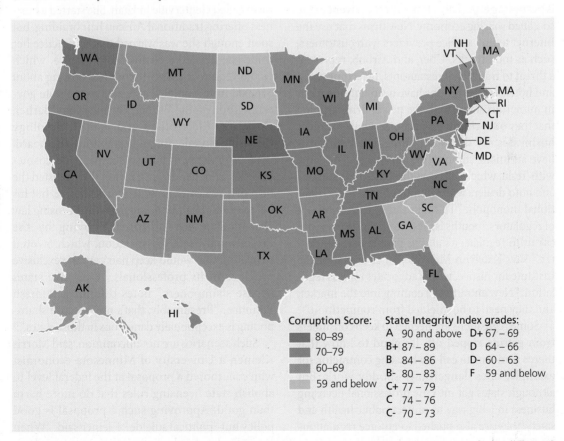

Corruption Score:
- 80–89
- 70–79
- 60–69
- 59 and below

State Integrity Index grades:

A 90 and above	D+ 67 – 69
B+ 87 – 89	D 64 – 66
B 84 – 86	D- 60 – 63
B- 80 – 83	F 59 and below
C+ 77 – 79	
C 74 – 76	
C- 70 – 73	

Source: State Integrity Investigation, The Center for Public Integrity (phone 202-466-1300), www.stateintegrity.org/your_state; Candace Hollingsworth (202.481.1216). Reproduced by permission of the Center for Public Integrity.

between ophthalmologists and opticians about what the regulations should be, a campaign contribution might make a difference because most people don't care."[69]

The adoption of bans on gifts and other ethical restraints has not stopped the lobbying industry or deterred interest groups. Too much is at stake in too many state capitals for corporations, unions, or cause activists not to play an active role. At the beginning of the 20th century, one or two powerful home-state companies dominated many state political cultures. State capitals remained old boys' clubs, where just a few powerful interests typically held sway, until about World War II. Since then, states have come to rival Washington in terms of the buzz of activity among competing interests.

This points to a little-discussed reality about regulation. Business owners love to complain about the burden regulatory compliance imposes on them, but many regulations come about because business groups have asked for them. That is becoming especially clear with the advent of the so-called sharing economy. New firms that use the Internet to link service providers with customers, such as food trucks, Uber, and Airbnb, represent a threat to traditional restaurants, taxi companies, and hotels. Those groups have been fighting it out in numerous states, with the newer firms arguing that they offer consumers a choice, while the older businesses say that such unregulated concerns have an unfair competitive advantage. The same with Tesla, which sells cars directly to consumers, and auto dealers who want to uphold their traditional monopoly. "The first thing that comes out of regulators' mouths is, 'It's never consumers who ask us to regulate; it's always people in the industry,'" says Katelynn McBride, an attorney for the Institute for Justice, which advocates for less regulation. "New entrants are coming into the market, and they need to be shielded from competition."[70]

Some regulations are needed to keep consumers from getting ripped off. It's good to know that there's someone to call if a housing contractor, for example, does dangerously shoddy work. But although states got into the professional licensing business in a big way to protect public health and safety, they are also pushed to enforce regulations by groups that want to set a bar high enough to discourage competition. Consider the case of

TABLE 6-1

Top Contributors to State Campaigns, by Sector, 2012

Sector	Contributions
General business (gambling, tobacco, etc.)	$350,025,574
Labor	$309,040,171
Finance, insurance, and real estate	$244,617,240
Lawyers and lobbyists	$176,099,869
Education and government agencies	$164,918,516
Health	$127,188,905
Energy and natural resources	$103,657,571
Construction	$87,326,457
Communication and electronics	$62,862,051
Transportation	$28,408,594

Source: National Institute on Money in State Politics.

Jestina Clayton, who moved at age 22 from a village in the West African nation of Sierra Leone to a town called Centerville in Utah. She started a business offering traditional African hair braiding, but soon enough she was warned that to practice her trade she needed a cosmetology license, which would require 2 years of schooling costing about $16,000 in tuition. She appealed to the state governing body—the Barber, Cosmetology/Barber, Esthetics, Electrology and Nail Technology Licensing Board—for an exemption. The board, made up mainly of licensed barbers and cosmetologists, shot her down. Clayton then enlisted the help of a sympathetic state representative, but his bill to exempt hair braiding from the licensing law was blocked by full-force lobbying by the Professional Beauty Association, which favored regulation that would keep hair care the exclusive province of its professionals. "Only five states license shampooers," notes columnist Ramesh Ponnuru. "Presumably, that's not because shampooing is exceptionally dangerous in those states."[71]

Such scenarios are not uncommon, said Morris Kleiner, a University of Minnesota economist who coauthored a proposal at the federal level to abolish state licensing rules that do more harm than good. Approving such a proposal is good policy but "political suicide," Kleiner said. "When you talk about reductions in licensing, you have every occupation from the plumbers to the CPAs to the electricians lining up to argue why regulation should not be reduced."[72]

Even when it comes to issues such as health and safety, there's plenty of intramural competition between groups competing for business. For instance, in 2014 Nebraska governor Dave Heineman vetoed a bill that would have allowed nurse practitioners to see patients without any professional agreement in place with a physician. Nurses argued that they'd be able to see more patients and address a shortage in care if they could operate independently, but doctors warned that there could be a threat to patient safety. It would also cut into their business. Orthopedic surgeons and podiatrists have faced off over who gets to treat ankle injuries, forcing legislators to debate whether the ankle is part of the foot. (The Colorado legislature decided it was, opening up the field to podiatrists.) Dog groomers fight veterinarians for the right to brush canine teeth.[73]

The active role of the states in regulating economic and social activities has induced some business interests, such as the pharmaceutical industry, to maintain lobbies that are just as powerful in the states as they are in Washington. Others, such as the aviation industry, have a major presence at the federal level but are weaker players in most states because state politics largely don't affect them. National companies that are not based in particular states are likely to hire local contract lobbyists to work in those states to lend clout to their causes. The consumer products company Johnson & Johnson has its own lobbyists but also maintains memberships in organizations in its home state, such as the New Jersey Chamber of Commerce, the state's Business and Industry Association, and the New Jersey Health Products Company Group. It also belongs to industry associations in California, Illinois, Massachusetts, and elsewhere. At the national level, Johnson & Johnson belongs to the Pharmaceutical Research and Manufacturers of America, the Health Care Industry Manufacturers' Association, and still other groups.[74]

When an industry has relatively little credibility, it often will turn to allies to represent the public face of its cause. Tobacco companies favor hiring lobbyists who have earned the respect of state legislators as former colleagues or by working for other, less controversial clients. They also seek other groups to take the lead on a lot of their fights. When a state considers legislation that will regulate smoking in public places, for example, the most public opponents are more likely to be restaurant groups rather than the tobacco industry. "We're going to participate in a very upfront way," said a spokesman for the Philip Morris tobacco company. "But like any other industry, we're going to look to people who share that point of view on any given issue" to take a role as well.[75]

As in the case of tobacco companies fighting smoking bans, lobbyists spend the majority of their time playing defense, trying to kill bills they believe would harm their companies or clients. Still, interest groups and their desires stir up much of the activity in state capitals. "Frankly, the legislature in New Jersey exists for the lobbyist," said one lobbyist there.[76] What he was suggesting is that the governor may want five or six bills passed during a session, while individual legislators may want one or two of their own passed as well. The remaining 99 percent of the thousands of bills introduced in a given year are a wish list of the wants and needs of the lobbyists and the interests they represent.

> When an industry has relatively little credibility, it often will turn to allies to represent the public face of its cause. Tobacco companies favor hiring lobbyists who have earned the respect of state legislators as former colleagues or by working for other, less controversial clients. They also seek other groups to take the lead on a lot of their fights.

That is why interest groups are an important part of the political landscape in every state. Certain groups play a disproportionate role in particular states—for example, gambling in Nevada or the poultry industry in Arkansas[77]—but the full range of interest groups has crucial influence over the workings of every state. Clive

S. Thomas and Ronald J. Hrebenar, two political scientists who have been studying interest group activity in the states for decades, rank the states according to which have policies that are most influenced by interest groups. In no state are interest groups subordinate to—that is, consistently outgunned by—other policy players, such as governors or political parties.

Those players are stronger in some states than in others. The relative weakness of political parties led Thomas and Hrebenar to argue that interest groups are most powerful in a few states in the South and West, such as Alabama, Nevada, and West Virginia.[78] Certain interest groups may hold greater sway at specific times. The importance of environmental issues, in particular, seems to ebb and flow. But Thomas and Hrebenar note that in the majority of states, the influence of interest groups as a whole remains fairly constant—and fairly strong.

The influence of interest groups is difficult to measure, but it is nonetheless quite apparent, part of the very air that policymakers breathe. Some groups may score a victory here and there:

dentists looking for a regulatory change or animal rights activists looking to ban cockfighting. Other groups have become a permanent part of the landscape, such as business lobbies concerned with taxes, transportation, and education.

There are some interest groups that are powerful everywhere because their members are everywhere. Groups such as teachers' unions and associations of car dealers, restaurant owners, and real estate agents hold particular sway because they have members in every legislative district, and legislators are more likely to be persuaded by individuals or employers from their home districts. Most lobbying by the National Association of Realtors, for example, is handled by volunteer members and state association staff rather than by hired contract lobbyists because realtors tend to be well connected in their communities. They also make it a point to have particular members of their professional community get to know individual legislators from their districts and keep them up to date about their issues of concern. Realtors, like members of other professions affected at the state policy level, also seek

Politicians in the past have worked hard to gain the support of unions, many of which are strong, outspoken, and well organized. While union support may still be sought after in many states, in others the tide has turned. Wisconsin union supporters staged mammoth protests in 2011 when Governor Scott Walker proposed ending collective bargaining rights for public employees.

office themselves in part-time legislatures. During the 2005–2006 session, no fewer than 22 people who made their livings in real estate also served as members of the Utah legislature—including the president of the National Association of Realtors.[79] In Texas, state representative Gary Elkins blocked a bill to regulate payday lending, despite the fact that he owns a chain of payday loan stores. Another state representative, Vicki Truitt, pestered him about his conflict of interest but became a lobbyist for ACE Cash Express, a payday loan company, 2 weeks after leaving office.

Taken together, interest groups are the means through which individual citizens and private companies, as well as governmental bodies, influence the policy decisions that affect their lives or ways of doing business. "I don't believe there are some states where interest groups are stronger and others where they're weaker," said Alan Rosenthal, a political scientist who was an expert on state politics at Rutgers University. "In every state, interest groups are important. That's the way interests are represented, through groups."[80]

Conclusion

The essential job of political parties is to nominate candidates for public office. The parties no longer control many government jobs, but despite changes in campaign finance laws, they have maintained their positions as crucial fundraising organizations. They also perform many other functions in American democracy. They aggregate and articulate political interests and create and maintain majorities within the electorate and within government. They are not the dominant organizing forces they once were, in part because voters and candidates—and nonparty fundraising organizations such as super PACs—have become more independent than they were decades ago. Parties, however, do still play important roles in recruiting political candidates, supporting them financially and logistically, and helping them market themselves to like-minded voters.

For the past 150 years, two major parties—the Democrats and the Republicans—have dominated politics in the United States. Few candidates not belonging to either of these parties have won office at any level of government, and in most cases, the victories of those few have been based on personal appeal rather than support for the third party they represented. The Republican and Democratic parties have been able to adapt to changing times and tastes in ways that have kept them in power, if not always in perfect favor.

With states regulating increasing numbers of industries, interest groups have proliferated so that there are now far more lobbyists than elected officials. Interest groups help push agendas subscribed to by individuals or corporations. Other interest groups push back. Their primary mission is to win as many political offices as possible; so the parties, with varying success, collate and mute the ideological agendas of their interest group allies. Parties cannot afford to have any one group's ideas play such a prominent role that other groups or voters are alienated. It is a difficult balancing act to try to appeal to the majority of voters at any given time while also standing for principles that are clear enough that most people are willing to support them.

The Latest Research

This chapter makes clear that political parties have critically important roles to play in democratic governance. How they go about fulfilling those roles has an enormous impact on politics and policy, in effect setting the boundaries of what will or can be done by the government. One aspect of how parties are executing those responsibilities has evolved into one of the dominant issues in contemporary American politics: the

(Continued)

(Continued)

increasing polarization of the two major parties. Much of the evidence for and discussion of the increasing partisanship of Democrats and Republicans, however, is concentrated on the federal level, especially on Congress, where bipartisanship has faded with the shrinking numbers of moderates from both sides of the aisle. Yet scholars of state politics are also intensely interested in the development and direction of political parties and their associated interest groups, and by employing the comparative method they have uncovered some fascinating insights about the polarized stances of political parties.

Indeed, the research discussed below suggests that if we want to know why political parties and interest groups are the way they are, polarized or not, we need a deeper understanding of what is happening outside government, especially at the local level. It is increasingly what happens there—especially in terms of interest group activity—that ultimately determines not just levels of partisanship but the very definition of what a political party is.

• •

• **Masket, Seth.** *No Middle Ground: How Informal Party Organizations Control Nominations and Polarize Legislatures.* Ann Arbor: University of Michigan Press, 2011.

In this provocative book, Masket, a political scientist at the University of Denver, takes a sustained look at what political parties are and what has caused the increasing partisanship in American politics. Traditionally, political scientists have viewed political parties as products of politicians. The basic argument is that political elites create formal organizations (i.e., political parties) to help them gain office, run government, and pursue particular sets of policies. Masket turns conventional wisdom on its head. Rather than centralized and hierarchical organizations, he argues, political parties, at least in the contemporary world, are characterized by what he terms informal party organizations (IPOs). These organizations, loose affiliations of individuals and interest groups, have enormous influence over primary elections. If elected officials—be they state legislators or members of Congress—want to keep their jobs, they need the support of these IPOs. This is because IPOs have the resources to mobilize enough voters to decide who wins in low-turnout primaries. This ends up distorting democratic representation. IPOs often have more extremely partisan viewpoints than do members of the general electorate, but an elected official who moderates his or her views once in office runs the risk of not making it through the next primary. Thus, politicians end up being creatures of (informal) political parties, rather than the other way around.

• **Bawn, Kathleen, Martin Cohen, David Karol, Seth Masket, Hans Noel, and John Zaller**. "A Theory of Political Parties: Groups, Policy Demands, and Nominations in American Politics." *Perspectives on Politics* 10 (2012): 571–597.

This article picks up on and develops a number of the ideas expressed in Masket's *No Middle Ground*. The central argument is that interest groups and activists are now the key actors in shaping political parties. Rather than political parties being tools of elected officials to help them win and keep office, parties are now dominated by interest groups and activists—essentially, the IPOs described in Masket's book—who are less interested in the preferences of voters than in their own narrow agendas. These groups focus their efforts on controlling the nomination process—that is, primary elections. This control provides them the whip they need to keep elected officials focused on narrow rather than general interests.

• **Iyengar, Shanto, Gaurav Sood, and Yphtach Lelkes.** "Affect, Not Ideology: A Social Identity Perspective on Polarization." *Public Opinion Quarterly* 76 (2012): 405–431.

Examining survey data over the past 40 years, the authors find an increasing level of hostility among partisans toward the other party. In 2008, for example, the average rating of the "out-party" was just above 30—a much lower rate of approval than the average rating of Catholics by Protestants, "big business" by Democrats, or homosexuals or people on welfare by Republicans. "Both Republicans and Democrats increasingly dislike, even loathe, their political opponents," the authors conclude. That makes governing difficult, since partisans are unlikely to trust the policies or even the facts presented by members of the other party. The reason isn't so much ideological differences between the parties or exposure to differing media sources or negative campaign ads. Instead, they contend, it is primarily affective—that is, "based on a primordial sense of partisan identity that is acquired very early in life and persists over the entire life cycle."

- **McGhee, Eric, Seth Masket, Boris Shor, Steven Rogers, and Nolan McCarty.** "A Primary Cause of Partisanship? Nomination Systems and Legislator Ideology." *American Journal of Political Science* 58 (2014): 337–351.

In an era of polarization, many have argued that opening up primary voting to nonparty members would force candidates to moderate their messages, rather than appealing to their own party's base. To test this idea, the authors compared electoral results under the different nominating systems used by every state over the past 20 years with a database of state legislative roll-call votes developed by Shor and McCarty. They found that there were consistent levels of polarization across time regardless of the way legislators were nominated. "The results of this analysis suggest that the openness of a primary election system has little to no effect on the ideological positions of the politicians it elects," they write. That is, Democrats remain liberal and Republicans remain conservative. If anything, they find that when primary systems are more open, more extreme candidates are nominated.

Chapter Review

Key Concepts

- candidate-centered politics (p. 160)
- cause lobbyist (p. 184)
- closed primary (p. 166)
- contract lobbyists (p. 182)
- crossover voting (p. 166)
- dealignment (p. 169)
- direct lobbying (p. 184)
- establishment (p. 157)
- factional splits or factions (p. 158)
- general elections (p. 166)
- independent expenditures (p. 177)
- indirect lobbying (p. 184)
- interest groups (p. 156)
- minority-party members (p. 169)
- nonpartisan ballots (p. 165)
- open primary (p. 166)
- party conventions (p. 166)
- patronage (p. 164)
- polarization (p. 160)
- political party (p. 155)
- political or party machines (p. 164)
- primary elections (p. 157)
- realignment (p. 170)
- responsible party model (p. 161)
- runoff primary (p. 166)
- soft money (p. 177)
- super PACs (p. 156)
- ticket splitting (p. 180)
- voter identification (p. 180)

Suggested Websites

- **ballotpedia.org.** A wiki providing information on candidates and ballot measures in all the states.

- **www.dnc.org.** Website of the Democratic National Committee.

- **www.electproject.org.** A website offering statistics and research on elections, run by Michael McDonald of the University of Florida.

- **fivethirtyeight.com.** Nate Silver's blog, now hosted by ESPN, covering electoral polling and politics at the national and state levels.

- **www.followthemoney.org.** Website of the National Institute on Money in State Politics, which tracks political donations and lobbying in all 50 states.

- **www.gop.com.** Website of the Republican National Committee.

- **influenceexplorer.com.** Website run by the Sunlight Foundation that provides data on campaign finance and lobbying expenditures.

- **www.irs.gov/Charities-&-Non-Profits/Political-Organizations/Political-Organization-Filing-and-Disclosure**. The Internal Revenue Service's political organization filing and disclosure website.

- **www.ncsl.org.** Website of the National Conference of State Legislatures.

- **www.opensecrets.org.** Website of the Center for Responsive Politics, a nonpartisan organization that tracks money in politics.

- **www.politicalmoneyline.com.** CQ Roll Call's website that provides information on campaign finance, lobbying and lobbyists, and parties and candidates.

- **www.publicintegrity.org.** Website of the Center for Public Integrity, which produces, among other investigative journalism reports, pieces on campaign finance and lobbying activity in the states and Washington, D.C.

⑤SAGE statestats

State Stats on Parties and Interest Groups

Explore and compare data on the states! Go to **edge.sagepub.com/smithgreenblatt5e** *to do these exercises.*

1. If you were a lobbyist for the oil industry, would you devote your time to working in North Dakota or in Louisiana? Why? Would your answer have been different ten years ago? Why?

2. What percentage of the population in Mississippi is enrolled in Medicaid? Based on this information alone, would you expect Mississippi to favor Democratic or Republican candidates for office? Is your expectation correct? Why or why not? Now, what percentage of the population in Wisconsin is enrolled in Medicaid? Why might Mississippi and Wisconsin have different political leanings considering this information?

3. How does the per capita state government tax revenue in New Hampshire compare to neighboring Vermont's? What about the state's history and politics led to this disparity? What are some of the possible implications?

4. How has the percentage of Hispanic residents in Colorado changed since 1995? What do you expect that this has done for Colorado's political leanings and why?

5. In the 1950s, Ray Bliss identified pockets of rural Americans who were not mobilizing to vote. Which states have the highest percentages of rural residents now? Which have the least? How do those states tend to lean politically? Why?

6. Which states have the most cattle? Which lobbying groups might you expect to find in these states?

Every state capitol attracts school groups, protesters, lobbyists, and people only casually interested in getting a glimpse of their government in action.

Legislatures

THE ART OF HERDING CATS

- Why do so many citizens think that legislatures accomplish so little—or accomplish the wrong things altogether?
- What constraints do legislatures face in making effective laws?
- Why are some legislators more powerful than others?

Minnesota and Wisconsin are neighboring states that have a lot in common: brutal winters, a shared German and northern European heritage, lots of dairy farming, and a love of recreational water sports. Until recently, their politics were pretty similar, too, with both states tending to elect moderately progressive politicians at the state level. Lately, though, their political paths have diverged. After Republicans took control of both the legislature and the governorship in Wisconsin in 2010, they enacted a conservative agenda, including changes in collective bargaining rights that gutted most public employee unions. In Minnesota, by contrast, Democrats took control of the political branches in 2012 and enacted laws their Wisconsin counterparts wouldn't even consider, including same-sex marriage rights and an expansion of Medicaid eligibility under the federal Affordable Care Act.

In both states, the partisan advantage is not great. Switching just a few thousand votes from one state to the other would change party control. In fact, Minnesota Democrats lost their state Senate majority in 2014—part of a huge victory for the GOP that year. Republicans now control all branches in half the states, compared with just seven held by Democrats, which is their lowest number since the Civil War. In many states, one party not only holds power but is completely dominant, with supermajorities of two thirds of the legislative seats or more. Politics at the state level is becoming a zero-sum game, with one party prevailing and the other losing, and with little interest in compromise. For decades, observers have talked about states as "laboratories of democracy," borrowing a

Chapter Objectives

After reading this chapter, you will be able to

- explain the role and activities of legislatures,
- discuss how legislatures are organized and how they operate,
- identify the characteristics of state legislators, and
- describe the relationship between legislators and public opinion.

phrase from Supreme Court justice Louis Brandeis, referring to experimentation with ideas that often blossom into national policy. Today, we have red labs and blue labs, with partisans pushing entirely different and opposite types of laws. Whether the topic is abortion, tax policy, voting rights, marijuana, or guns, Democratic "blue" states such as California and Connecticut are bound to take a different tack than are Republican "red" states such as Georgia and Tennessee.

While Congress barely functions, state legislators are able to move through ambitious, if mostly partisan, legislative programs. At the state level, most bills are still passed with broad, bipartisan support. But on controversial matters, Republicans and Democrats are pursuing entirely divergent agendas, with little need to compromise. "In many state legislatures, the minority has fewer opportunities to obstruct than they do in Congress," said Peverill Squire, a political scientist at the University of Missouri. "It does give the majority in most states a greater opportunity to exercise its will."[1]

Voters who prefer action to dysfunction should be pretty happy about all this. Whatever else you want to say about state politics these days, they are not sleepy. With so little consensus in the country about any number of issues, it might be better for states to be trying out different ideas than for Congress to come up with national solutions to many issues, suggests Lara Brown, a political scientist at George Washington University. Either one party would force through one-sided legislation that would create ire—as happened when the Affordable Care Act passed with strictly Democratic support—or Congress would come up with mushy compromises that would satisfy no one. "I'm not sure that people recognize the advantages that federalism does allow in a time as polarized as this is," Brown said.[2]

She may have a point. Approval ratings for Congress are barely into the double digits. By contrast, 57 percent of those surveyed by the Pew Research Center in 2013 approved of their state governments.[3] Not surprisingly, approval of state government was higher among Republicans in GOP-controlled states, while Democrats rated Democratic-led states more highly. Sizable minorities of voters in most states are likely to feel orphaned as their states pursue policies that aren't to their liking. This might be most apparent in "purple" states—those where voters are closely divided in terms of partisan loyalties. In North Carolina, Republicans control the state government and have enacted conservative legislation that triggered widely publicized "Moral Monday" protests organized by the National Association for the Advancement of Colored People. In Colorado, Democrats pushed through environmental and gun control measures that led to the recalls of two state senators in 2013. Even John Hickenlooper, the state's Democratic governor, conceded that the totality of his party's agenda was too much, too fast. "You go back and look at everything that got passed, and we don't see things we would change," Hickenlooper said. "But I think there was a sense in the state that it was just a lot of change. I don't mean that we would do anything differently, but I think it made people uncomfortable. Doing so much so fast in one year was a big bite to take."[4]

If partisan majorities are guilty of overreach—pushing policies that go further than most of the public can accept—they could be punished at the polls. In fact, voters even in one-sided states will still sometimes elect governors from the weaker party, to put a brake on the legislature. That happened in several states in 2014. But in most states, partisan majorities are pretty well entrenched. Few legislative seats are up for grabs, due to the fact that more and more voters are living in like-minded communities—a natural trend that is exacerbated by redistricting methods that aim to maximize support for a single party within most districts.

There have always been differences between states that favor low-tax, limited-government policies, such as Texas, and those that want government to play a more activist role, such as California. But polarization within and between states is increasing. Legislatures today are not so much places where compromises are made and consensus is formed as they are places where legislative leaders drive a particular agenda and punish colleagues who break with their party on key votes. The purpose of this chapter is to give you a sense of how legislators come to their decisions, who they are, what they do, and how they organize themselves in their institutions.

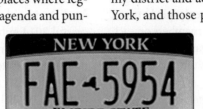

The Job of Legislatures

If Republicans hold 60 seats in the Indiana House of Representatives and Democrats have only 40, most of the time the Republicans are going to get their way. This is called **majority rule**.

But bills do not always pass according to predictable partisan majorities. On June 24, 2011, the New York state legislature voted to make the state the sixth to legalize gay marriage. The decision came as a significant surprise. Just 2 years earlier, when Democrats had the majority in the New York Senate, a bill to legalize gay marriage had failed on a lopsided vote. In the 2010 elections, Republicans won the edge in the New York Senate. As in most places, in New York Democrats are more likely than Republicans to favor gay marriage; yet, even with Republicans in charge, the legislation passed in the Senate because four Republicans joined with all but one of the chamber's Democrats in voting in favor.

Majority rule
The process in which the decision of a numerical majority is made binding on a group

The four Republicans had several reasons to break with their party. Polling showed that a strong majority of New Yorkers thought same-sex nuptials should be legal, so senators risked voter anger if they said no. Legalizing gay marriage was a top priority of the state's popular Democratic governor, Andrew Cuomo, and senators needed to stay in the governor's good graces to enact their own priorities. Still, the senators said that they had merely done what they thought was right. "I apologize for those who feel offended," said Mark Grisanti, one of the four Republicans. "I cannot deny a person, a human being, a taxpayer, a worker, the people of my district and across this state, the State of New York, and those people who make this the great state that it is the same rights that I have with my wife."[5]

Not surprisingly, some were offended. Social conservatives who oppose gay marriage play a key role in the Republican Party's coalition. "Marriage has always been, is now and always will be the union of one man and one woman in lifelong, life-giving union," the New York State Catholic Conference said in a statement. "Government does not have the authority to change this most basic of truths."[6] In 2012, the next time they were up for reelection, all four of the Republicans who had voted yes faced serious primary opposition from fellow Republicans, with foes spending hundreds of thousands of dollars to oust them. But gay marriage supporters also kicked in large amounts of campaign cash in their defense. One decided to retire rather than run again. Another lost in the Republican primary. A third lost to a Democratic opponent in the November election. As a result, when the legislature reconvened in 2013, Grisanti was the only one of the four left in the Senate.

The story of the four New York Republican senators demonstrates several key points about how legislatures operate today. Everyone understands that it is the job of the legislature to set policy for the state, in consultation with the governor—or sometimes despite the governor's wishes, if there are sufficient votes to override his or her veto. Nevertheless, the decisions that legislators make are, by their nature, political. It's difficult to please everybody, and often legislators have to balance competing interests. In this case, they had to choose between the desires of their party on one hand and the majority view of the state on the other. They had to choose which of two opposing interest groups they would offend, knowing that either choice would likely put their political careers at risk. And they had to consult their consciences, too.

Party caucuses in the state legislatures have grown further apart in recent years, with less agreement across party lines. The case of the New York gay marriage vote, in which just a few legislators broke with their party, is typical. For example, in Virginia in 2012, the legislature was weeks late completing its most basic job, writing a new state budget, because the Virginia Senate was evenly split between Democrats and Republicans—20 members on each side—and not a single member was willing to cross over and vote with the rival party.

> Everyone understands that it is the job of the legislature to set policy for the state, in consultation with the governor—or sometimes despite the governor's wishes, if there are sufficient votes to override his or her veto. Nevertheless, the decisions that legislators make are, by their nature, political. It's difficult to please everybody, and often legislators have to balance competing interests.

Bill sponsors seek to avoid such scenarios by engaging in **coalition building** or **logrolling**—finding ways to entice colleagues to support legislation by arguing that it would be in the best interest of their **districts**—or offering to swap their own vote on some future bill. Just as sponsors will try to build up the support they need for passage, an adamant opponent can stop a hated piece of legislation's progress through a chamber in many ways, including by mounting a **filibuster**, a kind of endless debate sometimes used in the U.S. Senate. With the Texas Senate running up against a midnight deadline to close out its business in 2013, Democratic state Senator Wendy Davis shot to national prominence by holding the floor for 11 hours with a filibuster against an abortion bill. Although she ran out the clock, the bill was soon passed in a special session (and Davis's celebrity did little to help her unsuccessful 2014 gubernatorial bid). Another way to derail legislation is to attach unwanted amendments, or **riders**, to a bill. The road to a bill's passage into law is twisty and sometimes full of unexpected hurdles. In 2013, Massachusetts Republicans blocked all legislative activity in the House for weeks by objecting to a change in the rules that allowed all members to look into "the can," a small metal box that sits on the Speaker's platform and contains copies of pending bills. John Dingell, D-Mich., the longest-serving member of the U.S. House of Representatives, perhaps best described the strange relationship between the actual substance of a bill and how it moves through the House when he said in 1984, "If you let me write procedure and I let you write substance, I'll screw you every time."[7]

All these complicated dynamics are why legislative leadership has sometimes been compared to the job of herding cats. "You come into the Senate every day with a wheelbarrow of 33 cats," writes William Bulger, a former president of the Massachusetts Senate. "Your job is to get the wheelbarrow with 17 of those cats to the other side of the chamber."[8]

Coalition building
The assembly of an alliance of groups to pursue a common goal or interest

Logrolling
A practice in which a legislator gives a colleague a vote on a particular bill in return for that colleague's vote on another bill

Districts
The geographical areas represented by members of a legislature

Filibuster
A debate that under U.S. Senate rules can drag on, blocking final action on the bill under consideration and preventing other bills from being debated

Riders
Amendments to a bill that are not central to the bill's intent

Denver Democratic representative Mark Ferrandino is the first openly gay lawmaker in Colorado to hold the title of House Speaker. He became Speaker in January 2013.

© Ed Andrieski/AP/Corbis

Legislatures were not designed to be simple. The congressional system was designed to be difficult enough to prevent new laws that have not been properly thought through and debated from bothering everybody. "The injury which may possibly be done by defeating a few good laws will be amply compensated by the advantage of preventing a number of bad ones," wrote Alexander Hamilton in *Federalist* No. 73.[9] Most state legislatures share the basic structure of the U.S. Congress, with a house chamber and a senate chamber, each of which must approve a bill before it can go to the governor to be signed into law. That means that even if a bill makes its way through all the circuitous steps of getting passed by the house, including **committee** fights and winning a majority in the chamber, it can easily die if the senate refuses to sign off on an identical version. "If we passed the Lord's Prayer, we'd send it to the Senate and they'd amend it and send it back," said Bob Bergren, Speaker of the Montana House.[10]

But as legislatures have grown more partisan, legislative leaders have been able to pass legislation without much **compromise**, counting on **rank-and-file members** to support party priorities. As political scientist Boris Shor notes, "About half of the states

are even more polarized than Congress—which is saying a lot."[11] Polarization—the inability of members of the two major parties to agree on much of anything—has stymied legislation in recent years in Congress, but it matters less now in states. When one party dominates a state, it is able to pass legislation pretty much to its heart's content.

What Legislatures Do

All state legislatures share four basic interrelated and often overlapping functions:

- *A lawmaking function:* They pass laws and create policy for their states.
- *A representative function:* They provide a means for various groups and individuals to have their interests represented in state policymaking.
- *A constituent service function:* They offer personalized constituent service to help residents sort out their problems with the state government.
- *An oversight function:* They oversee the activities of the governor and the executive branch and some private businesses through public hearings, budget reviews, and formal investigations.

Committee
A group of legislators who have the formal task of considering and writing bills in a particular issue area

Compromise
The result when there is no consensus on a policy change or spending amount but legislators find a central point on which a majority can agree

Rank-and-file members
Legislators who do not hold leadership positions or senior committee posts

Although state legislatures all address similar issues, including taxes, budgets, and a broad range of other matters (such as regulating office safety and requiring sex offenders to register their places of residence with police), differences in timing, state history, and political culture may cause one state's laws on a topic to differ widely from those of other states. Occasionally, legislatures are pressured to pass uniform laws, as when the federal government, through the National Minimum Drinking Age Act of 1984, insisted that the states raise their legal drinking ages to 21 or lose highway funding. Louisiana resisted the longest, adopting a minimum drinking age of 21 in 1987.

Often, laws are adapted to the local scene and are not easily molded to match other states' versions. Large insurance companies are regulated at the state level. They would love to have their agents qualified to sell in every state rather than having to take up to 50 different qualifying exams. "I'm still not sure what happens if Michigan says you can be an insurance agent if you can sign your name with your eyes shut, and New York says you've got to take a three-year course," said Alexander Grannis, chair of the insurance committee in the New York Assembly. "What happens if someone screws up—if we cancel a Michigan guy's license to practice here for malpractice, does that mean Michigan can retaliate and cancel a New Yorker's right to practice there?"[12]

Within a given state, the media and the public manage to register many failures of a legislature while sometimes failing to give the institution enough credit for its successes in balancing all the competing interests within the state. Ethics scandals generally receive greater coverage than do substantial debates; yet legislators debate and pass laws that cover everything from levels of Medicaid health insurance funding to clean water protections to aid for local governments to workers' compensation payments to the price of milk. In most legislatures, easily 90 percent of the bills receive almost no media attention and are of interest only to those they directly affect. The news media—and the voting public—pay attention only when issues that affect the broadest range of people are considered, such as increases (or cuts) in property tax rates. Legislators do not have the luxury of tuning out when complex and boring but important issues crop up.

One of the arguments against term limits is that legislators have to cope with many complicated issues, getting quickly up to speed on such topics as water rights and regional transportation plans. If they can serve for only limited terms, there is the potential that legislatures will end up reopening fights that had been settled through painful negotiations years earlier, because no one is around who remembers what the earlier lawmakers went through.

> State senators and representatives fight their biggest battles over budgets. Most of their power is derived from the fact that with the approval of the governor they can set fiscal policy, including tax rates.

State senators and representatives fight their biggest battles over budgets. Most of their power is derived from the fact that with the approval of the governor they can set fiscal policy, including tax rates. Dealing with how much money the state devotes to each of its programs is a way of revisiting all the problems that never go away. How much is enough to spend on education? How much of that education tab should the state pick up? Although public schools traditionally were funded by local property taxes, most states now pick up one third of the bill or more. How much money should be spent on health care? How long should prison terms be for all manner of crimes, and what should be done to reintegrate offenders into society once they've served their time? How big an investment should the state make in roads or public transportation? How much can be spent overall before the state is taxing individuals and businesses too highly? Practically every state has a legal requirement to balance its budget every year, so legislators debate how to make spending match what the state takes in through taxes—or at least how to make the numbers look as though they match on paper. State legislatures annually address hundreds of such issues, large and small.

Lawmaking

Legislatures tend to be reactive institutions. After more media attention was focused on the issue of high school football players' getting concussions, every single state passed legislation to address the issue. Most of these were largely designed to raise awareness of the problem, calling on schools to provide training and to remove players from the field who are suspected of having sustained a concussion. Some states have gone further, with 20 states requiring coaches to be trained in concussion recognition and awareness. A few are looking for ways to prevent such injuries before they occur. In 2010, for example, Massachusetts enacted a law that prevents coaches, trainers, or volunteers from encouraging or allowing students to engage in any technique that endangers the health of students, such as using a helmet as a weapon.

Most issues attract far less attention. The Texas state legislature grappled with more than 10,000 bills in 2013, while even much mellower Montana took up more than 1,000 that year.[13] Despite this amount of activity—or perhaps because of it—legislators generally do not go looking for issues to address. The typical bill is introduced for one of several reasons: It is a bill that has to be considered, such as the annual state budget; it is a bill dealing with a common problem modeled on another state's legislation; or it is something an individual or a group outside the legislature—such as constituents, the governor, or lobbyists—wants considered.

It may not always seem like it, but constituents can have a lot of influence in government. In Massachusetts, for instance, legislators are obliged to consider petitions to introduce bills on any topic a state resident wants. In 2014, Chloe Stirling, a 12-year-old girl who had gotten busted for baking and selling cupcakes, helped convince the Illinois legislature to pass a law limiting the authority of local governments to regulate the sale of baked goods. She testified before a committee and presented the governor with a plateful of cupcakes.

Governors and the executive branch are also powerful players in the legislative process, promoting ideas they want legislators to work on. Some of these bills are designed to address immediate problems quickly. For example, when the National Football League's Minnesota Vikings threatened to leave the state unless the team received financial help to build a new stadium, Governor Mark Dayton made the stadium bill a top priority. In 2012, he succeeded in persuading the legislature to commit $348 million in state funds to the project.

Finally, lobbyists representing a client such as a beer company or auto manufacturer often will promote draft legislation in the hope that a member of the legislature or general assembly—as the legislatures are known in Colorado, Georgia, Pennsylvania, and several other states—will sponsor it as a bill. True.com, an online dating service, convinced legislators in several states in 2006 to introduce legislation requiring such websites to conduct background checks of all their users. "I was shocked when I found out that dating services, which market themselves as finding someone's true soulmate, don't provide any kind of even cursory background checks," said Illinois state representative John Bradley, whose bill passed the state House that year. But, even though True.com's founder said he was motivated by an online meeting that ended in murder, his competitors were able to convince legislators that the bill was only a "PR stunt" designed to make True.com's services, which included background checks, look more enticing. They said there was no way of checking on customers, who everyone knew to be fibbers. "There's sort of a joke in the industry that the average person lies by 10 pounds and 10 years," said Eric Straus of Cupid.com.[14]

Although lobbyists promote bills, they also devote an enormous amount of energy to trying to kill bills. Part of the job of the legislative process is to act as a sort of referee among a lot of competing interests. Any proposed change in state law that someone views as a positive step is likely to adversely affect—or at least frighten—someone else. In 2011, the Kentucky Medical Association and the Kentucky Academy of Eye Physicians fought to kill a bill that would allow optometrists to perform laser eye surgeries. The

Illinois governor Pat Quinn is presented with cupcakes by Chloe Stirling, whose in-home cupcake business was shut down by the Madison County Health Department because she didn't have a license. The move garnered national attention and new state legislation to allow amateur bakers a limited number of sales without requiring a license.

groups argued that optometrists lack the right training to perform the surgery, but they were also defending their turf—they represent ophthalmologists, not optometrists. Their adversary, the Kentucky Optometric Association, proved to be too strong, however. The optometrists had hired 18 lobbyists to advocate for the legislation and had contributed campaign cash to all but one of the legislature's 138 members over the previous 2 years.[15] The bill passed. In Kentucky and elsewhere, disputes like this are common—doctors battle with nurse practitioners, or dentists disagree with dental hygienists. When a bill comes up for a vote, state legislators are forced to pick a side.

Legislators react most strongly to bills in which they have a personal stake or that they know will affect their constituents directly. Let's say that environmentalists are concerned about a river's water quality and want to require new water filters at a paper mill. The mill's owners, concerned that the cost of the filters will be exorbitant, warn that they will have to lay off 300 employees if the bill goes through. A legislator from that area will have to worry about whether creating a healthier environment is worth being accused of costing people their jobs. Legislators who live clear across the state from the river and its mill, however, will hold the the bill easily could be accused of deciding votes. The people directly affected—the company, the workers, and the downstream residents worried about pollution—will all try to portray themselves as standing for the greater good. If no side is clearly right and favoring one side over the other can do political damage, die. Legislators could then doing nothing when in reality they are merely reflecting the lack of statewide consensus about how to solve the problem.[16]

Representation

The bulk of the work legislators do involves formulating the law and trying to keep an eye on the executive branch, but legislators' primary responsibility is to provide **representation** for their constituents. Basically, they ensure that the interests of those for whom they speak are properly considered as part of decision making at the state level. For example, in 2012 California state representative Roger Dickinson introduced a bill to create a Public Employees Bill of Rights in the state. The legislation set out a host of new rules to help government workers, such as mandating that they could not be required to work extra when their colleagues were fired unless they were paid extra for their time. Some critics mocked the concept. California has had some of

Representation
Individual legislators acting as the voices of their constituencies within the house or senate

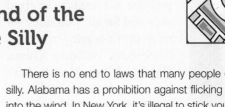

Taking on the Law in the Land of the Free . . . and the Home of the Silly

Rich Smith, a British journalism student, spent one Christmas Day playing board games. He came across a reference to an obscure law in Florida that made it illegal for divorced women to go parachuting on Sundays. Enchanted by this and a treasure trove of other dumb American laws, he decided to spend the summer after graduation driving across the United States and breaking every outdated or just plain absurd law he could find. "Tying giraffes to lampposts seemed a funnier way in which to become a felon" than arson or murder, Smith writes in his book about the spree, *You Can Get Arrested for That.*[a]

Smith and a friend attempted to break two dozen laws in all, succeeding in most cases. Many of the laws concerned personal behavior. Traveling east from San Francisco, Smith carried out his first successful crime by peeling an orange in a hotel room, an action illegal throughout California.

He then drove to Globe, Arizona, where it is illegal to play cards on the street against an American Indian, and did just that. He made sure to order plenty of garlic bread along with his pizza in Indianapolis, because in that city it is illegal to enter a theater within 3 hours of eating garlic. He also broke the law by eating watermelon in a cemetery in Spartanburg, South Carolina, and by sleeping on top of a refrigerator in Pennsylvania.

There is no end to laws that many people consider silly. Alabama has a prohibition against flicking boogers into the wind. In New York, it's illegal to stick your thumb against your nose and wiggle your fingers at someone. Montana men aren't allowed out in public with shaved chests on display, while New Mexico women can't go out in public if they haven't shaved.

The fashion police have made it illegal to wear a goatee in Massachusetts, so Smith grew one in plenty of time for his visit to that state. He also broke several laws concerning fishing, including his attempt to hunt down marine mammals in a lake in Utah and, of course, his blatant disregard for Chicago's ban on fishing while wearing pajamas. But he lacked sufficient skill to violate Tennessee's stricture against catching a fish with a lasso.

Although Smith managed to break numerous laws, several others defeated him. He failed to find a bathtub to carry illegally across the village green in Longmeadow, Massachusetts, and he couldn't persuade a woman in Iowa to kiss him for longer than 5 minutes (or at all).

Several of his crimes were witnessed by police or private security guards, but perhaps it's in the nature of "dumb" laws that they aren't rigorously enforced. The only time Smith and his buddy got into serious trouble was when they drove at 97 miles per hour in a 75-mile-per-hour zone in Wyoming. That time, they got nailed.

[a]Published by Three Rivers Press, New York, 2006.

the worst budget problems of any state. Why, the critics wondered, would the state offer new protections to government workers when it is already struggling to pay the salaries and benefits of its workforce and to maintain funding for basic services such as education and health care? "There is hardly a workplace in recession-battered America that has not been hit with layoffs," the *Modesto Bee* newspaper said in an editorial. "Private-sector workers regularly shoulder additional responsibilities along with pay cuts. It's how many deal with a drastically altered economic reality. Despite the valuable work that many of them do, government workers should not be shielded from such realities."[17] Dickinson, though, was just looking out for his constituents. His district is in Sacramento, California's capital, where state agencies are headquartered. The city is home to more public workers than any other in the state.[18]

Texas legislators approved a bill that would allow for random drug testing of thousands of high school athletes in an effort to stamp out steroid use.

If a problem is real and persistent enough, a state's legislature will address it eventually. Sometimes there is a general recognition that a long-festering problem just needs to be fixed once and for all. That does not mean the fix is going to be easy. Some states, including Kansas, Ohio, and Pennsylvania, have had to tweak their school funding formulas continually in response to state supreme court decisions that found their education systems inadequate.

Legislatures often finish their work on an issue not because of outside pressure but because of internal changes. New leaders in the Arizona Senate in 2001 brought with them solutions to long-standing issues that included understaffing in the state's highway patrol, underfunding of the state's mental health system, and provisioning for water through new contracts. Legislators even managed to repeal antiquated sex laws that made it a crime for unmarried couples to live together.[19] More recently, in 2008, Republicans won control of both legislative chambers in Tennessee for the first time since the Civil War. They quickly began pushing long-sought legislation in areas such as the regulation of guns, charter schools, and abortion. "I think every bad bill I've seen in my 10 years got resurrected this year and had a chance of passing," complained Mike Turner, chair of the House Democratic Caucus.[20] Two years later, the Republicans won even bigger legislative majorities and one of their own, Bill Haslam, was elected governor. They quickly enacted an ambitious agenda that included many party priorities, such as phasing out the inheritance tax, weakening teacher tenure, enacting tort reform, and overhauling civil service rules.

Not surprisingly, states with stagnant leadership or long-term control by one party or the other may have a harder time making breakthroughs. Changes in partisan control bring in new leaders and, with them, new agendas that reflect new priorities and different constituencies. After all,

before a bill can even get far enough to be debated, the idea for it must be developed. To get ideas for bills, legislators turn to each other, to staff, to colleagues in other states, and to outside sources such as companies with causes of their own or think tanks interested in pushing change. As the late Alan Rosenthal, who was a leading expert on state legislatures at Rutgers University, pointed out, "Legislation is becoming a national phenomenon."[21] National associations of legislators, such as the National Conference of State Legislatures and the American Legislative Exchange Council, promulgate ideas that quickly spread from state to state, as do bills pushed by national corporations and interest groups. And states may be addressing new issues that crop up on a similar time frame. In 2014, every state that was in session that year (which was all but four of them) saw legislation meant to address Common Core, a set of educational standards developed by states but promoted by the Obama administration and private groups such as the Gates Foundation. Common Core was adopted quickly by most states but soon grew controversial. About 20 percent of the legislation introduced that year was designed to slow or stop its implementation.

Sometimes private companies are able to go "venue shopping," finding sympathetic legislators in a state who will pass a law that may become a model for other states. But most ideas are still homegrown. Minnesota has an unusually fertile landscape when it comes to ideas for the legislature. More than 750 foundations are active in the state's public life. During the mid-1990s, 30 of them matched funds with the legislature to help nonprofit groups plan for federal budget cuts and changes in welfare law.[22] In addition, the state capital of St. Paul has the now-unusual benefit of being able to mine two major metropolitan daily newspapers—the *Pioneer Press* and the *Star Tribune*, which serves the capital's "twin city" of Minneapolis. Once upon a time, numerous communities were served by two or more competing newspapers. Today, consolidations and foldings have forced most areas to make do with one, if that. Fortunately for Minnesota's legislators, both of the Twin Cities' papers actively cover public policy. Perhaps partly as a result, the state was the first to ban smoking in restaurants, the first to allow schoolchildren to choose among public schools, the first to allow charter schools, and the first to enact requirements that people holding comparable jobs receive comparable pay. Such engagement from the media—and, by extension, interest from the public—has become fairly rare. We discuss how the media cover state legislatures a little later in this chapter.

Constituent Service

Aside from debating and passing laws, and ensuring that the interests of various groups are represented in decision making, legislators devote a good deal of time and energy to **constituent service**. They help clear up problems that citizens are having with public agencies or even private companies. They also act as liaisons between their constituents and unelected parts of the government in the executive branch, the bureaucracy that everyone knows and loves to hate.

Legislators and their staffs spend incredible amounts of their time dealing with constituent service requests, also known as **casework**.[23] Residents of a state may experience all manner of frustration coping with state laws or may merely want assistance in sorting through regulatory requirements. One of the advantages of being an **incumbent** is having the ability to dole out this kind of personalized help. While a recount battle dragged on in Minnesota for more than 6 months following the 2008 election, U.S. senator Amy Klobuchar, D-Minn., and her staff had to do the work of two senators—handling double the usual caseload of sorting through issues, from helping military veterans in the state navigate the federal bureaucracy "to adoptions that have been stalled out in Guatemala," she told MSNBC.[24]

At the state level, some legislators have staff members devoted solely to helping constituents.

This is particularly true in their district offices—offices located back home in the area they represent, as opposed to their capitol offices. Typical issues include tracking down deadbeat dads for child support, figuring out how constituents can receive proper health coverage under Medicaid programs, and determining which federal agency to contact with questions about military matters.

In one humorous case, Jim Townsend received a call from a constituent complaining that the grass in the median strip of a state road near his house had become overgrown. Townsend was not only a legislator but also the majority leader of the Oklahoma House. When he called the highway department, he expected action. He was promised prompt service, but the same constituent called him back 2 weeks later to report that nothing had been done. Townsend took matters into his own hands, putting his own riding mower in the back of his pickup truck and doing the mowing himself.[25] "I spend a tremendous amount of time on constituent service," said Tennessee senator Rosalind Kurita, D-Clarksville. "When we are in session, I probably make five or six calls a day and easily [write] that many e-mails and letters. To me, that is one of the most important things we do."[26]

No one objects to a senator like Kurita helping a 7-year-old boy who has outgrown his wheelchair figure out how to receive a new one through the state's health insurance program. The problem is that attempts to help individuals sometimes morph into policy decisions. That is, a legislator might not only write a letter to help a particular person but also write a bill that changes the way the state approaches a program, such as health insurance. Helping an individual may be all well and good, but changing the system based on the personal story of one constituent is not necessarily the best way to create policies that will affect thousands.

Undoubtedly, it is important for legislators to hear about the real-world experiences of their constituents. Because they cannot meet with everybody, however, they need to rely on reports and studies to get a complete picture. They otherwise might be swayed too greatly by personal interactions. The danger of politicians' having to raise significant campaign finance treasuries is not so much that their votes can be bought but

---

Constituent service
The work done by legislators to help residents in their voting districts

Casework
The work undertaken by legislators and their staffs in response to requests for help from constituents

Incumbent
A person holding office

FIGURE 7-1

HOW IT WORKS

A One-Eyed Frog's View of the Legislative Process, or How a Bill Really Became a Law in Minnesota

The mechanisms by which a bill becomes a law at the state level are similar to the mechanisms at work at the federal level. And we've all seen the flowcharts that outline the ins and outs: A bill goes in one side, gets debated, marked up, and reported out, and then comes out the other side as a real-life law to be implemented, or it gets returned to the legislature for an override, or it gets "killed." You'd be forgiven for thinking that beneath that abstraction lies a more complex and interesting process.

You'd be right. Below is a different flowchart, this one fleshing out what actually happened when a group of Minnesota teens brought to light the fact that the frog population in their area was turning up with extra limbs and missing eyes. About eight months and $151,000 later, the frogs were in much better shape.

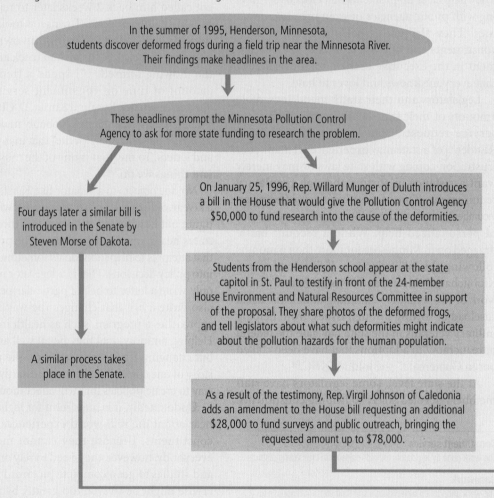

In the summer of 1995, Henderson, Minnesota, students discover deformed frogs during a field trip near the Minnesota River. Their findings make headlines in the area.

These headlines prompt the Minnesota Pollution Control Agency to ask for more state funding to research the problem.

Four days later a similar bill is introduced in the Senate by Steven Morse of Dakota.

On January 25, 1996, Rep. Willard Munger of Duluth introduces a bill in the House that would give the Pollution Control Agency $50,000 to fund research into the cause of the deformities.

Students from the Henderson school appear at the state capitol in St. Paul to testify in front of the 24-member House Environment and Natural Resources Committee in support of the proposal. They share photos of the deformed frogs, and tell legislators about what such deformities might indicate about the pollution hazards for the human population.

A similar process takes place in the Senate.

As a result of the testimony, Rep. Virgil Johnson of Caledonia adds an amendment to the House bill requesting an additional $28,000 to fund surveys and public outreach, bringing the requested amount up to $78,000.

Source: Minnesota House of Representatives Public Information Office, "Capitol Steps: How Six Bills Became Law."

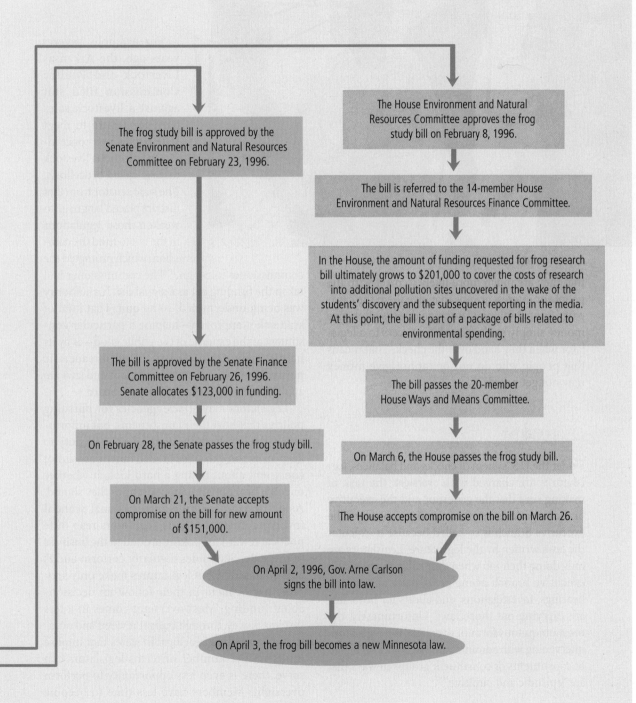

The frog study bill is approved by the Senate Environment and Natural Resources Committee on February 23, 1996.

The House Environment and Natural Resources Committee approves the frog study bill on February 8, 1996.

The bill is referred to the 14-member House Environment and Natural Resources Finance Committee.

In the House, the amount of funding requested for frog research bill ultimately grows to $201,000 to cover the costs of research into additional pollution sites uncovered in the wake of the students' discovery and the subsequent reporting in the media. At this point, the bill is part of a package of bills related to environmental spending.

The bill is approved by the Senate Finance Committee on February 26, 1996. Senate allocates $123,000 in funding.

The bill passes the 20-member House Ways and Means Committee.

On February 28, the Senate passes the frog study bill.

On March 6, the House passes the frog study bill.

On March 21, the Senate accepts compromise on the bill for new amount of $151,000.

The House accepts compromise on the bill on March 26.

On April 2, 1996, Gov. Arne Carlson signs the bill into law.

On April 3, the frog bill becomes a new Minnesota law.

Being mayor means constantly meeting with constituents, as Newark Mayor Cory Booker (front right) does here while running for the U.S. Senate in 2013.

For example, several years ago, the Arkansas Livestock and Poultry Commission filed suit against a livestock sales barn for failure to meet state regulations concerning an infectious livestock disease called brucellosis. The state senator from that district placed language to weaken those regulations in the bill to fund the commission, which prompted the commissioner to resign.[28] The commissioner had taken the funding cut as a signal that his authority was being undermined, so he quit. That kind of scattershot approach—helping a particular constituent at the expense of the public good—is by its nature inequitable. The point of bureaucratic norms is to make sure that regulations and laws are applied fairly and evenly across the board.

Legislators may attack agencies for pursuing policies that hurt their constituents, but unfortunately the legislative branch—despite its duty to keep an eye on executive branch functions—is not consistent about taking a hard look at whether ongoing programs are functioning as they should. Aside from unearthing an occasional scandal involving misspent funds, legislators reap little political reward for poking around in the business of the state. Staff aides regularly perform audits and evaluations, but legislatures make only sporadic use of them in their follow-up decisions about funding. Most oversight comes in a less systematic way, through budget reviews and occasional committee hearings. In states that impose limits on the number of terms legislators can serve, there is even less opportunity to perform oversight. Members have less time to become expert in any particular area, and so they often rely heavily on expert testimony from the very executive branch they are meant to oversee.

that they are much more likely to meet with the people or interest groups that give them the campaign contributions. Campaign donors often give money simply so they can have access to a legislator when they hand over the check. That means that people who do not or cannot give money may not get heard.

Oversight

Under the U.S. system of checks and balances, legislatures are charged with **oversight**, the task of making sure that the governor and the executive branch agencies are functioning properly. The executive branch is so called because it executes the laws written by the legislature. Legislators are only doing their job when they call governors and executive branch agencies to account through hearings, investigations, and audits for how they are carrying out those laws. Unfortunately, the most ubiquitous form of oversight is a legislator's intervening with administrative agencies on behalf of constituents or constituent groups in ways that are "episodic and punitive."[27]

Oversight
The legislature's role in making sure that the governor and executive branch agencies are properly implementing the laws

States Under Stress

Help Wanted: Must Enjoy High Stress, Low Pay, and Limited Autonomy

This decade has been marked by massive turnover among state legislators. The most recent round of redistricting and big GOP gains in 2010 meant that as legislative sessions got under way in 2013, roughly half the legislators in the country had 2 years of experience or less. Lots of newcomers were elected in 2014 as well, even in states that don't impose term limits.

Some of this has to do with legislative structures and salaries, which have led to changes in the types of people the office typically attracts—and the amount of time politicians are willing to serve.

For many states in the 20th century, serving in a legislature offered a slice of political power and a concentrated few weeks of social networking. The job hardly paid anything, but time wasn't much of a disincentive because the sessions frequently were over by springtime. As a result, the job attracted local civic leaders—lawyers, farmers, insurance brokers—who could afford to spend concentrated periods away from work and who took it as an honor that their fellow citizens desired their services.

All that began to change in the 1960s and even more in the 1970s with the movement to reform and professionalize legislatures, promoted and largely financed by the Ford Foundation. The foundation supported annual legislative sessions, enhanced staffing and technical capacity, and far greater transparency in communicating with the public. The reformers also called for higher salaries to reflect the new level of responsibility that state legislators should be taking on.

By 1980, many of the largest states had essentially bought into the reform model. Legislatures in California, Illinois, New York, Pennsylvania, and a handful of other places were meeting through most of the year, hiring professional staff to manage much of the workload, and ramping up legislators' pay significantly.

A few states, most of them small ones, rejected the reform model almost entirely, continuing to run short sessions with minimal staffing and old-fashioned pay scales. To this day, senators and representatives in New Hampshire receive $200 as compensation for 2 years of service, with no per diem included.

Left in between were midsized states, which chose to adopt most of the reform recommendations but declined to make corresponding adjustments in their members' pay. By the 1980s, most of these states were asking their members to give up substantial portions of their year to legislative sessions and postsession business, often making it difficult for them to hold private-sector jobs and paying them less than even the lower ranks of professional workers.

The result was that the old incentive structure disappeared. Service in a heavy-duty, low-paying institution ceased to be attractive to the Main Street business contingent that had signed up for it in earlier years. Instead, legislative careers began to attract a new cohort: the independently wealthy, citizen activists who were not the primary breadwinners in their families, and people engaged in low-paying professional jobs who could run without taking a significant pay cut. Being a legislator in the reform years meant accepting a financial squeeze, but for the politically ambitious, they could enjoy a good deal of influence.

In recent years, however, there's been less room for individual legislators to promote their pet causes. States' legislative leaders began reclaiming the power they had lost over the preceding decades. They raised leadership political action committee money to recruit favored candidates in competitive districts and maintained an influence over these new recruits once the legislative sessions convened. They began showing less tolerance for the mavericks and individualists who had acquired a substantial amount of power in the early reform years. Perhaps even more important, legislative politics started to take on a sharper partisan cast than had been the case before. The simplest way to explain state legislative politics in the past two decades is to say it has become more like congressional politics. Legislators vote more frequently in lockstep agreement with their party majorities than they used to, with opportunities for policy freelancing by individuals few and far between.

So it shouldn't be a surprise if significant numbers of legislators in heavily partisan states come to feel that there are more enjoyable, less stressful, and more lucrative ways they might be spending their time.

Source: Adapted from Alan Ehrenhalt, "The Evolution of State Legislatures Has Driven Some to Flee," *Governing*, September 2014, http://www.governing.com/columns/assessments/gov-state-legislature-evolution.html.

And for each program, it seems, there are not only agency officials but also program beneficiaries and lobbyists who will question the motives of legislators or staffers who seek to audit the program's work. In other words, there's often not much reward for a legislator in taking the job of oversight seriously. For example, in 2007, the North Carolina legislature created the Program Evaluation Division, which was charged with compiling a scorecard to show how state agencies were performing, in much the same way information about the performance of private companies might be compiled for investors. John Turcotte, the division's founding director, said his goal was to "target programs for evaluation that are important to the General Assembly and also look at all state government programs collectively to avoid legislative oversight gaps."[29] Turcotte's first report looked at agricultural research stations. North Carolina had the most of any state in the country—21, compared with only 11 in the much larger state of California—and Turcotte's group concluded that there was no economic or strategic justification for the state to support so many. "That report was like setting off a nuclear weapon in the area of Raleigh," he said. "Any time you question the necessity of an institution or a major component of a program, you will create massive opposition."[30]

Organization and Operation of Legislatures

The U.S. system of representative democracy was designed to be messy. In their book *Republic on Trial,* Alan Rosenthal and his coauthors argue that the institutions of democracy should be more popular because they work pretty well, but they concede, "The American political system was not designed for people to understand."[31] Legislatures were created because, even in colonial days, this country was too large and its problems too complex to be addressed by its vast numbers of individual citizens. We elect legislatures in our republican form of government to argue out our problems at appointed times and in a single space, in sessions at the capitol. The ranks of the legislatures have become far more diverse over the past 30 years. Although the average state legislator is still a white male, there are nearly 4 times as many African Americans and nearly 6 times as many women serving in legislatures today as there were in 1970. Also over the past 40 years or so, legislatures have become better equipped to do their job by hiring more and better-trained staffers. None of these changes, however, have made state legislatures any more popular with the public.

Bicameralism

Every state has a constitution that describes a body that can pass state laws. In every state but Nebraska, which has a unicameral (or one-house) legislature, the legislature is bicameral (or divided into two houses), pretty much like the U.S. Congress. As mentioned earlier in this chapter, one chamber is normally called either the house of representatives or the assembly and the other is called the senate. The Tenth Amendment of the U.S. Constitution reserves to the states all powers not given to the federal government, and state legislatures can write any state law that does not interfere with federal laws.

The house, or assembly, is considered more of a "people's house," with its members representing fewer people for shorter terms than do their colleagues in the senate. The house always has more members, known as state representatives, than the senate does. There are 163 representatives in the Missouri General Assembly, for example, but only 34 senators. There are some exceptions, but generally senators serve 4-year terms, whereas house members have to be reelected every 2 years. The two chambers operate independently, with separate leaders, committees, and agendas, although both chambers have to pass the same version of a bill before it can be sent to the governor to be signed into law or vetoed. Nebraska, with its unicameral legislature, is the one exception.

Legislative Leadership

Most state legislatures have essentially the same leadership structure, at least for their top positions.

TABLE 7-1

Total Number of State Legislators (House and Senate), 2014

State	Senate Members	House Members	Total Members
Alabama	35	105	140
Alaska	20	40	60
Arizona	30	60	90
Arkansas	35	100	135
California	40	80	120
Colorado	35	65	100
Connecticut	36	151	187
Delaware	21	41	62
Florida	40	120	160
Georgia	56	180	236
Hawaii	25	51	76
Idaho	35	70	105
Illinois	59	118	177
Indiana	50	100	150
Iowa	50	100	150
Kansas	40	125	165
Kentucky	38	100	138
Louisiana	39	105	144
Maine	35	151	186
Maryland	47	141	188
Massachusetts	40	160	200
Michigan	38	110	148
Minnesota	67	134	201
Mississippi	52	122	174
Missouri	34	163	197
Montana	50	100	150

State	Senate Members	House Members	Total Members
Nebraska	49	n/a	49
Nevada	21	42	63
New Hampshire	24	400	424
New Jersey	40	80	120
New Mexico	42	70	112
New York	63	150	212
North Carolina	50	120	170
North Dakota	47	94	141
Ohio	33	99	132
Oklahoma	48	101	149
Oregon	30	60	90
Pennsylvania	50	203	253
Rhode Island	38	75	113
South Carolina	46	124	170
South Dakota	35	70	105
Tennessee	33	99	132
Texas	31	150	181
Utah	29	75	104
Vermont	30	150	180
Virginia	40	100	140
Washington	49	98	147
West Virginia	34	100	134
Wisconsin	33	99	132
Wyoming	30	60	90
Total	1,971	5,411	7,382

Source: National Conference of State Legislatures, "2014 State and Legislative Partisan Composition," June 9, 2014, http://www.ncsl.org/documents/statevote/legiscontrol_2014.pdf.

MAP 7-1

Partisan Control of State Government, 1954

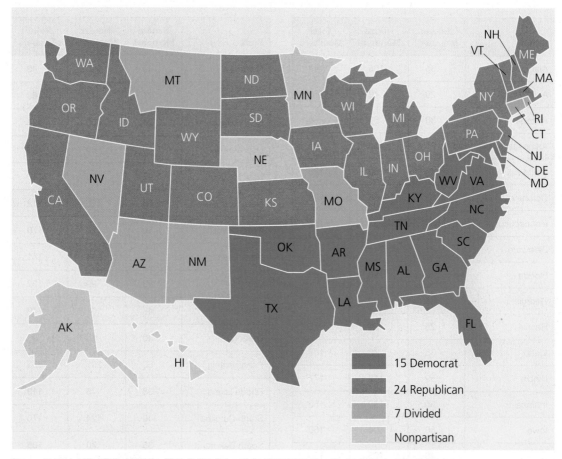

Source: All data from Carl Klarner Dataverse, "State Partisan Balance Data, 1937–2011," https://thedata.harvard.edu/dvn/dv/cklarner.

At the beginning of a session, each house votes in its Speaker. This is generally someone picked beforehand by a **caucus**, or meeting, of members of the majority party. The majority leader and the minority leader rank just below the Speaker of the house. *Majority* and *minority* here refer to the respective strengths of the major par ties. Either the Democratic or the Republican Party may hold the majority of seats in a chamber. (In 2014, fewer than two-dozen legislators—out of more than 7,000 nationwide—were indepen dents or members of third parties.) In the senate,

Caucus

All the members of a party—Republican or Democrat—within a legislative chamber; also refers to meetings of members of a political party in a chamber

the top leader is generally known as the president, president pro tempore (often shortened to presi-dent pro tem), or majority leader.

Certain aspects of the leadership positions remain constant across all the states. For example, a Speaker will typically preside over daily sessions of the house or assembly, refer bills to the appropriate committees, and sign legislation as it makes its way over to the senate or the governor's desk. Leaders appoint committee chairs (in some states, all the members of committees), set or change committee jurisdictions, and offer staff or legislative help to rank-and-file members. They also often help with campaigns, including providing financial support.

The amount of power invested in the office of Speaker or senate president does vary by state, however. In the Texas Senate, leadership powers

MAP 7-2

Partisan Control of State Government, 2014

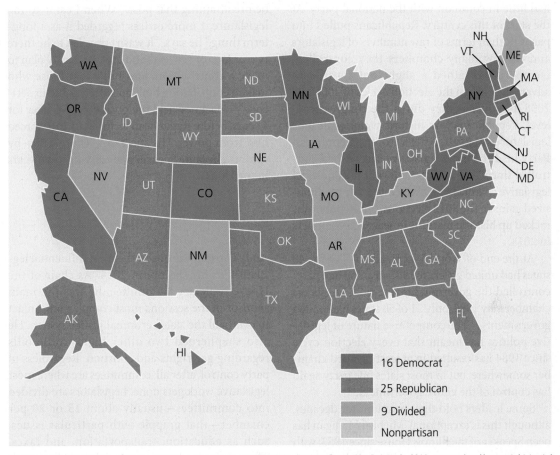

	16 Democrat
	25 Republican
	9 Divided
	Nonpartisan

Source: National Conference of State Legislatures, "2014 State and Legislative Partisan Composition," June 9, 2014, www.ncsl.org/documents/statevote/legiscontrol_2014.pdf.

are invested in the office of lieutenant governor. Lieutenant governors normally do not possess much formal power, but in Texas, they appoint the members of committees and committee chairs in the 31-member body and decide which bills are considered and when. In some older legislatures, such as those in New Jersey and Massachusetts, the Senate president performs all those functions, presides over debates, counts votes, and ensures member attendance. In California, those powers rest with the Senate president pro tem. But regardless of how the formal duties are divided up, usually there is one individual who emerges as holding the most power and speaking for the chamber in negotiating with the other chamber and the governor.

With the exception of Nebraska, where parties are actually banned from the nonpartisan

unicameral legislature, legislatures are divided along party lines (and even in Nebraska, the Democratic and Republican parties endorse candidates for the legislature, so it's well-known which lawmakers affiliate with which party). Not only does the majority party get to pick the top leader, but it gets to fill virtually all the important committee chairs as well. A party majority is worth much more than the comfort of knowing that your fellow Democrats or Republicans will help you outvote the opposition on most bills. Holding the leadership and chair positions means that the majority party gets to set the agenda—deciding which bills will be heard for a vote. From the 1950s into the early 1990s, Democrats held a 2-to-1 edge in the number of legislative seats and controlled many more chambers than did their

Republican counterparts. Much of the Democratic Party's dominance came from the South, where many of the Democrats were conservatives who had little in common with the national party. At the start of this century, Republicans pulled into parity both in terms of raw numbers of legislators and in how many chambers they controlled. Democrats regained a slight but significant advantage back in the election cycles of 2006 and 2008, but, just as they did at the congressional level, Republicans won historic victories in state legislatures in 2010. Afterward, the Republican Party held the most legislative seats it had controlled since 1928 and about 60 of the nation's 99 legislative chambers.[32] Democrats made medium-sized gains in the 2012 elections, but Republicans racked up historic margins in seats and chambers in 2014.

At the end of World War II, all but 7 of the 48 states had united governments, meaning one party controlled the governorship and both legislative chambers. By 1986, only 21 of 50 states had united governments.[33] The competitive nature of legislative politics has meant that every election cycle since 1984 has resulted in at least one tied chamber somewhere, but in most states one party again has control of the entire government.[34]

Some leaders hold their positions for decades, although this is exceptional. Michael Madigan has been Speaker of the Illinois House since 1983, with the exception of 2 years when his party lost power. Mike Miller started his run as president of the Maryland Senate back in 1987 and was still going strong in 2014. Fred Risser is the nation's longest-serving state legislator; he was elected to the Wisconsin Assembly in 1956 and then to the Wisconsin Senate in 1962, and has served in a variety of legislative leadership positions over the past 50 years, including stints as majority leader, minority leader, and Senate president. Lots of legislative experience can be an advantage in getting leadership positions, but it is by no means required. Climbing the leadership ladder can take no time at all in states with term limits, such as California and Florida, where House members can serve only 6 and 8 years, respectively, and Speakers are sometimes chosen as freshmen. In contrast, Joe Hackney, who became Speaker of the North Carolina House in 2007, had to serve more than a quarter century before attaining that post. "When I came to the legislature, I more or less regarded it as a long-term thing," he says. "It wasn't my plan to be there two or four or six years and quit. It was my plan to make a contribution, and I saw that those who make a contribution built up seniority and experience."[35] Hackney held the position of Speaker for 4 years, before Republican victories in 2010 forced him from power. His successor, Thom Tillis, by contrast, became Speaker after serving just 4 years in the House.

Committees

Andy Gipson was one of the most influential legislators in Mississippi in 2014. As chair of the House Judiciary Committee, he was the main sponsor of the session's most complex bill, an act to overhaul the state's criminal justice system. He also shepherded two other high-profile bills regarding gay rights and abortion. Regardless of party control, after all, committees are where most legislative work gets done. Legislators are divided into committees—usually about 15 or 20 per chamber—that grapple with particular issues, such as education, transportation, and taxes. Thousands of bills are introduced annually in each legislature. Most of these bills never reach the floor where the full house or senate meets. Basically, they never make it past the committee stage to be debated or voted on by the house or senate as a whole. Instead, they are sent to the appropriate committee, where they may be debated and amended but usually die without a hearing. Just as the senate president, house Speaker, or other leader sets the agenda for floor action on bills, so the committee chair decides which bills are going to be heard and receive priority treatment at the committee level.

Legislators try to serve on the committees where they will have the most influence. The most prestigious committees are the budget committees, which set tax and spending levels. Other

committees debate policies, but unless funding is provided to pay for those policies, they do not matter very much. Seats on a finance or appropriations committee are highly sought after, but members will also "request appointment to committees which will give them the most visibility and interest in their districts."[36] Thus, a senator from a rural district may want to serve on an agriculture committee. A representative who previously served on a city council may want a seat on the local government committee.

While any member can introduce legislation on any topic, members of the education committee, for example, are more likely to introduce and influence bills that affect schools. When an education bill is being debated in the full house or senate, other members, who have other specialties, will turn to members of the education committee for guidance about what the bill would do and how they should vote. The same holds true for other issues, such as transportation and health care.

Rank-and-File Members

Not every legislator, of course, can be a leader. The majority of legislators—those who provide leaders with their votes—are known as rank-and-file members of the legislature. And no legislator—leader or rank-and-file member—can be fully versed on the details of all the dozens of bills that confront him or her every day during a session. Legislators turn to many sources for information on how to vote. There is a classic notion, posited by the 18th century political philosopher and statesman Edmund Burke, that divides legislators into **delegates**, who vote according to the wishes of their districts, and **trustees**, who vote according to their own consciences.[37] Given the proliferation of legislation, however, members never hear from a single constituent on probably 90 percent of the bills they must consider. Instead,

they rely for guidance on staffers, other legislators, interest groups and lobbyists, executive branch officials, foundations, think tanks, and other sources.

That legislators cannot rely solely on their own judgment to vote is the source of many people's sense that legislators' votes can be bought—or at least rented. This is ironic, considering that political scientists note that most of the time most legislators are extremely attentive to their districts and vote according to their sense of their constituents' desires. Their primary goal, after all, is to win reelection. In addition, most states have made it tougher for lobbyists to get lawmakers' attention. It is difficult under the new ethics rules for a lobbyist to spring for a legislator's cup of coffee, much less treat him or her to lunch. In Kentucky, for example, there are fewer of the nightly receptions that once kept Frankfort well fed, and lobbyists are prohibited from making any personal contributions to candidates for the legislature. "A lot of the principal lobbyists are still here, so folks have had to learn to adapt," says Bobby Sherman, head of the Kentucky legislature's nonpartisan research staff. "It's more work for them. They have to build relationships in a different way, and information delivery is much more important."[38]

All this is necessary because, as with most things, times have changed. It used to be that rank-and-file members voted pretty much the way they were instructed by their party leaders. In Connecticut, the legislature of the early 1960s was an assemblage of party hacks—members beholden to the party chair for patronage. This meant that most of the legislature's important decisions were made in small meetings to which the public—or even most rank-and-file members—were not invited. Today, leaders still call the shots, but they are careful not to go against the wishes of their caucuses too often, knowing that they can be ousted if enough members want to go in a different direction. Leaders these days are no stronger than members want them to be; they often lead by listening. They have to pay attention to customer service, and their main customers are rank-and-file legislators. Leaders help other legislators intervene with the governor or the rest of the executive branch and help green-light bills to

---

Delegates
Legislators who primarily see their role as voting according to their constituents' beliefs as they understand them

Trustees
Legislators who believe they were elected to exercise their own judgment and to approach issues accordingly

build up political chits. "As long as it wasn't against the law, didn't require that I go to confession, or wouldn't break up my marriage, I did it," recalled Ralph Wright, a one-time Speaker of the Vermont House.[39]

Plenty of examples still exist, though, of members' caving in to party or leadership pressure—or being punished when they fail to do so. In 2014, Missouri Democratic representative Keith English was stripped of his positions on four House committees after he joined with Republicans to override Democratic governor Jay Nixon's veto of a tax-cut bill. English said he didn't take it personally. "Definitely, when you vote against the governor, or you vote against the Democratic position, there's retribution."[40] Conversely, businessman Rex Sinquefield gave campaign contributions totaling nearly $1 million to help oust four Republicans who had voted to sustain Nixon's veto.[41] The combination of leadership pressure and possible targeting by outside groups means the incentives for most legislators, most of the time, is to go along with what their party wants.

The pendulum has swung back toward greater power being held by legislative leaders. But they cannot simply bully their way through as they did a generation ago, for two reasons. Leadership offices control fundraising efforts designed to build or maintain majorities, but the leadership efforts are mainly directed at the relatively few contests that will make or break a majority. Dick Saslaw, the Democratic Senate president in Virginia, for example, spent about $1.5 million in campaign cash in 2011 trying to defend his party's narrow majority, funneling money to incumbents and challengers in the most competitive races.[42] Many rank-and-file members today can raise their own money and have greater access to expert advice for hire and separate sources of money, whether from political action committees run by industries or labor unions or elsewhere.

We have already touched on the other factor—members do not have to rely on leaders as much as they once did for information about bills or for help in writing legislation. The proliferation of lobbyists and the **professionalization** of legislatures have meant that members in many states have their own resources to draw on.[43]

Apportionment

One more issue that profoundly affects all legislators is **apportionment**. Following the nationwide census that occurs every 10 years, each state draws new lines for its legislative districts. In states with more than one member of Congress, congressional districts are redrawn as well. The **redistricting** process is the most naked exercise of political power in the states. Within the legal limits that exist—Supreme Court rulings in the 1960s set the requirement that districts be roughly even in population—the incumbent party will do everything it can to preserve its hold or, preferably, increase its numbers. Each party will seek to draw the maximum number of districts possible that are likely to elect members of its own party. The two major parties will fight each other as best they can to make certain that the other side does not gain the upper hand. "Just like there are no atheists in foxholes, there are no nonpartisans in redistricting," says Paul Green, director of the School of Policy Studies at Roosevelt University in Chicago. "You use whatever leverage you can."[44]

Travis County, Texas, where Austin is located, is one of the most Democratic jurisdictions in the state. President Obama won almost 64 percent of the vote in Travis County in 2008. In 2011 the Republican-controlled Texas legislature sliced and diced Travis County so that four of the five congressional districts that include parts of the county lean toward Republicans. They did that by packing Democrats into a single district that includes both parts of Austin and parts of San Antonio, three counties away—with the two halves connected only by a narrow strip of land. The district outline looked so strange on a map

---

Apportionment
The allotting of districts according to population shifts. The number of congressional districts that a state has may be reapportioned every 10 years, following the national census.

Redistricting
The drawing of new boundaries for congressional and state legislative districts, usually following a decennial census

---

Professionalization
The process of providing legislators with the resources they need to make politics their main career, such as making their positions full-time or providing them with full-time staff

MAP 7-3

The Upside-Down Elephant District

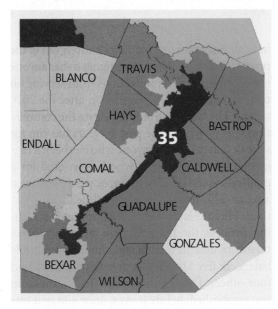

Texas's 35th Congressional District drew attention for its odd shape, the result of what many viewed as a partisan effort to redraw the district's lines.

Source: Texas Legislative Council.

that the *Washington Post* held a contest to describe it: the winning entry was "Upside-down elephant (spraying water)."[45] Travis County's government, among other groups, challenged the redistricting in court, but judges allowed the five-way split to go into effect for the 2012 elections.[46]

Political district boundaries that link disparate communities or have odd shapes that resemble earmuffs or moose antlers are known as **gerrymanders**, a term derived from the name of Elbridge Gerry, an early 19th-century governor of Massachusetts. **Malapportionment** occurs when districts violate the principle of equal representation. In the past, some state legislative districts could have many times the numbers of constituents in other districts. Votes in the smaller districts, in effect, counted for more. Relatively few people in, say, a sparsely populated rural district would have the same amount of representative clout in the

Gerrymanders
Districts clearly drawn with the intent of pressing partisan advantage at the expense of other considerations

Malapportionment
A situation in which the principle of equal representation is violated

legislature as many more people in a densely populated urban district.

As Texas's experience shows, the party in control of redistricting really does matter. Likewise, in 2006 in Ohio, Democrats won 60 percent of the vote in state Senate elections but gained only a single formerly Republican-held seat. Afterward, Republicans still had 21 members in the chamber, to the Democrats' 12. One big reason the Democratic votes didn't translate into more Democratic victories is that the GOP in Ohio had controlled the line-drawing process after the 2000 census. The Republicans had crafted Senate districts to give their party an edge.[47] Democrats typically do the same thing when they are in charge. In 2011 in Illinois, Democrats drew a new congressional map that imperiled more than half the state's Republican incumbents. Democrats loudly complained following the 2012 elections that although their candidates won more total votes in the U.S. House, the GOP came away with the majority. In North Carolina, for instance, Democrats took 51 percent of the statewide vote for the House but came away with just four of the 13 seats. Political scientists have been debating what share of such disparities can be attributed to redistricting and how much is due to the fact that Democrats tend to huddle together in more dense spaces, such as big cities, meaning they are naturally packed into more one-sided districts.

Legislatures define district boundaries in most states, but there are exceptions. Since the 1980s, Iowa's political maps have been created by the nonpartisan Legislative Services Agency. The agency uses computer software to draw 100 House districts and 50 Senate districts according to rules that keep population as equal as possible from district to district, avoid splitting counties, and keep the districts compact. In contrast to legislature-drawn maps, those drawn by the agency do not take into account party registration, voting patterns, or the political territory of incumbents. Largely as a result, partisan control of the Iowa legislature has flipped just about every 10 years since the agency was created.

While Iowa's system is unique, reformers elsewhere regularly try to find ways to prevent redistricting from flagrantly favoring one party over the other. Lately, the reformers have won some important victories. In Florida in 2010 voters

Jase Bolger stepped down from the Michigan House in 2014 due to term limits. He spent two of his three terms as Speaker, part of a trend of relatively junior members holding power in legislative chambers.

approved a constitutional amendment that mandated rules for redistricting, including forbidding the drawing of lines for the purpose of favoring incumbent officeholders or political parties. When the Republican-controlled Florida legislature nonetheless approved a new state Senate map that was seen as benefiting the GOP, the Florida Supreme Court rejected it on the grounds that it violated the 2010 amendment. Meanwhile, California approved a pair of citizen initiatives in 2008 and 2010 that took redistricting out of the hands of state legislators and entrusted it to an independent commission. These commissions may be in legal peril, as the U.S. Supreme Court in October 2014 agreed to hear a challenge against Arizona's redistricting commission. Depending on the outcome, redistricting could become the exclusive purview of state legislatures.

Independent commissions in some states, such as Washington, have succeeded in making redistricting somewhat less overtly partisan, but they have almost never taken politics entirely out of the process. California went to extremes to bar anyone with strong political motivations from serving on the new redistricting commission after the 2010 census. The law bars from serving on the commission anyone who in the past 10 years has run for state or federal office; anyone who has been a registered lobbyist; anyone who has worked for a political candidate, campaign, or party; and even anyone who has made large political contributions. Plus, the law specifies a complicated screening process for the selection of commission members, and the membership must be politically balanced: five Democrats, five Republicans, and four others. Despite that, once the commission was established, before it even drew a map it was accused of a political bias based on the consultants the members had hired to assist them. Those accusations gained some weight when an investigation by ProPublica journalists pointed to places where the commission had adopted district lines promoted by supposed "good government" groups that actually were run by Democratic operatives.[48] "It wasn't so much that the Democrats tried," says Douglas Johnson, a fellow at the Rose Institute of State and Local Government and one of the consultants the commission passed over. "Of course they tried. The surprise is that it worked."[49] Still, independent observers agreed that the new maps would allow for much more competitive elections than did the incumbent-protection plan lawmakers had enacted 10 years earlier.

Partisanship is the primary concern of redistricting, but it is not the only one. Issues of representation also play a big part. African Americans are overwhelmingly Democratic, but some joined with Republicans following the 1980 and 1990 censuses to create black majority districts, especially in the South. For African Americans, their deal with the GOP offered the advantage of creating districts in which African American candidates were likely to be elected. It wasn't that they joined the Republican Party, of course. They simply allied themselves with the

GOP to draw **majority-minority districts**, which guaranteed the election of more African Americans but also made the neighboring "bleached" districts more likely to elect Republicans. Following the Voting Rights Act of 1982, the federal Justice Department encouraged state legislators to create majority-minority districts whenever possible, until a series of U.S. Supreme Court decisions during the 1990s limited the practice. In a confusing and often contradictory series of rulings, the Court ruled that race could not be the "predominant" factor in redistricting.[50] In November 2014, the Court heard a case that turned on the question of whether Alabama had unconstitutionally classified African American voters by race when drawing legislative districts designed to have supermajority populations of blacks.

Redistricting also changes representation in ways that go beyond black and white. With each new round of redistricting, power shifts to places that are growing quickly and away from ones that are not. One of the major themes of the 2010 round of redistricting was a shift in power away from rural areas and to suburbs and exurbs that experienced far stronger population growth in the previous 10 years.[51] Alaska legislators were so concerned about having fewer lawmakers representing rural areas—and about the remaining rural districts becoming even more massive—that they submitted a constitutional amendment to voters in 2010 to add more seats to the legislature. One of the lawmakers supporting the change was State Senator Albert Kookesh, who represented the largest state legislative district in the country. From its southeastern corner, Kookesh's district extended 1,185 miles west—about the same distance as that from Jacksonville, Florida, to Minneapolis, Minnesota—and about 1,000 miles north—about the same as the distance from Phoenix, Arizona, to Portland, Oregon.[52] Getting around an area of that size cannot be done efficiently in a car; it's hard enough to do it by plane. "In order for me to get to one of my villages, Lime Village, I would have to go from Angoon to Juneau, Juneau to Anchorage,

Anchorage to Fairbanks, Fairbanks to Aniak, and Aniak to Lime Village," Kookesh said.[53] Alaska voters rejected the plan to add legislative seats.

State Legislators

In 2014, the Pew Research Center conducted a survey of that small fraction of the population that ever runs for public office. It found that office seekers are disproportionately white, male, and college educated. Men were 3 times more likely to run for office than were women, while whites made up 82 percent of those who had ever run for office—a higher number than their share of the population.[54] If you were to make a composite drawing of the average state legislator, he—and it would be a he—would be white and in his 50s or maybe 60s. He would have had at least some college education, have an income topping $50,000, describe himself as moderate or conservative, and have lived in the community he is representing for at least 10 years.[55] There are many, many exceptions to all the aspects of this composite. The type of person who runs for state legislative office has changed a good deal over the past 30 years—for example, there are far more women and African Americans in office and fewer lawyers—but nonetheless, the type of middle- to upper-middle-class American male described here still predominates.

The nation's 7,383 state legislators come from all backgrounds, particularly in the states where the house and senate meet for only part of the year. In states with full-time legislatures, such as California and Pennsylvania, the legislators tend, not surprisingly, to be career politicians who have served in local or other elected offices or perhaps as members of legislative staffs. In states with part-time legislatures, such as Arkansas and Indiana, members come from many different walks of life, devoting perhaps one third of their working hours to politics while earning their livings through some other means.

Professional Background

Some employers encourage the political hopes of their employees because they know legislative service can be good for business. This holds true especially for professions most directly affected

---

Majority-minority districts
Districts in which members of a minority group, such as African Americans or Hispanics, make up a majority of the population or electorate

by state lawmaking, such as big business. Buddy Dyer kept up his law practice while serving in the Florida Senate and in 2002 had to respond to complaints that the bills he proposed would have protected his industrial company clients from fines and lawsuits. His defense? "Probably not a bill that goes through the Legislature" did not affect one of his firm's clients.[56]

Other groups enjoy considerable representation within legislative bodies. State Senator Renee Unterman helped block a bill in the Georgia legislature in 2013 that would have required insurers to provide coverage for children with autism. As her day job, Unterman works as an executive with health insurance giant WellPoint. In 2006, Al Mansell stepped down from his leadership role as president of the Utah Senate to become president of the National Association of Realtors. He stayed in the Senate, however, sponsoring legislation that helped members of his profession. He was one of 22 people who worked in real estate who were serving in the Utah legislature at that time. "I've got people who are on county commissions, mayors, state senators," said Chris Kyler, CEO of the Utah Association of Realtors. "Our lieutenant governor was president of our state association about 20 years ago. Our people are involved in the parties, too. We've got precinct chairs and vice chairs and county delegates throughout the state."[57] The online news site *Texas Tribune* noted in 2013, "At the Capitol, lawmakers rarely recuse themselves from legislation that has an impact on their livelihoods for one simple reason: They don't have to."[58]

Consider public education. Teachers' unions are usually among the most active lobbying groups in any state, but schools do not necessarily have to rely on outsiders to influence the legislature. Teachers themselves are often members of legislatures, and employees of other institutions of higher learning also serve. In Maine, state law requires that teachers be granted leave from their jobs if they want to run for office. Maine's legislature meets for only 6 months every other year. But even that chunk of time is enough to play havoc with a person's work schedule, and there's a good deal of concern in the state that retirees are coming to dominate the legislative chamber.

The reality is that retired people account for only about 12 percent of state legislators nationwide.

About 15 percent of legislators are lawyers—a big decline from past decades. In New York, 60 percent of the assembly and 70 percent of the Senate used to be made up of lawyers.[59] Nowadays, the dominant group in legislatures nationwide comprises people with business backgrounds. They make up about 30 percent of today's legislators. The remaining half or so come from education, health care, real estate, insurance, and agriculture.

Demographic Diversity

The numbers of women legislators have risen dramatically since the "second wave" feminist era of the late 1960s and early 1970s, but they still do not reflect the female share of the overall population. In 1970, women held just 4 percent of all state legislative seats.[60] Their numbers doubled quickly, to 8 percent of all legislators, by 1975, and they climbed to 18 percent by 1991. The ranks of women legislators held steady at just over 20 percent for about a dozen years before spiking to 23.5 percent after the 2006 elections. The figure ticked up to just above 24 percent following the 2008 campaigns, about where it has remained ever since. Only six states—Arizona, Colorado, Minnesota, New Hampshire, Vermont, and Washington—could brag in 2007 that one third or more of their legislators were women.[61] But, in 2009, the New Hampshire Senate became the first legislative chamber in the nation to have a majority of women members. Women served as its president and majority leader, and another woman served as Speaker of the New Hampshire House.[62]

In 2014, a majority of the Democratic nominees for the Pennsylvania House were women. Still, women are much less likely than men to run for office. One program in New Haven, Connecticut, brings potential candidates together with members of Congress and their staff to offer 5 days of training in basics such as fundraising, making staffing decisions, and public speaking. The group has trained some 1,400 women over the past two decades.[63] But a 2013 American University study found that women remain less likely to run than men for various reasons, including lack of encouragement from their parents and less exposure to political information. The researchers found that men were 60 percent more likely than women to consider themselves "very qualified" for office; conversely, women were more than twice as likely as men to say they were "not at all qualified."[64]

The numbers of women entering state legislatures may not be growing exponentially, but the types of women holding house and senate seats have changed. In the old days of the 1970s—many years before most readers of this book were born—most women running for office came to politics later in life than did their male counterparts. They had not been tapped to run by party professionals or other "queenmakers." Instead, they jump-started their own careers, drawn into the policy realm by concern for their children's schools or their local communities. Men may know from the time they are in school that they want to run for office, says Barbara Lee, who runs a foundation dedicated to helping women run for office, but women often find out later in life that it is important to enter the game because of their specific concerns and experiences.[65] This dynamic has changed to some extent. Women now enter politics at ages comparable to those of men. Many still tend to care about particular issues (education, health care, and the environment) that are noticeably different from the top priorities of men (taxes and budgets), but sometimes they focus on such issues because they still find it harder than men to gain seats on the more powerful finance committees in representative numbers.

Back in the 1970s, when the first relatively large numbers of women legislators entered the capitols, they tended to be less politically ambitious than the men they served with, and thus less likely to enter the ranks of legislative leadership. They devoted more attention to constituent service matters and tended to serve on education, health, and welfare committees. They also tended to have less education than their male counterparts, and to come from jobs that were not as prestigious or well paying as those held by the men. During the 1980s, the average socioeconomic status of women legislators improved, and women served on a broader range of committees, but they mostly still focused on issues of women, family, and children.

By the 1990s, women legislators held about 15 percent of all legislative leadership positions but were still unlikely to serve on tax committees.[66] Their backgrounds had become more varied, and they had also become more conservative, although they still were more liberal than men—and significantly more likely than their male colleagues to initiate legislation.[67] Women also became more likely than men to get their priority bills through the legislative process successfully.[68]

Women legislators, however, do not alter the fundamental political dynamics in legislatures, perhaps because they remain a fairly small minority in most states. For example, women legislators are more likely than their male counterparts to favor reproductive rights, but they do not have an especially powerful impact on a given state's policy regarding this issue. Whether a state devotes much funding toward abortion programs or places a number of restrictions on such programs, including requiring parental notification in the case of minors seeking abortions, depends more on whether the state's overall political culture is liberal or conservative than on whether women make up a large minority of legislative caucuses.[69] Still, gender composition of a state legislature is a difference that makes a difference: Women legislators do tend to bring up issues and concerns that would not be raised by an all-male legislature.

This tendency is even truer of issues of concern to minorities. African Americans have made gains similar to those of women in legislatures over the past 40 years, growing from a microscopic minority to a larger minority, albeit one that still does not reflect their overall share of the population. The numbers of African American legislators have nearly quadrupled, to about 625—less than 10 percent of all the legislators nationwide. Hispanics are even more poorly represented, making up about 4 percent of state legislators, compared with 14 percent of the nation's population.

Although it can be both dangerous and wrong to generalize about any group, it has been observed that the interests of African Americans as a whole have long been fairly stable and predictable. "On questions of public policy, ideology, and candidate

A Difference That Makes A Difference

Continuing Rural Clout Demonstrates Value of Sticking Together

The number of legislative districts in rural America has been in decline for decades, even in farm states. By 2012, fully half the nation's population lived in the 39 largest metropolitan areas. That has made the job of legislators who represent rural areas a lot harder, but not impossible.

Instead, rural caucuses in many states have become masters of coalition politics, still able to punch well above their weight in numerous states. They provide a good illustration of how a well-organized minority that sticks together internally and finds common cause with others can still get its way a good amount of the time.

Consider Nevada. As is the case in many western states, the bulk of the population is concentrated in the major urban areas. Fully 2 million of the state's 2.7 million people live in Clark County, which includes Las Vegas. "Southern Nevada has had a majority of the legislators and now has a supermajority," said Jon Ralston, a prominent commentator on Nevada politics. "If the delegation [could] stick together, they could get anything they want."

That seldom seems to happen, though. If you looked at how state resources are allocated strictly in terms of where people live, Clark County is consistently shortchanged. For example, Nevada's antique school-funding formula awards lots of extra money to counties basically for being sparsely populated and remote. Clark County gets a little more than $5,000 per pupil from the state, while Esmeralda County—home to fewer than a thousand people—gets more than $17,000. That's an extreme case, but consider that the commission designed to study equity in school funding is also disproportionately made up of people from the more rural north. Things like that happen time and again in Nevada.

How? Rural delegations tend to stick together and take advantage of splits that are common within metropolitan areas. "The problem is the suburbs, which are often the biggest bloc, are fragmented and have not learned how to use their clout," said Lawrence Levy, dean of the National Center for Suburban Studies at Hofstra University in New York.

Generally, rural legislators are Republican, which means at times they are able to form partisan alliances that can run stronger these days than sectional ones. All kinds of horse-trading can happen when it's time to divvy up capital construction dollars, for example, and suburban areas are split. "Most of the Democratic legislators are clustered in the cities," said former Ohio GOP governor Bob Taft. "If you're trying to get Republican

choice," writes Kerry L. Haynie in his 2001 book on black state legislators, "African Americans have been the most cohesive and consistent policy subgroup in United States politics."[70] In short, the racial composition of state legislatures is also a difference that makes a difference. This is especially the case because state influence over issues important to African American legislators increased just as their numbers were increasing. Since the 1970s, decisions about many issues of importance to African Americans, including Medicaid, student aid, school lunch programs, community development, welfare, and environmental protection, have devolved from the federal level to the states.[71] In his study of how representatives in Arkansas, Illinois, Mississippi, New Jersey, and North Carolina acted in three different sessions, Haynie found that 55 to 82 percent of African American legislators introduced bills that addressed issues of particular interest to blacks. White legislators, by contrast, almost never introduced such legislation. In only one of the three years Haynie studied (1969, 1979, and 1989) did more than one quarter of nonblack legislators introduce even one bill of interest to African Americans.[72] It may sound obvious, but so-called black issues are much more likely to be addressed when African Americans are serving in state legislatures.

Black legislators, of course, do not focus solely or even mostly on issues that are specific to their

votes, that gives some clout to the Republican legislators who represent rural areas."

And, as the South did in Congress throughout much of the 20th century, rural areas are able to increase their clout simply by giving their representatives long careers and thus the power that seniority entails. That's despite the fact that a pair of Supreme Court decisions in the early 1960s—*Baker v. Carr* and *Gray v. Sanders*—ended the ability of rural areas to dominate state legislatures through the old system, in some states, of apportioning districts by counties rather than population.

Rural areas don't suffer the kind of image problems that big cities and wealthy suburbs tend to have in state capitols. In fact, the opposite is often true. People may not live in rural areas, but they're still inclined to see that the countryside receives its fair share—or maybe more—from the state. Individual legislators themselves may view the world through a split lens. With rural areas losing so much ground, many districts are split between half-empty rural counties and slices of suburbia that give them a population base.

A study by Gerald Gamm and Thad Kousser published in 2013 in the *American Political Science Review* found that major cities—those with populations above 100,000—have had little luck passing state legislation. From 1880 until 2000, passage rates for bills that benefited big cities directly were consistently a quarter to a third less likely to pass than were those that dealt with smaller cities and towns. "Year after year, while most bills affecting smaller districts pass, most big-city bills fail," Gamm and Kousser conclude.

After urban delegations got bigger, following the 1960s Supreme Court reapportionment decisions, the big-city batting average only got worse. As they became more numerous, metropolitan legislators were more likely to break ranks, splitting not just on partisan votes but on measures meant to help out their own areas. "It appears that legislators from the rest of the state follow the cues of the big-city delegation and split when its members divide, often dooming bills," according to Kousser and Gamm. That's not a problem rural legislators have had.

Source: Adapted from Alan Greenblatt, "Rural Areas Lose People but Not Power," *Governing*, April 2014, http://www.governing.com/topics/politics/gov-rural-areas-lose-people-not-power.html.

racial group. One reflection of this is that in recent years African American legislators have been voted into leadership roles by their colleagues in states with relatively few black voters. At the start of the 2009 legislative sessions, in the same month President Obama first took the oath of office, Colorado became the first state with a black Senate president and a black House Speaker simultaneously. Malcolm Smith was elected New York's first African American Senate president, and Steve Horsford became Nevada's first African American Senate majority leader that same year.

The fact that there are more African American legislators does not mean that voting trends have changed, however. Voting remains polarized along racial lines. Whites will support African American incumbents but are often reluctant to vote for black newcomers. The main reason for the growth in the number of black legislators, therefore, has been the creation of majority-black districts.[73]

Professional Versus Citizen Legislators

As discussed above, legislatures, strictly white male playgrounds in the past, have become more inclusive of women and minorities and more attentive to their concerns. But even bigger

TABLE 7-2

State House Demographic Diversity: Total Numbers and Percentages of Legislators Who Are Women, African American, and Hispanic

State	Total Number of Legislative Seats	Women State Legislators		African American State Legislators		Hispanic State Legislators	
		Total	Percentage of Total Seats	Total	Percentage of Total Seats	Total	Percentage of Total Seats
Alabama	140	20	14.3	34	24	0	0
Alaska	60	16	26.7	1	2	0	0
Arizona	90	32	35.6	2	2	17	19
Arkansas	135	23	17	15	11	0	0
California	120	32	26.7	9	8	28	23
Colorado	100	41	41	3	3	5	5
Connecticut	187	53	28.3	19	10	6	3
Delaware	62	16	25.8	5	8	1	2
Florida	160	41	25.6	25	16	17	11
Georgia	236	53	22.5	56	24	3	1
Hawaii	76	24	31.6	0	0	1	1
Idaho	105	28	26.7	0	0	1	1
Illinois	177	55	31.1	29	16	11	6
Indiana	150	30	20	13	9	1	1
Iowa	150	35	23.3	3	2	0	0
Kansas	165	41	24.8	6	4	4	2
Kentucky	138	25	18.1	7	5	0	0
Louisiana	144	18	12.5	29	20	0	0
Maine	186	55	29.6	0	0	0	0
Maryland	188	57	30.3	42	22	4	2
Massachusetts	200	49	24.5	8	4	5	3
Michigan	148	28	18.9	19	13	3	2
Minnesota	201	68	33.8	1	> 1	3	1
Mississippi	174	30	17.2	42	24	0	0
Missouri	197	43	21.8	12	6	1	1
Montana	150	40	26.7	0	0	1	1
Nebraska	49	10	20.4	1	2	1	2
Nevada	63	17	27	7	11	3	5
New Hampshire	424	137	32.3	1	> 1	2	< 1
New Jersey	120	36	30	10	8	5	4
New Mexico	112	32	28.6	2	2	44	39
New York	213	45	21.1	43	20	17	8

State	Total Number of Legislative Seats	Women State Legislators		African American State Legislators		Hispanic State Legislators	
		Total	Percentage of Total Seats	Total	Percentage of Total Seats	Total	Percentage of Total Seats
North Carolina	170	37	21.8	26	15	2	1
North Dakota	141	24	17	0	0	0	0
Ohio	132	31	23.5	16	12	0	0
Oklahoma	149	20	13.4	6	4	0	0
Oregon	90	27	30	3	3	1	1
Pennsylvania	253	45	17.8	21	8	1	< 1
Rhode Island	113	30	26.5	1	1	3	3
South Carolina	170	22	12.9	28	17	1	1
South Dakota	105	24	22.9	0	0	0	0
Tennessee	132	23	17.4	12	9	1	1
Texas	181	39	21.5	14	8	36	20
Utah	104	17	16.3	0	0	2	2
Vermont	180	73	40.6	1	1	0	0
Virginia	140	24	17.1	17	12	1	1
Washington	147	48	32.7	3	2	3	2
West Virginia	134	22	16.4	0	0	0	0
Wisconsin	132	34	25.8	8	6	1	1
Wyoming	90	14	15.6	0	0	2	2
Total	7,382	1,746	24	600	6	238	4

Sources: National Conference of State Legislatures (NCSL), "Number of African American Legislators 2009," available at www.ncsl.org/default.aspx?tabid=14781; NCSL; National Conference of State Legislatures, "2009 Latino Legislators," http://www.ncsl.org/Default.aspx?TabId=14766; National Conference of State Legislatures, "Women in State Legislatures for 2014," April 1, 2014, http://www.ncsl.org/legislators-staff/legislators/womens-legislative-network/women-in-state-legislatures-for-2014.aspx.

Note: Except for women state legislatures, percentages are rounded to the nearest whole number. Numbers are latest available; those for women legislators are from 2014, and those for African American and Hispanic legislators are from 2008.

changes in legislatures over the past 35 years have come in the very ways they do business. Whereas once legislatures were sleepy backwaters where not much got done—and even less got done ethically—now many chambers are highly professional operations. Most legislatures used to meet for short periods every other year. These days all but a handful meet every year and, in a few cases, nearly year-round. "No single factor has a greater effect on the legislative environment than the constitutional restriction on length of session," two leading legislative scholars wrote long ago.[74]

The most pronounced differences among the states are between "professional" legislatures that meet full-time, pay members high salaries, and employ large staffs, and "amateur," or "citizen," legislatures that meet part-time, have members who usually hold other jobs, and have smaller staffs. To some extent, all legislatures have become more professional. Even "amateur" legislators devote a third of their time to legislative work. In the early 1940s, the legislatures of only four states—New Jersey, New York, Rhode Island, and South Carolina—met in annual sessions, but the number meeting yearly has climbed continuously.[75] Today, only four states do not meet in regular annual sessions. Expenditures per legislator have increased above the rate of inflation in nearly every state, and today, the most professional legislatures have resources that rival those of the U.S. Congress.[76] Lately, however, that trend has slowed. The number of legislative staffers nationwide actually dropped from 1996 to 2009 after decades of increases.[77]

There are many variations among states as to how professional their legislatures are, and level of professionalism has profound impacts on legislatures' effectiveness, how much institutional strength they have compared with governors, and how popular they are with the public. Some disagreement still exists about whether professional legislators really do a better job than their citizen-legislator cousins. Typically, however, the more professional a legislature, the more effective it is at the essential jobs of drafting and passing laws and overseeing the governor and the executive branch. With the exception of Texas, the more populous states have highly professional legislatures. Such legislatures are able to provide more resources to their chambers, which allows these chambers to keep up with the wider variety of issues that arise in densely populated states in comparison with most of their less populous neighbors. Legislatures in some states, such as Pennsylvania and California, meet essentially year-round; in contrast, Montana's part-time legislature meets for only 90 days only in odd-numbered years.

More populous states have the money to invest in the full-time legislatures that are necessary for their governments to keep on top of issues facing these states' more complicated and developed economies and diverse populations. The reason that Texas, with a population second only to California's, has a part-time legislature lies in the state's distrust of government in general. Texas is one of only nine states that do not impose an income tax, and a legislature that meets only part-time every other year is in keeping with this general low-tax, low-service point of view. Other states have traditions of embracing more expansive government. States with strong progressive traditions, such as Michigan and Wisconsin, have long used full-time, professional legislators with substantial staffs at their command.

As distrust of government has spread to more state capitols, there have been some moves to reverse the trend toward better-staffed, more expensive, more professionalized legislatures. It was a sure sign of unhappiness with the Michigan legislature amid its struggles to pass budgets in a difficult economic time that serious, although ultimately unsuccessful, petition drives were launched in 2008, including one by a local area chamber of commerce, to turn it into a part-time body. In Pennsylvania, efforts to scale back the legislature's spending on itself grew out of a double-digit pay increase legislators approved for themselves at 2:00 A.M. on July 7, 2005. Since then, one perennial idea promoted by some in the state has been to save money by having fewer legislators. No one could accuse Pennsylvania's House members of serving their own career interests when they voted in 2012 for a constitutional amendment that would have cut the House from 203 to 153 members.[78] The Senate, which the amendment would have shrunk from 50 members to 38, did not act on the proposal. The House in 2014 tried again with a proposal that would again shrink its own numbers by 50 but the number of senators by just five. That didn't go any further, however. Also in 2014, a petition drive to shrink the legislature and cap legislative pay failed in Michigan, although organizers vowed to try again in 2016.

The northeastern states have maintained their traditional interest in hands-on government, which grew out of their old practices of self-government, including town hall meetings. These states boast some of the largest legislatures. The New Hampshire House is the most extreme example, with 400 members—one for every 3,300-or-so state residents. California's legislature is one of the best equipped and most professional in the country. It has to be, considering that each member of the assembly has more than 450,000 constituents.

Some states impose severe restrictions on the meeting times of their legislatures. In Colorado, the state constitution limits the House and the Senate to no more than 120 days per year. Sometimes such limits are honored mostly in the breach. The governor may insist that the legislature meet in special session to address a budget crisis or other issue that cannot wait until the next regular session. Or the legislature may simply carve out a little more time for itself, as happened in 2002 in North Carolina. House rules require that the chamber be shut down by 9:00 P.M.; so members stopped the clock one night at 8:50, essentially "freezing time," so they could continue debate until 3:35 A.M. and finish a session that had run for months longer than expected.[79]

Just like most of us, legislators feel intensely the pressure to get their work done on time. The fact that they have deadlines—for passing budgets or for adjournment—usually keeps them focused in much the same way that a final exam will make college students finally hit the books or do their serious Googling at term's end. Newspapers, however, routinely report on legislatures' missing their budget deadlines and often publish commentary critical of the practice. The reality is that a legislature is pretty cheap to operate—in no state does it cost much more than 0.5 percent of the state budget—but elected officials know that their overtime does not play well with voters.[80]

Mississippi's largest paper, the *Clarion Ledger*, for instance, ran a typical editorial condemning legislators for wasting money in a special session in 2008, even though the extra time cost the state

MAP 7-4

Full-Time, Hybrid, and Part-Time Legislatures

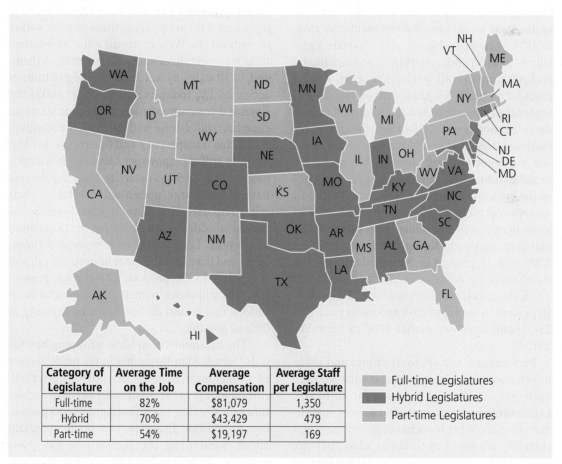

Category of Legislature	Average Time on the Job	Average Compensation	Average Staff per Legislature
Full-time	82%	$81,079	1,350
Hybrid	70%	$43,429	479
Part-time	54%	$19,197	169

Full-time Legislatures
Hybrid Legislatures
Part-time Legislatures

Source: Data compiled from the National Conference of State Legislatures, "Full- and Part-Time Legislatures," June 1, 2014, http://www.ncsl.org/research/about-state-legislatures/full-and-part-time-legislatures.aspx.

only $59,895 for the first day and $39,420 a day for each one after that. At that rate, the session would have had to drag on for weeks to add just 1 percent to the $90 million budget deficit the state faced the next year.[81] Such media coverage is one reason legislatures, even as they get more professional and better at their jobs, remain unpopular with the public. Map 7-4 shows the breakdown of full-time, hybrid, and part-time legislatures among the states.

The Citizens' Whipping Boy: Legislators and Public Opinion

Thirty or forty years ago, legislatures were, to put it bluntly, sexist, racist, secretive, boss ruled, malapportioned, and uninformed. Alabama's legislature was an extreme but representative case. In 1971, it ranked 50th out of the 50 state legislatures in independence, 50th in accountability, and 48th in overall performance in a Ford Foundation study. Yet, just 3 years earlier, 65 percent of the respondents in a statewide poll judged the institution favorably. By 1990, the legislature had freed itself of its institutional racism, secrecy, and malapportionment and was fully equipped to gather information and operate in a new state-of-the-art legislative facility. That year it received an approval rating of 24 percent.[82] Remarkably, some legislatures have fallen even further than that in recent years. During a leadership crisis in 2009, just 11 percent of New Yorkers said the state Senate was doing an excellent or good job.[83] The California legislature's approval rating fell to 10 percent in the fall of 2010 and never exceeded 23 percent from September 2008 to February 2012.[84]

Performance and approval ratings and other information about legislators and what they are up to are out there in the open for all to see. Legislatures are much more transparent institutions than the other branches of government and certainly are more open about what they are doing than are private-sector businesses or unions. This is not to say that many legislative

> Performance and approval ratings and other information about legislators and what they are up to are out there in the open for all to see. Legislatures are much more transparent institutions than the other branches of government and certainly are more open about what they are doing than are private-sector businesses or unions.

decisions are not still made behind closed doors, but they are acted on out in the open. Interested citizens can find out how their legislators have represented them by paging through their voting records on the Web, by reading the newsletters their representatives and senators mail to them, and, in 30 states, by watching their legislatures in action on TV. Today, every legislature makes the floor and committee proceedings of at least one chamber available for audio or video streaming.

All this transparency and openness—yet legislatures still manage to get a bad rap. It is a curious reality of U.S. political life. State legislatures have, by and large, gotten much better at their jobs. The diversity of their membership has moved steadily toward reflecting the population as a whole. Legislatures have reformed themselves and have become more honest, ethical, and competent in the process. The average person, however, still views them as out-of-control institutions that would do less harm by meeting as little as possible.

"The legislature is an ideal whipping boy (or girl)," writes Alan Rosenthal in his book *Engines of Democracy*. It is an institution, after all. Although it is made up of individuals, a legislature as a whole is not a flesh-and-blood person, like a governor. Everyone can easily complain about something the legislature has done recently—including legislators, many of whom campaign by promising to be the ones who will

Many state legislators attempt to keep their constituents informed about their doings through social media. On her Twitter feed, Texas Democratic state senator and candidate for governor Wendy Davis lets her supporters know where she'll be making appearances and what she thinks about events unfolding in the state.

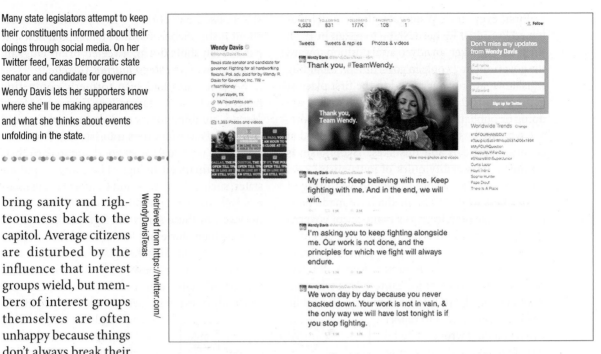

bring sanity and righteousness back to the capitol. Average citizens are disturbed by the influence that interest groups wield, but members of interest groups themselves are often unhappy because things don't always break their way. Finally, as Rosenthal writes, "people generalize from the worst cases, not the best cases." They do not assume that most legislators are like their own representative or senator, whom they tend to like; rather, they think most are like "the relative few who are convicted or indicted in a court of law, reprimanded by a state ethics commission, or are accused . . . in the media."[85]

If anything, legislators have become more unpopular than they were a generation ago. The increases in staff, in salaries, and in other professional tools that legislators have acquired in recent decades probably have made them better at their jobs. But as they have become more professional, legislatures also have become larger targets of disdain for a public that believes it has little or no use for professional or career politicians. Amateur legislatures hold a stronger appeal to deeply rooted American desires for limited government and limited governmental power.

To a large extent, the general public does not view large staffs and good salaries as ways of ensuring that legislators do their jobs in a professional manner. Instead, these increases in legislative resources are seen as yet more proof that politicians want to exploit their offices for personal gain. Rather than reacting strongly to policy issues, the public is quick to anger over such ethical questions as legislative pay raises and other perks for elected officials. "The public does not want the same thing out of a legislature that you think they might want," says John Hibbing, a University of Nebraska political scientist who has written about the unpopularity of legislatures. "The public wants a legislature whose members are not in a position to feather their own nests."[86]

Legislators have done a poor job of selling the idea that what they do is important and necessary in a democracy. "It's our fault" that the legislature is viewed as "dysfunctional," "sheep," and "not independent," says Richard Brodsky, a member of the New York Assembly. "We have never gotten the message out in a coherent way of what we do well and right."[87]

For their part, the media are more concerned with dramatizing conflicts than with explaining what are sometimes awfully dry policy matters; therefore, they have not helped legislators to make their case. A primary job of the media in a democracy is to report on what the government is up to, but less and less media attention is devoted to legislatures. Books about such media failings are even more tiresome, if you can believe it, than books about state and local government—but a few points are worth making here.

First, ever since Watergate, the scandal that forced President Richard Nixon to resign in 1974, the press has taken an adversarial position toward the government. People in government, including legislators, are not very good in the first place at getting out the good news about what they are doing or publicizing their successes. And reporters, who are by their nature skeptics, are good at covering scandals and mistakes. "Skepticism is not just a personality quirk of journalists," says one reporter. "It's a core value, the wellspring of all our best work."[88] The media have made boo-boo coverage practically the mainstay of government reporting. This is not true in 100 percent of cases, of course, but the press's general attitude toward government was summed up well a few years ago by a reporter in Pennsylvania who told a public official, "Your job is to manage the public business and mine is to report when you do it wrong."[89] To be fair, legislators do it wrong sometimes. Two former Speakers of the Pennsylvania House began sharing a jail cell in 2012 after they were convicted in separate corruption scandals. The legislature, in fact, put under the official portraits of four convicted former leaders plaques describing their crimes. A year doesn't go by without several legislators being charged with crimes. The *Sacramento Bee* couldn't resist pointing out that, with 3 out of the 40 California state senators arrested in 2014, the chamber had a higher arrest rate than any of the state's 25 largest cities.[90] In covering these scandals, though, what the press sometimes loses sight of is that the vast majority of legislators are law-abiding citizens who mostly try to do their best as public servants.

Reporters may be too cynical about what legislators are up to, but a bigger problem might be that there are so few reporters watching them. According to the Pew Research Center, the number of reporters covering state capitols full-time dropped by 35 percent between 2003 and 2014. Less than a third of all newspapers employed statehouse reporters, while less than 15 percent of local television stations had any. Students, who necessarily work part-time and have shorter tenures on the job, make up 14 percent of the total

statehouse news corps.[91] "Every time you tweet about Justin Bieber, another state capital newspaper bureau shuts down," tweeted Brian Duggan, an editor with the *Reno Journal-Gazette*.[92]

Several states had seen formerly competing papers, such as *The Tampa Bay Times* and *Miami Herald,* combine forces and share reporters and coverage. Fewer reporters translate into fewer stories about what legislators are doing to earn their taxpayer-financed livings. The more populous states, such as New York and California, still boast relatively sizable, if diminished, capitol press corps, but even in these states the legislatures lose out because their stories get lost in the clutter of other news. The South Dakota legislature, when it is in session, is a major source of news in that underpopulated state, whereas the Illinois General Assembly loses out to coverage of other activities in Chicago and the surrounding area.[93] As a result of diminished coverage, says Gary Moncrief, a political scientist at Boise State University, "I'm not sure the American public is very attuned to the inner workings of legislatures and the fact that they probably do work better today than thirty or forty years ago."[94]

Some of the slack has been taken up by new online-only publications, from blogs written by single activists or political junkies to nonprofit outlets with something closer to traditional newsrooms and staffs. Many of the nonprofits, such as *MinnPost, The Texas Tribune, The CT Mirror,* and *California Watch,* have gone quickly from startups to leading sources of news for state government officials, lobbyists, and fellow reporters. They've broken big stories, such as *California Watch*'s investigation of the earthquake risk of state schools. As newspapers can attest, however, good statehouse reporting does not guarantee a viable business model. These publications are counting on continued donations, ad revenue, and other more unconventional sources of funding to survive. "There's no question in my mind that with the right team of journalists and leadership, you can do consistent and high-quality journalism," says Robert Rosenthal, a former *New York Times* reporter and *Philadelphia Inquirer* editor who is now executive director of California's Center for Investigative Reporting. "How you keep that going financially, though, is still a huge question mark."[95] That became clear in 2013, when NPR ended an experiment in which it provided funding to eight groups of stations to expand coverage of state government issues. The network had hoped eventually to offer support in all 50 states, but it shut the project down after 2 years when it ran out of grant funding.

While fewer reporters are covering statehouses, legislators have found ways to cut out the middleman. Through social media sites such as Facebook, YouTube, and Twitter, legislators are able to communicate directly with their constituents and the wider world more easily than ever before. In a typical example, New Jersey senator Jim Whelan held a town hall meeting in July 2012 during which he answered questions from a radio host on the Senate Democrats' Ustream channel while simultaneously accepting tweeted questions from the public via his own Twitter feed. Afterward, the chat was posted on the Democrats' Ustream channel, their YouTube page, and Whelan's own YouTube page.[96] "The media are very fractured right now," said Connecticut senator Bob Duff. "I have to find many ways to communicate with my constituents."[97] Twitter has had a particularly profound effect on state capitols, allowing breaking news, policy arguments, and snarky comments to spread instantaneously. The direct interactions with the public that Twitter makes possible, however, have been a mixed blessing for legislators. Feuds that once would have been private—or wouldn't have had a venue at all—can now become public. For example, after New York Senate majority leader Dean Skelos criticized actor Alec Baldwin for supporting an income tax increase on the wealthy, the *30 Rock* star fired back on Twitter. "His partisanship doesn't bother me," Baldwin tweeted, using hashtags such as #noonelieslikedeanskelos. "It's that he's so dumb." Skelos didn't back down from the fight, tweeting back, "Hypocritical @AlecBaldwin rages against corporate greed yet is a paid spokesperson for corporate giant (Capital One Bank)."[98]

Many political figures have learned the hard way that some inside knowledge and some thoughts are best left untweeted. In 2009, when Democrats held an edge of only two seats in the Virginia Senate (21 to the Republicans' 19), Republicans nearly persuaded one Democratic senator, Ralph Northam, to leave his party's caucus. If Northam had switched sides, the Democrats' majority would have disappeared. But before the move was a done deal, Jeff Frederick, the chairman of the Virginia Republican Party, tweeted, "Big news coming out of Senate: Apparently one dem is either switching or leaving the dem caucus. Negotiations for power sharing underway." Democrats sprang into action, calling in Governor Tim Kaine to help persuade Northam to stick with the party. Ultimately, Northam agreed to stay with the Democrats. Some observers believed it was Frederick's premature tweet that alerted the Democrats and prevented them from closing the deal.[99] A couple of months later, Frederick was removed as party chairman.

The decline of general coverage and the rise of often partisan commentary and news sites on the Web are among the reasons that amateur legislatures are much more popular with their constituents than are more professional chambers. The urge to return legislatures to their more humble but lovable position as citizen institutions has been the main driver behind the term-limits movement. Limits on the number of terms an individual may serve in the house or senate have been approved in most of the states that allow ballot initiatives. As of 2014, there were 15 states with term limits. The limits range from a low of 6 years of service per legislative chamber in states such as Arkansas and Michigan to 12 years of service in Nevada, Oklahoma, and Louisiana.

Term limits are especially strict in states where the public thinks there has not been enough turnover in the legislature. "The lower the existing turnover rate in the legislature," a pair of political scientists concluded in 1996, "the harsher the term limits they tend to adopt."[100] In California, for example, Assemblyman Willie Brown became the poster child for a term-limits initiative because of his 14 years as Assembly Speaker. In 1990, California voters sent a strong message. When they limited terms, they also cut the legislature's budget and staffing levels by 40 percent—the third cut in 6 years. The same year, Colorado voters imposed 8-year term limits on legislators and limited sessions to no more than 120 days a year.

Policy in Practice

Outwit, Outlast, Outplay: Who Really Got the Best Deal With Term Limits?

The biggest change to hit state legislatures over the past quarter century has been the advent of term limits. In the 15 states with term limit laws—which were almost all approved through ballot initiatives by voters sick of career politicians—legislators are limited to serving no more than 6, 8, or 12 years in either the house or the senate. Although that may sound like a long time, it turns out not to be enough for most legislators to master all the complexities of understanding and formulating a wide range of policy.

Term limits have failed the public's goal of bringing in more "citizen legislators." Instead, legislators are constantly seeking their next political jobs rather than carving out decades-long careers in one chamber. Term limits also have failed to bring the anticipated and hoped-for substantial numbers of women and minorities into the legislative ranks. The total number of women legislators is up nationwide, but their ranks have actually been slower to grow in states that impose term limits.[a]

But if they haven't fulfilled all their promises, term limits have not been quite the disaster their opponents predicted either. One of the most common predictions— that with members serving so briefly, lobbyists hoarding institutional and policy knowledge would accrue all the power—appears to have missed the mark. Term limits pretty much have been a mixed bag for lobbyists, who must introduce themselves to a new, skeptical set of legislators every couple of years rather than relying on cozy relations with a few key committee chairs. "I don't know one lobbyist who thinks it's a good thing," said Rick Farmer, who wrote about term limits as an academic before going to work for the Oklahoma House. "If term limits are such a good thing for lobbyists, why do so many lobbyists hate them?"

It does seem clear, however, that legislators in term-limited states have lost power to the executive branch— the governors and their staff who actually know how to operate the machinery of government. "Agency heads can outwait and outlast anyone and everyone on the playing field and they have consolidated their power," said one southern legislator-turned-lobbyist. Las Vegas Democrat Tick Segerblom says he believes it's time to give term limits the boot. "We need all the brainpower and institutional knowledge we can get, and term limits deprives us of that," he said.[b]

Academic studies in term-limit states, including California, Colorado, and Maine, have found that legislators make far fewer changes to governors' budgets than they used to, representing many billions of dollars in legislative discretion that is no longer exercised. "The

In keeping with the public disdain for professional or full-time legislatures, policy competence in legislators is often viewed as a negative. The idea is that if they are too distracted by details and special interest wishes, they will never shut up and actually do something to serve the common good.[101] Political nominees are eager to appeal to this public sentiment. "I just want to get things done," one candidate said in 2002 in a typical statement. "Hewing to the party line—any party's line—does not interest me."[102] Why should anyone in a society as diverse and polarized as ours expect easy agreement among legislators about tax rates, budgets, health care, guns, or the envi

ronment? Legislators simply reflect the messiness of public opinion. No matter which way they decide an issue—even if it is only to decide to maintain the law as it stands—they are bound to make some people angry. People prefer decisions to be neat and simple and harmonious. Maybe that is why no one likes legislatures.

Conclusion

Legislatures have one of the toughest jobs in the political system. Imagine trying to get a hundred or more people—many of whom flat-out

crumbling of legislative power is clear across states," said Thad Kousser, a political scientist at the University of California, San Diego, and author of a book about term limits. "There's no more clear finding in the research than a shift in power where the legislature is becoming a less than equal branch of government."

For all that, it's become common to hear governors and other executive branch officials complain about term limits because the laws mean they lack negotiating partners whose knowledge and expertise they can count on. It seems that no one who works in a state capitol—or in the law and lobbying shops that surround any capitol—likes term limits.

But there is one group that still finds them attractive—the voting public. Polls suggest that as much as 75 percent of the public favors them. "With new people in office, you have people with real world experience," says Stacie Rumenap, president of U.S. Term Limits, a group that advocates limits. "Under term limits, you might have a schoolteacher sitting on the education committee."[c]

That sort of suggestion often is made about term limits—you get rid of the professional politicians and get people who know what the real problems are because they themselves are real. And while Idaho and Utah have repealed their limits, efforts to extend or weaken term limits have been rejected several times since 2002 by voters in Arkansas, Maine, California, Florida, Montana, and South Dakota. California voters did relax the state's term limits slightly in 2012.

The main effects of term limits, after all, are procedural. It's difficult to make a convincing case that term limits have made any one particular policy worse, let alone imperiled the quality of life in any state that observes them. The underlying complaint of term limits opponents—that they make legislators less powerful—is one reason many people supported them to begin with.

Source: Adapted from Alan Greenblatt, "The Truth About Term Limits," *Governing*, January 2006, 24.

[a]Peter Slevin, "After Adopting Term Limits, States Lose Female Legislators," *Washington Post*, April 22, 2007, A4.

[b]Quoted in Jeff Gillan, "Segerblom to Begin Long Process of Eliminating Term Limits," KSMV MyNews3.com, July 4, 2014, http://www.mynews3.com/content/news/story/segerblom-nevada-legislature-term-limits/5ZX-7SdA00q_-u9CO08YYQ.cspx.

[c]Interview with Stacie Rumenap, October 4, 2002.

oppose your preferred choice—to sign off on something as controversial as, say, a welfare bill. Now imagine trying to do that over and over again—researching; negotiating; meeting; balancing partisan interests, special interests, and constituent interests; and, finally, hammering out an agreement that no one is fully satisfied with and everyone is willing to criticize. That gives you some idea of the reality of a legislator's job.

Historically speaking, legislators today do their jobs more effectively and more fairly than legislators at any previous time. For this achievement, they are mistrusted and disliked. Why?

Ultimately, this is perhaps because a legislature can never give all the people everything they want. Democracy is simply not set up to do this, because people want very different things. Legislatures do not really create conflict; they simply reflect the disagreements that exist in the electorate. Or at least they do if the legislators are reasonably effective at representing the preferences of their constituencies. What democracy promises, and what state legislatures largely deliver, is not what everyone wants—on most issues, no such option exists. Rather, democracy is about reasonable compromises that most people can live with.

The Latest Research

This chapter has noted at various points the differences across legislatures that can make a difference. Term limits, partisanship and ideology, the sociodemographics of a legislature—all these can make a difference to legislative agendas, policy priorities, and whose political preferences do, or do not, get represented. Given the importance of these differences, it is not surprising that scholars are interested in their causes and consequences.

Below we summarize some of the latest research that employs the comparative method to explore how these legislative differences translate into power and policymaking.

• •

- **Birkhead, Nathaniel A**. "The Role of Ideology in State Legislative Elections." Prepared for presentation at State Politics and Policy Conference, Iowa City, IA, May 23–25, 2013. http://www.uiowa.edu/~stpols13/papers/Birkhead%20Ideology%20in%20State%20Legislative%20Elections.pdf.

How much do ideology and voting records actually matter when incumbent state legislators are up for reelection? They may have other interests than those of their district in mind when they vote, such as currying favor with party leaders or interest groups. If a legislator's voting record ends up being more extreme than the views of her district, will she be punished? Incumbent ideological extremity is associated with decreased electoral vote share in congressional elections, but individual state legislators and their voting habits receive less attention. Examining some 1,500 state legislative contests, Birkhead finds that ideological extremity does not seem overall to have a statistically significant effect on incumbents' vote totals, although Republicans (but not Democrats) are rewarded to a minor extent by voters for moderation.

- **Cummins, Jeff.** "The Effects of Legislative Term Limits on State Fiscal Conditions." *American Politics Research* 20 (2012): 1–26.

One of the themes running throughout this entire book, not just this chapter, is how battered state finances continue to be a major influence on policy and politics. This study analyzes state budgets between 1983 and 2008 and finds that as legislative turnover increases, budgets are more likely to head toward the red. This happens for several reasons. More experienced legislators may be better equipped to handle fiscal crises, in the same fashion a veteran pilot is better prepared for in-air emergencies. Legislators who have short time horizons are less likely to take into account the long-term implications of policy. The findings of this study have particular resonance given that term limits were increasing legislative turnover during and after the Great Recession.

- **Gamm, Gerald, and Thad Kousser**. "Contingent Partisanship: When Party Labels Matter—and When They Don't—in the Distribution of Pork in American State Legislatures." Paper presented at the American Political Science Association annual meeting, Chicago, IL, 2013. http://papers.ssrn.com/sol3/papers.cfm?abstract_id=2300304.

Legislatures often have authority to guide spending projects toward particular areas in a state. Examining budget decisions in six states during the first half of the 20th century, the authors found that states where power was divided between the two major parties were more likely to make spending decisions on a statewide basis, while one-party legislatures were more likely to direct money to specific districts—with the majority, of course, taking a larger share of such spending. In states where there was less competition or polarization between the parties, partisan identity mattered less than seniority or members' voting near the ideological center of the legislature when it came to receiving funds for their districts.

- **Reingold, Beth, and Adrienne R. Smith**. "Legislative Leadership and Intersections of Gender, Race, and Ethnicity in the American States." Paper presented at the annual meeting of the American Political Science Association, Washington, DC, August 26, 2014. http://papers.ssrn.com/sol3/papers.cfm?abstract_id=2487604.

A good deal of research has been done looking at the overall representation of women and minority groups in legislatures. Less examined has been the extent to which such groups have managed to obtain power within legislatures. Looking at half the state houses over a 10-year period, the authors conclude that the picture is mixed. Such groups are underrepresented at the top ranks of legislative leadership, such as Speaker or chairs of top committees, while overrepresented at lower leadership ranks, such as chairs of less prestigious committees. Women of color are the least likely to obtain positions of real power, regardless of seniority or other factors such as majority-party status.

Chapter Review

Key Concepts

- apportionment (p. 216)
- casework (p. 205)
- caucus (p. 212)
- coalition building (p. 198)
- committee (p. 199)
- compromise (p. 199)
- constituent service (p. 205)
- delegates (p. 215)
- districts (p. 198)
- filibuster (p. 198)
- gerrymanders (p. 217)
- incumbent (p. 205)

- logrolling (p. 198)
- majority-minority districts (p. 219)
- majority rule (p. 197)
- malapportionment (p. 217)
- oversight (p. 208)
- professionalization (p. 216)
- rank-and-file members (p. 199)
- redistricting (p. 216)
- representation (p. 202)
- riders (p. 198)
- trustees (p. 215)

Suggested Websites

- **www.alec.org.** Website for the American Legislative Exchange Council, an influential conservative organization that drafts model legislation. Both legislators and private-sector interests are members.

- **americanlegislatures.com**. A website maintained by two political scientists that offers voting data for state legislative chambers dating back 20 years.

$SAGE edge™
for CQ Press

Sharpen your skills with SAGE edge at edge.sagepub.com/smithgreenblatt5e. SAGE edge for students provides a personalized approach to help you accomplish your coursework goals in an easy-to-use learning environment.

- **www.csg.org.** Website for the Council of State Governments, which provides training and information to state government officials.

- **www.ncsl.org.** Website of the National Conference of State Legislatures; provides a wealth of information about legislative structures and procedures, as well as the major issues faced by legislators.

- **stateline.org.** A foundation-sponsored news service that provides daily news about state government.

$SAGE statestats

State Stats on Legislatures

Explore and compare data on the states! Go to ***edge.sagepub.com/ smithgreenblatt5e*** *to do these exercises.*

1. According to the ballots, in 2010, 54.3 percent of the eligible population turned out to vote in Washington State. What percentage of the eligible population reported voting? Why might there be a discrepancy here?

2. In 2012, the Virginia legislature was late in passing its state budget. What was its budget in 2010? Was this higher or lower than the national average? What is the problem with comparing the total budgets between states?

3. Utah has a very Republican state legislature, while Vermont has a very Democratic one. What is the difference in the state and local tax burden of these states? How might the partisan makeup of the state legislatures influence this?

4. State legislatures determine most of the budgetary allocations in their states, including spending on health programs such as Medicaid. Which state spends the largest percentage of its budget on Medicaid? Which spends the least? What might account for the differences?

5. How has the crime rate in your state changed since 2000? Is this what you expected? Why or why not?

6. Which states have the most farms? How might this affect the campaign strategy of someone running for state legislature?

AP Photo/Arthur D. Lauck, Pool

Louisiana governor Bobby Jindal used his executive power to order major spending cuts in the summer of 2012 to deal with the state's large budget shortfall. Although Louisiana's part-time legislators had gone home for the year, many objected to being cut out of the process, but they were wary of crossing the governor, who has the power to appoint top legislative leaders.

Governors and Executives

THERE IS NO SUCH THING AS ABSOLUTE POWER

- How did governors get to be such powerful players, when for much of American history their offices were weak?

- Why do some states still give their governors more pomp than power?

Bobby Jindal, the Republican governor of Louisiana, faced a big budget shortfall in the summer of 2012. The state's part-time legislature had gone home for the year, so Jindal decided to take care of the problem himself. He ordered nearly $1 billion in spending cuts, slashing some programs by 34.5 percent (reductions of 35 percent or more would have required legislative approval). He shut down major state-run facilities, including a prison and a mental hospital, in some cases giving local legislators less than an hour's notice before publicly announcing the shutdowns.

Needless to say, many legislators were unhappy. Some called for a special session to address the cuts. "I think legislators ought to be involved," said Dee Richard, a state representative. "Most of the cuts might be right, but we have no input."[1] Richard gained no traction with his call to bring the legislature back into session, however. Not only is Louisiana's legislature dominated by Republicans largely sympathetic to Jindal's desires, but the governor in that state gets to appoint top legislative leaders, including the House speaker and committee chairs. Legislators in Louisiana think carefully before crossing

After reading this chapter, you will be able to

- describe the various roles of the governor,
- identify the different types of power held by the governor,
- discuss who becomes governor and how, and
- identify other executive offices and their roles.

the governor. Even in states where the governors hold fewer cards than Jindal does, legislators hesitate to go up against them. "If you're a legislator and you look at the governor, he's calling the shots, whoever he is," Rutgers University political scientist Alan Rosenthal said—at the annual meeting of the National Conference of State Legislatures, no less.[2]

Governors are the prime political actors in virtually all states. The governor sets the agenda, largely determining which policy issues will be pursued and how the state budget will look. Governors are unique among state-level politicians in terms of the media attention they can attract. This helps them promote their causes, but they must rely on other institutional players if they are going to accomplish more than making speeches.

Recently, governors have become a lot better equipped to control the rest of the executive branch, and they are running states in fact as well as in theory. For more than 100 years after the founding of the American republic, governors were strong in title only, with little real power. Throughout the last decades of the 20th century, however, governors were given more and more formal control over the machinery of government at the same time as the federal government was shifting greater control of many programs, including welfare, to the states. Governors have longer terms than they once did and enjoy greater authority to appoint the top officials in virtually all government agencies. (Only New Hampshire and Vermont still have 2-year gubernatorial terms. The rest of the states have 4-year terms. Only Virginia limits its chief executive to a single consecutive term—although two-term limits are common among the states.) These changes were the results of changes in laws in many states that

were specifically designed to strengthen the office of governor in the hope of creating greater accountability and coherence in government. Governors are now, with few exceptions, not just the most famous politicians in their states but also the most powerful. "The weakest governor has a built-in advantage over the strongest legislature," said Rosenthal, who wrote a book on governors titled *The Best Job in Politics.*

Governors are like mini-presidents in their states. Like the president, the governor commands the lion's share of political attention in a state, is generally seen as setting the agenda for the legislative branch, and is basically the lead political actor—the figure most likely to appear on television on a regular basis. Also like the president, the governor tends to receive the blame or enjoy the credit for the performance of the economy.

> Governors are like mini-presidents in their states. Like the president, the governor commands the lion's share of political attention in a state, is generally seen as setting the agenda for the legislative branch, and is basically the lead political actor—the figure most likely to appear on television on a regular basis. Also like the president, the governor tends to receive the blame or enjoy the credit for the performance of the economy.

And, again like the president, the governor shares responsibility for running the government—implementing laws, issuing regulations, and doing the work of building the roads, maintaining the parks, and performing other public functions—with the help of a cabinet. Presidents appoint their cabinet officials to run the Departments of Defense and Agriculture and the like. Governors have help in running state-level departments of agriculture, finance, environmental protection, and so on. In most cases, the governor appoints officials to head these departments, but some other statewide officials, such as attorneys general, often are elected on their own and may even represent another party. We explore the roles of these other executive branch officials later in this chapter.

This chapter also answers these questions: How did governors get to be such powerful players, when for much of U.S. history their offices were weak? Why is this so? Why do some states still give their governors more pomp than power? We look at how the office of governor has changed over the years. We examine the types of powers governors can command by virtue of the office and which powers they must create out of the force of personality. We also look at what sorts of people get elected governor and how they get elected. Finally, we survey some of the other important statewide offices, such as lieutenant governor and attorney general.

The Job of Governor

Following the American Revolution, governors had very little power for one simple reason—distrust. Colonial governors, appointed by the British, had imposed unpopular taxes and exploited their positions to make themselves rich. Americans did not want to invest too much power in individuals who might turn into mini-dictators. There was no national president, after all, under the original Articles of Confederation. In the states, most of the power was disbursed among many individuals holding office in

---

Plural-executive system
A state government system in which the governor is not the dominant figure in the executive branch but, instead, is more of a first among equals, serving alongside numerous other officials who were elected to their offices rather than being appointed by the governor

legislatures and on state boards and commissions. Governors in all but three of the original states were limited to 1-year terms. Some early state constitutions gave more power to legislatures than to governors, while some adopted a **plural-executive system**, in which the governor was but one elected administrator among many. Governors were not given control over state departments and agencies. Separately elected individuals, boards, or commissions ran these instead. After his state's constitutional convention, one North Carolina delegate said that the governor had been given just enough power "to sign the receipt for his salary."[3]

The number of agencies grew as government became more complex toward the end of the 19th century. Lack of central control over these agencies, however, meant that states had difficulty functioning coherently. Governors still lacked the authority to perform in ways the public expected of them, given their position at the top of the political pyramid. This problem persisted well into the 20th century.

Lynn Muchmore, a political scientist, sums up the sorts of frustrations governors had as late as the 1980s in terms of getting various parts of government to act as they wished. Muchmore lays out a theoretical case of a governor elected on a platform of promoting growth in the state's rural areas and documents the difficulties he had in making good on those promises. In this scenario, the new governor found that the highway department, which was run by a separate commission, had decided a decade ago to complete urban segments of the state's road system. This decision siphoned money away from plans to develop better roads in rural areas. The board that oversaw the public colleges and universities had a policy of phasing out satellite campuses in favor of investing in three urban campuses. The state's department of commerce would not work in any county that did not have a local economic development corporation. Many rural counties lacked such corporations because they did not have the population or tax base to support them. And the state legislature had passed restrictions that denied new businesses breaks on rural utility rates.[4] Despite his promises, the governor's battle to help rural areas was an uphill one.

Not every scenario is so extreme, but it is often the case that state agencies not headed by people appointed by the governor—and therefore not answering to him or her—have their own constituencies and concerns. They do not have in mind the big picture of how the different parts of state government can best work together to promote the general good. Only the governor sees the whole field in that way.

In recent decades, governors have been granted greater powers, including much more power over appointments than they once had. This means that they are able to put their own teams in place to carry out their policies. They have become important symbols of their states, not only at home but also in other states and abroad as ambassadors who promote their states to businesses they hope to attract. YouTube is littered with clips of governors laying out their cases for why their states are the best.

Terry Sanford, a former governor of North Carolina, sums up the job of the contemporary governor well:

> The governor by his very office embodies his state. He must . . . energize his administration, search out the experts, formulate the programs, mobilize the support, and carry new ideas into action. . . . Few major undertakings ever get off the ground without his support and leadership. The governor sets the agenda for public debate; frames the issues; decides on the timing; and can blanket the state with good ideas by using his access to the mass media. . . . The governor is the most potent political power in the state.[5]

Governors must be multitaskers. They propose legislation, which has to win approval from the legislature. They can implement regulations that help clear up how those laws actually are applied to individuals, businesses, and other groups. Increasingly in recent years, governors have become the strongest advocates and public relations people for their states, traveling to promote tourism and help close deals with out-of-state trading partners that might locate offices or operations in their states. Below, we explore all these roles in some detail.

Chief Legislator

Just as the president does not serve in Congress, governors do not sit as members of state legislatures. Like the president, however, they have enormous influence over the work legislatures do. Governors outline their broad proposals in inaugural and annual state of the state addresses. They and their staffs then work with individual legislators and committees to translate these proposals into bills.

Some governors are better than others at getting what they want from legislatures. Why? Part of it is personal charm, but a lot of it has to do with the powers granted to a governor in a given state. In Texas, for instance, much of the influence that the executive branch holds over legislation is given to the lieutenant governor, who presides over the state Senate, not the governor. Governors vary in terms of how much authority they have in blocking bills they do not like through use of the **veto,** or rejection, of the bills. Those variations in authority help determine how much clout a governor has in the legislature. Ohio House Republicans debated their choice for Speaker in 2015 largely in terms of whether they could find a leader who would set goals working alongside Governor John Kasich, rather than merely responding to the governor's agenda.

Governors never get everything they want from state legislatures, but they do have a great deal of impact on which bills become laws. There are a number of reasons for this. Bills almost never become law without the governor's signature, and governors have veto power. Legislators can get around a veto, but that often means that they have to pass the bill again by a **supermajority vote.** Supermajority votes are usually votes of two thirds or more. That means a governor needs the support of only one third plus one vote in either chamber to sustain a veto. Because it is hard enough to get both legislative houses to agree on a bill in the first place, such a large vote against most governors rarely happens. If you can't pass a law without the governor's

Veto
The power to reject a proposed law

Supermajority vote
A legislative vote of much more than a simple majority, for instance, a vote by two thirds of a legislative chamber to override a governor's veto

California governor Jerry Brown speaks at a press conference in 2014. As with most governors, California's governor exercises considerable influence over the state's budget, and it is among the most critical bills he signs into law. Brown leads the way in setting goals for California's budget, and over the past few years, the legislature has followed.

AP Photo/Marco Ugarte

approval, it stands to reason that you will want to work with him or her to create a version of the bill that will win such approval.

Another factor that makes governors enormously influential in the legislative process is their command of state budgets. In nearly every state, the main responsibility for creating a state budget rests in the office of the governor. The governor proposes a budget that details the amounts of money that will go to every state agency, welfare program, highway department, and school district. There are often restrictions on how a state must spend much of its money from year to year, whether because of old laws or federal requirements. But the governor gets first crack at deciding how most of the state's money is going to be spent. As the budget picture began to improve for states following long years of diminished revenues after the financial crash of 2008, governors around the country began proposing tax cuts, increases in school spending, and freezes on college tuition. Governors don't get everything on their wish list, but they tend to set the general spending priorities for the state. In California, legislators expressed skepticism about the outlines of a budget proposed by Governor Jerry Brown in 2013, but in the end they followed his lead and gave him what he wanted in terms of tax policy, environmental spending, and a new funding formula for education. "As far as legislators are concerned," one political scientist wrote, "the ability to create the budget is so powerful that it becomes *the* major tool for a governor in achieving his legislative programs."[6]

While the legislature might set the overall dollar amount that goes to the transportation department, the governor might get to decide, for instance, whether bridges are going to be built in particular districts. To get those bridges—or any other goodies they might want—legislators often have to give the governor what he or she wants in terms of passing major initiatives. "Any legislator who says he needs nothing from the governor's office is either lying or stupid," according to one observer of the Alabama political scene.[7]

Head of State Agencies

Governors at one time had very little control over who ran their states' departments. This meant that people with other agendas could set policy on taxes or health care or other issues. Only about half the governors chose their own cabinet officials in 1969, but nearly all of them do today.[8] (From 1965 to 1979, 21 states embarked on comprehensive reorganizations of their executive branches.)[9] "Reformers had long advocated strengthening the governor's office by lengthening the governor's term of office, allowing consecutive succession in office, broadening the veto power, increasing appointment and removal power, and increasing budgetary authority," noted a trio of political scientists in 2010. "States have generally responded by adopting many of the reformers' propositions, and by late in the twentieth century, most governors enjoyed significantly enhanced formal powers."[10]

The power to appoint people to run state departments offers obvious benefits for governors.

They can pick their own people, who they know will pursue their policy preferences. If those people fail, they can be fired. Arguing for expanding the appointment power of New Hampshire governors, former legislator Marjorie Smith wrote in 2012:

> With the possible exception of Texas, New Hampshire's governor has power more limited than that of any other state's governor. We elect a governor with the expectation that she will shape the policy over the course of her term, but do not give her the power to name department heads who will carry out that policy.[11]

Just like any other boss, a governor may be disappointed in the performance of the people working for him or her. The ability to hire and fire people, however, as well as the ability to determine how much money the state's departments are going to get, means that the governor is truly the leader of the executive branch of government.

Chief Spokesperson for the State

In the fall of 2013, Colorado governor John Hickenlooper surveyed scenes of destruction caused by massive flooding in the Boulder area. He found a dramatic way to help: His helicopter stopped to pick up two groups of people who had been stranded by the storms. The Democrat was quick to applaud GOP representative Cory Gardner, who was riding with him (and would run for the U.S. Senate the following year), for spotting the residents, as well as his pilot for having the skill to make pinpoint landings. But Hickenlooper was still the one who got credit in the headlines.[12]

It's always this way with disasters. People don't expect governors to lead rescue missions personally, but they do expect them to take charge and rise rhetorically to the occasion. "It's sort of like a leadership pop quiz," said Andrew Reeves, a political scientist at Washington University in St. Louis who has studied disaster relief politics.[13] When governors rise to the occasion, they're heroes. If they don't, it can imperil both their reelection chances and their broader agenda. In 2010, Republican governor Chris Christie of New Jersey was lambasted for staying at Disney World for a family holiday trip after the state had been hit by a massive snowstorm. That was all forgotten when Christie won plaudits not only for his response to Superstorm Sandy in 2012 but for how he handled a boardwalk fire the following year. To deal with the latter, he canceled another Florida trip scheduled to celebrate his wife's 50th birthday. On Tuesday, the Newark *Star-Ledger* called him the "master of disaster," saying he "thrived amid chaos."[14] "One of the things Christie has been masterful at is having it appear that everything is being done by him," said John Weingart, a political scientist at Rutgers University. "He pulls it off and seems to be knowledgeable and in charge."[15]

A governor acts as the chief spokesperson and public face of a state's government in good times as well as bad. Governors didn't always think it was part of their job description to attract jobs and industry to their states, but they do now. The template was set for them by Luther Hodges, who served as governor of North Carolina from 1954 to 1961, before becoming U.S. secretary of commerce. Hodges created a business development corporation in his state to supply capital to businesses, changed the state's corporate income tax rates, and employed the expertise of nearby University of North Carolina, North Carolina State University, and Duke University in the creation of the 5,000-acre Research Triangle industrial park, which in turn led to the development of the state's high-tech infrastructure. "My administration was considered by many to be 'industry hungry,'" Hodges once said. "It was!"[16]

Governors regularly send out press releases about their role in helping land new jobs and companies through tax incentives, the creation of cooperative business ventures, and other economic development activities. When California-based Enquero Inc. announced it would create a new technology center in Lafayette, Louisiana, in 2014, Governor Jindal held a press conference and bragged that the state's technology sector had grown by 25 percent since 2008. Georgia governor Nathan Deal traveled to China in 2013 to announce that

Beijing-based TravelSky Technology Limited would invest $10 million in a new research and development center in his state. The day after his election in 2002, New Mexico governor Bill Richardson got on a plane to talk to executives in California's Silicon Valley in the hope of persuading them to set up operations in New Mexico. Once in office, Richardson proudly boasted that he called CEOs on a daily basis and "sucks up to them big time."[17]

Governors are also important lobbyists in Washington, seeking more federal money for their states. They are just about the only people lobbying in the nation's capital who can be sure that members of Congress and cabinet officials will meet with them directly rather than having them meet with staff.

Party Chief

Governors are also the leading figures in their parties within their states. U.S. senators arguably might be more influential figures, but governors are more important politically at home. Governors command more foot soldiers. A governor may be able to call on thousands of state workers, whereas a senator's staff numbers in the dozens at most. Not all of a governor's workers are loyal members of the same party—in fact, changes in patronage laws and the creation of a civil service system mean that governors appoint far fewer state employees than they did some decades ago. Governors, however, have more people whose jobs depend on them than do any other elected officials.

Governors often pick state party chairs of their liking. They help recruit and raise money for candidates for other statewide offices and the legislature. They use the media attention they attract to campaign for those they support. They are still the titular heads of their parties in their states, and no modern politician (who isn't already rich) can avoid the duties of raising campaign contributions.

With the Democratic and Republican governors associations having morphed into strictly campaign operations in recent years, governors are also taking a more partisan approach to politics outside their own borders. Even 20 years ago, governors who visited other states to campaign for their party's candidate would not speak ill of the incumbent. And that "host" governor would extend every courtesy, offering visiting

governors protection from state troopers. Today's governors are more willing to be openly critical of the other party. Andrew Cuomo said in a 2014 radio interview that "extreme conservatives who are right-to-life, pro-assault–weapon, anti-gay . . . have no place in the State of New York."[18] Although he was referring to the possible political fortunes of candidates with those views, his remark drew criticism, with some conservatives calling for a boycott of the state.

Commander in Chief of the National Guard

Even in this country's earliest days, when governors had few powers, each governor's military position was strong, "with all states designating him as commander-in-chief."[19] Southern governors perhaps most famously used their power to control the National Guard in resisting desegregation during the 1950s and 1960s. The National Guard in each state is a state agency, but the president has the power to federalize it, calling up units to perform federal service. That happened in the civil rights era, when the National Guard was ordered to work for the feds against governors who were resisting integration. Those serving in today's National Guard are more likely to fight alongside federal soldiers in such places as Iraq.

Governors do not use the National Guard as their private armies, however. Instead, they can call out units to respond to natural disasters or riots. Milton Shapp, governor of Pennsylvania during the 1970s, remembered his years in office in terms of emergency responses to floods, a pair of hurricanes, droughts, ice storms, fires, and a gypsy moth infestation, rather than in terms of lawmaking and policy agenda setting.[20] Still, the question of who controls the National Guard has become a politically potent one in recent years. The federal government pays for troop training and many of the National Guard's operations, and the Supreme Court has found that the feds—not governors—have the final say over where units are deployed.[21] In 2006 Congress passed a law that made it easier for the White House, rather than the statehouse, to take command of the National Guard during times of disaster. All 50 governors signed a letter protesting an earlier version of the law.

A Difference
That Makes A Difference

Contemporary Governors Are Becoming More Partisan

Republican governor Rick Scott, who was already executing prisoners faster than any Florida governor in modern times, signed a bill in 2013 designed to speed up the death penalty process. Six weeks earlier, Democratic governor Martin O'Malley had moved in the opposite direction: He signed a bill abolishing the death penalty, making Maryland the sixth state to end capital punishment in as many years.

This kind of difference is not unusual. On taxes, gun control, abortion, and a host of other issues, Democratic-controlled states are moving in entirely different directions than are their Republican-led neighbors. What is unusual is that governors are now often the ones leading the way. Traditionally, governors have been among the least partisan figures in big-league American politics, more likely to borrow ideas from their peers of other parties than ever to campaign against them. Many were willing to buck fashions in their own parties to balance their budgets or try to improve high school graduation rates. Compromise was simply part of their job description.

These days, whether fueled by their own presidential ambitions or pressured by interest groups that figure they can get more action in states than from a gridlocked Congress, governors have become more polarizing figures. "There just seems to be more of a partisan edge," said former Democratic U.S. representative Jim Matheson, whose father was a popular governor of Utah. "They seem to be infected along with everyone else, there's no question about it."

For decades, observers have talked about states as "laboratories of democracy," experimenting with ideas that often blossom into national policy. Today, we have red labs and blue labs, with partisan governors pushing entirely different and opposite types of laws. "The vast majority of states are deeply red or deeply blue, and they reflect that," said Larry Sabato, director of the University of Virginia's Center for Politics. "Governors used to be the most bipartisan group, but now they're as divided as everybody else."

Traditionally, once the campaign season was over, governors knew they had trains to run. The 50 governors saw themselves as belonging to a special breed—half the number of the U.S. Senate, the "world's most exclusive club," but with twice the accountability for solving problems. They collaborated with neighbors on border-crossing matters such as the environment while borrowing ideas from colleagues around the country on an ad hoc basis or through the National Governors Association (NGA).

"Governors used to clearly learn from each other at NGA meetings and follow up on projects," said John Weingart, director of the Center on the American Governor at Rutgers University. "They'd send their staff to look at interesting things being done in other states, regardless of party."

Now, governors are more likely to openly criticize one another's approaches to pensions or tax policy. Twenty years ago, NGA was considered one of the most powerful lobbying forces in Washington, speaking with the full authority of the most important politicians out in the country. The landmark welfare overhaul law of 1996, for instance, was largely built on state-level experiments.

The Powers of Governors

Anyone who follows sports understands that natural ability does not necessarily translate into success. Some players look great on paper—they're strong, they can run fast, they have whatever skills should help them dominate their sport. But, for whatever reason, these players sometimes squander their talents and are shown up by athletes who are weaker but who nevertheless have a greater understanding of the game, work harder, or simply find a way to win.

It is the same with governors. Some of them look incredibly strong on paper, and their states' constitutions give them powers that their neighbors can only envy. Nevertheless, states that

Today, with a more fractured group of governors, it's difficult for NGA to present a united front. Instead, the separate Democratic and Republican governors associations have become increasingly influential. The Republican Governors Association raised $117 million for the 2014 campaign cycle, the most recent big year for gubernatorial elections, while the Democratic Governors Association raised $55 million, according to the Center for Responsive Politics. "The transition moved quickly when the Democratic and Republican governor groups started taking positions on controversial issues, and then sought to have the NGA reflect their views," says Dave Freudenthal, a former Democratic governor of Wyoming, citing matters such as climate change and the Affordable Care Act, President Obama's health care law.

Meanwhile, the internal politics of many states have grown more partisan, with one party or the other coming to completely dominate the legislature. "It used to be, you'd run from one side or the other, but you were forced to govern more from the middle," said Ray Scheppach, a former NGA executive director. "Now, they do worry about primary challenges more, so it keeps them aligned in that partisan approach."

There was a time when it was common for governors to please just about everyone, earning approval ratings in the 70s or 80s. Scott Matheson, for instance, was one of the most popular governors in the country in the 1980s, even as a Democrat in Utah, in part because he worked well with Republicans such as Norman Bangerter, who served under him as state House Speaker and succeeded him as governor.

That sort of model still exists, but it's become more rare and doesn't bring with it national prominence. Instead, stars are born by taking ownership of some issue that excites the national party base—such as Republican governors who have taken on public employees' unions or talked about abolishing state income taxes, or Democrats' banning so-called assault weapons and signing gay-marriage laws. "Certainly those that want a national profile, they may well need to be partisan, just because of the way the nominating process works," said Bill Pound, executive director of the National Conference of State Legislatures. "They've got to get out and appeal to whatever base it is, on either side."

What would once have been seen as a no-brainer for governors—taking money from Washington—has become a bright dividing line. Many Republicans have objected on principle to accepting federal funds from the 2009 stimulus law or the Medicaid expansion at the heart of the Affordable Care Act.

"Being attractive to people in both parties used to be considered unambiguously a strength," says Weingart, the Rutgers professor. "Now, being seen as a moderate or someone who works well with the other party has not been a benefit in the last few cycles."

Bobby Jindal, the Republican governor of Louisiana, addressed members of his own party in a column in *Politico*, but he seemed to be channeling the attitude of many contemporary governors of both stripes: "Let's . . . get on offense," Jindal wrote, "and go kick the other guys around."

have set up the governor's office to be strong sometimes end up with weak governors. Conversely, states in which the governor's **formal powers** are weak sometimes can have individuals in that office who completely dominate their states' politics. They are able to exploit the **informal powers** of their office—they manage to create personal powers, as opposed to relying on relatively weak institutional powers.

Formal powers
The powers explicitly granted to a governor according to state law, such as being able to veto legislation and to appoint heads of state agencies

Informal powers
The things a governor is able to do, such as command media attention and persuade party members, based on personality or position, not on formal authority

More than 2,100 National Guard troops were called on to support relief efforts in New Jersey after Superstorm Sandy ravaged the state's coastline in 2012.

Below we outline the different types of powers governors actually do have—both the formal ones, those that come as part of the necessary equipment of the office, and the informal ones that these individuals create for themselves by using the office as a platform.

Formal Powers

Most governors have a wide variety of formal powers granted to them by state constitutions or other laws. Among the most important of these are the power to appoint officials to run state agencies, the power to veto legislation, the power to craft budgets, the power to grant pardons, and the power to call legislatures into session. We examine each of these aspects of a governor's job description in this section.

Power to Appoint. The first governors lacked **appointment powers.** They could not pick their own people to run state agencies, which made those agencies more independent. Nowadays, governors can pick their own teams, giving them greater authority to set policy. When John Engler served as governor of Michigan during the 1990s, for example, he put in place a series of appointees with a strong ideological commitment to limited government. These appointees helped him carry out his desire to shrink the state's government. Engler's contemporary, Ann Richards of Texas, set out to change the face of state government by changing the faces of the people within it, appointing women, African Americans, and Hispanics to replace the white men who had always run things in Austin.

Having loyal foot soldiers on your team rather than free agents is important for governors who want things done their way. This is not the only benefit the power of appointment carries with it,

however. Governors get to appoint dozens and sometimes thousands of people to full-time government jobs and to commissions and boards. For instance, if you are attending a public college, chances are that the governor appointed the board of governors of your school or university system. These are considered plum jobs, and giving them out is a way for a governor not only to influence policy but also to reward campaign contributors and other political allies.

Of course, there is a downside to the power of appointment, which is the risk of picking the wrong people. Earlier, we mentioned former Pennsylvania governor Milton Shapp, who remembered his administration mainly as a time of dealing with natural disasters. It is little wonder he prefers to remember his time in office that way, because many of his appointments turned into disasters of his own making. His secretary of property and supplies was sent to prison for contracting irregularities. The same fate befell a member of his turnpike authority. Other members of his administration came under ethical shadows as well. Even though Shapp himself was never touched by scandal, subsequent candidates—including the man who succeeded him as governor—ran campaigns against corruption. They won office by pledging to clean up Harrisburg.[22]

Power to Prepare State Budgets. The most powerful tool governors have may be their ability to shape their states' budgets. As we noted earlier in our discussion of Bobby Jindal's unilateral decision to cut $1 billion in spending, the power over the budget gives governors enormous influence in their dealings with the legislature. The same is true of their ability to maintain control over state agencies. In most states, agencies and departments submit their budget proposals to a central budget office that works as part of the governor's team. The governor's ability to deny them funds or shift money among departments helps make sure that agencies remain focused, at least to some extent, on the governor's priorities.

A governor can use the budget process to override old agency decisions, for example, to make sure that the transportation department fully funds bike trails that previously had been ignored. Even when an agency has some independence

---

Appointment powers
A governor's ability to pick individuals to run state government, such as cabinet secretaries

about how it spends its money, a governor can persuade officials to fund other priorities—such as a new law school at a state university—by threatening to withhold some percentage of their agency's overall budget. The governor's authority to set the terms of the budget varies by state. The governor of Texas can recommend a budget, but he or she has no authority to make the legislature grapple with it seriously. Compare that to Maryland, where legislators can only accept or defeat the governor's spending proposals; they can make no fresh additions of their own.

Power to Veto. In talking about the governor as chief legislator, we touched on the governor's ability to veto legislation in every state. (North Carolina's governor was the last to win this power, in 1997.) Legislators can override vetoes, but that rarely happens, because of supermajority vote requirements. Members of the governor's own party usually are reluctant to vote to override a veto. That means that if the governor's party holds just one third of the seats in a legislative chamber, plus one, a veto is likely to be sustained—meaning the governor wins.

Legislators, therefore, try to work with the governor or the governor's staff to craft a version of a bill that the governor will sign. There is little point in passing a bill if you know it is going to be rejected by the governor. Of course, legislatures sometimes pass a bill just to get it vetoed, to make the governor's opposition official and public. That happened often when Gary Johnson was governor of New Mexico during the 1990s. "During his eight years as New Mexico's governor, Gary Johnson competed in the Ironman Triathlon World Championship, won the America's Challenge Gas Balloon Race, played guitar with Van Halen's Sammy Hagar, and helped save a house when massive wildfires struck Los Alamos," political scientists Thad Kousser and Justin H. Phillips write in their 2012 book *The Power of American Governors.*[23] Yet, they note, he never succeeded in persuading legislators to enact items on his legislative agenda.

That didn't mean Johnson was irrelevant. Johnson, who ran as the Libertarian Party candidate for president in 2012, did not support any bill that increased the size of government, and so he ended up vetoing more than 700 bills. Legislators sent him bills that would increase funding for popular programs, such as education, in the hope that his vetoes would make him look bad. Whether that happened or not, Johnson almost always won the procedural battle. Not only was the legislature unable to override his vetoes except in one instance, but he also was reelected to a second term. All but six governors—those in Indiana, Nevada, New Hampshire, North Carolina, Rhode Island, and Vermont—have a power known as the line-item veto; that is, they can reject just a portion of a bill. If there is a bill funding education, for example, the governor can accept all of it except for an increase in funding for a school in the district of a legislator who is a political enemy. Governors can use the line-item veto to try to cut spending, as when New York governor George Pataki eliminated spending for more than 1,000 items from the state budget in

Governors Mike Pence of Indiana (from left to right), Scott Walker of Wisconsin, Nikki R. Haley of South Carolina, and Chris Christie of New Jersey attend a press conference of the Republican Governors Association, which serves both as a fundraising operation for campaigns and a forum for GOP governors to meet and share ideas. In recent years, governors have become more likely to copycat colleagues of their own party. While each serves as the head executive of his or her state, the amount of power each wields as governor varies.

States Under Stress

Governors Aren't Afraid to Grab Jobs From Other States

As he prepared to leave office, Texas governor Rick Perry had reasons to be satisfied. His state had consistently led the nation in job creation, with its economic growth outpacing the rest of the country's 2 to 1 over the preceding two decades, according to the Federal Reserve Bank of Dallas.

But Perry wanted more. During his last 2 years in office, the Republican seemed to spend as much time outside of Texas as he did in the state, traveling to New York, California, Illinois, Connecticut, and other states to encourage firms to move their operations to Texas.

Governors always want to recruit companies. Perry took an unusually public and aggressive approach, however. Not coincidentally, Perry chose for his tour states that had Democratic governors. He argued that the Texas model of low taxes and limited regulation were better for business. "When you grow tired of Maryland taxes squeezing every dime out of your business, think Texas, where we created more jobs than all other states combined," Perry said in radio and TV ads that ran in the state. "Maybe it's time to move your business to Texas."

When governors of the states he visited objected to both his presence and his policies—pointing out that Texas has large numbers of low-wage jobs and the highest percentage of residents without health insurance—Perry didn't shy away from the fight. When he visited Maryland in 2013, Democratic governor Martin O'Malley not only wrote an op-ed for the *Washington Post* touting his state's virtues over those of Texas but went on CNN's *Crossfire* to debate the Texan. After

O'Malley bragged about the "great companies" in his state, Perry said, "We'll recruit them."

"You're welcome to try," O'Malley said.

For all the media attention Perry's efforts garnered, they didn't always pan out. TexasOne, the public–private partnership that underwrote Perry's travels, claimed that its efforts helped convince companies to announce the creation of nearly 45,000 new jobs in Texas during the governor's last decade in office. But the *Dallas Morning News* noted in 2014 that "not all of those positions eventually materialized."

Perry caught his biggest fish that year when Toyota announced it would move its North American headquarters from California to the Dallas area, bringing with it roughly 4,000 jobs. The company didn't cite Perry's recruitment effort as its motivation for moving, but clearly it didn't hurt. An economic development fund overseen by the governor offered Toyota a $40 million incentive package to sweeten the deal. It beat out a $100 million package from North Carolina, whose commerce secretary told the Associated Press it was tough to compete against the lack of corporate or personal income taxes in Texas.

But Perry couldn't win them all. He missed out in 2014 on the chance to land a $5 billion battery factory planned by electric carmaker Tesla, which is based in California. Perry personally led negotiations with the company and went so far as to drive a Tesla Model S through Sacramento, California's state capital—a move the *Los Angeles Times* described as "stalking"—but Tesla decided to locate its plant in Nevada.

1998. The governor's ability to cut legislators' pet projects out of the budget forces most of them to support that governor's major initiatives. Congress tried to give the president line-item veto authority, but the U.S. Supreme Court ruled the practice unconstitutional in 1998.

When Tommy Thompson was governor of Wisconsin during the 1990s, he used the line-item veto to an unusual degree. Some governors can strike not only projects from bills but individual

words and letters as well. Thompson became notorious for vetoing just enough letters in a bill's wording to alter the meaning of the bill (see Chapter 3). The courts upheld his right to do so, but that power was soon curbed. Nevertheless, in 2005, Jim Doyle, the state's Democratic governor, was able to strike 752 words from a budget bill to cobble together a new 20-word sentence that shifted $427 million from transportation to education.[24] Prompted by Doyle's move—and by near-daily editorials in the *Wisconsin State Journal* newspaper and on the paper's website—the legislature in 2008 further restricted the governor's veto authority. The governor of Wisconsin can no longer stitch together words from different parts of a bill, but he or she can still delete words from individual sentences or change numbers—quickly converting $100 million to $10 million, for instance. "It seems like each governor gets more creative in their use of the partial veto, and this was clearly an abuse," said state senator Sheila Harsdorf, a sponsor of the successful anti-Frankenstein referendum. "When people saw that veto, it was pretty hard to justify."[25]

Power to Grant Pardons. One clichéd motif of old movies and television dramas was the depiction of a prisoner about to be put to death only to be spared by a last-minute pardon from the governor. Governors, like the president, can forgive crimes or commute (change) sentences if they feel that particular persons have been convicted unfairly. They sometimes act on the recommendations of pardon boards, but the decision to pardon is theirs alone and not reversible.

A famous example of the use of pardon power happened in Illinois in 2003. During his last week in office, Governor George Ryan pardoned four prisoners condemned to death and commuted the sentences of the other 167 death-row prisoners to life in prison. Ryan had grown concerned that the number of capital cases that were being overturned because of new evidence, such as DNA lab work, indicated that the death penalty was being unfairly and inequitably applied. He appointed a commission to study the application of the death sentence and became convinced that the state could not impose the death penalty with such absolute certainty that innocent people would not be put to death. The move gained Ryan international celebrity among death penalty opponents but was criticized by prosecutors and others at home.

Not all governors use their pardon powers in such a high-minded way. In Tennessee in 1979, Lamar Alexander was sworn in as governor 3 days early to prevent outgoing governor Ray Blanton from commuting the sentences of any more prisoners. Blanton already had granted 52 last-minute pardons, and the Federal Bureau of Investigation (FBI) had arrested members of his staff for extorting money to sell pardons, paroles, and commutations. More recently, outgoing governor Haley Barbour of Mississippi drew national condemnation by pardoning some 200 people during his final days in office in 2012, including five who were still in prison and five others who had worked in the governor's mansion. Despite a challenge from Mississippi's attorney general, the state Supreme Court quickly ruled that Barbour's actions had been perfectly in keeping with his power. In part because they fear political backlash if pardoned criminals should reoffend, the practice of pardoning has become increasingly rare among governors since the 1960s, with some governors currently in office never having pardoned anyone at all.[26]

Power to Call Special Sessions. Many legislatures meet only part-time and generally have fixed session schedules. When necessary or desired, however, every governor has the power to call legislatures into special session. Nearly half the nation's governors have the ability to set the agenda of a special session. This means that in such a session legislators can deal only with those issues that the governor wants addressed.

Special sessions can be useful for governors who want to deal with particular issues right away. In recent years, many governors have called special sessions when their states' revenues have fallen short so that the legislatures can help them cut spending. Sometimes a special session allows legislators to focus on a complex issue, such as changing medical malpractice liability laws. Such issues might get lost in the shuffle of a regular session, when most attention is devoted to passing a budget.

Although governors can call special sessions, they typically will not enjoy success unless they can work out deals on their pet bills in advance. "If a governor calls a special session without knowing what the outcome's going to be," said former Mississippi House Speaker Tim Ford, "it's chaos for everybody."[27] Arkansas governor Mike Beebe waited to call a special session in 2014 until legislative leaders assured him that they'd reached consensus on bills that addressed prison funding, the state lottery, and changes to the state employee health insurance system. The

TABLE 8-1

The Governors: Powers

State or Other Jurisdiction	Budget-Making Power		Item Veto Power			Item Veto—2/3 Legislators Present or 3/5 Elected to Override	Item Veto—Majority Legislators Elected to Override	Authorization for Reorganization Through Executive Order
	Full Responsibility	Shares Responsibility	Governor Has Item Veto Power on All Bills	Governor Has Item Veto Power on Appropriations Only	Governor Has No Item Veto Power			
Alabama	*(a)	...	*	...	...	...	*	...
Alaska	*	...	...	*	...	*	...	*
Arizona	*(a)	...	...	*	...	*	(b)	...
Arkansas	...	*	...	*	...	...	*	*
California	*(a)	...	...	*	...	*	...	*(c)
Colorado	...	*	...	*	...	*	...	*
Connecticut	...	*	...	*	...	*	...	...
Delaware	*(a)	...	*	...	...	*	...	*
Florida	...	*	...	*	...	*	...	*
Georgia	*	...	...	*	...	(b)	...	*
Hawaii	...	*	*	...	...	*	...	*
Idaho	(d)	(d)	...	*	...	*	...	*
Illinois	...	*	*	...	...	*	...	*
Indiana	*	...	...	...	*	...	...	*
Iowa	...	*	...	*	...	*	...	*
Kansas	*	...	...	*	...	*	...	*
Kentucky	*(a)	...	...	*(e)	...	*	*	*
Louisiana	...	*	...	*	...	...	*(f)	*(g)
Maine	...	*	...	*	...	...	*	...
Maryland	*	...	*	...	...	*	...	*
Massachusetts	*	...	*	...	...	...	*(f)	*(c)
Michigan	*(h)	...	...	*(e)	...	...	*(f)	*
Minnesota	...	*	...	*	...	...	*(f)	*(i)
Mississippi	...	*(j)	*	...	...	*	...	*
Missouri	*(a)	...	...	*	...	*	...	*
Montana	*	...	...	*	...	*(k)	...	*(l)
Nebraska	...	*	...	*	...	*(m)	...	...
Nevada	*	...	...	...	*	...	...	...
New Hampshire	*(a)	...	...	...	*	...	...	...
New Jersey	*(a)	...	...	*	...	...	*(f)	*(n)
New Mexico	*	...	...	*	...	*	...	...
New York	...	*	*	...	...	*	...	...
North Carolina	...	*	...	...	*	...	...	*(o)
North Dakota	*	...	...	*	...	*	...	*
Ohio	*	...	...	*	...	*	...	...
Oklahoma	...	*	...	*	...	...	*(f)	...
Oregon	...	*	...	*	...	*	...	*
Pennsylvania	*	...	...	*	...	*	...	...
Rhode Island	...	*	...	...	*	...	...	...

State or Other Jurisdiction	Budget-Making Power		Item Veto Power			Item Veto—2/3 Legislators Present or 3/5 Elected to Override	Item Veto—Majority Legislators Elected to Override	Authorization for Reorganization Through Executive Order
	Full Responsibility	Shares Responsibility	Governor Has Item Veto Power on All Bills	Governor Has Item Veto Power on Appropriations Only	Governor Has No Item Veto Power			
South Carolina	...	*	...	*	...	*	...	...
South Dakota	*	...	...	*	...	*(p)	...	*
Tennessee	...	*	...	*	...	...	*	*
Texas	...	*	...	*	...	*	...	*
Utah	...	*	...	*	...	*	...	*
Vermont	*	...	...	...	*	...	...	*
Virginia	*	...	...	*	...	*(p)	...	...
Washington	*	...	*(q)	...	...	*	...	...
West Virginia	*	...	...	*	...	*	...	...
Wisconsin	*(a)	...	...	*(r)	...	*	...	...
Wyoming	...	*	*	...	...	*	...	...
American Samoa	...	*	...	...	...	...	...	*
Guam	*	...	*	...	...	*	...	*
No. Mariana Islands	...	*	...	*	...	*	...	*
Puerto Rico	...	*	...	*	...	*	...	*(s)
U.S. Virgin Islands	*	...	...	*	...	*	...	*

Source: The Knowledge Center, The Council of State Governments' survey of governor's offices, December 2011. Reproduced by permission of The Council of State Governments.

Key:
*—Yes; provision for.
. . .—No; not applicable.

(a) Full responsibility to propose; legislature adopts or revises and governor signs or vetoes.
(b) Two thirds of members to which each house is entitled required to override veto.
(c) Authorization for reorganization provided for in state constitution.
(d) Legislature has full responsibility with regard to setting the state's budget.
(e) Governor may veto any distinct item or items appropriating money in any appropriations bill.
(f) Two thirds of elected legislators of each house to override.
(g) Only for agencies and offices within the governor's office.
(h) Governor has sole authority to propose annual budget. No money may be paid out of state treasury except in pursuance of appropriations made by law.
(i) Statute provides for reorganization by the commissioner of administration with the approval of the governor.
(j) Governor has the responsibility of presenting a balanced budget. The budget is based on revenue estimated by the governor's office and the Legislative Budget Committee.

(k) If the legislature is not in session when the governor vetoes a bill, the secretary of state must poll the legislature as to the question of an override, but only if the bill had passed by a vote of two thirds of the members present.
(l) The office of the governor shall continuously study and evaluate the organizational structure, management practices, and functions of the executive branch and each agency.
The governor shall, by executive order or other means within his authority, take action to improve the manageability of the executive branch. The governor may not, however, create an agency of state government by administrative action, except that the governor may establish advisory councils and must approve the internal organizational structures of departments.
(m) Three-fifths majority required to override line-item veto.
(n) Executive reorganization plans can be disapproved by majority vote in both houses of the legislature.
(o) Executive order must be approved by the legislature if changes affect existing law.
(p) Requires two thirds of legislators present to override.
(q) Governor has veto power of selections for nonappropriations and item veto in appropriations.
(r) In Wisconsin, governor has "partial" veto over appropriation bills. The partial veto is broader than item veto.
(s) Only if it is not prohibited by law.

legislature met and was able to pass the bills within 48 hours, and Beebe quickly signed them into law. Without a deal already in place, legislators who have been called into session will sit around reading newspapers and eating snacks while their leaders try to hammer out an agreement with the governor. They are likely to resent having to give up time from their regular jobs to sit idly in the capitol.

In 2011, the South Carolina legislature persuaded the state Supreme Court that Governor Nikki Haley didn't have the power to call the legislature into special session to take up bills she was insisting get consideration—bills that would have expanded her office's control over government operations. "She has to be mindful and respectful of the separation of powers," complained Glenn McConnell, the president of the state Senate. "She is not respectful of that."[28] Even though governors are able to call legislators into special session, they cannot necessarily make them do anything. In Iowa in 2002, Governor Tom Vilsack called the legislature back into session in the hope that it would increase funding for education and health, but the legislators adjourned after a single day without debating any bill. "We just came in and went home," said House majority leader Christopher Rants. Vilsack then signed a package of budget cuts he had accepted in meetings with legislators and went on to call a second special session later in the month.[29]

Informal Powers

The powers just outlined are spelled out in state constitutions and statutes. Governors either have line-item veto authority or they do not. Much of the outcome of a governor's program, however, depends on the governor's individual ability to wield informal powers—the ability to leverage the power and prestige of the office into real influence in a way that may not be replicated by successors. Governors may be personally popular, have a special gift for working with legislators, or have some other skills that help them do their jobs well but that are not based on any authority granted by the state. They can "exert leadership," as onetime South Carolina governor Richard Riley put it, using informal powers "such as negotiations, public relations and strategizing."[30]

Popular Support. One thing that will always help a governor is popular support. A governor who wins with 51 percent of the vote has all the same formal powers as a governor who wins with 75 percent, but the more popular governor is clearly going to have an edge. Legislators and other officials will accept more readily the need to go along with a popular governor's program because they believe that program is what most voters in the state want. This is especially true if the governor had strong support for election in their districts. When Haley Barbour ran for governor of Mississippi in 2003, he rarely made a speech without mentioning tort reform. He was able to convert his political support into a successful push for a law to curb trial lawyers, overcoming the resistance of House Democratic

leaders. Barbour then embarked on a "tort tour" to follow Mississippi's lead. "I think if a governor has strong popularity ratings, he's got a bigger **bully pulpit,**" said former Ohio governor Bob Taft. "If a governor is strong and popular, whether or not he's going to use the electoral power that gives him, legislators still think that he might use that either for or against them in their reelection."[31]

It is a long time between gubernatorial elections—4 years in most cases—so to maintain and build on their popularity, governors do all sorts of public relations work. They never fail to alert the press to all their good deeds, they constantly travel their states to appear in any number of forums—TV shows, groundbreakings, dedications, state fairs, church socials—where they can interact with the public, and they propose legislation that they believe will be popular. The fortunes of governors rise and fall with the health of the economy of their states, but individual governors can make themselves more or less popular depending on how well they appear to address the problems of the day.

Party Support in the Legislature. Having members of their own party dominate the legislature certainly helps governors get their agendas passed. Governors can be successful if the other party controls the legislature, but it is a lot tougher. The reasons are fairly obvious. Republican legislators want to see a Republican governor succeed, and the same holds true, obviously, for Democratic legislators serving under a Democratic governor. Voters perceive politicians who belong to the same party as being part of the same team; therefore, the political fortunes of these politicians will be tied together during the next election. Members of the same party are likely to hold similar positions on such issues as taxes, levels of social service spending, and the environment.

Governors are more likely to grant favors to legislators of their own party or raise money for them. This, in turn, makes those legislators more likely to support the governors' programs. Some

Bully pulpit
The platform from which a high-profile public official, such as governor or president, commands considerable public and media attention by virtue of holding office

governors curry favor with legislators because they used to be legislators themselves and still have friends in the house or senate. One-time Tennessee governor Ned McWherter, for example, was a longtime legislator before taking the top office. As governor, he concentrated his attention on a few pet initiatives, such as a major overhaul of the state Medicaid system, and went along with whatever his pals in the legislature were thinking on most other matters.

More typically, "each party attempts to strengthen the institution it commands and to weaken the institution controlled by the opposition," notes one political scientist.[32] In other words, a Republican holding the governorship will try to make that office more powerful at the expense of a Democratic legislature and vice versa. When power is shared under divided government, however, the two parties cannot just attack each other's programs. If they share power, they also share responsibility in the eyes of the voters, and so they have to work together to forge compromises on central issues such as the budget. Following the elections in 2012, however, fewer states had divided government. Power in both legislative chambers and the governorship was held by the same party in all but a dozen states. That number rose to 20 following the 2014 elections.

Ability to Communicate. We have already touched on the advantage governors have over legislators in regard to media exposure. There is no law that says newspapers and TV stations have to pay more attention to pronouncements from the governor—but that is what happens anyway. Pretty much anything legislators say and do takes a backseat. The governor is a single, well-known individual who is important to every voter in the state. A legislator, by contrast, even a powerful one, is just an individual legislator among 120 or 150 legislators and represents a district that makes up only a fraction of the state. Whereas a governor speaks clearly with one voice, Rosenthal notes, a legislature speaks with many—not just because it is made up of many individuals but also because there are differing points of view between the chambers and between the majority and

minority parties.[33] "In any squabble, the governor had a distinct edge over what amounted to a gang of unknowns in the legislature," writes former Vermont House Speaker Ralph Wright.[34]

Governors have to play both an inside game and an outside game. They have to appeal to capital insiders as well as to the public at large. A governor who makes every move based on the ability to turn it into a press release or who appeals to the public by bashing the "corruption" in the capital may score points with the media and the public but soon will have few friends in the legislature. In Illinois, Rod Blagojevich was elected governor thanks to his railing against the corruption of state government, and he did not change his theme song once he took office. He refused even to establish a permanent residence in the state capital of Springfield, instead commuting from his home in Chicago. "We're going to keep fighting to reform and change the system and give the people a government that stops spending their money like a bunch of drunken sailors," he said toward the end of his first year in office.[35] Needless to say, the legislators whom Blagojevich had likened to drunken sailors were not eager to cooperate with him any more than they had to—even though his own party had a majority in both chambers. They continued to feud with him throughout his tenure—one publicly called the governor "insane" in 2007[36]—and did not hesitate to impeach him in 2009 after federal investigators revealed tapes of phone conversations in which Blagojevich was caught trying to sell President Obama's U.S. Senate seat, which the governor had the power to fill following Obama's ascension to the White House.

But governors often enjoy the upper hand in their relations with the legislature. Roy Barnes, who served one term as governor of Georgia from 1999 until 2003, had said during his days in the state legislature, "When you are called down to the governor's office, it is a very impressive office, you're talking to the governor, and you know that he controls things that could be good or ill for your district. He controls grants, he controls roads, and other things."[37] In other words, the formal powers of the governor (the ability to control projects) merge with informal powers (the mystique

FIGURE 8-1

HOW IT WORKS

Merging Formal and Informal Gubernatorial Powers: Florida's Governor Crist Takes on Category 5 Insurance Problems

As powerful as they are, there are some things governors may not be able to control. The weather is one. The insurance industry may be another. Florida's Republican governor Charlie Crist tackled both in his first term as he worked behind the scenes and in front of the cameras to pass legislation to stem rising insurance costs in the state.

THE PROBLEM. The disastrous 2004 and 2005 hurricane seasons left many of Florida's homeowners with more than just flattened roofs: it landed them with crushing insurance bills. The cost of insuring a home more than doubled in 2006, and many residents considered leaving the state altogether. Joining a chorus of voices advocating for a host of insurance reforms, Governor Crist urged Floridians to stay put and promised to work with lawmakers to help bring down insurance rates.

That's no small feat. Insuring property in a state that saw nearly $36 billion in storm damages in one year alone is an expensive business—and regulating that industry is the state's responsibility. Even the industry's harshest critics understand that the premiums homeowners pay on a regular basis to insure their homes must keep pace with the amounts that agencies anticipate will be paid out in future claims. That's basic math. But, critics say, insurers' profits have soared in recent years. Some agencies have adopted such misleading or unfair practices as creating differently named subsidiary companies that offer different rates than their parent agencies. Others offer restricted insurance plans to Floridians (for example, they offer auto but not homeowners insurance). Still others refused to offer policies in that state, leaving many without coverage.

In their wake stands Citizens Property Insurance, a state-run agency created in 2002 by the Florida legislature as an insurance "safety net." Under its original rules, homeowners were allowed to switch to Citizens only if they had been denied coverage by a national company or if their premiums were quoted at more than 25 percent higher than Citizens's rates. By 2006, however, Citizens was set to become the insurer for more than half of all of Florida's homeowners—about 1.3 million policyholders—making it the state's largest insurance company rather than the agency of last resort.

With so many homeowners forced to pay exorbitant rates or cut loose from national policies altogether and Citizens stepping in to fill the gap, Governor Crist and Florida's lawmakers were made to reconsider the role that Citizens should (or could) play in wholesale insurance reform.

THE PROCESS. In January 2007 Crist called a weeklong special legislative session to try to hammer out a plan. Crist himself brought several aggressive measures to the table, including recommendations to lower threshold requirements for homeowners to get coverage through Citizens, to cap the agency's ability to raise rates, and to crack down on subsidiaries. He also asked for the power to appoint the company's director. But the hallmark of his plan was to make Citizens more competitive with private insurers. After the special session, the legislature continued the reform debate during its regular session.

Early predictions of Crist's likelihood of success were not good. The insurance lobby came on strong, as did a handful of legislators from his own party, who warned the public that increasing the role of the state-sponsored Citizens was tantamount to socialism and potentially could bankrupt the state. But having once been a state legislator himself, Crist knew how to work the ropes. His main advantage was his stratospheric popularity: he had plenty of political capital, and he wasn't shy about spending it.

To promote his plan, Crist put in rare appearances before several House and Senate committees and stumped to persuade homeowners that the promised rate relief wasn't an illusion. He also traveled to Washington, D.C., to help Florida lawmakers appeal for a national disaster relief fund to help defray costs to that state's homeowners.

Crist and his staff continued to work behind the scenes, too, with the governor's staff "buttonholing" legislators. State senator J. D. Alexander reported that "there had been some political arm-twisting," adding, "You don't go against a governor with a 77-percent approval rating."[a]

Both the House and Senate took up bills that included a number of Crist's original proposals; by the end of their regular session, they'd reached resolutions.

THE OUTCOMES. Crist got a lot of what he wanted. Legislators agreed to freeze Citizens's rates at 2006 levels through 2009. Policyholders will be allowed to choose coverage through Citizens if they receive quotes from national insurers that are more than 15 percent higher than Citizens's annual premiums. Other provisions also are in place to allow the agency to be more competitive with private insurers.

"You put the nail in the coffin this afternoon on the industry that was hurting our people. That's right and just fair and important, and you did it, and God bless you for fighting for the people of Florida," Crist told legislators. "I hear some groans from insurance lobbyists? Tough. That's right. We work for the people, not them."[b]

But Crist didn't get everything he asked for. Legislators killed an amendment giving him the power to appoint Citizens's director. Also rejected was a proposal that would have allowed the agency to write policies for auto, theft, and fire insurance that would have made it better able to amass greater financial reserves and offer lower premiums.

[a]Paige St. John, "Crist Still Pushing for Property-Insurance Legislation," *Tallahassee Democrat*, May 3, 2007, http://www.tallahassee.com/apps/pbcs.dll/article?AID=2007705030346.

[b]S. V. Date, "Session's End More Like Recess Than Finale," *Palm Beach Post*, 2007.

TABLE 8-2

Ranking of the Institutional Powers of Governors

State	Separately Elected Executive Branch Officials	Tenure Potential	Appointment Powers	Budgetary Powers	Veto Powers	Party Control	Total Score	Rank
Massachusetts	4	5	3	5	4	5	26	1
Alaska	2.5	4	3.5	5	2.5	3.5	21	2
Maryland	4	4	3	5	4	5	25	2
New Jersey	5	4	4	4	5	2	24	2
New York	4	5	3	2	5	3	22	2
West Virginia	2	4	3	5	2.5	4	20.5	2
Utah	4	5	3	2	2.5	5	21.5	7
Colorado	4	4	3	2	2.5	3	18.5	8
North Dakota	3	5	3.5	5	2.5	4	23	8
Illinois	4	5	3.5	2	5	4	23.5	10
Iowa	3	5	3.5	2	2.5	3	19	10
Nebraska	4	4	3	2	2.5	3	18.5	10
Pennsylvania	4	4	3	5	2.5	2	20.5	10
Tennessee	2	4	4.5	2	2	4	16.5	10
New Mexico	4	4	3.5	5	2.5	2	21	15
Arkansas	2	4	2	2	2	4	16	16
Connecticut	4	5	3	2	2.5	4	20.5	16
Florida	3	4	3	2	2.5	4	18.5	16
Maine	5	4	3	2	2	3.5	20	16
Michigan	4	4	3	4	4	4	23	16
Minnesota	4	5	3.5	2	2	4	20.5	16
Missouri	2	4	2.5	4	2.5	2	17	16
Ohio	4	4	3	5	2.5	4	22.5	16
Washington	1	5	4	5	5	4	24	16
Delaware	2	4	3	4	5	4	22	25
Montana	3	4	3	5	2.5	2	19.5	25
Oregon	1.5	4	2	2	2.5	3	15	25
Wisconsin	3	5	1.5	4	2.5	4	20	25
Arizona	2	4	2.5	4	2.5	4	20	29
Hawaii	5	4	2.5	2	5	5	23.5	29
Louisiana	2	4	4	2	2	3	17	29
California	1	4	2	4	2.5	4	17.5	32
Georgia	1	4	1.5	5	2.5	4	18	32

State	Separately Elected Executive Branch Officials	Tenure Potential	Appointment Powers	Budgetary Powers	Veto Powers	Party Control	Total Score	Rank
Idaho	1	5	2	1	2.5	5	16.5	32
Kansas	3	4	2.5	5	2.5	4	21	32
Kentucky	2.5	4	3	4	2.5	3	19	32
New Hampshire	5	2	2.5	4	0	3	16.5	32
Texas	2	5	1.5	2	2.5	4	17	32
Virginia	2.5	3	3.5	5	3	3	20	32
Wyoming	2	4	3	2	5	5	21	40
Nevada	2.5	4	2.5	5	0	4	18	41
South Carolina	1	4	2.5	2	2.5	4	16	41
South Dakota	3	4	3	5	3	4.5	22.5	41
Indiana	3	4	3.5	5	0	4	19.5	44
Mississippi	3	4	2	5	5	3	22	44
North Carolina	3	4	2.5	2	1.5	2	15	44
Alabama	1.5	4	2.5	4	4	4	20	47
Oklahoma	1	4	1.5	2	2	4	14.5	47
Rhode Island	4	4	3	2	0	1	14	49
Vermont	2	2	2.5	5	0	4	15.5	50

Source: Thad Beyle and Margaret Ferguson, "Governors and the Executive Branch," in *Politics in the American States*, 10th edition, eds. Virginia Gray and Russell L. Hanson (Washington, DC: CQ Press, 2012).

Separately elected executive branch officials: 5 = only governor or governor/lieutenant governor team elected; 4.5 = governor or governor/lieutenant governor team, with one other elected official; 4 = governor/lieutenant governor team with some process officials (attorney general, secretary of state, treasurer, auditor) elected; 3 = governor/lieutenant governor team with process officials, and some major and minor policy officials elected; 2.5 = governor (no team) with six or fewer officials elected, but none are major policy officials; 2 = governor (no team) with six or fewer officials elected, including one major policy official; 1.5 = governor (no team) with six or fewer officials elected, but two are major policy officials; 1 = governor (no team) with seven or more process and several major policy officials elected. **Source:** Council of State Governments, ed., *The Book of the States 2007* (Lexington, KY: Council of State Governments, 2007).

Tenure potential: 5 = 4-year term, no restraint on reelection; 4.5 = 4-year term, only three terms permitted; 4 = 4-year term, only two terms permitted; 3 = 4-year term, no consecutive election permitted; 2 = 2-year term, no restraint on reelection; 1 = 2-year term, only two terms permitted. **Source:** Council of State Governments, ed., *The Book of the States 2007* (Lexington, KY: Council of State Governments, 2007).

Appointment powers: In six major functional areas, including corrections, K–12 education, health, highways/transportation, public utilities regulation, and welfare. The six individual office scores are totaled and then averaged and rounded to the nearest 0.5 for the state score. 5 = governor appoints, no other approval needed; 4 = governor appoints, a board, council, or legislature approves; 3 = someone else appoints, governor approves or shares appointment; 2 = someone else appoints, governor and others approve; 1 = someone else appoints, no approval or confirmation needed. Budgetary power: 5 = governor has full responsibility, legislature may not increase executive budget; 4 = governor has full responsibility, legislature can increase by special majority vote or subject to item veto; 3 = governor has full responsibility, legislature has unlimited power to change executive budget; 2 = governor shares responsibility, legislature has unlimited power to change executive budget; 1 = governor shares responsibility with other elected official, legislature has unlimited power to change executive budget. **Sources:** Council of State Governments, ed., *The Book of the States 2007* (Lexington, KY: Council of State Governments, 2007); National Conference of State Legislatures, "Limits on Authority of Legislature to Change Budget," 1998.

Veto power: 5 = governor has item veto and a special majority vote of the legislature is needed to override a veto (three fifths of legislators elected or two thirds of legislators present); 4 = has item veto with a majority of the legislators elected needed to override; 3 = has item veto with only a majority of the legislators present needed to override; 2 = no item veto, with a special legislative majority needed to override a regular veto; 1 = no item veto, only a simple legislative majority needed to override a regular veto. **Source:** Council of State Governments, ed., *The Book of the States 2007* (Lexington, KY: Council of State Governments, 2007).

Party control: The governor's party—5 = has a substantial majority (75% or more) in both houses of the legislature; 4 = has a simple majority in both houses (under 75%), or a substantial majority in one house and a simple majority in the other; 3 = has split control in the legislature or a nonpartisan legislature; 2 = has a simple minority (25% or more) in both houses, or a simple minority in one and a substantial minority (under 25%) in the other; 1 = has a substantial minority in both houses. **Source:** National Conference of State Legislatures website, http://www.ncsl.org.

Score: Total divided by six to keep 5-point scale.

of the office) to influence legislators and other supplicants.

Becoming Governor and Staying Governor

We have described governors as the most powerful and important political actors in their states. It should come as little surprise, then, given the history of politics in this country, that middle-age white males have dominated the job. Women are being elected to governorships with greater frequency—only three women were elected governor during the nation's first two centuries—but plenty of states have yet to elect a woman for the top job.[38] In 2007, nine women served as governor, the highest number ever to serve at one time. (Their ranks have since been slightly depleted by retirements and presidential appointments; just five women governors were in office following the 2012 elections.) In 1873, P. B. S. Pinchback, the black lieutenant governor of Louisiana, was elevated to the post of acting governor for 43 days, but only two African Americans have ever been elected as governor of any state:[39] Douglas Wilder of Virginia held the job during the first half of the 1990s, and Deval Patrick was elected to the office in Massachusetts in 2006. David A. Paterson, who is African American and legally blind, became governor of New York following Eliot Spitzer's 2008 resignation due to a sex scandal. There have been a handful of Hispanic and Asian American governors, including Brian Sandoval of Nevada and Susana Martinez of New Mexico. In 2007, Bobby Jindal of Louisiana became the first Indian American to be elected governor; he was joined by Nikki Haley of South Carolina in 2010.

Many nonpoliticians have been elected governor, including movie action hero Arnold Schwarzenegger of California, former wrestler Jesse Ventura of Minnesota, and business executives Bruce Rauner of Illinois and Rick Scott of Florida. Most governors, however, have had a good deal of previous government experience. They have served in the U.S. Congress, the state legislature, or other statewide positions such as lieutenant governor, attorney general, or even state supreme court justice. Throughout the 20th century, in fact, only about 10 percent of governors had no prior elective experience.[40] Only a handful of independent or third-party candidates have been elected governor in recent years, including Lincoln Chafee of Rhode Island, who had served in the U.S. Senate as a Republican. In 2014, independent Bill Walker—a former Republican mayor of Valdez—won the Alaska gubernatorial election with the former Democratic nominee as his running mate.

One qualification for modern governors is quite clear—they must have the ability to raise money. Gubernatorial campaigns have become multimillion-dollar affairs, particularly in heavily populated states, where television ads are expensive to run because the media markets are competitive and costly. The total cost of the campaigns for the 37 governors' races in 2010 was $1.1 billion—the first time gubernatorial campaign costs exceeded $1 billion. Contributing mightily to that total were two self-funding candidates, both Republicans: Meg Whitman, the former head of eBay, who lost the California governorship despite spending $140 million of her own money; and hospital executive Rick Scott, who became governor of Florida thanks in part to his ability to devote $78 million in personal funds to his own campaign.

Factors Driving Gubernatorial Elections

Like the Winter Olympics, gubernatorial elections in most states have been moved to the second year of the presidential term in what are called off-year elections. Thirty-four states now hold their gubernatorial elections in the off year. Another five states—Kentucky, Louisiana, Mississippi, New Jersey, and Virginia—hold their elections in odd-numbered years. Nine states—Delaware, Indiana, Missouri, Montana, New Hampshire, North Carolina, North Dakota, Utah, and Vermont—hold their elections at the same time as the presidential contest. In addition, New Hampshire and Vermont, the only states that have clung to the old tradition of 2-year terms, hold elections for governor every even-numbered year.

The majority of governors are elected in even-numbered off years because states wanted to insulate the contests from getting mixed up in national issues. Many states from the 1960s to the 1980s moved their gubernatorial elections to the presidential midterm because they hoped this would allow voters to concentrate on matters of importance to the states, without having their attention diverted to federal issues brought up in presidential campaigns. This was the desire and the intent, but the plan has not been a 100 percent success. In gubernatorial elections the office of governor is often the biggest thing on the ballot; so voters use these races as a way of expressing their opinions about who is *not* on the ballot. "There is simply no question that the primary motivation was to reduce presidential coattails on the election for governor and to increase the voters' attention on state rather than national issues," says Larry J. Sabato, director of the University of Virginia's Center for Politics. "What changed? Party polarization increased. It is easier to link the president and governor (and Congress and state legislatures) because almost all Democrats now are liberal and almost all Republicans are conservative, at least on critical social, tax, and spending issues."[41] In 2002 and 2003, when Republican president George W. Bush was generally popular, Republicans did better than had been expected in gubernatorial contests. But as Bush's popularity sank, so did the ranks of Republican governors. Democrats in 2006 regained the majority of governorships for the first time since 1994, holding 28 states compared with the GOP's 22. Democratic gubernatorial candidates paid the price for Obama's midterm ebb in popularity in 2010, with the GOP that year gaining six governorships. The only governorship to change hands in 2012 was North Carolina's— Republican Pat McCrory won election to succeed an unpopular Democrat. McCrory had lost his bid for the office 4 years earlier and had jokingly blamed his loss on Obama to the president's face during a White House meeting in 2009, attributing his narrow loss to the Democrats' voter turnout efforts. Obama did some campaigning for Democratic governors in the closing weeks of the 2014 campaigns—a sharp contrast to U.S. Senate races, where the unpopular president was generally not welcome. That November proved to be a fairly volatile year for gubernatorial contests, with three

incumbents defeated and power changing hands in a total of six states.

Overall, however, gubernatorial races are still less prone to following national trends than, say, elections for the U.S. Senate. The reason? Voters understand that the governor's position is important in and of itself. The dominant concern in most gubernatorial contests is the state economy. Even the most powerful politicians have only limited control over the economy at best, but voters tend to reward or punish the incumbent party based on the state's economic performance. If a state is faring poorly or doing considerably worse than its neighbors, the incumbent party is likely to struggle.

Voters more often use party as a guide in lower-profile contests, such as state legislative races, but are better informed about individual gubernatorial candidates. One reason is the greater news coverage of the races. Another important factor is the amount of money that candidates for governor spend to publicize themselves. Candidates create extensive organizations that promote their campaigns and use all the modern techniques of political consultants, polling, and media buys. Voters are far more likely, even in less populous states, to get to know the candidates through TV ads and brochures than through speeches or other personal appearances. As noted above, gubernatorial elections are now a billion-dollar business, with individual races sometimes costing in excess of $100 million. Candidates and outside groups spent more than $80 million in the unsuccessful recall election of Wisconsin Republican Scott Walker in 2012 (roughly $14 for every man, woman, and child in Wisconsin.), more than doubling the previous gubernatorial record in that state.[42]

Keeping and Leaving Office

Despite all the potential for upsets, the office of governor is a pretty stable one these days. States used to change governors just about every chance they got, but that is no longer the case. According to political scientist Thad Beyle, states changed governors on average more than two times each

TABLE 8-3

Who's Who Among U.S. Governors, 2015

State	Governor	Party	Education (Highest Degree Obtained)	First Elected In[a]	Previous Political Life
Alabama	Robert Bentley	Republican	University of Alabama	2010	Member, Alabama State House of Representatives
Alaska	Bill Walker	Independent	University of Puget Sound (now Seattle University), J.D.	2014	Mayor of Valdez
Arizona	Doug Ducey	Republican	Arizona State University	2014	State treasurer
Arkansas	Asa Hutchinson	Republican	University of Arkansas, J.D.	2014	Undersecretary of Homeland Security (also, U.S. rep)
California	Jerry Brown	Democrat	Yale University (JD)	1974	California attorney general
Colorado	John Hickenlooper	Democrat	Wesleyan University	2010	Mayor of Denver
Connecticut	Dan Malloy	Democrat	Boston College (JD)	2010	Mayor of Stamford
Delaware	Jack Markell	Democrat	University of Chicago (MBA)	2008	State treasurer
Florida	Rick Scott	Republican	Southern Methodist University (JD)	2010	Started at the top as governor; previously a businessman
Georgia	Nathan Deal	Republican	Walter F. George School of Law (JD)	2010	Member, U.S. House of Representatives
Hawaii	David Ige	Democrat	University of Hawaii, MBA	2014	State senator
Idaho	C. L. "Butch" Otter	Republican	College of Idaho	2006	Member, U.S. House of Representatives
Illinois	Bruce Rauner	Republican	Harvard University, MBA	2014	Started at the top as governor; previously a businessman
Indiana	Mike Pence	Republican	Indiana University School of Law (JD)	2012	Member, U.S. House of Representatives
Iowa	Terry Branstad	Republican	University of Iowa	1982	Member, Iowa House of Representatives
Kansas	Sam Brownback	Republican	Kansas State University	2010	Member, U.S. Senate
Kentucky	Steve Beshear	Democrat	University of Kentucky (JD)	2007	Lieutenant governor
Louisiana	Bobby Jindal	Republican	Brown University (also Rhodes scholar at Oxford University)	2007	Member, U.S. House of Representatives
Maine	Paul LePage	Republican	University of Maine	2010	Mayor of Waterville
Maryland	Larry Hogan	Republican	Florida State University	2014	State secretary of appointments
Massachusetts	Charlie Baker	Republican	Northwestern University, MBA	2014	State administration and finance secretary
Michigan	Rick Snyder	Republican	University of Michigan (JD)	2010	Chair of the Michigan Economic Corporation
Minnesota	Mark Dayton	Democrat	Yale University	2010	Member, U.S. Senate
Mississippi	Phil Bryant	Republican	Mississippi College	2011	Lieutenant governor
Missouri	Jay Nixon	Democrat	University of Missouri (JD)	2008	Missouri attorney general
Montana	Steve Bullock	Democrat	Columbia University Law School (JD)	2012	Montana attorney general

State	Governor	Party	Education (Highest Degree Obtained)	First Elected In[a]	Previous Political Life
Nebraska	Pete Ricketts	Republican	University of Chicago, MBA	2014	Started at the top as governor; previously a businessman
Nevada	Brian Sandoval	Republican	Ohio State University	2010	District judge for the District of Nevada
New Hampshire	Maggie Hassan	Democrat	Northeastern School of Law (JD)	2012	President pro tempore and majority leader of New Hampshire State Senate
New Jersey	Chris Christie	Republican	Seton Hall University (JD)	2009	U.S. attorney for New Jersey
New Mexico	Susana Martinez	Republican	University of Oklahoma (JD)	2010	Elected district attorney
New York	Andrew Cuomo	Democrat	Albany Law School (JD)	2010	New York attorney general
North Carolina	Pat McCrory	Republican	Catawba College	2012	Appointed to Homeland Security Advisory Committee
North Dakota	Jack Dalrymple	Republican	Yale University	—	Lieutenant governor
Ohio	John Kasich	Republican	Ohio State University	2010	Member, U.S. House of Representatives
Oklahoma	Mary Fallin	Republican	University of Oklahoma	2010	Member, U.S. House of Representatives
Oregon	John Kitzhaber	Democrat	University of Oregon Medical School	1994	President, Oregon State Senate
Pennsylvania	Tom Wolf	Democrat	MIT, PhD	2014	State secretary of revenue
Rhode Island	Gina Raimondo	Democrat	Yale, J.D.	2014	State treasurer
South Carolina	Nikki Haley	Republican	Clemson University	2010	Member, South Carolina House of Representatives
South Dakota	Dennis Daugaard	Republican	Northwestern University (JD)	2010	Lieutenant governor
Tennessee	Bill Haslam	Republican	Emory University	2010	Mayor of Knoxville
Texas	Greg Abbott	Republican	Vanderbilt University, J.D.	2014	State attorney general
Utah	Gary Herbert	Republican	Brigham Young University (no degree)	—	Lieutenant governor
Vermont	Peter Shumlin	Democrat	Wesleyan University	2010	Member, Vermont House of Representatives
Virginia	Terry McAuliffe	Democrat	Georgetown University Law Center	2013	Started at the top as governor; previously a businessman
Washington	Jay Inslee	Democrat	Willamette University (JD)	2012	Member, U.S. House of Representatives
West Virginia	Earl Ray Tomblin	Democrat	University of Charleston	—	President, West Virginia Senate
Wisconsin	Scott Walker	Republican	Marquette University	2010	County executive of Milwaukee
Wyoming	Matthew Mead	Republican	University of Wyoming College of Law (JD)	2010	U.S. attorney for Wyoming

Source: National Governors Association, *Governors of the American States, Commonwealths and Territories, 2014* (Washington, DC: National Governors Association), http://www.nga.org/files/live/sites/NGA/files/pdf/BIOBOOK.PDF.

[a]Those individuals with no dates shown in this column (—) were not elected to the governorship when they first took that office; rather, each was elevated to the position after the elected governor left office for some reason.

during the 1950s. But now, turnover occurs on average just over once a decade.

It is not unusual to see governors get reelected by vote margins that top 70 percent. Not only are governors in charge of setting policy, but they also actually get things done. They educate children, build roads, and respond with help when miners get trapped. They also are much less likely than legislators to concern themselves directly with contentious social issues, such as gun owners' rights and gay marriage. In reviewing 2 years' worth of state of the state addresses, in which governors typically lay out their priorities for the year, political scientists Kousser and Phillips found that governors talked a lot about education and the economy but barely mentioned social issues—making just 15 proposals on such issues out of a total of 1,088.[43] Translation? Governors generally are viewed more favorably than legislators. From a constituent's standpoint, what do legislators do, after all, except vote?—and their votes tend to be highly partisan. Governors, on the other hand, have to compromise because of the number of people they must deal with and their role in running the state, not just arguing about policy. Even in these polarized times, voters occasionally will elect a governor from the less popular party in their state, to act as a brake on a one-party legislature, and many governors still seek to present themselves as centrists.

Governors are rarely booted out of office prematurely. In June 2004, Connecticut governor John Rowland resigned after being investigated by the legislature for accepting gifts from a contractor with business before the state. Faced with possible **impeachment** and a federal criminal investigation, Rowland, one of the nation's longest-serving governors at the time, chose to step down. Rod Blagojevich, the disgraced Illinois governor caught by the FBI on tape plotting to sell the appointment to President Obama's old Senate seat, continued to insist on his innocence even after he was impeached in 2009, but he was convicted in 2011 and sentenced to 14 years in prison.

Impeachment

A process by which the legislature can remove executive branch officials, such as the governor, or judges from office for corruption or other reasons

Recall election

A special election allowing voters to remove an elected official from office before the end of his or her term

In 2003, Gray Davis of California was the first governor forced to leave office by a **recall election** since Lynn Frazier of North Dakota was booted out more than 80 years earlier on charges of corruption. Voters felt that Davis had dug the state into such a deep hole financially that it would take years to recover. His liberal views on such issues as gay marriage also had stirred up controversy. Arnold Schwarzenegger won the special election held on the same day as Davis's recall.

Wisconsin's Scott Walker in 2012 became the first governor to survive a recall election. He had angered labor unions and Democrats by pushing through legislation a year earlier that eliminated collective bargaining rights for most public-sector workers. The unions and their allies had no difficulty gathering more than a million signatures calling for his recall, which in Wisconsin amounts to a "do-over" election—Walker had to run for office again in midterm. He was able to beat back a repeat challenge by his 2010 opponent, Milwaukee mayor Tom Barrett, in part because he was able to amass enormous sums for the campaign and in part because even some Democrats felt it would be wrong to remove a governor in the middle of his term over a policy dispute, as opposed to a personal failing such as corruption or gross incompetence.

Arizona governor Evan Mecham was impeached and convicted in 1987 for impeding an investigation and lending state money to a car dealership that he owned. The most recent previous conviction dates back to 1929, when Henry Johnston of Oklahoma was removed for general incompetence by a legislature with possible political motives. A few governors, including Fife Symington of Arizona (1997), Jim Guy Tucker of Arkansas (1996), and Guy Hunt of Alabama (1993), have resigned following criminal convictions. More recently, two governors have resigned amid sex scandals: Eliot Spitzer of New York (2008) and Jim McGreevey of New Jersey (2004).

A more common threat to gubernatorial staying power is term limits. Governors in 36 states are limited to either two terms or two consecutive terms in office. The only two states that have 2-year terms instead of 4-year terms—Vermont and New Hampshire—place no limits on the number of terms a governor may serve. Howard

Dean served five full terms as governor of Vermont before running for president in 2004.

A more common threat to gubernatorial staying power is term limits. Governors in 36 states are limited to either two terms or two consecutive terms in office.

So what do governors do once they leave office? Several of them, like Dean, run for higher offices, such as the presidency or a Senate seat. Four out of the five presidents elected prior to Barack Obama, in fact, were governors before winning the White House (see the box "A Difference That Makes a Difference: From State House to White House: Translating a Governorship Into a Presidency"). Governors also regularly run for the U.S. Senate. Eleven senators serving in 2014 previously had been governors.

Entering the Senate or serving as a cabinet official generally is considered a step up the professional ladder from being a governor. Many politicians, however, find that being governor—able to make and implement decisions, with a large staff and all the machinery of state government at their disposal—is the best job they'll ever have. Dirk

TABLE 8-4

Recall Rules

State	Grounds for Recall	Specific Signature Requirement	Petition Circulation Time	Election for Successor
Alaska	Yes	25%	Not specified	Successor appointed
Arizona	No	25%	120 days	Simultaneous (5)
California	No	12%	160 days	Simultaneous (6)
Colorado	No	25%	60 days	Simultaneous (6)
Georgia	Yes	15% (1)	90 days	Separate special
Idaho	No	20% (1)	60 days	Successor appointed
Illinois	No	15%	150 days	Separate special
Kansas	Yes	40%	90 days	Successor appointed
Louisiana	No	33.3% (1)	180 days	Separate special
Michigan	No	25%	60 days	Separate special
Minnesota	Yes	25%	90 days	Separate special
Montana	Yes	10% (1)	3 months	Separate special
Nevada	No	25%	60 days	Simultaneous (5)
New Jersey	No	25% (2)	320 days (4)	Separate special
North Dakota	No	25%	Not specified	Simultaneous (5)
Oregon	No	15% (3)	90 days	Successor appointed
Rhode Island	Yes	15%	90 days	Separate special
Washington	Yes	25%	270 days	Successor appointed
Wisconsin	No	25%	60 days	Simultaneous (5)

Source: Adapted from the National Conference of State Legislatures, "Recall of State Officials," September 11, 2013, http://www.ncsl.org/research/elections-and-campaigns/recall-of-state-officials.aspx#4.

Note: Signature requirement is percentage of votes cast in last election for official being recalled. Exceptions: (1) percentage of eligible voters at time of last election; (2) percentage of registered voters in electoral district of official sought to be recalled; (3) percentage of total votes cast in officer's district for all candidates for governor in last election; (4) applies to governor or U.S. senator; all others 160 days; (5) recall ballot consists of a list of candidates for the office held by the person against whom the recall petition was filed; the name of the officer against whom the recall was filed may appear on the list; and (6) recall ballot consists of two parts: the first asks whether the officer against whom the recall petition was filed should be recalled, and the second lists candidates who have qualified for the election; the name of the officer against whom the recall was filed may not appear on this list.

Kempthorne, who gave up a Senate seat to run for governor of Idaho in 1998, said that many of his colleagues regretted having to give up governorships to come to Washington and be just one more legislative voice among many. "They all said that being governor is the best job in the world," Kempthorne said on taking office. "I'm ready to find out."[44] Governor James Douglas took a post at Middlebury College rather than seeking federal office after he left the governorship in Vermont in 2011—one of a number of governors in recent years who have passed on the chance of continuing their careers in Washington. "Given the low repute in which Congress is now held, and its propensity to accomplish nothing or next to nothing, going to Washington is not a particularly appealing opportunity," he said.[45]

Many former governors in other positions complain that they never had it as good as back when they were running their states. "My worst day as governor was better than my best day as a United States senator," Thomas Carper, D-Del., said in 2009.[46] Wisconsin's Tommy Thompson openly lamented the second-guessing to which he was subjected as President George W. Bush's secretary of health and human services during a 2006 appearance before the National Governors Association, an organization he had once chaired. "When you're a Governor, you can wake up in the morning and you can have an idea and you can have somebody working on it by 11 o'clock in the morning," Thompson said. "When you go to Washington . . . I get up, get the same idea, go in. Then you have to vet it with 67,000 people who all believe sincerely they're smarter than you."[47]

An unusual number of governors sought to win back their old jobs in 2010, including Terry Branstad, who had previously served four terms as governor of Iowa during the 1980s and 1990s. He won, as did two other comeback governors on the West Coast—Jerry Brown of California and John Kitzhaber of Oregon. But Maryland's Bob Ehrlich and Georgia's Roy Barnes both lost their return runs that year. Charlie Crist, who served a single term as the Republican governor of Florida, sought to make a comeback in 2014 running as a Democrat. According to political scientist Eric Ostermeier, a grand total of 144 governors in American history have returned to power after some time out of office. Only five states—Hawaii, Kansas, Nevada, Utah, and Wyoming—have not reelected a "second-chance" governor.[48]

Other Executive Offices

Only the president is elected to the executive branch of the federal government. The vice president is the president's running mate and is elected as part of a package deal. The heads of all the cabinet departments—defense, transportation, energy, agriculture, and so on—are appointed by the president, subject to Senate approval. Voters do not get to say who gets in and who stays out.

Things work differently at the state level. The governor is the only statewide official elected in every state. Most states, however, also have several other statewide officials elected in their own right. This is a holdover from earlier times when the governor was not invested with much power and authority was distributed among a number of officeholders. Texas still has two dozen officials who are elected statewide, whereas New Jersey for many years elected only the governor. (That changed in 2009, when Garden State voters elected a lieutenant governor for the first time.) In 2013, the Maine House voted down a proposal to allow voters to select the state's treasurer, secretary of state, and attorney general, who are all picked by the legislature. Most states have handfuls of officials elected statewide; we outline the responsibilities of a few of them below.

Lieutenant Governor

The office of lieutenant governor traditionally has been seen as something of a joke. Lieutenant governors, it's been said, have nothing to do but wait for their governors to resign or die so they can accrue some real power. That situation has changed in some places in recent years. Some states, such as Georgia and Virginia, responded to budget shortfalls of recent years by slashing the budgets and limiting the powers of their lieutenant governors' offices. More states, however, have expanded the purview of the office, recognizing that the security demands created by the terrorist attacks of 2001 mean that there is plenty of work to go around and the skills of the second in command should be used more fully.

In Nebraska, for example, Governor Mike Johanns appointed Lieutenant Governor Dave Heineman to head all the state's homeland security efforts immediately after the September 11, 2001, terrorist attacks. Minnesota lieutenant governor Carol Molnau was given charge of the state's department of transportation after her election in 2002 and saved the state the $108,000-a-year expense of hiring a separate transportation secretary. Similarly, right after the 2003 election, Kentucky's new lieutenant governor, Stephen Pence, was named secretary of the department of justice, which put him in charge of public safety, corrections and law enforcement, the state police, and vehicle enforcement. Today, "it's rare that the lieutenant governor doesn't have some specific duties," says Julia Hurst, director of the National Lieutenant Governors Association.[49] In each of the cases just cited, power was granted to the lieutenant governor because of the desire of the governor. The next person to hold the office may have very different responsibilities or nothing to do at all. Lots of contemporary lieutenant governors seem dissatisfied or have been unsuccessful. Between 2012 and 2014, six lieutenant governors resigned, six saw campaigns for governor or senator crumble, and three decided not to run alongside the governor for reelection. Republican Lieutenant Governor Peter Kinder of Missouri complained that during his first 5 years serving alongside Democratic Governor Jay Nixon, "we've had one substantive discussion," and he wasn't even informed when the governor left the state.[50] Once, when similarly ignored Lieutenant Governor Gavin Newsom of California posed for a picture with a young boy who asked him what a lieutenant governor is, Newsom said, "I ask myself that every day."[51]

But in many states, the lieutenant governor's responsibilities are laid out by law. In Indiana, for example, the lieutenant governor's portfolio includes the departments of commerce and agriculture. In half the states, the lieutenant governor presides over the state senate, having varying degrees of authority in that chamber from state to state. In Texas and Mississippi, lieutenant governors play much more than a ceremonial role. Not only do they preside over the senate, but they also set the agenda and appoint senators to committees. In both states, the lieutenant governor often is referred to as the most powerful figure in the state, with authority in both the executive and legislative branches. In 1999, Alabama Democrats in the state Senate sought to strip control of their chamber along with other powers from Lieutenant Governor Steve Windom, a Republican. And they could have done it if only he had left the Senate floor, but Windom refused. To stay present in and to keep control of the chamber for that day, and thus for the rest of his term, he did what was necessary, even urinating into a plastic jug in the chamber.[52]

Twenty-five states elect their governors and lieutenant governors as part of the same ticket. (New Jersey opted for this model after two recent governors left office prematurely. As noted above, the state elected its first lieutenant governor in 2009.) In 18 other states, the two are elected separately. The other six states—Arizona, Maine, New Hampshire, Oregon, Tennessee, and Wyoming—don't elect lieutenant governors, although in Tennessee the Speaker of the Senate is given the title. Electing the governor and lieutenant governor separately can be a source of mischief, especially if the people elected are not from the same party. The lieutenant governor often assumes the powers of the governor when the boss is out of the state. During the 1970s, Republican Mike Curb of California had a lot of fun appointing judges and issuing **executive orders** while Democratic governor Jerry Brown was busy out of the state doing, among other things, his own presidential campaigning. In 2014, when Brown was again serving as governor, his travels led the state to work its way through almost the entire line of succession. California had four acting governors in as many days when Brown went

Executive orders
Rules or regulations with the force of law that governors can create directly under the statutory authority given them

A Difference
That Makes A Difference

From State House to White House: Translating a Governorship Into a Presidency

How big of an advantage is it to run for the presidency as a sitting governor, as opposed to some other position? For more than a quarter century prior to Barack Obama's election in 2008, it looked as though this advantage was about as big as they come. "If you live under a governor, you mainly care about his or her ability to govern," writes political scientist Larry J. Sabato. "If you don't, and you're in the political community, you primarily want to know whether a governor is presidential timber."[a]

Four of the previous five presidents had been governors: Jimmy Carter, Ronald Reagan, Bill Clinton, and George W. Bush. The one exception was George W. Bush's father, George H. W. Bush, who came to the Oval Office after serving as Reagan's vice president. Seventeen presidents in all had served earlier as governors.

Lately, though, governors have had bad luck. Former Massachusetts governor Mitt Romney lost to Obama in 2012, after beating Texas governor Rick Perry and former Minnesota governor Tim Pawlenty, among other opponents, in the GOP primaries.

Many recent presidential aspirants from among the gubernatorial ranks have seen their popularity plummet at home as they went courting voters in early-voting states such as Iowa and New Hampshire. Once his name began being floated regularly ahead of the 2016 campaign, Indiana governor Mike Pence sought to make clear that the Hoosier State remained his top priority. "Anytime I'm mentioned or talked to about the highest office in the land is deeply humbling, deeply humbling to me and my family," he told the Associated Press. "But my focus is Indiana."[b]

Obama's first race had been dominated by senators, including John McCain, Hillary Rodham Clinton, and Obama himself. (Obama had served 4 years in the U.S. Senate when he was first elected, after spending 8 years in the Illinois Senate.) They outpolled a large number of gubernatorial contenders that included Romney, Bill Richardson of New Mexico, Mike Huckabee of Arkansas, and Mark Warner of Virginia. Sarah Palin was serving as governor of Alaska when McCain picked her as his running mate (she resigned her post in Juneau the following year).

But if their recent track record isn't so great, compare governors to holders of other offices. No sitting U.S. senator before Obama had been elected president since John F. Kennedy in 1960. No member of the U.S. House has been elected since James Garfield, all the way back in 1880.

What makes governors such attractive candidates for the nation's most powerful office? And what makes legislators usually so *un*attractive?

For one thing, governors are the only politicians aside from presidents who have run governments that are anywhere near as complicated as the federal government. True, governors do not formulate foreign policy, but they do have to become experts in running departments that cover everything from taxes and education to public health and public safety. Governors have to run things. Members of Congress just vote. "Because the presidency is no place to begin to develop executive talents, the executive careerist clearly is preferable to the legislator," writes Sabato.[c]

to Mexico on a trade mission, with the lieutenant governor, state Senate president and Assembly Speaker all doing the duty before all but one traveled out of state.

Attorney General

Perhaps the statewide office that has undergone the greatest transformation in recent years is that of attorney general. Always referred to as the top law enforcement officer in the state, the attorney general sometimes has had duties that have been quite minimal because most criminal prosecutions are taken care of at the county level. But attorneys general have become major political players,

Furthermore, a legislator has to vote yes or no on thousands of issues, leaving a long paper trail. This trail is bound to contain more controversial elements than any governor's list of bridges built and budgets balanced. Opponents often distort legislators' records in smear campaigns that make use of attack ads and mudslinging. A vote for a $300 billion bill can become defined by one tiny provision it contained.

Also, Congress is a major part of "official" Washington, and senators and representatives can hardly say they have no connection with what occurs there. Conversely, governors running for the White House can always claim they are Washington "outsiders" who are going to sweep in and clean up the town. Former governor-turned-president Bill Clinton reportedly advised then-senator Joseph Biden, D-Del., that senators had to overcome big handicaps to run for president. Not only did they have their records to explain, but they also had forgotten how to speak the language of the average person. "When you get to Washington, the only people you talk to are the elites: elites in the press, elites among the lobbyists, elites that you hire on your own staff," Clinton told Biden. "You're not regularly talking to ordinary, everyday people."[d] Biden didn't listen to Clinton, launching his second bid for the presidency in 2008 and ultimately being elected at Obama's side as vice president. But, then, neither did Clinton's wife, who served as Obama's first secretary of state after losing to him in the 2008 primaries.

Still, the out-of-touch image of Congress and Washington in the public mind hampers members of Congress who seek national office. "It could probably be shown by facts and figures that there is no distinctly native American criminal class except Congress," Mark Twain wrote in his 1897 book *Following the Equator*. Governors running for national office invariably present themselves as fresh alternatives to the tired habits of Washington, promising to change the culture and tone of the nation's capital.

That they fail to do so is almost a given. That opens up the field for the next fresh face from the state of California or Arkansas or Texas. Within hours of Obama's reelection, attention turned to governors as potential candidates in 2016—particularly among Republicans but also among potential Democratic hopefuls not named Hillary Clinton.

---

[a]Larry J. Sabato, "Will a Governor Win the White House in 2016?" *Politico*, February 17, 2014, http://www.politico.com/magazine/story/2014/02/2016-elections-governor-white-house-103568.html.

[b]Quoted in Lou Jacobson, "Can Governors Balance National Ambitions With Concerns Back Home?" *Governing*, July 2014, http://www.governing.com/topics/politics/gov-going-national.html.

[c]Larry J. Sabato, *Goodbye to Good-Time Charlie: The American Governorship Transformed*, 2nd ed. (Washington, DC: CQ Press, 1983), 33.

[d]Quoted in E. J. Dionne Jr., "Govs 4, Senators 0. Tough Odds," *Washington Post*, January 4, 2004, E4.

---

finding new power by banding together in multistate consumer protection cases against financial firms, toy manufacturers, and drug companies, among many other examples. In 2014, for example, California attorney general Kamala Harris announced that her state would receive $103 million as part of a $7 billion settlement reached with banking giant Citigroup to resolve claims that it misled investors about mortgage-backed bonds.

The granddaddy of all such cases was the series of lawsuits filed against the tobacco companies during the mid-1990s. The attorneys general argued that the cigarette makers had engaged in fraud and caused a great deal of sickness and health conditions that the states had

Andrew Cuomo followed both Eliot Spitzer, his predecessor as state attorney general, and his father, Mario Cuomo, into the New York governor's mansion. He won the 2010 election and has since presided over the closing of a $10 billion budget deficit and the legalization of same-sex marriage.

© ZUMA Press, Inc./Alamy

ended up paying to treat through Medicaid and other programs. An initial agreement reached between the states and the industry was not ratified by Congress. Instead, in 1998 the attorneys general settled their lawsuits with the companies on their own. The tobacco companies agreed to pay the states an estimated $246 billion over 25 years. More recently, state attorneys general in 2012 reached a $25 billion settlement with home mortgage servicers—the largest joint federal–state settlement in history. Beginning in 2007, then New York State attorney general Andrew Cuomo won $13 million in settlements from lenders and universities that had violated state laws with their student loan policies. One of the first things Cuomo did after taking office as governor in 2011 was to use the money to set up a national student loan center that would offer "unbiased" financial advice to students and their parents.

Not surprisingly, there has been a backlash against these newly powerful officials. In part, this has been based on the fact that for many attorneys general the job has been a successful launching pad toward the governorship. In 2014, half a dozen former attorneys general were serving as governors, with about as many seeking the office in elections that year. "It seems to be considered the second most prominent and important position to governor," said veteran Arkansas newspaper columnist John Brummett. "The

other statewide offices are mostly clerical and pointless."[53] But the fight over control of the office of attorney general has largely been ideological. One of the great philosophical divides in U.S. politics is that between those with opposing views of how business should be regulated. On one side are those who believe that businesses have a right to conduct their affairs with a minimum of interference from state governments, which can only hinder their productivity and profits. On the other are those who believe just as strongly that conducting business in a state is a privilege that comes with a number of responsibilities that the state has the duty to enforce. The majority of state attorneys general over the past few years have acted as if they were members of the "privilege" camp, and that has fueled the rise of groups designed to combat what the business sector sees as excessive regulatory activism.

Attorneys general have traditionally been Democrats, their campaigns funded by trial lawyers. In recent years, the U.S. Chamber of Commerce and many other business groups have spent millions trying to defeat "activist" attorney general candidates. "Historically . . . attorney general races were off most business people's radar screens," says Bob LaBrant of the Michigan Chamber of Commerce. Today, "there's greater incentive to get involved in an attorney general race because of the increased involvement of attorneys general across the country in litigation against the business community."[54] The Republican Attorneys General Association was founded in 1999 to elect candidates who believe that their colleagues have gone too far in pursuit

TABLE 8-5

The Powers of State Offices

In Many States, Lieutenant Governors . . .	Secretaries of State . . .	Attorneys General . . .
Preside over the senate	File and/or archive state records and regulations, other corporate documents	Institute civil suits
Appoint committees	Administer uniform commercial code provisions	Represent state agencies and defend and/or challenge the constitutionality of legislative or administrative actions
Break roll-call ties	Publish state manual or directory, session laws, state constitution, statutes, and/or administrative rules and regulations	Enforce open meetings and records laws
Assign bills	Open legislative sessions	Revoke corporate charters
May be assigned special duties by governors	Enroll and/or retain copies of bills	Enforce antitrust prohibitions against monopolistic enterprises
Serve as cabinet members or members of advisory bodies	Register lobbyists	Enforce air pollution, water pollution, and hazardous waste laws in a majority of states
Serve as acting governors when the governors are out of state		Handle criminal appeals and serious statewide criminal prosecutions
		Intervene in public utility rate cases
		Enforce the provisions of charitable trusts

Sources: Compiled from Council of State Governments, ed., *The Book of the States 2003* (Lexington, KY: Council of State Governments, 2003), 215, 221, and 224; the National Association of Attorneys General, http://www.naag.org; and the National Lieutenant Governors Association, http://www.nlga.us.

of business regulations and the revenues such cases can generate. Their strategy appears to have worked—the number of GOP attorneys general climbed from 12 in 1999 to 20 by 2003; as of 2015 there are 26 GOP attorneys general and 24 Democrats.

Aside from taking a more active role in elections, corporations that might be subject to investigation by state attorneys general have also taken to courting them aggressively while they are in office, not just through campaign contributions but also with ongoing lobbying and personal appeals at lavish conferences—sometimes by former attorneys general who have been hired for the task. There are fewer disclosure requirements for attorneys general than for state legislators, and corporations with interests in banking, telecommunications, pharmaceuticals, and even energy drinks have spent millions to gain the ears of attorneys general and avoid exposure to costly litigation. "I don't fault for one second that corporate America is pushing back on what has happened," said John Suthers, a former Colorado attorney general, referring to multistate lawsuits

brought against various industries. "Attorneys general can do more damage in a heartbeat than legislative bodies can. I think it is a matter of self-defense, and I understand it pretty well, although I have got to admit as an old-time prosecutor, it makes me a little queasy."[55]

Partisan attorneys general have moved in different directions, and not only on business issues. In 2014, half a dozen Democratic attorneys general refused to defend their states' same-sex marriage bans in court. Republican attorneys general, meanwhile, had gotten into the habit of suing the federal government routinely over policy disputes in areas such as health care and the environment. During his 2014 campaign for governor, Texas attorney general Greg Abbott routinely boasted that his job consisted of going to the office, suing the Obama administration (which he did more than two-dozen times), and then heading home. "The AGs, who often attack the administration in packs, have done more than Republicans in Congress, statehouses, or anywhere else to block, cripple, undermine, or weaken Obama's initiatives," claimed the executive editor of *The Weekly Standard*.[56]

Other Offices

Every state elects its governor, and most states elect a lieutenant governor and attorney general. In terms of which other offices are held by elected officials—as opposed to officials appointed by the governor or by boards and commissions—the states vary widely. The theory behind electing many officials directly is that it gives the public a greater voice in shaping a variety of state programs, instead of just selecting a governor and leaving it all up to him or her.

In 2003, New Mexico governor Bill Richardson convinced voters to approve a referendum that gave him the power to name the state's top education official directly. Richardson knew he would receive the credit or blame for running the schools anyway, so he wanted to have the power to shape policy in that office by being the boss of the person who ran it. In 2013, Republican governor Mike Pence of Indiana attempted to make an end run around the Democrat elected as the state superintendent of public instruction by creating a new state education agency to set policy.

Only a few states, including Georgia, Montana, and Oregon, elect a state superintendent of education. In Nebraska, a state board of education is elected and the board in turn selects a superintendent. Several states, mostly in the South, directly elect a secretary of agriculture. An increasing number of states allow citizens to vote for an insurance commissioner. Most states elect a secretary of state who, in turn, regulates elections in those states. Overall, many states structure their executive branches similarly—if there isn't an elected agriculture secretary, there is certain to be an appointed one.

Some believe, however, that electing separate department heads makes too much of government political. A state treasurer who has to worry about getting reelected might not make politically unpopular but fiscally necessary decisions to make sure that the state's books are balanced. The other trouble with electing officials is that the departments they head will squabble over money and power instead of working together as part of a team to promote the greater good.

Election officials themselves have become controversial in some cases. Secretaries of state often oversee elections, and some have been accused of partisan bias in this role. Colorado secretary of state Scott Gessler came to his job after a career as one of the GOP's top campaign lawyers in the state. He was accused by Democrats of retaining a partisan bias in office, notably in participating in a fundraiser to pay off a campaign fine levied by his office. He was sued no fewer than eight times during his first year in office.[57] Similarly, Democrats in other states complained that GOP secretaries of state favored their parties by making changes to early-voting rules and implementing voter identification laws that they claimed were meant to suppress voting by those likely to vote Democratic. The formerly low-profile office attracted millions of dollars in super PAC spending in 2014, as each party saw increasing value in electing the person who controls elections. Iowa was one of the few states that saw voter turnout increase in 2012. Brad Anderson was proud of the role he played in encouraging turnout there as state director of President Obama's campaign. In 2014, he ran for secretary of state, saying, "I have a plan to make Iowa No. 1 in voter turnout."[58] The fact that a former Obama operative wants to run elections made some people nervous. But he was part of a trend of overtly partisan figures running for a job designed to be neutral when it comes to election administration.

Secretaries of state are the top election officers in 37 states, and many of them are therefore cautious about the dangers of appearing too partisan. In 2012, only 12 among the 37 endorsed a candidate for president. Ben Cannatti, a political consultant who advises Republican candidates for secretary of state, said concerns about potential bias among partisan officials in recounts or election enforcement are overblown. "The dozen secretaries of state who have endorsed either the president or Gov. Romney are doing so as political leaders in their states," Cannatti said in 2012. "It's neither surprising nor alarming. That's what politicians do. As public officials, they've taken an oath to uphold the law and run elections fairly in their states. To do anything else is politically and legally disastrous."[59]

Conclusion

How did governors become the most important political figures in their states? Over the years, their offices have become the centers of state power, with more and more authority given to them. The power of governors now matches, in most cases, the prestige they have always enjoyed. States have been involved in the difficult balancing act of trying to weigh the interests of direct citizen selection of leaders against the need to have professional people appointed to pursue a coherent policy promulgated by a single accountable leader. In recent decades the pendulum has mostly swung in favor of investing more power in the office of the governor.

Once weak, unable to set policy or budgets, governors have now become unquestioned leaders. They are able to select cabinets that run most of the state agencies according to the governors' priorities. Sometimes their staff picks prove to be embarrassments, but they are also able to fire such people in the hope of seeing their agendas pushed forward by more eager replacements. Many positions are designed with staggered terms so that governors cannot appoint their own people to every position. Strong governors, however, are able to combine their appointment powers with their ability to command attention from the

mass media to set the terms of political issues and the direction these issues take in their states. That clout extends to the judicial branch, with many governors able to appoint most state judges.

Their control of budgets and veto authority provide governors with enormous sway over the legislative branch as well. Although they never get everything they want from their legislatures, they almost always get more of what they want than do any individual legislators.

The unrivaled power of governors and their ability to command attention from the media and political donors make them the leading political actors at the state level. Their ability to put people to work in shaping policy and campaigns, as well as to raise money, makes them players in political races ranging from local and legislative contests all the way, in many instances, to the presidency.

Governors, in short, are the top dogs in the states. "As far as policy leadership goes," concludes Alan Rosenthal, "there may be big winners but there are no big losers among the nation's contemporary governors."[60]

The Latest Research

Understanding the evolving power and policy influence of governors through the comparative method has been a particular focus of political science for at least two decades. Much of this focus traces back to Thad Beyle, a professor at the University of North Carolina at Chapel Hill, who in the mid-1990s began developing and publishing quantitative measures of gubernatorial powers (see Table 8-2). Ever since, researchers have used these indexes to examine how gubernatorial power and what types of power translate into political and policy influence.

Gubernatorial powers, however, are constantly shifting. Institutional reforms—such as increases in staff and expansion of appointment powers—may change formal power. Informal power, of course, shifts every time a new governor is elected and brings his or her own personal characteristics to the job. How do these changes shape the ability of chief executives to get their agendas

enacted into law? Are these powers enough to give governors the tools they need to meet the increasingly heavy expectations voters place on them? Are those expectations—especially of the economic variety—realistic given that even the most powerful governor leads a state that is open to economic forces beyond his or her control? Political scientists search for systematic answers through the comparative method, examining differences in power and expectations to see whether they predict differences in political influence and policy success. Below we summarize some of the most recent research on the powers and expectations of governors.

• •

- **Crew, Robert E., Jr., and Christopher Lewis**. "Verbal Style, Gubernatorial Strategies, and Legislative Success." *Political Psychology* 32 (2011): 623–642.

(Continued)

(Continued)

As discussed above, one of the more interesting findings emerging from the study of executive power is that informal powers are at least as important as formal powers. This study takes an in-depth look at a particular dimension of the informal powers of Florida governors: verbal style. The central premise of the study is that speech making—the delivery of speeches such as the state of the state address—is an important governance tool. Speeches represent attempts at persuasion, opportunities to get important constituencies to buy into the governor's agenda. Communications scholars have developed a number of ways to measure how people use language persuasively, and this study appropriates one of these indexes to look at four dimensions of the verbal styles of governors: activity (language implying action), optimism (language reflecting praise or inspiration), certainty (language reflecting inflexibility), and realism (language reflecting tangible and immediate issues). The research finds that language and verbal style matter to policy. Governors with more optimistic and action-based verbal styles tend to have greater legislative success than do those whose verbal style is based more in certainty.

- **Crowley, George R., and William S. Reece.** "Dynastic Political Privilege and Electoral Accountability: The Case of U.S. Governors, 1950–2005." *Economic Inquiry* 51 (2013): 735–746.

Elections are meant to discipline politicians, making sure that the taxing and spending policies they pursue in office don't differ too widely from those preferred by a majority of voters. Incumbents have such strong advantages when it comes to reelection, however, that they may not be held as easily accountable. Are there factors that can mitigate incumbent advantage? The authors explore the factor of dynasties—that is, the sons and daughters of famous politicians' seeking the same or similar positions. Looking at a half-century's worth of governors, they find that those who face term limits are likely to tax and spend at higher rates; however, those who have politically active relatives tend to tax and spend at lower rates. Even governors who never have to face reelection again seem to temper their policies to brighten the prospects of their potential heirs.

- **Fredriksson, Per G., Le Wang, and Patrick L. Warren**. "Party Politics, Governors and Economic Policy." *Southern Economic Journal* 80 (2013): 106–126.

Who raises taxes the most? You may not be surprised to hear that Democratic governors push through higher tax increases than do their Republican counterparts. But something interesting happens when governors face term limits. Among governors who are not eligible to run for reelection, it's actually the Republicans who are more likely to raise taxes. Having studied tax policy changes from 1970 to 2007, the authors conclude that if a governor stays in office two terms, the tax rate at the end of his or her 8 years is likely to have changed by roughly the same amount, regardless of whether he or she is a Republican or Democrat. Just the timing of tax increases throughout the years is likely to have varied, depending on the governor's party.

- **Krupnikov, Yanna, and Charles Shipan**. "Measuring Gubernatorial Budgetary Power: A New Approach." *State Politics & Policy Quarterly* 12 (2012): 438–455.

The standard measure of formal gubernatorial powers used by political scientists is, as discussed above, that developed by Thad Beyle. This index has undergone a number of changes and updates as Beyle and others have sought to provide an ever more accurate indicator of the comparative power of governors. This study takes this development a step further: The authors argue that the standard power index suffers from some important measurement errors, and they propose an alternative. The specific focus is on measuring governors' budgetary powers. The authors' central criticism of Beyle's index is that, as typically constructed, its measures of budgetary power are comparable across states but not across time. This is because as part of its evolution and refinement, Beyle's index changed how budgetary powers were measured. This is potentially a problem for scholars using the comparative method, because they often do not look at differences that make a difference in one year but, rather, at differences that make a difference over multiple years. The authors of this study develop what they argue to be an index that is comparable from year to year as well as from state to state.

Chapter Review

Key Concepts

- appointment powers (p. 248)
- bully pulpit (p. 254)
- executive orders (p. 267)
- formal powers (p. 247)
- impeachment (p. 264)
- informal powers (p. 247)
- plural-executive model (p. 241)
- recall election (p. 264)
- supermajority vote (p. 242)
- veto (p. 242)

Suggested Websites

- **www.csg.org.** Website of the Council of State Governments, a forum for state officials to swap information on issues of common concern, such as drugs, water, and other policy matters.

- **library.cqpress.com.** The CQ Press Electronic Library, which features an online voting and elections collection with a component for gubernatorial elections.

- **www.naag.org.** Website of the National Association of Attorneys General, which has become increasingly prominent as state attorneys general have banded together on a number of high-profile cases.

- **www.nga.org.** Website of the National Governors Association, which shares information among governors and also lobbies the federal government on their behalf.

- **www.stateside.com.** Website of Stateside Associates, a lobbying firm that keeps close tabs on policies and actions in the states.

State Stats on Governors and Executives

*Explore and compare data on the states! Go to **edge.sagepub.com/ smithgreenblatt5e** to do these exercises.*

1. In 2003 the governor of Illinois commuted the death penalty for 167 prisoners and pardoned 4 more. How many death sentences have been overturned or commuted in the United States since 1973? Which state has had the most? The least? Might there be political or cultural explanations for these numbers?

2. In 2010 Arizona citizens voted to increase the sales tax rate by a penny. How has the per capita sales tax revenue in Arizona changed between 2005 and 2011? Does this make sense? What is a possible explanation?

3. The governor in most states can direct transportation funding toward specific projects, such as repairing deficient bridges. How many deficient bridges are there in your state? How does this compare to the national average? Do you think that this is something that should be prioritized in the budget?

4. The authors refer to governors as mini-presidents. Considering the population in some of the larger states, is this the case? How do the budgets of these larger states compare to those in the smaller states? What are the implications of these differences?

5. The governor of Maryland has more control over the state budget than any other governor. Has this power made Maryland's per capita outstanding debt better, worse, or similar to the surrounding states?

6. Which states have received the most money from grants for homeland security? Do these states need this money, or is it a political ploy?

DOWN WITH ACTIVIST JUDGES OVERTURNING THE WILL OF THE PEOPLE

OBAMACARE

CAGLECARTOONS.COM
CAGLECARTOONS.COM

Judges have increasingly found themselves in the midst of bitter partisan battles as they rule on cases related to important legislative issues such as voter identification. Some judicial decisions have raised accusations that "activist judges" are legislating from the bench. Judges often rule on cases concerning issues of great concern to legislators and the public, from gun rights and education to pipelines and death penalties, and their rulings will never please everyone.

ch. 9

Courts

TURNING LAW INTO POLITICS

- Why are some states' judges elected and some appointed?
- Why are some states' courts more likely than those in other states to impose the death penalty?
- What effects do state campaign finance rules have on judges and on the decisions they make?

Judges who make decisions in high-profile, politically charged cases can find themselves under pressure from all sides. Take, for example, Stephanie Stacy, a trial court judge in Lancaster County, Nebraska. In 2014 she ruled that the state's governor lacked the authority to green-light a passageway for a massive oil pipeline designed to carry crude from Canada's oil sands across Nebraska and on to refineries in Texas. This project, the Keystone XL pipeline, was opposed by Nebraska landowners and environmentalists worried about its potential to precipitate an ecological disaster. They were happy with Judge Stacy's ruling and saw her decision as a fair and reasonable application of the law. So did President Barack Obama. He cited her decision when he delayed a federal agency review of the pipeline, giving him the option of delaying a decision on a highly controversial project with electoral implications.

The governor and other supporters of the pipeline, which included state legislators, national Republican leaders, and some Democratic senators facing reelection, did not view Stacy's ruling as a fair and reasonable application of the law. U.S. Senate Energy and Natural Resources Committee chair Mary Landrieu, a Louisiana Democrat, called the decision "irresponsible, unnecessary and unacceptable." Others called it things not repeatable in a PG-rated college textbook, but the general gist was that Judge Stacy was making up laws rather than interpreting them. Stacy is far from the only judge to get an earful along these

After reading this chapter, you will be able to

- describe the role and structure of state courts,
- explain how judges are selected,
- summarize how judicial compensation is handled by the states,
- identify the players and elements present in state-level criminal court cases, and
- discuss the problems contributing to current changes in the courts.

lines in recent years. Angry political rhetoric and personal attacks have intruded on the once-quiet hallways of state courts in a big way. As Lee Epstein, a law and political science professor at Washington University, has suggested to her students, "Maybe the best definition of a judicial activist is a judge you don't like."[1]

Indeed, "activist judge!" is now something of a rallying cry for politicians when judges do not rubber-stamp their political and legislative goals. Organizations routinely decry "runaway courts" and judges "run amok" or "subverting the laws." Judges get it from both ends of the political spectrum. In 2012, liberal *New York Times* columnist Maureen Dowd, incorrectly assuming that the U.S. Supreme Court was poised to strike down President Obama's Patient Protection and Affordable Care Act, called the Court "hacks dressed up in black robes." When Chief Justice John Roberts surprised conservatives by upholding the act, conservative radio host Glenn Beck sold T-shirts with Roberts's face and the word "COWARD" boldly printed in yellow. For judges dealing with controversial political issues, it is a damned-if-you-do-and-damned-if-you-don't sort of deal.

Of course, railing against judges is nothing new. In 1954, when the U.S. Supreme Court, under Chief Justice Earl Warren, ordered an end to the practice of segregating schools by race, "Impeach Earl Warren" signs popped up along roadsides in many states. But, as former Supreme Court justice Sandra Day O'Connor has written, the "breadth of rage currently being leveled at the judiciary may be unmatched in American history."[2] In fact,

attacks against judges by politicians have moved beyond name-calling. According to the National Center for State Courts, judges faced more impeachment attempts in 2011 than in any previous year in history. In all but two instances, "the sole accusation was that the judges in question issued opinions that displeased members of the legislature."[3] In 2006, a handful of western states voted on ballot initiatives that were designed to rein in "out-of-control" judges. The most extreme was in South Dakota, where a group called JAIL 4 Judges advocated a state constitutional amendment to create special grand juries to punish judges for unpopular decisions. None of these initiatives passed, but they reflected a frustration felt by many regarding unpopular state court decisions.

Judges cannot avoid making decisions, which means they frequently find themselves in the position of having to decide cases that involve sensitive and polarizing issues, such as abortion, gun control, criminal sentencing, zoning laws, and school vouchers. Regardless of the decision and its legal merits, the losing side is increasingly likely to attribute its loss to the political beliefs of the judge. Thus, jurists such as Judge Stacy get criticized for "legislating from the bench"—that is, substituting their judgment for that of a democratically elected state legislature. Because this criticism can come from either end of the political spectrum, it is not always clear what—if anything—it means beyond the critics' not being happy with the outcome of a case. Judges face similar criticisms when they impose mandates so specific that they do indeed look a lot like legislation; examples include the Massachusetts Supreme Judicial Court's legalizing gay marriage and the New Jersey Supreme Court's imposing elaborate school financing formulas and requiring the creation of preschools in certain school districts.

Activist judge

A judge who is said to act as an independent policymaker by creatively interpreting a constitution or statute

Those sorts of decisions increasingly invite a political backlash. For example, following Massachusetts's lead, in 2009 the Iowa Supreme Court also legalized same-sex marriage in Iowa and did so in a unanimous decision. The next year, three of the seven justices who made that decision were up for a retention election. Historically, such elections are quiet up-or-down votes on a judge's qualifications. Not this time. Well-financed national organizations, including the National Organization for Marriage and the American Family Association, spent record sums opposing them, urging voters to unseat the justices with television ads accusing them of, among other things, "becom[ing] political and ignoring the will of the voters." The justices, as had been traditional in these kinds of races in the past, did not actively raise campaign money and made few public appearances in the period leading up to the election. They were all voted out. Another of Iowa's state justices, David Wiggins, faced the voters in 2012. Even though it was a nonpartisan election, the chair of the Republican Party in Iowa, A. J. Spiker, called on voters to remove Wiggins as punishment for his part in the decision legalizing same-sex marriage. *The New York Times* quoted Justice Wiggins's response to the campaign against him: "Our system is built on checks and balances between independent branches of government. Two of those branches are designed to be political. It is unfortunate that Mr. Spiker apparently thinks that all three branches should be political."[4] This time the results were different; 55 percent of Iowans voted to retain Wiggins on the supreme court despite his steadfast refusal to campaign for his job.

Federal judges—regardless of what they decide—are likely to be the next set of jurists accused of substituting politics for sound legal judgment on the question of gay marriage. In *United States v. Windsor* (2013), the U.S. Supreme Court overturned the federal Defense of Marriage Act, which excluded legally married same-sex couples from the definition of marriage for the purposes of more than 1,000 federal laws and programs, including Social Security survivor benefits, tax filings, immigration rights, and family leave. This decision did not directly address whether state laws and constitutions banning gay marriage conflicted with the federal constitution, though this possibility was clearly implied. Immediately, federal courts across the country exploded with constitutional challenges to same-sex marriage bans. Federal courts in states such as Idaho, Oklahoma, Texas, and Utah were soon ruling state bans unconstitutional, and getting predictably blasted for doing so. These decisions are being appealed—the issue will almost certainly have to be decided by the Supreme Court—but in the meantime, there may be plenty of federal judges feeling the same sort of political rhetorical heat that was recently burning their colleagues on the Iowa bench.

As the Iowa example shows, though, state judges have to deal with more than angry rhetoric. Unlike federal judges, many state jurists are elected, and those elections are starting to turn nasty. The U.S. Supreme Court's decision in *Citizens United v. Federal Election Commission* (2010), which invalidated laws placing limits on independent corporate and union campaign spending, did not specifically involve judicial elections, but concerns voiced by Justice John P. Stevens in his dissent have proved prophetic:

> The consequences of today's holding will not be limited to the legislative or executive context. The majority of the States select their judges through popular elections. At a time when concerns about the conduct of judicial elections have reached a fever pitch . . . the Court today unleashes the floodgates of corporate and union general treasury spending in these races.[5]

Dramatic increases in campaign spending have occurred in the 39 states that elect state court judges, more than doubling the amount spent in the previous decade. *Citizens United* heightened concerns about judicial spending by making it easier for unaffiliated groups to spend unlimited sums to elect judges. In 2012, the first judicial super PAC was created to support an incumbent state supreme court justice in a hotly contested race in North Carolina. This money frequently translates into mudslinging attack ads; the same pressure tactics used to influence those who make laws are now being directed at those who interpret laws. After all, from an interest group's standpoint, what is the point of getting laws passed if a judge will just declare them unconstitutional?

Judges are increasingly objecting to being used as political punching bags and are arguing for a renewed respect for the importance of an independent judicial branch. They emphasize that a judge's job is to provide a check on the other two branches of government and to protect minority rights, not to uphold the political sentiments of the day. Judges' actions in both of these vital roles will at times anger a majority of people, and judges cannot fulfill these roles if they are in fear for either their jobs or their lives, whether figuratively or literally. Again, former U.S. Supreme Court justice Sandra Day O'Connor, who has spoken out about the importance of judicial independence, has framed the significance of the issue: "It takes a lot of degeneration before a country falls into dictatorship, but we should avoid these ends by avoiding these beginnings."[6] Those angriest with judges' decisions tend to frame the issues in terms of accountability and democratic values rather than independence. They are outraged when judges interfere with what they regard as the political arena.

Ironically, at the same time that money is flooding into state court judicial elections, the state courts themselves are being starved of funds. Economic conditions across the country have led to plunging local tax revenues, and nearly all states have cut judicial branch funding. In many localities, budget cuts to local court systems have been so steep that they have placed, in the words of Georgia chief justice Carol Hunstein, "some court systems on the edge of an abyss."[7] While the judiciary is a separate and coequal branch of government, the courts depend on the political branches for funding. Dramatic budget cuts have led to closed courts, furloughed court workers, and a growing backlog of cases and delays, particularly for civil cases, which often are put on a back burner so the courts can deal with urgent criminal matters. The same economic conditions that have led to these budget shortfalls have led to an increase in recession-related lawsuits, including foreclosures. And many courts are short-staffed. Judge Glenn E. Grant, acting administrative director of the judiciary in New Jersey, warned in 2014 that the backlog of unresolved cases had increased between 2009 and 2013, even though new case filings had decreased by 9 percent during that period.[8]

Despite these multiple challenges, the work of the state courts continues. There is no single "right way" in which judges, justices, and courts operate. Each of the 50 states, the District of Columbia, and Puerto Rico has its own unique court system. Sometimes it seems as if every county in every state has its own way of doing things. From judicial selection to sentencing reform, states have organized their justice systems to meet the needs of the states' own unique political pressures and social dynamics.

> Sometimes it seems as if every county in every state has its own way of doing things. From judicial selection to sentencing reform, states have organized their justice systems to meet the needs of the states' own unique political pressures and social dynamics.

All this is of the utmost importance because it may affect public confidence in the state courts, institutions with a tremendous amount of power. This chapter provides an introduction to state court systems. First, we examine the types of courts and the different ways these courts are structured. Then the focus turns to the different ways state court judges are chosen and retained, and the controversies that these processes create. Many issues surround the various players in state justice systems, from prosecutors and defenders to victims and jurors; we explore these before turning to a discussion of some possible areas of reform.

The Role and Structure of State Courts

When people complained on old TV shows about how they felt abused or ripped off by their friends,

At the apex of most state court systems is a supreme court. State supreme court justices, such as the Supreme Court of California justices pictured here, typically have the final say on appeals from lower courts.

Supreme Court of California

those friends would often say, "Don't make a federal case out of it." In the real world of crime and legal conflict in the United States, there are actually relatively few federal cases, because such cases must involve violations of federal law, federal constitutional rights, or lawsuits that cross state borders. With the exception of celebrity trials such as the Casey Anthony murder case, state courts operate largely below the public's radar.

Yet they are enormously important institutions. The federal U.S. district courts hear several hundred thousand cases a year. By comparison, just over 100 million cases are filed in the lowest state courts every year. These courts have the awesome responsibility of resolving the vast majority of the nation's disputes. If you crash your car or your landlord evicts you, if you get divorced and fight for child custody, if your neighbor's tree lands in your yard, or if your employer won't pay you, any legal remedy you seek will be decided in a state court. State courts are also where virtually all criminal cases are tried, from drunk driving to murder, from misdemeanors to capital offenses. If you contest a traffic ticket, you will find yourself in a state court.

There are two basic kinds of court cases: criminal and civil. **Criminal cases** involve violations of the law, with the government prosecuting the alleged perpetrators, or criminals. Those found guilty usually go to jail. By contrast, **civil cases** involve disputes between two private parties, such as a dry cleaner and a customer with badly stained pants. In civil cases, individuals sue each other, usually for financial judgments. Both types of cases start out in **trial court**. If the parties in a case

cannot reach agreement through a **settlement** or a **plea bargain**, they go to trial.

Every trial has a winner and a loser. The losing side, if unhappy with the trial's outcome, can file an **appeal**. Most states have two levels of courts that hear appeals from trial court judgments. The appeal first goes to an **intermediate appellate court**, which reviews the original trial's record to see if any errors were made. After the appellate court has ruled, a party who still is not satisfied can attempt to appeal to the highest state court of appeals, usually called the **state supreme court**. In most states, this court does not automatically have to take an appeal; rather, it can pick and choose among cases. Typically, a state supreme court will choose to hear only those cases whose resolutions will require novel interpretation of the state constitution or clarification of the law. Such resolutions could set **precedent** that will have

Criminal cases
Legal cases brought by the state intending to punish violations of the law

Civil cases
Legal cases that involve disputes between private parties

Trial court
The first level of the court system

Settlement
A mutual agreement between parties to end a civil case before going to trial

Plea bargain
An agreement in which the accused in a criminal case admits guilt, usually in exchange for a promise that a particular sentence will be imposed

Appeal
A request to have a lower court's decision in a case reviewed by a higher court

Intermediate appellate court
A court that reviews court cases to find possible errors in their proceedings

State supreme court
The highest level of appeals court in a state

Precedent
In law, the use of the past to determine current interpretation and decision making

consequences well beyond the specifics of the case being appealed.

The state supreme court is the highest legal body in the state court system. This gives it the ultimate power to interpret the state constitution, and its decisions are almost always final. Only the U.S. Supreme Court outranks the highest state courts. Even the nine justices in Washington, D.C., however, cannot review—that is, come up with a new decision for—a state supreme court judgment unless that judgment conflicts with the U.S. Constitution or federal law.

When such federal issues are involved, there is no question that state courts must follow the rulings of the federal courts. The chief justice of the Alabama Supreme Court, Roy S. Moore, learned this lesson in 2003 after he oversaw the installation of a 2.5-ton monument to the Ten Commandments in the rotunda of the state supreme court building. Federal judges ruled that such a display violated the First Amendment's separation of church and state, and they ordered Moore to have the monument removed. He refused and ultimately was expelled from office by a state ethics panel for having tried to place himself above the law. In 2006, Justice Tom Parker, a former colleague of Moore's on the court, expressed anger at other Alabama Supreme Court justices for following the U.S. Supreme Court precedent that prohibits the use of the death penalty for crimes committed by minors. Justice Parker unsuccessfully urged his colleagues not to follow Supreme Court opinions "simply because they are precedents."[9]

Trial Courts

More than 103 million cases were filed in state courts in 2010, about one case for every three citizens. These numbers have stayed relatively constant over the past 10 years. More than half the cases involved traffic offenses. The number of civil and criminal cases was roughly equal—19 million and 20.4 million cases, respectively—and there were 8 million domestic and juvenile cases.[10] The vast majority of these millions of cases were resolved through plea bargains or settlements. Only a small minority ever went to trial.

When parties do go to trial, they appear before a state court judge in what is often referred to as a **court of first instance**. In this court, nothing has been determined and nothing is a "given." The trial is a blank canvas on which the parties can introduce documentary and physical evidence, such as fingerprints or DNA. Witnesses can testify as to what they saw or heard, and experts can try to help explain complex evidence.

The judge presides over the introduction of evidence; rules on objections, which occur when either of the parties thinks that the other party has said or done something improper, and issues of admissibility, that is, whether or not it is all right for specific evidence or facts to be included in the trial; and instructs the jury as to the relevant laws. The judge further instructs the jury members that they must apply the laws as stated to the facts as they find them. It is the jury, however, that must decide what the facts are. (In a **bench trial**, there is no jury and fact-finding is done by the judge.) The jury (or the judge in a bench trial) must decide who and what to believe and what happened. Unless the jury's final decision is based on a legal mistake, such as improper evidence, hearsay testimony (testimony based on rumor), or a misleading statement of the relevant law, the result typically will be upheld on appeal. The business of the trial court is to examine the facts to resolve the dispute. Subsequent appellate courts review the trial court's application of the law to those facts.

A key distinction among state courts is between **general jurisdiction trial courts** and **limited or special jurisdiction trial courts**. A general jurisdiction trial court hears any case not sent to a special court, whether it is civil or criminal. The kinds of cases that can be tried in special jurisdiction courts are statutorily limited. Some are limited to cases of less

---

Court of first instance
The court in which a case is introduced and nothing has been determined yet

Bench trial
A trial in which no jury is present and the judge decides the facts as well as the law

General jurisdiction trial courts
Courts that hear any civil or criminal cases that have not been assigned to a special court

Limited or special jurisdiction trial courts
Courts that hear cases that are statutorily limited by either the degree of seriousness or the types of parties involved

A Difference That Makes a Difference

The New Judicial Federalism

A century ago, state supreme courts were described as being so quiet that "you could hear the justices' arteries clog."[a] No one says this today, and the new judicial federalism is one big reason that is so.

This no longer so "new" doctrine describes a newfound reliance on state constitutions to protect those rights not covered by the U.S. Constitution. Under the principles of federalism, each state has its own justice system—distinct from those of its neighbors and from the federal system—and its own constitution. The U.S. Constitution is the supreme law of the land, and no state court can interpret its own state's constitution in a way that limits rights secured by the federal charter. States are free, however, to interpret their own constitutions any way they like, except for that single proviso.

For most of the country's history, state constitutions were overlooked. Rarely did the courts rely on them to overturn state laws, especially on the basis of civil rights. But starting in the early 1970s, state supreme courts increasingly began to use state constitutions as independent sources of rights. By 1986, U.S. Supreme Court justice William J. Brennan characterized the "rediscovery by state supreme courts of the broader protections afforded their own citizens by their state constitutions [as] . . . probably the most important development in constitutional jurisprudence in our time."[b]

In many legal areas, the actual impact of judicial federalism on civil liberties has not been all that sweeping. It is still true that most state court judges continue to interpret state constitutions in lockstep with interpretations of the U.S. Constitution. One scholar found, however, that in about one out of every three constitutional decisions, state courts extended rights beyond federal levels.[c] In some areas, such as the interpretation of the right to exercise religion freely and in search-and-seizure rulings, state courts, relying on their own constitutions, have continued to grant rights after the U.S. Supreme Court's interpretation of the Constitution took a more conservative and restrictive turn.

In other cases, state courts rely on unique constitutional provisions. For instance, state constitutions, unlike the federal document, often commit state governments to the achievement of particular policy ends. The New Jersey constitution requires a "thorough and efficient system of free public schools," the Illinois constitution requires the state to "provide and maintain a healthful environment for the benefit of this and future generations," and the New Mexico constitution requires the state to provide bilingual education. Relying on explicit provisions such as these, state supreme courts have ordered legislatures to restructure the way they finance public education when inequalities are so extreme that they rise to the level of a state constitutional violation. In a novel case, a California state trial court judge held in 2014 that the practice of granting lifetime tenure to public school teachers violated students' state constitutional right of equal access to a public education.

Today, the new judicial federalism is well established, with more and more cases raising state constitutional issues and sparking a renewed interest in these once-overlooked documents. State supreme court justices are more likely now to take a fresh look at their own constitutions than to slavishly follow the interpretations of the U.S. Supreme Court. Activists also have focused more attention on state constitutions, mounting campaigns to amend them to either extend or curtail rights.

[a]G. Alan Tarr, "The New Judicial Federalism in Perspective," *Notre Dame Law Review* 72 (1997): 1097.

[b]William J. Brennan, "State Constitutional Law," *National Law Journal* 9 (September 29, 1986): S-1.

[c]James N. G. Cauthen, "Expanding Rights Under State Constitutions: A Quantitative Appraisal," *Albany Law Review* 63 (2000): 1183, 1202.

seriousness, such as misdemeanors or civil cases that involve small amounts of money. Others are limited in regard to the types of parties involved, such as juvenile offenders or drug abusers.

Not all states make this distinction between types of trial courts. Illinois and California have no limited jurisdiction courts. In contrast, New York, the state with the largest number of judges,

FIGURE 9-1

HOW IT WORKS

State Court Structure in Illinois and New York

At a glance, it's easy to see why New York State's court system has been called Byzantine—just compare it with Illinois's (left). Although it encompasses 23 circuits with more than 850 justices, Illinois's single trial court system (its general jurisdiction courts) looks like a model of clarity and simplicity compared with New York's 10 different trial courts (the courts of general and limited jurisdiction). But the differences run deeper than what a simple organizational chart can reveal. New York's 300-year-old town and village justice court system, in particular, has been subject to loud and persistent criticism for cronyism, corruption, fiscal mismanagement, and plain old inefficiency. According to *New York Times* reporter William Glaberson, "the [town and village justice] courts have survived in part because the justices—most of them not even lawyers—have longstanding and deep ties to the upstate political system, and because of the substantial cost of replacing them with more professional courts."[a] With 2,300 justices involved at that level, this would indeed be a tall order.

What can be done? In 2006, New York's former chief judge Judith S. Kaye, the state's top advocate for court reform, recommended changes "across four broad areas: court operations and administration; auditing and financial control; education and training; and facility security and public protection."[b] A few of these proposed changes could be implemented right away, including requiring word-for-word records of court proceedings—a bona fide court transcript—to ensure fairness and the purchasing of recording equipment to make that possible. Other changes would require more sweeping institutional modifications. Judge Kaye called for state funds to help support the town and village justice courts, which are currently funded and operated locally. This change would require legislative approval. Her most aggressive recommendation—to simplify the trial court structure itself into a more common two-tiered organization—would require an amendment to the state's constitution. Legislators received the proposals coolly. A commission on state court reform backed some of Kaye's ideas in 2008 with its suggestion that the state eliminate as many as 500 of the justice courts, but New York had not instituted the changes by early 2010.[c]

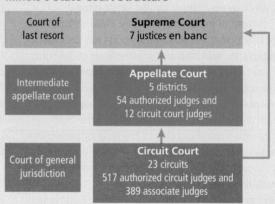

Illinois's State Court Structure

Court of last resort	**Supreme Court** 7 justices en banc
Intermediate appellate court	**Appellate Court** 5 districts 54 authorized judges and 12 circuit court judges
Court of general jurisdiction	**Circuit Court** 23 circuits 517 authorized circuit judges and 389 associate judges

is also the state that relies most heavily on limited jurisdiction courts. More than 3,000 of the state's 3,645 judges sit on limited jurisdiction courts.[11] (See Figure 9-1.) The majority of these limited jurisdiction courts are "town and village courts" or "justice courts." In states that do not rely on limited jurisdiction courts, appeals go directly to appellate courts. In states that make the distinction, some issues can be appealed from limited jurisdiction courts to general jurisdiction courts.

Appeals Courts: Intermediate Appeals and Courts of Last Resort

When one of the parties in a trial is dissatisfied with the outcome, that party can challenge the result by filing an appeal. As a general rule, an appeal cannot be based on mere dissatisfaction with the trial's result. An appellant does not get a free second chance to try his or her whole

New York State's Court Structure

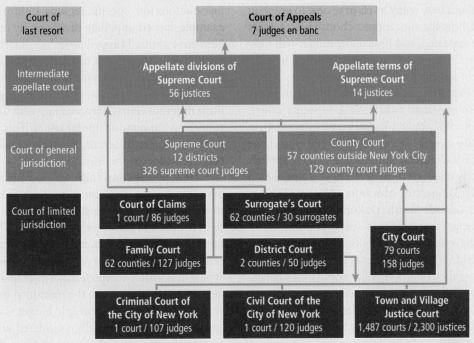

Court of last resort	**Court of Appeals** — 7 judges en banc
Intermediate appellate court	**Appellate divisions of Supreme Court** — 56 justices / **Appellate terms of Supreme Court** — 14 justices
Court of general jurisdiction	**Supreme Court** — 12 districts / 326 supreme court judges / **County Court** — 57 counties outside New York City / 129 county court judges
Court of limited jurisdiction	**Court of Claims** — 1 court / 86 judges / **Surrogate's Court** — 62 counties / 30 surrogates / **City Court** — 79 courts / 158 judges / **Family Court** — 62 counties / 127 judges / **District Court** — 2 counties / 50 judges / **Criminal Court of the City of New York** — 1 court / 107 judges / **Civil Court of the City of New York** — 1 court / 120 judges / **Town and Village Justice Court** — 1,487 courts / 2,300 justices

[a]William Glaberson, "Justice in Small Towns to Be Upgraded," *New York Times,* November 22, 2006, A1.

[b]Judith S. Kaye and Jonathan Lippman, *Action Plan for the Justice Courts* (Albany: State of New York Unified Court System, November 2006), https://www.nycourts.gov/publications/pdfs/ActionPlan-JusticeCourts.pdf.

[c]Joel Stashenko, "Study Supports Elimination of Hundreds of Justice Courts," *New York Law Journal* 240, no. 56 (2008): 2.

case. Appellate courts do not decide issues of guilt or innocence or ensure that trials were conducted perfectly. Instead, an appeal must be based on a claim that there were legal errors in the original trial. Further, it is not enough to show that an error occurred; the error had to have been **prejudicial**—that is, it had to have affected the outcome of the case. The appellant has to argue that there was a good chance the result would have been different if the error had not been made. This often is a very challenging argument to make.

To cite just one example, in 2006 the defense attorney representing the convicted murderer of an Indiana University freshman asked that the sentence be thrown out, arguing that the jurors may have been drinking during legal proceedings, given that some of the male jurors in the trial had

---

Prejudicial error
An error that affects the outcome of a case

painted their toenails and raced down a hotel hallway in a bailiff's backless high heels. "Two men with heels on, painting their toenails, it is not a normal activity unless they are intoxicated," the attorney said. The judge ruled against him, saying there was no indication of drunkenness in court or during the actual deliberations.[12]

There is no one way in which all the state appellate courts decide how to hear appeals from the trial courts. States have made different decisions about how many levels of review to grant an appeal, how the courts must choose which cases can be appealed, and how many judges will hear an appeal. These decisions combine to form the different appellate court structures.

For example, not all states have both an intermediate appellate court and a supreme court. Back in 1957, only 13 states had intermediate appellate courts. Today, only 11 states and the District of Columbia still resolve all their appeals with only one level of review. These states, which include Delaware, Montana, North Dakota, Rhode Island, South Dakota, Vermont, and Wyoming, have relatively small populations— seven have fewer than 1 million residents—and thus tend to have fewer cases to resolve than do more populous states. Smaller populations generally give rise to more manageable court caseloads. Nevada has the largest population of this group. Its Supreme Court says it is the busiest in the country, with a caseload double that of its neighboring states, leading to lengthy delays and backlogs. Establishing an appellate court, however, requires the voters to approve a constitutional amendment, and it has failed on the ballot three times. Unwilling to give up, its backers tried again—and succeeded—in 2014. Barbara Buckley, director at the Legal Aid Center of Southern Nevada, understood that voters could easily write off the vote as just another unnecessary layer of bureaucracy, but, when it comes down to it, she says, "it really doesn't matter what side you're on, whether you're on one side of the lawsuit or the other. Everybody wants it decided, right?"[13]

The majority of states recognize that the sheer volume of appeals makes it impossible for one appellate court to hear and resolve every appeal. To deal with burgeoning caseloads, almost all states have created another tier of review. In these states, appeals go first to an intermediate appellate court. Only after they have been reviewed at this level can they move on to the court of last resort, usually the state supreme court. The intermediate court makes it possible for the state judicial system to hear many more appeals and creates the possibility of a second level of appeal.

Intermediate appellate courts range in size from 3 judges (in Alaska) to 102 judges (in California). States with many judges at the intermediate appellate level usually divide the judges' jurisdictions into specific regions. California, for example, has six appellate divisions. By contrast, New Jersey, with 34 appellate judges, has the largest appellate court that is not divided into judicial regions.[14] Regional divisions help the courts operate smoothly, but they also create a danger. All these different courts may come up with different rulings on the same or similar issues. This has the potential to set different, possibly conflicting, precedents for future litigation.

State appellate courts also vary in whether they have **discretionary jurisdiction** or **mandatory jurisdiction**. In other words, in some states the courts have a right to pick and choose which cases they hear. In other states, judges must consider every case, the principle being that everyone has the right to an appeal. It is widely accepted that a loser in a single-judge court ought to have the right to at least one appeal to a court with multiple judges. This one appeal, however, is generally considered sufficient to correct any prejudicial errors made in the trial courts. Even in states in which the court of last resort has discretionary jurisdiction, appeals may be mandatory in capital punishment cases.

Two tiers of appellate courts allow petitioners the right to one appeal to the intermediate appellate court, followed by the possibility of a further appeal to the court of last resort. Such a structure allows the supreme court or other court of last resort to choose whether to hear cases that might have relevance beyond the parties in the cases, allowing the court to make the law clear to others.

One more variable in the state court system structure involves the number of judges at each level who hear a particular appeal. At the level of

---

Discretionary jurisdiction
The power of a court to decide whether or not to grant review of a case

Mandatory jurisdiction
The requirement that a court hear every case presented before it

Policy in Practice

State Appellate Court Organization: A Matter of Life or Death?

A national shortage of the drugs used by states to execute prisoners sentenced to die by lethal injection led to what was described by Bert Brandenburg, executive director of Justice at Stake, as a three-branch "governmental train wreck" in Oklahoma in 2014.[a] Oklahoma came up with its own experimental lethal drug cocktail but insisted that the composition and source be kept secret. This frightened Clayton Lockett, a death row inmate with an imminent execution. He challenged the state's secrecy.

The problem was that Oklahoma has two high courts, one for criminal matters and one for civil matters, and his issue appeared to fall right through the cracks. The Oklahoma Supreme Court wanted to handle the civil issue about the state's secrecy laws but thought that only the Oklahoma Court of Criminal Appeals could stay Lockett's execution. Seeing things differently, the Oklahoma Court of Criminal Appeals found that it had no jurisdiction to issue a stay when the concern didn't have anything to do with the petitioner's underlying conviction.

The two courts fought over this hot potato and, finally, the Oklahoma Supreme Court granted a stay of execution, angering both the justices on the court of criminal appeals and the governor, Mary Fallin, who said that the supreme court was acting outside its constitutional authority and she would ignore its stay of execution. Instead, she said that she would be guided only by the court of criminal appeals. Piling on, the legislature introduced articles of impeachment for the five justices who stayed the execution. In the midst of this intense political pressure, the state supreme court appeared to cave and, in a brief legal decision, dissolved its own stay 2 days after granting it.

The state moved quickly to execute Lockett, but the new lethal drugs led to a botched execution that drew intense national attention. Thirteen minutes after receiving the injection, Lockett appeared to regain consciousness and experience great pain. State officials called off the execution, but he died 27 minutes later of a heart attack.

Sources: Adapted from Ziva Bransetter, "Gov. Mary Fallin Issues 7-day Stay for Inmate's Execution," Tulsa World, April 23, 2014, http://www.tulsaworld.com/news/government/gov-mary-fallin-issues—day-stay-for-inmate-s/article_3743eedd-b94e-5971-be11-6bf773ea9eb6.html; Andrew Cohen, "Oklahoma Just Neutered Its State Supreme Court," The Week, April 29, 2014, http://www.theweek.com/article/index/260632/oklahoma-just-neutered-its-state-supreme-court; Andrew Spiropoulos, "Strategies Leading Up to the Botched Execution of an Oklahoma Death Row Inmate," Jurist, June 9, 2014, http://jurist.org/forum/2014/06/andrew-spiropoulous-oklahoma-death.php.

[a]Peter Hardin, "'Disgraceful Outcome' in Oklahoma Botched Execution, JAS Says," Gavel Grab blog, Justice at Stake, Washington, DC, April 30, 2014, http://www.gavelgrab.org/?p=71248.

either the appellate court or the court of last resort, judges may hear an appeal **en banc**, or all together, or they may sit in smaller **panels**, typically of three judges. Sitting in panels may be more convenient, because appellate courts sit simultaneously in different locations. This allows more appeals to be heard and makes the courts more convenient to the parties. However, as with regional divisions, this may also lead to problems of unifying doctrine when various courts at the same level reach different decisions.

States that use panels have a variety of techniques to limit the divergence of opinions among panels. These techniques include conferencing drafts of opinions en banc. This means that each panel's draft opinions are circulated among all the judges, even those not on that panel. Two states, Texas and Oklahoma, have created systems in which there are two supreme courts with different subject-matter jurisdictions rather than one

En banc
Appeals court sessions in which all the judges hear a case together

Panels
Groups of (usually) three judges who sit to hear cases in a state court of appeals

supreme court sitting in panels. In these states, one supreme court has largely civil jurisdiction and one supreme court hears only criminal appeals; each of these courts sits en banc. In Texas, the intermediate appellate court has both civil and criminal jurisdiction. In Oklahoma, the intermediate appellate court has only civil jurisdiction—all criminal appeals go directly to the court of last resort for criminal cases. A few states have created systems that have intermediate appellate courts with differing subject-matter jurisdictions and then a single court of last resort.

States have mixed and matched all these variables to come up with different ways to organize the appellate court review process. The most common pattern, adhered to by half the states, involves an intermediate appellate court, sitting in panels, which must consider all appeals. The decisions of these panels are then subject to review by a court of last resort, such as a supreme court, sitting en banc. Usually, this highest court hears just the cases it sees fit to hear. In states without an intermediate court of appeals, often the courts of last resort must hear all the cases that are sent to them. One such state, West Virginia, eliminated discretionary review for its supreme court in a historic change in 2010. In the next year, the number of appeals heard by the state's highest court more than tripled. In the District of Columbia, all appeals are heard by a court of appeals with nine justices, who often sit in panels of three and have mandatory jurisdiction over most cases.

In other words, no matter what state you are in, if you lose your case in court, you will have at least one chance—and sometimes more than one chance—to have your appeal heard. There is tremendous variation among states in courts and panels and rules; luckily, you need to know only the rules of the state where you file your case.

Selecting Judges

How judges are selected is a significant political decision. Historically, such decisions have generated tremendous controversy, and the controversy continues today. Why is there no clear consensus on this important issue? Controversy is perhaps inevitable. The judiciary is one of the pillars of the U.S. political system, but at the same time, we want to believe that judges are above politics. We like to think that they are independent and will rule only as justice requires, based on the specific facts presented and the applicable law. But, of course, judges are only human. That's why we want them held accountable for their decisions. These competing values—independence and accountability—tug judicial selection procedures in different directions. If independence is seen as more important than accountability, it makes sense to appoint judges for lifetime tenures. This is done in the federal system. If accountability is seen as more important than independence, it makes sense to elect judges. Elections are a key element of judicial selection at the state level. Yet they are not the only component; states have formulated a variety of selection systems in an effort to balance the competing values of independence and accountability. These specifics matter. How a state structures its courts and chooses its judiciary may affect the types of decisions made by individual judges and the confidence citizens have in their courts to provide fair trials.

Almost no two states select judges in the exact same way, although the states can be roughly divided into two camps of almost equal size. The first group includes states that choose judges through popular elections, either partisan or nonpartisan. In partisan elections, judicial candidates first run in party primaries, and then the winning candidates are listed on the general election ballot along with designations of their political parties. The names of candidates in nonpartisan elections appear on the ballot without any party labels. The second group consists of states that have appointed, rather than elected, judges. Under the appointment model, the governor or the legislature may appoint judges. In some states, only persons selected by a nominating committee are eligible for judicial appointments.

To make matters even more confusing, many states use different methods to choose judges at different levels of their judiciaries. A state might, for example, choose trial judges by popular election but

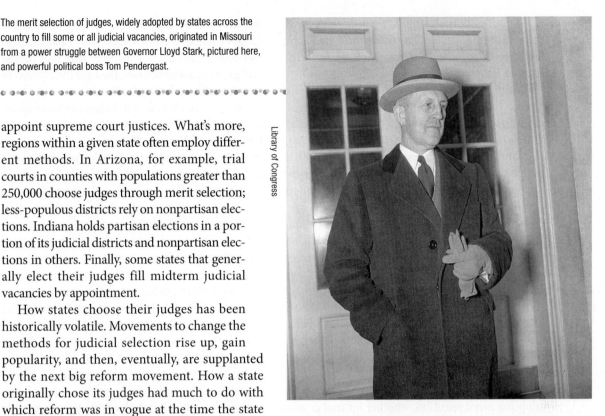

The merit selection of judges, widely adopted by states across the country to fill some or all judicial vacancies, originated in Missouri from a power struggle between Governor Lloyd Stark, pictured here, and powerful political boss Tom Pendergast.

Library of Congress

appoint supreme court justices. What's more, regions within a given state often employ different methods. In Arizona, for example, trial courts in counties with populations greater than 250,000 choose judges through merit selection; less-populous districts rely on nonpartisan elections. Indiana holds partisan elections in a portion of its judicial districts and nonpartisan elections in others. Finally, some states that generally elect their judges fill midterm judicial vacancies by appointment.

How states choose their judges has been historically volatile. Movements to change the methods for judicial selection rise up, gain popularity, and then, eventually, are supplanted by the next big reform movement. How a state originally chose its judges had much to do with which reform was in vogue at the time the state entered the Union and ratified its constitution. No single judicial reform has ever succeeded in completely replacing earlier methods, however, and so there is tremendous variation among the states in the way they select judges.

Under the U.S. Constitution, the president, with the advice and consent of the Senate, appoints all federal judges. Similarly, the original 13 states chose to appoint judges, giving the appointment power to one or both houses of the legislature or, less commonly, to the governor, either alone or with the consent of the legislature.[15]

Then, in the mid-1800s, during the presidency of Andrew Jackson—a period marked by distrust of government and a movement toward increased popular sovereignty—the appointive system came under attack. Every state that entered the Union between 1846 and 1912 provided for some form of judicial elections.[16] At the dawn of the 20th century, concern that judges were being selected and controlled by political machines led to a movement for nonpartisan elections. By 1927, 12 states employed this practice.[17]

During the second half of the 20th century, judicial reformers focused on persuading states to adopt a new method of choosing judges, referred to as **merit selection**. The variations of merit selection systems are discussed in detail in the following section on appointment. Basically, a merit system is a hybrid of appointment and election. It typically involves a bipartisan judicial nominating commission whose job is to create a list of highly qualified candidates for the bench. The governor appoints judges from this list, who must then face a **retention election**. The retention election for a newly appointed judge, which is usually set to coincide with the next general election, provides voters with a simple choice: to keep or not to keep the judge on the bench. If the vote

Merit selection
A hybrid of appointment and election that typically involves a bipartisan judicial nominating commission whose job is to create a list of highly qualified candidates for the bench from which the governor or legislature appoints judges. After serving a term, these judges are typically evaluated for retention either by the same commission or through uncontested popular elections.

Retention election
An election in which a judge runs uncontested and voters are asked to vote yes or no on the question of whether they wish to retain the judge in office for another term

is for retention, the judge stays on the bench. If the vote is against retention (this is rare), the commission goes back to work to come up with another list of candidates for the post.

Under some merit systems, all judges (not just newly appointed ones) must face periodic retention elections, although the length of term and other specifics vary from state to state. Missouri became the first state to adopt such a judicial selection method in 1940, which is why judicial merit selection is sometimes referred to as "the Missouri Plan." The movement enjoyed considerable success from the 1960s to the 1980s. The number of states that embraced merit selection for choosing supreme court justices grew from 3 in 1960 (Alaska, Kansas, and Missouri) to 18 by 1980.[18]

Recently, however, this approach appears to have lost momentum. About half the states still rely on merit selection to choose some or all of their judges, and no merit selection state has returned to selection through elections. However, since 1990, most states that have considered adopting merit selection, whether for trial courts or appellate-level courts, have rejected it. In Nevada, for example, the legislature sponsored a bipartisan ballot question in the 2010 election asking whether the Nevada constitution should be amended to adopt the Missouri Plan. It was rejected by 58 percent of the voters.[19] In recent years, several states have debated doing away with merit selection altogether—including Missouri, where it began. In 2012 proposals to overhaul existing merit selection systems went before voters in Arizona, Florida, and Mississippi; they all lost.[20] In the sections that follow, we discuss at length each method for selecting judges and the issues it raises. (Map 9-1 shows the system of selection for each state.)

Popular Elections

Why do some states elect judges? Elections allow greater popular control over the judiciary and more public accountability for judges. Proponents argue that such elections are compatible with this country's democratic traditions and that voters can be trusted to make choices for judges that are as good as those that legislators or mayors would

make. To these supporters, the appointment of judges smacks of elitism and raises worries about old-boy networks; that is, they fear that judges will get appointed because they are the cronies or political allies of elected officials.

Some argue that electing judges can increase the representation of women and minorities on the bench, but studies have found negligible differences in judicial diversity between selection methods.[21] Regardless of system, state judiciaries have grown slightly more diverse over time, but the percentages of minority and women judges continue to trail their numbers in the population at large. Nationwide, as of 2010, 43 (12 percent) state supreme court justices were members of minority groups and 111 (33 percent) were women.[22]

Those on the other side of the argument are critical of judicial elections in general, whether partisan or nonpartisan, asserting that such elections often become referendums on political issues rather than serving as forums that allow the public to evaluate the temperaments, backgrounds, and experience of the candidates. Opponents of judicial elections focus on what they see as the threat to the independence of the judiciary posed by the introduction of politics into the selection process and the danger that the need to solicit campaign contributions could make judges vulnerable to improper influence by donors. Further, opponents note that the tone of judicial elections has deteriorated substantially and in a manner that could damage the image of the judiciary. Given this, qualified candidates for office could choose not to run.

This is a debate about more than academic ideas, however. How a state chooses its judges has very real political impacts, with consequences for judicial impartiality, campaign fundraising, the role of interest groups, and the character of judicial campaigning. Some point to these problems as reasons to move away from selecting judges through judicial elections and toward a merit selection system. Others argue that there is no need to abandon elections altogether; rather, any problems can be addressed through targeted changes. Die-hard supporters of judicial election see the increased politicization of the process as a positive thing; they assert that greater competitiveness translates into more meaningful choices for voters.

MAP 9-1

Initial Judicial Selection, by Type of Court

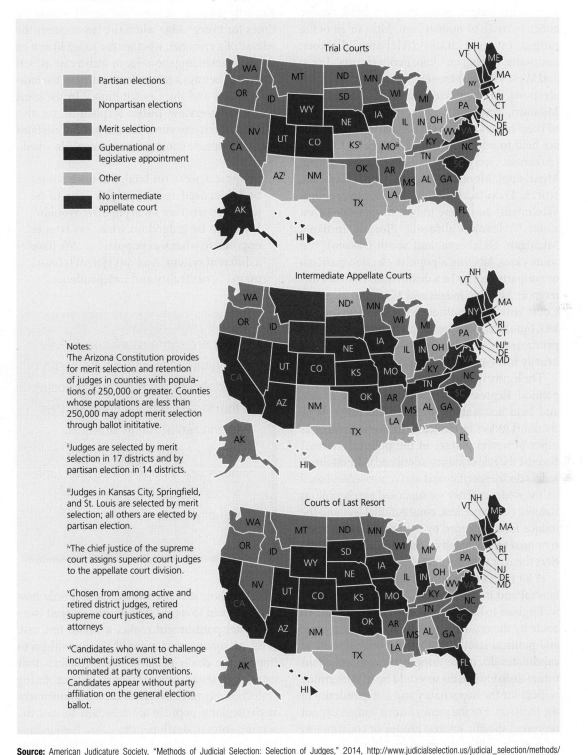

Legend:
- Partisan elections
- Nonpartisan elections
- Merit selection
- Gubernational or legislative appointment
- Other
- No intermediate appellate court

Trial Courts

Intermediate Appellate Courts

Courts of Last Resort

Notes:
[i]The Arizona Constitution provides for merit selection and retention of judges in counties with populations of 250,000 or greater. Counties whose populations are less than 250,000 may adopt merit selection through ballot inititative.

[ii]Judges are selected by merit selection in 17 districts and by partisan election in 14 districts.

[iii]Judges in Kansas City, Springfield, and St. Louis are selected by merit selection; all others are elected by partisan election.

[iv]The chief justice of the supreme court assigns superior court judges to the appellate court division.

[v]Chosen from among active and retired district judges, retired supreme court justices, and attorneys

[vi]Candidates who want to challenge incumbent justices must be nominated at party conventions. Candidates appear without party affiliation on the general election ballot.

Source: American Judicature Society, "Methods of Judicial Selection: Selection of Judges," 2014, http://www.judicialselection.us/judicial_selection/methods/selection_of_judges.cfm?state=.

Before we jump into a discussion of the consequences of judicial elections, we should note that it is important to remember that elections for state court judges, when they are held, can be either partisan or nonpartisan. Most or all of the judges in eight states (Alabama, Illinois, Louisiana, Michigan, Ohio, Pennsylvania, Texas, and West Virginia) are selected through partisan elections. Another five states (Indiana, Kansas, Missouri, New York, and Tennessee) select some of their judges this way.[23] Nonpartisan elections are held to select most or all judges in 13 states (Arkansas, Georgia, Idaho, Kentucky, Minnesota, Mississippi, Montana, Nevada, North Carolina, North Dakota, Oregon, Washington, and Wisconsin) and some judges in another seven states (Arizona, California, Florida, Indiana, Michigan, Oklahoma, and South Dakota).[24] In some cases, labeling a popular election partisan or nonpartisan may be a distinction without a difference. All Ohio judges and Michigan Supreme Court justices run without party labels on the ballots, but the candidates are chosen through party primaries or conventions, and the parties are heavily involved in judicial campaigns.

The legislative and executive branches are clearly political. Representatives of the people are chosen and held accountable through elections. Why shouldn't judges be elected in the same manner as other powerful players in the political system? Because the role of judges is designed to be different. Judges decide specific cases and controversies based on the evidence. They are supposed to rely only on statutes, case precedent, constitutional law, and the unique facts presented by each case. They are not supposed to rule based on the wishes of those who elect them or with the next election in mind.

A lot rides on the public's belief that judges are neutral and impartial. That belief underpins the willingness to bring disputes to the courts and to abide by the results—the keys to both economic and political stability. Judges cannot, as political candidates do, make campaign promises about future decisions; to do so would be to undermine respect for the impartiality and independence of the judiciary. For the same reasons, judges cannot represent specific interest groups or constituents or even the will of the majority. There are times when all judges, when doing their jobs properly, are compelled by the law to make unpopular judgments or to protect the rights of those without political power.

In 1999, U.S. Supreme Court justice Anthony Kennedy pointed out in an interview that there are times for every judge when the law requires the release of a criminal, whether the judge likes it or not. Characterizing the judge in such a case as "soft on crime" betrays a misunderstanding of the judicial process and the Constitution.[25] In the same television interview, Justice Stephen Breyer also expressed concerns about the way judicial elections require judges to court public opinion. He asked,

> Suppose I were on trial. Suppose somebody accused me. Would I want to be judged by whether I was popular? Wouldn't I want to be judged on what was true as opposed to what was popular? . . . We have a different system. And our system is based upon . . . neutrality and independence.[26]

> Why are some courts more likely than others to impose the death penalty? Some research indicates that state supreme court justices facing reelection in states in which capital punishment is particularly popular are reluctant to cast dissenting votes in death penalty cases.

Is this how it really works? Or is it only how it is *supposed* to work? The highly charged issue of capital punishment makes a useful test case. Why are some courts more likely than others to impose the death penalty? Some research indicates that state supreme court justices facing reelection in states in which capital punishment is particularly popular are reluctant to cast dissenting votes in death penalty cases. Researchers Paul Brace and Melinda Gann Hall found that, among politically comparable states, rulings to uphold death sentences are more likely in states with elected judges.[27] Not only that, but the closer supreme court justices are to reelection, the more likely they are to support capital punishment.[28]

Texas and Florida have at least one thing in common—hundreds of inmates on death row with a high volume of death penalty appeals. But the similarity stops there. Texas justices are elected in partisan elections, and they almost never reverse a death sentence. In Florida, however, supreme court justices are merit selected, and the court has one of the nation's highest reversal rates.[29] It is not misguided for a judge facing reelection to fear reversing a death sentence. There are numerous examples of state supreme court justices who were voted off the bench after they were labeled as soft for opposing the imposition of capital punishment in particular cases. This occurs even when the unpopular opinions are later held by the U.S. Supreme Court to be correct.[30]

The effects of judicial selection ripple out beyond those cases that tackle politically volatile issues such as capital punishment and raise

issues of improper influence on the judiciary. Law professor Stephen Ware reviewed all arbitration decisions made by the Alabama Supreme Court from 1995 to 1999. Justices there are selected through partisan elections, and this period encompassed a shift in the court majority from Democrats to Republicans. In virtually all cases—even those that involved bland issues of law that appeared ideologically neutral—Ware found a direct correlation between voting and campaign contributions.[31] The Democrats, funded mostly by lawyers who worked for the plaintiffs, opposed arbitration. The Republicans, financed primarily by business interests, favored it. In 2006, *The New York Times* published the results of an examination of campaign financing over 12 years in regard to the Ohio Supreme Court. The investigators found that justices routinely sat on cases after receiving campaign contributions from the parties involved or from groups that filed supporting briefs and that justices, on average, voted in favor of contributors 70 percent of the time, with one particular justice voting for his contributor 91 percent of the time.[32] A 2012 report published by the Center for American Progress collects illustrations from six states with particularly expensive judicial

elections: Alabama, Illinois, Michigan, Ohio, Pennsylvania, and Texas. The high courts in these states, the report notes, "are much more likely to rule in favor of big business and against individuals who have been injured, scammed or subjected to discrimination."[33] In one example, the Ohio legislature had passed three laws curtailing the right to sue an employer for on-the-job injuries. After the first two laws were held unconstitutional by the state supreme court, the insurance industry donated to judicial campaigns. The winning justices upheld the law on its third try.[34]

Okay, so this all sounds shady, but candidates running for judicial office must raise money. Frequently, this money comes from the very people who have vested interests in the outcomes of cases that are or will be before a judge. Describing judicial fundraising, Justice Paul E. Pfeifer, a Republican member of the Ohio Supreme Court, said, "I never felt so much like a hooker down by the bus station in any race I've ever been in as I did in a judicial race."[35] But the need to find dollars to run for a seat cannot supersede good judgment. In *Caperton v. Massey* (2009), the U.S. Supreme Court ruled that Justice Brent Benjamin of the West Virginia Supreme Court of Appeals should have recused himself from a case in which the chief executive officer of the lead defendant, after losing a $50 million verdict in the trial court, raised $3 million to elect Benjamin to the court that was hearing the case's appeal. Benjamin was the deciding vote in favor of the defendants. Chastising Justice Benjamin for not sitting out this appeal, the U.S. Supreme Court stated, "Just as no man is allowed to be a judge in his own cause, similar fears of bias can arise when . . . a man chooses the judge in his own cause." In Benjamin's case, the $3 million from the CEO of A. T. Massey Coal Co. represented about 60 percent of his electoral war chest[36]—another piece of evidence that the funds required to run a campaign have been skyrocketing, particularly in state supreme court races. From 2000 to 2009, candidates for state supreme court seats raised more than $200 million, more than double the $83 million they raised in the previous decade.[37] Much of the money raised by judicial candidates comes from corporations, lawyers, litigants, and other groups with interests in the outcomes of litigation.

Then *Citizens United v. Federal Election Commission* (2010) invalidated laws placing limits on corporate campaign contributions and opened the door to spending by outside organizations and super PACs. In its wake, spending has continued to increase, with more than $56 million spent in state high court elections in 2011–2012 alone, much of that coming from special interest groups and political parties.[38] Why do these groups contribute so much money to judicial elections? As with any other political donation, there is at least some truth to the cynic's sense that campaign contributions are a good investment. The president of the Ohio State Bar Association concluded, "The people with money to spend who are affected by court decisions have reached the conclusion that it's a lot cheaper to buy a judge than a governor or an entire legislature, and he can probably do a lot more for you."[39] When the judicial reform organization Justice at Stake surveyed 2,428 state court judges, one quarter said that campaign contributions influenced their decisions.[40]

Even if justices do not allow campaign contributions to affect their decisions, the appearance of conflict already has been created. A 2009 *USA Today*/Gallup poll found that 89 percent of voters believe campaign contributions to judges influence decisions.[41] This appearance of bias, whether actual bias exists or not, affects the confidence of citizens in the courts' ability to administer justice impartially. Single-issue interest groups may target a judge for a specific ruling on a topic such as capital punishment, abortion, or same-sex marriage. Groups may criticize or praise the judge, taking the case completely out of its legal context and transforming an election into a referendum on a political cause. Such groups have joined together in coalitions similar to those formed in other partisan political contests. Given the power of interest groups, Santa Clara University law professor Gerald Uelmen has observed that judicial independence is most endangered in states with growing death-row populations and rare executions, states with laws requiring parental consent for abortions by minors, and states that allow statutory enactments or constitutional amendments by initiative.[42] In two states, Ohio and Kentucky, these

three judicial land mines have come together. Both states elect supreme court justices in highly partisan and expensive races on a recurring basis.

Prior to 2002, judges' campaigns generally were subject to codes of judicial conduct that placed tight restrictions on campaigning to prevent judges from discussing topics that might later come before them on the bench. In *Republican Party of Minnesota v. White* (2002), however, the U.S. Supreme Court struck down such restrictions as violations of judges' free speech rights. Since then, interest groups such as the Christian Coalition of Georgia have asked judicial candidates to complete questionnaires, pressuring them to reveal their views on hot-button issues. The groups then target specific "bad" judges for removal. Some candidates themselves have run outspoken campaigns, stating their opinions on issues such as school funding that will clearly appear before the court.

Campaigns increasingly rely on 30-second TV spots, which can do little more than offer simplistic sound bites about complicated issues. According to Justice at Stake, in 2002 only 1 in 10 of these TV ads was negative; that number had risen to more than 1 in 5 by 2004. In 2010, judicial candidates themselves paid for only a quarter of the negative ads, with three out of every four attack ads being purchased by noncandidate groups, including special interests and political parties.[43] One notorious attack ad run by the Michigan Democratic Party in 2008 featured a "dramatization" portraying the Michigan chief justice as sleeping on the bench, an allegation that was never proven.[44] In 2010, a coalition of groups seeking to oust a sitting Illinois Supreme Court justice aired a radio ad with actors purporting to be some of the state's worst criminals, recounting their crimes in grisly detail and portraying the judge as taking their side.[45] In a North Carolina Supreme Court judicial primary in 2014, the Washington-based Republican State Leadership Committee gave $650,000 to Justice for All NC to air an attack ad against a sitting justice, claiming that she was "not tough on child molesters."[46] These kinds of ads do seem to make a difference. In 2004, 34 judicial elections featured some form of television advertising, and in 29 of them, the candidate with the most ad expenditures won.[47]

Added to this mix of expensive campaigns and 30-second TV spots is the fact that ordinary citizens have very little information with which to make informed choices about judicial races. Voters sometimes vote only for candidates at the top of the ticket, such as governors or senators, and leave the part of the ballot listing judicial candidates incomplete. A 2007 poll conducted by the Colorado League of Women Voters found that 52 percent of those who did vote in judicial elections admitted to being uninformed about the candidates. When these uninformed voters were asked to describe their voting strategies, the results were roughly evenly split between those who said they always voted to keep judges, always voted to remove them, or made random choices.[48] Lack of voter participation and uninformed voting both undermine the public's ability to keep the judiciary accountable and make judges more vulnerable to targeting by single-issue groups.

In partisan elections, an additional danger is that the political parties may expect favors from the candidates they put forward. In 1976, the Michigan Supreme Court decided a redistricting case in a way that favored Republicans. In the next election, the Democratic Party refused to renominate the court's Democratic chief justice.[49] Thomas Phillips, onetime chief justice of the Texas Supreme Court, has asked:

> When judges are labeled as Democrats or Republicans, how can you convince the public that the law is a judge's only constituency? And when a winning litigant has contributed thousands of dollars to the judge's campaign, how do you ever persuade the losing party that only the facts of the case were considered?[50]

Appointment

The systems used by states in which judges are appointed rather than elected can be divided into two general categories: **pure appointive systems** and merit selection systems that rely on nominating committees. Federal judges have always been selected through a pure appointive system. The president appoints judges who, if they are confirmed by the Senate, "shall hold their Offices during good Behavior." No state, however, employs precisely this method of judicial selection.

In three states—California, Maine, and New Jersey—the governor appoints state court judges without a nominating commission; that is, these governors are not limited in their selections to a list of names provided by someone else.[51] Judges' nominations still require some kind of second opinion, however. In Maine, the governor appoints judges subject to confirmation by a legislative committee, the decision of which may be reviewed by the state Senate. In New Jersey, the state Senate must confirm the governor's appointees, who then serve an initial 7-year term, after which the governor may reappoint them. California's governor appoints judges after submitting names to a state bar committee for evaluation, but the governor is not bound by the committee's recommendation. New Hampshire used to be on this list, but in 2013 the governor created a judicial selection commission through executive order and now is limited to appointing judges nominated by this commission.[52] Virginia is the only state in which the legislature appoints all state judges without a nominating committee. A majority vote of both houses of the Virginia General Assembly is required to appoint any judge.

Merit selection, initially endorsed by the American Bar Association in 1937, was conceived as a way to limit the intrusion of politics into judge selection and strike a balance between partisan election and lifetime appointment.[53] Under such a system, after an appointed judge serves an initial term, he or she must stand for a retention election. In this election, the judge runs unopposed. Voters may indicate only either yes or no on the question of whether the judge should be retained.

Most states that currently appoint judges rely on a method of merit selection through nominating committees. Twenty-four states and the District of Columbia rely on a merit selection plan for the initial selection of some or all judges. Another 10 states use such plans to fill midterm vacancies at some or all levels of the courts.[54]

What puts the *merit* into merit selection? It is misleading to describe merit selection as if it were

---

Pure appointive systems
Judicial selection systems in which the governor appoints judges alone, without preselection of candidates by a nominating commission

a single method for selecting judges, because the details vary considerably from state to state. At its core, it requires that the state assemble a nonpartisan nominating committee. This committee forwards a list of names from which either the governor or the legislature chooses a judge. How a partisan, distrustful legislature solves the problem of creating a nonpartisan committee differs in almost every state. Some states require parity of political party affiliation for the commission members. Others have adopted extremely complex methods to ensure the impartiality of nominating commissions. While the details of how a nominating committee is chosen may seem innocuous and dry, they have significant impact on just how successful a merit selection plan can be in minimizing the politicization of the judiciary. In 2012 three merit selection states—Arizona, Florida, and Missouri—held referendums on the issue of increasing the power of governors and legislatures in the selection of judges. These efforts mostly focused on giving executives or legislatures more power to influence merit system selection committees. While retaining the basic framework of a merit system, giving partisan actors a greater role in selection committee appointments nudges a merit system toward giving greater weight to political concerns than to judicial qualifications. For example, Missouri has had several failed attempts in recent years to revoke merit selection entirely and replace it with partisan elections. Opponents have since shifted tactics, focusing on an effort to give the governor the power to appoint a majority of the members of the judicial selection committee. The Missouri referendum did not pass, but such a move would have drastically increased the governor's power over who ends up sitting on the bench.

Even after the composition of a nominating commission has been determined, states have varying ways of choosing who will fill the most influential position, that of commission chair. In some states, including Maryland, New Hampshire, and Utah, the governor can exert considerable control over the commission through the ability to appoint its chair.[55] Other states, such as Alaska, Arizona,

Colorado, and Utah, designate the chief justice of the state supreme court as chair. Some states allow the commission to choose its own chair. New Mexico's constitution designates the dean of the University of New Mexico Law School as the chair of the state's judicial nominating commission.[56]

Usually, the governor chooses judicial appointees from a list forwarded by the nominating commission. In South Carolina and Connecticut, the nominating committee forwards a list of names to the legislature, which then meets in joint session to appoint judges by a majority vote.[57]

The ways judges are retained after they are appointed also vary by state. In most states, judges appointed through merit selection serve relatively short initial terms, usually 1 or 2 years. After that, they participate in retention elections. These special elections were conceived as a means to provide some public participation in the selection of judges while avoiding the intrusion of politics. This worked relatively well for some time, as retention elections appeared immune to the kind of big-money politics seen in partisan elections. But this all changed in the elections of 2009–2010, when incumbent justices in some states, notably Alaska, Colorado, Illinois, and Iowa, faced unprecedented and highly financed opposition in races as fiercely partisan as popular elections.

Some merit selection states have dispensed with elections altogether. For instance, in Connecticut, Delaware, and Hawaii, judges are reevaluated and reappointed by the judicial selection commission. In Vermont, after an initial appointment through merit selection, a judge receives an additional term as long as the General Assembly does not vote against it.[58]

Terms of Office

The length of a judge's tenure is another element in the balance between judicial independence and judicial accountability. In the federal court system, judges serve life terms "during good behavior"; that is, judges can be removed only through an impeachment process for cause. This life tenure is considered an important element, perhaps the most important element, in ensuring the independence of the federal judiciary.[59] There has never been a conviction of an impeached federal judge based solely on an unpopular judicial decision in the federal system.[60]

With only a few exceptions, state court judges serve fixed terms of office and must therefore seek reappointment or reelection. The rare exceptions are judges in Rhode Island, who serve life terms, and judges in Massachusetts and New Hampshire, who hold their positions until the age of 70. Judges in states with fixed terms typically serve for less than 10 years. New York trial court judges serve the longest terms among the states—14 years—and are required to retire at age 70.[61]

Shorter tenures bring with them the increased danger that political interests and pressures will intrude on judicial decision making. Longer terms allow for judges to be evaluated on more complete records; any particular controversial decisions may have weaker effects when there are long periods between elections. To look at this another way, research indicates that judges with longer terms of office are more willing to manifest partisanship than are judges with shorter terms. For example, researchers Brace and Hall found that, out of all the judges they studied, Democrats with long terms were least likely to support capital punishment, whereas Republicans with long terms were most likely to support it. This led them to conclude that "term length influences the willingness of individual justices to express their partisanship."[62]

Judicial Compensation

In addition to selection and tenure, compensation is one of the bellwethers for assessing independence of the judiciary. How a state determines the salaries of its judges and whether those salaries can be reduced makes a difference. The U.S. Constitution forbids reducing federal judicial salaries, as a protection for judges who make unpopular decisions. In 2012, Governor Chris Christie of New Jersey ran headlong into a similar state constitutional prohibition on lowering judicial pay. In his signature attempt to lower state expenditures, he sought to mandate increased pension and health benefit contributions from all state employees. Not so fast, said the state supreme court when it ruled in favor of the 375 state court judges who sued.[63] However, not all state constitutions include this proscription. In Florida, for instance, the constitution does not prevent the legislature from amending state laws to reduce salaries to discipline judges for unpopular decisions.[64] The Arkansas legislature in 2013 considered presenting voters with the option to end their state's guarantee that judicial salaries not be diminished and eliminate a provision requiring all circuit judges in the state to receive a uniform salary.

According to the National Center for State Courts, at least 20 states have created independent judicial compensation commissions to advise their legislatures on judicial salary levels. The goal of these commissions is to determine the amount necessary to retain and recruit qualified judges and to eliminate the need for judges to lobby for their own salaries. States without such commissions rely on a variety of methods to eliminate partisan bickering over judicial salaries. The District of Columbia links its judges' salary increases to those of federal judges. Judges' salaries in South Dakota are linked to annual increases of the salaries of other state employees. In Pennsylvania, judicial salary increases are tied to increases in the Consumer Price Index.[65] (See Table 9-1.)

Prosecution and Defense of Cases in State Courts

Criminal cases at the state court level most often involve a face-off between two state or county employees. The **prosecutor** pursues the case on behalf of the people and usually seeks the incarceration of the accused. Little difference exists among the states in the selection of the chief prosecutor; an elected county official almost always fills the position. The individual often is politically ambitious and views the job of chief prosecutor as

Prosecutor
A government official and lawyer who conducts criminal cases on behalf of the people

TABLE 9-1

Salaries and Rankings for Appellate and General-Jurisdiction Judges, 2013 (Dollars)

Courts of Last Resort		Intermediate Appellate Courts		Trial Courts	
Top Five		**Top Five**		**Top Five**	
California	218,237	California	204,599	Illinois	182,429
Illinois	211,228	Illinois	198,805	Alaska	181,440
Pennsylvania	199,606	Pennsylvania	188,337	Delaware	180,233
Alaska	196,224	Alaska	185,388	California	178,789
Delaware	190,639	Alabama	178,878	District of Columbia	174,000
Bottom Five		**Bottom Five**		**Bottom Five**	
Mississippi	122,460	Kentucky	130,044	Montana	113,928
Idaho	121,900	Oregon	122,820	South Dakota	113,688
South Dakota	121,718	Idaho	120,900	Mississippi	112,128
Montana	121,434	New Mexico	117,506	Maine	111,969
Maine	119,476	Mississippi	114,994	New Mexico	111,631

Source: Data compiled from the National Center for State Courts, "Salaries and Rankings for Appellate and General-Jurisdiction Judges," *Survey of Judicial Salaries* 38, no. 1 (January 1, 2013), http://www.ncsc.org/microsites/judicial-salaries-data-tool/home/~/media/microsites/files/judicial%20salaries/jud_2012.ashx.

a stepping-stone to higher elected office. For this reason, the policies of prosecutors tend to reflect the specific wishes of the county voters.

Private attorneys defend those individuals who can afford their services. In many cases, however, a **public defender**, an attorney also on the public payroll, represents the accused. Public defenders fulfill the state's constitutional requirement to provide indigent defense services—that is, defense services for those who are poor. There is much more variety in how states organize their systems of indigent defense than in their systems of prosecution. Some are organized into statewide systems of public defenders. Others have established statewide commissions that set guidelines for local jurisdictions, sometimes distributing limited state funds to local programs that follow specific standards. Still others delegate the responsibility of deciding how to provide and fund indigent defense entirely to the counties.

The competing values of state oversight and local control play out differently depending on the cultural and political realities of each state, as well as any practical concerns involved. Even some states with statewide public defenders' offices exclude rural areas where the case volume would make supporting such offices impracticable. In the current climate of runaway costs, increased caseloads, and widespread litigation-challenging programs, the trend has been toward more state oversight.

The Prosecutor

Commentators have gone so far as to say that the prosecutor has become the "most powerful office in the criminal justice system."[66] The prosecutor's office is run by an attorney referred to, depending on the state, as the chief prosecutor, district attorney, county attorney, commonwealth attorney, or state's attorney. Whatever the title, this lawyer represents the public in criminal and other cases. Most prosecutors are elected and typically serve 4-year terms. It is a daunting job, particularly in major metropolitan districts, where the top prosecutor manages hundreds of lawyers and support staffers, deals with horrific crimes, and balances the need to serve justice with the "unavoidable

Public defender
A government lawyer who provides free legal services to persons accused of crimes who cannot afford to hire lawyers

scrutiny of won-lost statistics that become a factor in re-election campaigns."[67] This focus on statistics may, according to one commentator, undergird some prosecutors' resistance to the use of postconviction DNA testing to determine conclusively if the correct person was incarcerated for a crime.[68]

The authority to prosecute comes from the state, but prosecutors' offices are essentially local. A prosecutor's authority is over a specific jurisdiction, usually a county. County governments fund these offices, although close to half of them also receive some portion of their budgets from state funds.[69] Nationwide, there are more than 2,000 state court prosecutors' offices, employing about 78,000 attorneys, investigators, and support staffers.[70] They handle more than 2 million felonies and 7 million misdemeanors a year.

Most chief prosecutors serve jurisdictions with fewer than 100,000 people. About one third of chief prosecutors' offices have a total staff of four or fewer.[71] The top 5 percent of prosecutors' offices, however, serve districts with populations of 500,000 or more. They represent almost half the entire U.S. population.[72] In 2001, these large offices handled about 66 percent of the nation's serious crimes and had a median budget of more than $14 million.[73] The Los Angeles County District Attorney's Office has the largest staff, consisting of more than 2,200 people, including more than 1,000 attorneys.[74] The types of cases handled by these offices grow increasingly complex as prosecutors' offices encounter high-tech crimes, including identity theft and credit card fraud, and take on homeland security responsibilities.

A state's chief prosecutors have enormous discretion in the conduct of most of their responsibilities. The prosecutor makes all decisions as to whether or not to prosecute, whom to prosecute, and with what cause of action to prosecute. Discretion in charging is, in the words of one scholar, "virtually unchecked by formal constraints or regulatory mechanisms, making it one of the broadest discretionary powers in criminal administration."[75] Charging decisions are enormously important, particularly in states where statutory guidelines set minimum sentences or where the same act can be subject to a number of different charges.

Several reasons exist for giving prosecutors such broad powers. One is the trend toward **legislative overcriminalization**, the tendency of legislatures to make crimes out of everything that people find objectionable.[76] By creating a large number of broadly defined crimes, legislatures have made it impossible for states to enforce all their criminal statutes, even as they have made it possible for prosecutors to charge a single act under multiple, overlapping provisions.[77] This ability to charge the same act in multiple ways gives a prosecutor tremendous leverage over a defendant. It is a powerful tool to coerce a guilty plea to a lesser charge through the process of plea bargaining.

A second reason prosecutors are given broad discretion is the need to individualize justice. Each case involves a unique set of facts and issues, and requires careful weighing of the evidence. To determine how best to spend limited resources, a prosecutor must balance the severity of the crime against the probability of sustaining a conviction. Prosecutors have been reluctant to publish general guidelines regarding their charging decisions. A Florida prosecutor stated that his office declines to prosecute cases of cocaine possession when the amount of cocaine involved is deemed too small. But he refused to say just how much is too small. Understandably, he worried that drug smugglers would package their shipments in smaller batches than this arbitrary limit and thus escape prosecution.[78]

There are some limits to prosecutorial authority, for instance, in regard to the trial process itself. In many jurisdictions, before proceeding to trial, the government first must obtain an **indictment**, a formal criminal charge, from a **grand jury**. The U.S. Supreme Court has noted that the grand jury historically has been regarded as the primary protection for the innocent. However,

---

Legislative overcriminalization
The tendency of government to make a crime out of anything the public does not like

Indictment
A formal criminal charge

Grand jury
A group of between 16 and 23 citizens who decide if a case should go to trial; if the grand jury decides that it should, an indictment is issued

only prosecutors and their witnesses appear before a grand jury; no members of the defense are present. Prosecutors are able to offer their interpretation of the evidence and the law and have no obligation to inform the grand jury of evidence of a defendant's innocence. Grand juries hear only one side of any given case and thus almost always indict. For this reason, no discussion of grand juries is complete without mention of the immortal quip by former New York state judge Sol Wachtler that a grand jury could "indict a ham sandwich." It is also part of the reason that many states have abolished the grand jury and now rely instead on a preliminary hearing in which a judge decides if enough evidence exists to warrant a trial.

At trial, a criminal jury must determine guilt beyond a reasonable doubt. The possibility of **jury nullification** exists if the jury does not believe a case should have been brought to court. Trials, however, rarely come into play as a check on the discretion of prosecutors—few cases actually end up going to trial. Most are resolved through plea bargaining. Plea bargaining is another area in which prosecutors have broad discretion. Judges rarely question or second-guess plea bargains reached between prosecutors and defendants. Prosecutors ultimately have to answer to the voters, because chief prosecutors are elected everywhere other than Alaska, Connecticut, New Jersey, and Washington, D.C.[79]

There are positive and negative aspects to subjecting the prosecution of local crimes to the political process. On the positive side, the person deciding which laws to enforce and how to enforce them is answerable to the people of that district. More worrying is that political pressures—rather than the facts of a case—may guide the exercise of prosecutorial discretion. Prosecutors, for example, may choose not to charge politically connected friends. Some attributed the multibillion-dollar savings and loan scandal of the 1980s and 1990s to the reluctance of prosecutors to subject their friends and political allies to criminal indictment.[80]

Discretion also can be misused when race enters the equation. Studies have shown that when the victim is white and the defendant is black, prosecutors are much more likely to seek the greatest possible punishment.[81] One researcher reviewed a national sample of outcomes in prosecutor elections revealing that a high percentage of races are uncontested, and, even when an incumbent faces a challenger, campaigns turn more on outcomes of a few high-profile cases than on overall larger patterns of outcomes.[82]

Defense Attorneys

Anyone with even a casual acquaintance with TV crime dramas knows that after the police make an arrest, they must inform the suspect of certain rights. One is that "you have the right to an attorney. If you cannot afford one, one will be appointed for you." This right derives from the Sixth Amendment of the U.S. Constitution: "In all criminal prosecutions, the accused shall enjoy the right . . . to have the assistance of counsel for his defense." In 1963, the U.S. Supreme Court found in *Gideon v. Wainwright* that this right to counsel is so fundamental and essential to a fair trial that the Constitution requires the state to provide a poor defendant with a lawyer at state expense. Nine years after *Gideon,* the Court extended this right to counsel to all criminal prosecutions, state or federal, **felony** or **misdemeanor**, that carry a possible sentence of imprisonment. The Court also has made it clear that the Sixth Amendment guarantees "the right to the *effective* assistance of counsel."[83] If an attorney is unprepared, drunk, or sleeping during a trial, that can be grounds for appeal.

No money came along with the constitutional mandate for counsel, and its scope is tremendous because most criminal defendants in the United States cannot afford to pay for legal services. In 1997, about three-quarters of state prison inmates reported that they had been represented by a

---

Jury nullification
A jury's returning a verdict of "not guilty" even though jurists believe the defendant is guilty. By doing so, the jury cancels out the effect of a law that the jurors believe is immoral or was wrongly applied to the defendant.

Felony
A serious crime, such as murder or arson

Misdemeanor
A less serious crime, such as shoplifting

court-appointed lawyer.[84] In 30 states, a public defender system is the primary method used to provide indigent criminal defendants with lawyers.[85] In 2007, 957 public defenders' offices across the country received almost 6 million cases, at a cost of $2.3 billion. Twenty-two states' public defenders' offices are funded almost exclusively by state sources, 11 use a combination of state and county funds, and 16 use only county funds.[86]

Not only did the mandate come with no funding, but it also lacked any specifications as to how indigent services must be provided. States and localities, as a consequence, have devised differing systems, with the quality of service provided varying tremendously. Three primary models have emerged throughout the nation, with most states employing public defender programs, **assigned counsel**, **contract attorneys**, or some combination of these. The method chosen may vary from county to county within a state, or a state may rely primarily on one type and use either of the other types for casework overload or the inevitable cases involving conflict of interest. Among the nation's 100 most populous counties in 1999 (the latest figures available), public defender programs were operating in 90 counties, assigned counsel programs in 89 counties, and contract programs in 42 counties.[87] Public defenders usually serve metropolitan areas, and assigned counsel programs and contract programs serve less-populous regions.

Public defenders' offices draw on salaried staffs of attorneys. They provide criminal legal defense services either as employees paid directly by the government or through public or private nonprofit organizations. Large public defenders' offices generally employ attorneys who are trained and supervised and who are supported by investigative, paralegal, and clerical staffers. The American Bar Association has observed, "When adequately funded and staffed, defender organizations employing full-time personnel are capable of providing excellent defense services."[88] The challenge is to fund and staff these offices adequately. In 2009, the Michigan Court of Appeals ruled in favor of criminal defendants who charged that three counties' public defense systems were so underfunded that they failed to provide adequate representation. Put simply, the defendants contended that the system was unconstitutional due to lack of funding—and the court agreed, sparking debate statewide about potential reforms.[89] In Washington, the state supreme court recently entered this debate by setting explicit limits on acceptable public defender workloads. The court set these limits after overturning convictions in a number of cases because of inadequate defenses provided by overburdened public defenders. In one such case, for instance, a 12-year-old boy convicted of sexually molesting a neighbor child was represented by a public defender who handled about 500 cases a year. The defender failed to investigate the case and only spoke with the boy to urge him to plead guilty. After the high court granted the boy a new trial, he was completely exonerated.[90]

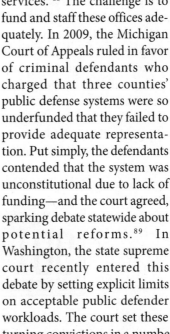

A 2005 survey of 2,485 Anchorage residents found that only 6.4 percent of respondents felt that defense attorneys were excellent at treating people fairly. Prosecutors and judges fared little better, at 8 and 13.3 percent, respectively.

Another type of system uses assigned counsel; here private attorneys are chosen and appointed to handle particular cases, either on a systematic or an ad hoc basis, and are paid from public funds. Depending on the state, individual judges, assigned counsel program offices, or the court clerk's office may make the appointments. In the oldest type of assigned counsel program, judges make ad hoc assignments of counsel. Sometimes the only basis for these decisions is whoever is in the courtroom at the time. These arrangements frequently are criticized for fostering patronage (the granting of jobs to political allies), particularly in counties with small populations. Counsel appointed by the judges they appear before may also be less willing to take strong opposing positions that could be perceived as biting the hand that feeds them.

Most states using assigned counsel appoint lawyers from a roster of attorneys available for

Assigned counsel
Private lawyers selected by the courts to handle particular cases and paid from public funds

Contract attorneys
Private attorneys who enter into an agreement with a state, county, or judicial district to work on a fixed-fee basis per case or for a specific length of time

assigned cases. These rosters are compiled in various ways. Generally, defense attorneys need do no more than put their names on a list to be appointed to cases. No review of their experience, qualifications, or competence is conducted. Some states, particularly those with organized plans administered by independent managers, may require that attorneys receive specific training before they can be included on the roster. Assigned counsel are generally paid either a flat fee or an hourly rate, in some cases subject to an overall fee cap. Many are paid at very low rates, such that only recent law school graduates or those who have been unsuccessful in the business of law will agree to take assignments.[91]

Contract attorney programs are another way states provide defense services. A state, county, or judicial district will enter into a contract for the provision of indigent representation. Such a contract may be awarded to a solo attorney, to a law firm that handles both indigent and private cases, to a nonprofit organization, or to a group of lawyers who have joined together to provide services under the contract. The contractor may agree to accept cases on a fixed-fee per case basis or to provide representation for a particular period of time for a fixed fee.

Fixed-fee contracts specify the total amount of compensation the lawyer will receive for work on all cases taken during a specified period of time. The contractor must accept all cases that come up during the duration of the contract. For this reason, some view the use of fixed-fee contracts as a quick fix that allows the funding body to limit costs and accurately project expenses for the coming year. However, such contracts have been criticized severely by the courts and by national organizations such as the American Bar Association, because to make a profit, the contracting attorney has to spend as little time as possible on each case.

Few states rely on contract attorneys to provide representation for all or even a majority of their indigent defense cases. More commonly, they use such attorneys to handle periods of public defender overload or when conflicts of interest arise. Sometimes, public defenders' offices will contract out specific categories of cases, such as juvenile or traffic offenses. Of the total amount spent on indigent criminal defense in the nation's 100 largest counties in 1999, only 6 percent was spent on contract programs.[92]

Regardless of the model used by a county or state, all indigent defense systems depend on adequate funding to successfully provide "effective assistance of counsel." Without such funding, the right to counsel becomes just another unfunded mandate, and justice for the rich becomes very different from justice for the poor. Inadequate funding leads to lawyers' carrying impossible caseloads. A 2013 documentary titled *Gideon's Army* shows young public defenders in Miami-Dade County, Florida, struggling to do right by their clients while carrying an average caseload of 500 felonies and 225 misdemeanors.[93]

A recent report found that the average time spent by a public defender with a client at arraignment is often less than 6 minutes and workloads are frequently multiples of the recommended 150 felony cases per year, concluding that, with these deficiencies, "it is impossible to represent individual clients while adhering to even minimal standards of professionalism."[94]

Overburdened lawyers make crucial decisions based on too little investigation of the facts and inevitably pressure clients to plead guilty. Innocent people plead guilty without really understanding their legal rights, under plea agreements that they only learned about from defenders they met just moments before and may never see again.[95] Many indigent defense systems are plagued by lack of funding and resources, high attorney workloads, and little or no oversight of the quality of services—problems that can and do result in the conviction of innocent people. "Providing genuinely adequate counsel for poor defendants would require a substantial infusion of money and indigent defense is the last thing the populace will voluntarily direct its tax dollars to fund," writes attorney David Cole. "Achieving solutions to this problem through the political process is a pipe dream."[96]

How secure would you feel if you were facing more than 20 years in jail for a felony you didn't commit, in Virginia, where your appointed lawyer could be paid a maximum of $1,235 to defend you?[97] If you didn't plead guilty quickly, your lawyer would lose money on your case. Recently, a wave of successful lawsuits against underfunded and over-burdened public defenders, assigned counsel programs, and contract attorneys by groups such as the American Civil Liberties Union have led legislators to enact reforms that "even the most skeptical observers admit have the potential to bring important changes to the process of criminal justice."[98] Some of these have led to successful injunctions or settlements, increased funding for indigent defense, and improved administration of such programs. Furthermore, the defense community and organizations such as the American Bar Association have been focusing on the need for standards for indigent criminal representation.

Juries

If you vote, pay a utility bill, or have a driver's license, you may be called to serve jury duty at some point in your life. You may be asked to decide whether a defendant in a capital case lives or dies; whether someone spends the rest of his or her life in prison; whether a civil plaintiff, injured and unable to work, should be able to collect damages; or whether a civil defendant must be bankrupted by the large amount of damages ordered to be paid. Service on a jury may require spending days or weeks listening to intricate scientific evidence and expert testimony, some of it conflicting, and deciding who is credible and who is not to be believed. Or you may spend one day in a large room with other potential jurors, break for lunch, and go home at the end of that day without ever hearing a single case.

The right to a jury trial in state criminal proceedings is granted by the Sixth Amendment. Not all criminal prosecutions trigger the right to a jury trial. Minor offenses involving potential sentences of less than 6 months do not require juries. Neither do juvenile proceedings, probation revocation proceedings, or military trials.

The jury's role in a trial is that of fact finder. The judge has to ensure a fair and orderly trial, but the jurors must determine the facts of the case. In some instances, parties may agree to forgo a jury trial and, instead, choose a bench trial, in which the judge serves as both judge and jury. In a criminal bench trial, the judge alone decides guilt or innocence.

> Stereotypes might lead you to think that juries are less capable than judges of separating emotion from reason or that juries decide cases more generously for injured plaintiffs or that grisly evidence in criminal cases may motivate juries to base their decisions on passion or prejudice. Not so.

Differences and similarities in how judges and juries rule have been the subject of much research and review. Stereotypes might lead you to think that juries are less capable than judges of separating emotion from reason or that juries decide cases more generously for injured plaintiffs or that grisly evidence in criminal cases may motivate juries to base their decisions on passion or prejudice. Not so. For instance, research shows that civil plaintiffs in product **liability** and medical malpractice cases have more success before judges in bench trials.[99]

Historically, juries in the United States have been composed of 12 people who must come to a unanimous verdict. Since 1970, however, a series of U.S. Supreme Court decisions has allowed states to move away from this standard.[100] In state jury trials, whether unanimity is required depends on the size of the jury. A conviction by a 12-member jury may be less than unanimous, whereas a six-member jury must have unanimity. A majority of states continue to require 12-member juries to make unanimous rulings in felony criminal cases, but seven states use six-member or eight-member juries for noncapital felonies. Two states, Louisiana and Oregon, do not require unanimous verdicts in such cases.[101] Most states provide for civil juries of six members or eight members. Those that still require 12 members typically allow the parties to civil cases to agree to smaller juries. Unanimity is not required in most civil trials; instead, most states provide for verdicts based on a supermajority of either five sixths or two thirds.

Liability
A legal obligation or responsibility

States develop and maintain master lists from which they identify potential jurors. Their sources include driver's licenses, motor vehicle registrations, telephone directories, tax rolls, utility customer lists, voter registration rolls, and lists of actual voters. It is very hard to avoid ever being called in for jury duty. Jurors must be residents of the county in which the court sits and must generally be at least 18 years old, although in Alabama and Nebraska the minimum age is 19 and in Mississippi and Missouri it is 21. States also usually have some sort of requirement regarding literacy and the ability to understand or communicate in English, or both. South Carolina requires that jurors have at least a sixth-grade education, and Tennessee explicitly excludes those of "unsound mind" and "habitual drunkards." Recently, states attempting to increase their juror pool have eliminated eclectic lists of professions that were previously exempt from jury duty. Clergy members, foot doctors, and embalmers must now serve their turn on juries in New York, and ferry boat captains no longer get a pass in Indiana. Most states also require that jurors not be convicted felons.

Defendants' Rights Versus Victims' Rights

A crime typically involves at least two actors: a perpetrator and a victim. Traditionally, the criminal justice system in the United States interposes the ideal of public prosecution between the two. That is, all crimes are crimes against the state. The prosecutor, representing the public and not any particular individual, sees that justice is done objectively and fairly. The public's interest, under this system, is distinct from the victim's interest in retribution.

Numerous provisions in the Bill of Rights balance the rights of criminal defendants against the powers of the state. These defendants' rights include the following:

- The right to be presumed innocent until proven guilty
- The right to be safe from arrest or searches and seizures unless the government has made a showing of probable cause
- The right to a lawyer
- The right to a jury trial

- The right to confront witnesses
- The rights to due process and the equal protection of laws
- If proven guilty, the right to punishment that is not cruel and unusual

In spelling out these rights, the framers sought to prevent the overreach of government power. They worried that innocent people otherwise might be railroaded into jail on charges they never had a chance to defend themselves against adequately. The Bill of Rights makes no mention of the rights of crime victims.

In the past three decades, the balance between defendants' rights and victims' rights has undergone a radical transformation. Defendants still have all the rights listed, but now state courts are increasingly balancing them against a new class of victims' rights. The movement advocating an increasing role in the courts for the victims of crime has become a formidable force and has achieved tremendous success in enacting legislation in all the states. The momentum started in 1982, when a president's task force on victims of crime described the U.S. justice system as "appallingly out of balance." That is not to say that victims were helpless—the number of state laws addressing victims' rights was already in the hundreds. By 1998, however, the number of crime victim–related statutes had soared to more than 27,000. Twenty-nine states had passed victims' rights constitutional amendments.[102]

Today, every state has either a constitutional amendment or a statutory scheme that protects victims' rights. Some predict that the next amendment to the U.S. Constitution will be a victims' rights amendment. Supporters of victims' rights frequently argue that the justice system favors defendants over victims and that, without modification, the system itself constitutes a second victimization. On the other hand, civil rights organizations fear that some victims' rights laws upset the system of checks and balances in the nation's criminal justice system and undercut the basic due-process protections designed to keep innocent people out of prison.

The specifics of victims' rights laws vary among the states. A variety of statutes and amendments guarantee that crime victims receive monetary compensation, notice of procedural developments in their cases, protection from offender harm, and more attentive treatment from the justice system.

The more controversial of such laws are directed toward providing victims with significantly greater involvement in actual prosecutions. This includes providing victims the right to confer with the prosecutor at all stages, including plea bargains; the right to attend all stages of the case, even if the victim will be called as a witness; and the right to introduce victim-impact statements at the sentencing phase of the trial.

Perhaps the most controversial and interesting of the victims' rights laws concern victim-impact evidence. This may be particularly true in capital cases, in which impact statements have been described as

> highly emotional, frequently tearful testimony coming directly from the hearts and mouths of the survivors left behind by killings. And it arrives at the precise time when the balance is at its most delicate and the stakes are highest—when jurors are poised to make the visceral decision of whether the offender lives or dies.[103]

In 1991, the U.S. Supreme Court reversed itself and ruled that impact statements that detailed the particular qualities of the victim and the harm caused to the victim's family could be admissible in capital sentencing hearings.[104] Today, all states allow victim-impact evidence at the sentencing phase of a trial. Most of the states with the death penalty allow it in capital trials.

Sentencing

The total U.S. prison population has ballooned in the past 30 years, rising from less than 320,000 in 1980 to a high of 2.3 million in 2008.[105] The trend might be reversing, as 2012 marked the fourth consecutive year of decline in total prison population, the first period of decline in four decades.[106] Corrections has been one of the fastest-growing items in state budgets, and, although it slowed considerably owing to widespread revenue shortfalls and limited state resources after 2008, it still averaged 31 percent of total state spending and 7.3 percent of state general fund budgets in 2010.[107]

In most states, after a jury finds a defendant guilty, the judge holds a separate sentencing hearing. In capital cases, the U.S. Supreme Court has held that only a unanimous jury, and not the judge, can sentence a defendant to death.[108] In many states, capital juries are instructed that a sentence of life in prison without the possibility of parole is an option. In noncapital cases, by contrast, it is almost always the judge who sets sentence. Only in Arkansas, Kentucky, Missouri, Oklahoma, Texas, and Virginia do juries choose the sentences of those they find guilty. In most of these states, the judge is free to reduce but not to increase the jury's sentence, except to comply with mandatory sentencing laws. Most of these states choose their judges through popular election; so having juries decide on sentences allows trial judges to evade political heat for sentencing.

Sentencing policy involves the balancing of value judgments, such as the perceived severity of the crime and of different punishments, with the relevance of mitigating circumstances. It must include consideration of the costs to the taxpayers and to society of incarceration. Surveys indicate that attitudes toward sentencing follow regional patterns, "with residents of New England demonstrating the greatest tendency to be lenient and residents of central southern states displaying the least leniency."[109] It is not surprising, then, that state sentencing laws vary and that the punishment a convict faces depends not just on what that person did but also on where the crime was committed. Voters in California and Oklahoma, for instance, view drug offenses differently. In California state courts, a cocaine dealer is subject to a 2- to 4-year prison term. The same offense in Oklahoma brings a minimum of 5 years and a maximum of life imprisonment.[110] While the Brooklyn, New York, district attorney announced in 2014 his decision to stop prosecuting first-time low-level marijuana offenses, personal possession of even the smallest amount in Louisiana, a state with some of the harshest marijuana laws in the country, can lead to 6 months in jail and a $500 fine, and a second offense could potentially lead to 5 years of incarceration.

The amount of discretion given to judges also varies from state to state. Depending on the type of crime and where the defendant is charged, the sentence can be a matter of "do the crime, do the time" or whatever the judge or parole board thinks is best.

Forty years ago, it was possible to talk of a predominant American approach to criminal sentencing. At all levels of the nation's criminal justice system, a concern for rehabilitation and deterrence led states to embrace **indeterminate sentencing.** Legislatures set very wide statutory sentencing margins within which judges had the discretion to impose sentences for imprisonment with little fear of appellate review. The sentencing was indeterminate because the parole board, not the judge, had ultimate control over the actual release date. Under this system, judges and parole boards had to apply their discretion to tailor punishments to the specific rehabilitative needs of individual defendants. This practice led to wide discrepancies in the sentences imposed on different persons convicted of the same crimes.

Indeterminate sentencing came under attack from several angles during the 1970s. The lack of guidance for judges led to the potential for discrimination in sentencing based on such factors as race, ethnic group, social status, and gender. There was also criticism of the ability of parole boards to determine successfully whether inmates had or had not been rehabilitated. Finally, rehabilitation lost favor as the country entered an era of tough-on-crime rhetoric and a "just deserts" theory of criminal sentencing.[111] Reformers sought to replace indeterminate sentencing with **determinate sentencing.** This led to the adoption of federal sentencing guidelines, a structured system of binding sentencing rules that greatly limited judicial discretion in sentencing in the federal courts.

Indeterminate sentencing does not necessarily mean more lenient sentencing. It just means that the actual amount of time served may vary depending on the judge or the findings of a parole board. For instance, before the charges were dropped, Los Angeles Lakers star Kobe Bryant was charged with felony sexual assault in Colorado. The sex offense statutes there are considered among the harshest in the country. Any sentence on a sex assault charge can mean the possibility of life imprisonment. The severity of the sentence depends in part on the results of a battery of tests administered to the convicted defendant. The judge uses these results in sentencing, and the parole board uses them to determine whether the prisoner is a continued threat. The tests include a penile plethysmograph test, which involves placing an electric band around the penis in an attempt to measure deviant thoughts as the person is shown images of abusive behaviors. Although the tests have been described as "very Clockwork Orangish" by Don Recht, former head of the Colorado Defense Bar, the results are studied carefully nonetheless. Under Colorado's indeterminate sentencing law, convicted sex offenders are released only when parole boards deem them safe to reenter society.

By the year 2000, all states had adopted at least some features of determinate sentencing, although in greatly differing degrees. When it comes to sentencing reform, "the states have served as hothouses of experimentation during the last thirty years, with so much activity that the diversity of provisions among the states has become exceedingly complex."[112] Some of the major reforms adopted included sentencing guidelines (either presumptive, meaning the judge can deviate with a good reason, or purely voluntary), **mandatory minimum sentences** that are imposed for conviction of specified crimes, **habitual offender laws,** and **truth-in-sentencing laws.** With the implementation of these reforms, the time served in prison by those convicted started increasing as a percentage of the sentence imposed. In 1993, the average portion of

---

Indeterminate sentencing
The sentencing of an offender, by a judge, to a minimum and a maximum amount of time in prison, with a parole board deciding how long the offender actually remains in prison

Determinate sentencing
The sentencing of an offender, by a judge, to a specific amount of time in prison depending on the crime

Mandatory minimum sentences
The shortest sentences offenders may receive upon conviction for certain offenses. The court has no authority to impose shorter sentences.

Habitual offender laws
Statutes imposing harsher sentences on offenders who previously have been sentenced for crimes

Truth-in-sentencing laws
Laws that give parole boards less authority to shorten sentences for good behavior by specifying the proportion of a sentence an offender must serve before becoming eligible for parole

a sentence that an offender spent in prison was 31.8 percent; that figure had increased to 46.7 percent by 2009.[113] The average length of an incarceration increased as well; offenders who were released from state prisons in 2009 served an average of almost 3 years behind bars, 9 months longer than served by those released in 1990.[114]

The most commonly adopted determinate sentencing reforms were mandatory minimum prison sentencing laws, adopted in some form by all 50 states and the District of Columbia.[115] These laws limited judicial discretion by requiring that individuals found guilty of specific crimes be incarcerated for no less than specified lengths of time. Such crimes may include drug possession or trafficking, drunk driving, and sexual offenses. The mandatory sentencing laws also may include "bump-ups" that take effect if certain acts enhanced the severity of the underlying crime—for instance, if weapons were involved or if the crime occurred near a school. If a crime involved the use of a deadly weapon, New Mexico requires an additional year for the first offense and three additional years for a second offense. The use of a firearm in the commission of a crime in Nevada requires a doubling of the sentence for the underlying crime. In Ohio, the use of a deadly weapon requires an additional term of 3 to 6 years.[116]

Habitual offender laws also became common among the states. These statutes impose more severe sentences for offenders who previously have been sentenced for crimes. By 1999, 24 states had enacted this kind of legislation, with California's "three strikes" law serving as a prototype. The California law states that if a defendant convicted of a felony has one prior conviction for a "serious" or "violent" felony, the sentence is doubled. Defendants convicted of a felony with two prior convictions for "serious" or "violent" felonies receive a life sentence without possibility of parole. Despite being severely criticized for its "unbending harshness," the law withstood constitutional challenges.[117] As originally written, according to Michael Romano, director of the Three Strikes Project, the law sentenced people to life in prison for relatively small crimes such as drug possession or petty theft. In 2004, a ballot proposition to revise the California law to impose a life term only if the third felony conviction is for a "serious or violent offense" failed. Supporters reintroduced the proposal for the 2012 elections, and this time it passed by a wide margin, leading to, within a year of the change, the release from prison of more than 1,000 inmates and an estimated savings for the state of $10 million in prison costs.[118] Convicted under Missouri's similar "prior and persistent drug offender" law, Jeff Mizanskey has been in jail since 1993, serving a life sentence for his third nonviolent marijuana possession charge.[119]

Another sentencing reform movement began in the 1990s as a reaction to the sometimes jarring disparity between the sentence handed down by a judge and the actual amount of time served in prison. These "truth-in-sentencing" laws reduce the amount of discretion parole boards have to shorten sentences for good behavior. They do this by specifying the proportions of sentences that offenders must serve before they may be considered for parole. The federal government encourages truth-in-sentencing laws by conditioning the states' receipt of federal prison construction funds on the requirement that certain violent offenders serve at least 85 percent of their sentences. With this carrot, almost all states and the District of Columbia adopted some form of truth-in-sentencing laws. Most, however, still have parole boards with some discretionary release authority and systems in which incarcerated felons can accumulate "good time" under specified formulas. Arkansas, Louisiana, Vermont, and Wyoming are among the many states that provide for a day of "good time" for each day—or less—served. North Dakota grants 5 days of "good time" for every month served.

These formulas also can be complicated by the accumulation of work or education credits. Some states, such as Illinois, have cut through the confusion by eliminating "good time" credits for certain serious offenses. Others have eliminated such credits altogether. Michigan eliminated "good time" for all felony offenses committed after December 2000, and the District of Columbia has not offered it since 1994.[120]

In the past few years, the pendulum appears to be swinging again on approaches to sentencing reform. In August 2013, Attorney General Eric

Holder released a new initiative outlining significant changes that, among other things, would end the use of mandatory lengthy sentences for nonviolent drug offenses in federal courts. "We of course," the report reads, "must remain tough on crime. But we must also be smart on crime."[121] This swing was necessitated in part by the considerable burden placed on the facilities and personnel of prison systems brought about by the reduction of judges' discretion and the increase in time spent by offenders in prison. Holder specifically sought to bring the federal government in line with "a growing movement at the state level to scrutinize the cost-effectiveness of our corrections system." In fact, a recent report by the Vera Institute of Justice shows that since 2000, at least 29 states have taken steps to roll back mandatory sentences and increase judicial discretion in sentencing. Most of these laws have been passed in the past 5 years alone, as states have increasingly recognized the consequences of the previous tough-on-crime sentencing policies. Indeed, states have been grappling with corrections costs that have roughly tripled in the past three decades and prisons that are dangerously overcrowded.

In California, atrocious conditions caused by prison overcrowding have become such a problem that the U.S. Supreme Court held in *Brown v. Plata* (2011) that California prisons violate the Eighth Amendment ban on cruel and unusual punishment. The Court ordered the release over the next several years of tens of thousands of prisoners to reduce overcrowding to 137.5 percent of capacity. For this reason, many nonviolent offenders find their prison terms greatly reduced. In November 2011, actress Lindsay Lohan served only 4 hours on a 3-day sentence for probation violations before being released to reduce overcrowding.

While few question that putting more people in prison for longer terms has played a role in the drop in crime rates since the 1990s, longer sentences have also been the primary drivers of increasing prison costs. In a 2012 report, the Pew Center on the States put the financial impact of longer prison stays at $10 billion for offenders released in 2009 alone; the report further suggested that a significant portion of nonviolent offenders could have served shorter stays with no

adverse impact on public safety.[124] In response to such research findings and increasingly tight state budgets, states are starting to take a step back on mandatory minimum sentencing. New York, for instance, has eliminated mandatory minimums for first- and second-time nonviolent drug offenses. In 2002, Michigan repealed most of its mandatory minimums for nonviolent drug offenders, a move that led to the closing of 20 prisons and has saved the state $41 million a year. According to the Vera Institute, by 2013, at least 17 states and the federal government had partially repealed or lessened the severity of mandatory sentences, and 13 had narrowed their sentence enhancements. In addition, most states are exploring sentencing options for their less serious offenders that are less severe than imprisonment but more severe than ordinary probation. The Department of Justice specifically praised Texas and Arkansas for reducing their prison populations by pioneering alternatives to incarceration for those convicted of low-level, nonviolent drug offenses.[125] By focusing on drug treatment and changes in parole policies, Texas was able to reduce its prison population by more than 5,000 inmates in 1 year. Another alternative to prison is house arrest. Offenders under house arrest are required to remain in their residences for the duration of their sentences. They often must wear electronic wrist or ankle bracelets that send continuous radio signals to verify their locations.

Many states rely on "intensive probation." This form of probation involves much closer supervision by parole officers, with smaller caseloads than the norm. In such a program, a parolee is typically required to hold a job, submit to urinalysis, pay restitution to victims, and perform community service. New legislation in Kentucky reserves prison for the most serious offenders and refocuses resources into such a community supervision program for a projected reduction in its prison population of more than 3,000 over the next decade and a savings of more than $400 million.[126] Other states have alleviated prison overcrowding by releasing prisoners to "halfway houses" that assist with their reintegration into the community. Young first-time offenders may be sentenced for short periods to "boot camps," where they are subjected to strict military-style discipline. Nonviolent offenders may be offered work release; weekend sentencing; alcohol, drug, or mental health treatment; or release subject to appearance at daily reporting centers.

How Courts Are Changing

How state courts are organized is not static or carved in stone. States constantly evaluate the practices and procedures of their criminal justice systems as they attempt to adapt to changing demographic, economic, and political conditions. This section discusses some reforms being adopted or at least being discussed in most states. Specialized courts to handle drug offenses or family matters are currently in vogue as ways to accommodate increasing caseloads and lower costs, as are attempts to streamline and speed up court dockets. Given the controversy surrounding judicial elections, particularly post–*Citizens United* (the Supreme Court decision that opened the door for unlimited campaign spending by super PACs), many states have not waited for major reforms to merit selection; instead, they have focused on modifying judicial elections to minimize the problems posed by the need for campaign contributions. Finally, this section addresses some of the pressures for court reform that stem from the lack of uniformity across the country and within individual states.

The Problem of Increasing Caseloads and Crowded Courts

Nationwide, violent crime rates are down. State courts, nonetheless, have found themselves on the front lines dealing with the results of societal problems such as substance abuse and family violence since the 1980s. From 1984 to 1999, the U.S. population grew by only 12 percent, but the number of juvenile criminal cases grew by 68 percent, and the number of domestic relations cases grew by 74 percent. Criminal cases, mostly misdemeanors, grew by 47 percent.[127]

In reaction to such growth, many states have created "problem-solving courts." These include community courts, domestic violence courts, mental health courts, and drug treatment courts. Their purpose is to deal decisively with low-level nonviolent crimes while reducing congestion in the general jurisdiction courts. The solutions often involve closely monitored treatment plans meant to stop the revolving door of recidivism, or relapse into criminal behavior. Drug courts, with their focus on judicially supervised treatment for nonviolent drug-addicted offenders, have been shown to contribute to the decline in violent crime and to save local and state governments millions of dollars annually from reduced incarceration rates. While it is difficult to determine the cost-effectiveness of drug courts, a definitive evaluation of a Portland, Oregon, court estimated that total savings from drug court participation were more than $5,000 per participant. With an annual caseload of 300 participants, the program saved the state more than $1.5 million per year.[128]

States also have been experimenting with integrated family courts. These courts, referred to as "one family/one judge" courts, adopt a holistic approach to all the issues that affect a single family in a single court system. Such integrated courts can address these issues more efficiently than can multiple courts, especially in cases where delays can leave children in foster-care limbo. Many individuals who appear in such family courts traditionally would have been forced, instead, to face multiple proceedings in different courts: assault charges in county court, custody disputes in family court, and divorce issues in yet another court. The current trend is to put all a family's problems before a single, informed judge to eliminate conflicting orders and multiple appearances. New York has estimated that its integrated domestic violence courts slashed the number of family court cases from more than 3,000 to fewer than 900 in its first 2 years, while reducing delay and duplication and increasing cost-effective case management.[129]

This increased focus on court administration and case management has not been confined to the criminal side of the court calendar. Until just a few

Recidivism
A return to, or relapse into, criminal behavior

years ago, crowded civil dockets and multiyear waiting periods were relatively common in many states. "Back in the 1980s, there was no incentive for an insurance company to settle a case for the first year," said Bill Sieben, who was then president of the Minnesota Trial Lawyers Association. "They knew the case wasn't even going to be nearing a trial for several years."[130] This is becoming less true as states focus on clearing their overcrowded and overly cumbersome civil dockets. Tom Phillips, former chief justice of the Texas Supreme Court, has attributed faster-clearing caseloads primarily to the rise of the managerial judge.[131] Most trial judges today may insist on strong case management systems, but a generation ago, when caseloads were smaller and more manageable, not many of them did.

In recent years, not content with merely handing down verdicts, forceful judges have seized control of their courts and made it clear that things will run according to their schedules, not at the convenience of lawyers who never seem quite ready to go to trial. "A very strong component of civil cases is, just set a trial date and the case will go away," said Kevin Burke, formerly the chief judge of the Hennepin County Court in Minnesota. "Left to their own devices, lawyers aren't necessarily going to manage it to a speedy resolution."[132]

State initiatives to speed up dockets, or court case schedules, have included an increased reliance on **alternative dispute resolution**. In certain types of cases, such resolution is now mandated, and lawyers are required to inform their clients about alternatives to standard court fights. These alternatives usually involve hashing things out in front of an expert mediator. Some courts have been creative in finding appropriately authoritative experts. Hennepin County courts, for instance, refer disputes involving dry cleaning—complaints about stained pants, torn dresses, and busted buttons—to a retired owner of a dry cleaning business for speedy resolution. An accountant may serve as mediator in the resolution of a financial dispute. These innovations increase the efficiency of the court system and free up trial judges for more complex cases.

Several states have experimented with the **rocket docket**, patterned after an innovation in a Virginia federal court. In essence, this fast-tracked docket imposes tight, unbending deadlines on lawyers for the handling of pretrial motions and briefs. In the Vermont Supreme Court, the rocket docket applies to cases that present no novel issue likely to add to the body of case law. Rather than all five justices sitting en banc to hear these cases, each month they split and rotate through a smaller and less cumbersome panel of three that is able to reach consensus more quickly. The panel releases its decisions on 99 percent of rocket-docket cases within 24 hours.

Rocket dockets are not always a panacea, however. Florida implemented the approach as thousands of home foreclosures began clogging the courts in late 2006. The foreclosure courts could clear 250 cases a day, each in a matter of minutes. But, although it represented a success for the state, attorneys found fault with the system. The few homeowners who attended the hearings had little time to be heard, and one review of 180 cases in Sarasota found that only one in four had complete paperwork. By late 2009, one judge found a way to slow the rapid-fire process, at least a bit—he gave any homeowners who showed up at the courthouse an additional 3 months to work to save their homes or to move.[133]

In Colorado, rapid population growth has led to mounting lawsuits, and courts increasingly have turned to **magistrates** to resolve less important cases. Often local officials or attorneys hired on contract, these magistrates have helped the state stay on top of an 85 percent increase in case filings despite only a 12 percent increase in the number of judges. A magistrate issues a preliminary decision that must then be upheld by a judge, but this is a formality in most

---

Alternative dispute resolution
A way to end a disagreement by means other than litigation. It usually involves the appointment of a mediator to preside over a meeting between the parties.

Rocket docket
Fast-tracked cases that often have limited, specific deadlines for specific court procedures

Magistrates
Local officials or attorneys granted limited judicial powers

cases. This modification is credited with enabling the state court system to handle routine cases efficiently and allowing more time for more complex cases, but some have complained to the Colorado Bar Association that this reliance on contract attorneys to serve as magistrates decreases the accountability of judges and does not yield sufficiently clear precedents to provide guidance to the attorneys who must practice before them.[134] Given these concerns, a task force on civil justice reform convened by then-governor Bill Ritter recommended that the state create additional district and county court judgeships to alleviate the caseload strain on the system.[135] A 2007 act created 43 new positions for judges across Colorado; however, in light of state revenue shortfalls, funding was provided for only 28.

The Reform of Judicial Selection

Nationally, 87 percent of all state judges face partisan, nonpartisan, or retention elections, or some mix of these.[136] As discussed earlier, the trend in recent years has been for these elections to become more and more like the elections for legislative and gubernatorial offices: loud, nasty, and expensive. Some fear that this will lead to a blurring of the distinction between the judicial and political branches of government and throw into question the independent decision making of the judiciary.

Indeed, two recent decisions from the U.S. Supreme Court may have brought politics closer than ever to the judicial election process. First, in *Republican Party v. White* (2002), a 5-to-4 majority ruled that the First Amendment does not allow the government "to prohibit candidates from communicating relevant information to voters during an election." This includes judicial candidates who wish to speak publicly about disputed legal matters. At the same time, the Court acknowledged the core responsibility of judges to "be willing to consider views that oppose [their] preconceptions, and remain open to persuasion when the issues arise in a pending case." Today, states that hold elections for judicial offices, such as Ohio, Pennsylvania, and Wisconsin, feature public debates among judicial candidates similar to those held for candidates for legislative office.

Then, in 2010, the Supreme Court ruled in the controversial *Citizens United v. Federal Election Commission* that laws placing limits on campaign spending by outside groups such as corporations and unions are unconstitutional. At the time, 24 states had laws banning independent expenditures in judicial elections; all were rendered moot by the holding in *Citizens United.* This ruling magnified the already growing debate about the impact of increased spending in judicial elections and the best method of judicial selection.

The major reform movement of the latter half of the 20th century involved the merit selection of judges, described previously. This movement initially was very successful, but, after roughly half the states adopted merit selection systems, it stalled. Since 1990, all the legislatures that have considered merit selection have rejected it. In the wake of *Citizens United,* a dozen state legislatures proposed moving away from selecting judges through popular elections, but none was successful. States seeking to adopt merit selection are confronted with both cultural and political obstacles. They face an ingrained cultural belief that elections are a critical part of our democracy that are not to be sacrificed without a fight. Combined with this is the political reality that in most states a change to merit selection would require the legislative supermajority and public approval necessary for a constitutional change.

Recognizing these barriers to the adoption of merit selection, reformers are focusing on improving popular judicial elections to minimize the threat they pose to judicial independence and impartiality. A 50-state survey commissioned by the California legislature reviewed state trends in the wake of *Citizens United* and the unprecedented level of interest-group activity in judicial elections.[137] In one trend, more than half the states have proposed more stringent reporting and disclosure of campaign contributions to increase the information available to voters. Iowa, for instance, passed a law requiring all political ads to run "paid for by" disclosures. Other states have focused on **recusal** and disqualification rules, which until recently have been very lenient, allowing judges to decide on their own whether

---

Recusal
The disqualification of a judge because of an actual or perceived bias or conflict of interest calling the judge's impartiality into question

States Under Stress

This Court Will Not Come to Order

In Birmingham, Alabama, domestic relations judge Suzanne Childers keeps a .38-caliber Smith & Wesson revolver under her bench. That and a can of pepper spray have served as protection for her courtroom since budget cuts eliminated two deputies' positions. Childers's story is extreme, but hers is not the only courtroom that has been left less safe as a result of the state and local fiscal crisis. In Massachusetts, open court officer positions were not filled between the end of 2008 and early 2010, and in Maine, metal detectors in courthouses go unstaffed. "It's a question of do you want to close courthouses and run [fewer] courthouses with full security? Or do you want to keep all your courthouses open and compromise on security?" said Mary Ann Lynch, a spokeswoman for Maine's court system.[a]

In many states, courts are opening later in the day, closing earlier, and shutting their doors entirely for several days per month. Kansas and Oregon have begun closing courts on Fridays, and one court in Georgia has stopped hearing civil matters altogether to focus time on critical criminal matters. In some parts of North Carolina and Ohio, cases have ground to a halt because the courts could not afford to buy more paper. With states facing severe budget shortfalls, almost every state court system is trying to get by with less. A survey conducted by the National Center for State Courts in 2011 estimated that at least 42 state court systems were facing cutbacks in their 2012 budgets, leading most courts to shrink staff and reduce hours.[b] Iowa, for instance, now has fewer employees in the judicial branch than it had 24 years ago, even though case filings in the state increased by 54 percent in the same period.[c] In California, budget cuts have led to the closing of so many courthouses that criminal defendants are increasingly pleading guilty to avoid making trips to courts that are now more than 200 miles away.[d]

The National Center for State Courts reported that the cuts would lead to increased backlogs in civil, criminal, and family court cases. Such backlogs lead inevitably to delays; in San Francisco, it can now "take up to a year from the time you first get a [traffic] ticket until you get a trial date," says Ann Donian, communications director for San Francisco Superior Court.[e]

Making matters worse, states expected that the very programs they had implemented to help alleviate backlogs—alternative dispute resolution and problem-solving courts—would themselves end up on the chopping block.

When budget cuts eliminated courtroom security guards, Jefferson County, Alabama, domestic court judge Suzanne Childers resorted to keeping a .38-caliber pistol under her desk during session for protection.

AP Photo/Bob Farley

---

[a]Quoted in Denise Lavoie, "Budget Cuts Force Tough Choices on Court Security," *Seattle Times,* January 10, 2010, http://seattletimes.nwsource.com/html/businesstechnology/2010758141_apuscourthousesecuritycuts.html.

[b]National Center for State Courts, "State Budget Cuts Threaten Public's Access to Courts," November 29, 2011.

[c]Alan Greenblatt, "Sue Me? Not a Chance This Year," NPR, April 12, 2012, http://www.npr.org/2012/04/12/150429441/sue-me-not-a-chance-this-year.

[d]Debra Cassens Weiss, "Make 200-Mile Trek to Courthouse or Plead Guilty? Some Defendants Choose the Latter," *ABA Journal,* July 9, 2014, http://www.abajournal.com/news/article/make_200-mile_trek_to_courthouse_or_plead_guilty_some_defendants_choose_the/.

[e]Quoted in Greenblatt, "Sue Me?"

they should recuse themselves from particular cases. Two kinds of recusal requirements have been proposed. Some require recusal if a case involves a contributor who has donated more than a specific cutoff amount to the judge's campaign, and other plans require that any recusal motion be heard by someone other than the challenged judge. Other states have focused on limiting permissible contributions to a judicial campaign. Minnesota, for instance, now limits contributions to $2,000 in election years. Some states have focused instead on limiting donations from certain donors. Florida proposed barring direct contributions by corporations, although, of course, *Citizens United* prevents the state from barring independent expenditures by corporations. New Mexico considered a flat ban on contributions and endorsements from lawyers.

Some states have focused their reform efforts on the dangers inherent in campaign financing and have experimented with public financing of judicial campaigns. They hope that this will reduce the potential of campaign contributions' influencing or creating the appearance of influencing outcomes. In 2002, North Carolina became the first state to provide full public financing of elections for appeals court and supreme court candidates who accept spending limits. All North Carolina's judicial candidates participated in the plan in 2010, and Judge Wanda Bryant stated, "I've run in two elections, one with the campaign finance reform and one without. I'll take 'with' any day, anytime, anywhere."[138] Despite its popularity and success, the North Carolina Campaign fund was repealed in 2013 as part of the state's massive election overhaul legislation. Passed in 2009, a similar law in Wisconsin had its funding cut shortly after passage. The experience of these states demonstrates one of the weaknesses of public financing of judicial elections: It leaves the independence of the judiciary dependent on continuing support from lawmakers, particularly if it relies on tax dollars.

Conclusion

State and local courts play a profound role in state governments. They resolve civil disputes and hand out justice in criminal cases. They also protect the citizens of their states from unconstitutional behavior by the political branches of government. Despite the importance of this role, or perhaps because of it, judicial systems differ tremendously from state to state. There are organizational differences from initial trial to final appeal. Judges in some states are elected by voters and in others are appointed by the governor. Such differences reflect each state's unique orientation toward the values of politics, law, judicial independence, and accountability.

The focus in this chapter has been on the players involved as a case works its way through the judicial system. In a criminal case, the elected prosecutor has tremendous freedom to decide which charges to bring against an accused criminal. Anyone charged with a crime has the right to an attorney, and the state must provide attorneys to those unable to afford their own. Usually the accused is represented by a public defender. If a plea bargain is not reached, the case goes to trial, and the fate of the accused rests in the hands of a panel of ordinary citizens who have been called to jury duty. Potential jurors are selected from a pool of individuals who may have done something as simple as paying a utility bill. This does not mean, however, that there is anything simple about a jury's task. Often, this group holds the future of another individual in its hands.

If an accused person is found guilty and sentenced to incarceration, the length of time the offender actually spends in jail depends a lot on how the values of rehabilitation, deterrence, and retribution have played out in a particular state's political system. Differences here can have an enormous impact. One state may try a nonviolent drug offender in a special drug court that focuses on treatment; another may try the same offense in a general trial court in which the judge has no choice under rigid minimum sentencing guidelines but to apply a sentence of lengthy incarceration.

None of the choices that states make in structuring their courts is fixed and unchanging. States are always responding to altered societal or political realities, experimenting with what works, and adapting to political movements. Some of the areas of reform and change examined in this chapter were triggered by the political rise of victims' rights movements, by the realities of changing caseloads, or by a perception that the selection of judges has become increasingly political.

The Latest Research

State courts, like state constitutions, are one of the aspects of government that remain relatively under-studied by political scientists. Although there is a long record of court studies, especially by law scholars, truly systematic research using the comparative method dates back only a few decades and is considerably less common than research examining state legislatures and executives. This is unfortunate because, as this chapter has explained in detail, state courts shoulder enormous responsibility for the administration of criminal and civil justice, and their decisions have far-reaching policy implications.

As this chapter makes clear, one of the perennial controversies in this branch revolves around how states can best select judges. Above we have given a flavor of the increasing politicization of the bench. Some champion this development as increasing democratic accountability, whereas others lament it as the courts losing their independence. Ultimately, which of these values is best to emphasize in selecting judges? Below we summarize some of the latest research on state courts. All these studies focus on the running theme of the impact of judicial elections, which are at the center of controversies regarding judicial selection.

• •

• **Bonneau, Chris, and Melinda Gann Hall.** *In Defense of Judicial Elections*. New York: Routledge, 2009.

An extended comparative examination of state supreme court elections, this book makes an empirical case that judicial elections have a number of benefits. The authors argue that judicial reforms aimed at depoliticizing the courts have had a number of potentially negative impacts. When states started moving toward Missouri Plan–type systems, judges' names were still showing up on ballots but without opponents or partisan labels. The net result was that voters knew virtually nothing about judicial candidates; the courts became so low profile, accountability was lost. This, however, did not make the judicial branch any

less political. The authors point to the justices of the U.S. Supreme Court as examples of judges who are appointed for life but clearly take on big political issues and decide them along roughly partisan lines. But at least the U.S. Supreme Court is high profile, and candidates for the Court are scrutinized closely in a relatively open process. There is little of this in a typical Missouri Plan setup. The authors find that competitive, partisan state supreme court elections do not just serve as accountability mechanisms; they confer more democratic legitimacy on the courts—voters trust the judges more because they know them and are more directly linked to them through the normal process of representative democracy.

• **Streb, Matthew, and Brian Frederick**. "When Money Cannot Encourage Participation: Campaign Spending and Rolloff in Low Visibility Judicial Elections." *Political Behavior* 33 (2011): 665–684.

One known way to increase voter turnout in legislative elections is to make those races partisan. Party labels give voters important information and a stake in the outcome of elections. Another known way to increase turnout in legislative races is to have competitive elections; competing candidates tend to spend more money and mobilize more voters. Do these same factors also increase turnout in judicial elections? This study takes a look at 172 appellate court elections between 2000 and 2008 and arrives at two key findings. First is a confirmation of the impact of partisan labels—if candidates for judicial office run on a party label, people are more likely to vote in that election. Second, and somewhat surprisingly, the authors find that campaign spending does not boost turnout significantly. In these low-visibility elections, even well-resourced candidates seem to struggle to get enough information to voters to make them confident in casting their ballots. The simplest and most basic piece of political information, partisanship, seems to be the important factor for increasing participation in judicial elections.

- **Canes-Wrone, Brandice, Tom S. Clark, and Jason P. Kelly**. "Judicial Selection and Death Penalty Decisions." *American Political Science Review* 108 (2014): 23–39.

These researchers examined an extensive data set of more than 12,000 state death penalty decisions between 1980 and 2006 in systems where judges are selected with partisan, nonpartisan, or retention elections, or by reappointment. Contrary to the conventional wisdom, they found that judges selected through non-partisan elections were significantly more influenced by popular support for the death penalty than were judges selected through partisan elections. This supports the "partisan signals" prediction that if party labels are missing from ballots, voters will rely more on information from the "new style" of expensive, policy-oriented judicial campaigns. Because of the extensive span of time covered by this study, it was able to highlight the changes brought by this new-style judicial campaigning and found that it has had a significant impact on judicial decision making. Judges facing retention elections, for instance, have become significantly less insulated from political pressures than they were previously.

- **Gibson, James, Jeffrey Gottfried, Michael DelliCarpini, and Kathleen Hall Jamieson**. "The Effects of Judicial Campaign Activity on the Legitimacy of the Courts: A Survey-Based Experiment." *Political Research Quarterly* 64 (2010): 545–558.

This study examines how citizens feel about the legitimacy of the Pennsylvania courts. The study's key contribution was a creative experiment in which different sets of people were randomly assigned to watch different kinds of campaign ads for judicial candidates, ranging from straightforward candidate endorsements by interest groups to negative attack ads. Overall, the authors found that elections have a positive impact—voters confer more legitimacy on the courts when judges periodically have to be approved by the voters. In contrast, some of the usual components of elections—that is, campaign ads—tend to decrease support for the courts. The positive overall impact of elections is larger than the negative impact of campaign ads, but one of the inferences that can be taken from this study is that while voters like the idea of judges being elected, they are less enthusiastic about judges actually acting like candidates for electoral office.

9

Chapter Review

Key Concepts

- activist judge (p. 280)
- alternative dispute resolution (p. 312)
- appeal (p. 283)
- assigned counsel (p. 303)
- bench trial (p. 284)
- civil cases (p. 283)
- contract attorneys (p. 303)
- court of first instance (p. 284)
- criminal cases (p. 283)

- determinate sentencing (p. 308)
- discretionary jurisdiction (p. 288)
- en banc (p. 289)
- felony (p. 302)
- general jurisdiction trial courts (p. 284)
- grand jury (p. 301)
- habitual offender laws (p. 308)
- indeterminate sentencing (p. 308)
- indictment (p. 301)

- intermediate appellate court (p. 283)
- jury nullification (p. 302)
- legislative overcriminalization (p. 301)
- liability (p. 305)
- limited or special jurisdiction trial courts (p. 284)
- magistrates (p. 312)
- mandatory jurisdiction (p. 288)
- mandatory minimum sentences (p. 308)
- merit selection (p. 291)
- misdemeanor (p. 302)
- panels (p. 289)
- plea bargain (p. 283)

- precedent (p. 283)
- prejudicial error (p. 287)
- prosecutor (p. 299)
- public defender (p. 300)
- pure appointive systems (p. 297)
- recidivism (p. 311)
- recusal (p. 313)
- retention election (p. 291)
- rocket docket (p. 312)
- settlement (p. 283)
- state supreme court (p. 283)
- trial court (p. 283)
- truth-in-sentencing laws (p. 308)

Suggested Websites

- **www.abanet.org.** Website of the American Bar Association, the largest voluntary professional association in the world, with a membership of more than 400,000.

- **www.ajs.org.** Website of the American Judicature Society, a nonpartisan organization with a national membership that works to maintain the independence and integrity of the courts, and increase public understanding of the justice system.

- **www.brennancenter.org.** Website of the Brennan Center for Justice, a nonpartisan center at New York University that conducts research and advocates on a range of judicial topics, including state court reform and campaign financing.

- **www.justiceatstake.org.** Website of the Justice at Stake campaign, a nonpartisan effort working to keep courts fair and impartial.

- **www.ncsc.org.** Website of the National Center for State Courts, an independent nonprofit organization that assists court officials to better serve the public.

- **www.ojp.usdoj.gov/bjs.** Website for the Bureau of Justice Statistics, which provides statistics and other information on a variety of justice system–related areas, including courts, sentencing, crimes, and victims.

$SAGE statestats

State Stats on Courts

*Explore and compare data on the states! Go to **edge.sagepub.com/ smithgreenblatt5e** to do these exercises.*

1. What is the per capita state and local government expenditure on corrections in your state? How does this compare with the national average? Do you think this amount is too little, too much, or just about right? Why?

2. Which state had the most authorized wiretaps in 2010? Which had the least? What factors may have contributed to this?

3. How many prisoners have been sentenced to death since 1973 versus how many have been executed in Texas? What about in Massachusetts? Why is there such a discrepancy?

4. Which state spends the most per capita on state-supported alcohol and drug prevention programs? Which state spends the least? What are the implications of these numbers for drug and alcohol–related arrests?

5. How much do trial court judges make in your state? Do you think that this is a fair salary considering the scope of the job? Would you raise or lower this amount? Are there some states where you think it is reasonable that for justices would make more money? Why?

6. What state has the highest occurrence of arrest-related deaths? Is this something we should be concerned about?

A swing in the park is not what usually springs to mind
when you mention bureaucracy. Public agencies,
however, come in many shapes and forms, including parks
and recreation departments. Public parks, believe it or not,
fit into the formal definition of a bureaucracy.

Bureaucracy

WHAT NOBODY WANTS BUT EVERYBODY NEEDS

- Why do we have so much bureaucracy?
- How good—or bad—a job does bureaucracy actually do?
- How does technology enable more efficient and effective bureaucracy?

Times were tough everywhere, but in 2012 the family of 13-year-old Nathan Duszynski had it tougher than most. His mom, Lynnette, suffers from epilepsy. Doug Johnson, his stepdad, was battling multiple sclerosis and lost his job as a paralegal. The family was barely squeezing by on $1,300 a month in disability benefits. Nathan figured he needed to do something to help support his folks.

The teenager had an entrepreneurial bent. He worked out a deal with a downtown sporting goods store in his hometown of Holland, Michigan. He would not only sell hot dogs in their parking lot but also get a sales commission for business he helped bring into the store. Nathan had a little money saved and invested it in a hot dog cart. This all sounds as though it's heading for a happy, heartwarming ending, right? Wrong. A villain was about to enter this story—a villain that shut down the hot dog stand, ending Nathan's nascent business before it really got started.

After reading this chapter, you will be able to

- identify the five organizational characteristics of a bureaucracy,
- explain how bureaucracy makes and implements policy,
- describe why rural states with smaller populations often have more bureaucracy than urban states with larger populations,
- relate the advantages and disadvantages of using a traditional bureaucracy to deliver public services,
- explain how the key organizational characteristics of bureaucracy help ensure neutral competence,
- compare the spoils system with the merit system,
- discuss how public labor unions and affirmative action have changed the merit system, and
- summarize new public management and attempts to incorporate private-sector management practices into the public sector.

Who was this villain? Who would stand in the way of a stand-up kid trying to do right by his family? Bureaucracy. Nathan's hot dog cart violated city zoning laws; a city bureaucrat spotted the violation and shut down the operation.[1] This is just one more example, as if we needed it, of everything that's wrong with government bureaucracy, right? Bureaucracy is overbearing, interfering, and a needless complication in citizens' lives, right?

Wrong. Nathan's story was picked up by the national media, which did indeed make City Hall out to be the villain. Yet if you take a little closer look, the bureaucracy was not quite the ogre it was made out to be. The city had a zoning regulation that banned food carts in the city's downtown area unless they were affiliated with a local restaurant. The reason was simple: ensuring fair competition. If you open up a hot dog restaurant downtown, you have to invest in property and pay taxes on it to fund everything from maintaining the roads to picking up the trash to paying a health inspector. Food carts do not bear those expenses; so the city regulates them downtown to ensure fair competition among food service providers.

The sorts of permits and regulations underlying the whole fuss are actually pretty reasonable. They are not designed to shut down people who are just trying to make a buck, let alone kids going above and beyond for their families. These sorts of rules are mostly about ensuring not just fair competition but public safety. Left unregulated, temporary vendors such as hot dog stands could operate anywhere at any time, creating the potential for traffic problems, neighborhood nuisances, and unscrupulous business practices. The "villainous" red tape that strangled Nathan's business highlights not bureaucracy's inherent silliness or uselessness but its paradoxical nature. On one hand, bureaucracy inevitably does mean rules and regulations that can be inconvenient at best and defy common sense at worst. Yet bureaucracy does not produce or enforce these rules just for fun. Like it or not, there are good reasons for the rules and good reasons for bureaucracy to enforce them.

Bureaucracy represents what is perhaps the political system's greatest contradiction. We do not particularly like it; yet we seem unable to live without it. Like a trip to the dentist, bureaucracy often is inconvenient, involves too much paperwork, and can result in a certain amount of pain. Ultimately, however, it turns out to be good for us.

This chapter explores this workhorse of the U.S. political system—the state and local bureaucracies that implement and manage most public programs and services. We discuss what bureaucracy is and why it plays such an important role. Most important, we use the comparative method to arrive at some explanations for why the American political system has so much bureaucracy when many citizens seem to value it so little.

What Is Bureaucracy?

For our purposes, **bureaucracy** consists of the public agencies and the public programs and services that these agencies implement and manage. Thus, **bureaucrats** are simply the employees of the public agencies. Most of these agencies—generically known as government bureaucracies—are located in the executive branches of state and local governments. Although these agencies vary greatly in terms of the programs and services they manage and deliver, the vast majority of them are organizationally similar. A specific set of organizational characteristics is associated with bureaucracy:

- *Division of labor.* Labor is divided according to task and function. Most large bureaucracies, for example, have separate technical, personnel, and financial specialists.
- *Hierarchy.* There is a clear vertical chain of command. Authority is concentrated at the top and flows down from superiors to subordinates.
- *Formal rules.* Bureaucracies are impartial rather than impulsive. They operate on the basis of rationally formulated guidelines and standardized operating procedures.
- *Maintenance of files and records.* Bureaucracies record their actions.
- *Professionalization.* Employees of bureaucratic agencies earn their jobs based on qualifications and merit.[2]

Virtually all large, complex organizations have these characteristics, not just government agencies. Wal-Mart and IBM have these characteristics and can thus be considered bureaucratic organizations, even though they are private companies. What separates a public bureaucracy such as the state department of motor vehicles or local school district from a private bureaucracy such as IBM is a difference in goals. In the end, what separates public bureaucracies from private bureaucracies is not what they are but what they do.

What Does Bureaucracy Do?

Public bureaucracies play two fundamental roles in state and local political systems. First, they are the key administrators in the democratic process. They are charged with carrying out the decisions and instructions of elected public officials. This is the central focus of the academic discipline of public administration. Their second role is more controversial. It involves trying to figure out exactly what those decisions and instructions are. Interpreting the will of elected officials can be a tricky a business; state laws and city ordinances can be complex and vague. The job of bureaucracy is to be specific and take action. Extracting specifics means that bureaucracies not only carry out the decisions of the democratic process; they also have a fairly important say in what those decisions are.

Bureaucracy as Policy Implementer

The first job of bureaucracy is to be the active manifestation of the will of the state. This is just a fancy way of saying that bureaucracy does what the government wants or needs done.[3] The whole process is known as **policy implementation**. Agencies implement policy by issuing grants and contracts, by enforcing laws and regulations, and by undertaking and managing programs directly. For example, when elected officials decide to build a new road, they do not adjourn the legislature to go survey land, drive bulldozers, and lay asphalt. A public agency negotiates to buy and survey the land. The agency either issues the contracts to build the road or takes on the job of construction using its own employees and

---

Bureaucracy
Public agencies and the programs and services they implement and manage

Bureaucrats
Employees of public agencies

Policy implementation
The process of translating the express wishes of government into action

Inside Erie County, New York, there are 3 cities, 25 towns, 15 villages, and almost 1,000 special fire, sewer, and lighting districts.

equipment. This is what makes private and public bureaucracy different: IBM and Wal-Mart exist to make money, whereas public agencies exist to serve the public interest by turning the decisions of elected officials into concrete reality.

The job of the bureaucracy is staggering in its scope and complexity. Citizens ask government for a lot: roads, education, health benefits, safe drinking water, parks, reliable power grids—the list is virtually endless. Governments respond by passing laws that create programs or policies, which then must be put into action and then managed or enforced. Governments respond, in other words, with bureaucracy. State and local bureaucracies manage not only state and local programs but federal programs as well. The federal government relies on state and local agencies to implement the vast majority of its welfare, education, and highway programs.[4]

> Citizens ask government for a lot: roads, education, health benefits, safe drinking water, parks, reliable power grids—the list is virtually endless. Governments respond by passing laws that create programs or policies, which then must be put into action and then managed or enforced.

In their roles as implementers, managers, and enforcers, state and local government bureaucracies shape the day-to-day lives of citizens more than does any other part of government.[5] The single largest form of bureaucracy in the United States is a fundamental part of virtually every community: public schools. Employing more than 3 million teachers, public schools serve about 50 million students and have a combined budget of $619 billion.[6]

Other public agencies regulate and set the licensing requirements for professions ranging from lawyer to bartender. Think of the need to ensure that professionals are qualified to deliver the services they sell. Look around at all the public libraries, swimming pools, and parks that offer recreational and educational opportunities at little or no cost. Think of programs for garbage removal, law enforcement, and fire protection. From the barber who is licensed to cut our hair to the street sweeper who is hired to clean the paths we walk, bureaucracy literally covers us from our heads to our toes.

Bureaucracy as Policymaker

The second fundamental role of the bureaucracy is more controversial than its job as the government's agent of implementation. Public bureaucracies not only help translate the will of a government into action but in many instances also actually determine the will of the government. Put bluntly, bureaucracies do not just implement policy; they also make it.[7] They do this in at least three ways.

The first way is through what has been called the power of the **street-level bureaucrat**. Street-level bureaucrats are the lower-level public employees who actually take the actions that represent government law or policy. In many cases, street-level bureaucrats have the discretion, or ability, to make choices about what actions they do or do not take. In making these choices, they are essentially making policy. For example, the street-level bureaucrat associated with speed limits is the traffic cop. This public employee is actually on the highway with a radar gun making certain that motorists abide by the speed limits specified by state or local law. The legislature may have passed a law setting a maximum highway speed of 65 miles per hour, but if the traffic cop decides to go after only those motorists doing 75 miles per hour or faster, what really is the speed limit that motorists must obey? And who has set that limit? Arguably, it is not the legislature but, rather, the street-level bureaucrat.[8]

Street-level bureaucrat
A lower-level public agency employee who actually takes the actions outlined in law or policy

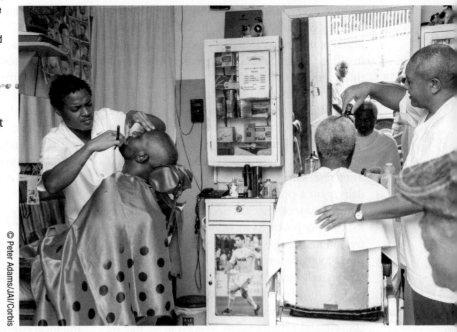

Cutting red tape? Most people do not associate barbers or beauticians with bureaucracy, yet most barbers and beauticians must be licensed and regulated by state and/or local government.

© Peter Adams/JAI/Corbis

This is not to suggest that street-level bureaucrats are power-hungry tyrants. In many cases, they have no choice but to make choices. On a road where speeding is common, it may be impossible to stop every lead foot putting pedal to the metal. Doesn't it make more sense to concentrate on the most flagrant offenders who pose the most risks to safety? Street-level bureaucrats have to balance the goals, laws, and regulations relevant to their agencies with the practical demands of the day-to-day situations they deal with. That often means making, not just implementing, policy.

The second way bureaucracies make policy is through rulemaking. **Rulemaking** is the process by which laws or mandates approved by legislatures are turned into detailed written instructions on what public agencies will or will not do.[9] Rules are necessary because most laws passed by legislatures express intention, but they do not specify the details of how to make that intention a reality. For example, the Nebraska state legislature created the Nebraska Games and Parks Commission to enforce a number of laws related to hunting, fishing, wildlife preservation, and boating. The details of enforcing those laws—such as setting permit fees, determining bag limits for particular types of fish, and designating no-wake zones on lakes—are rules established by the commission rather than laws passed by the legislature. This makes sense. The legislature would quickly become bogged down if it had to delve into the myriad details that must be addressed to put a public program into action. These details are left to individual agencies.

Once a rule is approved, it typically becomes

Rulemaking
The process of translating laws into written instructions on what public agencies will or will not do

part of the state's administrative code, which is the bureaucratic equivalent of state statutes. These rules have the force of law—violate them and you could face fines. Just ask anyone who has ever been caught fishing without a license. Given this, rules are not left to the discretion of the street-level bureaucrat. Most state agencies have to follow a well-defined process for making rules. This process includes seeking input from agency experts, holding public hearings, and, perhaps, listening to special interests. The Nebraska Games and Parks Commission is required to give public notice of any intention to create a rule and must hold a public hearing to allow interested parties to have their say. If this sounds a lot like the process of making laws in a legislature, that's because it is. Rulemaking is probably the most important political activity of bureaucracy. In effect, it is a large lawmaking operation that most citizens do not even know exists.

Finally, bureaucracies also contribute to policymaking directly by pursuing political agendas. Street-level discretion and rulemaking are *passive* policymaking in the sense that they involve bureaucrats' responding or not responding to something such as a speeding car or a newly signed bill. Yet bureaucracies and bureaucrats also take *active* roles in politics. They do so in a number of ways. At the state and local levels, the heads of many public agencies are elected. Such positions include everything from county sheriff to state attorney general. As elected officials, these agency heads often make campaign promises, and, once in office, they try to get their agencies to deliver on those promises.

The visibility and importance of these elected state and local agency heads increased with the rise of New Federalism. They now are widely recognized as critical players in the process of policy formulation, not just policy implementation.[10] Therefore, some agencies will be the tools used to deliver on a political agenda. It is also true that other bureaucrats, not just elected agency heads, try to influence policy. As we will see later in this chapter, unions are powerful political actors in many states, lobbying for better pay and benefits and getting actively involved in election campaigns.

The implementation and political roles of bureaucracy make it a particular target for citizen concern and, at times, scorn. It is easy to see that we need some bureaucracy. Somebody has to manage all those programs and services we want from government. Yet government bureaucracy has a terrible reputation for inefficiency, incompetence, and mismanagement.[11] Many question whether we have too much bureaucracy, and still others are concerned about the powerful political role of what are mostly unelected officials. Why do we have so much bureaucracy? How good a job does it really do? Could we get by with less of it? Is there a better way to run public programs and services? Is there too much bureaucracy and too little democracy in state and local government? These are reasonable questions that the comparative method can help answer.

What Is "Enough" Bureaucracy?

Most people believe that, whatever the merits of bureaucracy, there is too much bureaucracy in government and in our lives. Undeniably, state and local governments have a lot of bureaucracy. How much? Some insight into the size and scope of state and local agencies can be gleaned from Table 10-1, which lists the numbers of employees

TABLE 10-1

State and Local Government Employment by Function, 2012

Function	Total Individuals (in Thousands)	State Government (in Thousands)	Local Government (in Thousands)
Elementary and secondary education	8,037	67	7,970
Higher education	3,093	2,487	606
Hospitals	1,090	446	644
Police protection	1,017	107	909
Corrections	763	489	274
Streets and highways	560	240	320
Public welfare	549	247	303
Other government administration	429	62	366
Electric power and gas supply	94	4	90
Judicial and legal	456	183	273
Financial administration	432	173	258
Fire protection	429	0	429
Natural resources	208	159	49
Social insurance	83	83	0
State liquor stores	10	10	0
Other	514	201	313
All functions	19,809	5,329	14,480

Source: U.S. Department of Commerce, *Statistical Abstract of the United States, 2012* (Washington, DC: U.S. Census Bureau, 2012).

on state and local government payrolls by function. Combined, state and local governments have more than 19 million full-time and part-time employees. Most of these—about 14 million—are employees of local rather than state governments.[12] Whether at the local or state level, the vast majority of these individuals work in what we would recognize as a bureaucracy.

The numbers contained in Table 10-1 confirm that there are a lot of state and local bureaucrats, but numbers alone give little insight into whether there is too much or too little bureaucracy. In reality, the size of the bureaucracy and the extent of its role in the day-to-day life of any given individual vary from state to state and locality to locality for two main reasons. First, in each locality, citizens make different kinds of demands on each state and local government agency. Some localities need more of one particular resource, whereas others need less. In Eden Prairie, Minnesota, the public demands more cross-country ski trails, and in Yuma, Arizona, the citizens need more public swimming pools. As a result, the size and role of the public sector can vary significantly from place to place—more demand equals more bureaucracy.

Second, there is no universally agreed-on yard-stick for measuring what constitutes a "reasonably" sized bureaucracy. Where one person sees a bloated public sector overregulating citizens' lives, a second sees the same set of agencies providing important public goods and services. At the very least, to compare the size of bureaucracy across states and localities, we need to explore not just the total number of public employees but also the size of a specific public sector relative to the size of the public it serves. Table 10-2 shows one way to do this. It lists the states with the five largest and the five smallest bureaucracies as measured by the number of government employees for every 10,000 citizens.

By this measure, it looks as though more urban and populous states such as California, Pennsylvania, and Michigan have smaller bureaucracies than do more rural, less populous states such as Alaska, Nebraska, and Wyoming. How can this be? Why on earth would Wyoming have more bureaucracy than Illinois? The answer is actually pretty simple. Fewer people do not necessarily mean less demand on the government. Even the most rural state still needs an educational system, roads, police and fire protection, as well as social welfare agencies to help

TABLE 10-2

States With the Most and the Least Bureaucracy by Number of Employees

State	State and Local Employees (per 10,000 Citizens)
Top Five	
Wyoming	893
Alaska	761
Vermont	677
Kansas	669
Nebraska	652
Bottom Five	
Pennsylvania	458
California	457
Michigan	455
Arizona	434
Nevada	374

Source: SAGE State Stats database, http://library.cqpress.com/statestats/document.php?id=series-2631; "States With Most Governing Employees: Per Capita Rates by Job Type," *Governing*, 2012, http://www.governing.com/gov-data/public-workforce-salaries/states-most-government-workers-public-employees-by-job-type.html.

administer programs such as Medicaid. These are all labor-intensive propositions. Indeed, they may be even more labor-intensive in rural states. To understand why, consider education. All states are required to support and maintain public elementary and secondary education systems, but in a rural state with a widely dispersed population, an educational system either has to build lots of small schools or figure out a way to transport lots of students over considerable distances to a smaller number of large schools. In contrast, more urban, densely populated states can take advantage of the economies of scale that come with centralized locations. Basically, less bureaucracy is needed where the citizens being served are close by.

The same tale is told when we use expenditures—in this case, the amount of money states spent for services—to measure the size of bureaucracy. Alaska and Wyoming are both among the five states with the largest bureaucracies as measured by both number of employees and per capita expenditure. (See Table 10-3.)

TABLE 10-3

States With the Most and the Least Bureaucracy by Expenditures

State	State and Local Expenditures (Dollars Per Capita)
Top Five	
Alaska	20,292
New York	15,400
Wyoming	15,313
California	12,143
Massachusetts	11,463
Bottom Five	
Oklahoma	8,117
Arkansas	8,089
Indiana	8,085
Georgia	7,959
Idaho	7,619

Source: SAGE State Stats database, http://library.cqpress.com/statestats/document.php?id=series-2303.

Expenditures and employees tell us something about the size of the bureaucracy, but they do not tell us much about its influence or power over the daily lives of citizens. An undermanned bureaucracy with a small budget still can have considerable impact on the interests of an individual. If you have ever spent time in a university financial aid office, you probably already understand the point here—when people complain about bureaucracy being too big, they often mean the red tape and rules that come with it, not its budget or payroll. For the number of forms you fill out at the financial aid office, you may feel that the bureaucracy owes you a free meal, but there is only so much money in the pot. It is very easy to recognize this sort of thing as a central part of bureaucracy; it is very hard to measure it objectively. The lack of good measures of "red tape" or "rules" makes drawing comparisons difficult. If there are no comparative measures, it is harder to use the comparative method to help show why some bureaucracies have more influence than others.

Despite this, there is little doubt that public bureaucracies play a more powerful role in the day-to-day lives of citizens in large urban areas than they do in less populous rural areas. Why? It is not because bureaucracy is more power hungry in cities but, rather, because more-concentrated populations require more rules. Building codes are more critical in urban areas because of the associated fire-safety and health risks—a problem with one building can pose risks for those working or living in the surrounding buildings. Building regulations thus tend to be more detailed, and the enforcement of these rules tends to be a higher priority in urban than in rural areas. In this sense, urban areas do have more bureaucracy than rural areas.

Measuring Bureaucratic Effectiveness: It Does a Better Job Than You Think

So far, our application of the comparative method has given us a sense of how big bureaucracy is and why it is so big—because characteristics such as urbanization and geography result in different demands being placed on government. These different demands translate into public agencies of different sizes and with varying levels of involvement in our day-to-day lives. What the comparative method has not told us is how good (or bad) of a job public agencies do. The widespread belief is that such agencies are, at best, mediocre managers of public programs and services.[13] Although this negative stereotype is held by many, for the most part it is wrong. Public agencies, as it turns out, are very good at what they do.

How good? Well, in many cases, they are at least as good as, if not better than, their private-sector counterparts. The assumption is that the private sector is more efficient and more effective than the public sector, but numerous studies have found that this assumption is based more on stereotypes than on facts.[14] For example, **contracting out** is a term used to describe having private or nonprofit organizations rather than government agencies deliver public services. The basic idea is that rather than

---

Contracting out
Government hiring of private or nonprofit organizations to deliver public goods or services

using an expensive and inefficient bureaucracy to provide a public good or service, the job is awarded to an outside organization through a competitive bidding process. The bidder that can do the best job with the least charge to the taxpayer gets the business, and government reaps the efficiency benefits of the market. At least, that's the theory. The record of contracting out in practice is much more mixed. While it certainly works well in some circumstances, it is far from being a magic bullet.

For example, faced with rising health care costs and a reluctance to increase student fees on top of rising tuition bills, a number of colleges and universities have experimented with contracting out student health care services. These attempts to privatize student health care services have met with very mixed success. The University of Northern Colorado outsourced its student health center in 2003, but the large health care provider that took over the operation asked to be released from its contract a few years later when it found it couldn't make a profit. Auburn University outsourced its student health center in 1999, but one of the private companies that won the contract went bust in 2001. These teething problems, though, were overcome, and the health center privatization is generally recognized as a success at Auburn. Not so at the University of Denver, where an experiment with privatization was largely a failure. The health care company that took over the university's student health care services seemed to focus too much on its bottom line and too little on the outreach services central to the original health center's mission. The university brought its health center back in-house and funded it with student fees.[15]

Some of the problems associated with contracting out often include a loss of accountability and transparency, difficulty in specifying contracts to cover all possible contingencies (e.g., who bears the costs if bad weather delays road construction), and a clash of public service versus make-a-profit value systems. All this can create conflict between private contractors and governments, conflict that can be messy, litigious, and expensive. After experimenting with contracting out, some governments—like the University of Denver—end up deciding that it causes more headaches than it's worth. This is a pretty common experience; local governments that

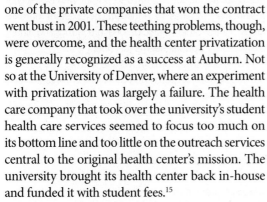

contract out services frequently bring those services back in-house after a year or two.[16] A public bureaucracy might be old-fashioned, but it generally can be counted on not just to get the job done but also to be responsive to its elected bosses rather than its profit–loss statement.

Although popularly viewed as inferior to their private-sector counterparts, public agencies actually come out equal to or better than the private sector on a wide range of employee characteristics used to identify effective organizations. Public- and private-sector employees are roughly equal in terms of their job motivation, their work habits, and their overall competence. Compared with private-sector employees, however, public-sector employees tend to have higher levels of education, express a greater commitment to civic duty and public service, abide by more stringent codes of ethical behavior, and are more committed to helping other people.[17] Various studies have shown that over the past 30 years state and local agencies have become more productive and more professional, and they have done so during an era when they have shouldered an increasing share of the burden for delivering programs and services from the federal government.[18]

There is wide variation between and within the states when it comes to how well public bureaucracies are managed. Good management has an enormous impact on the capacities and effectiveness of programs and agencies. States that engage in prudent, long-range fiscal planning are better positioned to deal with economic downturns, and they generally can deliver programs more efficiently. States that do a better job of attracting qualified employees with a strong commitment to public service almost certainly are going to be rewarded with more effective public agencies. States that make training their employees a priority are likely to enjoy similar benefits. The bottom line is that well-managed public agencies lower costs and improve results, whereas the reverse is true for badly managed agencies.[19]

So how can we tell if agencies are being well managed or not? This is not exactly clear. During the past decade or two, there have been numerous efforts to come up with some at least semiobjective performance evaluations of public-sector bureaucracies. These efforts, however, are rarely

Policy in Practice

Privatizing an Entire City

Measured by the size of its workforce, the city of Weston, Florida, has tripled the size of its bureaucracy in the past decade. Still, nobody complained. Actually, it's doubtful whether many residents even noticed. The city of 65,000 had three employees in 2007. These days it has nine.

How can a city of 65,000 have only nine public employees? Easy. Rather than having public agencies provide public services, Weston hires out the job to private contractors. The city is basically set up to answer the question: What if there were no public bureaucracy?

If Weston is anything to judge by, the answer to that question is that there will be a big private bureaucracy. Weston may employ only nine people, but running the city also requires nearly 300 full-time "dedicated staff." These all work in city facilities and act like city employees, but they work for private contractors. The big advantage of this setup is that city managers do not have to worry about labor issues. There are no salary disputes with unions, and layoffs are the contractors' problem, not the city's.

From the day-to-day perspective of the citizen, though, there's not much difference. Weston still has a pretty big bureaucracy (roughly a full-time staffer for every 215 residents), and the funds to pay for that bureaucracy still come out of the taxpayer's pocket. The difference is that the money goes to a middleman—the contractor—to purchase a service, rather than going directly toward hiring a public employee to provide that service.

Only a handful of cities have privatized their bureaucracies to the same extent as Weston. Sandy Springs, Georgia, a suburb of Atlanta, is one of them. Sandy Springs is a municipality with 94,000 residents and seven employees at city hall. Actually, that's not quite true. It doesn't have a city hall; the government of Sandy Springs operates out of an office complex in an industrial park. Sandy Springs has contracted out—effectively privatized—just about every public service, program, and facility possible, and that includes its center of operations.

You name the program or service—business licensing, building permits, trash collection—and it's handled not by a public bureaucracy but by a private company hired to do the job. The municipal court's administrative staff all work for a private company, and the judge is a private-practice attorney who temps as a judge for a hundred bucks an hour.

Like Weston, Sandy Springs's decision to privatize big chunks of the public sector means it escapes some big traditional costs associated with old-fashioned bureaucracies. The city has no pension obligations, for example, and it doesn't have to bother with building or maintaining facilities to house its nonexistent bureaucrats. While other municipalities are struggling financially, Sandy Springs seems just fine.

While effectively turning over the running of a city to a set of corporations seems to have worked in Weston and Sandy Springs, it is not without controversy. For example, Sandy Springs is a relatively affluent and white area within Fulton County, which tends to be poorer and has a high minority population. When Sandy Springs incorporated in 2005, some saw the town as basically seceding from Fulton County to ensure that local tax revenues were not spent in more needy areas of the county. There are losers to the privatization as well as winners; the incorporation of Sandy Springs has cost Fulton County revenues, which means that traditional public agencies that serve needier areas do so with fewer resources.

Sources: Ryan Holeywell, "How Weston, Florida, a City of 65,000, Gets By on 9 Employees," *Governing*, May 14, 2012, http://www.governing.com/blogs/view/How-.html; David Segal, "A Georgia Town Takes the People's Business Private," *New York Times*, June 23, 2012.

comprehensive and comparative; in other words, they tend to focus on agencies in one city or one state. While states and localities have expended enormous effort and energy toward creating performance evaluation metrics, it is not at all clear that they have done much good. Performance measures generally indicate that public bureaucracies are doing reasonably good jobs. More worrying is the increasing evidence that performance measures don't seem to change much, even when they do highlight problems. A big claim of the performance measurement movement was that these metrics would help create a virtuous circle; they would clarify agency objectives and measure performance on those objectives, and the resulting data could be used to improve management practices to improve performance, thus resulting in more effective and efficient goal achievement. One recent study on performance evaluations at the municipal level gloomily concluded that, despite all the associated effort and expense, we know little about the impact, if any, of all the efforts to "grade" public agencies and "we may need to ask ourselves how much it matters how much effort should continue to be placed in promoting it."[20]

This lesson may be reflected in what was probably the biggest and truly comprehensive evaluation effort for state-level public agencies. The idea behind the Government Performance Project (GPP) was to hold state governments publicly accountable for the quality of management within their jurisdictions and prod them into making improvements.[21] Starting in 1999, the GPP did this by researching management practices and performance in four areas (money, people, infrastructure, and information) and issuing states grades for performance in each area. The GPP was not around long enough to have any lasting impact. The last grades were issued in 2008—just before the Great Recession hit and shook up the budgets, objectives, and management practices of public agencies in ways the GPP never did.

Is There a Better Way to Run Public Programs and Services?

Looking at bureaucracy comparatively, we learn how big it really is, we see why it is so big, and we might even get some insight into how well it performs. But is a traditional bureaucracy really the best way to run public programs and services? Do we really need less democracy and more bureaucracy? Do we really need 19 million people on the state and local government payrolls? The short answer is no. As we have already discussed, public services and programs could be contracted out through a competitive bidding process and delivered by the private sector. Public agencies could be staffed and run by political party loyalists or special-interest supporters. Things could be done differently. Before we abandon the traditional public bureaucracy, however, it is worth considering why public agencies are so, well, bureaucratic.

Remember the key characteristics of bureaucratic organizations listed earlier? (Here's a reminder: division of labor, hierarchy, formal rules, keeping records, and professionalization.) These turn out to be important advantages when it comes to running public programs and services. For one thing, bureaucracies tend to be impartial because they operate using formal rules, not partisan preference, bribes, or arbitrary judgment. If you need some form of license or permit, if your shop is subject to some form of environmental or business regulation, or if you are trying to receive benefits from a public program, it does not matter to the bureaucracy if you are rich or poor, liberal or conservative, an influential high roller or an average citizen. What matters to the bureaucracy are the rules that define the application process, eligibility, and delivery of the necessary service or program. Following bureaucratic rules can be maddening, but these rules do help ensure that public agencies are more or less impartial.

The bureaucratic characteristics of hierarchy and record keeping help hold public agencies accountable. Public agencies are expected to be accountable for their actions. They have to justify to legislatures, executives, the courts, and citizens why they do what they do.[22] An action at a lower level of bureaucracy almost always can be appealed to a higher level. Students at most colleges and universities, for example, can appeal their grades. In such appeals, the bureaucrat responsible for issuing the grade—the instructor—is expected to justify to the appeals board and the dean why the grade represents a fair and reasonable application of the rules of the class and the grading policies of the university. Setting rules, requiring records, and setting up a clear chain of authority all help ensure that bureaucrats and bureaucracies do not exceed their authority or act unfairly. If they do, these same factors provide a means for holding the bureaucrat or bureaucracy accountable.

Professionalization is another bureaucratic characteristic that is desirable in public agencies because it promotes competence and expertise. To get a job in most state and local bureaucracies, what you know is more important than who you know. Getting a job as a professor at a state university requires a specific set of professional qualifications. The same is true for an elementary school teacher, an accountant at the Department of Revenue, or a subway operator. Of course, setting and enforcing such qualifications as the basis for employment and promotion means another set of rules and regulations. These qualifications also help ensure that merit—rather than partisan loyalty, family connections, or political influence—is the basis for an individual's gaining public-sector employment.

The great irony of public bureaucracy is that the very characteristics that help ensure neutrality, fairness, and accountability also produce the things people dislike about bureaucracy: red tape and inefficiency. Formal rules help guarantee equity and fairness, but—as anyone who has spent time filling out forms and waiting in line can attest—they can be a pain. Enforcing rules, or "going by the book," may mean bureaucracy is fair, but it is not particularly flexible. Treating everyone the same is an advantage from an equity standpoint, but the fact is that not everyone *is* the same. Surely there are ways to make bureaucracy more responsive to the individual? Well, yes, there are. But the history of bureaucratic reform in the United States suggests that the cures are often worse than the problem. Although going through this history is not a particularly comparative exercise, it is a necessary step toward understanding why bureaucracy is the way it is.

State Bureaucracy: From Patronage to Professionalism

Public agencies have undergone a remarkably radical transformation during the past century.

They have become more professionalized, more organized, and more able to shoulder a large share of the political system's responsibilities.

For much of the early history of the United States, there was little in the way of state and local bureaucracy. State and local government functions that we now take for granted, such as public schools, libraries, and fire protection, were left largely to the private sector. In most cases, this meant they did not exist at all or were available only to those who could afford them. Public education is the single largest public program undertaken by state and local governments. Yet public education in the contemporary sense did not exist until the last half of the 19th century, roughly 100 years after the nation's founding. As the nation grew, however, so did the demands on government. The country needed to build roads, regulate commerce, clean the streets, and curtail crime. And taxes had to be collected to make all this happen. There was no centralized plan to expand public bureaucracy—it evolved in fits and starts as governments took on the jobs citizens wanted done.

At the federal level, staffing the bureaucracy was initially a job for which only the educated elite were considered qualified. This example often was followed at the state and local levels. Public service was seen as an obligation of the aristocratic class of a community or state. This "gentlemen's" system of administration was swept away following the election of Andrew Jackson to the presidency in 1828.

Jackson believed in the **spoils system**—that is, the right of an electoral winner to control who worked for the government. The intent was to democratize government and make it more accountable by having regular citizens who supported the electoral winners run the government agencies. This process of giving government jobs to partisan loyalists is called **patronage**.

Instead of producing a more democratic bureaucracy, the spoils system and patronage invited corruption. Following Jackson's example,

---

Professionalization
The rewarding of jobs in a bureaucratic agency based on applicants' specific qualifications and merit

Spoils system
A system under which an electoral winner has the right to decide who works for public agencies

Patronage
The process of giving government jobs to partisan loyalists

Political machines were powerful organizations that dominated many state and local governments for parts of the 19th and 20th centuries. Their power was based on their ability to control government jobs, awarding these positions to supporters or, as this cartoon suggests, to the highest bidder.

● ○ ●○ ● ○ ●○ ○ ○ ●○ ○ ● ○ ●○ ○ ●○ ● ○ ●○ (

Library of Congress

electoral winners used positions in the administrative arms of many state and local governments as ways to pay off political favors or to reward partisan loyalty. Perhaps the most famous examples are the big-city political machines that flourished well into the 20th century and produced some of the most colorful characters ever to wield power in state and local politics. As discussed in Chapter 6, political or party machines were organizations headed by party committees or party bosses. A committee or boss led a subset of ward or precinct leaders whose job it was to make sure voters in their districts supported the machine-endorsed candidates. Supporters of the machine were, in turn, rewarded with government jobs and contracts. They also were often expected to contribute a set percentage of their salaries to the machine.[23] This created a well-regulated cycle, or machine—votes in one end, power and patronage out the other.

Political machines dominated politics in many urban areas and even whole states in the 19th and early 20th centuries. They produced some of the most fascinating characters in U.S. political history: Boss Tweed of New York, Tom Pendergast of Kansas City, and Gene Talmadge of Georgia, to name just a few. These men wielded enormous power, aided in no small part by their ability to dole out government jobs and contracts. Some machines survived well into the 20th century. Mayor Richard Daley of Chicago ran what many recognize as a political machine well into the 1960s.

While the machines made for lively politics and brought almost unlimited power to their leaders, they were often corrupt. Machine politics meant

that getting a government job was based on whom you knew rather than what you knew. Job security lasted only as long as you kept in your political patron's good graces or until the next election. Understandably, then, there was a tremendous incentive to make the most of a government position. Kickbacks and bribery inevitably made their way into many state and local agencies.

The founders of the modern conception of government bureaucracy were the progressive reformers of the late 19th and early 20th centuries. They wanted a lasting solution to the gross dishonesty and inefficiency they saw in public administration. Toward this end, these reformers created a new philosophy. At its center was the idea that the administrative side of government needed to be more insulated from the political arena.[24] Reformers promoted **neutral competence**, the idea that public agencies should be the impartial implementers of democratic decisions, not partisan extensions of whoever happened to win the election.

To achieve these ends, progressive reformers began to push for public agencies to adopt the formal characteristics of bureaucratic organizations.

Neutral competence
The idea that public agencies should be the impartial implementers of democratic decisions

This was accomplished in no small part through lobbying for the merit system as an alternative to the spoils system. In a **merit system**, jobs and promotions are awarded on the basis of technical qualifications and demonstrated ability instead of given out as rewards for political loyalty. A merit system also makes it harder for public employees to be dismissed without due cause. But this does not mean a guaranteed job. The idea is to create a system within which public employees can be fired only for failing to do their jobs and not because they missed a payment to a political boss. The overall goal was to make government bureaucracies less political and more professional.

The federal government shifted from the spoils system to the merit system in 1883 with the passage of the Pendleton Act. The main features of this merit system were (1) competitive examination requirements for federal jobs, (2) security from political dismissals (i.e., people could not be fired simply because they belonged to the "wrong" party or supported the "wrong" candidate), and (3) protection from being coerced into political activities (so workers were no longer expected or required to contribute a portion of their salaries to a political party or candidate). The basic principles of merit systems have since been expanded to include equal pay for equal work; recruitment, hiring, and promotion without regard to race, creed, national origin, religion, marital status, age, or disability; and protection from reprisals for lawful disclosure of lawbreaking, mismanagement, abuse of authority, or practices that endanger public health—called whistle-blower laws.

States and localities once again followed the example of the federal government and began shifting from spoils systems to merit systems. New York State was the first to do so, adopting a merit system in the same year that the Pendleton Act became law. In 1935, the federal Social Security Act made merit systems a requirement for related state agencies if they wished to receive federal grants. This stimulated another wave of merit-based reforms of state and local bureaucracies. By 1949, nearly half the states had created merit-based civil service systems. Fifty years later, virtually all states and many municipalities had adopted merit systems. All this helped professionalize state and local bureaucracies, and turned what had been sinkholes of patronage and corruption or marginally competent old-boy networks into effective instruments of democratic policymaking.

Politics and the Merit System

Although using merit as the basis for public bureaucracy has effectively created agencies that are competent and professional, it has its drawbacks. Remember the two key roles of the bureaucracy, policy implementation and policymaking? Merit systems have positive and negative implications for both.

In some ways, merit-based bureaucracy is a victim of its own success. The whole idea of shifting to a merit system was to insulate public agencies and their employees from undue political influence. We want bureaucrats to work for the public interest, not for the interests of party bosses. We want bureaucrats to apply rules neutrally, not to interpret them through the lens of partisan prejudices. To a remarkable extent, merit systems have had exactly that effect. Rules are rules, and bureaucracies more or less competently and impartially enforce them regardless of which party controls the legislature or who sits in the governor's mansion. The merit system has undoubtedly been an enormous positive for the policy implementation role of bureaucracy.

The impact of merit systems on the policymaking role of bureaucracy is more open for debate. Merit systems did not eliminate the political role of the bureaucracy; they merely changed it. Under the spoils system, bureaucracy was an agent of a particular boss, party, or political agenda, and it favored the supporters of electoral winners. The merit system cut the connection between the ballot box and the bureaucracy. Distancing bureaucracy from elections, however, can make it less accountable to the democratic process—a big concern if bureaucracy is policymaker as well as policy implementer.

Merit system

A system used in public agencies in which employment and promotions are based on qualifications and demonstrated ability; such a system blends very well with the organizational characteristics of bureaucracy

Once distanced from the ballot box, public agencies and public employees discovered their own political interests and began to pursue them with vigor. Organized interests outside the bureaucracy also began to realize that being able to influence lawmaking and, especially, rulemaking offered enormous political opportunities. All you have to do is get your favored policy written into the rules, and bureaucracy will enforce it well beyond the next election. These sorts of developments raise serious questions about the drawbacks of the merit system. As examples of how these concerns play out in state and local agencies, let us consider two issues: public labor unions and affirmative action.

Public Labor Unions

Public-sector labor unions are a relatively new political force. Unions were almost exclusively a private-sector phenomenon until the 1960s. This changed in 1962 when President John F. Kennedy issued an executive order that recognized the right of federal employees to join unions and required federal agencies to recognize those unions. The 1960s and 1970s saw a considerable expansion in the number of state and local employees joining unions. Today, roughly 3 to 4 times as many public-sector as private-sector workers belong to unions.[25]

The reasons for the expansion in public-sector union membership are not hard to fathom. For much of their history, public employees received lower wages than did their private-sector counterparts. Public employees also had limited input with regard to personnel decisions. Despite the merit system, many still saw favoritism and old-boy networks as having too much influence in pay and promotion decisions. Public-sector labor unions pushed for the right to engage in **collective bargaining**, a process in which representatives of labor and management meet to negotiate pay and benefits, job responsibilities, and working conditions. The

Collective bargaining
A process in which representatives of labor and management meet to negotiate pay and benefits, job responsibilities, and working conditions

vast majority of states allow at least some public unions to bargain collectively.

What should not be missed here is that the outcomes of collective bargaining are important policy decisions. They are decisions in which the voter—and sometimes the legislator—has little say. Negotiations about pay and benefits for public employees are, in a very real sense, negotiations about taxes. A raise won by a public employee represents a claim on the taxpayer's pocketbook. And it is a claim that is worked out not in an open democratic process but often in closed-door negotiations.

And it is not just money. Collective bargaining agreements can result in fairly complex rules about what public employees are and are not expected to do. Such rules reduce both the flexibility of agency managers, who are constrained from redirecting personnel from their assigned jobs, and the responsiveness of bureaucracy to legislatures and elected executives.

Labor unions have given public employees more than just collective bargaining muscle; they also have started to do some heavy lifting in electoral politics. Unions that are able to deliver their members' votes can have a powerful say in who holds office. Understandably, people seeking public office pay attention to the policy preferences of public-sector unions. By raising money, mobilizing voters, and even running independent campaigns, unions exercise considerable political clout. Consider the Wisconsin Education Association Council (WEAC). This teachers union, long recognized as an important political actor in the state, has a well-thought-out set of legislative goals and supports candidates accordingly.[26] It also spends its money strategically. In 2011, a series of state senate recall elections was triggered in part by bitter fights over proposed reforms to the state's collective bargaining laws (see discussion below). In that election cycle, WEAC spent roughly half a million dollars on state political campaigns.[27] That made the union the biggest-spending political action committee in state politics.

The boots-on-the-ground political organization combined with big bucks translates into considerable political clout for public labor unions, enough to shape how the merit system actually works. A basic principle of the merit system is that competence is supposed to be rewarded. Expertise and job performance are supposed to be the bases of promotion and pay increases. In contrast, unions tend to advocate seniority—the length of time spent in a position—as the basis for promotions and pay increases. Public employees with more experience may—and often do—deserve such rewards, but it is not always the most senior employee who is the most productive or who contributes the most to an agency's success. Even in the absence of unions, seniority plays a considerable role in the pay and benefits of public employees. This is much to the chagrin of critics who view civil service protections as failing the public interest. For example, some critics view tenure at colleges and universities as a system that rewards laziness and allows "deadwood"—unproductive faculty members—to collect healthy paychecks.[28]

In recent years there have been several efforts to curtail the power of public unions, especially their rights to collective bargaining. The two most high-profile efforts to take on public unions were spearheaded by Scott Walker and John Kasich, the governors of Wisconsin and Ohio, respectively. Walker and Kasich were both elected in the so-called Republican Red Tide of 2010, and both came to office promising to shrink government and curb its power. They championed enormously controversial proposals to roll back the collective bargaining rights of public employee unions. Walker's proposals triggered huge demonstrations, recall elections, and legal attacks in both state and federal courts. Despite the political acrimony, restrictions on collective bargaining remained intact. In Ohio, Kasich backed a similar measure to restrict the collective bargaining rights of public unions. Among other things, the Ohio law would have prevented public employees from striking and would have restricted their right to bargain collectively for wages and benefits. Opponents

spearheaded a drive to overturn the law, which culminated in a statewide referendum in which the legislation was decisively defeated (the vote was 61 percent in favor of overturning the law).

Walker and Kasich ignited political firestorms because their efforts were viewed by many as thinly disguised attempts at union busting. Yet there is a growing recognition that merit systems are overdue for reform. At the heart of state merit systems are civil service rules, which spell out how employees of public agencies are to be hired, fired, and promoted. Pretty much everyone agrees with the general intent behind these rules—that is, to ensure that public agencies are staffed with people who are qualified and good at their jobs, and to protect them from arbitrary discrimination or retribution. In many cases, however, these rules have become incredibly complex and convoluted.

For example, consider civil service exams. Such exams are used to determine hiring and promotion opportunities, and are designed to identify the people best suited for these opportunities. So far, so good. This sounds like the merit system in action; if you want to be a firefighter or social worker or whatever, then part and parcel of the application or promotion process is a test designed to figure out who are the most knowledgeable firefighters or social workers. The problem is that scores on these tests have become increasingly subject to legal "adjustments." In Massachusetts, for example, civil service test scores can be readjusted on the basis of more than a dozen "preferences." In other words, your test grade is effectively curved if you meet one of those preferred characteristics. Affirmative action, or giving priority based on minority-group membership, is probably the best known and most controversial of these (see discussion below). In Massachusetts, though, preferred groups also include veterans, children of police officers or firefighters injured in the line of duty, and widows of veterans killed in the line of duty. Recalculate test scores on a long list of such preferences and the results of those civil service exams can seem pretty distorted. In 2009, Boston was hiring 25 firefighters and none of the people who scored a 100 percent on the civil service exam even made the top 200 list of candidates. One individual

---

Seniority
The length of time a worker has spent in a position

who scored a 100 percent was ranked number 1,837.[29] Those sorts of results lead many people to argue that civil service rules need reforming to put merit at the center of the merit system.

Affirmative Action

Public unions show how a political role for bureaucracy can be generated internally—public employees get organized and pursue their interests in the political arena. Yet bureaucracies can be politicized from the outside as well. Consider **affirmative action**, the set of policies used to get government to make a special effort to recruit and retain certain categories of workers who, historically, have been underrepresented, to achieve better and fairer representation. It is illegal for government agencies to have employment, evaluation, or promotion practices that discriminate on the basis of race, age, color, creed, gender, physical disability, or other characteristics not related to the job or job performance. Although such discrimination has been banned outright, public bureaucracies are not particularly diverse in a number of these factors, especially race and gender.

About 54 percent of state and local government employees are males, and about 68 percent are white. Males hold roughly 62 percent of the top management jobs in public agencies, and more than 80 percent of the individuals—male or female—in these positions are white. In contrast, racial and ethnic minorities tend to be much more concentrated in lower-ranking positions. They constitute about 19 percent of the top management jobs in state and local government but more than 46 percent of the service and maintenance positions.[30] Consider the New York Police Department (NYPD), which in 2005 had about 680 officers at the rank of captain or above. Of these, about 10 percent were minorities.[31] That proportion clearly did not reflect the overall population of New York City, which was more than 50 percent minority.

The lack of diversity in the management ranks of the NYPD is probably not the result of the outright racism of individuals. A bigger problem is that the nondiscriminatory hiring practices that form the foundation of the merit system are passive; they ensure access to hiring opportunities but make no guarantees about jobs or promotions. In choosing who should be hired or promoted, the merit system is predicated on looking at factors such as experience, qualifications, and performance on civil service exams. This strict approach, though, does not account for gender, race, or ethnicity, and this is potentially a problem because minorities historically have had fewer educational opportunities. Less education means fewer qualifications. This translates into a tougher time gaining access to jobs. The end result is that, even if race is not an explicit factor in hiring and promoting, whites tend to have more education and better connections in bureaucratic hierarchies.[32] This strikes many as unfair.

One of the remedies offered to address this unfairness is affirmative action, a set of policies that, in essence, constitute proactive attempts to increase diversity. Such policies are highly controversial—are they necessary to remove institutionalized racism from the merit system, or are they simply a way for certain groups to profit from a double standard that makes a mockery of the merit system? Defenders argue that such policies are necessary because of the political role of the bureaucracy.

More than the desire for multiracial balance stands behind this argument. A fairly long-standing theory in the field of public administration suggests that more diverse bureaucracies actually may be more effective. According to the theory of **representative bureaucracy**, public agencies that reflect the diversity of the communities they serve are more likely to account for the interests of all groups when managing programs and delivering services.[33] To serve a diverse and democratic society well, a bureaucracy should include affirmative action as an important part of its hiring and promoting practices. Remember our street-level bureaucrat, the traffic cop deciding which speeders to stop? What if all the traffic cops were white and most of the speeders stopped were black—or vice versa? Regardless of who was going how fast, this sort of situation would likely create friction. Some may view the agency as unfair, which could

---

Affirmative action
A set of policies designed to help organizations recruit and promote employees who are members of disadvantaged groups

Representative bureaucracy
The idea that public agencies that reflect the diversity of the communities they serve will be more effective

Policies to help organizations recruit and promote historically underrepresented groups such as women and/or African Americans, broadly known as affirmative action, create more diversity in public agencies. Such policies are controversial, with critics arguing that they undercut the principle of technical competence at the heart of the merit system.

make the bureaucracy's job harder. If traffic cops are ethnically diverse, the bureaucracy will be less likely to be seen as playing favorites and will be better able to focus on its job.

Opponents of affirmative action reject such arguments. Males and whites often resent establishing preferential recruitment and promotion policies for women and for racial and ethnic minorities. Some see the policies as little more than reverse discrimination. From this perspective, affirmative action represents the success of special interests in getting their favored agendas written into the law and the rules that run bureaucracies. In a merit system, technical qualifications and job performance—not race or gender—are supposed to drive personnel decisions in the ideal bureaucracy. Opponents of affirmative action argue that it produces quotas and favoritism for certain groups. In effect, affirmative action has bureaucracy wage politics on behalf of the favored groups. Speeders should be stopped, and the race or gender of the driver and of whoever issues the ticket should be irrelevant.

Which of these viewpoints is correct is a matter of fierce debate. Whatever the underlying pros and cons, the fight comes down to what is the best way to recruit and promote public employees, and who—if anyone—should be given preferential treatment. This is ultimately a political fight about who gets government jobs. That fight took center stage in June 2009, when the U.S. Supreme Court ruled that the city of New Haven, Connecticut, discriminated against 19 white and Hispanic firefighters when it threw out their scores on an exam that would have qualified them for promotions, fearing a lawsuit from minority employees. But despite the case's high profile—U.S. Supreme Court justice Sonia Sotomayor ruled on the case as an appellate court judge—the ruling left this area of employment law as gray as ever, ensuring that the fight will go on.[34]

If Not Merit . . . Then What?

At least in theory, traditional bureaucracy and the merit system have some clear advantages: equity, competence, and something approaching neutrality. They also have disadvantages: a measure of red tape and inefficiency, a lack of flexibility and accountability, and a political role that makes many uncomfortable. No clear answer exists on whether the pros outweigh the cons or vice versa, but this has not stopped the nearly constant search for a better way to do things. Bureaucratic reform is a perennial issue in American politics.

Many of the reform efforts are variations on a single theme that reflects a popular belief that government would be better if it were run more like a business. In practice, this means introducing competition into the delivery of public programs and services, making the organizations that deliver these goods and services less hierarchical, and making greater use of the private sector to deliver public services.[35] The idea is to introduce the benefits of the market into the public sector, which in theory could lead to more efficiency through lower costs while increasing responsiveness, because competition means paying attention to your customers or going out of business. The great difficulty facing reformers is how to get these benefits without leaving behind the advantages of the traditional, tried-and-true merit-based bureaucracy.

Over the past two decades, reformers have made a sustained effort to try to change the entire philosophy of delivering public programs and services from the use of a traditional bureaucracy to the use of a more business-based model. Although these reforms come in many different packages, collectively they often are described as new public management. New public management has six core characteristics that have been widely pursued and adopted by state and local governments:

1. A focus on productivity that emphasizes "doing more with less"—that is, providing public services with fewer resources

2. A market orientation that looks increasingly to the private sector to deliver public services, typically done through a process of competitive bidding, during which private companies vie to gain a government contract to run a public program

3. A drive to improve customer satisfaction with public services

4. A decentralization of decision-making power, an effort to push policymaking choices as close as possible to the people who are going to be affected by them

5. A movement to improve the government's capacity to make, implement, and manage public policy and public programs

6. An effort to maintain accountability—that is, to make the government deliver on its service promises[36]

These characteristics all sound fairly positive when presented as a simple list. In practice, however, they have proven to be a mixed bag. The basic problem with trying to run government more like a business is that government is simply not a business. For the most part, we as citizens do not like rules and red tape—until there is a problem or a scandal. Then we want to know what went wrong and who is to blame. We want government agencies to act more like a business until bureaucracy takes a calculated risk—as businesses do routinely—and loses taxpayer money. We want bureaucrats to be given the freedom to be flexible and make choices—until those choices result in favoritism or program failure. We like the idea of competition and the profit motive; we like it until a private company contracted to provide public services puts profit above the public interest.

> The basic problem with trying to run government more like a business is that government is simply not a business.

Although most efforts to make government bureaucracy more market-like have produced very mixed results, they have done little to reduce the widespread belief that government is best run as a business. This belief has spawned a veritable alphabet soup of business-oriented reform movements. Reinventing government (REGO) stresses making public agencies entrepreneurial. Total quality management (TQM) emphasizes having public programs and services designed and shaped by the clients who actually consume those services, and focuses on preventing problems rather than reacting to them. Management by objectives (MBO) and performance-based management (PBM) are approaches that focus on setting goals and achieving them. There are many other such movements. All originated in private-sector management trends that do not fully account for the unique problems of the public sector. Support and enthusiasm for making government more like a

FIGURE 10-1

Quarterly Changes in State and Local Government Employment, 2009–2014

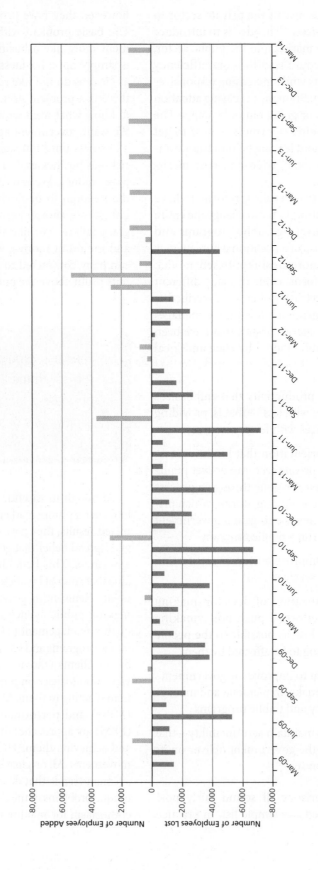

Source: "State and Local Government Employment: Monthly Data," *Governing*, last updated September 5, 2014, http://www.governing.com/gov-data/monthly-government-employment-changes-totals.html.

States Under Stress

The End of the Cushy Government Job

State employees in Florida recently received their first pay raise in 7 years. Lucky them. City workers in Philadelphia have not had a pay increase since 2007. State workers in New Mexico must feel as though they are rolling in it; they recently received a whopping 1 percent pay raise.

This is an all-too-common story. A 2013 survey of senior state and local officials by *Governing* magazine found that more than 40 percent of them reported pay freezes in the preceding 12 months. Nine percent reported pay cuts. Freezes in public-sector pay raises were a common response to the budget pressures of the Great Recession of 2008–2009. Seven or eight years later, many public employees are still waiting for a thaw.

The implications of these long-term pay freezes are far-reaching for public agencies and the services they provide. Watching increases in the cost of living shrink paychecks year after year is not exactly a recipe for good employee morale. But more than that, it is making retaining and recruiting qualified people to work in the public sector more difficult.

Especially hard-hit are public employees who are not members of public unions. Because of collective bargaining agreements, governments are often contractually obligated to honor pay increases for union members. Not so nonunion employees, who are often found in management positions and jobs requiring high levels of education.

Some public agency managers, their paychecks stagnant for the better part of a decade, have found themselves earning less than the unionized employees they supervise. Some are even leaving management in favor of union jobs to increase their salaries. Individuals with advanced skill sets, especially engineers and information technology (IT) professionals, are simply abandoning jobs in the public sector for the higher-paying private sector.

This all raises some big questions about the future of public agencies. While higher-paying jobs have always been available in the private sector, working for a public agency used to involve a decent paycheck, good benefits, and a high degree of job security. For many states and localities, that is simply no longer the case. The pay is low, and the benefits and job security are under pressure as state governments seek to roll back collective bargaining rights.

Some states have started to grasp that if they do not start being more competitive in the labor market, they may face a real personnel crisis. North Carolina, for example, created a special fund to help retain workers in high-demand fields. This is critical for retaining employees in, say, a critical state data center if Google or Facebook moves in next door and starts offering top dollar for skilled IT workers.

Such programs certainly help but are not a long-term solution. For one thing, they create the possibility of a two-speed pay scale. If you work for a public agency and your skill set is in demand in the private sector, you get a pay raise. If you work for a public agency that provides vital services (law enforcement, firefighting, social work) but does not have a Google or Facebook competing for your services, well, maybe you go 5 or 6 years without a pay raise.

Sources: Adapted from Charles Chieppo, "Paying the Price to Keep Government's Best Workers," *Governing*, June 2014; Mike Maciag, "The Implication of Long-Term Pay Freezes for States, Localities," *Governing*, June 2013.

business tend to fade when these systems are put into practice and it becomes apparent that there are good reasons government is not run like the typical 9-to-5 corporation.

As the problems with these proffered replacements for traditional bureaucracy become clear, public agencies gravitate back to their tried-and-true bureaucratic ways of doing things, at least until they get swept up in the next big reform movement. Some of these movements are counterproductive from the beginning because they spread more confusion than efficiency and leave public managers with vague or complicated sets of guidelines that are difficult to implement and based on concepts that are hard to understand.

Another big drawback to trying to replace the traditional merit-based bureaucracy is that the advantages of such a bureaucracy get overlooked until they are no longer there. Many of the attempts to radically reform the bureaucracy by either making agencies more like businesses or eliminating the merit system end up doing little more than returning public programs and services to the spoils system.[37]

This is not to say that it is impossible to implement long-lasting changes in public bureaucracies. Indeed, the Great Recession brought about some of the biggest and potentially longest-lasting changes to public agencies in at least a generation. One of the most obvious of these changes is that, personnel-wise, public agencies have been shrinking. Cash-strapped state and local governments started shedding jobs shortly after the financial crunch hit in 2008 and were still handing out pink slips at a fairly steady clip more than 5 years later. Between January 2009 and May 2014, state government shed 144,000 employees and local government an additional 485,000.[38] If citizens really want smaller government, then over the past few years they've gotten it. Flint, Michigan, cut 23 of its 88 firefighters and closed two fire stations. Dallas, Texas, laid off 4 percent of its workforce (500 people) as a money-saving measure; especially hard-hit were the city's libraries. San Jose, California, cut employee compensation by 10 percent, fired 30 managers, and shut down 22 community centers. Even as the populations they serve increased, state and local bureaucracy shrank by roughly 3 percent between 2009 and 2013.

The impacts of the shrinking public-sector workforce show up in different ways. Some governors have used the financial crisis as leverage to consolidate and centralize the executive branch. For example, Kansas governor Sam Brownback folded the largely independent Kansas Health Policy Authority (which historically administered Medicaid) into the state health department, the latter being more under the direct control of his administration. Other governors have been actively seeking to merge different bureaucracies into bigger agencies that report directly to the chief executive.[39]

That consolidation of power will last long after the economy has fully recovered from the Great Recession. Public agencies facing big losses in human resources are also experimenting with volunteers and other ways to maintain their previous levels of services. The biggest impact, however, may be in who will work in the public sector in the future. As a result of structural changes brought on by the fiscal crisis—changes such as limits on collective bargaining rights and generally lower levels of public service provision—it seems clear that going forward there will be fewer public workers, and they will likely be paid less and have less job security than did such workers in the past. Further, they will not have the generous pensions and benefits that historically have helped motivate people to seek careers in public service. Some scholars suggest that the end result may be a public sector that has not just less-compensated but also less-qualified employees, and greater employee turnover.[40]

Conclusion

Although bureaucracy is often despised and disparaged, it is clear that the effectiveness of government bureaucracy is underestimated, and bureaucratic agencies do not get the credit they actually deserve. A wide range of state and local agencies support and deliver the programs and services that make up social and economic life as we know it. The comparative method shows us that bureaucracy is big—but only as big as we want it to be. If we want less bureaucracy, we can choose to make fewer demands on government. For the most part, bureaucracies do their jobs remarkably well. In contrast to the popular stereotype, most public agencies tackle difficult jobs that are unlikely to be done better by any other alternative. Perhaps the most astonishing thing about bureaucracy is how much we take it for granted. Public schools, safe drinking water, working utility grids, and roads are simply there. We rarely contemplate what astounding administrative and logistical feats are required to make these aspects of everyday life appear so mundane.

Indeed, perhaps the one thing that makes us pay attention to the upside of bureaucracy is when that bureaucracy is not there. There are fewer bureaucrats on state and local government payrolls today than there were 5 or 6 years ago. Some may think that is a good thing in the abstract—who could argue against having fewer expensive government bureaucrats to support with our tax dollars? In reality, though, what this means is fewer police, fewer teachers, fewer librarians, and big difficulties in maintaining prerecession levels of public goods and services. The high cost of those services has prompted an ongoing debate about what government should do, and it may result in a shift of more of what was traditionally considered public administration toward the private sector.

Bureaucratic reform movements, at least in some ways, should be viewed with skepticism.

Criticizing the bureaucracy is a traditional sport in American politics, and a lot of reforms turn out to be little more than fads that quickly fade when the pleasing rhetoric meets the real-life challenge of delivering the goods. Some reforms are almost certainly overdue for state civil service systems that have evolved away from ensuring neutral competence and toward favoring seniority and similar preferences. How to do that without making public employees vulnerable to retribution or discrimination, though, remains a tricky and controversial proposal. Regardless of how such reform plays out, however, one thing will almost certainly remain constant: Whatever the government is and whatever it does, it will rely on bureaucracy to get it done.

The Latest Research

As discussed above, the Great Recession had an enormous and potentially long-lasting impact on public agencies. Most obviously, public-sector payrolls shrank as states and localities shed hundreds of thousands of employees in an attempt to keep the books balanced. By 2014 that exodus was tapering off, but it was clear that things were not just going to return to the way they were. The big question, of course, was what was going to happen? Would agencies stay lean and try to keep doing with less? Would they engage in more contracting out? Would the shattered traditional notion of a secure government-sector job make it more difficult for agencies to recruit the best and the brightest into careers in public service? What about representation—did the massive disruption in employment leave bureaucracies more or less representative of the constituencies they serve? These are big questions that social scientists have been busily studying, and the research reviewed below offers some perspective on what the answers might be.

- **Levine, Heliss, and Eric Scorsone.** "The Great Recession's Institutional Change in the Public

Employment Relationship: Implications for State and Local Governments." *State and Local Government Review* 43 (2011): 208–214.

The Great Recession made the pay and benefits of public employees a white-hot political issue. Rightly or wrongly, government employees were sometimes accused of being more insulated from economic problems than were their counterparts in the private sector. This chapter discussed the bitter fights that broke out in Wisconsin and Ohio over labor relations in the public sector, fights that were repeated on a less heated scale in many states and localities. Does all this mean that the public labor sector is undergoing a dramatic and long-term shift? If so, what does it imply? Levine and Scorsone take a crack at answering these questions. They conclude that the Great Recession has brought about one of the biggest changes in public employment in 50 years. The fallout of that change is probably lower pay and fewer benefits for government employees. As a result, public agencies of the future may struggle to attract a high-quality labor pool, which may in turn have implications for the quality if not the cost of public goods and services.

(Continued)

(Continued)

- **Joaquin, M. Ernita, and Thomas J. Greitens**. "Contract Management Capacity Breakdown? An Analysis of U.S. Local Governments." *Public Administration Review* 72 (2012): 807–816.

  At least in theory, contracting out allows governments to leverage the power of the marketplace to deliver goods and services more efficiently. In practice, as the discussion of university health services in this chapter made clear, contracting out has a mixed track record. Sometimes it works, sometimes it doesn't. This study tries to figure out what some of the underlying causes of this variation might be. Specifically, the authors look at "capacity," essentially the ability of local governments to effectively manage these contracts, which are often made with the private sector. Disturbingly, they conclude that there has been a long-term trend toward the diminishment of this capacity. This may be a result of a combination of decreasing competition and the highly complex and demanding nature of the contracts. Contracting out seems to have increased the need for public officials to undertake often very demanding evaluation responsibilities, even as their capacity to fulfill those responsibilities has shrunk. Given the huge toll the Great Recession took on the public sector, it seems that such capacity is unlikely to begin increasing in the foreseeable future.

- **Nicholson-Crotty, Jill, Jason Grissom, and Sean Nicholson-Crotty**. "Bureaucratic Representation, Distributional Equity, and Democratic Values in the Administration of Public Programs." *Journal of Politics* 73 (2011): 582–596.

One of the key concepts discussed in this chapter is that of representative bureaucracy, or the idea that bureaucracies that sociodemographically mirror the constituencies they serve will do a better job of representing constituents' interests in the provision of public goods and services. Needless to say, this has been a controversial theory given its potential implications of a merit/diversity trade-off. While there is considerable research suggesting that increasing minority representation in bureaucracy leads to better service and outcomes for the same minorities in the community served by that bureaucracy, virtually no research has examined the potential trade-offs of such outcomes. Goods and services can be limited and divisible—in other words, there's only so much of something, and if one person gets it, then another person does not. This is a comparative study—the unit of analysis is a national sample of elementary schools—that looks at the racial and ethnic breakdown of gifted and talented (G&T) students. There are only so many G&T seats to go around. Does more white teachers mean more white G&T students and fewer black and Hispanic G&T students? Does more black teachers mean more black students and fewer white and Hispanic students? Through careful research, the authors found that increasing minority representation does not necessarily lead to such predictable winners and losers. What it generally results in is more distributional equity; in other words, the G&T seats are spread out more proportionally relative to race. This suggests that a more diverse bureaucracy may be a fairer bureaucracy.

Chapter Review

Key Concepts

- affirmative action (p. 337)
- bureaucracy (p. 323)
- bureaucrats (p. 323)
- collective bargaining (p. 335)
- contracting out (p. 328)
- merit system (p. 334)
- neutral competence (p. 333)
- patronage (p. 332)

SAGE edge™
for CQ Press

Sharpen your skills
with SAGE edge at
edge.sagepub.com/
smithgreenblatt5e.
SAGE edge for
students provides a
personalized approach
to help you accomplish
your coursework goals
in an easy-to-use
learning environment.

SAGE statestats

- policy implementation (p. 323)
- professionalization (p. 332)
- representative bureaucracy (p. 337)
- rulemaking (p. 332)
- seniority (p. 336)
- spoils system (p. 332)
- street-level bureaucrat (p. 324)

Suggested Websites

- **www.aspanet.org.** Website of the American Society for Public Administration, the largest professional association for those who work for or study public agencies.

- **www.governing.com.** Web version of *Governing* magazine, which is dedicated to covering state and local issues; includes numerous stories and other resources on agency leaders and performance, e-government, and more.

- **www.pewstates.org.** State and consumer initiatives section of the website of the Pew Charitable Trusts, home to a number of analyses of government effectiveness and efficiency, including the Government Performance Project.

State Stats on Bureaucracy

*Explore and compare data on the states! Go to **edge.sagepub.com/ smithgreenblatt5e** to do these exercises.*

1. What is the average salary for a full-time government worker in California? Why might a state such as California need to have relatively high wages for government workers? Now, compare this with a state that has lower salaries. Is the difference reasonable? Why or why not?

2. How many state government employees are there in your state? If, for example, budget cuts forced a 5 percent reduction in the government workforce, how many people would lose their jobs?

3. Which state has the highest number of law enforcement agencies? Why might they have so many, even though they may not have the highest population? Does this number lead to an increased or a reduced crime rate? Why do you think this is?

4. How does your state compare to the average in terms of per capita state and local government expenditures on welfare programs? How do you think this would translate into the workforce that is necessary to administer these programs?

5. How many K-12 public school teachers are there in your state? Do you normally think of teachers as part of the bureaucracy? Why or why not? Does the number of teachers tell us anything about the performance of schools in your state?

6. What is the average salary for a state employee in your state? What other industries have a similar average?

AP Photo/Julio Cortez

The ancient Greeks pledged allegiance to their cities, not to any nation-state. There are plenty of people who still make formal commitments to serve local government, including police officers and firefighters. Pictured here is the swearing-in ceremony for new cadets of the Newark Fire Department; these individuals will go on to work as municipal firefighters and in other posts throughout the city.

Local Government

FUNCTION FOLLOWS FORM

- Why do local governments vary so much within and between states?
- How and why have local governments changed over the years?
- What are the positive and negative aspects of Dillon's Rule?
- How has the Great Recession affected local governments?

Ancient Greeks did not pledge allegiance to ancient Greece. The nation-state as we know it didn't really exist in that time and place. What did exist were city-states, places such as Athens and Sparta, and it was to those city-states that Greek citizens pledged patriotic loyalty and civic duty. And boy, did they take those promises seriously.

The Athenian Oath, recited by the citizens of Athens more than 2,000 years ago, is still cited as a model code for civic duty and responsibility. Citizens who took this oath pledged: "We will never bring disgrace on this our City by an act of dishonesty or cowardice . . . We will revere and obey the City's laws, and will do our best to incite a like reverence and respect in those above us who are prone to annul them or set them at naught."[1]

Americans don't quite reach that level of civic commitment to their cities, but attitudes toward local government in the 21st century are not as far from the ancient Greek ideal as you might imagine. The United States has a long tradition of strong local government, which is unsurprising given the political system's founding principles of division and decentralization of power. Woven tightly into the country's political fabric is a mistrust of centralized power. Americans generally prefer to keep government as close as possible to citizens, where they can keep an eye on it.

Government does not get any closer to the citizens than local government—the cities, counties, and other political jurisdictions that exist at the substate level. It is this level of

After reading this chapter, you will be able to

- identify the three main types of local government and how they are different,
- describe the three basic forms of county government,
- explain the four basic governance systems used by municipalities,
- summarize Dillon's Rule and how it shapes the relationship between state and local governments,
- discuss how politics and political participation are different at the local level compared with the state and federal levels of government, and
- describe how the Great Recession changed local governments.

government that Americans tend to trust the most, and it is this level of government that citizens generally want to have more rather than less power. In 2013, only about 28 percent of Americans had favorable opinions of the federal government. More than twice as many had favorable opinions of state (57 percent) and local (63 percent) government.[2] What accounts for these differences? Clearly, part of the explanation is the perceived poor performance of the federal government in dealing with important issues. Maybe more important is the general notion that local governments not only do a good job but also are less profligate spenders of the taxpayers' money. In bang-for-buck assessments, local governments are seen as doing more with less in comparison with state and federal governments, which suggests that Americans, as a general rule, prefer, value, and trust government down at the grassroots level.[3] Given those attitudes, it is somewhat paradoxical that local government is, technically speaking, the weakest level of government. The federal government and state governments are sovereign powers, equal partners in the federal system that draw their powers from their citizens. Pull a state out of the federal system and view it independently, however, and what you find is not a federal system but a unitary system. (See Figure 11-1.) Hierarchically speaking,

as discussed in some depth in this chapter, states are superior to local governments. Local governments are not sovereign; they can exercise only the powers granted to them from the central authority of the states.

An individual state, however, is a strange sort of unitary system. Whereas a state government is clearly the seat of power, below the state are an astonishing number and variety of political jurisdictions, many of them piled on top of one another and related to one another in no clear organizational fashion. Many of them operate independently of one another even when they occupy the same geographical space and provide services to the same citizens. For example, a city and a school district may overlap each other entirely but have different governance structures, different leaders, and different purposes. One of these governments is not the boss of the other; the city cannot tell the school district what its tax rate should be any more than the school district can tell the city to build another library.

FIGURE 11-1

Substate "Unitary" System

State-Level Unitary System

At the state level, state government grants power to local governments.

Strong attachments to localities are not unusual. Detroit has faced its fair share of troubles in recent years, dealing with everything from fiscal stress to underperforming sports teams. Being the center of America's iconic automobile industry gives Detroiters a strong identity and a rallying point for community pride.

© Jim West/Alamy

It is down here in the crazy quilt of local governments that much of the grunt work of the political system takes place. Local governments provide law enforcement, roads, health services, parks, libraries, and schools; they are mostly responsible for regulating (or even providing) utilities, such as sewer and water; they run airports, public transportation systems, mosquito control programs, and community recreation centers. The list goes on—and on. Collectively, these are the public services we encounter most in our daily lives, generally take for granted, and almost certainly could not get along without. No wonder citizens tend to think that local governments give them good value for their money (well, at least compared with what they get from state and federal governments).

Local governments, however, go well beyond just providing services. They must make political and philosophical decisions that affect their residents' quality of life and reinforce community values. In short, local governments are worth getting to know. This chapter examines the powers, responsibilities, and specific forms of local government; how and why these forms evolved; how they differ by state and region; and how the political process works within the astonishing number and variety of substate governments.

The Many Faces of Local Government

The importance of local governments to the American political system is evident, on one level, from their sheer numbers. According to the U.S. Census Bureau, at last count in 2012, roughly 90,000 local governments were operating in the United States. (See Table 11-1.) That works out to roughly one local government for every 3,550 people.[4]

The forms these local governments take, the responsibilities and powers they exercise, and the numbers of particular kinds that exist in given geographical or demographic areas vary wildly from state to state. The number of local governments within a state's boundaries, for example, depends on the state's history, culture, and administrative approach to service delivery. New England states have a tradition of active civic participation and social spending that accommodates a large number of local governing units. By contrast, the South has much less of a tradition of civic engagement in local government, and even today a relatively small number of powerful county leaders dominate such services as school governance.

In terms of differences, local governments make state governments look as though they were all stamped from the same cookie cutter. Take the average of 3,550 people for each local

TABLE 11-1

Number of Government Units, Ranked by State and Type

State	All Government	County	Municipal	Town or Township	School Districts	All Special Districts
Alabama	1,208	67	461	—	132	680
Alaska	177	14	148	—	—	15
Arizona	674	15	91	—	242	568
Arkansas	1,556	75	502	—	239	979
California	4,425	57	482	—	1,025	3,886
Colorado	2,905	62	271	—	180	2,572
Connecticut	643	—	30	149	17	464
Delaware	339	3	57	—	19	279
Florida	1,650	66	410	—	95	1,174
Georgia	1,378	153	535	—	180	690
Hawaii	21	3	1	—	—	17
Idaho	1,168	44	200	—	118	924
Illinois	6,963	102	1,298	1,431	905	4,132
Indiana	2,709	91	569	1,006	291	1,043
Iowa	1,947	99	947	—	366	901
Kansas	3,826	103	626	1,268	306	1,829
Kentucky	1,338	118	418	—	174	802
Louisiana	529	60	304	—	69	165
Maine	840	16	22	466	99	336
Maryland	347	23	157	—	—	167
Massachusetts	857	5	53	298	84	501
Michigan	2,875	83	533	1,240	576	1,019
Minnesota	3,672	87	853	1,784	338	948
Mississippi	983	82	298	—	164	603
Missouri	3,768	114	954	312	534	2,388
Montana	1,265	54	129	—	319	1,082
Nebraska	2,581	93	530	417	272	1,541
Nevada	191	16	19	—	17	156
New Hampshire	541	10	13	221	166	297
New Jersey	1,344	21	324	242	523	757
New Mexico	863	33	103	—	96	727
New York	3,453	57	614	929	679	1,853
North Carolina	973	100	553	—	—	320
North Dakota	2,685	53	357	1,313	183	962
Ohio	3,842	88	937	1,308	668	1,509
Oklahoma	1,852	77	590	—	550	1,185
Oregon	1,542	36	241	—	230	1,265

State	All Government	County	Municipal	Town or Township	School Districts	All Special Districts
Pennsylvania	4,897	66	1,015	1,546	514	2,270
Rhode Island	133	—	8	31	4	94
South Carolina	678	46	270	—	83	362
South Dakota	1,983	66	311	907	152	699
Tennessee	916	92	345	—	14	479
Texas	5,147	254	1,214	—	1,079	3,679
Utah	622	29	245	—	41	348
Vermont	738	14	43	237	291	444
Virginia	518	95	229	—	1	194
Washington	1,900	39	281	—	295	1,580
West Virginia	659	55	232	—	55	372
Wisconsin	3,128	72	596	1,255	440	1,205
Wyoming	805	23	99	—	55	683

Source: U.S. Census Bureau, *2012 Census of Governments,* http://www.census.gov/govs/cog/.

government. That number can be misleading because local governments are not evenly spread out demographically. Hawaii has relatively few local governments. Think of a municipality such as a city as a type of corporation, specifically an organization incorporated under state law to provide government services to a community. Think of a county as just a geographic subdivision of state government. By those definitions, Hawaii has no incorporated **municipalities,** just four **counties** and the consolidated city-county government of Honolulu. Georgia, on the other hand, has 153 counties, and all of them are vested with municipal-like powers. The same types of local governments can serve wildly different sorts and sizes of population. The city of New York, for example, has a resident population of more than 8 million. The city of Hove Mobile Park, North Dakota, has a population of one. No, that's not a typo. Hove Mobile Park is an incorporated municipality whose entire population consists of an elderly woman living in a trailer park.[5]

Municipalities
Political jurisdictions, such as cities, villages, or towns, incorporated under state law to provide governance to defined geographical areas; more compact and more densely populated than counties

Counties
Geographical subdivisions of state government

Local governments are not evenly spread out geographically, either. They range from villages covering less than a square mile to counties that cover nearly 125,000 square miles. Within or adjacent to their borders may be mountains, deserts, beaches, urban centers, or vast stretches of nothingness. These differences help explain why some local governments are interested in maintaining subways and others worry about maintaining clean beaches.

Political and cultural traditions also vary at the local level. For instance, the degree of loyalty that citizens display toward a local governing entity often depends on whether they personally identify with the area or whether they ignore their membership and regard the area as an artificial construct. Put another way, a Manhattanite probably feels more community pride than, say, a user of the Buncombe County, North Carolina, Metropolitan Sewer District.

Despite all these differences, however, there are only three general forms of local government in the United States: counties, municipalities, and special districts. Counties traditionally are viewed as geographical and administrative subdivisions of states. The exact definition of a municipality varies from state to state, although municipalities generally are political units that are distinguished geographically from counties

Illinois has 6,963 local governments—the most of any state.

by being more compact and are distinguished legally by being independent corporations rather than "branch offices" of the state government. Special districts cover a huge range of local governments. Typically, special districts are single-purpose governments. Unlike counties and cities, which are general-purpose governments, special districts usually are created to provide a specific public service rather than a range of services. School districts are a good example. These are geographically defined local units of government created to provide educational services. Other special districts include water management and sewage treatment districts.

The Organization and Responsibilities of Local Governments

Even within each of the three basic categories of local government, there is considerable variation in organizational structure, autonomy, and responsibilities. These categories are distinct enough, however, to wrangle those roughly 90,000 local governments in the United States into a general understanding of what local governments are and why they take on the forms they do.

Between the County Lines

To learn what county government is all about, you might find it instructive to take a trip to your local county courthouse. There you are likely to find signs pointing you toward a variety of self-explanatory government offices: district attorney, coroner, sheriff, treasurer, and the like. You also may find signs for offices whose purposes are not quite so self-evident. President Harry Truman once walked into the courthouse in Allegheny, Pennsylvania, and was taken aback by one of the signs he saw. "What the hell is a prothonotary?" he famously asked. Well, a prothonotary,

Mr. President, is the chief record keeper of a civil court. Truman's bewilderment over this obscure county office encapsulates some of the confusion over what county government is and what it does. People might be asked to vote on a prothonotary come election time, but chances are only a small minority knows what the heck a prothonotary is or why the position is necessary.[6]

In your particular courthouse, the prothonotary might travel under a less mysterious title, such as clerk of the civil court. Regardless, however, the office of prothonotary points out what county government is often about: the unglamorous, but undoubtedly necessary, administration of state government functions. Civil courts and criminal courts for the most part function under the framework of state rather than county authority. Yet at the county courthouse, the court's record keeper, prosecutor, and judge are typically county-level elective offices. It is the county government that represents the local face of the state government.

The unglamorous utilitarian governing unit known as the county grew out of a 1,000-year-old tradition brought over from England, where it was known as the shire. (Many English county names still carry this suffix; one of the authors of this book was born in the county of Oxfordshire.) In the United States, counties "are nothing more than certain portions of the territory into which the state is divided for the more convenient exercise of the powers of government," wrote U.S. Supreme Court chief justice Roger B. Taney in *Maryland ex. rel. Washington County v. Baltimore & Ohio Railroad Co.* (1845).[7] Centralizing day-to-day governance for an entire state in the state capital was, and largely still is, simply impractical. Thus, states divided themselves into smaller geographical units—counties—and created a governance structure within each to provide a local "branch office" of the state government.

Called parishes in Louisiana and boroughs in Alaska, more than 3,000 counties are drawn on the maps of the remaining 48 states. How many county governments reside within a state varies wildly. Rhode Island and Connecticut are the only states that have no county governments (as geographically compact states, they have no need for such administrative subunits of state government). Some states have just a handful. Delaware, for example, has only three counties. Supporting the claim that everything is bigger in Texas, that state has 254 counties—the most in the nation.

Geographically speaking, counties are typically the largest local governments, although, like their numbers, their sizes can vary enormously. Arlington County, Virginia, covers 42 square miles, which is on the smallish side. North Slope Borough, Alaska, encompasses 142,224 (mostly uninhabited) square miles. Measured by population, counties range from 10 million people in Los Angeles County, California, to 90 people in Kalawao County, Hawaii. (See Tables 11-2 and 11-3.)

Because among substate governments counties generally cover the largest amounts of geographical territory, they bear much of the burden of providing services widely, if not lavishly. The majority of the million citizens in California's Sacramento County, for example, live in unincorporated territory. This means that their property is not part of any city, town, or township that can provide municipal services. Hence, the burden

TABLE 11-2

Twenty-Five Largest U.S. Counties by Population, 2013

Rank	County, State	Population Estimates
1	Los Angeles County, California	10,017,068
2	Cook County, Illinois	5,240,700
3	Harris County, Texas	4,336,853
4	Maricopa County, Arizona	4,009,412
5	San Diego County, California	3,211,252
6	Orange County, California	3,114,363
7	Miami-Dade County, Florida	2,617,176
8	Kings County, New York	2,592,149
9	Dallas County, Texas	2,480,331
10	Queens County, New York	2,296,175
11	Riverside County, California	2,292,507
12	San Bernardino County, California	2,088,371
13	King County, Washington	2,044,449
14	Clark County, Nevada	2,027,868
15	Tarrant County, Texas	1,911,541
16	Santa Clara County, California	1,862,041
17	Broward County, Florida	1,838,844
18	Bexar County, Texas	1,817,610
19	Wayne County, Michigan	1,775,273
20	New York County, New York	1,626,159
21	Alameda County, California	1,578,891
22	Philadelphia County, Pennsylvania	1,553,165
23	Middlesex County, Massachusetts	1,552,802
24	Suffolk County, New York	1,499,738
25	Sacramento County, California	1,462,131

Source: U.S. Census Bureau, "2013 Population Estimates," http://factfinder2.census .gov/faces/tableservices/jsf/pages/productview.xhtml?src=bkmk

TABLE 11-3

Twenty-Five Smallest U.S. Counties by Population, 2013

Rank	County, State	Population
1	Kalawao County, Hawaii	90
2	Loving County, Texas	95
3	King County, Texas	285
4	Kenedy County, Texas	412
5	Arthur County, Nebraska	458
6	Blaine County, Nebraska	482
7	Petroleum County, Montana	506
8	McPherson County, Nebraska	526
9	Loup County, Nebraska	576
10	Grant County, Nebraska	633
11	Borden County, Texas	637
12	Yakutat City and Borough, Alaska	642
13	San Juan County, Colorado	692
14	Harding County, New Mexico	693
15	Thomas County, Nebraska	699
16	Treasure County, Montana	700
17	Mineral County, Colorado	721
18	Hooker County, Nebraska	738
19	Banner County, Nebraska	759
20	Wheeler County, Nebraska	759
21	Slope County, North Dakota	761
22	Logan County, Nebraska	763
23	McMullen County, Texas	764
24	Keya Paha County, Nebraska	790
25	Kent County, Texas	807

Source: U.S. Census Bureau, "2013 Population Estimates," http://factfinder2 .census.gov/faces/tableservices/jsf/pages/productview.xhtml?src=bkmk

falls on the county to provide these residents with such services as law enforcement, parks and recreation, and storm water management.

The autonomy and authority of county governments also vary considerably from state to state. There are some regional patterns to such differences. For example, in the Northeast, local government traditionally is centered in towns and villages. These are the units of government that attract the most participation, make the most high-profile decisions, and are the focus of the most attention. County governments in this region are historically viewed as just the local offices of state government, representing a form of government and governance more remote than the village board.

In the South, counties are also technically creatures of state government in that they were formed and granted their authority by state legislatures; yet county governments in other regions are much more likely to be a central focus of local government than are counties in the South. County government tends to be the form of local government that wields the most political power and policy influence, and thus it tends to be the focus of local political elites. The reason for these differences primarily has to do with the more urban nature of the Northeast compared with the historically more rural South. Rural areas by definition lack substantial urban centers, which means they lack large and powerful city or village governments. County governments thus occupy the center of local government, and the county seat—the place where county government is physically located—becomes the locus of local politics.

Counties are distinct from municipalities (which are discussed in depth later), although the distinctions have blurred. County governments are historically rural governments that help conduct state government business. The quintessential county government is a keeper of public records (such as property deeds, birth and death certificates, and mortgages) and an administrator of property taxes, local road maintenance, election results certification, criminal courts, and jails run by county sheriffs. The typical U.S. municipality, on the other hand, performs such day-to-day functions as police and fire protection, sewage disposal, sanitation, and the maintenance of public parks and other infrastructure facilities, including stadiums, airports, and convention centers.

In the messy real world, however, such clear distinctions often disappear. Many modern county governments—particularly urban ones—have their official fingers in these classic city functions as well. In many regions there is substantial overlap between county and city functions, and county and city governments operate cheek by jowl. For example, in Phoenix, Arizona, the city hall is directly across the street from the Maricopa County administration building.

As a general rule, however, counties tend to be kept on a tighter leash by state governments than are municipalities (especially large urban cities). In New Hampshire, for example, state legislators still approve county budgets. In Texas, state government mandates that each county appoint a county judge-at-large and four commissioners, regardless of whether the county's population numbers in the hundreds or the millions. Counties, in other words, are still in theory and often in practice the administrative subunits of state government.

County governments, like all other subnational governments, became more dependent on federal grants after the economic woes of 2008 and 2009, but they have always had independent sources of revenue. The primary funding source controlled by county governments is the property tax, which historically accounts for about 30 percent of county government income. Like everything else about local government, however, there is considerable variation in where county governments get their money and what they spend it on. In 2012, real estate taxes accounted for about 60 percent of revenues in Fairfax County, Virginia, with another 16 percent of the county's revenue coming from personal property taxes. Orange County, California, in contrast, got only about 14 percent of its revenue from sales and property taxes combined; its biggest source of income was intergovernmental transfers—that is, money from the state and federal governments.[8]

Just as there are huge variations among counties in terms of revenue, there are similar variations in spending priorities. Where county governments focus their spending depends on geography, politics, and relations with neighboring jurisdictions.

A significant chunk of county spending goes to basic social services; public welfare, hospitals, and other health care programs account for about 60 percent of county government expenditures. Other categories of expenditure range from roads to sewers to schools to general administration.[9]

The Structure of County Government.

There are three basic forms of county government: commission, council-executive, and commission-administrator. What differentiates the three forms is the degree of separation between legislative and executive powers and who is responsible for the day-to-day administration of the executive side of government.

The most common form is the **county commission system**, which concentrates legislative and executive functions and powers into an elected board of commissioners. For example, the commission exercises legislative powers by passing county ordinances and approving the budget. Further, it wields executive powers, as it is responsible for a broad range of hiring and firing decisions and exercises considerable control over many administrative offices.

Depending on the state and the county, members of these county-level legislatures may be called county commissioners, supervisors, selectmen, county board members, or judges. In Louisiana, these locally elected legislators are called parish jurors. In New Jersey, the county legislatures are called boards of chosen freeholders. Whatever their official titles, commissioners are typically members of small groups elected to serve staggered 2- or 4-year terms.

The most significant reform of county government since its inception has been the separation of executive and legislative powers through the creation of an independent county-level executive office. A county government using a **council-executive system** typically has an independently elected officer who serves as the county-level equivalent of a governor. County executives frequently have the power to veto ordinances passed by the board of commissioners and the authority to appoint key department heads. Thus, the main difference between the commission and council-executive forms of county government is the approach to separation of powers. (See Figure 11-2.)

The **commission-administrator system** of county government stands somewhere between the commission and council-executive forms. In this form of government, an elected commission retains most legislative and executive powers but appoints a professional administrator to actually run the government. County administrators usually serve at the pleasure of the commissioners—that is, they can be hired and fired as the county commissioners see fit. In practice, commissioners typically delegate considerable powers to administrators, including the powers to hire and fire department heads and to prepare a budget for the commission's approval.

Commission-administrator and, to an even greater extent, council-executive structures have been popular reforms to the traditional commission form of county government. Diffuse and ineffective decision making and outright corruption were the primary reasons for the shift away from commissions in the 20th century. Reformers were concerned that under the commission approach, power was so diffuse that county governments tended to drift in the absence of clear leadership; also, commissioners too often appointed their friends to important positions. As a result, an increasing number of counties, as many as 15 percent, now are run by elected county executives who exert firm leadership on policy and hiring. This reduces the role of the commissioners to something closer to an advisory level. Another 12 percent of counties are led by appointed administrators. State policymakers have contributed to this trend—Arkansas, Kentucky, and Tennessee now mandate that their counties be headed by elected executives.

County commission system

A form of county governance in which executive, legislative, and administrative powers are vested in elected commissioners

Council-executive system

A form of county governance in which legislative powers are vested in a county commission and executive powers are vested in an independently elected executive

Commission-administrator system

A form of county governance in which executive and legislative powers reside with an elected commission, which hires a professional executive to manage the day-to-day operations of government

FIGURE 11-2

HOW IT WORKS

The Structure of County Government

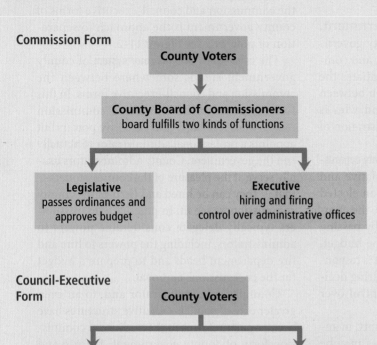

Commission Form

County Voters

County Board of Commissioners
board fulfills two kinds of functions

Legislative
passes ordinances and
approves budget

Executive
hiring and firing
control over administrative offices

The three basic forms of county government differ in the division of powers and in who is responsible for day-to-day administration of county government. In the commission form, voters elect county commissioners who exercise legislative and executive powers and exercise considerable authority over day-to-day administration. In the council-executive form, voters elect commissioners who exercise legislative powers and independently elect a county executive who wields executive powers and serves as the chief administrator. In the commission-administrator form, voters elect commissioners who retain most legislative and executive powers. However, they hire a professional manager to handle day-to-day administration of county government.

Council-Executive Form

County Voters

County Board of Commissioners
retains most legislative type functions

← can veto ordinances

County Executive
can appoint department heads for

County Offices

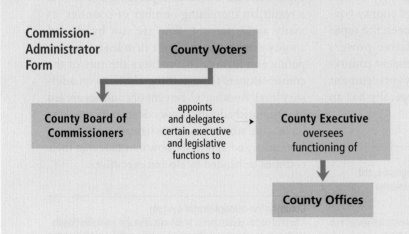

Commission-Administrator Form

County Voters

County Board of Commissioners

appoints and delegates certain executive and legislative functions to →

County Executive
oversees functioning of

County Offices

Although such reforms have reduced entrenched corruption, even today there are examples of county governments going very badly astray. When this happens, states have been known to step in and, in effect, put these county governments out of business. For example, in 1997, the Massachusetts House of Representatives voted to abolish the government of Middlesex County, which it believed had become a corrupt, debt-ridden, and expensive administrative burden. The state retained a handful of county-based positions (e.g., the sheriff, district attorney, and register of deeds) as independently elected offices, but it simply absorbed much of the rest of the county government. Still today, the most populous county in the state of Massachusetts (roughly 1.5 million residents) does not have a county government.

Most counties, however, continue to have representative forms of government that include elected heads of a broad range of administrative and executive offices. These typically include a district attorney, a sheriff, a treasurer, a clerk of records, and, yes, sometimes even a prothonotary.

Municipalities

A municipality is a political jurisdiction formed by an association of citizens to provide self-governance within a clearly defined geographical area. Municipalities encompass two basic forms of government: townships and cities. Cities are corporations. In other words, they are legal entities incorporated under state law for the purpose of self-government at the local level. This is a central difference between counties and cities. Counties were created by the state from the top down; states mandated these political jurisdictions and delegated to them certain powers and functions. Cities are bottom-up creations. A local community seeks the authority of self-governance by incorporating itself as a legal entity with certain powers and responsibilities under state law. Such corporate municipal governments also may be called villages, towns, or boroughs (although, somewhat confusingly, *towns* and

boroughs in some states can also refer to nonincorporated governments).

Townships (or towns) constitute an interesting category of local government that all but defies general description. In some states, townships are little more than geographical subdivisions of counties vested with little in the way of responsibility or power. In other states, townships are vested with a considerable range of responsibilities and essentially function as mini-county governments. They typically are run by boards of commissioners or township supervisors—a county commission form of government in miniature. These more active townships typically are responsible for such functions as snowplowing rural roads.

In still other states, townships exercise as much power as cities do, if not more. This is particularly true in the New England states, where the township is the traditional form of local governance. These kinds of townships function as municipalities. Like cities, they are bottom-up institutions, political entities formed by groups of local citizens for the purpose of self-governance. Many are incorporated, like cities, and some of them have been working units of government longer than the United States has been in existence. The Maine town of Dover-Foxcroft, for example, was incorporated in 1769, 7 years before the Declaration of Independence was approved.[10] Townships, in other words, can be viewed as being like counties, like cities, or like large geographical spaces with little in the way of governance structure within them. Which of these descriptions is accurate depends on state law and the traditions of local governance.

What distinguishes cities and city-like townships from counties and county-like townships is that they are formed by associations of citizens rather than brought to life as designated subunits of states. Municipalities are general-purpose governments that provide a range of public services and address a variety of political issues at the local level. They are brought into existence because

---

Cities

Incorporated political jurisdictions formed to provide self-governance to particular localities

Townships

Local governments whose powers, governance structure, and legal status vary considerably from state to state. In some states, townships function as general-purpose municipalities; in others, they are geographical subdivisions of counties with few responsibilities and little power.

FIGURE 11-3

Strong Mayor–Council Form of Government

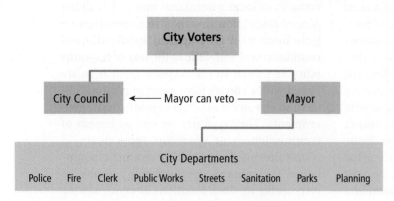

Source: John P. Pelissero, "The Political Environment of Cities in the Twenty-First Century," in *Cities, Politics, and Policy: A Comparative Analysis,* ed. John P. Pelissero (Washington, DC: CQ Press, 2003), 15.

FIGURE 11-4

Weak Mayor–Council Form of Government

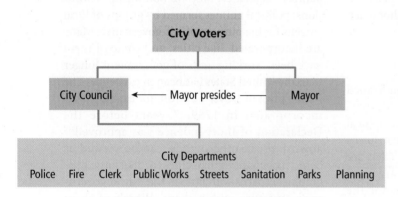

Source: John P. Pelissero, "The Political Environment of Cities in the Twenty-First Century," in *Cities, Politics, and Policy: A Comparative Analysis,* ed. John P. Pelissero (Washington, DC: CQ Press, 2003), 15.

typically a **city council**. A strong role often is played by an appointed administrator, or **city manager**, who is given the day-to-day responsibility for running municipal operations. Municipal governance systems can be divided into four basic types: the mayor-council system, the city manager system, the commission system, and the town meeting system.

Mayor-Council Systems

One of the most common forms of municipal governance is the **mayor-council system**. It is distinguished by a separation of executive and legislative powers. According to the International City/County Management Association (ICMA), about 43 percent of U.S. cities use this system. Executive power is vested in a separately elected mayor, although the powers a mayor is actually allowed to exercise vary considerably.

Mayor-council systems can be broken down into **strong mayor** and **weak mayor systems**. (See Figures 11-3 and 11-4.) In discussions of city governance, these terms have less to do with a politician's personality than with the powers that a given mayor enjoys when stacked up against the powers

groups of citizens, usually those concentrated in compact urban areas, want to exercise a degree of political self-determination over their community. Accordingly, they incorporate, bringing to life a legal entity—a municipality—that grants them the right to a broad degree of self-governance.

Governance arrangements vary even more at the municipal level than at the county level. In municipalities, there is variation in the powers of the executive, or **mayor**, and the legislature,

Mayor
The elected chief executive of a municipality

City council
A municipality's legislature

City manager
An official appointed to be the chief administrator of a municipality

Mayor-council system
A form of municipal governance in which there is an elected executive and an elected legislature

Strong mayor system
A municipal government in which the mayor has the power to perform the executive functions of government

Weak mayor system
A municipal government in which the mayor lacks true executive powers, such as the ability to veto council decisions or appoint department heads

of the city council and the bureaucracy. Under the strong mayor system, the executive is roughly the municipal-level equivalent of a governor. Strong mayors exercise a great deal of power, and typically they have the authority to make appointments to key city offices, to veto council decisions, to prepare budgets, and to run the day-to-day operations of municipal government in general.

The strong mayor system is most common in the Northeast and the Midwest. One example of a strong mayor in action is Carleton S. Finkbeiner, who was elected mayor of Toledo, Ohio, in 1994. Early in his tenure, he overrode resistance from school authorities and placed uniformed police officers in every junior high school and high school as a way to reduce violence. The policy took some cops off the streets, but it also created trust between police and students. Further, this preventive approach reduced drug and gang problems by providing mentors and role models for students. The U.S. Conference of Mayors cited the program as an example of best practice in 2000.[11] What Finkbeiner demonstrated was the ability of a strong mayor to make important policy decisions independently. Making such decisions can often be controversial, although it doesn't seem to have hurt Finkbeiner. He served three full terms as mayor between 1994 and 2010.

A weak mayor system retains the elected executive, but this is more of a ceremonial than a real policymaking office. In a weak mayor system, the executive, as well as legislative, power is wielded by the council. Executives in weak mayor systems still can exercise considerable influence, but they have to do this by using their powers of persuasion rather than the authority vested in their office. In many cities where mayors have limited powers, individuals with strong personalities are nevertheless able to exert huge influence. They do this by fostering cooperative relationships with their powerful city managers. Examples are Pete Wilson, the mayor of San Diego in the 1970s, and Henry Cisneros, the mayor of San Antonio in the 1980s.

In both strong and weak mayor systems, the council serves as the municipal-level legislature and can wield extensive policymaking power. No major policy or program can get far in a city without massaging from the city council. Councils average 6 members, but in many large jurisdictions, 12 to 14 members are elected. Los Angeles, for example, has 15. Chicago has a whopping 50 council members, and New York City has 51. These individuals exert a major influence over a city's livability. They steer policies on such vital issues as zoning and urban renewal, as well as the provision of a wide range of public services—everything from law enforcement and fire protection to libraries and parks.

> Like legislatures at the state and federal levels, however, councils are subject to conflict, gridlock, and disagreement with the executive branch. While some councils are exemplars of good democratic governance, others are notorious for their levels of self-interest and corruption.

Like legislatures at the state and federal levels, however, councils are subject to conflict, gridlock, and disagreement with the executive branch. While some councils are exemplars of good democratic governance, others are notorious for their levels of self-interest and corruption. Illinois politics has long had a reputation for high levels of corruption—two recent Illinois governors are currently serving prison terms for various forms of malfeasance—and the Chicago city council has played its part in that reputation. The council consists of 50 aldermen, each elected from a neighborhood **ward**. Between the late 1970s and 2009, 30 Chicago aldermen were convicted of federal crimes ranging from extortion to income tax evasion.[12] While few other councils can rival that level of criminal activity, council

Ward
A division of a municipality, usually representing an electoral district of the city council

FIGURE 11-5

Council-Manager Form of Government

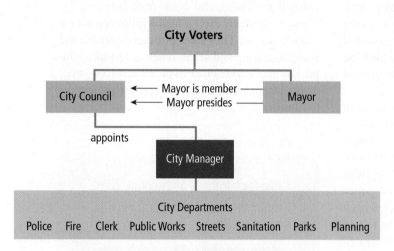

Source: John P. Pelissero, "The Political Environment of Cities in the Twenty-First Century," in *Cities, Politics, and Policy: A Comparative Analysis,* ed. John P. Pelissero (Washington, DC: CQ Press, 2003), 16.

members in many cities report that they are frustrated with the more typical legislative issues of gridlock and conflict, which are exacerbated by interest group pressure and media coverage.[13] In some cases all it takes is just one or two individuals to hold up their hands or raise objections in council chambers, and entire city operations can grind to a halt.

Council-Manager Systems

Rather than separating executive and legislative functions, the **council-manager system** is based on the principle of separating the political and administrative functions of government. In such a system, a council makes policy decisions but places the implementation of those decisions in the hands of a professional administrator, usually called a city manager, hired by the council. (See Figure 11-5.)

The origins of this system are in the Progressive reform movement that swept through government at all levels beginning at the end of the 19th century. As discussed elsewhere in the context of

Council-manager system
A form of municipal governance in which the day-to-day administration of government is carried out by a professional administrator

state-level party politics, a century ago political machines ran the typical large city in the United States. Places such as Boston, Chicago, and New York were governed by charismatic politicians who took advantage of their ties to ethnic minorities, such as the Irish or the Italians. Patronage jobs were given out to their personal friends, whose chief qualification was that they were campaign supporters. Elections were fraught with partisanship, which produced high incumbent reelection rates. Many machine insiders got themselves elected as city commissioners and were given authority to run individual departments, including police, fire, and sanitation services. This resulted in politically powerful, but often corrupt and incompetent, municipal governments.

During the first half of the 20th century, reform groups began pressuring city governments to become more professionalized and less politicized. The National Municipal League (now the National League of Cities), which focused on small- to medium-size cities, was one such group. The U.S. Conference of Mayors, whose members head larger cities, and the ICMA were two others. In the belief that the top vote-getters in a given city may not be the best managers, the National Municipal League drafted a model charter that laid out the powers of mayors, city councils, and administrators.

In 1913, Dayton, Ohio, became the first major U.S. city to create a position for a strong manager, largely in response to suburbanization (the establishment of residential communities on the outskirts of the city) and the rise of an educated middle class. The idea was that a government run by a professional city manager would be less prone to corruption and partisan favoritism than one led by the classic big-city mayor. Such managers are generally more interested in implementing organizational systems than they are in glad-handing voters and trolling for campaign cash.

This reform movement by no means eliminated the urban political machines or the power wielded by strong executives. For example,

Richard J. Daley, mayor of Chicago from 1955 to 1976, continued to run the city with unequaled influence, even though Chicago had a supposedly independent city council. He swayed his city council members, the national Democratic Party, and the Chicago-area delegation to the U.S. Congress. Even today there are a handful of mayors with political influence that extends far beyond municipal borders. For example, Rahm Emanuel, Daley's modern-day successor, continues the tradition of high-profile and powerful Chicago mayors. Prior to being elected mayor in 2011, Emanuel was President Barack Obama's chief of staff, and before that he was a member of the House of Representatives and chair of the Democratic Caucus in that chamber. While Emanuel does not have Daley's political machine, his political résumé and national-level political network, and the clout that these imply, make him a formidable mayor.

Worries about mayors or city councils wielding political power for their own interests rather than the public interest were at least part of the motivation behind the notion of a city manager. This is an individual who is appointed, not elected, and who, at least in theory, can counter the powers of commissioners or city council members with nonpartisan technical administrative expertise. In some cities, this manager is paired with a mayor. In such cases, the mayor acts as more of a ceremonial figurehead and seldom blocks anything that the manager or the council members want. Supported by a legislative body that is elected by popular vote and meets about every 2 weeks to deal with policy issues, the manager is empowered to hire and fire all city employees, set pay scales, prepare an annual budget that is approved by elected officials and implemented by staff, and make policy recommendations.

Today, the council-manager system of city government is used by roughly half of municipalities with populations of more than 2,500. It is most popular in medium-size cities, primarily in the South and the West. The reason council-manager systems tend to be concentrated in cities of medium size is that smaller cities cannot afford to pay a full-time manager's salary and big cities tend to want a more partisan mayor. However, there are exceptions to this rule. Large cities that use a council-manager system include Dallas, Texas, and San Diego and San Jose, California.[14]

And the trend toward professionalization continues. A survey conducted by the ICMA showed that the proportion of city managers with advanced degrees rose from 27 percent in 1971 to 73 percent in 1995. Managers are also less likely to use volunteer committees to farm out work and more likely to use professional staffs. They supervise the systems that provide detailed financial controls and report transparency. For example, in Phoenix, Arizona, the city manager issues a monthly report detailing performance measures for every municipal department, ranging from fire service response times to the public housing occupancy rate to hits on the public library's website.[15]

Commission Systems

Similar to their county-level counterparts, **city commission systems** concentrate executive and legislative powers into a single elected body. These bodies make key policy decisions in the same way a legislature does. Yet each commissioner is also the head of an executive department. Commissioners run for office not as representatives in a legislative body but as the heads of particular city departments: commissioner for public safety, commissioner for public works, and so on. Most commission systems also have a mayor. The position usually is held by a commissioner chosen to preside over commission meetings; it is not an independent executive office but more of ceremonial position.

As a form of municipal (as opposed to county) governance, the commission system originated in Galveston, Texas, in the early 1900s. Galveston had suffered a devastating hurricane that killed thousands and left the city in ruins. The existing city government proved ineffective in dealing with the aftermath of this disaster. In response, the Texas legislature approved a completely new form of municipal government—the commission system—to try to deal with the huge task of rebuilding the city. It proved successful; Galveston was rebuilt and put back on the civic track.

City commission system
A form of municipal governance in which executive, legislative, and administrative powers are vested in elected city commissioners

This success led other municipalities to follow Galveston's lead and adopt the commission form of governance. The commission system's success, however, has been limited, and only a relative handful of cities currently operate under it. Its main drawbacks are two. First, the merging of elected and administrative positions leads to commissioners' becoming the entrenched advocates of their departments. Second, winning an election and administering a large bureaucracy are very different skills. Good politicians, in other words, do not always make good department heads.

Only about 2 percent of municipalities with populations greater than 2,500 use the commission form of government.[16] The drawbacks of commission governments are much the same as the drawbacks of commission systems at the county level—executive authority is so diffuse it tends to produce a government with no real direction. Because commissioners serve as the heads of their own departments, with no real central authority above their positions, commission systems at the municipal level function as legislatures consisting of elected executives. This can make coordinating departments difficult and providing a strong sense of direction for the government overall even harder.

Town Meetings

The **town meeting form of government** is largely unique to the United States and is mostly found in towns in New England states (in New England, towns are basically municipalities, although they may also have some of the functions traditionally associated with county government in other states). Although not a particularly widespread form of local governance, it is probably the oldest, and it is certainly the most democratic. Its origins are rooted in the religious communities that made up early colonial settlements in New England. A high premium was put on consensus in these communities, and the town meeting evolved as a means to reach such widespread agreement.

Town meeting form of government
A form of governance in which legislative powers are held by the local citizens

Town meetings allowed citizens to have a direct role in deciding which laws they would pass and who would be responsible for implementing and enforcing these laws. In many cases, the politics were worked out before the actual meetings took place, with neighbors talking to neighbors across their fences and in taverns. The grassroots agreements hashed out in these informal discussions then were expressed as community consensus in the town meeting.[17]

What all this boils down to is that the legislative functions are concentrated in the citizens themselves. A town meeting is convened through a warrant, or an announcement of the date, time, and place of the meeting and the items to be discussed. It is open to all community citizens, and all have an equal vote in matters of town policy. Such legislative power often is exercised directly; for example, budgets are approved by town meetings. Some authority, however, may be delegated to a representative board, whose members are called selectmen. The board of selectmen exercises whatever authority is granted to it and is responsible for seeing that policies enacted in the town meeting are carried out.

Towns also have incorporated some elements of the council-manager system by voting to hire professional managers to handle the administrative side of government. The manager system seems to work well with this type of government; for example, roughly 30 percent of the towns in Maine—most of them small communities with fewer than 2,500 residents—have managers but hold town meetings as well.[18]

The town meeting is probably the most idealized form of government that has ever existed in the United States. Thomas Jefferson, for example, saw this grassroots democratic approach to self-governance as "the wisest invention ever devised by man."[19] Alexis de Tocqueville, the 19th-century French aristocrat who wrote one of the most celebrated analyses of the American political system, referred to towns as the "fertile germ" of democracy.[20] For even modestly large communities, however, this approach simply isn't practical. A gathering of citizens that runs into the thousands would be too unwieldy, and the likelihood of getting broad agreement from such a large group on any number of policy issues is pretty low.

The town meeting form of government is largely unique to the United States and even in the United States is mostly confined to the Northeast. In this form of local governance, legislative powers are vested in citizens, who exercise those powers during town meetings of local residents. Here, residents in Burke Hollow, Vermont, are meeting to discuss local issues.

This goes a long way toward explaining why this approach is largely confined to smaller communities in New England.

© Nathan Benn/CORBIS

Special Districts

Special districts, for the most part, are fundamentally different from the other forms of local government already discussed. Counties and municipalities are general-purpose governments that provide a broad range of public services within their given jurisdictions. Special districts, on the other hand, are mostly single-purpose governments. They are created to provide specific services that are not being provided by a general-purpose government.

With few exceptions, special districts exist outside the consciousness of the average citizen. More than 50,000 special districts have been created across the country—and often across borders of other units of government—to administer single programs or services. Still, most people know very little about these governments. The single biggest exception to this general rule of special district anonymity is the school district; there are roughly 14,000 independent school districts in the United States. Public schools are often one of the best-known and most widely used local public institutions. Few might know a lot about a school district's politics, but a lot of people will

know teachers, students, and administrators, how the school sports teams are doing, and which schools have good or poor reputations for academic performance. That level of knowledge and intimacy drops off quickly for other types of special districts. Among the most numerous forms of special districts are sewer and water system districts, which account for about one third of special districts nationwide. Few people know much at all about these sorts of districts—many may be completely unaware of their existence.

Other types of special districts administer fire and housing services, public transportation, soil conservation, mosquito control, and even libraries. Commuters may not know it, but hundreds of thousands of them use some pretty well-known special districts every day. The Port Authority of New York and New Jersey, Boston's Massachusetts Bay Transportation Authority, and the Washington Metropolitan Area Transportation Authority of the District of Columbia collectively cover hundreds of square miles and cross dozens of government borders.

Why use special districts to provide single programs or services? Why not just have the county or municipality add those services to its governing portfolio? Well, in certain situations, single-purpose governments can seem like

---

Special districts
Local governmental units created for a single purpose, such as water distribution

Oklahoma was one of five territories to gain statehood in the 20th century. At one point, American Indians initiated efforts to create a state from land in the Indian and Oklahoma territories. Today, the state is home to the most members of recognized tribes in the country, and, like other native groups in the United States, many of these have their own government and judicial systems.

attractive solutions to political and practical problems. For example, special districts sometimes are implemented as a way of heading off threats of political annexation of one local government by another. They also are used as a tool for community and business improvement. Freed of local tax authority, administrators of special districts often can get infrastructure items built and services provided without dipping into any one locality's funds. For example, farmers in special water districts, particularly in the West, are eligible for discounted federal loans to help them with irrigation. In addition, special districts can use private-sector business techniques in management, such as paying market rates instead of government rates to contractors.

Working Within Limits: The Powers and Constraints of Local Government

Local governments, regardless of their particular form, differ from state and federal governments in a fundamentally important way—they are not sovereign. This means that local governments draw their power not from the citizens they serve but from the government immediately above them—the state government (this is why states considered in isolation are referred to as unitary governments in the introduction to this chapter).

This is not to say that local governments are powerless. Far from it. Local governments are charged with the primary responsibility for delivering a broad range of public services (such as education, law enforcement, roads, and utilities), and they have broad authority to levy taxes and

pass regulations and ordinances (an ordinance is a law passed by a nonsovereign government). Local governments can also exercise the power of eminent domain. Yet, despite all their responsibilities and powers (not to mention their sheer numbers), not all forms of local governments are, at least technically, equal partners in government. They are subordinate to the state governments that grant their power.

Why is this the case? The short answer is the Tenth Amendment to the U.S. Constitution. Local governments are not mentioned anywhere in the U.S. Constitution, which divides power between the federal and state governments. Despite the long-standing cultural practice of having strong local governments, legally these governments fall under the purview of the Tenth Amendment's guarantee of state sovereignty. This means the power to determine the scope of authority of local governments is among the powers "reserved to the States respectively, or to the people." In other words, states get to say what localities can and cannot do. They set the limits and define the terms.

Dillon's Rule

The legal doctrine that defines the division of power between state and local governments is known as **Dillon's Rule**, named for Iowa Supreme Court justice John F. Dillon. In addition to having a fine legal mind, Dillon was a highly respected and well-read scholar of local government. An argument he formulated in 1868 has served ever since as the basis for understanding and justifying the power—or, more accurately, the lack of power—of local government. Dillon's Rule is built on the legal principle of *ultra vires,* which means "outside one's powers." In a nutshell, it states that local governments are limited to the powers expressly granted to them by their state and to those powers indispensable to the stated objectives and purposes of each local government.

Dillon's Rule
The legal principle that says local governments can exercise only the powers granted to them by state government

> Dillon's Rule is built on the legal principle of *ultra vires*, which means "outside one's powers." In a nutshell, it states that local governments are limited to the powers expressly granted to them by their state and to those powers indispensable to the stated objectives and purposes of each local government.

What Dillon essentially did was build a legal argument that the Tenth Amendment secures power for the states but not for local governments. As Dillon himself put it in his famous 1868 ruling in *City of Clinton v. Cedar Rapids and Missouri Railroad,* local governments are "mere tenants at the will of their respective state legislatures." The rule has structured legal thinking on the power of local governments ever since, although it has always had its critics. It was challenged as early as the 1870s, when Missouri legislators rewrote the state constitution specifically to allow municipalities a degree of independence from the constraints of state government.[21]

For the most part, however, Dillon's Rule holds. In a nutshell, state power trumps local government power, which means that state legislatures invariably win power struggles with local governments. In Virginia, for example, antitax lawmakers continually prevent localities from restructuring their tax systems to raise revenue. It should come as no surprise that ambitious state legislators hoard power over their county and city counterparts. States have the authority to limit even traditionally exercised local government powers, such as eminent domain, or the right to take private property without the owner's consent.

Yet, although Dillon's Rule says state governments can grant powers to local governments and retract those powers as they see fit, Dillon himself felt that it would be a bad idea for state governments to take full advantage of this legal authority. The bottom line is that the division of labor between local and state governments, broadly speaking, works. It makes sense, Dillon argued, for states to respect local government autonomy because of cultural tradition and sheer practicality. Accordingly, the independence and powers that state governments grant to localities vary considerably. Some state governments are more willing than others to let local governments make their own decisions. Many of these differences can be explained by state culture and degree of citizen participation. Idaho and West Virginia reserve the most local powers to the state; Oregon and Maine give localities the most freedom.[22]

The powers granted to substate political jurisdictions, in other words, reflect the cultural traditions, politics, and practicalities of governance unique to each state. This variation is a difference that can make a difference. For example, it can make a difference in taxes. What local governments can or cannot tax, and by how much, is structured by state law. For example, Virginia allows cities with populations greater than 5,000 to operate independently from the counties of which they are a part. It also gives these communities the right to impose sales taxes on meals, lodging, and cigarettes. On the other hand, counties in Virginia rely heavily on a single revenue source—property taxes—to pay their bills.[23] This can pose a serious dilemma for county leaders. When the housing market is booming, many homeowners watch their property assessments, and hence their annual taxes, rise relentlessly. In many cases, the property taxes rise faster than their incomes. These homeowners, subsequently, take out their annoyance with the tax increases on county leaders come election time.

And taxes are not the only issue. State governments can, and sometimes do, place regulatory limits on local government in areas ranging from taxes to titles, from personnel to pensions. For example, the city of Buffalo, New York, is prevented from controlling the salaries and pensions of its uniformed workers because of New York state labor laws. The state limits the pool of candidates the city can consider when hiring managers and requires a lengthy and involved hearing process before a city employee can be fired.

The lack of local government sovereignty embodied in Dillon's Rule has added to the financial struggles of many substate governments. In addition to limiting the revenues of local governments by limiting their taxing authority, states can require these governments to provide programs or services. Such unfunded mandates can put a severe squeeze on city and county governments. For example, in 2011 the New York State Association of Counties estimated that its members had spent more than $11 billion to implement or manage policies or programs imposed on them by the state.[24] In effect, what this means is that the state is creating programs and forcing counties to deliver and pay for them. As these counties are heavily reliant on property taxes as a primary revenue source, they are put in the tough position of increasing very unpopular levies to pay for programs over which they have relatively little control.

Financial challenges created by economic recession, unfunded mandates, poor decisions, and collapsing property values have in recent years provided blunt examples of the difference in sovereignty between state and local governments. In some cases states have pushed aside financially struggling local government authorities and taken over their governance responsibilities. More than half the states have laws allowing them to exercise some degree of direct supervision over financially stressed localities. Harrisburg, Pennsylvania; Central Falls, Rhode Island; and Nassau County, New York, all went bankrupt in the past few years and ended up with state-appointed rather than locally elected leaders calling the shots on a range of important decisions. In Michigan a number of struggling cities have been effectively taken over by the state, with state-appointed administrators assuming virtually all the powers typically vested in local officials (see the box "States Under Stress: Suspending Democracy in Michigan").

Home Rule

Dillon's Rule establishes a clear legal hierarchy between state and local governments. Local governments are unquestionably subordinate to state governments; yet states, if they so choose, can grant considerable autonomy to local governments. Many states make such grants of autonomy formal by giving local governments **home rule**, or the freedom to make local decisions without interference from state government. Home rule typically is enshrined in a **charter**, which spells out the powers and purposes of the local government. In effect, a charter is the municipal equivalent of a constitution.

The movement for such charters started in the 19th century and peaked in the early 1970s. Charters can be adopted only after voters approve a council-approved or citizen-written petition. Of the 48 states that use a county form of government, 36 allow charters or some form of home rule, according to the National Association of Counties. This can free these communities from both state and county obligations. Even under home rule, however, the state may place some strict limits on local governmental autonomy. And even those who might be thought of as natural advocates of home rule support keeping a measure of state control. For instance, city or county employees may prefer state protections to giving the local mayor or city manager too much authority. Antitax groups often fear that independent cities free of state regulation will raise new taxes.

Home rule can be granted in two basic forms. Legislatures may approve home rule in **general act charters**, which apply to all cities, or in **special act charters**, each of which affects only one community. Either type can be initiated by state legislators, local councils, or citizens' groups. In cases of citizen initiatives, advocates gather the requisite number of signatures on petitions, which are then

---

Home rule
The right of a locality to self-government, usually granted through a charter

Charter
A document that outlines the powers, organization, and responsibilities of a local government

General act charters
Charters that grant powers, such as home rule, to all municipal governments within a state

Special act charters
Charters that grant powers, such as home rule, to a single municipal government

States Under Stress

Suspending Democracy in Michigan

Over the past few years, democracy has, if not ended, been temporarily suspended in at least nine Michigan municipalities and school districts. These local governments were all struggling financially and were effectively put into receivership by the state. The upshot was a shift in power from elected local leaders to an emergency manager appointed by the state.

Probably the best known of these emergency managers is Kevyn Orr, a Washington, D.C., lawyer appointed to run the day-to-day operations of the city of Detroit, which filed for bankruptcy in 2013. The state gave Orr fairly sweeping powers to try to solve Detroit's long-accumulating fiscal difficulties. This puts elected officials in a bit of an awkward position. Detroit mayor Mike Duggan and the Detroit city council were elected to deal with those problems, but Orr mostly calls the shots. And Orr works for the governor, not the voters of Detroit.

This perceived trampling of democratic rights can create big tensions between states and local governments that are, for all intents and purposes, being run by emergency managers. After all, what's the point of running for an elective office that brings little decision- or policymaking power? Why bother voting for a candidate who cannot follow through on his or her campaign promises? This sort of situation can breed not just tension between governments but also disillusionment and apathy about the democratic process among voters and elected officials. In the 2013 Detroit municipal elections, the then-incumbent mayor (Dave Bing) and five of the nine city council members did not even bother running, and only 25 percent of registered voters showed up to the polls.

These sorts of conflicts are not unique to Detroit. Pontiac, Michigan, strongly resisted a state takeover in 2009, and Flint, Michigan, elected a mayor in 2011 only to see that official quickly and effectively replaced by an emergency manager. The loss of local decision making isn't the only thing local officials resent. The specific job that emergency managers are given is to get local government finances in order. That frequently means cutting budgets, eliminating jobs, reducing retirement benefits, and raising taxes. Not only are those decisions often unpopular, but they also can have an impact that will last long after the emergency manager has gone.

Despite the apparent affront to democracy, many residents of the governments being run by state overseers reluctantly admit that it was necessary. "I didn't like the idea of an emergency manager, but it's obvious things wouldn't correct themselves on their own," said Jenise Verde, 48, of Detroit.

To be successful, though, emergency managers have to negotiate a delicate balance of local concerns and the need to make tough decisions. Joyce Parker did two stints as an emergency manager for local governments in Michigan, in Ecorse in 2009 and Allen Park in 2012. She says communication is important, being upfront about the challenges and the role the emergency manager plays. Engaging the community is critical, and that includes elected officials, city workers, labor unions, and civic, business, and religious leaders.

Local elected officials do not have to be completely frozen out. While under Michigan law emergency managers have broad powers to act in place of the mayor and council, they can assign some responsibilities to elected officials if they so choose. In 2014, Duggan lobbied hard to get Orr—a former classmate at the University of Michigan law school—to let elected officials get back into the business of helping govern the city they were elected to run.

Judiciously sharing power, being transparent, and keeping an open-door policy can make things easier, but there really is no way to sugarcoat a lot of the decisions emergency managers are making in Michigan. In some cases they are trying to deal with fiscal problems decades in the making, and that unavoidably means painful decisions—so painful that they are not being put to a vote.

Source: Adapted from Stephen C. Fehr, "New Detroit Mayor Trying to Secure Power," *Governing*, December 2013.

converted into legislation or language for a ballot referendum that is put before voters.

For example, in 2000, a ballot question for the city of Signal Hill, California, asked voters whether the city should become a locally governed charter city, as opposed to a general-law city that would be governed by all statewide laws. The question explained that the charter would serve as the city's constitution, giving it full control over its municipal affairs.

The ballot text specified that municipal affairs included the "regulation of municipal utilities; procedures for bidding and contracting; regulation of parks, libraries, and other facilities; salaries of officers and employees; parking regulations; franchise and other fees; taxation; and zoning and election procedures." It also noted that the charter could exempt the city from some state sales taxes.

The city would remain subject to state law on "matters of statewide importance," however. This basically meant environmental regulations, general plan requirements, open-meeting laws, public records, and redevelopment. Despite the complexity of the issue and the uncertainty about the fiscal impact of home rule, the charter city ballot question passed with 86 percent of the vote.[25] The lopsided vote highlights that, at least in principle, American voters are supportive of local government autonomy even though such autonomy brings new responsibilities.

Although voters generally support the notion of local government autonomy and generally oppose state or federal governments' making decisions on behalf of local communities, there are benefits to state or federal oversight. What is lost in local control can be offset by the deeper pockets of the larger, sovereign governments. Much of what local leaders wish to accomplish requires infusions of funds from Washington and state capitals. Those intergovernmental sources of revenue are especially critical during hard economic times, when the traditional local government sources of funding, such as property and sales taxes, tend to take a hit. With oversight, at least local governments also get some cold, hard cash. The superior capacity of state governments and the federal government to raise revenues is another limit on the powers of localities.

The important point here is that there are trade-offs that go along with greater local government autonomy. County officials, for example, are responsible for the building and maintenance of extensive road systems, as well as for enforcing traffic and safety laws on those roads. That's an expensive proposition, and counties generally welcome state and federal money to support these critical public services. Yet the Golden Rule—he who has the gold makes the rules—means that those funds inevitably come with strings. The obligations that come with the money, in the form of state or federal mandates, are not nearly as popular as the cash. This sets up a love–hate relationship between local authorities and the state and federal governments above them. In addition, state and federal governments cause frustration by restricting the decision-making freedom of local authorities. Restrictions and conditions, however, are often the price of the intergovernmental grants that underwrite important local government functions.

Participation in Local Government

Local governments are distinguished from state and federal governments not only by their power (or lack thereof) but also by their politics. Comparatively speaking, state and federal politics are dominated by political parties, which contest elections, mobilize voters, and organize government. Things are different down at the local level, where more than two thirds of governments are nonpartisan. Since the decline of the big-city political machines of the early 20th century, candidates for county boards and city councils run on their personal competence for the most part rather than on ideology or past affiliation. Only about a quarter of city councils hold partisan elections, according to ICMA.[26] Yet in some cities, party labels that have been abolished officially continue to play a role unofficially. This has occurred in Chicago, where city government has been officially nonpartisan since the 1930s but where Democrats continue to dominate the heavily African American city.

Council members usually run in **ward or district elections**. The advantage of organizing such elections on the basis of defined geographical areas is that they assure each neighborhood of having a local on

Ward or district elections
Elections in which voters in municipal wards vote for candidates to represent them on councils or commissions

the city council who knows the streets and residents by name. This is especially important for minorities, who may be grouped together by housing patterns. Very large cities, however, have to balance the desire to have districts small enough that council members really know the neighborhood concerns with the practical matter of having a municipal legislature that has a reasonable number of members. In some places, the populations of council districts are themselves the equivalent of midsize cities. Los Angeles, for examples, is split into 15 city council districts. Given the city's population of roughly 3.8 million, that means each district has something like a quarter million constituents.

Other jurisdictions permit candidates to run in **at-large elections**. This means that they can hail from any part of the jurisdiction. The advantage of having candidates run at-large, and the reason most cities opt for it, is that it makes room for the largest possible pool of highly qualified and talented people who, presumably, look at the interests of the city as a whole rather than just the parochial interests of their own wards or neighborhoods. Some city charters require a combination of ward representatives and at-large members. But the use of at-large elections can get controversial. In 1991 in Dallas, court-ordered redistricting required a switch from an at-large system to one in which 14 city council members were chosen by districts. The result was that more Hispanics and African Americans won seats.

There is perhaps no better example of the unique nature of local politics than the town meetings that define local governance in New England. Usually held twice a year when the elected council or clerk issues a warrant, or agenda, these gatherings epitomize direct democracy in action. Citizens can do everything from passing a budget to opposing a developer's plan for a new golf course. There simply is no equivalent to this comprehensive citizen legislature at the state or federal level, nor, as a practical matter, could there be.

One of the paradoxes of local government is that, although it is the level of government that citizens support the most, it is also the level of government in which they participate the least. The voter turnout in local elections is often half the national turnout average of 55 percent in a presidential election. This reflects a general indifference among many citizens toward the prosaic affairs of local government. Neighborhood volunteer and community development organizations, although generally run by articulate and dedicated activists, often involve as little as 3 to 12 percent of the local population.[27]

Yet the absence of popular fervor over local issues does not mean that local offices are not important. Indeed, politics at this level can have implications for state and even national politics. For example, local government offices often serve as proving grounds for up-and-coming politicians who go on to higher office at the state or national level. New immigrants, particularly Asians and Latinos, increasingly are working their way into public office on this level. By the end of the 20th century, one third of all cities with more than 200,000 residents had elected either a Hispanic or an African American mayor.[28] In 2007, there were more than 5,000 elected Hispanic or Latino officials, with the majority holding local offices and with many of those in state and federal offices coming from local government backgrounds. Representative Nydia Velázquez, D-N.Y., for example, was the first Puerto Rican American woman elected to Congress and served as the chair of the influential Congressional Hispanic Caucus. She began her career as a member of the New York City Council.

The increase in black local officials during the final third of the 20th century was dramatic. According to the Washington-based Joint Center for Political and Economic Studies, from 1970 to 2001 the number of black mayors rose from 48 to 454, the number of black city council members rose from 552 to 3,538, and the number of black county commissioners rose from 64 to 820.

Women also have made great gains in local government, although they remain far from matching their proportion as half the total population. According to the Center for American Women and Politics in Washington, D.C., in January 2012, 1,248 mayors of cities

At-large elections
Elections in which city or county voters vote for council or commission members from any part of the jurisdiction

Local Focus

Political Participation, or the Lack Thereof, in Local Politics

Low voter turnout is a perennial concern in American politics. The presidency is typically decided by roughly 55 percent of eligible voters, and that tends to be a national high-water mark in terms of political participation. In midterm elections, turnout drops off sharply—in those years, only about 40 percent of eligible voters decide who controls Congress. This helps explain why a president can easily take the White House even though more than half the voting-eligible population either did not vote for him (they didn't bother to show up) or actively voted against him.

While the turnout numbers at the national level are the cause of considerable hand-wringing after every election, from the perspective of turnout in local elections, those numbers look more like a reason for celebration than worry. Take Los Angeles mayor Eric Garcetti, who was elected in 2013. Only 23 percent of eligible Angelenos showed up to the polls in the 2013 municipal election. So while Garcetti took a healthy 54 percent of votes cast, he swept into the most powerful elective office in the city with only 12 percent of eligible voters actually casting a ballot in his favor.

If you can get elected as mayor of the nation's second-largest city with the active support of only 12 percent of registered voters, imagine what proportion of the electorate you need to cruise to victory in a low-profile school board election (hint: not much). The bottom line is that a small minority of citizens—those who actually participate—have a massively disproportionate say in who runs local governments.

This is not just because of low voter turnout. Nationwide citizen participation in local government more generally is abysmally low. A study by the National Research Center, a firm that conducts citizen surveys for more than 200 communities, found that less than 1 in 5 citizens had contacted a local elected official in the previous 12 months, and only 1 in 4 had bothered to attend a public meeting.

As a large majority of citizens have basically checked out of local government, it means that in many city halls the extremists on any given issue dominate debate and deliberation. Those who do show up to sparsely attended meetings tend to be the same cast of characters week after week. It is this vocal and engaged minority that local governments are disproportionately likely to respond to, because, well, they actually show up and speak out.

Who are these people? The National Research Center's data suggest that they are far from a representative group. For one thing, those who participate in local government are not young. Roughly three quarters of the people who report contacting local elected officials are over 55. Nearly half are over 65. Roughly a quarter to a third of those over 55 report attending a public meeting. For the under-25 crowd, the number was about 10 percent. Those who participate are also more likely to be longer-term residents and better off financially.

Is there anything that can be done to improve participation in local politics? Some localities are experimenting with unconventional approaches to increasing citizen engagement. For example, when the city of Rancho Cordova, California, debated permitting more residents to raise chickens on their properties, it launched an open town hall. More than 500 residents joined in the interactive forum to make or review public statements. "It is noisy and smelly enough with pigeons, turkeys, feral cats, and untended dogs without adding chickens to the mix," wrote one resident. The city drafted an ordinance that incorporated this sort of input and e-mailed it to all the forum's subscribers for review.

Other communities are also trying to creatively piggyback on the ease and convenience of communicating through social media as a means to get citizens civically involved. While there are success stories here and there, it is not clear that these efforts are having much of an impact in terms of engaging big numbers of residents who would not normally participate. Most citizens might say they like and trust local government—at least to a greater extent than they do state and federal governments—but apparently not enough to actually get involved.

Sources: Adapted from Mike Maciag, "The Citizens Most Vocal in Local Government," *Governing*, July 2014, http://www.governing.com/topics/politics/gov-national-survey-shows-citizens-most-vocal-active-in-local-government.html; "Study: Off-Year Local Elections Reduce Voter and Minority Turnout," *Governing*, October 2013, http://www.governing.com/news/local/Study-Finds-Downsides-for-Off-Year-Local-Elections.html.

Although their ranks in high office are far below the roughly 50 percent of the population they represent, women hold some of the most important leadership positions in local government. Here, Houston mayor Annise Parker campaigns for reelection.

AP Photo/Pat Sullivan

with populations of more than 30,000 were women. These included the mayors of Baltimore, Maryland; Fresno, California; and Las Vegas, Nevada. Annise Parker has been elected mayor of Houston, Texas—the fourth-largest city in the United States—three times.

Where partisan affiliations are allowed at the local level, there have been some historically important divisions among voters. For example, Democratic candidates have tended to draw votes from minority groups, Catholics, and the liberal intelligentsia. Republicans have tended to draw votes from WASPs (white Anglo-Saxon Protestants), big business, and law-and-order enthusiasts. The payoff for winning local office is more likely to come in the form of visibility and personal satisfaction than in cold, hard cash. Mayors, many of whom work part-time, earn an average of less than $10,000 per year. Former New York City mayor Michael Bloomberg shelled out more than $100 million to win a third term in 2009, but he declined to take a salary; he worked for a token $1 per year. Typically, mayors of big cities get considerably more than that. Los Angeles mayor Antonio Villaraigosa's annual salary was more than a quarter million dollars, although, like many city employees, he was actually paid less than his official wage in his last few years in office (his second term ended in June 2013). This was because of his administration's policy of mandating furloughs, or unpaid leaves of absence, for city workers as a budget-balancing measure. Like other city employees, the mayor did not get paid on furlough days. Council members generally earn less than mayors. In most small and medium-size cities, being a member of the city council is more of a public service than a part-time job. Even in large mayor-council cities—where being a member of the city council is a full-time job—compensation can be less than $40,000 per year.[29]

On the other hand, the job of professional city or county manager tends to be a fairly well-compensated, white-collar position. According to payscale.com (a website devoted to compensation analysis), city managers across a number of states ranged between $47,000 and $151,000 per year in 2014 (check out the compensation numbers yourself at www.payscale.com/research/US/Job=City_Manager/Salary/by_State). The weekly average workload for council members in small, medium, and large cities is 20, 25, and 42 hours, respectively. The typical proportion of their time that council members spend doing services for constituents has risen to 35 percent. In larger cities with mayor-council systems, more than 90 percent of elected officials have staffs at their disposal, compared with only 50 percent in smaller cities, according to the National League of Cities.[30]

Many citizens oppose large salaries for their local officials, particularly at the school board level, because they feel that the nominal fees the officials receive are not an hourly wage but, rather, a stipend that honors public spiritedness.

Given the low pay and relatively high workloads, it is not surprising that 66 percent of city council members surveyed by the National League of Cities said they wanted a raise. Many citizens oppose large salaries for their local officials, particularly at the school board level, because they feel that the nominal fees the officials receive are not an hourly wage but, rather, a stipend that honors public spiritedness.

The Road Ahead

The forms and functions of local governments have evolved through myriad permutations, nearly all of them designed to produce leaders and practices that maximize both efficiency and responsiveness to voters. Yet few local governments can go it alone. In the first 5 years of the 21st century, local governments suffered considerably as recession squeezed their budgets. By 2006, most local governments had significantly improved their fiscal outlooks, helped by a hot real estate market that improved property tax revenues. The real estate market, however, began to cool in 2006, signaling that market forces were about to put downward pressure on the growth of property tax revenues. That pressure became an overwhelming force in 2008 and 2009 as the national housing bubble burst, the country slid into the deepest economic recession since the Great Depression, and local governments faced a fiscal crisis.

In response to plunging sales and property taxes, local governments were forced to take some drastic actions. A survey by the Center for State and Local Government Excellence reported that a few years after the start of the recession, nearly 70 percent of state and local governments had enacted hiring freezes, more than 40 percent had laid off workers, and roughly one third had instituted furloughs and reformed employee benefits packages to reduce costs.[31] A similar survey by ICMA highlighted the sweeping changes that the Great Recession brought specifically to local government. More than 80 percent of those responding to the ICMA survey said the financial crisis had affected their local governments' operations and

that in response city and county managers were making hard choices about deferring capital projects and maintenance, increasing fees, and cutting some services altogether. Tellingly, the overwhelming majority of respondents (67 percent) reported that the changes forced by the Great Recession were not temporary; local government management professionals saw the wrenching contractions as a new "business norm" for the foreseeable future. Indeed, local governments were consistently shedding jobs until 2013–2014, and even when they did start hiring again, their payrolls did not recover to prerecession levels. In mid-2014, total local government employment was estimated at about 14.1 million, or roughly 3.5 percent smaller than 5 years earlier.[32] As Jason Gage, city manager of Salina, Kansas, put it: "Some of the changes we've implemented will continue once the recession ends. We will continue to emphasize performance, explore ways to restrict staffing, and this has been a wake up call to pay close attention to our daily expenditures."[33]

ICMA director Robert O'Neill Jr. says that there is a silver lining to the Great Recession's brutal impact on local governments: the possibility of creative destruction. O'Neill argues that the fiscal crisis has forced local governments to become more efficient, more adaptable, and more focused on seeking out new and creative ways to address long-standing problems. Although local governments may be smaller in the postrecession era, they are likely to be tougher and better equipped to address bigger problems with fewer people, less cash, and more creativity. Experiencing a fiscal crisis of historic proportions is forcing localities to question everything about their way of doing business, and, O'Neill argues, that's not necessarily a bad thing for the long term.[34]

Despite the rough ride over the past few years, the long-term durability of governments at the town, city, county, and special district levels continues to be seen in the variety of ways each responds to its own unique circumstances, not just economic trends but the full array of particular traits and challenges unique to every locality. There is no shortage of candidates willing to pay the price in time, sweat, and sacrificed income that it takes to make a go of it in the modern world of local elected offices. These small-scale leaders continue to debate and organize to provide valued services using a process consistent with a loftier vision of democracy. Tocqueville noted nearly 200 years ago that democracy in America is practiced unusually effectively at the local level, where "inhabitants with the same interests" manage to provide "all the elements of a good administration."[35] At least in this way, recession or not, local government hasn't changed much at all.

Conclusion

Alexis de Tocqueville viewed local governments in the United States as sort of mini-republics. He saw them as civic entities in which citizens were closest to government and in which government reflected accurately what citizens desired. In many ways, that perspective is still valid. Local governments wield actual power, and they are responsible for important programs and services. They come in a bewildering variety of types, many of which reflect state or regional history, culture, and preferences. Taken as a whole, all these differences can seem confusing. Yet in any single place—your hometown or local county—the government and what it does or does not do probably seem perfectly reasonable and natural.

Local government certainly remains the most common form of government in the United States,

and it is still the form of government the average citizen is most likely to come into contact with on a day-to-day basis. Counties, municipalities, and special districts build and maintain roads, police those roads, run schools, manage libraries, and provide other programs and services too numerous to list. And they do all this while employing very different approaches to government. Some are run by powerful executives, others are run by more egalitarian councils or commissions, and still others are mostly run by professional managers.

Yet local government is far from ideal. These mini-republics are constrained by Dillon's Rule. They tend to have relatively low voter turnout for elections. The idiosyncrasies of local government structure can mean that someone with no real administrative experience may be elected to run a complicated bureaucracy with a multimillion-dollar budget.

Local governments today face significant challenges, most notably an uncertain fiscal future. Part of the fallout of the Great Recession seems to be a "new normal" characterized by relatively stagnant property and sales tax revenues. Yet while revenue is stubbornly slow to grow, demand for local government services remains high. The conflicting pressures of restrained revenues and high demand for services are forcing local governments to take a hard look at doing things differently or not doing them at all. That makes tough choices unavoidable. Just because the politics is local does not mean it is less difficult.

The Latest Research

Despite their numbers and importance to the day-to-day lives of citizens, local governments are surprisingly understudied by political scientists. Certainly, systematic comparative studies on local governance are few and far between in the discipline's major journals. Part of the reason for this may be the astonishing variety of local governments and their sometimes bewildering numbers of responsibilities. It is hard to say something

generalizable about local governments because, unlike state governments, they are not necessarily comparable units. A county, a school district, and a municipality not only have different responsibilities, but they may also be organized and run very differently. Yet one thing common to all governments is the need for accountability. Local governments exist to provide certain goods and services, and some do a better job of it than others.

(Continued)

(Continued)

Given the myriad forms of governance and responsibilities, who holds these governments accountable for doing a decent job and how? All the studies described below examine this general question. Given the numbers and variety, it is not surprising to find that accountability in local government comes in many different forms.

• • • • • • • • • • • • • • • • • • • •

- **Arnold, R. Douglas, and Nicholas Carnes.** "Holding Mayors Accountable: New York's Executives From Koch to Bloomberg." *American Journal of Political Science* 56 (2012): 949–963.

This study seeks to answer a simple question: How do citizens evaluate the performance of municipal executives? This question is important—one of the things we have learned from our study of state executives is that popular support is a key component of informal power, which is arguably the most important tool governors have for making policy and influencing the public agenda. Although such questions seem basic and have been the subject of intense study at the level of state executives, we have no comparable basis of knowledge at the local level. We are not even sure if citizens hold mayors accountable for the quality of municipal services or city life in general. Arnold and Carnes sought to fill that gap by doing the first-ever study to track mayoral approval across time, analyzing how approval ratings change in response to local conditions and whether that level of public opinion has electoral implications. They did this by examining responses on 150 public opinion surveys, administered over a 25-year period, that included questions on mayoral approval in New York City. They found that New Yorkers hold the mayor accountable for levels of crime and economic conditions—when crime rates go up and economic conditions worsen, mayoral approval dips. Those approval ratings translate into votes. What this study suggests is that citizens treat local executives the same way they treat state executives. Even if the relevant conditions are clearly beyond a mayor's control—a weakening national economy, for example—citizens hold the mayor accountable and punish him or her at the polls if conditions do not improve.

- **Tekniepe, Robert, and Christopher Stream.** "You're Fired! County Manager Turnover in Large American Counties." *American Review of Public Administration* 42 (2012): 715–729.

While the Arnold and Carnes study noted above examined how citizens hold elected executives accountable, Tekniepe and Stream examined how elected officials hold hired bureaucrats accountable. As discussed in this chapter, county-manager systems are common forms of government at the county level. County managers are hired to run the day-to-day operations of county government, which makes them responsible for delivering the same sorts of public services that elected executives (such as mayors) are held accountable for. As the Arnold and Carnes study shows, if crime rates go up or local economic conditions take a turn for the worse, voters are more likely to vote to fire the executive in the next election. But what about county managers, technocrats who take on many of the day-to-day responsibilities of executive office but are hired by elected officials, not by the voters—do county managers get pushed out for the same sorts of reasons? This study suggests that the answer is no. Unlike mayors, county managers do not generally lose their positions because of local economic conditions. County manager turnover seems to have less to do with local quality-of-life considerations and much more to do with local political conditions. Tekniepe and Stream found that the best predictor of involuntary departure by a county manager was turnover in the county board or a shift in county board leadership. They conclude that political volatility seems to be the biggest threat to county manager job security.

- **Martell, Christine, and Robert Kravchuck.** "The Liquidity Crisis: The 2007–2009 Market Impacts on Municipal Securities." *Public Administration Review* 72 (2012): 668–677.

Markets, like elections and county boards, are also instruments of accountability. Investors will reward or punish bond issuers depending on their financial management history, their fiscal condition, and how they intend to use the funds raised by bonds. This study makes an interesting comparison study to the two just described because it looks at how local governments were punished by the securities market following the Great Recession. This happened even though local governments didn't necessarily do anything wrong.

The bursting of a housing market bubble froze credit markets, making it difficult for local governments to raise cash from those markets and harder for them to finance public projects such as building sewers or roads. This problem was exacerbated by a big drop in property values. As we've learned, local governments depend heavily on property taxes as a primary source of revenue. As that revenue source contracted, municipal bonds became riskier investments and made it even harder for local governments to get projects financed. The upshot is that financial managers at the local level have had to reexamine how they do business. As access to credit gets harder, retaining the confidence of investors through prudent fiscal management becomes more important.

- **Holbrook, Thomas M., and Aaron Weinschenk**. "Campaigns, Mobilization, and Turnout in Mayoral Elections." *Political Research Quarterly* 67 (2014): 42–55.

The ultimate form of accountability for local governments is the same mechanism that holds all representative governments accountable: voters. We know there is at least one glaring issue with this form of accountability at the local level—as discussed in the text, voters simply do not seem to be that engaged with local government. Yet while we know voter turnout is low at the local level, we are not really sure why. Is it because elections are mostly nonpartisan? Because municipal ballots are often in off-year (nonpresidential) elections? Does it have anything to do with the sorts of campaigns that are run at the local level? Part of the problem in comprehensively answering these questions is the difficulty in putting together truly comparative studies; we cannot understand what differences make a difference if we haven't got the necessary data. This is a rare study that overcomes this problem. It is an analysis based on 340 mayoral elections that took place over time in 144 large, comparable cities. It identifies a broad range of variables that effect turnout in mayoral elections. Partisan elections increase turnout, and so does increased campaign spending—but only increased spending by challengers rather than incumbents. The timing of an election matters, but the relative wealth and sociodemographics of a municipality do not. If you want to increase local turnout, this study implies a clear set of policies that could do exactly that: Use partisan ballots, switch election timing to presidential election years, and promote more competitive challengers to incumbent office holders.

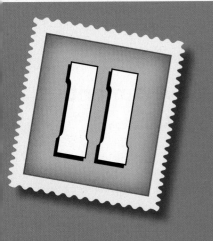

Chapter Review

Key Concepts

- at-large elections (p. 369)
- charter (p. 366)
- cities (p. 357)
- city commission system (p. 361)
- city council (p. 358)
- city manager (p. 358)
- commission-administrator system (p. 355)
- council-executive system (p. 355)
- council-manager system (p. 360)
- counties (p. 351)
- county commission system (p. 355)
- Dillon's Rule (p. 364)
- general act charter (p. 366)
- home rule (p. 366)
- mayor (p. 358)
- mayor-council system (p. 358)

- municipalities (p. 351)
- special act charters (p. 366)
- special districts (p. 363)
- strong mayor system (p. 358)
- town meeting form of government (p. 362)

- townships (p. 357)
- ward (p. 359)
- ward or district elections (p. 368)
- weak mayor system (p. 358)

Suggested Websites

- **www.brookings.edu.** Website of the Brookings Institution, one of Washington, D.C.'s, oldest think tanks, which pursues independent, nonpartisan research in such areas as metropolitan policy and governance.

- **www2.icma.org/main/sc.asp.** Website of the International City/County Management Association, whose mission is to create excellence in local government by developing and fostering professional local government management worldwide.

- **www.naco.org.** Website of the National Association of Counties, the only national organization that represents county governments in the United States.

- **www.natat.org.** Website of the National Association of Towns and Townships, which seeks to strengthen the effectiveness of town and township governments by exploring flexible and alternative approaches to federal policies to ensure that smaller communities can meet federal requirements.

- **www.nlc.org.** Website of the National League of Cities, the oldest and largest national organization representing municipal governments in the United States.

- **www.usmayors.org.** Website of the U.S. Conference of Mayors, which is the official nonpartisan organization of the 1,183 U.S. cities with populations of 30,000 or more.

⑤SAGE statestats

State Stats on Local Government

Explore and compare data on the states! Go to **edge.sagepub.com/ smithgreenblatt5e** *to do these exercises.*

1. How did local government spending across the states change between 2000 and 2011? Where did it change the most and the least? What might account for some of the changes?

2. How did local government tax revenue change in the states between 2000 and 2010? Where did it change the most? The least? What might account for some of the changes?

3. Which state has the highest level of local government direct general expenditures? Which has the least? How does state population affect these expenditures? Why?

4. What is the homeownership rate in your state? How do changes in this rate affect the local governments' budgets? What does the homeownership rate in states that have been relatively financially secure even during the recession, such as North Dakota, look like? Is there a connection?

5. What is the average value of new housing units in your state? Now, compare your state to a state that neighbors yours. How do these numbers affect local government budgets? Should governments encourage people to buy more expensive houses?

6. What county has the highest-paid county government employees? What is the average? Does this seem like a reasonable wage?

AP Photo/Shiho Fukada

Critics of urban governance argue that there is a hole in local government. Not a hole quite as literal as this one but, rather, the general absence of meaningful regional government. While many issues—such as transportation and highway maintenance—are essentially regional in nature, there is a notable lack of regional political jurisdictions.

ch. 12

Metropolitics

The Hole Problem of Government

- What is the "hole" in government?
- Why do the decisions of one local government affect the decisions of other local governments?
- Why do patterns of growth create pressure for new forms of local government?

Allegheny County, Pennsylvania, has a lot of governments. There is the county government, of course. You've probably also heard of the county seat, Pittsburgh, a city famed for football (the Steelers are six-time Super Bowl champs), ketchup (the headquarters of the H. J. Heinz Company), and steel (in the early 20th century, Pittsburgh accounted for half the nation's steel manufacturing). Pittsburgh is a major metropolitan city, with a general-purpose government organized under a mayor-council system. Chances are, however, that you can't name even a tiny fraction of all the governments in Allegheny County, even if you live there. If you can, you have a remarkably good memory. Shoehorned into this single county are 130 municipalities, 101 special districts, and 44 school districts. That's more than 270 governments—everything from the city of Pittsburgh to the West Mifflin Sanitary Sewer Municipal Authority to the Allegheny County Hospital Development Authority. Allegheny County is one of the densest concentrations of local governments in the United States.[1]

In Allegheny County there is, on average, one government for every 2.67 square miles, or every 4,511 residents.[2] All those political jurisdictions add up to a lot of differences, and, you guessed it, those differences make a difference. Hundreds of police and fire departments operate within the county.[3] No one has actually managed a full tally of all the different public works departments, library systems, purchasing operations, and the like,

After reading this chapter, you will be able to

- describe the "missing level of government" and the difficulties its absence creates for local governance,
- identify the key characteristics of sprawl and how they shape urban development patterns,
- summarize the negative impacts of sprawl and metropolitan growth,
- discuss current approaches to creating regional governance,
- contrast the Tiebout model with efforts to reform metropolitan governance by creating regional governments, and
- describe the big challenges of "rural metropolitics" and how they differ from the big challenges of metropolitics in more urban areas.

but there's no doubt that there are lots of them. You get the point. There are a lot of differences. And how do they make a difference? Well, in taxes for one thing. Municipal property taxes, for example, vary wildly across the county. In 2014, someone owning property valued at $100,000 in Pine Township, on the county's northern edge, paid $99.80 in annual municipal property taxes. A similarly valued property in the city of Pittsburgh cost its owner $756 in municipal property taxes.[4] In other words, the municipal property tax burden can vary by a factor of 7 or 8 depending on where the property is located within the county's borders. Of course, not everybody pays taxes for the same public services. What public services are available, and the quality of those services, also varies from place to place.

Keeping up with all this variation can cause a headache. So can trying to make rational sense of it. The problem with large urban areas such as Pittsburgh and its immediate surrounding areas is that their fragmented political systems are not really designed to deal with the realities of governing. In Allegheny County, a lot of governments are engaged in providing the same services, and each has its own political leaders, governance structure, and bureaucracy. Some say this is a bad thing. Splitting the responsibilities of local government into literally hundreds of small slices adds up to a lot of redundant inefficiency.

It also makes it incredibly difficult to coordinate an effective response to a wide range of problems that have multijurisdictional causes and consequences. Consider traffic. Authorizing, say,

the construction of a new industrial park means there will be a lot of new commuters. Chances are that many of these commuters will live in other communities, which they will drive through on their way to work. Those communities will face increased pressure on their transportation infrastructures and will have to deal with the expensive consequences of a more heavily used transportation system. In other words, a decision by one local government can have important implications for other local governments. This not only makes coordination difficult, but it can also lead to a lot of hard feelings and conflict.

Other individuals, however, say, "*Vive la différence.*" Pittsburgh and Allegheny County are like most other major metropolitan areas in that for a lot of people they are pretty terrific places to work, live, attend school, and raise a family. So what if there are a lot of local governments? The positive side to having a lot of different municipalities, townships, and counties—with their different tax rates and levels of public services—is choice, and lots of it. All those differences mean people can choose to live in a place that has the right mix of taxes and public services to suit their individual preferences. Of course, this assumes that they actually have the resources and the knowledge to make such choices, an assumption that more than one political scientist has questioned. Consider that in the larger Pittsburgh metropolitan area, which extends beyond Allegheny County, there are nearly a thousand local governments.[5] So if you are considering a move to the Pittsburgh area and want to comprehensively comparison-shop taxes and public services, good luck—we hope you have a lot of spare time and access to a super-computer.

Chapter 11 discussed the different forms of local government and various ways of organizing local government. This chapter focuses more on the importance and difficulty of coordinating all those localities. Most Americans live in urban areas like Allegheny County, areas where local governments are very close together and, at times, piled on top of one another. The central economic and social problems that governments must address in these areas are regional rather than local in nature. Yet the United States has no tradition, and few examples, of regional government. It has quite a few local governments with limited abilities and limited incentives to act regionally. How to fashion coherent responses to regional problems is the central challenge of local governance in urban areas. This problem has become particularly acute in the wake of the Great Recession. The federal government is increasingly recognizing that local economies are defined by metro regions rather than by the sometimes arbitrary geographical lines of states or localities. Boosting the economy means targeting these metro areas for grants and other programs, which can be difficult when there is little or no governance infrastructure specifically designed to tie the polyglot mix of local governments into a coherent policy agenda. It raises questions about how governments below the state level are organized, as well as fundamental questions of political power, especially questions that deal with who has the authority to make policy and who has to pay for it.

It is not just densely populated places such as Allegheny County that are dealing with these sorts of problems. Rural areas are facing the same governance challenges, although for different reasons. Rural areas are being forced to grapple with regional-level coordination issues because shrinking populations cannot provide the tax base needed to support general-purpose governments in small communities. Thus, local governments in rural areas, like local governments in urban areas, are feeling their way toward more cooperative arrangements, sharing the burden of providing public services, and even considering mergers. So, urban or rural, the biggest challenge for everyone is dealing with a world in which the problems are regional but the governments are local.

The Missing Level of Government

You might not have noticed, but according to some scholars there is a hole in the organizational structure of the federal system. The basic organization of the federal government and the powers and responsibilities of state and federal governments are covered by the U.S. Constitution. The organization of the state governments and the powers and responsibilities of state and local governments are covered by individual state constitutions. The hole is at the regional level. There is nothing in the U.S. Constitution, and virtually nothing in state constitutions, that addresses even the notion of regional government, let alone its organization or powers and responsibilities.

In some ways this is understandable. The federal arrangement set up by the Constitution is the bedrock of the U.S. political system and is deeply woven into the fabric of society. No one seriously proposes to fundamentally alter this arrangement. Even though it stands on less legal authority—local governments, remember, are not sovereign—there is a strong tradition of local government. People tend to be oriented toward their local communities and tend to place more faith in city hall than in the state or national capitol. In contrast, there are no strong legal foundations for regional governments and no strong tradition of regional government either. Regional government is the poor relation of the U.S. political system: little thought of and, outside the community of urban scholars and a handful of officials, not much loved.

Yet the majority of local governments in the United States are, like the hundreds of governments in Allegheny County, embedded in larger metropolitan regions. These regions have similar policy challenges and problems that have common sources and call for common solutions. This absence of some sort of regional umbrella government has

MAP 12-1

Pittsburgh Metropolitan Statistical Area (MSA) and Surrounding MSAs

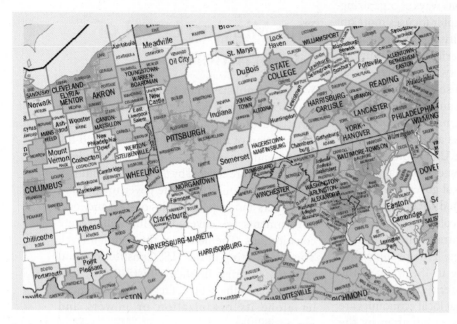

Source: U.S. Census Bureau, Population Division.

communities having a high degree of social and economic integration with that core." It is important to note that this definition goes on to specify that a metropolitan area comprises "one or more entire counties."[7]

For data-gathering and reporting purposes, the federal government formally defines metropolitan areas using the concept of the **metropolitan statistical area (MSA)**, an area made up of a city of 50,000 or more people, together with adjacent urban communities that have strong ties to the central city. As of 2013, there were 381 MSAs in the United States (and 7 more in Puerto Rico). More than 80 percent of U.S. residents live in such metropolitan areas, with 30 percent living in central cities.[8] These metros are where some of the most important policy challenges of the 21st century are not just concentrated but irretrievably interconnected. Consider traffic congestion. According to metro scholar Bruce Katz, roughly 60 percent of all the vehicular miles logged in the United States occur in the top 100 metropolitan areas. This reflects not just the population concentration of those areas or just the challenges of traffic congestion and maintaining transportation infrastructure but also the effects of such concentration on global warming (that much traffic produces a lot of greenhouse gases) as well as on global trade, shipping, and freight.[9]

Local governments in these metros, like it or not, simply cannot confine their problems or their ambitions within their own borders, any more than

been called a "fundamental flaw in America's governance structure." This is due to the fact that "metropolitan regions have become the most important functional units of economic and social life in almost all modern societies."[6] Labor and jobs, for example, rarely are concentrated in a single local political jurisdiction. The bottom line is that localities are intertwined economically and socially but are governed as if such matters can be isolated within the preexisting geographical boundaries of political jurisdictions.

The basic problem, then, is that political geography no longer lines up with economic and social geography. The center of economic and social life in the United States is increasingly less a city or a county and more a larger metropolitan area. The U.S. Office of Management and Budget defines a **metropolitan area** as a region with "a large population nucleus, together with adjacent

---

Metropolitan area

A populous region typically comprising a city and surrounding communities that have a high degree of social and economic integration

Metropolitan statistical area (MSA)

An area with a city of 50,000 or more people, together with adjacent urban communities that have strong ties to the central city

TABLE 12-1

Metropolitan Statistical Areas at a Glance, 2013

Ten Largest MSAs by Population, 2010	Rank
New York–Northern New Jersey–Long Island, NY–NJ–PA	1
Los Angeles–Long Beach–Santa Ana, CA	2
Chicago–Joliet–Naperville, IL–IN–WI	3
Dallas–Fort Worth–Arlington, TX	4
Houston–Sugar Land–Baytown, TX	5
Philadelphia–Camden–Wilmington, PA–NJ–DE–MD	6
Washington–Arlington–Alexandria, DC–VA–MD–WV	7
Miami–Fort Lauderdale–Miami Beach, FL	8
Atlanta–Sandy Springs–Marietta, GA	9
Boston–Cambridge–Quincy, MA–NH	10
Ten Smallest MSAs by Population, 2010	**Rank**
Grants Pass, OR	371
Pocatello, ID	372
Kokomo, IN	373
Great Falls, MT	374
Casper, WY	375

	Rank
Hinesville, GA	376
Danville, IL	377
Columbus, IN	378
Walla-Walla, WA	379
Lewiston, ID–WA	380
Carson City, NV	381
Top Ten MSAs by Percentage Change, 2010–2013	**Rank**
The Villages, FL	1
Midland, TX	2
Austin–Round Rock, TX	3
Odessa, TX	4
Bismarck, ND	5
Auburn–Opelika, AL	6
Crestview–Fort Walton Beach–Destin, FL	7
Myrtle Beach–Conway–North Myrtle Beach, SC–NC	8
Columbus, GA	9
Casper, WY	10

Source: U.S. Census Bureau, "Population Estimates: Metropolitan and Micropolitan Statistical Area Totals Dataset; Population and Estimated Components of Change: April 1, 2010 to July 1, 2013," https://www.census.gov/popest/data/metro/totals/2013/CBSA-EST2013-alldata.html.

they can independently control global trade or air pollution. In metros, the cities, their suburbs, and the counties in which they are geographically located all blend together into a dense urban concentration. The vast majority of Americans live, work, and play in such urban areas, more often than not crossing local government jurisdictions as they go from one of these activities to another. But there are even bigger units to consider. These dense metropolitan areas often bump into each other, forming an even larger urban geographical area referred to as a **megaregion**. A megaregion is an urban area made up of several large cities and their surrounding urban areas—in effect, a string of MSAs. Megaregions represent a new type of urban geography, a merging of metropolitan areas into a massive interlocking economic and social system.

Megaregion

An urban area made up of several large cities and their surrounding urban areas that creates an interlocking economic and social system

Megaregions may spill across multiple counties or even multiple states, but there is typically no overarching institution at this level with anything like the powers of a municipal, let alone a state, government. Instead, within megaregions are dozens and dozens of governments trying to balance local and regional interests, with mixed success. All these different governments share a set of common interests because a decision by any one jurisdiction in a megaregion has implications for other jurisdictions. This interdependence fuels an increasing recognition of the need for local governments to coordinate with one another in policy and decision making on everything from transportation infrastructure to economic development to public housing.

Achieving that sort of coordination is incredibly difficult in the United States because of the relative lack of regional government. Because these metropolitan areas span not just county but also state and even national borders, exercising any form of centralized planning over their growth and operation is incredibly difficult. As in Allegheny County, in megaregions literally hundreds of governments are making thousands of decisions, often with little coordination or thought to their regional effects. Not only does this fragmentation of political authority make it hard to address regional problems, but it is arguably the cause of some of those problems.

Take, for example, the rise of so-called **edgeless cities**. These are sprawling, unplanned office and retail complexes that are not pedestrian-friendly and often become ghost towns at night. They do have obvious economic attractions—they mean jobs, sales taxes (people who work in them buy stuff, even if it is just gas and incidentals at a convenience store), and also property taxes (office complexes are valuable properties).

Yet, whatever local benefits they produce, they also export a set of costs to the larger region. Most of the people who work in edgeless cities commute home to greener residential areas. This means that such developments segregate and put considerable geographical distance between where people live and where they work. The end results—traffic congestion and smog—affect all communities in the region, but individually there is not much any local government can do about such problems.

Sprawl: How Metropolitan Regions Grow

The fragmented nature of governance in metropolitan areas creates an interconnected set of problems that are difficult to address in a systematic and coordinated fashion. To understand the causes and consequences of these problems, as well as the challenges involved in effectively addressing them, it helps to have a little historical background on the roots of metropolitan growth.

Metropolitan areas (and certainly megaregions) are a relatively new concept. As recently as the 1920s, scholars recognized that the growth of

suburbs, rapid and easily accessible transportation, and new forms of communication were transforming urban areas into a new social and economic phenomenon. They also recognized that existing forms of local government were ill equipped to deal with this new urban reality, and some even went so far as to call for a new form of metropolitan government to address the gap between state and local political jurisdictions.[10]

It was not until after World War II, however, that the country really saw the explosive growth of metropolitan areas and the broad-scale governance problems that accompanied it. In some ways, this growth was inevitable. A population boom created enormous pressure for new development, and that development typically took place on the peripheries of large cities or urban areas in the form of low-density suburban housing and commercial developments. This created an interrelated set of problems that can be traced to the catchall phenomenon of **sprawl**. Although the term *sprawl* is often used generically to refer to the rapid growth of any metropolitan area, most urban scholars consider it to be a particular type of growth. There is no universal definition of sprawl, but this type of growth does have a set of specific characteristics: single-use zoning, low-density development, leapfrog development, car-dependent living, and fragmentation of land-use powers. We discuss each in turn below.

Single-Use Zoning. One of the central political powers of local government is control over land use. This power is typically exercised through **zoning laws**. These laws can allow land to be used for a mix of commercial, recreational, and residential development or for single uses, when land is used for single-purpose developments. Local governments in metropolitan areas have tended to favor the latter approach. The end result has been the geographical separation of the places where people work, live, and play.

Low-Density Development. The growth of metropolitan areas has been defined not only by

---

Sprawl
The rapid growth of a metropolitan area, typically as a result of specific types of zoning and development

Zoning laws
Regulations that control how land can be used

Edgeless cities
Office and retail complexes without clear boundaries

single-use development but also by **low-density development**. In effect, local governments have exercised their powers over land use to dictate that the growth in metropolitan areas will be out rather than up. Rather than multifamily developments such as high-rise condominiums and apartments, suburbs and other urban municipalities have favored single-family developments. These developments make for lower population densities, but obviously they also require more land. For example, the population of the Milwaukee, Wisconsin, metropolitan area increased roughly 3 percent between 1970 and 1990, but geographically the metro area increased by 38 percent. Los Angeles is a classic case of how low-density development can consume vast stretches of land. Population-wise, Los Angeles grew about 45 percent between 1970 and 1990; land-wise, it grew by 300 percent.[11]

Leapfrog Development. In **leapfrog development** practices, developments jump—or leap-frog—over established developments, leaving undeveloped or underdeveloped land between developed areas. This puts a particular strain on infrastructure—not just roads but also water and sewer facilities. When new development bypasses undeveloped land, utilities have to be stretched out farther to serve the newly developed areas.

Leapfrog development is partially driven by the economic incentives of developers. Most established municipalities like to create uniform requirements for developments within their own jurisdictions, for example, by enforcing specific building codes. They may even impose what are sometimes called **impact fees**. Municipalities charge builders of new housing or commercial developments impact fees to help offset the costs of extending services such as parks,

schools, law enforcement, and fire protection services to these developments. A new housing development, for instance, may require the building of a new fire station, and impact fees can help offset that cost. It is not hard to see, then, why developers often favor building in unincorporated areas, typically on land with geographical separation from municipal borders that is still close enough to make for an easy commute to the urban center. The land in unincorporated areas tends to be cheaper, and there are fewer regulations to deal with.

Car-Dependent Living. Developing metropolitan areas through single-use, low-density developments means that citizens have to be highly mobile. Getting from a suburban home to a job in a commercial office development and from home to the kids' soccer game on the weekend pretty much requires an automobile. In low-density housing developments, it is often impossible—or at least impractical—to do something such as "run to the corner store." Getting a six-pack to watch the game or a bag of sugar to bake cookies, even arranging a play date for the kids, requires transportation. Because public transportation systems are, for the most part, not set up for convenient and efficient transportation across large, multijurisdictional geographical areas, having a car becomes a necessity for anyone living in a metropolitan area.

Between 1950 and 1990, the population of the United States increased by about 40 percent, but the number of miles traveled in cars increased 140 percent. The imbalance between population growth and the growth in automobile use is a direct consequence of how land has been developed in metropolitan areas. The rise of **car-dependent living** exacts an environmental toll. Governments have done a reasonably good job of controlling "point" sources of pollution (concentrated sources of pollutants that tend to be limited in number, such as factories and power plants) over the past three decades or so. However, nonpoint sources of pollution are harder to identify and control because they consist of many sources,

---

Low-density development
Development practices that spread (rather than concentrate) populations across the land

Leapfrog development
Development practices in which new developments jump—or leapfrog—over established developments, leaving undeveloped or underdeveloped land between developed areas

Impact fees
Fees that municipalities charge builders of new housing or commercial developments to help offset the costs of extending services.

Car-dependent living
A situation in which owning a car for transportation is a necessity; an outcome of low-density development

One of the consequences of urban development patterns is traffic congestion. Because people tend to live in one place and work in another, commuting by car is a daily ritual for millions of Americans.

© Cameron Davidson/Corbis

each putting out a relatively small amount of pollutants but collectively having a large-scale impact on the environment. Cars are a classic example of a nonpoint source of pollution and are a major cause of air-quality problems in metropolitan areas.[12]

Fragmentation of Land-Use Powers. A key characteristic of sprawl is the division of powers among local political jurisdictions, in particular the power over land use. Local governments frequently have strong incentives to use these powers in a way that provides benefits for those within the particular local jurisdiction but creates costs for neighboring communities.

The basic characteristics described above have defined the growth and development of many major metropolitan areas in the United States during the past half-century or so. The result has been largely unplanned growth (growth with no systematic coordination to balance local benefits with regional costs) spread out across ever-larger geographical regions, gobbling up previously rural areas and replacing them with low-density, single-use developments.

The Cons of Metropolitan Growth

By now it should be fairly obvious that the characteristic sprawl-like growth of metropolitan areas over the past 50 or 60 years has contributed to, and in some cases is a primary cause of, problems such as traffic congestion and smog. According to many academics who study urban politics and growth, these same development patterns produce a wide range of other problems as well. These problems include the concentration of poverty and crime in certain neighborhoods, segregation by race and class, and inequality in public services, fiscal resources, and political power.

As new low-density housing developments began popping up around core cities after World War II, the middle and upper classes began moving from the cities to the suburbs. There were "push" and "pull" reasons for the migration of the better-off classes to the suburbs. One reason was the lure of the lifestyle—the home with the white-picket fence on a leafy suburban lane—that "pulled" people out of the city. Another was the racial desegregation of public schools in the 1960s and 1970s; increasing numbers of less-well-off nonwhites began to make up an even greater proportion of urban schools, acting as an incentive for whites to move, "pushing" them out to the suburbs.

The racial—and perhaps racist—undertones of this demographic shift have been repeatedly noted by academics.[13] Because the middle and upper classes were largely white, this demographic phenomenon became known as **white flight**. As whites left the dense, multiuse neighborhoods of cities for the lure of single-family homes on large lots in suburbia, minorities became concentrated in the core urban areas. Because racial minorities also were much more likely to be less socioeconomically well-off than whites, this meant that inner-city neighborhoods became poorer.

White flight
A demographic trend in which the middle and upper classes leave central cities for predominantly white suburbs

Local Focus

The End of Sprawl?

One of the unanticipated consequences of the Great Recession is a slowing, and in some cases an outright reversal, of urban sprawl. The reasons for this are complex, and the next boom economy may push development patterns back toward sprawl. Still, there is no doubt that at least in some geographic areas, the Great Recession turned growth patterns away from those characterized by sprawl.

Some of this is simple economics. The Great Recession hammered many local economies nationwide, but the suburbs got hammered hardest. One report looked at job losses in 100 metro areas and found that the farther away the area was from a central business district, the larger the loss in employment there. Between 2000 and 2007, job growth was likely to be found in areas 10 to 35 miles away from a central business district. The Great Recession ended that, with jobs becoming more concentrated in central business cores. And where there are jobs, people will follow.

It is not just employment opportunities, though. There is evidence of a significant shift in the attitudes of Americans. More and more, they prize walkable working and living. This trend has become so prominent that developers in places such as the Washington, D.C., suburbs in Virginia and Maryland are less interested in picket fences and big houses and are instead concentrating on projects such as building condos close to train stations.

Indeed, this trend has become so prominent that a handful of cities—including Washington, D.C., New York, and Boston—are said by urban scholars to be "witnessing the end of sprawl." The far-flung suburban office parks are becoming less and less attractive to employees who want a different lifestyle than having a house in one place, a job in another, a long commute in between, and no sense of community in either.

The benefits of more compact and connected metro areas are backed by a number of studies. One study by the University of Utah's Metropolitan Research Center found that the more compact a metro area, the greater the economic mobility in that area. There are also other benefits. People who live in more compact and more connected places tend to have lower rates of obesity and higher life expectancies. When you spend less time sitting in a car and more time outside walking and talking, apparently not just your job prospects improve but also your health.

All this is not lost on an increasing number of people who are turning away from traditional suburban lifestyles, with their clear separation of home, work, leisure, and community, and toward something that combines all this into a more geographically compact area. This sort of trend undercuts most of the classic characteristics of sprawl discussed in the text. These sorts of spaces are much more likely to be high-density developments with multiuse zoning that require much less reliance on an automobile to get through the day.

So are we really "witnessing the end of sprawl"? That question is impossible to answer, at least in the foreseeable future. Are we seeing some important shifts in urban development patterns? That question is much easier to answer: Yes. How those development trends evolve over the next decade or two will ultimately tell us whether sprawl is ending or just taking a postrecession pause.

Sources: Adapted from Chris Kardish, "Study Ranks Metro Areas by Sprawl," *Governing*, April 2014; Mike Maciag, "Suburbs Suffered Most Job Losses During Recession, Report Finds," *Governing*, April 2013; Daniel C. Vock, "Some Cities Are Spurring the End of Sprawl," *Governing,* June 2014.

As the city neighborhoods became poorer, the remaining middle-class residents felt more pressure to move to the suburbs, and a self-reinforcing trend set in; the poor and ethnic minorities became increasingly concentrated in core city neighborhoods. In the past couple of decades, this trend has started to occur in the suburbs themselves. Minorities who managed to get far enough up the socioeconomic ladder to move to an inner-ring suburb have triggered another round of white flight; as these comparatively less-white, less-well-off people move into the inner-ring suburbs, the better-off move farther out. The end result is the increasingly racial and socioeconomic homogeneity of particular political jurisdictions.

This leads to certain local political jurisdictions that are well-off and have property values that support high-quality public services. Middle- and upper-class suburbs, for example, tend to have high-quality public schools. So do **exurbs**, or municipalities in more rural settings that serve as bedroom communities, with residents commuting to jobs in the cities or suburbs during the day and returning to their homes after work. This tends to be in stark contrast to some inner-city neighborhoods and inner-ring suburbs in which poverty is concentrated. Property values are low in such neighborhoods, which means that they cannot support high-quality public services.

It is important to note that the end result is economic *and* racial segregation based on housing patterns. This trend is made apparent by school districts. In some urban areas, for example, African Americans make up less than 3 percent of the total population but constitute 70 percent of the enrollment in school districts.[14] These are invariably schools that serve poor communities, where crime and other social problems place enormous strains not just on public education but also on social and economic opportunities in general. While people can, and do, experience challenge and struggle out in the suburbs, suburban communities are much more likely to have the fiscal capacity to support such public services as good school systems. And because good schools play an important role in determining where the middle class wants to live, again this becomes a self-reinforcing trend.

In other words, here is a difference that makes a big difference to the quality of life of millions of people. Place matters because wealth is segregated by communities across metropolitan regions,

> Place matters because wealth is segregated by communities across metropolitan regions, communities that are themselves concentrated in different political jurisdictions. As one well-known study of metropolitan politics and policy concludes, where you live in a given metropolitan area both affects your quality of life and shapes your social and economic opportunities.

communities that are themselves concentrated in different political jurisdictions. As one well-known study of metropolitan politics and policy concludes, where you live in a given metropolitan area both affects your quality of life and shapes your social and economic opportunities. Place affects access to jobs, public services, level of personal security (crime tends to be higher in some socioeconomically stressed neighborhoods), availability of medical services, and even the quality of the air we breathe (the people commuting in from the exurbs contribute to urban smog but escape to the cleaner rural air after the workday is done).[15]

Take the issue of jobs. Even with the suburbs getting hammered by the recession (see the box "Local Focus: The End of Sprawl?"), there are still a lot of jobs generated there. For example, think of the big-box stores such as Wal-Mart and Home Depot that dot suburban landscapes—even in the hard economic times of recent years, they still represent a lot of jobs. The people who most desperately need those jobs, and the social and economic opportunities they represent, are concentrated in poorer inner-city neighborhoods. Three quarters of all welfare recipients live either in the central cities or in poorer rural areas.[16] These people cannot move to the suburbs, where the jobs are, because they cannot afford the expensive homes that typify low-density, single-use housing developments.

Exurbs

Municipalities in rural areas that ring suburbs. They typically serve as bedroom communities for the prosperous, providing rural homes with easy access to urban areas.

Buying and operating a car also are expensive propositions that can levy a harsh financial toll on those less well-off. That leaves public transportation, which is often an inefficient way to cover the huge geographical spaces that separate inner-city homes from suburban workplaces.

Critics of the consequences of sprawl argue that the end result will be metropolitan areas that continue to promote and reinforce economic and racial segregation and create disparities in tax bases that lead to huge differences in the quality of public services among local political jurisdictions. On top of that, from a regional perspective, the patterns of metropolitan growth are economically inefficient (jobs and the labor market are disconnected) and environmentally dangerous (all those cars pump out a lot of toxic emissions).[17]

Government Reform in Metropolitan Areas

Racial and economic segregation, inequities in tax bases and public services, and, above all, political fragmentation that creates difficulty in coordinating rational and effective responses to regional challenges—the problems of governance in metropolitan areas are well-known. But what can be done about them?

A number of strategies have been developed for rationalizing government in metropolitan areas, all of which have been either implemented or considered to various degrees in virtually all major urban areas. The reform perspective pushes for such rationalization and begins with the assumption that the key problems and challenges of governance in metropolitan areas are regional in nature and, as such, should be addressed regionally. Proponents also tend to argue that many of the problems have been created by political fragmentation in the first place, in that there are lots of smaller governments making decisions that may produce local benefits but export the costs to other jurisdictions. If the root cause of these problems is political fragmentation, government consolidation is the obvious solution.

Reform perspective
An approach to filling gaps in service and reducing redundancies in local governments that calls for regional-level solutions

In other words, new regional governing structures should be created to fill the hole in the federal system, governments that are better positioned to respond effectively to the interconnected problems of large metropolitan areas.[18]

There is no universal response to filling that hole, however. Instead, there are a number of different strategies that range from creating new pan-regional governments to eliminating long-standing local jurisdictions.

Regional Governments

Adherents of the reform perspective are strong advocates of creating regional authorities to address regional problems. This can be done in a couple of ways. First, new government structures can be created to sit above existing political jurisdictions and be given the authority to oversee regional land-use planning. This sort of approach has been popular with a number of civic activists from the reform tradition. Former Albuquerque mayor David Rusk, former Minnesota state representative Myron Orfield, and syndicated columnist Neal Pierce have all been popular champions of pan-regional planning authorities.

A couple of well-known examples of such regional planning authorities are frequently cited by advocates as examples of the benefits of taking a top-down approach to land-use regulation. One of the best known of these is the Metropolitan Service District in Portland, Oregon, known simply as Metro. Metro is a true regional government that covers Clackamas, Multnomah, and Washington counties and the 25 municipalities in the Portland metropolitan area; all told, its jurisdiction extends across about 1.5 million people, or about 40 percent of Oregon residents. It is governed by an elected legislature (a six-member council) and an elected executive (the council president).[19] Metro exercises real regulatory authority in areas such as land-use planning, regional transportation, recycling and garbage disposal, and a host of other policy areas that are regional rather than local in nature.

A number of academic observers have concluded that the Portland top-down approach to regional planning has reaped considerable benefits not seen in metropolitan areas that have no comparable regional governance. For example, white flight has been markedly lower in Portland than in other cities. In contrast to the pattern seen in many other major cities, in Portland the middle class—especially young, highly educated individuals—tend to settle in the central city rather than in the suburbs or nonmetropolitan areas.[20]

One of the notable characteristics of the Portland Metro is the presence of an **urban growth boundary (UGB)**. A UGB controls the density and type of development by establishing a boundary around a given urban area. Land inside the UGB is slated for high-density development; land outside the UGB is slated for lower-density, rural sorts of development. In effect, this type of planning regulation forces cities to grow vertically rather than horizontally and, thus, sets limits on sprawl and the problems it generates.

Critics of UGBs argue that they have a significant downside. By limiting the land available for development, UGBs drive up prices for land in particular and real estate in general. The end results are high property values and limited supplies of affordable housing. This does not seem to have happened in Portland, however, at least to any extreme. In fact, property values there are considered reasonable compared with the rest of the West Coast. Reformers have pointed to the success of the UGB in Portland to promote the adoption of similar policies in other urban areas. Three states—Oregon, Tennessee, and Washington—now mandate cities to establish UGBs.

Regional Councils

Although Metro is a true regional government, it is also a very rare example—the vast majority of metropolitan areas in the United States lack any form of regional government with comparable authority and policymaking power. There are, however, a large number of regional planning authorities that provide at least a rudimentary form of coordination among the local governments packed into their metropolitan areas.

Probably the most common attempt to rationalize local policymaking across multijurisdictional metropolitan areas is the formation of regional councils. A **regional council** is "a multi-service entity with state- and locally-defined boundaries that delivers a variety of federal, state, and local programs while carrying out its function as a planning organization, technical assistance provider, and 'visionary' to its member local governments."[21]

Regional councils are made up of member governments, such as municipalities and school districts, although other nonprofit, civic, private, or academic organizations also may be included. They originated in the 1960s and 1970s as vehicles for delivering state and federal programs to regional areas. Since then, they have grown to become an important means of making and coordinating region-wide policy and planning in such areas as land use, transportation, economic development, housing, and social services. Regional councils are a way to recognize that decisions made in one community can trigger domino effects in neighboring communities and that it therefore makes sense to address some problems regionally rather than locally. There are 516 such bodies in the United States, and of the roughly 39,000 general-purpose local governments in the country (which include counties, cities, municipalities, villages, boroughs, towns, and townships), about 35,000 are served by regional councils.[22]

A related form of regional authority is the **metropolitan planning organization (MPO)**. MPOs are regional organizations that decide how federal transportation funds are allocated within their regional areas. MPOs are interesting because they represent a specific recognition by federal law that regions—as opposed to localities—are central functional policy units. The Intermodal Surface Transportation Efficiency Act of 1991 mandated that every metropolitan region had to identify an institution (an MPO)

Urban growth boundary (UGB)
A border established around an urban area that is intended to control the density and type of development

Regional council
A planning and advisory organization whose members include multiple local governments; often used to administer state and federal programs that target regions

Metropolitan planning organization (MPO)
A regional organization that decides how federal transportation funds are allocated within that regional area

to serve as the central coordinating authority for federal transportation funds in that area. These MPOs have the responsibility of developing transportation plans and programs for their metropolitan regions. Every transportation project involving federal money—which is to say virtually every major transportation project—has to be approved by an MPO. Some MPOs administer billions of dollars in federal transportation grants, and control over such large amounts of money, coupled with the MPOs' authority over critical transportation programs, translates into major political clout.[23] There is even a nascent effort to coordinate the decision making of MPOs within megaregions, which would extend their influence on transportation infrastructure policy across even wider geographic areas.

Regional councils and MPOs, however, should not be confused or equated with Portland's Metro. They are more a vehicle for intergovernmental cooperation than an actual form of government with executive and legislative authority independent of local government interests. Formal organizations of local governments in metropolitan areas have existed in some form or another for decades; regional councils and MPOs are just the more common and better-known examples. Hashing out roles and responsibilities, not to mention making decisions, involves a complicated—and often contentious—give-and-take among the local governments that constitute the membership of these regional bodies.

Intergovernmental institutions such as regional councils are, at best, confederal sorts of regional governments that are creatures of the often conflicting interests of their members. This complicates decision making and makes it harder for these bodies to exert firm regulatory authority over critical areas such as land use. Still, in most parts of the country, they come the closest to filling the hole in the organizational structure of the federal system. A move in this direction has been growing support for regional planning efforts that promote **smart growth**, development practices that emphasize more efficient infrastructure and less dependence on automobiles. Smart growth is reflected in regional, or even single-jurisdiction, policies that promote mixed-use developments that are pedestrian- and bicycle-friendly, emphasize building community rather than just structures of bricks and mortar, and consciously account for development's impact on the environment.

The bottom line on regional councils and MPOs is that, for the most part, there is a considerable mismatch between their governance capacities and the need for effective and coordinated responses to regional issues. As one study of regional councils concludes, "Despite the efforts of progressive reformers to push strategies encouraging . . . strong, centralized regional government institutions, most regional institutions find it difficult to address issues affecting the quality of life in a metropolitan area."[24]

> One of the lessons to emerge from the massive economic stimulus effort initiated by the federal government in response to the Great Recession was that the existing mechanisms of disbursement—state and local governments—sometimes do not effectively connect federal dollars with their intended policy targets. Part of this disconnect is clearly due to the lack of effective regional governance.

Despite their obvious limitations, these councils are currently the only politically viable regional governance mechanisms that "most local jurisdictions can use to address multiple and cross-cutting issues."[25] And the power and role of regional councils and MPOs may be increasing because of a shift in philosophy at the federal level. One of the lessons to emerge from the massive economic stimulus effort initiated by the federal government in response to the Great Recession was that the existing mechanisms of disbursement—state and local

---

Smart growth
Environmentally friendly development practices, particularly those that emphasize more efficient infrastructure and less dependence on automobiles

governments—sometimes do not effectively connect federal dollars with their intended policy targets. Part of this disconnect is clearly due to the lack of effective regional governance. The overarching intent of the federal government in providing the stimulus money was to stimulate the economy, and that meant targeting metro areas, where much of the nation's economic activity takes place. Yet, for the most part, there were no effective, general-purpose regional governments available to implement that sort of region-wide policy goal. Because of the "hole" in government, most of the stimulus dollars went to states and localities that were scrambling to get their individual shares of the federal pie. Powerful metro-level governments with the ability to effectively address key issues across political jurisdictions got less stimulus money for the simple reason that they largely do not exist. In response, the federal government began an effort to tie federal grants to increased regional cooperation, which puts regional councils and MPOs in a good position to increase their governance capacities in the future.

Many local governments also engage in looser, informal cooperative arrangements rather than creating formal institutions such as regional councils or MPOs. This sort of cooperation is known as an **interjurisdictional agreement (IJA)**, an increasingly common form of intergovernmental cooperation. An IJA may take the form of a binding agreement. For example, a town may contract with the county for law enforcement services or for dispatch services. Other IJAs may be much more informal and rest on nothing more than good-faith agreements between two or more local governments to provide a service jointly or to work together on planning or management issues. No one really knows how many IJAs there are or how effective they are in promoting successful integrated responses to regional problems. Given the shortcomings of more formal institutions such as regional councils and MPOs, however, IJAs often represent one of the few viable alternatives for multijurisdictional governance.[26]

Government Consolidation

One way to regularize or rationalize governance in a metropolitan region is to create a pan-regional institution. As already discussed, such an institution can take the form of a new level of government (such as Portland's Metro) or a formal institution of intergovernmental cooperation, such as a regional council. A second approach is to reduce the number of governments through merger or consolidation. This is typically done through the merging of a city with a county.

On the face of it, this makes a good deal of sense. Cities and urban counties share the same geographical space and provide similar services. A classic example is law enforcement services. Think of an urban county sitting on top of a large city. The county will have a sheriff's office; the city will have a police department. Each can have its own jails, dispatch centers, training facilities, and purchasing departments. It strikes many that there is a lot redundancy and inefficiency in duplicating these services in such close quarters. Why not consolidate at least some of these functions? That is exactly what Des Moines, Iowa, and Polk County did with their city and county jails. The county and city jails sat on opposite sides of the Des Moines River—directly across from each other—and consolidating facilities and operations just seemed to make sense.

If consolidating operations can reduce redundancy and improve efficiency, why not go whole hog and merge municipal and county governments into a single government? Cities and counties often duplicate bureaucracies and paperwork; so there seems to be an obvious logic to **city–county consolidation**. With as many as 75 percent of all major urban areas in the United States contained within single counties, it would seem to make sense that such mergers would be common and easy. But they aren't, and it doesn't.

According to the National Association of Counties, of the nation's more than 3,000 counties, only about 40 (roughly 1 percent) have consolidated with cities. Since 1990, there have been only about 45 formal proposals to consolidate city and county

---

Interjurisdictional agreement (IJA)
A formal or informal agreement between two or more local governments to cooperate on a program or policy

City–county consolidation
The merger of separate local governments in an effort to reduce bureaucratic redundancy and service inefficiencies

governments, and only about a dozen have actually passed.[27] Unsuccessful efforts include the attempts to merge Gainesville, Florida, with Alachua County and Spokane, Washington, with Spokane County.

Despite the glacial pace of city–county consolidation, it is an idea that has been around for a long time. The earliest consolidation dates back to 1805, when the city of New Orleans was consolidated with New Orleans Parish (remember, in Louisiana counties are called parishes). The practice even enjoyed an era of popularity in the 1960s and 1970s. Proposals for consolidation often come in response to state initiatives or regional challenges. For example, the citizens of Jacksonville, Florida, in Duval County, were experiencing industrial waste in their river, underachieving high schools, and clashes between city and county officials during the 1960s. Local business leaders lobbied the state legislature for help. The legislature created a commission that proposed a consolidation plan. The plan was approved in 1967 by the legislature and, subsequently, by the voters in a referendum.

For the most part, this merger has worked for the two governments involved. But even after the merger, there were municipalities in Duval County (Atlantic Beach, Baldwin, Jacksonville Beach, and Neptune Beach) but outside Jacksonville city limits that continued as independent local governments. These communities periodically have considered splitting off from Jacksonville/Duval and forming a new county (Ocean County) as a means to recover a county government less tied to the city of Jacksonville. Thus far, however, these efforts have not progressed beyond the discussion stage, and all these municipalities remain a part of Duval County.

Still, only a few dozen mergers in 200 years leaves a lot of cities and counties sitting right on top of each other, duplicating services. Why haven't city–county consolidations happened more often? The answer in part has to do with who supports and who opposes the mergers when they are proposed.

Consolidation typically is favored by business groups and others who favor efficiency in government spending and regulation over local control of government. These individuals seek a reorganization of government to reduce bureaucratic redundancy and to allow communities to speak "with one voice." The politics of consolidations, however, are tricky. Middle-class suburbanites may be concerned that mergers will benefit mostly downtown residents while raising taxes in the suburbs; inner-city minorities may fear their voting power will be diluted. Elected officials reflect these concerns and perhaps add some of their own. Consolidated governments mean fewer elected politicians and, most likely, fewer public employees. This creates internal pressure to resist merger movements.

There is also plain, old-fashioned community loyalty. The point has been made before about the strong tradition of local government in the United States. People identify with their local governments and tend to trust them (at least compared with state and federal governments). There is no tradition of regional government, and citizens and public officials treat these new and unknown entities with a degree of mistrust.

All this combines to make city–county consolidations a tough political undertaking, even when most objective observers agree they make a good deal of sense. Allegheny County and the City of Pittsburgh, for example, have been flirting with the issue of consolidation for more than a decade. A series of blue-ribbon panels, committees, and commissions have studied the pros and cons of an Allegheny–Pittsburgh consolidation, and they have mostly come to the same conclusion. "There's no question you could save money and provide much better service," states David O'Laughlin, who served on one such panel.[28]

There has been some progress. The city and county have managed to consolidate some operations, including 911 call centers, fingerprinting duties, and some court functions. But a full-scale merger, despite its apparent advantages, still seems a long way off. In 2006, yet another panel was formed to study city–county consolidation, and in 2008, it recommended that a merger take place. As of 2014, there was still no merger. Allegheny County and the hundreds of governments within its borders sometimes cooperate and sometimes feud, but they retain their local political independence. The bottom line is that local governments as a general

TABLE 12-2

Consolidated City–County Governments, 2011

City–Counties Operating Primarily as Cities		Metropolitan Governments Operating Primarily as Cities		Areas With County-Like Offices in Other Governments (City, Township, Special District, State)	
Alaska	City and borough of Anchorage	Tennessee	Hartsville and Trousdale County	Florida	County of Duval (City of Jacksonville)
	City and borough of Juneau		Lynchburg and Moore County	Georgia	County of Clarke (City of Athens) County of Echols (City of Statenville) County of Greley (City of Tribune)
	City and borough of Sitka		Nashville and Davidson County		County of Muscogee (City of Columbus)
	City and borough of Yakutat				County of Richmond (City of Augusta) County of Quitman (City of Georgetown) County of Webster (City of Preston)
California	City and county of San Francisco			Hawaii	County of Kalawao (State of Hawaii)
Colorado	City and county of Broomfield			Indiana	County of Marion (City of Indianapolis)
	City and county of Denver			Kentucky	Lexington-Fayette Urban County
Hawaii	City and county of Honolulu			Louisiana	Parish of East Baton Rouge (City of Baton Rouge)
Kansas	Unified Government of Wyandotte County and City of Kansas City				Parish of Lafayette (City of Lafayette)
Montana	Anaconda–Deer Lodge County				Parish of Orleans (City of New Orleans)
	Butte–Silver Bow County				Terrebonne Parish Consolidated Government
				Massachusetts	County of Nantucket (Town of Nantucket)
					County of Suffolk (City of Boston)
				New York	Counties of Bronx, Kings, New York, Queens, and Richmond (all part of the City of New York)
				Pennsylvania	County of Philadelphia (City of Philadelphia)

Source: National League of Cities, "List of Consolidated City-County Governments," 2011, http://www.nlc.org/build-skills-and-networks/resources/cities-101/city-structures/list-of-consolidated-city-county-governments.

rule do not want to share customers and definitely do not want to put themselves out of business.[29]

Like a good marriage, the consolidation of a city and a county depends critically on partners that trust each other and can make equal contributions to the merger. For example, Phoenix, Arizona, has won awards for its state-of-the-art management innovations. Surrounding Maricopa County, in contrast, has a reputation for management inefficiency. Good luck getting those two governments down the aisle.[30]

Policy in Practice

Is Merging Worth It?

Wouldn't it make sense to combine some of the more than 90,000 local governments in the United States? Wouldn't this reduce duplication of services and gain economies of scale? Wouldn't the new governments be better able to deal with the realities of the 21st century than are cities and counties whose boundaries were drawn when it took a daylong buggy ride to get from one to the other? Maybe.

The evidence on the benefits of consolidating city and county governments is mixed, at least when it comes to reducing government expenditures. Although efficiency is often touted as one of the big payoffs of consolidation, the numbers contradict that claim as much as they support it, according to Kurt Thurmaier, director of the Division of Public Administration at Northern Illinois University. Sometimes, for example, only the major cities within the county are included, and when employee salaries and benefits within the combining jurisdictions are brought in line with each other, the rounding tends to be up, not down.

Things have worked out better for Kansas City, Kansas, and Wyandotte County, according to Dennis Hays, who has been administrator of that unified government since it was created 17 years ago (and who before that was the city's administrator for 3 years). Before the consolidation, he says, "we were slipping into the deep abyss, and if we hadn't done consolidation when we did, who knows where we'd be?" Since then, according to Hays, the quality of services has improved, thanks to economies achieved when duplicative departments were merged. Taxes have been cut by 15 percent, and the combined workforce has been reduced by 20 percent. But in Hays's view, having a single policymaking body willing to take on the tough decisions has made the biggest difference, resulting in real improvements to the local quality of life. "We are an older blue-collar community, and now we are seeing young people wanting to move into Wyandotte for the first time in decades."

Nashville, Tennessee, is in the process of celebrating 50 years of consolidation with Davidson County.

Mayor Karl Dean, the combined government's sixth mayor since consolidation, believes that the overwhelming majority of his constituents see the merger as a key component of the success the city has had, including not experiencing the population exodus that a lot of cities have. In addition to efficient service delivery, Dean says, the consolidation has allowed Nashville to deal with issues such as economic development and securing sports teams without involving a lot of small political jurisdictions. And consolidation has provided a larger tax base, something that's critically important in efforts to improve services while holding down costs. As another bit of evidence of the success of consolidation, Dean notes that once or twice a year someone from another city asks Nashville how to do it.

The answer, of course, is that consolidations are politically very difficult to pull off. Somebody has to give up power, and consolidations usually require a vote of the electorate in each of the combining jurisdictions. So it shouldn't be surprising that there have been many more defeats than victories. From 1921 to 1996, there were 132 formal consolidation attempts with only 22 successes, according to a history of consolidations by Pat Hardy of the University of Tennessee's Municipal Technical Advisory Service. In the 1990s alone, there were 13 unsuccessful referendums on consolidation.

Little wonder that many pundits keep declaring the idea dead. Yet it keeps coming up. Since 1805, when New Orleans combined with Orleans Parish, there have been 33 city–county consolidations, according to Hardy's research, with about two per decade since World War II and four in the 1990s. The most recent consolidation was that of Louisville, Kentucky, and Jefferson County in 2003.

Consolidation is not a cure-all, but in the end structure does matter. Where would New York City be today if it were still five separately governed boroughs? Marrying political sovereigns is hard, but no consolidated government has ever divorced.

Source: Mark Funkhouser, "Cities, Counties and the Urge to Merge," *Governing,* October 2012.

Despite the inherent difficulties, in the past few years there has been a renewed interest in consolidation, especially by state governments. A good deal of this interest has been driven by economic pressures stemming from the Great Recession. In Michigan, for example, there are nearly 2,000 municipalities, more than 1,000 fire departments, more than 600 police departments, and a similar number of school districts. Michigan is a state that was particularly hard-hit by the recession; as discussed in Chapter 11, a number of its local governments fell into such precarious financial positions that they were effectively taken over by the state. The massive bureaucratic duplication at the local level did not make a whole lot of sense to Governor Rick Snyder when he took office in 2011. Snyder, whose background is primarily as a business executive and venture capitalist, saw all that government as inefficient and made attempts to trim it down. While the governor cannot force local governments to merge, he can create incentives to do exactly that. He made hundreds of millions of dollars in state aid for cities contingent on the elimination of duplication in areas such as fire departments and trash collection.[31]

Similar proposals were floated around the country in the past few years as elected officials sought ways to make government cheaper and more efficient in an era of scarcity. These proposals, however, generally have met the same fate as Snyder's—they have run into strong opposition at the local level. People are all in favor of smaller government, it appears, as long as it is not their government. People are loath to give up local control and tradition, and, besides, the evidence for the promised efficiencies of consolidation seems mixed (see the box "Policy in Practice: Is Merging Worth It?").

Annexation

Rather than forming new governments like Portland's Metro or merging old ones, another option for dealing with the problems of sprawl, traffic congestion, and uneven economic development is to make the existing political jurisdictions bigger. **Annexation** is the legal

---

Annexation
The legal incorporation of one jurisdiction or territory into another

incorporation of one jurisdiction or territory into another. Usually, the jurisdiction that does the annexing is the more politically powerful, whereas the "annexee" is weaker and may not be enthusiastic about becoming the latest addition to a larger municipal neighbor. This approach is relatively common in the South and West, regions where there are large tracts of unincorporated land adjacent to major cities. Cities such as El Paso, Houston, and Phoenix have annexed hundreds of square miles and, in doing so, have turned themselves into regional governments by sheer geographical size. Oklahoma City, for example, has more than 600 square miles within its city limits, with much of that added over the years through annexations.[32]

Annexation is principally a tool used by municipalities that want to control development along their peripheries and engage in planned expansions of their tax bases. Remember that cities like to place uniform requirements on area developers, leading developers to favor unincorporated areas where land is cheaper and there are fewer regulations. One way cities can put a stop to developers' avoiding regulation and impose a more coherent and orderly plan on metropolitan growth is simply to annex that unincorporated land.

A city government that wishes to annex a tract of land must organize the citizens of the unincorporated area to sign a petition. Some communities seek to expand by annexing prospectively, working to incorporate still-undeveloped parcels of land farther out from suburban parcels already being transformed from woods or farmland into subdivisions. This, in turn, may alienate rural landowners, including farmers, who value their traditional identity as separate from that of the city.[33] Annexation, in short, can create a lot of conflict, with some residents of unincorporated areas seeing it as a land grab that threatens to develop their rural communities out of existence.

Given this sort of conflict, it should not be too surprising to find that states make it tough for cities to annex new land. For example, in 1963 the California legislature created 58 local agency formation commissions as boundary watchdogs to discourage annexation. Among other things, these commissions are supposed to discourage urban sprawl. However, because urban sprawl pretty much describes metropolitan growth in the past four decades in large parts of the state, many Californians believe that these commissions are too weak to deal with rapid suburbanization.

Annexation can make sense from a big-picture perspective in that it can help impose the orderly expansion of urban municipalities, but there is no getting around the fact that it creates losers as well as winners. And the losers often are not interested in losing at all. For example, in Ohio, townships and counties are pushing for more say over annexations, deliberately trying to limit the ability of municipalities to gobble up unincorporated land in the name of development.[34]

Annexation also has natural limits—there has to be land available to annex. Although municipalities tend to have the upper hand over sparsely populated, unincorporated territories, if they bump up against another city, it's a different story. Unlike cities in the South and West, cities in the North and East are more likely to be ringed by incorporated suburbs; in effect, core cities are fenced in by other cities, with no real option to expand. Pittsburgh, for example, covers about 58 square miles—a fraction of Oklahoma City's 600-plus square miles. Outside of a merger with Allegheny County, it is unlikely that Pittsburgh is going to grow to anywhere near the geographical size of Oklahoma City.

The Case Against Reform: Public Choice and the Tiebout Model

Although metropolitan areas undoubtedly have problems, not everyone agrees that these problems require stronger regional governments. Indeed, some argue that at least a few of the underlying problems have been exaggerated, or at least not balanced adequately against the benefits of metropolitan growth.

Backing this argument is the fact that cities are, for the most part, pretty decent places to live. Core cities have not been swirling down into a uniform death spiral of relentless flight to the suburbs, leaving poverty, racial segregation, and crime. In many MSAs, the core cities remain the economic and social hubs of their regions. Scholars and musicians, business leaders and actors—people in a wide range of fields are still more likely to be attracted to the city to pursue their opportunities and dreams than to an exurb or single-use housing tract. Core cities remain exciting places—centers of innovation and culture, shopping and business activity.

So, despite the undeniable downsides to long-time growth patterns in metropolitan areas, there are also some positives, at least for some people. First and foremost are the quality-of-life benefits. That house in the suburbs can be a pretty darn nice house, in a pretty darn nice neighborhood. Good-quality schools are not hard to find in the suburbs, and neither are relatively crime-free developments with nice parks and maybe even a golf course nearby. This looks pretty attractive to those who have the means to take advantage of such opportunities. The same developments that often are castigated by academic critics of urban planning (or the lack thereof) can be job-generating machines.

For example, many consider Levittown in Nassau County, New York, to be the original "cookie-cutter" modern suburban housing development. Eventually totaling more than 17,000 homes, Levittown was built in an unincorporated area in the late 1940s and early 1950s. It was, literally, a community built from the ground up. First came the housing development; then public services (schools and parks) followed. Levittown served as a model for suburban growth across the United States, and what is notable about it for present purposes is that it was designed as an affordable housing development. The houses were nothing fancy—brand-new they cost less than $8,000, which even by the standards of the early 1950s was a good price for a single-family home. What they offered was not economic segregation for the moneyed class but, instead, the

In June 2006, Anaheim, California, became the first major U.S. city to go wireless. Residents can subscribe to the service on a monthly basis, and visitors can purchase temporary usage capabilities.

Gentrification, the physical rehabilitation of urban areas, is a double-edged sword. It can improve property values and attract new investment, but it can also disrupt long-standing local communities and cultures. In the Harlem neighborhood of New York, pictured here, African rhythm drummers who have been a fixture since the 1960s were forced to relocate after the residents of nearby new and expensive condominiums filed noise complaints.

American Dream of homeownership for a generation of World War II veterans.[35]

And the middle and upper classes have not abandoned every neighborhood in every city. Indeed, some decaying urban areas have undergone a renaissance, with old warehouses being turned into upscale condos and downtown neighborhoods becoming the focus of thriving cultural scenes. This process of physical rehabilitation of urban areas, which attracts investment from developers and drives up property values, is known as **gentrification**. Gentrified neighborhoods do present something of a double-edged sword, however. Although gentrification clearly can resuscitate decaying areas, the rise in property values means that poorer people (the original residents) can no longer afford to live there. In essence, gentrification creates pockets of middle-class wealth within cities. These pockets may be growing. Long commutes and the falling values of suburban properties brought on by the Great Recession have made city living more attractive to younger, middle-class people. This is the demographic that started heading to the suburbs 50 or 60 years ago. We may be seeing the beginning of that demographic's return to a more urban lifestyle.

In short, there is a glass–half-full perspective that sees innovation and vitality, high standards of living, and social and economic opportunities in the cities; this contrasts with a glass–half-empty perspective that focuses on segregation, smog, and economic inequality. There are also strong theoretical arguments against any large-scale movement to replace multiple local jurisdictions with larger regional governance structures.

> In short, there is a glass–half-full perspective that sees innovation and vitality, high standards of living, and social and economic opportunities in the cities; this contrasts with a glass–half-empty perspective that focuses on segregation, smog, and economic inequality.

The public choice model of politics views governments and public services in market terms. In this model, governments are seen as producers of public services and citizens are seen as consumers. As in most markets, competition among producers is seen as a good thing. With lots of local

---

Gentrification
The physical rehabilitation of urban areas, which attracts investment from developers and drives up property values

Public choice model
A model of politics that views governments and public services in market terms; governments are seen as producers of public services, and citizens are seen as consumers

jurisdictions, citizens can choose their favored "producers" by moving to the cities or towns that have the mixes of taxes and public services that suit them best. If local governments fail to satisfy individual citizen consumers—in other words, if their taxes go too high or their public services drop too low—the citizens can vote with their feet and move to other jurisdictions with more attractive tax–public service packages.

Multiple jurisdictions mean multiple producers, a set of competing "products" in the form of different mixes of taxes and public services. That competition keeps governments responsive to their constituents and puts pressure on the governments to be efficient and to keep the quality of public services as high as possible and taxes as low as possible. If local governments are inefficient—that is, their taxes are high and their public services are poor—they risk having their constituents move to other jurisdictions that offer better deals.

From a public choice perspective, concentrating local governments into regional governments, either through formal or informal mechanisms, risks a considerable downside. Government consolidation basically represents the creation of monopoly service providers and brings with it all the problems of monopolies that are well understood from private markets: lack of response to consumers, high costs, and indifferent quality.

This perspective on local government was most famously articulated by Charles Tiebout in the 1950s. The **Tiebout model** of local government calls for a metro area made up of a series of micropolitical jurisdictions. If each jurisdiction can control its tax-service package, fully mobile citizens will respond to the available packages by gravitating to the one that suits them best. Or, as Tiebout put it, the mobility of citizens will provide "the local public goods counterpart to the private market's shopping trip."[36]

In addition to highly mobile citizens, the Tiebout model requires informed citizens. If people do not know what different governments are offering in the way of alternative tax-service packages, they are not

going to be very good local government "shoppers," and local governments may be able to take advantage of that ignorance by becoming lazy and inefficient producers of public goods and services.

If the mobility and information requirements are met, the Tiebout model makes a strong theoretical case for political fragmentation in metropolitan areas, obviously arguing against the reform perspective of pushing for government consolidation. From the Tiebout model perspective, a regional government or a merged city and county government represents a big monopoly, which is likely to produce a large, inefficient bureaucracy that is unresponsive to citizens and has little incentive to keep quality high and costs low.

The "if" on the mobility and information requirements, however, is a big one. A number of scholars have argued that citizens are neither fully mobile nor fully informed. The constraints on mobility are fairly obvious: Where you can live is determined by how much money you can earn. This means the well-off, if they so choose, can be fairly mobile. The less well-off, on the other hand, are more likely to find their mobility limited by their pocketbooks. They simply cannot afford to move to better neighborhoods, even if they want to, because property prices are too high. There are some important implications here. The Tiebout model, remember, makes a good case that local governments will be responsive to people who have a real exit option, in other words, people who can pack up and move if they do not like what the local government is doing. If those people are defined by wealth, it means governments in metropolitan areas are likely to be more responsive to the concerns of the well-off than to those of the poor.

The requirement that citizens be informed also turns out to be a fairly restrictive burden on using the Tiebout model as a practical template for metropolitan governance. Studies show that citizens are not particularly mobile and pretty uninformed about local services. Indeed, if anything, citizens known more about local services when they live in an area with a single centralized local government compared with areas where there are lots of local governments.[37] These findings raise considerable questions about whether the Tiebout model can serve as a practical guide to governance in metropolitan areas.

Tiebout model

A model of local government based on market principles wherein a metro area is made up of a series of micropolitical jurisdictions that, on the basis of their services and costs, attract or repel certain citizens

Regardless, the Tiebout model demonstrates that there is at least a theoretical case to be made for political fragmentation in metropolitan areas. Coupled with high suburban standards of living and gentrification in the core cities, there is a reasonable counterargument to the calls for more centralized government in metropolitan areas.

Rural Metropolitics

Rural governments frequently face a different set of challenges from those that confront the urban areas discussed thus far. For example, some rural counties are dealing with shrinking and aging populations, as younger people shift from rural agricultural areas to more metropolitan areas in search of educational, social, and economic opportunities.

Consider that nationwide there are roughly 300 counties with fewer than 25,000 people that lost at least 10 percent of their population between 2000 and 2010.[38] At least in part, this reflects a population exodus that tracks a massive consolidation in agriculture as family farms give way to vast corporate operations. Fewer farms means fewer agricultural jobs, which means that younger people move to the cities, where the jobs are, leaving smaller rural communities with fewer shoppers, fewer schools, and fewer businesses. That is a recipe for decline that can be hard to reverse.

Rather than white flight, rural states with agriculture-based economies such as Iowa, Kansas, and Nebraska face **rural flight**, the movement of the young and the middle class to more urban areas. Although the underlying cause is different, the end result can be pressure for a solution that sounds familiar to any veteran of the political battles over urban growth—regional government. Iowa, for example, is a mostly rural state. It has a population of roughly 3 million and more than 1,000 general-purpose governments. If special districts (schools and the like) are included, Iowa has something like one government per 1,600 residents. Most counties in Iowa do not have a lot of people; what they have is a lot of government.

Rural flight
The movement of youth and the middle class from rural areas to more urban areas

(See Map 12-2 for county-by-county population changes in Iowa.)

That makes government tremendously inefficient; in rural areas, there are redundant layers of government sitting on stagnant tax bases. That puts upward pressure on property taxes, and it also creates incentives to make government more efficient. Consolidating governments is one way to do this, and it is an option that increasingly is being considered in rural states. Schools are typically among the first sets of merger candidates. As student populations decrease in a rural community, it is harder to fund a comprehensive K–12 school system. If there is another community within busing distance, it can make a good deal of financial sense for the two communities to split educational services—for example, to have elementary schools in both communities, the junior high in one town, and the high school in the other.

These sorts of pressures have made for a steady stream of school district consolidations in rural states. As recently as the mid-1980s, for example, Nebraska had more than 1,000 public school districts. As of 2014, it had 249. In a 30-year span, three quarters of school districts in Nebraska consolidated or went out of business.[39] It is not hard to fathom the economics behind this massive contraction of governments. School consolidations make financial sense from the standpoint of the statewide taxpayer; larger districts can take advantage of economies of scale, rationalize class sizes, and lower per-pupil spending. From a community perspective, however, school consolidations are less about dollars and cents than about identity, or even survival. A rural community that loses its school loses a central social and cultural institution, and the loss of teachers also means losing a significant chunk of a town's middle class. Many see the loss of a school, especially a high school, as a devastating blow to a rural community.

When economics come up against strong loyalties to local governments, the local loyalties often win, but those victories mean higher property taxes and fewer public services. Back in 2005, then-Iowa-governor Tom Vilsack tried to do something about his state's surplus of government, arguing that Iowans simply could not support that level of public infrastructure. Vilsack proposed a truly

MAP 12-2

Population Changes by County, Iowa, 2010–2013

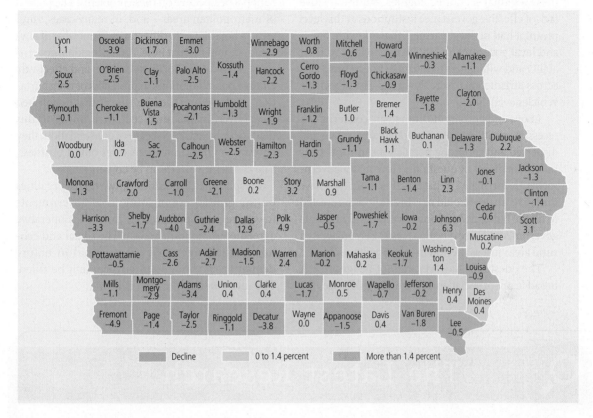

Lyon 1.1	Osceola −3.9	Dickinson 1.7	Emmet −3.0		Winnebago −2.9	Worth −0.8	Mitchell −0.6	Howard −0.4	Winneshiek −0.3	Allamakee −1.1

Decline   0 to 1.4 percent   More than 1.4 percent

Source: Iowa State University, "Population Percentage Change: April 1, 2010 to July 1, 2013," http://www.icip.iastate.edu/sites/default/files/uploads/images/thematic_maps/popchg_estimates.jpg.

radical solution—replacing the grab bag of hundreds of local governments with about 15 regional governments. These regional governments, Vilsack reasoned, would be not only cheaper but also better positioned to drive economic development in rural areas. His plan landed with a thud; it got little support at the local level and a chilly reception in the legislature.[40] Iowans preferred higher taxes and/or lower levels of service to losing their traditional local governments, a preference that is almost certainly still prevalent in most rural states.

Rural flight is a demographic phenomenon whose causes and consequences tend to attract less scholarly and media attention than do white flight and the problems it causes for core cities and urban areas. The governance and political issues raised by rural flight, however, clearly have distinct parallels with the broader story of metropolitics told in larger urban areas.

Conclusion

The central issue of metropolitics—and its rural equivalent—boils down to the gap that exists between local and state governments. Local governments were founded and organized in a horse-and-buggy era, and those organizational structures do not always make for a rational fit with 21st century realities. This gap became particularly noticeable during the Great Recession. Dense urban concentrations, or metros, are where most economic activity in the United States is located, and this activity is integrated and interconnected across a region rather than confined within a single local government's borders. It was natural for the federal government to focus its stimulus efforts on these regional economic engines, but the relative lack of effective governance institutions at this level meant it had no local partners to work with. States and local governments, which vary wildly in their ability and willingness to integrate policy functions across jurisdictions, were the only politically viable vehicles available.

Above and beyond the immediate concerns of a recession, political fragmentation in urban areas and dispersed and shrinking populations in rural areas raise a tough set of questions: How many governments are too many? What exactly should they have the power to do? Should new institutions be created to fill the hole between local governments and state government? These questions resist easy answers in rural areas just as they do in metropolitan ones.

The questions, however, cannot be ignored. A broad array of social and economic challenges are essentially regional in nature, and the hole in government organization means that in most places there is no strong central government taking a regional perspective on these problems. The politics of metropolitan areas—and, in many cases, rural areas—boils down to differences about what, if anything, should fill that hole. A true regional government, with the authority to develop and effectively enforce policy solutions to problems of transportation, land use, and the like, means that established local governments must cede their power to this new government. In the case of consolidation, they have to, in effect, put themselves out of business. The politics involved can be contentious.

Despite the difficulties, however, the realities on the ground are pushing local governments toward regional perspectives through cooperative agreements and joint action. The social and economic challenges that are regional in nature demand that the hole in government be filled. The unanswered question is how.

The Latest Research

Local government in the United States is organized for a 19th century social and economic environment, not for its 21st century equivalent. As this chapter has made crystal clear, we have many local governments, often crammed into the same metropolitan area, all making decisions that affect one another and the broader region with varying levels of cooperation and coordination. While there is more-or-less universal agreement on these points, there is less agreement on what a 21st century model of local governance should look like. Should it involve more city–county consolidation and a move to true regional governments, like Portland's Metro? Or do we want less centralization and more fragmentation, a concentrated effort to create a flexible and efficient market for public services along the lines of the Tiebout model? As the studies described below suggest, the latest research on these questions gives conflicting answers.

- **Faulk, Dagney, and Georg Grassmueck**. "City-County Consolidation and Local Government

Expenditures." *State and Local Government Review* 44 (2012): 196–205.

One of the central arguments for reducing the number of local governments is efficiency. Supporters say consolidation can make government more efficient and less costly by eliminating duplication of services and increasing economies of scale. This argument has taken on particular resonance during the past half-decade, as cash-strapped local governments have begun dusting off old consolidation proposals and debating whether they might offer an obvious means to do more with less. Yet evidence for the promised cost savings of consolidation is pretty mixed. This study is worth noting because of its powerful comparative-method research design. Faulk and Grassmueck examine two groups of cities and counties: One group consolidated, and the other considered but ultimately rejected consolidation. This allows them to make an apples-to-apples comparison of local government expenditures. The key finding of this study is actually a nonfinding: There was no difference in per capita expenditures between the consolidated and the unconsolidated groups. The authors conclude that consolidated governments might be able to produce better public services, but consolidation does not make those services any cheaper.

- **Hendrick, Rebecca, Benedict Jimenez, and Kamna Lal.** "Does Local Government Fragmentation Reduce Local Spending?" *Urban Affairs Review* 47 (2011): 467–510.

This makes for an interesting companion piece to the study just reviewed. The research team looks at local government spending in 126 metropolitan regions covering 538 counties. The key research question is whether greater fragmentation in these regions leads to higher spending. The answer is yes . . . and no. One of the key findings is that geographical areas with more single-purpose governments have higher levels of local government spending. This seems to support the argument for consolidation; the obvious implication is that merging the responsibilities of those single governments into fewer general-purpose governments will reduce spending. Yet another key finding of this study is that areas with more centralized governments also have higher spending. The takeaway story here is that the costs and benefits of fragmentation versus centralization are not clear-cut. Neither the many governments along the lines of the Tiebout model nor the fewer governments recommended by metro advocates are one-size-fits-all solutions. The pros and cons of more versus fewer governments depend on what sorts of governments (e.g., single-purpose vs. general-purpose) are involved, as well as on the political, economic, and social context.

- **Leland, Suzanne, and Kurt Thurmaier.** "Political and Functional Local Government Consolidation: The Challenges for Core Public Administration Values and Regional Reform." *American Review of Public Administration* 44, no. 4 (2014): 29S–46S.

A big contribution of this research article is a study of studies. It provides an in-depth review of research on the adoption, implementation, and results of local government consolidations. What emerges from this review is a clear signal that consolidations are rarely approved when they are proposed and results are mixed in the rare instances when consolidation actually takes place. The key stumbling block in both instances is politics; consolidation, to citizens and public officials, typically creates fears not just of a loss of political power but of an erosion of local identity. Rather than fighting these often unwinnable political battles, the authors push for an alternate approach that emphasizes acceptance of shared sovereignty and multilevel governance. What this means is that rather than local governments' disappearing, they would cede some of their authority to intergovernmental bodies that could operate on a regional scale. So, for example, to bring regional coherence to zoning, local governments would relinquish their zoning powers to a regional zoning board or commission. The local governments would remain intact and would have representation on that board, but the board itself would exercise sovereign power over zoning across jurisdictions in the region.

- **Bowman, Ann O'M., and Richard Kearney.** "Are U.S. Cities Losing Power and Authority? Perceptions of Local Government Actors." *Urban Affairs Review* 48 (2012): 528–546.

This is not a study of the pros and cons of consolidation versus fragmentation but, rather, a study of the distribution of power. As we learned from the discussion of Dillon's Rule in Chapter 11, local governments are not sovereign—they wield only those powers that states allow them to have. This raises an interesting question given the focus and theme of this chapter. If there really is no functioning level of regional government between states and localities, will states take on the job themselves? Especially given the social, economic, and political stakes (all discussed above), will states leave local governments to keep going their own way, or will they start to exercise their sovereign authority and start to lessen the power of local authorities? Bowman and Kearney get at this question by surveying state and local government officials to get their perspectives on the evolution of state–local relationships. Their findings show that state officials generally see a reasonable distribution of power, with local officials given a more or less appropriate balance of authority and discretion. The authors report that the view from local officials is decidedly different: "From the perspective of city managers . . . the past decade has been one of loss of power and discretionary authority accompanied by encumbering (state) mandates in numerous policy areas." Lacking meaningful regional government structures, perhaps states are taking on that job themselves.

Chapter Review

Key Concepts

- annexation (p. 396)
- car-dependent living (p. 385)
- city–county consolidation (p. 392)
- edgeless cities (p. 384)
- exurbs (p. 388)
- gentrification (p. 398)
- impact fees (p. 385)
- interjurisdictional agreement (IJA) (p. 392)
- leapfrog development (p. 385)
- low-density development (p. 385)
- megaregion (p. 383)
- metropolitan area (p. 382)
- metropolitan planning organization (MPO) (p. 390)
- metropolitan statistical area (MSA) (p. 382)
- public choice model (p. 398)
- reform perspective (p. 389)
- regional council (p. 390)
- rural flight (p. 400)
- smart growth (p. 391)
- sprawl (p. 384)
- Tiebout model (p. 399)
- urban growth boundary (UGB) (p. 390)
- white flight (p. 386)
- zoning laws (p. 384)

Suggested Websites

- **www.ampo.org.** Website of the Association of Metropolitan Planning Organizations (AMPO), the national organization for MPOs. AMPO is mainly oriented toward transportation issues, but the site includes downloadable studies and publications on a range of issues facing metropolitan areas.

- **www.metro-region.org.** Website of Portland, Oregon's, Metro, a rare example of a true regional government in the United States; includes the history of Metro's formation and information on a range of its activities.

- **www.narc.org.** Website of the National Association of Regional Councils, an organization of metropolitan planning organizations that seeks to promote cooperation between governments; covers urban, suburban, and rural governments.

State Stats on Metropolitics

*Explore and compare data on the states! Go to **edge.sagepub.com/ smithgreenblatt5e** to do these exercises.*

1. There are a large number of local governments in Allegheny County, Pennsylvania. How does Pennsylvania stack up against the rest of the country in terms of the number of elected officials? Is this surprising? Why or why not?

⑤SAGE edge™
for CQ Press

Sharpen your skills with SAGE edge at edge.sagepub.com/ smithgreenblatt5e. SAGE edge for students provides a personalized approach to help you accomplish your coursework goals in an easy-to-use learning environment.

⑤SAGE statestats

2. Kansas City is unique in that it is actually made up of two cities, Kansas City, Missouri, and Kansas City, Kansas. Say you live in Kansas City, Kansas, and work in Kansas City, Missouri. Should you gas up your car close to home or close to work? Why? What are the implications of this?

3. How did the number of public high schools in Nebraska change between 2001 and 2011? Why did this change occur? What (if anything) should the state and local governments in Nebraska do about this?

4. New York, northern New Jersey, and portions of Pennsylvania make up the largest metropolitan statistical area in the United States. What is the average household income in these states? What might this tell us about the relationship among these states? Do we have enough information here to make this analysis?

5. One of the drawbacks of metropolitan growth is the dependence on cars that it creates. Which states have the most cars per driver? Which have the least? Why is there such a large difference? Do these same states have the highest and lowest amount of pollutions released? If not, why?

6. What was the percentage change in the population of Fargo, North Dakota, between 2000 and 2010? What accounts for this change?

K–12 education is one of the single largest categories of expenditure for state and local governments. That means when budgets get tight, schools suffer. Cuts to public education in Kansas drew protests not just from educators, but from parents, students and other supporters of public schools.

Education

READING, WRITING, AND REGULATION

- Why are some school systems so much stronger than others?
- Why do curricula vary so much from state to state?
- Why are there so many different brands of school reform?
- Why has the federal government increased its involvement in education, traditionally a function of local and state governments?

President Lyndon B. Johnson once called education "the answer to all our national problems."[1] There's nothing too shocking about expressing this sentiment—faith in education's power to cure a wide variety of social and economic ills has long been broadly shared by American citizens. What is notable is who was saying it: the president of the United States. Historically speaking, public education has been almost exclusively the province of states and localities, not the federal government. Yet if education is going to be considered the cure for *national* problems, it inevitably attracts the attention—some might say the meddling—of the federal government. And it has. Johnson's administration led some of the first major federal forays into regulating public education, and successors have expanded those expeditions into this most traditional of state and local policy jurisdictions. As a result, public education has evolved into a classic example of the push and pull of federalism. Although public education systems are legally under the jurisdiction of states (public education systems are legally authorized by state constitutions), federal policy interests and the dollars and mandates that come with them have given the national government an ever-increasing role in governing neighborhood schools.

After reading this chapter, you will be able to

- describe key education policymakers and how they help shape and implement education policy,
- explain why per-pupil spending varies so much,
- summarize how educational performance is measured and what those measures say about public school performance,
- describe aims and objectives such as No Child Left Behind and the Common Core State Standards,
- discuss key alternatives to public schools, and
- identify key interest groups seeking to influence education policy.

This increasing federal role has dismayed a number of state officials, who over the past decade or so have fought vigorously to limit the federal government's growing role in public education. Nowhere is this made clearer than in the controversial history of the **No Child Left Behind Act (NCLB)**, a federal law that has been at the center of education policy reform debates for more than a decade. Passed in 2002 with broad bipartisan support, NCLB was the signature domestic policy program of President George W. Bush. The central goals motivating the legislation—to improve academic achievement, to eliminate gaps in educational achievement and opportunity between white and minority students, and to hold schools more accountable for student achievement—were broadly shared. The means used to achieve those goals, however, put different levels of government on a collision course. NCLB relied heavily on a mandated regime of standardized tests, set minimum standards of proficiency for passing those tests, and required schools to have all demographic groups reach that proficiency standard or risk being branded as "failing." This required states to implement expensive new curriculum and testing systems that were not always welcomed, especially when the federal government failed to live up to its promises to help cover the costs. In addition to funding squabbles and disagreements about the

educational merits of "teaching to the test," a battery of critics argued that the standards set by NCLB were unrealistic and impossible to meet. Effectively, NCLB told states that all their public school students had to be above average by 2014 or the states' schools would be punished. Needless to say, 2014 came and went without states meeting what some called the Lake Wobegon mandate, named after the fictional Minnesota town of novelist and radio personality Garrison Keillor, who described a place where "all the women are strong, all the men are good-looking, and all the children are above average."

States recognized well in advance of 2014 that they were not likely to meet the goals of NCLB. In 2011, Montana superintendent of public instruction Denise Juneau said her state was fed up with NCLB and was not going to impose unrealistic and possibly harmful performance targets on its school system. "We're not asking for permission," said Juneau. "We're just telling them we won't raise our annual objectives."[2] Idaho, South Dakota, and Utah soon followed suit. Rather than punish states for backing away from NCLB mandates, the administration of President Barack Obama began granting them waivers, essentially freeing them from NCLB requirements as long as they had plans to improve education performance. As of 2014, the vast majority of states had obtained such waivers.[3]

The NCLB controversy and the interest and involvement of all levels of government reflect the broad acceptance of President Johnson's claim that all the nation's social and economic problems

No Child Left Behind Act (NCLB)
Federal law enacted in January 2002 that introduced new accountability measures for elementary and secondary schools in all states receiving federal education aid

have a solution in education. It wasn't always this way. Up until the 20th century, there wasn't much of a public education system for anyone to be interested or involved in. Luckily, one intensely interested and involved person was Horace Mann, a 19th century Massachusetts education chief who is widely recognized as the father of the American **common school**, which remains the basis of the American system of public education. At a time when schooling was reserved mostly for children whose families were able to afford tutors or boarding schools, Mann's common-school concept represented radical reform. As the first secretary of Massachusetts's **state board of education**, the one-room schoolhouses that Mann inspected were crude and ill equipped. Many of the teachers were poorly paid and lacked training, and regular attendance by students was not required by law. Through personal advocacy and his widely circulated writings, Mann did much to build up state government as the primary actor in the fledgling experiment of public education in the United States. Mann's ideas evolved from radical reform of public education as we know it today, a system of taxpayer-funded schools governed and regulated primarily through state law.

States being states, there are big differences across education systems, in everything from funding to curricular requirements to investment in infrastructure. Yep, you guessed it—these differences make a difference. The physical state of a classroom, the salary and qualifications of the teacher running that classroom, and what a student has to do to pass that class can vary widely from state to state. There are some constants, however. All states have laws requiring all taxpayers, not just families with school-age children, to support society's bid for an educated citizenry. All states also have to live with the burden of expectations that comes with the sentiments expressed by President Johnson. Education is seen not just as a solution to all national problems but as the basis for individual social and economic opportunity. Education is thus an area of governance that brings out panic in some parents who feel that their children's entire futures are at stake with every report card. It is an area that allows ambitious political candidates to make names for themselves by vowing to hold schools more accountable and promising to get better results in the classroom from taxpayer dollars. Politicians get involved in education policymaking despite occasional resistance by professional educators, who value their autonomy and resent burdensome regulation.

The high political stakes surrounding education are not unique to the 21st century or to NCLB. For decades, state and federal lawmakers have been expressing concern that public education in the United States is underperforming and that this underperformance hinders the nation's social and especially economic fortunes. In 1983 the administration of President Ronald Reagan commissioned a study of education in the United States; the resulting report, titled *A Nation at Risk,* created a firestorm with its declaration that the mediocrity of public schools invited the defeat of the United States by a foreign power. NCLB is just one example of a near-continuous education reform effort that was sparked by that report and generally focuses on themes such as **back to basics**, new curriculum **standards**, and **high-stakes standardized testing**.

In this chapter we take an in-depth look at education policy. This perennial obsession of parents, reformers, and lawmakers, held up by presidents as the answer to all our problems, is the focus of much friction in the federalist system and is one of the primary policy responsibilities of state and local governments.

Common school
In a democratic society, a school in which children of all income levels attend at taxpayer expense

State board of education
Top policymaking body for education in each of the 50 states, usually consisting of appointees selected by the governor

Back to basics
A movement against modern education "fads," advocating a return to an emphasis on traditional core subjects such as reading, writing, and arithmetic

Standards
In education, fixed criteria for learning that students are expected to reach in specific subjects by specific grade years

High-stakes standardized testing
Testing of elementary and secondary students in which poor results can mean either that students fail to be promoted or that the school loses its accreditation

Organization and Leadership: Schools Have Many Bosses

The United States is one of the few industrialized countries with no national ministry of education. The federal government does have a cabinet-level education agency—the U.S. Department of Education—but its regulatory and funding authority is limited. The agency was created in 1978 as the fulfillment of a campaign promise by President Jimmy Carter, and its existence has been controversial ever since. Many critics, especially conservatives and Republicans, argue that education is not the federal government's policy concern and that Washington has no business sticking its large bureaucratic nose into a primary concern of the states. In 1980 Ronald Reagan campaigned on an explicit promise to abolish the Department of Education, and nearly a quarter-century later, 2012 Republican presidential nominee Mitt Romney was campaigning on a promise to shrink the agency drastically if not kill it outright. The department has proven to be remarkably resistant to such plans; yet its survival and expansion over the past three decades have not centralized governance over education at the federal level. The primary authority for running schools remains with the 50 states. The reason education is controlled by states rather than the federal government is the Tenth Amendment, which dictates that the powers not delegated by the Constitution to the federal government are reserved for the states. In effect, that means regulatory authority over education ultimately rests with the states. The big exception to this is the District of Columbia, which technically is a federal city and not a state; its board of education derives its funds from the city's appropriation from Congress.

In contrast to the Johnny-come-lately federal government, states have been taking on the task of schooling their citizens for a very long time. For example, in 1857, Minnesota's constitution proclaimed that because the "stability of a Republican form of government depends upon the intelligence of the people, it is the duty of the legislature to establish a general and uniform system of public schools."[4] In other words, the consensus was that creating a well-educated population not only helps individual citizens prosper but also helps entrench the democratic process. Indeed, most state constitutions justify their provisions for taxpayer-supported education systems and compulsory school attendance laws not by citing economic reasons but by arguing that democracy needs an educated citizenry to function.[5]

> Legend has it that a national education chief in Europe can look at a clock on any given weekday and know precisely which lesson is being taught in classrooms across the country at that moment.

Fifty varying traditions make for a lot of bosses in a democratic approach to education. A system that permits local innovations and variations is a far cry from the systems in use in other countries. Legend has it that a national education chief in Europe can look at a clock on any given weekday and know precisely which lesson is being taught in classrooms across the country at that moment. This is not the case in the United States, where education systems can be very different from state to state.

Generally speaking, state legislatures working with state **departments of education** are the major players dealing with state education policy questions and large-scale resource issues. A state legislature can raise teacher salaries statewide, equalize funding among districts, and set up health benefits and retirement plans for the state's pool of teachers. It can borrow money by floating state bonds to provide schools with construction funds, which commits taxpayers to long-term debts. The states are also the main players in

---

Departments of education
State-level agencies responsible for overseeing public education

Special interests frequently target school board elections. In 2014, South Carolina state senator Mike Flair pushed to change that state's biology curriculum to be more critical of the theory of evolution and, his critics argued, to promote the teaching of creationism in science classes.

AP Photo/Mary Ann Chastain

determining **teacher licensure procedures.** For example, they determine whether or not teacher candidates must take standardized tests and how schools are awarded **accreditation.** States also set curricular standards and graduation requirements.

The more complex state decisions are proposed and implemented by an experienced educator who is the chief state school officer. Such an official may be appointed by the governor, as in Iowa, Maine, and New Jersey, or by a state board of education, as in Louisiana, Utah, and Vermont. In some states, the top school official is elected, whether on a partisan ballot, as in North Carolina and Oklahoma, or on a nonpartisan ballot, as in North Dakota and Oregon. This official works closely with the state board of education, the members of which are also appointed or elected, depending on the state. The members of a state's board usually represent all the regions of the state.

While regulatory authority over education is concentrated at the state level, the actual administration of schools is widely decentralized. Most public schools are not run directly by the state but by **local education agencies (LEAs),** which have been formed in nearly 15,000 **school districts** scattered over cities, counties, and townships. School districts are staffed with full-time professionals, but they carry out policies set by **school boards** or other locally elected officials.

The extent of policymaking authority enjoyed by each LEA or district is determined by the state's legislature, and this is a difference that can make a difference. In Horace Mann's region of New England, local control is strong. In contrast, the population of states in the Deep South traditionally has been poor and rural. Many southern citizens are suspicious of government and untutored in its workings. As a result, the legislatures of these states have retained a more centralized role.

Even within states, there are huge differences in economies, traditions, and demographics. Think of rural, mountainous Northern California versus densely populated, arid Southern California. Also, Northern Virginia, an affluent suburban area of Washington, D.C., that tends to favor active government, is very different from Virginia's rural areas, in which folks tend to favor limited government.

The degree of flexibility in education that states can give to localities depends greatly on scale. It also depends on how passionate local citizens are about participating in school governance. The

Teacher licensure procedures
The processes states use to qualify teacher candidates to work in school districts; requirements for licensing typically include attainment of certain academic degrees, work experience, and adequate performance on adult standardized tests

Accreditation
A certification process in which outside experts visit a school or college to evaluate whether it is meeting minimum quality standards

Local education agencies (LEAs)
School districts, which may encompass cities, counties, or subsets thereof

School districts
Local administrative jurisdictions that hire staff and report to school boards on the management of area public schools

School boards
Elected or appointed bodies that determine major policies and budgets for school districts

nation's school districts are a patchwork quilt, the parts of which evolved as individually as the states themselves. Texas, for example, contains more than 1,000 school districts. These vary widely, from the liberal college town of Austin to the conservative business center of Dallas. In contrast, Hawaii has one school district covering the whole state.

School boards are quintessentially U.S. democratic institutions that got their start in the Progressive Era at the end of the 19th century. These citizen boards were envisioned as a way to end the spoils system. Individuals would no longer be able to show partisan and political favor by awarding school jobs to their followers. This would make way for the shared pursuit of effective public education.

Looking back now, that promise seems quaint; various groups have long targeted school board elections to further special interests rather than the public interest. In Virginia, school board elections were actually abolished in the early 1950s because southern white traditionalists feared that too many candidates were sympathetic to the then-growing school desegregation movement. It was not until 1992 that elected members once again replaced appointed members. More recently, conservative Christian political activists have zeroed in on school board elections as battlegrounds for their agenda of promoting school prayer, eliminating sex education, and introducing the teaching of "intelligent design" as a curricular counterweight to science classes that teach evolution.

Some critics say school boards actually produce fewer school improvements than they do campaign bumper stickers. That is one reason they were curbed by city governments during the 1990s in Boston, Chicago, Cleveland, and Detroit, and a little later in New York.[6] Faced with stagnating test scores and an exodus of families to private or parochial schools, urban leaders argued that emergency action to arrest the decline of the schools was more important than the democracy of a thousand voices.

The idea is that a centralized authority figure, such as a mayor or school chief, is more visible and thus more accountable than are low-profile school board members, who are often more worried about getting reelected than about making difficult decisions. Members appointed by an elected mayor are more likely to take decisive action and worry less about glad-handing, returning campaign favors, and seeking reelection. The jury is still out on such propositions, and proposals to abolish elected school boards tend to appear only in districts that are in dire straits.

To be fair, most school boards are genuinely focused on their responsibilities, but they often face formidable challenges. Keep in mind that by law a public school must accept all students who live within its jurisdiction. This makes planning tricky, because different student populations can have wildly differing needs, including accommodations for pupils who speak little English or have disabilities. Many school boards do not have taxing authority, but most prepare budgets for approval by the county board or city council, which must balance education spending against spending on police and fire protection and transportation. The board hires the superintendent, who hires the principals, who in turn hire the teachers.

Money Matters

Public education is funded almost exclusively by state and local governments; indeed, public education is by far the largest single category of spending for these governments. About 28 cents of every dollar spent by state and local governments goes to primary (K–12) education.[7] On average, states funded 44 percent of school budgets in 2011–2012, with 44 percent coming from local jurisdictions and just 12 percent from the federal government.[8]

Many states and localities raise school funds from income taxes and sales taxes. Twenty-seven states earmark lottery funds for education, although the budgetary impact of this often controversial revenue source is debatable. While lotteries no doubt can provide funds to support public schools, those moneys tend to be a modest fraction of overall education budgets. The lottery in California, for example, covers about 1 percent of the state's education spending.[9] While education is funded by a diverse revenue stream, the biggest and often most controversial source of school funds is local property taxes. These taxes are paid by homeowners and businesses based on the assessed value of their homes and businesses, usually a percentage of each $100 in assessed value.

There is logic to using property values as a basis for education funding. All taxpayers in a given community are believed to benefit from a high-quality school system—it helps maintain attractive real estate values and contributes to an educated workforce. And property taxes are progressive, meaning that homeowners whose property is worth more pay more in nominal amounts, although all pay the same percentage. Most mortgage companies inconspicuously collect these tax funds for homeowners. The money is then kept in the homeowners' personal escrow accounts until the taxes are due.

The downside of property taxes is that, as property values gain in value, the assessment and corresponding property taxes also rise—irrespective of whether a homeowner's income is rising along with it. This vicious circle is what fueled passage of California's famous Proposition 13 in 1978. This statewide ballot measure capped property taxes and ignited a tax revolt in other states.

An even deeper problem with funding schools through property taxes is that wealthier districts are able to keep theirs at an attractively low percentage rate and still produce enough revenue dollars to support good schools. For example, in affluent Beverly Hills, California, property was—and still is—very expensive. Yet the tax rate cited in *Serrano v. Priest* (1971), a famous school-funding equity case, was only $2.38 per $100 in assessed value. Place this up against the $5.48 per $100 in the low-income Baldwin Park area. There the schools were demonstrably inferior, and the community was able to spend only half the amount spent in Beverly Hills. The California Supreme Court agreed that families in Baldwin Park were being denied a "fundamental right" to good-quality schools.[10] The court ordered the legislature to find a way to make school funding more equitable.

A slightly different principle was spelled out by the U.S. Supreme Court in the 1973 ruling in *San Antonio Independent School District v. Rodriguez*. In this case, attorneys for a largely Mexican American population found that their clients were paying a tax rate 25 percent higher than that paid by people in nearby affluent school districts. These less-affluent districts, however, were able or willing to fund schools with only 60 percent of the amount enjoyed by wealthy San Antonio neighborhoods. Here the Supreme Court acknowledged the disparities but ruled that equal school funding is not a federal constitutional right: "The Equal Protection Clause does not require absolute equality or precisely equal advantages," the justices wrote. Despite this ruling, the precedent was set. State courts began to see themselves as protectors of poor and rural students, and the movement for school funding equity at the state level gathered more steam.

Vermont has the fewest enrolled public school students (88,000 in fall 2014). California has the most (6,268,600).

These two cases launched a decades-long period of constitutional litigation on school funding that has spread to nearly every state. It pits the principle of local control against pressures to close the gap between wealthy and poor districts. Jurists, educators, parents, and tax activists continue to fight about the key to school equity.

In the 1970s, the courts in most states, as in California, ruled in favor of greater equalization among districts. After some judicial setbacks, the momentum slowed in the 1980s before gaining ground again in the courts of the 1990s. Nowhere was this drama played out more visibly than in Vermont, where a 1997 state supreme court ruling prompted the legislature to enact the controversial Act 60. This law forces wealthier districts that want to upgrade their schools to share their added funds with schools in poor districts.

Understandably, citizens in affluent districts like to see their tax dollars spent in their own communities, and they will lobby and push to keep their schools the best. Many middle-class and upper-class taxpayers say they paid extra for their homes so their children could attend schools that do not lack for essentials. Citizens in poor districts, by contrast, argue that dilapidated school buildings, meager resources, and teachers at the low end of the profession's already low pay scale are the chief reasons for the achievement gap between their children and those in wealthier districts. (See Map 13-1.) They assert that resources should be distributed among all districts so all students receive an essentially equitable level of education. Should

MAP 13-1

Spending per Student, Fiscal Year 2012

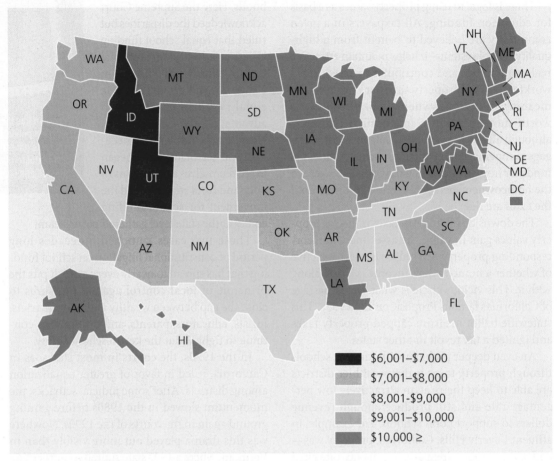

Legend:
- $6,001–$7,000
- $7,001–$8,000
- $8,001–$9,000
- $9,001–$10,000
- $10,000 ≥

Source: Mark Dixon, U.S. Census Bureau, "Public Education Finances: 2012," Table 11, http://www2.census.gov/govs/school/12f33pub.pdf.

individuals from less-affluent areas be denied access to a good education? Must funneling more resources into disadvantaged communities require "penalizing" affluent communities?

Responses among state legislatures to court orders on school funding have varied. The issue has not always broken down easily along conservative–liberal lines. Indeed, the percentage of per-pupil expenditures has risen most steeply during periods of conservative ascendancy, such as the 1920s and 1950s.[11] This demonstrates the degree to which creating quality schools is a near-universal value.

Researchers examining the role money plays in learning have created models that attempt to factor in such variables as a school's percentage of student dropouts, graduation rates, teacher salaries, and enrollment. These models also look at the percentage of children living in poverty and those in female-headed households, how many students have disabilities and how many of these have severe disabilities, and how many students possess limited English proficiency.[12] Few believe that pouring money into a school district will automatically produce improvements. As a result, they also attempt to consider such human factors as the degree of cooperation among teachers, rates of absenteeism, and the extent of disruptive behavior in classrooms.

Most important, researchers try to isolate precisely how moneys are best spent inside schools to derive the most benefit. Areas in which increased funding translates into student learning gains, according to one study, include instruction,

States Under Stress

Suing for Funding in Kansas

Lawsuits on education financing have consumed Kansas politics for 40 years. There's nothing unusual about states' being sued for undersupporting public education. Most states have some constitutional or statutory obligation to contribute financially to public education; supporters of public education at the local level—parents, students, and the policymakers who have to set and levy property taxes—often think that contribution is too modest. The upshot is that the vast majority of states are dragged into court over this issue at one time or another. Kansas, though, takes this scenario to another level. No matter what the state's legislators are talking about at a given moment, school finance hangs over them like a menacing storm cloud that just won't go away.

In 2014 the legislature was sent scrambling to comply with a state supreme court decision declaring that school funding levels (a) were too low and (b) varied way too much from one school district to another. The cost of complying with the ruling was somewhere in the neighborhood of $130 million. That merely set the stage for the next big legal battle over whether the state's entire public education system was inadequate to meet the needs of Kansas's children.

At the root of much of this conflict is a mandate in the state's constitution that "the legislature shall make suitable provision for finance of the educational interests of the state." Dating back to at least 1973, the state has been sued for failing to meet that standard. In the 1990s, for example, per-pupil spending in some districts was 4 or 5 times higher than in other districts. The constitutional implications of that imbalance prompted the legislature to shore up minimum state aid per student. Another legal kerfuffle in 2005 led the legislature to kick in an extra $147 million to fund public education.

In the past 6 or 7 years, two things happened to bring the conflict over state aid for public schools in Kansas to a particularly acrimonious peak. First the recession hit in 2008. Then in 2011 Republicans took full control of the state government on a promise to cut taxes. The net result was a hefty cut in state aid; per-pupil state aid fell by roughly 15 percent, from $4,492 to $3,838 (overall, per-pupil spending in Kansas dropped by roughly 17 percent in inflation-adjusted dollars between 2008 and 2014). The state was sued for failing to adequately fund public schools and, again, lost. This time, though, the courts were not just saying that the state needed to pony up more cash to meet its legal obligations; they were strongly hinting that money was not the only problem—the whole system for determining state aid might fail constitutional muster.

And so the fight wages on. Kansas has been embroiled in a four-decade debate about how to finance schools, with no end in sight as of mid-2014. Barring some unlikely outbreak of feasible consensus and practical compromise, it is a pretty safe bet that some version of this same conflict will be playing out in Topeka 40 years from now.

Source: Adapted from Alan Ehrenhalt, "Have Judges Overstepped Their Authority on Education?" *Governing*, June 2014.

---

central office administration, and teacher/student ratios. Areas in which spending more has demonstrated less of a payoff include school-level administration, overall **capital outlays**, and salaries for teachers with advanced degrees.[13]

Capital outlays
A category of school funding that focuses on long-term improvements to physical assets

Since the movement for new standards and accountability gained ground in the 1990s, school funding battles have shifted from an emphasis on equalization toward an effort to achieve adequacy, or what is required to get students to meet high standards.[14] To determine how much per-pupil spending is adequate for a school district, some states convene a panel of experts who use their professional judgment to pick the resources needed by schools, determine the costs of acquiring these resources, and then adjust their recommendations in favor of the needier districts. Examples of such states are Maine, Oregon, and Wyoming. Other states use the **successful schools model**, wherein groups of schools whose students have done well according to state standards are examined for their average per-pupil costs, which are then applied across the state. Examples of these states are Illinois, Mississippi, and Ohio.[15]

Successful schools model
An education model that uses observed spending levels in the highest-performing schools as the basis from which to calculate necessary spending in other, lower-performing schools

The funding appropriated by state legislatures depends on the input expected of localities. In New York State, for example, disparities in per-pupil spending between affluent and less-affluent districts can amount to thousands of dollars.[16] The amounts also vary by regional costs of living and by states' philosophies on the proper reach of government.

Furthermore, affluent suburban communities often differ from their urban counterparts in funding priorities. Parents in downtown Detroit or Cleveland, for example, may want extra moneys for crime prevention and building upgrades, whereas suburbanites in places such as Bloomfield Hills, Michigan, and Shaker Heights, Ohio, want more money spent on computer technology and extracurricular programs.

MAP 13-2

Projected Student Enrollment in Public Schools by State, 2014

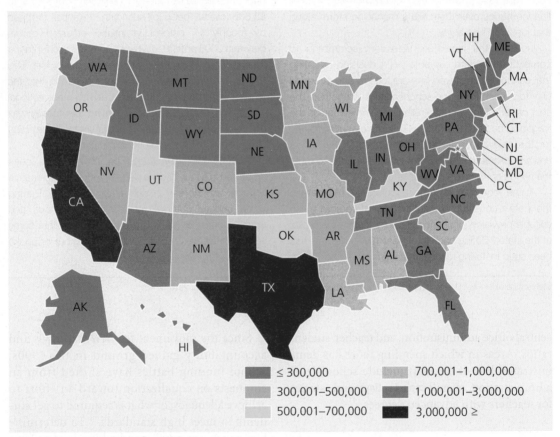

Legend:
- ≤ 300,000
- 300,001–500,000
- 500,001–700,000
- 700,001–1,000,000
- 1,000,001–3,000,000
- 3,000,000 ≥

Source: National Center for Education Statistics, *Digest of Education Statistics* (Washington, DC: Institute of Education Sciences, U.S. Department of Education, 2013), Table 203.20, "Enrollment in Public Elementary and Secondary Schools, by Region, State and Jurisdiction: Selected Years, Fall 1990 Through Fall 2023," http://nces.ed.gov/programs/digest/d13/tables/dt13_203.20.asp.

Rural districts in states such as South Dakota or Wyoming have their own problems. They may have trouble raising teacher salaries, for example, if it means pushing those salaries out of line with comparable local salaries in other professions.

Looking strictly at per-pupil spending, the state offering the least in 2012 was Utah, at $6,206. The state spending the most was New York, at $19,552. School funding suffered considerably as a result of the tough economic times ushered in by the Great Recession. It is estimated that in the 2013–2014 school year, 35 states were spending less per student in inflation-adjusted dollars than they did in 2008. Fourteen of those states saw per-pupil expenditures drop by at least 10 percent, and seven states (Alabama, Arizona, Idaho, Kansas, Oklahoma, South Carolina, and Wisconsin) cut education spending by more than 15 percent. In contrast, only a single state—oil-rich North Dakota—has increased per-pupil expenditures by more than 10 percent. Even though the recession was technically long over by 2014, cuts to education were still coming. In 2013–2014, 15 states cut per-student spending and 7 states increased spending not at all or by less than 1 percent. Only two states, Florida and Oregon, increased spending by more than 5 percent in 2013–2014. The impact of all this cutting is hard to overstate, and not just in purely educational terms—between 2008 and 2013, local school districts also cut more than 320,000 jobs.[17]

The Pressure to Perform

Except in the minds of some nostalgists, it is doubtful there ever was a halcyon era of consensus among education's disparate stakeholders. For example, traditionalists who hark back to the classic education taught in the early 20th century seem to forget that in 1900, only 6 percent of children in the United States finished high school. Back then, the best that most could count on was a solid job in, say, manufacturing. For many, college wasn't an option.[18] The bottom line is that there are far too many views about the nation's public schools for all parties ever to agree that public education achieved some satisfactory level of quality at *any* point in time. Today's charge that schools are going to the proverbial hell in a handbasket has been a rallying call for education reformers going back to at least the 1940s and 1950s.

> Traditionalists who hark back to the classic education taught in the early 20th century seem to forget that in 1900, only 6 percent of children in the United States finished high school. Back then, the best that most could count on was a solid job in, say, manufacturing. For many, college wasn't an option.

These days, the most frequently cited evidence for public school underperformance is comparisons of standardized test scores. The claim is that test scores within the United States are falling, or at least not increasing, and/or that American students come out poorly in international comparisons of test performance. These charges are nothing new. In 1983, Reagan administration education secretary Dr. Terrell Bell published a high-profile and highly controversial report titled *A Nation at Risk*. It is worth pointing out that *A Nation at Risk* was a research report that employed the comparative method. It compared states on a wide variety of performance metrics in four broad areas (curriculum content, learning expectations, teaching, and time) and reported that not many states fared well in these comparisons. When states were compared with other nations, they looked even worse. The publication of this comparative research report sparked an education reformation movement that is still ongoing. In spite of all the resources and energy consumed by this education reform movement, the worry that public schools are not up to standard has not changed much at all. In 2008, the U.S. Department of Education published a 25-year follow up to *A Nation at Risk*. Its big conclusion was this: "If we were 'at risk' in 1983, we are at even greater risk now."[19]

There are certainly some empirical reasons for all this worry. It is true that school test scores have been relatively stagnant for many years. It is hard to argue that a yawning achievement gap has not persisted between the preponderance of African American and Hispanic students at the lower end of the achievement scale and the frequently more-affluent whites and Asian Americans near the top. Yet test scores are not locked into a downward spiral. There is a glass–half-full perspective to public education in America. Look at the nation's ever-replenishing supply of successful entrepreneurs. Look at the country's proliferation of Nobel Prize winners. Look at how American corporations continue to compete and succeed in the world economy. If public education plays a foundational role in supporting the economy and promoting new knowledge, America's schools must be doing something right. Americans seem to recognize this. In 2013, polls showed that strong majorities of citizens gave their local schools a grade of A or B, and nearly three quarters said they had trust and confidence in the teachers in those schools. Tellingly, though, less than 20 percent of Americans would give public schools nationally a grade of A or B. Citizens seem to think that for the most part their local schools are doing a pretty good job but, given all the bad news they hear about education, everyone else's schools must be in serious trouble.[20]

Teaching to the Test

Although increasingly controversial, the main performance indicator for schools remains not grades, not responses to satisfaction surveys, not performance on oral exams but scoring on standardized tests—an indicator that has taken on new significance in the era of NCLB. Critics bemoan the trend of "teaching to the test," which skews classroom time toward the subjects covered on these tests, often at the expense of classes such as art and music.[21]

A thriving commercial testing industry has grown up to supply schools with inexpensive, mass-produced tests for quick computerized scoring of large numbers of students from kindergarten to 12th grade. Familiar giants in this multibillion-dollar industry include the Comprehensive Test of Basic Skills, the Iowa Test of Basic Skills, and the Stanford Achievement Test (SAT; note that this is not the SAT formerly known as the Scholastic Assessment Test, which many of you took when applying to colleges).

Each publisher has developed procedures to continually rotate questions, keep the tests statistically valid and as free as possible of cultural bias, and minimize scorekeeping errors—and all for good reason. When things go awry, lawsuits can result. Some of these tests are **criterion-referenced tests**, intended to measure mastery of a given subject as defined by state standards. Most, however, are **norm-referenced tests**, meaning that students are graded on how well they approach the mean student score on that same test administered across the country.[22]

A large number of states have developed their own tests, and these continue to be permitted under NCLB, largely because advocates of local control mounted strong resistance to proposals made in the 1990s for a national student test. Florida has its Florida Comprehensive Assessment Test, Texas has its State of Texas Assessments of Academic Readiness, and Virginia has its Standards of Learning. Students in most states are familiar with these sorts of tests, which have become academic rites of passage in most public grade schools—even though critics question whether these tests are properly aligned with curricula and whether they provide any useful comparison with schools in other states, or with previous cohorts of students in the same state who took earlier versions of these tests.

In an effort to provide some uniformity and continuity in testing, the federal government has

---

Criterion-referenced tests
Standardized tests designed to gauge students' level of mastery of a given set of materials

Norm-referenced tests
Standardized tests designed to measure how students' mastery of a set of materials compares with that of a specially designed sampling of students determined to be the national "norm" for that age group

administered its own test since 1969—the National Assessment of Educational Progress (NAEP). Nicknamed "the nation's report card," it is administered in volunteer sample districts to students in Grades 4, 8, and 12. Over the years, NAEP scores have remained essentially flat, with subgroups' scores rising and falling. For example, scores on mathematics and reading were a bit higher for 9- and 13-year-olds but not significantly different for 17-year-olds.[23]

Another key performance indicator coordinated by the U.S. Department of Education is the Trends in International Mathematics and Science Study (TIMSS). Designed to compare the academic achievement of students in dozens of countries, the 2011 TIMSS (the latest for which data are available) found, for example, that the scores for U.S. fourth- and eighth-graders exceeded the TIMSS averages for both math and science. That's the good news. The bad news is that the United States only once cracked the top 10 in the international rankings compiled by TIMSS—U.S. eighth-graders were ranked 10th in science. U.S. school reform advocates frequently point out this sort of superior test performance by students in many other countries as a sign of the urgent need for the United States to introduce more resources and more accountability measures.[24]

Many of the countries that participate in TIMSS run schools that have established rigid tracks, one for college-bound elite students and one for the remainder, who normally attend vocational schools. In the United States, all students have an equal opportunity to advance, at least in theory. Most students applying to college endure the stomach-churning test known as the SAT, as well as the less widely used ACT (used primarily in the Midwest). Designed by the private nonprofit Educational Testing Service and run by the private nonprofit College Board, the SAT is designed to be a predictor of college achievement. The test has been renamed and recalibrated on several occasions. What began as the Scholastic Aptitude Test became the Scholastic Assessment Test and now is known simply as the SAT. Thirty years of annual scores from this test have prompted much anguish.

In the early 1980s, a study found that the average SAT scores had fallen by 81 points from 1963 to 1977—from 478 down to 429 on the verbal test and from 502 to 470 on the math test. During the 1990s and early part of the 21st century, however, the College Board had reason to be upbeat; in an August 2003 report, the board reported the highest level of math scores in 35 years. Then the College Board revised the test once again, adding a writing section and including higher-level math. In 2013, average scores on the revised test were 496 in critical reading, 514 in mathematics, and 488 in writing. Those scores had remained essentially flat since 2008.[25]

Standardized tests are not the only benchmark used to measure the performance of the education system; high school graduation rates are also widely used. Graduation rates, however, have some inherent drawbacks as a comparative measure. Historically, the states have applied a patchwork of methods for determining these rates, and at the district or school level experts have long pointed out the temptation to calculate rates by simply subtracting the number of dropouts from the number collecting a diploma. That approach can result in misleading figures, because some dropouts transfer to other schools in a general equivalency diploma (GED) program, get their GEDs on their own, or are incarcerated.

It is often difficult to account for these missing students because they can be hard to track down. Furthermore, states and districts have little incentive to invest scarce resources to rectify such gaps in their accounting, because the poor performance of these students can contribute to the perception of "failure" on the part of school or district. Unsurprisingly, few states spend the money

---

National Assessment of Educational Progress (NAEP)
The only regularly conducted, independent survey of what a nationally representative sample of students in Grades 4, 8, and 12 know and can do in various subjects; known as "the nation's report card"

Trends in International Mathematics and Science Study (TIMSS)
A regularly updated study launched by the United States in 1995 that compares the performance in science and mathematics of students in 46 countries

---

General equivalency diploma (GED) program
A program offering a series of tests that an individual can take to qualify for a high school equivalency certificate or diploma

required to perform longitudinal studies of the fates of such students. Some districts have even deliberately ignored these students in an effort to make their graduation rates look higher than they really are. Most famously, in 2003, city high schools in Houston, Texas, were found to be spectacularly underreporting dropout rates to appear to be performing better under the state's accountability plan. The officially reported citywide dropout rate was 1.5 percent, when in reality the rate was somewhere between 25 and 50 percent.[26]

For these reasons and others, graduation rates are not fully reliable. In 2005, the governors of all 50 states signed on to a formula proposed by the National Governors Association: divide the number of students receiving diplomas in a given year by the number of students entering ninth grade for the first time that same year. However, few states implemented the change, leading U.S. secretary of education Margaret Spellings to issue a regulation in October 2008 mandating that a single dropout rate formula be used across the country; despite this regulation, states continue to employ different definitions.[27] One long-used measure of the dropout rate nationally is the percentage of 16- through 24-year-olds who are not enrolled in school and have not earned a high school diploma, a GED, or an equivalent certificate. Using that definition, the dropout rate in the United States was 6.6 percent in 2012, although it varied considerably across demographic groups. For example, the rate among white Americans was 4.3 percent, while that for Hispanics was 12.7 percent.[28]

Many Brands on the School Reform Shelf

It is one thing to theorize about how to improve schools and quite another to implement real-world programs that get results. Decades of promising techniques—and sometimes utopian promises—have rotated through solutions that span site-based management, early-reading programs, and smaller class sizes, to name just a few. No consensus has materialized, only more debate. Still, the main schools of thought on school reform can be boiled down to those addressed in the sections below.

Standards and Accountability

The **standards movement** first drew attention at a 1989 education summit in Charlottesville, Virginia. Attended by President George H. W. Bush and state governors, including future president Bill Clinton, the summit created a national panel to set and monitor education targets that would become **Goals 2000**, or the Educate America Act. That same year, the Kentucky Supreme Court struck down that state's entire education system, which prompted the enactment of the **Kentucky Education Reform Act** the following year. This paved the way for the standards movement nationwide.

The premise of the standards movement was simple: define what students should be able to do at each grade in each subject, aligning tests to that content, and then evaluate students on those standards. Professional associations, starting with the National Council of Teachers of Mathematics, began producing grade-appropriate standards. As momentum built in the early 1990s, the Clinton administration worked to give the movement a national framework in its reauthorization of the **Elementary and Secondary Education Act**, originally passed in 1965.

Site-based management
A movement to increase freedom for building administrators such as school principals to determine how district funds are spent at individual schools

Standards movement
An effort to create benchmarks of adequate learning in each subject for each grade level so that students and teachers can be evaluated on the mastery of this predetermined material

Goals 2000
The Educate America Act, signed into law in March 1994, which provided resources to states and communities to ensure that all students could reach their full potential

Kentucky Education Reform Act
The 1990 law passed in response to court findings of unacceptable disparities among schools in Kentucky; considered the most comprehensive state school reform act to date

Elementary and Secondary Education Act
Federal law passed in 1965 as part of President Johnson's Great Society initiative; steered federal funds to improve local schools, particularly those attended primarily by low-income and minority students

Prodding from governors and the business community produced considerable progress on the integration of a standards-based approach. Fully 49 states laid out standards, with Iowa being the lone holdout, and by summer 2002, 47 states were issuing "report cards" on student achievement. Not quite half were breaking the data down by racial subgroups, level of income, and/or limited English proficiency. Among teachers, according to an *Education Week* survey, 8 in 10 reported that their curricula were now more demanding; 6 out of 10 said their students were writing more.

The standards movement reached something of a threshold in 2009 with the beginning of a coordinated effort by states to formulate a uniform, national set of academic standards. This effort, known as the **Common Core State Standards (CCSS)**, was backed by the National Governors Association and the Chief Council of State School Officers. The basic idea is to develop a consistent, rigorous set of standards aligned with the academic skill sets students need to get good jobs or pursue higher-education opportunities.[29] The hope is that the CCSS will provide a consistent and uniform framework that will replace the often idiosyncratic academic standards and testing programs currently used by states. By 2013, 45 states and the District of Columbia had committed to CCSS, with standardized testing on the standards set for the 2014–2015 school year. Although this is a state-based and state-led initiative, the effort reflects an increasing push to impose a more centralized and uniform set of achievement expectations on schools nationwide.[30]

Just as it started to be implemented, however, CCSS and the whole standards movement encountered a strong political backlash. Some critics argued that there was little evidence of what CCSS would or would not do to improve education and that such a massive reform of curricula in schools should not be undertaken in the absence of proof that it would actually work. Others did not like the one-size-fits-all approach embraced by CCSS—they wanted states to remain free to do whatever they decided was best. Some parents grew alarmed when some students who were earning good grades did poorly on the new standardized tests. Others were suspicious of new approaches to old subjects that came with CCSS or worried about the retooling teachers had to go through to teach the new curricula. Some worried about the growing clout of companies that produced the tests and administrative bungling in implementing CCSS (e.g., many states adopted the new standards without updating high school graduation requirements that did not comply with them). President Obama's administration strongly supported CCSS, which only seemed to spur opposition in some state governments controlled by conservative Republicans. At least eight states introduced anti-CCSS bills—Alabama, Georgia, Indiana, Kansas, Michigan, Missouri, Pennsylvania, and South Dakota—all of them in Republican-controlled legislatures.

Most of these bills failed, but as of 2014 they seemed to signal an emerging political conflict over the future of education in the United States. On one side are those who increasingly see CCSS as a stalking horse for a federal takeover of public education; on the other are those who see CCSS as a long-overdue attempt to haul the entire public education system into the 21st century. The battle lines here do not fall along neat ideological or party lines. Tea Party conservatives tend to oppose CCSS, but many business groups support it. At its 2014 convention, the American Federation of Teachers—a labor union with a million members nationwide—considerably softened its long-standing support of CCSS, giving its members leeway not only to critique the standards but even to try to rewrite them from scratch. The reasoning for the union's change of heart on CCSS was that "the promise of Common Core has been corrupted by political manipulation, administrative bungling, corporate profiteering and an invalid scoring system designed to ensure huge numbers of kids fail."[31] This was a sentiment shared by people across the ideological spectrum. Despite the growing opposition, CCSS was set to be fully implemented in most states for the 2014–2015 school year.

Common Core State Standards (CCSS)
An education initiative that creates a uniform set of learning expectations in English and math for students at the end of each grade. Though participation is voluntary, most states have joined this initiative.

Policy in Practice

What's Really Going on With the Common Core?

Not sure what the Common Core is or what all the fuss is about? Don't worry, you're not alone. Here are some common questions and answers that will hopefully clarify things.

What is the Common Core?

The Common Core State Standards set out guidelines for what students from kindergarten through 12th grade should know in English and math. They were created by the Council of Chief State School Officers, which includes representatives from the top education officers in each state; the National Governors Association; and Achieve, an education policy nonprofit group. The idea behind the Common Core was that public education needed to improve to meet the demands of a globally competitive economy. It was voluntarily adopted by 45 states.

Why are people so upset about the Common Core?

For many reasons. In most states, adoption of the Common Core did not require approval by state lawmakers but only by state education agencies and/or chief education officers. One side effect of this was that many people heard of the new standards only as they were about to be implemented. As these new requirements often turned out to be controversial (see main text), state legislatures increasingly began to feel pressure to pause, modify, or even scrap the Common Core standards.

Was the Common Core mandated by the federal government?

No. States voluntarily opted into the program, and a handful of states (e.g., Texas, Nebraska) have chosen not to adopt the Common Core. President Obama's administration has been a strong supporter of the initiative,

and the federal government spent $348 million helping develop standardized tests aligned to the Common Core; however, this is not a federal program.

How does the Common Core compare with previous standards?

There are different perspectives on this. A Fordham Institute report says the Common Core standards are clearer and more rigorous than existing standards in the vast majority of states. A team of researchers at the University of Pennsylvania concluded that the Common Core standards were not a significant improvement over existing state standards. Researchers at Michigan State found that states with standards that looked more like Common Core standards did better on the National Assessment of Educational Progress (or "the nation's report card").

Is there evidence that Common Core standards will increase student achievement?

As the Common Core has not been fully implemented, no one knows if it will significantly increase student achievement nationally.

Why are some people so opposed to national standards in education?

Public education has always been a function of state and local government in the United States, and there has always been resistance to ceding any significant degree of control over education policy to the federal government. The Common Core is the closest the United States has ever come to national educational standards and is viewed by some as a pathway for a federal takeover of public education.

Source: Adapted from Adrienne Lu, "What's Really Going on With the Common Core?" *Governing*, December 6, 2013, http://www.governing.com/news/headlines/What-Going-on-with-the-Common-Core.html.

School reform efforts have brought a new focus on test scores as proof of student improvement and achievement. Standardized tests have become common nationwide, and students increasingly must pass exams to advance in grade or to graduate.

© Marmaduke St. John/Alamy

Recruiting Good Teachers

Research has demonstrated that the single most important factor in student learning—more important than curriculum, family income, student health, or parental involvement—is good teaching.[32] Economists have even quantified the effect, estimating that the best teachers give their students an extra year's worth of learning and perhaps increase their standardized test scores by 50 points.[33] Such gains are seen particularly with minority students, many of whom enter school with a social or economic disadvantage.

While the importance of teachers is recognized, finding qualified teachers and holding on to them can be a problem for schools. This problem is particularly pronounced in high-poverty schools, which tend to suffer from heavy staff turnover. More generally, there are notable shortages of teachers in certain subject areas, including special education, mathematics, science, bilingual education, and technology.[34] This is in part due to the fact that teacher salaries often are too low to attract candidates who can earn more at high-tech firms and corporations. School districts must make do, then, with whomever they have to teach the necessary courses. The use of teachers by school districts, however reluctantly, to instruct in areas in which they do not hold degrees affects between 4 and 16 percent of high school students in the liberal arts, according to the Department of Education.[35]

One piece of NCLB aims at improving this record. It originally called for all teachers of core subjects to be "fully qualified," defined broadly as holding a teaching license and showing command of the subjects they teach, by the 2005–2006 school year. When the U.S. Department of Education realized that most states were unlikely to meet this deadline, it declared them compliant if they could demonstrate "good faith and effort" toward meeting the goal. All but seven states passed that test.[36] A survey of states and school districts revealed, however, that few believe the NCLB requirement has significantly improved teacher quality.[37]

Colleges and universities that have schools of education are working to improve the quality of their graduates and to provide aspiring educators with more substantive knowledge and less jargon and abstract pedagogy. Many current researchers believe that teachers with the most content knowledge in their fields are most effective in raising student achievement.[38]

Alternative licensure programs that provide appropriate training, mentoring, and testing to interested individuals now are permitted in 24 states and the District of Columbia. Examples of such programs include Troops to Teachers, which opens up classroom jobs to former military personnel, and Teach for America, which involves recent college graduates who want to fight poverty. Thousands of teachers enter the profession through these programs each year.

Perhaps the biggest obstacle to recruiting good, qualified teachers has already been discussed earlier in the chapter—stressed education budgets mean that tens of thousands of teachers have lost their jobs over the past 5 or 6 years. The benefits of hiring new well-qualified teachers are unlikely to be realized if schools do not have the money to keep the teachers they already have.

Many Schools, Few Resources

On average, the salaries of teachers in rural school districts are 88 percent of the salaries of their nonrural counterparts. While rural schools do have lower crime and dropout rates than do urban schools, teachers in rural districts—home to 19 percent of public school students—must also contend with the perpetual challenges of few opportunities for professional development, limited curricula, and threats of school and district consolidation.[39]

The consolidation of small rural schools has been controversial since it began back in the days of Horace Mann and his one-room schoolhouse. The practice, often pursued by states and districts in search of cost savings, picked up steam throughout the 20th century. According to the National Center for Education Statistics (NCES; part of the U.S. Department of Education), the nation's 117,108 school districts in the 1937–1938 school year had been cut back to 13,924 by 2007–2008. During that same period, enrollment grew from 25.5 million students to 49.2 million.[40] States continue to propose consolidation plans, despite conflicting evidence of the strategy's success.[41] West Virginia closed more than 300 schools between 1990 and 2005, and Iowa consolidated 14 percent of its districts during the same period.[42] And proposals for consolidations increased later in the decade as municipal and state budgets plunged steeply downward. Through its consolidation law, Maine has cut 75 school districts, resulting in hundreds of thousands of dollars in savings. Other states are eyeing yet more drastic measures. Mississippi governor Haley Barbour asked a blue-ribbon committee to develop a plan for cutting districts by one third, and in 2009,

Pennsylvania governor Edward G. Rendell recommended reducing the state's school districts from 500 to 100, although his plan failed to gain traction among legislators.[43]

Backlash against further consolidation, accompanied by the continuing realization that cost savings need to be made, has some districts and states rethinking their strategies and turning, yet again, to technology. Distance learning is more than just correspondence courses; it encompasses videoconferencing and online learning modules, and can vastly expand learning opportunities for both students and teachers.[44] This is not to say that computers are a panacea for all the ills plaguing rural school districts—after all, they still have to come up with the money to invest in the technology—but proponents argue that distance learning is a strong alternative to closing schoolhouse doors.

Choosing Wisely: Alternatives to Public Schools

The issue of school choice, always guaranteed to stir up emotions, has been brought to the forefront of the education debate by NCLB. Under NCLB, schools that fail to make adequate yearly progress for two consecutive years are deemed "in need of improvement," giving parents the right to transfer their children to another public school. NCLB has not led to a high volume of student transfers; polls show that the public would rather reform the public school system from within. Alternatives such as charter schools and voucher programs excite varying levels of support.[45] Nevertheless, reformers continue to promote school choice, and increasing numbers of parents are taking advantage of the options available. The percentage of students attending their assigned public schools fell from 80 percent in 1993 to 73 percent in 2007.[46]

Charter Schools

Entrepreneurs who want to launch their own schools with public money have been applying to run **charter schools** since the early 1990s. These schools reflect less an educational philosophy than a variation on school governance. Charter schools range in theme from Montessori to the fact-based niche curriculum called Core Knowledge to ranching to online (distance) learning. Sponsors have included former public and private school principals, parent groups, universities, social service agencies, and nonprofits such as the YMCA. By 2011, nearly 5,000 charter schools had sprung up nationwide, with more than 1.7 million students enrolled.[47]

In principle, students who attend charter schools are given the same per-pupil expenditure as are students in mainstream schools, although the founders often must scrounge to find facilities. The willingness of a state to encourage the establishment of charter schools depends on the condition of its public schools and the energies of would-be charter school founders. Some states set up special chartering boards, whereas others allow local school boards to approve the applications.

State charter laws vary widely. Arizona's loose regulations provide start-up funds, a 15-year authorization, and the freedom for existing private schools to convert to charter status. Kansas's strict charter law, in contrast, provides no start-up funds and allows only a 5-year term before a charter school must seek a renewal.[48]

Backers see charter schools as laboratories of innovation that bypass staid bureaucracies and satisfy the parental desire for choice. Evidence of the academic achievement of charter schools is modestly favorable but not spectacular. Some have been forced to close due to corruption, such as embezzlement by administrators, or because they have failed to attract enough students or to maintain physical facilities. In one high-profile case, California's largest charter school operator announced in August 2004 that it would be closing at least 60 campuses amid an investigation into its academic and financial practices, leaving 10,000

students stranded just weeks before the start of the school year.[49] In addition, critics worry that charter schools will balkanize public education and that states may exploit them as a way to avoid dealing with unionized teachers. Some observers fear that these schools may present administrative headaches to those school superintendents charged with monitoring them to prevent abuses of funds. Critics of charter schools also worry that they have the potential to drain funding from traditional schools—every student who walks out the door of a traditional public school to a charter school takes taxpayer dollars with him or her.

To determine whether particular charter school models should be scaled up and duplicated throughout the country, researchers do not just want to know whether a charter's own students' test scores improve; they want to know if the schools these children's families chose to leave are using the departures as an incentive to do better.[50] To that end, studies have been carried out. Advocates of charter schools, including the George W. Bush administration, suffered a blow in August 2006 when a long-awaited study of test scores by the U.S. Department of Education revealed that fourth-graders in charter schools scored significantly lower than did their peers in traditional public schools.[51]

But there are also plenty of individual charter school success stories. Especially in some larger urban areas, charter schools have become a common and desirable alternative to traditional public schools. In 2010, 99 of the 181 public schools in Washington, D.C., were charter schools, and students in these charter schools have scored comparatively well on standardized tests.[52]

Some studies suggest that tracking students over time might provide additional favorable findings. Tom Loveless, director of the Brown Center on Education Policy at the Brookings Institution, conducted a 2-year study of 569 charter schools in 10 states. He found that, although charter school students do score lower on state tests, over time they progress faster than do students in traditional public schools. Other proponents believe that students in charter schools also score lower initially, in part, because they were further behind to begin with in their previous,

---

Charter schools
Public schools, often with unique themes, managed by teachers, principals, social workers, or nonprofit groups. The charter school movement was launched in the early 1990s.

traditional schools.[53] A comparison study by Stanford University researchers of charter and traditional public schools in 15 states and Washington, D.C., found that charter school students experiencing poverty and English-language learners earned higher scores than did their traditional school counterparts. Across all students, however, 37 percent of charter schools fared worse than the traditional schools.[54]

Vouchers

School vouchers, a more radical reform than charter schools, have been proposed in some form since the 1950s. The idea of the school voucher movement is simple: Rather than give money to schools, governments give families a public grant (a voucher) that can be used to enroll their children at any accredited school—not just public schools but also private and parochial (religious) schools. Supporters argue that voucher programs create real markets for educational services, providing parents with real choices and breaking up the "monopoly" of public education bureaucracy. The goal is that the competitive market forces will force schools to innovate and respond to consumer demand or face going out of business. More recently, many have advanced the argument that vouchers serve a civil rights function in that they can rescue low-income black families from failing schools in low-income neighborhoods.

Opponents worry that vouchers spell the beginning of the end of society-wide efforts to maintain and improve universal public education. They note that private schools can be selective about which students they accept. In addition, the proposed amounts for vouchers are often less than half the actual tuition charges at many schools. In some communities, the number of available slots at area private schools is insufficient for the number of interested applicants. Voucher proponents aren't without counterarguments, however. They assert that the programs create competition that forces public schools to

School voucher movement
A movement, dating back to the 1950s, to allow taxpayer dollars to be given to families for use at whatever public, private, or parochial schools they choose

improve and that they give lower-income students opportunities they might not otherwise have.[55]

Critics also object to the widespread participation of religious schools in voucher programs. Many are uncomfortable with the idea that, through vouchers, taxpayer funds go to institutions that support the inculcation of particular sets of religious beliefs. Despite these concerns, in June 2002, the U.S. Supreme Court ruled that vouchers can go to a religious school as long as the school's chief purpose is education—in other words, a school that offers a comprehensive secular curriculum, albeit with religious rituals and instructors, as opposed to a Sunday school or Bible study school.

Despite the Supreme Court ruling that vouchers can be used to fund parochial-school tuitions, there remains widespread concern that vouchers threaten the historic separation between church and state. For example, many state ballot initiatives proposing voucher programs have been defeated at least partially on concerns that they would divert money from traditional public schools and send it to parochial schools. Such proposals were defeated in Michigan and California in 2000 and in Utah in 2007.[56] A 2012 Florida initiative to repeal that state's ban on using public dollars to purchase services from religious service providers also failed. And while the U.S. Supreme Court has ruled that voucher programs do not necessarily violate the U.S. Constitution, this does not necessarily mean that such programs are allowable under all state constitutions. In 2006, the Florida Supreme Court struck down the state's voucher program, a key part of then-governor Jeb Bush's education plan, as unconstitutional. Efforts to reinstate part of the program at the ballot box in 2008 failed when the court rejected the questions due to technicalities.[57]

Despite mixed political support, some voucher programs have been in place for decades. Probably the two best known are programs that, at least initially, were aimed at long-troubled and racially isolated schools in Cleveland, Ohio, and Milwaukee, Wisconsin. Cleveland's voucher program, which served 5,800 students during the 2005–2006 school year, was folded into Ohio EdChoice. This statewide voucher program offers up to 60,000 renewable scholarships to

Charter schools have grown across the country as alternatives to traditional public schools. President Obama has made school competition, including the encouragement of charter schools, a hallmark of his proposals to reform the No Child Left Behind Act and the nation's education system.

© Brooks Kraft/Corbis

students attending schools considered in "academic emergency" or on "academic watch," the state's two lowest rankings for school performance.[58]

Milwaukee's program offers vouchers to low-income families (family income may not exceed 300 percent of the federal poverty level). These vouchers can be used to enroll students in more than 100 private schools that participate in the program. The program included only secular schools when it started, but in 1995 it expanded to include parochial schools, a measure protected by the 2002 Supreme Court ruling. By 2006, religiously affiliated schools constituted about 70 percent of the participating schools. In 2006, Wisconsin governor Jim Doyle signed a bill to raise the number of vouchers issued annually from 15,000 to 22,500 in exchange for increased accountability on the part of schools accepting vouchers, including standardized testing and accreditation.[59] In 2013–2014, the maximum voucher amount that could be received by families was $7,856.

Whether students who use vouchers experience achievement gains is a matter of fairly intense debate. Dozens—likely hundreds—of studies have produced mixed evidence. Studies backed by advocacy groups, unsurprisingly, have found significant gains for voucher students.[60] More academic studies have a much more mixed record, with some showing significant gains and others showing no impact. A 2012 study of the Milwaukee school choice program, for example, shows that voucher students have slightly higher reading test scores than do comparable nonvoucher students

but found no differences in math test scores between these groups.[61] Generally speaking, the weight of evidence from the nearly quarter-century experiment in Milwaukee shows that in terms of academic achievement, voucher programs produce little improvement over traditional public schools.[62]

Homeschooling

A major school reform movement gaining popularity is **homeschooling**. In 1999, according to a survey by the U.S. Department of Education, an estimated 850,000 students were being taught at home. By 2012, that number had jumped to more than 1.7 million, according to NCES.[63]

As the movement has grown, homeschooling parents have organized sports leagues, field trips, proms, and graduation ceremonies. Supporters of homeschooling have even organized a legal defense network and a sophisticated lobbying effort. And there are plenty of homeschooling

---

Homeschooling
The education of children in the home; a movement to grant waivers from state truancy laws to permit parents to teach their own children

success stories, including Harvard acceptances and solid scores on standardized tests.

Homeschooling advocates are a diverse group, but the two main strands are fundamentalist Christians and "free-school" advocates who favor more student choice of subject matter. Parents who can make the time to homeschool like the security and personal imprint they can leave on their youngsters. An NCES study found that 30 percent of homeschooling parents surveyed wanted the flexibility to teach their children moral or religious lessons. Another 31 percent cited concerns about the environment of traditional schools.[64]

Of course, throughout the history of this country, there always have been those who have chosen to teach their children at home. The modern homeschooling movement, however, really started taking off in the 1980s. State governments have accommodated homeschoolers to varying degrees. Some require a parent to have a bachelor's degree to homeschool. Others require parents to submit their curricula for approval, and still others give parents the choice of giving their children standardized tests selected by the school district or hiring their own qualified evaluators.

Michael Farris, cofounder of the Home School Legal Defense Association, based in Purcellville, Virginia, has been at the forefront of the national movement. His organization ranks states based on how tightly or loosely they regulate homeschooling. States with no requirements for homeschoolers to notify state authorities include Idaho, Michigan, and Texas. States with low regulation include Alabama, Kentucky, and Mississippi. Most other states in the Southeast moderately regulate homeschooling, whereas most states in New England regulate more intensively.[65]

Critics fear that homeschooled students miss important opportunities for social development and that many parents are not qualified to teach. They also worry that some homeschooling parents isolate their children and instill in them religious prejudice. Some state and local officials consider homeschooling an inconvenience. It forces them to come up with policies on home visits, gauge assessments that may be out of sync with conventional report-card grades, and wrestle with dilemmas such as whether a homeschooled student can play in the public high school band.

Can't Tell the Players Without a Program: Groups That Influence Public Education

When the Texas Supreme Court struck down school funding disparities in *Edgewood Independent School District v. Kirby* (1989), it declined to specify a precise solution to the problem. Instead, it opted to launch a dialogue with legislators and education officials. In Kentucky, the state supreme court was even more an activist—it declared the state's school system unconstitutional and not adequate as "an efficient system of public schools." The court went on to lay out a set of goals and ability standards to be pursued.[66]

In both cases, the courts knew that no legal ruling on the subject of education would hold sway without public support and buy-in from key stakeholders. That meant going far beyond a small elite of education officials. In Texas, for example, the Mexican American Legal Defense and Educational Fund played an influential role in developing and supporting the state's new education reforms.

In Kentucky, the legislation and landmark school reform program that resulted from the state court's ruling gained ground largely because of support from such players as newspaper editorialists and a group of education and business leaders called the Prichard Committee for Academic Excellence. Such groups as these are common participants in the educational debate and are part of the following roster of familiar players in the education dramas that unfold across the country.

Teachers Unions

For decades, the major **teachers unions** have been the National Education Association (NEA),

Teachers unions
Public-sector unions that organize employees at all educational levels to form state and local affiliates. In the United States, the two major teachers' unions are the National Education Association and the American Federation of Teachers, both headquartered in Washington, D.C.

which boasts 3.2 million members, and the American Federation of Teachers (AFT), which reported more than 1.5 million members as of 2012.[67] These groups organize employees from the preschool level to the K–12 level to the university level to form state and local affiliates. They engage in collective bargaining, lobby for resources, and seek to upgrade teacher professionalism through training and publications.

For years these two unions, both headquartered in Washington, D.C., have flirted with a merger, but style differences always intervene. The AFT was quicker than the NEA to join the school reform parade, for example, by participating in the creation of standards and charter schools. By the late 1990s, however, both had turned sour on the school choice movement, which they consider a threat to public education and their members' livelihoods. They have been critical, too, of NCLB, with the NEA leading the charge in lawsuits challenging the federal government's administration of the law. As we have already seen, teachers unions have provided mixed support for the Common Core initiative. The AFT's initial enthusiasm for the Common Core, for example, soured over its frustration that the whole initiative was devolving into a political football. Regardless of their specific policy stands, both unions align themselves with the Democratic Party, one reason most Republicans blame them for obstructing school reform.

Parent Groups

The **National PTA**, with 5 million members, bills itself as the "largest volunteer child advocacy organization in the United States."[68] For decades, this umbrella group for local parent–teacher associations and organizations was stereotyped as a klatch of moms putting on bake sales. Today, however, the PTA has school-based state and national organizations that combine to form a sophisticated lobbying and policy force. For the most part, the organization works to boost parent

involvement and to encourage parent–teacher cooperation.

The National PTA has strict rules about remaining nonpartisan. Despite this, local PTAs' occasional endorsements of state legislative candidates based on school funding commitments have gotten some in hot water. Other parent groups have emerged over the years to focus on narrower school-related issues, such as the school desegregation efforts of the Mississippi-based Parents for Public Schools.

National Political Parties

For much of the latter part of the 20th century, education was Democratic Party turf, at least on the national level. This was because Democrats traditionally wanted to expand government spending to close the gap between affluent and low-income schools. Republicans, on the other hand, emphasized local control and social issues, such as efforts to overturn the ban on school prayer. During the Reagan administration, Republicans vowed to abolish the federal Department of Education set up by President Carter. Many of them opposed proposals made during the mid-1990s to introduce a national standardized test. They based their protests on the need to preserve local control of schools.

By 2000, however, Texas governor George W. Bush moved the Republicans dramatically to the center of the education debate while campaigning for the Oval Office. His eventual victory in enacting NCLB, which is modeled in part on the system used since the early 1990s in Texas and borrows its name from the liberal Children's Defense Fund, was attributable to support from key Democratic lawmakers. President Bush's brother, former Florida governor Jeb Bush, is another Republican who has spearheaded important education reforms that have become part of the national debate about public schooling. Jeb Bush has championed grading schools on the basis of student performance on standardized tests, establishing mandatory grade standards, instituting merit pay for teachers, and pushing alternatives to traditional public schools, not just charters and vouchers but also online "virtual" schools.[69]

National PTA

An umbrella organization founded in 1897 consisting of state-based and school-based parent–teacher associations of volunteers who work to improve and support schools

While Republicans' efforts in some areas have resulted in bipartisan agreement, their efforts to woo Democrats to their side on the more controversial proposals for school vouchers have been less successful, due to the strong support that Democrats depend on from antivoucher teachers unions and the Democrats' general skepticism about market-based alternatives to government programs.

Business Groups

Corporations and small businesses have been among the most vocal in pushing for school reform. They cite what they perceive as a decline in the writing and math skills of young job applicants as industry has become more complex technologically. Business leaders, such as former Intel chairman Craig Barrett, have joined with business groups, such as the Business Roundtable and the National Alliance of Business, to meet with governors, educators, and school reform activists to press for higher standards for students and teachers. The Business Coalition for Student Achievement, led by the Business Roundtable and the U.S. Chamber of Commerce, has issued recommendations to improve NCLB, including

a call to improve teacher quality, to focus on college and workplace readiness, and to strengthen science, math, and technology curricula.[70] Through his foundation, Microsoft chairman Bill Gates has been active in promoting a wide range of education reforms, including supporting the CCSS projects.

Professional and Advocacy Groups

Within the education "establishment," each of the managerial groups—administrators, principals at the elementary and secondary levels, and school boards—has its own association. The official decision makers in these groups usually win their jobs through a prerequisite set of academic credentials, years of experience in the classroom, and dues paid on the front lines of management.

Also influencing public education are research groups such as the Education Trust, which is based in Washington, D.C., and performs research to encourage those in higher education to help with elementary and secondary school reforms. And then there are the advocacy groups, such as the Center for Education Reform, which promotes school choice, and the Public Education Network, which organizes local funds to improve public engagement in school reform.

Conclusion

Although each state has its own internal timeline for success, NCLB, as envisioned and enacted under the Bush administration, required that all schools bring every single student to proficiency by the 2013–2014 school year. That bold, bipartisan vision was not realized. While the goal of educational improvement was widely shared, there were always mixed opinions at the state level, not just about the realism and feasibility of NCLB but also about the expanded role of the federal government in this most traditional of state policy arenas. President Obama's administration granted waivers to most states to release them from at least some mandates of NCLB, but it is a safe bet that those debating school performance, accountability, and funding, as well as teacher quality, will continue to invoke, with passion, lofty themes of democracy and civic ideals. Efforts to strengthen the federal role in public education will continue to run up against the centuries-old tradition of local control. Advocates of increased funding targeting the poor will still lock horns with those who stress reforms in pedagogy and new incentives. The growing controversy over the Common Core initiative is just the latest chapter in a very long story of reform.

If Horace Mann is watching from school reformers' heaven, he probably isn't surprised that the ancient debates over school reform remain unsettled. The governance of the U.S. public education system is rooted in local control and wide variations in state and community traditions. This guarantees that it always will be characterized by diverse approaches and active political maneuvering. The quest for the ideal school continues to be more art than science. The results? They are as glorious—and as messy—as democracy itself.

The Latest Research

Education is such a sprawling, perennially high-profile topic that it should come as no surprise that a very large research industry is devoted to examining its every dimension and nuance. Many political scientists, economists, and sociologists study education issues, as do many more researchers from exclusively education-based disciplines such as educational psychology—not to mention the large number of scholars in university teaching colleges and departments who not only train educators but also conduct studies on everything from curricular development to best practices in educational administration. Entire academic journals are devoted to research in education (e.g., *American Journal of Education, American Educational Research Journal*). Given this, it is all but impossible for us to summarize here anything but a narrow slice of the latest education research.

That said, one of the more interesting developments in the latest research is the current direction of debates over the effectiveness of the market-based reforms that have provided much of the intellectual firepower behind the standards and accountability movement discussed in this chapter. These reforms—most of which are

discussed above—include such things as the strong focus on standardized testing and the introduction of competition through charter schools and vouchers. For more than 20 years, dueling studies have claimed to provide evidence to support or contradict the efficacy of such reforms. While a lot of that continues, over the past half-decade or so, scholars have been increasingly paying attention to what the mixed messages of all this research mean. Do the inconsistent reports on the efficacy of these reforms, or the lack thereof, mean that the evidence on the impacts is not clear, even though some of the reforms have been in place for decades? Does it mean that the studies are, consciously or unconsciously, being conducted to serve political agendas rather than to get at objective assessments of what works and what does not? Are the studies' results simply being cherry-picked by key players in the reform debate who ignore contradicting evidence and the often careful caveats that study authors place on the interpretation of their findings? Given the high stakes involved for state governments, which have often invested heavily in these reforms, these are important questions. Below we discuss some representative

(Continued)

(Continued)

research looking hard for answers, especially in trying to understand the actual payoffs of charter schools, which have been touted in many states and on both sides of the aisle in the federal government as effective alternatives to traditional public schools.

• •

• **Ravitch, Diane**. *Reign of Error*. New York: Vintage, 2013.

Any discussion of the hard questions being asked about the market-based reform movement and the research that supports it has to include the latest book by Ravitch, an education historian and policy scholar at New York University and former assistant U.S. secretary of education. She was initially a supporter of many of the reforms championed by charter and voucher advocates and an early backer of NCLB; however, she has come to question the evidence supporting the effectiveness of such reforms, and this book lays out her case. Long respected on all sides of the education reform debate, Ravitch has rocked the conversation with this book, which is a stinging indictment of many of the market-like reforms she once championed.

• **Henig, Jeffrey**. *The End of Exceptionalism in American Education: The Changing Politics of School Reform*. Cambridge, MA: Harvard Education Press, 2013.

Henig is one of the most widely known political scientists studying education policy. His latest book is an analysis of the shift in the focus of education policymaking in the United States over the past 50 years. A half-century ago, education policy was largely the exclusive province of local and state school boards. Today, it is on the agenda of pretty much every branch and level of government—legislatures, courts, and executives at local, state, and federal levels. This shift has led to a big change in how schools are organized, funded, and evaluated, along the way politicizing education in new and different ways. These changes have big implications for how education relates to the social, political, and economic environments in the United States.

• **Betts, Julian R., and Richard C. Atkinson**. "Better Research Needed on the Impact of Charter Schools." *Science* 335 (2012): 171–172.

This article, published in one of the premier academic research journals, is coauthored by an economist and a former director of the National Science Foundation. Betts and Atkinson argue that although the past two presidential administrations have been enthusiastic supporters of charter schools, the evidence backing that advocacy is thin. They suggest that most studies of charter schools suffer from a range of methodological and sampling problems that make it hard to generalize the results, let alone use those results to reach a consensus on the efficacy of such schools. Betts and Atkinson argue that more randomized field trials—studies in which students are essentially assigned to traditional public or charter schools by lottery—are needed to produce better scientific evidence on the pros and cons of charter schools. They also call on states to make it easier for researchers to access student-level data on test scores. Without access to good data, they argue, researchers cannot arrive at valid and reliable estimates of reform impacts.

• **Imberman, Scott**. "Achievement and Behavior in Charter Schools: Drawing a More Complete Picture." *Review of Economics and Statistics* 93 (2011): 416–435.

This article reports on a study of the impact of charter schools that is notable for the particularly rich data set employed. It compares student outcome measures from charter and noncharter schools not just on academics—math, reading, and language—but also on a long list of behavioral outcomes, such as attendance rates, substance abuse, and disciplinary infractions. Imberman examined data on dozens of schools from 1994 to 2007, as well as hundreds of thousands of observations from individual students—a very strong foundation for empirical analysis. Imberman's findings? Charter schools do not seem to improve test scores much, but they do seem to have a positive behavioral impact, promoting increased attendance and better student discipline.

Chapter Review

Key Concepts

- accreditation (p. 411)
- back to basics (p. 409)
- capital outlays (p. 415)
- charter schools (p. 425)
- Common Core State Standards (CCSS) (p. 421)
- common school (p. 409)
- criterion-referenced tests (p. 418)
- departments of education (p. 410)
- Elementary and Secondary Education Act (p. 420)
- general equivalency diploma (GED) program (p. 419)
- Goals 2000 (p. 420)
- high-stakes standardized testing (p. 409)
- homeschooling (p. 427)
- Kentucky Education Reform Act (p. 420)
- local education agencies (LEAs) (p. 411)

- National Assessment of Educational Progress (NAEP) (p. 419)
- National PTA (p. 429)
- No Child Left Behind Act (NCLB) (p. 408)
- norm-referenced tests (p. 418)
- school boards (p. 411)
- school districts (p. 411)
- school voucher movement (p. 426)
- site-based management (p. 420)
- standards (p. 409)
- standards movement (p. 420)
- state board of education (p. 408)
- successful schools model (p. 416)
- teacher licensure procedures (p. 411)
- teachers unions (p. 428)
- Trends in International Mathematics and Science Study (TIMSS) (p. 419)

Suggested Websites

- **www.aasa.org.** Website of the American Association of School Administrators. Founded in 1865, AASA has more than 13,000 members worldwide. Its mission is to support and develop individuals dedicated to the highest-quality public education for all children.

- **www.aft.org.** Website of the American Federation of Teachers, which represents the economic, social, and professional interests of classroom teachers. The AFT has more than 3,000 local affiliates nationwide, 43 state affiliates, and more than 1.3 million members.

- **www.cep-dc.org.** Website of the Center on Education Policy, a national independent advocate for more effective public schools.

- **www.ed.gov.** Website of the U.S. Department of Education, which oversees the federal government's contributions to public education.

- **www.edexcellence.net.** Website of the Thomas B. Fordham Institute, whose mission is to advance the understanding and acceptance of effective reform strategies in primary and secondary education.

- **www.edreform.com.** Website of the Center for Education Reform, a national organization dedicated to the promotion of more choices in education and more rigorous education programs.

- **www.edweek.org.** Website of *Education Week*, a weekly publication devoted to primary and secondary education and funded by Editorial Projects in Education. *Education Week* publishes *Quality Counts*, an annual evaluation of K–12 education in all 50 states.

- **nationsreportcard.gov**. Website of the National Assessment of Educational Progress, the program that administers standardized tests to Grades 4, 8, and 12 across the United States.

- **www.nea.org.** Website of the National Education Association, which is dedicated to advancing public education. The organization has 2.8 million members across every level of education, from preschool to university graduate programs, and affiliates in every state, as well as in more than 13,000 local communities across the United States.

- **www.nsba.org.** Website of the National School Boards Association, a not-for-profit federation of state associations of school boards across the United States.

$SAGE statestats

State Stats on Education

*Explore and compare data on the states! Go to **edge.sagepub.com/ smithgreenblatt5e** to do these exercises.*

1. How did the per capita amount of revenue that states receive from the federal government change from 2000 to 2010? What accounts for this change?

2. How did the average public school eighth-grade math scores change in Montana from 2005 to 2007? What about from 2007 to 2011? Do you think that the state's exemption from the No Child Left Behind Act will change this trend?

3. In 2013, which state had the highest average ACT composite score? Which had the lowest? What are some of the variables that might cause this difference? Do these same states have higher average income levels? Discuss the possible connection between the two.

4. For the most recent year available, which state has the largest percentage of its schools operating as charter schools? Which has the smallest? Why is there such a difference?

5. In 2000, what was the national average salary for a public elementary or secondary school teacher straight out of college? How does your state compare? Is this enough? Why or why not? Do teacher salaries correlate with student performance? Why or why not?

6. Which state had the highest dropout rate for black students in 2010? Was this surprising? Why or why not?

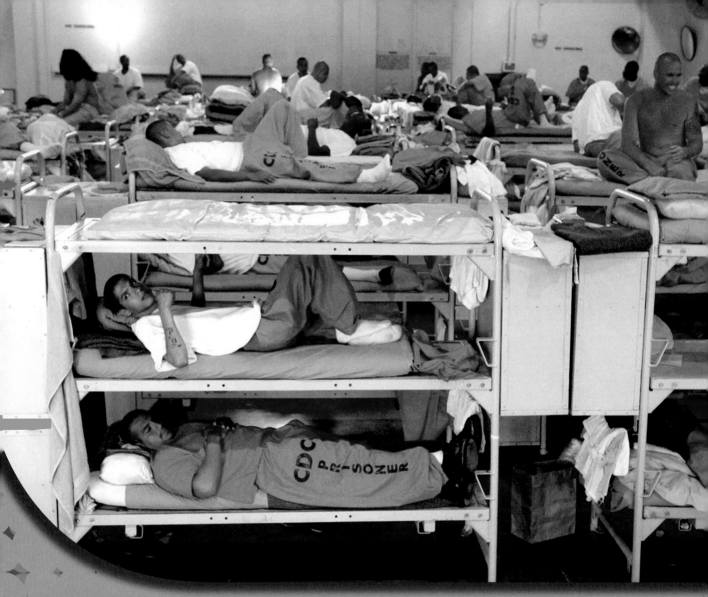

California's 33 adult prisons house some 115,000 inmates, making it the largest penal system in the country. Since 2006, the state has been reducing its inmate population in response to a U.S. Supreme Court ruling that conditions violated the U.S. Constitution's prohibition on cruel and unusual punishment. Since then, California has revised laws to reduce admissions, reworked, and moved tens of thousands of low-level offenders to county jails. While progress has been made, the California Department of Corrections and Rehabilitation budget for 2013–2014 still amounted to some $9.1 billion dollars.

ch. 14

Crime and Punishment

- What factors contribute to the poor relationship between police and minority communities?
- Why does the United States incarcerate a higher proportion of its population than does any other developed country?
- What options are state and local governments considering to reduce both imprisonment and crime?

At 11:51 A.M. on Saturday, August 9, 2014, the 911 dispatch center in Ferguson, Missouri, received a call about a convenience store robbery. According to the caller, a young black male had stolen a box of cigars and then assaulted the sales clerk. The dispatcher directed a police officer to the scene, where he intercepted an 18-year-old African American teenager, Michael Brown. Exactly what happened next remains a matter of debate; certain facts, though, are undisputed. There was a confrontation of some sort, multiple shots were fired, and when the shooting stopped, Michael Brown was lying face-down on the pavement. A subsequent autopsy found that he'd been shot six times.

Police backup arrived within minutes, as did an ambulance. Brown was immediately pronounced dead. For 4 hours, Brown's body was left lying in the street while police investigated the scene and horrified onlookers gathered. Rumors spread that the teenager had been shot in the back.

The next day, St. Louis County police chief Joe Belmar called a morning news conference. He announced that Brown had attacked the officer and that during the struggle,

After reading this chapter, you will be able to

- outline the basic public perceptions of the criminal justice system and its inequalities,
- describe the origins and legacies of the American penal and policing systems,
- discuss the evolution of the criminal justice system to one of mass incarceration, and
- identify contemporary issues and debates on crime and punishment.

Brown had reached for the officer's gun. One shot was fired inside the car and two shots were fired outside. Brown's family disagreed. That evening, they held a candlelight vigil. While the gathering was largely peaceful, some of the demonstrators were angry. Some protestors smashed car windows and looted local stores.

The police responded in force, deploying officers in riot gear and armored trucks. Reporters from *The Washington Post* and *The Huffington Post* were detained at a nearby McDonald's by police carrying assault rifles. For years, certain reporters on the public safety beat had sounded the alarm about the "militarization" of the police, much of it fueled by surplus war material left over from the wars in Iraq and Afghanistan. Photographs from Ferguson seemed to suggest that those fears had come to pass. The photographs of heavily armed police officers in body armor pointing semiautomatic weapons at civilians fueled a nationwide debate about police tactics and the relationship between law enforcement agencies and minority communities.[1]

The killing of Michael Brown was not an isolated incident. Although concrete numbers are hard to find, the best estimate is that U.S. police kill more than 400 people a year. Compared with other developed countries, that's a high number. In Great Britain (a country whose population is a fifth that of the United States) the corresponding number was zero. In Japan (a country of 127 million), police have killed two people—in the past 6 years. Brown was just one of the two people killed by Ferguson police that month. Indeed, in many high-crime neighborhoods in this country, police killings of civilians happen with such frequency that there's even a name for it—"death by cop."[2]

Over the course of the past generation, violent crime rates have fallen by nearly 50 percent from their highs in the early 1990s. Most of the decline occurred between 1992 and the mid-2000s. Since then crime rates have drifted gently downward in most parts of the country. The exception is in America's biggest cities. In New York and Los Angeles, the cities that were once seen as the most dangerous places in the country, crime rates have continued to fall. Since the early 1990s, both New York and Los Angeles have seen their homicide rates decline by 80 percent. What this means in terms of lives saved is profound. In the early 1990s, New York had more than 2,000 homicides a year. By 2012 it had only 414 homicides (most of them people of color). Most of the lives saved were those of young minority men, particularly African Americans, who, though constituting just 12 percent of the population, account for nearly half its murder victims. The homicide decline means that hundreds if not thousands of young men who might otherwise have been killed are alive today.[3]

The reasons for this crime decline remain a subject of debate. Criminologists generally agree that the nation's high incarceration rate contributed something to the crime decline (although New York experienced one of the most dramatic crime declines while also shrinking its prison population). Others have pointed to factors such as the changing nature of the drug market, the aging of the U.S. population, improved trauma procedures in hospital emergency rooms, legalized abortion, and the phaseout of leaded gasoline.[4] The clear implication of many of these findings was that the police don't deserve all or perhaps even most of the credit for the crime decline. However, the continuing decline in New York and Los Angeles has led some scholars to rethink such beliefs. In his book *The City That Became Safe: New York's Lessons for Urban Crime and Its Control*, Franklin Zimring credited new policing tactics via a process of elimination. "There are simply no other changes in policy, social conditions, or economics that could plausibly explain the city's much better than typical performance in the crime drop years of the 1990s and in the nine years after the general crime decline stopped," concluded Zimring, a law professor at the University of California, Berkeley.[5]

You might expect that more than a decade of declining crime would translate into higher public regard for the police—but it hasn't. Research conducted by the Pew Charitable Trusts shows that different ethnic groups perceive the criminal justice system in starkly different ways. A 2014 Pew Research Center study found that just 10 percent of African Americans believed that police did an "excellent" or "good" job of treating blacks and whites equally, compared with 38 percent of whites. The result is a conundrum: Levels of crime have fallen to lows not seen since the early 1960s, and the communities that have benefited most from the fall in violent crimes are minority communities. Yet minority mistrust of the criminal justice system remains high. Why?[6]

The way the police conduct themselves is part of the answer. Since the early 1990s, many big-city police departments have embraced the tactic of "stopping, questioning, and frisking" potential suspects in dangerous, high-crime neighborhoods, a practice widely known as "**stop and frisk.**"

The scale of "stop and frisk" in certain cities can be hard to grasp. Columbia professor Jeffrey Fagan and his colleagues found that 18- and 19-year-old African Americans residing in New York City had a 78 to 80 percent chance of being stopped in 2006. Latino teenagers of the same age had a 35 to 40 percent chance of being stopped. For white teenagers, the numbers were between 1 and 13 percent. In Los Angeles, the black stop rate is 3,400 stops higher than the white stop rate. It's hardly surprising that many African Americans see this as **racial profiling**.

There is also the problem of the mass imprisonment of uneducated men, particularly men of color. Bruce Western, a sociologist at Harvard University, has calculated that white men born between 1965 and 1969 who do not earn a high school degree have an 11 percent chance of ending up in prison. "This means that for certain men—black men without a high school degree—imprisonment is modal in statistical terms," notes Yale Law School professor Tracey Meares. "In everyday language, it is normal. For these men, going to prison is an ordinary life experience along one's life course trajectory, just like graduation, marriage, a first job, or having children is for everybody else."[7]

This is a chapter about crime and punishment. It's a story that is at once darker than *Dexter* and more unexpected than *Orange Is the New Black*. We'll talk about the American penal and policing system's origins and then discuss how the crime explosion of the early 1960s led to a crackdown whose effects we are still dealing with today. We'll also discuss one of the most hopeful developments of our current era—the bipartisan effort to rethink how states approach the issue of incarceration. Along the way we'll examine how the court system operates differently for different segments of society, even as the flow of money (less from states, more from political donors) remakes the system as a whole. We'll examine what the future of punishment and policing might look like. Finally, we'll consider one of the biggest potential changes of the quarter-century, the end of the war on drugs. If the "war" is over, what might peace look like?

Private Wrongs, Public Justice

Americans are fascinated with crime. Books about private eyes, criminals, and the courts regularly top the best-seller lists. Television shows about cops, drug dealers, and even serial killers are staples. In fact, anyone who watches TV has a pretty good idea of how the criminal justice system in the United States works: The police enforce the law and make arrests, but they do not have the power to punish—that authority rests with the state. District attorneys initiate prosecutions. Elected at the county level—except in Alaska, Connecticut, and New Jersey, where they are appointed by the governor—these

---

Stop and frisk
A police tactic that allows police officers to stop, question, and search citizens under a set of narrowly defined circumstances

Racial profiling
The allegation that police target minorities when enforcing the law

individuals represent the state's interests in criminal cases. As discussed in Chapter 9, defendants are represented by defense attorneys, often public defenders, and most of the time they agree to plea bargains without ever going to trial.

If a case does go to trial, a jury decides the guilt or innocence of the accused. If the accused is found guilty—and most defendants are—then a circuit judge metes out a penalty in accordance with relevant law. Judges may be appointed or elected, depending on the state, but their responsibilities are the same in this situation. A defendant who believes he or she received an unfair trial may file an appeal request with an appeals court or even with the state supreme court.

That is the U.S. criminal justice system, as seen on *CSI* or *Law & Order*. It's a pretty accurate picture, as far as it goes. The problem is, it doesn't go far enough. In fact, Americans' seeming familiarity with the system obscures some basic facts about it. Take, for instance, the fact that punishment is a public function.

One of the most (pardon the pun) arresting features of the U.S. criminal justice system is that the state initiates and dispenses punishment for such crimes as homicide, assault, robbery, and burglary. To Americans, this seems entirely natural. Crime is thought of as an offense not just against an individual but against society itself. As a result, the state initiates the punishment—and the punishment can be severe. It can take the form of imprisonment or **probation**. Punishment deemed to be cruel and unusual, such as torture, is not allowed under the U.S. Constitution, but for homicide, the death penalty is still an option.

People in the United States are aware of the differences between civil and criminal affairs. Civil disputes are private. Your neighbor knocks down your fence and then refuses to put it back up or pay to repair it. You've never much liked that neighbor, so you decide to sue. The state offers a forum for the dispute—the court—and sees that any penalty is carried out, but the dispute is between two private individuals and their

lawyers. You don't expect the county district attorney to initiate criminal proceedings against your neighbor over a broken fence. No matter how precious your fence or how guilty your neighbor, the state will not lock your neighbor away. In short, a civil offense is against only an individual.

A look at the historical record reveals something interesting: The distinctions that Americans see as natural are, in fact, not at all universal. For most of human history, from ancient Greece to monarchical Europe, private prosecution was the norm.[8] In medieval Britain, the attorney general initiated cases only for the king. Justices of the peace began prosecutions only when there was no private individual to initiate punishment.

Until relatively recently, the governments of most nations simply set the rules for how offended parties should pursue justice. Their role was essentially that of umpire. Governments had to fight long and hard to establish that they had the *exclusive* right to punish wrongdoers.[9] A key figure in this transference of the right of retaliation from the wronged party to the state was the public prosecutor. For reasons that historians still do not fully understand, public prosecutors first appeared in North America—in Great Britain's Atlantic colonies.

On the whole, the state's successful monopoly on punishment has brought enormous benefit to the United States. Conflicts such as the famous one between the Hatfields and McCoys notwithstanding, the nation is essentially free of ongoing feuds or vendettas.

Liberty and Justice for All? Systemwide Racial Inequalities

In recent years, however, the legitimacy of the criminal justice system has come under withering criticism. Perhaps the most forceful critique is that our criminal justice system is racist. In her best-selling book *The New Jim Crow: Mass Incarceration in the Age of Colorblindness*, Ohio State University law school professor Michelle

Probation
Supervised punishment in the community

Alexander examines how minorities have fared under the U.S. criminal justice system.

The answer is, not well. By 2006, 5 percent of all black males in the United States were serving time either in a state prison or in a city or county jail. That stood in sharp contrast to the 1 percent of white males jailed during the same period. Nearly one third of all black males ages 20 to 29 were either in prison or under some form of supervision, such as probation or **parole**. One study estimated that in 1997 black males had a 32 percent chance of going to prison at some point in their lives. In contrast, Hispanic males had a 17 percent chance of being imprisoned, and white males had a 5.9 percent chance.[10]

The primary cause of this difference in treatment is the **war on drugs**—and, specifically, the war on crack cocaine. "Drug offenses alone account for two-thirds of the rise in the federal inmate population and more than half of the rise in state prisoners between 1985 and 2000," notes Alexander. About 500,000 of the nearly 2.5 million people incarcerated today are serving time for a drug offense—versus fewer than 50,000 people in 1980. "Nothing," she concludes, "has contributed more to the systematic **mass incarceration** of people of color in the United States than the War on Drugs."

But in Alexander's view, the war on drugs wasn't the real issue; the real issue was racism. "The War on Drugs, cloaked in race-neutral language, offered whites opposed to racial reform a unique opportunity to express their hostility toward blacks and black progress, without being exposed to the charge of racism," writes Alexander.

Had the war on drugs really been about drugs, she continues, then "the drug war could have been waged primarily in overwhelmingly white suburbs or on college campuses. SWAT teams could have rappelled from helicopters in gated suburban communities and raided the homes of high school lacrosse players known for hosting coke and ecstasy parties after their games. . . . All of this could have happened as a matter of routine in white communities, but it did not." The so-called crack "epidemic" was, in Alexander's opinion, a sensationalized media phenomenon that was created by the far right.[11]

That goes too far for many of the people who saw crack's impact firsthand. Indeed, David Kennedy, a professor at the John Jay College of Criminal Justice, disagrees. In his book *Don't Shoot: One Man, A Street Fellowship, and the End of Violence in Inner-City America*, Kennedy responds to the claim that "crack sparked a 'moral panic': that it was never really that bad, that the public and political and law enforcement response was just a fevered overreaction," with a single, italicized epithet—"*Bullshit*." Kennedy got a firsthand look at the crack epidemic 25 years ago, at Nickerson Gardens, a thousand-unit housing project in Los Angeles. "I've never been so scared before or since," writes Kennedy of the day spent walking through the housing development with two Los Angeles Police Department (LAPD) patrol officers. (In fact, Kennedy's LAPD companions would later tell him that the dealers had been scared of *him*; they had seen a white guy in a suit in the projects and thought, "Fed.")

But while Kennedy rejects Alexander's belief that the criminal justice system is a tool of racist oppression, he shares her belief that something has gone terribly wrong with the way this country polices its inner-city communities. "We are destroying the village in order to save it," he writes.[12]

The war on drugs is just part of the problem; the other problem is how law enforcement operates. Some critics have argued that police operate with insufficient zeal in high-crime neighborhoods. In her book *Ghettoside: A True Story of Murder in America*, Jill Leovy, founder of the Los Angeles murder blog *The Homicide Report*, explores the long history of official indifference to black-on-black crime. "African-Americans have suffered from . . . a lack of effective criminal justice

The feud between the Hatfields of West Virginia and the McCoys of Kentucky came to involve the U.S. Supreme Court and the National Guard before the families agreed to end the conflict in 1891.

Parole
Supervised early release from prison

War on drugs
An effort by the federal government to treat drug abuse as a law enforcement rather than public health problem

Mass incarceration
The phrase used to describe the United States' striking high rate of imprisonment

An alleged drug dealer sits on the ground in handcuffs after being caught fleeing from police in 2005. Critics of the war on drugs claim that it unfairly targeted racial minorities, who suffered disproportionately under its policies.

and this, more than anything, is the reason for the nation's long-standing plague of black homicides," she writes. Leovy notes that in Los Angeles County blacks are killed at 2 to 4 times the rate of Latinos (even Latinos residing in the same high-crime neighborhoods as African Americans) and at 12 times the rate of whites. Yet black homicides rarely receive top priority.[13] It's a valuable perspective. The more common argument, however, is that law enforcement in minority communities operates with excessive, indiscriminate zeal. Central to the perception that law enforcement operates unfairly is the practice of "stopping, questioning, and frisking" residents in high-crime neighborhoods.

Principle Versus Practice in Common Law

Americans are governed by a mixture of formal (statutory) law and case (or common) law. Statutes are laws enacted by the sovereign. The most famous example is the Napoleonic Code, drafted by the French emperor Napoleon Bonaparte in the early 19th century. Most countries today have statutes and justice systems where disputes are adjudicated by a magistrate. The United States has statutes, too, of course, at both the state and federal levels of government. But the U.S. justice system is also rooted in the English common law.

The common law is made up of legal opinions written by judges that recognize commonly accepted community practices, and it evolves gradually over time as a community's ideas change. Forty-nine states operate within this common-law tradition. (The exception is Louisiana. As a former French colony, the state instead operates under the Napoleonic Code.) Common law makes the U.S. system quite unlike the legal systems of most other countries. In most of the world, law is enacted by a single sovereign power: a legislature, a monarch, or some combination. The United States has both statutes and a body law.

Many of the other institutions that characterize the U.S. criminal justice system have their roots in the English system as well. County sheriffs are the most notable example. At more than 1,000 years old, the office of sheriff is the oldest law enforcement office within the common-law system. The king of England appointed a representative called a reeve to act on behalf of the king in each shire or county. *Shire reeve,* or king's representative, became *sheriff* as the English language changed.

The United Kingdom also gave us the model for today's police. European cities had night watchmen since the Middle Ages, but it was not until then–British home secretary Sir Robert Peel established the Metropolitan Police in 1829 that a recognizably modern police force with uniforms, a regular chain of command, and a philosophy of interacting with the citizenry that prefigures community policing came into being. (British police officers are called "Bobbys" in his

Common law
Law composed of judges' legal opinions that reflects community practices and evolves over time

> The common law is made up of legal opinions written by judges that recognize commonly accepted community practices, and it evolves gradually over time as a community's ideas change. Forty-nine states operate within this common-law tradition.

Perhaps our most important inheritance from the common-law tradition is the institution of the jury. Serving on a jury is *the* defining act of citizenship. It is just about the only thing every citizen must do. (Men between the ages of 18 and 25 must also register with the Selective Service in the event that the government needs to reinstitute a military draft.) In most states, ignoring a jury summons is a crime. Failing to appear for jury duty without being properly exempted constitutes contempt of court and may present a somewhat less appealing opportunity to experience the criminal justice system, such as fines or even imprisonment. Unless you commit a crime or have the misfortune of being one of the roughly 5 million people who fall victim to a crime every year, serving on a jury probably will be your primary interaction with the criminal justice system.[15]

In 2012, Colorado and Washington became the first two states to legalize marijuana.

honor.) U.S. cities such as Philadelphia, Boston, and New York quickly followed suit. These police departments were only the most visible part of American law enforcement. County sheriffs make up the vast bulk of the law enforcement capacity in the United States, and states operate law enforcement agencies, too, from state highway patrol departments to more specialized bureaus of investigation that operate much like the Federal Bureau of Investigation (FBI).

The existence of multiple agencies with jurisdictional overlap can lead to confusion. The United States is a federation in which the federal government and the state governments are both sovereign. Congress and the state legislatures each make laws—as do county and city governments, though these typically operate under the jurisdiction of the states. Citizens must obey these laws or risk punishment. Yet sometimes states enact laws that contradict federal laws.

Take the issue of marijuana, for example. In 2012, Washington and Colorado legalized the recreational use of marijuana for adults. Cities such as Philadelphia have decriminalized the possession of small amounts of marijuana. Possession, which had once been a misdemeanor offense, is now punishable with a $25 civil fine. It's like a cheap parking ticket. Yet the possession of marijuana remains a federal offense. Colorado is collecting taxes on marijuana growers (who must submit to a whole range of regulations), but the federal Drug Enforcement Administration could still arrest them.[14]

As discussed in Chapter 9, there are two types of juries. In most states east of the Mississippi River, a grand jury determines whether there is sufficient evidence for the state to prosecute someone for a crime. In states west of the Mississippi, the district attorney usually has the authority to indict someone and take that person to trial. Presented with a less clear instance of wrongdoing, a prosecutor also may impanel an investigative grand jury to study the evidence and determine exactly who should be targeted for prosecution. Once a grand jury or the district attorney has indicted an individual, another trial begins and another jury is formed to hear the case.

So what is the role of a juror? Most jurors are given clear instructions by the presiding judge. The word **verdict** comes from the Latin phrase *vera dicere,* "to speak the truth." Jurors usually are told that their role is to determine exactly what the truth of a case is. They are to apply the law, regardless of whether they personally agree with it or not. As a result, the role of the juror often is that of

Verdict
A jury's finding in a trial

Local Focus

The NYPD Derives Twenty-First Century Goals From Nineteenth Century England

Current New York Police Department (NYPD) commissioner Bill Bratton has had an unusual career in policing. Between 1992 and 1994, he led the NYPD under then-mayor Rudolph Giuliani. During this time period, the department was known for its embrace of an assertive style that reflected the ideas of "broken windows" policing (discussed in more detail toward the end of this chapter). Between 2002 and 2007, Bratton led the LAPD. In late 2013, he was once again appointed commissioner of the NYPD.

In 1992, Bratton's job was to reduce crime and restore order. Today, it is to keep crime low while restoring relations between the NYPD and all of New York's communities. New York's commish has found a surprising inspiration for this new assignment.

Since returning as New York City's police commissioner in 2014, Bratton has made no secret of his admiration for another famous policeman, Sir Robert Peel. Indeed, Bratton has spoken of Sir Robert with such frequency that prominent New Yorkers have had to go back to their history books.

"I have heard the commissioner refer to him continually, which made me look him up," the Reverend Al Sharpton told *The New York Times*. Bratton has expressed particular admiration for Peel's famous "Nine Principles of Policing," going so far as to tell reporters, "I carry these with me everywhere." Here are Peel's principles:

- "The basic mission for which the police exist is to prevent crime and disorder."
- "The ability of the police to perform their duties is dependent upon public approval of police actions."

- "Police must secure the willing cooperation of the public in voluntary observance of the law to be able to secure and maintain the respect of the public."
- "The degree of cooperation of the public that can be secured diminishes proportionately to the necessity of the use of physical force."
- "Police seek and preserve public favor not by catering to the public opinion but by constantly demonstrating absolute impartial service to the law."
- "Police use physical force to the extent necessary to secure observance of the law or to restore order only when the exercise of persuasion, advice and warning is found to be insufficient."
- "Police, at all times, should maintain a relationship with the public that gives reality to the historic tradition that the police are the public and the public are the police; the police being only members of the public who are paid to give full-time attention to duties which are incumbent on every citizen in the interests of community welfare and existence."
- "Police should always direct their action strictly towards their functions and never appear to usurp the powers of the judiciary."
- "The test of police efficiency is the absence of crime and disorder, not the visible evidence of police action in dealing with it."

In a city struggling to build closer relations between the police and minority communities, it's easy to see the appeal of Peel's principles—even if scholars say that it was in fact Sir Robert's successor who articulated them.

Sources: Joseph Goldstein and J. David Goodman, "A London Guide for One Police Plaza," *New York Times*, April 15, 2014, http://www.nytimes.com/2014/04/16/nyregion/a-london-guide-for-1-police-plaza.html?_r=0; "Sir Robert Peel's Nine Principles of Policing," *New York Times*, April 15, 2014, http://www.nytimes.com/2014/04/16/nyregion/sir-robert-peels-nine-principles-of-policing.html.

a cog—albeit a very important one—in the criminal justice machine. But in fact, the jury system is at the heart of America's criminal justice process.

The history of the jury system underscores the importance of the checks that Americans, as inheritors of the English common-law tradition, have historically placed on the state, and the awesome powers and responsibilities that our system of justice gives to a group of citizens duly empaneled and sworn to uphold the law. But it is also clear that for a significant portion of the U.S. population, the system has gone terribly wrong.

Prison Nation

The first aspect that is striking about the U.S. system is how many people we incarcerate. In 2012, some 2.2 million Americans were in jail or prison, a rate of incarceration 5 times the average of the developed world. Just how many people is that? By one estimate, a quarter of the world's prisoners are housed in the United States, a country with just 5 percent of the world's population. Another 4.7 million Americans are on probation or parole.[16]

The U.S. system is arguably cruel. Only China, Iraq, Iran, and Saudi Arabia execute more people than does the United States. These are not typically countries Americans like to be grouped with. The United States also holds 25,000 inmates in nearly complete isolation in so-called **supermax prisons**, despite compelling evidence that doing so increases violence and leads to mental illness. An additional 50,000 to 80,000 residents are held in restrictive segregation units, which closely resemble supermax units.[17] Then there is the regular system. Some 41,000 inmates in this country are serving life sentences without parole; in England, that number is just 41. Not surprisingly, all this prison use is expensive. In 2010, the United States spent $80 billion on jails and prisons—about $280 per person.[18]

The second standout characteristic of the U.S. justice system is how much more punishment minorities experience. On average, black men receive sentences that are 20 percent longer than the sentences whites and Latinos receive for similar offenses. According to an estimate by the Bureau of Justice Statistics, at current rates of imprisonment, 1 in 3 black men will serve time in prison in their lifetimes. University of Washington professor Becky Pettit found that on any given day in 2008, 1 in 9 black men was incarcerated and that a full 37 percent of young, black, male high school dropouts were behind bars.[19]

But incarceration is only the most visible part of the problem. Increasingly, governments don't just punish offenders; they profit from them. Consider Orange County, California. It outsourced its "supervised electronic confinement program" to a private company that monitors movements, oversees case management, and tests participants for drug and alcohol use—all for free. The catch is that the company then charges probationers $35 to $100 a month, a sum that can be challenging to pay. To some, this is smart and fair. Others, such as journalist Thomas Edsall, have described it as "poverty capitalism." "In this unique sector of the economy," writes Edsall, "costs of essential government services are shifted to the poor."[20]

This dynamic is perhaps most evident in the criminal justice system. Consider the case of Nicole Bolden, a 32-year-old single mother of four who got into a car accident in the town of Florissant, which is near Ferguson outside of St. Louis, after another driver made an illegal U-turn. Bolden had four outstanding arrest warrants in other jurisdictions, all for failing to appear in court for minor traffic violations. Bolden hadn't appeared, she said, because she didn't have the money to pay the fine and feared she might be jailed if she appeared in court. It's a common misconception. The fact is, you can't be jailed for lacking the money to pay a fine, but you can be jailed for failing to appear for a court date. You can also be fined again for not showing, which is what happened to Bolden. Arrested and unable to pay her $1,700 bond, Bolden spent 2 weeks in jail, during which time she was given a psychological evaluation and put on suicide watch. She missed a job interview, fell behind in her studies, and had little contact with her kids before finally having her day in court.

Such cases are far from unique. St. Louis County has 90 municipalities. According to *The Washington Post*, some communities there earn as much as 40 percent of their municipal budgets from court fees. St. Louis attorneys even have a term for these types of offenses: "poverty offenses."[21]

Supermax prisons
High-security prisons designed to house violent criminals

A Difference
That Makes A Difference

Jury Power: What the Courts Don't Want You to Know

The origins of the modern jury go back to the early 1200s, when the English Crown enlisted the most notable men in local communities across England into administrative divisions called "hundreds." Twice a year, the king's circuit court judges would meet with these hundreds of notable individuals and ask them to identify people in each village who had violated the king's peace. Fines and other forms of punishment were then administered accordingly.

By the 14th century, it had become clear that this approach was subject to abuse. As a result, it was decided that jury verdicts had to be unanimous. By the mid-16th century, justices of the peace had the power to investigate accusations, take statements from the accused and the accuser, and indict potential criminals. Justices of the peace still had to present their findings to a jury, but they increasingly attempted to direct juries' verdicts by providing instructions on how they should proceed.

But sometimes juries refused to play along. This was particularly true when it came to enforcing laws about religion. In 1670, William Penn, a Quaker, was brought to trial for illegally preaching to the public. Under English law, only state-sanctioned Anglican priests could preach publicly. Penn admitted that he had broken the law, but he argued that the law itself was illegal. He asked the jury to acquit him. It did, despite instructions from the presiding judge to enforce the law.

The Crown was profoundly displeased, because, in a sense, the jury's challenge raised a very fundamental question: Who really held sovereign power? When a jury could set aside laws made by the queen in Parliament, the clear implication was that the jury, not the government, was the ultimate power in society. To demonstrate where power really lay, the Crown fined all 12 jury members.

Juryman Bushel, however, refused to pay. His appeal went to the court of Chief Justice Robert Vaughan, who ruled in favor of the stubborn juror. Vaughan's opinion established something remarkable: Juries truly became the final authority in the English justice system. This had been rather vague until that moment, and so Vaughan's ruling marked a turning point in judicial history. Today, the practice whereby juries set aside laws or penalties that they disagree with is known as jury nullification. In the United States, the right to a trial by jury is one of a citizen's basic constitutional rights, enshrined in the Sixth Amendment of the U.S. Constitution.

Penn went on to establish the colony of Pennsylvania in North America. Like him, jury nullification also jumped across the Atlantic. In the tumultuous years leading up

For young men with criminal records in high-crime areas, it's even worse. Sociologist Alice Goffman's book *On the Run: Fugitive Life in an American City* followed a group of young men and women, as well as their extended families and romantic partners, in inner-city Philadelphia over the course of 4 years. She describes "hidden systems of policing and supervisions" that "are transforming poor black neighborhoods into communities of suspects and fugitives," where "a climate of fear and suspicion pervades everyday life, and many residents live with the daily concern that the authorities will seize them and take them away."[22]

Michelle Alexander, as we discussed above, sees this as deliberate—the latest manifestation of deep-rooted American racism. A close look at the history of our society's embrace of punishment suggests another possible interpretation—unintended consequences.

The Crime Explosion and the War on Drugs

The story begins in the 1960s. In 1962, the United States experienced 4.2 murders per 100,000

to the Revolutionary War, American juries repeatedly refused to convict John Hancock and other agitators who were brought to trial on charges of smuggling, because they viewed the defendants' activities as principled acts of defiance rather than crimes. During the 1850s, juries in the North regularly refused to enforce the Fugitive Slave Act, which had been passed at the insistence of the South in 1850 and made it illegal for anyone to assist a runaway slave. Southern anger at northern "lawlessness" and northern anger at southern "overreach" became major issues of contention in the years leading up to the Civil War.

The practice of jury nullification and the spirit of civil disobedience that inspired it also inspired other, less savory actions. For instance, in the 1950s and 1960s, many white juries in the South would not convict white citizens who assaulted and sometimes killed civil rights workers. The federal government responded by enacting new guidelines for jury selection that made juries more representative of the community as a whole. Women, minorities, and poor whites began to sit on juries after centuries of exclusion.

Despite the important role that jury nullification has played in U.S. history, authorities have never been eager to publicize this right. Many states bar defense lawyers and judges from even mentioning that jurors may set aside a law. Still, state constitutions in Georgia, Oregon, Indiana, and Maryland include provisions guaranteeing the right of jurors to "judge" or "determine" the law in "all criminal cases." Courts in those states have held that a jury has the power—but not the right—to acquit a guilty person but that jurors should not be told that they may ignore or nullify the law. As in the days of Juryman Bushel, the state remains uneasy about the discretion that juries enjoy.

Does the fact that jurors can find whatever they want mean that they should? Not necessarily. Chief Justice Vaughan upheld the right of an English jury to reject laws promulgated by a thoroughly undemocratic monarchical government. In contrast, the United States today is a democracy in which nearly every adult citizen has the right to vote. Today, jury nullification can be seen as a profoundly undemocratic act. After all, laws are passed by democratically elected bodies. However, it is also a right that jurors continue to enjoy. It may be a secret, but under the U.S. system of law, the jury is still sovereign.[a]

---

[a] Danielle S. Allen, *The World of Prometheus: The Politics of Punishing in Democratic Athens* (Princeton, NJ: Princeton University Press, 1999), 7.

---

residents. By 1964, the homicide rate had climbed to 6.4; by 1972, it had risen to 9.4. And that was just the homicide rate. Another category of violent crime, robberies, had risen far more sharply. In 1959, the rate was 51.2 for every 100,000 residents; by 1968, the rate had nearly tripled. Crime, the political scientist James Q. Wilson concluded, "had assumed epidemic proportions." (See Figure 14-1.)

Wilson looked primarily to cultural changes to explain this explosion in criminality. However, he and University of Chicago economist Gary Becker posited another cause as well: Crime was rising because the risk of punishment was falling. Crime was up, but the number of prison beds was down. By 1974, the "average" punishment per committed burglary was 4 days of incarceration. The average punishment per committed aggravated assault was 8 days; for robbery, 28. In short, crime increasingly "paid." That gave rise to a straightforward solution: Incarcerate more people for longer periods of time.

It was an idea that resonated with voters. From 1968 to 1990, "crime" consistently polled as American voters' top domestic concern. As a result, states went on a prison-building spree.

FIGURE 14-1

The Rise and Fall of Crime Rates: Aggravated Assault, Robbery, and Homicide Rates per 100,000 Residents, 1960–2012

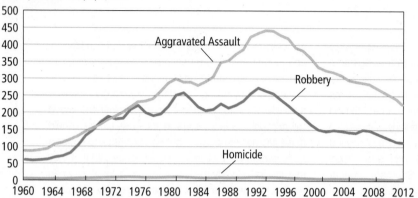

Source: "Estimated Number and Rate (per 100,000 Inhabitants) of Offenses Known to Police, by Offense, United States, 1960–2012," in *Sourcebook of Criminal Justice Statistics*, School of Criminal Justice, University at Albany, 2013, http://www.albany.edu/sourcebook/pdf/t31062012.pdf.

States also increased punishment in other ways. Between 1975 and 2002, all 50 states adopted mandatory sentencing laws that curbed judicial discretion by mandating minimum sentences. Many also enacted "three strikes" laws, which led to lengthy convictions for repeat offenders, even if their third crime was comparatively minor. By 1996, the United States had regained the level of punitiveness (calculated by dividing crimes committed by punishment given out) of 1962, the year before the crime spike of the 1960s began. By 1996, crime was beginning to fall.[23] (See Figure 14-2.)

But the prison-building didn't stop. Between 1985 and 2008, state prison populations nearly tripled. According to the Vera Institute of Justice, corrections spending rose even faster, by more than 600 percent. It now makes up 7 percent of state general fund spending. By 2008, some 2.3 million Americans were in prison or jail—that's 1 percent of the adult population. Another 5 million were under court supervision on probation or parole. Some 40 percent of the inmates were black. What had happened?[24]

Part of the answer has to do with the war on drugs. In 1971, President Richard Nixon declared

war on illegal drugs. "If we cannot destroy the drug menace in America, then it will surely in time destroy us, Nixon told a joint session of Congress. "I am not prepared to accept this alternative."[25]

The war did not go well. By 1978, one third of all kids ages 12 to 17 admitted to having tried an illegal drug.[26] Faced with a seemingly unstoppable rise in violence, more and more states responded by increasing the penalties for dealing and possessing drugs. Nelson Rockefeller, the liberal Republican governor of New York State, led the way. In 1973, Rockefeller and the state legislature agreed to impose new drug laws that were among the toughest in the nation. Anyone found in possession of 4 ounces or more of a narcotic such as heroin or cocaine faced the likelihood of a mandatory 15-year prison sentence. Selling as little as 2 ounces of the same narcotic could result in a similar penalty. The hope was that such harsh penalties would drive up drug prices and deter potential users. New York's strategy was an application of **deterrence theory**, the belief that if the punishment is severe enough, it will keep people from committing the crime. Other states and many cities quickly followed suit. State legislatures upped the penalties for the possession of illegal narcotics, and local and county law enforcement officers focused their resources on catching dealers.[27]

It didn't work. The tough new penalties directed against drug users had a minor effect at best on drug use. What they did succeed in doing was putting a lot more people in jail. In 1973, New York State incarcerated about 10,000 people. By 1980, that number had reached 20,000. To many,

Deterrence theory
A theory advanced by criminologists that harsh penalties will deter people from committing crimes

FIGURE 14-2

U.S. Incarceration Rate, 1920–2012

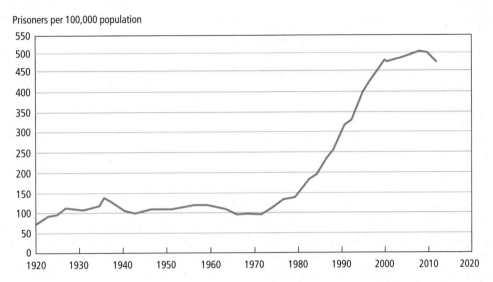

Prisoners per 100,000 population

Source: M. W. Cahalan, *Historical Corrections Statistics in the United States, 1850–1984* (Washington, DC: U.S. Department of Justice, 1986); E. Anne Carson and Daniela Golinelli, "Prisoners in 2012: Trends in Admissions and Releases, 1991–2012," Table 18, Bureau of Justice Statistics, Washington, DC, December 2013, revised September 2, 2014, http://www.bjs.gov/content/pub/pdf/p12tar9112.pdf; E. Anne Carson and William J. Sabol, "Prisoners in 2011," Bureau of Justice Statistics, Washington, DC, December 2012, http://www.bjs.gov/content/pub/pdf/p11.pdf; William J. Sabol, Heather C. West, and Matthew Cooper, "Prisoners in 2008," Bureau of Justice Statistics, Washington, DC, December 2009, revised June 30, 2010, http://www.bjs.gov/content/pub/pdf/p08.pdf.

it seemed that things could hardly get worse—but by the mid-1980s, they did.

In the early 1980s, intrepid drug dealers discovered that they could add baking soda and water to high-quality powder cocaine and bake the resulting solution to create small rocks. These rocks could be smoked in homemade pipes. Nicknamed "crack," for the crackling sound the rocks make when broken, the drug could be bagged in small portions that could be sold for as little as $5 each. Before, cocaine had been a yuppie drug, available only to those with the right connections and the right amount of cash. Now a teenager could buy it for less than a week's allowance.

Crack delivered a potent high at a bargain price. As a result, it quickly found users—with devastating results. Highly concentrated, it created a craving in most users that was so intense they would do shocking things to get more. Some crack addicts abandoned their children. Some began engaging in prostitution to get money to support their habits. Crack addicts broke into condemned buildings and stripped them of their

contents, even the plumbing pipes, just to make more money to buy crack.

To serve this new market, open-air drug markets sprang up on street corners across urban America. In drug-infested neighborhoods, teenagers often occupied the perfect dealing niche. Many were juveniles and thus were hard to arrest or at least to prosecute. Because the profits were so large, dealing drugs on a street corner was often a violent business. Street-level dealers became popular robbery targets; so they started carrying handguns. Neighborhood fistfights and gang brawls turned into running gun battles. Homicide rates, which had been rising slowly for years, skyrocketed. More than half the males arrested in nine major cities in 1988 tested positive for cocaine. In Washington, D.C., the figure was 59 percent, up from 14 percent in 1984. In Manhattan, the figure was more than 80 percent. A 1987 survey found that police classified more than a third of murders and two thirds of robberies and burglaries as drug-related.[28]

Getting Tough on Crime Through Sentencing

State and local government officials responded to this frightening surge in violence and crime in much the same way that legislators had responded to drug use concerns a decade earlier: They imposed tough new penalties for the use and possession of crack. Many states also made fundamental changes to their sentencing practices. For most of the post–World War II era, courts across the United States had enjoyed considerable leeway in determining the severity of the punishments they delivered. In academic-speak, this was known as indeterminate sentencing (see Chapter 9).

By the 1980s, however, the public's rising fears led to more strident demands to get tough on crime. Most judges obliged, if only to placate voters. Federal judges are nominated by the president and approved by the Senate for life service; however, most states rely at least in part on elections to select judges—even state supreme court justices.[29]

Stories of judges' releasing hardened criminals with little more than a slap on the wrist resulted in a growing number of states' moving toward determinate sentencing. "Truth-in-sentencing" laws were passed. These restricted judges' ability to set penalties and curtailed parole boards' freedom to release prisoners early. All 50 states passed mandatory sentencing laws. Many states went even further. Fourteen states abolished discretionary parole and parole boards altogether. In 1994, California voters approved a "three strikes" law, under which individuals arrested and convicted of three felony crimes were to be imprisoned for a minimum of 25 years, if not for the rest of their lives. In 2004, the U.S. Supreme Court further constrained judges' sentencing flexibility but also set the stage for potentially shorter sentences when it ruled that only juries, not judges, can increase sentences beyond the maximums suggested by sentencing laws.

Crackdowns on crack cocaine and other drugs, the broadening of offenses classified as felonies, the introduction of mandatory sentencing, and a tendency toward longer sentences in general soon led to a surge in prisoners. States expanded their prison systems accordingly. Between 1983 and 1990, California added 21,000 prison beds at a cost of $3.2 billion. During that same period, New York added 17,780 cells. And the prison building was only getting started. The increased reliance on incarceration had a big effect on state budgets. In 1978, state governments spent about $5 billion on maintaining prisons and jails. By 2007, prison spending had risen to $44 billion, or 10 percent of state expenditures. More than 1 in every 100 U.S. adults were under lock and key.[30] Spending has since ticked down a bit, but states still spend an average of 7 percent of total general revenue funds—$1 out of every $14—on prisons.[31]

Problems of a Prison Nation

Nowhere are the problems posed by the growth of the prison state more evident than in California. In 1994, California voters enacted a "three strikes" law in response to the horrific murder of 12-year-old Polly Klaas by a convicted felon with a long criminal record. The law imposed a sentence of 25 years to life for almost every crime, no matter how minor, if the defendant had two prior convictions for crimes defined as serious or violent by the California Penal Code. Serious crimes included drug possession and burglary. The result was a surge in prisoners (including a man in Torrance who was given a 25-year sentence for stealing a slice of pizza)—and more prison beds, of course. The state auditor would estimate that in the 12 years before its emendation in 2012, "three strikes" cost the state $19 billion. Some 45 percent of the people affected were African American.

By 1990, California's prisons were severely overcrowded, a condition that in time led to two lawsuits alleging that overcrowding and inadequate health care amounted to a violation of the U.S. Constitution's ban on cruel and unusual punishment. By the early 21st century, the state was spending about $8 billion a year to incarcerate some 173,000 prisoners. Forget the image of cellblocks: State facilities were so overcrowded that triple-height bunk beds spilled out into hallways and filled gymnasiums. A significant number of the inmates were mentally ill. Some of these prisoners were held in telephone-booth-sized cages pending sentencing. An outside investigation found that an average of one inmate a week was dying of maltreatment or neglect.

In 2006, a federal judge in San Francisco appointed someone to oversee the prison health system. The overseer found that it would cost the state $8 billion to meet constitutional requirements, money the state legislature failed to provide. In August 2009, a panel of federal judges ruled that overcrowding in California's prisons was so severe that it endangered the health and safety of inmates and prison staff in a way that violated the U.S. Constitution's prohibition on cruel and unusual punishment. The court ruled that California must reduce its prison population by 137.5 percent in 2 years' time. In concrete terms, that means that the state had to cut its inmate population by some 33,000 prisoners to bring the overall number down to 110,000.[32]

The state appealed the decision to the U.S. Supreme Court, but 2 years later, the court upheld the ruling. Citing conditions whereby suicidal inmates were held in "telephone-booth-sized cages without toilets," Justice Anthony Kennedy, writing for a 5-to-4 majority, declared that a "prison that deprives prisoners of basic sustenance, including adequate medical care, is incompatible with the concept of human dignity and has no place in civilized society."

In response, the state decided to move prisoners from state-run prisons to county jails, a process known as "realignment." But Democratic governor Jerry Brown resisted efforts to slow the influx of new prisoners into the system. When the Democratic-controlled legislature passed a bill that would change simple drug possession from a felony to a "wobbler"—a crime local prosecutors could decide to prosecute as a felony or a misdemeanor, depending on the circumstances—Brown vetoed it, promising instead to propose comprehensive reforms. But instead of unveiling the reforms, 1 year later, Brown proposed increasing California's $9-billion-a-year corrections budget by half a billion to build more prisons.[33]

In 2012, California reduced its prison population by 15,000 inmates. It was a big number but not enough to meet the target set by the panel of judges. At first, the state sought a delay. When that was not granted, Governor Brown declared that he would no longer comply with the order, claiming that "prison crowding no longer poses safety risks to prison staff or inmates, nor does it inhibit the delivery of timely and effective health care services to inmates." Today, California's prison system is widely seen as one of the nation's most troubled—ruinously expensive, cruel, and criminogenic.[34] In 2014, California voters approved a ballot measure that should reduce the prison populations, with many non-violent crimes, including drug possession, no longer treated as felonies.

It has been not a pretty picture; however, a growing number of states are taking action to avoid California-style dysfunction. It is a trend that started in an unlikely place—Texas, which is famous for its tough-on-crime culture. While all 50 states saw incarceration rates rise dramatically, beginning in the 1970s, Texas outdid them all (with the possible exception of Louisiana). The Lone Star State incarcerates roughly 1,000 out of every 100,000 people. (In contrast, the state with the lowest level of incarceration, Maine, locks up 300 people per 100,000.) Its prison system, second in size only to California's, holds more people than do the prison systems of Germany, France, Belgium, and the Netherlands—combined. And that's not counting the roughly 700,000 people the state supervises who are on probation or parole. It also executes more prisoners than any other state. Indeed, since 1976, when the U.S. Supreme Court reinstated the death penalty, Texas alone has carried out roughly a third of the country's executions.[35]

The Bipartisan Search for Solutions

Not surprisingly, between 1985 and 2005, Texas built prisons with gusto, increasing its inmate population from roughly 64,000 in 1993 to 154,000 in 2007. That year the Texas Department of Criminal Justice approached the state legislature with a request for $523 million in additional funding for three new prisons, which would allow the prison population to grow to more than 168,000 by 2012. The department had good reason to expect a positive response. The chairman of the Senate Criminal Justice Committee, John Whitmire, was a conservative Democrat from Houston and the author of Texas's famously tough penal code. His counterpart in the House, Jerry Madden, was a conservative Republican from Plano. Governor Rick Perry and Lieutenant Governor David Dewhurst were onboard.

A Difference
That Makes A Difference

The Slow Death of Capital Punishment

In 1972, the U.S. Supreme Court found that the application of the death penalty in many states had been cruel, arbitrary, and unconstitutional. A moratorium, or indefinite delay, was placed on all executions. Four years later, the Court lifted the moratorium. By then, the states had passed sentencing guidelines that addressed the Court's concern that the death penalty was being applied in an arbitrary fashion. Today, the statutes of 33 states allow prosecutors to request the death penalty. (The federal death penalty, of course, can apply anywhere in the country.) More than 1,300 prisoners have been executed since capital punishment was reinstated, and another 3,152 people were on death row in October 2012, according to the Death Penalty Information Center.

The fact that most states sanction capital punishment does not mean that they use it in similar ways. Some counties and states are much more enthusiastic in its use than are others. For example, suburban counties tend to apply the death penalty with more zeal than do urban counties. In 2009, San Mateo County, a suburb of San Francisco, had 17 people on California's death row; by contrast, San Francisco itself, a larger city with twice as many murders, had sentenced only four people to death.

During the 1990s, the scientific breakthrough of DNA testing shook up the capital punishment systems. In state after state, lawyers and public interest groups convinced courts and prosecutors to reexamine forensic evidence. They found that many people had been convicted of crimes they had not committed. By December 2012, postconviction DNA testing had cleared 301 Americans, according to the Innocence Project at the Cardozo School of Law at Yeshiva University. Eighteen of these people had been sentenced to death; 70 percent of the total were persons of color. The impact of this new research has been felt. In January 2000, Illinois governor George Ryan, a Republican and avowed supporter of capital punishment, became the first governor in the nation to halt executions in his state.

Other states began examining the most widely used method of execution—lethal injection—after the U.S. Supreme Court ruled in June 2006 that lower courts must consider the possibility that the

But instead of OK'ing the request, Whitmire and Madden did something unexpected. They teamed up to convince the legislature, governor, and lieutenant governor to spend $241 million on treatment, mental health, and rehabilitation instead. These programs are designed to help ex-felons stay out of prison following release by providing them with help such as drug treatment and job training. Some 95 percent of prisoners, after all, will return to their home communities at some point after their incarceration ends.

By all accounts, this approach has been working. In the 3 years that followed the adoption of the legislature's reform package, Texas's prison population declined by some 15,000 prisoners. (It had been expected to rise.) Probation **recidivism** fell by nearly a quarter, probation violations plummeted, and overall crime rates declined. Instead of adding thousands of prison beds, the state was able to close three adult and six juvenile prisons. "This is not a Republican or Democratic issue," said Madden. "It's about what's smart for Texas."[36]

Whitmire and Madden's pioneering work in Texas did something remarkable: It made corrections reform a bipartisan issue. Since 2007,

---

Recidivism
The tendency of criminals to relapse into criminal behavior and be returned to prison

process can be cruel and painful, a finding that would make the procedure unconstitutional. Several states proposed adding an anesthesiologist to monitor executions and confirm that the three-drug process, intended to sedate, paralyze, and finally kill the prisoner, was working properly. There was just one problem—anesthesiologists balked at presiding over executions because that would go against their Hippocratic Oath to "do no harm." States also began to lose access to the drugs most typically used to induce unconsciousness, stop breathing, and stop the heart. In 2014, a series of botched executions in which inmates retained or appeared to retain consciousness or feel pain while dying raised pointed questions about whether death by lethal injection is an efficient standard after all. In light of these challenges, some experts are calling for a return to other execution methods, including the electric chair and the firing squad. "We've known for a long time that there are better methods, but states don't want to look bad and horrifying," says Deborah Denno, a law professor at Fordham University who has written about the death penalty.

Instead, states have slowed down. In 2014 the United States executed the fewest prisoners since 1994, a third fewer prisoners than at capital punishment's peak of 98 in 1999. With crime falling and a wide range of options to choose from (thanks to the curtailment of mandatory sentencing laws), prosecutors and judges simply have more choices. Texas offers a case in point. For years, it accounted for a third of all executions nationwide, but in 2005, the Lone Star State introduced the possibility of life-without-parole sentences for the first time. "When that happened," said Craig Watkins, district attorney for Dallas County, "you saw a decrease in prosecutors even bringing death-penalty cases. . . . Now you have a choice. Before, you didn't."

Sources: Nathan Koppel and Chris Herring, "Lethal Injection Draws Scrutiny in Some States," *Wall Street Journal,* October 15, 2009, A13; "The Slow Death of the Death Penalty," *The Economist,* April 26, 2014.

legislatures in some 26 states have passed corrections reform packages. Some of the most ambitious packages have been enacted in the most conservative states, including such states as Arkansas, Georgia, Kentucky, Mississippi, Missouri, Ohio, Oklahoma, and South Carolina. An analysis by the nonprofit group GiveWell suggests that these reforms will reduce state prison populations by 11 percent in 5 years' time and save states billions of dollars. Prominent conservatives such as former House Speaker Newt Gingrich and Tea Party stalwart Mike Lee, a Republican senator from Utah, have even teamed up to form a conservative group, "Right on Crime," to promote smart penal policies. In the process, corrections reform has become the rare issue on which policymakers from both parties can agree.[37]

Governments at both the state and federal level are also beginning to reduce the number of people entering the correctional system. In 2010, Congress passed the Fair Sentencing Act, which reduced the punishment disparities between crack and powder cocaine. Some 29 states have passed legislation scaling back mandatory sentence laws, and in 2012, California voters approved a ballot initiative to curb "three strikes and you're out." The result has been a small decrease in state prison populations since 2010. But progress remains uneven. One of the states that corrections reformers are most disappointed with is California.

AP Photo/Harry Cabluck

Texas representative Jerry Madden (R-Richardson; left) and Senator John Whitmire (D-Houston) worked together on a bipartisan effort in 2007 to convince the Texas executive and legislature to implement measures focused on rehabilitation more than incarceration of those within the state's criminal justice system. Since their success, more than half of U.S. states have enacted similar reforms.

Political scientists talk a lot about culture and its impact on policy—and with good cause. As discussed previously, different states and localities do have very different political cultures; so it should come as no shock that they define some crimes differently and punish them differently. However, there is considerable evidence to suggest that differences in punishment are distinctly related to issues of race. For instance, studies have shown that the percentage of African American residents in a state's population correlates closely with the severity of penalties meted out in its criminal justice system. The more black residents a state has, the tougher its laws tend to be.[38] States in the Deep South, which have the largest proportion of African American residents, imprison people at much higher rates than do states in other parts of the country. (See Map 14-1.) Social scientists question the degree to which what is supposed to be an objective, color-blind criminal justice system—one that is administered largely by whites—systematically disadvantages blacks.[39]

Corrections isn't the only part of the criminal justice system that has seen stirrings of reform. Over the course of the past decade, the often-neglected field of probation has become one of the most interesting areas of crime control. The most significant experiment has played out in

Hawaii. It is called Hawaii's Opportunity Probation with Enforcement—HOPE for short.

Probation, of course, is an alternative punishment to incarceration. In a typical year, some 4.1 million people move onto or off of probation. (Parolees account for the other 800,000 under community supervision in a typical year. These are people leaving prison.) In theory, probationers are supervised by probation officers. In practice, most probation officers have such large caseloads that close oversight is impossible. As a result, few systems function well. Nationwide, about a third of probationers complete their sentences or are discharged early.[40]

A significant number of people on probation miss appointments or incur minor infractions with few immediate consequences—until the probationer is stopped for some minor offense, probation is revoked, and he or she abruptly returns to jail. Steven Alm saw the system firsthand as a circuit judge in Honolulu. As a judge, one of his roles was to revoke probation. But when Alm read the motions put before him, he saw page after page of violations: 10 or more missed appointments, dirty drug tests, failure to show up for treatment. In most cases, all this misbehavior had essentially been ignored. Then, all of a sudden, he was being asked to send the violator to prison for 5, 10, or even 20 years for another violation.

"This is absolutely a crazy way to try to change anyone's behavior," Alm concluded. Think about a parent who ignores bad behavior and then, suddenly and in a seemingly arbitrary fashion, decides to brutally spank the misbehaving child. That was essentially what the justice system was doing. So in 2004 Alm decided to try an experiment. In place of the existing practice, he proposed a kind of correctional time-out—brief but immediate punishment. Anybody found violating any term of his or her probation would be returned to a jail cell for a few days.

MAP 14-1

Incarceration Rates per 100,000 Population, 2013

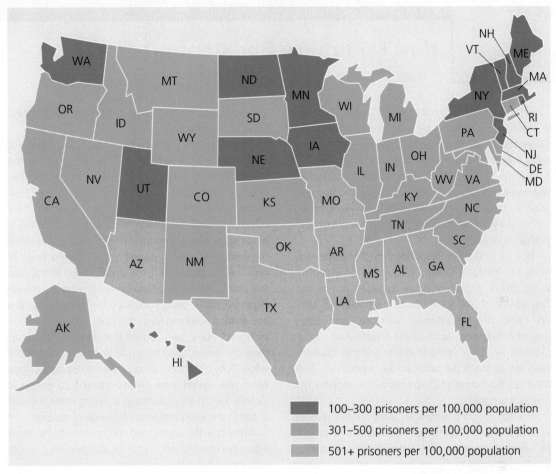

100–300 prisoners per 100,000 population

301–500 prisoners per 100,000 population

501+ prisoners per 100,000 population

Source: E. Ann Carson, "Prisoners in 2013," Bureau of Justice Statistics, September 2014, Table 6, http://www.bjs.gov/content/pub/pdf/p13.pdf.

Note: No 2013 data were available on Nevada; data displayed for Nevada are as of 2011.

Thirty-four probationers were placed under Alm's supervision. Eighteen were sex offenders; the others were chronic transgressors who had been on probation for a variety of felony offenses. Many had substance abuse problems—about 40 percent routinely failed even prescheduled drug tests. That was 7 years ago. Today, Alm's initiative encompasses nearly 1,500 of the roughly 8,000 probationers on Oahu. With very little dedicated public funding, it has achieved extraordinary results: In its first 5 years of operation, it claimed an 80 percent reduction in missed appointments, an 86 percent reduction in the incidence of drug use, and, based on the best current estimates, a 50 percent reduction in recidivism. A randomized

evaluation in 2012 found that the program "produced dramatic, positive results." "There may not be another intervention that could have a more dramatic impact on crime, drug use and prison spending," says Adam Gelb, who heads the Pew Center on the States's Public Safety Performance Project.[41]

What is particularly striking about HOPE is how few resources are needed to enforce compliance. In game theory terms, Hawaii has moved from a high-violation, high-punishment equilibrium to a low-violation, low-punishment equilibrium. In short, it tipped, just as in Boston and other cities where Kennedy-style intervention operations worked. Not surprisingly, the National Institute of Justice

Policy in Practice

How Far to Take Gun Control?

A few days before Christmas in 2012, the nation was plunged into grief by a tragedy in Newtown, Connecticut. A gunman killed 20 children—first-graders, ages 6 and 7—along with six adults at Sandy Hook Elementary School, before killing himself. It was not the first mass shooting the nation had witnessed that year, but the death of young children in their neighborhood school revived the gun control debate in a way that nothing had in years.

Not all politicians responded in the same way, however. President Obama pledged to do everything in his power to prevent future tragedies of this sort. Democrats in the U.S. Senate pledged to bring up bans on assault-style weapons and large-capacity magazines such as the shooter had used in Connecticut. Lawmakers in states such as California pledged to respond with similar measures, while localities such as San Diego rushed to expand gun buyback programs.

But not everyone embraced these traditional types of restrictions on firearms or newer ideas for tagging or taxing ammunition. The National Rifle Association (NRA) responded to the shooting by calling for armed personnel and police to be put in every school—an idea that legislators in some states, such as Missouri and Tennessee, had already talked about. "It's magnified in the moment, but I expect red states will vote to expand gun rights and the blue states will seek to enact gun control legislation," said Scott Melzer, an expert on

gun politics at Albion College in Michigan, in the days following the shooting.[a]

Would tougher gun control laws save lives? For some people, the answer is obvious. In 2011, the United States suffered 11,000 gun-related homicides. Countries with strict gun control laws, such as Great Britain and Japan, had well under 50 apiece. For others, the very suggestion of outlawing handguns is outrageous. Many gun owners view individual firearms ownership as a basic constitutional right—a point of view the Supreme Court has upheld twice in the past few years. The Second Amendment proclaims, "A well-regulated militia being necessary for the security of a free state, the right to keep and bear arms shall not be infringed." Some have argued that allowing citizens to carry concealed weapons would improve overall public safety. They claim that the country would be safer if more Americans carried guns. The massacre of 32 people at Virginia Tech in 2007 led some states to make it easier to carry concealed weapons on college campuses.

In general, the courts have not agreed with this more expansive interpretation of the Constitution. As a result, the extent of your right to bear arms depends very much on where you live. Thirty-five states essentially require law enforcement agencies to provide concealed weapon licenses to any law-abiding citizens who apply. Ten states give law enforcement agencies the discretion to issue or deny concealed weapons licenses based on a variety of factors. Illinois was the last state that banned concealed

recently announced plans to replicate HOPE. Programs are getting under way in Clackamas County, Oregon; Essex County, Massachusetts; Saline County, Arkansas; and Tarrant County, Texas.

HOPE is just one of the innovative ways judges, court districts, and states are attempting to keep people out of the prison system. The past decade has also seen a tremendous growth in **drug courts**, special tribunals that offer nonviolent drug offenders a

chance at reduced or dismissed charges in exchange for their undergoing treatment or other rehabilitation, an initiative that got under way during the

---

Drug courts
Special tribunals that offer nonviolent drug offenders a chance at reduced or dismissed charges in exchange for their undergoing treatment or other rehabilitation; an alternative forum for sentencing nonviolent drug offenders

weapons altogether, but its law was struck down in 2012. In Alaska, Arizona, Vermont, and Wyoming, no permit is needed to carry a concealed weapon.

Both sides of the gun debate believe that they argue for actions that will increase public safety. The advocates of gun ownership point out that localities with strict gun control laws often have very high crime rates and all that bans on handguns do is ensure that only criminals have guns. The advocates of gun control acknowledge the problems but counter that the real problem is that borders are porous and other surrounding jurisdictions often have very weak gun control laws. In fact, according to criminologist Garen Wintemute at the University of California, Davis, a dispassionate look at the evidence seems to support the key claims of both sides. Studies have shown that certain types of gun restrictions—waiting periods, background checks, and some level of screening for gun buyers—work. In Wintemute's words, "They reduce rates of criminal activity involving guns and violence among people who are screened out and denied purchase of a gun—about 25 percent to 30 percent of those who are screened."[b] Other types of restrictions, such as gun "buybacks," do not. Buybacks often encourage people to turn in only old, sometimes inoperable guns.

Some measures, such as requiring gun manufacturers to install trigger locks on new handguns, are still too new to allow researchers to evaluate the effects. However, the argument for treating gun violence as a public health problem is a strong one. Gun wounds, most of which are accidental, are among the leading causes of death in the United States.[c] At the same time, there is no evidence to suggest that gun control laws reduce violent crime. This raises an intriguing question: How can gun control laws work and yet not work at the same time?[d] One possible reason it's hard to say: "The N.R.A. has blocked most efforts at serious gun research, going so far as to restrict access to the highly informative data available from Justice Department traces of guns used in crimes," according to The New York Times.[e]

[a]Quoted in Alan Greenblatt, "When It Comes to Politics, States Are Barely United," NPR, http://www.npr.org/blogs/itsallpolitics/2012/12/26/168068305/when-it-comes-to-politics-states-are-barely-united.

[b]Quoted in Jeremy Travis and Michelle Waul, Reflections on the Crime Decline: Lessons for the Future? Proceedings From the Urban Institute Crime Decline Forum (Washington, DC: Urban Institute Justice Policy Center, August 2002), 16, http://www.urban.org/uploadedpdf/410546_crimedecline.pdf.

[c]For a discussion of the public health approach to gun violence, see David Hemenway, Private Guns, Public Health (Ann Arbor: University of Michigan Press, 2004). For statistics related to injuries and fatalities by year, see the U.S. Centers for Disease Control and Prevention's National Center for Injury Prevention and Control, http://www.cdc.gov/injury/index.html.

[d]Wintemute's answer: "The resolution of that apparent paradox is that under current criteria so few people are denied the purchase of a firearm under Brady and its state-level analogs relative to the number of people who purchase guns every year that an impact on that select group is too small at the population level to be noticed." Quoted in Travis and Waul, Reflections on the Crime Decline, 16.

[e]Gary Gutting, "The N.R.A.'s Blockade on Science," New York Times, December 20, 2102, http://opinionator.blogs.nytimes.com/2012/12/20/the-blockade-on-science-on-gun-violence/.

Clinton administration. As of December 2011, more than 2,600 drug courts were operating across all 50 states. National Institute of Justice researchers found evidence that the programs are successful in both reducing recidivism and lowering long-term costs. The researchers report that enrolling a participant in a drug court program saves more than $12,000 in criminal justice and victimization costs.[42]

Drug courts are closely connected to the **community, or restorative, justice movement.** This movement's basic goal is to give neighborhoods a voice in determining which kinds of criminals prosecutors

Community, or restorative, justice movement
A movement that emphasizes nontraditional punishment, such as community service

should pursue. Sometimes restorative justice involves sentences that are tailored to fit both the crime and the perpetrator. A woman convicted of stealing from a nursing home patient may have to fill vases with potpourri for a senior center, for instance, or an artist convicted of drunk driving may have to paint a picture for the organization whose lawn she drove over. Although such sentences are sometimes belittled as not just soft but mushy on crime, some communities have found that they are more effective than traditional probation in leading perpetrators to commit fewer offenses in the future. In practice, community justice initiatives range from the modest (placing prosecutors in local police stations, where they can see the neighborhood needs firsthand) to the ambitious (alternative courts that may require juvenile offenders to apologize to the people they have harmed and perform community service in an attempt to rectify the harm done by the crime committed).

Issues to Watch

The growth of drug courts and the increasing willingness of the criminal justice system to experiment with such innovative approaches to compliance as HOPE are among the most visible signs of a pivot away from attempting to deter drug production, distribution, and use via punishment. Even more significant changes seem likely in the years to come.

The End of the War on Drugs

The war on drugs began with the decision to criminalize the use of illicit drugs and to punish not just the production and distribution of drugs but also possession and use with severe criminal penalties. Today, authorities at both the federal and state levels are turning away from criminal sanctions. Instead, they are embracing a public health approach. Michael Botticelli (aka the "drug czar"), the acting head of the Office of National Drug Control Policy, has spoken openly and frequently of the Obama administration's "very clear pivot" toward treating illegal drug use as a public health issue that should be addressed with prevention and treatment, not a "war." Botticelli

has also spoken openly about his own criminal record (for drunken driving) and about how alcoholism brought him to the brink of eviction and total ruin. (He has been sober for 25 years.)

The drugs that authorities are targeting are also changing. Cocaine use has fallen sharply since 2002. So have alcohol and nicotine use. During this same time period, illicit prescription drug use and heroin use have risen sharply. Overdoses—mainly of prescription painkillers—are now the leading cause of accidental death in the United States.[43]

Legalization of Marijuana

While the drug "war" may be winding down, exactly what the peace will look like remains uncertain. Take the issue of marijuana: Use has risen since 2007; so has public support for decriminalization if not legalization. In 1990, less than 20 percent of Americans supported legalization. Today, more than 50 percent do. Not surprisingly, since 2007 the marijuana arrests have fallen sharply—by nearly 40 percent, according to an analysis of crime data by Keith Humphreys, a Stanford University psychiatrist and former senior drug policy adviser to the Obama administration. At the same time, the number of people smoking marijuana has increased by 20 percent.[44]

The more meaningful metric, though, is total pot consumption. (See Figure 14-3 for Colorado's consumption.) Survey results suggest that a small number of people consume the vast majority of marijuana; in fact, people who use marijuana more than 21 times a month account for 89 percent of total marijuana consumption. Not coincidentally, these heavy if not daily users tend to be less educated and poorer; many also have mental health issues. From a public health viewpoint, this has clear policy implications. People who occasionally use marijuana are not a major public health concern. Daily users are. A strong case can be made that the number of heavy users should be minimized through high taxes that discourage heavy consumption, caps on THC content (to reduce marijuana dependency), and limits on advertising and points of sale in vulnerable communities. Of course, marijuana entrepreneurs would like to have the exact opposite. Indeed, it would be logical for them to agitate for a regulatory regime similar to that in place for alcohol (a drug that is also heavily dependent for sales on a small number of heavy drinkers)—that is, low taxes, massive advertising, and lots of liquor stores in America's poorest, least educated neighborhoods.

To date, only Alaska, Colorado, and Washington have actually legalized marijuana. Another 22 states allow for medicinal use. If, however, as seems likely, the trend toward legalization continues, state legislatures (and perhaps Congress) will ultimately have to decide what kind of regulatory structure will prevail. In doing so, states will have to weigh their desire for revenues from marijuana taxes—a stream of revenue that would benefit from increases in consumption—against public health needs.[45]

Policing's Race Problem

Policing is also a profession at the crossroads. Despite nearly two decades of falling crime, police relations with minority communities are strained. Central to the perception that law enforcement operates unfairly is the practice of stopping, questioning, and frisking residents in high-crime neighborhoods. It's a common tactic with a troubled history. Prior to the 1960s, police departments employed tactics that would outrage most citizens today. Police routinely (and sometimes arbitrarily) arrested people for "vagrancy." To apprehend criminals, big-city police departments would blockade entire neighborhoods, stopping and searching all cars and pedestrians entering or leaving the area. In 1968, however, the Supreme Court established a new method of conduct in *Terry v. Ohio*. The case concerned a Cleveland detective, Martin McFadden, who observed two men who seemed to be casing a store in the neighborhood. Detective McFadden confronted the men, identified himself as a police officer, and asked the men for their names. Their response was unclear, so McFadden spun one of the men around and patted down his outside clothing. He felt a revolver. The officer ordered the men to line up against the wall. There he patted down another man, finding another gun. All three were taken to the local police station. There two were arrested for illegally carrying a concealed weapon. At trial, the defense argued that Detective McFadden's actions amounted to an unconstitutional search and seizure.

FIGURE 14-3

Colorado's Marijuana Consumption

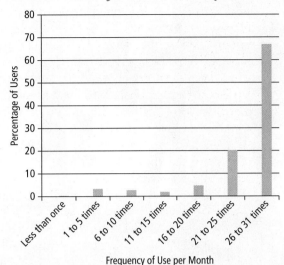

Source: Miles K. Light, Adam Orens, Brian Lewandowski, and Todd Pickton, "Market Size and Demand for Marijuana in Colorado," Table 8, prepared for the Colorado Department of Revenue, Marijuana Policy Group, 2014.

The Supreme Court disagreed. "Where a reasonably prudent officer is warranted in the circumstances of a given case in believing that his safety or that of others is endangered, he may make a reasonable search for weapons of the person believed by him to be armed and dangerous," wrote Chief Justice Earl Warren in his decision. A new type of police interaction with the citizenry— "stop and frisk"—was born.[46]

"Stop and frisk" soon became a familiar—and often resented—ritual in many high-crime, minority communities. Nowhere was it embraced with more enthusiasm than in New York City. There the tactic of stopping and frisking large numbers of people was bound up with a concept known as "broken windows." The idea, as elaborated by the political scientist James Q. Wilson and criminologist George Kelling in the early 1980s, was that minor kinds of disorder, such as shoplifting and vandalism, often give rise to much more serious types of disorder and crime, such as robbery and arson. The two social scientists went on to make a larger point about policing. Those police officers whom researchers in the 1950s observed walking around and resolving disputes actually might have been doing something important. By their very presence, they had been maintaining order. It was time, Wilson and Kelling wrote, to go back to the past.[47]

Two police officers stop and frisk a group of young men in Orange, New Jersey. Critics of the practice allege that police departments often stop young minority men in high-crime neighborhoods without probable cause, a practice they say constitutes unconstitutional "racial profiling." Some police departments, however, defend the practice, saying the ability to stop, question, and frisk people in situations where officers have reason to be concerned about their safety is constitutional and appropriate.

© Aristide Economopoulos/Star Ledger/Corbis

Wilson and Kelling argued for a dramatic break from the **professional model of policing**. This approach to fighting crime emphasizes squad cars and quick response times; police departments across the country embraced it during the 1970s. The reason for this was an important new innovation—the 911 emergency number. Cops who had once walked the beat and played the role of friendly neighborhood supervisor now were put into squad cars. Response time—how quickly the police responded to a call for assistance—became the criterion by which departments were judged as successes or failures. It was an all-or-nothing situation because there simply were not enough police officers available to monitor neighborhoods *and* answer emergency calls.

Wilson and Kelling's article caused a sensation among policymakers and the public; however, the criminologists weren't interested in exploring the "broken windows" theory, which held that enforcement of minor violations would help make a community feel more secure and better policed. In 1983, the National Institute of Justice prepared to fund an experimental assessment of the proposition that reducing disorder could reduce crime. At the last minute, the

project was rejected. Not until 1990 was the idea tested on a large scale. That's when Boston police chief Bill Bratton took command of the New York City transit department (the nation's seventh-largest police force).

Bratton thought of his job as a police chief as akin to that of a doctor treating a sick patient. In his previous jobs, many of which had involved turnarounds, he had begun to develop what he thought of as a doctor's kit for damaged police departments. For example, he thought that morale was important; so when he arrived in New York, he improved both the transit police's uniforms (adding commando-style sweaters) and weapons (issuing modern Glocks, a distinct improvement on the old revolvers). Bratton also upgraded the department's radio system so the transit cops could communicate underground.

But the most celebrated aspect of Bratton's tenure as transit chief was his embrace of **broken windows policing**. Along with Kelling, who was working as a consultant for the transit police, he emphasized catching fare beaters. The transit cops who, following his orders, started arresting turnstile jumpers made a surprising discovery: 1 in 7 was wanted on an outstanding warrant, and 1 in 21 was carrying a weapon. In short, enforcing the law was also an excellent way to arrest felons and fugitives, which in turn drove down crime rates and public fear. Bratton's subway successes vindicated broken windows as a policing strategy and put Bratton on track to become Rudy Giuliani's commissioner of the NYPD in 1994.[48]

Professional model of policing
An approach to policing that emphasizes professional relations with citizens, police independence, police in cars, and rapid responses to calls for service

Broken windows policing
Policing that emphasizes maintaining public order, based on the theory that unattended disorder breeds crime

Bratton's immediate predecessors at the NYPD had promoted **community policing**, an approach to policing that emphasized police officers' forming relationships with neighborhood residents and engaging with them in collaborative problem solving. But exactly what community policing entailed had always been somewhat vague. Bratton disagreed with the idea that young cops who'd grown up in places such as Staten Island or Long Island could go into New York's most challenging neighborhoods and problem solve. Instead, he expected the captains of New York City's 77 precincts to take responsibility for reducing crime.

Bratton's book about his time in New York, *Turnaround*, provides a comprehensive account of the many changes he made to the NYPD and its operations. The key innovation, however, was a new computerized crime-mapping system known as CompStat. This system allowed the police to map crime in virtual real time, identify patterns or problems, and then shift resources and devise solutions accordingly. Before the creation of CompStat, the NYPD compiled crime statistics every quarter. CompStat provided fresh numbers every week and allowed police commanders to look for crime patterns and "hot spots." It also encouraged officers to try new tactics and introduced an element of accountability into policing.[49]

The New Criminal Frontier

Bratton left the NYPD after only 2 years as commissioner. By the time he left, crime was down 40 percent. Not surprisingly, police departments around the country rushed to adopt his tactics. Yet exactly what New York had done was somewhat unclear. In his book *The City That Became Safe*, Zimring reports that broken windows was a tactic that was only occasionally used by the NYPD during Bratton's tenure. Yet many outsiders seemed to view an extreme version of broken windows as its essence. They called it "zero tolerance": The idea was that the police should enforce every law, no matter how minor. Kelling saw this approach as a disaster waiting to happen. "Broken windows has always been a negotiated sense of order in a community, in which you negotiate with residents about what is

appropriate behavior in an area," said Kelling. "If you tell your cops, 'We are going to go in and practice zero tolerance for all minor crimes,' you are inviting a mess of trouble."[50]

Yet to some extent that is what the NYPD itself did. Misdemeanor arrests rose by roughly 70 percent over the course of the 1990s and continued to climb in the years that followed. Mayor Michael Bloomberg and his police commissioner Ray Kelly justified the tactics as a form of deterrence: If there was a high probability of interacting with a police officer, youth would not carry guns. Without ready access to firearms, the seemingly petty disputes that ignited so many conflicts in high-crime neighborhoods would be less likely to turn violent. Intent on driving crime down, the NYPD steadily increased the number of stops. In 2002, the NYPD made 97,296 stops. By 2011, the number of stops had risen to 685,724. Ninety percent of the stops involved blacks and Latinos. Only 2 percent resulted in arrests. Critics alleged that this constituted "racial profiling"; the police responded that this was where the crime was.[51]

In 2008, a class action lawsuit was filed against the department, and in August 2013, federal judge Shira A. Scheindlin ruled that the police department resorted to a "policy of indirect racial profiling" as it increased the number of stops in minority communities. That has led to officers' routinely stopping "blacks and Hispanics who would not have been stopped if they were white." Scheindlin appointed a monitor to reform the department's stop-and-frisk practices. But just 2 months later, an appeals court stayed her order and removed her from the case, saying that Judge Scheindlin "ran afoul" of the judiciary's code of conduct by compromising the "appearance of impartiality surrounding this litigation" by actively seeking to hear the 2008 case in her courtroom.[52]

In January 2014, newly elected mayor Bill de Blasio announced that the NYPD would voluntarily adopt Judge Scheindlin's remedies. The department had already scaled back police contacts with citizens—with no adverse effects on the city's homicide rates. De Blasio also appointed a new police commissioner, Bill Bratton. During his time away

The first police car went on patrol in Akron, Ohio, in 1899. It was electric powered and could reach a speed of 16 miles per hour.

Community policing
An approach that emphasizes police officers' forming relationships with neighborhood residents and engaging with them in collaborative problem solving

Police wearing riot gear point weapons at a man before arresting him on August 11, 2014. He was among the many protesters who gathered in Ferguson, Mo., following the shooting death of Michael Brown by a local police officer. Protests continued for months and spread around the country after grand juries decided not to indict that officer or another police officer in New York who killed Eric Garner using a forbidden chokehold.

from New York, Bratton had served as chief of the LAPD for 7 years. There he oversaw a remarkable improvement in the LAPD's relationship with Los Angeles's black community. By the time he left in 2009, surveys showed that 83 percent of Angelenos believed that the LAPD was doing a good or excellent job, up from 71 percent 2 years earlier. The percentage of residents saying that the police in their communities treated members of all racial and ethnic groups fairly "almost all the time" or "most of the time" rose from 44 percent in 2005 to 51 percent in 2009. When asked to assess personal experiences, a majority of every racial and ethnic group in Los Angeles reported that most LAPD officers treated them, their friends, and their family with respect. Bratton accomplished this while driving crime down dramatically—especially violent crime. The crime rate during his final year in Los Angeles was 54 percent lower than it had been during his predecessor's final year.

De Blasio is clearly hoping that New York can accomplish something similar. Yet the future of policing remains cloudy. Many police chiefs believe that it is important to develop stronger relationships with all the communities they serve. Yet "community policing" remains more a slogan than a program. Meanwhile, the advance of technology has spurred interest in new approaches to crime fighting, such as predictive policing. Using computers that analyze where crimes have occurred in the past, police departments in Santa Cruz, Los Angeles, Chicago, and Shreveport are now attempting to predict where future crimes will occur. To some, that represents exciting progress. To others, it summons up images of a *Blade Runner*-esque

future, where airborne drones monitor high-crime neighborhoods and police apprehension occurs before the actual crime.[53]

Conclusion

Today, America's prison system is in flux. A 2009 study by the human rights group Amnesty International found that more than 20,000 prisoners continued to be held in conditions of extreme isolation in supermax prisons. According to a Justice Department survey of former inmates released in 2012, nearly 10 percent of prisoners suffer sexual abuse while incarcerated in state prisons, local jails, or postrelease treatment centers. Nearly 4 percent said they were forced to have nonconsensual sex with another prisoner, while more than 5 percent reported incidents involving facility staff. For many of these prisoners, rape may be just the beginning. Male prisoners who are passive or effeminate may end up as slaves, forced to do menial jobs and sometimes "rented out" to other inmates to be used sexually.[54]

The United States also leads the world in the execution of people with mental impairments. An estimated 56 percent of state prisoners and 64 percent of local jail inmates suffer from mental health disorders, including serious conditions such as schizophrenia, bipolar disorder, and depression. That's more than a million mentally ill prisoners and inmates—far more than the number of patients in mental hospitals.[55]

But there is hope, too. A growing number of states are embracing corrections reform and showing that there are smarter ways to reduce crime and punishment than mere severity in the process. A destructive and unsuccessful war on drugs is coming to an end. The criminal justice system as a whole has wakened to its problems with race, even if the search for solutions is just beginning. Will the future bring the return of Officer Friendly or *The Attack of the Drones*? The decisions voters and politicians make over the course of the coming years will decide.

The Latest Research

- **Donahue, John J. III, and Steven D. Levitt.** "The Impact of Legalized Abortion on Crime." National Bureau of Economic Research Working Paper 8004, November 2000. http://www.nber.org/papers/w8004.pdf?new_window=1.

- **Drum, Kevin.** "America's Real Criminal Element: Lead." *Mother Jones*, January–February 2013.

- **Mielke, Howard, and Sammy Zahran**. "The Urban Rise and Fall of Air Lead (Pb) and the Latent Surge and Retreat of Societal Violence." *Environment International* 43 (August 2012): 48–55.

Scholars continue to debate the causes of the crime drop that began in 1992. A decade and a half ago, *Freakonomics* coauthor Steven Levitt (along with John Donahue) startled readers with the argument that legalized abortion reduced crime. More recently, journalist Drum has drawn on research by Rick Nevin, Jessica Wolpaw Reyes, Howard Mielke, and Sammy Zahran to identify another external change that may have affected the crime rate—the removal of lead from gasoline in the 1970s. High exposure to lead is associated with lower IQs for children and a whole raft of behavioral problems. By introducing leaded gasoline in the 1940s and '50s, the argument goes, industry unwittingly exposed a broad swath of children to this dangerous element, increasing the likelihood of criminal activity. The crime drop in the 1990s occurred when a generation with less exposure to lead grew up.

• •

- **Zimring**, **Franklin.** *The City That Became Safe: New York's Lessons for Urban Crime and Its Control.* New York: Oxford University Press, 2011.

The role of the police in the crime drop also remains controversial. This is particularly true of the NYPD. Politicians and police commissioners from Rudolph Giuliani and Bill Bratton to Michael Bloomberg and Ray Kelly have all pointed to police tactics as a primary cause of the crime decline (and a primary reason for the public to support them). Not surprisingly, skeptics have argued that New York City's crime rate plummeted within *weeks* of Giuliani and Bratton's arrival. However, the most comprehensive examination of New York City's crime decline to date concludes that policing did play an important critical role. "The estimates of the independent impact of changes in policing in New York City exceed 30 percent for robbery and burglary, 20 percent for auto theft, and are also substantial for homicide and rape," Zimring writes. "Police make a difference."

- **Meares, Tracey, Tom Tyler, and Jacob Gardner**. "Lawful or Fair? How Cops and Laypeople View Good Policing." Yale Law School, Public Law Working Paper No. 255, August 11, 2014.

Mass incarceration and racial profiling have become hot-button issues, thanks largely to the mounting evidence that current imprisonment levels are not deterring crime but are instead turning entire communities against law enforcement. In response, academics have begun to explore the concept of procedural fairness. This paper draws on surprising research about court decisions finding that people's satisfaction with the court system hinged more on how they were treated than on the outcomes. Psychologist Tom Tyler called this "procedural fairness." Tyler's research has spawned a rapidly growing body of research into issues of fairness and legitimacy, one that has found that firsthand experiences of fairness increase civilians' belief that police authority is legitimate and enhance their willingness to cooperate.

- **Benson**, Michael L., Leanne Fiftal Alarid, Velmer S. Burton, and Francis T. Cullen. "Reintegration or Stigmatization? Offenders' Expectations of Community Re-Entry." *Journal of Criminal Justice* 39 (2011): 385–393.

A survey of 1,031 adult males convicted in Texas confounds expectations about whether ex-prisoners will feel stigmatized after serving their sentences. Although prior researchers had found that offenders experience the criminal justice system as degrading

(Continued)

(Continued)

and stigmatizing, this survey found that most of the men surveyed expected to be accepted and helped by friends and family upon their release. Some worried about finding employment, but even in an era of mass incarceration, most were optimistic about their prospects, regardless of race. The findings suggest that young adult offenders in particular are good prospects for reentry and restorative justice programs that take advantage of their willingness to accept responsibility for lawbreaking and building relationships that will move them away from crime.

- **Papachristos, Andrew V., Anthony A. Braga, and David M. Hureau**. "Social Networks and the Risk of Gunshot Injury." *Journal of Urban Health* 89, no. 6 (December 2012): 992–1003.

The stories we tell about crime and punishment tend to be black and white. We talk about guilt and innocence, about criminals and victims. Yet that viewpoint hides a surprising fact about violent crime: Criminals and victims are often the same people. In recent years, criminologists have moved from analyzing the geography of crime (crime "hot spots") and toward analyzing networks of crime. What they have found is that the world of homicide is often a very intimate one. As Papachristos, Braga, and Hureau put it, "the closer one is to a gunshot victim, the greater the probability of one's own victimization." Using this and similar research, police in Chicago have begun mining arrest data to identify people whose networks put them at risk for homicide and to contact them to warn them of the risks they face—21st century policing, indeed.

Chapter Review

Key Concepts

- broken windows policing (p. 460)
- common law (p. 442)
- community policing (p. 461)
- community, or restorative, justice movement (p. 457)
- deterrence theory (p. 448)
- drug courts (p. 456)
- mass incarceration (p. 441)
- parole (p. 441)
- probation (p. 440)
- professional model of policing (p. 460)
- racial profiling (p. 439)
- recidivism (p. 452)
- stop and frisk (p. 439)
- supermax prisons (p. 445)
- verdict (p. 443)
- war on drugs (p. 441)

Suggested Websites

- **www.aclu.org.** The American Civil Liberties Union offers extensive research on crime issues from a civil liberties perspective.

- **www.bjs.gov.** The Bureau of Justice Statistics pulls together a wide variety of information on the criminal justice system.

- **www.fbi.gov.** Website of the Federal Bureau of Investigation offers information on national and international criminal activities as well as crime prevention tips. Its Uniform Crime Report is the best source of information on felony and violent crime nationwide.

- **www.manhattan-institute.org.** Website of the Manhattan Institute includes archived articles from the institute's *City Journal,* which addresses such issues as the effectiveness of various policing strategies.

- **www.ncjrs.gov.** Website of the National Criminal Justice Reference Service provides statistics on a variety of topics involving crime.

- **www.nij.gov.** Website of the National Institute of Justice, the research, development, and evaluation agency of the U.S. Department of Justice; the agency researches crime control and justice issues, particularly at the state and local levels.

- **www.pewtrusts.org/en/projects/public-safety-performance-project.** The Pew Center on the States's Public Safety Performance Project offers up-to-date information on corrections reform and on the crime–prison connection.

- **www.sentencingproject.org.** Website of the Sentencing Project offers data and information about racial disparities in the U.S. criminal justice system.

- **www.urban.org/Justice/index.cfm.** The nonpartisan Washington, D.C.–based Urban Institute offers an excellent collection of criminal justice research.

- **www.vera.org.** Website of the Vera Institute of Justice, a nonprofit organization that conducts research, demonstration projects, and technical assistance to improve the justice system.

State Stats on Crime and Punishment

*Explore and compare data on the states! Go to **edge.sagepub.com/smithgreenblatt5e** to do these exercises.*

1. In 2009, what percentage of the population in Washington were marijuana users? What was the percentage in Colorado? How do you think these numbers influenced the recent passage of recreational marijuana use laws?

2. It costs about $90,000 more per year, per prisoner to keep someone on death row in California rather than in regular confinement. In 2010, how many death row prisoners did California have? How much per year would California save by commuting these sentences to life in prison?

3. What is the reported crime rate at colleges and universities in your state? Do you think that this is an accurate number? Why or why not?

4. In 2001, what was the average, national, annual operating cost of correctional facilities per state prisoner? How does your state compare? Does this seem like a reasonable amount to you? Why or why not?

5. How many drug laboratories were seized in your state in1999? How did this change by 2006? What might account for this change?

6. What was the average time between property crimes in Florida in 2012? How does this compare to the national average? Can this statistic be used to evaluate the quality of law enforcement in Florida?

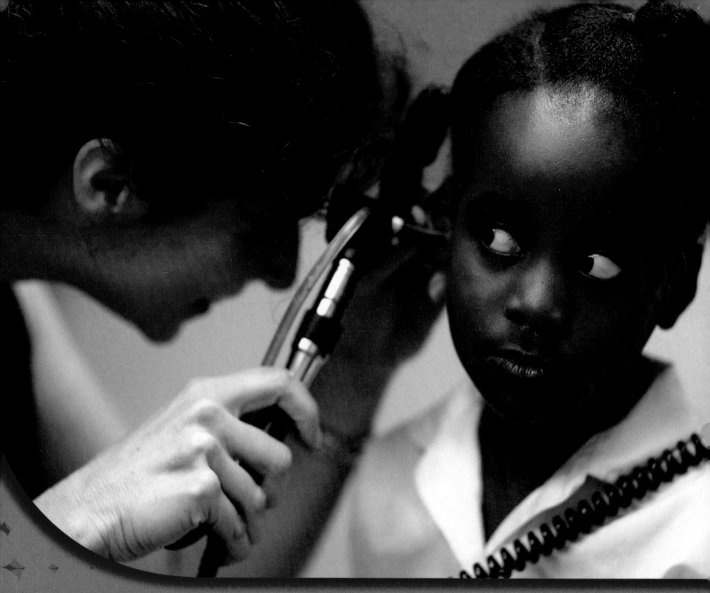

Undeniably, the patients aren't the only ones who are sick in the U.S. health care system. The system itself needs more than an aspirin and an apple a day to heal itself, and it remains to be seen whether the federal healthcare reform package will provide that solution. Meanwhile, states and localities continue to pick up the slack. Here, Dr. Gwen Wurm, a pediatrician with the University of Miami Health System, checks 5-year-old Christina Brownlee's ears in October 2007.

Health and Welfare

STATE, HEAL THYSELF!

- Why does access to health care vary so widely across the country?
- How will federal health care reform affect states, cities, and counties?
- What roles do state and local governments play in maintaining public health?

A dam O'Neal decided to walk. He is the mayor of Belhaven, North Carolina, and soon after the hospital in his town shut down in July 2014, O'Neal started off on a 273-mile walk to Washington, D.C., where he hoped to draw attention to the plight of rural hospitals. The closure of Pungo District Hospital in his eastern North Carolina town meant that townspeople had to travel 75 miles to the nearest emergency room. O'Neal shared the story of a woman who had died 4 days after the hospital closed, just as a Medevac helicopter arrived an hour after it was called to airlift her for treatment. "Before, she would have been given nitroglycerin, put in the back of an ambulance and been to a hospital in about 25 minutes," O'Neal said. "In that hour that she lived, she would have received 35 minutes of emergency room care and she very well could have survived."[1]

O'Neal described himself as a conservative Republican; yet he had come to Washington to make the argument that his state and others should accept the Medicaid expansion included as part of the Affordable Care Act. That 2010 federal law, a top priority of President Barack Obama, was intended to expand access to health care in part by providing more people with health insurance—including millions under **Medicaid**, the

---

Medicaid
A joint state and federal health insurance program that serves low-income mothers and children, the elderly, and people with disabilities

joint federal–state health insurance program for the poor and disabled. The U.S. Supreme Court upheld the law in 2012 but threw out a provision that required states to implement the Medicaid expansion or lose funding for their traditional Medicaid programs.

Nearly half the states refused to expand the program. Republicans have been pretty much unanimous in their disdain for the law since it was passed. The Medicaid expansion appeared to be a good deal—the federal government would pick up 100 percent of the cost for the first 3 years, from 2014 to 2016, and no less than 90 percent after that—but many Republican officials decided that they couldn't afford it anyway. Already, Medicaid eats up a sizable percentage of state budgets (states pay, on average, 43 percent of traditional Medicaid costs, and total spending on the program nation-wide was $415 billion in 2012).[2] Rather than make Medicaid bigger, a number of Republican governors and legislators argued that the program had to be made more efficient. And some were skeptical that the federal government would pay its promised share. It wouldn't be the first time Washington started a program and then left states to make up the difference when funding dropped. "We believe in the end the track record of the federal government has been to pull away from their commitments to the states," said Governor Scott Walker of Wisconsin. "We believe confidently going forward this federal government is likely to renege from its promises on Medicaid to the states. And we won't be exposed to that."[3]

Not taking the money was costing Wisconsin money, however. Rather than having the federal government pick up 100 percent of the costs for some Medicaid patients, Wisconsin was paying about 40 percent of the costs for those covered under traditional Medicaid rules—which amounted to about $100 million a year for the state. And lots of other Wisconsin residents who might be receiving coverage found themselves ineligible.

It's people like that who were causing problems for hospitals such as Pungo. These hospitals are required to provide emergency medical care, regardless of ability to pay. One study found that in the first 4 months of the Medicaid expansion, uncompensated care of patients without insurance dropped by 30 percent at 465 hospitals in 30 states that had embraced the new program. In states that hadn't expanded Medicaid, the amount of uncompensated care was essentially unchanged.[4] The big price tag of uncompensated care is one reason hospitals have been pressing states to accept the Medicaid expansion.

Some of the Affordable Care Act's provisions are popular, such as the requirement that insurers allow parents to keep their children on their plans up until age 26. (Formerly, young people could be dropped at 18.) A survey by the Commonwealth Fund in 2013 found that 7.8 million Americans between the ages of 19 and 25 were enrolled on a parent's plan and that most of them wouldn't have been able to do so prior to passage of the law. As a result, the number of young adults without health insurance had declined by 2014 from 3 million to 1 million.[5] Other parts of the law have remained controversial, such as a mandate for employers, including religious organizations, to provide contraceptive coverage. Also, Obama misled Americans in claiming that they'd be able to keep their present doctors and insurance plans if they liked them; the law's mandates resulted in insurers' canceling some plans.

Still, even some Republican governors and legislators are seeing that, no matter how much they may hate the Affordable Care Act, often called Obamacare, it makes sense in terms of cash flow. After all, their residents pay federal taxes—and thus underwrite the Medicaid expansion—even if their state doesn't participate. Not surprisingly, overall Medicaid costs are expanding fastest in states that have accepted the expansion, but costs were rising at a rate 50 percent lower for those states themselves in 2014 and 2015 than for the states that blocked expansion. "Most states, those that have not expanded Medicaid, are probably going to do it over the next 3 to 4 years," Ray Scheppach, a former executive director of the National Governors Association, said in 2014. "They're getting increasing pressure from their health care communities."[6] States such as Pennsylvania, Utah, and Tennessee that initially resisted the expansion have already started to rethink their positions. State Representative Steve Crouse, the Republican who chairs the Alabama Ways and Means General Fund Committee, favors repealing the Affordable Care Act but argues that as long as it's the law it would make sense for his state to bring in the Medicaid dollars. The net gain for his state if it accepted the expansion would be $935 million between 2013 and 2022, according to an Urban Institute study. It's "the hand we've been dealt by the feds," Clouse said.[7]

Obamacare remains widely unpopular with the public, but it's settling in as a fact of life for policymakers. When it comes to health policy, it always boils down to money. Back during the 1980s, President Ronald Reagan's administration floated the idea of having the federal government pay the entire cost of Medicaid in exchange for states' fully funding welfare, which is also a joint federal–state responsibility. It went nowhere, in part because governors and other state officials balked. In a sense, they are replaying that argument today, with some state leaders happy to take money from Washington but others sensing that there may be hidden costs for them down the road.

The argument surrounding Obamacare isn't all about dollars and cents; partly, it reflects a difference in ideology. One of the ongoing arguments in American politics is over how much—and how best—to help the poor. Giving people handouts, such as through welfare—the cash assistance program also known as **Temporary Assistance for Needy Families (TANF)**—only enables them to remain mired in poverty, argue many conservative politicians and others. "I am not interested in growing entitlements, especially through an already broken and unsustainable Medicaid program dictated to the states by Washington," said Georgia Republican governor Nathan Deal. "I am interested in real economic development where Georgians are better equipped to provide for themselves and their families, rather than having to rely on government welfare programs like Medicaid."[8]

In Kansas, Republican governor Sam Brownback refused to implement the Medicaid expansion and also cut his state's TANF caseload by about a third through changes in eligibility benefits. Rather than giving poor people a "pittance," he said, government policies should prod them into finding work. "Our country has spent billions of dollars and decades supporting a welfare system that has shown no improvement getting people out of poverty," Brownback says. "Instead of focusing on spending more money on a system that creates dependency, we need to reform our welfare system to provide the opportunity for people to learn the skills to be self-sufficient, which is what we are doing here in Kansas."[9]

Many states—and not just ones run by Republicans—have cut social service programs, even during recent years of recession. Government cannot cure all social ills. Many believe it shouldn't even try, but over the years Americans have come to count on the various levels of government to provide many benefit programs. Chief among these is health care. The Affordable Care Act relies primarily on employers and private insurance companies to expand coverage, stopping short of the type of government-funded health coverage that liberals favor and that is common in other rich nations. But the act

Temporary Assistance for Needy Families (TANF)
The next-generation welfare program (passed in 1996) that provides federal assistance in the form of block grants to states, which have great flexibility in designing their programs

represents the latest and one of the most important expansions of the government's role in regulating and underwriting health care in this country.

Government's Role in Health

It doesn't take a fresh act of Congress for government to play a central role in the health of the American people. One of the most important functions of government is protecting **public health**. Public health is the area of medicine that deals with the protection and improvement of citizen health and hygiene through government agencies.

State and local governments also have taken the lead in responding to public health crises. In practice, this includes responses as simple as making sure an ambulance or fire truck is dispatched to a 911 call and as complex as managing an epidemic. A century ago, the latter might have involved yellow fever, cholera, or influenza. In 1918, it involved a flu **pandemic** that killed an estimated 600,000 Americans and 100 million people worldwide.[10] Such diseases pose continued threats. As a result, state and local governments spend an increasing amount of time planning for such crises and carrying out drills intended to simulate public health emergencies.

Just how active state and local governments should be on issues that affect the public health is often a source of heated debate. According to the U.S. Centers for Disease Control and Prevention (CDC), smoking tobacco causes more than 480,000 deaths a year in the United States.[11] In addition, a growing percentage of Americans are overweight or suffer from **obesity**. Some state and local officials have made combating obesity a major priority. They have pushed for educational programs for parents and, for children, have restored physical education classes and removed

soft drink machines from schools. Others resist the idea that obesity is a problem that should be addressed through government policy.

The scope of public health programs varies from state to state. Some states are generous providers of assistance to their low-income citizens to cover the expenses associated with illness and hospitalization. Other states are much more restrictive. The explanations for these differences are explored in this chapter.

For all the variation among state and local governments, it is clear that over the course of the past two decades many of these governments have become much more assertive concerning public health. Forty years ago, most states were minor players in the nation's health care system. The proponents of expanded health coverage and health care reform looked to the federal government for solutions. A decade of inaction and partisan division in Washington in the 1990s shifted some of the most important—and most difficult—health care issues to the state and local governments. Since then, the lawmakers tackling tough issues such as the rising rate of obesity, rising prescription drug costs, the need to provide long-term care, the spread of the human immunodeficiency virus (HIV) and other sexually transmitted diseases, and the problem of illicit drug use have been more likely to be sitting in the state capitols than under the Capitol dome in Washington, D.C. When the federal government acted after decades of debate over health care reform in early 2010 to pass the Affordable Care Act, the center of power might reasonably have been expected to shift back to Washington.

But states continue to play a central role even under the federal health care reform regime. Aside from the Supreme Court's ruling that placed the decision of whether to expand Medicaid in the states' hands, the law left the states some important powers. The Affordable Care Act attempts to expand health insurance by creating state health insurance exchanges, online marketplaces where consumers can choose among different health insurance plans. The exchanges represent an alternative to employer-provided insurance. For low-income and middle-income people, the cost of insurance purchased through the exchanges is subsidized by federal tax credits. In following the exchange model, the Affordable Care Act borrowed from ideas that had already

---

Public health
Area of medicine that addresses the protection and improvement of citizen health and hygiene through the work of government agencies

Pandemic
An outbreak of a disease that spreads across a large geographical area and affects a high proportion of the population

Obesity
The medical condition of being excessively overweight; defined as having a body mass index of more than 25

been tried at the state level. Massachusetts established a health insurance exchange in a law enacted under Governor Mitt Romney in 2006 to expand access to health insurance.

Under the federal law, states themselves can run the exchanges if they choose. States that administer the exchanges themselves will get to make important choices, such as whether to allow every health insurance plan that meets basic criteria into the exchange or to provide more structure to consumers' options.[12] Most states opted not to set up their own exchanges, and legal challenges left it unclear whether residents of states without their own exchanges would remain eligible for federal coverage subsidies. In addition to the exchanges, the Obama administration announced in December 2011 that states will have broad discretion to make another key decision under the law: what level of coverage a health insurance plan must, at a minimum, meet to count as health insurance.[13] In addition, states have taken the lead in rethinking such safety-net programs as welfare, which provides cash payments to needy families. In 1996, Congress abolished the existing **Aid to Families with Dependent Children (AFDC)**, or welfare, program and replaced it with a system of block grants to the states, called Temporary Assistance for Needy Families (TANF). These grants gave state governments the leeway to design their own personalized, work-oriented, time-limited welfare programs. The result has been a profusion of sometimes very different welfare-to-work programs.

The Influence of Culture

How state governments define public health has a lot to do with the distinctive political cultures of their regions. All public health officials would agree that certain issues, such as terrorism and acquired immune deficiency syndrome (AIDS), are important public health issues. No one would argue that a flu epidemic or the contamination of a major watershed would not also qualify.

Other topics are not so easily categorized. Is gun violence a public health issue? Researchers at the CDC think so. They point out that gun-related deaths, most of which are accidental, are the country's second leading cause of death. The American Medical Association now advises doctors to talk with patients about the proper handling and storage of any guns they may own. Many gun owners, however, vehemently reject the idea that guns are a public health issue.

On other health fronts, some cities have attempted to reduce the transmission of dangerous blood-borne illnesses, such as HIV and Hepatitis C, by providing drug addicts with clean needles. Others have rejected these needle exchange programs, charging that they give rise to disorder and crime and send the message that intravenous drug use is acceptable.

Then there is the always controversial question of sexual health and education. Should parents, educators, and other adult role models emphasize **abstinence** with teenagers or teach them to use condoms? Or is instruction in a variety of options that include both abstinence and birth control the answer? What role should government play in providing access to contraception?

As we have seen before, often different policies reflect very different political cultures. Oregon has granted terminally ill patients the right to physician-assisted suicide. Most other states continue to classify such an action as a felony, even if it is rarely prosecuted. North Dakota passed legislation to ban abortions after 6 weeks of pregnancy, while Arkansas imposed a ban after 12 weeks. Both laws were quickly overturned in 2014, but those state legislatures had made their preferences known.

Different states have very different notions about the roles state governments should fill. Wisconsin's innovative early attempts at welfare reform in the late 1980s and early 1990s laid the groundwork for the federal decision to junk AFDC altogether in 1996 and return most welfare responsibilities to the states. A number of states have debated bills to require random drug testing

---

Aid to Families with Dependent Children (AFDC)
The original federal assistance program for women and their children, started under Roosevelt's New Deal

Abstinence
Refraining from sexual activity, usually intercourse

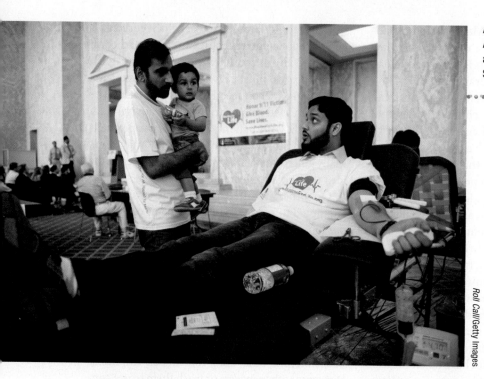

At a federal building in Washington, the Ahmadiyaa Muslim Community holds an annual blood drive in memory of the September 11, 2001, terrorist attacks.

Roll Call/Getty Images

back coverage in certain ways. In 2012, for example, Florida cut the number of days most Medicaid patients could spend in hospitals from 45 to 23, and Maine eliminated coverage for podiatry, optometry, and dental care.[15] In 2011, California tried to end a well-regarded adult day-care program for Medicaid patients that had succeeded in keeping seniors and people with disabilities out of nursing homes. Lawmakers were tempted by the possibility of saving $145 million immediately, even though having more people in nursing homes would likely have cost the state more money in the long term.[16] After opponents of the cuts sued, the state agreed to maintain a more modest program.

As these examples illustrate, the states and the federal government have been tugging Medicaid in opposite directions since 2010. Through the Affordable Care Act, the federal government is attempting to expand health insurance to tens of millions of additional Americans. Yet many states' inclination has been to cut back to save money. That tension helps explain why some states are reluctant to agree to expand their Medicaid programs under the Affordable Care Act—a decision the Supreme Court's 2012 ruling left in the hands of states.

In one sense, the Medicaid expansion is a tremendous deal for states. As noted earlier, under the Affordable Care Act, the federal government will pay the full cost of the expansion through 2016, then taper its share back to 90 percent by 2020. Taking the deal doesn't just mean more people will have health coverage; it also means billions of dollars will be pumped into states' economies via their health care systems. In certain ways, states are likely to save money: If fewer

of people receiving welfare or unemployment benefits. States such as Massachusetts and Maine sought to expand health care coverage to nearly every resident in advance of the passage of federal health care reform in 2010, whereas other states have shown no great enthusiasm for providing health care to low-income citizens.

Yet even states that have shown little interest in taking on new responsibilities have found that health care is *the* unavoidable issue. This is due largely to Medicaid, the joint state–federal health insurance program for low-income mothers and children, the elderly, and people with disabilities. When Congress created it in 1965, it was supposed to be a modest program that served only a small number of extremely poor people. But it didn't work out that way.

As soon as it was created, Medicaid expenditures started growing quickly—and never stopped. As of May 2014, Medicaid provided health insurance and services to more than 65 million Americans—an all-time high. States now devote an average of about 24 percent of their general revenue funds to Medicaid.[14]

The Affordable Care Act largely forbids states to reduce the number of people who are eligible for Medicaid, but it doesn't stop them from scaling

A Difference That Makes A Difference

Some States Fail at Setting Up Health Exchanges

The Obama administration's plan to expand access to health insurance depends greatly on the states. But not all states are enjoying the same rate of success in carrying out this mission—even among those that support the Affordable Care Act.

The 2010 law calls on states to set up health exchanges that allow individuals and companies to browse different insurance policies and pick the one that suits them best, often with a federal subsidy for people with limited incomes. The goal was for the exchanges to be as easy to use as a travel website such as Orbitz or Expedia.

That hasn't always been the case, however. Since only 16 states opted to create exchanges of their own, the federal government created one for citizens elsewhere, only to see its site (HealthCare.gov) widely lambasted for its many bugs and failures upon its launch in 2013.

Some of the states that set up exchanges struggled as well. Maryland officials were leading supporters of the Affordable Care Act, making theirs the second state to pass a law creating an exchange after the federal act had passed. But the state's website crashed once it was launched.

By the next morning, a grand total of four people had managed to sign up for insurance. State officials were so amazed that anyone had navigated the system successfully that they contacted each of them to make sure they were real people. Weeks later, thousands of Marylanders were facing frozen computer screens and error messages. Comparatively few were able to sign up.

The reasons for this failure were long in the making. The state devoted $170 million to the project; yet no one seemed to be in charge. The state's health secretary, human resources secretary (who was in charge of Medicaid), and the official running the exchange itself all tried to make decisions together, creating what one official called a "three-headed monster."

The exchange was supposed to be able to link data from Medicaid and agencies such as the Department of Motor Vehicles, but coordination with those agencies—and among contractors working on the project—was poor. Project managers came and went, even as new software was being added to the system months before the launch.

Maryland wasn't the only state to fail to set up a health exchange of its own. Problems were so bad in Oregon that the state resorted to paper applications and federal prosecutors launched an investigation into what had gone wrong.

But some states did have smooth rollouts. Kentucky, for example, received 7,000 completed insurance applications within the first 2 days of the launch of its site. New York signed up 40,000 people the first week, while Connecticut was able to sign up some 79,000 residents the first few months, half of whom hadn't previously had insurance.

Connecticut avoided serious problems by testing its systems early. The state limited the number of services its site would handle upon its launch, leaving some functions for later. The development team was serious about deadlines—not the case in Maryland—and emphasized the functionality of the site.

Connecticut simply did a better job of testing features and connectivity to other systems (including the federal hub that verifies some information) before going live than did some other states or the federal government. "I got a lot of pushback," said Jim Wadleigh, the chief information officer for Connecticut's health insurance exchange. "A lot of people weren't happy with me, but I was able to find some things that would've been a problem if we waited, so I got a little start on the rest of the country by being able to do that."

Connecticut's success was recognized in other places. Maryland ended up using Connecticut's system to insure its residents, and Kevin Counihan, the head of the Connecticut exchange, was hired by the Obama administration in 2014 to run HealthCare.gov.

people are uninsured, fewer will seek treatment in hospital emergency rooms and stick the state with the bill. On the other hand, the Medicaid expansion is so large that even the remaining 10 percent would mean millions of dollars a year in fresh costs for many states. Given the precarious condition of many states' budgets, adding any new costs is a difficult sell.[17]

There is a political dimension to the debate over the Medicaid expansion, too. In Republican-controlled states, many political leaders are generally philosophically opposed to raising taxes to pay for more generous government services. Many of those leaders have been opposed to the federal health care law from the start. Immediately after the Court's ruling, a group of Republican governors came out against expanding Medicaid.

Although Medicaid is the states' biggest immediate health care expense, it is hardly their only one. States provide health insurance to their own employees and, in many cases, to their former employees after they retire. As with employee pension costs, paying for retired state employees' health care costs has emerged over the past decade as one of the states' leading long-term budget challenges. Traditionally, states have paid for the retiree health care bill that shows up each year, rather than setting aside money in advance. The looming bill is so large in coming decades, though—as of 2010, states had promised $627 billion more in retiree health care than they had assets set aside—that many states are starting to rethink that strategy.[18] In 2012, West Virginia, which has a long-term bill of $10 billion, became the first state to dedicate a specific amount of tax money for retiree health care, committing $30 million per year. West Virginia also did what many other states have done: It made retiree health care benefits less generous for future retirees. State and local employees have gone along with the changes reluctantly. "Does it give me heartburn?" Josh Sword, political director of the American Federation of Teachers–West Virginia, asked. "Sure. But at the end of the day, the state cannot continue to afford this level of benefit."[19]

States are also responsible for providing health care for inmates in state prisons. No state has struggled more with inmate health care than California, where state prisons have long been massively overcrowded. In 2006, a federal judge said that one inmate a week was dying unnecessarily because of the low quality of care, a violation of the U.S. Constitution's prohibition of cruel and unusual punishment. The judge took control of the prisoner health care system away from the state and placed it in the hands of an independent receiver. Since then, the state has made some gradual improvements—improvements that have come at a cost. The state spends well above $10,000 per prisoner each year for medical care, far more than most other states.[20] Still, the changes have not been enough to convince federal courts that the problems are solved. In 2011, the U.S. Supreme Court upheld an order that California cut its prison population of 142,000 by more than 30,000 as a way to improve care, although it allowed the state 2 years to implement the order and indicated that more time could be requested.[21] The state got another 2-year extension in 2014.

County and city governments spend significant amounts on health care as well. In many parts of the country, hospitals and clinics funded by counties and cities continue to function as a critical social safety net for people without health insurance. These are people who earn too much to qualify for Medicaid but too little to be able to pay for private health insurance. Cities and counties also run the facilities that were tested during the 2009 H1N1 influenza pandemic, and if the United States ever experiences a large-scale biological attack, such facilities will determine how well this society survives.

How Government Got Into the Health Care Biz

Any serious discussion of health care soon arrives at a basic question: Who should pay for what? Over the past two decades, answers to this question have varied widely. During the early 1990s, the solution offered by many Democrats was that the federal government should provide health insurance to everyone who does not have it. By the early 21st century, however, a lot of those same Democrats were arguing that the state governments, not the federal government, should lead the way.

Universal—or nearly universal—coverage, they stated, should be created through the gradual extension of existing health insurance programs, notably Medicaid. Such programs should be expanded to encompass various populations not currently eligible for them. In contrast, some Republicans argued that health insurance should be extended through federal tax credits. How much health insurance should be provided has been another hotly contested topic. When President Obama entered office with a Democratic-majority Congress in 2009, his party once again saw the federal government as the best venue for action, leading to the Affordable Care Act.

It wasn't always so complicated. For most of the nation's history, elected officials believed that the government should serve as the health and welfare provider of last resort for society's poorest and sickest members. The level of government that officials had in mind, however, was not the federal government and not even state governments. It was local government.

The role of local governments in health and welfare goes back to the very beginning of U.S. history. In colonial America, local communities maintained almshouses to feed and clothe people who could not care for themselves and who had no families to care for them. Back then, few distinctions were made among the sick, the mentally ill, and people without means of support. As sociologist Paul Starr has noted, almshouses "received dependent persons of all kinds, mixing together promiscuously the aged, the orphaned, the insane, the ill, the debilitated."[22] Those with infectious diseases, such as typhoid fever and cholera, were sent into quarantine in pesthouses to survive as best they could.

That began to change in the 19th century. By the middle of the century, elected officials, social reformers, and physicians—who were just beginning to establish medicine as a respectable profession—came to believe that mixing juveniles, beggars, the mentally ill, widows, and others in almshouses was no longer the best course of action. In effect, physicians and public officials began to distinguish between the sick and the destitute. A new institution was needed—the hospital.

From the early to mid-1800s, cities such as Philadelphia and New York transformed some of their almshouses into hospitals.[23] Privately organized charitable hospitals, many run by religious groups, appeared in many cities, too. Even state governments made modest forays into health care. By 1860, most states had established mental hospitals and homes for the blind and the deaf.

Like almshouses, the first hospitals were institutions for unfortunates without money or family. For people with family or money, a house call from the doctor was the preferred form of medical care. According to Starr, "Almost no one who had a choice sought hospital care."[24] Hospitals were regarded with dread, and rightly so. They were dangerous places, in part because of the medical and hygienic practices of the time. Sick people were safer at home. The few who became hospital patients did so because of special circumstances. They might be seamen in strange ports, travelers, the homeless, or the solitary aged, individuals who, whether traveling or destitute, were unlucky enough to fall sick without family, friends, or servants to care for them.[25]

Hospitals and physicians made a spirited effort to improve their image. Hospitals moved their sickest residents—as well as patients who were dissolute or morally objectionable—to other institutions. In 1847, for instance, Bellevue Hospital in New York decided to move the penitentiary and almshouse off its grounds and concentrate on medical care.[26] The hospital was beginning to emerge as a distinct institution.

The Idea of a Social Safety Net

The arrangement described above continued in the United States until well into the 20th century. The duty of providing health care and welfare remained firmly in the hands of local governments. States assisted those with mental illnesses and people with disabilities. The federal government ran a compulsory health insurance system for the merchant marine so that sick sailors could get care in any port, and provided pensions and health care to military veterans.

By the end of the 19th century, a new idea was percolating in progressive circles. Many social reformers came to believe that the federal government should take a much larger role in securing health care and pensions for the working class.

The idea first arose in Germany. In 1883, the conservative government of German chancellor Otto von Bismarck created the world's first compulsory sickness and unemployment insurance fund, which required employees and employers to set aside money to cover the costs of medical treatment for workers. Bismarck later created a compulsory retirement program, the cost of which was divided among employees, employers, and the national government, in much the same way that the Social Security system operates in the United States today. These innovations were momentous in the development of the state. Before Bismarck, most talk of health care, unemployment insurance, and pensions had come from socialists and communists. He showed that conservative capitalist countries could enact such programs, too. Indeed, they could take the lead in developing a generous social safety net. Over the course of the next 30 years, other European countries followed Germany's lead.

The United States, however, did not. During the heyday of the Progressive movement in the early 20th century, discussions about national health insurance were widespread. Eventually, opposition from physicians and from the country's largest labor union, the American Federation of Labor (the forerunner of today's AFL-CIO), fearful of government control of the health care system, effectively derailed the idea. During the 1920s, many states took the first small steps toward creating a social safety net by setting up workers' compensation funds for injured workers. However, amid the affluence of the times, there was little support for a more ambitious social safety net.[27] That changed with the start of the Great Depression.

The Birth of the American Safety Net

On Thursday, October 24, 1929, the stock market in New York City collapsed in what *The New York Times* called "the most disastrous trading day in the stock market's history."[28] By spring 1933, it was clear that the United States had entered an unprecedented economic slump—the Great Depression.

In response to this economic disaster, the federal government for the first time took on some of the social safety-net functions that European governments had pioneered decades earlier.[29] In 1935, President Franklin Delano Roosevelt and Congress teamed up to pass the Social Security Act. This act established two social safety-net programs. The first was a joint federal–state program of unemployment compensation. The second was a federally run program of retirement benefits for senior citizens, which soon would be known simply as Social Security.

The federal government also created AFDC, the purpose of which was to provide monetary assistance to widowed women with children, women who had been abandoned by their husbands, and women who were in some way incapacitated. Funded by the federal government, the program was administered by the states.

The Roosevelt administration briefly considered adding a compulsory health insurance program to the Social Security Act. However, given the medical industry's continued vehement opposition to such a program due to fear of too much government control, the proposal was eventually dropped as too controversial. Instead, the Social Security Act provided federal grants to help states pay for programs for the disabled and the aged and to provide child welfare services, public health services, and vocational rehabilitation.[30] As a result, responsibility for providing a health care safety net remained in the hands of state and local governments.

A Multibillion-Dollar Afterthought

State governments became major participants in the U.S. safety-net system almost by accident. After the assassination of President John F. Kennedy in 1963, Lyndon B. Johnson ascended to the Oval Office. Johnson and congressional Democrats were determined to pass legislation that would cover hospital costs for senior citizens. Congressional Republicans, however, had a different proposal in

With the strong backing of President Lyndon Johnson, Congress created Medicare in 1965. The federal health insurance program for the elderly has proven to be wildly popular. Pictured here is John Gardner, Johnson's secretary of health, education, and welfare. His outline for implementing Medicare notably says nothing about who is covering the costs.

© Corbis

IMPLEMENTING MEDICARE

1. Getting the People 65 or Over Ready
2. Getting Hospitals and Other Institutions Ready
3. Arranging for Participation of Physicians
4. Tooling Up for Internal Operations

mind. They supported a voluntary health insurance program that would cover the cost of physician visits for seniors. In 1965, the two parties decided to compromise in classic Washington fashion—by doing both. The result was **Medicare**, the federal health insurance program for the elderly.

But Congress didn't stop there. While it was on a roll, it also created Medicaid. Despite their similar names, Medicare and Medicaid are very different programs. Medicare is run and paid for entirely by the federal government. As with Social Security, every senior who worked for 10 years and paid taxes—or whose spouse worked for 10 years and paid taxes—is eligible to participate, as are people with certain types of disabilities. The program is financed in part by a payroll tax. Most retirees, however, take far more out of Medicare than they contributed during their working years.[31] Understandably, Medicare almost immediately became a popular program.

Medicaid, on the other hand, is a joint state–federal program that is paid for in part by the general revenue funds of state and local governments. The federal government does pick up most of the cost, however. On average, it covers nearly 60 percent of Medicaid expenditures; for poorer areas, the percentage is higher. Arkansas, Idaho, Kentucky, Mississippi, South Carolina, and West Virginia all receive at least 70 percent of their Medicaid expenditures from the federal government.[32] Wealthier states split the cost 50–50. The federal government's share will rise for states that take the Medicaid expansion under the Affordable Care Act. States do not have to participate in Medicaid; however, since 1982—when Arizona finally signed on—all states do.

Therefore, Medicaid is not an unfunded mandate; the federal government does not force states to participate in it. It is, however, an **entitlement program**; that is, it does create legally enforceable rights. In fact, it is a double entitlement program. First, states have a right to a certain amount of federal money for Medicaid every year; second, individuals who meet eligibility thresholds are entitled to Medicaid services, regardless of the cost. States are required to provide coverage to certain populations, including children in families with income below the **poverty line or poverty threshold**, and parents who qualify for TANF.[33]

Beyond these basics, the states enjoy considerable leeway when setting those eligibility standards.

Medicare
The federal health insurance program for elderly citizens

Entitlement program
A government-run program that guarantees unlimited assistance to those who meet its eligibility requirements, no matter how high the cost

Poverty line or poverty threshold
An annual income level, set by the federal government, below which families cannot afford basic necessities

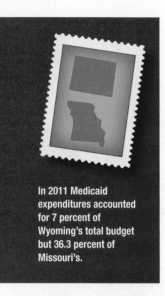

In 2011 Medicaid expenditures accounted for 7 percent of Wyoming's total budget but 36.3 percent of Missouri's.

(See Table 15-1.) They have created health care safety nets with very different levels of generosity. As of July 2014, Arkansas was the least generous state in the country. It allowed only those earning less than 13 percent of the federal poverty level—the threshold set by the U.S. Census Bureau to measure poverty—to receive Medicaid. That means that a working parent with two children who earned more than $214 a month—slightly more than $2,560 a year—earned too much to qualify. Few states want to be stingy when it comes to health coverage, but they need to balance their budgets, and paring back eligibility levels is one way to make the numbers work, especially when Medicaid expenditures increase by double-digit percentages every year.

The most generous state was Minnesota. It allowed families earning up to 200 percent of the federal poverty level to receive Medicaid benefits.

In other words, a working parent with two children could earn up to $3,298 a month—more than $39,500 a year—and still qualify for Medicaid.[34] Even controlling for the fact that most parts of Arkansas have considerably lower costs of living than does Minnesota, that is a dramatic difference. The United States may have one safety net for seniors, but for everyone else, it is a country with many different safety nets. One of the goals of the Affordable Care Act was to set the same baseline of at least 133 percent of the poverty level for Medicaid eligibility, but with many states not participating in the program expansion, that is not the case.

Oops! The Unexpected Cost of Health Insurance

Medicare and Medicaid were structured very differently, but the two programs soon revealed a common trait. They both quickly proved to be fantastically expensive. From 1965 to 1970, the annual rate of increase in state and federal health expenditures was 20.8 percent.[35] By fiscal year 2012, the federal government and state governments spent nearly $415 billion annually on Medicaid alone.

TABLE 15-1

Amount a Working Parent With Two Children Applying for Publicly Funded Coverage May Earn and Still Be Eligible for Medicaid (as of July 1, 2014)

State	Monthly Income-Eligibility Threshold (Dollars)	Annual Income-Eligibility Threshold (Dollars)	Percentage of 2014 Federal Poverty Line
Alabama	214	2,568	13
Alaska	2,660	31,920	129
Arizona	2,193	26,316	133
Arkansas	2,193	26,316	133
California	2,193	26,316	133
Colorado	2,193	26,316	133
Connecticut	3,232	38,784	196
Delaware	2,193	26,316	133
District of Columbia	3,562	42,744	216
Florida	495	5,940	30
Georgia	577	6,924	35
Hawaii	2,523	30,276	133
Idaho	396	4,752	24

State	Monthly Income-Eligibility Threshold (Dollars)	Annual Income-Eligibility Threshold (Dollars)	Percentage of 2014 Federal Poverty Line
Illinois	2,193	26,316	133
Indiana	330	3,960	20
Iowa	2,193	26,316	133
Kansas	544	6,528	33
Kentucky	2,193	26,316	133
Louisiana	313	3,756	19
Maine	1,649	19,788	100
Maryland	2,193	26,316	133
Massachusetts	2,193	26,316	133
Michigan	2,193	26,316	133
Minnesota	3,298	39,576	200
Mississippi	363	4,356	22
Missouri	297	3,564	18
Montana	775	9,300	47
Nebraska	940	11,280	57
Nevada	2,193	26,316	133
New Hampshire	2,193	26,316	133
New Jersey	2,193	26,316	133
New Mexico	2,193	26,316	133
New York	2,193	26,316	133
North Carolina	742	8,904	45
North Dakota	2,193	26,316	133
Ohio	2,193	26,316	133
Oklahoma	693	8,316	42
Oregon	2,193	26,316	133
Pennsylvania	544	6,528	33
Rhode Island	2,193	26,316	133
South Carolina	1,022	12,264	62
South Dakota	957	11,484	58
Tennessee	1,732	20,784	105
Texas	247	2,964	15
Utah	841	10,092	51
Vermont	2,193	26,316	133
Virginia	808	9,696	49
Washington	2,193	26,316	133
West Virginia	2,193	26,316	133
Wisconsin	1,567	18,804	95
Wyoming	924	11,088	56

Source: Centers for Medicare and Medicaid Services, "State Medicaid and CHIP Income Eligibility Standards," July 1, 2014, http://www.medicaid.gov/medicaid-chip-program-information/program-information/downloads/medicaid-and-chip-eligibility-levels-table.pdf; Centers for Medicare and Medicaid Services, "State Medicaid and CHIP Income Eligibility Standards Expressed in Monthly Income, Household Size of Three," July 1, 2014, http://www.medicaid.gov/medicaid-chip-program-information/program-information/downloads/medicaid-and-chip-eligibility-levels-table_hhsize3.pdf.

Note: The federal poverty level for a family of three was $19,790 for the 48 contiguous states and Washington, D.C.; $24,740 for Alaska; and $22,760 for Hawaii. Monthly and annual income thresholds are rounded to the nearest dollar.

As Medicaid spending soared, another disturbing trend was becoming evident. The number of women with children receiving financial assistance under AFDC was soaring, too. After two decades of slow growth, the number of AFDC beneficiaries took off in the late 1960s, rising from slightly more than 2 million recipients in 1960 to more than 10 million recipients by 1972.

The composition of AFDC recipients also was changing. The widows of the 1940s were being replaced by divorced and separated women with children as well as single mothers who had never been married. By 1979, single mothers made up nearly 80 percent of all AFDC recipients.[36]

As the group benefiting from welfare changed, the program became increasingly unpopular with the public. During the late 1970s and early 1980s, Reagan and other conservative politicians railed against what they saw as the excesses of the welfare state. They evoked images of "welfare queens" who drove Cadillacs and paid for steak dinners with fat rolls of food stamps.[37] Reagan's welfare queen proved to be more myth than reality, but it was arguably true that the United States had created a set of permanent dependents of the sort that Roosevelt had warned against when he called government relief "a narcotic, a subtle destroyer of the human spirit."[38]

The Devolution Revolution

The supporters of Reagan weren't the only people who were fed up. State and local officials were, too. Many were frustrated by the high-handed way the federal government administered welfare and Medicaid. Medicaid was theoretically a joint state–federal program, but the federal government always held the whip over state governments. The Centers for Medicare and Medicaid Services (CMS) is the federal agency responsible for administering both Medicare and Medicaid. Formerly called the Health Care Financing Administration, this agency monitors state governments in much the same way that a reform-school principal might monitor juvenile offenders.

Of course, the federal government sometimes had reason to be suspicious. Many states, most notably Louisiana, have long sought to shift as many Medicaid expenses to the federal side of the ledger as possible. Despite sometimes questionable actions on the part of states, even federal officials began to come around during the 1980s to the idea that perhaps the states should be given greater freedom to experiment with their welfare and Medicaid programs. In the late 1980s, the U.S. Department of Health and Human Services, the parent organization of CMS, began to grant states demonstration waivers that allowed them to experiment with how they provided welfare and health care. By 2006, every state had received at least one waiver for a portion of its Medicaid program. States were able to extend or augment health insurance for more than 7 million individuals who otherwise would not have been eligible to receive it.[39] Recently, with the Affordable Care Act, the federal government has taken the lead role in offering health insurance to more people. States, however, are at the forefront of a different type of innovation. They have experimented with new ways to coordinate care in the hope of improving patients' health outcomes and saving money simultaneously.

Welfare Reform

One of the first states to take advantage of federal flexibility was Wisconsin. In 1987, Tommy Thompson entered the governor's office, and one of his first acts was to bring together about a dozen people for lunch at the state executive mansion to discuss one of the most contentious topics in American politics—welfare reform. Thompson's first lunch underscored that he was eager to think outside the box and achieve real reform. Unlike most governors, Thompson didn't invite policy wonks or advocates, either pro or con. Instead, he invited welfare mothers so he could hear firsthand about the obstacles that made it difficult for them to get and keep jobs.[40]

Thompson took the answers he got that day and, during his subsequent yearly lunches, set out to radically reorient welfare in Wisconsin. In doing so, he managed to avoid the dead ends that previous reformers had encountered. In the past, most states had attempted to move welfare recipients into the job market by providing training and education opportunities. All these programs were expensive, and only some were successful. Thompson decided to focus on getting welfare recipients jobs—any jobs. Virtually all welfare recipients were required to work. If a recipient was unable to find a job, then a subsidized position or one in community service was made available. In addition, if a welfare recipient needed child care during the workday or transportation to get to work, the state provided it.

Essentially, Thompson subverted one of the major arguments for ending welfare—namely, that welfare recipients were free riding on the taxpaying public. In doing so, he actually increased funding for child care, health care, and transportation. Once recipients were working, they were provided with one-on-one job counseling, education, training, and other support services.[41] The program also sought to use dollars to promote better behavior. Funds were cut off to the parents of truant children. Also, marriage incentives were created for teenage parents.

By forcing welfare recipients to get jobs *in addition to* offering them the support they realistically needed to enter the job market, Thompson disarmed both conservative and liberal critics and pointed the way to workable reforms to the system. Other states soon followed suit. Work requirements were strengthened and time limits on benefits were imposed. New assistance with child care and transportation was offered. By summer 1996, more than 40 states had received statewide waivers that allowed them to vary the work requirements for AFDC recipients.[42]

Thompson's reforms, coercive or otherwise, were remarkably effective. Providing services such as child care and transportation increased per capita welfare costs in the short run, but in the long run it paid off. State welfare costs fell by about 65 percent over the course of the decade. The state saved more than $1 billion. Such successes later earned Thompson the position of secretary of health and human services under President George W. Bush.

In 1996, Congress and President Bill Clinton formally embraced the reforms that the states had

initiated and replaced AFDC with TANF. As part of this new program, the Personal Responsibility and Work Opportunity Reconciliation Act put a 5-year cap on federal payments to welfare recipients. It also required states to put a large portion of welfare recipients to work.

The new legislation was most notable, however, for what it did not require. Gone were most of the requirements that the federal government sign off on the state plans. TANF gave states the freedom to set benefit levels, eligibility requirements, and financial incentives and penalties as they saw fit.

Arizona in 2014 was gearing up to become the 11th state with stand-alone agencies devoted to child welfare.

TANF also converted welfare from an entitlement program to a block grant program. In the past, people who met eligibility guidelines had been legally entitled to welfare, no matter the cost. Now, the federal government would provide only a finite amount of money to the states. At first, the federal payout was quite generous. The intent was to give states plenty of funds to devise and implement the support programs of their choice. Over time, however, the federal contribution grew smaller and smaller.

The number of welfare recipients declined sharply, from about 6 million in 1996 to less than 4 million by 2008. Poverty rates for single-parent households also fell during this period. By and large, the alarming outcomes predicted by opponents of the welfare reform bill failed to materialize, although caseloads began creeping northward through 2009 as national unemployment topped 10 percent.[43] Still, even as the economy remained weak in 2012, fewer people were receiving TANF benefits than in 2005. That stands in contrast to entitlement programs such as food stamps, which grew rapidly during the recession and its aftermath.[44]

The Feds Falter

When Bill Clinton took office in 1993, he and his administration were prepared to let states take the

MAP 15-1

TANF Income Eligibility Thresholds, 2013

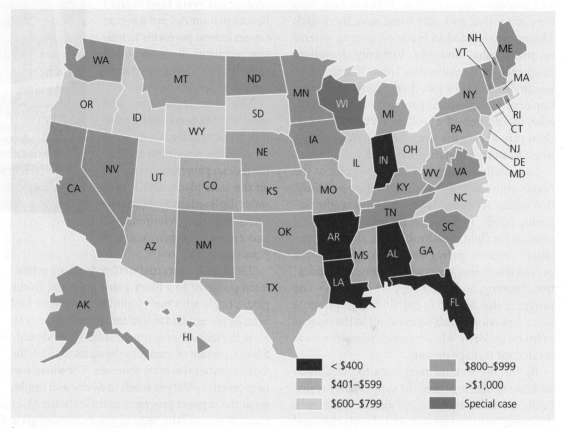

< $400	$800–$999
$401–$599	>$1,000
$600–$799	Special case

Source: Urban Institute, "TANF Policy Tables," Welfare Rules Database, Table I.E.3, "Standards for Estimating Eligibility, July 2013," http://anfdata.urban.org/wrd/tables.cfm.

lead on welfare reform. After all, the president's previous job had been governor of Arkansas. However, the president and his wife, Hillary Rodham Clinton, did see the problem of the uninsured as primarily a federal one. In early 1994, Clinton introduced the Health Security Act. This was legislation that would have provided universal health insurance to all Americans.

Senate Republicans initially countered with a proposal that would have extended health insurance coverage dramatically but would still have fallen short of universal health insurance. Clinton rejected this counterproposal, vowing to veto any measure that failed to provide 100 percent coverage.[45] Politics being politics, the two major parties were unable to find common ground. Nine months later, the Clinton health insurance proposal went down in defeat.[46]

Fast-forward more than 15 years. In 2010, the year Congress approved the Affordable Care Act, 50 million Americans lacked health insurance—fully 16 percent of the population.[47] (See Map 15-2 for the more recent uninsured rates by state.) The Kaiser Commission on Medicaid and the Uninsured has estimated that some 20 percent of uninsured residents are noncitizens, who often work in low-wage jobs that do not include health coverage.[48]

The Rise of the Health Care State

The collapse of health care reform efforts in the 1990s at the federal level left states in a tricky position. They were being squeezed between the

MAP 15-2

Rates of Uninsurance Among Nonelderly, 2012

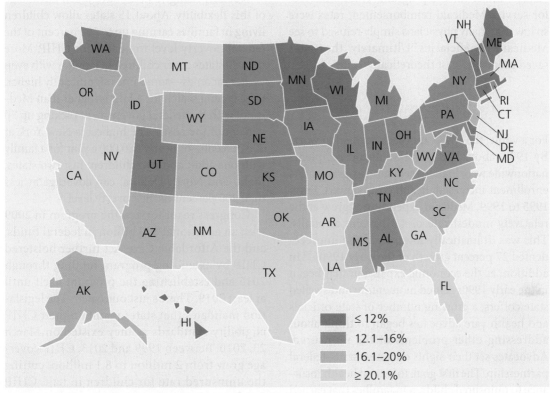

≤ 12%	
12.1–16%	
16.1–20%	
≥ 20.1%	

Source: Kaiser Family Foundation, "Health Insurance Coverage of Nonelderly 0–64," 2013, http://kff.org/other/state-indicator/nonelderly-0-64/.

pincers of the rising costs of state Medicaid programs and the rising demands for assistance from citizens struggling with prescription drug costs and a lack of health insurance. Finally, in the mid-1990s, states found what looked like a good way both to contain costs and to expand coverage—managed care.

Proponents of **managed care** originally saw health maintenance organizations (HMOs) as a way to improve the quality of care patients received. Most medical care that patients receive in the United States is poorly coordinated. Different doctors often cannot easily share a patient's medical records. In addition, physicians have little incentive to offer preventive services because they

get paid for dealing with sickness. Paul Ellwood, the physician who coined the phrase *health maintenance organization* in the early 1970s, believed that HMOs would rationalize and coordinate the medical care that patients received. This would improve the quality of health care for members of an HMO; moreover, HMOs would reduce costs by emphasizing preventive health care.

Under managed care, instead of paying doctors a fee for each service provided, states typically paid an HMO a flat fee for each Medicaid patient enrolled in a plan. The fees that states offered HMOs were designed to be lower than the expenses the states would have incurred if patients had remained in a traditional fee-for-service Medicaid program. HMOs agreed to these lower rates because they believed that, even with lower reimbursement rates, they would still be able to squeeze inefficiencies out of the system and turn a profit.

Managed care
An arrangement for the provision of health care whereby an agency acts as an intermediary between consumers and health care providers

Medicaid recipients benefited, too. They were able to join health plans that gave them access to physicians and services that often had been unavailable under the old program. Traditional fee-for-service Medicaid reimbursement rates were so low that many physicians simply refused to see Medicaid beneficiaries. Ultimately, the states saved money, at least theoretically.

A Promising Beginning

For a while, the HMO approach seemed to work. By 1998, about half of all Medicaid recipients nationwide were in managed-care programs.[49] As enrollment increased, health costs slowed. From 1995 to 1999, Medicaid expenditures grew at the relatively modest rate of 4.3 percent annually. This was dramatically lower than the unprecedented 27 percent growth of the early 1990s.[50] In addition, as the economic expansion that began in the early 1990s gained momentum and swelled state coffers, a growing number of state officials and health care advocates began to think about addressing other problems of the uninsured. Advocates set their sights on a new state–federal partnership. The first goal: to extend health insurance to uninsured children in families that earned too much to qualify for Medicaid but too little to pay for health care on their own.

In August 1997, Congress created the **Children's Health Insurance Program (CHIP)** at the behest of President Clinton. CHIP was designed to provide health insurance to roughly 6.5 million children in low-income families without health insurance.[51] As with Medicaid, CHIP would be designed and administered by the states and paid for primarily by the federal government. The federal government would spring for about 80 percent of total costs.

The states were given considerable flexibility in designing their child health programs. They were free to fold CHIP into their Medicaid programs or create stand-alone CHIP programs. As with Medicaid, they determined the eligibility

---

Children's Health Insurance Program (CHIP)
A joint federal–state program designed to expand health care coverage to children whose parents earned income above the poverty line but still were too poor to afford insurance

levels. They also could cap CHIP enrollments and force recipients to pay some of the costs for the health insurance they received.[52]

Not surprisingly, states have taken advantage of this flexibility. About 15 states allow children living in families earning up to 200 percent of the federal poverty level to qualify for CHIP. More than 20 states cover children in families with even higher incomes—sometimes significantly higher. (The federal match for CHIP is higher than Medicaid, with the federal government picking up 70 percent of the cost.) The highest is New York at 400 percent—or nearly $80,000 a year for a family with one adult and two children. Just two states, Idaho and North Dakota, cap coverage at less than 200 percent of the poverty level.[53]

Congress reauthorized the program in 2009 with an additional $33 billion in federal funds, and the Affordable Care Act further bolstered CHIP by extending program funding through 2015 and establishing the program itself until at least 2019. There's just one catch: The legislation mandates that states maintain their CHIP eligibility standards as they existed on March 23, 2010. Between 1999 and 2013, CHIP coverage grew from 2 million to 8.1 million, cutting the uninsured rate for children in half. CHIP funding was set to run out in 2015, barring action by Congress. There was considerable debate about how best to provide coverage to children, given the ways the insurance landscape had changed following the passage of the Affordable Care Act.

The Safety Net Widens

What effects do these different policies have on the residents of these states? Researchers have found a strong correlation between having health insurance and access to and use of health care services.[54] In addition, giving more people more access to public health care is one direct way to increase their health care use. Some research shows that expanding Medicaid results in lower death rates and that Medicaid participants report being in better health.[55] Thanks to the Affordable Care Act, the number of uninsured Americans is expected to drop by half, from about 45 million in 2012 to 23 million by 2023, according to CMS.

Not having health insurance does not necessarily translate into no health care. Government-supported community health centers provide health care to more than 20 million uninsured Americans in thousands of communities across the country every year. These clinics treat people regardless of their ability or inability to pay.[56] In addition, hospitals are required to provide treatment to people who come into their emergency rooms whether these people can pay or not. As noted at the beginning of this chapter, that is why many hospitals support expanding Medicaid and other provisions of the Affordable Care Act.

> Many public hospitals border high-crime neighborhoods and provide essential advanced emergency and trauma services, as well as outpatient clinics for these same communities. These are critically important functions. They are not, however, very profitable ones.

Along with community health centers, public hospitals have long assumed a particularly important role in providing services to the uninsured. For many low-income individuals, the emergency room of a public hospital is their first and only way to access medical care. Many public hospitals border high-crime neighborhoods and provide essential advanced emergency and trauma services, as well as outpatient clinics for these same communities. These are critically important functions. They are not, however, very profitable ones. Uncompensated care—medical care provided to the uninsured that they do not pay for themselves—cost the medical system $85 billion in 2013.[57] In 2008, 16 percent of public hospitals' costs were uncompensated, compared with 5.8 percent for hospitals nationwide, according to the National Association of Public Hospitals and Health Systems.[58]

The result is that public hospitals have a tough time staying open. Between 1996 and 2002, the number of public hospitals in the nation's 100 largest cities fell from 730 to 645.[59] The recent recession crunched them even further; public hospital systems across the country cut back on programs, including mental health services, pharmacies, and oncology clinics. New York cut 400 positions from its public hospitals in 2009.[60]

Although the Affordable Care Act has helped address the problem of uncompensated care, particularly in those states participating in the Medicaid expansion, it has exacerbated another problem—lack of physicians. "The Affordable Care Act will add hundreds of thousands of people to the rolls of the insured. That's good," said Dr. G. Richard Olds, the founding dean of the medical school at the University of California, Riverside. "But where are the primary care physicians going to come from to serve that population?"[61]

A majority of the counties even in a well-served state such as California do not have enough primary care doctors, according to guidelines set by the American Medical Association. The Association of American Medical Colleges warns that the nation will be short 100,000 doctors by 2020. Admittedly, this association has a vested interest in promoting the training of more doctors. In many states, the gap in care is being made up partially by expanded use of nurse practitioners and other health professionals who are not physicians. But, remember from our discussion of interest groups in Chapter 7, doctors do not necessarily care for other clinicians providing care on their turf.

Lack of access to care is certainly not an issue limited to cities and suburbs. Rural areas long have been plagued by fragmented health care systems and shortages of doctors and nurses. Even worse, rural residents tend to be older and poorer than their urban and suburban counterparts, factors that often translate into a greater need for health care services.[62] It's not a formula for a healthy population.

Missouri tried a novel approach to addressing this problem in 2014, passing a law to allow graduates fresh out of medical school to practice primary care in underserved areas under the supervision of a "collaborating physician." Every state had required physicians to complete a year's residency in a teaching hospital before practicing primary care. The Missouri State Medical Association promoted the bill, but the American Medical Association formally opposed special licensing pathways for physicians who aren't enrolled in an accredited postgraduate program or have at least a year of additional education in the United States under their belt. The reason is simple, said Atul Grover, the chief public policy officer at the Association of American Medical Colleges: Their education is often grounded in theoretical and academic work with the assumption that a future doctor will spend time in a residency afterward. "That education is designed to pair them up with residency," he said. "It's not designed to pair them up with immediate independent practice."[63]

Beyond Managed Care

The use of managed care in Medicaid programs is alive and well. As of 2010, 71 percent of Medicaid patients were enrolled in managed-care plans.[64] The trend has been for states to shift ever more patients into managed care, with Florida, Illinois, and South Carolina all deciding in 2011 to virtually end traditional fee-for-service Medicaid. Yet, more and more, states are deciding that managed care on its own isn't enough.

The accountable care organization (ACO) is one possible successor to the HMO. ACOs are partnerships of health care providers—including primary care doctors, specialists, and sometimes hospitals—that agree to a set budget for serving all the health and long-term care needs of a defined group of patients. In other words, ACOs are a lot like HMOs, except that health care providers themselves, rather than third-party entities, manage the care they provide. Under the ACO model, the health care providers have a financial incentive to work together to keep patients healthy, to treat those who are sick efficiently, and to help patients who have chronic illnesses control the effects of their diseases. If costs fall below a set budget, the ACO shares in the profits. If costs exceed the budget, some ACOs share in the losses. Budgets are set based on the overall

health of the population to be served, and payments are tied to quality measurements.[65]

At a basic level, an ACO gives doctors, hospitals, and clinics the responsibility to provide care for a group of patients within a specified budget. If health care providers better coordinate care to provide good quality for less money, they can share in the savings. ACOs started out as mostly a private-sector phenomenon. As recently as 2010, only 41 such practices existed. By 2014, that number had exploded to at least 600. ACOs have already started to take root in Medicare; now they're making their way into Medicaid.

Borrowing heavily from the ACO model, in 2011 Oregon approved a law to move close to a million people—including Medicaid enrollees, but also teachers and other government employees—into coordinated care organizations.[66] "We have the opportunity to do something that no other state has done, and something that has eluded our nation for decades," Oregon governor John Kitzhaber said at the time. "That is creating a system that actually improves the health of the population at a cost we can afford."[67]

Minnesota is one of the other leaders behind the accountable care movement. It launched an initiative in 2013 to test ACOs in Medicaid. For the first year, the setup was pretty straightforward: The state let provider groups set risk terms they were comfortable with. Any savings realized were shared with those ACOs that came in under budget—that is, those that provided care for less than the targeted amount. By 2014, some larger health systems had to pay the state back if they went over budget. Managing that risk is much easier for larger providers, with several revenue streams and control over every segment of care. The larger systems that are taking on downside risk in the second year are building toward a 15 percent goal—meaning they split savings or overages with the state up to 15 percent above or below their spending goal. "They wanted to ease us into it so they could increase the trust level that would allow us to take risk in the following year," said Greg Klugherz, the chief financial officer at St. Cloud Hospital, a facility 60 miles northwest of Minneapolis. He sees the risk-sharing change as strengthening the system's focus

A Difference That Makes A Difference

States Try New Approaches to Limit Abortion

Abortion opponents know they have a problem. As long as *Roe v. Wade*—the 1973 Supreme Court decision that affirmed the right to abortion—remains in effect, abortion cannot be banned outright. Arkansas and North Dakota found that out in 2014, when federal courts struck down laws that banned abortion after a certain number of weeks of pregnancy.

Many abortion foes believe that continuing to press the courts on the underlying legal question is the best and most moral strategy. But others have come to embrace an approach that, rather than seeking to eliminate abortions, chips away at access to the procedure. In recent years, numerous GOP-controlled states have imposed hundreds of new restrictions on clinics, such as requiring their physicians to have admitting privileges at neighboring hospitals and stricter building standards.

In Ohio, 4 of the state's 14 abortion clinics closed once such restrictions were put in place, with others remaining in legal peril. The goal of this strategy is not to ban abortion—"There are things that are banned that occur every day," said Mike Gonidakis, president of Ohio Right to Life—but to end it. "Abortion is legal, so you must have incremental legislation to save as many babies as we can," he said.

Abortion rights supporters, of course, objected. After Ohio passed its law requiring clinics to have patient transfer agreements in place with nearby hospitals, it passed another barring public hospitals from entering into such agreements. "When they initially put into the law the requirement of a transfer agreement, they said

it was for the good of the women," said Jerry Lawson, CEO of Planned Parenthood of Southwest Ohio, which operates clinics in Cincinnati and Dayton. "Then they turn around and pass a law that says public hospitals can't have transfer agreements," he said. "Now, which is it—are you worried about the women, or are you interested in preventing abortions?"

The new laws have been so good at preventing abortion—or at least forcing clinics to close—that some federal courts became wary of them. The Supreme Court in 2013 refused to block a Texas law that requires clinic physicians to have hospital admitting privileges, but lower courts subsequently found that if women live too far from clinics able to meet such requirements, that puts an undue burden on their right to abortion.

A Mississippi law that would have forced the state's only clinic to close was blocked for this reason in 2014. Texas, which was expected to see its total number of clinics drop from 40 to fewer than 10 once its law was fully implemented, saw several clinics closed once the law took effect. The Supreme Court soon ruled they could reopen pending the final disposition of the case. A federal judge had ruled that too many women would live more than 150 miles from an operating clinic, which too greatly restricted their access. The state countered that most of the population would live close enough to drive to a clinic. "Driving distances of 150 miles are not an undue burden, and 10 percent is not a large fraction," the state argued in a legal filing seeking to go ahead and close most of the state's clinics.

---

on long-time priorities, such as reducing hospital-acquired infections.[68]

Time for Reform

The defeat of federal health care reform in the 1990s left the states in charge of efforts to expand

health insurance coverage. Maine and Massachusetts unveiled universal (or near-universal) health care plans that served as precursors to the federal health care reform bill passed in 2010.

When Dirigo Health, Maine's plan, began in 2004, 14 percent of the state's residents lacked health insurance and 80 percent of the uninsured worked for small businesses that could not afford to provide coverage. Private insurers agreed to provide coverage, which the state would administer and, for the first year, subsidize. In the first phase of enrollment, geared toward small businesses and self-employed workers, 250 businesses and 1,000 individuals signed up.[69] By late 2006, however, researchers found that, even though the program had enrolled more than 16,000 Mainers, it had reduced the state's uninsured population by less than 10 percent. They also reported that the state had raised insufficient funds to support Dirigo.[70] The plan ultimately ran into financial problems and capped enrollment well below its original goal.[71] "The time has passed for states to go it alone; DirigoChoice helps prove that," wrote Maine representative Sharon Anglin Treat, chair of the state's Joint Standing Committee on Insurance and Financial Services, in a letter to the editor of *The Wall Street Journal* in 2009.[72]

Maine's experience did not stop Massachusetts from launching an even more ambitious plan of its own. The plan required every resident of the state to have health insurance by July 2007 or face tax penalties. Under the law, every resident below the federal poverty line can receive insurance fully subsidized by the state; subsidies are extended on a sliding scale to those earning between 100 and 300 percent of the established federal poverty line. Businesses that do not provide health insurance are required to pay the state $295 per employee per year; this money is used to fund the coverage subsidies. However, calling the Massachusetts plan "universal health care" isn't exactly accurate. State officials estimated that the law would extend health insurance coverage to as much as 95 percent of the state's population. They expected that the remaining residents would accept the tax penalties rather than pay for insurance that may still be too expensive, despite the government subsidies.[73]

By 2008, just 6.1 percent of the state's population was uninsured, the lowest rate in the nation. But Massachusetts was beginning to suffer under the strains of the initiative's expense. The Massachusetts Taxpayers Foundation estimated that the program added more than $700 million per year in annual costs, which the state split 50–50 with the federal government. The state cut its payments to hospitals for uncompensated care and raised its cigarette tax by $1 a pack, but, coupled with declining revenues, its efforts weren't sufficient to close the gap.[74] In response, Massachusetts adopted an ambitious, multifaceted new plan in 2012 designed to limit the state's expenses. Among other things, the plan now limits by law how fast the state's health care costs are allowed to rise and redirects more patients into managed care, ACOs, and other arrangements that are designed to spend less by improving coordination.[75]

Shortly after taking office, President Obama declared that the federal government would, once again, take on health care reform. Members of Congress invoked the Massachusetts program often during their debates; those in favor of reform pointed to its success in reducing the uninsured population, while those opposed singled out its costs. Ultimately, after nearly a year of hearings and speeches, President Obama signed the Affordable Care Act into law on March 23, 2010. Major federal health care changes had finally been accomplished, but the debate was far from over.

Issues to Watch

Passing federal health care reform legislation was just the first step. States will continue to grapple with the law's effects inside their borders, and they must continue to address a number of other burgeoning challenges, including those discussed below.

Health Information Technology

In an age when laptops and smartphones are ubiquitous, anyone who has had to fill out identical paperwork for multiple doctors has probably wondered why those documents couldn't be saved electronically and shared. The federal government and states are working with private health care providers to enable them to do just that, through a number of health information technology (IT) initiatives. These initiatives seek to integrate electronic medical records, prescription

California hosts an informative Covered California event to mark the opening of the state's health insurance exchange in 2013. Health care exchanges throughout the 50 states are a result of President Obama's health care reform law known as the Affordable Care Act, the latest health care reform effort undertaken by the federal government, with the goal of providing coverage to millions of uninsured Americans.

ordering, and other critical patient documents, and facilitate the sharing of files among doctors and hospitals. A 2005 study by the RAND Corporation found that health IT could save the country as much as $77 billion annually in efficiencies.[76] Most of the technology that the initiatives need already exists, but the states and the federal government must still convince private practitioners to participate, identify national standards to match technologies across state lines, address patient privacy concerns, and find a way to pay for it all.[77]

The 2009 federal stimulus bill included nearly $26 billion for health IT for Medicare, Medicaid, and the general population. A small fraction of that money—about $560 million—was made available in competitive grants to states to help them pay for the development of health information exchanges, the backbone of the nationwide network. The stimulus funding produced some

quick results. By November 2011, 34 percent of doctors had access to basic electronic health records, up from 22 percent 2 years earlier. By May 2011, every state had a coordinator in charge of health IT.[78]

While the stimulus funds provided some seed money to states, they were temporary. That means states need an ongoing revenue stream to keep their health information exchanges operational. Starting in 2008, Vermont began generating its funds through a fee the state charges insurance companies. Within a year, the fee had pumped enough money into the state to pay for an electronic medical records system for physicians who are not affiliated with hospitals (independent practitioners often cannot afford the average $44,000 start-up cost).[79] Tennessee is an example of a state that has been less successful in finding a financially viable way to sustain its health information exchanges. Beginning in 2005, a regional health information organization began serving eastern Tennessee. At one point, 1,500 doctors had signed up. Yet the organization couldn't persuade enough local health care providers to pay join-up fees to make the financing work—area hospitals chose not to participate. The organization shut down in 2011.[80]

Two major health insurers in California, Blue Shield of California and Anthem Blue Shield, announced they would provide $80 million in "seed money" toward a new health database that they hoped would reduce repetitive tests and procedures.[81] Similar efforts earlier had foundered due to technical difficulties, and, as you would expect when organizations talk about bundling millions of patient records together, privacy protections remain a concern.

Long-Term Care

Unlike private-sector health insurance plans, state Medicaid programs have an additional responsibility. Medicaid provides long-term care to the elderly and other services to people with disabilities. These services can range from providing nursing-home care for low-income Medicaid recipients to developing rehabilitation plans for people with disabilities. All these services are extremely expensive. Although the elderly and disabled make up only about 25 percent of the people enrolled in Medicaid, they account for two thirds of total Medicaid spending.[82] More than 10 million Americans now use some form of long-term care.[83]

Moreover, the cost of long-term care is growing fast. According to the Congressional Budget Office, caring for elderly and disabled Medicaid beneficiaries accounted for more than 72 percent of the program's cost increases between 1975 and 2002. States' long-term care bills hit $147 billion in 2009 and may reach as much as $346 billion by 2040.[84]

Demographics are largely driving those cost increases. According to the U.S. Census Bureau, the number of people 85 years of age and older will grow by 40 percent by 2020. By 2040, that population is expected to grow by more than 250 percent, to 15.4 million people.[85] As it does, the number of people with serious disabilities will almost certainly increase. Many of these people will be unable—or unwilling—to pay for long-term care on their own.

Some states, such as Oregon, have kept costs down by shifting the elderly away from expensive care in nursing homes and toward less-expensive at-home care and assisted-living centers. Seniors overwhelmingly prefer such alternatives to nursing homes. The federal government has encouraged states' efforts in this direction despite opposition from the strong nursing-home lobby. The percentage of Medicaid long-term care spending that went to noninstitutional care more than tripled between 1995 and 2010, rising to 45 percent.[86] The Affordable Care Act will use financial incentives to move states more aggressively toward the provision of home-based services.

Despite the expense to states, the long-term care coverage provided under Medicaid comes with a big drawback. To qualify, a patient must have almost nothing in assets. Examples abound of long-term care patients' spending down hundreds of thousands of dollars in life savings before they qualify for Medicaid.[87] The Affordable Care Act attempted to find a new model. It created the first national long-term care insurance plan, a voluntary program to be financed through payroll deductions.[88] During the debate over the law, however, Republicans who were concerned about the potential cost of the program succeeded in convincing Congress to include a provision requiring the federal government to design the program in such a way that it would pay for itself over the course of 75 years. In October 2011, the Obama administration conceded that making the program financially solvent wasn't possible and abandoned it.

The Return of Public Health

The states have become major players in the field of health care. However, local governments at both the county and city levels continue to play important roles as well. In many parts of the country, local governments, unlike state governments, are direct health care providers.

In the wake of the terrorist attacks of September 11, 2001, many government officials have come to view the public health system in a new light. Individuals in this field now are seen as the first responders to possible biological terrorism, pandemics, and natural disasters such as hurricanes. During the initial response to the Ebola outbreak in 2014, hospitals, cities, and state governments seemed to struggle, unclear on proper protocols for treating patients, as well as the question of whether or not to quarantine health providers who had potentially been exposed to the disease. Rules and strategies regarding protective gear, use of isolation wards, and handling of blood changed rapidly as new cases emerged. Responding to novel health threats is always a challenge. States and cities seem at first to fall back on a generic playbook, whether a crisis is caused by measles or a dirty bomb. "To think the first patients would go flawlessly are an overestimation of our systems," said Dr. Craig Smith, medical director for infectious disease at University Hospital in Augusta, Georgia, in response to Dallas's handling of the first case of Ebola diagnosed in the United States. "I would expect there would be a few stumbles."[89]

Another controversial issue in many communities involves sexual health and education. One in nine girls between the ages of 16 and 19 becomes pregnant outside of marriage; yet a considerable number of parents remain opposed to their children learning about sexuality in the classroom. These parents helped resurrect abstinence-only sex education programs, which have received $1 billion in federal funding since 1998, when only 2 percent of schools offered such programs. By 2002, the proportion of schools teaching abstinence as the only way to avoid sexually transmitted diseases and pregnancy had risen to 23 percent.[90] Congressional Democrats allowed the program to expire in June 2009, but it was partially revived as part of a federal health care reform compromise. The bill will provide $250 million over 5 years for abstinence education—if states can provide 75 percent matching funds. It also allocates $375 million for comprehensive sex education.[91]

Evaluations of abstinence-only programs report conflicting findings that are often used by both proponents and opponents to advance their positions. One recent study conducted by a Pennsylvania State University researcher found that, compared with counterparts who had taken comprehensive sex education classes, fewer middle-school students who were enrolled in an abstinence-only education program engaged in sexual activity within 2 years. Further, more students in both groups remained sexually inactive in comparison with students who had no sex education at all.[92] Regardless of the teaching

method, the statistics seem headed in the right direction: In 2010, the rate of births to teenage mothers fell to the lowest level since the 1940s.[93]

The states are also battlegrounds in the debate over access to contraception. At least 26 states have passed laws that require insurers that cover prescription drugs to include coverage of contraceptives. Twenty-one of the states, however, allow exemptions for employers who oppose such coverage for religious reasons.[94] In this way, the states foreshadowed a debate that would take place in early 2012 at the federal level. The Affordable Care Act requires health insurance to cover contraceptives. Initially, the Obama administration said that even religious groups with objections to contraception coverage would be required to provide it to their employees. But, facing a backlash even from some of its allies, the administration decided on a compromise instead. Religious organizations themselves wouldn't be required to provide contraception, but employees of the religious groups would still be offered the coverage directly from their health insurance companies. This deal borrowed directly from the states: It was called the "Hawaii rule" because it mimicked a policy in that state.[95] Many religious conservatives weren't satisfied with the deal, however, including some in state capitols. Arizona approved a law in May 2012 to permit religious employers not to cover contraception and, in so doing, directly challenged the federal mandate.[96] In 2014, the Supreme Court ruled that closely held private companies (those with five or fewer owners) could not be required to provide contraceptive coverage.

What Is Good Health Anyway?

As if these issues were not enough, local health officials are increasingly wrestling with another question we have not yet touched on in this chapter: What exactly constitutes a health issue anyway?

Consider obesity. More than one third of all adult Americans are considered obese. Media attention has turned to this issue as an ever-growing list of health studies proclaim just how out of shape

MAP 15-3

Obesity Trends Among U.S. Adults, 2013

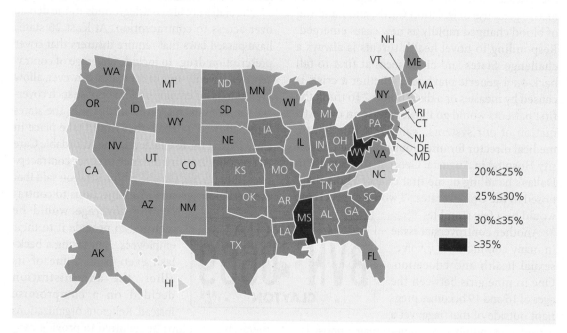

Source: Centers for Disease Control, "Overweight and Obesity: Obesity Prevalence Maps," 2013, http://www.cdc.gov/obesity/data/prevalence-maps.html.

Americans are. The films *Super Size Me* (2004) and *Fast Food Nation* (2006) address people's obsession with fast food. (See Map 15-3.) Kids are getting heavier, too. In the past two decades, the number of overweight and obese children has nearly tripled. Today, according to the CDC, roughly 18 percent of children between the ages of 6 and 11 are overweight—up from just 4 percent in the early 1970s. The number is 18 percent for adolescents between the ages of 12 and 19, too; that is also a significant change from the early 1970s, when just 6 percent of teens weighed too much.[97]

Obesity contributes to a variety of ailments, among them heart disease, certain types of cancer, diabetes, stroke, arthritis, breathing problems, and psychological disorders such as depression. Overweight individuals suffer from these and other related conditions at much higher rates than do people who are not overweight. Indeed, in the United States alone, researchers attribute about 112,000 deaths each year to obesity.[98] In 2003, obesity in the United States cost about $92.6 billion in medical spending.[99] Researchers at Emory University have estimated that if the United States

could curb the rate of increase of obesity, the nation could save $821 per adult by 2018.[100]

In 2006, New York City reignited the debate over government's role in promoting healthy eating habits when it banned the use of trans fats (some of the most dangerous fats) in city restaurants. Soon after, other cities and states began to consider similar legislation. Parent groups and health organizations demanded better, healthier fast-food options, and the fast-food restaurants quickly took notice. McDonald's, the world's largest fast-food chain, received such a negative rap for its unhealthy products that it was under strong pressure to take immediate action. It began expanding its "healthy" meal options with great fanfare, shooting commercials showing Ronald McDonald rollerblading and exercising with children instead of sitting in the restaurant eating, and posting fact sheets on its website announcing how much healthy food it had sold worldwide. Wendy's, KFC, Chili's, and other restaurant chains began using oils free of trans fats for frying.

One of New York City's next public health initiatives required chain restaurants to post calorie

Local Focus

The High-Stakes Battle Over High School Cafeterias

A well-known politician or celebrity can direct attention to an issue, but such support might also lead opponents to personalize their attacks on an initiative. Both those dynamics came into play once Michelle Obama made more-nutritious school lunches a personal priority.

The First Lady helped persuade Congress in 2010 to pass more stringent nutrition requirements. The federal government subsidizes free and reduced-cost meal programs. School districts could lose that funding if they didn't follow the new guidelines, which phased in requirements for lower-sodium foods and more servings of fresh fruits and vegetables.

The idea that schools should serve healthier fare was a no-brainer to some people. Just as kids are taught math and history in the classroom, they should be learning better eating habits in the cafeteria, said Ginny Ehrlich, director of the childhood obesity project at the Robert Wood Johnson Foundation.

After the law passed, the percentage of schools that offered lots of prepackaged foods but nothing by way of produce went down fast. But many people objected. They felt that local schools didn't need the federal government—or Michelle Obama—telling them what to serve. The First Lady became something of a lightning rod, repeatedly described as a "tyrant" by conservative blogs. "By leaving the program, we will not be required to follow these onerous guidelines, pushed by and large by Michelle Obama, who last I checked had been elected by no one," Rick Petfalski, school board president of the Muskego-Norway district in Wisconsin, told the *Milwaukee Journal Sentinel*.

The First Lady did not shy away from the controversy. She said that companies that make big money selling processed and packaged foods are unwilling to give up their profits, even at the expense of children's good eating habits. "We are currently spending $10 billion a year—did you hear that, $10 billion a year—on our school lunch programs," she said in 2014 at a White House lunch with schoolchildren who won a healthy recipe contest. "So it's not surprising that there are certain interests that are resisting change and trying to take us back to the old ways of doing business, because for them there's a lot of money on the line."

But aside from complaining about heavy-handed mandates, some school leaders felt that the nutrition standards championed by Michelle Obama simply didn't work. That is, students weren't eating the meals. If you dine at your school's cafeteria, are you more drawn to the kale or the ice cream? Lots of districts ended up complaining about the waste and expense involved in students' throwing uneaten produce straight into the trash.

They also said that their budgets were being hurt by students' choosing altogether not to buy their meals in the cafeteria. At C. W. Baker High School in Baldwinsville, New York, the number of students buying lunch dropped from an average of 650 per day to about 400 once the standards were implemented. "With the changes in the kinds of lunches we were able to provide to students, they just wouldn't eat it," said David Hamilton, superintendent of the Baldwinsville district. "They would turn right around and throw out produce that we had purchased maybe at quite a cost to us. In upstate New York, produce is not cheap."

Ehrlich argued that while it took some students time to adjust to less-fatty, less-salty meals, most of them did come around. The Robert Wood Johnson Foundation sponsored two surveys in 2014 that found a majority of schools were selling as many lunches as they had before the standards were implemented, and the number of kids complaining about their choices had gone way down. "There is some element of growing pains in this, but we're really trying to showcase the success stories and the bright spots," Ehrlich said.

Hamilton, the educator in upstate New York, says it's fine to offer kids more-nutritious choices, but districts should be able to do so on their own timetable. After he removed Baker High from the federal program, he installed a salad bar in time for the 2014–2015 school year. "It's a mistake to say it's either a federal program and its requirements, or it's going to be corn chips with nacho cheese on them," he said.

counts on their menus, based on the theory that if diners eating fast food knew how many calories were in their meals, they would eat less. Some research showed that the calorie labels didn't succeed in encouraging consumers to eat less, at least initially.[101] Nonetheless, the Affordable Care Act nationalized the concept, requiring all chain restaurants with at least 20 locations to post calorie counts. Even before the rule went into effect, McDonald's announced that it was updating its menus at its 14,000 locations nationwide to include calorie labels.

Not all efforts by states and localities to discourage the consumption of fast food and junk food have gone so smoothly. In 2010, several states, including California, Kansas, New York, Rhode Island, and Washington, engaged in spirited debates about new taxes on soft drinks. Every state has a cigarette tax, and research shows that these taxes have succeeded in helping discourage young people from starting smoking. The idea behind the proposed soda taxes was that they would have the same effect—reducing consumption of unhealthy sugary beverages while raising money for states. Yet most of the states didn't end up enacting soda taxes. Washington did approve such a tax, only to have voters repeal it in November 2010. The soda industry fought back against the efforts to tax its products by portraying the efforts as examples of overly intrusive government. "It's government digging into the grocery cart of people," said Chris Gindlesperger, director of communications at the American Beverage Association.[102] Once again, New York City wasn't willing to let the issue rest. In September 2012, the city's board of health banned the sale of many sugary beverages by restaurants, movie theaters, and other vendors in containers larger than 16 ounces. Soon after, the beverage industry sued to block the rule. In 2014, voters in Berkeley, California, approved the nation's first local tax on sugary drinks.

Conclusion

State and local governments have played an important role in providing health care and assistance to the poorest members of society for a long time. They also have the responsibility to protect and promote public health. Things changed in the 1960s, however, when Congress passed legislation that created the Medicare program for the elderly and the Medicaid program for low-income Americans. This set into motion a process that continues to this day. In recent decades, Medicaid has emerged as one of the most expensive and most important functions of state government.

States have been forced to look for ways to save money on one hand and extend health insurance coverage on the other. Despite the difficulty in reconciling these tasks, some state governments have achieved notable successes. The Children's Health Insurance Program, known as CHIP, has made health insurance available to most American children, and in some cases experimental programs have brought coverage to their parents as well. Even after the passage of federal health care reform legislation in March 2010, states continue to be at the center of health care expansion in the United States. Thanks to a June 2012 ruling by the U.S. Supreme Court, states get to decide whether or not to expand Medicaid under the law. At stake in those choices are many billions of dollars and health insurance for millions of Americans.

At the same time, state and local governments are grappling with new public health challenges. Illnesses such as influenza show that local governments still have a role to play in guarding public health. The threat of biological and chemical terrorism also presents local public health officials

> One of New York City's public health initiatives required chain restaurants to post calorie counts on their menus, based on the theory that if diners eating fast food knew how many calories were in their meals, they would eat less. The Affordable Care Act nationalized the concept, requiring all chain restaurants with at least 20 locations to post calorie counts.

with a grave responsibility. In addition, governments' expenses continue to mount for treating diseases caused by obesity and smoking. All this means that health care will almost certainly continue to be a major concern of state and local governments for the foreseeable future.

The Latest Research

As we have seen in this chapter, the federal Affordable Care Act is an attempt to provide health insurance to tens of millions of Americans—an attempt in which, willingly or unwillingly, states will be intimately involved. It will be years before anyone is able to say with confidence whether the law has succeeded or failed. It became clear almost as soon as the law's major provisions took effect in 2014 that its goals of expanding insurance coverage had significant effects. Supporters of the law also cheered initial reports that overall health spending increased by relatively low amounts. But it was not clear whether enduring savings would be possible as more people sought care.

And not every state was seeing the same results. Following the Supreme Court's ruling in 2012, states get to decide whether or not to expand their Medicaid programs under the law. The Medicaid expansion is one of the central ways the act attempts to expand health insurance coverage to nearly every American, but for many state officials, whether or not to pursue it has proved to be a difficult choice. Many policymakers who were initially resistant to the law have grudgingly come to see that increased federal spending on Medicaid could be beneficial to their states; yet the law remains politically unpopular.

• •

- **Baicker, Katherine, Sarah L. Taubman, Heidi L. Allen, Mira Bernstein, Jonathan H. Gruber, Joseph P. Newhouse, Eric C. Schneider, Bill J. Wright, Alan M. Zaslavsky, and Amy N. Finkelstein.** "The Oregon Experiment—Effects of Medicaid on Clinical Outcomes." *New England Journal of Medicine* 368 (2013): 1713–1722.

Academic researchers have been studying the question of what effects the Affordable Care Act may have by looking at Medicaid expansions that predate the law. Oregon offered a limited expansion of its Medicaid program in 2008 by holding a lottery that chose 30,000 names from a waiting list of nearly 90,000 individuals. Those chosen could enroll in Medicaid if they met its eligibility requirements. The researchers conducted 12,000 in-person interviews 2 years after the lottery. They found that increased Medicaid coverage led to an increase in medical spending due to increases in the number of prescription drugs received and office visits made. They did not find significant change in the number of visits to emergency rooms or hospital admissions. Thanks to increases in preventive care and health screenings, patients were more likely to receive diagnoses of and treatments for diabetes; risk for depression was also substantially decreased. But Medicaid coverage appeared to have no significant effect in terms of other matters such as hypertension, cholesterol levels, smoking, and obesity.

- **Chua, Kao-Ping, and Benjamin D. Sommers.** "Changes in Health and Medical Spending Among Young Adults Under Health Reform." *Journal of the American Medical Association* 311 (2014): 2437–2439.

How have young adults fared under the Affordable Care Act? The law allows parents to keep children on their plans until the age of 26. That provides young adults greater access to health care at lower cost (about 18 percent less on an annual basis). Prior to the law's passage, about 63 percent of those ages 19 to 25 were covered by health insurance. That number increased to 69 percent after the law passed. Looking

(Continued)

(Continued)

at data from surveys between 2002 and 2011, Chua and Sommers found that young adults were more likely to report better physical and mental health after the federal law passed in 2010, although only slightly. Thirty-one percent reported excellent physical health, compared with 27 percent before the law was passed. The researchers also found that for slightly older adults—those ages 26 to 35—there was a slight decline in the percentage of individuals reporting excellent physical and mental health.

- **Sommers, Benjamin D., and Arnold M. Epstein.** "Why States Are So Miffed About Medicaid: Economics, Politics, and the 'Woodwork Effect.'" *New England Journal of Medicine* 365 (2011): 100–102.

While the Medicaid expansion could offer substantial benefits to newly insured people, those benefits come with a cost. Sommers and Epstein show that the cost to states is much greater than just the portion they have to pay for the population that is newly eligible for the program. They predict that many of the roughly 9 million people who already were eligible for Medicaid but had not signed up will "come out of the woodwork" and enroll once the Affordable Care Act kicks in. The law's promise of near-universal coverage will make more people realize Medicaid is available to them—even people who would have been eligible all along. While the federal government has promised to pay 90 percent of the cost of the newly eligible population under the law, states will bear a larger share for new enrollees who were eligible all along. By identifying this effect, Sommers and Epstein help explain why some governors and legislators are worried that the Medicaid expansion will cost more than their states can afford.

- **Sommers, Benjamin D., and Sara Rosenbaum.** "Issues in Health Reform: How Changes in Eligibility May Move Millions Back and Forth Between Medicaid and Insurance Exchanges." *Health Affairs* 30 (2011): 228–236.

Under the Affordable Care Act, whether someone receives coverage through Medicaid or through subsidized private health insurance depends on that individual's income. Sommers and Rosenbaum identify a potential problem with that: A person's income changes over time. If people are bouncing back and forth between Medicaid and private insurance, they may become confused or frustrated or face disruptions in coverage—disruptions that could put their health at risk. By studying individuals' historical income data over time, Sommers and Rosenbaum show that many millions of people are likely to be bouncing back and forth. Aside from posing an administrative challenge for patients, this "churning" could also pose administrative challenges for states, since states run Medicaid and many states will run the health insurance exchanges where individuals will buy subsidized coverage. How well the new health care law works will depend in part on whether states can meet this administrative challenge. In making this point, Sommers and Rosenbaum offer an important lesson: To a substantial extent, health care reform will end up being what states make of it.

Chapter Review

Key Concepts

- abstinence (p. 473)
- Aid to Families with Dependent Children (AFDC) (p. 473)
- Children's Health Insurance Program (CHIP) (p. 486)
- entitlement program (p. 479)
- managed care (p. 485)
- Medicaid (p. 469)
- Medicare (p. 479)
- obesity (p. 472)
- pandemic (p. 472)
- poverty line or poverty threshold (p. 479)
- public health (p. 472)
- Temporary Assistance for Needy Families (TANF) (p. 471)

Suggested Websites

- **www.americashealthrankings.org.** Website of America's Health Rankings, a 20-year project tracking health indicators at the state level.
- **www.astho.org.** Website of the Association of State and Territorial Health Officials.
- **www.familiesusa.org.** Website of FamiliesUSA, a liberal advocacy group that promotes a more activist government policy.
- **www.healthyamericans.org.** Website of Trust for America's Health, a nonprofit organization dedicated to protecting public health.
- **www.kaiserhealthnews.org.** Website of Kaiser Health News, a nonprofit news organization covering state and federal health care issues, funded by the Kaiser Family Foundation.
- **www.kff.org.** Website of the Henry J. Kaiser Family Foundation; offers a wealth of detail on state health care initiatives in general and Medicaid in particular. See, especially, kff.org/statedata for detailed information on states.
- **www.naccho.org.** Website of the National Association of County and City Health Officials.

State Stats on Health and Welfare

Explore and compare data on the states! Go to ***edge.sagepub.com/ smithgreenblatt5e*** *to do these exercises.*

1. Which state spent the largest percentage of its gross domestic product on health programs in 2009? Which state spent the least? Why do some states spend more than others?

2. How did health care spending in your state change between 2000 and 2009? What might account for this change?

3. In 2011, which states had the largest percentages of their populations aged 85 or older? What are the implications for these states' health care spending? Does political culture make a difference?

4. How did the population over years of age change in Delaware between 1997 and 2011? How might this affect health care spending?

5. What was the national average Medicaid expenditure per enrollee in 2002? How does your state compare with others? Why might there be so much variation between states?

6. What state has the highest per capita rate of alcohol consumption? Why might this be?

California state senator Fran Pavley, left, talks with a local woman about the restoration and protection of the Los Angeles River. Pavley is one of many state politicians whose efforts can help urge bigger changes, such as when the Obama administration announced it would establish tighter regulations on tailpipe emissions, following one of Pavley's initiatives.

Environment and Climate Change

THINKING GLOBALLY, ACTING LOCALLY

- How did states become important voices on a global problem?
- Why has climate change become a partisan issue?

States have long taken different approaches to environmental protection. Coastal states such as California and Maine traditionally put a higher premium on clean air and clean water than do the industrial states of the Midwest and coal-producing states such as West Virginia and Kentucky. Over the past decade, however, when questions about climate change have at times been a top-priority concern, the differences between states have seemed to become more pronounced. In addition to regional differences in priorities and willingness to spend large sums of money, climate questions have become—like so many other issues—a matter of partisan debate.

When the Obama administration unveiled a plan in 2014 that called on states to reduce their carbon emissions from power plants by 30 percent from 2005 levels by the year 2030, it was applauded in some of the Democratic-led states that had already made major efforts to increase energy efficiency, and perhaps even seen as insufficiently bold to address the challenge at hand. The northeastern states participating in a carbon-reduction compact known as the Regional Greenhouse Gas Initiative had already slashed their combined carbon dioxide emissions by more than 30 percent from 2005 levels and were upping their target to 45 percent. "The announcement is a little bit of a non-event here in New England,"

After reading this chapter, you will be able to

- discuss the various measures states have taken to protect the environment,
- explain the aim and impact of enacting green policies in building construction and jobs,
- relate the role of adaptation in dealing with climate change, and
- identify contemporary issues, debates, and agreements on the environment.

said Dan Dolan, president of the New England Power Generators Association.[1]

In more conservative states, however, officials saw the announcement as one more regulatory intrusion from the federal Environmental Protection Agency (EPA) that would cost jobs. Two months after the plan was announced, a coalition of attorneys general from a dozen coal-reliant states sued to block it, arguing that the EPA was overstepping its authority under the Clean Air Act. The agency's proposed rule would have "devastating effects on West Virginia jobs and its economy" by forcing some coal-fired plants to close, argued Patrick Morrisey, that state's attorney general.[2] States including Kansas, Kentucky, and West Virginia moved swiftly to pass laws directing their environmental agencies to develop carbon emission plans that would consider the "unreasonable costs" of compliance for power plants.

Republicans have argued that the Obama administration and its Democratic allies in the states have been too eager to impose costs on some industries, while steering money to favored "green" businesses that have proven to be boondoggles. The solar panel company Solyndra, which defaulted on more than $500 million worth of government loans in 2011, has remained a prominent part of the litany of GOP complaint about President Obama's policies and management. "What are the costs of us going on these crusades, these environmental crusades?" asked Trip Pittman, a Republican state senator in Alabama, who calls federal research on climate "bad science" and "fearmongering." "We've elevated environmentalism into some kind of religion."[3]

Republicans continue to stress the importance of taking care not to make changes that could cost big money and jobs. "I do think it's sensible for a Republican candidate to express skepticism about this headlong rush . . . a lot of Democrats seem to be having to kill the coal industry," said Dick Wadhams, a former chair of the Colorado Republican Party.[4] But, like a lot of other GOP officials, Wadhams cautioned that climate change is a real issue. Many Republican candidates during the 2014 election season criticized the Obama administration's approach and some continued to express skepticism about whether human activity was contributing to climate change, but some Republicans expressed concern about how the nation would respond to apparent changes in weather patterns. "I don't think it would be wise for a Republican to shut the door on a discussion of climate change," Wadhams said.

That may be in part because the scientific consensus about climate change and its effects becomes firmer every year—and more dire. The proof may also be all around us. "Extreme weather" conditions, such as severe droughts in California, Texas, and the Midwest, along with a proliferation of powerful storms, had politicians talking about climate change in more urgent tones. The state of Louisiana has already lost its distinctive boot shape as more and more land has been swallowed by the Gulf of Mexico. One town, Isle de Jean Charles, was settled in the early 1800s but is expected to be not just abandoned but underwater by 2016. It was the subject of a documentary in 2014 and the inspiration for the feature film *Beasts of the Southern Wild*. It became known as "the Louisiana town devoured by climate change." "If nothing is done to stop the hemorrhaging, the state predicts as much as another 1,750 square miles of land—an area larger than Rhode Island— will convert to water by 2064," writes Brett Anderson, a reporter for the New Orleans *Times-Picayune*. "An area approximately the size of a football field continues to slip away every hour."[5]

In 2014, the Pentagon released a report concluding that climate change poses immediate national security threats, leading to increased risks from terrorism, infectious disease, poverty, food shortages, and extreme weather. The report described ways the military would have to adapt to increased droughts, storms, and rising sea levels.[6] A draft UN report that same year said that global warming had already cut grain production by several percentage points' worth and warned that sea levels could rise, periods of high heat would increase, and other climate issues would worsen unless greenhouse gas emissions were brought under control. Scientists and even the White House were careful to assert that no single episode of extreme weather—no storm, no flood, no record-breaking heat wave, and no drought—could be attributed specifically to global climate change. But weather everywhere seemed to be impacted by the continuing buildup of greenhouse gases. "The new reality in New York is we are getting hit by 100-year storms every couple of years," said Andrew Cuomo, the state's Democratic governor.[7] In 2014, he signed a law known as the Community Risk and Resiliency Act that amended a number of statutes to require consideration of the impact of climate change for many projects and permits. The state's Public Service Commission ordered Consolidated Edison, which serves New York City and some of its suburbs, to spend $1 billion on upgrading its equipment and physical plants to prevent future damage from flooding and other weather events.

How to address the effects of climate change—if not climate change itself—has become a top challenge for states and localities. It's true that roughly half the states have taken little to no action related to climate change, either because they are concerned that the price of addressing the issue, through limiting energy use, is simply too high or because their leaders and political cultures remain skeptical that global warming is anthropogenic (i.e., caused largely by human activity). In general, states have lately come to concentrate less on limiting energy consumption than on promoting the development of energy resources. Numerous states have been undergoing booms in oil and natural gas production in recent years.

Many states, however, have put in place new measures meant to limit reliance on fossil fuels. More than half the states have adopted renewable energy portfolio standards requiring utilities to rely on renewable sources such as wind and solar energy to generate a significant share of their electricity (25 percent in most states) in future years. "They're committed to moving forward on various measures that they've already started in the absence of federal action," says Jessica Shipley, a fellow at the Center for Climate and Energy Solutions. "Definitely, states are still working hard on climate, in conjunction with federal action."[8]

This represents an important new role for states, which traditionally have taken a backseat to federal efforts when it comes to environmental issues. The major environmental laws of the early 1970s, such as the Clean Air and Clean Water Acts, set out strict federal guidelines that states had to follow. In contrast to this "command and control" model, in which the federal government called all the shots, in the area of climate change the American states are leading, influencing not only federal policy under Obama but also efforts in many other countries through state partnerships with regions and provinces in other nations.

Approaches to climate change, then, have become a particularly interesting exercise in federalism. States have sought to fill the vacuum left by the absence of federal leadership on an issue that state leaders themselves realize calls for a national—indeed, international—set of solutions. "States have been tripping all over themselves to show national leadership on this issue," says Barry G. Rabe, a professor of public policy at the University of Michigan. "California, I would argue, has made as heavy an investment in time and treasury into climate change as any government on Earth, including the European Union."[9]

In short, inaction by the federal government and differences across states and localities have resulted in significant obstacles to a coordinated response to environmental problems, especially problems associated with global warming. Climate change is certain to remain an important issue among states and localities, but whether a subset of the subnational governmental units of the

United States can make a significant impact on greenhouse gas emissions in the absence of further action at the national and international levels remains very much in question. California Democratic governor Jerry Brown said that no matter what aggressive efforts his state might undertake, it represents only 1 percent of the global problem. "We have to get other states and other nations on a similar path forward," Brown said. "That is enormously difficult because it requires different political jurisdictions, different political values, to unite around this one challenge of making a sustainable future."[10]

In this chapter, we consider some of the specific environmental policy challenges facing states and localities. These include substantive policy topics such as regulating tailpipe emissions and promoting renewable energy, but they also include the problems that the federal system itself poses to comprehensive action on climate change, as well as the widening partisan divide that further fragments state and local government action on the environment.

New Jersey has 116 Superfund sites, uncontrolled or abandoned places where hazardous waste is located. That's the most of any state.

States Get Serious About the Environment

Unlike education, crime, taxes, and budgets, the environment is a relatively recent policy concern for state and local governments. Indeed, it is a relatively recent policy concern for the federal government. The modern environmental movement got its start in the 1960s and led to a concerted federal response in the early 1970s. This included the passage of landmark laws regarding air and water quality, and the creation of the U.S. Environmental Protection Agency (EPA). Enforcing and expanding those responsibilities has made environmental policy one of the central responsibilities of the federal and, increasingly, state and local governments. "Today,

after nearly four decades, environmental protection is the most heavily funded regulatory responsibility in the United States," writes Marc Allen Eisner, a political scientist at Wesleyan University.[11]

At the heart of contemporary environmental debates is **climate change**, which has become a hot issue not just among national (and international) policymakers but also for state and local officials. It's worth remembering, however, that policymakers at all levels have taken this issue seriously for a relatively short time. "We're still very much at the embryonic stage of dealing with climate change in this country," said John Cahill, who worked on environmental legislation as an aide to former New York governor George Pataki.[12]

The federal government has, to put it mildly, a mixed record in dealing with the climate change challenge. Environmentalists derided President George W. Bush for not seriously addressing **global warming**, but Bush's predecessor's record was not notably stronger. Congress rejected President Bill Clinton's 1993 proposal to impose a tax on energy, and the Senate passed a unanimous resolution in 1997 that it would reject U.S. participation in the **Kyoto Protocol** if it harmed the U.S. economy.

At least initially, states followed the skeptical approach of the federal government. It soon became clear, however, that many states were eager to address the problem of global warming, particularly after Bush's formal rejection of the Kyoto Protocol in 2001. "Ironically . . . American states may be emerging as international leaders at the very time the national government continues to be portrayed as an international laggard on global climate change," Rabe wrote in 2004.[13]

Most of these initial state-level efforts were largely symbolic, lacking specific mandates or resources. Unlike the federal government, however, some states actually put teeth into their efforts. As early as 1989, New Jersey governor Thomas Kean, a Republican, signed an executive order instructing all state agencies to take the lead

---

U.S. Environmental Protection Agency (EPA)
The federal agency charged with protecting the environment

Climate change
A shift in global temperatures

Global warming
Rising average temperatures worldwide

Kyoto Protocol
A 1997 international treaty that sought to reduce emissions of greenhouse gases

Montokoling, New Jersey, mayor George C. Nebel, left, and state commissioner of environmental protection Bob Nevin, right, respond to the continuing cleanup process in the aftermath of 2012's Superstorm Sandy. Extreme weather such as Sandy has prompted officials to take a more serious look at threats from climate change.

AP Photo/Mel Evans

in reducing **greenhouse gases**. In 2001, Massachusetts governor Jane Swift, also a Republican, issued a rule limiting a variety of pollutants from six major power plants, including the nation's first **carbon dioxide** standards. "The new, tough standards will help ensure older power plants in Massachusetts do not contribute to regional air pollution, acid rain and global warming," Swift said.[14] Her action was soon copied in New Hampshire.

Indeed, it was actually a state government—California's—rather than the federal government that emerged as the leader in addressing climate change–related policies. California stepped into this policy arena not simply because of its green-leaning political constituencies or its large economy or its role as a national cultural trendsetter, although all these factors certainly played their roles. As the only state allowed to set air pollution controls stricter than those mandated by federal law (thanks to a provision in the **Clean Air Act**), California occupies a unique policymaking niche in the federal system. That law—written at a time during the early 1970s when Southern California was notorious for its **smog**—gives California the authority to regulate any such pollutant as long as the state can get a waiver from the EPA. Other states are then allowed to follow California's rules. There was strong pressure from environmentalist forces within California to move on the issue of greenhouse gases following the 1998 elections, with both the legislature and the governor's mansion in Democratic hands for the first time in two decades. Thus, on a series of important environmental issues, California began to act. Other states, following California's lead, began experimenting with innovative environmental policies. One of the biggest obstacles the states faced in these efforts was the federal government.

Regulating Vehicles

In 2002, California lawmakers enacted a measure to regulate **tailpipe emissions**, or greenhouse gases released from vehicles, which in 1999 accounted for 37 percent of carbon dioxide emissions in the state.[15] The idea came from Bluewater Network, a San Francisco environmental group that has since become part of Friends of the Earth, a global organization. The group found its sponsor in Fran Pavley, a Democratic freshman state representative willing to take on the fight when more prominent legislators were avoiding it. "We were happy at that point to find any progressive author,

Greenhouse gases
Emissions—primarily carbon dioxide but also other gases such as methane—that are believed to contribute to global warming

Carbon dioxide
A naturally occurring gas, the prevalence of which is increased by the burning of fossil fuels

Clean Air Act
The law, initially enacted in 1970, that provides authority for federal regulation of air pollution

Smog
A type of air pollution; the word comes from the combination of *smoke* and *fog*.

Tailpipe emissions
Greenhouse gases released by cars and other vehicles

because we knew it would be a difficult bill," said Bluewater executive director Russell Long.[16]

The legislation survived a committee challenge and was ready to reach the floor by the middle of 2001, but Pavley held off on a vote until 2002 so she could broaden her backing. Carmakers and oil companies spent an estimated $5 million attempting to sink it, and she was ardently attacked by talk-radio hosts for impinging on the freedom of Californians to drive SUVs and other large vehicles.

Pavley responded with polls demonstrating overwhelming popular support for the bill, even among SUV owners. She also got help from water-quality districts, religious leaders, technology executives from Silicon Valley, and celebrities such as Paul Newman, Tom Hanks, and former president Bill Clinton, who made calls to wavering lawmakers.

Her bill's progress was also helped immeasurably by legislative leaders who showed the former civics teacher some parliamentary tricks to ensure its passage. One was to put language into the bill all in capital letters highlighting the fact that the California Air Resources Board would not have the power to ban SUVs or other specific types of vehicles, as bill opponents were warning would be the case in their advertisements. One of Pavley's colleagues called these the "We Really Mean It" amendments. The substance of the bill was not changed, but the amendments were "put in to clarify it for the public," Pavley said. "Admittedly, in all the years I taught 'how a bill becomes law,' we didn't talk about that possibility."[17]

But her law did require the Air Resources Board to adopt "cost-effective" and "reasonable" restrictions on carbon dioxide emissions from cars and light trucks by 2005, with automakers having until 2009 to comply. Not surprisingly, carmakers fought the law through numerous court challenges.

More than a dozen other states enacted laws saying they would abide by California's rules once they were approved, and several others pledged to do so, but the Bush administration refused to grant California the necessary waiver. "All we asked for was permission to enforce, because the rules were all in place," California Air Resources Board spokesman Stanley Young said in a 2008 interview. "We've been ready for 2 years on Pavley. The rules

were fully fleshed out. They were formally adopted back in 2005, and we're ready to move on them as soon as we get the green light."[18]

Challenging the Environmental Protection Agency

In the face of federal reluctance to regulate greenhouse gas emissions, several environmentalist groups as early as 1999 had petitioned the EPA to use its authority under the Clean Air Act to regulate the gases. The agency denied it had such authority and also argued that the link between greenhouse gases and climate change was not firmly established.

Massachusetts and 11 other states appealed the EPA's denial. In April 2007, the Supreme Court ruled 5 to 4 in the states' favor, noting that they had standing to bring such a case due to the "risk of catastrophic harm" they faced as sovereign entities. Justice John Paul Stevens wrote that the EPA had provided "no reasonable explanation for its refusal to decide whether greenhouse gases cause or contribute to climate change." In his dissent, Chief Justice John G. Roberts Jr. argued that it was an issue better decided by Congress and the executive branch.[19] But the Court's majority had determined that carbon dioxide was indeed an air pollutant under the federal Clean Air Act.

The 2007 Supreme Court decision set the political stage for Congress to enforce a new mileage standard for cars and light trucks. In December 2007, President Bush signed into law requirements that a car manufacturer's entire fleet average 35 miles per gallon by 2020.

Just hours after that bill was signed, however, EPA administrator Stephen L. Johnson dashed hopes that the *Massachusetts v. EPA* decision would lead the agency to approve California's waiver application for enforcement of the Pavley bill. "The Bush administration is moving forward with a clear national solution, not a confusing patchwork of state rules, to reduce America's climate footprint from vehicles," Johnson said in a statement.[20]

California had been granted more than 50 waivers under the Clean Air Act, which allowed it to develop such innovations as the catalytic converter, which reduces tailpipe emissions; tighter fuel caps to reduce gasoline evaporation; and computerized detectors to warn when a car's smog controls are not working. California's standards have often been adopted by other states and, thus, by carmakers. "If not for California's leadership, I think it's fair to say that cars wouldn't be as clean as they are today," said Ron Burke, Midwest climate change director for the Union of Concerned Scientists. "We would have suffered through more bad air days over the last 30 years."[21]

The *Los Angeles Times* reported that EPA staff had urged Johnson to grant the waiver. "California met every criteria . . . on the merits. The same criteria we have used for the last 40 years on all the other waivers," one EPA staffer told the *Times*. "We told him [Johnson] that."[22] Technical and legal staff of the EPA also reportedly advised Johnson he would likely lose a legal challenge. The *St. Petersburg Times* reported that during the late summer and fall, secretary of transportation Mary Peters had quietly urged members of Congress and some governors to let the EPA know her department opposed the waiver request.[23]

As noted earlier, the waiver had to wait until President Obama granted it—representing the federal government's first step toward regulating greenhouse gases. Under rules finalized in April 2010 by the EPA and the Department of Transportation, emission and mileage standards for new vehicles would require an average performance of 35.5 miles per gallon by 2016. "The rules are expected to cut emissions of carbon dioxide and other heat-trapping gases about 30 percent from 2012 to 2016," *The New York Times* reported.[24] The Obama administration estimated that the new standards would add $985 to the price of a car but would save the consumer $4,000 in fuel costs over the life of the vehicle.

Canada adopted identical standards the same day. The federal rules were largely based on the California law, but they also reflected an agreement hammered out with carmakers.

Cap and Trade

Cars are not the only source of greenhouse gas emissions. In 2006, Fran Pavley and other California lawmakers were promoting a piece of legislation, known as AB 32, that sought to address the stationary sources of pollution, such as power plants, oil refineries, and cement plants. The law aims to reduce industrial carbon dioxide emissions by 25 percent by 2020. AB 32 represents the first imposition of statewide enforceable limits on greenhouse gas emissions that includes penalties for noncompliance. The legislation is the first in the nation to require a cap-and-trade system to address greenhouse gases.

Cap and trade puts an overall limit—or cap—on the emission of a pollutant, such as carbon dioxide. Once the limit is set, polluters are given or sold some number of emissions allowances—in essence, permits to pollute. The amount of pollution they can release—say, 1,000 tons of carbon dioxide at a power plant—is slowly reduced over time. If they come in below their limits, they can sell or trade their excess permits; if not, they have to pay fines or buy extra permits from other polluters. That's the trade part. Late in 2012, California held its first auction of 23.1 million carbon emission permits, which sold for $10.09 apiece. When the law took effect at the beginning of 2013, California became the world's second-largest carbon market, after the European Union.[25]

Cap-and-trade systems have been used by the federal government and by other states to address environmental concerns. Congress created such a system to address acid rain in the 1990 Clean Air Act. (Acid rain is rain that contains a high concentration of sulfur dioxide; it is blamed for polluting lakes and streams.)

Ten states in the Northeast and Mid-Atlantic— Connecticut, Delaware, Maine, Maryland, Massachusetts, New Hampshire, New Jersey, New York, Rhode Island, and Vermont—signed on to a cooperative effort known as the Regional

With its 2007 Next Generation Energy Act, the Minnesota state legislature adopted the strategic goal of reducing the state's greenhouse gas emissions by at least 80 percent of 2005 levels by 2050.

Cap and trade
A system for limiting pollution by assigning allowances to polluters, who can sell their excess permits if they succeed in reducing their emissions

Greenhouse Gas Initiative (RGGI), which uses cap and trade. (New Jersey dropped out in 2011, a decision by Republican governor Chris Christie that has remained controversial with legislators and the courts.) These states have capped carbon dioxide emissions from their power sectors, requiring gradual reductions that will bring emissions down 10 percent by 2018.

Governors from seven states began RGGI negotiations in 2003, reached a formal agreement in 2006 (with the last three states, Maryland, Massachusetts, and Rhode Island, signing on the following year), and began auctioning pollution permits to power companies in 2009. The history of RGGI includes many touch-and-go moments when states dropped out of or rejoined the program. RGGI stayed afloat based on the hope that, once carbon emissions carried a price, utilities would burn less coal, oil, and natural gas because it would be in their economic interest to do so, which would then make carbon-free alternatives comparatively more attractive.

The early auctions were considered a success, but not everyone is convinced that the most optimistic scenarios about reducing emissions will play out as intended. The region-by-region approach has left open plenty of opportunities for undermining the system.

In the Northeast, for example, it would be easy enough for a big industrial customer in New York, which is part of RGGI, to look for cheaper power generated by coal-fired plants in Pennsylvania or Ohio, which are not part of the initiative. If that occurs, said Kenneth Pokalsky, a regulatory analyst for the Business Council of New York State, "we'll have the worst of both worlds: higher energy costs in New York to implement a program that has no discernible impact on worldwide greenhouse gas emissions."[26]

The other regional initiatives have not been as productive as RGGI. The midwestern regional initiative outlined a cap-and-trade system, with an advisory group releasing its final recommendations and model rules in May 2010, but the states involved then failed to follow through on their greenhouse gas reduction goals through the accord. The Western Climate Initiative, originally comprising seven states and four Canadian provinces, appeared bolder in its approach than did RGGI, targeting not just carbon dioxide but other greenhouse gases as well, but every U.S. member state, save California, had dropped out of the Western Climate Initiative by 2012. The three regional initiatives joined forces in 2012 with the creation of North America 2050: A Partnership for Progress, a group of 16 states and four Canadian provinces designed to share ideas and techniques for moving toward a low-carbon economy. California has since signed climate deals with China and Mexico, but those agreements only lay the groundwork for increased cooperation, as opposed to setting any binding targets for new reductions in greenhouse gas emissions.

A cap-and-trade proposal was central to the approach taken by the 2009 bill passed by the U.S. House, but the concept itself became highly charged over the course of congressional debate. Critics derided the idea, calling it "cap and tax" and claiming that it would add billions to the nation's energy costs.

As White House counsel under President George H. W. Bush, C. Boyden Gray was an architect of the 1990 Clean Air Act cap-and-trade program designed to address acid rain. Nevertheless, he added his voice to the chorus of complaints about the cap-and-trade model proposed by federal climate change legislation. "The proponents always say they're copying the highly successful cap-and-trade program of the Clean Air Act and they're most decidedly not, because they've thrown in this auction function," Gray said. "It's purely a revenue function, and that becomes a tax. You pull 2 or 3 trillion dollars out of the economy and that's what people are objecting to."[27] In 2014, the U.S. Conference of Mayors—a group that has long supported climate efforts—dropped its call for Congress to pass a cap-and-trade bill, due to differences of opinion within the group's own ranks. "Rather than split mayors up over partisan disagreements, we wanted to focus on actually doing something," said Democratic mayor Bill Finch of Bridgeport, Connecticut, cochair of the group's climate task force.[28]

In March 2010, in a move seen largely as a response to complaints that a cap-and-trade bill would hurt the economy by raising energy prices,

MAP 16-1

Renewable and Alternative Energy Portfolio Standards, 2014

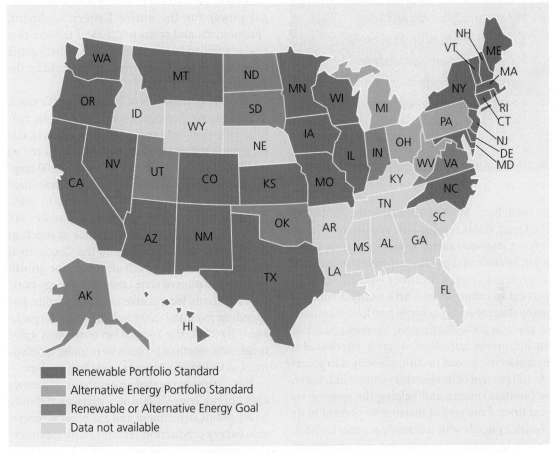

Renewable Portfolio Standard
Alternative Energy Portfolio Standard
Renewable or Alternative Energy Goal
Data not available

Source: Center for Climate and Energy Solutions, "Renewable and Alternative Energy Portfolio Standards," 2014, http://www.c2es.org/node/9340.

Obama outlined a plan to open up much of the East Coast to offshore oil drilling. His proposal would have ended a longtime moratorium on offshore oil exploration. The West Coast would remain closed to drilling and exploration, as would the East Coast from New Jersey northward. But opening up oil exploration from Delaware down to the central coast of Florida covered 167 million acres of ocean.[29] Obama's move, which included more environmental protections than a similar idea previously floated by President George W. Bush, was mainly cheered by oil companies and supporters of increased domestic energy production—as well as by state officials, who welcomed the chance to share in oil-extraction tax revenues.

But within 3 weeks, an offshore oil rig exploded 40 miles off the Louisiana coast. (This occurred in the Gulf of Mexico, an area that had long been open to oil drilling, not in the newly designated area.) The resulting catastrophic oil spill effectively ended any chance for an expansion of offshore drilling for a time, but in 2011, the Obama administration announced a proposal for a new 5-year plan. It opened up new areas in the Gulf of Mexico and Alaska to oil drilling but barred development along the East Coast and West Coast. Overall, domestic oil production during Obama's first term grew by more than 10 percent.

Promoting Renewable Energy

Meanwhile, all but a dozen states are pushing forward on another front intended to reduce greenhouse gas emissions and lower U.S. dependence

> Critics charge that an emphasis on renewable energy sources is not a panacea. Despite heavy public investment and tax breaks, renewable energy production remains more expensive than energy produced using coal. It also remains less reliable.

on fossil fuels. Most states outside the South and the Great Plains regions now require utilities to rely on **renewable energy** sources, such as wind, solar, biofuels, and geothermal power, to generate a significant share of electricity—usually up to 25 percent in future years. That's nearly 3 times as many states as had renewable portfolio standards in place in 2004. Burlington, Vermont, reached an important milestone when it purchased a hydroelectric project in 2014, allowing it to generate 100 percent of its electricity from wind, water, or biomass sources and helping the state on its way toward the goal of meeting 90 percent of its electricity needs with renewable sources by 2050. "It's an important step in the process of weaning ourselves from foreign oil," said Rhode Island state senator David E. Bates, who helped push through legislation in 2004 that requires a 20 percent renewable energy portfolio in his state by 2020. "We provided incentives for companies to produce renewable energy. We also took great pains to make it a workable formula. You can't tell a national grid to produce green energy in twenty years without making sure the energy is available."[30] A decade after Bates's bill passed, Rhode Island passed a law aiming to reduce greenhouse gas emissions by 45 percent below 1990 levels by 2035 and by 80 percent by 2050.

Meeting the required targets remains quite a challenge, however, especially in coal-dependent regions such as the South and the Midwest. Coal

Renewable energy
Power generated using natural sources that can be replenished, such as wind and solar energy, as opposed to nonrenewable fossil fuels

is used to generate about half the nation's electricity. As governor of West Virginia, Joe Manchin touted wind energy but noted in 2008 that his state's coal production is the key source of electrical power for the entire Eastern Seaboard. "Economists and scientists . . . will tell you that coal is going to be the primary factor that's going to power this nation and most of the world for the next thirty to fifty years."[31]

According to the Global Wind Energy Council, U.S. wind energy capacity has been growing rapidly, with wind turbines installed by 2013 capable of generating more than 60,000 megawatts of additional electricity. That's up from 17,000 megawatts of capacity as recently as 2007. Investment in geothermal energy grew 26 percent in 2009, thanks largely to public investment. A total of 188 projects in 15 states could produce as much as 7,875 megawatts, according to the Geothermal Energy Association, which attributed the growth to a combination of state renewable energy portfolio standards, federal investment tax credits, and spending from the 2009 federal stimulus package.[32] By 2012, the association noted that 4,500 megawatts' worth of projects were under development in California, Nevada, and Oregon alone.

But critics charge that an emphasis on renewable energy sources is not a panacea. Despite heavy public investment and tax breaks, renewable energy production remains more expensive than energy produced using coal. It also remains less reliable. "Over the past 15 years, I've participated in or seen many of the analyses of the economic impact of reducing greenhouse gases," said Margo Thorning, senior vice president of the American Council for Capital Formation, a Washington think tank. "In every case there is a slower economy and less overall employment, even though new green jobs are created. The reason that happens is that renewables are more expensive."[33]

Some of the states' requirements are not realistic anyway, according to public policy professor Barry Rabe. He notes that California set a renewable energy standard for utilities of 20 percent by 2010, which the state could not meet. (It was at 11 percent at the end of 2009.) Legislators in 2010 debated raising the standard to 33 percent by 2020, which Republican governor Arnold Schwarzenegger also sought by executive order. Rabe called it "hubris" for states to

A Difference
That Makes A Difference

Why Texas Harvests More Wind Than California Does

Although many states have taken aggressive steps to reduce greenhouse gases, not all of them have. More than half the states now require utilities to generate a percentage of their power from renewable sources such as wind and solar energy, but this is an idea that has yet to gain traction in the Southeast, which has traditionally sought weaker environmental protections. States in the industrial Midwest, meanwhile, are wary of ideas that would limit their use of coal.

The differences in approaches among the states are especially clear when two or more are trying to accomplish similar goals. Nowhere is this more apparent than in the different ways Texas and California have pursued their renewable energy goals.

Despite being an oil state, Texas was actually the first state to set a target for renewable energy. Texas quickly met its goal, set in 1999, of generating 2,000 megawatts of power through renewable sources by 2009. In 2005, the legislature created more ambitious targets—8,800 megawatts by 2015 and 10,000 by 2025. By 2014, Texas was generating 12,755 megawatts, nearly 3 times the wind capacity of the second- and third-ranked states, Iowa and California.

Lots of states are home to plenty of wind and land. But Texas had one additional advantage—lack of regulation. Texas developers have minimal dealings with the state and are able to cut the development deals they need with local officials.

California, by contrast, has built few big wind farms since the 1980s because of the costs and delays caused by the need to comply with environmental regulations, including concerns about the fact that wind turbines often kill birds.

Regulation and environmental worries have also slowed efforts in California to build large solar plants in the Mojave Desert. Environmentalists were divided about the construction of Green Path North, a $2 billion transmission line intended to convey geothermal and solar energy from remote desert areas near the Salton Sea to the 5 million customers served by the Los Angeles Department of Water and Power. Residents in San Bernardino County worried that the project would defile some natural scenery and increase the risk of forest fires with colossal steel towers and ugly high-voltage power lines. Indeed, the project was abandoned in 2010.

Most environmentalists concede that California, to meet its greenhouse gas reduction targets, will have to step up its generation of renewable energy—and expand its capacity for transmitting that power across long distances. But development fights such as the one over Green Path North are one reason the state has concentrated much of its efforts not in the area of power generation but in the area of conservation.

The state is aggressively pushing energy efficiency. A 2008 law allows local governments to create assessment districts to provide low-cost, long-term financing for homeowners who install solar panels or upgrade their heating and air-conditioning units. "Strict building codes and energy-saving requirements for home appliances and light bulbs—measures that have been largely ignored by Texas—make an excellent fit for California, where residents are used to being regulated," reports *The New York Times*.[a]

---

[a]Kate Galbraith, "California and Texas: Renewable Energy's Odd Couple," *New York Times,* October 18, 2009, 3.

---

create ever-tougher but elusive standards for the future.[34] But Schwarzenegger's successor, Democrat Jerry Brown, signed a bill in 2011 codifying the 33 percent target for 2020.

Terry Tamminen, who served as an energy and environmental adviser to Schwarzenegger, argues that ambitious targets have helped move things in the right direction. "Everyone forgets that the original law set the target at 2017, so by accelerating the date we've moved it up by at least 5 years," he said in a 2009 interview.[35] By 2014, Matt Rodriguez said that the state was on track to meet its goals for reduction of greenhouse gas and the renewable energy target.[36] Running for reelection that year, Governor Brown said he intended to set carbon standards for 2030 that would be "far more stringent."[37]

Cutting Back on Coal

At the same time that states are promoting generation of energy from renewable sources, some are also simply clamping down on coal. Construction was canceled on nearly 100 coal-fired power plants in 2008 and 2009 because of environmental concerns. The Texas energy giant TXU Corporation shelved 8 out of 11 planned coal plants, investing heavily in wind energy instead. Only 3 of 10 plants that were once planned for southern Illinois remained active.[38]

Nowadays, wherever a coal-fired plant is proposed, the Sierra Club or an allied group steps forward with a lawsuit to block it.[39] Environmentalists believe that delays, and their concomitant costs, can only serve to move power generation away from coal. "Each time you step back and reassess the politics and economics of coal," said Bob Eye, a Sierra Club attorney and former counsel to the Kansas Department of Health and Environment (KDHE), "things are more difficult for the coal plant proponents."[40]

In 2007, Rod Bremby, KDHE secretary, blocked a pair of massive coal-fired power plants. Citing that year's *Massachusetts v. EPA* Supreme Court decision (which sought to force the EPA to regulate greenhouse gases), Bremby overruled his own staff and rejected Sunflower Electric Power Corporation's application to build a $3.6 billion power plant project outside Holcomb. Bremby was the first regulator to block a power plant strictly out of concern for climate change and without getting specific statutory cover from the legislature. "To approve the permit didn't seem a reasonable option, given that carbon dioxide is a pollutant and we're talking about 11 million tons of carbon," he said.[41] Since Bremby's original decision, more than 120 power plants have been retired or new projects have seen their permits denied, delayed, or withdrawn for reasons similar to the ones he cited.

A lot of this had to do with environmentalists' complaints and regulation, but another factor was at work as well. Thanks to a boom in **fracking**, natural gas prices dropped in 2012 below $3 per million British thermal units (BTUs), down from about $8 in 2008, and some gas-fueled plants were able to generate electricity for about 2 cents per kilowatt, or less than half what it costs to run many coal-fired operations. That year, "natural gas pulled even with coal as a fuel source for power plants," according to *The Washington Post,* with coal usage down 17 percent and natural gas up 27 percent.[42] The trend of electric companies' shutting down coal-fired plant capacity was set to continue at least through 2016.

Fracking itself remains controversial. New technologies have made it possible to extract oil from rock as thick as concrete through horizontal drilling and fracking, which involves pumping a mixture of water, sand, and chemicals into the ground to extract natural gas and oil. As a result, states such as North Dakota have experienced an energy boom. The high price tag of those extraction techniques means they're economically feasible only now that the price of a barrel of crude oil at times hovers around $100. Oil companies are rushing to tap the ground before the cheap pre-boom leases they signed with mineral rights owners expire, and North Dakota is reaping the benefits. By the end of 2010, the state had more than 6,000 wells capable of producing oil and gas, and an additional 20,000 wells could be drilled within the next 10 or 20 years, followed by more than 30 years of pumping oil.

In the summer of 2014, the unemployment rate in North Dakota was less than 3 percent—the lowest in the nation and less than half the national rate. For the past hundred years, the number of people in North Dakota has remained virtually stagnant. It's the only state in the country that had more residents in 1930 than it does today. Now the population is booming in the western part of the state; the state added 50,000 residents between 2010 and 2013, boosting its total population by 8 percent. "This boom is just wild and crazy," said Ward Koeser, mayor of Williston, the largest city in the center of the oil activity. "It's more than you can fathom."[43]

North Dakota isn't the only state to use fracking for its economic rewards. Early forms of

---

Fracking
A process in which water, sand, and chemicals are pumped into the ground to enable the extraction of natural gas and oil

fracking have been around since 1947, but the vast increase in its use in recent years has made fracking perhaps the top environmental concern facing states, and they differ in how they balance the risks and rewards.

The benefits of fracking are readily apparent. According to the Heritage Foundation, the process has been used to retrieve more than 7 billion barrels of oil and more than 600 trillion cubic feet of natural gas. One trillion cubic feet of natural gas is enough to heat 15 million homes for 1 year. Fracking has made it possible to tap the Marcellus Shale in the Mid-Atlantic region, one of the richest natural gas deposits in the world. This rock formation lies more than a mile beneath the earth's surface, and until fracking came along, there was no economical way to extract the gas. Ohio Republican governor John Kasich has referred to the formation as "a gift from heaven."

All this exploration has helped lower energy prices and create jobs. But along with its benefits, fracking presents many potential environmental hazards. Industry officials insist that their processes are safe, but environmentalists are worried that the chemicals released in fracking pollute both air and groundwater. A federal Department of Energy study released in 2014 found no evidence that chemicals or brine water contaminated drinking water at a site in western Pennsylvania. After 18 months of monitoring—the first time an energy company allowed independent researchers to study a drilling site—the scientists found that chemical-laced fluids used to free gas stayed almost a mile below drinking water supplies. A separate study in 2014 found that faulty well construction, not fracking itself, caused water pollution near drilling sites.

Still, some are worried just about the amount of water that fracking requires. Each well can use up to 5 million gallons of water per year—in some parts of the country, even more. In Carroll County, Ohio, alone, the state has issued permits to drill 161 wells. Across the state, as many as 2,250 wells could be drilled to get at the Utica Shale by 2015.

In addition to concerns about water consumption and pollution, activists who say "no fracking way" point to the increase in seismic activity in states such as Colorado and Texas where fracking has been employed. The problem seems to be the wastewater—the water that has been used in fracking and then retrieved and injected into waste wells. The waste wells can be thousands of feet deep, under high pressure that can build up for months or years, eventually causing earthquakes. A study released in 2014 said that the 2,500 small earthquakes over the previous 5 years in Jones, Oklahoma, were likely triggered by oil and gas extraction. The largest earthquake in the state's history, a 5.7-magnitude quake in 2011 that damaged about 200 buildings, was "likely caused by fluid injection," according to scientists from the University of Oklahoma, Columbia University, and the U.S. Geological Survey.

Scientists say that the earthquake risk caused by fracking could be reduced by regulations demanding more careful placement and construction of wells. Following a series of earthquakes in 2011, Ohio instituted a moratorium on new wastewater injection permits. It resumed issuing the permits the following year, after putting more safeguards in place.

In general, the fracking boom has been so rapid that it has seen comparatively little regulation. A study released in 2012 by OMB Watch, a research and advocacy group, found that only 13 of the 30 states engaged in natural gas drilling had passed legislation related to fracking. Hundreds of other bills were under consideration in other states.

Some government officials, however, have demanded further study before allowing fracking to proceed. Even as neighboring states such as Pennsylvania were going full steam ahead with fracking, Maryland governor Martin O'Malley, a Democrat, placed a de facto moratorium on the practice in 2011, pending completion in 2014 of a $1.5 million study by the state Department of the Environment. The report warned that fracking would cause air pollution and create jobs that were dangerous for workers.

Another Democrat, New York governor Andrew Cuomo, had appeared to be ready to give fracking the green light, but after 7 years of study, he decided to put off lifting the state's moratorium, pending still more review. Antifracking

An oil worker returns home from a day of work in Bakken, North Dakota. The state's fracking boom has caused its economy and population to surge, but environmental concerns and the potential risk of increased seismic activity have resulted in calls for more regulation and antifracking protests.

protesters had been stalking Cuomo for months—not just at speaking engagements but at his home and office—while celebrities such as Lady Gaga lined up to express their disapproval of fracking. "I literally see them everywhere I go," Cuomo said of the hydraulic fracturing opponents in 2014. "One of my daughters joked, we were pulling up to an event and she said, 'We must be in the wrong place. There's no fracking protesters.'"[44]

Limiting Land Use

In addition to addressing the consumption of energy directly, states are looking at ways to cut back on individuals' use of fuel. Many environmentalists blame sprawl—the growth of suburban and exurban communities far from central cities and existing transit and transportation infrastructure—for contributing to the greater consumption of natural resources.

Tom Adams, president of the California League of Conservation Voters, argues that his state must cut down on sprawl to meet its long-term environmental goals. In 2008, the state took a big step in the direction that Adams favored by enacting a major new land-use law.

Typically, land-use policies are decided at the local level, with cities or counties passing zoning laws, or ordinances, that, for instance, keep industrial sites separate from residential areas or require that no more than one house be built on each quarter acre of land. Some areas impose only loose zoning restrictions—or none at all, as in Houston. But state governments often do influence land-use policy, if only through their transportation programs. Numerous states, led by Maryland, have enacted policies in recent years aimed at cutting down on sprawl—saying that the state will not build infrastructure outside approved development areas, for instance. Most such laws have proved to be largely toothless.

California's 2008 law, known as SB 375, goes further than most. SB 375 directs the California Air Resources Board to come up with targets for reducing emissions from cars and trucks. Regional planning boards will then rewrite their master growth plans in ways that seek to meet those targets—for instance, by planning more housing near existing mass-transit lines. The regions that come closest to the goals will be rewarded with extra federal and state transportation dollars.

It's no surprise that SB 375 was backed by environmentalists, but it also had the support of California's home builders, who liked the prospect

Sprawl
The rapid growth of a metropolitan area, typically as a result of specific types of zoning and development

Zoning laws
Regulations that control how land can be used

Local Focus

Local Governments Pay the Price for Fracking Boom

The shale gas market is an economic boon for the 30-odd states that permit fracking. The severance tax that states impose on the process adds up. In 2010, it generated more than $11 billion. The flow of that revenue goes straight into state and federal treasuries, as does increased corporate income tax revenue from energy companies profiting from fracking.

Localities, however, enjoy no such benefits. Instead, they get stuck with all the fracking problems: noise from blasting, storage of toxic chemicals, degraded water sources, and heavy truck traffic, as well as the rising costs of cleaning up the detritus fracking leaves behind. North Dakota counties affected by hydraulic fracturing have reported to the state Department of Mineral Resources' Oil and Gas Division that traffic, air pollution, job-site and highway accidents, sexual assaults, bar fights, prostitution, and drunk driving have all increased.

In addition, fracking, in many cases, negatively impacts property values, which in turn depresses property tax revenue. For property owners who own the rights to the oil and gas on their land, the effects of drilling can be offset by royalty payments. But localities have no revenue offset if properties lose value.

According to a 2013 survey by business researchers at the University of Denver, persons bidding on homes near fracking locations reduced their offers by as much as 25 percent. In North Texas, the Wise County Central Appraisal Review Board reduced the appraised value of a family's home and 10-acre ranchette by more than 70 percent. The board agreed to the extraordinary reduction as a result of numerous environmental problems related to fracking just 1 year after the first drilling rig went up on the property.

Although a number of states want to expand fracking, localities have some leverage. They control land-use policies, zoning, and property rights. In New York, the state's highest court upheld the right of two of the Empire State's local governments to establish zoning laws that keep out fracking companies. The court's 5-to-2 decision was based solely on reaffirming the towns' rights to make their own zoning choices. In its ruling, the majority noted that the towns had engaged in a "reasonable exercise" of their zoning authority, that they had "studied the issue and acted within their home-rule powers in determining that gas drilling would permanently alter and adversely affect the deliberately cultivated small-town character of their communities."

In Colorado, where the cities of Boulder, Broomfield, Fort Collins, and Lafayette have adopted antifracking measures, Governor John Hickenlooper in 2014 announced the appointment of a task force to develop recommendations that would reduce land-use conflicts when oil and gas facilities are located near homes, schools, businesses, and recreation areas. He also asked the Colorado Oil and Gas Conservation Commission to dismiss litigation challenging the city of Longmont's ban on hydraulic fracturing and to call on all parties to withdraw ballot initiatives on the topic.

Ironically, one of the earliest local–state challenges came from Exxon's chief executive officer. As a homeowner in an upscale community in Bartonville, Texas, the CEO found himself at odds with a local fracking operation. He filed suit to block construction of a water tower near his home—a tower that would increase fracking in the area—alleging that it would create "a noise nuisance and traffic hazards."

Source: Adapted from Frank Shafroth, "Fracking's Financial Losers," *Governing*, September 2014, 62.

of greater predictability in the zoning process. One of the main goals of the bill is to induce localities to coordinate their major planning tasks: transportation, land use, and housing. Few had been doing that. In addition, SB 375 provides relief from certain air-quality standards that had, perversely, discouraged developers from undertaking infill projects. "Builders thrive on certainty, knowing what the rules are," said Tim Coyle of the California Building Industry Association.[45] Local

Manny Diaz (right), attends a green certification ceremony. As Miami mayor, Diaz promoted Miami 21, a redevelopment plan intended to manage growth and sustainability for the city in the 21st century. It was approved by the City Commission in 2009 after much debate.

jurisdictions as California and Maryland. In 2012, the Republican Party made opposition to Agenda 21 part of its official platform.

Still, the notion that sprawl is bad both for the environment and for the health of communities has become fashionable over the past decade—perhaps nowhere more so than in Miami. That's surprising because, when it comes to building and construction, Miami had always been a wide-open town, home to endless rows of towering condo buildings. In late 2009, the city council approved a new zoning code that is likely to have a profound effect on development. Ardently promoted by Miami mayor Manny Diaz but drafted in large part by architect Elizabeth Plater-Zyberk, the code embraces the **New Urbanism** principles that made Plater-Zyberk and Andrés Duany (her husband and professional partner) famous.

The new code, known as Miami 21, seeks to encourage street-level pedestrian activity and reduce automobile dependence. The hope is that neighborhoods will fit within a comfortable scale, with plenty of shops out front and buildings that conform to fixed height limits, with upper-story setbacks from the street. At the same time, the goal is to create corridors with enough density that public transit will be viable. But the most important idea may be the decision to focus on entire neighborhoods rather than on individual projects.

New Urbanism codes have been adopted in various places around the country for new projects in previously unbuilt areas (greenfields) and

governments also supported the law; it provides incentives and creates a policymaking framework, but it doesn't create specific mandates for any individual region. "It's really a very important piece of legislation," said Peter Kasabach of New Jersey Future, a smart-growth group. "How we develop our land is going to impact our greenhouse gas targets. A lot of folks think that if we drive hybrids or change our lightbulbs, we'll be okay. But a significant amount of our greenhouse gas targets will be met by how we get around and reduce vehicle miles traveled."[46]

But various regions of California have struggled to meet requirements under the law. For instance, a judge ruled in 2012 that a transportation plan put forward by the San Diego Association of Governments relied too much on temporary measures such as telecommuting to meet specific emission reduction targets, with the pace of reductions achieved slipping over time (from 14 percent per capita in 2020 to 9 percent by 2050). In addition, Tea Party activists and other conservatives have come to oppose such zoning restrictions, seeing them as a challenge to private-property rights. One particular document that has drawn their ire is Agenda 21, a sustainability program adopted by the United Nations back in 1992. Police have been called out to quell protests against the plan even in such pro-zoning

New Urbanism
A design movement that seeks to promote walkable communities through transit-oriented, mixed-use development

for specific areas undergoing redevelopment, such as riverfronts. But Miami became the first city of any size to attempt to apply these principles throughout its borders.

Advocates of the approach are making grand claims about its potential to transform much of the landscape and have explicitly promised that it will make Miami far more environmentally friendly as well. "A whole city is changing its strategy consistent with this idea of preventing climate change," says Armando Carbonell, chair of the Department of Planning and Urban Form at the Lincoln Institute of Land Policy.[47]

Miami was horrendously overbuilt during the overheated housing market that collapsed in 2007. It is home to thousands of foreclosed condos. "Our economic condition stinks down here," Truly Burton, a lobbyist for the Builders Association of South Florida, said bluntly after the code had passed.[48] Developers, looking for a hedge against the next downturn, over the past couple of years have taken advantage of Miami 21's mixed-use provisions to help convert all-condo buildings into combined live–work spaces, which has succeeded in increasing residency in areas such as the city's downtown and Wynwood arts district.

Going Green

In addition to regulating power sources and emissions, some states and localities have set new rules in recent years to promote greater energy efficiency in buildings, as well as the creation of so-called green jobs that would contribute to the health of the environment. We'll explore in the section below the still-hazy definition of what constitutes a green job, but many local officials have been insisting on more green buildings. Newly elected Pittsburgh mayor Bill Peduto called in 2014 for energy audits of all municipal buildings every 10 years, for example. But Peduto and other mayors are looking beyond their cities' own buildings to push for greener infrastructure in the private sector as well.

Green Building

In 2008, Chicago mayor Richard Daley unveiled what *The New York Times* described as "perhaps the most aggressive plan of any major American city to reduce heat-trapping gases."[49] The plan, which aimed to cut Chicago's carbon output by 25 percent by 2020, focuses on tougher **building codes**.

"Green" building codes have drawn significant attention among local governments seeking to cut back on carbon emissions. Buildings account for 40 to 50 percent of a city's energy demands. Buildings use 25 percent of the drinking water and produce 35 percent of the solid waste, mostly in the form of construction materials. And buildings produce anywhere from 30 to 70 percent of municipal carbon emissions, according to the American Institute of Architects. Many cities have received grants from former president Bill Clinton's foundation to rewrite their codes, but far more are pursuing such strategies on their own. In 2012, nearly 25,000 local officials attended the Greenbuild conference in San Francisco sponsored by the U.S. Green Building Council.

The trend has exploded in recent years. From 2003 to 2009, the number of cities with green building programs grew by more than 600 percent, from 22 to 138, according to the American Institute of Architects. By 2009, 20 percent of municipalities with populations of more than 50,000 had adopted such programs.

By and large, cities' green building programs are based on the standards of the council's rating system, known as LEED (Leader in Energy and Environmental Design). To encourage developers to build green, cities are offering tax incentives, reductions in permit fees, and access to grants for projects that meet certain environmental benchmarks. Some cities offer bonus density allowances; a green building project might be exempt from height restrictions, for example. But the most popular incentive by far is expedited permitting for green projects. This policy has proven extremely attractive to cities, because they can implement it at virtually no cost to themselves.

Some cities are going further and actually requiring energy-efficient construction through their building codes. In 2006, Washington, D.C.,

---

Building codes
Rules regarding the standards for structures; they mainly have to do with safety issues but sometimes also include requirements for things such as exterior pedestrian walkways

became the first major U.S. city to mandate green construction for all private buildings of at least 50,000 square feet, beginning in 2012. And in 2007, Boston became the first city actually to implement a green requirement for private construction and renovation projects.

Since then, a handful of other cities have adopted similar mandates. In 2009, the New York City Council began requiring the owners of the city's largest buildings to perform energy audits and upgrade lighting, and the council is considering more rules regarding the heating and insulation of individual apartments. In 2008, San Francisco adopted the strictest codes of any U.S. city so far, requiring green standards for any residential building taller than 75 feet and commercial buildings of more than 5,000 square feet. That same year, California became the first state to include green environmental standards, such as requirements to recycle construction waste, reduce the use of polluting materials, and improve energy efficiency in new structures, in its statewide building code; these rules took effect in 2010.

Builders routinely have said that they support the goals of such regulations, but they have often also complained that they are too costly. Nevertheless, increased energy efficiency of new and existing structures has become a primary goal for all levels of government. In 2007, in response to requests from the U.S. Conference of Mayors and other groups, Congress authorized up to $2 billion annually in block grants for state and local programs designed to save energy. That authorization went unfunded until the 2009 enactment of the American Recovery and Reinvestment Act (ARRA), the federal stimulus bill. ARRA included $3.2 billion for energy-efficiency block grants for states and localities and an additional $5 billion in funding for Department of Energy **weatherization** efforts, much of which also amounted to grants for the states.

Weatherization, at least for the first year after ARRA passed, became a case study in the difficulties of quickly ramping up an entirely new program within the federal system. Neither the states nor the federal government had ever devoted much money to weatherization, and suddenly both were spending billions. In addition, because the work relied on great numbers of local providers—such as nonprofit groups and individual contractors—many states were slow to get projects under way.

For example, Washington State fell badly behind schedule during the first year of its stepped-up weatherization efforts. By summer's end, local agencies had weatherized just 10 percent of the units the state had planned. The problem drew the attention of Democratic governor Christine Gregoire's office, which helped untangle some of the regulatory and labor law problems that were hampering efforts. By the end of 2009, the state had exceeded its targeted goals.

In general, however, the boom in green building codes hasn't exactly triggered a green building boom. In 2009, Seattle employed incentives to encourage 12 developers to build projects that would generate all their own electricity and use only water that fell onsite. Three years later, just one such project was under construction, and only two more were in the planning stages.

Green Jobs

Another area where environmentalists and others have made grand promises—which, at least initially, look overblown—is the notion of **green jobs**. Just what a green job is has been hard to define. Clearly, making wind turbines would qualify. But most of the jobs that are labeled "green" are positions that already exist and bear only tangential relationships to the environment. A study done for the state of Colorado counted some Wal-Mart employees as green because a percentage of the products the retailer sells are certified by Energy Star, the federal government's program to rate the efficiency of appliances. Cashiers, janitors, accountants, secretaries, lawyers, and even government officials—all can be categorized as "green" workers if their work touches energy efficiency in almost any way.[50]

Weatherization
The practice of protecting buildings from the elements (e.g., by installing insulation) both to improve their habitability and to cut down on energy use

---

Green jobs
Occupations that contribute to environmental sustainability

However you define green jobs, generating them—another central goal of ARRA—has been slower than some promised. Many people still are counting on green-collar jobs not only to revive the economy but also to restore the manufacturing sector in places where it has long been in decline. "American cities have suffered more than anyone from the loss of manufacturing jobs," said Minneapolis mayor R. T. Rybak. "Cities have become the green incubators for America."[51]

> However you define green jobs, generating them—another central goal of ARRA—has been slower than some promised. Many people still are counting on green-collar jobs not only to revive the economy but also to restore the manufacturing sector in places where it has long been in decline.

Plenty of studies have suggested that there will be an explosion of investment and job creation in the green sector. The Apollo Alliance, a coalition of business, labor, and environmental groups, estimates that a $300 billion investment over 10 years would create 3.3 million jobs in renewable energy, hybrid cars, and infrastructure replacement.[52] The U.S. Conference of Mayors forecasts there will be 4.2 million green jobs by 2038 and suggests that cities and towns prepare to compete for them.[53]

According to Fran Pavley, the California state senator, $3.3 billion, or about 60 percent of the venture capital devoted to clean technology in the country, was invested in her state in 2009.[54] "Everything that is good for global warming is good for jobs," Van Jones, who served briefly as a White House adviser and wrote the 2008 book *The Green Collar Economy,* said in a 2008 conference call with reporters. "Buildings do not weatherize themselves, wind turbines do not construct themselves, solar panels do not install themselves. Real people are going to have to get up in the morning and do these things."

However, despite all its apparent promise, the interest in green technology has not yet translated into either mass employment or a huge economic windfall. The Brookings Institution estimated that only 100,000 new green jobs were created between 2003 and 2010. "People are talking about this in the future, but it's not happening today," said Eric Crawford, president of Greenman Alliance, a Milwaukee-based recruiting firm. "Everyone wants a green job," but the demand for such jobs totally outstrips the supply.[55] The Bureau of Labor Statistics released a definition of "green jobs" in 2010; 2 years later, it found that just under 2 million people were employed by companies engaged in "green goods and services," although that number ticked up above 3 million in its latest survey. (See Map 16-2.)

And government investment in clean technology has not always reaped large dividends. Under New Jersey's energy master plan, solar power should account for more than 2 percent of the Garden State's electricity by 2020. But by mid-2008, solar systems were generating only 0.07 percent of current energy needs, despite the fact that the state had already handed out more than $170 million in rebates to encourage their installation. The state revised its goals for solar power in 2010. "We need to do things differently because ratepayers can't keep paying for rebates indefinitely," said Jeanne M. Fox, president of New Jersey's Board of Public Utilities.[56]

"This idea that we're going to have a massive environmental WPA—it's not going to help the economy, it's going to hurt the economy," said Myron Ebell, director of energy and global warming policy at the Competitive Enterprise Institute. (WPA, the Works Progress Administration, was a Depression-era jobs program.) Putting government money into green energy would not create great economic returns, Ebell suggested, because—at least so far—renewable energy is more expensive than dirty fuels such as coal; it also means directing dollars away from other fields entirely. "I believe just on a very simple analysis that there is no question it will take net

MAP 16-2

Green Goods and Services Jobs as a Percentage of Total Employment in a State, 2013

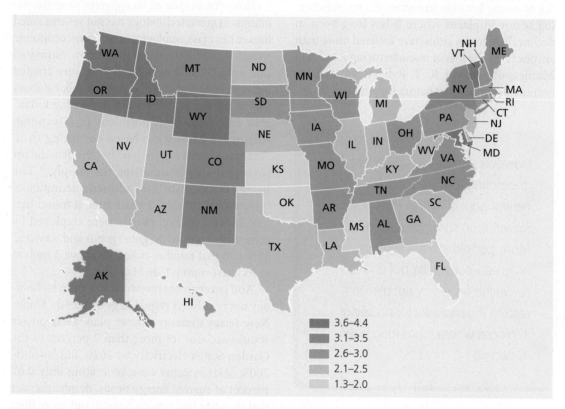

Legend:
- 3.6–4.4
- 3.1–3.5
- 2.6–3.0
- 2.1–2.5
- 1.3–2.0

Source: U.S. Bureau of Labor Statistics, "Table 4: Green Goods and Services (GGS) Employment by State, Annual Averages," March 19, 2013, http://www.bls.gov/news.release/ggqcew.t04.htm.

Note: The GGS scope consists of industries that may produce green goods and services within one or more of the following five groups: (1) energy from renewable sources; (2) energy-efficiency equipment, appliances, buildings, and vehicles, and goods and services that improve the energy efficiency of buildings and the efficiency of energy storage and distribution; (3) pollution reduction and removal, greenhouse gas reduction, and recycling and reuse of goods and services; (4) organic agriculture, sustainable forestry, and soil, water, and wildlife conservation; and (5) governmental and regulatory administration and education, training, and advocacy goods and services.

jobs out of the economy and it will be a net economic harm," Ebell said.[57]

A 2010 study from the McKinsey Global Institute suggests that clean energy will ultimately have less in common with manufacturing sectors than with the semiconductor industry, which once promised to generate millions of high-tech jobs but, instead, mainly employs robots. Green jobs employ only 0.6 percent of the U.S. workforce—a number the McKinsey report suggests won't grow by much. "The bottom line is that these 'clean' industries are too small to create the millions of jobs that are needed right away," said James Manyika, a McKinsey director.[58]

But even if the critics are correct, the goal of green investment is not only to stimulate the economy but also to help clean up the environment. In a column published in *The New York Times* just after the November 2008 election, former vice president Al Gore called for large governmental investments in clean energy as the optimum way to address climate change—a shift from his traditional focus on increased regulation of carbon pollution.[59] "With his op-ed, Gore has reversed the longstanding green-lobby prioritization of regulation first and investment second," wrote Michael Shellenberger and Ted Nordhaus for the *New Republic*.[60]

Adaptation

In 2006, the U.S. Army Corps of Engineers proposed a plan to help protect Long Beach, home to 33,000 people on a barrier island just off of Long Island, New York. The plan involved the erection of sand dunes and the elevation of beaches along more than 6 miles of coast to protect the island. But the project would have cost $98 million, and the city would have had to chip in a $7 million share. And people just didn't like the idea of having their ocean views obscured and giving up their nice, wide, flat beaches. So the city council voted unanimously to block the project.

It was a decision Long Beach came to regret. In 2012, the storm known as Sandy did some $200 million worth of property damage to the town. Neighboring communities on the barrier island had approved construction of 15-foot-high dunes and were able to avoid suffering catastrophic losses in the storm.[61]

The effects of Superstorm Sandy in 2012 and other high-impact weather events turned the attention of some policymakers away from the question of how to prevent climate change and toward planning for coping with its effects. If climate change is already having real impacts—and will continue to do so, even if efforts to reduce greenhouse gas emissions succeed—state and local governments have little choice but to deal with these effects. So how should state and local governments begin to adapt to the resulting problems, such as flooding, coastal erosion, and species loss? Should they, for example, build higher seawalls to offset rising sea levels? Many officials in areas affected by Sandy became believers, but facing price tags potentially reaching into the hundreds of billions of dollars, some remained skeptical. "I don't think there's any practical way to build barriers in the oceans," New York City mayor Michael Bloomberg said in 2012. "Even if you spent a fortune, it's not clear to me that you would get much value for it."[62]

Up until 2007 or so, most environmentalists dismissed talk about **adaptation** to climate change.

Adaptation
Taking steps to prepare for and deal with the effects of climate change

Their concern seemed to be that shifting the policy debate away from efforts to prevent climate change by cutting down on carbon emissions amounted to conceding to conservatives' denials that human activity causes global warming. They also felt that planning for the effects brought about by climate change was defeatist. "It was seen as a potential smokescreen behind which high-emission countries could hide so they wouldn't have to make binding agreements to reduce," said Nathan Hultman, a professor of science, technology, and international affairs at Georgetown University.[63]

Some advocates still argue that discussion about how to adapt to climate shifts amounts to a distraction from the larger project of reducing emissions. "There are people out there working on adaptation, but I have to say the overwhelming effort is to try to reduce our emissions," said Tom Adams, president of the California League of Conservation Voters. "At this point, some fairly significant climate impacts are inevitable, but a lot of us feel that this is a genuine planetary emergency, and it's imperative that we cut emissions."[64] But the notion that talking about adaptation is just a smokescreen to conceal the lack of effort to reduce greenhouse gases seems to be fading away. There's a growing recognition among those concerned about global warming that even if carbon emissions were reduced to zero tomorrow—which clearly isn't going to happen—there is already enough carbon dioxide in the air to guarantee more changes to come. The Intergovernmental Panel on Climate Change, which shared the 2007 Nobel Peace Prize with former vice president Al Gore, has stressed the importance of adaptation in its recent reports, and in 2007 a group of scientists published an article in the journal *Nature* titled "Lifting the Taboo on Adaptation."[65]

As a practical matter, policymakers are increasingly concerned about how to plan for

On January 1, 2010, stores selling food or beverages in the District of Columbia began charging a 5-cent user fee on every paper or plastic bag. The money collected goes to cleaning the Anacostia River, and the law is meant to encourage shoppers to provide their own reusable bags.

Environmentalists hope that the conversion to cleaner energy technologies such as wind power will not only curb carbon emissions but also provide a new source of jobs. Here, Cerro Coso Community College instructor Mike Cervantes explains safety procedures to students about to make their first climb on a wind turbine in Tehachapi, California. His students enrolled in the technical course after being laid off from auto or construction work.

the climate-related changes their communities are facing. **Resilience** has become a big buzzword for civic leaders who are looking for ways their communities can cope with and bounce back from environmental changes that are already widely evident—not just shocks such as fires and floods but ongoing differences in areas such as the availability of fresh water. The Rockefeller Foundation is running a program to offer assistance to 100 cities around the world that are finding ways to become more resilient. While noting the importance of British Columbia's first-on-the-continent carbon tax, Vancouver mayor Gregor Robertson said his city is striving not only to reduce greenhouse gases through greener building codes and the like but also preparing for the damage existing emissions are already causing. "The successful cities of the future will be those making the investments and changes necessary to adapt to the impacts of climate change," he wrote. "Climate change poses a serious risk to global economic and social stability, and resilient cities will prove to be attractive draws for people and capital."[66] For his part, President Obama has stressed the importance of building resilience in forums such as the United Nations (which has its own urban resilience program) and international climate treaty negotiations that began in 2015.

According to an online clearinghouse of state efforts compiled by the Georgetown Climate Center, fewer than half the states in 2014 were attempting to protect themselves from the effects of climate change.[67] Not surprisingly, the issue has drawn the most attention in areas along coastlines, such as in Maryland and Oregon. In 2011, the city of Boston released a climate action plan to prepare for sea levels' rising 2 to 6 feet by the end of the century, depending on the rate of polar ice melt. Added to a hurricane storm surge, some models show parts of Boston under 10 feet of water. Researchers have warned city officials that by midcentury such storms could happen every 2 to 3 years. In 2014, Massachusetts officials announced a $50 million resiliency plan that included projects to rebuild sea walls, repair dams, and help coastal communities rebuild natural defenses against storm surges. That same year, Washington Democratic governor Jay Inslee signed an executive order updating the state's emission limits and creating a cap-and-trade program modeled on California's, stressing the need for the state to reduce energy use and also adapt to the effects of climate change. "This is not a hypothetical thing for governors on the West Coast—this is fire alarms and floods," he said.

Resilience
Like *adaptation*, a term borrowed from biology to describe efforts to prepare for effects of climate change

"It's not a next-century issue. This is a next half-hour issue."[68]

But because climate change will manifest itself differently in different locales, adaptation questions are drawing attention all over. For instance, government officials in Vermont have been working with the state university to begin crafting plans to help the forestry and farming industries cope with the local effects of climate change.

In parts of the nearby Cascade Range in Washington State, snowpack has declined by as much as 60 percent. In response, King County, which includes Seattle, has begun planning backward from 2050, formulating plans to adapt to the climate change effects that are seen as likely to occur even if carbon emissions are cut significantly between now and then. For example, officials expect coastal erosion problems associated with rising sea levels, health effects such as new infectious diseases and heat stroke, increasing numbers of forest fires, and ecological issues affecting salmon. In 2007 the county council agreed to a tax inspired by such looming dangers, part of county executive Ron Sims's $335 million plan to bolster river levees and reduce flood risks. The county is now building climate change risks into all its long-term planning and policy development. "We're learning to define ourselves not in 2009 terms but in 2050 terms," said Sims, who went on to serve with the federal Department of Housing and Urban Development. "We're making decisions based on something that has not occurred yet."[69]

Like most environmentalists, Ron Burke, the Midwest climate change director for the Union of Concerned Scientists, says that both responses to climate change—reduction of carbon emissions, or **mitigation**, and adaptation—are important. Still, he says, "If you had to argue one versus the other, which I don't think is really helpful, I think mitigation is a higher priority given the urgency with which we need to create these reductions. You see that reflected in how most cities and states are going about their planning. They're definitely

doing the mitigation piece first and then moving onto adaptation."[70]

One of the world's biggest adaptation efforts is taking place in the Netherlands. The Dutch are spending billions to create "floating communities" that can rise with floodwaters and to otherwise reengineer their long coastline. They expect to spend $100 per year per person on climate-proofing over the next century, according to *The Washington Post*. Although some say their efforts are excessive, according to *The Post*, U.S. officials have consulted with the Dutch about how to protect New Orleans and other low-lying coastal areas.[71]

Relatively few jurisdictions in the United States have turned their full attention to adaptation and planning questions. Even normally proactive California has barely paid attention to adaptation issues and is unprepared for the flooding, coastal erosion, and loss of wildlife habitat predicted to occur in coming decades as the results of higher temperatures.[72] Only in 2008 did Governor Arnold Schwarzenegger issue an executive order directing state agencies to identify the state's biggest vulnerabilities to rising sea levels and draft an "adaptation strategy."[73] That strategy, formally adopted in 2009, was revised in 2012. The California Coastal Commission may require all waterfront communities to include forecasts for extreme flooding and sea-level rise in their plans; those that don't comply risk losing some state funds. In 2012, the San Francisco Bay Conservation and Development Commission amended its San Francisco Bay Plan to make sure projected sea-level rise is accounted for by new projects, such as a planned $1.5 billion development on Treasure Island, which rests in the bay midway between San Francisco and Oakland.

States and local governments face a practical challenge when it comes to crafting adaptation plans. Much of the science in this area has been, not surprisingly, global in scope. Thus, planning for climate change's local impacts will require experts to downscale the large-scale data to make them applicable to and useful for communities. According to Sims, it is imperative for states, cities, and counties to accept the need to make decisions based on scientific modeling rather than

---

Mitigation
Reduction of emissions of greenhouse gases and other steps taken to curb the forces that cause climate change

historical experience. "With all the discussion we've had on global warming, I am stunned that people haven't realized that it's actually going to occur," he said in 2007. "The ice caps are melting now. They're not going to refreeze next year because we reduce our emissions. We're going to live in that world. So plan for it."[74]

> States and local governments face a practical challenge when it comes to crafting adaptation plans. Much of the science in this area has been, not surprisingly, global in scope. Thus, planning for climate change's local impacts will require experts to downscale the large-scale data to make them applicable to and useful for communities.

Issues to Watch

Growing Partisanship and Skepticism

Not everyone believes we are going to be living in a world forever altered by climate change. In 2012, James Lawrence Powell, executive director of the National Physical Science Consortium, searched 13,950 peer-reviewed articles on climate change dating back to 1991. He found that only 24 rejected the idea of human-caused global warming.[75] Nevertheless, public opinion polls in recent years have shown that Americans are increasingly skeptical about the alarm bells that have been sounding about climate change. A Gallup Poll in March 2014 found that 51 percent of Americans worried about global warming "a great deal" or "a fair amount"— well below the peak of 72 percent in 2000.[76] Polling by Gallup and other groups has consistently found that the public does not consider global warming in particular and the environment in general nearly as important as other issues, such as the economy.

A series of small controversies helped shift opinions on climate change in recent years, including a mistake about glacier loss in the Himalayas in a report by the Intergovernmental Panel on Climate Change and a scandal involving European climate scientists whose e-mails, suggesting they had withheld contradictory data, were hacked into and released. Official inquiries subsequently cleared the scientists of any serious wrongdoing, but the damage was done.[77]

Just as a series of mild winters in the Northern Hemisphere and a batch of devastating hurricanes had contributed to fears about global warming in earlier years, an unusually cold and snowy winter in 2010 eased such concerns for some. Senator Jim DeMint, R-S.C., an opponent of climate change legislation, tweeted in the midst of a series of large snowfalls in the Washington, D.C., region, "It's going to keep snowing until Al Gore cries 'uncle.'"[78] Those concerned about global warming tended to make the opposite point during the heat of summer.

Media attention devoted to the climate change issue turned largely into disquisitions about whether all these points raised by skeptics had been blown out of proportion and why climate scientists, who appeared to have won the argument about whether global warming was real, now appeared to be on the defensive on the public relations front.

But advocates for measures addressing climate change were losing ground in Congress, as well. A cap-and-trade system that was the centerpiece of the climate change bill passed by the U.S. House in June 2009 appeared dead even before the major Senate climate change bill was introduced in April 2010. Interior Secretary Ken Salazar said during a March 2010 CNBC interview, "I think the term 'cap and trade' is not in the lexicon anymore."[79]

At the state level in 2010, a number of legislatures debated legislation that highlighted the skepticism about global warming—notably a resolution adopted in South Dakota urging schools to offer "balanced teaching" about global warming, saying that it "is a scientific theory rather than a proven fact." In 2012, conservative groups led by the American Legislative Exchange Council and the Heartland Institute attempted to persuade legislators to roll back renewable energy requirements, which they claimed would come at a cost to consumers.

What is most striking for political scientists, as opposed to climate scientists, is not only how much the ground has shifted on this issue but also how partisan it has become. As climate change began to emerge as an issue of pressing concern a few years ago, it was associated with Democrats such as Al Gore, and many of the leading doubters were Republicans, such as James Inhofe of Oklahoma, who chairs the Senate Environment and Public Works Committee when the GOP holds the majority.

Yet many of the voices calling loudest for a policy response were Republicans. Senator John McCain, R-Ariz., the GOP presidential nominee in 2008, had sponsored cap-and-trade legislation. Some of the most prominent governors cheerleading for action on the issue were Republicans, including Arnold Schwarzenegger of California, George E. Pataki of New York, Charlie Crist of Florida (who later switched to the Democratic Party), Jon Huntsman Jr. of Utah, and Tim Pawlenty of Minnesota. It was still easier to muster support for climate change legislation among Democrats than among Republicans at all levels of government, but the issue was far less partisan in nature than, say, health care or taxes.

By the 2010 midterm election season, however, it was hard to find a Republican who was raising climate change as an issue—unless it was to denounce it. Some Republicans who had advocated tough environmental measures are leaving the scene, such as Schwarzenegger, who signed a landmark California law capping carbon emissions in 2006 but was term-limited out of office as governor in 2010. Others have switched their position, now advocating more of a market response and shying away from strict governmental controls. That's especially true of Republicans reaching for higher office—including the presidency. Insisting on caps on energy use has become something of a nonstarter for GOP candidates. The March 2012 Gallup poll showed that only half as many Republicans as Democrats were worried about global warming.

"You see growing sentiment that climate change has been exaggerated," said Karlyn Bowman, a polling expert at the American Enterprise Institute, a conservative think tank. Still, she added, she is struck by the growing partisan divide on the issue: "The Republican–Democrat and conservative–liberal differences are quite large."[80]

Opposition to cap-and-trade legislation nearly became official Republican Party dogma. It was one of 10 items on a list that some members of the Republican National Committee wanted candidates to be required to take a stand on; candidates would receive party backing only if they agreed to at least eight. The committee ultimately rejected the idea of such a "purity test," but party candidates have needed no such official sanction to express their disapproval of cap and trade. Sarah Palin had always expressed skepticism that climate change was human-made, but when she was governor of Alaska, she thought her state should prepare for its effects. In late 2010, however, she tweeted that climate science was "bogus."[81]

In 2008 Republican governor Pawlenty of Minnesota appeared with Janet Napolitano, then the Democratic governor of Arizona, in a nationwide radio advertisement criticizing Congress for not addressing climate change. But appearing on NBC's *Meet the Press* in February 2010, Pawlenty, who was briefly a candidate for the presidential nomination in 2012, said, "Cap and trade . . . would be a disaster." "With Tim Pawlenty, I guess he sees that there's a need to talk about climate change in a more skeptical frame to make himself more appealing in a Republican primary," said Jim DiPeso, vice president for policy and communications at Republicans for Environmental Protection.[82]

Other GOP politicians also seem to have experienced their own changes of heart. As a state senator, Scott Brown voted in 2008 in support of Massachusetts's participation in the Regional Greenhouse Gas Initiative (RGGI). During his successful campaign in a special U.S. Senate election in 2010, however, Brown expressed doubts about the science underpinning global warming theories. He explained his new position by saying that RGGI hadn't worked.

Similarly, Marco Rubio, as Speaker of the Florida House, declared in 2007 that "this nation—and ultimately the world—is headed toward emission caps."[83] He backed the idea of creating a state cap-and-trade program the following year. In his 2010 campaign for the U.S. Senate, however, Rubio blasted Crist, his primary opponent, for having pushed the cap-and-trade idea. Rubio said that he doesn't believe the scientific evidence for human-influenced climate change.

It's true that Senator Lindsey Graham, R-S.C., worked on drafting the main Senate climate change bill in 2010 with John Kerry, D-Mass., and Joseph Lieberman, I-Conn. But Graham attracted no other Republicans to the effort and was widely castigated back home in South Carolina for his work. The Charleston County GOP passed a resolution condemning Graham for undermining "Republican leadership and party solidarity for his own benefit."[84] Graham withdrew his support from the bill just before it was introduced because, he said, he was angry about Democratic plans to move immigration legislation onto the Senate floor ahead of it.

This leads straight to a chicken-and-egg question: Are many Republican leaders growing more skeptical about climate change legislation because of concerns raised by their political base? Or are GOP voters following a shift among top officials and the conservative media? "Many ordinary citizens take their cues on complex political issues from leaders of the political party that they identify with," said DiPeso.[85]

But Daniel J. Weiss, senior vice president of the League of Conservation Voters, thinks it is public opinion that is leading the leaders in this case. He cited the frequent attacks against global warming legislation efforts launched by Rush Limbaugh and commentators on Fox News Channel. "That has really riled up their highly conservative base," Weiss said.[86]

He also noted that elected officials are well aware of the opposition to congressional climate change legislation led by energy companies and the U.S. Chamber of Commerce. In 2012, fossil-fuel companies devoted more than $150 million to advertising focused on energy issues. "If you're a Republican," Weiss asked, "would you really stand up to them and risk getting on their wrong side when they have so much money to spend?"[87]

Billionaire investor Tom Steyer sought to level the playing field in 2014, spending millions to promote candidates who took climate change seriously or defeat those who didn't. He spent upwards of $70 million during the 2014 campaign season, including more than $10 million supporting Charlie Crist in his effort to get reelected as Florida's governor, running as a Democrat. As the scientific evidence mounted, some Republicans, such as Crist's opponent, Florida governor Rick Scott, began again to treat climate change as a real issue. "I do think privately—and some not so privately—Republicans are coming to the point where this has been an issue that's been pretty much settled with regard to the science," said Steve Chabot, a GOP former member of Congress from Ohio. "A lot of it has to do with people calming down and saying let's have a conversation."[88]

But for the most part GOP officials continued to downplay the risk. The top Republican leaders in Congress, such as Senator Mitch McConnell of Kentucky and House Speaker John Boehner of Ohio, said either that the jury was still out on whether the planet is in fact warming or that Obama administration proposals to grapple with the issue would hurt the economy. They continued to hammer at the president for delaying a decision about approving the Keystone XL pipeline. Environmentalists warned that the pipeline would increase the flow of dirty oil from Canadian tar sands and thus worsen greenhouse gas emissions, but Republicans described the pipeline delays as a job killer. "Those of us who disagree with [the president] on this issue do not deny climate change; we simply suggest that his priorities are wrong," said Kentucky Republican representative Ed Whitfield at a House hearing in 2014 at which GOP members of Congress pushed back against Democratic claims that they are "climate deniers."[89]

International Agreements

Just a couple of weeks after he was elected president in November 2008, Barack Obama offered a

Local Focus

Cities Seek to Prepare for Local Climate Effects

As is true throughout the Midwest, summer storms have gotten worse in Dubuque, Iowa, leading to flash floods along the Mississippi River. Water speeds downhill toward the Bee Branch Creek, a partially buried waterway that flows beneath several neighborhoods before emptying into the Mississippi. Often, the storms dump so much rain that the creek's concrete channels cannot contain the runoff. Water spills over streets, across backyards, and into basements. It can push open manhole covers, spray out from fire hydrants, and carry away parked cars.

Six times between 1999 and 2014, Dubuque has been declared a presidential disaster area. One storm in 2011 dumped nearly 11 inches of rain on the city in less than 24 hours. The city estimates that since 1999 floods in the Bee Branch Creek watershed have caused $70 million in damage to homes and businesses. Mayor Roy Buol worries that climate change, which has raised the average U.S. temperature by 1.5 degrees since 1895, will only make the storms worse. So Buol and other Dubuque leaders are planning for $200 million in infrastructure improvements to give the city resilience in the face of global warming and natural disasters.

Dubuque is not alone. Cities love their waterfronts, but in an era of fierce storms and rising sea levels, they are investing heavily in infrastructure improvements designed to help them ride out the next storm. It's expensive—Miami Beach is planning to spend $300 million on new storm-water pumping stations alone—but increasingly necessary. "We have approximately $22 billion worth of property value in the seven square miles that make up Miami Beach," said Eric Carpenter, the city's public works director. When you're looking at it from a perspective of having $22 billion in assets, coming up with half a billion dollars to become resilient becomes a little bit more manageable."

South Florida is considered one of the regions most vulnerable to climate change. To address rising sea levels, four area counties have formed a compact to come up with recommendations—more than 100 so far—including a surface water reservoir. By reducing flooding, the reservoir would help cope with extreme storms, such as the one that dumped 22 inches of rain on Palm Beach County on a single day in January 2014.

Just the first phase of the reservoir could cost $150 million, however. Local governments don't have enough extra money to take on such projects alone. "Everything that Norfolk needs to do is $1 billion," said Lori Crouch, a spokeswoman for that southeastern Virginia city. "We don't have $1 billion."

That's why a lot of cities and counties are drawing up wish lists—so they have projects in mind that they can start working on once they receive federal and state aid after disasters strike. "Every time there is a disaster, you use the money you get from the disaster to build up your long-term resiliency," said Niek Veraart, an infrastructure consultant.

Rebuilding after one disaster offers a unique opportunity to learn and prepare for the next. Still, it would be better to put resilience measures in place before the next disaster strikes, rather than afterward. But while it can be hard to secure funds to prevent bad things from happening, money almost inevitably starts to flow once disasters occur. Cities have learned that they can't simply rebuild what was lost but also have to think about making changes that will prevent repetition of the same type of destruction.

Even as cities plan for their wetter, potentially more devastating futures, they are hoping that federal policymakers will provide more forethought—and dollars—to their cause. Coastal communities account for 45 percent of the nation's economy; so the fate of many regions and industries is tied to their survival. "No one could afford to do these projects on their own, [so we] will be looking for financial resources either at the state or federal level," said Jennifer Jurado, director of environmental planning in Broward County, Florida. "As a nation, we can't afford to just allow individual localities to figure it out."

Source: Adapted from Daniel C. Vock, "A Climate of Change," *Governing*, September 2014, http://www.governing.com/topics/transportation-infrastructure/gov-climate-change-cities-resiliency.html.

videotaped address to state leaders gathered at a climate change policy summit in California. "When I am president, any governor who's willing to promote clean energy will have a partner in the White House," he said.[90] When Obama came into office, he made it clear that climate change was among his highest priorities.

That was welcome news to those assembled, an audience of policymakers who had felt frustrated by the lack of attention that global warming had received under President George W. Bush. Some were openly emotional, believing Obama's remarks signaled a new day. Many state and local leaders had gotten involved in climate change policy only because of the lack of federal action—a state of affairs they felt certain was at its end.

But by the time of Obama's election, it was clear that many states and localities were already too invested in the issue simply to cede the ground to Washington. They became highly vocal lobbyists during deliberations in Congress, as well as in international forums. In contrast to the general run of environmental issues, where policies have largely been set by the federal government even though responsibilities are carried out by the states, climate change had become an issue in which states and localities had already claimed their ground. In large part because its effects are felt differently in different locales, many states and cities had become convinced of the need to formulate their own strategies and plans, even if the logjam in Washington looked as though it was ready to be broken.

As it turned out, state leaders who believed greenhouse gas emissions needed to be lowered were still acting on their own. Obama and other world leaders failed to reach any serious agreement at a summit in Copenhagen in December 2009, the purpose of which had been to revamp and update the international treaty on greenhouse gases that had been written in Kyoto a dozen years earlier. A 2-week UN meeting in Doha at the end of 2012 led to little agreement beyond the idea of extending the old Kyoto Protocol. The U.S. and China did announce a climate agreement in November 2014 and renewed UN talks on climate were scheduled to take place in Paris at the end of 2015. Knowing he was unlikely to get approval of any treaty through the Senate, Obama floated the idea well ahead of those negotiations of a "name-and-shame" strategy that would taunt countries into cutting their emissions.

For all the dire predictions, climate was not an issue that seemed to gain or retain traction in domestic politics. Climate was essentially a nonissue in the presidential campaign of 2012. During the presidential debates, Republican candidate Mitt Romney criticized Obama's spending on clean energy companies more than once, while Obama criticized Romney for bragging that as governor of Massachusetts he had shut down coal-fired power plants. They never addressed climate change directly. Candy Crowley of CNN, who moderated one of the debates, said afterward that she had prepared a "question for all of you climate change people. We just, we knew that the economy was still the main thing." All that meant in retrospect that, ultimately, the more significant news out of the California climate change policy summit in 2008 was not Obama's statement but agreements reached between American states and provinces in other countries. At that meeting, governors from 13 states and regional leaders from four other nations signed a declaration to work together to combat global warming. Under a separate agreement, California, Illinois, and Wisconsin pledged to work with the governors of six provinces within Indonesia and Brazil to help slow tropical deforestation and land degradation through joint projects and incentive programs. "When California passed its global warming law two years ago, we were out there on an island, so we started forming partnerships everywhere we could," Governor Schwarzenegger said.[91] But, as noted earlier, the multistate regional initiatives have had difficulty meeting their own goals.

In 2009, Schwarzenegger and subnational leaders from Algeria, Canada, France, and Nigeria announced that they had formed the Club of 20 Regions, later known as the R20 Regions of Climate Action, to lobby their respective national governments on climate change policies and to implement those policies and any international agreements more quickly. The group, which has received the blessing of the United Nations, launched officially in 2010.

MAR •*Massachusetts*• 11
432 EY3
•*The Spirit of America*•

"When Obama got elected, there was a bit of a pause because we thought we'll have federal legislation and an international agreement," said Terry Tamminen, Schwarzenegger's former state EPA secretary. "But the lack of agreement in Copenhagen and, so far, the lack of an agreement in Washington has inspired states to keep going. The frustration level by the states and regions is such that they're going to be launching an alternative to try to get things going internationally."[92]

Conclusion

Climate change has seen considerable policy debate and innovation at the state and local levels over the past decade. In some ways, this is surprising. Global warming, by its name and nature, is an issue that should seek solutions on an international level as opposed to a subnational one. And states historically have left policy on most environmental issues up to Washington.

But the opposition of the Bush administration to serious curbs on energy use at a time when global warming concerns were at their height led many state and local leaders to chart their own courses. Not all states are convinced that promoting renewable energy sources or curbing carbon emissions is the right or even a necessary course. And there are plenty of critics who charge that most of the policies pursued at the state and local levels have been largely symbolic. It's easy to set targets that won't take effect for several years. And an increasingly loud chorus of voices maintains that even effective measures will not be worth the high cost that they might impose on the economy.

Many states and cities, however, have taken real action to curb their own energy use and to promote conservation and renewable energy sources throughout their economies. They have done this in spite of years of inaction at the national level and in spite of the difficulties in coordinating policy responses that are inherent in the federal system. Despite the challenges, having gotten into this game, many state and local governments clearly intend to stay. They remain frustrated by the inability of Congress to enact legislation in this area. And, even when Washington does act, they will want to be able to pursue policies and programs that by now are pretty well entrenched.

The Latest Research

This chapter has illustrated the ways many states have emerged as policy leaders on climate issues. For decades, the federal government was the driver on environmental policy, but lack of anything like consensus in Washington in recent years has allowed states to take various approaches (including none at all) to addressing climate change. Policy innovations among individual states and regional consortiums have provided frameworks not just for the erstwhile efforts of the Obama administration but for efforts at the provincial level in other countries as well.

States have sought ways of addressing climate change only over the past couple of decades, with many important laws passed only in the past few years. Perhaps for that reason, scholarship in this field has emerged relatively slowly, certainly in comparison with other long-standing state and local government concerns, such as budgets, political parties, and crime. This has proven to be a robust field of inquiry nonetheless, as academics can grapple not only with policy innovations and their efficacy but also with a number of questions regarding federalism and intergovernmental relations, since climate is a topic that is inherently cross-jurisdictional in scope.

• •

- **Bierbaum, Rosina, Joel B. Smith, Arthur Lee, Maria Blair, Lynne Carter, F. Stuart Chapin III, Paul Fleming, et al.** "A Comprehensive

(Continued)

(Continued)

Review of Climate Adaptation in the United States: More Than Before, But Less Than Needed." *Mitigation and Adaptation Strategies for Global Change* 18 (2013): 361–406.

Just what are states and localities doing to adapt to climate change effects? Not as much as they need to, the authors conclude. At all levels of government, as well as the private sector, there is more planning than action, with fairly few concrete measures put in place. Those that have been adopted amount to incremental changes, not major transformations of the kind that may be needed in some areas. Lots of barriers having to do with money, policy, and institutional constraints, as well as lack of firm knowledge about what the climate has in store for particular places, still impede more ambitious efforts. Lacking financial and staff resources, many governments are shoehorning adaptation planning into existing frameworks, such as public health, water management, and hazard mitigation programs. "Most adaptation actions are currently in the initial phase, with many actors focusing on identifying the relevant climate risks and conducting current and future risk and vulnerability assessments of their assets and resources," the authors write.

- **Javeline, Debra**. "The Most Important Topic Political Scientists Are Not Studying: Adapting to Climate Change." *Perspectives on Politics* 12 (2014): 420–434.

Decisions about responding to climate change are political in nature. Political scientists could help inform such debates by conducting research about adaptation and its costs, social justice questions, and federalism, since different levels of government are bound to be involved. But phrases such as "climate change adaptation" barely occur in political science journals and are even more rarely discussed in depth. To encourage research, Javeline summarizes the basic science that scholars would need to know and offers up a plethora of questions and topics that invite further

study. "Adaptation studies sorely need the contributions of political scientists from almost every subfield," she concludes.

- **Krause, Rachel M.** "Political Decision-Making and the Local Provision of Public Goods: The Case of Municipal Climate Protection in the U.S." *Urban Studies* 49 (2012): 2399–2417.

Many examinations of local climate change efforts barely look beyond the question of whether cities participate in networks devoted to the topic. Examining original survey data, Krause looks at what makes a city more likely to engage in specific climate protection efforts. Rather than financial support from other levels of government or the likely local impact of climate change (for instance, because of location along a coast), the biggest factors appear to be both the municipal government's own capacity for formulating and implementing policy and the human resources available locally, in terms of both per capita income and, especially, levels of higher education.

- **Wolinsky-Nahmias, Yael, ed.** *Changing Climate Politics: U.S. Policy and Civic Action.* Los Angeles: CQ Press, 2015.

Much of the research devoted to climate change has been scientific in nature. This edited volume offers a comprehensive overview of U.S. climate change policy, arguing that the federal government has largely been absent, save for court action. The collapse of federal climate strategies has led states and localities to take on more expansive roles. After outlining their efforts, including state-led cap-and-trade programs and municipal efforts to inventory and reduce greenhouse gas emissions, contributors look at the broader impact of climate change on society. They examine not just political issues such as activists' pushing for stronger environmental policies through ballot measures and other means but also effects on consumer behavior.

16

Chapter Review

Key Concepts

- adaptation (p. 523)
- building codes (p. 519)
- cap and trade (p. 509)
- carbon dioxide (p. 507)
- Clean Air Act (p. 507)
- climate change (p. 506)
- fracking (p. 514)
- global warming (p. 506)
- green jobs (p. 516)
- greenhouse gases (p. 507)
- Kyoto Protocol (p. 506)

- mitigation (p. 525)
- New Urbanism (p. 518)
- renewable energy (p. 511)
- resilience (p. 524)
- smog (p. 507)
- sprawl (p. 516)
- tailpipe emissions (p. 507)
- U.S. Environmental Protection Agency (EPA) (p. 506)
- weatherization (p. 520)
- zoning laws (p. 516)

$SAGE edge™
for CQ Press

Sharpen your skills with SAGE edge at edge.sagepub.com/smithgreenblatt5e. SAGE edge for students provides a personalized approach to help you accomplish your coursework goals in an easy-to-use learning environment.

Suggested Websites

- **www.aspanet.org.** Official website of the American Society for Public Administration, the largest professional association for those who work for or study public agencies.

- **www.governing.com.** Web version of *Governing* magazine, which is dedicated to covering state and local issues. Includes numerous stories and other resources on agency leaders and performance, e-government, and more.

- **www.pewtrusts.org/en/topics/state-policy.** Home to a number of analyses about government effectiveness and efficiency, including the Government Performance Project.

$SAGE statestats

State Stats on Environment and Climate Change

*Explore and compare data on the states! Go to **edge.sagepub.com/smithgreenblatt5e** to do these exercises.*

1. Which states have the highest per capita energy consumption? Is this surprising? Why or why not? Now, look at which states have the lowest number of housing units per square mile. How might these two things be related?

2. In 2011, which states were responsible for the most pollution from fossil fuel emissions? The least? What is it about these states that might explain this?

3. Which state decreased its pollution from fossil fuel emissions the most from 1996 to 2000? Which state increased the most? Why is there so much variation? Does political culture influence this?

4. Which state has the most hazardous waste sites? To what extent should cleaning up these sites be a priority?

5. In 1995, which states used the most water? Even though we do not have more recent data, how do you think this might be different now?

6. In what part of the United States are most of the nation's coal mines located? What does this mean for environmental efforts in this area?

Notes

Chapter 1

1. Kei Kawashima-Ginsberg and Nancy Thomas, "Civic Engagement and Political Leadership Among Women—A Call for Solutions" (fact sheet, Center for Information and Research on Civic Learning and Engagement, Tufts University, Medford, MA, May 2013), http://www.civicyouth.org/wp-content/uploads/2013/05/Gender-and-Political-Leadership-Fact-Sheet-3.pdf.

2. National Center for Education Statistics, "Total Fall Enrollment in Degree-Granting Institutions, by Control and Level of Institution: 1970 through 2012," in *Digest of Education Statistics* (Washington, DC: National Center for Education Statistics, October 2013), http://nces.ed.gov/programs/digest/d13/tables/dt13_303.25.asp.

3. National Center for Education Statistics, "Revenues of Public Degree-Granting Postsecondary Institutions, by Source of Revenue and Level of Institution: 2005–06 through 2011–12," in *Digest of Education Statistics* (Washington, DC: National Center for Education Statistics, January 2014), http://nces.ed.gov/programs/digest/d13/tables/dt13_333.10.asp.

4. Alan Greenblatt, "Tuition? UC Riverside Students Say Bill Me Later," *Governing*, April 2012, www.governing.com/topics/education/gov-tuition-uc-riverside-students-say-bill-me-later.html.

5. National Center for Education Statistics, "Fast Facts: Financial Aid," 2014, http://nces.ed.gov/fastfacts/display.asp?id=31.

6. National Center for Education Statistics, "Fast Facts: Back to School Statistics," 2014, http://nces.ed.gov/fastfacts/display.asp?id=372.

7. Kenneth J. Meier, *Politics and the Bureaucracy* (Pacific Grove, CA: Brooks/Cole, 1993), 2.

8. Christopher Z. Mooney, "Why Do They Tax Dogs in West Virginia? Teaching Political Science Through Comparative State Politics," *PS: Political Science & Politics* 31 (June 1998): 199–203.

9. J. F. Chriqui, S. S. Eidson, and F. J. Chaloupka, "State Sales Tax on Regular Soda (as of January 2014)" (fact sheet, Bridging the Gap Program, Health Policy Center, Institute for Health Research and Policy, University of Illinois at Chicago, 2014), http://www.bridgingthegapresearch.org/_asset/s2b5pb/BTG_soda_tax_fact_sheet_April2014.pdf.

10. Based on a standard ordinary least squares regression analysis in which average tuition bills at public 4-year universities are the dependent variable and state appropriations as thousands of dollars per enrolled student are the dependent variable. Data taken from Thomas D. Snyder and Sally A. Dillow, *Digest of Education Statistics 2010* (Washington, DC: National Center for Education Statistics, Institute of Education Sciences, U.S. Department of Education, April 2011), http://nces.ed.gov/pubs2011/2011015.pdf.

11. U.S. Census Bureau, "State and County QuickFacts," http://quickfacts.census.gov/qfd/index.html.

12. Richard Morrill, "The Urban US: Growth and Decline," *NewGeography*, April 11, 2012, http://www.newgeography.com/content/002769-the-urban-us-growth-and-decline.

13. Associated Press, "Not So Sunny: Florida's Growth Rate Continues to Slide, Census Reports," *Naples Daily News*, http://www.naplesnews.com/news/2010/jun/10/not-so-sunny-floridas-growth-rate-continues-slide-.

14. Daniel J. Elazar, *American Federalism: A View From the States* (New York: Crowell, 1966). This book has gone through three editions, the most recent of which was published in 1984.

15. Ibid., 88.

16. Maureen Moakley, "New Jersey," in *The Political Life of the American States*, ed. Alan Rosenthal and Maureen Moakley (New York: Praeger, 1984), 222.

17. Quoted in Robert D. Putnam, *Bowling Alone: The Collapse and Revival of American Community* (New York: Simon & Schuster, 2000), 293.

18. Russell Hanson, "Political Culture Variations in State Economic Development Policy," *Publius: The Journal of Federalism* 21, no. 2 (1991): 63–81; Kevin B. Smith, *The Ideology of Education: The Commonwealth, the Market, and America's Schools* (Albany: State University of New York Press, 2003).

19. Bureau of Economic Analysis, "Per Capita Real GDP by State," 2014, http://bea.gov/iTable/iTable.cfm?reqid=99&step=1.

20. Phillip W. Roeder, *Public Opinion and Policy Leadership in the American States* (Tuscaloosa: University of Alabama Press, 1994); J. Wolak and C. K. Palus, "The Dynamics of Public Confidence in U.S. State and Local Government," *State Politics & Policy Quarterly* 10 (2010): 421–445.

21. Bruce Wallin, "State and Local Governments Are American Too," *Political Science Teacher* 1 (1988): 1–3.

22. U.S. Census Bureau, "Government Employment and Payroll," 2012, http://www.census.gov/govs/apes.

23. Jeffrey L. Barnett and Phillip M. Vidal, "State and Local Government Finances Summary: 2011," July 2013, http://www2.census.gov/govs/local/summary_report.pdf.

24. Evan J. Ringquist and James C. Garand, "Policy Change in the American States," in *State and Local Politics*, ed. Ronald E. Weber and Paul Brace (New York: Chatham House, 1999).

25. David Osborne and Ted Gaebler, *Reinventing Government: How the Entrepreneurial Spirit Is Transforming the Public Sector* (New York: Plume, 1993).

Chapter 2

1. Cass Sunstein, "The Return of States' Rights," *American Prospect*, November 30, 2002, http://www.prospect.org/cs/articles?article=the_return_of_states_rights.

2. James Collier and Christopher Collier, *Decision in Philadelphia* (New York: Random House, 1986).

3. Quoted in ibid., 3.

4. Ellen Perlman, "The Preemption Beast: The Gorilla That Swallows State Laws," *Governing*, August 1994, 46–51.

5. Quoted in Harry N. Scheiber, "The Condition of American Federalism: An Historian's View," in *American Intergovernmental Relations*, ed. Laurence J. O'Toole Jr. (Washington, DC: CQ Press, 2000), 71.

6. Ibid.

7. Kala Ladenheim, "History of U.S. Federalism," March 16, 1999, http://www.cas.sc.edu/poli/courses/scgov/History_of_Federalism.htm.

8. Scheiber, "Condition of American Federalism."

9. Ellis Katz, "American Federalism, Past, Present and Future," *Issues of Democracy* 2, no. 2 (1997), http://www.ucs.louisiana.edu/~ras2777/amgov/federalism.html.

10. Paul L. Posner, *The Politics of Unfunded Mandates: Whither Federalism?* (Washington, DC: Georgetown University Press, 1998), 13.

11. National Conference of State Legislatures, "Mandate Monitor," http://www.ncsl.org/state-federal-committees/scbudg/mandate-monitor-overview.aspx.

12. Timothy Conlon, "Federalism and Competing Values in the Reagan Administration," *Publius: The Journal of Federalism* 16, no. 4 (1986): 29–47.

13. Thomas J. Anton, "New Federalism and Intergovernmental Fiscal Relationships: The Implications for Health Policy," *Journal of Health Politics, Policy and Law* 22, no. 3 (1997): 691–720.

14. Richard L. Cole and John Kincaid, "Public Opinion and American Federalism: Perspectives on Taxes, Spending, and Trust," *Spectrum: The Journal of State Government* 74, no. 3 (2000): 14–18.

15. "Same-Sex Marriage: Federal and State Authority," *Congressional Digest* 75 (November 1996): 263.

16. Peter Harkness, "Potomac Chronicle: Obama and the States," *Governing*, January 1, 2009, 18.

17. Barton Aronson, "The Rising Tide of Federalism," CNN.com, February 1, 2001, http://www.cnn.com/2001/LAW/02/columns/fl.aronson.federalism.02.01.

18. Alan Ehrenhalt, "Devolution in Reverse," *Governing*, December 1, 2008, 8.

19. Michael S. Greve, *Real Federalism: Why It Matters, How It Could Happen* (Washington, DC: AEI Press, 1999), 17.

20. Jeffrey G. Homrig, "*Alden v. Maine*: A New Genre of Federalism Shifts the Balance of Power," *California Law Review* 89, no. 1 (2001): 183–205.

21. David G. Savage, "Justices Rule U.S. Can Ban Medical Pot," *Los Angeles Times*, June 7, 2005.

22. John Dinan, "The State of American Federalism 2007–2008: Resurgent State Influence in the National Policy Process and Continued State Policy Innovation," *Publius: The Journal of Federalism* 38, no. 3 (2008): 381–415.

23. Brady Baybeck and William Lowry, "Federalism Outcomes and Ideological Preferences: The U.S. Supreme Court and Preemption Cases," *Publius: The Journal of Federalism* 30, no. 1 (2000): 73–96.

Chapter 3

1. Referendum A, Colorado, 2004.

2. Shauna Reilly and Sean Richey, "Ballot Question Readability and Roll-Off: The Impact of Language Complexity," *Political Research Quarterly* 64 (2011): 59–67.

3. Donald Kettl, "Governor Rehnquist," *Governing*, July 1999.

4. Alan Tarr, *Understanding State Constitutions* (Princeton, NJ: Princeton University Press, 1998), 6–8.

5. Christopher Hammons, "Was James Madison Wrong? Rethinking the American Preference for Short, Framework-Oriented Constitutions," *American Political Science Review* 93, no. 4 (1999): 837.

6. Ibid., 840.

7. Ibid. See also John G. Kester, "Amendment Time," *Washingtonian*, March 1995.

8. Janice C. May, "Trends in State Constitutional Amendment and Revision," in *The Book of the States 2003*, ed. Council of State Governments (Lexington, KY: Council of State Governments, 2003), 8.

9. Robert J. Taylor, ed., *Massachusetts, Colony to Commonwealth* (New York: Norton, 1961).

10. Quoted in Willi Paul Adams, *The First American Constitutions: Republican Ideology and the Making*

of the State Constitutions in the Revolutionary Era (Chapel Hill: University of North Carolina Press, 1980), 53.

11. Quoted in ibid., 61.

12. Quoted in ibid., 207.

13. Tarr, *Understanding State Constitutions,* 121.

14. W. B. Stouffer, Cynthia Opheim, and Susan Bland Day, eds., *State and Local Politics: The Individual and the Governments* (New York: HarperCollins, 1996).

15. Bruce Sundlun, "R.I.'s Martyr for Democracy," *Providence Journal-Bulletin,* August 11, 2002.

16. Delaware is the only state that does not refer constitutional amendments to the electorate as a whole. The legislature may enact constitutional amendments on its own if a measure receives support in two consecutive legislative sessions.

17. Council of State Governments, ed., *The Book of the States 2001* (Lexington, KY: Council of State Governments, 2001), 5. In South Carolina, a majority of both houses of the legislature must vote to approve a constitutional amendment a second time, after it has passed a popular referendum, before it can go into effect.

18. Initiative and Referendum Institute, http://www .iandrinstitute.org. The institute's website includes detailed time lines of initiative and referendum activity in each state.

19. Juan B. Elizondo Jr., "Ratliff: Time to Rewrite Constitution; Lawmaker Joined by Watchdog," *Austin American-Statesman,* October 28, 1999.

20. Council of State Governments, ed., *The Book of the States 2003* (Lexington, KY: Council of State Governments, 2003), 3–4.

21. Isaiah J. Ashe, "Alabama Constitutional Revision Commission Finishes Work With Disappointing Results in Key Areas," *AL.com,* October 14, 2013, http://www.al.com/opinion/index.ssf/2013/10/ alabama_constitutional_revisio.html.

22. Warren Richey, "Unique Law Lets Florida Voters Make Changes to Constitution," *Christian Science Monitor,* May 8, 1998.

23. Quoted in Alan Ehrenhalt, "Vermont's Judicial Distillery," *Governing,* February 2000, http://www.gov erning.com/topics/mgmt/Vermonts-Judicial-Distill ery.html.

24. Hammons, "Was James Madison Wrong?" 839.

25. Joni James, "Voters Hold Key to Big Shake-Up in State Cabinet: The Revision Would Eliminate Three Posts, Give the Governor More Power, and Shift Control of Education Policy," *Orlando Sentinel,* October 20, 1998, D1.

26. Stuart MacCorkle and Dick Smith, *Texas Government* (New York: McGraw-Hill, 1960).

27. Daniel Elazar, *American Federalism: A View From the States,* 3rd ed. (New York: Harper & Row, 1984), 115.

28. Hammons, "Was James Madison Wrong?" 846.

29. See ibid. for a more complete argument along these lines.

30. Melinda Gann Hall, "State Judicial Politics: Rules, Structures, and the Political Game," in *American State and Local Politics,* ed. Ronald Weber and Paul Brace (New York: Chatham House, 1999), 136.

31. National Conference of State Legislatures, "Gubernatorial Veto Authority With Respect to Major Budget Bill(s)," December 2008, http://www.ncsl .org/IssuesResearch/BudgetTax/Gubernatorial VetoAuthoritywithRespecttoMajor/tabid/12640/ Default.aspx.

32. Andrew Taylor, "Line Item Budget Barely Trims Spending at State Level," *Denver Rocky Mountain News,* January 15, 1995.

33. Scott Milfred, "Some Want to Clip Gubernatorial Wings: A Resolution in the Legislature Would Curtail Wisconsin Governor's Exceptionally Broad Veto Power," *Wisconsin State Journal,* September 23, 2001, A1.

34. Virginia Gray, Herbert Jacob, and Kenneth N. Vines, eds. *Politics in the American States: A Comparative Analysis* (Boston: Little, Brown, 1983).

35. In 2003, the U.S. Supreme Court invalidated laws prohibiting sodomy. Until that time, Alabama, Florida, Idaho, Louisiana, Massachusetts, Mississippi, North Carolina, South Carolina, Utah, and Virginia had laws that explicitly prohibited sodomy. Kansas, Oklahoma, and Texas prohibited same-sex sodomy only. LAMBDA Legal Defense and Education Fund website, http://www.lambda.org.

36. James Madison, *Federalist* No. 10, in Alexander Hamilton, James Madison, and John Jay, *The Federalist Papers,* ed. Charles Kesler and Clinton Rossiter (New York: Penguin Putnam, 1961), 76.

37. Ibid. Hamilton, Madison, and Jay envisioned other safeguards as well. One was the well-known principle of the separation of powers among the three branches of government. The other was the large size of the republic itself. Previous theorists of democracy had worried about republics that became too large to govern. In *Federalist* No. 10, Madison makes the novel claim that a more extensive republic would be less likely to succumb to factionalism than were the smaller republics of old.

38. Quoted in David Broder, *Democracy Derailed: Initiative Campaigns and the Power of Money* (New York: Harcourt, 2000), 27.

39. Ibid.

40. Initiative and Referendum Institute, "The History of Initiative and Referendum in the United States," http://www.iandrinstitute.org.

41. Richard Ellis, *Democratic Delusions: The Initiative Process in America* (Lawrence: University Press of Kansas, 2002).

42. Broder, *Democracy Derailed.*

43. Keon S. Chi, "Emerging Trends Shaping State Governments: 2005 and Beyond," in *The Book of the*

States 2005, ed. Council of State Governments (Lexington, KY: Council of State Governments, 2005).

44. "California Ballot Initiative Petition Signature Costs," Ballotpedia, 2014, http://ballotpedia.org/wiki/index.php/California_ballot_initiative_petition_signature_costs.

45. Broder, *Democracy Derailed,* 1.

46. Lawrence F. Keller, "Municipal Charters," *National Civic Review* 91, no. 1 (2002): 155–161.

Chapter 4

1. Phil Oliff, Chris Mai, and Vincent Palacios, "States Continue to Feel Recession's Impact," Center on Budget and Policy Priorities, June 27, 2012, http://www.cbpp.org/cms/index.cfm?fa=view&id=711.

2. Lucy Dadayan and Donald J. Boyd, "Recession or No Recession, State Tax Revenues Remain Negative," Rockefeller Institute of Government, Albany, NY, January 2010, 3.

3. Kathryn Tormey, "Federal Assistance, Cost-Cutting Measures Helping Curb Fiscal Impact of Medicaid on States," *Stateline Midwest* 19, no. 10 (2010), http://knowledgecenter.csg.org/kc/content/federal-assistance-cost-cutting-measures-helping-curb-fiscal-impact-medicaid-states.

4. Tax Foundation, "State and Local Tax Burdens: All States, One Year, 1977–2011," October 23, 2012, http://taxfoundation.org/article/state-and-local-tax-burdens-all-states-one-year-1977-2009.

5. These figures and many that follow come from U.S. Department of Commerce, *Statistical Abstract of the United States, 2012* (Washington, DC: U.S. Census Bureau, 2012), http://www.census.gov/compendia/statab, and refer to the fiscal year that concluded in 2008, one of the most recent years for which such data are available.

6. Ibid., Table 453.

7. National Governors Association and National Association of State Budget Officers, *The Fiscal Survey of States* (Washington, DC: National Governors Association and National Association of State Budget Officers, fall 2009), vii, http://www.nasbo.org/sites/default/files/fsfall2009.pdf.

8. U.S. Department of Commerce, *Statistical Abstract,* Table 436.

9. Federation of Tax Administrators, "State Excise Tax Rates on Cigarettes," January 1, 2014, http://www.taxadmin.org/fta/rate/cigarette.pdf.

10. Estimated sales tax calculated at Minnesota online sales tax calculator for Bloomington, Minnesota, http://www.revenue.state.mn.us/businesses/sut/Pages/SalesTaxCalculator.aspx.

11. Tax Foundation, "A Sales Tax Word of Warning in Hawaii, New Mexico, South Dakota, and Wyoming," September 30, 2011, http://taxfoundation.org/blog/sales-tax-word-warning-hawaii-new-mexico-south-dakota-and-wyoming.

12. Katherine Barrett, Richard Greene, Michele Mariani, and Anya Sostek, "The Way We Tax: A 50-State Report," *Governing,* February 2003, http://www.schouse.gov/archives/citizensinterestpage/TRAC/TheWayWeTax-A50StateReport.pdf.

13. Donald Bruce, William F. Fox, and LeAnn Luna, "State and Local Sales Tax Revenue Losses from E-Commerce," Center for Business and Economic Research, University of Tennessee, Knoxville, April 13, 2009, http://cber.bus.utk.edu/ecomm/ecom0409.pdf.

14. Cited in Penelope Lemov, "The Untaxables," *Governing,* July 2002.

15. Alan Greenblatt, "The Sales Tax Goes Online," *Governing,* December 2005.

16. Streamlined Sales Tax Governing Board, "Frequently Asked Questions," 2011, http://www.streamlinedsalestax.org/index.php?page=faqs.

17. Saul Hansell, "Court to Amazon: Keep Paying Sales Tax," Bits Blog, *New York Times,* January 13, 2009, http://bits.blogs.nytimes.com/2009/01/13/court-to-amazon-keep-collecting-sales-tax-to-new-yorkers.

18. Ben Tracy, "Amazon Is Now Collecting California Sales Tax," CBS News, September 15, 2012, http://www.cbsnews.com/news/amazon-is-now-collecting-california-sales-tax/.

19. Jeffrey L. Barnett and Phillip M. Vidal, "State and Local Government Finances Summary: 2011," U.S. Department of Commerce, July 2013, http://www2.census.gov/govs/local/summary_report.pdf.

20. U.S. Department of Commerce, *Statistical Abstract,* Tables 451 and 455.

21. Tax Foundation, *Facts and Figures 2014: How Does Your State Compare?* (Washington, DC: Tax Foundation, 2014), Table 31, http://taxfoundation.org/article/facts-figures-2014-how-does-your-state-compare.

22. U.S. Department of Commerce, *Statistical Abstract,* Table 455.

23. Barnett and Vidal, "State and Local Government Finances Summary: 2011."

24. Alan Greenblatt, "The Loathsome Local Levy," *Governing,* October 2001.

25. Barnett and Vidal, "State and Local Government Finances Summary: 2011."

26. Fifteen states allow certain localities to impose income taxes as well, but for the most part, income tax receipts are a minor source of funds for cities and counties.

27. U.S. Department of Commerce, *Statistical Abstract,* Table 453.

28. Tax Foundation, *Facts and Figures 2014,* Table 13.

29. U.S. Department of Commerce, *Statistical Abstract,* Table 436.

30. Ibid.

31. National Governors Association and National Association of State Budget Officers, *Fiscal Survey of States*, 18.

32. U.S. Department of Commerce, *Statistical Abstract,* Table 436.

33. National Association of State Budget Officers, "Summary: NASBO State Expenditure Report," December 20, 2011, http://www.nasbo.org/sites/default/files/Summary%20-%20State%20Expenditure%20Report.pdf.

34. Ibid.

35. U.S. Department of Commerce, *Statistical Abstract,* Table 455.

36. Alan Greenblatt, "Enemies of the State," *Governing,* June 2002.

37. Elizabeth Malm and Gerald Prante, *Annual State–Local Tax Burden Rankings FY 2011* (Washington, DC: Tax Foundation, April 2014), 3, http://taxfoundation.org/sites/taxfoundation.org/files/docs/Burdens_2014_Final.pdf.

38. Tax Foundation, *Facts and Figures 2014,* Tables 19 and 31.

39. Tax Foundation "Income Per Capita by State, Fiscal Year 2010," February 16, 2012, http://taxfoundation.org/article/income-capita-state-fiscal-year-2010.

40. Tax Foundation, "State and Local Tax Burdens."

41. See the Mayflower Compact for further insights into the mind-set of the founders of the Massachusetts Bay Colony, http://www.pilgrimhallmuseum.org/ap_mayflower_compact.htm.

42. John E. Petersen, "Guide to Municipal Finance: Credit Raters Make Their Mark," *Governing,* June 2005.

43. Penelope Lemov, "The Muni Market in 2012," *Governing,* January 12, 2012, http://www.governing.com/columns/public-finance/col-municipal-bond-market-2012.html.

44. For a detailed discussion of the state budget process, see National Association of State Budget Officers, *Budget Processes in the States* (Washington, DC: National Association of State Budget Officers, 2008).

45. These states are Connecticut, Hawaii, Indiana, Kentucky, Maine, Minnesota, Montana, Nebraska, Nevada, New Hampshire, North Carolina, North Dakota, Ohio, Oregon, Texas, Virginia, Washington, Wisconsin, and Wyoming. Ron Snell, "State Experiences With Annual and Biennial Budgeting," National Conference of State Legislatures, April 2011, http://www.ncsl.org/issues-research/budget/state-experiences-with-annual-and-biennial-budgeti.aspx.

46. Robert Zahradnik, "Rainy Day Funds: Opportunities for Reform," Center on Budget and Policy Priorities, March 9, 2005, http://www.cbpp.org/3-9-05sfp.htm.

47. "Government Spending Details: Spending per Capita," usgovernmentspending.com, February 2012, http://www.usgovernmentspending.com/year_spending_2013USdn_15dc2n#usgs302.

48. "State and Local Government Employment: Monthly Data," *Governing,* 2014, http://www.governing.com/gov-data/public-workforce-salaries/monthly-government-employment-changes-totals.html; U.S. Department of Commerce, *Statistical Abstract,* Table 436.

49. Cheryl H. Lee, Robert Jesse Willhide, and Edwin Pome, "State Government Finances Summary Report: 2012," U.S. Department of Commerce, January 23, 2014, http://www2.census.gov/govs/state/12statesummaryreport.pdf.

50. U.S. Department of Commerce, *Statistical Abstract,* Table 456.

51. "Table 1: State Fiscal Support for Higher Education, by State, Fiscal Years 2006–07, 2009–10, 2010–11, and 2011–12," in *Grapevine* (Normal: College of Education, Illinois State University, 2013).

52. National Association of State Budget Officers, *State Expenditure Report: Fiscal Year 2008* (Washington, DC: National Association of State Budget Officers, December 2009), 47.

53. National Association of State Budget Officers, *State Expenditure Report: Examining Fiscal 2011–2013 State Spending* (Washington, DC: National Association of State Budget Officers, 2013), http://www.nasbo.org/publications-data/state-expenditure-report/archives.

54. Henry J. Kaiser Family Foundation, "Federal and State Share of Medicaid Spending, FY 2012," September 16, 2013, http://www.statehealthfacts.org/comparemaptable.jsp?ind=636&cat=4.

55. Georgetown University Health Policy Institute, "Medicaid and CHIP Programs," January 1, 2013, http://ccf.georgetown.edu/facts-statistics/medicaid-chip-programs.

56. Cynthia Miller, "Leavers, Stayers, and Cyclers: An Analysis of the Welfare Caseload," Manpower Demonstration Research Corporation, New York, November 2002. For a full discussion of the effects of welfare reform, see also Alan Weil, "Ten Things Everyone Should Know about Welfare Reform," no. A-52, Urban Institute, Washington, DC, May 9, 2002.

57. U.S. Department of Health and Human Services, "A.1: Federal TANF and State MOE Expenditures Summary by ACF-196 Spending Category, FY 2012," http://www.acf.hhs.gov/sites/default/files/ofa/fy2012_expenditures.pdf.

58. U.S. Department of Commerce, *Statistical Abstract,* Table 436.

59. National Association of State Budget Officers, *State Expenditure Report: Examining Fiscal 2011–2013 State Spending*, 55.

60. Joseph Henchman, "Gasoline Taxes and User Fees Pay for Only Half of State and Local Road Spending," Tax

Foundation, Washington, DC, January 3, 2014, http://taxfoundation.org/article/gasoline-taxes-and-user-fees-pay-only-half-state-local-road-spending.

61. Ibid.

62. National Association of State Budget Officers, *State Expenditure Report: Examining Fiscal 2011–2013 State Spending*, 65.

63. Pew Charitable Trusts, "The Fiscal Health of State Pension Plans: Funding Gap Continues to Grow," April 2014, http://www.pewtrusts.org/en/research-and-analysis/analysis/2014/04/08/the-fiscal-health-of-state-pension-plans-funding-gap-continues-to-grow.

64. Greenblatt, "Enemies of the State."

65. Bill Piper, *A Brief Analysis of Voter Behavior Regarding Tax Initiatives: From 1978 to March 2000* (Washington, DC: Citizen Lawmaker Press, n.d.).

66. This section is adapted from the February 2003 *Governing* special issue on state tax systems; see Barrett et al., "The Way We Tax."

Chapter 5

1. Quoted in Steven Laccino and Lizette Alvarez, "New G.O.P. Bid to Limit Voting in Swing States," *New York Times*, March 29, 2014, http://www.nytimes.com/2014/03/30/us/new-gop-bid-to-limit-voting-in-swing-states.html.

2. Justin Levitt, "A Comprehensive Investigation of Voter Impersonation Finds 31 Credible Incidents Out of One Billion Ballots Cast," *Washington Post*, April 30, 2014, http://www.washingtonpost.com/blogs/wonkblog/wp/2014/08/06/a-comprehensive-investigation-of-voter-impersonation-finds-31-credible-incidents-out-of-one-billion-ballots-cast/.

3. Michael McDonald, Twitter post, August 6, 2014, https://twitter.com/ElectProject/status/497034025081798656.

4. Richard L. Hasen, "How to Predict a Voting Rights Decision," *Slate*, October 10, 2014, http://www.slate.com/articles/news_and_politics/jurisprudence/2014/10/supreme_court_voting_rights_decisions_contradictions_in_wisconsin_ohio_north.html.

5. Government Accountability Office, "Issues Related to State Voter Identification Laws," report to Congressional requesters, September 2014, http://www.gao.gov/assets/670/665966.pdf.

6. Quoted in Lisa Mascaro, "GOP-Backed Limits on Voting Lead to Spirited Backlash From Democrats," *Los Angeles Times*, October 9, 2014, http://www.latimes.com/nation/la-na-voting-backlash-20141010-story.html.

7. Thom File, "The Diversifying Electorate—Voting Rates by Race and Non-Hispanic Origin in 2012 (and Other Recent Elections)," Current Population Survey Report P20-568, U.S. Census Bureau, May 2013, https://www.census.gov/prod/2013pubs/p20-568.pdf.

8. Nate Cohn, "Southern Whites' Loyalty to Republicans Nearing That of Blacks to Democrats," *New York Times*, April 23, 2014, http://www.nytimes.com/2014/04/24/upshot/southern-whites-loyalty-to-gop-nearing-that-of-blacks-to-democrats.html.

9. Earl Black and Merle Black, *Divided America: The Ferocious Power Struggle in American Politics* (New York: Simon & Schuster, 2007), 10.

10. Gary Langer, "'Own Rep' Rating Hits a Record Low, Marking the Public's Political Discontent," Langer Research Associates, August 5, 2014, http://www.langerresearch.com/uploads/1144a43ThreeMonthsOut.pdf.

11. Quoted in Aaron Blake, "Obama Blames Lack of African American, Latino Turnout for Democrats' Midterm Woes," *Washington Post*, April 10, 2014, http://www.washingtonpost.com/blogs/post-politics/wp/2014/04/10/obama-democrats-lose-in-midterms-because-african-americans-latinos-young-people-dont-turn-out-to-vote/.

12. Chris Evans, "It's the Autonomy, Stupid: Political Data-Mining and Voter Privacy in the Information Age," *Minnesota Journal of Law, Science & Technology* 13 (2012): 868.

13. Steven Hill, *Fixing Elections: The Failure of America's Winner Take All Politics* (New York: Routledge, 2002), 119.

14. Caroline J. Tolbert, John A. Grummel, and Daniel A. Smith, "The Effects of Ballot Initiatives on Voter Turnout in the American States," *American Politics Research* 29, no. 6 (2001): 625–648.

15. Interview with Rhodes Cook, December 11, 2006.

16. Kevin J. Coleman, Thomas H. Neale, and Joseph E. Cantor, "The Election Process in the United States," Congressional Research Service, Washington, DC, July 6, 1995, 69.

17. National Conference of State Legislatures, "Straight-Ticket Voting," May 23, 2014, http://www.ncsl.org/research/elections-and-campaigns/straight-ticket-voting.aspx.

18. Election Data Services, *The Election Data Book: A Statistical Portrait of Voting in America* (Lanham, MD: Bernan Press, 1992), appendix.

19. Vauhini Vara, "'Instant Runoff' Faces Test," *Wall Street Journal*, October 21, 2011, http://online.wsj.com/article/SB10001424052970204774604576631212229446284.html.

20. Kay Lawson, "How State Laws Undermine Parties," in *Elections American Style*, ed. A. James Reichley (Washington, DC: Brookings Institution, 1987), 241.

21. Cited in William C. Binning, Larry E. Esterly, and Paul A. Sracic, *Encyclopedia of American Parties, Campaigns, and Elections* (Westport, CT: Greenwood Press, 1999), 95.

22. Quoted in Reid Wilson, "Runoff Elections a Relic of the Democratic South," *Washington Post*, June 4,

2012, http://www.washingtonpost.com/blogs/govbeat/wp/2014/06/04/runoff-elections-a-relic-of-the-democratic-south.

23. E-mail correspondence with Richard Winger, July 24, 2012.

24. Paul Singer, "For Third-Party Candidates, Playing Field Is Uneven by State," *USA Today*, July 10, 2012, http://usatoday30.usatoday.com/news/politics/story/2012-07-08/third-party-ballot-access/56098480/1.

25. Lawson, "How State Laws Undermine Parties," 246.

26. E-mail from Richard Winger, June 1, 2014.

27. Quoted in Jesse McKinley, "California Puts Vote Overhaul on the Ballot," *New York Times*, May 27, 2010, A1.

28. Larry Sabato, Twitter post, December 24, 2011, https://twitter.com/BuzzFeedBen/statuses/150620246800220162.

29. Binning et al., *Encyclopedia of American Parties*, 95.

30. Quoted in Dan Eggen and Amy Goldstein, "Voter-Fraud Complaints by GOP Drove Dismissals," *Washington Post*, May 14, 2007, A4.

31. Andrew Hacker, "Obama: The Price of Being Black," *New York Review of Books*, September 25, 2008, http://www.nybooks.com/articles/21771.

32. Megan Reisz, "Register to Vote Through Facebook?" *Christian Science Monitor*, July 18, 2012, http://www.csmonitor.com/Innovation/2012/0718/Register-to-vote-through-Facebook-Washington-reveals-new-app.

33. Phone interview with Curtis Gans, September 4, 2003.

34. Phone interview with Steven Hill, September 11, 2003.

35. Mark Hugo Lopez, "The Latino Electorate in 2010: More Voters, More Non-Voters," Pew Research Center's Hispanic Trends Project, April 26, 2011, http://www.pewhispanic.org/2011/04/26/the-latino-electorate-in-2010-more-voters-more-non-voters.

36. Jens Manuel Krogstad, "Hispanics Punch Below Their Weight in Midterm Elections," Pew Research Center, April 2, 2014, http://www.pewresearch.org/fact-tank/2014/04/02/hispanics-punch-below-their-weight-in-midterm-elections/.

37. Interview with Ruy Teixeira, April 2006.

38. Robert D. Putnam, *Bowling Alone: The Collapse and Revival of American Community* (New York: Simon & Schuster, 2000).

39. Barbara G. Salmore and Stephen A. Salmore, *New Jersey Politics and Government*, 2nd ed. (Lincoln: University of Nebraska Press, 1998), 128.

40. Quoted in Danielle Todesco, "New Mexico Governor, Attorney General, Battle over Emails," *KOB Eyewitness News*, July 6, 2012, http://www.kob.com/article/stories/S2680886.shtml.

41. Susanne Craig, "With $613 Million at Stake, an Albany Rivalry Is Said to Escalate," *New York Times*, January 16, 2014, http://www.nytimes.com/2014/01/16/nyregion/cuomo-and-schneiderman-prepare-to-fight-over-jpmorgan-settlement.html.

42. Stephen Dinan, "Conservative Super PAC to Fund Secretary of State Hopefuls," *Washington Times*, January 22, 2014, http://www.washingtontimes.com/news/2014/jan/22/conservative-super-pac-to-fund-secretary-of-state-/.

43. Quoted in Alan Greenblatt, "Where Campaign Money Flows," *Governing*, November 2002, 44.

44. Alan Greenblatt, "The Avengers General," *Governing*, May 2003, 54.

45. Quoted in Reid Wilson, "Republican Group Will Focus on Judicial Races," *Washington Post*, April 29, 2014, http://www.washingtonpost.com/blogs/govbeat/wp/2014/04/29/republican-group-will-focus-on-judicial-races.

46. Zach Patton, "Robe Warriors," *Governing*, March 2006, 34.

47. Quoted in Brian Haas, "TN Supreme Court Battle Brings National Money, Scrutiny," *The Tennessean*, August 5, 2014, http://www.tennessean.com/story/news/politics/2014/08/04/tn-supreme-court-battle-brings-national-money-scrutiny/13550987.

48. Initiative and Referendum Institute at the University of Southern California website, http://www.iandrinstitute.org.

49. John F. Camobreco, "Preferences, Fiscal Policy, and the Initiative Process," *Journal of Politics* 60, no. 3 (August 1998): 822.

50. Reid Wilson and Niraj Chokshi, "Ballot Initiatives Become Pricey Playgrounds of Parties and Corporations," *Washington Post*, August 27, 2014, http://www.washingtonpost.com/blogs/govbeat/wp/2014/08/27/ballot-initiatives-become-pricey-playgrounds-for-corporations-and-political-parties/.

51. Presentation at the annual meeting of the National Conference of State Legislatures, Chicago, IL, August 9, 2012.

52. Quoted in James Dao, "Same-Sex Marriage Key to Some G.O.P. Races," *New York Times*, November 4, 2004, P4.

53. Simon Jackman, "Same-Sex Marriage Ballot Initiatives and Conservative Mobilization in the 2004 Election," presentation, http://jackman.stanford.edu/papers/risspresentation.pdf.

54. Quoted in Alan Greenblatt, "Some Presidential Politics Is Local," *New York Times*, October 10, 2004, sec. 4, 5.

55. National Conference of State Legislatures, "Recall of State Officials," September 11, 2013, http://www.ncsl.org/research/elections-and-campaigns/recall-of-state-officials.aspx.

56. Ryan Holeywell, "The Rise of the Recall Election," *Governing*, April 2011, http://www.governing.com/topics/politics/rise-recall-election.html.

57. Seth Masket, "The Recall Is the New Normal," *Pacific Standard*, September 17, 2013, http://www.psmag

.com/navigation/politics-and-law/recall-election-now-thing-permanent-campaign-election-66344/.

58. Alan Greenblatt, "Total Recall," *Governing,* September 2003, 27.

59. Phone interview with Randall Gnant, August 7, 2003.

60. V. O. Key, *Public Opinion and American Democracy* (New York: Knopf, 1964), 7.

61. Interview with Doug Duncan, November 15, 2006.

62. Interview with Mike Haridopolos, August 8, 2012.

63. Rob Gurwitt, "The Demise of the Public Hearing," *Governing,* October 2013, http://www.governing.com/topics/mgmt/gov-demise-of-public-hearing.html.

64. See, especially, Robert S. Erikson, Gerald C. Wright, and John D. McIver, *Statehouse Democracy: Public Opinion and Policy in the American States* (New York: Cambridge University Press, 1993).

65. Paul Brace, Kellie Sims-Butler, Kevin Arceneaux, and Martin Johnson, "Public Opinion in the American States: New Perspectives Using National Survey Data," *American Journal of Political Science* 46, no. 1 (January 2002): 173–189.

66. Susan Herbst, "How State-Level Policy Managers 'Read' Public Opinion," in *Navigating Public Opinion: Polls, Policy, and the Future of American Democracy,* ed. Jeff Manza, Fay Lomax Cook, and Benjamin I. Page (New York: Oxford University Press, 2002), 176.

67. Logan Dancey and Paul Goren, "Party Identification, Issue Attitudes, and the Dynamics of Political Debate," *American Journal of Political Science* 54 (July 2010): 686–699.

68. Phone interview with Greg Shaw, September 3, 2003.

69. Phone interview with Paul Brace, September 10, 2003.

Chapter 6

1. Quoted in Peter Overby, "Outside Group Mirrors Successful Strategies of Political Parties," NPR, August 22, 2014, http://www.npr.org/blogs/itsallpolitics/2014/08/22/342354175/outside-group-mirrors-successful-strategies-of-political-parties.

2. Shane Goldmacher, "This Man Is the Future of Super PACs," *National Journal,* May 5, 2014, http://www.nationaljournal.com/magazine/this-man-is-the-future-of-super-pacs-20140505.

3. Quoted in Karen Tumulty, "Super PACs' Spending Isn't Always Welcomed by Candidates They Support," *Washington Post,* August 5, 2014, http://www.washingtonpost.com/politics/super-pacs-spending-isnt-always-welcomed-by-candidates-they-support/2014/08/04/ecc36ed6-18ed-11e4-9349-84d4a85be981_story.html.

4. Nicholas Confessore, "Secret Money Fueling a Flood of Political Ads," *New York Times,* October 10, 2014, http://www.nytimes.com/2014/10/11/us/politics/ads-paid-for-by-secret-money-flood-the-midterm-elections.html.

5. Reity O'Brien, "Secretive Groups Spend Millions to Influence State Elections," Center for Public Integrity, October 9, 2014, http://www.publicintegrity.org/2014/10/09/15896/secretive-groups-spend-millions-influence-state-elections.

6. Seth Masket, "Are the Parties Devolving?" Mischiefs of Faction, March 3, 2014, http://www.mischiefsoffaction.com/2014/03/are-parties-devolving.html.

7. David A. Graham, "Really, Would You Let Your Daughter Marry a Democrat?" *Atlantic,* September 27, 2012, http://www.theatlantic.com/politics/archive/2012/09/really-would-you-let-your-daughter-marry-a-democrat/262959/.

8. Ed Kilgore, "Diagnosing Dems," *Blueprint,* May 17, 2006, http://www.dlc.org/ndol_cid527.html?contentid=253867&kaid=127&subid=171.

9. Quoted in Mark Leibovich, "The Tea-Party Primary," *New York Times Magazine,* January 10, 2010, 29.

10. John Celock, "Steve Morris, Kansas Senate President, Blames Moderates' Defeat on Conservative Attack Ads," *Huffington Post,* August 8, 2012, http://www.huffington post.com/2012/08/08/steve-morris-kansas-senate-koch-brothers_n_1757928.html.

11. Martin Gilens and Benjamin I. Page, "Testing Theories of American Politics: Elites, Interest Groups, and Average Citizens," *Perspectives on Politics* 12, no. 3 (2014): 575, doi:10.1017/S1537592714001595.

12. Quoted in Jeff Greenfield, "Hayes's Ride," *Washington Monthly,* March 2003.

13. Alvin Kess, *Politics in New York State* (Syracuse, NY: Syracuse University Press, 1965), 29.

14. David R. Mayhew, *Placing Parties in American Politics: Organization, Electoral Settings, and Government Activity in the Twentieth Century* (Princeton, NJ: Princeton University Press, 1986), esp. 24.

15. Quoted in Bertil L. Hanson, "County Commissioners of Oklahoma," *Midwest Journal of Political Science* 9 (1965): 396.

16. Joel H. Sibley, "The Rise and Fall of American Political Parties, 1790–1990," in *The Parties Respond: Changes in the American Party System,* ed. L. Sandy Maisel (Boulder, CO: Westview Press, 1990), 9.

17. Mayhew, *Placing Parties in American Politics,* 185.

18. John F. Bibby and Thomas M. Holbrook, "Parties and Elections," in *Politics in the American States: A Comparative Analysis,* 7th ed., ed. Virginia Gray, Russell L. Hanson, and Herbert Jacobs (Washington, DC: CQ Press, 1999), 71.

19. John F. Bibby, "State and Local Parties in a Candidate-Centered Age," in *American State and Local Politics: Directions for the 21st Century,* ed. Ronald E. Weber and Paul Brace (New York: Chatham House, 1999), 198.

20. Rhodes Cook, "Republican Brawls Through the Century Helped Define Party for Years to Come," *Congressional Quarterly Weekly Report,* April 6, 1996, 942.

21. John R. Schmidt and Wayne W. Whalen, "Credentials Contests at the 1968—and 1972—Democratic National Conventions," *Harvard Law Review* 82 (May 1969): 1456.

22. Alan Greenblatt, "History: Winds of War Blew Through Chicago," *Congressional Quarterly Weekly Report,* August 17, 1996, 23.

23. Quoted in Joe Wagner, "Former Mayor John Coyne of Brooklyn, 97, Remembered as Influential Politician," *Plain Dealer,* July 21, 2014, http://www.cleveland.com/metro/index.ssf/2014/07/post_239.html.

24. Quoted in Alan Greenblatt, "Wired to Win," *Governing,* October 2006, 26.

25. Bibby, "State and Local Parties," 199.

26. Sasha Issenberg, "A More Perfect Union," *MIT Technology Review,* December 16, 2012, http://www.technologyreview.com/featuredstory/508836/how-obama-used-big-data-to-rally-voters-part-1/.

27. Peter W. Wielhower and Brad Lockerbie, "Party Contacting and Political Participation, 1952–90," *American Journal of Political Science* 38 (February 1994): 213.

28. See John H. Kessel, "Ray Bliss and the Development of the Ohio Republican Party During the 1950s," in *Politics, Professionalism, and Power: Modern Party Organization and the Legacy of Ray C. Bliss,* ed. John C. Green (Lanham, MD: University Press of America, 1994), 49–50.

29. "Major Party Candidates With Major Party Competition in the November 2014 State Legislative Elections," Ballotpedia, 2014, http://ballotpedia.org/Major_party_candidates_with_major_party_competition_in_the_November_2014_state_legislative_elections.

30. Malcolm E. Jewell and Sarah M. Morehouse, *Political Parties and Elections in American States,* 4th ed. (Washington, DC: CQ Press, 2001), 22–23.

31. Ruy Teixeira, ed., *America's New Swing Region: Changing Politics and Demographics in the Mountain West* (Washington, DC: Brookings Institution Press, 2012), 43.

32. Alan Greenblatt, "How California Is Turning the Rest of the West Blue," NPR, August 29, 2013, http://www.npr.org/blogs/itsallpolitics/2013/08/29/216150644/how-california-is-turning-the-rest-of-the-west-blue.

33. Jason Szep, "Youth Turnout in Election Biggest in 20 Years," Reuters, November 8, 2006.

34. Emily Hoban Kirby and Kei Kawashima-Ginsberg, "The Youth Vote in 2008," Center for Information and Research on Civic Learning and Engagement, August 17, 2009, http://www.civicyouth.org/PopUps/FactSheets/FS_youth_Voting_2008_updated_6.22.pdf.

35. Alan Ehrenhalt, "Political Pawns," *Governing,* July 2000, 20.

36. Quoted in Alan Greenblatt, "Citizens United's Corporate Candidate," *Governing,* May 2012, http://www.governing.com/topics/politics/gov-citizen-uniteds-corporate-candidate.html.

37. Leon D. Epstein, *Political Parties in the American Mold* (Madison: University of Wisconsin Press, 1986), 155.

38. Michael P. McDonald, "Partisan Voter Registration Totals," *Huffington Post,* October 13, 2010, http://www.huffingtonpost.com/michael-p-mcdonald/partisan-voter-registrati_b_761713.html.

39. Jewell and Morehouse, *Political Parties and Elections,* 76.

40. Bibby, "State and Local Parties," 198.

41. Bibby and Holbrook, "Parties and Elections," 70.

42. Ibid., 71.

43. Thomas B. Edsall, "Would Stronger Parties Mean Less Polarization?" *New York Times,* October 21, 2014, http://www.nytimes.com/2014/10/22/opinion/would-stronger-parties-mean-less-polarization.html.

44. Alan Greenblatt, "Soft Money: The Root of All Evil or a Party-Building Necessity?" *Congressional Quarterly Weekly Report,* September 26, 1997, 2064.

45. Quoted in Ruth Marcus, "Party Spending Unleashed; Justices Say Independence From Candidate Is Key," *Washington Post,* June 27, 1996, A1.

46. Don Van Natta Jr. and Richard A. Oppel Jr., "Parties Set Up Groups to Elude Soft Money Ban," *New York Times,* November 2, 2002, A1.

47. Agustín Armendariz and Aron Pilhofer, "McCain-Feingold Changes State Party Spending," Center for Public Integrity, May 26, 2005, http://www.publicintegrity.org/2005/05/26/5836/mccain-feingold-changes-state-party-spending.

48. Jim Rutenberg, "Money Talks," *New York Times Magazine,* October 19, 2014, 31.

49. Interview with Larry J. Sabato, May 2002.

50. Pew Research Center for the People and the Press, *Partisan Polarization Surges in Bush, Obama Years* (Washington, DC: Pew Research Center, June 4, 2012), http://www.people-press.org/2012/06/04/partisan-polarization-surges-in-bush-obama-years/.

51. Dana Milbank, "Where Have All the Candidates Gone?" *Washington Post,* May 15, 2012, http://www.washingtonpost.com/opinions/where-have-all-the-candidates-gone/2012/05/15/gIQA6ZRISU_story.html.

52. Quoted in Guy Taylor, "Third-Party Candidacies: Rarely Successful, Often Influential," *Washington Times,* November 12, 2012, http://www.washingtontimes.com/news/2012/nov/6/third-party-candidacies-rarely-successful-often-in.

53. Quoted in Joel Siegel, "Party's Over for Liberals," *Daily News,* February 24, 2003, 20.

54. Jeffrey M. Jones, "Record-High 42% of Americans Identify as Independent," Gallup, January 8, 2014, http://www.gallup.com/poll/166763/record-high-americans-identify-independents.aspx.

55. Larry M. Bartels, "Partisanship and Voting Behavior, 1952–1996," *American Journal of Political Science* 44 (January 2000): 35.

56. Ibid., 36–37.

57. Bruce E. Keith, David B. Magleby, Candice J. Nelson, Elizabeth Orr, Mark C. Westlye, and Raymond E. Wolfinger, *The Myth of the Independent Voter* (Berkeley: University of California Press, 1992).

58. Interview with Jane Jech, August 17, 2012.

59. Quoted in Alan Greenblatt, "Politics and Marketing Merge in Parties' Bid for Relevance," *Congressional Quarterly Weekly Report,* August 16, 1997, 1967.

60. Frank J. Sorauf, *Political Parties in the American System* (Boston: Little, Brown, 1964), 13.

61. Clive S. Thomas and Ronald J. Hrebenar, "Interest Groups in the States," in *Politics in the American States: A Comparative Analysis,* 8th ed., ed. Virginia Gray and Russell L. Hanson (Washington, DC: CQ Press, 2004), 114–115.

62. Leah Rush, "Hired Guns," Center for Public Integrity, December 20, 2007, updated August 19, 2011, http://www.publicintegrity.org/2007/12/20/5895/influence-booming-business.

63. Virginia Gray and David Lowery, "Interest Representation in the States," in Weber and Brace, *American State and Local Politics,* 267.

64. Quoted in Alan Rosenthal, *The Third House: Lobbyists and Lobbying in the States,* 2nd ed. (Washington, DC: CQ Press, 2001), 17.

65. Alex Stuckey, "St. Louis Doctor's Crusade Finally Ends With Tanning Bed Bill," *St. Louis Post-Dispatch,* May 20, 2014, http://www.stltoday.com/news/local/govt-and-politics/st-louis-doctor-s-crusade-finally-ends-with-tanning-bed/article_7ea484ae-9a3b-54f4-9559-3cd85a66552b.html.

66. Lee Drutman, "The Complexities of Lobbying: Toward a Deeper Understanding of the Profession," *PS: Political Science & Politics* 43, no. 4 (October 2010): 835.

67. Richard L. Hall and Molly E. Reynolds, "Targeted Issue Advertising and Legislative Strategy: The Inside Ends of Outside Lobbying," *Journal of Politics* 74, no. 3 (July 2012): 888–902.

68. Christopher Swope, "Winning Without Steaks and Cigars," *Governing,* November 2000. See also Rob Gurwitt, "Cookie-Jar Clampdown," *Governing,* April 2007.

69. Phone interview with John Weingart, August 18, 2010.

70. Quoted in Alan Greenblatt, "Illinois Declares Truce in Cupcake War," NPR, June 6, 2014, http://www.npr.org/2014/06/06/319413152/illinois-declares-truce-in-cupcake-war.

71. Ramesh Ponnuru, "Is Your Fortune Teller Licensed?" *Bloomberg View,* March 28, 2014, http://www.bloombergview.com/articles/2014-03-28/is-your-fortune-teller-licensed.

72. Quoted in Jacob Goldstein, "So You Think You Can Be a Hair Braider?" *New York Times,* June 12, 2012, http://www.nytimes.com/2012/06/17/magazine/so-you-think-you-can-be-a-hair-braider.html.

73. Rosenthal, *Third House,* 78.

74. Ibid., 45.

75. Quoted in Alan Greenblatt, "Secondhand Spokesmen," *Governing,* April 2002, http://www.governing.com/topics/health-human-services/Secondhand-Spokesmen.html.

76. Quoted in Rosenthal, *Third House,* 61.

77. Clive S. Thomas and Ronald J. Hrebenar, "Lobby Clout," *State Legislatures,* April 1999.

78. Thomas and Hrebenar, "Interest Groups in the States," 121–122.

79. Alan Greenblatt, "Real Power," *Governing,* June 2006, 46.

80. Phone interview with Alan Rosenthal, February 6, 2007.

Chapter 7

1. Quoted in Rex Santus, "With Congress Deadlocked, NCSL Says Eyes Are on State Legislatures," *Denver Post,* August 8, 2014, http://www.denverpost.com/politics/ci_26295129/congress-deadlocked-ncsl-says-eyes-are-state-legislatures.

2. Phone interview with Lara Brown, March 6, 2014.

3. Pew Research Center for the People and the Press, "State Governments Viewed Favorably as Federal Rating Hits New Low," Pew Research Center, Washington, DC, April 15, 2013, http://www.people-press.org/2013/04/15/state-goverrmnents-viewed-favorably-as-federal-rating-hits-new-low.

4. Zach Patton, "John Hickenlooper: The Man in the Middle," *Governing,* August 2014, http://www.governing.com/topics/politics/gov-colorado-hickenlooper.html.

5. Quoted in Nicholas Confessore and Michael Barboro, "New York Allows Same-Sex Marriage, Becoming Largest State to Pass Law," *New York Times,* June 24, 2011, http://www.nytimes.com/2011/06/25/nyregion/gay-marriage-approved-by-new-york-senate.html?pagewanted=all.

6. Quoted in ibid.

7. Quoted in Philip D. Duncan and Christine C. Lawrence, *Congressional Quarterly's Politics in America 1998* (Washington, DC: CQ Press, 1997), 755.

8. William M. Bulger, *While the Music Lasts: My Life in Politics* (Boston: Houghton Mifflin, 1996), 71.

9. Alexander Hamilton, *Federalist* No. 73, http://thomas.loc.gov/home/fedpapers/fed_73.html.

10. Bob Bergren, presentation at the Council of State Governments western regional meeting, October 7, 2009.

11. Boris Shor, "How States Are Polarized and Getting More Polarized," *Washington Post*, January 14, 2014, http://www.washingtonpost.com/blogs/monkey-cage/wp/2014/01/14/how-u-s-state-legislatures-are-polarized-and-getting-more-polarized-in-2-graphs/.

12. Quoted in Rob Gurwitt, "The Riskiest Business," *Governing*, March 2001, 21.

13. "Filed House Bills," Texas Legislature, September 6, 2014, http://www.capitol.state.tx.us/Reports/Report.aspx?LegSess=83R&ID=housefiled; "Filed Senate Bills," Texas Legislature, September 6, 2014, http://www.capitol.state.tx.us/Reports/Report.aspx?LegSess=83R&ID=senatefiled; "2013 Montana Session Statistics," State Net, November 29, 2013, http://statenet.com/resources/session_statistics.php?state=MT.

14. Quoted in Alan Greenblatt, "The Date-Checking Game," *Governing*, October 2006, 17.

15. Tom Loftus, "Optometrists' Kentucky Political Donations Exceed $400,000," *Louisville Courier-Journal*, February 15, 2011, http://www.courier-journal.com/article/20110215/NEWS01/302150097/Optometrists-Kentucky-political-donations-exceed-400-000?gcheck=1&nclick_check=1.

16. Judith C. Meredith, *Lobbying on a Shoestring*, 2nd ed. (Dover, MA: Auburn House, 1989), 4.

17. "Government Workers Don't Need Even More Protections," *Modesto Bee*, February 17, 2012.

18. Melissa Maynard, "A Bill of Rights for State Workers?" Stateline, April 3, 2012, http://www.pewstates.org/projects/stateline/headlines/a-bill-of-rights-for-state-workers-85899380541.

19. Greenblatt, "Fit to Be Tied," *Governing*, August 2001, 20.

20. Quoted in Andy Sher, "GOP Claims Strides on Issues," *Chattanooga Times Free Press*, June 21, 2009, A1.

21. Alan Rosenthal, *Engines of Democracy: Politics and Policymaking in State Legislatures* (Washington, DC: CQ Press, 2009), 310.

22. Virginia Gray and David Lowery, "Where Do Policy Ideas Come From? A Study of Minnesota Legislators and Staffers," *Journal of Public Administration Research and Theory* 10 (January 2000): 573–597.

23. See Gary F. Moncrief, Joel A. Thompson, and Karl T. Kurtz, "Old Statehouse Ain't What It Used to Be," *Legislative Studies Quarterly* 21, no. 1 (February 1996): 57–72.

24. MSNBC interview with Amy Klobuchar, July 1, 2009.

25. Rosenthal, *Engines of Democracy*, 84.

26. Interview with Rosalind Kurita, October 7, 2002.

27. Alan Rosenthal, *Governors and Legislatures: Contending Powers* (Washington, DC: CQ Press, 1990), 187.

28. Diane D. Blair, *Arkansas Politics and Government* (Lincoln: University of Nebraska Press, 1988), 182, cited in Rosenthal, *Governors and Legislatures*.

29. Katherine Barrett and Richard Greene, "B&G Interview: Questions for John Turcotte," *Governing*, February 1, 2008, http://www.governing.com/column/bg-interview-questions-john-turcotte.

30. John Turcotte, presentation at the annual meeting of the National Conference of State Legislatures, July 21, 2009.

31. Alan Rosenthal, Burdett Loomis, John Hibbing, and Karl Kurtz, *Republic on Trial: The Case for Representative Democracy* (Washington, DC: CQ Press, 2003), 26.

32. Karen Hansen, "Red Tide," *State Legislatures*, December 2010, 14.

33. Wes Clarke, "The Divided Government and Budget Conflict in the U.S. States," *Legislative Studies Quarterly* 23, no. 1 (February 1998): 5.

34. National Conference of State Legislatures, "In Case of a Tie . . . ," 2014, http://www.ncsl.org/legislatures-elections/legislatures/incaseofatie.aspx.

35. Quoted in Alan Greenblatt, "Reformer in Power," *Governing*, January 2009, 20.

36. Meredith, Lobbying on a Shoestring, 34.

37. Edmund Burke, "The English Constitutional System," in *Representation*, ed. Hannah Pitkin (New York: Atherton Press, 1969).

38. Quoted in Christopher Swope, "Winning Without Steak and Cigars," *Governing*, November 2000, 40.

39. Quoted in Rosenthal, *Engines of Democracy*, 237.

40. Quoted in Bill Reker, "Rep. English Stripped of Committee Positions After Tax Cut Vote," KMOX, May 8, 2014, http://stlouis.cbslocal.com/2014/05/08/democrat-loses-committee-spots-after-tax-cut-vote/.

41. "Sinquefield Money Flows in Fallout Over Tax Cut Fight," *St. Louis Post-Dispatch*, July 7, 2014, http://www.stltoday.com/news/local/govt-and-politics/sinquefield-money-flows-in-fallout-over-tax-cut-fight/article_46c4506f-f603-5ce4-b3a9-1d4dd76de2e9.html.

42. Virginia Public Access Project, "Saslaw for Senate—Richard: Money Out," http://www.vpap.org/committees/profile/money_out_vendors/1696?start_year=2011&end_year=2011&lookup_type=year&filing_period=all&filter_expend=all&order=amount.

43. Richard A. Clucas, "Principal-Agent Theory and the Power of State House Speakers," *Legislative Studies Quarterly* 26, no. 2 (May 2001): 319–338.

44. Quoted in Alan Greenblatt, "The Mapmaking Mess," *Governing*, January 2001, 23.

45. Aaron Blake, "Name That District Winner: 'Upside-Down Elephant,'" *Washington Post*, The Fix blog, August 12, 2011, http://www.washingtonpost.com/

blogs/the-fix/post/name-that-district-winner-upside-down-elephant/2011/08/11/gIQABOTABJ_blog.html#pagebreak.

46. Nolan Hicks, "New Congressional Redistricting Maps Very Close to Greg Abbott's Plan," *Houston Chronicle,* Texas on the Potomac blog, February 28, 2012, http://blog.chron.com/txpotomac/2012/02/new-congressional-redistricting-maps-very-close-to-greg-abbotts-plan.

47. Alan Ehrenhalt, "Party Lines," *Governing,* January 2007, 11.

48. Olga Pierce and Jeff Larson, "How Democrats Fooled California's Redistricting Commission," ProPublica, December 21, 2011, http://www.propublica.org/article/how-democrats-fooled-californias-redistricting-commission.

49. Quoted in Josh Goodman, "Why Redistricting Commissions Aren't Immune From Politics," Stateline, January 27, 2012.

50. Greenblatt, "The Mapmaking Mess," 22.

51. Josh Goodman, "Farming for Votes," *Governing,* November 2010, 46, http://www.governing.com/topics/politics/future-redistricting-rural-america.html.

52. Josh Goodman, "Introducing America's Largest State Legislative District," *Governing,* Politics blog, February 11, 2010, http://www.governing.com/blogs/politics/Introducing-Americas-Largest-State.html.

53. Quoted in Sean Cockerham, "Lawmakers Spar Over Adding Seats to Legislature," *Alaska Dispatch News,* February 2, 2010, http://www.adn.com/2010/02/02/1121936/lawmakers-spar-over-adding-districts.html.

54. Seth Motel, "Who Runs for Office? A Profile of the 2%," Fact Tank, Pew Research Center, Washington, DC, September 3, 2014, http://www.pewresearch.org/fact-tank/2014/09/03/who-runs-for-office-a-profile-of-the-2/.

55. Rosenthal et al., *Republic on Trial,* 69.

56. Quoted in Howard Troxler, "Choice for Attorney General Not So Easy," *St. Petersburg Times,* October 18, 2002, 1B.

57. Quoted in Alan Greenblatt, "Real Power," *Governing,* June 2006, 46.

58. Jay Root, "For John Carona, Conflicts and Interests," *Texas Tribune,* May 20, 2013, http://www.texastribune.org/2013/05/20/conflicts-and-interests-sen-john-carona/.

59. Otis White, "Making Laws Is No Job for Lawyers These Days," *Governing,* June 1994, 27.

60. Kathleen Dolan and Lynne E. Ford, "Change and Continuity Among Women Legislators: Evidence From Three Decades," *Political Research Quarterly* 50 (March 1997): 137–152.

61. Center for American Women and Politics, "Women in State Legislatures 2007," December 2007, http://www.cawp.rutgers.edu/fast_facts/levels_of_office/documents/stleg07.pdf.

62. Renee Loth, "The Matriarchy up North," *Boston Globe,* April 30, 2009, 15.

63. Gwen Moran, "How a Nonprofit Is Teaching Women to Run for Office," *Fast Company,* August 26, 2014, http://www.fastcompany.com/3034778/strong-female-lead/how-a-nonprofit-is-teaching-women-to-run-for-office.

64. Jennifer L. Lawless and Richard L. Fox, *Girls Just Wanna Not Run: The Gender Gap in Young Americans' Political Ambition* (Washington, DC: Women and Politics Institute, March 2013), http://www.american.edu/spa/wpi/upload/girls-just-wanna-not-run_policy-report.pdf.

65. Interview with Barbara Lee, October 8, 2002.

66. Thomas H. Little, Dana Dunn, and Rebecca E. Deen, "A View From the Top: Gender Differences in Legislative Priorities Among State Legislative Leaders," *Women and Politics* 22, no. 4 (2001): 29–50.

67. Donald E. Whistler and Mark C. Ellickson, "The Incorporation of Women in State Legislatures: A Description," *Women and Politics* 20, no. 2 (1999): 84.

68. Ibid.

69. Michael B. Berkman and Robert E. O'Connor, "Do Women Legislators Matter? Female Legislators and State Abortion Policy," *American Politics Quarterly* 21, no. 1 (January 1993): 105.

70. Kerry L. Haynie, *African American Legislators in the American States* (New York: Columbia University Press, 2001), 19.

71. Ibid., 2.

72. Ibid., 25.

73. Bernard Grofman and Lisa Handley, "Impact of the Voting Rights Act on Black Representation in Southern State Legislatures," *Legislative Studies Quarterly* 16 (1991): 111–128.

74. Malcolm E. Jewell and Samuel C. Patterson, *The Legislative Process in the States* (New York: Random House, 1966), 138.

75. William Pound, "State Legislative Careers: Twenty-Five Years of Reform," in *Changing Patterns in State Legislative Careers,* ed. Gary F. Moncrief and Joel A. Thompson (Ann Arbor: University of Michigan Press, 1992).

76. James D. King, "Changes in Professionalism in U.S. State Legislatures," *Legislative Studies Quarterly* 25, no. 3 (May 2000): 327–343.

77. National Conference of State Legislatures, "Size of State Legislative Staff: 1979, 1988 1996, 2003, 2009," June 2009, http://www.ncsl.org/legislatures-elections/legisdata/staff-change-chart-1979-1988-1996-2003-2009.aspx.

78. Josh Goodman, "Pennsylvania Takes Step Toward Smaller Legislature," Stateline, April 11, 2012, http://www.pewstates.org/projects/stateline/headlines/pennsylvania-takes-step-toward-smaller-legislature-85899381094.

79. Wade Rawlins, "Lawmakers Adjourn," *News and Observer* (Raleigh), October 4, 2002.

80. Ellen Perlman, "The 'Gold-Plated' Legislature," *Governing*, February 1998, 37.

81. Editorial, *Clarion Ledger*, April 21, 2008, 6A.

82. Alan Ehrenhalt, "An Embattled Institution," *Governing*, January 1992, 30.

83. Marist Poll, "6/30: NY State Senate Unrest Irks Voters," June 30, 2009, http://maristpoll.marist.edu/630-ny-state-senate-unrest-does-not-sit-well-with-voters/.

84. Field Poll, "Brown's Job Rating Remains Favorable. Very Poor Appraisal of the Legislature. Yet, Voters Oppose Having Lawmakers Work Part-Time," February 25, 2012, 6.

85. Rosenthal, *Engines of Democracy*, 19.

86. Interview with John Hibbing, October 15, 2002.

87. Quoted in Nicholas Confessore, "Perception of Being Slighted Stoked Revolt by Lawmakers," *New York Times*, February 9, 2007, B7.

88. William Powers, "The Saturation Fallacy," *National Journal*, September 7, 2002, 2565.

89. Jonathan Walters, "How to Tame the Press," *Governing*, January 1994, 30.

90. Phillip Reese, "Arrest Rate in California Senate Higher Than Arrest Rate in All of State's Cities," *Sacramento Bee*, August 26, 2014, http://www.sacbee.com/2014/08/26/6655649/arrest-rate-in-california-senate.html.

91. Jodi Enda, Katerina Eva Matsa, and Jan Lauren Boyles, *America's Shifting Statehouse Press* (Washington, DC: Pew Research Journalism Project, July 10, 2014), http://www.journalism.org/2014/07/10/americas-shifting-statehouse-press/.

92. Brian Duggan, Twitter post, January 29, 2014, https://twitter.com/brianduggan/status/428669730329612288.

93. Peverill Squire, "Professionalization and Public Opinion of State Legislatures," *Journal of Politics* 55, no. 2 (1993): 479–491.

94. Interview with Gary Moncrief, October 2, 2002.

95. Quoted in Rob Gurwitt, "Can Nonprofit News Survive?" Stateline, June 9, 2011.

96. New Jersey Senate Democrats, "Media Advisory—Senator Whelan to Hold 'Twitter Town Hall' Live on Monday," July 6, 2012.

97. Quoted in Jon Kuhl, "Tools of the Trade: Social Media Rules!" *State Legislatures*, June 2013, http://www.ncsl.org/bookstore/state-legislatures-magazine/tools-of-the-trade_june-2013.aspx.

98. Glenn Blain, "Alec Baldwin Engages in Twitter War With State GOP Leader Dean Skelos," *New York Daily News*, October 27, 2011, http://www.nydailynews.com/news/politics/alec-baldwin-engages-twitter-war-state-gop-leader-dean-skelos-article-1.968221.

99. Jason Linkins, "Jeff Frederick's Twitter Use Foils GOP Virginia Senate Coup," *Huffington Post*, February 10, 2009, http://www.huffingtonpost.com/2009/02/10/jeff-fredericks-twitter-u_n_165769.html.

100. Anita Chadha and Robert A. Bernstein, "Why Incumbents Are Treated So Harshly: Term Limits for State Legislators," *American Politics Quarterly* 24 (1996): 363–376.

101. Patricia Lopez, "Coleman's Journey Crosses Typical Divide," *Minneapolis Star Tribune*, October 16, 2002.

102. Quoted in Rob Gurwitt, "Southern Discomfort," *Governing*, October 2002, 32.

Chapter 8

1. Interview with Dee Richard, September 5, 2012.

2. Quoted in Alan Greenblatt, "When Governors Don't Play Nice," *Governing*, November 2012, 9.

3. Quoted in Larry J. Sabato, *Goodbye to Good-Time Charlie: The American Governorship Transformed*, 2nd ed. (Washington, DC: CQ Press, 1983), 4.

4. Lynn R. Muchmore, "The Governor as Manager," in *Being Governor: The View From the Office*, ed. Thad Beyle and Lynn R. Muchmore (Durham, NC: Duke University Press, 1983), 83.

5. Terry Sanford, *Storm Over the States* (New York: McGraw-Hill, 1967), 185–188, quoted in Eric B. Herzik and Brent W. Brown, "Symposium on Governors and Public Policy," *Policy Studies Journal* 17 (1989): 761.

6. E. Lee Bernick, "Gubernatorial Tools: Formal vs. Informal," *Journal of Politics* 42 (1979): 661.

7. Quoted in Alan Rosenthal, *Governors and Legislatures: Contending Powers* (Washington, DC: CQ Press, 1990), 14.

8. Muchmore, "Governor as Manager," 13.

9. Brian Balogh, "Introduction: Directing Democracy," in *A Legacy of Innovation: Governors and Public Policy*, ed. Ethan G. Sribnick (Philadelphia: University of Pennsylvania Press, 2008), 9.

10. Ann O'M. Bowman, Neal D. Woods, and Milton R. Stark II, "Governors Turn Pro: Separation of Powers and the Institutionalization of the American Governorship," *Political Research Quarterly* 63, no. 2 (June 2010): 307.

11. Marjorie Smith, "NH's Executive Branch Needs Reform," *Manchester Union-Leader*, August 1, 2012, 7.

12. "Colorado Gov. John Hickenlooper's Helicopter Stops to Rescue Flood-Stranded Families," CBS News, September 15, 2013, http://www.cbsnews.com/news/colorado-gov-john-hickenloopers-helicopter-stops-to-rescue-flood-stranded-families/.

13. Quoted in Alan Greenblatt, "In Emergencies, Politicians Are Expected to Master Disaster," NPR, September 17, 2013, http://www.npr.org/blogs/itsallpolitics/2013/09/17/223389847/in-emergencies-politicians-are-expected-to-master-disaster.

14. Jenna Portnoy, "Once Again, Christie Thrives Amid Chaos as Seaside Fire Reminiscent of Sandy,"

Star-Ledger, September 17, 2013, http://www.nj.com/politics/index.ssf/2013/09/christie_sandy_response.html.

15. Quoted in Greenblatt, "In Emergencies."

16. Quoted in Jon C. Teaford, "Governors and Economic Development," in Sribnick, *Legacy of Innovation,* 113.

17. Quoted in Alan Greenblatt, "Governing in the Fast Lane," *Governing,* January 2004, 28.

18. David Freedlander, "Governor Cuomo: 'Extreme Conservatives Have No Place in New York,'" *The Daily Beast,* January 22, 2014, http://www.thedailybeast.com/articles/2014/01/22/governor-cuomo-extreme-conservatives-have-no-place-in-new-york.html.

19. Sabato, Goodbye to Good-Time Charlie, 4.

20. See Muchmore, "Governor as Manager."

21. Alan Greenblatt, "Tug of War," *Governing,* August 2004, 32.

22. Rob Gurwitt, "The Governor's People," *Governing,* March 1991, 28.

23. Thad Kousser and Justin H. Phillips, *The Power of American Governors* (New York: Cambridge University Press, 2012), 26.

24. Daniel C. Vock, "Govs Enjoy Quirky Veto Power," Stateline, April 24, 2007.

25. Quoted in Alan Greenblatt, "Killing Frankenstein," *Governing,* June 2008, 17.

26. Maggie Clark, "Governors Balance Pardons With Politics," Stateline, February 8, 2013.

27. Quoted in Alan Greenblatt, "Why Are We Meeting Like This?" *Governing,* August 2002, 40.

28. Quoted in Kim Severson, "South Carolina Supreme Court Rules Against Governor in Legislative Feud," *New York Times,* June 7, 2011, 14.

29. Ibid.

30. Quoted in Alan Rosenthal, *The Best Job in Politics: Exploring How Governors Succeed as Policy Leaders* (Washington, DC: CQ Press, 2013), 28.

31. Quoted in Kousser and Phillips, *Power of American Governors,* 40.

32. Laura A. Van Assendelft, *Governors, Agenda Setting, and Divided Government* (Lanham, MD: University Press of America, 1997), 1.

33. Rosenthal, *Best Job in Politics,* 29.

34. Ralph Wright, *Inside the Statehouse: Lessons From the Speaker* (Washington, DC: CQ Press, 2005), 88.

35. Quoted in Alan Greenblatt, "States of Frustration," *Governing,* January 2004, 26.

36. Quoted in Alan Greenblatt, "Rod Reeling," *Governing,* September 2007, 18.

37. Quoted in Van Assendelft, *Governors, Agenda Setting, and Divided Government,* 71.

38. Jan Reid, "The Case of Ann Richards: Women in Gubernatorial Office," in *A Legacy of Leadership: Governors and American History,* ed. Clayton McClure Brooks (Philadelphia: University of Pennsylvania Press, 2008), 185.

39. Raphael J. Sonenshein, "Can Black Candidates Win Statewide Elections?" *Political Science Quarterly* 105 (1990): 219.

40. Rosenthal, *Best Job in Politics,* 58.

41. Quoted in Alan Greenblatt, "All Politics Is National," *Governing,* October 2012, 28.

42. Wisconsin Democracy Campaign, "Recall Race for Governor Cost $81 Million," July 25, 2012, updated January 31, 2013, http://www.wisdc.org/pr072512.php.

43. Kousser and Phillips, *Power of American Governors,* 83.

44. Quoted in Thomas Clouse, "Kempthorne at the Helm," *Idaho Statesman,* January 5, 1999, 1A.

45. Quoted in Lou Jacobson, "Where Have All the Governors Gone?" *Governing,* March 4, 2013, http://www.governing.com/blogs/politics/Where-Have-All-the-Governors-Gone.html.

46. Quoted in Brian Friel, "For Governors in Congress, No More King of the Hill," *National Journal,* June 27, 2009.

47. Quoted in Clayton McClure Brooks, "Afterword: Governing the Twenty-First Century," in Brooks, *Legacy of Leadership,* 219.

48. Eric Ostermeier, "A Brief History of Ex-Governors Returning to Power," *Smart Politics,* September 2, 2014, http://blog.lib.umn.edu/cspg/smartpolitics/2014/09/a_brief_history_of_ex-governor.php.

49. Interview with Julia Hurst, January 5, 2004.

50. Quoted in Jo Mannies, "Kinder Says He's Tired of Being Ignored by Governor," St. Louis Public Radio, January 22, 2014, http://news.stlpublicradio.org/post/kinder-says-hes-tired-being-ignored-governor.

51. Quoted in Michael J. Mishak, "Gavin Newsom a Rising Star Who's in Eclipse as Lt. Governor," *Los Angeles Times,* July 15, 2013, http://www.latimes.com/local/la-me-gavin-newsom-20130715-dto-htmlstory.html.

52. Associated Press, "The Decatur Daily on Windom Candidacy," October 4, 2001.

53. Quoted in Josh Goodman, "The Second Best Job in the State," *Governing,* April 2009, 34.

54. Quoted in Alan Greenblatt, "Where Campaign Money Flows," *Governing,* November 2002, 44.

55. Quoted in Eric Lipton, "Lobbyists, Bearing Gifts, Pursue Attorneys General," *New York Times,* October 28, 2014, http://www.nytimes.com/2014/10/29/us/lobbyists-bearing-gifts-pursue-attorneys-general.html.

56. Fred Barnes, "The Last Redoubt," *Weekly Standard,* July 22, 2013, http://www.weeklystandard.com/articles/last-redoubt_739263.html.

57. Megan Verlee, "Secretaries of State at Center of Election Battles," NPR, January 18, 2012, http://www.npr.org/2012/01/18/145351397/secretaries-of-state-at-center-of-election-battles.

58. Quoted in Alan Greenblatt, "Once Obscure State Job Is Now Attracting Millions of Campaign Dollars," NPR, February 21, 2014, http://www.npr.org/blogs/itsallpolitics/2014/02/19/279659009/once-obscure-state-job-is-now-attracting-millions-of-campaign-dollars.

59. Quoted in Louis Jacobson, "Secretaries of State Still Juggling Politics, Elections," *Governing*, Politics blog, September 21, 2012, http://www.governing.com/blogs/politics/gov-secretaries-state-juggling-politics-elections.html.

60. Rosenthal, *Best Job in Politics*, 199.

Chapter 9

1. Quoted in Scott Shane, "Ideology Serves as a Wild Card on Court Pick," *New York Times*, November 4, 2005, A1.

2. Sandra Day O'Connor, "The Threat to Judicial Independence," *Wall Street Journal*, September 27, 2006, A18.

3. Bill Raftery, "2011 Year in Review: Record Number of Impeachment Attempts Against Judges for Their Decisions," Gavel to Gavel, December 27, 2011, http://gaveltogavel.us/site/2011/12/27/2011-year-in-review-record-number-of-impeachment-attempts-against-judges-for-their-decisions.

4. Quoted in "Politics, Intolerance, Fair Courts" (editorial), *New York Times*, August 10, 2012.

5. *Citizens United v. Federal Election Commission*, 558 U.S. (2010) (Stevens, dissenting).

6. O'Connor, "Threat to Judicial Independence," A18.

7. Quoted in Steven M. Puiszis, ed., *Without Fear or Favor in 2011: A New Decade of Challenges to Judicial Independence and Accountability* (Chicago: DRI—The Voice of the Defense Bar, 2011), 5.

8. Martin Bricketto, "NJ Judiciary Chief Warns of Vacancy Related Backlogs," Law360, April 30, 2014, http://www.law360.com/articles/533238/nj-judiciary-chief-warns-of-vacancy-related-backlogs.

9. Tom Parker, "Alabama Justices Surrender to Judicial Activism," *Birmingham News*, January 1, 2006, 4B.

10. R. LaFountain, R. Schauffler, S. Strickland, and K. Holt, *Examining the Work of State Courts: An Analysis of 2010 State Court Caseloads* (Williamsburg, VA: National Center for State Courts, 2012), http://www.courtstatistics.org/Other-Pages/~/media/Microsites/Files/CSP/DATA PDF/CSP_DEC.ashx.

11. David Rottman and Shauna M. Strickland, *State Court Organization, 2004* (Washington, DC: Bureau of Justice Statistics, 2004), http://www.bjs.gov/content/pub/pdf/sco04.pdf.

12. Diana Penner, "Judge: Jurors Antics Harmless," *Indianapolis Star*, November 30, 2006, 1.

13. Will Stone, "Nevada Court Quagmire Waits—and Waits—for Voters to Solve it," NPR, March 18, 2014, http://www.wbur.org/npr/291172155/nevada-court-quagmire-waits-and-waits-for-voters-to-solve-it?ft=3&f=291172155.

14. Court Statistics Project, "State Court Structure Charts," National Center for State Courts, 2013, http://www.courtstatistics.org/Other-Pages/State_Court_Structure_Charts.aspx.

15. Sari S. Escovitz, *Judicial Selection and Tenure 4* (Chicago: American Judicature Society, 1975).

16. Caleb Nelson, "A Re-Evaluation of Scholarly Explanations for the Rise of the Elected Judiciary in Antebellum America," *American Journal of Legal History* 37 (April 1993): 190–224.

17. Larry C. Berkson, "Judicial Selection in the United States: A Special Report," *Judicature* 64, no. 4 (1980): 176–193, updated 1999 by Seth Andersen.

18. G. Alan Tarr, "Rethinking the Selection of State Supreme Court Justices," *Willamette Law Review* 39, no. 4 (2003): 1445.

19. Doug McMurdo, "Voters Reject Changing Judge Selection," *Las Vegas Review-Journal*, November 3, 2010.

20. William Raftery, " Judicial Selection in the States," Trends in State Courts, National Center for State Courts, December 2013, http://www.ncsc.org/sitecore/content/microsites/future-trends-2013/home/Monthly-Trends-Articles/Judicial-Selection-in-the-States.aspx.

21. Ciara Torres-Spelliscy, Monique Chase, and Emma Greenman, *Improving Judicial Diversity* (New York: Brennan Center for Justice, New York University School of Law, 2008), http://brennan.3cdn.net/96d16b62f331bb13ac_kfm6bplue.pdf.

22. American Judicature Society, "Judicial Selection in the States: Diversity of the Bench," 2010, http://www.judicialselection.us/judicial_selection/bench_diversity/index.cfm?state.

23. American Judicature Society, "Judicial Selection in the States," 2014, http://www.judicialselection.us.

24. Ibid.

25. "Justice for Sale: Interview, Justices Stephen Breyer and Anthony Kennedy," *Frontline*, PBS, http://www.pbs.org/wgbh/pages/frontline/shows/justice/interviews/supremo.html.

26. Ibid.

27. Paul Brace and Melinda Gann Hall, "Studying Courts Comparatively: The View From the American States," *Political Research Quarterly* 48 (1995): 5. See also Paul Brace and Brent D. Boyea, "State Public Opinion, the Death Penalty, and the Practice of Electing Judges," *American Journal of Political Science* 52, no. 2 (2008): 360–372.

28. Brace and Hall, "Studying Courts Comparatively."

29. Gerald F. Uelmen, "Crocodiles in the Bathtub: Maintaining the Independence of State Supreme Courts in an Era of Judicial Politicization," *Notre Dame Law Review* 72 (1997): 1135–1142.

30. Ibid., 1133, 1137.

31. Stephen J. Ware, "Money, Politics and Judicial Decisions: A Case Study of Arbitration Law in Alabama," *Journal of Law and Politics* 15 (1999): 645.

32. Adam Liptak and Janet Roberts, "Campaign Cash Mirrors a High Court's Rulings," *New York Times,* October 1, 2006.

33. Billy Corriher, *Big Business Taking Over State Supreme Courts: How Campaign Contributions to Judges Tip the Scales Against Individuals* (Washington, DC: Center for American Progress, August 2012), 2.

34. Ibid., 14.

35. Quoted in Liptak and Roberts, "Campaign Cash," sec. 1, 1.

36. "*Caperton v. Massey,*" Brennan Center for Justice, New York University School of Law, New York, June 8, 2009, http://www.brennancenter.org/content/resource/caperton_v_massey.

37. Justice at Stake, "Money and Elections," 2014, http://www.justiceatstake.org/issues/state_court_issues/money__elections.cfm.

38. John Light, "Dark Money's New Frontier: State Judicial Elections," October 31, 2013, http://billmoyers.com/2013/10/31/dark-moneys-new-frontier-state-judicial-elections/.

39. Quoted in Sheila Kaplan, "Justice for Sale," *Common Cause Magazine,* May–June 1987, 29–30.

40. Justice at Stake, "National Surveys of American Voters and State Judges," February 14, 2002, http://www.justiceatstake.org/media/cms/PollingsummaryFINAL_9EDA3EB3BEA78.pdf.

41. Joan Biskupic, "*Caperton v. AT Massey Coal Co*: Supreme Court Case With the Feel of a Best Seller," *USA Today,* February 16, 2009.

42. Uelmen, "Crocodiles in the Bathtub."

43. Adam Skaggs, Maria da Silva, Linda Casey, and Charles Hall, *The New Politics of Judicial Elections 2009–10: How Special Interest "Super Spenders" Threatened Impartial Justice and Emboldened Unprecedented Legislative Attacks on America's Courts* (Washington, DC: Justice at Stake Campaign, Brennan Center for Justice, and National Institute on Money and State Politics, October 2011), 16.

44. Brennan Center for Justice, "Buying Time—2010," analysis, September 9, 2010.

45. David Kidwell, "Attack Ads Target Illinois Supreme Court Justice," *Chicago Tribune,* October 21, 2010.

46. Erik Eckholm, "Outside Spending Enters Arena of Judicial Races," *New York Times*, May 5, 2014.

47. Zach Patton, "Robe Warriors," *Governing,* March 2006.

48. Colorado League of Women Voters, "Colorado Voter Opinions on Judiciary, 2007," November 25, 2008, Institute for the Advancement of the American Legal System, University of Denver, 4, http://iaals.du.edu/images/wygwam/documents/publications/Nov252008.JudicialWars.pdf.

49. David B. Rottman, Anthony Champagne, and Roy A Schotland, *Call to Action: Statement of the National Summit on Improving Judicial Selection* (Williamsburg, VA: National Center for State Courts, 2002).

50. Quoted in Mark A. Behrens and Cary Silverman, "The Case for Adopting Appointive Judicial Selection Systems for State Court Judges," *Cornell Journal of Law and Public Policy* 11, no. 2 (Spring 2002): 282.

51. American Judicature Society, "Judicial Selection in the States," 2014.

52. Ibid.

53. Berkson, "Judicial Selection in the United States."

54. Ibid.

55. Behrens and Silverman, "Case for Adopting," 303.

56. Ibid.

57. Rottman et al., *Call to Action.*

58. American Judicature Society, "Methods of Judicial Selection: Selection of Judges," 2014, http://www.judicialselection.us/judicial_selection/methods/selection_of_judges.cfm?state=.

59. Luke Bierman, "Beyond Merit Selection," *Fordham Urban Law Journal* 29 (2002): 851, 864–865.

60. American Bar Association, "An Independent Judiciary: Report of the Commission on Separation of Powers and Judicial Independence," 1997, 48–49; Henry J. Abraham, *The Judicial Process: An Introductory Analysis of the Courts of the United States, England, and France,* 6th ed. (New York: Oxford University Press, 1993), 42, cited ibid.

61. American Judicature Society, "Methods of Judicial Selection."

62. Brace and Hall, "Studying Courts Comparatively," 24.

63. MaryAnn Spoto, "Court Sides With Judges in Pension Dispute," *Star-Ledger,* July 25, 2012.

64. Drew Noble Lanier and Roger Handberg, "In the Eye of the Hurricane: Florida Courts, Judicial Independence, and Politics," *Fordham Urban Law Journal* 29 (2002): 1033.

65. National Center for State Courts, "How States Set Salaries," Judicial Salary Tracker, July 2013, http://www.ncsc.org/microsites/judicial-salaries-data-tool/home/Special-Reports/How-States-Set-Salaries/Map.aspx.

66. Robert L. Misner, "Recasting Prosecutorial Discretion," *Journal of Criminal Law and Criminology* 86 (1996): 741.

67. Steve Weinberg, "Inside an Office: An Elected Prosecutor Explains," Center for Public Integrity, June 26, 2003, http://www.publicintegrity.org/2003/06/26/5521/inside-office.

68. Daniel S. Medwed, "The Zeal Deal: Prosecutorial Resistance to Post-Conviction Claims of Innocence," *Boston University Law Review* 84 (2004): 125–183.

69. Steven W. Perry, *Prosecutors in State Courts 2005,* Bureau of Justice Statistics Bulletin NCJ-213799 (Washington, DC: U.S. Department of Justice, July 2006).

70. Ibid.

71. Misner, "Recasting Prosecutorial Discretion."

72. Carol J. DeFrances, *State Court Prosecutors in Large Districts 2001,* Bureau of Justice Statistics Special Report NCJ-191206 (Washington, DC: U.S. Department of Justice, December 2001).

73. Ibid. "About two-thirds of Part I Uniform Crime Report (UCR) offenses reported to the police in 1998 occurred in the prosecutorial district served by these offices" (2).

74. Los Angeles County District Attorney's Office website, http://da.co.la.ca.us.

75. Shelby A. Dickerson Moore, "Questioning the Autonomy of Prosecutorial Charging Decisions: Recognizing the Need to Exercise Discretion—Knowing There Will Be Consequences for Crossing the Line," *Louisiana Law Review* 60 (Winter 2000): 374.

76. Wayne R. LaFave, "The Prosecutor's Discretion in the United States," *American Journal of Comparative Law* 18 (1970): 532, 533.

77. Misner, "Recasting Prosecutorial Discretion."

78. Telephone interview with Kenneth Noto, deputy chief of the narcotics section at the U.S. Attorney's Office for the Southern District of Florida, in William T. Pizzi, "Understanding Prosecutorial Discretion in the United States: The Limits of Comparative Criminal Procedure as an Instrument of Reform," *Ohio State Law Journal* 54 (1993): 1325n88.

79. Perry, *Prosecutors in State Courts 2005.*

80. Moore, "Questioning the Autonomy."

81. Tushar Kansal, "Racial Disparity in Sentencing: A Review of the Literature," Sentencing Project, Washington, DC, January 2005, http://www.sentencingproject.org/doc/publications/rd_sentencing_review.pdf.

82. Ronald F. Wright, "How Prosecutor Elections Fail Us," *Ohio State Journal of Criminal Law* 6 (2009): 581–610.

83. *McMann v. Richardson,* 397 U.S. 759, 771 n.14 (1970). ("The right to counsel is the right to the effective assistance of counsel.")

84. Caroline Wolf Harlow, "Defense Counsel in Criminal Cases," Bureau of Justice Statistics Special Report NCJ-179023, U.S. Department of Justice, Washington, DC, November 2000, Table 16, http://www.bjs.gov/content/pub/pdf/dccc.pdf.

85. Steven K. Smith and Carol J. DeFrances, "Indigent Defense," Bureau of Justice Statistics Selected Findings NCJ-158909, U.S. Department of Justice, Washington, DC, February 1996, http://bjs.ojp.usdoj.gov/content/pub/pdf/id.pdf.

86. Lynn Langton and Donald J. Farole Jr., "Public Defender Offices, 2007—Statistical Tables," Bureau of Justice Statistics Selected Findings NCJ-228538, U.S. Department of Justice, Washington, DC, November 2009 (revised June 17, 2010), http://www.bjs.gov/content/pub/pdf/pdo07st.pdf.

87. Carol J. DeFrances and Marika F. X. Litras, "Indigent Defense Services in Large Counties 1999," Bureau of Justice Statistics Bulletin NCJ-184932, U.S. Department of Justice, Washington, DC, November 2000, http://www.bjs.gov/content/pub/pdf/idslc99.pdf.

88. Criminal Justice Standards Committee, *Standards for Criminal Justice: Providing Defense Services,* 3rd ed. (Chicago: American Bar Association, 1992).

89. Carol Lundberg, "Justice for All," *Michigan Lawyers Weekly,* June 22, 2009.

90. Gene Johnson, "State High Court Limits Public Defender Caseloads," *Seattle Times,* June 15, 2012.

91. Adele Bernhard, "Take Courage: What the Courts Can Do to Improve the Delivery of Criminal Defense Services," *University of Pittsburgh Law Review* 63 (2002): 305.

92. DeFrances and Litras, "Indigent Defense Services in Large Counties."

93. *Gideon's Army,* documentary, directed by Dawn Porter (Montclair, NJ: Trilogy Films, 2013), http://gideonsarmythefilm.com/.

94. Thomas Giovanni, *Community-Oriented Defense: Start Now* (New York: Brennan Center for Justice, 2012), 2, http://www.brennancenter.org/sites/default/files/legacy/publications/COD_WEB.pdf.

95. Stephen B. Bright and Sia M. Sanneh, "Fifty Years of Defiance and Resistance to *Gideon v. Wainwright,*" *Yale Law Journal* 122, no. 8 (June 2013): 2106–2720, http://www.yalelawjournal.org/essay/fifty-years-of-defiance-and-resistance-after-gideon-v-wainwright.

96. David Cole, No Equal Justice: *Race and Class in the American Justice System* (New York: New Press, 1999), 92.

97. State of Virginia, Chart of Allowances, July 2014, http://www.courts.state.va.us/courtadmin/aoc/fiscal/chart.pdf Virginia recently created a fund from which attorneys could petition to exceed the cap, but the fund rarely lasts for the whole year.

98. Andrew Rachlin, "Rights of Defense," *Governing,* January 2007.

99. Kevin Clermont and Theodore Eisenberg, "Trial by Jury or Judge: Transcending Empiricism," *Cornell Law Review* 77 (1992): 1124.

100. See *Williams v. Florida,* 399 U.S. 78 (1970), approving six-member juries; and *Apodaca v. Oregon,* 406 U.S. 404 (1972), allowing nonunanimous verdicts.

101. Rottman and Strickland, *State Court Organization.*

102. U.S. Department of Justice, Office of Justice Programs, Office for Victims of Crime, "Executive Summary," in *New Directions From the Field: Victims' Rights and Services for the 21st Century* (Washington, DC: Government Printing Office, 1998).

103. Wayne A. Logan, "Through the Past Darkly: A Survey of the Uses and Abuses of Victim Impact Evidence in Capital Trials," *Arizona Law Review* 41 (1999): 177–178.

104. See *Payne v. Tennessee,* 501 U.S. 808 (1991), which reversed *Booth v. Maryland,* 482 U.S. 496 (1987).

105. "1 in 31: The Long Reach of American Corrections," Pew Center on the States, Washington, DC, March 2009, http://www.pewtrusts.org/en/about/news-room/press-releases/0001/01/01/one-in-31-us-adults-are-behind-bars-on-parole-or-probation.

106. Lauren E. Glaze and Erinn J. Herberman, "Correctional Populations in the United States, 2012," Bureau of Justice Statistics, Washington, DC, December 19, 2013, http://www.bjs.gov/content/pub/pdf/cpus12.pdf.

107. National Association of State Budget Officers, *2010 State Expenditure Report: Examining Fiscal 2009–2011 State Spending* (Washington, DC: National Association of State Budget Officers, 2011), 52.

108. In *Ring v. Arizona,* 536 U.S. 584 (2002), the Supreme Court invalidated Arizona's capital sentencing procedures, holding that the jury, not the judge, must find the aggravating factors necessary to impose the death penalty. Similar procedures in Colorado, Idaho, Montana, and Nebraska also were ruled unconstitutional.

109. Michael M. O'Hear, "National Uniformity/Local Uniformity: Reconsidering the Use of Departures to Reduce Federal-State Sentencing Disparities," *Iowa Law Review* 87 (2002): 756.

110. Ibid., 749.

111. Robert Mosteller, "New Dimensions in Sentencing Reform in the Twenty-First Century," *Oregon Law Review* 92 (2003): 16–17.

112. Marguerite A. Driessen and W. Cole Durham Jr., "Sentencing Dissonances in the United States: The Shrinking Distance Between Punishment Proposed and Sanction Served," *American Journal of Comparative Law* 50 (2002): 635.

113. Thomas P. Bonczar, "National Corrections Reporting Program: Sentence Length of State Prisoners, by Offense, Admission Type, Sex, and Race," Bureau of Justice Statistics, Washington, DC, 2009, Table 9, http://bjs.ojp.usdoj.gov/index.cfm?ty=pbdetail&iid=2056.

114. "Sensible Sentences for Nonviolent Offenders" (editorial), *New York Times,* June 14, 2012, http://www.nytimes.com/2012/06/15/opinion/sensible-sentences-for-nonviolent-offenders.html?_r=0.

115. Bureau of Justice Assistance, "1996 National Survey of State Sentencing Structures," NCJ-169270, Washington, DC, 1998, Exhibit 1-1, https://www.ncjrs.gov/pdffiles/169270.pdf.

116. Rottman and Strickland, *State Court Organization.*

117. Driessen and Durham, "Sentencing Dissonances in the United States."

118. Ram Subramanian and Ruth Delaney, "Playbook for Change? States Reconsider Mandatory Sentences," Vera Institute of Justice, February 11, 2014, http://www.vera.org/pubs/mandatory-sentences-playbook-for-change.

119. Lindsey Bever, "Missouri Man Serving Life in Prison for Pot While Some States Have Legalized It," *Washington Post,* July 11, 2014, http://www.washingtonpost.com/news/morning-mix/wp/2014/07/11/missouri-man-serving-life-in-prison-for-pot-while-some-states-have-legalized-it/?tid=hp_mm&hpid=z3.

120. Ibid.

121. "Smart on Crime: Reforming the Criminal Justice System for the 21st Century," Department of Justice, Washington, DC, August 2013, 2, http://www.justice.gov/ag/smart-on-crime.pdf.

122. Ibid., 1.

123. Subramanian and Delaney, "Playbook for Change?"

124. Pew Center on the States, "Time Served: The High Cost, Low Return of Longer Prison Terms," June 2012, http://www.cdcr.ca.gov/realignment/docs/Report-Prison_Time_Served.pdf.

125. "Attorney General Eric Holder Delivers Remarks at the Annual Meeting of the American Bar Association's House of Delegates," August 12, 2013, San Francisco, http://www.justice.gov/iso/opa/ag/speeches/2013/ag-speech-130812.html.

126. Ibid.

127. Brian Ostrom, Neal Kauder, and Robert LaFountain, *Examining the Work of the State Courts, 1999–2000: A National Perspective From the Court Statistics Project* (Williamsburg, VA: National Center for State Courts, 2000).

128. National Institute of Justice, *Drug Courts: The Second Decade* (Washington, DC: National Institute of Justice, 2006), 32–36, http://www.ncjrs.gov/pdffiles1/nij/211081.pdf.

129. Judith S. Kaye, "The State of the Judiciary, 2003: Confronting Today's Challenge," annual address, Albany, NY, January 13, 2003, 4.

130. Quoted in Alan Greenblatt, "Docket Science," *Governing,* June 2001, 40.

131. Ibid.

132. Quoted in ibid. For more on his reforms to the Hennepin County courts, see also the profile of Kevin Burke in "Court Reform," *Governing,* November 2004.

133. Todd Ruger, "'Rocket Docket' Can Be Slowed," *Sarasota Herald-Tribune,* September 27, 2009, BN1; Todd Ruger, "Two Minutes, and Home Goes Away," *Sarasota Herald-Tribune,* May 14, 2009, A1.

134. Greenblatt, "Docket Science."

135. Rebecca A. Koppes Conway, Timothy M. Tymkovich, Troy A. Eid, Britt Weygandt, and Anthony van Westrum, "Report of the Committee on Magistrates in the Civil Justice System," Governor's Task Force on Civil Justice Reform, October 1, 2000.

136. Rottman et al., *Call to Action.*

137. Carmen Lo, Katie Londenberg, and David Nims, "Spending in Judicial Elections: State Trends in the

Wake of *Citizens United*," report prepared for the California Assembly Judiciary Committee, Spring 2011, http://gov.uchastings.edu/public-law/docs/judicial-elections-report-and-appendices-corrected.pdf.

138. Quoted in Bert Brandenburg, "Protecting Wisconsin's Court from Special Interest Pressure," *Milwaukee Journal Sentinel,* March 27, 2007, http://www.jsonline.com/news/opinion/29460844.html.

Chapter 10

1. "Mich. Boy Homeless After City Shuts Down Hot Dog Stand," CBS News, August 10, 2012, http://www.cbsnews.com/news/mich-boy-homeless-after-city-shuts-down-hot-dog-stand/.

2. H. H. Gerth and C. Wright Mills, *Max Weber: Essays in Sociology* (New York: Oxford University Press, 1943).

3. Ronald C. Moe and Robert S. Gilmour, "Rediscovering Principles of Public Administration: The Neglected Foundation of Public Law," *Public Administration Review* 55, no. 2 (March–April 1995): 135–146.

4. John J. Gargan, "Introduction and Overview of State Government Administration," in *Handbook of State Government Administration,* ed. John J. Gargan (New York: Marcel-Dekker, 2000).

5. Jerrell D. Coggburn and Saundra K. Schneider, "The Quality of Management and Government Performance: An Empirical Analysis of the American States," *Public Administration Review* 63, no. 2 (March–April 2003): 206–213.

6. National Center for Education Statistics, "Fast Facts: Back to School Statistics," 2014, http://nces.ed.gov/fastfacts/display.asp?id=372.

7. Charles Barrilleaux, "Statehouse Bureaucracy: Institutional Consistency in a Changing Environment," in *American State and Local Politics,* ed. Ronald E. Weber and Paul Brace (New York: Chatham House, 1999).

8. Michael Lipsky, *Street-Level Bureaucracy* (New York: Russell Sage Foundation, 1980).

9. Cornelius Kerwin, *Rulemaking: How Government Agencies Write Law and Make Policy,* 3rd ed. (Washington, DC: CQ Press, 2003).

10. Deil S. Wright, Chung-Lae Cho, and Yoo-Sun Choi, "Top-Level State Administrators: Changing Characteristics and Qualities," in *The Book of the States 2002,* ed. Council of State Governments (Lexington, KY: Council of State Governments, 2002).

11. Charles T. Goodsell, *The Case for Bureaucracy: A Public Administration Polemic,* 4th ed. (Washington, DC: CQ Press, 2003).

12. U.S. Department of Commerce, *Statistical Abstract of the United States, 2012* (Washington, DC: U.S. Census Bureau, 2012), Table 461, "Governmental Employment and Payrolls: 1982 to 2009," http://www.census.gov/compendia/statab/2012/tables/12s0461.pdf.

13. Goodsell, *Case for Bureaucracy.*

14. George W. Downs and Patrick D. Larkey, *The Search for Government Efficiency* (Philadelphia: Temple University Press, 1986).

15. Kevin Abourezk, "University Health Privatization a 'Mixed Bag,'" *Lincoln Journal-Star,* September 27, 2012, http://journalstar.com/news/local/education/university-health-privatization-a-mixed-bag/article_bd064c84-4524-5581-8f07-37512ebf7ee1.html.

16. Scott Lamothe and Meeyoung Lamothe, "The Dynamics of Local Service Delivery Arrangements and the Role of Nonprofits," *International Journal of Public Administration* 29 (2006): 769–797.

17. J. Norman Baldwin, "Public Versus Private Employees: Debunking Stereotypes," *Review of Public Personnel Administration* 12 (Winter 1991): 1–27.

18. Barrilleaux, "Statehouse Bureaucracy," 106–107.

19. John J. Dilulio Jr., Gerald Garvey, and Donald F. Kettl, *Improving Government: An Owner's Manual* (Washington, DC: Brookings Institution, 1993).

20. Mary Bryna Sanger, "Does Measuring Performance Lead to Better Performance?" *Journal of Policy Analysis and Management* 32 (2013): 200.

21. Pew Center on the States, "The Government Performance Project," 2010, http://www.pewstates.org/projects/government-performance-project-328600.

22. Barbara Romzek and Melvin Dubnick, "Accountability in the Public Sector: Lessons From the Challenger Tragedy," *Public Administration Review* 47, no. 3 (May–June 1987): 227–238.

23. Alfred Steinberg, *The Bosses* (New York: Macmillan, 1972).

24. Dwight Waldo, *The Administrative State* (New York: Holmes and Meier, 1948).

25. "Union Membership Edges Up, but Share Continues to Fall," *Monthly Labor Review,* January 1999, 1–2.

26. WEAC's legislative goals are described on its website, http://www.weac.org/Issues_Advocacy.aspx.

27. Wisconsin Democracy Campaign, "Hijacking Special Elections and Recall 2011," March 21, 2011, updated January 14, 2014, http://www.wisdc.org/index.php?module=cms&page=3122.

28. Charles J. Sykes, *Profscam: Professors and the Demise of Higher Education* (New York: St. Martin's Press, 1989).

29. Charles Chieppo, "The Civil Service Systems Governments Need for the Modern Era," *Governing,* September 2013.

30. U.S. Department of Commerce, *Statistical Abstract of the United States, 2012,* Table 463, "State and Local Government—Full-Time Employment and Salary by Sex and Race and Ethnic Group: 1980 to 2009," http://

www.census.gov/compendia/statab/2012/tables/
12s0464.pdf.

31. Jennifer 8. Lee, "In Police Class, Blue Comes in Many Colors," *New York Times,* July 8, 2005.

32. C. J. Chivers, "For Black Officers, Diversity Has Its Limits," *New York Times,* April 2, 2001.

33. Sally Selden, *The Promise of Representative Bureaucracy: Diversity and Responsiveness in a Government Agency* (Armonk, NY: M. E. Sharpe, 1997).

34. Steven Greenhouse, "Supreme Court Ruling Offers Little Guidance on Hiring," *New York Times,* June 29, 2009; Adam Liptak, "Supreme Court Finds Bias Against White Firefighters," *New York Times,* June 29, 2009.

35. Donald F. Kettl, *The Global Public Management Revolution: A Report on the Transformation of Governance* (Washington, DC: Brookings Institution Press, 2000).

36. H. George Frederickson, Kevin B. Smith, Christopher W. Larimer, and Michael J. Licari, *The Public Administration Theory Primer,* 2nd ed. (Boulder, CO: Westview Press, 2012), 227.

37. James S. Bowman and Jonathan P. West, "Ending Civil Service Protections in Florida Government: Experiences in State Agencies," in *American Public Service: Radical Reform and the Merit System,* ed. James S. Bowman and Jonathan P. West (Boca Raton, FL: CRC Press, 2007).

38. "State and Local Government Employment: Monthly Data," *Governing,* last updated September 5, 2014, http://www.governing.com/gov-data/public-work-force-salaries/monthly-government-employment-changes-totals.html.

39. Melissa Maynard, "New Governors Drive to Reorganize Agencies," *Stateline,* June 6, 2011, http://www.pewstates.org/projects/stateline/headlines/new-governors-drive-to-reorganize-agencies-85899375045.

40. Helisse Levine and Eric Scorsone, "The Great Recession's Institutional Change in the Public Employment Relationship: Implications for State and Local Governments," *State and Local Government Review* 42 (2011): 208–214.

Chapter 11

1. This translation of the oath is available on the National League of Cities website, http://www.nlc.org/build-skills-and-networks/resources/cities-101/city-factoids/the-athenian-oath.

2. Pew Research Center for the People and the Press, "State Governments Viewed Favorably as Federal Rating Hits New Low," Pew Research Center, Washington, DC, April 15, 2013, http://www.people-press.org/2013/04/15/state-govermnents-viewed-favorably-as-federal-rating-hits-new-low/.

3. Richard Cole and John Kincaid, "Public Opinion on U.S. Federal and Intergovernmental Issues in 2006," *Publius: The Journal of Federalism* 36, no. 3 (2006): 443–459.

4. This figure is based on an estimated total population of 300 million.

5. City-Data.com website, http://www.city-data.com/city/Hove-Mobile-Park-North-Dakota.html.

6. David Y. Miller, *The Regional Governing of Metropolitan America* (Boulder, CO: Westview Press, 2002).

7. Quoted in Jonathan Walters, "Cry, the Beleaguered County," *Governing,* August 1996.

8. County Executive Office, Orange County, California, "OC Annual Budget FY 2011–12," http://ocgov.com/gov/ceo/deputy/finance/budget/fy2012/budget; Department of Management and Budget, Fairfax County, Virginia, "FY 2012 Adopted Budget," http://www.fairfaxcounty.gov/dmb/fy2012/adopted/overview/10_budget_summary.pdf.

9. National Association of Counties, "A Brief Overview of County Government," August 2003, http://www.naco.org/Counties/learn/Pages/Overview.aspx.

10. Miller, *Regional Governing of Metropolitan America,* 26.

11. U.S. Conference of Mayors website, http://www.usmayors.org.

12. Thomas J. Gradel, Dick Simpson, and Andris Zimelis, with Kirsten Byers and Chris Olson, "Curing Corruption in Illinois: Anti-Corruption Report Number 1," Department of Political Science, University of Illinois, Chicago, February 3, 2009, http://pols.uic.edu/political-science/chicago-politics/anti-corruption-reports.

13. National League of Cities, "Serving on City Councils," Research Brief on America's Cities, no. 2003-5, Washington, DC, September 2003.

14. Roger L. Kemp, ed., *Model Government Charters: A City, County, Regional, State, and Federal Handbook* (Jefferson, NC: McFarland, 2003), 10.

15. These monthly reports are archived and available online at https://www.phoenix.gov/citygovernment/phoenix-facts.

16. William Hansell, "Evolution and Change Characterize Council-Manager Government," *Public Management* 82 (August 2000): 17–21.

17. Michael Zuckerman, *Peaceable Kingdoms: The New England Towns of the 18th Century* (New York: Knopf, 1970).

18. Miller, *Regional Governing of Metropolitan America,* 41.

19. Quoted in Anwar Syed, *The Political Theory of the American Local Government* (New York: Random House, 1966), 40.

20. Alexis de Tocqueville, *Democracy in America: A New Translation,* trans. George Lawrence, ed. J. P. Mayer (New York: HarperCollins, 2000), 33.

21. Penelope Lemov, "Infrastructure Conference Report: Building It Smarter, Managing It Better," *Governing*, October 1996, 40.

22. Ann O. Bowman, "Urban Government," in *Handbook of Research on Urban Politics and Policy in the United States*, ed. Ronald K. Vogel (Westport, CT: Greenwood Press, 1997), 133.

23. Kemp, Model Government Charters, 59.

24. New York State Association of Counties, "State Programs Funded by County Property Taxes," December 2011, http://www.rensco.com/pdfs/smn/NYSAC%20County%20Mandates%20Report2.pdf.

25. League of Women Voters of California's Smart Voter website, http://smartvoter.org.

26. National League of Cities, "Partisan vs. Nonpartisan Elections," http://www.nlc.org/build-skills-and-networks/resources/cities-101/city-officials/partisan-vs-nonpartisan-elections.

27. Elaine B. Sharpe, "Political Participation in Cities," in *Cities, Politics, and Policy: A Comparative Analysis*, ed. John P. Pelissero (Washington, DC: CQ Press, 2003), 81.

28. Lana Stein, "Mayoral Politics," in Pelissero, *Cities, Politics, and Policy*, 162.

29. National League of Cities, "City Councils," 2013, http://www.nlc.org/build-skills-and-networks/resources/cities-101/city-officials/city-councils.

30. Ibid.

31. Center for State and Local Government Excellence, *The Great Recession and State and Local Government Work Force* (Washington, DC: Center for State and Local Government Excellence, 2010).

32. "State and Local Government Employment: Monthly Data," *Governing*, September 5, 2014, http://www.governing.com/gov-data/monthly-government-employment-changes-totals.html.

33. Quoted in International City/County Management Association, "How It Plays in Peoria: The Fiscal Crisis on Local Governments," September 14, 2009, http://icma.org/en/Article/4884/How_It_Plays_in_Peoria_The_Impact_of_the_Fiscal_Crisis_on_Local_Governments.

34. Robert J. O'Neill Jr., "An Opportunity for Creative Destruction," *Governing*, October 2009, http://www.governing.com/column/opportunity-creative-destruction.

35. Tocqueville, *Democracy in America*, 63.

Chapter 12

1. Rae Archibald and Sally Sleeper, *Government Consolidation and Economic Development in Allegheny County and the City of Pittsburgh* (Santa Monica, CA: RAND Corporation, 2008); Christopher Briem, "A Primer on Local Government Fragmentation and Regionalism in the Pittsburgh Region," http://www.briem.com/frag/PittsburghIndex.htm.

2. Figures calculated from U.S. Census Bureau data, 2013, http://quickfacts.census.gov/qfd/states/42/42003.html.

3. Advisory Commission on Intergovernmental Relations, "Metropolitan Organization: The Allegheny County Case," February 1992, http://www.briem.com/files/ACIRAlleghenyCounty.pdf.

4. Allegheny County, Pennsylvania, "Municipality Map," http://www.alleghenycounty.us/munimap/index.asp.

5. Archibald and Sleeper, *Government Consolidation*, ix.

6. Anthony Downs, "The Devolution Revolution: Why Congress Is Shifting a Lot of Power to the Wrong Levels," Policy Brief no. 3, Brookings Institution, July 1996, http://www.brookings.edu/research/papers/1996/07/governance-downs.

7. Office of Management and Budget, "2010 Standards for Delineating Metropolitan and Micropolitan Statistical Areas," *Federal Register* 75, no. 123 (June 28, 2010), http://www.whitehouse.gov/sites/default/files/omb/assets/fedreg_2010/06282010_metro_standards-Complete.pdf.

8. Office of Management and Budget, OMB Bulletin No. 13-01, February 28, 2013, http://www.whitehouse.gov/sites/default/files/omb/bulletins/2013/b-13-01.pdf.

9. Bruce Katz, "A Nation in Transition: What the Urban Age Means for the United States," speech presented at the Urban Age Conference, New York, May 4, 2007, http://www.brookings.edu/speeches/2007/0504communitydevelopment_katz.aspx.

10. David Y. Miller, *The Regional Governing of Metropolitan America* (Boulder, CO: Westview Press, 2002), 1.

11. David Cieslewits, "The Environmental Impacts of Sprawl," in *Urban Sprawl: Causes, Consequences, and Policy Responses*, ed. Gregory D. Squires (Washington, DC: Urban Institute Press, 2002).

12. Ibid.

13. See, for example, Myron Orfield, *American Metropolitics: The New Suburban Reality* (Washington, DC: Brookings Institution Press, 2002).

14. Ibid., 41.

15. Peter Dreier, John Mollenkopf, and Todd Swanstrom, *Place Matters: Metropolitics for the Twenty-First Century* (Lawrence: University Press of Kansas, 2001).

16. Ibid., 67.

17. Orfield, *American Metropolitics*, 10.

18. G. Ross Stephens and Nelson Wikstrom, *Metropolitan Government and Governance: Theoretical Perspectives, Empirical Analysis, and the Future* (New York: Oxford University Press, 1999).

19. "What Is Metro?" http://www.oregonmetro.gov/regional-leadership/what-metro.

20. Heike Mayor and John Provo, "The Portland Edge in Context," in *The Portland Edge: Challenges and Successes in Growing Communities,* ed. Connie P. Ozawa (Washington, DC: Island Press, 2004).

21. National Association of Regional Councils, "What Is a Regional Council or Council of Governments?" 2013, http://narc.org/about-narc/cogs-mpos/.

22. National Association of Regional Councils, "History," 2013, http://narc.org/about-narc/about-the-association/history.

23. Miller, *Regional Governing of Metropolitan America,* 103.

24. James F. Wolf and Tara Kolar Bryan, "Identifying the Capacities of Regional Councils of Government," *State and Local Government Review* 41 (2010): 61.

25. Ibid., 67.

26. Simon Andrew, "Recent Development in the Study of Interjurisdictional Agreements: An Overview and Assessment," *State and Local Government Review* 41 (2010): 133–142.

27. National Association of Counties, "City-County Consolidation Proposals, 1921–Present," 2010, http://www.naco.org/Counties/learn/Documents/City%20County%20Consolidations.01.01.2011.pdf.

28. Quoted in Jeffrey Cohan, "Reports Outline Options in Merging Pittsburgh-Allegheny County Services," *Pittsburgh Post-Gazette,* April 2, 2004.

29. Lara Brenckle, "City, County Study Merger . . . Again," *Pittsburgh Tribune-Review,* October 20, 2006.

30. National League of Cities, "Serving on City Councils," Research Brief on America's Cities, no. 2003-5, Washington, DC, September 2003.

31. Kate Linebaugh, "Threats to Town Halls Stir Voter Backlash," *Wall Street Journal,* June 8, 2011.

32. David Rusk, *Cities Without Suburbs,* 2nd ed. (Washington, DC: Woodrow Wilson Center Press, 1995).

33. Ann O. Bowman, "Urban Government," in *Handbook of Research on Urban Politics and Policy in the United States,* ed. Ronald K. Vogel (Westport, CT: Greenwood Press, 1997), 139.

34. Rob Gurwitt, "Annexation: Not So Smart Growth," *Governing,* October 2000.

35. Barbara Kelly, *Expanding the American Dream: Building and Rebuilding Levittown* (Albany: State University of New York Press, 1993).

36. Charles Tiebout, "A Pure Theory of Local Expenditures," *Journal of Political Economy* 64, no. 5 (October 1956): 422.

37. William Lyons, David Lowery, and Ruth Hoogland DeHoog, *The Politics of Dissatisfaction: Citizens, Services, and Urban Institutions* (Armonk, NY: M. E. Sharpe, 1992).

38. Dante Chinni, "Rural Counties Are Losing Population and Aging, but Are They Really 'Dying'?" PBS NewsHour, March 4, 2011, http://www.pbs.org/newshour/rundown/2011/03/-as-the-2010-census.html.

39. Nebraska Department of Education, "2013–2014 Number of Districts/Systems," updated August 2, 2013, http://www.education.ne.gov/dataservices/PDF/2013_14_District_Listing.pdf.

40. Alan Greenblatt, "Little Mergers on the Prairie," *Governing,* July 2006, 49–50.

Chapter 13

1. Quoted in David Tyack and Larry Cuban, *Tinkering Toward Utopia: A Century of Public School Reform* (Cambridge, MA: Harvard University Press, 1995), 2.

2. Quoted in Alan Greenblatt, "New Headaches for 'No Child Left Behind,'" *Governing,* November 2011, http://www.governing.com/topics/education/new-headaches-for-no-child-left-behind.html.

3. "NCLB Waivers: A State-by-State Breakdown," *Education Week,* March 20, 2013, updated October 6, 2014, http://www.edweek.org/ew/section/infographics/nclbwaivers.html.

4. Quoted in Michael A. Rebell, "Fiscal Equity Litigation and the Democratic Imperative," *Journal of Education Finance* 24, no. 1 (1998): 23–50.

5. Ibid.

6. Charles Mahtesian, "Too Much Democracy," *Governing,* January 24, 2000.

7. Jeffrey Barnett and Phillip Vidal, "State and Local Government Finances Summary: 2010," Governments Division Brief, U.S. Census Bureau, September 2012, http://www2.census.gov/govs/estimate/summary_report.pdf.

8. National Center for Education Statistics, "Revenues and Expenditures for Public Elementary and Secondary School Districts: School Year 2010–11 (Fiscal Year 2011)," http://nces.ed.gov/pubs2013/2013344.pdf.

9. Armen Keteyian, "Where Does Mega Millions Money Go After the Jackpot?" CBS News, March 30, 2012, http://www.cbsnews.com/8301-18563_162-57407364/where-does-mega-millions-money-go-after-the-jackpot.

10. Rebell, "Fiscal Equity."

11. Tyack and Cuban, *Tinkering Toward Utopia,* 47.

12. William Duncombe, John Ruggiero, and John Yinger, "Alternative Approaches to Measuring the Cost of Education," in *Holding Schools Accountable: Performance-Based Reform in Education,* ed. Helen F. Ladd (Washington, DC: Brookings Institution Press, 1996), 338. See also Christopher B. Swanson, "Ten Questions (and Answers) About Graduates, Dropouts, and NCLB Accountability," Urban Institute, October 21, 2003, http://www.urban.org/publications/310873.html.

13. Harold Wenglinsky, "School District Expenditures, School Resources, and Student Achievement: Modeling

the Production Function," in *Developments in School Finance, 1997: Does Money Matter?* ed. William J. Fowler Jr. (Washington, DC: National Center for Education Statistics, 1998).

14. Allan Odden, "Equity and Adequacy in School Finance Today," *Phi Delta Kappan* 85 (October 2003): 120–125.

15. Margaret Ritsch, ed., *Money Matters: A Reporter's Guide to School Finance* (Washington, DC: Education Writers Association, 2003), 5.

16. Education Trust, "Funding Gaps 2006," 2006, based on 2003–2004 U.S. Department of Education and U.S. Census Bureau data.

17. Michael Leachman and Chris Mai, "Most States Funding Schools Less Than Before the Recession," Center on Budget and Policy Priorities, Washington, DC, revised May 20, 2014, http://www.cbpp.org/files/9-12-13sfp.pdf.

18. "Quality Counts 2003: If I Can't Learn From You...," *Education Week* XXII, no. 17 (January 9, 2003): 22, http://www.edweek.org/media/ew/qc/archives/QC03full.pdf.

19. U.S. Department of Education, "A Nation Accountable: Twenty-Five Years After *A Nation at Risk*," April 2008, 1, http://www2.ed.gov/rschstat/research/pubs/accountable/accountable.pdf.

20. William J. Bushaw and Shane J. Lopez, "The 45th Annual PDK/Gallup Poll of the Public's Attitudes Toward the Public Schools: Which Way Do We Go?" *Phi Delta Kappan* 95 (September 1, 2013): 9–25.

21. William J. Bushaw and John A. McNee, "Americans Speak Out: Are Educators and Policy Makers Listening?" *Phi Delta Kappan* 91 (September 2009): 8–23.

22. Jennifer McMurrer, "Instructional Time in Elementary Schools: A Closer Look at Changes for Specific Subjects," Center on Education Policy, February 2008, http://www.arteducators.org/research/InstructionalTimeFeb2008.pdf.

23. National Center for Education Statistics, *The Nation's Report Card: Trends in Academic Progress 2012* (Washington, DC: Institute of Education Sciences, U.S. Department of Education, June 2013), http://nces.ed.gov/nationsreportcard/subject/publications/main2012/pdf/2013456.pdf.

24. National Center for Education Statistics, "Trends in International Mathematics and Science Study: Overview," http://nces.ed.gov/timss/index.asp.

25. College Board, "2013 College-Bound Seniors: Total Group Profile Report," 2013, http://media.collegeboard.com/digitalServices/pdf/research/2013/TotalGroup-2013.pdf.

26. Rebecca Leung, "The 'Texas Miracle,'" CBS News, January 6, 2004, http://www.cbsnews.com/stories/2004/01/06/60II/main591676.shtml.

27. Sam Dillon, "U.S. to Require States to Use a Single School Dropout Formula," *New York Times*, April 1, 2008.

28. National Center for Education Statistics, *Digest of Education Statistics* (Washington, DC: Institute of Education Sciences, U.S. Department of Education, 2013), Table 219.70, "Percentage of High School Dropouts Among Persons 16 Through 24 Years Old (Status Dropout Rate), by Sex and Race/Ethnicity: Selected Years, 1960 Through 2012," http://nces.ed.gov/programs/digest/d13/tables/dt13_219.70.asp.

29. Common Core State Standards Initiative, "Mission Statement," http://www.corestandards.org.

30. Dylan Scott, "States Begin Implementing Common Core Standards," *Governing*, View blog, February 7, 2012, http://www.governing.com/blogs/view/States-Begin-Task-of-Implementing-Common-Core-Standards.html.

31. Stephanie Simon, "Teachers Union Takes on Common Core," *Politico*, July 11, 2014, http://www.politico.com/story/2014/07/american-federation-of-teachers-common-core-108793.html?hp=r5.

32. Kati Haycock, "Good Teaching Matters: How Well-Qualified Teachers Can Close the Gap," *Thinking K–16* 3, no. 2 (1998).

33. Economists Steven G. Givkin and Eric A. Hanushek, cited (along with researcher William Sanders) in "Quality Counts 2003," 10.

34. U.S. Department of Education, *Teaching Shortage Areas Nationwide Listing: 1990–1991 Through 2012–2013* (Washington, DC: U.S. Department of Education, 2012).

35. John Wirt, Susan Choy, Patrick Rooney, Stephen Provasnik, Anindita Sen, and Richard Tobin, *The Condition of Education 2004: Out-of-Field Teacher in Middle and High School Grades* (Washington, DC: National Center for Education Statistics, 2004).

36. Bess Keller, "Most States Pass Federal Review on Highly Qualified Teachers," *Education Week*, August 17, 2006.

37. Diane Stark Rentner, Caitlin Scott, Nancy Kober, Naomi Chudowsky, Victor Chudowsky, Scott Joftus, and Dalia Zabala, "From the Capital to the Classroom: Year 4 of the No Child Left Behind Act," Center on Education Policy, March 2006, www.cep-dc.org/displayDocument.cfm?DocumentID=301.

38. Michael Allen, *Eight Questions on Teacher Preparation: What Does the Research Say?* (Denver, CO: Education Commission of the States, July 2003).

39. Vicki Hobbs, *The Promise and the Power of Distance Learning in Rural Education* (Arlington, VA: Rural School and Community Trust, 2004), http://www.ruraledu.org/user_uploads/file/Promise_and_the_Power.pdf; Jerry Johnson and Marty Strange, *Why Rural Matters 2009: State and Regional Challenges and Opportunities* (Arlington, VA: Rural School and Community Trust, 2009).

40. Thomas D. Snyder and Sally A. Dillow, *Digest of Education Statistics 2009* (Washington, DC: U.S. Department of Education, 2010), Tables 84 and 86.

41. See studies such as Erin McHenry-Sorber, "School Consolidation in Pennsylvania: An Analysis of Governor Rendell's Policy Proposal," *Beacon,* summer 2009. One study of school consolidation in New York State between 1985 and 1997 by researchers at Syracuse University found substantially reduced operating costs, but only when the smallest districts were consolidated; see William Duncombe and John Yinger, "Does School District Consolidation Cut Costs?" Center for Policy Research, Working Paper no. 33, January 2001, http://www.maxwell.syr.edu/uploadedFiles/cpr/publications/working_papers2/wp33.pdf.

42. Joe Bard, Clark Gardener, and Regi Wieland, "Rural School Consolidation Report," prepared for the National Rural Education Association Executive Board, University of Oklahoma, Norman, April 1–2, 2005.

43. Melissa Maynard, "Still Too Many Schools?" *Stateline,* March 22, 2010.

44. Hobbs, Promise and the Power.

45. Lowell C. Rose and Alec M. Gallup, "38th Annual Phi Delta Kappa/Gallup Poll of the Public's Attitudes Toward the Public Schools," *Phi Delta Kappan* 88, no. 1 (September 2006): 41–57.

46. Sarah Grady, Stacey Bielick, and Susan Aud, *Trends in the Use of School Choice: 1993 to 2007* (Washington, DC: U.S. Department of Education, 2010).

47. National Charter School Resource Center, "Frequently Asked Questions," http://www.charterschoolcenter.org/page/frequently-asked-questions.

48. Education Commission of the States, "Charter Schools: Online Database," 2014, http://www.ecs.org/html/educationIssues/CharterSchools/CHDB_intro.asp.

49. Erika Hayasaki, "Charter Academy Shuts 60 Schools," *Los Angeles Times,* August 16, 2004, http://articles.latimes.com/2004/aug/16/local/me-charter16.

50. Charles S. Clark, "Charter Schools," *CQ Researcher,* December 20, 2002; Brian P. Gill, P. Michael Timpane, Karen E. Ross, and Dominic J. Brewer, *Rhetoric Versus Reality: What We Know and What We Need to Know About Vouchers and Charter Schools* (Santa Monica, CA: RAND Corporation, 2001), xviii.

51. National Center for Education Statistics, "America's Charter Schools: Results From the NAEP 2003 Pilot Study," Washington, DC: Institute of Education Sciences, U.S. Department of Education, December 2004, http://nces.ed.gov/nationsreportcard/pdf/studies/2005456.pdf.

52. Dan Keating and Theola Labbé-DeBose, "Charter Schools Make Gains on Tests," *Washington Post,* December 15, 2008. This article and a variety of multimedia resources about the Washington, D.C., charter schools are available at http://www.washingtonpost.com/wp-srv/metro/specials/charter/index.html.

53. Diana Jean Schemo, "Nation's Charter Schools Lagging Behind, U.S. Test Scores Reveal," *New York Times,* August 17, 2003, http://www.nytimes.com/2004/08/17/education/17charter.html?hp.

54. Center for Research on Education Outcomes, *Multiple Choice: Charter School Performance in 16 States* (Stanford, CA: Stanford University, Center for Research on Education Outcomes, June 2009), http://credo.stanford.edu/reports/MULTIPLE_CHOICE_CREDO.pdf.

55. Kenneth Jost, "School Vouchers Showdown," *CQ Researcher,* February 15, 2002.

56. See William A. Fischel, "Why Voters Veto Vouchers: Public Schools and Community-Specific Social Capital," *Economics of Governance* 7, no. 2 (2006): 109–132.

57. Josh Hafenbrack, "Update: Florida Supreme Court Strikes Voucher, Property Tax Amendments From the Ballot," *Orlando Sentinel,* Central Florida Political Pulse blog, September 3, 2008.

58. Ohio Department of Education, "EdChoice Scholarship Program," http://education.ohio.gov/Topics/Other-Resources/Scholarships/EdChoice-Scholarship-Program.

59. Amanda Paulson, "Milwaukee's Lessons on School Vouchers," *Christian Science Monitor,* May 23, 2006.

60. John Robert Warren, "Graduation Rates for Choice and Public School Students in Milwaukee, 2003–2008," School Choice Wisconsin, February 2010, http://www.schoolchoicewi.org/data/currdev_links/2010-Grad-Study-1-31-2010.pdf.

61. John F. Witte, Deven Carlson, Joshua M. Cowen, David J. Fleming, and Patrick J. Wolf, *MPCP Longitudinal Educational Growth Study: Fifth Year Report,* Report of the School Choice Demonstration Project (Fayetteville: University of Arkansas, Department of Education Reform, 2012).

62. National Education Policy Center, "Reports, Reviews Offer Little to Commend Milwaukee Voucher Schools," April 19, 2012, http://nepc.colorado.edu/newsletter/2012/04/review-Milwaukee-Choice-Year-5. U.S. General Accounting Office, *School Vouchers: Publicly Funded Programs in Cleveland and Milwaukee,* GAO 01-914 (Washington, DC: U.S. General Accounting Office, 2001), 4; Zachary M. Seward, "Long-Delayed Education Study Casts Doubt on Value of Vouchers," *Wall Street Journal,* July 15–16, 2006.

63. National Center for Education Statistics, "Number and Percentage of All Students Ages 5–17 Who Were Homeschooled and Homeschooling Rate, by Selected Characteristics, 2011–2012," http://nces.ed.gov/pubs2013/2013028/tables/table_07.asp.

64. National Center for Education Statistics, *The Condition of Education* (Washington, DC: U.S. Department of Education, 2005).

65. Home School Legal Defense Association, "State Laws," http://www.hslda.org/laws/default.asp.

66. Matthew H. Boswell, *Courts as Catalysts: State Supreme Courts and Public School Finance Equity* (Albany: State University of New York Press, 2001), 125.

67. See the NEA and AFT websites, http://www.nea.org and http://www.aft.org.

68. National PTA, "About PTA," http://www.pta.org/about/?navItemNumber=503.

69. John O'Connor, "Jeb Bush: The Once and Future Reformer," StateImpact, NPR, 2014, http://stateimpact.npr.org/florida/tag/jeb-bush.

70. Business Coalition for Student Achievement, "Who We Are," 2012, http://www.biz4achievement.org/about_the_coalition/.

Chapter 14

1. Mark Berman, "Washington Post reporter arrested in Ferguson," *Washington Post*, August 31, 2014; "Timeline: Michael Brown Shooting in Ferguson, Mo.," *USA Today*, August 14, 2014, http://www.usatoday.com/story/news/nation/2014/08/14/michael-brown-ferguson-missouri-timeline/14051827/; Josh Voorhees, "Everything That Went Wrong in Ferguson," *Slate*, August 21, 2014, http://www.slate.com/articles/news_and_politics/politics/2014/08/ferguson_police_timeline_a_comprehensive_chronological_accounting_of_the.html.

2. "Overkill," *Economist*, August 23, 2014; Michael Wine, "Race and Police Shootings: Are Blacks Targeted More?" *New York Times*, August 30, 2014.

3. Jill Leovy, *Ghettoside: A True Story of Murder in America* (New York: Spiegel & Grau, 2015), vii.

4. John J. Donohue III and Steven D. Levitt, "The Impact of Legalized Abortion on Crime," *Quarterly Journal of Economics* CXVI, no. 2 (May 2001), http://pricetheory.uchicago.edu/levitt/Papers/DonohueLevittTheImpactOfLegalized2001.pdf; Kevin Drum, "America's Real Criminal Element: Lead," *Mother Jones*, January–February 2013, http://www.motherjones.com/environment/2013/01/lead-crime-link-gasoline; Anthony R. Harris, Stephen H. Thomas, Gene A. Fisher, and David J. Hirsch, "Murder and Medicine: The Lethality of Criminal Assault 1960–1999," *Homicide Studies* 6, no. 2 (2002): 128–166.

5. Franklin Zimring, *The City That Became Safe: New York's Lessons for Urban Crime and Its Control* (New York: Oxford University Press, 2012), 132–133.

6. Pew Research Center for the People and the Press, "Few Say Police Forces Nationally Do Well in Treating Races Equally," Pew Research Center, Washington, DC, August 25, 2104, http://www.people-press.org/2014/08/25/few-say-police-forces-nationally-do-well-in-treating-races-equally/.

7. Tracey Meares, "The Legitimacy of Police Among Young African-American Men," *Marquette Law Review* 92, no. 4 (2009), http://digitalcommons.law.yale.edu/cgi/viewcontent.cgi?article=1527&context=fss_papers.

8. Danielle S. Allen, *The World of Prometheus: The Politics of Punishing in Democratic Athens* (Princeton, NJ: Princeton University Press, 1999), 3.

9. For a brilliant discussion of how this transformation came to pass, see Sir Frederick Pollock and F. W. Maitland, *History of English Law Before the Time of Edward I* (Cambridge, UK: Cambridge University Press, 1969).

10. Allen J. Beck and Thomas P. Bonczar, "Lifetime Likelihood of Going to State or Federal Prison," Bureau of Justice Statistics, March 1997, http://bjs.gov/content/pub/pdf/Llgsfp.pdf.

11. Michelle Alexander, *The New Jim Crow: Mass Incarceration in the Age of Colorblindness* (New York: New Press, 2010), 5–6, 50–53.

12. David M. Kennedy, *Don't Shoot: One Man, a Street Fellowship, and the End of Violence in Inner-City America* (New York: Bloomsbury, 2011), 18.

13. Leovy, *Ghettoside*, xvi.

14. For a comprehensive statement of the administration's position on marijuana, see Drug Enforcement Administration, "The DEA Position on Marijuana," U.S. Department of Justice, Washington, DC, April 2013, http://www.justice.gov/dea/docs/marijuana_position_2011.pdf.

15. Marc Mauer, "The Crisis of the Young African American Male and the Criminal Justice System," presentation to the U.S. Commission on Civil Rights, Washington, DC, April 15–16, 1999, 6.

16. Glenn Loury, "Prison's Dilemma," *Washington Monthly*, January–February 2013, http://www.washingtonmonthly.com/magazine/january_february_2013/features/prisons_dilemma042048.php?page=all; Laura M. Maruschak and Thomas P. Bonczar, "Probation and Parole in the United States, 2012," Bureau of Justice Statistics, December 2013, revised April 22, 2014, http://www.bjs.gov/content/pub/pdf/ppus12.pdf.

17. The degree to which states put inmates in isolation units varies widely. As of 1999, Arizona, Colorado, Maine, Nebraska, New York, Nevada, Rhode Island, and Virginia all kept between 5 and 8 percent of their prison population in isolation. In contrast, Indiana had 85 supermax beds; Georgia had only 10. See Atul Gawande, "Hellhole: The United States Holds Tens of Thousands of Inmates in Long-Term Solitary Confinement. Is This Torture?" *New Yorker*, March 30, 2009.

18. Eduardo Porter, "In the U.S., Punishment Comes Before the Crimes," *New York Times*, April 29, 2014; "The Slow Death of Capital Punishment," *Economist*, April 26, 2014.

19. Becky Pettit, "Black Progress? Not When You Include the Incarcerated," *Washington Post*, November 13, 2012, http://www.washingtonpost.com/blogs/the-rootdc/post/black-progress-not-when-you-include-the-incarcerated/2012/11/13/1412b6b2-2da0-11e2-9ac2-1c61452669c3_blog.html.

20. Thomas Edsall, "The Expanding World of Poverty Capitalism," *New York Times*, August 26, 2014, http://www.nytimes.com/2014/08/27/opinion/thomas-edsall-the-expanding-world-of-poverty-capitalism.html?_r=0.

21. Ibid.; Radley Balko, "How Municipalities in St. Louis County, Mo., Profit From Poverty," *Washington Post*, September 3, 2014, http://www.washingtonpost.com/news/the-watch/wp/2014/09/03/how-st-louis-county-missouri-profits-from-poverty/.

22. Alice Goffman, *On the Run: Fugitive Life in an American City* (Chicago: University of Chicago Press, 2014).

23. The rise in incarceration levels almost certainly had something to do with the crime decrease. Estimates of what percentage of the crime reduction it accounts for range from 10 to 40 percent. See Steven Levitt, "Understanding Why Crime Fell in the 1990s: Four Factors That Explain the Decline and Six That Do Not," *Journal of Economic Perspectives* 18, no. 1 (2004): 163–190.

24. Lauren Glaze and Thomas Bonczar, "Probation and Parole in the United States, 2008," Bureau of Justice Statistics, Washington, DC, December 2009.

25. German Lopez, "Everything You Need to Know About the War on Drugs," *Vox*, October 6, 2014, http://www.vox.com/cards/war-on-drugs-marijuana-cocaine-heroin-meth/war-on-drugs-goals.

26. This figure—from the Office of National Drug Control Policy—does not include alcohol, which is, of course, the most popular drug of all.

27. See Robert MacCoun and Peter Reuter, *Drug War Heresies: Learning From Other Vices, Times, and Places* (New York: Cambridge University Press, 2001), 26, 29.

28. "Crack; A Disaster of Historic Dimension, Still Growing," *New York Times*, May 28, 1989.

29. Kathleen Hunger, "Money Mattering More in Judicial Elections," *Stateline*, May 12, 2004.

30. Pew Center on the States, "One in 100: Behind Bars in America 2008," February 28, 2008, http://www.pewtrusts.org/en/research-and-analysis/reports/2008/02/28/one-in-100-behind-bars-in-america-2008.

31. "Crack; A Disaster of Historic Dimension," *New York Times*; National Association of State Budget Officers, *State Expenditure Report, 2008* (Washington, DC: National Association of State Budget Officers, 2009), 58.

32. Mike Nizza, "California's $8 Billion Surprise," *New York Times*, August 13, 2008; Jennifer Steinhauer, "Prisons Push California to Seek New Approach," *New York Times*, December 11, 2006.

33. Keith Humphreys, "California's Strange, Tragic Embrace of Prisons," *Reality-Based Community*, August, 13, 2014, http://www.samefacts.com/2014/08/drug-policy/californias-strange-enduring-embrace-of-prisons/.

34. Andrew Cohen, "California's Prison Crisis Is Now a Constitutional Crisis," *The Atlantic*, April 14, 2013, http://www.theatlantic.com/national/archive/2013/04/californias-prison-crisis-is-now-a-constitutional-crisis/274852/; Don Thompson, "Supreme Court Upholds Order for California to Cut Prison Population," *Huffington Post Politics*, May 23, 2011, http://www.huffingtonpost.com/2011/05/23/supreme-court-orders-cali_n_865503.html.

35. Marie Gottshalk, "American Hell," *New Republic*, June 28, 2010.

36. John Buntin, "The Correctionists," *Governing*, 2010, http://www.governing.com/poy/jerry-madden-john-whitmire.html; Betsy Woodruff, "Bipartisan Prison Reform: Many Conservatives and Liberals Agree: We're Putting Too Many People in Jail," *National Review Online*, January 20, 2014, http://www.nationalreview.com/article/368877/bipartisan-prison-reform-betsy-woodruff.

37. "Pew Public Safety Performance Project," GiveWell, http://www.givewell.org/labs/causes/criminal-justice-reform/Pew-Public-Safety-Performance-Project.

38. Kevin Smith, "The Politics of Punishment: Evaluating Political Explanations of Incarceration Rates," *Journal of Politics* 66, no. 3 (2004): 925.

39. Katherine Beckett, *Making Crime Pay: Law and Order in Contemporary Politics* (New York: Oxford University Press, 1997).

40. Maruschak and Bonczar, "Probation and Parole in the United States, 2012."

41. John Buntin, "Swift and Certain: Hawaii's Probation Experiment," *Governing*, October 31, 2009, http://www.governing.com/topics/public-justice-safety/Swift-and-Certain-Hawaiis.html; Kevin McEvoy, "HOPE: A Swift and Certain Process for Probationers," *National Institute of Justice Journal*, no. 269 (March 26, 2012), http://www.nij.gov/journals/269/pages/hope.aspx.

42. National Institute of Justice, "Do Drug Courts Work? Findings From Drug Court Research," U.S. Department of Justice, Office of Justice Programs, May 12, 2008.

43. Katie Zesima, "Drug Czar Approaches Challenge From a Different Angle: As a Recovering Alcoholic," *Washington Post*, August 26, 2014.

44. E. J. Dionne Jr. and William A. Galston, "The New Politics of Marijuana Legalization," Brookings Institution Governance Studies, Washington, DC, May 2013; Marc Fisher, "Even as Marijuana Gains

Ground, Some Tightly Enforce Laws," *Washington Post*, June 21, 2014.

45. Keith Humphreys, "Three Ways of Looking at Marijuana Consumption Data," *Reality-Based Community*, July 21, 2014, http://www.samefacts.com/2014/07/drug-policy/three-ways-of-looking-at-marijuana-consumption-data/.

46. *Terry v. Ohio*, U.S. Supreme Court, 392 US 1 (1968).

47. James Q. Wilson and George L. Kelling, "Broken Windows: The Police and Neighborhood Safety," *Atlantic Monthly*, March 1982.

48. John Buntin, "The LAPD Remade: How William Bratton's Police Force Drove Crime Down—and Won Over Los Angeles's Minorities," *City Journal*, Winter 2013.

49. For an account of how CompStat was created and how it is used, see John Buntin, *Assertive Policing, Plummeting Crime: The NYPD Takes on Crime in New York City,* Kennedy School of Government Case Study (Cambridge, MA: Harvard University, August 1999).

50. Quoted in Buntin, "LAPD Remade."

51. New York Civil Liberties Union, "Stop and Frisk Facts," http://www.nyclu.org/node/1598.

52. Joseph Goldstein, "Judge Rejects New York's Stop-and-Frisk Policy," *New York Times*, August 12, 2013; Joseph Goldstein, "Court Blocks Stop-and-Frisk Changes for New York Police," *New York Times*, October 31, 2013.

53. Buntin, "LAPD Remade."

54. Robert Weisberg and David Mills, "Violence Silence: Why No One Really Cares About Prison Rape," *Slate,* October 1, 2003, http://www.slate.com/id/2089095. See also Human Rights Watch, *No Escape: Male Rape in U.S. Prisons* (New York: Human Rights Watch, 2001), http://www.hrw.org/reports/2001/prison/report.html.

55. Doris J. James and Lauren E. Glaze, "Mental Health Problems of Prison and Jail Inmates," Bureau of Justice Statistics Special Report, NCJ 213600, U.S. Department of Justice, September 2006, http://www.bjs.gov/content/pub/pdf/mhppji.pdf.

Chapter 15

1. Quoted in Tony Pugh, "An N.C. Mayor Treks 273 Miles to Help Rural Hospitals," McClatchy, July 28, 2014, http://www.mcclatchydc.com/2014/07/28/234665_an-nc-mayor-treks-273-miles-to.html.

2. "Total Medicaid Spending," Kaiser Family Foundation, September 16, 2013, http://kff.org/medicaid/state-indicator/total-medicaid-spending/.

3. Quoted in Patrick Marley, "Wisconsin Loses $206 Million by Not Fully Expanding BadgerCare," *Milwaukee Journal Sentinel*, August 17, 2014, http://www.jsonline.com/news/statepolitics/wisconsin-loses-206-million-by-not-fully-expanding-badgercare-b99331674z1-271552321.html.

4. Chris Kardish, "Uncompensated Care Dropping Fast in Medicaid Expansion States," *Governing*, June 17, 2014, http://www.governing.com/topics/health-human-services/gov-uncompensated-care-dropping-fast.html.

5. David Blumenthal and Sara R. Collins, "Health Care Coverage Under the Affordable Care Act—A Progress Report," *New England Journal of Medicine* 371 (July 17, 2014): 275–281.

6. Phone interview with Ray Scheppach, October 17, 2014.

7. Quoted in Tony Pugh, "States That Decline to Expand Medicaid Give Up Billions in Aid," McClatchy, September 2, 2014, http://www.mcclatchydc.com/2014/09/02/238367/states-that-decline-to-expand.html.

8. Quoted in Misty Williams, "Left Behind By Obamacare, and the State," *Atlanta Journal-Constitution*, April 5, 2014, http://www.myajc.com/news/news/left-behind-by-obamacare-and-the-state/nfRj8/.

9. Quoted in Alan Greenblatt, "Can Tough Love Help Reduce Poverty?" *Governing*, November 2013, http://www.governing.com/topics/health-human-services/gov-can-tough-love-help-reduce-poverty.html.

10. John Barry, *The Great Influenza: The Epic Story of the Deadliest Plague in History* (New York: Viking Penguin, 2004).

11. U.S. Centers for Disease Control and Prevention, "Tobacco-Related Mortality," last updated February 6, 2014, http://www.cdc.gov/tobacco/data_statistics/fact_sheets/health_effects/tobacco_related_mortality/.

12. Kaiser Family Foundation, "Establishing Health Insurance Exchanges: An Overview of State Efforts," May 2, 2013, http://kff.org/health-reform/issue-brief/establishing-health-insurance-exchanges-an-overview-of/.

13. Robert Pear, "Health Care Law Will Let States Tailor Benefits," *New York Times*, December 16, 2011, http://www.nytimes.com/2011/12/17/health/policy/health-care-law-to-allow-states-to-pick-benefits.html?_r=2&.

14. National Association of State Budget Officers, "Summary: NASBO State Expenditure Report," Washington, DC, November 21, 2013, 2, http://www.nasbo.org/sites/default/files/State%20Expenditure%20Report-Summary.pdf.

15. Christine Vestal, "States Push to Contain Health Costs," *Stateline*, June 15, 2012, http://www.pewstates.org/projects/stateline/headlines/states-push-to-contain-health-costs-85899398539.

16. Christine Vestal, "In California, Adult Day Care Program Is Threatened With Extinction," *Stateline*, June

10, 2011, http://www.pewstates.org/projects/stateline/headlines/in-california-adult-day-care-program-is-threatened-with-extinction-85899376889.

17. Christine Vestal, "For Some States, Medicaid Expansion May Be a Tough Fiscal Call," *Stateline*, July 11, 2012, http://www.pewstates.org/projects/stateline/headlines/for-some-states-medicaid-expansion-may-be-a-tough-fiscal-call-85899404110.

18. Pew Center on the States, "The Widening Gap Update," June 2012, http://www.pewtrusts.org/en/research-and-analysis/reports/0001/01/01/the-widening-gap-update.

19. Quoted in Stephen C. Fehr, "West Virginia Tackles Retiree Health Costs," *Stateline*, March 13, 2012, http://www.pewtrusts.org/en/research-and-analysis/blogs/stateline/2012/03/13/west-virginia-tackles-retiree-health-costs.

20. Mac Taylor, "Providing Constitutional and Cost-Effective Inmate Medical Care," California Legislative Analyst's Office, April 19, 2012, http://www.lao.ca.gov/reports/2012/crim/inmate-medical-care/inmate-medical-care-041912.pdf.

21. Daniel B. Wood, "Supreme Court Orders California to Slash Prison Population by More than 30,000," *Christian Science Monitor*, May 23, 2011, http://www.csmonitor.com/USA/Justice/2011/0523/Supreme-Court-orders-California-to-slash-prison-population-by-more-than-30-000.

22. Paul Starr, *The Social Transformation of American Medicine* (New York: Basic Books, 1992), 149.

23. Ibid., 72.

24. Ibid.

25. Ibid.

26. NYU Langone Medical Center, "Bellevue Hospital," http://emergency.med.nyu.edu/patient-care/bellevue-hospital.

27. Samuel Gompers, the head of the AFL, viewed compulsory health insurance as "paternalistic" and worried that it might weaken the labor movement by causing workers to look to employers instead of to unions for benefits. Starr, *Social Transformation of American Medicine*, 254–255.

28. "Stocks Collapse in 16,410,030-Share Day, but Rally at Close Cheers Brokers," *New York Times*, October 30, 1929.

29. Scholars such as Theda Skocpol have argued that the federal government's first major foray into safety-net programs actually came much earlier, in the form of lavish pensions for Union veterans of the Civil War. Theda Skocpol, "America's First Social Security System: The Expansion of Benefits for Civil War Veterans," *Political Science Quarterly* 108 (Spring 1993): 85–86.

30. "Social Security," in *Columbia Encyclopedia*, 6th ed. (New York: Columbia University Press, 2001).

31. Jay Bhattacharya and Darius Lakdawalla, "Does Medicare Benefit the Poor? New Answers to an Old Question," Working Paper w9280, National Bureau of Economic Research, Cambridge, MA, October 2002.

32. Kaiser Commission on Medicaid and the Uninsured, "An Overview of Changes in the Federal Medical Assistance Percentages (FMAPs) for Medicaid," July 2011, http://www.kff.org/medicaid/upload/8210.pdf.

33. Center for Budget and Policy Priorities, "Policy Basics: Introduction to Medicaid," updated May 8, 2013, http://www.cbpp.org/cms/index.cfm?fa=view&id=2223.

34. All Medicaid eligibility figures from Centers for Medicaid and Medicare Services, "State Medicaid and CHIP Income Eligibility Standards," July 1, 2014, http://www.medicaid.gov/medicaid-chip-program-information/program-information/downloads/medicaid-and-chip-eligibility-levels-table.pdf; Centers for Medicaid and Medicare Services, "State Medicaid and CHIP Income Eligibility Standards Expressed in Monthly Income, Household Size of Three," July 1, 2014, http://www.medicaid.gov/medicaid-chip-program-information/program-information/downloads/medicaid-and-chip-eligibility-levels-table_hhsize3.pdf.

35. John Klemm, "Medicaid Spending: A Brief History," *Health Care Financing Review* 22, no. 1 (2000). For more recent data, see the Kaiser Family Foundation's State Health Facts website, http://www.statehealthfacts.org.

36. By 1983, the number of single mothers had fallen back to about 50 percent of AFDC recipients. By 1992, that number had crept back up to 55 percent. National Research Council, *Evaluating Welfare Reform in an Era of Transition*, ed. Robert A. Moffitt and Michele Ver Ploeg (Washington, DC: National Press, 2001), 17.

37. Steven Roberts, "Food Stamps Program: How It Grew and How Reagan Wants to Cut It Back," *New York Times*, April 4, 1981.

38. Quoted in Lou Cannon, *Governor Reagan: His Rise to Power* (New York: Public Affairs, 2003), 349. Of course, Roosevelt made this statement to argue for government-funded work programs—a measure that Reagan never supported as president.

39. Andy Schneider, *Medicaid Resource Book* (Washington, DC: Kaiser Commission on Medicaid and the Uninsured, July 2002), 97–98.

40. "Public Officials of the Year: Leading in Good Times and in Bad," *Governing*, December 1997.

41. Charles Mahtesian, "Captains of Conservatism," *Governing*, February 1995.

42. National Research Council, *Evaluating Welfare Reform*, 19.

43. Administration for Children and Families, "TANF: Total Number of Recipients, Fiscal Year 2009," U.S. Department of Health and Human Services, Washington, DC, January 28, 2010. Caseload data are

available at http://www.acf.hhs.gov/programs/ofa/programs/tanf/data-reports.

44. Pamela M. Prah, "Why Are Welfare Rolls Flat, While the Food Stamp Program Grows Rapidly?" *Stateline*, July 2, 2012, http://www.pewtrusts.org/en/research-and-analysis/blogs/stateline/2012/07/02/why-are-welfare-rolls-flat-while-the-food-stamp-program-grows-rapidly.

45. For a comprehensive account of this health care debate, see Haynes Johnson and David Broder, *The System: The Way of American Politics at the Breaking Point* (Boston: Little, Brown, 1996).

46. Ibid.

47. U.S. Census Bureau, "Income, Poverty and Health Insurance Coverage in the United States: 2011," September 12, 2012, http://www.census.gov/newsroom/releases/archives/income_wealth/cb12-172.html.

48. Kaiser Commission on Medicaid and the Uninsured, "The Uninsured: A Primer—Key Facts About Health Insurance on the Eve of Coverage Expansions," October 23, 2013, http://kff.org/uninsured/report/the-uninsured-a-primer-key-facts-about-health-insurance-on-the-eve-of-coverage-expansions/.

49. Christopher Swope, "The Medicaid Windfall: Enjoy It While It Lasts," *Governing*, September 1998.

50. Medicaid expenditures grew at an annual rate of 27.1 percent from 1990 to 1992. Kaiser Commission on Medicaid and the Uninsured/Alliance for Health Care Reform, "Medicaid 101 Briefing Charts," Washington, DC, February 28, 2003.

51. Kaiser Commission on Medicaid and the Uninsured, "Enrolling Uninsured Low Income Children in Medicaid and SCHIP," Washington, DC, May 2002.

52. National Conference of State Legislatures, "NCSL Resources—SCHIP General Information," Washington, DC, 2009.

53. Kaiser Family Foundation, "Income Eligibility Limits for Children's Separate CHIP Programs by Annual Incomes and as a Percent of Federal Poverty Level, January 2013," http://kff.org/other/state-indicator/income-eligibility-separate-chip-prog/.

54. John Holahan and Brend Spillman, "Health Care Access for Uninsured Adults: A Strong Safety Net Is Not the Same as Insurance," Urban Institute, Washington, DC, January 15, 2002, http://www.urbaninstitute.org/UploadedPDF/310414_anf_b42.pdf.

55. Benjamin D. Sommers, Katherine Baicker, and Arnold M. Epstein, "Mortality and Access to Care Among Adults After State Medicaid Expansions," *New England Journal of Medicine* 367 (2012): 1025–1034. Also see Amy Finkelstein, Sarah Taubman, Bill Wright, Mira Bernstein, Jonathan Gruber, Joseph P. Newhouse, Heidi Allen, and Katherine Baicker, "The Oregon Health Insurance Experiment: Evidence From the First Year," National Bureau of Economic Research Working Paper 17190, July 2011, http://www.nber.org/papers/w17190.pdf.

56. National Association of Community Health Centers, "Health Centers at a Glance: Research Snapshots and Infographics," 2013, http://www.nachc.com/Research%20Snapshots.cfm.

57. Teresa A. Coughlin, John Holahan, Kyle Caswell, and Megan McGrath, "Uncompensated Care for the Uninsured in 2013: A Detailed Examination," Kaiser Family Foundation, May 30, 2014, http://kff.org/uninsured/report/uncompensated-care-for-the-uninsured-in-2013-a-detailed-examination/.

58. Obaid S. Zaman, Linda C. Cummings, and Sari Siegel Spieler, *America's Public Hospitals and Health Systems, 2008* (Washington, DC: National Public Health and Hospital Institute, 2010).

59. Katherine Vogt, "Public Hospitals Seen Slipping Away, Changing Into Other Entities," American Medical News, September 12, 2005, http://www.ama-assn.org/amednews/2005/09/12/bise0912.htm.

60. Kevin Sack, "Immigrants Cling to Fragile Lifeline at Safety-Net Hospital," *New York Times,* September 24, 2009, A16.

61. Quoted in David Westphal, Emily Bazar, John Gonzales, Richard Kipling, Deborah Schoch, and Lauren M. Whaley, "California Faces Headwinds in Easing Doctor Shortages," Center for Health Reporting, California Healthcare Foundation, June 29, 2012, http://centerforhealthreporting.org/article/california-faces-headwinds-easing-doctor-shortages.

62. Agency for Healthcare Research and Quality, "Challenges Facing Rural Health Care," U.S. Department of Health and Human Services, November 7, 2012, https://innovations.ahrq.gov/perspectives/challenges-facing-rural-health-care?id=3752.

63. Quoted in Chris Kardish, "Missouri's Unprecedented Push to Ease the Doctor Shortage," *Governing*, July 22, 2014, http://www.governing.com/topics/health-human-services/gov-missouri-medical-residency-law.html.

64. Kaiser Family Foundation, "Medicaid Managed Care Enrollees as a Percent of State Medicaid Enrollees," July 1, 2010.

65. Christine Vestal, "Accountable Care Explained: An Experiment in State Health Policy," *Stateline*, October 11, 2012, http://www.pewstates.org/projects/stateline/headlines/accountable-care-explained-an-experiment-in-state-health-policy-85899422676.

66. Quoted in John Buntin, "Coordinating More Care in Oregon," *Governing*, August 23, 2011, http://www.governing.com/topics/health-human-services/coordinating-more-care-oregon.html.

67. Quoted in John Buntin, "What Experts Think of Five Medicaid-Savings Strategies," *Governing*, August 31, 2011, http://www.governing.com/topics/

health-human-services/what-experts-think-five-medicaid-savings-strategies.html.

68. Quoted in Chris Kardish, "How Can States Fix Their Medicaid Programs?" *Governing*, September 2014, http://www.governing.com/topics/health-human-services/gov-states-fix-medicaid.html.

69. Katherine Barrett, Richard Greene, and Michele Mariani, "Insurance Coverage: Access Denied," *Governing*, February 2004; "Dirigo Agency Reaches Deal With Anthem to Extend DirigoChoice," Associated Press, September 22, 2006; Penelope Lemov, "Maine's Medical Gamble," *Governing*, November 2004.

70. Debra J. Lipson, James M. Verdier, and Lynn Quincy, "Leading the Way? Maine's Initial Experience in Expanding Coverage Through Dirigo Health Reforms," Mathematica Policy Research, December 2007, http://www.mathematica-mpr.com/~/media/publications/PDFs/dirigooverview.pdf.

71. "No Maine Miracle Cure," *Wall Street Journal*, August 21, 2009, http://online.wsj.com/article/SB10001424052970204619004574322401816501182.html.

72. Sharon Anglin Treat, "Competing Lessons From Maine's Health Insurance Plan," *Wall Street Journal*, August 25, 2009, A14.

73. Anna C. Spencer, "Massachusetts Going for Full Coverage," *State Health Notes*, April 17, 2006.

74. Richard Wolf, "Mass. Has Lessons for Health Care Debate," *USA Today*, July 23, 2009.

75. Christine Vestal, "Massachusetts Tackles Health Costs," *Stateline*, August 16, 2012, http://www.pewstates.org/projects/stateline/headlines/massachusetts-tackles-health-costs-85899411644.

76. RAND Corporation, "Health Information Technology: Can HIT Lower Costs and Improve Quality?" RAND Health Research Highlights, 2005, http://www.rand.org/content/dam/rand/pubs/research_briefs/2005/RAND_RB9136.pdf.

77. Ellen Perlman, "Digitally Dazed," *Governing*, June 2007, http://www.governing.com/topics/health-human-services/Digitally-Dazed.html.

78. David Blumenthal, "Implementation of the Federal Health Information Technology Initiative," *New England Journal of Medicine* 365 (2011): 2426–2431.

79. Ellen Perlman, "Finding the Money for Health IT," *Governing*, October 6, 2009, http://www.governing.com/hidden/Finding-the-Money-for.html.

80. Darrell M. West and Allan Friedman, "Health Information Exchanges and Megachange," Brookings Institution, February 8, 2012, http://www.brookings.edu/~/media/Research/Files/Papers/2012/2/08%20health%20info%20exchange%20friedman%20west/0208_health_info_exchange_west.pdf.

81. Tim Logan and Stuart Pfeifer, "Insurance Giants Creating Massive Database of Patient Records," *Los Angeles Times*, August 4, 2014, http://www.latimes.com/business/la-fi-insurance-database-patient-records-20140804-story.html.

82. Kaiser Family Foundation, "Distribution of Medicaid Enrollees by Enrollment Group, FY2010," http://kff.org/medicaid/state-indicator/distribution-by-enrollment-group/; Kaiser Family Foundation, "Distribution of Medicaid Payments by Enrollment Group, FY2010," http://kff.org/medicaid/state-indicator/payments-by-enrollment-group/.

83. Molly O'Malley Watts, "The Community Living Assistance Services and Supports (CLASS) Act," Kaiser Commission on Medicaid and the Uninsured, October 2009, http://kaiserfamilyfoundation.files.wordpress.com/2013/01/7996.pdf.

84. Christine Vestal, "Hope for the Long Term," *Stateline*, April 15, 2010, http://www.pewtrusts.org/en/research-and-analysis/blogs/stateline/2010/04/15/hope-for-the-long-term.

85. Ibid.

86. Kaiser Commission on Medicaid and the Uninsured, "Medicaid and Long-Term Care Services and Supports," June 2012, http://www.kff.org/medicaid/upload/2186-09.pdf.

87. See, for example, William Galston, "Live Long and Pay for It: America's Real Long-Term Cost Crisis," *The Atlantic*, September 12, 2012, http://www.theatlantic.com/business/archive/2012/09/live-long-and-pay-for-it-americas-real-long-term-cost-crisis/262247.

88. Vestal, "Hope for the Long Term."

89. Quoted in Sharon Begley and Yasmeen Abutaleb, "Cities, States Scramble After Dallas's Ebola Missteps Expose Planning Gaps," Reuters, October 11, 2014, http://www.reuters.com/article/2014/10/11/us-health-ebola-planning-idUSKCN0I00CT20141011.

90. Jane Brody, "Abstinence-Only: Does It Work?" *New York Times*, June 1, 2004; Nicholas Kristof, "Shaming Young Mothers," *New York Times*, August 23, 2002.

91. Erik W. Robelen, "Program Promoting Sexual Abstinence Gets Resurrected; Instructional Approach Winds Up in Health-Care Law," *Education Week*, April 7, 2010, 6.

92. Faye Flam, "Study Offers Nuanced View of Abstinence Education: Penn's Sex-Education Study," *McClatchy-Tribune Business News*, February 16, 2010.

93. Brady E. Hamilton and Stephanie J. Ventura, "Birth Rates for U.S. Teenagers Reach Historic Lows for All Age and Ethnic Groups," NCHS Data Brief No. 89, Centers for Disease Control and Prevention, April 2012, http://www.cdc.gov/nchs/data/databriefs/db89.pdf.

94. National Conference of State Legislatures, "Insurance Coverage for Contraception Laws," updated February 2012, http://www.ncsl.org/issues-research/health/insurance-coverage-for-contraception-state-laws.aspx.

95. Helene Cooper and Laurie Goodstein, "Rule Shift on Birth Control Is Concession to Obama Allies," *New York Times*, February 10, 2012, http://www.nytimes

.com/2012/02/11/health/policy/obama-to-offer-accommodation-on-birth-control-rule-officials-say.html?_r=2&pagewanted=all&.

96. Jessica Arons and Elizabeth Rich, "State Efforts to Reject Contraceptive Coverage Laws on Religious Grounds," Center for American Progress, July 30, 2012, http://www.americanprogress.org/wp-content/uploads/issues/2012/07/pdf/state_contraception.pdf.

97. Cynthia Ogden and Margaret Carroll, "Prevalence of Obesity Among Children and Adolescents: United States, Trends 1963–1965 through 2007–2008," U.S. Centers for Disease Control and Prevention, June 2010, http://www.cdc.gov/nchs/data/hestat/obesity_child_07_08/obesity_child_07_08.pdf.

98. Todd Zwillich, "CDC: Obesity Is Still an Epidemic," *WebMD Health News,* June 2, 2005, http://www.webmd.com/diet/news/20050602/cdc-obesity-is-still-epidemic.

99. Eric A. Finkelstein, Ian C. Fiebelkorn, and Guijing Wang, "National Medical Spending Attributable to Overweight and Obesity: How Much, and Who's Paying?" *Health Affairs,* May 14, 2003.

100. United Health Foundation, American Public Health Association, and Partnership for Prevention, "The Future Costs of Obesity: National and State Estimates of the Impact of Obesity on Direct Health Care Expenses," November 2009, http://www.fightchronicdisease.org/sites/fightchronicdisease.org/files/docs/CostofObesityReport-FINAL.pdf.

101. Anemona Hartocoolis, "Calorie Postings Don't Change Habits, Study Finds," *New York Times,* October 6, 2009, http://www.nytimes.com/2009/10/06/nyregion/06calories.html?_r=1&.

102. Quoted in Josh Goodman, "Spread of Soda Taxes Fizzles," *Stateline,* February 14, 2012, http://www.pewstates.org/projects/stateline/headlines/spread-of-soda-taxes-fizzles-85899375415.

Chapter 16

1. Quoted in Brian Dowling, "New England Leading the Way in Capping Carbon Emissions," *Hartford Courant,* June 3, 2014, A1.

2. Neela Banerjee, "12 States Sue the EPA Over Proposed Power Plant Regulations," *Los Angeles Times,* August 4, 2014, http://www.latimes.com/business/la-fi-epa-lawsuit-20140805-story.html.

3. Quoted in Toluse Olorunnipa, "Alabama's Climate Change Deniers Refuse to Save the State," *Bloomberg Businessweek,* May 22, 2014, http://www.businessweek.com/articles/2014-05-22/alabamas-climate-change-deniers-refuse-to-save-the-state.

4. Quoted in Alex Roarty, "Republicans Are Talking Differently About Climate Change," *National Journal,* June 18, 2014, http://www.nationaljournal.com/politics/republicans-are-talking-differently-about-climate-change-20140618.

5. Brett Anderson, "Louisiana Loses Its Boot," *Medium,* September 8, 2014, http://cmedium.com/matter/louisiana-loses-its-boot-b55b3bd52d1e.

6. Office of the Deputy Under Secretary of Defense for Installations and Environment, "2014 Climate Change Adaptation Roadmap," Department of Defense, Alexandria, VA, June 2014, http://www.acq.osd.mil/ie/download/CCARprint.pdf.

7. Quoted in Dan Vock, "A Climate of Change," *Governing,* September 2014, 28.

8. Phone interview with Jessica Shipley, November 18, 2009.

9. Phone interview with Barry Rabe, December 8, 2008.

10. Quoted in Jennifer Medina, "Climate Issues Moved to Fore in California by Governor," *New York Times,* May 20, 2014, A12.

11. Marc Allen Eisner, *Governing the Environment: The Transformation of Environmental Regulation* (Boulder, CO: Lynne Rienner, 2007), 1.

12. Phone interview with John Cahill, December 5, 2008.

13. Barry G. Rabe, *Statehouse and Greenhouse: The Emerging Politics of American Climate Change Policy* (Washington, DC: Brookings Institution Press, 2004), xiv.

14. Quoted in ibid., 77.

15. Alan Greenblatt, "Fran Pavley: Legislative Prodigy," *Governing,* September 2002, 80.

16. Quoted in ibid.

17. Phone interview with Fran Pavley, September 3, 2002.

18. Phone interview with Stanley Young, November 21, 2008.

19. Quoted in Linda Greenhouse, "Justices Say EPA Has Power to Act on Harmful Gases," *New York Times,* April 8, 2007, A1.

20. Quoted in John M. Broder and Felicity Barringer, "EPA Says 17 States Can't Set Greenhouse Gas Rules for Cars," *New York Times,* December 20, 2007, A1.

21. Phone interview with Ron Burke, November 20, 2008.

22. Quoted in Janet Wilson, "EPA Chief Is Said to Have Ignored Staff," *Los Angeles Times,* December 21, 2007, A30.

23. Craig Pittman, "Crist Blasts EPA's Ruling," *St. Petersburg Times,* December 21, 2007, 1A.

24. John M. Broder, "Limits Set on Pollution From Autos," *New York Times,* April 2, 2010, B1.

25. "California Greening," *The Economist,* November 24, 2012, 36.

26. Quoted in Tom Arrandale, "Carbon Goes to Market," *Governing,* September 2008, 26.

27. Phone interview with C. Boyden Gray, April 5, 2010.

28. Quoted in J. B. Wogan, "Mayors Group Scraps Cap-and-Trade Support," *Governing,* July 8, 2014, http://

www.governing.com/topics/transportation-infrastructure/gov-mayors-group-scraps-cap-and-trade-in-new-climate-plan.html.

29. John M. Broder, "Obama to Open Offshore Areas to Drilling," *New York Times,* March 31, 2010, A1.

30. Quoted in Chelsea Waugaman, "Voltage Charge," *Governing,* November 2005, 76.

31. Quoted in Mannix Porterfield, "Manchin Wants Aggressive Renewable Energy Policy," (Beckley, WV) *Register-Herald,* October 20, 2008.

32. Michael Burnham, "Public Spending Drives Robust Growth in U.S. Geothermal Industry, Report Says," *New York Times,* April 13, 2010, http://www.nytimes.com/gwire/2010/04/13/13greenwire-public-spending-drives-robust-growth-in-us-geo-72049.html.

33. Phone interview with Margo Thorning, November 13, 2008.

34. Phone interview with Rabe.

35. Phone interview with Terry Tamminen, October 22, 2009.

36. Mark Hertsgaard, "The U.S. May Not Be Leading on Climate Change, but California Is," *Bloomberg Businessweek,* September 9, 2014, http://www.businessweek.com/articles/2014-09-09/u-dot-s-dot-may-not-be-leading-on-climate-but-california-is.

37. Quoted in Juliet Williams, "Brown Wants Higher Carbon Standards," Associated Press, October 17, 2014.

38. Michael Hawthorne, "How Coal Got a Dirty Name," *Chicago Tribune,* July 9, 2008, 1.

39. Judy Pasternak, "Coal at Heart of Climate Battle," *Los Angeles Times,* April 14, 2008, A1.

40. Phone interview with Bob Eye, May 15, 2008.

41. Quoted in Alan Greenblatt, "Guarding the Greenhouse," *Governing,* July 2008, 21.

42. Steven Mufson, "The Coal Killer," *Washington Post,* November 25, 2012, G1.

43. Quoted in Ryan Holeywell, "North Dakota's Oil Boom Is a Blessing and a Curse," *Governing,* August 2011, http://www.governing.com/topics/energy-env/north-dakotas-oil-boom-blessing-curse.html.

44. Quoted in Jon Campbell, "Cuomo: Fracking Protesters Are 'Everywhere,'" *PressConnects,* September 10, 2014, http://www.pressconnects.com/story/news/local/new-york/2014/09/09/new-york-fracking-cuomo-protest/15351419/.

45. Quoted in Alan Greenblatt, "Confronting Carbon," *Governing,* December 2008, 14.

46. Quoted in ibid.

47. Quoted in Alan Greenblatt, "Miami's Vision," *Governing,* November 2009, 15.

48. Quoted in ibid.

49. Dirk Johnson, "Chicago Unveils Multifaceted Plan to Curb Emissions of Heat-Trapping Gases," *New York Times,* September 19, 2008, A13.

50. Christopher Swope, "Lofty Goals," *Governing,* March 2009, 22.

51. Phone interview with R. T. Rybak, 2008.

52. Apollo Alliance, "The New Apollo Program: Clean Energy, Good Jobs," September 2008, http://www.bluegreenalliance.org/apollo/programs/new-apollo/file/Program.NewApolloProgram_Report.pdf.

53. "Current and Potential Green Jobs in the U.S. Economy," *Global Insight,* October 2008.

54. Phone interview with Pavley, 2009.

55. Phone interview with Eric Crawford, November 20, 2008.

56. Quoted in Anthony DePalma, "New Jersey Dealing With Solar Policy's Success," *New York Times,* June 25, 2008, B1.

57. Phone interview with Myron Ebell, November 19, 2008.

58. Quoted in Rana Foroohar, "The Real Green Revolution," *Newsweek,* April 12, 2010, 25.

59. Al Gore, "The Climate for Change," *New York Times,* November 9, 2008, WK10.

60. Michael Shellenberger and Ted Nordhaus, "A New Inconvenient Truth," *New Republic,* November 17, 2008, http://www.newrepublic.com/article/politics/new-inconvenient-truth.

61. Mireya Navarro and Rachel Nuwer, "Resisted for Blocking the View, Dunes Prove They Blunt Storms," *New York Times,* December 4, 2012, A1.

62. Quoted in Alan Feuer, "Protecting the City, Before Next Time," *New York Times,* November 4, 2012, MB1.

63. Quoted in Alan Zarembo and Thomas H. Maugh II, "U.N. Says It's Time to Adapt to Warming," *Los Angeles Times,* November 17, 2007, A1.

64. Phone interview with Tom Adams, November 18, 2008.

65. Roger Pielke Jr., Gwyn Prins, Steve Rayner, and Daniel Sarewitz, "Lifting the Taboo on Adaptation," *Nature* 445 (February 8, 2007): 597–598.

66. Gregor Robertson, "Cities Can Lead on Climate Change to Build a More Resilient Future," *Development in a Changing Climate,* World Bank, September 15, 2014, http://blogs.worldbank.org/climatechange/cities-can-lead-climate-change-build-more-resilient-future.

67. Georgetown Climate Center, "State and Local Adaptation Plans," Georgetown Law, 2014, http://www.georgetownclimate.org/adaptation/state-and-local-plans.

68. Quoted in Medina, "Climate Issues Moved to Fore," A12.

69. Quoted in Christopher Swope, "Local Warming," *Governing,* December 2007, 25.

70. Quoted in Alan Greenblatt, "Confronting Warming," *CQ Researcher,* January 9, 2009, 10.

71. Anthony Faiola and Juliet Eilperin, "Dutch Defense Against Climate Change: Adapt," *Washington Post,* December 6, 2009, A1.

72. Louise Bedsworth and Ellen Hanak, "Preparing California for a Changing Climate," Public Policy Institute of California, San Francisco, November 2008.

73. Chris Bowman, "California Bulks Up Defenses Against Tide of Global Warming," *Sacramento Bee*, November 24, 2008, A1.

74. Quoted in Swope, "Local Warming," 25.

75. James Lawrence Powell, "Why Climate Deniers Have No Scientific Credibility," *DesmogBlog*, November 15, 2012, http://www.desmogblog.com/2012/11/15/why-climate-deniers-have-no-credibility-science-one-pie-chart.

76. Rebecca Riffkin, "Climate Change Not a Top Worry in the U.S.," Gallup Politics, March 12, 2014, http://www.gallup.com/poll/167843/climate-change-not-top-worry.aspx.

77. Karla Adam and Juliet Eilperin, "Panel Clears 'Climate-Gate' Scientists," *Washington Post*, April 15, 2010, A6.

78. Quoted in Bill McKibben, "Record Snows on a Warming Planet," *Washington Post*, February 14, 2010, B1.

79. Quoted in Rachel Slajda, "Salazar: 'Cap and Trade' Not in the Lexicon Anymore," *Talking Points Memo*, March 31, 2010, http://tpmdc.talkingpointsmemo.com/2010/03/salazar-cap-and-trade-not-in-the-lexicon-anymore.php.

80. Phone interview with Karlyn Bowman, March 23, 2010.

81. Quoted in Alan Greenblatt, "How Republicans Learned to Reject Climate Change," NPR, March 25, 2010, http://www.npr.org/templates/story/story.php?storyId=125075282.

82. Phone interview with Jim DiPeso, March 23, 2010.

83. Quoted in William March, "Rubio Questions Climate Change," *Tampa Tribune*, February 13, 2010, 7.

84. Quoted in Andy Barr, "S.C. GOP Castigates Lindsey Graham," *Politico*, November 13, 2009, http://www.politico.com/news/stories/1109/29476.html.

85. Phone interview with DiPeso.

86. Phone interview with Daniel J. Weiss, March 19, 2010.

87. Ibid.

88. Quoted in Anthony Adragna, "Many Republicans Privately Support Action on Climate," *Bloomberg BNA*, August 15, 2014, http://www.bloomberg.com/news/2014-08-15/many-republicans-privately-support-action-on-climate.html.

89. Quoted in Nathanael Massey, "Democrats, Republicans Spar Over 'Climate Denier' Label During House Hearing on EPA Carbon Rule," *ClimateWire*, Energy & Environmental Publishing, September 10, 2014, http://www.eenews.net/stories/1060005538.

90. Quoted in Samantha Young, "Schwarzenegger Opens Climate Summit With Obama," Associated Press, November 19, 2008.

91. Quoted in John M. Broder, "Obama Affirms Climate Change Goals," *New York Times*, November 19, 2008, A4.

92. Phone interview with Terry Tamminen, March 29, 2010.

Glossary

abstinence: Refraining from sexual activity, usually intercourse (Chapter 15)

accreditation: A certification process in which outside experts visit a school or college to evaluate whether it is meeting minimum quality standards (Chapter 13)

activist judge: A judge who is said to act as an independent policymaker by creatively interpreting a constitution or statute (Chapter 9)

ad hoc federalism: The process of choosing a state-centered or nation-centered view of federalism on the basis of political or partisan convenience (Chapter 2)

adaptation: Taking steps to prepare for and deal with the effects of climate change (Chapter 16)

affirmative action: A set of policies designed to help organizations recruit and promote employees who are members of disadvantaged groups (Chapter 10)

Aid to Families with Dependent Children (AFDC): The original federal assistance program for women and their children, started under Roosevelt's New Deal (Chapter 15)

alternative dispute resolution: A way to end a disagreement by means other than litigation. It usually involves the appointment of a mediator to preside over a meeting between the parties. (Chapter 9)

American Recovery and Reinvestment Act (ARRA): A $787 billion federal government package intended to stimulate economic growth during the recession of 2008–2009 (Chapter 4)

annexation: The legal incorporation of one jurisdiction or territory into another (Chapter 12)

appeal: A request to have a lower court's decision in a case reviewed by a higher court (Chapter 9)

appointment powers: A governor's ability to pick individuals to run state government, such as cabinet secretaries (Chapter 8)

apportionment: The allotting of districts according to population shifts. The number of congressional districts that a state has may be reapportioned every 10 years, following the national census. (Chapter 7)

appropriations bills: Laws passed by legislatures authorizing the transfer of money to the executive branch (Chapter 3)

assigned counsel: Private lawyers selected by the courts to handle particular cases and paid from public funds (Chapter 9)

at-large elections: Elections in which city or county voters vote for council or commission members from any part of the jurisdiction (Chapter 11)

back to basics: A movement against modern education "fads," advocating a return to an emphasis on traditional core subjects such as reading, writing, and arithmetic (Chapter 13)

balanced budget: A budget in which current expenditures are equal to or less than income (Chapter 4)

ballot initiatives: Processes through which voters directly convey instructions to the legislature, approve a law, or amend the constitution (Chapter 3)

bench trial: A trial in which no jury is present and a judge decides the facts as well as the law (Chapter 9)

bicameral legislatures: Legislatures made up of two chambers, typically a house of representatives, or assembly, and a senate (Chapter 3)

Bill of Rights: The first 10 amendments to the Constitution, which set limits on the power of the federal government and set out the rights of individuals and the states (Chapter 2)

blanket primary: An initial round of voting in which candidates from all parties appear on the same ballot, with the top two vote-getters proceeding on to the general election (Chapter 5)

block grants: Federal grants-in-aid given for general policy areas that leave states and localities with wide discretion over how to spend the money within the designated policy area (Chapter 2)

bonds: Certificates that are evidence of debts on which the issuer promises to pay the holders a specified amount of interest for a specified length of time and to repay the loans on their maturity (Chapter 4)

broken windows policing: Policing that emphasizes maintaining public order, based on the theory that unattended disorder breeds crime (Chapter 14)

budget deficits or shortfalls: Cash shortages that result when the amount of money coming into the government falls below the amount being spent (Chapter 4)

budget process: The procedure by which state and local governments assess revenues and set budgets (Chapter 4)

building codes: Rules regarding the standards for structures; they mainly have to do with safety issues but sometimes also include requirements for things such as exterior pedestrian walkways (Chapter 16)

bully pulpit: The platform from which a high-profile public official, such as governor or president, commands considerable public and media attention by virtue of holding office (Chapter 8)

bureaucracy: Public agencies and the programs and services that they implement and manage (Chapter 10)

bureaucrats: Employees of public agencies (Chapter 10)

candidate-centered politics: Politics in which candidates promote themselves and their own campaigns rather than relying on party organizations (Chapter 6)

cap and trade: A system for limiting pollution by assigning allowances to polluters, who can sell their excess permits if they succeed in reducing their emissions (Chapter 16)

capital investments: Investments in infrastructure, such as roads (Chapter 4)

capital outlays: A category of school funding that focuses on long-term improvements to physical assets (Chapter 13)

carbon dioxide: A naturally occurring gas, the prevalence of which is increased by the burning of fossil fuels (Chapter 16)

car-dependent living: A situation in which owning a car for transportation is a necessity; an outcome of low-density development (Chapter 12)

casework: The work undertaken by legislators and their staffs in response to requests for help from constituents (Chapter 7)

categorical grants: Federal grants-in-aid given for specific programs that leave states and localities with little discretion over how to spend the money (Chapter 2)

caucus: All the members of a party—Republican or Democrat—within a legislative chamber; also refers to meetings of members of a political party in a chamber (Chapter 7)

cause lobbyist: A person who works for an organization that tracks and promotes an issue, for example, environmental issues for the Sierra Club or gun ownership rights for the National Rifle Association (Chapter 6)

centralized federalism: The notion that the federal government should take the leading role in setting national policy, with state and local governments helping implement the policies (Chapter 2)

charter: A document that outlines the powers, organization, and responsibilities of a local government (Chapter 11)

charter schools: Public schools, often with unique themes, managed by teachers, principals, social workers, or nonprofit groups. The charter school movement was launched in the early 1990s. (Chapter 13)

Children's Health Insurance Program (CHIP): A joint federal–state program designed to expand health care coverage to children whose parents earned income above the poverty line but still were too poor to afford insurance (Chapter 15)

cities: Incorporated political jurisdictions formed to provide self-governance to particular localities (Chapter 11)

city commission system: A form of municipal governance in which executive, legislative, and administrative powers are vested in elected city commissioners (Chapter 11)

city council: A municipality's legislature (Chapter 11)

city–county consolidation: The merger of separate local governments in an effort to reduce bureaucratic redundancy and service inefficiencies (Chapter 12)

city manager: An official appointed to be the chief administrator of a municipality (Chapter 11)

civil cases: Legal cases that involve disputes between private parties (Chapter 9)

Clean Air Act: The law, initially enacted in 1970, that provides authority for federal regulation of air pollution (Chapter 16)

climate change: A shift in global temperatures (Chapter 16)

closed primary: A nominating election in which only voters belonging to that party may participate. Only registered Democrats can vote in a closed Democratic primary, for example. (Chapter 6)

coalition building: The assembling of an alliance of groups to pursue a common goal or interest (Chapter 7)

collective bargaining: A process in which representatives of labor and management meet to negotiate pay and benefits, job responsibilities, and working conditions (Chapter 10)

colonial charters: Legal documents drawn up by the British Crown that spelled out how the colonies were to be governed (Chapter 3)

commission-administrator system: A form of county governance in which executive and legislative powers reside with an elected commission, which hires a professional executive to manage the day-to-day operations of government (Chapter 11)

committee: A group of legislators who have the formal task of considering and writing bills in a particular issue area (Chapter 7)

Common Core State Standards (CCSS): An education initiative that creates a uniform set of learning expectations in English and math for students at the end of each grade. Though participation is voluntary, most states have joined this initiative. (Chapter 13)

common law: Law composed of judges' legal opinions that reflects community practices and evolves over time (Chapter 14)

common school: In a democratic society, a school in which children of all income levels attend at taxpayer expense (Chapter 13)

community policing: An approach that emphasizes police officers' forming relationships with neighborhood residents and engaging with them in collaborative problem solving (Chapter 14)

community, or restorative, justice movement: A movement that emphasizes nontraditional punishment, such as community service (Chapter 14)

compact theory: The idea that the Constitution represents an agreement among sovereign states to form a common government (Chapter 2)

comparative method: A learning approach based on studying the differences and similarities among similar units of analysis (such as states) (Chapter 1)

compromise: The result when there is no consensus on a policy change or spending amount but legislators find a central point on which a majority can agree (Chapter 7)

concurrent powers: Powers that both federal and state governments can exercise. These include the power to tax, borrow, and spend. (Chapter 2)

confederacy: Political system in which power is concentrated in regional governments (Chapter 2)

constituent service: The work done by legislators to help residents in their voting districts (Chapter 7)

constitutional amendments: Proposals to change a constitution, typically enacted by a supermajority of the legislature or through a statewide referendum (Chapter 3)

constitutional convention: An assembly convened for the express purpose of amending or replacing a constitution (Chapter 3)

constitutional revision commissions: Expert committees formed to assess constitutions and suggest changes (Chapter 3)

contract attorneys: Private attorneys who enter into an agreement with a state, county, or judicial district to work on a fixed-fee basis per case or for a specific length of time (Chapter 9)

contract lobbyists: Lobbyists who work for different causes for different clients, in the same way that a lawyer represents more than one client (Chapter 6)

contracting out: Government hiring of private or nonprofit organizations to deliver public goods or services (Chapter 10)

cooperative federalism: The notion that it is impossible for state and national governments to have separate and distinct jurisdictions and that both levels of government must work together (Chapter 2)

council-executive system: A form of county governance in which legislative powers are vested in a county commission and executive powers are vested in an independently elected executive (Chapter 11)

council-manager system: A form of municipal governance in which the day-to-day administration of government is carried out by a professional administrator (Chapter 11)

counties: Geographical subdivisions of state government (Chapter 11)

county commission system: A form of county governance in which executive, legislative, and administrative powers are vested in elected commissioners (Chapter 11)

court of first instance: The court in which a case is introduced and nothing has been determined yet (Chapter 9)

criminal cases: Legal cases brought by the state intending to punish violations of the law (Chapter 9)

criterion-referenced tests: Standardized tests designed to gauge students' level of mastery of a given set of materials (Chapter 13)

crosscutting requirements: Constraints that apply to all federal grants (Chapter 2)

crossover sanctions: Federal requirements mandating that grant recipients pass and enforce certain laws or regulations as a condition of receiving funds (Chapter 2)

crossover voting: Members of one party voting in another party's primary. This practice is not allowed in all states (Chapter 6)

dealignment: The lack of nationwide dominance by any one political party (Chapter 6)

delegates: Legislators who primarily see their role as voting according to their constituents' beliefs as they understand them (Chapter 7)

departments of education: State-level agencies responsible for overseeing public education (Chapter 13)

determinate sentencing: The sentencing of an offender, by a judge, to a specific amount of time in prison depending on the crime (Chapter 9)

deterrence theory: A theory advanced by criminologists that harsh penalties will deter people from committing crimes (Chapter 14)

devolution: The process of taking power and responsibility away from the federal government and giving it to state and local governments (Chapter 1)

Dillon's Rule: The legal principle that says local governments can exercise only the powers granted to them by state government (Chapter 11)

direct democracy: A system in which citizens make laws themselves rather than relying on elected representatives (Chapter 3)

direct lobbying: A form of lobbying in which lobbyists deal directly with legislators to gain their support (Chapter 6)

discretionary jurisdiction: The power of a court to decide whether or not to grant review of a case (Chapter 9)

discretionary spending: Spending controlled in annual appropriations acts (Chapter 4)

districts: The geographical areas represented by members of a legislature (Chapter 7)

dividend: A payment made to stockholders (or, in Alaska's case, residents) from the interest generated by an investment (Chapter 4)

drug courts: Special tribunals that offer nonviolent drug offenders a chance at reduced or dismissed charges in exchange for their undergoing treatment or other rehabilitation; an alternative forum for sentencing nonviolent drug offenders (Chapter 14)

dual constitutionalism: A system of government in which people live under two sovereign powers. In the United States, these are the government of their state of residence and the federal government. (Chapter 3)

dual federalism: The idea that state and federal governments have separate and distinct jurisdictions and responsibilities (Chapter 2)

edgeless cities: Office and retail complexes without clear boundaries (Chapter 12)

electorate: The population of individuals who can vote (Chapter 3)

Elementary and Secondary Education Act: Federal law passed in 1965 as part of President Johnson's Great Society initiative; steered federal funds to improve local schools, particularly those attended primarily by low-income and minority students (Chapter 13)

en banc: Appeals court sessions in which all the judges hear a case together (Chapter 9)

entitlement: A service that government must provide, regardless of the cost (Chapter 4)

entitlement program: A government-run program that guarantees unlimited assistance to those who meet its eligibility requirements, no matter how high the cost (Chapter 15)

enumerated powers: Grants of authority explicitly given by the Constitution (Chapter 2)

establishment: The nexus of people holding power over an extended period of time, including top elected officials, lobbyists, and party strategists (Chapter 6)

estate taxes: Taxes levied on a person's estate or total holdings after that person's death (Chapter 4)

excise or sin taxes: Taxes on alcohol, tobacco, and other similar products that are designed to raise revenues and reduce use (Chapter 4)

exclusive powers: Powers given by the Constitution solely to the federal government (Chapter 2)

executive orders: Rules or regulations with the force of law that governors can create directly under the statutory authority given them (Chapter 8)

expenditures: Money spent by government (Chapter 4)

exurbs: Municipalities in rural areas that ring suburbs. They typically serve as bedroom communities for the prosperous, providing rural homes with easy access to urban areas (Chapter 12)

factional splits or factions: Groups that struggle to control the message within a party; for example, a party may be split into competing regional factions (Chapter 6)

federalism: Political system in which national and regional governments share powers and are considered independent equals (Chapter 2)

felony: A serious crime, such as murder or arson (Chapter 9)

filibuster: A debate that under U.S. Senate rules can drag on, blocking final action on the bill under consideration and preventing other bills from being debated (Chapter 7)

fiscal federalism: The system by which federal grants are used to fund programs and services provided by state and local governments (Chapter 4)

fiscal year: The annual accounting period used by a government (Chapter 4)

focused consumption taxes: Taxes that do not alter spending habits or behavior patterns and therefore do not distort the distribution of resources (Chapter 4)

formal powers: The powers explicitly granted to a governor according to state law, such as being able to veto legislation and appoint heads of state agencies (Chapter 8)

Fourteenth Amendment: Constitutional amendment that prohibits states from depriving individuals of the rights and privileges of citizenship, and requires states to provide due process and equal protection guarantees (Chapter 2)

fracking: A process in which water, sand, and chemicals are pumped into the ground to enable the extraction of natural gas and oil (Chapter 16)

franchise: The right to vote (Chapter 3)

full faith and credit clause: Constitutional clause that requires states to recognize each other's public records and acts as valid (Chapter 2)

general act charter: A charter that grants powers, such as home rule, to all municipal governments within a state (Chapter 11)

general elections: Decisive elections in which all registered voters cast ballots for their preferred candidates for a political office (Chapter 6)

general equivalency diploma (GED) program: A program offering a series of tests that an individual can take to qualify for a high school equivalency certificate or diploma (Chapter 13)

general jurisdiction trial courts: Courts that hear any civil or criminal cases that have not been assigned to a special court (Chapter 9)

general obligation bonds: Investments secured by the taxing power of the jurisdiction that issues them (Chapter 4)

general revenue sharing grants: Federal grants-in-aid given with few constraints, leaving states and localities almost complete discretion over how to spend the money (Chapter 2)

general welfare clause: Constitutional clause that gives Congress an implied power through the authority to provide for the "general welfare" (Chapter 2)

gentrification: The physical rehabilitation of urban areas, which attracts investment from developers and drives up property values (Chapter 12)

gerrymanders: Districts clearly drawn with the intent of pressing partisan advantage at the expense of other considerations (Chapter 7)

gift taxes: Taxes imposed on money transfers made during an individual's lifetime (Chapter 4)

global warming: Rising average temperatures worldwide (Chapter 16)

Goals 2000: The Educate America Act, signed into law in March 1994, which provided resources to states and communities to ensure that all students could reach their full potential (Chapter 13)

grand jury: A group of between 16 and 23 citizens who decide if a case should go to trial; if the grand jury decides that it should, an indictment is issued (Chapter 9)

grants-in-aid: Cash appropriations given by the federal government to the states (Chapter 2)

green jobs: Occupations that contribute to environmental sustainability (Chapter 16)

greenhouse gases: Emissions—primarily carbon dioxide but also other gases such as methane—that are believed to contribute to global warming (Chapter 16)

habitual offender laws: Statutes imposing harsher sentences on offenders who previously have been sentenced for crimes (Chapter 9)

high-stakes standardized testing: Testing of elementary and secondary students in which poor results can mean either that students fail to be promoted or that the school loses its accreditation (Chapter 13)

home rule: A form of self-governance granted to towns and cities by the state (Chapter 3); the right of a locality to self-government, usually granted through a charter (Chapter 11)

homeschooling: The education of children in the home; a movement to grant waivers from state truancy laws to permit parents to teach their own children (Chapter 13)

impact fees: Fees that municipalities charge builders of new housing or commercial developments to help offset the costs of extending services (Chapter 12)

impeachment: A process by which the legislature can remove executive branch officials, such as the governor, or judges from offices for corruption or other reasons (Chapter 8)

implied powers: Broad, but undefined, powers given to the federal government by the Constitution (Chapter 2)

income taxes: Taxes on wages and interest earned (Chapter 4)

incumbent: A person holding office (Chapter 7)

independent expenditures: Funds spent on ad campaigns or other political activities that are run by a party or an outside group without the direct knowledge or approval of a particular candidate for office (Chapter 6)

indeterminate sentencing: The sentencing of an offender, by a judge, to a minimum and a maximum amount of time in prison, with a parole board deciding how long the offender actually remains in prison (Chapter 9)

indictment: A formal criminal charge (Chapter 9)

indirect lobbying: A form of lobbying in which lobbyists build support for their cause through the media, rallies, and other ways of influencing public opinion, with the ultimate goal of swaying legislators to support their cause (Chapter 6)

individualistic culture: A political culture that views politics and government as just another way to achieve individual goals (Chapter 1)

informal powers: The things a governor is able to do, such as command media attention and persuade party members, based on personality or position, not on formal authority (Chapter 8)

insurance trust funds: Money collected from contributions, assessments, insurance premiums, and payroll taxes (Chapter 4)

interest groups: Individuals, corporations, or associations that seek to influence the actions of elected and appointed public officials on behalf of specific companies or causes (Chapter 6)

intergovernmental transfers: Funds provided by the federal government to state governments and by state governments to local governments (Chapter 4)

interjurisdictional agreement (IJA): A formal or informal agreement between two or more local governments to cooperate on a program or policy (Chapter 12)

intermediate appellate court: A court that reviews court cases to find possible errors in their proceedings (Chapter 9)

interstate commerce clause: Constitutional clause that gives Congress the right to regulate interstate commerce. This clause has been broadly interpreted to give Congress a number of implied powers. (Chapter 2)

Jim Crow laws: Legislative measures passed in the last decade of the 19th century that sought to systematically separate blacks and whites (Chapter 3)

judicial federalism: The idea that the courts determine the boundaries of state–federal relations (Chapter 3)

judicial review: The power of courts to assess whether a law is in compliance with the constitution (Chapter 3)

jury nullification: A jury's returning a verdict of "not guilty" even though jurists believe the defendant is guilty. By doing so, the jury cancels out the effect of a law that the jurors believe is immoral or was wrongly applied to the defendant. (Chapter 9)

Kentucky Education Reform Act: The 1990 law passed in response to court findings of unacceptable disparities among schools in Kentucky; considered the most comprehensive state school reform act to date (Chapter 13)

Kyoto Protocol: A 1997 international treaty that sought to reduce emissions of greenhouse gases (Chapter 16)

laboratories of democracy: A metaphor that emphasizes the states' ability to engage in different policy experiments without interference from the federal government (Chapter 1)

leapfrog development: Development practices in which new developments jump—or leapfrog—over established developments, leaving undeveloped or underdeveloped land between developed areas (Chapter 12)

legislative overcriminalization: The tendency of government to make a crime out of anything the public does not like (Chapter 9)

liability: A legal obligation or responsibility (Chapter 9)

limited or special jurisdiction trial courts: Courts that hear cases that are statutorily limited by either the degree of seriousness or the types of parties involved (Chapter 9)

line-item veto: The power to reject a portion of a bill while leaving the rest intact (Chapter 3)

local education agencies (LEAs): School districts, which may encompass cities, counties, or subsets thereof (Chapter 13)

logrolling: The practice in which a legislator gives a colleague a vote on a particular bill in return for that colleague's vote on another bill to be considered later (Chapter 7)

low-density development: Development practices that spread (rather than concentrate) populations across the land (Chapter 12)

magistrates: Local officials or attorneys granted limited judicial powers (Chapter 9)

majority-minority districts: Districts in which members of a minority group, such as African Americans or Hispanics, make up a majority of the population or electorate (Chapter 7)

majority rule: The process in which the decision of a numerical majority is made binding on a group (Chapter 7)

malapportionment: A situation in which the principle of equal representation is violated (Chapter 7)

managed care: An arrangement for the provision of health care whereby an agency acts as an intermediary between consumers and health care providers (Chapter 15)

mandatory jurisdiction: The requirement that a court hear every case presented before it (Chapter 9)

mandatory minimum sentences: The shortest sentences that offenders may receive upon conviction for certain offenses. The court has no authority to impose a shorter sentence. (Chapter 9)

mass incarceration: The phrase used to describe the United States' striking high rate of imprisonment (Chapter 14)

mayor: The elected chief executive of a municipality (Chapter 11)

mayor-council system: A form of municipal governance in which there is an elected executive and an elected legislature (Chapter 11)

Medicaid: A joint state and federal health insurance program that serves low-income mothers and children, the elderly, and people with disabilities (Chapter 15)

Medicare: The federal health insurance program for elderly citizens (Chapter 15)

megaregion: An urban area made up of several large cities and their surrounding urban areas that creates an interlocking economic and social system (Chapter 12)

merit selection: A hybrid of appointment and election that typically involves a bipartisan judicial nominating commission whose job is to create a list of highly qualified candidates for the bench from which the governor or legislature appoints judges. After serving a term, these judges are typically evaluated for retention either by the same commission or through uncontested popular elections. (Chapter 9)

merit system: A system used in public agencies in which employment and promotion are based on qualifications and demonstrated ability; such a system blends very well with the organizational characteristics of bureaucracy (Chapter 10)

metropolitan area: A populous region typically comprising a city and surrounding communities that have a high degree of social and economic integration (Chapter 12)

metropolitan planning organization (MPO): A regional organization that decides how federal transportation funds are allocated within that regional area (Chapter 12)

metropolitan statistical area (MSA): An area with a city of 50,000 or more people, together with adjacent urban communities that have strong ties to the central city (Chapter 12)

minority-party members: Politicians or officials associated with the party that is out of power, for instance, Democrats in a chamber where the GOP holds the majority of seats (Chapter 6)

misdemeanor: A less serious crime, such as shoplifting (Chapter 9)

mitigation: Reduction of emissions of greenhouse gases and other steps taken to curb the forces that cause climate change (Chapter 16)

model constitution: An expert-approved generic or "ideal" constitution that states sometimes use as a yardstick against which to measure their existing constitutions (Chapter 3)

moralistic culture: A political culture that views politics and government as the means to achieve the collective good (Chapter 1)

municipal bonds: Bonds issued by states, counties, cities, and towns to fund large projects as well as operating budgets. Income from such bonds is exempt from federal taxes and from state and local taxes for the investors who live in the state where they are issued. (Chapter 4)

municipal charter: A document that establishes operating procedures for a local government (Chapter 3)

municipalities: Political jurisdictions, such as cities, villages, or towns, incorporated under state law to provide governance to defined geographical areas; more compact and more densely populated than counties (Chapter 11)

National Assessment of Educational Progress (NAEP): The only regularly conducted, independent survey of what a nationally representative sample of students in Grades 4, 8, and 12 know and can do in various subjects; known as "the nation's report card" (Chapter 13)

National PTA: Umbrella organization founded in 1897 consisting of state-based and school-based parent–teacher associations of volunteers who work to improve and support schools (Chapter 13)

national supremacy clause: Constitutional clause that states that federal law takes precedence over all other laws (Chapter 2)

nation-centered federalism: The belief that the nation is the basis of the federal system and that the federal government should take precedence over the states (Chapter 2)

natural law or higher law: A set of moral and political rules based on divine law and binding on all people (Chapter 3)

necessary and proper clause: Constitutional clause that gives Congress an implied power through the right to pass all laws considered "necessary and proper" to carry out the federal government's responsibilities as defined by the Constitution (Chapter 2)

neutral competence: The idea that public agencies should be the impartial implementers of democratic decisions (Chapter 10)

New Federalism: The belief that states should receive more power and authority and less money from the federal government (Chapter 2)

New Urbanism: A design movement that seeks to promote walkable communities through transit-oriented, mixed-use development (Chapter 16)

No Child Left Behind Act (NCLB): Federal law enacted in January 2002 that introduced new accountability measures for elementary and secondary schools in all states receiving federal education aid (Chapter 13)

nonpartisan ballots: Ballots that do not list candidates by political party; still often used in local elections (Chapter 6)

nonpartisan election: An election in which the candidates do not have to declare party affiliation or receive a party's nomination; local offices and elections are often nonpartisan (Chapter 5)

norm-referenced tests: Standardized tests designed to measure how students' mastery of a set of materials compares with that of a specially designed sampling of students determined to be the national "norm" for that age group (Chapter 13)

nullification: The process of a state's rejecting a federal law and making it invalid within state borders (Chapter 2)

obesity: The medical condition of being excessively overweight; defined as having a body mass index of more than 25 (Chapter 15)

office group (Massachusetts) ballot: A ballot in which candidates are listed by name under the title of the office they are seeking (Chapter 5)

open primary: A nominating election that is open to all registered voters regardless of their party affiliations (Chapter 6)

oversight: The legislature's role in making sure that the governor and executive branch agencies are properly implementing the laws (Chapter 7)

pandemic: An outbreak of a disease that spreads across a large geographical area and affects a high proportion of the population (Chapter 15)

panels: Groups of (usually) three judges who sit to hear cases in a state court of appeals (Chapter 9)

parole: Supervised early release from prison (Chapter 14)

party column (Indiana) ballot: A ballot in which the names of candidates are divided into columns arranged according to political party (Chapter 5)

party conventions: Meetings of party delegates called to nominate candidates for office and establish party agendas (Chapter 6)

patronage: The practice of elected officials' or party leaders' handing out jobs to their friends and supporters rather than hiring people based on merit (Chapter 6); the process of giving government jobs to partisan loyalists (Chapter 10)

plea bargain: An agreement in which the accused in a criminal case admits guilt, usually in exchange for a promise that a particular sentence will be imposed (Chapter 9)

plenary power: Power that is not limited or constrained (Chapter 3)

plural-executive model: A state government system in which the governor is not the dominant figure in the executive branch but, instead, is more of a first among equals, serving alongside numerous other officials who were elected to their offices rather than being appointed by the governor (Chapter 8)

plurality: The highest number of votes garnered by any of the candidates for a particular office but short of an outright majority (Chapter 5)

polarization: A split among elected officials or an electorate along strictly partisan lines (Chapter 6)

policy implementation: The process of translating the express wishes of government into action (Chapter 10)

political culture: The attitudes and beliefs broadly shared in a polity about the role and responsibility of government (Chapter 1)

political party: Organization that nominates and supports candidates for elected offices (Chapter 6)

political or party machines: Political organizations controlled by small numbers of people and run for partisan ends. In the 19th and 20th centuries, these organizations controlled party nominations for public office and rewarded supporters with government jobs and contracts. (Chapter 6)

poverty line or poverty threshold: An annual income level, set by the federal government, below which families cannot afford basic necessities (Chapter 15)

precedent: In law, the use of the past to determine current interpretation and decision making (Chapter 9)

preemption: The process of the federal government's overriding areas regulated by state law (Chapter 2)

prejudicial error: An error that affects the outcome of a case (Chapter 9)

primary elections: Elections that determine a party's nominees for offices in general elections against other parties' nominees. Participation in a primary election is sometimes limited to voters registered as members of that particular party. (Chapter 6)

privileges and immunities clause: Constitutional clause that prohibits states from discriminating against citizens of other states (Chapter 2)

probation: Supervised punishment in the community (Chapter 14)

professional model of policing: An approach to policing that emphasizes professional relations with citizens, police independence, police in cars, and rapid responses to calls for service (Chapter 14)

professionalization: The process of providing legislators with the resources they need to make politics their main career, such as making their positions full-time or providing them with full-time staff (Chapter 7); the rewarding of jobs in a bureaucratic agency based on applicants' specific qualifications and merit (Chapter 10)

progressive tax system: A system of taxation in which the rate paid reflects ability to pay (Chapter 4)

prosecutor: A government official and lawyer who conducts criminal cases on behalf of the people (Chapter 9)

public choice model: A model of politics that views governments and public services in market terms; governments are seen as producers of public services, and citizens are seen as consumers (Chapter 12)

public defender: A government lawyer who provides free legal services to persons accused of crimes who cannot afford to hire lawyers (Chapter 9)

public health: Area of medicine that addresses the protection and improvement of citizen health and hygiene through the work of government agencies (Chapter 15)

pure appointive systems: Judicial selection systems in which the governor appoints judges alone, without preselection of candidates by a nominating commission (Chapter 9)

racial profiling: The allegation that police target minorities when enforcing the law (Chapter 14)

rank-and-file members: Legislators who do not hold leadership positions or senior committee posts (Chapter 7)

ratification: A vote of the entire electorate to approve a constitutional change, referendum, or ballot initiative (Chapter 3)

realignment: The switching of popular support from one party to another (Chapter 6)

recall: A way for voters to oust an incumbent politician prior to the next regularly scheduled election; they collect signatures to qualify the recall proposal for the ballot and then vote on the ouster of the politician (Chapter 5)

recall election: A special election allowing voters to remove an elected official from office before the end of his or her term (Chapter 8)

recidivism: A return to, or relapse into, criminal behavior (Chapter 9); the tendency of criminals to relapse into criminal behavior and be returned to prison (Chapter 14)

Reconstruction: The period following the Civil War when the southern states were governed under the direction of the Union army (Chapter 3)

recusal: The disqualification of a judge because of an actual or perceived bias or conflict of interest calling the judge's impartiality into question (Chapter 9)

redistricting: The drawing of new boundaries for congressional and state legislative districts, usually following a decennial census (Chapters 5 and 7)

referendums: Procedures that allow the electorate either to accept or reject a law passed by the legislature (Chapter 3)

reform perspective: An approach to filling gaps in service and reducing redundancies in local governments that calls for regional-level solutions (Chapter 12)

regional council: A planning and advisory organization whose members include multiple local governments; often used to administer state and federal programs that target regions (Chapter 12)

regressive taxes: Taxes levied on all taxpayers, regardless of income or ability to pay; tend to place proportionately more of a burden on those with lower incomes (Chapter 4)

renewable energy: Power generated using natural sources that can be replenished, such as wind and solar energy, as opposed to nonrenewable fossil fuels (Chapter 16)

representation: Individual legislators' acting as the voices of their constituencies within the house of representatives or senate (Chapter 7)

representative bureaucracy: The idea that public agencies that reflect the diversity of the communities they serve will be more effective (Chapter 10)

representative government: A form of government in which citizens exercise power indirectly by choosing representatives to legislate on their behalf (Chapter 2)

resilience: Like adaptation, a term borrowed from biology to describe efforts to prepare for effects of climate change (Chapter 16)

responsible party model: The theory that political parties offer clear policy choices to voters, try to deliver on those policies when they take office, and are held accountable by voters for the success or failure of those policies (Chapter 6)

retention election: An election in which a judge runs uncontested and voters are asked to vote yes or no on the question of whether they wish to retain the judge in office for another term (Chapter 9)

revenue bonds: Investments secured by the revenue generated by a state or municipal project (Chapter 4)

revenues: The money governments bring in, mainly from taxes (Chapter 4)

riders: Amendments to a bill that are not central to the bill's intent (Chapter 7)

rocket docket: Fast-tracked cases that often have limited, specific deadlines for specific court procedures (Chapter 9)

rulemaking: The process of translating laws into written instructions on what public agencies will or will not do (Chapter 10)

runoff primary: An election held if no candidate receives a majority of the vote during the regular primary. The two top finishers face off again in a runoff to determine the nominee for the general election. Such elections are held only in some states, primarily in the South. (Chapter 6)

rural flight: The movement of youth and the middle class from rural areas to more urban areas (Chapter 12)

sales taxes: Taxes levied by state and local governments on purchases (Chapter 4)

school boards: Elected or appointed bodies that determine major policies and budgets for school districts (Chapter 13)

school districts: Local administrative jurisdictions that hire staff and report to school boards on the management of area public schools (Chapter 13)

school voucher movement: A movement, dating back to the 1950s, to allow taxpayer dollars to be given to families for use at whatever public, private, or parochial schools they choose (Chapter 13)

secession: The process of a government's or political jurisdiction's withdrawing from a political system or alliance (Chapter 2)

secret (Australian) ballot: A ballot printed by a state that allows voters to pick and choose among different candidates and party preferences in private (Chapter 5)

seniority: The length of time a worker has spent in a position (Chapter 10)

separation of powers: The principle that government should be divided into separate legislative, executive, and judicial branches, each with its own powers and responsibilities (Chapter 3)

settlement: A mutual agreement between parties to end a civil case before going to trial (Chapter 9)

severance taxes: Taxes on natural resources removed from a state (Chapter 4)

site-based management: A movement to increase freedom for building administrators such as school principals to determine how district funds are spent at individual schools (Chapter 13)

smart growth: Environmentally friendly development practices, particularly those that emphasize more efficient infrastructure and less dependence on automobiles (Chapter 12)

smog: A type of air pollution; the word comes from the combination of smoke and fog (Chapter 16)

sociodemographics: The characteristics of a population, including size, age, and ethnicity (Chapter 1)

soft money: Money not subject to federal regulation that can be raised and spent by state political parties. A 2002 law banned the use of soft money in federal elections. (Chapter 6)

sovereign immunity: The right of a government not to be sued without its consent (Chapter 2)

special act charters: Charters that grant powers, such as home rule, to a single municipal government (Chapter 11)

special districts: Local governmental units created for a single purpose, such as water distribution (Chapter 11)

spoils system: A system under which an electoral winner has the right to decide who works for public agencies (Chapter 10)

sprawl: The rapid growth of a metropolitan area, typically as a result of specific types of zoning and development (Chapters 12 and 16)

standards: In education, fixed criteria for learning that students are expected to reach in specific subjects by specific grade years (Chapter 13)

standards movement: An effort to create benchmarks of adequate learning in each subject for each grade level so that students and teachers can be evaluated on the mastery of this predetermined material (Chapter 13)

state board of education: Top policymaking body for education in each of the 50 states, usually consisting of appointees selected by the governor (Chapter 13)

state-centered federalism: The belief that states are the basis of the federal system and that state governments should take precedence over the federal government (Chapter 2)

state supreme court: The highest level of appeals court in a state (Chapter 9)

states' rights: The belief that states should be free to make their own decisions with little interference from the federal government (Chapter 2)

stop and frisk: A police tactic that allows police officers to stop, question, and search citizens under a set of narrowly defined circumstances (Chapter 14)

straight ticket: Originally, a type of ballot that allowed voters to pick all of one party's candidates at once; today, voting a straight ticket refers to voting for all of one party's candidates for various offices—for instance, voting for all Democrats or all Republicans (Chapter 5)

street-level bureaucrat: A lower-level public agency employee who actually takes the actions that represent law or policy (Chapter 10)

strong mayor system: A municipal government in which the mayor has the power to perform the executive functions of government (Chapter 11)

successful schools model: An education model that uses observed spending levels in the highest-performing schools as the basis from which to calculate necessary spending in other, lower-performing schools (Chapter 13)

super PACs: Political action committees that can spend unlimited funds on behalf of political candidates but can not directly coordinate their plans with those candidates (Chapter 6)

supermajority vote: A legislative vote of much more than a simple majority, for instance, a vote by two thirds of a legislative chamber to override a governor's veto (Chapter 8)

supermax prisons: High-security prisons designed to house violent criminals (Chapter 14)

tailpipe emissions: Greenhouse gases released by cars and other vehicles (Chapter 16)

tax burden: A measurement of taxes paid as a proportion of income (Chapter 4)

tax capacity: A measure of the ability to pay taxes (Chapter 4)

tax effort: A measure of taxes paid relative to the ability to pay taxes (Chapter 4)

teacher licensure procedures: The processes states use to qualify teacher candidates to work in school districts; requirements for licensing typically include attainment of certain academic degrees, work experience, and adequate performance on adult standardized tests (Chapter 13)

teachers unions: Public-sector unions that organize employees at all educational levels to form state and local affiliates. In the United States, the two major teachers unions are the National Education Association and the American Federation of Teachers, both headquartered in Washington, D.C. (Chapter 13)

Temporary Assistance for Needy Families (TANF): The next-generation welfare program (passed in 1996) that provides federal assistance in the form of block grants to states, which have great flexibility in designing their programs (Chapter 15)

Tenth Amendment: Constitutional amendment guaranteeing that a broad, but undefined, set of powers be reserved for the states and the people (Chapter 2)

ticket splitting: Voters' or districts' voting for different parties' nominees for different offices—for instance, supporting a Republican for president while supporting a Democrat for Congress (Chapter 6)

Tiebout model: A model of local government based on market principles wherein a metro area is made up of a series of micropolitical jurisdictions that, on the basis of their services and costs, attract or repel certain citizens (Chapter 12)

town meeting form of government: A form of governance in which legislative powers are held by the local citizens (Chapter 11)

townships: Local governments whose powers, governance structure, and legal status vary considerably from state to state. In some states, townships function as general-purpose municipalities; in others, they are geographical subdivisions of counties with few responsibilities and little power (Chapter 11)

traditionalistic culture: A political culture that views politics and government as the means of maintaining the existing social order (Chapter 1)

Trends in International Mathematics and Science Study (TIMSS): A regularly updated study launched by the United States in 1995 that compares the performance in science and mathematics of students in 46 countries (Chapter 13)

trial court: The first level of the court system (Chapter 9)

trustees: Legislators who believe they were elected to exercise their own judgment and to approach issues accordingly (Chapter 7)

truth-in-sentencing laws: Laws that give parole boards less authority to shorten sentences for good behavior by specifying the proportion of a sentence an offender must serve before becoming eligible for parole (Chapter 9)

unfunded mandates: Federal laws that direct state action but provide no financial support for that action (Chapter 2)

unicameral legislatures: Legislatures that have only one chamber. Nebraska is currently the only state with a unicameral legislature. (Chapter 3)

unitary systems: Political systems in which power is concentrated in a central government (Chapter 2)

urban growth boundary (UGB): A border established around urban areas that is intended to control the density and type of development (Chapter 12)

U.S. Environmental Protection Agency (EPA): The federal agency charged with protecting the environment (Chapter 16)

user fees: Charges levied by governments in exchange for services. Such fees constitute a type of hidden tax. (Chapter 4)

variance: The difference between units of analysis on a particular measure (Chapter 1)

verdict: A jury's finding in a trial (Chapter 14)

veto: The power to reject a proposed law (Chapter 8)

voter identification: When a voter identifies strongly with one of the major parties, he or she is considered a Democrat or a Republican; many voters, however, are considered weakly aligned with either major party (Chapter 6)

voter turnout: The percentage of voting-eligible citizens who register to vote and do vote (Chapter 5)

war on drugs: An effort by the federal government to treat drug abuse as a law enforcement rather than public health problem (Chapter 14)

ward: A division of a municipality, usually representing an electoral district of the city council (Chapter 11)

ward or district elections: Elections in which voters in municipal wards vote for candidates to represent them on councils or commissions (Chapter 11)

weak mayor system: A municipal government in which the mayor lacks true executive powers, such as the ability to veto council decisions or appoint department heads (Chapter 11)

weatherization: The practice of protecting buildings from the elements (e.g., by installing insulation) both to improve their habitability and to cut down on energy use (Chapter 16)

white flight: A demographic trend in which the middle and upper classes leave central cities for predominantly white suburbs (Chapter 12)

zoning laws: Regulations that control how land can be used (Chapters 12 and 16)

Index

Note: In page references, f indicates figures, m indicates maps, and t indicates tables.

Abbott, Greg, 271
Abortion:
    average state opinions on, 147
    crime decline and, 438
    interest groups and, 296
    judges and, 280
    legalized, 463
    by minors, 296
    Mississippi and, 214
    new approaches to limiting, 489
    parental notification for, 144
    Republicans and, 142, 173, 204
    women legislators and, 221
    See also Reproductive rights
Abramowitz, Alan I., 123
Abstinence, 473, 473n, 493
Accountability:
    bureaucracy and, 329, 331, 332, 339
    bureaucracy/merit system and, 338–339
    federalism and, 34
    funding public education and, 415
    governors and, 240
    judicial, 282, 292, 298, 313, 315, 316
    local governments and, 373–375
    NCLB and, 408
    policing and, 461
    public education and, 409, 419, 430–431
    school boards and, 412
    school voucher programs and, 427
    selecting judges and, 290, 297
    through elections, 294
Accountable Care Organization (ACO), 488
Accreditation, 411, 411n
Activism:
    conservative Christian political, 412
    judicial federalism and, 61
    political, 156
Activist judges, 280, 280n
Adams, John, 40, 64–65, 73
Adams, Tom, 516, 523
Adaptation, 523, 523n
Ad hoc federalism, 47–49, 48
    root of, 54–55
    taken to a new extreme, 50–51
    U.S. Supreme Court and, 51–54
    See also Federalism
Affirmative action, 337, 337n
    California and, 81
    civil service test scores and, 336–337, 338

merit system and, 335, 337–338
    opponents of, 338
    sociodemographics and, 8
Affordable Care Act, 33–34
    CHIP and, 486
    Congress approved, 484
    conservatives and, 49
    contraceptives and, 493
    controversial, 471
    eating healthy and, 496
    federal government and, 477
    goals of, 480
    government's roll in protecting public health
        and, 472
    health care expenditures and, 107–108
    health insurance exchange and, 472–473, 475
    home-based services and, 492
    lack of physicians and, 487
    latest research on, 497–498
    Medicaid expansion and, 107, 469–470, 470–471,
        474, 476, 479
    one-sided legislation and, 196
    opt-outs and, 51, 54–55
    two-speed federalism and, 50
    uninsured Americans and, 486–487
    See also Health insurance
African Americans:
    Alabama's state constitution and, 72f
    at-large elections and, 369
    black majority districts and, 218–219
    differences in punishment and, 454
    direct democracy and, 139
    as governors, 260
    homicide rates for, 442
    imprisonment of, 445
    as legislators, 210
    local governments and, 369
    as murder victims, 438
    political parties and, 158
    in prisons/jails, 441
    public education and, 426
    racial profiling of, 439, 461
    school test scores and, 418
    as state legislators, 221–223, 224–225t
    three strikes laws and, 450
    in urban areas, 388
    voter identification and, 134
    voter registration for, 129
    voter turnout for, 131–132
    voting and, 66, 118, 119, 120, 130
    white men replaced by, 248
    See also Minorities; Slavery

Beyle, Thad, 261, 273, 274
Bible Belt, 102, 144
Bicameralism, 210
Bicameral legislatures, 65, 65n
Biden, Joseph, 269
Bieber, Justin, 230
Biggs, Chris, 134
Bill of Rights, 36
    rights of defendants/victims and, 306
    state constitutions and, 61, 65
    state/federal governments and, 38
    See also U.S. Constitution
Bing, Dave, 367
Blagojevich, Rod, 255, 264
Blanket primary, 128n, 166
Blanton, Ray, 251
Block grants, 45n, 46
    TANF and, 108
    welfare reform and, 483
    See also Grants
Bloomberg, Michael, 127, 156, 371, 461, 463, 523
Bluewater Network, 507
Boehner, John, 528
Bolden, Nicole, 445
Bonds, 102, 102n
Botticelli, Michael, 458
Bowling Alone, 133
Bowman, Karlyn, 527
Bowser, Jennie, 80
Boyd, Donald, 96
Brace, Paul, 148, 294
Bradley, John, 201
Brandeis, Louis, 18, 33, 196
Brandenburg, Bert, 289
Branstad, Terry, 266
Bratton, Bill, 444, 460, 461, 462, 463
Bremby, Rod, 514
Brennan, William, 61
Brennan, William J., 286
Breyer, G., 177
Breyer, Stephen, 294
Brock, Ken, 168, 169
Broder, David, 81–82
Brodsky, Richard, 229
Broken windows policing, 444, 460, 460n
Brookings Institution, 425, 521
Brown, Jerry, 80, 243, 266, 267, 451, 506, 513, 514
Brown, Lara, 196
Brown, Michael, 437–438
Brown, Roy, 111
Brown, Scott, 527
Brown, Willie, 231
Brownback, Sam, 161, 471
Brown v. Plata, 310
Bruce, Donald, 93
Brummett, John, 270
Bryant, Kobe, 308
Bryant, Wanda, 315
Buckley, Barbara, 288
Buckley v. Valeo, 177
Budget deficits, 90, 90n
Budget process, 104, 104n

Budgets:
    ACOs and, 488
    balanced, 105, 105n, 161
    budget committees and, 214–215
    California's, 111, 243
    court fees and, 445
    fastest-growing items in state, 307
    freezes in public-sector pay raises and, 341
    governors and, 240, 243, 246, 273
    health care and, 480
    incarceration and, 450
    latest research on, 112–113
    legislators and, 200, 201
    mandatory minimum sentencing and, 310
    Medicaid and, 470
    Michigan legislature and, 226
    powers of governors and, 248–249
    public education and, 412
    recruiting good teachers and, 424
    restraints on state/local, 110
    review of, 208
    sentencing laws and, 310
    state courts and, 314
    state/local politics and, 5
    states', 476
    town meeting form of government and, 362
    See also Economic issues; Finances; Great Recession of 2008-2009; Money
Building codes, 519, 519n
Bulger, William, 198
Bullock, Bob, 78
Bullock, Charles, 126
Bully pulpit, 254, 254n
Buol, Roy, 529
Bureaucracy, 321–322, 323n
    business-based model and, 339
    charter schools and, 425
    government consolidation and, 393, 396
    history of, 332
    inefficient, 399
    irony of public, 332
    key characteristics of, 331
    latest research on, 343–344
    legislators and, 205
    local governments and, 373, 380
    management of, 329
    measuring effectiveness of, 328–332
    merit-based, 334–339
    new public management and, 339
    organizational characteristics of, 323
    oversight and, 208
    performance measures and, 329–331
    picket-fence federalism and, 44
    as policy implementer, 323–324
    as policymaker, 324–326
    political role of, 337
    privatizing and, 328–329, 330
    professionalized, 332
    public education and, 410, 426
    radically reforming, 342
    replacing traditional merit-based, 339, 341–342
    representative, 337, 337n, 344

roles of, 334
state/local government employment and, 326–327, 326t
state stats on, 345
states with the most/least, 327t, 328t
too much or too little, 326–327
traditional, 331, 338, 339, 341
what it does, 323–326
what it is, 323
Bureaucrats, 323, 323n
Bureau of Labor Statistics, 521
Burke, Edmund, 215
Burke, Kevin, 312
Burke, Ron, 509, 525
Bush, George H. W., 52, 268, 420
Bush, George W., 47, 54, 78
  charter schools and, 425
  climate change and, 506
  departure from New Federalism by, 47–48
  Electoral College and, 79–80
  electoral votes and, 120
  environmental protection and, 508, 511
  global warming and, 530
  gubernatorial elections and, 261
  NCLB and, 408
  public education and, 429
  voter turnout and, 121–122
  won a majority of the popular vote, 158
Bush, Jeb, 426, 429
Bush v. Gore, 53

Cahaba River Society, 103
Cahill, John, 506
Calhoun, John, 40
California:
  adaptation issues in, 525
  Agenda 21 and, 518
  annexation in, 396
  appeals courts in, 288
  attorney general of, 269
  ballot access laws in, 126
  ballot initiatives in, 80–81, 141
  blanket primary system in, 128
  budget of, 90
  bureaucracy in, 327
  cap-and-trade and, 509, 510
  charter schools in, 425
  Clean Air Act and, 508–509
  constitutional conventions and, 70–71
  constitutional revision commissions and, 71
  constitution of, 62, 63, 77, 83
  county governments in, 353–354
  courts in, 314
  education in, 5
  electoral votes and, 120
  environmental protection in, 503, 507
  federalism and, 33
  funding public education in, 412
  governor of, 260, 264, 266
  gun control in, 456
  health care in, 474
  health insurers in, 492

home rule and, 111
immigrants and, 172–173
Internet sales taxes and, 93
judicial selection in, 297
land-use policy in, 516–517, 518
leadership powers in, 213
legislators of, 226
legislators/public opinion and, 228
lieutenant governor of, 267
no limited jurisdiction courts in, 285
political machines in, 165
political parties in, 159
prison population in, 310, 450–451
prisons health care in, 476
prisons in, 450, 453
property taxes in, 80, 95
Proposition 13 in, 80–81, 95, 141, 413
public education in, 411
recall in, 145
redistricting commission in, 218
reforms in, 165–166
renewable energy in, 512
representation and, 202–203
sales taxes in, 92
school voucher programs in, 426
selecting judges in, 294
sentencing in, 307, 309
severe droughts in, 504
smaller government in, 342
sociodemographics and, 8
soda taxes in, 496
state legislators in, 219
state senators arrested in, 230
Stockton, 89
styles of ballots in, 124
taxes in, 111, 354
term limits and, 214, 232, 233
top-two primary systems in, 166
voting in, 121, 125, 130
wind farms in, 513
California Air Resources Board, 508
California Coastal Commission, 525
California Democratic Party v. Jones, 166
California League of Conservation Voters, 523
California Supreme Court, 413
California Watch, 230
Campaign finance, 176–178
  detailed information about, 182
  interest groups and, 156
Candidate-centered politics, 160, 160n
Cannatti, Ben, 272
Cantor, Dan, 180
Cap and trade, 509–511, 509n
Caperton v. Massey, 295
Capital investments, 102, 102n
Capital outlays, 415, 415n
Capital punishment, 147, 251, 284, 289
  interest groups and, 296
  slow death of, 452–453
  state supreme court justices and, 294–295
  terms of judges and, 299
  See also Death penalty; Punishment

mandates, 5–6
NCLB and, 408
school testing and, 418, 421
standards, 409
Cutler, Eliot, 179

Daley, Richard, 333, 361, 519
Dallas Morning News, 250
Dark money groups, 157
Davis, Gray, 145, 264
Davis, Paul, 161
Davis, Wendy, 198
Dayton, Mark, 201
Deal, Nathan, 471
Dealignment, 169–170, 169n
Dean, Howard, 264–265
Dean, Karl, 395
Death penalty, 246, 284, 289, 294
average state opinions on, 147
DNA testing and, 452
for homicide, 440
lethal injection and, 452–453
mental illness and, 462
popular support for, 317
powers of governors and, 251
Texas and, 451
U.S. Supreme Court on, 307
victim-impact statements and, 307
See also Capital punishment
Death Penalty Information Center, 452
Death taxes, 92, 96
Debt, state, 106t
Decision making:
county governments and, 355
decentralization of, 339
local governments and, 368, 391
megaregions and, 383, 384
public education and, 430
representation and, 202–205
Deep South:
budget decisions in, 111
incarceration rates in, 454
juries in, 447
political culture in, 13
public education in, 411
Defense attorneys, 302–305, 440
Defense of Marriage Act, 47, 281
Delaware:
appeals courts in, 288
cap-and-trade and, 509
constitution of, 68, 71
county governments in, 352–353
geography/taxes and, 101
gross domestic product of, 14
gubernatorial elections in, 260
judicial selection in, 298
political parties in, 165
Delegates, 215, 215n
DeMint, Jim, 526
Democracy:
bureaucracy and, 323, 331, 332
constitutions and, 63

cornerstone of American, 134
elections and, 120, 123–124, 313
environmental protection and, 503, 504, 507
fundamental aspect of, 117
hijacked, 161–162
jury nullification and, 447
laboratories of, 18, 18m, 21, 33, 195–196, 246
local governments and, 372–373
national committees and, 159
party organization in Ohio by, 162f, 163f
political parties and, 158
public education and, 410, 412, 431
pure, 79
regulating, 126, 128
representative, 79, 210
suspending, 367
town meeting form of government
and, 362
See also Direct democracy
Democracy North Carolina, 118
Democratic Farmer-Labor Party, 180
Democrats:
climate change and, 527
conservative, 214
electoral differences among states and, 7
gubernatorial elections and, 261
health care and, 476
Minnesota and, 195
money raised at state level by, 177
one-party states and, 132–133
policymaking and, 19
public education and, 429
religion and, 160
selecting judges and, 295
Southern states and, 120
support for, 118–119, 159
two-speed federalism and, 50
voter identification and, 117–118
voting and, 121
yellow-dog, 172
Demographics:
long-term care and, 492
tax variations and, 101
voter turnout and, 130–131
Department of Education. *See* U.S. Department of
Education
Department of Energy, 520
Department of Housing and Urban
Development, 525
Department of Transportation, 509
Desegregation, 245, 429
Determinate sentencing, 308–309, 308n
Deterrence theory, 448, 448n
de Tocqueville, Alexis, 13
Devolution, 18, 18m
Dewhurst, David, 160, 451
Diaz, Manny, 518
Dickinson, Roger, 202
Dillon, John F., 364
Dillon's Rule, 364–366, 364n, 373
Dingell, John, 198
DiPeso, Jim, 527

average state legislators and, 219
ballot initiatives and, 139, 140, 144
bilingual, 8
bureaucracy and, 324, 327
in California, 80
changing state constitutions and, 73
charter schools and, 424–426
compulsory school attendance laws and, 410
consolidation and, 424
control over public, 47
cooperative federalism and, 41
deep cuts to, 90–91
desegregation of public, 38
distance learning and, 424, 425
dropout rates and, 420, 424, 445
education committees and, 215
eliminating sex, 412
federal takeover of, 421, 422
funding for, 8, 19, 90, 98, 106–107
government's role in, 5–6
governors and, 243, 264
graduation rates and, 419–420
groups that influence, 428–430
history of public, 332
inequality in, 35
interest groups and, 188
latest research on, 431–432
legislators and, 200, 214
lottery funds for, 412
organization and leadership of, 410–412
picket-fence federalism and, 44
political culture and, 13
powers of governors and, 248, 249, 250–251, 254
professional/advocacy groups and, 430
property taxes and, 94–95, 412–413, 415
of public-sector employees, 329
recruiting good teachers for, 423–424
reformation movement and, 417
regulatory authority over, 411
in rural areas, 16
school prayer and, 429
sociodemographics and, 9
spending on, 412–417, 414m
standardized testing and, 409, 411, 417, 418–420
state constitutions and, 60, 63, 77
state expenditures for, 106–107
state funding for, 90
state government's subsidy to higher, 7–8
state/local governments and, 16
state/local politics and, 4–5
states' being sued for undersupporting, 415
state's economy and, 14–15
state superintendent of, 272
stats on, 434
taxpayers and, 5
teachers' unions and, 428–429. See also Teachers' unions
technology and, 424
voter turnout and, 132
voucher programs and, 280, 424, 426–427
welfare reform and, 483
See also Schools; U.S. Department of Education

Education Trust, 430
Education Week, 421
Effective tax rate, 94
Ehrlich, Bob, 266
Ehrlich, Ginny, 495
Eighth Amendment, 310
Eisner, Marc Allen, 506
Elazar, Daniel, 10, 11, 22, 75, 102, 120
    average state opinion and, 147
    voter turnout and, 130
Elderly. *See* Senior citizens
Elections, 120–133
    at-large, 369
    ballots and, 124, 125
    congressional, 157
    constitutional conventions and, 70
    council-mayor format and, 133
    democracy and, 123–124
    direct democracy and, 139, 141, 144–145
    distancing bureaucracy from, 334
    district, 368–369, 368n
    executive branches of government and, 133, 136–137
    fundraising and, 139, 178f
    general, 166, 166n
    gubernatorial, 260–261
    judges and, 290, 297, 299, 307, 313, 315, 450
    judicial, 281, 291, 292, 294–297
    latest research on, 149–151
    legal offices and, 137–139
    local governments and, 368, 373
    negative advertising and, 123
    nonpartisan, 294
    one-party states and, 132–133
    partisan, 298
    popular, 292, 294–297
    primary, 126
    ratifications and, 71
    recall, 336
    reduction of federal grants and, 49
    regulating, 176
    retention, 281, 291, 291n, 298, 317
    runoff, 126
    school board, 412
    secretary of state and, 272
    signatures and, 126
    state high court, 296
    state supervision of, 123–125
    voter turnout and, 121–123, 370
    ward/district, 368–369, 368n
    what they are used for, 133
    See also Primary elections; Voters/voting
Electoral College, 36
    Florida's, 53
    representative government and, 79–80
    third parties/independents and, 179
    voting and, 120
Electorate, 60, 60n
Elementary and Secondary Education Act, 420, 420n
    Title I of, 94
Eleventh Amendment, 53
Elkins, Gary, 189
Ellwood, Paul, 485

gubernatorial elections in, 260
immigration laws and, 48
lieutenant governor of, 267
partisan elections in, 291
powers of governors in, 249
public education in, 421
selecting judges in, 294
state legislators in, 219
voting in, 129–130
Indiana ballot, 124, 124n
Indian Americans, 260
Indictment, 301, 301n
Indirect lobbying, 184, 184n
Individualistic culture, 10–11, 10n
Inequality:
    federalism and, 35
    in metropolitan regions, 386
Informal Party Organizations (IPOs), 190
Informal powers, 247, 247n, 273, 274
Information Technology (IT), 490–492
Inhofe, James, 527
Initiative and Referendum Institute, 111
Inmates. *See* Prisoners
Innocence Project, 452
Inslee, Jay, 524
Instant-Runoff Voting (IRV), 124–125
Institute for Women's Policy Research (IWPR), 12
Institutions:
    bottom-up, 357
    constitutions and, 61
    federalism and, 33
    grants to support, 41
    health care, 477
    intergovernmental, 391
    out-of-control, 228
    pan-regional, 392n
    state courts as, 283
    See also Military; Religion; Universities
Insurance commissioner, 272
Insurance trust funds, 97–98
Interest groups, 155–157, 156, 156n, 189
    affirmative action and, 338
    attack ads by, 296
    ballot initiatives and, 81–82, 141
    conservative, 138
    dark money, 157
    Democratic Party and, 160
    electing judges and, 292
    funding for, 174
    governors and, 246
    hijacked democracy and, 161–162
    importance of, 187
    incumbents and, 185
    judges and, 281–282
    judicial elections and, 296
    legislators and, 198
    legislators/public opinion and, 229
    lobbying by, 181, 184. *See also* Lobbying/lobbyists
    overtaken by deep-pocketed, 174
    policymaking and, 19
    political parties and, 181–182
    public opinion and, 147

rank-and-file members and, 215
school boards and, 412
selecting judges and, 294, 296
state constitutions and, 83
state stats on, 192–193
supporting candidates by, 160
types of, 181–182
voting and, 119
See also Super PACs
Intergovernmental Panel on Climate Change, 523, 526
Intergovernmental transfers, 98
Interjurisdictional Agreement (IJA), 392, 392n
Intermediate appellate court, 283, 283n, 288, 290
Intermodal Surface Transportation Efficiency
    Act of 1991, 390
International City/County Management Association
    (ICMA), 358, 360, 361, 368, 372
Internet:
    lobbying and, 182
    public opinion and, 146
    regulating, 201
    taxes and, 93, 112
    voting and, 130
    voting records of legislators on, 228
Interstate commerce, 49–51
Interstate commerce clause, 50–51, 50n
    public schools and, 52–53
Iowa:
    chief state school officer in, 411
    constitutional conventions and, 70
    constitution of, 68
    government consolidation in, 392
    governor of, 254, 266
    judicial selection in, 298
    political maps in, 217
    population changes by county in, 401m
    public education in, 421
    rural flight in, 400, 401m
    same-sex marriage in, 76
    voter turnout in, 130, 272
Iowa Supreme Court, 281
Iowa Test of Basic Skills, 418

Jackman, Simon, 144
Jackson, Andrew, 40, 291, 332
JAIL 4 Judges, 280
Jails:
    black males in, 441
    cost of, 445, 450
    government consolidation and, 392
    realignment and, 451
    See also Prisons
Jarvis, Howard, 80
Javits, Jacob, 180
Jech, Jane, 181
Jefferson, Thomas, 39, 158, 362
Jenness v. Fortson, 128
Jim Crow laws, 66, 66n
Jindal, Bobby, 239, 247, 248, 260
Jobs:
    agricultural, 400
    cushy government, 341

homeschooling in, 428
lieutenant governor of, 267
Medicaid in, 479
public education in, 428
selecting judges in, 294
sentencing in, 307, 310
Kentucky Education Reform Act, 420, 420n
Kentucky Optometric Association, 202
Kerry, John, 528
Key, V. O., 126
Keystone XL pipeline, 279, 528
Kilgore, Ed, 142
Kinder, Peter, 267
King, Gary, 136, 137
Kitzhaber, John, 266, 488
Klaas, Polly, 450
Kleiner, Morris, 186–187
Klobuchar, Amy, 205
Klugherz, Greg, 488
Knox, John, 72f
Koch, Charles, 155–156
Koch, David, 155–156
Koch Industries, 155–156, 161
Koeser, Ward, 514
Kookesh, Albert, 219
Kousser, Thad, 223, 249
Kurita, Rosalind, 205
Kyler, Chris, 220
Kyoto Protocol, 48, 506, 506n, 530

Laboratories of democracy, 18, 18m, 21, 33
Labor unions. *See* Teachers' unions; Unions
LaBrant, Bob, 138, 270
La Follette, Robert M., 80
Landrieu, Mary, 279
Langone, Kenneth G., 171
Latinos:
    homicide rates for, 442
    imprisonment of, 445
    local governments and, 369
    voter turnout and, 122
    See also Hispanics
Law enforcement:
    federalism and, 34
    local governments and, 349
    states and, 54
    See also Police
Law Enforcement Alliance of America, 138
Law & Order, 440
Law(s):
    abortion, 489
    about religion, 446
    anticorruption, 165
    ballot access, 126, 128
    benefiting political parties, 126, 128
    bureaucracy and, 323, 324
    campaign finance, 176–177, 189
    case, 442
    changes in patronage, 245
    changes in voting, 149
    changes to immigration, 156
    charter, 425

common, 442, 442n, 444–445
compulsory school attendance, 410
constitutional, 294
curtailment of mandatory sentencing, 453
differences in election, 120
drug, 448
due process, 38
election, 120, 150
employment, 338
environmental, 504, 505
ethics, 184
federal, 35
federal antidiscrimination, 50–51
federalism and, 33
federal residence, 28
federal/state, 443
formal, 442
governors and, 242
gun control, 49, 456–457. *See also* Gun control
habitual offender, 308, 309
higher, 61–62, 61n
immigration, 28–29, 48
Jim Crow, 66, 66n
land-use, 516
legislators and, 199, 200
lemon, 33
licensing, 186
mandatory sentencing, 147–148, 307, 308–310,
    448, 453
McCain-Feingold campaign finance, 177
medical malpractice liability, 251
minimum prison sentencing, 308–309
minimum-wage, 45, 122, 144
motor voter, 129, 130
natural, 61–62, 61n
obscure, 203
open-meeting, 368
oversight and, 208
preventing bad, 199
prison sentencing, 183
professional legislators and, 226
public education and, 409, 412
regulating political parties, 176
search/seizure, 459
stand-your-ground gun, 50
state constitutions and, 83
states and, 38
state sentencing, 307
street-level bureaucrats and, 324–325
subverting, 280
supreme, 49
three strikes, 448, 450
truth-in-sentencing, 308, 308n, 309, 450
victims' rights, 306–307
voter identification, 117, 118, 119, 120,
    134, 272
welfare, 204. *See also* Welfare
whistle-blower, 334
zoning, 280, 384, 384n, 516, 516n
See also Minimum-wage laws
Lawson, Jerry, 489
Lawson, Kay, 126

limits set on the federal government's, 52
of local governments, 19–21, 82, 348, 348f,
349, 364–368
of localities, 368
of mayors, 358–359, 360
mistrust of centralized, 347
naked exercise of political, 216
of national/state governments, 39f
overreach of government, 306
party machines and, 333
plenary, 62, 62n
political parties/interest groups and, 174
presidents and, 245
of public unions, 336
redistricting and, 219
separation of, 65, 65n
shared, 174, 255
of state governments, 348f
states as independent decision makers and, 32
study of executive, 274
systems of, 29–31, 30f
term limits and, 232–233
in times of crisis, 48
traditionalistic culture and, 11, 13
tyranny and, 32
U.S. Constitution and, 62
weak institutional, 247
See also Executive powers; Legislative powers
Power of American Governors, The, 249
Precedent, 283–284, 283n
Preemption, 35, 35n
Prejudicial error, 287, 287n
Presidents:
appoints judges, 297
electing, 36, 266
selecting judges and, 291
Primary elections, 157, 157n
party affiliation requirements for voting
in, 167m
political parties and, 159, 166
See also Elections
Prisoners:
amount of, 448
changing behavior of, 454
corrections reforms and, 452–453
court-appointed lawyers for, 302–303
execution of, 246, 289, 462. *See also* Death penalty
isolation of, 559n17
mentally ill, 462
pardons for, 248, 251
parole of, 308, 441, 441n, 445, 448
rehabilitation of, 456
right to counsel for, 302, 304
sentencing of, 307–311
sexual abuse of, 462
treatment for, 452
truth-in-sentencing laws and, 450
See also Probation; Sentencing
Prisons, 302
black males in, 441
building, 447, 448
cost of, 445, 450

funding for, 91, 251, 309, 451
governor sent to, 264
health care in, 476
incarceration rates in, 438, 441, 445, 449f,
454, 455m
legislators and, 200
mandatory sentencing laws and, 147–148, 307,
308–310, 448
overcrowding in, 450–451
pardons and, 248, 251
population of, 307
reforms and, 452–453
sentencing laws and, 183
spending on, 108
supermax, 445, 445n, 462, 559n17
See also Jails; Punishment
Privacy issues:
health care and, 491
state constitutions and, 79
voters and, 119
Private property:
eminent domain and, 38
rights, 144, 517, 518
social conservatives and, 160
See also Property taxes
Privileges and immunities clause, 36
Probation, 440, 440n
amount of people on, 445, 448
black males on, 441
reforms and, 454
Professional Beauty Association, 186
Professionalization, 216, 216n, 331–332, 332n
Professional model of policing, 460, 460n
Program Evaluation Division, 210
Progressive Era:
direct democracy and, 80
political parties following, 165–166
school boards and, 412
state constitutions and, 63
Progressive movement, 139
council-manager systems and, 360
health insurance and, 478
Progressive Party, 179
Progressive tax system, 95, 95n
Property rights, 144, 517, 518
Property taxes, 92, 93–95, 379
ballot initiatives and, 80
county governments and, 354
downside of, 413
edgeless cities and, 384
education and, 94–95, 412–413, 415
fracking and, 517
home rule and, 110–111
legislators and, 200
local governments and, 366, 372, 373, 375
municipal, 380
in rural areas, 400
senior citizens and, 95, 101
in Virginia, 365
See also Taxes
Proposition 2½, 95
Proposition 13, 80–81, 95, 141, 413

Rogowski, Jon C., 123
Romano, Michael, 309
Romney, Mitt, 119, 127, 175, 268, 410
  environmental issues and, 530
  health insurance exchange and, 472–473
  voter identification and, 135
  voter turnout and, 122
Roosevelt, Franklin Delano, 42, 158, 161, 170, 478
  U.S. Supreme Court and, 49
Roosevelt, Theodore, 161, 168
Rosenthal, Alan, 189, 210, 228, 229, 239, 240, 273
Rosenthal, Robert, 230
Rothfuss, Chris, 175
Rove, Karl, 121
Rowland, John, 264
Rubio, Marco, 528
Rulemaking, 325, 325n
Rumenap, Stacie, 233
Runoff primary, 166, 166n
Rural areas:
  annexation and, 396
  assigned counsel in, 303
  bureaucracy in, 327, 328
  county governments in, 354
  funding public education in, 413, 417
  government in, 400–401
  governors and, 241
  health care in, 469, 487
  legislative districts in, 222–223
  metropolitan growth and, 386
  public defenders in, 300
  public education in, 411, 424
  regional-level coordination issues in, 381
  shrinking populations in, 402
  voting and, 121
  welfare in, 388
Rural flight, 400, 400n, 401
Rusk, David, 389
Rutenberg, Jim, 177
Ryan, George, 251, 452
Rybak, R. T., 521

Sabato, Larry J., 128, 178, 246, 261, 268
Sacramento Bee, 230
Salazar, Ken, 526
Sales taxes, 92–93, 111
  Internet and, 112
  property taxes and, 94
  state, 90
  See also Taxes
Same-sex marriage:
  attorneys general and, 271
  ballot initiatives and, 139, 541n53
  ban on, 144
  changing state constitutions and, 73
  Defense of Marriage Act and, 47, 281
  governors and, 247, 264
  Hawaii/Vermont and, 47
  interest groups and, 296
  in Iowa, 281
  judges and, 280

Medicaid and, 195
New York and, 197, 198
state constitutions and, 61, 76, 84
states and, 55
states' rights and, 48
two-speed federalism and, 50
voter turnout and, 121, 122
San Antonio Independent School District v. Rodriguez, 413
San Diego Association of Governments, 518
Sandoval, Brian, 260
Sandy Hook Elementary School, 456
Sanford, Terry, 242
Santorum, Rick, 127
Saslaw, Dick, 216
Saunders, Kyle L., 123
Scheindlin, Shira A., 461
Scheppach, Ray, 247, 471
Schneiderman, Eric, 137
Scholastic Assessment Test (SAT), 419
School boards, 411–412, 411n
School districts, 411, 411n
  consolidations of, 400, 424
  government consolidation and, 396
  local governments and, 20–21
  operate under state constitutions, 82
  recruiting good teachers in, 423
  regional councils and, 390
  special districts and, 363
Schools:
  alternatives to, 424–428
  capital investments and, 102
  charter, 424–426, 425n, 431–432
  common, 409, 409n, 422
  county governments and, 355
  funding for, 91, 200, 296
  global warming and, 526
  good-quality, 397
  government's roll in protecting public health and, 472
  governors and, 243
  high-poverty, 423
  high school cafeterias and, 495
  home, 427–428, 427n
  inequality in, 35
  interstate commerce clause and, 52–53
  local governments and, 349, 373
  parochial, 426, 427
  powers of governors and, 248
  private, 425, 426, 427
  projected student enrollment in, 416m
  property taxes and, 80, 94–95
  racial desegregation of public, 386
  replaced, 248
  in rural areas, 400
  school choice and, 424, 430
  state expenditures for, 106–107
  taxpayer-funded, 409
  in upper-class suburbs, 388
  vouchers and, 280, 424
  See also Education

collective bargaining and, 335
concurrent powers and, 35
corporate income, 244
county governments and, 354
death, 92, 96
discriminatory, 36
dog, 7
edgeless cities and, 384
effective rate for, 94
on energy, 506
estate, 92, 96
excise, 91–92, 91n, 111
federalism and, 34
focused consumption, 92
fracking and, 517
funding public education and, 412
gasoline, 108
gift, 92, 96, 111
government consolidation and, 393, 395
government's roll in protecting public health
  and, 472
governors and, 243, 244
green building projects and, 519
for health care in Massachusetts, 490
home rule and, 366, 368
immigration and, 28
income/sales/property, 42, 90
inheritance, 204
interest groups and, 188
latest research on, 112–113
legislators and, 200, 214
local governments and, 19–20, 365, 380–381
low, 197
marijuana, 443, 458–459
Medicaid and, 471
Medicaid expansion and, 476
Medicare and, 479
metropolitan growth and, 389
motor vehicle, 92
national bank and, 38
nominal rate for, 94
on oil/gas production, 99, 511
payroll, 97–98
per person, 91
plunging local, 282
political culture and, 13
poll, 129, 134
primary, 91–92
property as payment for, 31
pros/cons of property, 95
public education and, 412
public service packages and, 398–399
regional economic differences and, 14
regressive, 92
renewable energy and, 512
rural areas and, 381, 400
sales, 8
severance, 96, 96n
sin, 91–92, 91n, 111
on soft drinks, 496
state constitutions and, 63
state/local, 38, 90, 91

tax committees and, 221
tax cuts and, 90
tax-exempt social welfare organization and, 155–156
tax penalties and, 490
term limits and, 274
Texas model of low, 250
types of, 111
unpopular, 241
See also Income taxes; Property taxes; Sales taxes
Taxpayers:
California education and, 5
charter schools and, 425
departments of education and, 410
education and, 5
federalism and, 34
public education and, 409, 410
retiree pensions and, 110
school voucher programs and, 426
sentencing and, 307
sociodemographics and, 8–9
voting and, 65
welfare reform and, 483
Teacher licensure procedures, 410–411, 411n
Teachers' unions, 428–429, 428n
ballot initiatives and, 141
in California, 80
charter schools and, 425
interest groups and, 188
lobbying by, 220
policymaking and, 19
See also Unions
Teach for America, 423–424
Tea Party, 142, 143
conservatives/libertarians and, 160
grassroot supporters of, 157
land-use policy and, 518
public education and, 421
Technology:
clean, 521
crime and, 462
distance learning and, 424, 425
fracking, 514
health information, 490–492
Technology Review, 169
Teixeira, Ruy, 132
Television:
attack ads on, 296
governors and, 260
Temporary Assistance for Needy Families (TANF),
  108, 471, 471n, 473
income eligibility thresholds for, 484m
welfare reform and, 483
Ten Commandments, 284
Tennessee:
constitution of, 68, 79
county governments in, 355
elections in, 128
government consolidation in, 395
governor of, 255
gun control in, 456
health information exchanges in, 491–492
income taxes in, 96

governors and, 243
in individualistic cultures, 11
interest groups and, 188
land-use policy and, 516–517, 518
legislators and, 200, 214
lieutenant governors and, 267
local governments and, 349, 380
in metropolitan areas, 382, 389
MPOs and, 390–391
picket-fence federalism and, 44
powers of governors and, 248, 250–251
railroads and, 42
regional councils and, 390
regional governments and, 402
spending on, 108, 110
sprawl and, 516
state/local politics and, 6
states and, 54
taxes and, 96
welfare reform and, 483
See also Highway construction; Roads
Trends in International Mathematics and
    Science Study (TIMSS), 419, 419n
Trial courts, 283, 283n, 284–286
    appeals courts and, 288
Tribe of Florida v. Florida, 53
Troops to Teachers, 423
Truitt, Vicki, 189
Truman, Harry, 352
Trump, Donald, 171
Trustees, 215, 215n
Truth-in-sentencing laws, 308, 308n
Tucker, Jim Guy, 264
Tuition:
    bureaucracy and, 329
    electoral differences among states and, 7
    geography affects, 16
    governors and, 243
    school voucher programs and, 426
    sociodemographics and, 9
    state government's subsidies and, 7
    state/local politics and, 5
    state's economy and, 15
Turcotte, John, 210
Turnaround, 461
Turner, Mike, 204
Turzai, Mike, 135
Tweed, Boss, 333
Twenty-Fourth Amendment, 129
Twenty-Sixth Amendment, 129
Twitter, 231
    See also Social media
Two-speed federalism, 50–51
    See also Federalism
Tyler, Tom, 463

Uelmen, Gerald, 296
Unemployment:
    benefits, 473–474
    insurance, 478
    in North Dakota, 514
    rates, 90

welfare reform and, 483
    See also Employment
Unfunded mandates, 45, 45n, 47, 110–111
    Medicaid and, 479
    See also Mandates
Unicameral legislatures, 65, 65n
    in Nebraska, 210, 213
Union of Concerned Scientists, 525
Unions, 143
    campaign finance and, 177
    collective bargaining rights and, 174, 195, 264
    Democrats and, 169
    extorting funds from, 164
    freezes in public-sector pay raises and, 341
    governors and, 264
    health insurance and, 478
    limits on campaign spending by, 313
    lobbyists and, 181
    political parties and, 158
    public employee, 195, 247
    public labor, 335–337
    seniority and, 336
    See also Collective bargaining; Teachers' unions
Unitary systems, 29, 29n
    Constitutional Convention and, 32
    local governments and, 348f
United Nations:
    Agenda 21 and, 518
    report on climate change by, 505
    resilience and, 524
United States v. Darby Lumber Co, 49
United States v. Lopez, 52
United States v. Morrison, 53
United States v. Windsor, 281
Universities:
    financing, 91
    funding/tuition and, 8
    governors and, 241
    land-grant colleges and, 41
    political culture and, 13
    private, 5
    state/local politics and, 5
    See also Colleges
University System of Georgia, 147
Unterman, Renee, 220
Upside-down elephant, 216–217, 217m
Urban areas:
    bureaucracy in, 328
    charter schools in, 425
    city-county consolidation and, 392
    county governments and, 354
    governors and, 241
    local governments in, 381, 383
    municipalities in, 357–358
    party machines and, 333
    physical rehabilitation of, 398
    political fragmentation in, 402
    problem with large, 380
    public education in, 424
    school districts in, 388
Urban Growth Boundary (UGB), 390, 390n
U.S. Army Corps of Engineers, 523

U.S. Army engineers, 41
U.S. Census Bureau, 492
  local governments and, 349
  measuring poverty by, 480
  voting and, 118
U.S. Centers for Disease Control and
      Prevention (CDC), 472, 494
U.S. Chamber of Commerce, 138, 142, 270
U.S. Conference of Mayors, 359, 360
  cap-and-trade and, 510
  green building projects and, 520, 521
U.S. Congress:
  approval ratings for, 196
  approved national bank, 39
  budget deficits/shortfalls and, 90
  campaign finance and, 176–177
  child health programs and, 486
  environmental protection and, 508
  governors and, 260
  green building projects and, 520
  implied powers and, 35–36
  Internet sales taxes and, 93
  laws passed by, 49
  line-item veto and, 250
  national debt and, 63
  National Guard/governors and, 245
  powers of, 49–50
  public education and, 410
  unfunded mandates and, 45, 110
  Washington, D.C. and, 19, 20
U.S. Constitution:
  Congress and, 20
  cruel/unusual punishment and, 440, 450, 451,
      452–453, 476
  defining marriage and, 73
  elections and, 124
  federalism and, 34
  federal judicial salaries and, 299
  federal power and, 53
  interpretation of, 38, 40
  local governments and, 364
  national economy and, 38
  national supremacy clause in, 49
  nation-centered interpretation of, 52
  original purpose of, 62
  power and, 35–38
  provisions for federalism in, 37t
  public education and, 410
  ratified, 30
  regional governments and, 381
  representative government and, 79
  right to a trial by jury and, 446
  right to counsel and, 302
  right to privacy and, 79
  school voucher programs in, 426
  selecting judges and, 291
  silent on the powers of the states, 36
  state constitutions and, 61, 62–63
  state/local politics and, 7
  states powers and, 30–31, 210
  state supreme courts and, 284
  supremacy clause in, 28

victims' rights amendments in, 306
voting for African Americans and, 66
voting rights and, 129
See also Bill of Rights
U.S. Department of Education, 410, 410n
  charter schools and, 425
  homeschooling and, 427
  performance indicator and, 419
  recruiting good teachers and, 423
  Republicans vowed to abolish, 429
  at risk education and, 417–418
  See also Education
U.S. Department of Energy, 520
U.S. Department of Health and Human Services, 482
U.S. Department of Housing and Urban
      Development, 525
U.S. Department of Transportation, 509
U.S. district courts, 283
U.S. Drug Enforcement Agency, 34
U.S. Environmental Protection Agency (EPA), 506, 506n
U.S. Green Building Council, 519
U.S. House:
  cap-and-trade and, 510
  climate change and, 526
  voter turnout and, 123
U.S. Justice Department, 134
U.S. Office of Management and Budget, 382
U.S. secretary of agriculture, 272
U.S. secretary of state, 124, 135–136, 137, 272
U.S. Senate:
  endless debate sometimes used in, 198
  former governors in, 265–266
  gun control and, 456
  judges confirmed by, 297
  representative government and, 79
  selecting judges and, 291
  Tea Party movement and, 142
  voter turnout and, 123
U.S. Senate Energy and Natural Resources
      Committee, 279
U.S. Supreme Court:
  abortion and, 489
  ad hoc federalism and, 51–54
  affirmative action and, 338
  Affordable Care Act and, 474
  blanket primary and, 166
  campaign finance and, 177
  campaign spending and, 281, 311, 313
  capital punishment and, 295
  changing federal constitution by, 76
  collecting signatures and, 128
  conflict of interest and, 139
  contraceptive coverage and, 493
  counties and, 352
  counting votes and, 127
  death penalty and, 307, 451, 452
  death penalty for crimes committed by minors and, 284
  defense attorneys for the poor and, 302
  dual federalism and, 42
  environmental protection and, 508
  federalism and, 49–54
  funding public education and, 413

WASPs (White Anglo-Saxon Protestants), 371
Watergate, 230
Watkins, Craig, 453
Weak mayor systems, 358–359, 358f, 358n
Weatherization, 520, 520n
Weekly Standard, The, 271
Weicker, Lowell, 179
Weingart, John, 244, 246
Weiss, Daniel J., 528
Welfare:
    African Americans and, 222
    bureaucracy and, 324
    central cities/rural areas and, 388
    county governments and, 355
    drug testing and, 473–474
    federal funds for, 98
    federal government and, 42
    governors and, 240, 243
    inequality in, 35
    law that ended, 47
    limits on, 147–148
    picket-fence federalism and, 44
    reform, 482–483, 539n56
    sociodemographics and, 8
    spending on, 108
    states and, 482
    states rethinking, 473
    state stats on, 499–500
    waivers and, 51
    See also Poverty
WellPoint, 220
Western, Bruce, 439
Western Climate Initiative, 510
West Virginia:
    ballot access laws in, 126
    environmental protection in, 503, 504
    governor of, 512
    health care in, 476
    interest groups and, 188
    local government powers in, 365
    Medicaid in, 479
    public education in, 424
    selecting judges in, 294
    sociodemographics and, 8
    supreme court in, 290
    taxing dogs in, 7
West Virginia Supreme Court of Appeals, 295
Whelan, Jim, 231
Whig Party, 158
White flight, 386, 386n
    minorities in suburbs and, 387–388
    regional planning and, 389n
White House:
    climate change and, 505
    lobbying by, 182
    National Guard/governors and, 245
White males:
    affirmative action and, 337
    Alabama's state constitution and, 72f
    changing state constitutions and, 66
    as governors, 260
    as legislators, 210, 219

in prisons/jails, 441
replaced, 248
voting for, 65–66
Whites:
    affirmative action and, 337–338
    color-blind criminal justice system and, 454
    discrimination against, 338
    dropout rates of, 420
    imprisonment of, 445
    NCLB and, 408
    racial desegregation of public schools and, 386
    school board elections and, 412
    school test scores and, 418
    voter registration for, 129
    voter turnout for, 131, 132
    voting and, 118, 119
Whitfield, Ed, 528
Whitman, Meg, 260
Whitmire, John, 451, 452
Wickard v. Filburn, 50
Wiggins, David, 281
Wilder, Douglas, 260
Wilson, James Q., 447, 459–460
Wilson, Pete, 359
Wilson, Woodrow, 168
Wind energy, 512, 514
Windom, Steve, 267
Winger, Richard, 126
Wintemute, Garen, 457
Winthrop, John, 64
Wisconsin:
    constitution of, 68, 75, 78
    elections for judicial offices in, 313
    governor of, 251, 264, 336, 470
    high school cafeterias in, 495
    interest groups in, 174
    labor relations in the public sector in, 343
    Medicaid and, 470
    political culture in, 10, 13
    professional legislators of, 226
    public education in, 417
    public financing of elections in, 315
    school voucher programs in, 426, 427
    selecting judges in, 294
    slavery and, 40–41
    third parties/independents in, 179
    voter turnout for, 122
    voting in, 118, 130
    welfare reform in, 482–483
Wisconsin Education Association Council (WEAC), 335
Wisconsin State Journal, 250–251
Women:
    affirmative action and, 337, 338
    allowed to own property, 75
    electing judges and, 292
    as governors, 260
    as legislators, 210, 219, 220–221, 224–225t
    local governments and, 369, 371
    political culture and, 12t
    protecting violence against, 29
    term limits and, 232
    violence against, 53